WELCOME TO
EXPLORING STRATEGY

Strategy is an exciting subject. It's about the overall direction of all kinds of organisations, from multinationals to entrepreneurial start-ups, from charities to government agencies, and many more. Strategy raises the big questions about these organisations – how they grow, how they innovate and how they change. As a manager of today or tomorrow, you will be involved in shaping, implementing or communicating these strategies.

Our aim in writing *Exploring Strategy* is to give you a comprehensive understanding of the issues and techniques of strategy, and to help you get a great final result in your course. Here's how you might make the most of the text:

- Explore hot topics in cutting-edge issues such as competitive strategy, corporate governance, innovation and entrepreneurship, international strategy, strategic change and acquisitions and alliances.

- Consider the 'key debates' and the different strategy 'lenses' to get new perspectives and set you on your way to better grades in your assignments and exams.

- Follow up on the recommended readings at the end of each chapter. They're specially selected as accessible and valuable sources that will enhance your learning and give you an extra edge in your course work.

After you've registered with the access code included in this book, visit *Exploring Strategy* at **www.pearsoned.co.uk/mystrategylab** to find essential student learning material including:

- The **Strategy Experience simulation**, which gives you practical hands-on experience of strategic decision-making in organisations. As a Director of the Board, you must deal with opportunities as they arise, and your decisions will affect the company's performance. Choose wisely!

- A **personalised study plan** based on feedback that identifies your strengths and weaknesses, then recommends a tailored set of resources that will help to develop your understanding of strategy.

- **Audio** and **video resources**, including case studies on IKEA, Land Rover and the Eden Project, that put a spotlight on strategy in practice.

We want *Exploring Strategy* to give you what you need: a comprehensive view of the subject, an ambition to put that into practice, and – of course – success in your studies. We hope that you'll be as excited by the key issues of strategy as we are!

So, read on and good luck!

Gerry Johnson
Richard Whittington
Kevan Scholes

Gerry Johnson, BA, PhD is Emeritus Professor of Strategic Management at Lancaster University School of Management and a Senior Fellow of the UK Advanced Institute of Management Research (AIM). He has also taught at Strathclyde Business School, Cranfield School of Management, Manchester Business School and Aston University. He is the author of numerous books and his research has been published in many of the foremost management research journals in the world. He also serves on the editorial boards of the *Academy of Management Journal*, the *Strategic Management Journal* and the *Journal of Management Studies*. He is a partner in the consultancy partnership Strategy Explorers (see www.strategyexplorers.com) where he works with senior management teams on issues of strategy development and strategic change.

Richard Whittington MA, MBA, PhD is Professor of Strategic Management at the Saïd Business School and Millman Fellow at New College, University of Oxford. He is author or co-author of nine books and has published many journal articles. He serves on the editorial boards of *Organization Science, Organization Studies*, the *Strategic Management Journal* and *Long Range Planning*, amongst others. He has had full or visiting positions at the Harvard Business School, HEC Paris, Imperial College London, the University of Toulouse and the University of Warwick. He is a partner in Strategy Explorers and active in executive education and consulting, working with organisations from across Europe, the USA and Asia (see www.strategyexplorers.com). His current research is focused on strategy practice and international management.

Kevan Scholes MA, PhD, DMS, CIMgt, FRSA is Principal Partner of Scholes Associates – specialising in strategic management. He is also Visiting Professor of Strategic Management and formerly Director of the Sheffield Business School, UK. He has extensive experience of teaching strategy to both undergraduate and postgraduate students at several universities. In addition, his corporate management development work includes organisations in manufacturing, many service sectors and a wide range of public service organisations. He has had regular commitments outside the UK – including Ireland, Australia and New Zealand. He has also been an advisor on management development to a number of national bodies and is a Companion of The Chartered Management Institute.

EXPLORING STRATEGY

NINTH EDITION

GERRY JOHNSON
Lancaster University Management School

RICHARD WHITTINGTON
Saïd Business School, University of Oxford

KEVAN SCHOLES
Sheffield Business School

With the assistance of
STEVE PYLE

Financial Times
Prentice Hall
is an imprint of

Harlow, England • London • New York • Boston • San Francisco • Toronto
Sydney • Tokyo • Singapore • Hong Kong • Seoul • Taipei • New Delhi
Cape Town • Madrid • Mexico City • Amsterdam • Munich • Paris • Milan

Pearson Education Limited
Edinburgh Gate
Harlow
Essex CM20 2JE
England

and Associated Companies throughout the world

Visit us on the World Wide Web at:
www.pearsoned.co.uk

First edition published under the Prentice Hall imprint 1984
Fifth edition published under the Prentice Hall imprint 1998
Sixth edition published under the Financial Times Prentice Hall imprint 2002
Seventh edition 2005
Eighth edition 2008
Ninth edition 2011

ISBN: 978-0-273-73549-6 (text only)
ISBN: 978-0-273-73202-0 (text and cases)

British Library Cataloguing-in-Publication Data
A catalogue record for this book is available from the British Library

Library of Congress Cataloging-in-Publication Data
A catalog record for this book is available from the Library of Congress

10 9 8 7 6 5 4 3 2 1
14 13 12 11

Typeset in 9.5/13.5pt Photina by 35
Printed and bound by Rotolito Lombarda, Italy

BRIEF CONTENTS

EXPLORING STRATEGY ONLINE

A wide range of supporting resources are available at:

PEARSON mystrategylab™

Register to create your own personal account using the access code supplied with your copy of the book,* and access the following teaching and learning resources:

Resources for students

- **A dynamic eText** of the book that you can search, bookmark, annotate and highlight as you please
- **Self-assessment questions** that identify your strengths before recommending a personalised study plan that points you to the resources which can help you achieve a better grade
- **Key concept audio summaries** that you can download or listen to online
- **Video cases** that show managers talking about strategic issues in their own organisations
- **Revision flashcards** to help you prepare for your exams
- **A multi-lingual online glossary** to help explain key concepts
- Guidance on **how to analyse a case study**
- **Links** to relevant sites on the web so you can explore more about the organisations featured in the case studies
- **Classic cases** – over 30 case studies from previous editions of the book
- The **Strategy Experience simulation** gives you hands-on experience of strategic analysis and putting strategy into action

Resources for instructors

- **Instructor's manual**, including extensive teaching notes for cases and suggested teaching plans
- **PowerPoint slides**, containing key information and figures from the book
- **Secure testbank**, containing over 600 questions
- Support for the **Strategy Experience simulation** with guidance on the aims and objectives of the simulation, and instructions on how to set up simulation groups that enable you to monitor your student's performance

Also, the following instructor resources are available off-line:

- Instructor's manual in hard copy, with CD containing PowerPoint slides and classic cases
- Video resources on DVD

For more information, please contact your local Pearson Education sales representative or visit **www.pearsoned.co.uk/mystrategylab**

*If you don't have an access code, you can still access the resources.
Visit **www.pearsoned.co.uk/mystrategylab** for details.

CONTENTS

PART II
STRATEGIC CHOICES

CASE STUDIES

LIST OF ILLUSTRATIONS
AND KEY DEBATES

ILLUSTRATIONS

KEY DEBATES BY CHAPTER

LIST OF FIGURES

LIST OF TABLES

PREFACE

We are delighted to offer this ninth edition of *Exploring Strategy*. With sales of previous editions above 900,000, we believe we have a well-tried product. Yet the strategy field is constantly changing. For this edition, therefore, we have thoroughly refreshed each chapter, with new concepts, new cases and new examples throughout. Here we would like to highlight four substantial changes, while recalling some of the classic features of the book.

The ninth edition's principal innovations are:

- **Our new title, *Exploring Strategy*:** we have dropped the reference to 'Corporate' in the title in order to reflect the wide scope the book has always had. To some, 'corporate' implied a focus on large, multi-business commercial organisations. *Exploring Strategy* is for all organisations, including small entrepreneurial businesses, not-for-profits and public sector organisations too.

- **A new chapter on Mergers, Acquisitions and Alliances:** mergers and acquisitions are an important method for many strategies, particularly diversification and internationalisation, and they often grab the headlines. Alliances too are a crucial feature of contemporary business. We have recognised the importance of these methods by granting them a new chapter of their own.

- **A separate chapter on Strategy Evaluation:** in the end, strategies have to be evaluated, not just described. This chapter introduces key evaluation techniques, financial and non-financial, encouraging students to apply them and assess their usefulness on real cases.

- **A new web-based strategy simulation, the Strategy Experience:** our simulation of an international advertising company gives students the chance to apply strategy frameworks in action, either individually or in teams. The simulation also provides teachers with an effective method of assessment and feedback. You can find this simulation at **www.MyStrategyLab.com**.

At the same time, *Exploring Strategy* retains its longstanding commitment to a comprehensive and real-world view of strategy. In particular, this entails a deep concern for:

- **Process:** we believe that the human processes of strategy, not only the economics of particular strategies, are central to achieving long-term organisational success. Throughout the book, we underline the importance of human processes, but in particular we devote Part III to processes of strategy formation, implementation and change.

- **Practice:** we conclude the book with a chapter on the Practice of Strategy (Chapter 15), focused on the practicalities of managing strategy. Throughout the book, we introduce concepts and techniques through practical illustrations and applications, rather than abstract descriptions.

Many people have helped us with the development of this new edition. Steve Pyle has taken leadership in coordinating the case collection. We have consulted carefully with our Advisory Board, made up of experienced adopters of the book. Many other adopters of the book provide more informal advice and suggestions – many of whom we have had the pleasure of meeting at our annual teachers' workshops. This kind of feedback is invaluable. Also, our students and clients at Sheffield, Lancaster and Oxford and the many other places where we teach are a constant source of ideas and stimulus. We also gain from our links across the world, particularly in Ireland, The Netherlands, Denmark, Sweden, France, Canada, Australia, New Zealand, Hong Kong, Singapore and the USA. Many contribute directly by providing case studies and illustrations and these are acknowledged in the text. But for other kinds of contributions we particularly thank Julia Balogun, Phyl Johnson, John Kind, Donald MacLean, Sam McPherson, Lance Moir, David Pettifer, Rob Pieters and Basak Yakis-Douglas.

Finally, we thank those organisations that have been generous enough to be written up as case studies. We hope that those using the book will respect the wishes of the case study organisations and *not* contact them directly for further information.

Gerry Johnson (gerry.johnson@lancaster.ac.uk)
Richard Whittington (richard.whittington@sbs.ox.ac.uk)
Kevan Scholes (KScholes@scholes.u-net.com)
May 2010

ADVISORY BOARD

Special thanks are due to the following members of the Advisory Board for their valued comments:

Clive Choo	Nanyang Technological University
David Oliver	HEC Montréal
Emiel Wubben	Wageningen University
Eric Cassells	Oxford Brookes University
Erik Wilberg	BI Oslo
Heather Farley	University of Ulster
Kenneth Wiltshire	University of Queensland
Laure Cabantous	Nottingham University
Lisa Barton	Cardiff University
Ludovic Cailluet	IAE Toulouse
Marian Crowley-Henry	Dublin Institute of Technology
Martin Lindell	Hanken School of Economics
Matthew Hinton	The Open University
Michael Mayer	University of Bath
Michael O'Keefe	King's College London
Moira Fischbacher-Smith	University of Glasgow
Shigefumi Makino	The Chinese University of Hong Kong

EXPLORING STRATEGY

This ninth edition of *Exploring Strategy* builds on the established strengths of this best-selling textbook. A range of in-text features and supplementary features have been developed to enable you and your students to gain maximum added value from the teaching and learning of strategy.

- **Outstanding pedagogical features**. Each chapter has clear learning outcomes, practical questions associated with real-life illustrations and examples which students can easily apply to what they have learnt.
- **Flexibility of use**. You can choose to use either the Text and Cases version of the book, or – if you don't use longer cases (or have your own) – the Text-only version. The provision of Key Debates, Commentaries and Strategy 'Lenses' allow you to dig deeper into the tensions and complexity of strategy.

The two versions are complemented by a concise version of the text, *Fundamentals of Strategy*, and instructors also have the option of further customising the text. Visit **www.pearsoned.co.uk/CustomPublishing** for more details.

- **Up-to-date materials**. As well as a new chapter on mergers, acquisitions and alliances, we have fully revised the other chapters, incorporating new research and updating references so that you can easily access the latest research.
- **Encouraging critical thinking**. As well as the Strategy Lenses, we encourage critical thinking by ending each chapter with a 'key debate', introducing students to research evidence and theory on key issues of the chapter and encouraging them to take a view.

Our 'three circles' model – depicting the overlapping issues of strategic position, strategic choices and strategy-in-action – also challenges a simple linear, sequential view of the strategy process.

- **Case and examples**. A wide range of Illustrations, Case Examples and (in the Text and Cases version) longer Case Studies are fresh and engage with student interests and day-to-day experience. The majority of these are entirely new to this edition; we have extensively revised the remainder. Finally, we draw these examples from all over the world and use examples from the public and voluntary sectors as well as the private.
- **Teaching and learning support**. You and your students can access a wealth of resources at **www.pearsoned.co.uk/mystrategylab**, including the following:
  For students
  - **The Strategy Experience** simulation, which puts the student in the driving seat and allows them to experience the real world of strategic decision-making.
  - A personalised study plan that helps students focus their attention and efforts on the areas where they're needed the most.
  - Flashcards, a multilingual glossary, and weblinks for revision and research.

For instructors

- An Instructor's Manual which provides a comprehensive set of teaching support, including guidance on the use of case studies and assignments, and advice on how to plan a programme using the text.

- PowerPoint slides.

- A test-bank of assessment questions.

- Classic Cases from previous editions of the book.

In addition to the website, a printed copy of the Instructor's Manual is also available.

- **Video resources on DVD**. A DVD has been specially created for in-class use and contains briefings on selected topics from the authors, and material to support some of the case studies in the book:

1 'With the Experts' (the authors explain key concepts)
   Strategy in Different Contexts
   Porter's five forces
   Core Competencies
   Strategic Drift and the Cultural Web

2 Case Study organisations
   SABMiller – international development
   eBay – success and sustainability
   Amazon.com – business-level strategy
   Manchester United – football club or business?
   easyJet – competitive strategy
   Marks & Spencer – two CEOs on managing turnaround

You can order and find out more about these resources from your local Pearson Education representative (**www.pearsoned.co.uk/replocator**).

- **Teachers' workshop**. We run an annual workshop to facilitate discussion of key challenges and solutions in the teaching of strategic management. Details of forthcoming workshops can be found at **www.pearsoned.co.uk/ecsworkshop**.

GUIDED TOUR

→ Setting the scene

The **'three circles' navigational diagram** shows where you are in the three-part structure that underpins the book.

Key terms are identified at the beginning of each chapter.

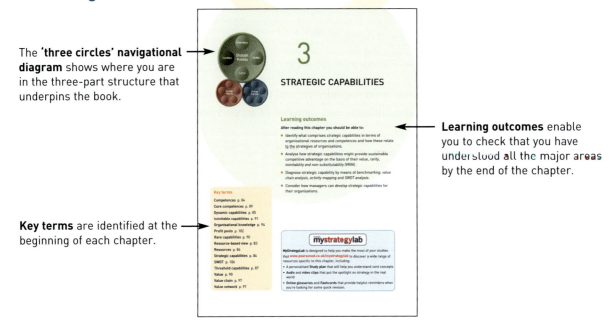

Learning outcomes enable you to check that you have understood all the major areas by the end of the chapter.

→ Strategy in the real world

Illustrations showcase the application of specific strategic issues in the real world so you can identify and relate theory to practice.

Video cases enable you to engage with and learn from the experience of senior managers responsible for determining and implementing strategy.

The **Case example** at the end of each chapter allows exploration of topics covered in the chapter.

→ **Critical thinking and further study**

The **Key debate** at the end of each chapter invites you to reflect on topical and contentious questions of strategy.

Work and **Video assignments** at the end of each chapter provide stimulating questions which encourage you to explore key concepts and applications.

Commentaries at the end of each part of the book present a view of strategy through four 'lenses' to help you see strategic issues in different ways.

→ Check your understanding with *

Thus the long-term
ong-term direction of
amines the practical
nt levels of strategy;
statement'.

Key concept icons in the text direct
you to audio and other resources in
MyStrategyLab where you can check
and reinforce your understanding of
key concepts.

These terms are also included in the
Glossary, found in **MyStrategyLab**.
(The Glossary is also translated into
Chinese, Dutch, French, Norwegian
and Swedish.) You can test your
understanding of these key terms
using **Flashcards** on the website.

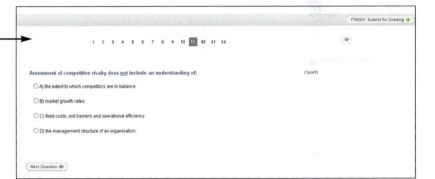

Need a little extra help?
Self-assessment tests will
help you to identify the areas
where you need to improve . . .

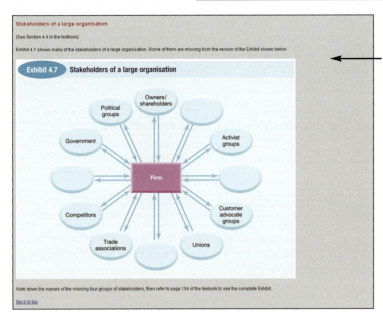

. . . and the **Personalised study plan**
will direct you to the specific resources
that can help you achieve a better grade.

***Don't forget to register using your
access code at:**
www.pearsoned.co.uk/mystrategylab

The **Strategy Experience simulation** included in **MyStrategyLab**, puts you in the position of a strategic decision maker. You are the Director of the Board at WRSX Group, a global advertising and marketing communications business.

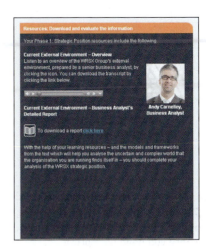

Multimedia resources and briefing documents help you to build an understanding of the WRSX Group's strategic position, as well as the choices that are available to the organisation.

You apply your knowledge in the boardroom, where you are faced with a number of scenarios. Here you must make tough decisions that will shape the company's future.

Success will depend on how well you understand and can apply the concepts that are covered in *Exploring Strategy*. Choose wisely!

EXPLORING STRATEGY

1

INTRODUCING STRATEGY

Learning outcomes

After reading this chapter you should be able to:

● Summarise the strategy of an organisation in a *'strategy statement'*.

● Identify key issues for an organisation's strategy according to the *Exploring Strategy* model.

● Distinguish between *corporate*, *business* and *operational* strategies.

● Understand how different people contribute to strategy *at work*.

● Appreciate the contributions of different academic disciplines and *theoretical lenses* to practical strategy analysis.

PEARSON **mystrategylab**

MyStrategyLab is designed to help you make the most of your studies.

Visit **www.pearsoned.co.uk/mystrategylab** to discover a wide range of resources specific to this chapter, including:

● A personalised **Study plan** that will help you understand core concepts

● **Audio** and **video clips** that put the spotlight on strategy in the real world

● **Online glossaries** and **flashcards** that provide helpful reminders when you're looking for some quick revision.

1.1 INTRODUCTION

Strategy is about key issues for the future of organisations. For example, how should Google – originally a search company – manage its entry into the market for mobile phones? Should universities concentrate their resources on research excellence or teaching quality or try to combine both? How should a small video games producer relate to dominant console providers such as Nintendo and Sony? What should a rock band do to secure revenues in the face of declining CD sales?

All these are strategy questions. Naturally they concern entrepreneurs and senior managers at the top of their organisations. But these questions matter more widely. Middle managers also have to understand the strategic direction of their organisations, both to know how to get top management support for their initiatives and to explain their organisation's strategy to the people they are responsible for. Anybody looking for a management-track job needs to be ready to discuss strategy with their potential employer. Indeed, anybody taking a job should first be confident that their new employer's strategy is actually viable. There are even specialist career opportunities in strategy, for example as a strategy consultant or as an in-house strategic planner, often key roles for fast-track young managers.

This book takes a broad approach to strategy, looking at both the economics of strategy and the people side of managing strategy in practice. It is a book about 'Exploring', because the real world of strategy rarely offers obvious answers. In strategy, it is typically important to explore several options, probing each one carefully before making choices. The book is also relevant to any kind of organisation responsible for its own direction into the future. Thus the book refers to large private-sector multinationals and small entrepreneurial start-ups; to public-sector organisations such as schools and hospitals; and to not-for-profits such as charities or sports clubs. Strategy matters to almost all organisations, and to everybody working in them.

1.2 WHAT IS STRATEGY?[1]

In this book, **strategy is the long-term direction of an organisation**. Thus the long-term direction of Nokia is from mobile phones to mobile computing. The long-term direction of Disney is from cartoons to diversified entertainment. This section examines the practical implication of this definition of strategy; distinguishes between different levels of strategy; and explains how to summarise an organisation's strategy in a 'strategy statement'.

1.2.1 Defining strategy

Defining strategy as the long-term direction of an organisation implies a more comprehensive view than some influential definitions. Figure 1.1 (over page) shows the strategy definitions of three leading strategy theorists: Alfred Chandler and Michael Porter, both from the Harvard Business School, and Henry Mintzberg, from McGill University, Canada. Each points to important but distinct elements of strategy. Chandler emphasises a logical flow from the determination of goals and objectives to the allocation of resources. Porter focuses on deliberate choices, difference and competition. On the other hand, Mintzberg uses the word 'pattern' to allow for the fact that strategies do not always follow a deliberately chosen and logical plan, but can

Figure 1.1 Definitions of strategy

'the determination of the long-run goals and objectives of an enterprise and the adoption of courses of action and the allocation of resource necessary for carrying out these goals'

Alfred D. Chandler

'Competitive strategy is about being different. It means deliberately choosing a different set of activities to deliver a unique mix of value'

Michael Porter

'a pattern in a stream of decisions'

Henry Mintzberg

'the long-term direction of an organisation'

Exploring Strategy

Sources: A.D. Chandler, *Strategy and Structure: Chapters in the History of American Enterprise*, MIT Press, 1963, p. 13; M.E. Porter, 'What is strategy?', *Harvard Business Review*, 1996, November–December, p. 60; H. Mintzberg, *Tracking Strategy: Toward a General Theory*, Oxford University Press, 2007, p. 3.

emerge in more ad hoc ways. Sometimes strategies reflect a series of incremental decisions that only cohere into a recognisable pattern – or 'strategy' – after some time.

All of these strategy definitions incorporate important elements of strategy. However, this book's definition of strategy as 'the long-term direction of an organisation' has two advantages. First, the long-term direction of an organisation can include both deliberate, logical strategy and more incremental, emergent patterns of strategy. Second, long-term direction can include both strategies that emphasise difference and competition, and strategies that recognise the roles of cooperation and even imitation.

The three elements of this strategy definition – the long term, direction and organisation – can each be explored further. The strategy of News Corporation, owner of social networking company MySpace, illustrates important points (see Illustration 1.1):

● *The long term*. Strategies are typically measured over years, for some organisations a decade or more. The importance of a long-term perspective on strategy is emphasised by the 'three horizons' framework in Figure 1.2 (over page). The **three horizons framework suggests that every organisation should think of itself as comprising three types of business or activity, defined by their 'horizons' in terms of years.** *Horizon 1* businesses are basically the current core activities. In the case of News Corporation, Horizon 1 businesses include the original print newspapers. Horizon 1 businesses need defending and extending but the expectation is that in the long term they will likely be flat or declining in terms of profits (or whatever else the organisation values). *Horizon 2* businesses are emerging activities that should provide new sources of profit. In News Corporation, those include the various internet initiatives, principally MySpace. Finally, there are *Horizon 3* possibilities, for which nothing is sure.

ILLUSTRATION 1.1

MySpace becomes part of a bigger network

Social networking site MySpace presents opportunities and challenges for the global media conglomerate News Corporation.

The social networking site MySpace was founded in California in 2003 by MBA graduate Chris DeWolfe and rock musician Tom Anderson. From the first, the networking site was strong on music, and helped launch the careers of the Arctic Monkeys and Lily Allen. By 2005, it had 22 million members, with more page views than Google. That was the point when the multinational media conglomerate News Corporation bought it for $580m (€406m).

News Corporation started in Australia in the newspaper business, acquiring the *Times* newspaper group in the United Kingdom and the *Wall Street Journal* in the United States. It also diversified into television (for example Fox News and BSkyB) and film, including 20th Century Fox, responsible for the hit film *Avatar*. Its chairman is Rupert Murdoch, whose family owns a controlling interest: Rupert Murdoch's son James is expected to succeed him at the top.

In 2005, with media audiences increasingly moving to the internet, Rupert Murdoch declared his ambition to create 'a leading and profitable internet presence'. The acquisition of MySpace seemed a good fit. Chris DeWolfe and Tom Anderson were retained at the head of MySpace, but within a new division providing oversight for all News Corporation's internet interests. Ross Levinsohn, long-time News Corporation insider and head of the new division, told the *Financial Times*: 'The MySpace guys were really freaked out that we were going to come in and turn it into Fox News. One of the things we said was: "We're going to leave it alone"'.

Some adjustments had to be made. Tom Anderson told *Fortune* magazine: 'Before, I could do whatever I wanted. Now it takes more time to get people to agree on things. All the budget reviews and processes. That can be a pain. But it's not stopping us.' News Corporation was able to fund a more robust technology platform to cope with the thousands of new users MySpace was getting each day. In 2006, MySpace signed a three year advertising contract with Google worth $900m, which paid for the original acquisition with money left over. Executives summed up MySpace's distinctive positioning by saying: 'Your mom uses Facebook'.

But business then got tougher. Facebook overtook MySpace in terms of unique visitors in 2008. News Corporation executives complained about the excessive new initiatives at MySpace and the failure to prioritise: DeWolfe and Anderson were even considering launching their own film studio. Then Rupert Murdoch announced a target of $1bn in advertising revenues for 2008, without consulting DeWolfe. MySpace missed the target by about 10 per cent. The push from News Corporation to increase advertisements on MySpace, and a reluctance to remove pages with advertising from the site, began to make MySpace increasingly less attractive for users.

During 2009, MySpace's share of the social networking market fell to 30 per cent, from a peak of 66 per cent. The company missed the online traffic targets set by the Google contract. Losses were expected to be around $100m. In March, Chris DeWolfe was removed as Chief Executive of MySpace. The new Chief Executive was Alan Van Natta, from Facebook. Van Natta told the *Financial Times* that MySpace was no longer competing with Facebook: 'we're very focused on a different space . . . MySpace can foster discovery [of music, films and TV] in a way that others can't'.

Sources: M. Garnham, 'The rise and fall of MySpace', *Financial Times*, 4 December 2009; P. Sellers, 'MySpace Cowboys', *Fortune*, 29 August 2006; S. Rosenbusch, 'News Corp's Place in MySpace', *Business Week*, 19 July 2005.

Questions

1 How valuable is MySpace's distinctive position in the social networking market?

2 How should News Corporation have managed MySpace?

Figure 1.2 Three horizons for strategy

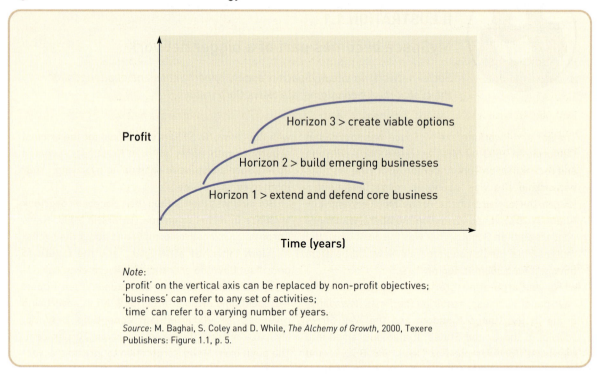

Note:
'profit' on the vertical axis can be replaced by non-profit objectives;
'business' can refer to any set of activities;
'time' can refer to a varying number of years.

Source: M. Baghai, S. Coley and D. While, *The Alchemy of Growth*, 2000, Texere
Publishers: Figure 1.1, p. 5.

These are typically risky Research & Development projects, start-up ventures, test-market pilots or similar, some of which may fuel growth in the future even if most are likely to fail. For a fast-moving internet organisation like MySpace, *Horizon 3* might only be a couple of years from the present time. In a pharmaceutical company, where the R&D and regulatory processes for a new drug take many years, *Horizon 3* might be a decade ahead. While timescales might differ, the basic point about the 'three horizons' framework is that managers need to avoid focusing on the short-term issues of their existing activities. Strategy involves pushing out Horizon 1 as far as possible, at the same time as looking to Horizons 2 and 3. Strategy for Horizons 2 and 3 will involve a good deal of *uncertainty*.

● *Strategic direction*. Over the years, strategies follow some kind of long-term direction or trajectory. The strategic direction of News Corporation is from print to internet media, as represented by MySpace. Sometimes a strategic direction only emerges as a coherent pattern over time. Typically, however, managers and entrepreneurs try to set the direction of their strategy according to long-term *objectives*. In private-sector businesses, the objective guiding strategic direction is usually maximising profits for shareholders. Thus Rupert Murdoch's acquisition of MySpace was driven by the objective to create a leading and profitable presence on the internet. However, profits do not always set strategic direction. First, public-sector and charity organisations may set their strategic direction according to other objectives: for example, a sports club's objective may be to move up from one league to a higher one. Second, even in the private sector profit is not always the sole criterion for strategy. Thus controlling families (such as perhaps News Corporation's Murdoch family) may sometimes sacrifice the maximisation of profits for family objectives, for example passing down the management of the business to the next generation. The objectives behind strategic direction always need close scrutiny.

- *Organisation.* In this book, organisations are not treated as discrete, unified entities. Organisations involve complex relationships, both internally and externally. This is because organisations typically have many internal and external *stakeholders*, in other words people and groups that depend on the organisation and upon which the organisation itself depends. Internally, organisations are filled with people, typically with diverse, competing and more or less reasonable views of what should be done. At MySpace, the News Corporation executives clashed over strategic direction with MySpace founder Chris DeWolfe. In strategy, therefore, it is always important to look *inside* organisations and to consider the people involved and their different interests and views. Externally, organisations are surrounded by important relationships, for example with suppliers, customers, alliance partners, regulators and shareholders. For MySpace, the relationship with Google was critical. Strategy therefore is also crucially concerned with an organisation's external *boundaries*: in other words, questions about what to include within the organisation and how to manage important relationships with what is kept outside.

Because strategy typically involves managing people, relationships and resources, the subject is sometimes called 'strategic management'. This book takes the view that managing is always important in strategy. Good strategy is about managing as well as strategising.

1.2.2 Levels of strategy

Inside an organisation, strategies can exist at three main levels. Again they can be illustrated by reference to MySpace and News Corporation (Illustration 1.1):

- **Corporate-level strategy is concerned with the overall scope of an organisation and how value is added to the constituent businesses of the organisational whole**. Corporate-level strategy issues include geographical scope, diversity of products or services, acquisitions of new businesses, and how resources are allocated between the different elements of the organisation. For News Corporation, diversifying from print journalism into television and social networking are corporate-level strategies. Being clear about corporate-level strategy is important: determining the range of businesses to include is the *basis* of other strategic decisions.

- **Business-level strategy is about how the individual businesses should compete in their particular markets** (for this reason, business-level strategy is often called 'competitive strategy'). These individual businesses might be stand-alone businesses, for instance entrepreneurial start-ups, or 'business units' within a larger corporation (as MySpace and Fox are inside News Corporation). Business-level strategy typically concerns issues such as innovation, appropriate scale and response to competitors' moves. In the public sector, the equivalent of business-level strategy is decisions about how units (such as individual hospitals or schools) should provide best-value services. Where the businesses are units within a larger organisation, business-level strategies should clearly fit with corporate-level strategy.

- **Operational strategies are concerned with how the components of an organisation deliver effectively the corporate- and business-level strategies in terms of resources, processes and people**. For example, MySpace engineers had to keep developing enough processing capacity to cope with the strategy of rapid growth. In most businesses, successful business strategies depend to a large extent on decisions that are taken, or activities that occur, at the operational level. Operational decisions need therefore to be closely linked to business-level strategy. They are vital to successful strategy implementation.

This need to link the corporate, business and operational levels underlines the importance of *integration* in strategy. Each level needs to be aligned with the others. The demands of integrating levels define an important characteristic of strategy. Strategy is typically *complex*, requiring careful and sensitive management. Strategy is rarely simple.

1.2.3 Strategy statements

David Collis and Michael Rukstad[2] at the Harvard Business School argue that all entrepreneurs and managers should be able to summarise their organisation's strategy with a 'strategy statement'. **Strategy statements** **should have three main themes: the fundamental *goals* that the organisation seeks, which typically draw on the organisation's stated mission, vision and objectives; the *scope* or domain of the organisation's activities; and the particular *advantages* or capabilities it has to deliver all of these**. These various contributing elements of a strategy statement are explained as follows, with examples in Illustration 1.2:

- *Mission*. This relates to goals, and refers to the overriding purpose of the organisation. It is sometimes described in terms of the apparently simple but challenging question: '*what business are we in?*'. The mission statement helps keep managers focused on what is central to their strategy.

- *Vision*. This too relates to goals, and refers to the desired future state of the organisation. It is an aspiration which can help mobilise the energy and passion of organisational members. The vision statement, therefore, should answer the question: '*what do we want to achieve?*'.

- *Objectives*. These are more precise and ideally quantifiable statements of the organisation's goals over some period of time. Objectives might refer to profitability or market share targets for a private company, or to examination results in a school. Objectives introduce discipline to strategy. The question here is: '*what do we have to achieve in the coming period?*'.

- *Scope*. An organisation's scope or domain refers to three dimensions: customers or clients; geographical location; and extent of internal activities ('vertical integration'). For a university, scope questions are twofold: first, which academic departments to have (a business school, an engineering department and so on); second, which activities to do internally themselves (vertically integrate) and which to externalise to subcontractors (for example, whether to manage campus restaurants in-house or to subcontract them).

- *Advantage*. This part of a strategy statement describes how the organisation will achieve the objectives it has set for itself in its chosen domain. In competitive environments, this refers to the *competitive* advantage: for example, how a particular company or sports club will achieve goals in the face of competition from other companies or clubs. In order to achieve a particular goal, the organisation needs to be better than others seeking the same goal. In the public sector, advantage might refer simply to the organisation's capability in general. But even public-sector organisations frequently need to show that their capabilities are not only adequate, but superior to other rival departments or perhaps to private-sector contractors.

Collis and Rukstad suggest that strategy statements covering goals, scope and advantage should be no more than 35 words long. Shortness keeps such statements focused on the essentials and makes them easy to remember and communicate. Thus for News Corporation, a strategy statement might be: 'to build a leading and profitable presence in both old and new media, drawing on competitive advantages in terms of the scale, diversity and international

ILLUSTRATION 1.2

Strategy statements

Both Nokia, the Finnish telecommunications giant, and University College Cork, based in the West of Ireland, publish a good deal about their strategies.

Nokia Vision and Strategy

Our vision is a world where everyone can be connected. Our promise is to help people feel close to what is important to them.

The businesses of Nokia

- Compelling consumer solutions with devices and services
- Strong infrastructure business with Siemens Networks

Our competitive advantage is based on scale, brand and services

- Scale-based assets and capabilities
- Leading brand
- Build further competitive advantage by differentiating our offering through services

Our business strategy

- Maximize Nokia's lifetime value to consumer
- Best mobile devices everywhere
  - Take share and drive value across price brands and geographies
  - Enhance and capture market growth in emerging markets
- Context-enriched services
  - Take share of the internet services market by delivering winning solutions
  - Take share of business mobility market

University College Cork (UCC), Strategic Plan 2009–2012

University College Cork (UCC) . . . is sited in Ireland's second city . . . UCC's motto *'Where Finbarr taught let Munster learn'* binds us to the sixth-century monastery and place of learning established by St. Finbarr . . . UCC was established in 1845 as one of three Queen's Colleges . . . The campus today is home to over 18,000 students including 2,000 international students from 93 countries. . . . A third of our staff are from overseas. Our strategic alliances with world-ranking universities in Asia, Europe and North America ensure that we learn from and contribute to the best standards of teaching, learning and research.

Vision

To be a world-class university that links the region to the globe.

Mission

In an environment which gives parity of esteem to teaching, learning and research and where students are our highest priority, the University's central roles are to create, preserve and communicate knowledge and to enhance intellectual, cultural, social and economic life locally, regionally and globally.

Targets by 2012 (selected from 'Teaching, Learning and the Student Experience')

- Achieve a first year retention rate of 93% or greater
- Increase the proportion of students at post-graduate level from 19% to 30%
- Increase flexible/part-time provision to 15% of undergraduate entrants

Sources: www.nokia.com; www.ucc.ie.

Questions

1 Construct short strategy statements covering the goals, scope and advantage of Nokia and University College Cork. How much do the different contexts matter?

2 Construct a strategy statement for your own organisation (university or employer). What implications might this statement have for your particular course or department?

range of our businesses'. The strategy statement of American financial advisory firm Edward Jones is more specific: 'to grow to 17,000 financial advisers by 2012 by offering trusted and convenient face-to-face financial advice to conservative individual investors through a national network of one-financial adviser offices'. Of course, such strategy statements are not always fulfilled. Circumstances may change in unexpected ways. In the meantime, however, they can provide a useful guide both to managers in their decision-making and to employees and others who need to understand the direction in which the organisation is going. The ability to give a clear strategy statement is a good test of managerial competence in an organisation.

As such, strategy statements are relevant to a wide range of organisations. For example, a small entrepreneurial start-up will need a strategy statement to persuade investors and lenders of its viability. Public-sector organisations need strategy statements not only for themselves, but to reassure external clients, funders and regulators that their priorities are the right ones. Voluntary organisations need to communicate persuasive strategy statements in order to inspire volunteers and donors. Thus organisations of all kinds frequently publish materials relevant to such strategy statements on their websites or annual reports. Illustration 1.2 provides published materials on the strategies of two very different organisations: the technology giant Nokia from the private sector and the medium-sized University College Cork from the public sector.

(1.3) WORKING WITH STRATEGY

A theme so far is that almost all managers are concerned with strategy to some extent or another. Strategy is certainly a key issue for top management, but it is not just their preserve. Middle and lower-level managers have to meet the objectives set by their organisation's strategy and observe the constraints imposed by it. Managers have to communicate strategy to their teams, and will achieve greater performance from them the more convincing they are in doing so. Indeed, as responsibility is increasingly decentralised in many organisations, middle and lower-level managers play a growing part in shaping strategy themselves. Because they are closer to the daily realities of the business, lower-level managers can be a crucial source of ideas and feedback for senior management teams. Being able to participate in an organisation's 'strategic conversation' – engaging with senior managers on the big issues facing them – is therefore often part of what it takes to win promotion.[3]

Strategy, then, is part of many managers' work. However, there are specialist strategists as well, in both private and public sectors. Many large organisations have in-house strategic planning or analyst roles.[4] Typically requiring a formal business education of some sort, strategic planning is a potential career route for many readers of this book, especially after some operational experience. Strategy consulting has been a growth industry in the last decades, with the original leading firms such as McKinsey & Co., the Boston Consulting Group and Bain joined now by more generalist consultants such as Accenture, IBM Consulting and PwC, each with its own strategy consulting arm.[5] Again, business graduates are in demand for strategy consulting roles.[6]

The interviews in Illustration 1.3 (see over page) give some insights into the different kinds of strategy work that managers and strategy specialists can do. Galina, the manager of an international subsidiary, Masoud, working in a governmental strategy unit, and Chantal, a strategy consultant, all have different experiences of strategy, but there are some common themes also. All find strategy work stimulating and rewarding. The two specialists, Masoud and Chantal, talk more than Galina of analytical tools such as scenario analysis, sensitivity analysis and hypothesis testing. Galina discovered directly the practical challenges of real-world strategic planning, having to adapt the plan during the first few years in the United Kingdom. She emphasises the importance of flexibility in strategy and the value of getting her managers to see the 'whole picture' through involving them in strategy-making. But Masoud and Chantal too are concerned with much more than just analysis. Chantal emphasises the importance of gaining 'traction' with clients, building consensus in order to ensure implementation. Masoud likewise does not take implementation for granted, continuing to work with departments after the delivery of recommendations. He sees strategy and delivery as intimately connected, with people involved in delivery needing an understanding of strategy to be effective, and strategists needing to understand delivery. For him, strategy is a valuable stepping-stone in a career, something that will underpin his possible next move into a more operational role.

Strategy, therefore, is not just about abstract organisations: it is a kind of work that real people do. An important aim of this book is to equip readers to do this work better.

(1.4) STUDYING STRATEGY

This book is both comprehensive and serious about strategy. To understand the full range of strategy issues, it is important to be open to the perspectives and insights of many academic disciplines, particularly economics, sociology and psychology. To be serious about strategy means to draw as far as possible on rigorous research about these issues. This book aims for an evidence-based approach to strategy, hence the articles and books referenced at the end of each chapter.[7]

This book therefore covers equally the three main branches of strategy as a subject: strategy *context*, strategy *content* and strategy *process*. Each of these is important to effective strategy-making, and each is underpinned by research streams whose characteristic analytical approaches can be applied to practical strategy issues as well. Figure 1.3 shows the three branches and the respective research streams: these are listed in the approximate historical order of their emergence as strong research streams, the arrows representing the continuously

Figure 1.3 Strategy's three branches

Context (internal and external)	Content (strategic options)	Process (formation and implementation)
Research: Industry analysis Cultural analysis Resource-based view	**Research:** Choice and performance	**Research:** Strategic planning Choice and change Strategy-as-practice

ILLUSTRATION 1.3

Strategists

For Galina, Masoud and Chantal, strategy is a large part of their jobs.

Galina

After a start in marketing, Galina became managing director of the British subsidiary of a Russian information technology company at the age of 33. As well as developing the strategy for her local business, she has to interact regularly with the Moscow headquarters:

'Moscow is interested in the big picture, not just the details. They are interested in the future of the business.'

The original strategic plans for the subsidiary had had to be adapted heavily:

'When we first came here, we had some ideas about strategy, but soon found the reality was very different to the plans. The strategy was not completely wrong, but in the second stage we had to change it a lot: we had to change techniques and adapt to the market. Now we are in the third stage, where we have the basics and need to focus on trends, to get ahead and be in the right place at the right time.'

Galina works closely with her management team on strategy, taking them on an annual 'strategy away-day' (see Chapter 15):

'Getting people together helps them see the whole picture, rather than just the bits they are responsible for. It is good to put all their separate realities together.'

Galina is enthusiastic about working on strategy:

'I like strategy work, definitely. The most exciting thing is to think about where we have come from and where we might be going. We started in a pub five years ago and we have somehow implemented what we were hoping for then. Strategy gives you a measure of success. It tells you how well you have done.'

Her advice is:

'Always have a strategy – have an ultimate idea in mind. But take feedback from the market and from your colleagues. Be ready to adjust the strategy: the adjustment is the most important.'

Masoud

Aged 27, Masoud is a policy advisor in a central government strategy unit in the United Kingdom. He provides analysis and advice for ministers, often on a cross-departmental basis. He typically works on projects for several months at a time, continuing to work with responsible service departments after the delivery of recommendations. Projects involve talking to experts inside and outside government, statistical analysis, scenario analyses (see Chapter 2), sensitivity analyses (see Chapter 11), hypothesis testing (see Chapter 15) and writing reports and making presentations. As he has progressed, Masoud has become increasingly involved in the management of strategy projects, rather than the basic analysis itself.

Masoud explains what he likes most about strategy work in government:

developing nature of each. In more detail, the three branches and the characteristic analytical approaches of their main research streams are as follows:

- *Strategy context* refers to both the internal and the external contexts of organisations. All organisations need to take into account the opportunities and threats of their external environments. *Industry analysis* took off as a research tradition in the early 1980s, when Michael Porter showed how the tools of economics could be applied to understanding what makes industries attractive (or unattractive) to operate in.[8] From the 1980s too, *cultural*

'I like most the challenge. It's working on issues that really matter, and often it's what you are reading about in the newspapers. They are really tough issues; these are problems facing the whole of society.'

He thinks people should get involved in strategy:

'I would encourage people to do strategy, because it gets to the heart of problems. In all organisations, having some experience of working on strategy is very valuable, even if it is not what you want to major on your whole career.'

Masoud is considering moving into service delivery as the next step of his career, because he sees knowledge of strategy and knowledge of operations as so interconnected:

'Part of doing strategy is you have to understand what can be delivered; and part of doing delivery is you have to understand the strategy.'

Chantal

Chantal is in her early thirties and has worked in Paris for one of the top three international strategy consultancies since graduating in business. Consulting was attractive to her originally because she liked the idea of helping organisations improve. She chose her particular consultancy because

'I had fun in the interview rounds and the people were inspiring. I pictured myself working with these kinds of topics and with these kinds of people.'

Chantal enjoys strategy consulting:

'What I like is solving problems. It's a bit like working on a mystery case: you have a problem and then you have to find a solution to fit the company, and help it grow and to be better.'

The work is intellectually challenging:

'Time horizons are short. You have to solve your case in two to three months. There's lots of pressure. It pushes you and helps you to learn yourself. There are just three to four in a team, so you will make a significant contribution to the project even as a junior. You have a lot of autonomy and you're making a contribution right from the start, and at quite a high level.'

Consulting work can involve financial and market modelling (see Chapters 2 and 11), interviewing clients and customers, and working closely with the client's own teams. Chantal explains:

'As a consultant, you spend a lot of time in building solid fact-based arguments that will help clients make business decisions. But as well as the facts, you have to have the ability to get traction. People have to agree, so you have to build consensus, to make sure that recommendations are supported and acted on.'

Chantal summarises the appeal of strategy consulting:

'I enjoy the learning, at a very high speed. There's the opportunity to increase your skills. One year in consulting is like two years in a normal business.'

Source: interviews (interviewees anonymised).

Questions

1 Which of these strategy roles appeals to you most – manager of a business unit in a multinational, in-house strategy specialist or strategy consultant? Why?

2 What would you have to do to get such a role?

---

analysts have used sociological insights into human behaviour to point to the importance of shared cultural understandings about appropriate ways of acting. In the internal context, cultural analysts show that strategies are often influenced by the organisation's specific culture. In the external context, they show how strategies often have to fit with the surrounding industry or national cultures. *Resource-based view* researchers focus on internal context, looking for the unique characteristics of each organisation.[9] According to the resource-based view, the economic analysis of market imperfections, the psychological analysis of perceptual or emotional biases, and the sociological analysis of organisational cultures should reveal the particular characteristics (resources) that contribute to an organisation's specific competitive advantages and disadvantages.

- *Strategy content* concerns the content (or nature) of different strategies and their probability of success. Here the focus is on the merits of different strategic options. *Strategy and Performance* researchers started by using economic analysis to understand the success of different types of diversification strategies. This research continues as the enduring central core of the strategy discipline, with an ever-growing list of issues addressed. For example, contemporary Strategy and Performance researchers examine various new innovation strategies, different kinds of internationalisation and all the complex kinds of alliance and networking strategies organisations adopt today. These researchers typically bring a tough economic scrutiny to strategy options. Their aim is to establish which types of strategies pay best and under what conditions. They refuse to take for granted broad generalisations about what makes a good strategy.

- *Strategy process*, broadly conceived, examines how strategies are formed and implemented. Research here provides a range of insights to help managers in the practical processes of managing strategy.[10] From the 1960s, researchers in the *Strategic Planning* tradition have drawn from economics and management science in order to design rational and analytical systems for the planning and implementing of strategy. However, strategy involves people: since the 1980s, *Choice and Change* researchers have been pointing to how the psychology of human perception and emotions, and the sociology of group politics and interests, tend to undermine rational analysis. The advice of these researchers is to accept the irrational, messy realities of organisations, and to work with them, rather than to try to impose textbook rationality. Finally, *Strategy-as-Practice* researchers have recently been using micro-sociological approaches to closely examine the human realities of formal and informal strategy processes.[11] This tradition focuses attention on how people do strategy work, and the importance of having the right tools and skills.

From the above, it should be clear that studying strategy involves perspectives and insights from a range of academic disciplines. Issues need to be 'explored' from different points of view. A strategy chosen purely on economic grounds can easily be undermined by psychological and sociological factors. On the other hand, a strategy that is chosen on the psychological grounds of emotional enthusiasm, or for sociological reasons of cultural acceptability, is liable to fail if not supported by favourable economics. As underlined by the four strategy lenses to be introduced later, one perspective is rarely enough for good strategy. A complete analysis will typically need the insights of economics, psychology and sociology.

THE *EXPLORING STRATEGY* MODEL

This book is structured around a three-part model that encompasses issues of context, content and process equally. **The *Exploring Strategy* Model** includes understanding *the strategic position* of an organisation (context); assessing *strategic choices* for the future (content); and managing *strategy in action* (process). Figure 1.4 shows these elements and defines the broad coverage of this book. Together, the three elements provide a practical template for studying strategic situations. The following sections of this chapter will introduce the strategic issues that arise under each of these elements of the Exploring Strategy Model. But first it is important to understand why the model is drawn in this particular way.

Figure 1.4 The *Exploring Strategy* Model

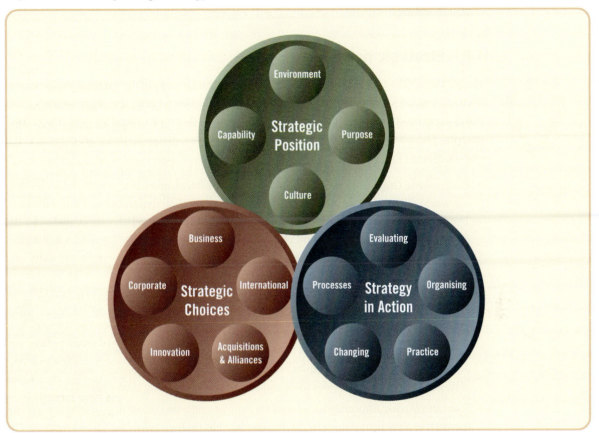

Figure 1.4 could have shown the model's three elements in a linear sequence – first understanding the strategic position, then making strategic choices and finally turning strategy into action. Indeed, this logical sequence is implicit in the definition of strategy given by Alfred Chandler (Figure 1.1) and many other textbooks on strategy. However, as Henry Mintzberg recognises, in practice the elements of strategy do not always follow this linear sequence. Choices often have to be made before the position is fully understood. Sometimes too a proper understanding of the strategic position can only be built from the experience of trying a strategy out in action. The real-world feedback which comes from launching a new product is often far better at uncovering the true strategic position than remote analysis carried out in a strategic planning department at head office.

The interconnected circles of Figure 1.4 are designed to emphasise this potentially non-linear nature of strategy. Position, choices and action should be seen as closely related, and in practice none has priority over another. It is only for structural convenience that this book divides its subject matter into three sections; the book's sequence is not meant to suggest that the process of strategy must follow a logical path of distinct steps. The three circles are overlapping and non-linear. The evidence provided in later chapters will suggest that strategy rarely occurs in tidy ways and that it is better not to expect it to do so.

However, the Exploring Strategy Model does provide a comprehensive and integrated framework for analysing an organisation's position, considering the choices it has and putting strategies into action. Each of the chapters can be seen as asking fundamental strategy questions and providing the essential concepts and techniques to help answer them. Working systematically through questions and answers provides the basis for persuasive strategy recommendations.

1.5.1 Strategic position

The strategic position is concerned with the impact on strategy of the external environment, the organisation's strategic capability (resources and competences), the organisation's goals and the organisation's culture. Understanding these four factors is central for evaluating future strategy. These issues, and the fundamental questions associated with them, are covered in the four chapters of Part I of this book:

- *Environment*. Organisations operate in a complex political, economic, social and technological world. These environments vary widely in terms of their dynamism and attractiveness. The fundamental question here relates to the *opportunities* and *threats* available to the organisation in this complex and changing environment. Chapter 2 provides key frameworks to help in focusing on priority issues in the face of environmental complexity and dynamism.

- *Strategic capability*. Each organisation has its own strategic capabilities, made up of its *resources* (e.g. machines and buildings) and *competences* (e.g. technical and managerial skills). The fundamental question on capability regards the organisation's *strengths* and *weaknesses* (for example, where is it at a competitive advantage or disadvantage?). Are the organisation's capabilities adequate to the challenges of its environment and the demands of its goals? Chapter 3 provides tools and concepts for analysing such capabilities.

- *Strategic purpose*. Although sometimes unclear or contested, most organisations claim for themselves a particular purpose, as encapsulated in their *vision, mission* and *objectives*. The strategic purpose is a key criterion against which strategies must be evaluated. The third fundamental question therefore is: what is the organisation's strategic purpose; what does it seek to achieve? Here the issue of *corporate governance* is important: which stakeholders does the organisation primarily serve and how should managers be held accountable for this? Questions of purpose and accountability raise issues of *corporate social responsibility* and *ethics*: is the purpose an appropriate one and are managers achieving it? Chapter 4 provides concepts for addressing these issues of purpose.

- *Culture*. Organisational cultures can also influence strategy. So can the cultures of a particular industry or particular country. The impact of these influences can be *strategic drift*, a failure to create necessary change. The fundamental question here, therefore, is: how does culture shape strategy? Answering this typically requires an understanding of the organisation's *history*. Chapter 5 demonstrates how managers can analyse, challenge and sometimes turn to their advantage the various cultural influences on strategy.

Applying the Exploring Strategy Model to the positioning of News Corporation (Illustration 1.1) raises the following issues. News Corporation was threatened by an environmental shift from print to the internet. It also lacked the capabilities to develop a social networking business on its own. The company was determined to grow its internet business fast, setting demanding goals that MySpace struggled to meet. Finally, there appeared to be culture clashes between the traditional family-owned conglomerate and the young entrepreneurial start-up.

1.5.2 Strategic choices

Strategic choices involve the options for strategy in terms of both the *directions* in which strategy might move and the *methods* by which strategy might be pursued. For instance, an organisation might have a range of strategic directions open to it: the organisation could diversify into new products; it could enter new international markets; or it could transform its existing products and markets through radical innovation. These various directions could be pursued by different methods: the organisation could acquire a business already active in the product or market area; it could form alliances with relevant organisations that might help its new strategy; or it could try to pursue its strategies on its own. Typical strategic choices, and the related fundamental questions, are covered in the five chapters that make up Part II of this book, as follows:

- *Business strategy*. There are strategic choices in terms of how the organisation seeks to compete at the individual *business level*. Typically these choices involve strategies based on *cost* (for example, economies of scale) or *differentiation* (for example, superior quality). Crucial is deciding how to win against competitors (for this reason, business strategy is sometimes called 'competitive strategy'). The fundamental question here, then, is how should the business unit compete? Key dilemmas for business-level strategy, and ways of resolving them, are discussed in Chapter 6.

- *Corporate strategy and diversification*. The highest level of an organisation is typically concerned with corporate-level strategy, focused on questions of portfolio scope. The fundamental question in corporate-level strategy is therefore which businesses to include in the portfolio. This relates to the appropriate degree of *diversification*, in other words the spread of products and markets. Corporate-level strategy is also concerned both with the relationship between the various businesses that make up the corporate portfolio of the business and with how the corporate 'parent' (owner) adds value to the individual businesses. Chapter 7 provides tools for assessing diversification strategies and the appropriate relationships within the corporate portfolio.

- *International strategy*. Internationalisation is a form of diversification, but into new geographical markets. It is often at least as challenging as product or service diversification. Here the fundamental question is: where internationally should the organisation compete? Chapter 8 examines how to prioritise various international options and identifies key methods for pursuing them: export, licensing, direct investment and acquisition.

- *Innovation and entrepreneurship*. Most existing organisations have to innovate constantly simply to survive. Entrepreneurship, the creation of a new enterprise, is an act of innovation too. A fundamental question, therefore, is whether the organisation is innovating appropriately. Chapter 9 considers key choices about innovation and entrepreneurship, and helps in selecting between them.

- *Acquisitions and alliances*. Organisations have to make choices about methods for pursuing their strategies. Many organisations prefer to grow 'organically', in other words by building new businesses with their own resources. Other organisations might develop through mergers and acquisitions or strategic alliances with other organisations. The fundamental question here, then, is whether to buy another company, ally or to go it alone. How to choose between these alternative methods is discussed in Chapter 10.

Again, issues of strategic choice are live in the case of News Corporation and MySpace (Illustration 1.1). The Exploring Strategy Model asks the following kinds of questions here. Should MySpace compete against Facebook by emphasising its music strengths? Should a newspaper company try to enter the new social networking market and, if it does, is an acquisition the best method? How should News Corporation add value to its entrepreneurial new business? And should MySpace be allowed to continue to innovate in its old loosely disciplined style?

1.5.3 Strategy in action

Managing strategy in action is about how strategies are formed and how they are implemented. The emphasis is on the practicalities of managing. These issues are covered in the five chapters of Part III, and include the following, each with their own fundamental questions:

- *Strategy evaluation*. Once a set of strategic options has been established, it is time to evaluate their relative merits. The fundamental evaluation questions are as follows: are the options *suitable* in terms of matching opportunities and threats; are they *acceptable* in the eyes of significant stakeholders; and are they *feasible* in terms of the *capabilities* the organisation has available? Chapter 11 introduces a range of financial and non-financial techniques for evaluating suitability, acceptability and feasibility.

- *Strategy development processes*. Strategies are often developed through formal *planning* processes. However, while formal planning is important, in practice the strategies an organisation actually pursues are often *emergent* – in other words, accumulated patterns of ad hoc decisions, bottom-up initiatives and rapid responses to the unanticipated. Given the scope for emergence, the fundamental question is: what kind of strategy process should an organisation have? Should it try to plan strategy in detail or should it leave plenty of opportunities for emergence? Chapter 12 considers how strategic planning processes should be designed and the degree to which organisations should allow for other processes of strategy development.

- *Organising*. Once a strategy is developed, the organisation needs to organise for successful implementation. Each strategy requires its own specific configuration of *structures* and *systems*. The fundamental question, therefore, is: what kinds of structures and systems are required for the chosen strategy? Chapter 13 introduces a range of structures and systems and provides frameworks for deciding between them.

- *Leadership and strategic change*. In a dynamic world, strategy inevitably involves change. Managing change involves *leadership*, both at the top of the organisation and lower down. There is not just one way of leading change, however: there are different *styles* and different *levers* for change. So the fundamental question is: how should the organisation manage necessary changes entailed by the strategy? Chapter 14 therefore examines options for leading and managing change, and considers how to choose between them.

- *Strategy practice*. Inside the broad processes of strategy development and change is a lot of hard, detailed work. The fundamental question in managing this work is: who should do what in the strategy process? Chapter 15 thus provides guidance on which *people* should be included in the process; what *activities* they have to do; and which *methodologies* can help them do it. These kinds of practicalities are a fitting end to the book and essential equipment for those who will have to go out and participate in strategy work themselves.

Table 1.1 The strategy checklist

Fourteen fundamental questions in strategy		
Strategic position	**Strategic choices**	**Strategy in action**
• What are the environmental opportunities and threats? • What are the organisation's strengths and weaknesses? • What is the basic purpose of the organisation? • How does culture shape strategy?	• How should business units compete? • Which businesses to include in a portfolio? • Where should the organisation compete internationally? • Is the organisation innovating appropriately? • Should the organisation buy other companies, ally or go it alone?	• Which strategies are suitable, acceptable *and* feasible? • What kind of strategy-making process is needed? • What are the required organisation structures and systems? • How should the organisation manage necessary changes? • Who should do what in the strategy process?

With regard to strategy-in-action, the Exploring Strategy Model raises the following kinds of questions for News Corporation and MySpace. Should MySpace move towards a more disciplined strategy development process? Was it wise to organise MySpace under the authority of a divisional head responsible for all the existing internet businesses of News Corporation? Was this divisional head, Ross Levinson, the right person to provide leadership to the entrepreneurial MySpace? Which change levers were available to the new Chief Executive from Facebook, Alan Van Natta?

Thus the Exploring Strategy Model offers a comprehensive framework for analysing an organisation's position, considering alternative choices, and selecting and implementing strategies. In this sense, the fundamental questions in each chapter provide a comprehensive checklist for strategy. These fundamental questions are summed up in Table 1.1. Any assessment of an organisation's strategy will benefit from asking these questions systematically. The frameworks for answering these and related questions can be found in the respective chapters.

The logic of the Exploring Strategy Model can be applied to our personal lives as much as to organisations. We all have to make decisions with long-run consequences for our futures and the issues involved are very similar. For example, in pursuing a career strategy, a job-seeker needs to understand the job market, evaluate their strengths and weaknesses, establish the range of job opportunities and decide what their career goals really are (positioning issues). The job-seeker then chooses particular jobs and makes some applications (choice issues). Finally, the job-seeker takes a job and starts to work for their next promotion or job move (strategy-in-action). Just as in the non-linear, overlapping Exploring Strategy Model, work experience will frequently amend the original strategic goals. Putting a career strategy into action produces better understanding of strengths and weaknesses and frequently leads to the setting of new ambitions.

1.5.4 Exploring strategy in different contexts

The Exploring Strategy Model can be applied in many contexts, though in each context the typical balance of strategic issues may differ. For example, just within News Corporation

(Illustration 1.1), fast-growing challenger MySpace is likely to have quite different issues from static traditional newspapers such as *The Times*, even though both businesses are dealing with the internet. In applying the Exploring Strategy Model, it is therefore useful to ask what kinds of issues are likely to be particularly significant in the specific context being considered. To illustrate this general point, this section shows how issues arising from the Exploring Strategy Model can vary in three important contexts.

- *Small businesses.* With regard to positioning, small businesses will certainly need to attend closely to the environment, because they are so vulnerable to change. But, especially in small entrepreneurial and family businesses, the most important positioning issue will often be strategic purpose: this will not necessarily just be profit, but might include objectives such as independence, family control, handing over to the next generation and maybe even a pleasant lifestyle. The range of strategic choices is likely to be narrower: it is rare for a small business to make an acquisition itself, though small businesses may have to decide whether to allow themselves to be acquired by another business (as MySpace was). Some issues of strategy-in-action will be different, for example strategic change processes will not involve exactly the same challenges as for large, complex organisations.

- *Multinational corporations.* In this context, positioning in a complex global marketplace will be very important. Each significant geographical market may call for a separate analysis of the business environment. Likewise, operating in many different countries will raise positioning issues of culture: variations in national culture imply different demands in the marketplace and different managerial styles internally. Strategic choices are likely to be dominated by international strategy questions about which geographies to serve. The scale and geographical reach of most multinationals point to significant issues for strategy-in-action, particularly those of organisational structure and strategic change.

- *Public sector and not-for-profits.* Positioning issues of competitive advantage will be important even in these contexts. Charitable not-for-profits typically compete for funds from donors; public-sector organisations, such as schools and hospitals, often compete on measures such as quality or service. The positioning issue of purpose is likely to be very important too. In the absence of a clear, focused objective such as profit, purpose in the public sector and not-for-profits can be ambiguous and contentious. Strategic choice issues may be narrower than in the private sector: for example, there may be constraints on diversification. Strategy-in-action issues often need close attention, leadership and strategic change typically being very challenging in large public-sector organisations.

In short, while drawing on the same basic principles, strategy analysis is likely to vary in focus across different contexts. As the next section will indicate, it is often helpful therefore to apply different lenses to strategy problems.

1.6 THE STRATEGY LENSES

KEY CONCEPT

www.pearsoned.co.uk/mystrategylab

Strategy lenses

Exploring means looking for new and different things. Exploring strategy involves searching for new angles on strategic problems. A comprehensive assessment of an organisation's strategy needs more than one perspective. **The strategy lenses are ways of looking at strategy issues differently in order to generate many insights.** Looking at problems in different ways will raise new issues and new solutions. Thus, although the lenses are drawn from academic research on strategy, they should also be highly practical in the job of doing strategy.

The four lenses are introduced more fully immediately after this chapter and will provide the framework for separate *commentaries* on each of the three parts of this book. This section introduces them briefly as follows:

- *Strategy as design.* This takes the view that strategy development can be 'designed' in the abstract, as an architect might design a building using pens, rulers and paper. The architect designs, and then hands over the plans for the builders actually to build. This design lens on strategy encourages a large investment in planning and analysis before making final decisions. It tends to exclude improvisation in strategy development and underplay the unpredictable, conservative or political aspects of human organisations. Taking a design lens to a strategic problem means being systematic, analytical and logical.

- *Strategy as experience.* The experience lens recognises that the future strategy of an organisation is often heavily influenced by its experience and that of its managers. Here strategies are seen as driven not so much by clear-cut analysis as by the taken-for-granted assumptions and ways of doing things embedded in people's personal experience and the organisational culture. Strategy is likely to build on and continue what has gone on before. Insofar as different views and expectations within the organisation exist, they will be resolved not through rational optimisation, as in the design lens, but through messy compromises and ad hoc deals. The experience lens suggests that the personal experience and interests of key decision-makers need to be understood. It sets low expectations of radical change.

- *Strategy as variety.*[12] Neither of the above lenses is likely to uncover radical new ideas in strategy. Design approaches risk being too rigid and top-down; experience builds too much on the past. How then are radical new ideas discovered? The variety lens sees strategy not so much as planned from the top as emergent from within and around organisations as people respond to an uncertain and changing environment with a variety of initiatives. New ideas bubble up through unpredictable and competitive processes. The variety lens therefore emphasises the importance of promoting diversity in and around organisations, in order to allow the seeding of as many genuinely new ideas as possible. Somebody with a variety lens would look for future strategies at the bottom and the periphery of organisations. They should be ready for surprises.

- *Strategy as discourse.* Managers spend most of their time talking, persuading and negotiating. They are always using language, or what is here called 'discourse'. The discourse lens points to how command of strategy discourse becomes a resource for managers by which to shape 'objective' strategic analyses to their personal views and to gain influence, power and legitimacy. Treating strategy as a discourse focuses attention on the ways managers use language to frame strategic problems, make strategy proposals, debate issues and then finally communicate strategic decisions. For believers in the discourse lens, strategy 'talk' matters. The discourse lens tries to look under the surface of strategy to uncover the personal interests and politicking in organisations. Taking a discourse lens thus encourages a somewhat sceptical view.

None of these lenses is likely to offer a complete view of a strategic situation. The point of the lenses is to encourage the exploration of different perspectives: to look at the situation first from one point of view (perhaps design) and then from another. These lenses help in recognising how otherwise logical strategic initiatives might be held back by cultural experience; in checking for unexpected ideas from the bottom or the periphery of the organisation; and in seeing through the formal strategy discourse to ask whose interests are really being served.

SUMMARY

- Strategy is the long-term direction of an organisation. A 'strategy statement' should cover the *goals* of an organisation, the *scope* of the organisation's activities and the *advantages* or *capabilities* the organisation brings to these goals and activities.

- *Corporate-level strategy* is concerned with an organisation's overall scope; *business-level strategy* is concerned with how to compete; and *operational strategy* is concerned with how resources, processes and people deliver corporate- and business-level strategies.

- Strategy work is done by *managers* throughout an organisation, as well as specialist *strategic planners* and *strategy consultants*.

- Research on strategy *context*, *content* and *process* shows how the analytical perspectives of economics, sociology and psychology can all provide practical insights for approaching strategy issues

- The Exploring Strategy Model has three major elements: understanding the *strategic position*, making *strategic choices* for the future and managing *strategy-in-action*.

- Strategic issues are best seen from a variety of perspectives, as exemplified by the four *strategy lenses* of *design, experience, variety* and *discourse*.

WORK ASSIGNMENTS

✳ *Denotes more advanced work assignments.* * *Refers to a case study in the Text and Cases edition.*

1.1 Drawing on Figure 1.2 as a guide, write a strategy statement for an organisation of your choice (for example, your university), drawing on strategy materials in the organisation's annual report or website.

1.2 Using the *Exploring Strategy* Model of Figure 1.4, map key issues relating to strategic position, strategic choices and strategy into action for either the Lego case* or an organisation with which you are familiar (for example, your university).

1.3 Go to the website of one of the major strategy consultants such as Bain, the Boston Consulting Group or McKinsey & Co. (see reference 5 below). What does the website tell you about the nature of strategy consulting work? Would you enjoy that work?

1.4✳ Using Figure 1.3 as a guide, show how the elements of strategic management differ in:

    (a) a small business (e.g. Ekomate*, Leax* or Web Reservations*)

    (b) a large multinational business (e.g. Marks & Spencer*, SABMiller*, Sony*)

    (c) a non-profit organisation (e.g. NHS Direct* or Queensland Rail*).

RECOMMENDED KEY READINGS

It is always useful to read around a topic. As well as the specific references below, we particularly highlight:

- For general overviews of the strategy discipline, R. Whittington, *What Is Strategy – and Does it Matter?*, 2nd edition, International Thompson, 2000; and H. Mintzberg, B. Ahlstrand and J. Lampel, *Strategy Safari: a Guided Tour through the Wilds of Strategic Management*, Simon & Schuster, 2000.

- Two accessible articles on what strategy is, and might not be, are M. Porter, 'What is strategy?', *Harvard Business Review*, November–December 1996, pp. 61–78; and F. Fréry, 'The fundamental dimensions of strategy', *MIT Sloan Management Review*, vol. 48, no. 1 (2006), pp. 71–75.

- For contemporary developments in strategy practice, business newspapers such as the *Financial Times*, *Les Echos* and the *Wall Street Journal* and business magazines such as *Business Week*, *The Economist*, *L'Expansion* and *Manager-Magazin*. See also the websites of the leading strategy consulting firms: www.mckinsey.com; www.bcg.com; www.bain.com.

REFERENCES

1. The question 'What is strategy?' is discussed in R. Whittington, *What Is Strategy – and Does it Matter?*, International Thomson, 1993/2000 and M.E. Porter, 'What is strategy?', *Harvard Business Review*, November–December 1996, pp. 61–78.

2. D. Collis and M. Rukstad, 'Can you say what your strategy is?', *Harvard Business Review*, April 2008, pp. 63–73.

3. F. Westley, 'Middle managers and strategy: microdynamics of inclusion', *Strategic Management Journal*, vol. 11, no. 5 (1990), 337–51.

4. For insights about in-house strategy roles, see D. Angwin, S. Paroutis and S. Mitson, 'Connecting up strategy: are strategy directors a missing link?', *California Management Review*, vol. 51, no. 3 (2009).

5. The major strategy consulting firms have a wealth of information on strategy careers and strategy in general: see www.mckinsey.com; www.bcg.com; www.bain.com.

6. University careers advisers can usually provide good advice on strategy consulting and strategic planning opportunities. See also www.vault.com.

7. For reviews of the contemporary state of strategy as a discipline, see H. Volberda, 'Crisis in strategy: fragmentation, integration or synthesis', *European Management Review*, vol. 1, no. 1 (2004), pp. 35–42; and J. Mahoney and A. McGahan, 'The field of strategic management within the evolving science of strategic organization', *Strategic Organization*, vol. 5, no. 1 (2007), 79–99.

8. See M.E. Porter, 'The Five Competitive Forces that shape strategy', *Harvard Business Review*, January 2008, pp. 57–91.

9. The classic statement of the resource-based view is J. Barney, 'Firm resources and sustained competitive advantage', *Journal of Management*, vol. 17, no. 1 (1991), pp. 91–120.

10. Two recent collections in the strategy process tradition are G. Szulanski, J. Porac and Y. Doz (eds), *Strategy Process: Advances in Strategic Management*, JAI Press, 2005; and S. Floyd, J. Roos, C. Jacobs and F. Kellermans (eds), *Innovating Strategy Process*, Blackwell, 2005.

11. For recent samples of Strategy-as-Practice research, see the special issues edited by P. Jarzabkowski, J. Balogun and D. Seidl, 'Strategizing: the challenge of a practice perspective', *Human Relations*, vol. 60, no. 1 (2007) and R. Whittington and L. Cailluet, 'The crafts of strategy', *Long Range Planning*, vol. 41, no. 3 (2008).

12. In earlier editions, this lens was called the 'ideas lens'.

Glastonbury – from hippy weekend to international festival

Steve Henderson, Leeds Metropolitan University

Glastonbury Festival has become a worldwide attraction for music fans and artists alike. In 2009, Bruce Springsteen was added to the long list of acts (from Paul McCartney to Oasis) that have appeared at the festival. It started in 1970 when 1,500 hippy revellers gathered on a farm near Glastonbury Tor to be plied with free milk and entertainment from a makeshift stage. Now, Glastonbury is a major international festival that attracts over 150,000 attenders. Without any knowledge of the line-up, the tickets for the 2010 Festival sold out in days.

In those early days, the Festival was developed by local farmer, Michael Eavis, whose passion for music and social principles led to a weekend of music as a means of raising funds for good causes. It was a social mission rooted in the hippy counter-culture of the 1960s and events such as Woodstock. Today, the Glastonbury Festival attender finds that those early days of hippy idealism are a long way off. The scale of the organisation demands strong management to support the achievement of the festival's social aims.

At first, the statutory requirements for an event held on private land were minimal. Jovial policemen looked over hedges whilst recreational drugs were sold from tables near the festival entrance as if this was just a slightly unusual village fête. Needless to say, the festival began to attract the attention of a number of different groups, especially as legislation around the running of events tightened. Eavis struggled with local residents who hated the invasion of their privacy; with hippy activist groups who felt that their contribution in helping at the festival gave them a sense of ownership; with drug dealers carrying on their activities on the fringes of the festival; and fans climbing over the fences to get free access.

The festival's continued expansion has resulted in a festival with over ten stages covering jazz, dance, classical, world music and other genres. Added to this, there is comedy, poetry, circus, theatre and children's entertainment alongside more esoteric street theatre performances. Much of this is organised into specific grassy field areas where, for example, the Dance Village uses a number of tents dedicated to different types of dance music. Indeed, such is the range of entertainment

Source: Getty Images.

on offer that some attenders spend the whole weekend at the festival without seeing a single live music act. Though the Eavis family remain involved with the main programme, much of the other entertainment is now managed by others. Reflecting this shift towards more diverse entertainment, the name of the festival was changed from Glastonbury Fayre (reflecting the ancient cultural heritage of the area) to the Glastonbury Festival for Contemporary Performing Arts.

In some years, the festival is forced to take a year off to allow the farmland to recover from the trampling of thousands of pairs of feet. Not only is this wise on an agricultural front but also gives the local residents a rest from the annual invasion of festival goers. Despite this, the festival has met with a number of controversies such as when a large number of gatecrashers spoilt the fun in 2000. This caused the festival to be fined due to exceeding the licensed attendance and excessive noise after the event. Furthermore, health and safety laws now require the event management to have a 'duty of care' to everyone on the festival site. To address these health and safety concerns, support was sought from Melvin Benn who ran festivals for the Mean Fiddler organisation. With a steel fence erected around the perimeter, Melvin Benn helped re-establish the festival in 2002 after a year off.

Ownership of the festival remained with the Eavis family but Melvin Benn was appointed Managing Director. However, concerns arose in 2006 when his employer, Mean Fiddler, was taken over by major music promoters, Live Nation and MCD Productions. In a worrying move, Live Nation announced that they would entice a number of major artists to appear on the weekend normally used by Glastonbury at a new UK festival called Wireless. Based in London, this seemed set to offer a city-based alternative to Glastonbury. At much the same time, Live Nation announced that they would launch their own online ticket agency to support the sales of their music events. This shift in power between the major music promoters indicated not only their interest in the ownership of key events but their desire to control income streams.

Elsewhere in the world of live entertainment, the success of Glastonbury had not gone unnoticed and the festival market showed considerable growth. Some of the other festivals tried to capitalise on features that Glastonbury could not offer. For example, Glastonbury was famous for its wet weather with pictures of damp revellers and collapsed tents being commonplace. Live Nation's city-based Wireless festival offered the opportunity to sleep under a roof at home or hotel, as opposed to risking the weather outdoors. Alternatively, Benicassim in southern Spain offered a festival with an excellent chance of sunshine and top acts for the price of a low cost airline ticket. Other festivals noted that Glastonbury attenders enjoyed the wider entertainment at the event. In doing this, they realised that many festival goers were attracted by the whole social experience. So, sidestepping major acts and their related high fees, smaller festivals were created for just a few thousand attenders. These offered entertainment in various formats, often in a family-friendly atmosphere. Sometimes described as boutique festivals, Freddie Fellowes, organiser of the Secret Garden Party, describes this type of festival as a chance 'to be playful, to break down barriers between people and create an environment where you have perfect freedom and perfect nourishment, intellectually and visually'. Festival Republic, the rebranded Mean Fiddler, created a boutique festival on a larger scale with their Latitude festival. Similarly, Rob da Bank, a BBC DJ, put together Bestival on the Isle of Wight where the attenders are encouraged to join in the fun by appearing in fancy dress. Quite clearly, audiences are now being presented with a wide range of festivals to consider for their leisure time entertainment.

Many of these festivals attract sponsors with some becoming prominent by acquiring naming rights on the festival. Others have low profile arrangements involving so-called 'contra' deals as opposed to sponsorship payments. For example, Glastonbury has official cider suppliers who typically boost their brand by giving the festival a preferential deal on their products in exchange for publicity. Though these commercial relationships are sometimes spurned by the smaller festivals that see the branding as an intrusion on their fun environment, larger festivals often need such relationships to survive. In order to attract sponsors, large festivals are turning to radio and television broadcasters as a means to expand the audience and offer wider exposure for the sponsor. Indeed, in 2009, the BBC sent over 400 staff members down to Glastonbury for broadcasting aimed at satisfying the interest of the armchair viewer/listener.

With such huge demand for their talents, artists can have a lucrative summer moving between festivals. Similarly, audiences can make lengthy treks to their favourite festivals. For some, this has caused environmental concerns with Glastonbury's rural location, poor transport links and large audience being cited as a specific problem. On the other hand, artists are not only finding that the festivals offer a good source of income but that private parties and corporate entertainment have emerged as alternative, often greater, income opportunities. One newspaper claimed that George Michael pocketed more than £1.5m (~€1.65m; ~$2.25m) to entertain revellers at the British billionaire retailer Sir Philip Green's 55th birthday party in the Maldives. Hence, for many artists, the summer has become a case of 'cherry picking' their favourite festivals or seeking out the most lucrative opportunities.

Over time, the shift from small, homespun event to corporate-controlled festival has provided awkward situations for Michael Eavis – from the difficulties with establishment figures who felt the event was out of control to the demands of counter-cultural groups such as the travelling hippies. However, along the way, the festival has maintained its aim of supporting charities like CND and, later, Greenpeace, Oxfam and a number of local charities. In the mind of the audience, this helps position the festival as a fun event with a social conscience. The continued expansion and shift in management of the festival has freed Michael Eavis to be the figurehead for the event and to pursue the original social mission of the festival.

Given this growing and increasingly competitive market, there is much to consider for the festivals involved. In recent years, Glastonbury has sold all its tickets and made donations to its favoured causes, confirming the financial viability of its current business model. Indeed, the festival's iconic status has traditionally meant that it is a rite of passage for many young music fans. Yet, in 2008, Eavis publicly registered concern over the age of the Glastonbury audience suggesting that selling tickets by phone would help attract a younger audience. Maybe Eavis was concerned by comments such as those in *The Times* newspaper that cruelly declared Glastonbury as suited to the 'the hip-op generation' and questioned whether young people thought it was 'cool' to go to the same music events as their parents. On the other hand, their parents belong to the 'baby boomer' generation that grew up with popular music and festivals like Glastonbury. So, there is no real surprise that they would enjoy this eclectic event. Whatever disturbed Eavis, he announced that Jay-Z, an American rap artist, was to headline in order to help attract a younger audience. With sales slower compared with previous sell-out years, he later stated 'We're not trying to get rid of anybody. The older people are fantastic, but we do need young people coming in as well.' Then, reflecting on the 2008 festival in 2009, Michael Eavis displayed concerns over the future of the festival saying 'Last year I thought that maybe we'd got to the end and we'd have to bite the bullet and fold it all up. A lot of the bands were saying Glastonbury had become too big, too muddy and too horrible.'

With such an established festival as Glastonbury, one would expect the management might be looking to leverage its brand with, for example, further events. Yet, the comments of Michael Eavis suggest not only a lack of clarity about the target audience but also concern over whether it can persist. Furthermore, Eavis seems nervous about the festival's appeal to artists who have lots of opportunities to make appearances over the summer. Audiences and artists are the two key factors that underpin financial success at these events, as successful festival promoters are well aware.

Sources: The history of Glastonbury is charted on its website (http://www.glastonburyfestivals.co.uk/history) whilst ownership and finances are available through Companies House.

Most of the background to the festival and related market has been drawn from online news resources such as the BBC, Times Online and the *Guardian*, or industry magazines such as *Music Week*.

More information on UK Festivals is available from Mintel.

Questions

1 Sticking to the 35 word limit suggested by Collis and Rukstad in section 1.2.3, what strategy statement would you propose for the Glastonbury Festival?

2 Carry out a 'three horizons' analysis (section 1.2.1) of the Glastonbury Festival, in terms of both existing activities and possible future ones. How might this analysis affect their future strategic direction?

3 Using the headings of environment, strategic capability, strategic purpose and culture seen in section 1.5.1, identify key positioning issues for the Glastonbury Festival and consider their relative importance.

4 Following on from the previous question and making use of section 1.5.2, what alternative strategies do you see for the Glastonbury Festival?

5 Converting good strategic thinking into action can be a challenge: examine how the Glastonbury Festival has achieved this by considering the elements seen in section 1.5.3.

COMMENTARY
THE STRATEGY LENSES

Chapter 1 showed that there are different academic disciplines underpinning the way strategy is understood. Exploring the subject in terms of different perspectives is helpful because it provides *different insights* on issues relating to strategy and the management of strategy. Think of everyday discussions you have. It is not unusual for people to say: 'But if you look at it this way . . .'. Taking one view can lead to a partial and perhaps biased understanding. A fuller picture, giving different insights, can be gained from multiple perspectives. In turn these different insights can prompt thinking about different *options or solutions* to strategic problems. There is, therefore, both conceptual and practical value in taking a multi-perspective approach to strategy.

This commentary builds on different perspectives on strategy to develop four *lenses* through which strategy in organisations can be viewed. They are:

- **Strategy as design** **views strategy development as a logical process of analysis and evaluation** to establish a clear picture of an organisation's strategic position as a basis for deciding future strategy and planning its implementation. So strategy viewed through the design lens emphasises the use of tools and concepts that encourage such objective analysis for making strategy. It is also the most commonly held view about how strategy is developed and what managing strategy is about.

- **Strategy as experience** **views strategy development as the outcome of people's (not least managers'), taken-for-granted assumptions and ways of doing things**. Strategy through the experience lens therefore puts people and their experience centre stage in strategy development.

- **Strategy as variety*** **is the view that strategy bubbles up from new ideas arising from the variety of people in and around organisations**. The variety lens therefore helps explain why some organisations may be more innovative than others. It also suggests that, if innovation is specially important, managing strategy is about creating the organisational context to benefit from such variety, foster the emergence of ideas and develop them as they emerge. Whereas the design lens suggests strategy develops in terms of planned direction from the top, the emphasis here is more on bottom-up strategy development. From this point of view it is important to look to the periphery and bottom of the organisation to discover the organisation's future strategy.

- **Strategy as discourse** is **the view that the language is important as a means by which managers communicate and explain and change strategy, but by which they also gain influence and power and establish their legitimacy and identity**. The discourse lens suggests it is important to unpick the language managers use to justify their strategy in order to uncover hidden assumptions and political interests: the view that language is a resource.

---

* In earlier editions the variety lens was called the 'ideas lens'. The authors believe, however, that the word 'variety' more accurately encapsulates the concepts explained in this section.

The rest of this commentary explains the lenses in more detail. In so doing, the discussion suggests how the lenses relate to and shed light on three key dimensions of managing strategy:

- *Rationality.* The extent to which the development of strategy is a rationally managed act. Of course the design lens assumes this is the case, but the other lenses raise questions about it.

- *Innovation and change.* The extent to which the management of strategy is likely to develop innovatory, change-oriented organisations; or conversely, consolidate strategies rooted in past experience, established ways of doing things and existing power structures.

- *Legitimacy.* How strategy and the involvement in the management of strategy provide a basis of power, authority and influence in their organisations.

The lenses are then used in commentaries at the end of each part of the book to identify implications that arise through viewing the content of the chapters in these different ways and to encourage readers to reflect on the issues that have been raised.

Strategy as design

The design lens builds on two main premises. The first is that managers are, or should be, rational decision-makers. The second is that they should be taking decisions about how to optimise economic performance of their organisations. The principles of economics and the guidelines provided by the decision sciences support and feed the notion that this is what strategic management is all about. Moreover most managers would probably agree that is what they are there to do.

Rational choice implies that managers can and should be able to weigh the benefits and disbenefits of different strategic options on the basis of evidence that informs them of likely outcomes of decisions they make.[1] This is the way strategic management is often explained in textbooks, by tutors and indeed by managers. Stated more fully, the assumptions typically underpinning a *design* view of strategy are as follows. First, in terms of *how strategic decisions are made*:

- *Systematic analysis.* Although there are many influences on an organisation's performance, careful analysis can identify those most likely to influence the organisation significantly. It may be possible to forecast, predict or build scenarios about future impacts so that managers can think through the conditions in which their organisation is likely to operate.

- *Strategic positioning.* This analysis provides a basis for the matching of organisational strengths and resources with changes in the environment so as to take advantage of opportunities and overcome or circumvent threats.

- *Analytic thinking precedes and governs action.* Strategy-making is often seen as a *linear process.* Decisions about what the strategy should be in terms of its content come first and are managed down through the organisation. Decisions about what the strategy should be are therefore separate from and precede its implementation.

- *Objectives* should be clear and explicit and the basis upon which *options are evaluated.* Given a thorough analysis of the factors internal and external to the organisation to inform management about the strategic position of the organisation, a range of options for future strategic direction are then considered and evaluated in terms of the objectives and that analysis. A strategic decision is then made on the basis of what is considered to be optimal, given all these considerations.

Second, the design lens makes assumptions about the *form and nature of organisations*:

- *Organisations are hierarchies.* It is the responsibility of top management to plan the destiny of the organisation. They make important decisions, and lower levels of management, and eventually the rest of the organisation, carry out these decisions and implement the strategy decided at the top.

- *Organisations are rational systems.* Since the complexity organisations face can be understood analytically such that logical conclusions are reached, the associated assumption is that people in the organisation will adopt and accept such logic. The system can be controlled rationally too. *Control systems* (for example, budgets, targets, appraisals) provide the means by which top management can measure whether or not others in the organisation are meeting expected objectives and behaving in line with the strategy.

- *Organisations are mechanisms* by which strategy can be put into effect. They are analogous to engineered systems or, perhaps, machines. So how an organisation is structured and controlled (see Chapter 13) needs to be suited to the strategy. Mechanisms to ensure that strategy is, indeed, being considered rationally and dispassionately are also needed.

Implications for management

Managers often talk as if strategy comes about – or *should* come about – much as the design lens suggests: it is seen as valuable by managers. Arguably there are five main reasons for this:

- *Dealing with complexity and uncertainty.* Strategy as design provides a means of coping with and talking about complex and uncertain issues in a rational, logical and structured way. Indeed there are many *concepts*, *tools* and *techniques* to help managers with this.

- *Management power and legitimacy.* Managers, particularly CEOs, face complex and often challenging situations. The assumptions, tools and techniques of design provide them with ways in which they can feel in control and exercise control in such circumstances.

- Rationality is *deeply rooted* in our way of thinking and in our systems of education. We also live in a world in which science and reasoned solutions to the problems we face seem to surround us and provide many benefits. In this sense the design lens is embedded in our human psyche. So, for example, even when managers admit that strategy is not actually developed in ways the design lens suggests, they often think it should be.

- *Stakeholder expectations.* Important stakeholders such as banks, financial analysts, investors and employees may expect and value such an approach. So it is an important means of gaining their support and confidence.

- *The language of strategy.* In many respects the design lens, especially in its emphasis on analysis and control, is the orthodox approach to strategy development most commonly written about in books, taught at business schools and verbalised by management when they discuss the strategy of their organisations. So it is a useful language to know (see the discourse lens below).

In summary, the design lens is a useful way of viewing the management of strategy on the basis of *analysis and planning*. The associated assumption is that change and innovation can, or at least should be able to, be achieved through such rational and mechanistic approaches. However, the emphasis on analysis and control may well result in conformity rather than innovation. Indeed insights from the experience and ideas lenses that follow help explain why this is so. As Figure C.i also shows, since a rational/analytic approach is typically seen as being

Figure C.i Design lens

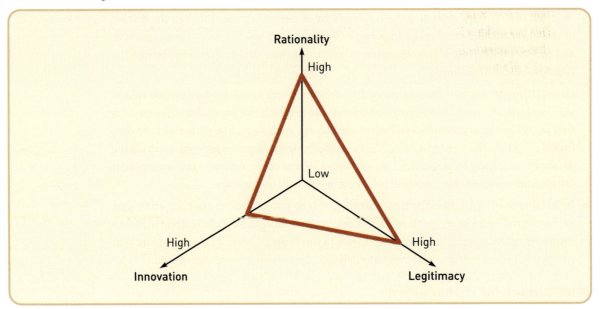

central to the management of strategy, those who see their role like this may also be seen as, or seek to position themselves as, credible, influential (and therefore legitimate) strategists.

This book argues that the design lens is indeed a useful explanation of how strategy is managed but is not sufficient. Other lenses provide insights that are also useful.

Strategy as experience

Much of the evidence from research on how strategies actually develop gives a different picture than that seen through the design lens. As early as the 1950s, Nobel prize winner Herbert Simon and management theorist Charles Lindblom[2] pointed out that rational decision-making models were unrealistic. It is not possible to obtain the information necessary to achieve the sort of exhaustive analysis required; it is not possible to predict an uncertain future; there are limits in terms of cost and time in undertaking such analysis; organisations and environments are changing continually, so it is not possible for managers to take long-term decisions at a point in time. There are also psychological limitations on managers themselves which mean that they cannot be expected to weigh the consequences of all options or be the objective analysts such rationality would expect – a point which is discussed more fully below. The best that can be expected is what Simon termed 'bounded rationality'; managers do the best they can within the limits of their circumstances, knowledge and experience. The experience lens recognises this boundedness in **viewing strategy development as the outcome of people's individual and collective taken-for-granted assumptions and ways of doing things.**

Individual experience and bias[3]

Managers make sense of their complex world by drawing on their previous experience. Human beings function in their everyday lives not least because they have the cognitive capability to make sense of problems or issues they encounter. They recognise and make sense of these on the basis of past experience and what they come to believe to be true about the world. More formally, how we interpret issues we face can be explained in terms of the mental (or cognitive) models we build over time to help make sense of our situations. Managers are no exception to this. When they face a problem they make sense of it in terms of their mental models. This has major advantages. They are able to relate such problems to prior events and therefore have comparisons to draw upon. They can interpret one issue in the light of another. Making sense of situations in this way is fast and, most often, efficient. Indeed, if managers did not have such mental models they could not function effectively; they would meet each situation as though they were experiencing it for the first time.

There are, however, downsides. Mental models simplify complexity. It is not possible for managers to operate in terms of 'perfect knowledge'. Understanding the effects of such *simplification processes* is important. Even if managers have a very rich understanding of their environment, they will not bring that complex understanding to bear for all situations and decisions. They will access part of that knowledge.[4] This is called *selective attention*: selecting from total understanding the parts of knowledge that seem most relevant. Managers also use *exemplars* and *prototypes*. For example, commonly competitors become prototypical. Television company executives came to see other television companies – even specific channels – as their competitors. They therefore readily accepted that satellite broadcasting could introduce new competition because it would introduce new television channels. However, they failed to see that the Internet and sites such as YouTube would become an alternative to watching television. There is also the risk that the 'chunk' of information most often used becomes the only information used and that stimuli from the environment are selected to fit these dominant representations of reality. Information that squares with other television channels being the competitors is taken on board, whilst information counter to that is not. Sometimes this distortion can lead to severe errors as managers miss crucial indicators because they are, in effect, scanning the environment for issues and events that are familiar or readily recognisable.[5]

In summary, there are three important points:

- *Cognitive bias is inevitable*. The idea that managers approach problems and issues of a strategic nature entirely dispassionately and objectively is unrealistic.

- *The future is likely to be made sense of in terms of the past*. Managers typically make sense of new issues in the context of past issues; so when it comes to strategic decisions they are likely to resolve a problem in much the same way as they dealt with a previous one seen as similar. This is one explanation of why strategies tend to develop incrementally from prior strategy (see section 5.2.1).

- Nonetheless, *experience may confer legitimacy and power*. Managers with extensive experience may well be seen as experts or have significant influence in an organisation.

However, managers do not operate purely as individuals; they work and interact with others in organisations, and at this collective level there are also reasons to expect similar tendencies.

Collective experience and organisational culture

How people make sense of situations and issues is not just a matter of individual cognition, but has a collective aspect to it. In this context cultural influences are important: indeed culture was defined by the anthropologist Clifford Geertz as 'socially established structures of meaning'.[6] Central to the concept of culture is the importance of what is 'taken for granted' in terms of assumptions and in terms of activities or practices – 'the way we do things around here'. In everyday life, for example, there are assumptions such as those about the role of the family in bringing up children and about behaviour within the family. These assumptions and associated ways of behaving differ between societies in different parts of the world. In organisational life, an equivalent example might be assumptions about top management, their roles and how they should behave. These also differ, for example between Western firms and Japanese firms. Taken-for-granted aspects of culture also exist at different levels: for example, within a managerial function such as marketing or finance; an organisational unit such as a business; or more widely a professional grouping, such as accountants, an industry sector or even a national culture. The important point here is that these assumptions and taken-for-granted ways of behaving influence strategy in three ways.

First, cultural influences help to explain why managers within a group – an organisation or a department, for example – may see things in similar ways and respond to situations similarly. Second, given this, they help explain why such managers may adhere to familiar strategies and be reluctant to change them. However, third, differences in culture also explain why different groups see things differently. Japanese managers may see things differently from European managers or marketing managers differently from accountants. In turn, and together with the differences in people's personal experience and biases, this helps explain why the management of strategy is often characterised by a good deal of bargaining and negotiation to reconcile such differences.

Implications for management

The experience lens, then, puts people, their experience and the culture in which they work at the centre of strategy development. Figure C.ii summarises its implications in relation to the three dimensions of strategic management. Rationality, in the sense of the careful weighing of options in a search for optimal solutions, is not the emphasis; rather strategies develop as managers try to relate their experience, individual and collective, to the strategic issues that they face. Managers' experience may, however, be seen by colleagues as relevant and important and therefore bestow a high degree of legitimacy. However, strategic change or innovation is likely to be problematic. It should not be assumed that analysis or reasoned argument necessarily

Figure C.ii Experience lens

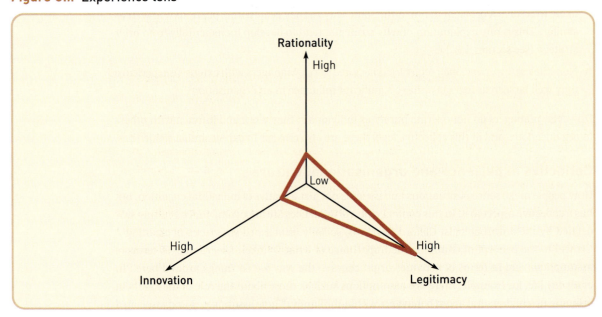

changes deeply embedded assumptions or ways of doing things; readers need only think of their own experience in trying to persuade others to rethink their religious beliefs or, indeed, allegiances to sports teams to realise this.

In turn this provides insights into two other important phenomena associated with managing strategy:

- *Strategic drift* is a risk. If managers are 'captured' by their own and their colleagues' experience the strategy of the organisation gradually drifts away from the realities of its environment and towards an internally determined view of the world. This can lead to significant performance downturn and, potentially, the demise of the organisation (see section 5.2).

- *Bargaining and negotiation* may take place between managers on the basis of different interpretations of events according to their past experience or cultural differences. This is the more likely, since managers' personal reputation and standing are likely to be based partly on such experience. This perspective is reflected in discussions of strategy development as a political process (sections 4.5.2 and 14.4.5).

Strategy as variety

The extent to which the two lenses described so far help explain innovation is rather limited. The variety lens helps explain innovative strategies, processes and products; and how organisations faced with fast-changing environments and short decision horizons, such as those in high-technology businesses or the fashion industries, cope with the speed of change and innovation required.

The variety lens builds on complexity theory[7] and evolutionary theory.[8] McKinsey consultant Shona Brown and Stanford academic Kathy Eisenhardt[9] have shown these are helpful when it comes to explaining the conditions that help generate innovation. The basic tenets of evolutionary theory – variation, selection and retention – provide an understanding of how organisational context is important in relation to the generation of new ideas and how managers may help shape that context. The emphasis of complexity theory on how systems cope with uncertainty in non-linear ways adds to that understanding. Viewed through the variety lens, top-down design and direction of strategy is de-emphasised. Rather, strategies are seen as emerging from ideas that bubble up from the variety in and around organisations.

The importance of variety

New ideas are generated in conditions of variety whereas conditions of uniformity give rise to fewer new ideas. Whether the concern is with species, as in the natural world, people in societies or indeed ideas in organisations,[10] uniformity is not the norm; there exists variety. There is an ever-changing environment, different types of businesses, a variety of groups and individuals, a variety of their experience and ideas, and there are deviations from routine ways of doing things.[11] Evolution helps explain how any living system, including an organisation, evolves through natural selection acting upon such variation.

Variety is likely to be greatest where the environment is changing fastest. For example, in our biological world there has been the rapid development of new strains of viruses given the advances in modern medicine to fight them. There are parallels with regard to organisations. Organisations in industry sectors that are developing and fragmented tend to be more innovative than those in mature and concentrated industries,[12] because of the variety of ideas that exist in such dynamic conditions. Take the example of the microelectronics industry. It is a fast-changing industry. This has spawned many different types of businesses, from hardware manufacturers through to software boutiques and firms engaged in applications of such technology. Within these organisations, in turn, there develop new ideas as people interpret opportunities and potential applications differently.

A good deal of this variety occurs naturally and quite likely outside managers' direct control. Since sensing of its environment takes place throughout an organisation, new ideas quite likely come from low down in an organisation, not just from the top.[13] Such ideas will be more or less well informed, may not be well formulated and, at the individual level at least, they may be very diverse. Complexity theorist Bill McKelvey refers to this as the 'distributed intelligence' of an organisation.[14] Moreover, innovation in large organisations often comes from outside their boundaries, perhaps from smaller businesses.[15]

Managers may seek to generate such variety and some of the ways they do this are discussed below. Variation may not, however, always be intentional. In the natural world, change and newness come about because of *imperfections* – a mutation of a gene, for example – that may provide the basis for a 'fitter' organism in a changing environment. In organisations, ideas are also copied imperfectly between individuals, groups or organisations. Some of these will give rise to innovations better suited to the changing environment. A research chemist's idea may be taken up by a marketing executive but interpreted differently from the original idea. Managers in one organisation may seek to copy the strategy of another, but will not do things in exactly the same way. Some of these imperfect copies will not be successful; but others may be. A famous example is Post-its, which originated in an 'imperfect' glue being applied to paper, but resulted in a semi-adhesive for which the researcher saw market potential. There may also be surprises and unforeseen circumstances in the environment; for example the unexpected skills or views introduced by new appointees or unintended consequences arising from management initiatives.

Figure C.iii Variety lens

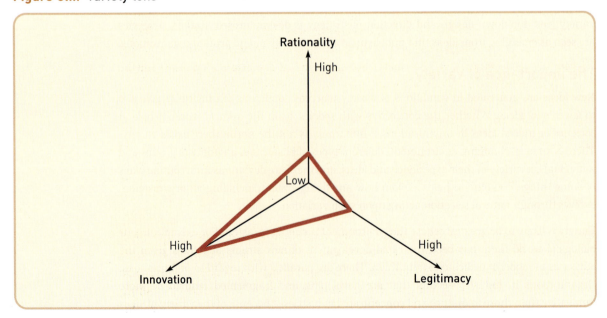

Selection and retention

The implication of the design lens is that the selection of a strategy is a matter of deliberate choice to optimise some sort of outcome, for example competitive advantage leading to enhanced profits. The variety lens and evolutionary theory in particular do not deny the deliberate acts of managers. They do suggest, however, that selection is 'blind'[16] in the sense that outcomes cannot be known. Managers may exercise judgement and choice, indeed may use or refer to management tools to do so, but the strategies that develop are also the result of other processes of selection and retention. These include:

- *Experience and culture*. People's experience and the culture of an organisation act as filters of ideas that do not 'fit'. Formal processes of control, planning and evaluation act to regularise what ideas will and will not go forward. The self-interest of powerful managers may block ideas counter to their own. So pressures for conformity may see off potential new ideas.

- *Functional benefit*. An idea may meet the needs of environmental and market forces. However, many of these (from climate changes to competitor responses) can at best be partially known. There may, however, be other functions such as serving the interests of individuals within the organisation, for example in furthering career aspirations.

- *Alignment*. An idea is likely to be more successful if it aligns with other successful ideas, for example because it is what other organisations are doing or it fits the culture and experience of the organisation itself.

- *Attraction*. Some strategic ideas, by their very nature, are more or less attractive than others.[17] For example, ideas that are altruistic tend to spread and get adopted most.[18] In line with this, complexity theory emphasises the need for sufficient support or 'positive feedback', and some ideas are more likely to attract this than others. For example, a new product idea in a science-based company persisted despite strong evidence of its lack of commercial viability because it addressed 'green' issues and its potential benefits interested colleagues in other divisions and friends and families of the managers developing it.

- *Retention*. As well as processes of selection, there are processes of retention. 'Retention occurs when selected variations are preserved, duplicated or otherwise reproduced',[19] leading to their future repetition. One key factor here is the extent to which ideas become routinised and thus retained. Routinisation varies from formal procedures (for example, job descriptions), accounting and control systems, management information systems, training, organisation structuring, to the formal or informal standardisation of work routines and the eventual embedding of such routines in the culture of the organisation.

Implications for management[20]

A key insight from the variety lens is that managers need to be wary of assuming they can directly control the generation and adoption of new ideas. However, managers can foster new ideas and innovation by *creating the context* and conditions where they are more likely to emerge.

First, they can do this by considering what the appropriate *boundaries* are for the organisation. The more the *boundaries between the organisation and its environment* are reduced, the more innovation is likely to occur. For some high-technology businesses it is difficult to see quite what their boundaries are. They are networks, intimately linked to their wider environment. As that environment changes, so do the ideas in the network. For example, in Formula One motor racing the different teams are intimately linked with the wider motor industry as well as other areas of advanced technology. As a result of this networking new ideas get imitated (but changed) very rapidly. In contrast, where people are insulated from the environment, perhaps by relying on particular ways of doing things, as in a highly rule-based bureaucracy, an organisation will generate less variety of ideas and less innovation.

Second, managers can promote behaviours likely to encourage new ideas in at least five ways:

- *Interaction and cooperation* within organisations encourage variety and the spread of ideas. There is a danger that organisational structures become too established such that people's relationships become too predictable and ordered; rather, ideas tend to be generated more where there are 'weak ties' based on less established relationships.[21] However, there may be limits to this. Too many 'connections' may lead to an over-complex system.[22] All this may help explain why so much effort is spent by managers in changing organisational structures in the search for the most appropriate working environment (see Chapter 13).

- *Questioning and challenge* of 'received wisdom' are important. For example, large organisations often move executives across businesses or divisions with the specific intention of encouraging new ideas and challenging prevailing views.

- *Experimentation* is important. This may take different forms. Some organisations have formal incentive programmes to encourage experimentation. Others have established it as part of their culture. For example, Google gives staff 20 per cent of their time to pursue their own projects. Strategic experiments at an organisational level, such as alliances and joint ventures, are also ways in which organisations may try out possible strategy developments and generate new ideas without over-commitment.

- *Adaptive tension.* Some complexity theorists argue that innovation and creativity emerge when there is sufficient order to make things happen but not when there is such rigidity of control as to prevent such innovation. This is the idea of 'adaptive tension' or 'edge of chaos'.[23] Innovation occurs most readily when the organisation never quite settles down into a steady state or equilibrium and volatility arising from variation is given sufficient rein (see Figure C.iv), though of course not to the extent that the organisation cannot function.

- *Order-generating rules.* Complexity theory also suggests there is no need for elaborate control to create sufficient order for an organisation to work effectively; that ordered patterns of behaviour can come about through just a few 'order-generating rules' or 'simple rules'. In organisations in which innovation is important, managers need to be very clear about the very few overarching requirements that have to be met, but then allow flexibility and latitude in how they are achieved. Table C.i summarises the types of rules identified as important in organisations facing fast-changing environments[24] and gives some examples of how they take form and their effects.

Finally, top management need to consider their role in developing strategy. They need to be able to discern promising ideas, monitor how they 'function' and 'fit' (see above) as they develop, be sensitive to their outcome and impact, and mould the most promising into coherent strategies. Strategy development by top management is therefore more about *'pattern recognition'* than formal analysis and planning. Managers need to develop the competences to do this rather than being over-reliant on the formal tools and techniques of the design lens.

Figure C.iv Adaptive tension

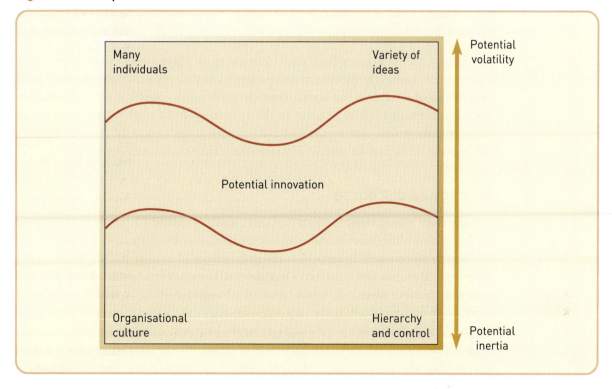

Table C.i Simple rules

Turbulent markets require strategic flexibility to seize opportunities – but flexibility can be disciplined. Different types of simple rules help.

Type	Purpose	Example
How-to rules	Spell out key features of how a process is executed – 'What makes our process unique?'	Dell focus on focused customer segments. So a Dell business must be split in two when its revenue hits $1 billion.
Boundary rules	Focus managers on which opportunities can be pursued and which should not	In Miramax movie-picking process, every movie must: i) revolve around a central human condition, such as love; ii) have a main character appealing but deeply flawed; iii) have a clear story line.
Priority rules	Help managers rank the accepted opportunities	Intel's rule for allocating manufacturing capacity: allocation is based on a product's gross margin. (See Illustration 12.5).
Timing rules	Synchronise managers with the pace of emerging opportunities and other parts of the company	Nortel's product development time must be less than 18 months, which forces it to move quickly into new opportunities.
Exit rules	Help managers decide when to pull out of yesterday's opportunities	In Oticon, the Danish hearing aid company, if a key team member – manager or not – chooses to leave a project for another within the company, the project is killed.

Source: Reprinted by permission of *Harvard Business Review*. Exhibit adapted from 'Strategy as simple rules' by K.M. Eisenhardt and D.N. Sull, January 2001. Copyright © 2001 by the Havard Business School Publishing Corporation. All rights reserved.

In addition, since new ideas are unlikely to emerge fully formed – indeed they may be the result of 'imperfect copying' – managers have to learn to tolerate such imperfection and allow for failures if they want innovation.

In summary, the variety lens helps an understanding of where innovative strategies come from. It de-emphasises the directive role of managers and their rationality and therefore poses questions about whether or not top management really have control over strategic direction to the extent the design lens suggests. In this respect and in its emphasis on the dispersed nature of ideas, it also questions the legitimacy of top management as the strategic directors and source of the success (or failure) of organisations. Figure C.iv summarises this.

Strategy as discourse

In many ways management is about discourse. Managers spend 75 per cent of their time communicating with others[25] in gathering information, persuading others of a course of action or following up decisions. In particular, the management of strategy has a high discursive component. Managers and consultants talk about strategy and strategy is written as formal plans and mission or vision statements, explained in annual reports and in newspaper releases. Efforts to get managerial colleagues, employees and other stakeholders to buy into strategy are also fundamentally discursive; and managers use the language of strategy for their own ends, to gain influence and establish their legitimacy as strategists. The ability to use discursive re-sources effectively can, then, be an advantage and competence for a manager (see Chapter 15 on strategy practice which discusses strategy 'conversations'). Looking at strategy develop-ment in terms of strategy as discourse therefore provides insight into how the language of strategy is used by managers to persuade others, to gain influence and power or establish their identity as strategists.[26]

Discourse and rationality

As discussion of the design lens pointed out, rationality is a central component of the orthodox language of strategy. From a management point of view, then, appearing rational is key to making strategy: 'To be rational is to make persuasive sense.'[27] Strategic management must seem more than just hunch and intuition; it should be more like science and the models like scientific models. As such, managers familiar with such logic can call on it and employ it to justify the 'rightness' of their arguments and views. Indeed typically, even when managers find themselves unable to achieve the goals of strategy – unable, for example, to achieve competitive advantage – they do not deny the logic of the strategy, merely the ability of the organisation to achieve it.[28] They may employ this language because they are themselves persuaded of the logic of a strategy, because they believe that by doing so their arguments will carry more weight with others, because it is the typical way in which strategy is com-municated or because, by so doing, it positions them as an authority on the subject.

Discourse and influence

The language of strategy has characteristics that make it convincing to others.[29] Strategy is not only written about in impressive documents – strategic plans or annual reports, for example – but also written about important phenomena such as markets, competitors and customers. It is often associated with 'heroic' chief executives or successful firms. Strategy discussions take place in important places such as boardrooms or strategy away-days. There is also evidence that the employment of strategy discourse works. Managers consciously employ the vocabulary and concepts of strategy to effect change,[30] to justify and legitimise strategies that are to be followed,[31] or to ensure conformity to the right ways to manage strategy.[32] In other words, managers draw on the concepts of strategy and the apparent 'rightness' of strategy concepts to convince others they should comply.

Discourse, identity and legitimacy

How managers talk about strategy also positions them in relation to others, either by their own deliberate choice or as a result of how they are perceived. Discourse is therefore also related to the identity and legitimacy of managers. The common use of the language of rationality has been highlighted above. At other times or in other circumstances managers may also employ different discourse. For example, in trying to get a strategy implemented at an operational level down the line a manager may draw on previous experience as a 'hands-on worker'. In other circumstances reference to prior experience in turning around an organisation may matter. In other contexts the language of the 'visionary leader' or the innovative entrepreneur may be employed.

Strategy discourse may also be consciously or unconsciously employed by managers – particularly top managers – to provide certain benefits for themselves.[33] It helps legitimise a manager as a knowledgeable strategist, employing the right concepts, using the right logic, doing the right thing and being at the forefront of management thinking. It also provides the sense of centrality, of 'making a difference' to the most important aspects of organisational survival. Since over time different strategy discourses have been more or less fashionable, some elements of discourse are likely to be more effective than others at different times. In the 1960s and 1970s it was the language of corporate or strategic planning; in the 1980s there was more of an emphasis on organisational culture; and latterly strategy has become discussed and communicated more in terms of capabilities and competences.

Discourse as power

In turn the discourse of strategy is linked to power and control. By understanding the concepts of strategy, or being seen to do so, it is top managers or strategy specialists who are positioned as having the knowledge about how to deal with the really difficult problems the organisation faces. The possession of such knowledge gives them power over others who do not have it. It 'allows managers to imagine themselves as controllers of . . . economic life'.[34]

Thus the discourse of strategy can also operate as social control. Groups may adopt particular ways of thinking, behaving and speaking about strategy. For example, some organisations, especially firms of consultants, have developed their own discourse on strategy. Or there may develop ways of approaching strategic issues that are embedded in particular discourse. For example, the need to cut costs may be indisputable in certain circumstances. However, it can foster a mindset in which cutting becomes the norm such that it is difficult to propose a strategy that would not lead to reduced costs. Similarly, 'offshoring' and 'the world is flat' have become common terms amongst Western businesses, helping to legitimise the transfer of work from highly paid employees in home countries to cheaper labour in Asian countries. Such discourse may become so taken-for-granted, so difficult to question or change that it becomes a powerful influence on behaviour. In this sense discourse is associated with power when it attracts followers and is self-reproducing and self-reinforcing.

Figure C.v Discourse lens

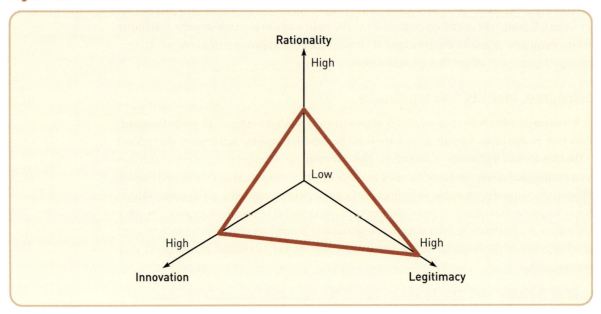

Implications for management

In summary, as shown in Figure C.v, the discourse lens raises the question of the extent to which managers rely on the appearance, rather than the reality, of rational argument. Discourse is used not only to justify strategies, but as ways of seeking power, identity, recognition (and therefore legitimacy). The extent to which such discourse promotes innovation and change will depend on the motivations of the managers and the nature of the language used, though there is evidence that language can play an important role in the management of change.

The fundamental lesson for managers is that the language of strategy they employ matters. The discourse lens highlights this, provides a way of considering how this is so and in practical terms offers concepts and cues by which managers can manage more effectively, for example:

- *Discourse and context.* Different strategy discourses are likely to be more or less effective in different contexts and circumstances. How a strategy is explained and justified to a potential investor may call for a major emphasis on logic and reason under-pinning a financial case. A similarly rational approach may be needed to persuade fellow managers, but perhaps with an additional component related to the benefits in terms of their own interests, future influence and standing. A similar explanation to the workforce of an organisation will have to address the implications for job security, but perhaps also needs to be expressed in ways that reinforce confidence in management. A press release on strategy will likely need to give thought to the main headlines or 'sound bites'. Careful thought needs to go into how strategy is explained and justified to whom.

- *Discourse and the management of strategic change.* Strategy discourse plays an especially important role in the diffusion of innovations, new management practices and the management of change.[35] In particular, different forms of language may be more or less useful in achieving the adoption and retention of new practices. Language that appeals to emotion and self-interest may help adoption, but a reliance on this may lead to the early rejection of new practices. A more rational approach may mean that it takes longer to achieve adoption but will be less likely to result in early rejection. Language that appeals to or relates to accepted ways of doing things may, however, help ensure retention.

- *Common discourse.* It may be beneficial to seek to develop a common language of strategy in an organisation. This is a common reason for management development programmes in relation to strategy. The argued benefit is that managers can then communicate on the basis of a common set of generally understood concepts, terms and tools of strategy which makes strategy debate more effective. It is also a role management educators provide in the diffusion of strategy concepts and language, of course.

- *A critical perspective for managers.* A critical perspective on the discourse of strategy should prompt managers and students alike to question just how substantial concepts and models to do with strategy really are. Are they really based on sound evidence and theory; do they really make a difference? Or are they a discourse being employed because it seems to be what is expected; because it is 'the language of strategists'; or a way for managers to gain power and influence? In this sense, seeing strategy as discourse can prompt the healthy questioning of concepts, ideas and assumptions that might otherwise be taken for granted.

Conclusion

The core assumptions and the key implications of the four lenses of design, experience, variety and discourse are summarised in Table C.ii. They are not offered here as an exhaustive list. They are an attempt to encapsulate different approaches and insights into the complex

Table C.ii A summary of the strategy lenses

	Strategy as:			
	Design	**Experience**	**Variety**	**Discourse**
Strategy develops through . . .	A logical process of analysis and evaluation	People's experience, assumptions and taken-for-granted ways of doing things	Ideas bubbling up from the variety of people in and around organisations	Managers seeking influence, power and legitimacy through the language they use
Assumptions about organisations	Mechanistic, hierarchical, rational systems	Cultures based on experience, legitimacy and past success	Complex and potentially diverse organic systems	Arenas of power and influence
Role of top management	Strategic decision-makers	Enactors of their experience	'Coaches', creators of context and pattern-recognisers	Exercising or gaining power and influence over others
Key implications	Undertake careful and thorough analysis of strategic issues	Recognise that people's experience is central and needs to be built upon but also challenged	If innovation is important look for ideas bubbling up from the bottom and periphery of the organisation	Unpick the language used by managers to uncover hidden assumptions and political interests

concept of strategy. Indeed, the suggestion is that you may usefully extend your exploration of different lenses yourself. It should be apparent in what you have read so far that the lenses presented here actually include several perspectives themselves. For example, the experience lens builds on explanations from cognition, sociology and cultural anthropology and the variety lens builds on both evolutionary theory and complexity theory. So, within these lenses there are finer-grained insights that can be gained and the references and key readings should help with that. In addition there are whole books written that provide multiple perspectives on strategy, from the four that Richard Whittington[36] offers to the ten of Henry Mintzberg and his co-authors.[37]

However, there are two overarching messages that come through consistently. The first is the one with which this commentary began: in considering a topic like strategy, it helps to take more than one perspective. The second is that, in so doing, there is a need to question the conventional wisdom of strategy encapsulated in the design lens. In particular the central tenet of managers at the top planning and directing strategy through machine-like organisations is too limited a view of what strategic management is about.

In the rest of the book the four lenses are employed in commentaries at the ends of Parts I, II and III in particular to examine critically the coverage of each part and consider the management implications.

REFERENCES

1. A useful review of the principles of rational decision making can be found in J.G. March, *A Primer on Decision Making: How Decisions Happen*, Simon & Schuster, 1994, Chapter 1, Limited liability, pp. 1–35.
2. See H.A. Simon, *The New Science of Management Decision*, Prentice Hall, 1960; and C.E. Lindblom, 'The science of muddling through', *Public Administration Review*, vol. 19 (1959), pp. 79–88.
3. For a thorough explanation of the role of psychological processes in strategy see G.P. Hodgkinson and P.R. Sparrow, *The Competent Organization*, Open University Press, 2002.
4. For a review of these points see the introduction to J. Dutton, E. Walton and E. Abrahamson, 'Important dimensions of strategic issues: separating the wheat from the chaff', *Journal of Management Studies*, vol. 26, no. 4 (1989), pp. 380–95.
5. See A. Tversky and D. Kahnemann, 'Judgments under uncertainty: heuristics and biases', *Science*, vol. 185 (1975), pp. 1124–31.
6. See C. Geertz, *The Interpretation of Culture*, Basic Books, 1973, p. 12.
7. For a fuller discussion of complexity theory in relation to strategy see R.D. Stacey, *Strategic Management and Organizational Dynamics: The Challenge of Complexity*, 3rd edition, Pearson Education, 2000; and B. Burnes, 'Complexity theories and organizational change', *International Journal of Management Reviews*, vol. 7 issue 2 (2005), 73–90.
8. For a systematic discussion of the implications of evolutionary theory on management see H. Aldrich, *Organizations Evolving*, Sage, 1999.
9. See S.L. Brown and K.M. Eisenhardt, *Competing on the Edge*, Harvard Business School Press, 1998.
10. An excellent discussion of the development of ideas (or what the authors refer to as 'memes') and the relationship of this to the role and nature of organisations can be found in J. Weeks and C. Galunic, 'A theory of the cultural evolution of the firm: the intra-organizational ecology of memes', *Organization Studies*, vol. 24, no. 8 (2003), pp. 1309–52.
11. M.S. Feldman and B.T. Pentland, 'Reconceptualizing organizational routines as a source of flexibility and change', *Administrative Science Quarterly*, vol. 48 (2003), 94–118, show how 'performative' variations from standardised (they call them ostensive) routines may create variation which creates organisational change.
12. See Z.J. Acs and D.B. Audretsch, 'Innovation in large and small firms – an empirical analysis', *American Economic Review*, vol. 78, September (1988), pp. 678–90.
13. See G. Johnson and A.S. Huff, 'Everyday innovation/ everyday strategy', in G. Hamel, G.K. Prahalad, H. Thomas and D. O'Neal (eds), *Strategic Flexibility – Managing in a Turbulent Environment*, Wiley, 1998, pp. 13–27. Patrick Regner also shows how new strategic directions can grow from the periphery of organisations in the face of opposition from the centre; see 'Strategy creation in the periphery: inductive versus deductive strategy making', *Journal of Management Studies*, vol. 40, no. 1 (2003), pp. 57–82.
14. Bill McKelvey, a complexity theorist, argues that the variety within this distributed intelligence is increased because individual managers seek to become better

informed about their environment: see B. McKelvey, 'Simple rules for improving corporate IQ: basic lessons from complexity science', in P. Andriani and G. Passiante (eds), *Complexity, Theory and the Management of Networks*, Imperial College Press, 2004.

15. See E. von Hippel, *The Sources of Innovation*, Oxford University Press, 1988.

16. The concept of blind selection is explained more fully in the chapter by D. Barron on evolutionary theory in the *Oxford Handbook of Strategy*, ed. D. Faulkner and A. Campbell, Oxford University Press, 2003.

17. See Weeks and Galunic, reference 10.

18. The role of altruism and other bases of attraction is discussed by Susan Blackmore in *The Meme Machine*, Oxford University Press, 1999.

19. See Aldrich, reference 8, p. 30.

20. For other implications see some of the references above. In particular Stacey (7), Brown and Eisenhardt (9) and McKelvey (14).

21. See M.S. Granovetter, 'The strength of weak ties', *American Journal of Sociology*, vol. 78, no. 6 (1973), pp. 1360–80.

22. See McKelvey, reference 14.

23. This is the term used by Brown and Eisenhardt, reference 9, amongst others.

24. This discussion is based on research by K.M. Eisenhardt and D.N. Sull, reported in 'Strategy as simple rules', *Harvard Business Review*, vol. 79, no. 1 (2001), pp. 107–16.

25. H. Mintzberg, *The Nature of Managerial Work*, Harper & Row, 1973.

26. In the *Handbook of Discourse Analysis* (ed. D. Schiffrin and H. Hamilton, Blackwell, 2001) T.A. Van Dijk writes: 'Critical Discourse Analysis primarily studies the way social power abuse, dominance and inequality are enacted, reproduced and resisted by text and talk in the social and political context' (p. 352).

27. S.E. Green Jr, 'A rhetorical theory of diffusion', *Academy of Management Review*, vol. 29, no. 4 (2004), pp. 653–69.

28. D. Knights, 'Changing spaces: the disruptive impact of a new epistemological location for the study of management', *Academy of Management Review*, vol. 17, no. 3 (1992), pp. 514–36.

29. D. Barry and M. Elmes, 'Strategy retold: toward a narrative view of strategic discourse', *Academy of Management Review*, vol. 22, no. 2 (1997).

30. For example, see C. Hardy, I. Palmer and N. Phillips, 'Discourse as a strategic resource', *Human Relations*, vol. 53, no. 9 (2000), p. 1231 and L. Heracleous and M. Barrett, 'Organizational change as discourse: communicative actions and deep structures in the context of information technology implementation', *Academy of Management Journal*, vol. 44, no. 4 (2001), pp. 755–78.

31. R. Suddaby and R. Greenwood, 'Rhetorical strategies of legitimacy', *Administrative Science Quarterly*, vol. 50 (2005), pp. 35–67. Also J. Sillence and F. Mueller, 'Switching strategic perspective: the reframing of accounts of responsibility', *Organization Studies*, vol. 28, no. 2 (2007), pp. 175–6.

32. L. Oakes, B. Townley and D.J. Cooper, 'Business planning as pedagogy: language and institutions in a changing institutional field', *Administrative Science Quarterly*, vol. 43, no. 2 (1998), pp. 257–92.

33. D. Knights and G. Morgan 'Corporate strategy, organizations and subjectivity', *Organization Studies*, vol. 12, no. 2 (1991), pp. 251–73.

34. A. Spicer, 'Book review of *Recreating Strategy*', *Organization Studies*, vol. 25, no. 7 (2004), p. 1256.

35. For example see Hardy, Palmer and Phillips (30 above).

36. R. Whittington, *What Is Strategy – and Does it Matter?*, 2nd edition, Thomson, 2000.

37. H. Mintzberg, B. Ahlstrand and J. Lampel, *Strategy Safari*, Prentice Hall, 1998.

PART I
THE STRATEGIC POSITION

This part explains:

- How to analyse an organisation's position in the external environment.

- How to analyse the determinants of strategic capability – resources, competences and the linkages between them.

- How to understand an organisation's purposes, taking into account corporate governance, stakeholder expectations and business ethics.

- How to address the role of history and culture in determining an organisation's position.

INTRODUCTION TO PART I

This part of the book is concerned with understanding the strategic position of the organisation. There are four chapters, organised around two themes. The first theme is the organisation's strategic *potential*, in other words what it *can* do. The second theme is the organisation's strategic *ambitions*, what it actually *seeks* to do, sometimes deliberately and sometimes not so deliberately (see Figure I.i).

Strategic potential is addressed as follows:

- Chapter 2 considers how different environments can be more or less rich in opportunities or hostile, imposing threats and constraints.
- Chapter 3 considers how each organisation has its own particular strategic capabilities (resources and competences), and how these can enable or constrain strategies.

Organisational ambitions are addressed in the following two chapters:

- Chapter 4 is about how the expectations of powerful groups can shape an organisation's purpose, often expressed in terms of vision and mission statements for example.
- Chapter 5 examines how an organisation's culture and history may shape the ambitions of an organisation, often in semi-conscious and hard-to-change ways.

There is an important strategic dilemma that runs through Chapters 2 and 3. How much should managers concentrate their attention on the external market position and how much should they focus on developing their internal capabilities? On the external side, many argue that environmental factors are what matter most to success: strategy development should be primarily about seeking attractive opportunities in the marketplace. Those favouring a more internal approach, on the other hand, argue that an organisation's specific strategic capabilities should drive strategy. It is from these internal characteristics that distinctive strategies and superior performance can be built. There can be a real trade-off here. Managers

Figure I.i Strategic position

who invest time and resources in developing their external market position (perhaps through acquiring companies that are potential competitors) have less time and resources to invest in managing their internal capabilities (for example, building up research and development). The same applies in reverse. This trade-off between the internal and the external is discussed explicitly in Chapter 2's Key Debate at the end of that chapter.

Chapters 4 and 5 raise another underlying issue. To what extent should managers' ambitions for their organisations be considered as free or constrained? Chapter 4 explains how the expectations of investors, regulators, employees and customers can often influence strategy. Chapter 5 raises the constraints on managers exercised by organisational history and culture. Managers may be only partially aware of these kinds of constraints and are often in danger of underestimating the hidden limits to their ambitions.

Understanding the extent of managers' freedom to choose is fundamental to considering the issues of strategic choice that make up Part II of this book. But first Part I provides a foundation by exploring the question of strategic position.

2

THE ENVIRONMENT

Learning outcomes

After reading this chapter, you should be able to:

● Analyse the broad macro-environment of organisations in terms of political, economic, social, technological, environmental ('green') and legal factors (*PESTEL*).

● Identify key drivers in this macro-environment and use these key drivers to construct alternative *scenarios* with regard to environmental change.

● Use *Porter's five forces* analysis in order to define the attractiveness of industries and sectors and to identify their potential for change.

● Identify successful *strategic groups*, valuable *market segments* and attractive *'Blue Oceans'* within industries.

● Use these various concepts and techniques in order to recognise *threats* and *opportunities* in the marketplace.

(2.1) INTRODUCTION

The environment is what gives organisations their means of survival. It creates opportunities and it presents threats. For example, the success of Apple's iPhone created rich market opportunities for the writers of mobile phone apps. On the other hand, the rise of electronic encyclopaedias such as Microsoft's Encarta and online Wikipedia nearly destroyed the market for the traditional print market-leader, *Encyclopaedia Britannica*, after two hundred years of existence. Although the future can never be predicted perfectly, it is clearly important that entrepreneurs and managers try to analyse their environments as carefully as they can in order to anticipate and – if possible – influence environmental change.

This chapter therefore provides frameworks for analysing changing and complex environments. These frameworks are organised in a series of 'layers' briefly introduced here and summarised in Figure 2.1.

- *The macro-environment* is the highest-level layer. This consists of broad environmental factors that impact to a greater or lesser extent on almost all organisations. Here, the PESTEL framework can be used to identify how future issues in the *political, economic, social, technological, environmental ('green') and legal* environments might affect organisations. This PESTEL analysis provides the broad 'data' from which to identify *key drivers of change*. These key drivers can be used to construct *scenarios* of alternative possible futures.

- *Industry, or sector*, forms the next layer within this broad general environment. This is made up of organisations producing the same products or services. Here the *five forces* framework

Figure 2.1 Layers of the business environment

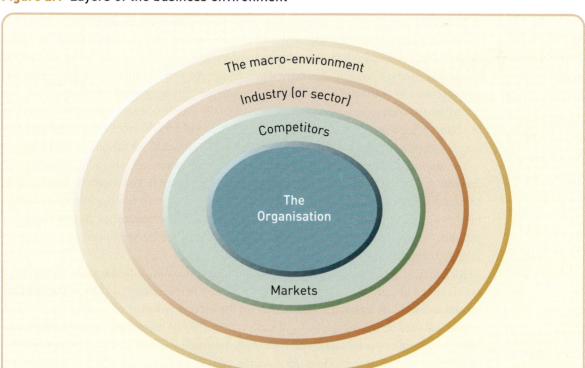

is particularly useful in understanding the attractiveness of particular industries or sectors and potential threats from outside the present set of competitors. The Key Debate at the end of this chapter addresses the importance of industry factors, rather than business-specific factors, in determining success.

● *Competitors and markets* are the most immediate layer surrounding organisations. Here the concept of *strategic groups* can help identify different kinds of competitors. Similarly, in the marketplace, customers' expectations are not all the same. They have a range of different requirements the importance of which can be understood through the concepts of *market segments* and *critical success factors*.

This chapter works through these three layers in turn, starting with the macro-environment.

2.2 THE MACRO-ENVIRONMENT

The three concepts in this section – PESTEL, key drivers and scenarios – are interrelated tools for analysing the broad macro-environment of an organisation. PESTEL provides a wide overview; key drivers help focus on what is most important; and scenarios build on key drivers to explore different ways in which the macro-environment might change.

2.2.1 The PESTEL framework

The **PESTEL framework** categorises environmental influences into six main types: political, economic, social, technological, environmental and legal. Thus PESTEL provides a comprehensive list of influences on the possible success or failure of particular strategies.[1] In particular, Politics highlights the role of governments; Economics refers to macro-economic factors such as exchange rates, business cycles and differential economic growth rates around the world; Social influences include changing cultures and demographics, for example ageing populations in many Western societies; Technological influences refer to innovations such as the internet, nano-technology or the rise of new composite materials; Environmental stands specifically for 'green' issues, such as pollution and waste; and finally Legal embraces legislative constraints or changes, such as health and safety legislation or restrictions on company mergers and acquisitions. Illustration 2.1 provides examples of PESTEL factors for the airline industry.

For managers, it is important to analyse how these factors are changing, drawing out implications for their organisations. Many of these factors are linked together. For example, technology developments may simultaneously change economic factors (for example, creating new jobs), social factors (facilitating more leisure) and environmental factors (reducing pollution). As can be imagined, analysing these factors and their interrelationships can produce long and complex lists.

Rather than getting overwhelmed by a multitude of details, it is necessary to step back eventually to identify the key drivers for change. **Key drivers for change** are the environmental factors likely to have a high impact on the success or failure of strategy. Typical key drivers will vary by industry or sector. Thus a retailer may be primarily concerned with social changes driving customer tastes and behaviour, for example forces encouraging out-of-town shopping, and economic changes, for example rates of economic growth and employment. Public-sector managers are likely to be especially concerned with social change (for example, an ageing population), political change (changing government funding and policies) and

ILLUSTRATION 2.1

PESTEL analysis of the airline industry

Environmental influences on organisations can be summarised within six categories. For the airline industry, an initial list of influences under the six PESTEL analysis categories might include the following:

Political

- Government support for national carriers
- Security controls
- Restrictions on migration

Economic

- National growth rates
- Fuel prices

Social

- Rise in travel by elderly
- Student international study exchanges

Technological

- Fuel-efficient engines and airframes
- Security check technologies
- Teleconferencing for business

Environmental

- Noise pollution controls
- Energy consumption controls
- Land for growing airports

Legal

- Restrictions on mergers
- Preferential airport rights for some carriers

Questions

1 What additional environmental influences would you add to this initial list for the airline industry?
2 From your more comprehensive list, which of these influences would you highlight as likely to be the 'key drivers for change' for airlines in the coming five years?

legislative change (introducing new requirements). Identifying key drivers for change helps managers to focus on the PESTEL factors that are most important and which must be addressed as the highest priority. Many other changes will depend on these key drivers anyway (for example, an ageing population will drive changes in public policy and funding). Without a clear sense of the key drivers for change, managers will not be able to take the decisions that allow for effective action.

2.2.2 Building scenarios

When the business environment has high levels of *uncertainty* arising from either complexity or rapid change (or both), it is impossible to develop a single view of how environmental influences might affect an organisation's strategies – indeed it would be dangerous to do so. Scenario analyses are carried out to allow for different possibilities and help prevent managers from closing their minds about alternatives. Thus scenarios offer plausible alternative views of how the business environment might develop in the future, based on key drivers for change about which there is a high level of uncertainty.[2] Scenarios typically build on PESTEL analyses and key drivers for change, but do not offer a single forecast of how the environment will change. The point is not to predict, but to encourage managers to be alert to a range of possible futures.

Illustration 2.2 shows an example of scenario planning for the global financial system to 2020. Rather than incorporating a multitude of factors, the authors focus on two key drivers which (i) have high potential impact and (ii) are uncertain: geo-economic power shifts and international coordination on financial policy. Both of these drivers may produce very different futures, which can be combined to create four internally consistent scenarios for the next decade. The authors do not predict that one will prevail over the others, nor do they allocate relative probabilities. Prediction would close managers' minds to alternatives, while probabilities would imply a spurious kind of accuracy.

Scenario analyses can be carried out as follows:[3]

- *Identifying the scope* is an important first step. Scope refers to the subject of the scenario analysis and the time span. For example, scenario analyses can be carried out for a whole industry globally, or for particular geographical regions and markets. They can be for a decade or so (as in Illustration 2.2) or for just three to five years ahead.

- *Identifying key drivers for change* comes next. Here PESTEL analysis can be used to uncover issues likely to have a major impact upon the future of the industry, region or market.

- *Selecting opposing key drivers* is crucial in order to generate a range of different but plausible scenarios. Typically scenario analyses select from the various key drivers for change two key drivers which both have high uncertainty and have the potential for producing significantly divergent or opposing outcomes. In the oil industry, for example, political stability in the oil-producing regions is one major uncertainty; another is the capacity to develop major new oilfields, thanks to new extraction technologies or oilfield discoveries.

- *Developing scenario 'stories'*: as in films, scenarios are basically stories. Having selected opposing key drivers for change, it is necessary to knit together plausible 'stories' that incorporate both key drivers and other factors into a coherent whole. Thus in Illustration 2.2, the Fragmented protectionism scenario brings together in a consistent way failure to achieve international coordination and a slow rate of geo-economic shift: nationalistic protectionist measures in the West would prevent coordination at the same time as delaying the rise of the Asian economies. But completing the 'story' of Fragmented protectionism would also involve incorporating other consistent factors: for example, slow economic growth resulting from barriers to trade; possible military conflicts due to lack of international cooperation; and illiberal domestic politics associated with nationalism.

- *Identifying impacts* of alternative scenarios on organisations is the final key stage of scenario building. Fragmented protectionism would obviously have a very negative impact for most multinational corporations. Rebalanced multilateralism on the other hand would favour multinationals, especially those from the rising Asian economies. It would be important for an organisation to carry out *robustness checks* in the face of each plausible scenario and develop *contingency plans* in case they happen.

ILLUSTRATION 2.2

Scenarios for the global financial system, 2020

Founded in 1971, the World Economic Forum (www.weforum.org) is a not-for-profit organisation based in Geneva dedicated to developing new thinking amongst political, business and society leaders from countries worldwide. Participants at its famous annual Davos meetings have included German Chancellor Angela Merkel, Microsoft founder Bill Gates and South African President Nelson Mandela. As the world wrestled with the financial crisis of 2008–9, the World Economic Forum proposed to the 2009 Davos meeting four long-range scenarios for how the global financial system might develop to 2025. These scenarios were developed through eight separate workshops involving over 250 financial executives, regulators, policy-makers and senior academics.

The scenarios were based on two key drivers, each governed by a great deal of uncertainty. The first key driver was the pace of geo-economic power shifts, in particular from the traditional centres of economic power in the United States and Europe to the emerging ones in Asia and elsewhere. The second key driver was the degree of international coordination of financial policy, referring to issues such as banking regulation and currency policies. It was the

upsides and downsides of these key drivers that defined the following four scenarios.

Re-engineered Western-centrism proposes a world in which the power-shift from the West is reasonably slow and policy-makers manage to coordinate a stable financial framework in which to navigate change. This is a comforting scenario for many Western companies. The *Rebalanced multilateralism* scenario envisages a more rapid shift from the West, but none the less policy-makers are able to co-ordinate change. For most Western companies, this is challenging but manageable, with Asia continuing to value their participation. More limiting is the *Financial regionalism* scenario. Here policy-makers are unable to find global agreement and the world splits into three major blocs, an American one, a European one and an increasingly powerful Asian one. Western companies are obliged to adopt very different strategies and structures for each of the three main blocs. The final scenario of *Fragmented protectionism* is daunting. Here nationalistic protectionism slows the shift from the West, but also reduces economic growth and leads to the collapse of the integrated Eurozone. All kinds of international business suffer from volatility, conflict and controls.

The World Economic Forum made no forecast about which scenario was more probable. But in presenting the alternatives, it aimed to get policy-makers to see the need for serious action, at the same time as warning business leaders that 'business as usual' was not a likely prospect.

Source: http://www.weforum.org/pdf/scenarios/ TheFutureoftheGlobalFinancialSystem.pdf.

	Slow geo-economic shift	Rapid geo-economic shift
Harmonised financial coordination	Re-engineered Western-centrism	Rebalanced multilateralism
Discordant financial coordination	Fragmented protectionism	Financial regionalism

Question

Over which of the two drivers – the geo-economic power shift and policy coordination – do companies have the most influence? How should they exercise this influence?

Because debating and learning are so valuable in the scenario building process, and they deal with such high uncertainty, some scenario experts advise managers to avoid producing just three scenarios. Three scenarios tend to fall into a range of 'optimistic', 'middling' and 'pessimistic'. Managers naturally focus on the middling scenario and neglect the other two, reducing the amount of organisational learning and contingency planning. It is therefore typically better to have two or four scenarios, avoiding an easy mid-point. It does not matter if the scenarios do not come to pass: the value lies in the process of exploration and contingency planning that the scenarios set off.

 2.3 INDUSTRIES AND SECTORS

The previous section looked at how forces in the macro-environment might influence the success or failure of an organisation's strategies. But the impact of these general factors tends to surface in the more immediate environment through changes in the competitive forces surrounding organisations. An important aspect of this for most organisations will be competition within their industry, sector or market. **An industry is a group of firms producing products and services that are essentially the same.**[4] Examples are the automobile industry and the airline industry. Industries are also often described as 'sectors', especially in public services (for example, the health sector or the education sector). Industries and sectors are often made up of several specific markets. **A market is a group of customers for specific products or services that are essentially the same (for example, a particular geographical market)**. Thus the automobile industry has markets in North America, Europe and Asia, for example.

This section concentrates on industry analysis, starting with Michael Porter's *five forces framework* and then introducing techniques for analysing the *dynamics* of industries. However, while the following section will address markets in more detail, this section will refer to markets and most of the concepts apply similarly to markets and industries.

2.3.1 Competitive forces – the five forces framework

KEY CONCEPT
Porter's five forces framework

Porter's five forces framework[5] **helps identify the attractiveness of an industry in terms of five competitive forces: the threat of entry, the threat of substitutes, the power of buyers, the power of suppliers and the extent of rivalry between competitors.** These five forces together constitute an industry's 'structure' (see Figure 2.2), which is typically fairly stable. For Porter, an attractive industry structure is one that offers good profit potential. His essential message is that where the five forces are high, industries are not attractive to compete in. There will be too much competition, and too much pressure, to allow reasonable profits.

Although initially developed with businesses in mind, the five forces framework is relevant to most organisations. It can provide a useful starting point for strategic analysis even where profit criteria may not apply. In the public sector, it is important to understand how powerful suppliers can push up costs; amongst charities, it is important to avoid excessive rivalry within the same market. Moreover, once the degree of industry attractiveness has been understood, the five forces can help set an agenda for action on the various critical issues that they identify: for example, what should be done to control excessive rivalry in a particular industry? The rest of this section introduces each of the five forces in more detail. Illustration 2.3 on the evolving steel industry provides examples.

Figure 2.2 The five forces framework

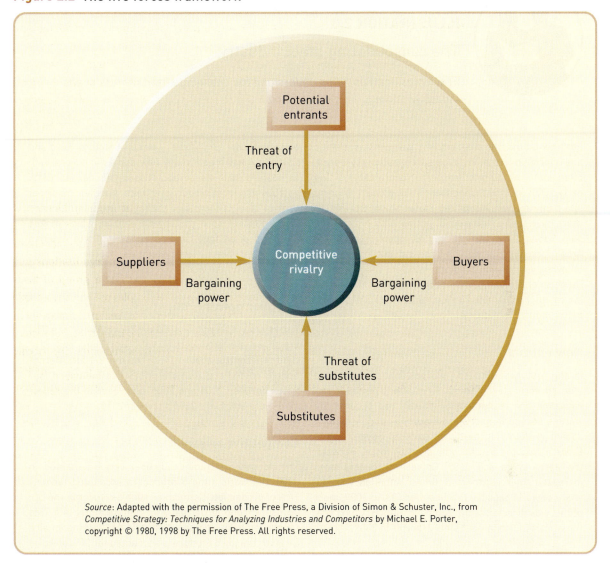

The threat of entry

How easy it is to enter the industry obviously influences the degree of competition. The greater the threat of entry, the worse it is for incumbents (existing competitors) in an industry. An attractive industry has high barriers to entry in order to reduce the threat of new competitors. **Barriers to entry are the factors that need to be overcome by new entrants if they are to compete in an industry**. Typical barriers are as follows:

● *Scale and experience*. In some industries, *economies of scale* are extremely important: for example, in the production of automobiles or the advertising of fast-moving consumer goods. Once incumbents have reached large-scale production, it will be very expensive for new entrants to match them and until they reach a similar volume they will have higher unit costs. This scale effect is increased where there are high *investment requirements* for entry, for example research costs in pharmaceuticals or capital equipment costs in automobiles. Barriers to entry also come from *experience curve* effects that give incumbents a cost

ILLUSTRATION 2.3

The consolidating steel industry

Five forces analysis helps understand the changing attractiveness of an industry.

For a long time, the steel industry was seen as a static and unprofitable one. Producers were nationally-based, often state-owned and frequently unprofitable – the early 2000s saw 50 independent steel producers going into bankruptcy in the United States alone. But recent years have seen a turnaround. During 2006, Mittal Steel paid $35bn (~€24.5bn) to buy European steel giant Arcelor, creating the world's largest steel company. The following year, Indian conglomerate Tata bought Anglo-Dutch steel company Corus for $13bn. These high prices indicated considerable confidence in the prospects of a better industry structure.

New entrants

In the last two decades, two powerful groups have entered world steel markets. First, after a period of privatisation and reorganisation, Russia had become the world's second largest steel exporting country (behind Japan) in 2009, led by giants such as Severstal and Evraz. China too had become a major force. Between the early 1990s and 2009, Chinese producers have increased their capacity six times. Although Chinese share of world capacity reached over 40% in 2009, most of this was directed at the domestic market. China was the word's fourth largest steel exporter in 2009.

Substitutes

Steel is a nineteenth century technology, increasingly substituted for by other materials such as aluminium in cars, plastics and aluminium in packaging and ceramics and composites in many high-tech applications. Steel's own technological advances sometimes work to reduce need: thus steel cans have become about one third thinner over the last few decades.

Buyer power

The major buyers of steel are the global car manufacturers. Car manufacturers are sophisticated users, often leading in the technological development of their materials. In North America at least, the decline of the once dominant 'Big Three' – General Motors, Ford and Chrysler – has meant many new domestic buyers, with companies such as Toyota, Nissan, Honda and BMW establishing local production plants. Another important user of steel is the metal packaging industry. Leading can producers such as Crown Holdings, which makes one third of all food cans produced in North America and Europe, buy in large volumes, coordinating purchases around the world.

Supplier power

The key raw material for steel producers is iron ore. The big three ore producers – Vale, Rio Tinto and BHP Billiton – control about 70% of the market for internationally traded ore. Iron ore prices had multiplied four times between 2005 and 2008, and, despite the recession, were still twice 2005's level in 2010.

Competitive rivalry

The industry has traditionally been very fragmented: in 2000, the world's top 5 producers accounted for only 14% of production. Companies such as Nucor in the US, Thyssen-Krupp in Germany as well as Mittal and Tata responded by buying up weaker players internationally. By 2009, the top 5 producers accounted for 20% of world production. New steel giant ArcelorMittal alone accounted for about 10% of world production, with one fifth of the European Union market. None the less, despite a cyclical peak in 2008 and a slump in 2009, the world steel price was basically the same in 2010 as in 2005.

Questions

1 In recent years, which of the five forces has become more positive for steel producers, which less so?

2 Explain the acquisition strategies of players such as Mittal, Tata and Nucor.

3 In the future, what might change to make the steel industry less attractive or more attractive?

INDUSTRIES AND SECTORS **57**

advantage because they have learnt how to do things more efficiently than an inexperienced new entrant could possibly do (see section 6.3.1). Until the new entrant has built up equivalent experience over time, it will tend to produce at higher cost.

- *Access to supply or distribution channels.* In many industries manufacturers have had control over supply and/or distribution channels. Sometimes this has been through direct ownership (vertical integration), sometimes just through customer or supplier loyalty. In some industries this barrier has been overcome by new entrants who have bypassed retail distributors and sold directly to consumers through e-commerce (for example, Dell Computers and Amazon).

- *Expected retaliation.* If an organisation considering entering an industry believes that the retaliation of an existing firm will be so great as to prevent entry, or mean that entry would be too costly, this is also a barrier. Retaliation could take the form of a price war or a marketing blitz. Just the knowledge that incumbents are prepared to retaliate is often sufficiently discouraging to act as a barrier. This dynamic interaction between incumbents and potential new entrants will be discussed more fully in section 2.3.2 below.

- *Legislation or government action.* Legal restraints on new entry vary from patent protection (e.g. pharmaceuticals), to regulation of markets (e.g. pension selling), through to direct government action (e.g. tariffs). Of course, organisations are vulnerable to new entrants if governments remove such protection, as has happened with deregulation of the airline industry.

- *Differentiation.* Differentiation means providing a product or service with higher perceived value than the competition; its importance will be discussed more fully in section 6.3.2. Cars are differentiated, for example, by quality and branding. Steel, by contrast, is by-and-large a commodity, undifferentiated and therefore sold by the ton. Steel buyers will simply buy the cheapest. Differentiation reduces the threat of entry because of increasing customer loyalty.

The threat of substitutes

Substitutes are products or services that offer a similar benefit to an industry's products or services, but by a different process. For example, aluminium is a substitute for steel in automobiles; trains are a substitute for cars; television and videogames are substitutes for each other. Managers often focus on their competitors in their own industry, and neglect the threat posed by substitutes. Substitutes can reduce demand for a particular type of product as customers switch to alternatives – even to the extent that this type of product or service becomes obsolete. However, there does not have to be much actual switching for the substitute threat to have an effect. The simple risk of substitution puts a cap on the prices that can be charged in an industry. Thus, although Eurostar has no direct competitors in terms of train services from Paris to London, the prices it can charge are ultimately limited by the cost of flights between the two cities.

There are two important points to bear in mind about substitutes:

- *The price/performance ratio* is critical to substitution threats. A substitute is still an effective threat even if more expensive, so long as it offers performance advantages that customers value. Thus aluminium is more expensive than steel, but its relative lightness and its resistance to corrosion give it an advantage in some automobile manufacturing applications. It is the ratio of price to performance that matters, rather than simple price.

- *Extra-industry effects* are the core of the substitution concept. Substitutes come from outside the incumbents' industry and should not be confused with competitors' threats from within the industry. The value of the substitution concept is to force managers to look outside their own industry to consider more distant threats and constraints. The higher the threat of substitution, the less attractive the industry is likely to be.

The power of buyers

Buyers are the organisation's immediate customers, not necessarily the ultimate consumers. If buyers are powerful, then they can demand cheap prices or product or service improvements liable to reduce profits.

Buyer power is likely to be high when some of the following conditions prevail:

- *Concentrated buyers.* Where a few large customers account for the majority of sales, buyer power is increased. This is the case on items such as milk in the grocery sector in many European countries, where just a few retailers dominate the market. If a product or service accounts for a high percentage of the buyers' total purchases their power is also likely to increase as they are more likely to 'shop around' to get the best price and therefore 'squeeze' suppliers than they would for more trivial purchases.

- *Low switching costs.* Where buyers can easily switch between one supplier and another, they have a strong negotiating position and can squeeze suppliers who are desperate for their business. Switching costs are typically low for weakly differentiated commodities such as steel.

- *Buyer competition threat.* If the buyer has the capability to supply itself, or if it has the possibility of acquiring such a capability, it tends to be powerful. In negotiation with its suppliers, it can raise the threat of doing the suppliers' job themselves. This is called *backward vertical integration* (see section 7.5), moving back to sources of supply, and might occur if satisfactory prices or quality from suppliers cannot be obtained. For example, some steel companies have gained power over their iron ore suppliers as they have acquired iron ore sources for themselves.

It is very important that *buyers* are distinguished from *ultimate consumers*. Thus for companies like Procter & Gamble or Unilever (makers of shampoo, washing powders and so on), their buyers are retailers such as Carrefour or Tesco, not ordinary consumers (see discussion of the 'strategic customer' in 2.4.2). Carrefour and Tesco have much more negotiating power than an ordinary consumer would have. The high buying power of such supermarkets has become a major source of pressure for the companies supplying them.

The power of suppliers

Suppliers are those who supply the organisation with what it needs to produce the product or service. As well as fuel, raw materials and equipment, this can include labour and sources of finance. The factors increasing supplier power are the converse to those for buyer power. Thus *supplier power* is likely to be high where there are:

- *Concentrated suppliers.* Where just a few producers dominate supply, suppliers have more power over buyers. The iron ore industry is now concentrated in the hands of three main producers, leaving the steel companies, still relatively fragmented, in a weak negotiating position for this essential raw material.

- *High switching cost.* If it is expensive or disruptive to move from one supplier to another, then the buyer becomes relatively dependent and correspondingly weak. Microsoft is a powerful supplier because of the high switching costs of moving from one operating system to another. Buyers are prepared to pay a premium to avoid the trouble, and Microsoft knows it.

- *Supplier competition threat.* Suppliers have increased power where they are able to cut out buyers who are acting as middlemen. Thus airlines have been able to negotiate tough contracts with travel agencies as the rise of online booking has allowed them to create a direct route to customers. This is called *forward vertical integration*, moving up closer to the ultimate customer.

Most organisations have many suppliers, so it is necessary to concentrate the analysis on the most important ones or types. If their power is high, suppliers can capture all their buyers' own potential profits simply by raising their prices. Star football players have succeeded in raising their rewards to astronomical levels, while even the leading football clubs – their 'buyers' – struggle to make money.

Competitive rivalry

These wider competitive forces (the four arrows in the model in Figure 2.2) all impinge on the direct competitive rivalry between an organisation and its most immediate rivals. Thus low barriers to entry increase the number of rivals; powerful buyers with low switching costs force their suppliers to high rivalry in order to offer the best deals. The more competitive rivalry there is, the worse it is for incumbents within the industry.

Competitive **rivals** **are organisations with similar products and services aimed at the same customer group (i.e. not substitutes).** In the European airline industry, Air France and British Airways are rivals; trains are a substitute. As well as the influence of the four previous forces, there are a number of additional factors directly affecting the degree of competitive rivalry in an industry or sector:

- *Competitor balance.* Where competitors are of roughly equal size there is the danger of intensely rivalrous behaviour as one competitor attempts to gain dominance over others, through aggressive price cuts for example. Conversely, less rivalrous industries tend to have one or two dominant organisations, with the smaller players reluctant to challenge the larger ones directly (for example, by focusing on niches to avoid the 'attention' of the dominant companies).

- *Industry growth rate.* In situations of strong growth, an organisation can grow with the market, but in situations of low growth or decline, any growth is likely to be at the expense of a rival, and meet with fierce resistance. Low growth markets are therefore often associated with price competition and low profitability. The *industry life cycle* influences growth rates, and hence competitive conditions: see section 2.3.2.

- *High fixed costs.* Industries with high fixed costs, perhaps because requiring high investments in capital equipment or initial research, tend to be highly rivalrous. Companies will seek to spread their costs (i.e. reduce unit costs) by increasing their volumes: to do so, they typically cut their prices, prompting competitors to do the same and thereby triggering price wars in which everyone in the industry suffers. Similarly, if extra capacity can only be added in large increments (as in many manufacturing sectors, for example a chemical or glass factory), the competitor making such an addition is likely to create short-term over-capacity in the industry, leading to increased competition to use capacity.

- *High exit barriers.* The existence of high barriers to exit – in other words, closure or disinvestment – tends to increase rivalry, especially in declining industries. Excess capacity persists and consequently incumbents fight to maintain market share. Exit barriers might be high for a variety of reasons: for example, high redundancy costs or high investment in specific assets such as plant and equipment that others would not buy.

- *Low differentiation.* In a commodity market, where products or services are poorly differentiated, rivalry is increased because there is little to stop customers switching between competitors and the only way to compete is on price.

Types of industry

Five forces analysis helps to identify four main types of industry structure. In practice, particular industries are typically not pure representatives of these types, but nonetheless it is helpful to have these broad categories in mind in order to compare the attractiveness of industries and likely broad patterns of competitive behaviour within them. These four types are:

- *Monopolistic industries.* A **monopoly is formally an industry with just one firm and therefore no competitive rivalry**. Because of the lack of choice between rivals, there is potentially very great power over buyers and suppliers. This can be very profitable. In practice, pure monopolies are rare because government regulators typically prohibit them. However, firms may still have 'monopolistic power' where their dominance over other firms in the industry is very great, as for example Google which in early 2010 had 65 per cent of the American search market, against Yahoo's 17 per cent and Microsoft's 11 per cent. Such monopolistic power gives firms considerable leverage in negotiating prices with buyers and suppliers. Thus Google has strong price-setting power in the internet advertising business.

- *Oligopolistic industries.* An **oligopoly is where just a few firms dominate an industry, with the potential for limited rivalry and great power over buyers and suppliers**. The iron ore market is an oligopoly, dominated by Vale, Rio Tinto and BHP Billiton (see Illustration 2.3). Where there are just two oligopolistic rivals, as for Airbus and Boeing in the civil airline industry, the situation is a duopoly. In theory, oligopoly can be highly profitable, but much depends on the extent of rivalrous behaviour, the threat of entry and substitutes and the growth of final demand in key markets. Oligopolistic firms have a strong interest in minimising rivalry between each other so as to maintain a common front against buyers and suppliers.

- *Hypercompetitive industries.* **Hypercompetition occurs where the frequency, boldness and aggression of competitor interactions accelerate to create a condition of constant disequilibrium and change**.[6] Under hypercompetition, rivals tend to invest heavily in destabilising innovation, expensive marketing initiatives and aggressive price cuts, with negative impacts on profits. Hypercompetition often breaks out in otherwise oligopolistic industries. Thus the global mobile phone industry has some oligopolistic characteristics, with Nokia holding 35 per cent share, Samsung 21 per cent and LG 11 per cent in 2009. However, Samsung and LG are increasing their share aggressively, and there are many strong challengers, including the innovative Apple iPhone and Google's Nexus One. Competitive moves under conditions of hypercompetition are discussed in section 6.4.2.

- *Perfectly competitive industries.* **Perfect competition exists where barriers to entry are low, there are many equal rivals each with very similar products, and information about competitors is freely available**. Few markets are absolutely perfectly competitive, but many are highly so. In these conditions, firms are unable to earn more profit than the bare minimum required to survive. Competition focuses heavily on price, because competitors typically cannot fund major innovations or marketing initiatives. Minicab services in large cities often come close to perfect competition. Entrepreneurs should beware entering industries with low barriers to entry, as these are liable to be perfectly or highly competitive and good profits will be very hard to earn.

Implications of five forces analysis

The five forces framework provides useful insights into the forces at work in the industry or market environment of an organisation. It is important, however, to use the framework for more than simply listing the forces. The bottom line is an assessment of the attractiveness of the industry. The analysis should conclude with a judgement about whether the industry is a good one to compete in or not.

The analysis should next prompt investigation of the *implications* of these forces, for example:

- *Which industries to enter (or leave)?* The fundamental purpose of the five forces model is to identify the relative attractiveness of different industries: industries are attractive when the forces are weak. Entrepreneurs and managers should invest in industries where the five forces work in their favour and avoid, or disinvest from, markets where they are strongly against.

- *What influence can be exerted?* Industry structures are not necessarily fixed, but can be influenced by deliberate managerial strategies. For example, organisations can build barriers to entry by increasing advertising spend to improve customer loyalty. They can buy up competitors to reduce rivalry and increase power over suppliers or buyers. Influencing industry structure involves many issues relating to *competitive strategy* and will be a major concern of Chapter 6.

- *How are competitors differently affected?* Not all competitors will be affected equally by changes in industry structure, deliberate or spontaneous. If barriers are rising because of increased R&D or advertising spending, smaller players in the industry may not be able to keep up with the larger players, and be squeezed out. Similarly, growing buyer power is likely to hurt small competitors most. Strategic group analysis is helpful here (see 2.4.1).

Although originating in the private sector, five forces analysis can have important implications for organisations in the public sector too. For example, the forces can be used to adjust the service offer or focus on key issues. Thus it might be worth switching managerial initiative from an arena with many crowded and overlapping services (e.g. social work, probation services and education) to one that is less rivalrous and where the organisation can do something more distinctive. Similarly, strategies could be launched to reduce dependence on particularly powerful and expensive suppliers, for example energy sources or high shortage skills.

Key issues in using the five forces framework

The five forces framework has to be used carefully and is not necessarily complete, even at the industry level. When using this framework, it is important to bear the following three issues in mind:

- *Defining the 'right' industry.* Most industries can be analysed at different levels, for example different markets and even different segments within them (see 2.4.2 below). For example, the airline industry has different geographical markets (Europe, China and so on) and it also has different segments within each market (e.g. leisure, business and freight). The competitive forces are likely to be different for each of these markets and segments and can be analysed separately. It is sometimes useful to conduct industry analysis at a disaggregated level, for each distinct segment or market. The overall picture for the industry as a whole can then be assembled.

- *Converging industries.* Industry definition is often difficult too because industry boundaries are continuously changing. For example, many industries, especially in high-tech arenas, are converging. Convergence is where previously separate industries begin to overlap or merge in terms of activities, technologies, products and customers.[7] Technological change has brought convergence between the telephone and photographic industries, for example, as mobile phones have come to include camera and video functions. For a camera company like Kodak, Nokia and Samsung could even be considered direct competitors.

- *Complementary organisations.* Some analysts argue that industry analyses need to include a 'sixth force', the existence of organisations that are complementors rather than simple competitors. **An organisation is your complementor: (i) if customers value your product more when they have the other organisation's product than when they have the product alone; (ii) if it's more attractive for suppliers to provide resources to you when they are also supplying the other organisation than when they are supplying you alone.**[8] An example of the first is Microsoft Windows software and McAfee computer security: each is better because of the other. An example of the second is airlines in relationship to an aircraft supplier such as Boeing: Boeing invests more in innovation because of the existence of many airline companies as potential customers. Complementarity implies a significant shift in perspective. While Porter's five forces sees organisations as battling against each other for share of industry value, complementors may *cooperate* to increase the total value available[9]. If Microsoft and McAfee keep each other in touch with their technological developments, they increase the value of both their products. Opportunities for cooperation can be seen through a **value net: a map of organisations in a business environment demonstrating opportunities for value-creating cooperation as well as competition.** In Figure 2.3, Sony is a complementor, supplier and competitor to Apple's iPod. Sony and Apple have an interest in cooperating as well as competing.

2.3.2 The dynamics of industry structure

Industry structure analysis can easily become too static: after all, structure implies stablility.[10] However, the previous sections have raised the issue of how competitive forces change *over time*. The key drivers for change are likely to alter industry structures and scenario analyses can be used to understand possible impacts. An illustration of changing industry structure, and the competitive implications of this, is provided by the Illustration 2.4 on the UK charity sector. This section examines three additional approaches to understanding change in industry structure: the *industry life cycle* concept; *comparative five forces analyses*; and the notion of *hypercompetitive cycles of competition*.

The industry life cycle

The power of the five forces typically varies with the stages of the industry life cycle. The industry life cycle concept proposes that industries start small in their development stage, then go through period of rapid growth (the equivalent to 'adolescence' in the human life cycle), culminating in a period of 'shake-out'. The final two stages are first a period of slow or even

Figure 2.3 The value net

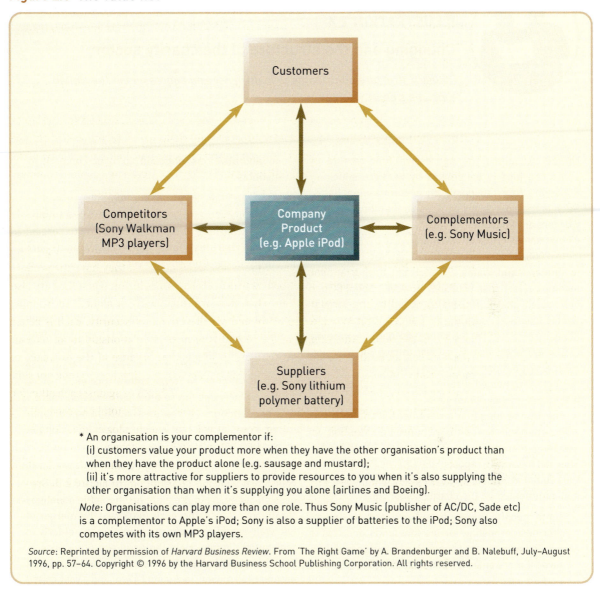

* An organisation is your complementor if:
 (i) customers value your product more when they have the other organisation's product than when they have the product alone (e.g. sausage and mustard);
 (ii) it's more attractive for suppliers to provide resources to you when it's also supplying the other organisation than when it's supplying you alone (airlines and Boeing).

Note: Organisations can play more than one role. Thus Sony Music (publisher of AC/DC, Sade etc) is a complementor to Apple's iPod; Sony is also a supplier of batteries to the iPod; Sony also competes with its own MP3 players.

Source: Reprinted by permission of *Harvard Business Review*. From 'The Right Game' by A. Brandenburger and B. Nalebuff, July–August 1996, pp. 57–64. Copyright © 1996 by the Harvard Business School Publishing Corporation. All rights reserved.

zero growth ('maturity'), and then the final stage of decline ('old age'). Each of these stages has implications for the five forces.[11]

The *development stage* is an experimental one, typically with few players, little direct rivalry and highly differentiated products. The five forces are likely to be weak, therefore, though profits may actually be scarce because of high investment requirements. The next stage is one of high growth, with rivalry low as there is plenty of market opportunity for everybody. Buyers may be keen to secure supplies of the booming new product and may also lack sophistication about what they are buying, so diminishing their power. One downside of the growth stage is that barriers to entry may be low, as existing competitors have not built up much scale, experience or customer loyalty. Another potential downside is the power of suppliers if there is a shortage of components or materials that fast-growing businesses need for expansion. The *shake-out stage* begins as the growth rate starts to decline, so that increased rivalry forces the

ILLUSTRATION 2.4

Chugging and the structure of the charity sector

Industry structure contributes to inefficiency and aggression in the United Kingdom's charity sector.

The charity sector has become controversial in the United Kingdom. The aggressive fund-raising of some charities is epitomised by workers soliciting donations from shoppers on a commission basis. Such is their perceived aggression that these charity workers are known as 'chuggers', compared with the violent street-crime of 'muggers'.

In 2008, there were 189,000 charities registered in England and Wales, 95 per cent having annual incomes of less than £500,000. However, about 80 per cent of all charity income is raised by the largest twenty charities, headed by Cancer Research UK (2008 income, £355m (~€390m; ~$532m)). According to *Charity Market Monitor*, in 2008, the top 300 charities averaged a 0.9 per cent increase in income, but the largest 10 managed income growth of 2.3 per cent (excluding impact of mergers).

The United Kingdom government introduced the 2006 Charities Act with the specific intention of assisting mergers between independent charities. This had followed a report of the Charity Commission, the regulator for charities in England and Wales, that had commented on the charity sector thus:

> Some people believe that there are too many charities competing for too few funds and that a significant amount of charitable resource could be saved if more charities pooled their resources and worked together. . . .
>
> The majority of charities are relatively small, local organisations that rely entirely on the unpaid help of their trustees and other volunteers. They may have similar purposes to many other charities but they are all serving different communities. The nature of these charities suggests that there are less likely to be significant areas of overlap . . . It is the much larger, professionally run, charities which, because of their size, tend to face charges of duplication, waste and over-aggressive fund-raising. Whilst there are some clear advantages to be had from a healthy plurality of charities, which are constantly refreshed by new charities pursuing new activities, there are also big benefits of public

confidence and support to be had from showing collaborative, as opposed to over-competitive, instincts.

Local authorities in particular were frustrated by duplication and waste, as they increasingly commission local charities to deliver services. With respect to small charities, local authority budgets are relatively large. One charity sector chief executive, Caroline Shaw, told *Charity Times* as she pursued more cooperation between local charities:

> 'Without a doubt there is increased competition when it comes to [local authority] commissioning . . . Our driving force has really been to try to create a more effective service for front line organisations; to offer more projects, more diverse services, more effective services. There's a huge amount [of charities] all fighting for funding. I really think that people should be looking at working more closely together.'

During 2008, more than 230 charity mergers were registered with the Charity Commission. As the recession began to put pressure on charitable donations throughout the sector, early 2009 saw the merger of two well-established charities helping the elderly in the United Kingom, Help the Aged and Age Concern. The new charity, Age UK, has a combined income of around £160 million, including £47 million a year raised through fundraising, and over 520 charity shops.

Sources: 'RS 4a – Collaborative working and mergers: Summary', http://www.charity-commission.gov.uk/publications/rs4a.asp; *Charity Times*, 'Strength in Numbers', August 2007; *Charity Market Monitor*, 2009.

Questions

1 Which of Porter's five forces are creating problems for the United Kingdom's charity sector?

2 What type of industry structure might the charity industry be moving towards? What would be the benefits and disadvantages of that structure?

Figure 2.4 The industry life cycle

weakest of the new entrants out of the business. In the *maturity stage*, barriers to entry tend to increase, as control over distribution is established and economies of scale and experience curve benefits come into play. Products or service tend to standardise. Buyers may become more powerful as they become less avid for the industry's products or services and more confident in switching between suppliers. Market share is typically crucial at the maturity stage, providing leverage against buyers and competitive advantage in terms of cost. Finally, the *decline stage* can be a period of extreme rivalry, especially where there are high exit barriers, as falling sales force remaining competitors into dog-eat-dog competition. Figure 2.4 summarises some of the conditions that can be expected at different stages in the life cycle.

It is important to avoid putting too much faith in the inevitability of life-cycle stages. One stage does not follow predictably after another: industries vary widely in the length of their growth stages, and others can rapidly 'de-mature' through radical innovation. The telephony industry, based for nearly a century on fixed-line telephones, de-matured rapidly with the introduction of mobile and internet telephony. Anita McGahan of Toronto University warns of the 'maturity mindset', which can leave many managers complacent and slow to respond to new competition.[12] Managing in mature industries is not necessarily just about waiting for decline. However, even if the various stages are not inevitable, the life-cycle concept does remind managers that conditions are likely to change over time. Especially in fast-moving industries, five forces analyses need to be reviewed quite regularly.

Comparative industry structure analyses

The industry life cycle underlines the need to make industry structure analysis dynamic. One effective means of doing this is to compare the five forces over time in a simple 'radar plot'.

Figure 2.5 Comparative industry structure analysis

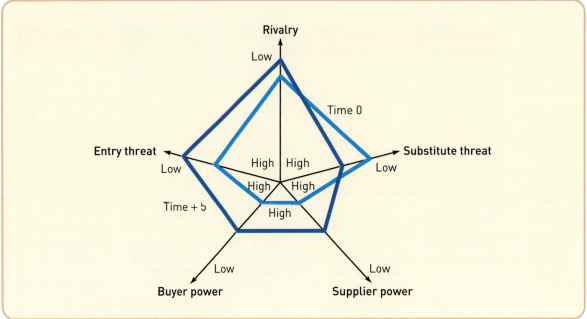

Figure 2.5 provides a framework for summarising the power of each of the five forces on five axes. Power diminishes as the axes go outwards. Where the forces are low, the total area enclosed by the lines between the axes is large; where the forces are high, the total area enclosed by the lines is small. The larger the enclosed area, therefore, the greater is the profit potential. In Figure 2.5, the industry at Time 0 (represented by the light blue lines) has relatively low rivalry (just a few competitors) and faces low substitution threats. The threat of entry is moderate, but both buyer power and supplier power are relatively high. Overall, this looks like only a moderately attractive industry to invest in.

However, given the dynamic nature of industries, managers need to look forward – here five years represented by the dark blue lines in Figure 2.5. Managers are predicting in this case some rise in the threat of substitutes (perhaps new technologies will be developed). On the other hand, they predict a falling entry threat, while both buyer power and supplier power will be easing. Rivalry will reduce still further. This looks like a classic case of an industry in which a few players emerge with overall dominance. The area enclosed by the blue lines is large, suggesting a relatively attractive industry. For a firm confident of becoming one of the dominant players, this might be an industry well worth investing in.

Comparing the five forces over time on a radar plot thus helps to give industry structure analysis a dynamic aspect. Similar plots can be made to aid diversification decisions (see Chapter 7), where possible new industries to enter can be compared in terms of attractiveness. The lines are only approximate, of course, because they aggregate the many individual elements that make up each of the forces into a simple composite measure. Notice too that if one of the forces is very adverse, then this might nullify positive assessments on the other four axes: for example, an industry with low rivalry, low substitution, low entry barriers and low supplier power might still be unattractive if powerful buyers were able to demand highly discounted prices. With these warnings in mind, such radar plots can nonetheless be both a useful device for initial analysis and an effective summary of a final, more refined analysis.

Figure 2.6 Cycles of competition

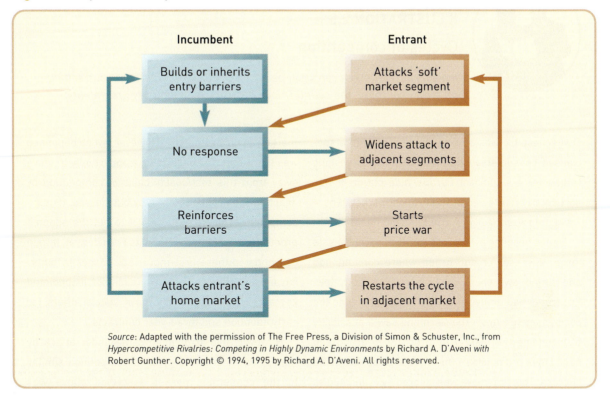

Competitive cycles[13]

In most industries, competitors constantly interact in terms of competitive moves: price cuts are matched and innovations imitated. These sequences of move and counter-move are called *cycles of competition*. If these cycles of competition become very rapid and aggressive, then industry structure becomes unstable. The industry may fall into a state of hypercompetition, implying low profitability for most competitors (see 2.3.1 above).

Figure 2.6 shows a cycle of competition involving various moves and counter-moves between competitors over time. The starting point is a new entrant attacking an incumbent's established market, apparently protected by inherited entry barriers. The new entrant sensibly attacks a particularly 'soft' (unprotected) segment of the overall market. If receiving no strong competitive response from the incumbent (i.e. no retaliation), the new entrant widens its attack to adjacent segments of the incumbent's market. There is a danger of increased industry rivalry and rapidly falling industry profits. In Figure 2.6, the incumbent finally responds by increasing entry barriers, perhaps by reinforcing customers' loyalty through increased differentiation. The new entrant counters with a price war. The final resort of the incumbent is to attack the new entrant's home market, hoping to do enough damage there to persuade the new entrant to back off. Thus rivalry increases in that home industry as well. The incumbent meanwhile does its best to raise barriers to entry at home.

Illustration 2.5 demonstrates a similar cycle of competition in an international context. Here moves and counter-moves by organisations and their competitors take place simultaneously in several locations. So a competitive move in one arena, the German company's aggressive move into France, did not trigger off a counter-move in that arena (France), but in its competitor's home territory (Germany).

ILLUSTRATION 2.5

Cycles of competition

Industry attractiveness can easily be undermined by rivalrous behaviour, setting off a cycle of move and countermove destructive of industry profitability.

Deutschespitze was a German company with a specialised consumer goods product that was wishing to become a significant Europe-wide player. It was particularly interested in the French market, where Francotop was the highly profitable dominant player.

Deutschespitze's first competitive move was to target a consumer age group where consumption and brand awareness in France were both low. Francotop had limited their marketing efforts to the over-25 age groups – the Germans saw a possibility of extending the market into the 18–25 group and aimed their promotional efforts at the group with some success. This first move was ignored by Francotop as it did not impact on its current business. However, from this bridgehead Deutschespitze's second move was to attack Francotop's key older market. This triggered Francotop to launch an advertising campaign reinforcing brand awareness in its traditional segments, hoping to confine the German company to its initial niche.

Deutschespitze responded by counter-advertising and price reductions – undermining the margins earned by its French rival. Competition then escalated with a counter-attack by Francotop into the German market. This wider competitive activity played itself out resulting in the erosion of both of the original strongholds and a progressive merger of the French and German markets. With falling barriers between the two markets, profits fell.

It is possible at this stage that this whole cycle of competition could have repeated itself in an adjacent

market, such as the UK. However, what happened was that Deutschespitze saw an opportunity to move away from this *cost/quality* basis of competition by adapting the product for use by businesses. Its core competences in R&D allowed it to get the adapted product to market faster than its French rival. It then consolidated these first-mover advantages by building and defending barriers. For example, it appointed key account salesmen and gave special offers for early adoption and three-year contracts.

However, this stronghold came under attack by the French firm and a cycle of competition similar to the consumer market described above was triggered. The German firm had built up enough financial reserves to survive a price war, which they then initiated. It was willing and able to fund losses longer than the French competitor – which was forced to exit the business user market.

Questions

1 Which moves were likely to trigger intensely rivalrous behaviour and which were better calculated to minimise destructive competition?

2 How might the French firm have prevented this cycle of competition from breaking out in the first place?

2.4 COMPETITORS AND MARKETS

An industry or sector may be too high a level to provide for a detailed understanding of competition. The five forces can impact differently on different kinds of players. To return to the earlier example, Hyundai and Porsche may be in the same broad industry (automobiles), but they are positioned differently: they are protected by different barriers to entry and competitive moves by one are unlikely to affect the other. It is often useful to disaggregate. Many industries contain a range of companies, each of which has different capabilities and competes on different bases. These competitor differences are captured by the concept of *strategic groups*. Customers too can differ significantly and these can be captured by distinguishing between different *market segments*. Thinking in terms of different strategic groups and market segments provides opportunities for organisations to develop highly distinctive positionings within broader industries. The potential for distinctiveness is further explored through '*Blue Ocean*' thinking, the last topic in this section.

2.4.1 Strategic groups[14]

Strategic groups **are organisations within an industry or sector with similar strategic characteristics, following similar strategies or competing on similar bases**. These characteristics are different from those in other strategic groups in the same industry or sector. For example, in the grocery retailing industry, supermarkets, convenience stores and corner shops each form different strategic groups. There are many different characteristics that distinguish between strategic groups but these can be grouped into two major categories (see Figure 2.7).[15]

Figure 2.7 Some characteristics for identifying strategic groups

It is useful to consider the extent to which organisations *differ* in terms of **characteristics** such as:

Scope of activities

- Extent of product (or service) diversity
- Extent of geographical coverage
- Number of market segments served
- Distribution channels used

Resource commitment

- Extent (number) of **branding**
- **Marketing effort** (e.g. advertising spread, size of salesforce)
- Extent of **vertical integration**
- Product or service **quality**
- **Technological leadership** (a leader or follower)
- **Size** of organisation

First, the *scope* of an organisation's activities (such as product range, geographical coverage and range of distribution channels used). Second, the *resource commitment* (such as brands, marketing spend and extent of vertical integration). Which characteristics are relevant differs from industry to industry, but typically important are those characteristics that separate high performers from low performers.

Strategic groups can be mapped on to two-dimensional charts – for example, one axis might be the extent of product range and the other axis the size of marketing spend. One method for choosing key dimensions by which to map strategic groups is to identify top performers (by growth or profitability) in an industry and to compare them with low performers. Characteristics that are shared by top performers, but not by low performers, are likely to be particularly relevant for mapping strategic groups. For example, the most profitable firms in an industry might all be narrow in terms of product range, and lavish in terms of marketing spend, while the less-profitable firms might be more widely spread in terms of products and restrained in their marketing. Here the two dimensions for mapping would be product range and marketing spend. A potential recommendation for the less-profitable firms would be to cut back their product range and boost their marketing.

Figure 2.8 shows strategic groups amongst Indian pharmaceutical companies, with research and development intensity (R&D spend as a percentage of sales) and overseas focus (exports and patents registered overseas) defining the axes of the map. These two axes do

Figure 2.8 Strategic groups in the Indian pharmaceutical industry

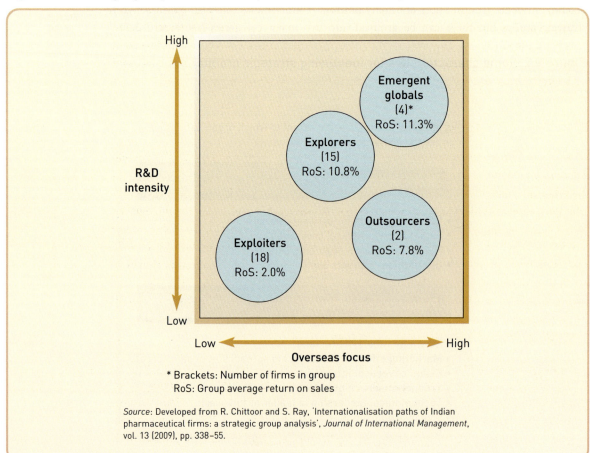

* Brackets: Number of firms in group
RoS: Group average return on sales

Source: Developed from R. Chittoor and S. Ray, 'Internationalisation paths of Indian pharmaceutical firms: a strategic group analysis', *Journal of International Management*, vol. 13 (2009), pp. 338–55.

explain a good deal of the variation in profitability between groups. The most profitable group is the Emergent Globals (11.3 per cent average return on sales), those with high R&D intensity and high overseas focus. On the other hand, the Exploiter group spends little on R&D and is focused on domestic markets, and only enjoys 2.0 per cent average return on sales.

This strategic group concept is useful in at least three ways:

- *Understanding competition.* Managers can focus on their direct competitors within their particular strategic group, rather than the whole industry. They can also establish the dimensions that distinguish them most from other groups, and which might be the basis for relative success or failure. These dimensions can then become the focus of their action.

- *Analysis of strategic opportunities.* Strategic group maps can identify the most attractive 'strategic spaces' within an industry. Some spaces on the map may be 'white spaces', relatively under-occupied. In the Indian pharmaceutical industry, the white space is high R&D investment combined with focus on domestic markets. Such white spaces might be unexploited opportunities. On the other hand, they could turn out to be 'black holes', impossible to exploit and likely to damage any entrant. A strategic group map is only the first stage of the analysis. Strategic spaces need to tested carefully.

- *Analysis of mobility barriers.* Of course, moving across the map to take advantage of opportunities is not costless. Often it will require difficult decisions and rare resources. Strategic groups are therefore characterised by 'mobility barriers', obstacles to movement from one strategic group to another. These are similar to barriers to entry in five forces analysis. Although movement from the Exploiter group in Indian pharmaceuticals to the Emergent Global group might seem very attractive in terms of profits, it is likely to demand very substantial financial investment and strong managerial skills. Mobility into the Emergent Global group will not be easy. As with barriers to entry, it is good to be in a successful strategic group into which there are strong mobility barriers, to impede imitation.

2.4.2 Market segments

The concept of strategic groups discussed above helps with understanding the similarities and differences in terms of competitor characteristics. The concept of market segment looks at the other side, differences in customer needs. A **market segment**[16] **is a group of customers who have similar needs that are different from customer needs in other parts of the market**. Where these customer groups are relatively small, such market segments are often called 'niches'. Dominance of a market segment or niche can be very valuable, for the same reasons that dominance of an industry can be valuable following five forces reasoning. However, dominance of market segments is typically less secure than that of a whole industry, as entry from competitors in adjacent market segments is likely to be relatively easy. For long-term success, strategies based on market segments must keep customer needs firmly in mind.

Three issues are particularly important in market segment analysis, therefore:

- *Variation in customer needs.* Focusing on customer needs that are highly distinctive from those typical in the market is one means of building a secure segment strategy. Customer needs vary for a whole variety of reasons – some of which are identified in Table 2.1. Theoretically, any of these factors could be used to identify distinct market segments. However, the crucial bases of segmentation vary according to market. In industrial markets, segmentation is often thought of in terms of industrial classification of buyers: steel producers might segment

Table 2.1 Some bases of market segmentation

Type of factor	Consumer markets	Industrial/organisational markets
Characteristics of people/organisations	Age, sex, race Income Family size Life-cycle stage Location Lifestyle	Industry Location Size Technology Profitability Management
Purchase/use situation	Size of purchase Brand loyalty Purpose of use Purchasing behaviour Importance of purchase Choice criteria	Application Importance of purchase Volume Frequency of purchase Purchasing procedure Choice criteria Distribution channel
Users' needs and preferences for product characteristics	Product similarity Price preference Brand preferences Desired features Quality	Performance requirements Assistance from suppliers Brand preferences Desired features Quality Service requirements

by automobile industry, packaging industry and construction industry, for example. On the other hand, segmentation by buyer behaviour (for example, direct buying versus those users who buy through third parties such as contractors) or purchase value (for example, high-value bulk purchasers versus frequent low-value purchasers) might be more appropriate. Being able to serve a highly distinctive segment that other organisations find difficult to serve is often the basis for a secure long-term strategy.

● *Specialisation* within a market segment can also be an important basis for a successful segmentation strategy. This is sometimes called a 'niche strategy'. Organisations that have built up most experience in servicing a particular market segment should not only have lower costs in so doing, but also have built relationships which may be difficult for others to break down. Experience and relationships are likely to protect a dominant position in a particular segment. However, precisely because customers value different things in different segments, specialised producers may find it very difficult to compete on a broader basis. For example, a small local brewery competing against the big brands on the basis of its ability to satisfy distinctive local tastes is unlikely to find it easy to serve other segments where tastes are different, scale requirements are larger and distribution channels are more complex.

● *Strategic customers.* It is crucial to understand whose needs matter. **The strategic customer is the person(s) at whom the strategy is primarily addressed because they have the most influence over which goods or services are purchased.** As above, for a food manufacturer, it is the retailers' needs that matter most directly, not simply the ultimate consumers of the food. It is retailers who pay the manufacturer and decide what to stock. Retailers care about price and quality because consumers do, so the manufacturer must take these needs into account. But retailers also care about delivery convenience and reliability. For a food manufacturer, therefore, the strategic customer is the retailer: the retailer's needs, not just the ultimate consumers' needs, should shape strategy. In the public sector, the strategic customer is very often the agency that controls the funds or authorises use rather than the user of the service. In public health care, therefore, it is hospitals, not patients, that are the strategic customers of pharmaceutical companies.

2.4.3 Blue Ocean thinking

The more differentiated views of competitors and customers embodied in strategic groups and market segments can be taken a step further by 'Blue Ocean' thinking. As developed by W. Chan Kim and Renée Mauborgne at INSEAD, **Blue Oceans** **are new market spaces where competition is minimised.**[17] Blue Oceans contrast with 'Red Oceans', where industries are already well defined and rivalry is intense. Blue Oceans evoke wide empty seas. Red Oceans are associated with bloody competition and 'red ink', in other words financial losses.

Blue Ocean thinking therefore encourages entrepreneurs and managers to be different by finding or creating market spaces that are not currently being served. Strategy here is about finding *strategic gaps*, opportunities in the environment that are not being fully exploited by competitors. The strategy canvas is one framework that can effectively assist this kind of Blue Ocean thinking. A **strategy canvas compares competitors according to their performance on key success factors in order to develop strategies based on creating new market spaces.** Figure 2.9 shows a strategy canvas for three engineering components companies, highlighting the following three features:

● **Critical success factors** (CSFs) **are those factors that are either particularly valued by customers or which provide a significant advantage in terms of cost.** Critical success factors are therefore likely to be an important source of competitive advantage or disadvantage. Figure 2.9 identifies five established critical success factors in this engineering components

Figure 2.9 Strategy canvas for electrical components companies

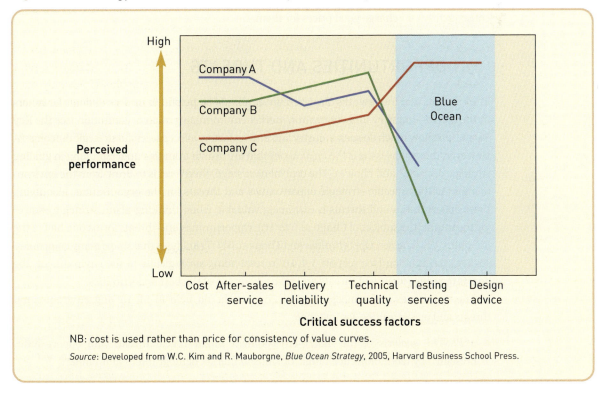

NB: cost is used rather than price for consistency of value curves.

Source: Developed from W.C. Kim and R. Mauborgne, *Blue Ocean Strategy*, 2005, Harvard Business School Press.

market (cost, after-sales service, delivery reliability, technical quality and testing facilities). Note there is also a new sixth critical success factor, design advisory services, which will be discussed under the third subhead, value innovation.

● **Value curves are a graphic depiction of how customers perceive competitors' relative performance across the critical success factors**. In Figure 2.9, companies A and B perform well on cost, service, reliability and quality, but less well on testing. They do not offer any design advice. Company C has a radically different value curve, characteristic of a 'value innovator'.

● **Value innovation is the creation of new market space by excelling on established critical success factors on which competitors are performing badly and/or by creating new critical success factors representing previously unrecognised customer wants**. Thus in Figure 2.9, company C is a value innovator in both senses. First, it excels on the established customer need of offering testing facilities for customers' products using its components. Second, it offers a new and valued design service advising customers on how to integrate their components in order for them to create better products.

Company C's strategy exemplifies two critical principles in Blue Ocean thinking: *focus* and *divergence*. First, Company C focuses its efforts on just two factors, testing and design services, while maintaining only adequate performance on the other critical success factors where its competitors are already high performers. Second, it has created a value curve that significantly diverges from its competitors' value curves, creating a substantial strategic gap, or Blue Ocean, in the areas of testing and design services. This is shrewd. For Company C, beating Companies A and B in the areas where they are performing well anyway would require major investment and likely provide little advantage given that customers are already highly satisfied. Challenging A and B on cost, after-sales service, delivery or quality would be a Red Ocean strategy. Far better is to concentrate on where a large gap can be created between competitors. Company C faces little competition for those customers who really value testing and design services, and consequently can charge good prices for them.

 ## 2.5 OPPORTUNITIES AND THREATS

The concepts and frameworks discussed above should be helpful in understanding the factors in the macro-, industry and competitor/market environments of an organisation (see the Key Debate: just how much do such industry and market factors affect successful strategic outcomes?). However, the critical issue is the *implications* that are drawn from this understanding in guiding strategic decisions and choices. The crucial next stage, therefore, is to draw from the environmental analysis specific strategic opportunities and threats for the organisation. Identifying these opportunities and threats is extremely valuable when thinking about strategic choices for the future (the subject of Chapters 6 to 10). Opportunities and threats forms one half of the Strengths, Weaknesses, Opportunities and Threats (SWOT) analyses that shape many companies' strategy formulation (see section 3.4.4). In responding strategically to the environment, the goal is to reduce identified threats and take advantage of the best opportunities.

The techniques and concepts in this chapter should help in identifying environmental threats and opportunities, for instance:

● a *PESTEL analysis* of the macro-environment might reveal threats and opportunities presented by technological change, or shifts in market demographics and similar;

KEY DEBATE

How much does industry matter?

A good start in strategy must be to choose a profitable industry to compete in. But does simply being in the right industry matter more than having the right kinds of skills and resources?

This chapter has focused on the role of the environment in strategy-making, with particular regard to industries. But the importance of industries in determining organisational performance has been challenged in recent years. This has led to a debate about whether strategy-making should be externally-orientated, starting with the environment, or internally-orientated, starting with the organisation's own skills and resources (the focus of Chapter 3).[1]

Managers favouring an external approach look primarily *outside* the organisation, for example building market share in their industries through mergers and acquisitions or aggressive marketing. Managers favouring an internal approach concentrate their attention *inside* the organisation, fostering the skills of their people or nurturing technologies, for example. Because managerial time is limited, there is a real trade-off to be made between external and internal approaches.

The chief advocate of the external approach is Michael Porter, Professor at Harvard Business School and founder of the Monitor Consulting Group. An influential sceptic of this approach is Richard Rumelt, a student at Harvard Business School but now at University of California Los Angeles. Porter, Rumelt and others have done a series of empirical studies examining the relative importance of industries in explaining organisations' performance.

Typically, these studies take a large sample of firms and compare the extent to which variance in profitability is due to firms or industries (controlling for other effects such as size). If firms within the same industry tend to bunch together in terms of profitability, it is industry that is accounting for the greater proportion of profitability: an external approach to strategy is supported. If firms within the same industry vary widely in terms of profitability, it is the specific skills and resources of the firms that matter most: an internal approach is most appropriate.

The two most important studies in fact find that more of the variance in profitability is due to firms rather than industries – firms account for 47 per cent in Rumelt's study of manufacturing (see the figure).[2] However, when Porter and McGahan included service industries as well as manufacturing, they found a larger industry effect (19 per cent).[3,4]

Per cent of variance in profitability due to:

The implication from this work is that firm-specific factors generally influence profitability more than industry factors. Firms need to attend carefully to their own skills and resources. However, the greater industry effect found in Porter and McGahan's study of both manufacturing and services suggests that industry's importance varies strongly by industry. External influences can matter more in some industries than others.

References:
1. E.H. Bowman and C.E. Helfat, 'Does corporate strategy matter?', *Strategic Management Journal*, vol. 22, no. 1 (2001), pp. 1–14.
2. R.P. Rumelt, 'How much does industry matter?', *Strategic Management Journal*, vol. 12, no. 2 (1991), pp. 167–85.
3. M.E. Porter and A.M. McGahan, 'How much does industry matter really?', *Strategic Management Journal*, vol. 18, Summer Special Issue (1997), pp. 15–30.
4. M.E. Porter and A.M. McGahan, 'The emergence and sustainability of abnormal profits', *Strategic Organization*, vol. 1, no. 1 (2003), pp. 79–108.

Question

Porter and McGahan's study suggests that some industries influence member firms' profitabilities more than others: in other words, their profitabilities bunch together. Why might some industries have a larger influence on their members' profitability than others?

- identification of *key drivers for change* can help generate different scenarios for managerial discussion, some more threatening, others more favourable;

- a *Porter five forces analysis* might for example identify a rise or fall in barriers to entry, or opportunities to reduce industry rivalry, perhaps by acquisition of competitors;

- *Blue Ocean* thinking might reveal where companies can create new market spaces; alternatively it could help identify success factors which new entrants might attack in order to turn 'Blue Oceans' into 'Red Oceans'.

While all these techniques and concepts are important tools for understanding environments, it is important to recognise that any analysis is likely to be somewhat subjective. Entrepreneurs and managers often have particular blinkers with regard to what they see and prioritise.[18] Techniques and concepts can be helpful in challenging existing assumptions and encouraging broader perspectives, but they are unlikely to overcome human subjectivity and biases completely.

SUMMARY

- Environmental influences can be thought of as layers around an organisation, with the outer layer making up the *macro-environment*, the middle layer making up the *industry or sector* and the inner layer *strategic groups* and *market segments*.

- The macro-environment can be analysed in terms of the *PESTEL factors*, from which *key drivers of change* can be identified. Alternative *scenarios* about the future can be constructed according to how the key drivers develop.

- Industries and sectors can be analysed in terms of the *Porter five forces* – barriers to entry, substitutes, buyer power, supplier power and rivalry. Together, these determine industry or sector attractiveness.

- Industries and sectors are dynamic, and their changes can be analysed in terms of the *industry life cycle*, *comparative five forces radar plots* and *hypercompetitive cycles of competition*.

- In the inner layer of the environment, *strategic group* analysis, *market segment* analysis and the *strategy canvass* can help identify strategic gaps or opportunities.

- *Blue Ocean* strategies characterised by low rivalry are likely to be better opportunities than *Red Ocean* strategies with many rivals.

VIDEO ASSIGNMENT

Visit *MyStrategyLab* and watch the *Hiscox* case study.

1 Describe recent environmental changes in the insurance industry in terms of Porter's five forces. What else needs to be factored into an environmental analysis?

2 Assess Hiscox's strategic position in this environmental context.

WORK ASSIGNMENTS

✻ *Denotes more advanced work assignments.* * *Refers to a case study in the Text and Cases edition.*

2.1   For an organisation of your choice carry out a PESTEL analysis and identify key drivers for change. Use Illustration 2.1 as a model.

2.2✻   For the same organisation as in 2.1, and using Illustration 2.2 as a model, construct four scenarios for the evolution of its environment. What implications are there for the organisation's strategy?

2.3   Drawing on section 2.3, carry out a five forces analysis of the pharmaceutical industry* or Vodafone's position in the mobile phone industry*. What do you conclude about that industry's attractiveness?

2.4✻   Drawing on section 2.3, and particularly using the radar plot technique of Figure 2.5, choose two industries or sectors and compare their attractiveness in terms of the five forces (a) today; (b) in approximately three to five years' time. Justify your assessment of each of the five forces' strengths. Which industry or sector would you invest in?

2.5   With regard to section 2.4.1 and Figure 2.8, identify an industry (for example, the motor industry or clothing retailers) and, by comparing competitors, map out the main strategic groups in the industry according to key strategic dimensions. Try more than one set of key strategic dimensions to map the industry. Do the resulting maps identify any under-exploited opportunities in the industry?

2.6✻   Drawing on section 2.4.3, and particularly on Figure 2.10, identify critical success factors for an industry with which you and your peers are familiar (for example, clothing retailers or mobile phone companies). Using your own estimates (or those of your peers), construct a strategy canvas comparing the main competitors, as in Figure 2.10. What implications does your strategy canvas have for the strategies of these competitors?

Integrative assignment

2.7   Carry out a full analysis of an industry or sector of your choice (using for example PESTEL, scenarios, five forces and strategic groups). Consider explicitly how the industry or sector is affected by globalisation (see Chapter 8, particularly Figure 8.2 on drivers) and innovation (see Chapter 9, particularly Figure 9.2 on product and process innovation).

RECOMMENDED KEY READINGS

● The classic book on the analysis of industries is M.E. Porter, *Competitive Strategy*, Free Press, 1980. An updated view is available in M.E. Porter, 'The five competitive forces that shape strategy', *Harvard Business Review*, vol. 86, no. 1 (2008), pp. 58–77. An influential development on Porter's basic ideas is W.C. Kim and R. Mauborgne, *Blue Ocean Strategy: How to Create Uncontested Market Space and Make Competition Irrelevant*, Harvard Business School Press, 2005.

● For approaches to how environments change, see K. van der Heijden, *Scenarios: The Art of Strategic Conversation*, 2nd edition, Wiley, 2005, and the work of Michael Porter's colleague, A. McGahan, *How Industries Evolve*, Harvard Business School Press, 2004.

● A collection of academic articles on the latest views on PEST, scenarios and similar is the special issue of *International Studies of Management and Organization*, vol. 36, no. 3 (2006), edited by Peter McKiernan.

REFERENCES

1. PESTEL is an extension of PEST (Politics, Economics, Social and Technology) analysis, taking more account of environmental ('green') and legal issues. For an application of PEST analysis to the world of business schools, relevant also to PESTEL, see H. Thomas, 'An analysis of the environment and competitive dynamics of management education', *Journal of Management Development*, vol. 26, no. 1 (2007), pp. 9–21.

2. For a discussion of scenario planning in practice, see K. van der Hiejden, *Scenarios: The Art of Strategic Conversation*, second edition, Wiley, 2005. For how scenario planning fits with other forms of environmental analysis such as PESTEL, see P. Walsh, 'Dealing with the uncertainties of environmental change by adding scenario planning to the strategy reformulation equation', *Management Decision*, no. 43, vol. 1 (2005), pp. 113–22 and G. Burt, G. Wright, R. Bradfield and K. van der Heijden, 'The role of scenario planning in exploring the environment in view of the limitations of PEST and its derivatives', *International Studies of Management and Organization*, vol 36, no. 3 (2006), pp. 50–76.

3. Based on P. Schoemaker, 'Scenario Planning: a tool for strategic thinking'. *Sloan Management Review*, vol. 36 (1995), pp. 25–34. Variations on this approach are offered in the sources in reference 2 above.

4. See M.E. Porter, *Competitive Strategy: Techniques for Analysing Industries and Competitors*, Free Press, 1980, p. 5.

5. An updated discussion of the classic framework is M. Porter, 'The five competitive forces that shape strategy', *Harvard Business Review*, vol. 86, no. 1 (2008), pp. 58–77. C. Christensen, 'The past and future of competitive advantage', *Sloan Management Review*, vol. 42, no. 2 (2001), pp.105–9 provides an interesting critique and update of some of the factors underlying Porter's five forces.

6. This definition is from R. D'Aveni, *Hypercompetition: Managing the Dynamics of Strategic Manoeuvring*, Free Press, 1994. p. 2. In his later book, *Strategic Supremacy: How Industry Leaders Create Spheres of Influence*, Simon and Schuster International, 2002, he gives examples of strategies that can help defend a strong position in conditions of hypercompetition.

7. See: L. Van den Berghe and K. Verweire, 'Convergence in the financial services industry', *Geneva Papers on Risk and Insurance*, vol. 25, no. 2 (2000), pp. 262–72; A. Malhotra and A. Gupta, 'An investigation of firms' responses to industry convergence', *Academy of Management Proceedings*, 2001, pp. G1–6.

8. A. Brandenburger and B. Nalebuff, 'The right game', *Harvard Business Review*, July–August 1995, pp. 57–64.

9. See: K. Walley, 'Coopetition: an introduction to the subject and an agenda for research', *International Studies of Management and Organization*, vol. 37, no. 2 (2007), pp. 11–31. On the dangers of 'complementors', see D. Yoffie and M. Kwak, 'With friends like these', *Harvard Business Review*, vol. 84, no. 9 (2006), pp. 88–98.

10. There is a good discussion of the static nature of the Porter model, and other limitations, in M. Grundy, 'Rethinking and reinventing Michael Porter's five forces model', *Strategic Change*, vol. 15 (2006), pp. 213–29.

11. A classic academic overview of the industry life cycle is S. Klepper, 'Industry life cycles', *Industrial and Corporate Change*, vol. 6, no. 1 (1996), pp. 119–43. See also A. McGahan, 'How industries evolve', *Business Strategy Review*, vol. 11, no. 3 (2000), pp. 1–16.

12. A. McGahan, 'How industries evolve', *Business Strategy Review*, vol. 11, no. 3 (2000), pp. 1–16.

13. For a full discussion of the dynamics of competition see: R. D'Aveni (with R. Gunther), *Hypercompetitive Rivalries*, Free Press, 1995. For a critical overview of various recent perspectives on hypercompetition and turbulence, plus cases, see J. Slesky, J. Goes and O. Babüroglu, 'Contrasting perspectives of strategy making: applications in hyper environments, *Organization Studies*, vol. 28, no. 1 (2007), pp. 71–94.

14. For recent examples of strategic group analysis, see G. Leask and D. Parker, 'Strategic groups, competitive groups and performance in the UK pharmaceutical industry', *Strategic Management Journal*, vol. 28, no. 7 (2007), pp. 723–45; and W. Desarbo, R. Grewal and R. Wang, 'Dynamic strategic groups: deriving spatial evolutionary paths', *Strategic Management Journal*, vol. 30, no. 8 (2009), 1420–39.

15. These characteristics are based on Porter, reference 4 above.

16. A useful discussion of segmentation in relation to competitive strategy is provided in M.E. Porter, *Competitive Advantage*, Free Press, 1985, Chapter 7. See also the discussion on market segmentation in P. Kotler, G. Armstrong, J. Saunders and V. Wong, *Principles of Marketing*, 3rd European edition, Financial Times Prentice Hall, 2002, Chapter 9. For a more detailed review of segmentation methods see: M. Wedel and W. Kamakura, *Market Segmentation: Conceptual and Methodological Foundations*, 2nd edition, Kluwer Academic, 1999.

17. W.C. Kim and R. Mauborgne, 'How strategy shapes structure', *Harvard Business Review*, September 2009, 73–80.

18. P. Schoemaker and G. Day, 'How to make sense of weak signals', *Sloan Management Review*, vol. 50, no. 3 (2009), pp. 81–9.

CASE EXAMPLE

Global forces and the Western European brewing industry

Mike Blee and Richard Whittington

This case is centred on the European brewing industry in Western Europe and examines how the increasingly competitive pressure of operating within global markets is causing consolidation through acquisitions, alliances and closures within the industry. This has resulted in the growth of the brewers' reliance upon super-brands.

In the early years of the 21st century, European brewers faced a surprising paradox. The traditional centre of the beer industry worldwide and home to the world's largest brewing companies, Europe, was turning off beer. Beer consumption was falling in the largest markets of Germany and the United Kingdom, while burgeoning in emerging markets around the world. In 2008, Europe's largest market, Germany, ranked only 5th in the world, behind China, the United States, Brazil and Russia. China, with 12% annual growth between 2003 and 2008, had become the largest single market by volume, alone accounting for 23% of world consumption (Euromonitor, 2010).

Table 1 details the overall decline of European beer consumption. Decline in traditional key markets is due to several factors. Governments are campaigning strongly against drunken driving, affecting the propensity to drink

Source: Alamy Images/Picturesbyrob.

Table 1 European beer consumption by country and year (000 hectolitres)

Country	1980	2000	2003	2007
Austria	7651	8762	8979	9100
Belgium	12945	10064	9935	9137
Denmark	6698	5452	5181	4840
Finland	2738	4024	4179	4073
France	23745	21420	21168	18781
Germany‡	89820	103105	97107	91000
Greece	N/A	4288	3905	4600
Ireland	4174	5594	5315	5193
Italy	9539	16289	17452	17766
Luxembourg	417	472	373	429
Netherlands	12213	13129	12771	12910
Norway*	7651	2327	2270	2670
Portugal	3534	6453	6008	6200
Spain	20065	29151	33451	35658
Sweden	3935	5011	4969	4900
Switzerland*	4433	4194	4334	4489
UK	65490	57007	60302	51300

* Non-EU countries; ‡ 1980 excludes GDR. Figures adjusted.

Source: Based on information from www.Brewersofeurope.org.

beer in restaurants, pubs and bars. There is increasing awareness of the effects of alcohol on health and fitness. Particularly in the United Kingdom, there is growing hostility to so-called 'binge drinking', excessive alcohol consumption in pubs and clubs. Wines have also become increasingly popular in Northern European markets. However, beer consumption per capita varies widely between countries, being four times higher in Germany than in Italy, for example. Some traditionally low consumption European markets have been showing good growth.

The drive against drunken driving and binge drinking has helped shift sales from the 'on-trade' (beer consumed on the premises, as in pubs or restaurants) to the off-trade (retail). Worldwide, the off-trade increased from 63% of volume in 2000 to 67% in 2008. The off-trade is increasingly dominated by large supermarket chains such as Tesco or Carrefour, who often use cut-price offers on beer in order to lure people into their shops. More than one fifth of beer volume is now sold through supermarkets. German retailers such as Aldi and Lidl have had considerable success with their own 'private-label' (rather than brewery-branded) beers. Pubs have suffered: in the United Kingdom, an estimated 50 pubs closed per week during the recessionary year 2009. However, although on-trade volumes are falling

Table 2 Imports of beer by country

Country	Imports 2002 (% of consumption*)	Imports 2008 (% of consumption)
Austria	5.1	6.6
Belgium	4.74	12.8
Denmark	2.6	10.5
Finland	2.3	10.1
France	23	31.4
Germany	3.1	7.6
Greece	4.1	6.5
Ireland	NA	16.8
Italy	27.2	33.5
Luxembourg	NA	43.1
Netherlands	3.2	18.6
Norway	5.4	3.7
Portugal	1.1	0.6
Spain	11.7	8.6
Sweden	NA	23.4
Switzerland	15.4	17.6
United Kingdom	10.9	17.7

Note: Import figures do not include beers brewed under licence in home country; also countries vary in measuring per cent of consumption.

Source: Based on information from www.Brewersofeurope.org.

in Europe, the sales values are generally rising, as brewers introduce higher-priced premium products such as non-alcoholic beers, extra cold lagers or fruit-flavoured beers. On the other hand, a good deal of this increasing demand for premium products is being satisfied by the import of apparently exotic beers from overseas (see Table 2).

Brewers' main purchasing costs are packaging (accounting for around half of non-labour costs), raw material such as barley, and energy. The European packaging industry is highly concentrated, dominated by international companies such as Crown in cans and Owens-Illinois in glass bottles. In the United Kingdom, for example, there are just three can makers: Ball Packaging Europe, Crown Bevcan and REXAM.

Acquisition, licensing and strategic alliances have all occurred as the leading brewers battle to control the market. There are global pressures for consolidation due to over-capacity within the industry, the need to contain costs and benefits of leveraging strong brands. For example, in 2004, Belgian brewer Interbrew merged with Am Bev, the Brazilian brewery group, to create the largest brewer in the world, InBev. In 2008, the new InBev bought the second largest brewer, the American Anheuser-Busch, giving it nearly 20 per cent of the world market. In 2002, South African Breweries acquired the Miller Group (USA) and Pilsner Urquell in the Czech Republic, becoming SABMiller. SABMiller in turn bought Dutch specialist Grolsch in 2007. Smaller players in the fast-growing Chinese and Latin American markets are being snapped up by the large international brewers too: in 2010, Dutch Heineken bought Mexico's second largest brewery, FEMSA. On the other hand, medium-sized Australian brewer Fosters has withdrawn from the European market. The European Commission fined Heineken and Kronenbourg in 2004 for price-fixing in France, and Heineken, Grolsch and Bavaria in 2007 for a price-fixing cartel in the Dutch market.

Table 3 lists the world's top ten brewing companies, which accounted for about 60 per cent of world beer volumes in 2009. However, there remain many specialist, regional and microbreweries, for example Greene King (see below). Germany, with its pub-brewing tradition (the Brauhaus), still has 1319 separate breweries owned by 583 separate brewing companies. None the less, market concentration has increased in Western Europe: in 2000, the top two players (Heineken and Interbrew) had 19.3 per cent of the market; in 2009, the top two players, Heineken and Carlsberg, held 28.5 per cent of the Western European market, with A-B InBev accounting for a further 10.6 per cent.

Three brewing companies

The European market contains many very different kinds of competitor: this section introduces the world's largest brewer and two outliers.

Table 3 The world's top ten brewery companies by volume: 2000 and 2009

2000		2009	
Company	Share global volume %	Company	Share global volume %
Anheuser-Busch (US)	8.8	A-B InBev (Belgium)	19.5
AmBev (Brazil)	4.6	SABMiller (UK)	9.5
Heineken (Dutch)	4.3	Heineken (Dutch)	6.9
Interbrew (Belgium)	4.0	Carlsberg (Danish)	5.9
Miller (US)	3.6	China Resources (China)	4.5
SAB (South Africa)	3.3	Tsingtao (China)	3.1
Modelo (Mexico)	2.7	Modelo (Mexico)	2.9
Coors (US)	2.0	Molson Coors (US)	2.8
Asahi (Japan)	2.0	Beijing Yanjing (China)	2.5
Kirin (Japan)	1.9	FEMSA (Mexico)	2.3

Source: Euromonitor International, 2010.

Anheuser-Busch InBev (Belgium)

A-B InBev has roots going back to 1366, but has transformed itself in the last decade with a series of spectacular mergers. First, InBev was created in 2004 from the merger of Belgian InterBrew and Brazilian AmBev. As well as making it the second largest brewing company in the world, this merger gave it a significant position in the Latin American soft drinks market. Then in 2008 InBev acquired the leading American brewer Anheuser-Busch for $52bn (~€36.4bn), making the company indisputably the world leader. The company now has nearly 300 brands, led by such well-known international beers as Beck's, Budweiser and Stella Artois. The company has nearly 50 per cent share of the US market, and owns 50 per cent of Mexico's leading brewer, Modelo, famous for its global Corona brand. In 2008, the new A-N InBev had four of the top ten selling beers in the world, and a number one or number two position in over 20 national markets. However, the company has been reducing its stake in the Chinese market in order to raise funds to pay for the Anheuser-Busch acquisition and to meet local monopoly authority concerns. It also sold its Central and Eastern beer operations in 2009.

The company is frank about its strategy: to transform itself from the biggest brewing company in the world to the best. It aims to do this by building strong global brands and increasing efficiency. Efficiency gains will come from more central coordination of purchasing, including media and IT; from the optimisation of its inherited network of breweries; and from the sharing of best practice across sites internationally. A-B InBev is now emphasising organic growth and improved margins from its existing business. Its declared intention is to be 'The Best Beer Company in a Better World'.

Greene King (United Kingdom)

Established in 1799, Greene King is now the largest domestic British brewer, owner of famous brands such as Abbot, IPA and Old Speckled Hen. It has expanded through a series of acquisitions including Ruddles (1995), Morland (1999) and Hardys and Hansons (2006). Acquisition is typically followed by the closure of the acquired brewery, the termination of minor brands and the transfer of major brand production to its main brewery in Bury St. Edmunds. This strategy has led to critics calling the company 'Greedy King'. IPA is the UK's top cask ale, with over 20 per cent of the on-trade market, and Old Speckled Hen is the top premium UK ale with more than one eighth of the multiple retailer market. Greene King is unusual amongst contemporary breweries in operating many of its own pubs, having added to its original chain several acquisitions (notably Laurels

with 432 pubs and Belhaven with 271). Greene King now operates nearly 2000 pubs across the United Kingdom, with a particularly dominant position in its home region of East Anglia. The company is also active in restaurants. Business is effectively confined to the UK market. In 2009, Greene King raised £207m (~€228m; ~$310m) on the financial markets in order to fund further acquisitions. Greene King explains its success formula in brewing thus: 'The Brewing Company's continued out-performance is driven by a consistent, focused strategy: most importantly, we brew high quality beer from an efficient, single-site brewery; [and] we have a focused brand portfolio, minimising the complexity and cost of a multibrand strategy.'

Tsingtao (China)

Tsingtao Brewery was founded in 1903 by German settlers in China. After state ownership under Communism, Tsingtao was privatised in the early 1990s and listed on the Hong Kong Stock Exchange in 1993. In 2009, the Japanese Asahi Breweries held 19.9 per cent of the shares, purchased from A-B InBev (which also sold the remainder of its original stake – 7 per cent – to a Chinese private investor). Tsingtao has 13 per cent market share of its home market but has long had an export orientation, accounting for more than 50 per cent of China's beer exports. Tsingtao Beer was introduced to the United States in 1972 and is the Chinese brand-leader in the US market. A bottle of Tsingtao appeared in the 1982 science fiction film *Blade Runner*. Tsingtao set up its European office in 1992 and its beer is now sold in 62 countries. The company has described its ambition thus: 'to promote the continuous growth of the sales volume and income to step forward (sic) the target of becoming an international great company'.

Sources: Ernst & Young, The Contribution Made by Beer to the European Economy, 2009; Euromonitor International, Global Alcoholic Drinks: Beer – Opportunities in Niche Categories, April, 2009; Euromonitor, Strategies for Growth in an Increasingly Consolidated Global Beer Market, February 2010.

Questions

1 Using the data from the case (and any other sources available), carry out for the Western European brewing industry (i) a PESTEL analysis and (ii) a five forces analysis. What do you conclude?

2 For the three breweries outlined above (or breweries of your own choice) explain:

   (a) how these trends will impact differently on these different companies; and

   (b) the relative strengths and weaknesses of each company.

3

STRATEGIC CAPABILITIES

Learning outcomes

After reading this chapter you should be able to:

- Identify what comprises *strategic capabilities* in terms of organisational *resources* and *competences* and how these relate to the strategies of organisations.

- Analyse how strategic capabilities might provide sustainable competitive advantage on the basis of their *value*, *rarity*, *inimitability and non-substitutability (VRIN)*.

- Diagnose strategic capability by means of *benchmarking*, *value chain analysis*, *activity mapping* and *SWOT analysis*.

- Consider how managers can *develop strategic capabilities* for their organisations.

Key terms

Competences p. 84

Core competences p. 89

Dynamic capabilities p. 85

Inimitable capabilities p. 91

Organisational knowledge p. 94

Profit pools p. 102

Rare capabilities p. 90

Resource-based view p. 83

Resources p. 84

Strategic capabilities p. 84

SWOT p. 106

Threshold capabilities p. 87

Value p. 90

Value chain p. 97

Value network p. 97

(3.1) INTRODUCTION

Chapter 2 outlined how the external environment of an organisation can create both strategic opportunities and threats. However, Nokia, Sony and Motorola have all sought to compete in the same market for mobile phones and develop their businesses within the same technological environment, but with markedly different success. Nokia has been relatively successful consistently. Sony has found it more difficult to compete effectively of late. And Motorola's performance has been such that it has considered withdrawing altogether despite being an early innovator in the market. It is not so much variations in the environment which explain these differences in performance, but the differences in their *strategic capabilities* in terms of the *resources and competences* they have or have tried to develop. It is the strategic importance of such capabilities that is the focus of this chapter.

The key issues posed by the chapter are summarised in Figure 3.1. Underlying these are two key concepts. The first is that organisations are not identical, but have different capabilities; they are 'heterogeneous' in this respect. The second is that it can be difficult for one organisation to obtain or copy the capabilities of another. For example, competitors cannot readily obtain or access Nokia's experience built up over decades of success. The implication for managers is that they need to understand how their organisations are different from their rivals in ways that may be the basis of achieving competitive advantage and superior performance. These concepts underlie what has become known as the **resource-based view** (RBV) of strategy[1] (though it might more appropriately be labelled the 'capabilities view'): **that the competitive advantage and superior performance of an organisation is explained by the distinctiveness of its capabilities**. RBV has become very influential in strategy and this chapter draws on it a good deal. It should be borne in mind, however, that there are different treatments of the topic.

Figure 3.1 Strategic capabilities: the key issues

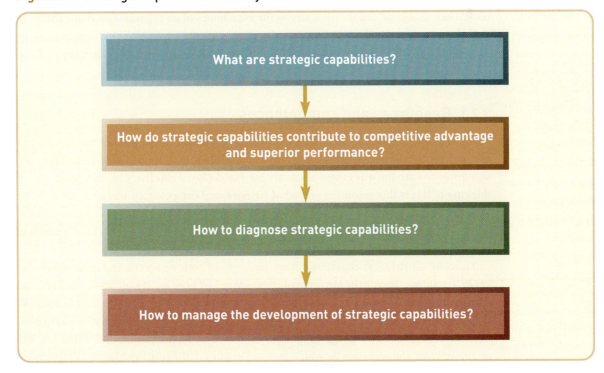

So, whilst the terminology and concepts employed here align with RBV, readers will find different terminology used elsewhere.

The chapter has four further sections:

- Section 3.2 discusses the foundations of *strategic capability*; in particular what is meant by *resources, competences* and the related concept of *dynamic capabilities.* It also draws a distinction between *threshold capabilities* required to be able to compete in a market and *distinctive capabilities* that may be a basis for achieving competitive advantage and superior performance.

- Section 3.3 explains the ways in which distinctive capabilities may contribute to the *developing and sustaining of competitive advantage* (in a public-sector context the equivalent concern might be how some organisations sustain relative superior performance over time). In particular, the importance of the *Value, Rarity, Inimitability and Non-substitutability (VRIN)* of capabilities is explained.

- Section 3.4 moves on to consider different ways strategic capability might be analysed. These include *benchmarking, value chain analysis* and *activity system mapping.* The section concludes by explaining the use of *SWOT* analysis as a basis for pulling together the insights from the analyses of the environment (explained in Chapter 2) and of strategic capabilities in this chapter.

- Finally section 3.5 discusses some of the key issues in managing the *development of strategic capabilities* through internal and external development and the management of people.

(3.2) FOUNDATIONS OF STRATEGIC CAPABILITY

Given that different writers, managers and consultants use different terms and concepts it is important to understand how concepts relating to strategic capabilities are used in this book. Here **strategic capabilities** means **the capabilities of an organisation that contribute to its long-term survival or competitive advantage**. However, to understand and to manage strategic capability it is necessary to explain its components and the characteristics of those components.

3.2.1 Resources and competences

There are two components of strategic capability: resources and competences. **Resources are the assets that organisations have or can call upon** (e.g. from partners or suppliers); **competences are the ways those assets are used or deployed effectively**. A shorthand way of thinking of this is that resources are 'what we *have*' and competences are 'what we *do well*'. Other terms are common. For example, Gary Hamel and C.K. Prahalad refer to *core competences* and many writers use the term *intangible assets* as an umbrella term to include intangible resources such as brands and business systems as well as competences.

Typically all strategic capabilities have elements of both resources and competences as Table 3.1 shows. Resources are certainly important but how an organisation employs and deploys its resources matters at least as much. There would be no point in having state-of-the-art equipment if it were not used effectively. The efficiency and effectiveness of physical or financial resources, or the people in an organisation, depend, not just on their existence, but on the systems and processes by which they are managed, the relationships and cooperation

Table 3.1 Components of strategic capabilities

Strategic capability		
Resources: what we have, e.g.		**Competences: what we do well, e.g.**
Machines, buildings, raw materials, products, patents, data bases, computer systems	Physical	Ways of achieving utilisation of plant, efficiency, productivity, flexibility, marketing
Balance sheet, cash flow, suppliers of funds	Financial	Ability to raise funds and manage cash flows, debtors, creditors etc.
Managers, employees, partners, suppliers, customers	Human	How people gain and use experience, skills, knowledge, build relationships, motivate others and innovate

Long-term survival and competitive advantage

between people, their adaptability, their innovatory capacity, the relationship with customers and suppliers and the experience and learning about what works well and what does not. Illustration 3.1 shows examples of how executives explain the importance of the resources and capabilities of their different organisations.

3.2.2 Dynamic capabilities[2]

If they are to provide a basis for long-term success, strategic capabilities cannot be static; they need to change. University of Berkeley economist David Teece has introduced the concept of **dynamic capabilities**, by which he means **an organisation's ability to renew and recreate its strategic capabilities to meet the needs of changing environments**. He argues that the capabilities that are necessary for efficient operations: 'maintaining incentive alignment, owning tangible assets, controlling costs, maintaining quality, optimizing inventories – are necessary but . . . are unlikely to be sufficient for sustaining superior performance'.[3] Moreover he acknowledges the further danger that capabilities that were the basis of competitive success may over time be imitated by competitors, become common practice in an industry or become redundant as its environment changes. Harvard's Dorothy Leonard-Barton also warns of the danger that, despite a changing environment, such capabilities can become 'rigidities'.[4] Chapter 5 deals with some of the problematic consequences of this. So, the important lesson is that if capabilities are to be effective over time they need to change; they cannot be static.

In this context, Teece suggests that there are three generic types of dynamic capabilities: those concerned with *sensing* opportunities and threats, those concerned with *seizing* opportunities and those concerned with *re-configuring* the capabilities of an organisation. This view of dynamic capabilities relates directly to the framework for this book. Sensing capabilities is to do with understanding an organisation's strategic position; seizing opportunities relates to making strategic choices; and re-configuration is to do with enacting strategies.

Dynamic capabilities may take the form of relatively formal organisational systems, such as recruitment and management development processes, or major strategic moves, such as

ILLUSTRATION 3.1

Strategic capabilities

Executives emphasise different strategic capabilities in different organisations.

The Goddard Space Center

Flight Center NASA's Goddard Space Flight Center manages many aspects of the space agency's missions and lays claim to some unique resources. For example, its 42-foot-tall acoustic test chamber can produce sounds of up to 150 decibels to allow technicians to expose payloads to launch noise. The high bay clean room, which can accommodate two space shuttle payloads, circulates nine million cubic feet of air every minute through its filters to prevent contaminants damaging spacecraft components – essential to space missions since cleaning of such contaminants in space is highly problematic. And its 120-foot-diameter high-capacity centrifuge with two 1250-horsepower motors can accelerate a 2.5-ton payload up to 30Gs.

Royal Opera House, London

Tony Hall, Chief Executive of the Royal Opera House:

> 'World-class' is neither an idle nor boastful claim. In the context of the Royal Opera House the term refers to the quality of our people, the standards of our productions and the diversity of our work and initiatives. Unique? Unashamedly so. We shy away from labels such as 'elite', because of the obvious negative connotations of exclusiveness. But I want people to take away from here the fact that we are elite in the sense that we have the best singers, dancers, directors, designers, orchestra, chorus, backstage crew and administrative staff. We are also amongst the best in our ability to reach out to as wide and diverse a community as possible.[2]

Maersk

Maersk is the the leading container shipping company in the world. Its fleet comprises more than 500 vessels and it has over 300 offices in 125 countries across the world. They also operate container terminals in 50 locations. Maersk emphasise the value and comparative rarity of their size, not least in terms of it providing a reliable and comprehensive coverage for customers worldwide. Their website emphasises size in a number of novel ways: for example:

> If all Maersk Line containers were placed one after the other, they would reach about 19,000 km. This is more than the distance from Copenhagen, Denmark to Perth, Australia, via Cape Town, South Africa or almost half of the earth's circumference.

However, Brian Godsafe, a Customer Service Director emphasises other capabilities. He explained that Maersk Line's stated top priority is: 'to provide you, our customers, with services you can count on to satisfy your own customers and grow your business'. Since Maersk are connected to so many markets around the world, customers are able to use them for multiple rather than singular trades. In terms of sales service, Maersk have a dedicated account manager for every regular customer, empowered to deal with their requests. Moreover this is replicated throughout the world. So, for example, there is a dedicated customer service team for each client based in the UK but this team is duplicated in locations around the world. In this way their global clients have touch points into their business all around the world. Many other companies just do not have that advantage.[3]

Sources: (1) Goddard Space Center website. (2) *Annual Review*, 2005/6, p. 11. (3) Pearson Strategy Documentaries.

Questions

1 Categorise the range of capabilities highlighted by the executives in terms of section 3.2 and Tables 3.1 and 3.2.

2 To what extent and why might these capabilities be the basis of *sustained* competitive advantage?

3 For an organisation of your choice undertake the same exercise as in questions 1 and 2 above.

acquisitions or alliances, by which new skills are learned and developed. For example, Stanford's Kathy Eisenhardt[5] has shown that successful acquisition processes can bring in new knowledge to organisations. However, this depends on high-quality pre- and post-acquisition understanding of how the acquisition can be integrated into the new organisation so as to capture synergies and bases of learning from that acquisition. As Teece acknowledges, then, dynamic capabilities are likely to have foundations in less formal, behavioural aspects of organisations, such as the way in which decisions get taken, personal relationships, and entrepreneurial and intuitive skills. Illustration 3.2 provides an example in the context of a new business venture.

3.2.3 Threshold and distinctive capabilities

A distinction also needs to be made between strategic capabilities that are at a threshold level and those that might help the organisation achieve competitive advantage and superior performance. Table 3.2 summarises these distinctions.

Threshold capabilities are those needed for an organisation to meet the necessary require- ments to compete in a given market and achieve parity with competitors in that market. Without such capabilities the organisation could not survive over time. Indeed many start-up businesses find this to be the case. They simply do not have or cannot obtain the resources or competences needed to compete with established competitors. Identifying threshold require- ments is, however, also important for established businesses. By the end of the first decade of the 21st century BP faced declining oil output in countries such as the US, the UK and Russia. BP's board regarded securing new sources of supply as a major challenge. In 2008/9 some high-profile financial institutions went bankrupt or were bailed out by huge government funding because they did not have the financial resources to meet their debts as recessionary pressures grew. There could also be changing *threshold resources* required to meet minimum customer requirements: for example, the increasing demands by modern multiple retailers of their suppliers mean that those suppliers have to possess a quite sophisticated IT infrastruc- ture simply to stand a chance of meeting retailer requirements. Or they could be the *threshold competences* required to deploy resources so as to meet customers' requirements and support particular strategies. Retailers do not simply expect suppliers to have the required IT infras- tructure, but to be able to use it effectively so as to guarantee the required level of service.

Identifying and managing threshold capabilities raises two significant challenges:

● *Threshold levels of capability will change* as critical success factors change (see section 2.4.3) or through the activities of competitors and new entrants. To continue the example, suppliers

Table 3.2 Threshold and distinctive capabilities

	Resources	Competences
Threshold capabilities Required to be able to compete in a market	Threshold resources	Threshold competences
Distinctive capabilities Required to achieve competitive advantage	Distinctive resources	Distinctive competences

ILLUSTRATION 3.2

Building dynamic capabilities in a new venture

Networks and partnerships can be a source of dynamic capabilities and learning for firms and for managers.

HMD Clinical is an Edinburgh-based clinical technological new venture that seeks to make large-scale clinical trials more efficient for drug development companies. HMD initially provided bespoke services using telephony technology (for example, interactive voice recognition) to monitor clinical trials. However, this was problematic, principally due to human error. HMD therefore sought to develop a product based on another technology – radiofrequency identification. HMD felt this would also offer the prospect of market diversification, especially through international expansion. However, making changes to the company's product market domain called for capabilities to expand or modify HMD's current configuration of resources and capabilities – in other words, for dynamic capabilities.

HMD decided to partner with a large established firm, which HMD saw as a potential source of legitimacy, resources and opportunities: Sun Microsystems, a multinational corporation with a significant presence in Scotland. Co-founder Ian Davison commented, 'There's a certain cachet in being associated with a big company.' Sun was interested in HMD's product idea and within months there was progress in establishing the alliance. Davison believes that considerable benefit was derived by HMD: 'We got what we wanted out of the relationship because we managed to build a prototype using the Sun technology.' HMD's experience also illustrates the building of dynamic capabilities at various levels.

Opportunities arose for mutual learning. From HMD's perspective, the venture benefited from exposure to new technological ideas. Of particular advantage was Sun's ability to tap into its widespread resources and capabilities elsewhere in the UK and beyond (for example, Western Europe). Also, Sun's reputation opened doors for HMD. When the prototype was built, HMD made a joint sales call with Sun to a prospective international customer and a demonstration was subsequently held on Sun's Scottish premises. Such activities facilitated experiential learning about processes such as product development and sales.

There were also further benefits for HMD:

● *Product development.* In developing a prototype with Sun, HMD engaged in integrating resources and capabilities to achieve synergies; for example, its own customer-centric technological knowledge in the clinical trials domain was combined with Sun's hardware technology architecture.

● *Alliancing.* Through inputs from a public sector intermediary, HMD gained vital knowledge about formal aspects of alliancing, such as the legalities of sharing intellectual property; equally, HMD came to appreciate the utility of informal social networking in ensuring the smooth progress of joint activity.

● *Strategic decision making.* HMD was able to build new thinking within the firm in terms of, for example, the identification of external knowledge sources as evident from subsequent decisions to expand the alliance to include a third partner.

At the individual level within HMD managers also learned 'new tricks' by engaging in informal routines such as brainstorming sessions and everyday activities such as negotiating. Managers claimed that such learning would help HMD approach its next alliance by replicating certain aspects while modifying others. Davison commented: 'In future we would approach this sort of relationship in a broadly similar manner [but] I think we would attempt to set some clearer company goals and boundaries at the outset.'

Prepared by Shameen Prashantham, Department of Management, University of Glasgow.

Questions

1 At what levels could dynamic capabilities benefit organisations?

2 How do network relationships, such as strategic partnerships, potentially contribute to dynamic capability development?

3 What other joint activity within, and across, organisations could give rise to dynamic capabilities? How?

4 Can dynamic capability development be deliberately planned? How?

to major retailers did not require the same level of IT and logistics support a decade ago. But the retailers' drive to reduce costs, improve efficiency and ensure availability of merchandise to their customers means that their expectations of their suppliers have increased markedly in that time and continue to do so. So there is a need for those suppliers continuously to review and improve their logistics resource and competence base just to stay in business.

- *Trade-offs* may need to be made to achieve the threshold capability required for different customers. For example, businesses have found it difficult to compete in market segments that require large quantities of standard product as well as market segments that require added-value specialist products. Typically, the first requires high-capacity, fast-throughput plant, standardised highly efficient systems and a low-cost labour force; the second a skilled labour force, flexible plant and a more innovative capacity. The danger is that an organisation fails to achieve the threshold capabilities required for either segment.

While threshold capabilities are important, they do not of themselves create competitive advantage or the basis of superior performance. These are dependent on an organisation having distinctive or unique capabilities that are of value to customers and which competitors find difficult to imitate. This could be because the organisation has *distinctive resources* that critically underpin competitive advantage and that others cannot imitate or obtain – a long-established brand, for example. Or it could be that an organisation achieves competitive advantage because it has *distinctive competences* – ways of doing things that are unique to that organisation and effectively utilised so as to be valuable to customers and difficult for competitors to obtain or imitate. Gary Hamel and C.K. Prahalad[6] argue that the distinctive competences that are especially important are likely to be: 'A bundle of constituent skills and technologies rather than a single, discrete skill or technology'. They use the term **core competences** to emphasize **the linked set of skills, activities and resources that, together, deliver customer value, differentiate a business from its competitors and, potentially, can be extended and developed**. For example as markets change or new opportunities arise. There are, then, also similarities here to Teece's conceptualisation of dynamic capabilities.

KEY CONCEPT

Core competences

Bringing these concepts together, a supplier that achieves competitive advantage in a retail market might have done so on the basis of a distinctive resource such as a powerful brand, but also by distinctive competences such as the building of excellent relations with retailers. However, it is likely that what will be most difficult for competitors to match and will therefore be the basis of competitive advantage will be the multiple and linked ways of providing products, high levels of service and building relationships – its core competence.

Section 3.3 that follows discusses in more depth the role played by distinctive resources and competences in contributing to long-term, sustainable competitive advantage. Section 3.4 then explores further the importance of linkages of activities.

 3.3 **'VRIN' STRATEGIC CAPABILITIES AS A BASIS OF COMPETITIVE ADVANTAGE**

How, then, does a strategist consider on what bases organisational capabilities might be the foundation for sustainable competitive advantage and superior economic performance? As argued above, this is unlikely if the organisation is no different from its rivals and therefore has nothing that provides a basis for earning greater profits. Threshold capabilities may achieve parity with competitors but not advantage over those competitors. This section considers four key criteria by which capabilities can be assessed in terms of their providing a basis for achieving such competitive advantage: **v**alue, **r**arity, **i**nimitability and **n**on-substitutability – or *VRIN*.[7]

3.3.1 V – value of strategic capabilities

Strategic capabilities are of value when they provide potential competitive advantage in a market at a cost that allows an organisation to realise acceptable levels of return (in the case of the private sector).[8] There are four components here:

- *Taking advantage of opportunities and neutralising threats*: the most fundamental question is whether the capabilities provide the potential to address the opportunities and threats that arise in the organisation's environment.

- *Value to customers*: it may seem an obvious point to make that capabilities need to be of value to customers, but in practice it is often ignored or poorly understood. For example, managers may seek to build on capabilities that *they* may see as valuable but which do not meet customers' critical success factors (see section 2.4.3). Or they may see a distinctive capability as of value simply because it is distinctive. Having capabilities that are different from other organisations' is not, of itself, a basis of competitive advantage. So the discussion in sections 3.3.2 and 3.3.3 and the lessons it draws are important here.

- *Providing potential competitive advantage*: the capabilities do, nonetheless, need to be capable of delivering a product or service that competitors do not currently have or do not currently emphasise.

- *Cost*: the product or service needs to be provided at a cost that still allows the organisation to make the returns expected of it (e.g. by investors). The danger is that the cost of developing the capabilities to deliver what customers especially value is such that products or services are not profitable.

Managers should therefore consider carefully which of their organisation's activities are especially important in providing such value and which are of less value. Value chain analysis and activity mapping explained in sections 3.4.2 and 3.4.3 can help here.

3.3.2 R – rarity

If competitors have similar capabilities they can respond quickly to the strategic initiative of a rival. This has happened in competition between car manufacturers as they have sought to add more accessories and gadgets to cars. As soon as it becomes evident that these are valued by customers, they are introduced widely by competitors who typically have access to the same technology. **Rare capabilities**, on the other hand, **are those possessed uniquely by one organisation or by a few others**. Here competitive advantage might be longer-lasting. For example, a company may have patented products or services that give it advantage. Service organisations may have rare resources in the form of intellectual capital – perhaps particularly talented individuals. Some libraries have unique collections of books unavailable elsewhere; a company may have a powerful brand; or retail stores may have prime locations. In terms of competences, organisations may have unique skills developed over time or have built special relationships with customers or suppliers not widely possessed by competitors. However, there are two important points to bear in mind about the extent to which rarity might provide competitive advantage:

- *Meeting customer need*: again rarity, of itself, is of little value unless the resources or capabilities lead to outputs in the form of products or services that meet customer needs and are therefore of value to them.

- *Sustainability*: rarity could be temporary. For example, uniquely talented individuals may be an advantage but can also be a risk. In 2009 the financial press reported increasing concerns about Apple, given the health of its CEO Steve Jobs, with headlines such as: 'Can Apple survive without Steve Jobs?'[9] Moreover it may be dangerous to assume that resources and capabilities that are rare will remain so. If an organisation is successful on the basis of something distinctive, then competitors will very likely seek to imitate or obtain that distinctiveness. So it may be necessary to consider other bases of sustainability.

3.3.3 I – inimitability

It should be clear by now that the search for strategic capability that provides sustainable competitive advantage is not straightforward. Having capabilities that are valuable to customers and relatively rare is important, but this may not be enough. Sustainable competitive advantage also involves identifying **inimitable capabilities** – **those that competitors find difficult to imitate or obtain**. For example, the competitive advantage of some professional service organisations is built around the competence of specific individuals – such as a doctor in 'leading-edge' medicine, individual fund managers, the manager of a top sports team or the CEO of a business. However, since these individuals may leave or join competitors, this resource may be a fragile basis of advantage. More sustainable advantage may be found in capabilities that exist for recruiting, training, motivating and rewarding such individuals or be embedded in the culture that attracts them to the organisation – so ensuring that they do not defect to 'competitors'.

At the risk of over-generalisation, it is unusual for competitive advantage to be explainable by differences in the tangible resources of organisations, since over time these can usually be acquired or imitated. Advantage is more likely to be determined by the way in which resources are deployed and managed in terms of an organisation's activities; in other words on the basis of competences.[10] For example, it is unlikely an IT system will improve an organisation's competitive standing of itself, not least because competitors can probably buy something very similar in the open market. On the other hand the capabilities to manage, develop and deploy such a system to the benefit of customers may be much more difficult to imitate. This is likely to be so if two conditions are met:

- *Superior performance*: the capabilities lead to levels of performance of product or service that are significantly better than competitors';

- *Linked competences*: if the capability integrates activities, skills and knowledge both inside and outside the organisation in distinct and mutually compatible ways. It is then the *linkages* of the activities that go to make up capabilities that can be especially significant. There are four reasons why such linkages may make capabilities particularly difficult for competitors to imitate. These are summarised in Figure 3.2 and are now briefly reviewed.

Figure 3.2 Criteria for the inimitability of strategic capabilities

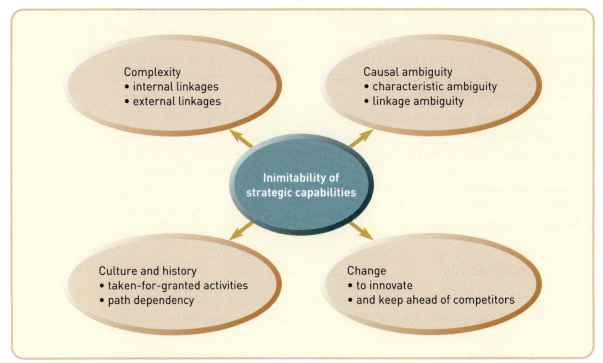

Complexity

The capabilities of an organisation may be difficult to imitate because they are complex. This may be for two main reasons.

- *Internal linkages.* There may be linked activities and processes that, together, deliver customer value. The discussion of activity systems in section 3.4.3 below explains this in more detail and shows how such linked sets of activities might be mapped so that they can be better understood. However, even if a competitor possessed such a map, it is unlikely that it would be able to replicate the sort of complexity it represents. This is not only because of the complexity itself but because, very likely, it has developed on the basis of custom and practice built up over years and is specific to the organisation concerned.

- *External interconnectedness.* Organisations can make it difficult for others to imitate or obtain their bases of competitive advantage by developing activities together with the customer such that the customer becomes dependent on them. This is sometimes referred to as *co-specialisation.* For example, an industrial lubricants business moved away from just selling its products to customers by coming to an agreement with them to manage the applications of lubricants within the customers' sites against agreed targets on cost savings. The more efficient the use of lubricants, the more both parties benefited. Similarly software businesses can achieve advantage by developing computer programs that are distinctively beneficial to specific customer needs.

Causal ambiguity[11]

Another reason why capabilities might be difficult to imitate is that competitors find it difficult to discern the causes and effects underpinning an organisation's advantage. This is called *causal ambiguity.* Causal ambiguity may exist in two different forms:[12]

- *Characteristic ambiguity.* Where the significance of the characteristic itself is difficult to discern or comprehend, perhaps because it is based on tacit knowledge or rooted in the organisation's culture. For example, the know-how of the buyers in a successful fashion retailer may be evident in the sales achieved for the ranges they buy year after year. But it may be very difficult to comprehend just what that know-how is, so competitors will find it difficult to imitate.

- *Linkage ambiguity.* Where competitors cannot discern which activities and processes are dependent on which others to form linkages that create core competences. The expertise of the fashion buyers is unlikely to be lodged in the one individual or even one function. It is likely that there will be a network of suppliers, intelligence networks to understand the market and links with designers. Indeed in some organisations the managers themselves admit that they do not fully comprehend the linkages throughout the organisation that deliver customer value. If this is so it would certainly be difficult for competitors to understand them.

Culture and history

Competences may become embedded in an organisation's culture. So coordination between various activities occurs 'naturally' because people know their part in the wider picture or it is simply 'taken for granted' that activities are done in particular ways. We see this in high-performing sports teams, in teams that work together to combine specialist skills as in operating theatres; but also, for example, in how some firms integrate different activities in their business to deliver excellent customer service. Linked to this cultural embeddedness is the likelihood that such competences have developed over time and in a particular way. The origins and history by which competences have developed over time are referred to as *path dependency.*[13] This history is specific to the organisation and cannot be imitated (see section 5.3.1). As explained in Chapter 5 there is, however, a danger that culturally embedded competences built up over time become so embedded that they are difficult to change: they become rigidities.

Change

The concept of dynamic capabilities is relevant here. If an organisation builds a basis of competitive advantage on resources or capabilities that change as the dynamics of a market or the needs of customers change, they will be more difficult for competitors to imitate. Indeed, arguably, organisations that wish to be market leaders, to innovate and create new markets must do so on the basis of dynamic capabilities. They are, in effect, continually seeking to stay ahead of their competitors by evolving new bases of doing so.

3.3.4 N – non-substitutability[14]

Providing value to customers and possessing competences that are rare and difficult to imitate may mean that it is very difficult for organisations to copy them. However, the organisation may still be at risk from substitution. Substitution could take two different forms:

- *Product or service substitution.* As already discussed in Chapter 2 in relation to the five forces model of competition, a product or service as a whole might be a victim of substitution. For example, increasingly e-mail systems have substituted for postal systems. No matter how complex and culturally embedded were the competences of the postal service, it could not avoid this sort of substitution.

Figure 3.3 VRIN

- *Competence substitution.* Substitution might, however, not be at the product or service level but at the competence level. For example, task-based industries have often suffered because of an over-reliance on the competences of skilled craft workers that have been replaced by expert systems and mechanisation.

In summary and from a resource-based view of organisations, managers need to consider whether their organisation has strategic capabilities to achieve and sustain competitive advantage. To do so they need to consider how and to what extent it has capabilities which are (i) valuable to buyers, (ii) rare, (iii) inimitable and (iv) non-substitutable.

As Figure 3.3 shows, there is an additive effect here. Strategic capabilities provide sustainable bases of competitive advantage the more they meet all four criteria. If such capabilities for competitive advantage do not exist, then managers need to consider if they can be developed. How this might be done is considered in section 3.5 below.

3.3.5 Organisational knowledge as a basis of competitive advantage

A good example of how both resources and competences may combine to produce competitive advantage for an organisation is in terms of organisational knowledge.[15] **Organisational knowledge is the collective intelligence, specific to an organisation, accumulated through both formal systems and the shared experience of people in that organisation.**

The reasons why organisational knowledge is seen as especially important illustrate many of the points made above. As organisations become larger and more complex, the need to share what people know becomes more and more important but increasingly challenging. So organisations that can share knowledge especially well may gain advantage over those that do not. Computerised information systems are available or have been developed by organisations to codify technological, financial and market data that are *valuable* to them; indeed without which they probably could not compete effectively. However, the technology which forms the basis of information systems is hardly *rare*; it is widely available or can be developed. It is therefore less likely that organisations will achieve competitive advantage through such resources and more likely that it will be achieved through the way they manage and develop organisational knowledge more broadly. This may be to do with the competences they employ to utilise and develop

ILLUSTRATION 3.3

Sandvik's rapid production capabilities

Different strategic capabilities might be valuable, rare, inimitable or non-substitutable.

Swedish-based global industrial group Sandvik manufactures products for companies operating in a wide range of industries including medical technology. In a 2009 press release, it announced it had:

> invested in a technologically advanced direct metal laser sintering machine (DMLS) in order to provide rapid production capabilities to its customers, unique amongst contract manufacturers.
>
> Sandvik is now significantly reducing the time required to cost-effectively develop working prototypes, which means its customers can bring new innovations to market far more quickly than was previously possible. Sandvik is also exploiting the powder-based technique used by the DMLS machine to manufacture to almost any design, thereby removing limitations previously imposed on design teams within medical device OEMs (original equipment manufacturers). In an industry where innovation and speed to market are crucial differentiators, these benefits represent a real commercial advantage to OEMs.
>
> Through this investment and the enhanced capabilities it brings, Sandvik has further strengthened its position as a strategic partner to medical technology companies, helping them improve their competitiveness.

Tord Lendau, President Sandvik MedTech, explained:

> 'Medical device OEMs operate in a highly competitive market. We want to leverage Sandvik's long experience within powder metallurgy to deliver real value to OEMs and so must continuously introduce new manufacturing techniques, which is why we have made this significant investment. . . . Medical device manufacturers can now capitalise on enhanced capabilities and improve the speed to market of their new designs and innovations.'

The press release continued:

> The new capabilities provided by the DMLS machine are ideal for the production of working prototypes of medical devices and for complex custom-made instruments.

It quoted John Reynolds, a special projects manager at Sandvik:

> 'Prototyping is an important stage in the creation of a new device, since it provides the opportunity to explore the design and make the necessary adjustments prior to full production. However, most rapid prototyping processes do not produce a working model while those that do are time consuming and more expensive. . . . By using the DMLS machine we can bring to bear rapid production techniques that enable us to quickly and cost-effectively manufacture a working prototype. This means our customers can present a working model to their customers in a fraction of the time it would take with conventional manufacturing techniques and bring the final design to market far quicker. . . . We can also now manufacture almost any design the OEM can create, irrespective of the complexity of the geometry. This means our customers' design teams are not constrained by the manufacturing limitations previously typical in the industry. They have the flexibility to respond with precision to the individual preferences of any one surgeon or the specific needs of a patient.'

The press release concluded:

> By enhancing its capabilities through this significant investment and combining it with its materials and manufacturing expertise, Sandvik is helping OEMs achieve real competitive advantage in a challenging market.

Source: www.smt.sandvik.com/sandvik. © AB Sandvik Materials Technology.

Questions

1 Assess the bases of Sandvik's strategic capabilities using the VRIN criteria.

2 Which are the key strategic capabilities which provide, or could provide, Sandvik with sustainable competitive advantage?

information technology. But it is also likely to be about how they draw on and develop the accumulated and dispersed experience-based knowledge in the organisation.

The distinction between *explicit* and *tacit organisational knowledge* made by Ikijuro Nonaka and Hiro Takeuchi[16] helps explain why this is important in terms of achieving competitive advantage. Explicit or 'objective' knowledge is transmitted in formal systematic ways. It may take the form of a codified information resource such as a systems manual or files of market research and intelligence. In contrast, tacit knowledge is more personal, context-specific and therefore hard to formalise and communicate. For example it could be the knowledge of a highly experienced sales force or research and development team; or the experience of a top management team in making many successful acquisitions. It is therefore not only distinctive to the organisation, but likely to be *difficult to imitate* or obtain for the reasons explained in 3.3.3 above. Such knowledge may have been developed over the years by '*communities of practice*'[17] developing and sharing information because it is mutually beneficial to them. It may also be continually changing as their experience changes. It will also be difficult for competitors to comprehend precisely because it is context specific, experiential and dispersed (and therefore complex and causally ambiguous).

Many organisations that have tried to improve the sharing of knowledge by relying on IT-based systems have come to realise that, while some knowledge can usefully be codified and built into computer-based systems, it may be very difficult to codify the knowledge that truly bestows competitive advantage.

DIAGNOSING STRATEGIC CAPABILITIES

So far this chapter has been concerned with explaining concepts associated with the strategic significance of organisations' resources and capabilities. This section now provides some ways in which strategic capabilities can be understood and diagnosed.

3.4.1 Benchmarking[18]

Benchmarking is used as a means of understanding how an organisation compares with others – typically competitors. Many benchmarking exercises focus on outputs such as standards of product or service, but others do attempt to take account of organisational capabilities.

Broadly, there are two approaches to benchmarking:

- *Industry/sector benchmarking.* Insights about performance standards can be gleaned by comparing performance against other organisations in the same industry sector or between similar service providers against a set of performance indicators. Some public-sector organisations have, in effect, acknowledged the existence of strategic groups (see section 2.4.1) by benchmarking against similar organisations rather than against everybody: for example, local government services and police treat 'urban' differently from 'rural' in their benchmarking and league tables. An overriding danger of industry norm comparisons (whether in the private or the public sector) is, however, that the whole industry may be performing badly and losing out competitively to other industries that can satisfy customers' needs in different ways. Another danger with benchmarking within an industry is that the boundaries of industries are blurring through competitive activity and industry convergence. For example, supermarkets have entered retail banking and the benchmarking processes of the traditional retail banks probably need to reflect this.

- *Best-in-class benchmarking.* Best-in-class benchmarking compares an organisation's performance or capabilities against 'best-in-class' performance – wherever that is found – and therefore seeks to overcome some of the above limitations. It may also help challenge managers' mindsets that acceptable improvements in performance will result from incremental changes in resources or competences. It can therefore encourage a more fundamental reconsideration of how to improve organisational capabilities. For example, British Airways improved aircraft maintenance, refuelling and turnaround time studying the processes surrounding Formula One Grand Prix motor racing pit stops.[19] Xerox benchmarked its distribution capabilities against LL Bean, a mail order company. A police force wishing to improve the way in which it responded to emergency telephone calls studied call-centre operations in the banking and IT sectors.

The importance of benchmarking is, then, not so much in the detailed 'mechanics' of comparison but in the impact that these comparisons might have on reviewing capabilities underlying performance. But it has two major limitations:

- *Surface comparisons.* If benchmarking is limited to comparing inputs (resources) and outputs or outcomes, it does not directly identify the reasons for relative performance in terms of underlying capabilities. For example, it may demonstrate that one organisation is poorer at customer service than another but not show the underlying reasons. However, it could encourage managers to seek out these reasons and hence understand how capabilities could be improved.

- *Measurement distortion.* Benchmarking can lead to a situation where '*you get what you measure*' and this may not be what is intended strategically. It can therefore result in changes in behaviour that are unintended or dysfunctional. For example, the university sector in the UK has been subjected to rankings in league tables on research output. This has resulted in academics being 'forced' to orient their published research to certain types of academic journals that may have little to do directly with the quality of the education in universities.

3.4.2 The value chain and value network

The **value chain** describes the categories of activities within an organisation which, together, **create a product or service.** Most organisations are also part of a wider **value network**, **the set of inter-organisational links and relationships that are necessary to create a product or service.** Both are useful in understanding the strategic position of an organisation.

KEY
CONCEPT

Value chain
and value
network

The value chain

If organisations are to achieve competitive advantage by delivering value to customers, managers need to understand which activities their organisation undertakes are especially important in creating that value and which are not. It can, then, be used to model the value system of an organisation. The important point is that the concept of the value chain invites the strategist to think of an organisation in terms of sets of activities. There are different frameworks for considering these categories: Figure 3.4 is a representation of a value chain as developed by Michael Porter.[20]

Primary activities are directly concerned with the creation or delivery of a product or service. For example, for a manufacturing business:

- *Inbound logistics* are activities concerned with receiving, storing and distributing inputs to the product or service including materials handling, stock control, transport, etc.

Figure 3.4 The value chain within an organisation

● *Operations* transform these inputs into the final product or service: machining, packaging, assembly, testing, etc.

● *Outbound logistics* collect, store and distribute the product to customers; for example, warehousing, materials handling, distribution.

● *Marketing and sales* provide the means whereby consumers or users are made aware of the product or service and are able to purchase it. This includes sales administration, advertising and selling.

● *Service* includes those activities that enhance or maintain the value of a product or service, such as installation, repair, training and spares.

Each of these groups of primary activities is linked to *support activities* which help to improve the effectiveness or efficiency of primary activities:

● *Procurement*. Processes that occur in many parts of the organisation for acquiring the various resource inputs to the primary activities. These can be vitally important in achieving scale advantages. So, for example, many large consumer goods companies with multiple businesses nonetheless procure advertising centrally.

● *Technology development*. All value activities have a 'technology', even if it is just know-how. Technologies may be concerned directly with a product (e.g. R&D, product design) or with processes (e.g. process development) or with a particular resource (e.g. raw materials improvements).

● *Human resource management*. These transcend all primary activities and are concerned with recruiting, managing, training, developing and rewarding people within the organisation.

● *Infrastructure*. The formal systems of planning, finance, quality control, information management and the structure of an organisation.

The value chain can be used to understand the strategic position of an organisation in three ways.

- As a *generic description of activities* it can help managers understand if there is a cluster of activities providing benefit to customers located within particular areas of the value chain. Perhaps a business is especially good at outbound logistics linked to its marketing and sales operation and supported by its technology development. It might be less good in terms of its operations and its inbound logistics. The value chain also prompts managers to think about the role different activities play. For example, in a local family-run sandwich bar, is sandwich making best thought of as 'operations' or as 'marketing and sales', given that its reputation and appeal may rely on the social relations and banter between customers and sandwich makers? Arguably it is 'operations' if done badly but 'marketing and sales' if done well.

- In *analysing the competitive position of the organisation* using the VRIN criteria as follows:

  V Which value creating activities are especially significant for an organisation in meeting customer needs and could they be usefully developed further?

  R To what extent and how does an organisation have bases of value creation that are *rare*? Or conversely are all elements of their value chain common to their competitors?

  I What aspects of value creation are difficult for others to *imitate*, perhaps because they are *embedded* in the activity systems of the organisation (see section 3.4.3 below)?

  N What aspects of the value chain are or are not vulnerable to substitution? For example, the production and distribution of CDs was seen as a key value-creating activity by firms such as EMI in the music industry; but the availability of music downloads via the internet has dramatically reduced the value of such activities.

- To *analyse the cost and value of activities*[21] of an organisation. This could involve the following steps:

  - *Identifying sets of value activities.* Figure 3.5 might be appropriate as a general framework here or a value chain more specific to an organisation may be needed. The important thing is to ask (a) which separate categories of activities best describe the operations of the organisation and (b) which of these are most significant in delivering the strategy and achieving advantage over competitors? For example, it is likely that in a branded pharmaceutical company research and development and marketing activities will be crucially important.

  - *Relative importance of activity costs internally.* Which activities are most significant in terms of the costs of operations? Does the significance of the costs align with the significance of the activities? Which activities most add value to the final product or service (and in turn to the customer) and which do not? It can also be important to establish which sets of activities are linked to or are dependent on others and which, in effect, are self-standing. For example, organisations that have undertaken such analyses often find that central services have grown to the extent that they are a disproportionate cost to internal sets of activities and to the customer.

  - *Relative importance of activities externally.* How does value and the cost of a set of activities compare with the similar activities of competitors? For example, although they are both global oil businesses, BP and Shell are different in terms of the significance of their value chain activities. BP has historically outperformed Shell in terms of exploration; but the reverse is the case with regard to refining and marketing.

● *Where and how can costs be reduced?* Given the picture that emerges from such an analysis it should be possible to ask some important questions about the cost structure of the organisation in terms of the strategy being followed (or that needs to be followed in the future). For example, is the balance of cost in line with the strategic significance of the elements of the value chain? Can costs be reduced in some areas without affecting the value created for customers? Can some activities be outsourced (see section 7.5.2), for example those that are relatively free-standing and do not add value significantly? Can cost savings be made by increasing economies of scale or scope; for example, through central procurement or consolidating currently fragmented activities (e.g. manufacturing units)?

The value network

A single organisation rarely undertakes in-house all of the value activities from design through to the delivery of the final product or service to the final consumer. There is usually specialisation of roles so, as Figure 3.5 shows, any one organisation is part of a wider *value network*. There are questions that arise here that build on an understanding of the value chain itself.

● *What are the activities and cost/price structures of the value network?* Just as costs can be analysed across the internal value chain, they can also be analysed across the value network: Illustration 3.4 shows this in relation to fish farming. Value network analysis

ILLUSTRATION 3.4

A value network for Ugandan chilled fish fillet exports

Even small enterprises can be part of an international value network. Analysing it can provide strategic benefits.

A fish factory in Uganda barely made any profit. Fish were caught from small motorboats owned by poor fishermen from local villages. Just before they set out they would collect ice and plastic fish boxes from the agents who bought the catch on their return. The boxes were imported, along with tackle and boat parts. All supplies had to be paid for in cash in advance by the agents. Sometimes ice and supplies were not available in time. Fish landed with insufficient ice achieved half of the price of iced fish, and sometimes could not be sold to the agents at all. The fish factory had always processed the fillets in the same way – disposing of the waste back into the lake. Once a week, some foreign traders would come and buy the better fillets; they didn't say who they sold them to, and sometimes they didn't buy very much.

By mapping the value chain it was clear that there were opportunities for capturing more value along the chain and reducing losses. Together with outside specialists, the fish factory and the fishing community developed a strategy to improve their capabilities, as indicated in the figure, until they became a flourishing international business, The Lake Victoria Fish Company, with regular air-freight exports around the world.

You can see more of their current operations at http://www.ufpea.co.ug/, and find out more about the type of analytical process applied at www.justreturn.ch.

(The approximate costs and prices given represent the situation before improvements were implemented.)

Questions

1 Draw up a value chain or value network for another business in terms of the activities within its component parts.

2 Estimate the relative costs and/or assets associated with these activities.

3 What are the strategic implications of your analysis?

Figure 3.5 The value network

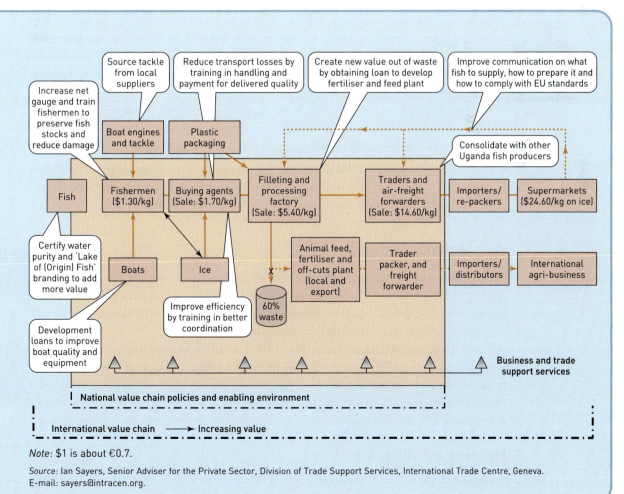

Note: $1 is about €0.7.

Source: Ian Sayers, Senior Adviser for the Private Sector, Division of Trade Support Services, International Trade Centre, Geneva. E-mail: sayers@intracen.org.

was used by Ugandan fish farmers as a way of identifying what they should focus on in developing a more profitable business model.

- *Where are the profit pools?*[22] **Profit pools refer to the different levels of profit available at different parts of the value network**. Some parts of a value network may be inherently more profitable than others because of the differences in competitive intensity (see section 2.3.1). For example, in the computer industry microprocessors and software have historically been more profitable than hardware manufacture. The strategic question becomes whether it is possible to focus on the areas of greatest profit potential? Care has to be exercised here. It is one thing to identify such potential; it is another to be successful in it given the capabilities an organisation has. For example, engineering firms may recognise the greater profit potential in providing engineering consulting services in addition to or instead of manufacturing. Nonetheless many have found it difficult to develop such services successfully either because their staff do not have consultancy capabilities or because their clients do not recognise the firms as having them.

- The *'make or buy'* decision for a particular activity is critical given some of the above questions. This is the *outsourcing* decision. Increasingly outsourcing is becoming common as a means of lowering costs. Of course, the more an organisation outsources, the more its ability to influence the performance of other organisations in the value network may become a critically important capability in itself and even a source of competitive advantage. For example, the quality of a cooker or a television when it reaches the final purchaser is not only influenced by the activities undertaken within the manufacturing company itself, but also by the quality of components from suppliers and the performance of the distributors. There is, of course, the converse question: which activities most need to be part of the internal value chain because they are central to achieving competitive advantage? For example, Howard Schultz,[23] the founder, argued that the benefit to Starbucks of owning and controlling most activities in its value chain was because its competitive advantage lay in the quality of its coffee, which it needed to guarantee.

- *Partnering.* Who might be the best partners in the parts of the value network? And what kind of *relationships* are important to develop with each partner? For example, should they be regarded as suppliers or should they be regarded as alliance partners (see section 10.4)?

3.4.3 Activity systems

The discussion so far highlights the fact that all organisations comprise sets of capabilities but that these are likely to be configured differently across organisations. It is this variable configuration of capabilities that makes an organisation and its strategy more or less unique. So for the strategist, understanding this matters a good deal.

Value chain analysis can help with this, but so too can understanding the activity systems of an organisation. As the discussion above in section 3.3 has made clear, the way in which resources are deployed through the organisation actually takes form in the activities pursued by that organisation; so it is important to identify what these activities are, why they are valuable to customers, how the various activities fit together and how they are different from competitors'.

Mapping activity systems

A number of the writers,[24] including Michael Porter, have written about the importance of mapping activity systems and shown how this might be done.

The starting point is to identify what Porter refers to as 'higher order strategic themes'. In effect these are the ways in which the organisation meets the critical success factors determining them in the market. The next step is to identify the clusters of activities that underpin each of these themes and how these do or do not fit together. The result is a picture of the organisation represented in terms of activity systems such as that shown in Illustration 3.5. This shows an activity systems map for the Scandinavian strategic communications consultancy, Geelmuyden.Kiese.[25] At the heart of its success is its knowledge, built over the years, of how effective communications can influence 'the power dynamics of decision making processes'. However, as Illustration 3.5 shows, this central theme is related to other higher-order strategic themes, each of which is underpinned by clusters of activities. Three points need to be emphasised here:

- *Relationship to the value chain.* The various activities represented in an activity map can also be seen as parts of a value chain. The in-house methodology is, in effect, part of Geelmuyden.Kiese's operations; their recruitment practices are a component of their human resource management; their stance on integrity and insistence on openness rather than suppression of the information part of their service offering; and so on. However, activity systems mapping encourages a greater understanding of the complexity of strategic capabilities – important if bases of competitive advantage are to be identified and managed.

- *The importance of linkages and fit.* An activity systems map emphasises the importance of different activities that create value to customers pulling in the same direction and supporting rather than opposing each other. So the need is to understand (a) the fit between the various activities and how these reinforce each other and (b) the fit externally with the needs of clients. There are three implications:

  - The danger of *piecemeal change* or tinkering with such systems which may damage the positive benefits of the linkages that exist.

  - The consequent *challenge of managing change.* When change is needed the implication is that change to one part of the system will almost inevitably affect another; or, put another way, change probably has to be managed to the whole system.

  - The need to understand where there is an *absence of fit* which can be extremely damaging. For example, the Institute of Public Policy Research produced a report in 2009 pointing to the way in which failures to link up different arms of government was doing potential damage to the UK's national security.[26]

- *Relationship to VRIN.* It is these linkages and this fit that can be the bases of sustainable competitive advantage. In combination they may be *valuable* to clients, truly distinctive and therefore *rare.* Moreover, whilst individual components of an activity system might be relatively easy to imitate, in combination they may well constitute the complexity and causal ambiguity rooted in culture and history that makes them *difficult to imitate.*

However, it is not just at the conceptual level that activity maps are important; they can also be directly helpful in the management of strategy.

- *Disaggregation.*[27] Useful as an activity map is, the danger is that, in seeking to explain capabilities underpinning their strategy, managers may identify capabilities at too abstract a level. If the strategic benefits of activity systems are to be understood greater disaggregation is likely to be needed. For example, managers may talk of 'innovation' or 'putting the customer first' as a basis for 'good service'. These terms are too generic; they are umbrella descriptors of activities that exist at an even more operational level than those shown in the

ILLUSTRATION 3.5

Activity systems at Geelmuyden.Kiese

The strategic capabilities of an organisation can be understood and analysed in terms of linked activities (an activity system).

Geelmuyden.Kiese is a Scandinavian strategic communications consultancy – an extension of what has traditionally been known as public relations services (PR). Their clients include organisations in the financial, oil, energy, pharmaceuticals and health care sectors. These clients typically approach Geelmuyden.Kiese when they have a problem, the solution of which critically depends on effective external or internal communication. In this context, their services include facilitation of contacts with public agencies, officials and government, investor relations, media relations, communication campaigns for new product launches, crisis management and in-company communication on key strategic issues.

At the heart of the company's success is the knowledge they have built up since their founding in 1989 of the dynamics of decision making processes, often within influential bodies such as government and, linked to this, 'how effective communication may move power within those decision making processes'. This knowledge is underpinned by some key aspects in the way in which they do business (also see Figure 3.6).

- They seek to *work at a strategic level* with their clients, prioritising those clients where such work is especially valued. Here they employ their own in-house methodology, developed on the basis of years of experience and systematically review the assignments they undertake both internally and on the basis of client surveys.

- They take a clear stance on *integrity of communication*. They always advise openness of communication rather than suppression of information and only deal with clients that will accept such principles. They often take a stance on this approach in controversial and high profile issues in the public domain.

- Staff are given high degrees of *freedom* but with some absolute criteria of *responsibility*. In this regard there are strict rules for handling clients' confidential information and strict sanctions if such rules are broken.

- *Recruitment* is based on ensuring that such responsibility can be achieved. It is largely on the basis of values of openness and integrity but also humour. The emphasis tends to be on recruiting junior personnel and developing them. Geelmuyden.Kiese has learned that this is a better way of delivering its services than recruiting established 'high profile' consultants. Combined with its mentoring system for competence development of junior staff, they therefore believe that it offers the *best learning opportunities* in Scandinavia for young communications consultants.

- Geelmuyden.Kiese also offers *strong financial incentives* for top performance within the firm. Such performance includes rewards for the development of junior personnel but is also based on the internal evaluation of leadership qualities and performance.

activity map. If an activity map is to be useful for the purposes of managing activities then managers need to identify specific activities at an operating level that are manageable. To take an example from Illustration 3.5, there is the recognition that the mentoring of junior staff by partners is important; but the map itself does not show specifically how this is done. Managers need to delve further and further into explanations of how specific activities support other activities so as to eventually 'deliver' customer benefit. There are computer programs in existence that can be used for this purpose;[28] or it may be done more basically, for example by mapping activities on a large blank wall by using Post-its.[29]

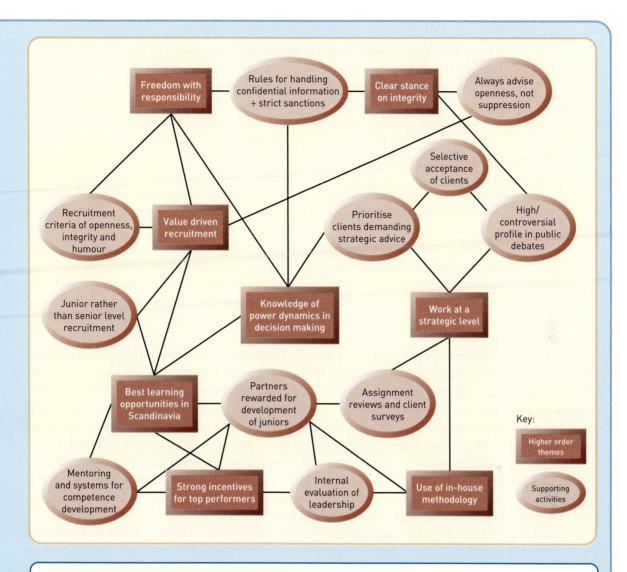

Questions

1 Assuming Geelmuyden.Kiese managers are correct that they have capabilities that provide competitive advantage:
   a What would competitors find difficult to imitate and why?
   b Are there any activities that could be done away with without threatening that advantage?

2 If disaggregation (see section 3.4.3) is important, suggest what even more specific activities underpinning those in the activity map that might be important.

● *Superfluous activities.* Just as in value chain analysis, but at a more detailed level, the question can be asked: are there activities that are not required in order to pursue a particular strategy? Or how do activities contribute to value creation? If activities do not do this, why are they being pursued by the organisation? Whether Ryanair used activity mapping or not, they have systematically identified and done away with many activities that other airlines commonly have. They are also continually seeking further activities that can be eliminated or outsourced to reduce cost.

3.4.4 SWOT[30]

It can be helpful to summarise the key issues arising from an analysis of the business environ-ment and the capabilities of an organisation to gain an overall picture of its strategic position. **SWOT summarises the strengths, weaknesses, opportunities and threats likely to impact on strategy development** that arise from such analyses. This can also be useful as a basis against which to generate strategic options and assess future courses of action.

The aim is to identify the extent to which strengths and weaknesses are relevant to, or capable of dealing with, the changes taking place in the business environment. Illustration 3.6 takes the example of a pharmaceuticals firm (Pharmcare).[31] It assumes that key environmental impacts have been identified from analyses explained in Chapter 2 and that major strengths and weaknesses have been identified using the analytic tools explained in this chapter. A scoring mechanism (plus 5 to minus 5) is used as a means of getting managers to assess the interrelationship between the environmental impacts and the strengths and weaknesses of the firm. A positive (+) denotes that the strength of the company would help it take advantage of, or counteract, a problem arising from an environmental change or that a weakness would be offset by that change. A negative (−) score denotes that the strength would be reduced or that a weakness would prevent the organisation from overcoming problems associated with that change.

Pharmcare's share price had been declining because investors were concerned that its strong market position was under threat. This had not been improved by a merger that was proving problematic. The pharmaceutical market was changing with new ways of doing busi-ness, driven by new technology, the quest to provide medicines at lower cost and politicians seeking ways to cope with soaring health-care costs and an ever more informed patient. But was Pharmcare keeping pace? The strategic review of the firm's position (Illustration 3.6a) confirmed its strengths of a flexible salesforce, well-known brand name and new health-care department. However, there were major weaknesses, namely relative failure on low-cost drugs, competence in information and communication technology (ICT) and a failure to get to grips with increasingly well-informed users.

However, in the context of this chapter, if this analysis is to be useful, it must be remembered that the exercise is not absolute but relative to its competitors. So SWOT analysis is most useful when it is comparative – if it examines strengths, weaknesses, opportunities and threats in relation to competitors. When the impact of environmental forces on competitors was analysed (Illustration 3.6b), it showed that Pharmcare was still outperforming its traditional competitor (Company W), but potentially vulnerable to changing dynamics in the general industry structure courtesy of niche players (X and Y).

There are two main dangers in a SWOT exercise:

- *Listing.* A SWOT exercise can generate very long lists of apparent strengths, weaknesses, opportunities and threats, whereas what matters is to be clear about what is really important and what is less important. So prioritisation of issues matters.

- *A summary, not a substitute.* SWOT analysis is an engaging and fairly simple tool. It is also useful in summarising and consolidating other analysis that has been explained in Chapters 2 and 3. It is not, however, a substitute for that analysis. There are two dangers if it is used on its own. The first is that, in the absence of more thorough analysis, managers rely on preconceived, often inherited and biased views. The second is again the danger of a lack of specificity. Identifying very general strengths, for example, does not explain the underlying reasons for those strengths.

ILLUSTRATION 3.6

SWOT analysis of Pharmcare

A SWOT analysis explores the relationship between the environmental influences and the strategic capabilities of an organisation compared with its competitors.

(a) SWOT analysis for Pharmcare

	Environmental change (opportunities and threats)					
	Health care rationing	Complex and changing buying structures	Increased integration of health care	Informed patients	+	−
Strengths						
Flexible salesforce	+3	+5	+2	+2	12	0
Economies of scale	0	0	+3	+3	+6	0
Strong brand name	+2	+1	0	−1	3	−1
Health care education department	+4	+3	+4	+5	+16	0
Weaknesses						
Limited competences in biotechnology and genetics	0	0	−4	−3	0	−7
Ever lower R&D productivity	−3	−2	−1	−2	0	−8
Weak ICT competences	−2	−2	−5	−5	0	−14
Over-reliance on leading product	−1	−1	−3	−1	0	−6
Environmental impact scores	+9	+9	+9	+10		
	−6	−5	−14	−12		

(b) Competitor SWOT analyses

	Environmental change (opportunities and threats)				
	Health care rationing	Complex and changing buying structures	Increased integration of health care	Informed and passionate patients	Overall impact
Pharmcare *Big global player suffering fall in share price, low research productivity and post-mega-merger bureaucracy*	−3 Struggling to prove cost-effectiveness of new drugs to new regulators of health care rationing	+6 Well-known brand, a flexible salesforce combined with a new health care education department creates positive synergy	−3 Weak ICT and lack of integration following mergers means sales, research and admin. are all underperforming	−2 Have yet to get into the groove of patient power fuelled by the Internet	−2 Declining performance over time worsened after merger
Company W *Big pharma with patchy response to change, losing ground in new areas of competition*	−4 Focus is on old-style promotional selling rather than helping doctors control costs through drugs	−4 Traditional salesforce not helped by marketing which can be unaccommodating of national differences	+0 Alliances with equipment manufacturers but little work done across alliance to show dual use of drugs and new surgical techniques	+4 New recruits in the ICT department have worked cross-functionally to involve patients like never before	−4 Needs to modernise across the whole company
Organisation X *Partnership between a charity managed by people with venture capital experience and top hospital geneticists*	+3 Potentially able to deliver rapid advances in genetics-based illnesses	+2 Able possibly to bypass these with innovative cost-effective drug(s)	+2 Innovative drugs can help integrate health care through enabling patients to stay at home	+3 Patients will fight for advances in treatment areas where little recent progress has been made	+10 Could be the basis of a new business model for drug discovery – but all to prove as yet
Company Y *Only develops drugs for less common diseases*	+3 Partnering with big pharma allows the development of drugs discovered by big pharma but not economical for them to develop	0 Focus on small market segments so not as vulnerable to overall market structure, but innovative approach might be risky	+2 Innovative use of web to show why products still worthwhile developing even for less common illnesses	+1 Toll-free call centres for sufferers of less common illnesses Company, like patients, is passionate about its mission	+6 Novel approach can be considered either risky or a winner, or both!

Questions

1 What does the SWOT analysis tell us about the competitive position of Pharmcare with the industry as a whole?

2 How readily do you think executives of Pharmcare identify the strengths and weaknesses of competitors?

3 Identify the benefits and dangers (other than those identified in the text) of a SWOT analysis such as that in the illustration.

Prepared by Jill Shepherd, Segal Graduate School of Business, Simon Fraser University, Vancouver, Canada.

Figure 3.6 The TOWS matrix

		Internal factors	
		Strengths (S)	Weaknesses (W)
External factors	Opportunities (O)	**SO Strategic options** Generate options here that use srengths to take advantage of opportunities	**WO Strategic options** Generate options here that take advantage of opportunities by overcoming weaknesses
	Threats (T)	**ST Strategic options** Generate options here that use srengths to avoid threats	**WT Strategic options** Generate options here that minimise weaknesses and avoid threats

SWOT can also help focus discussion on future choices and the extent to which an organisation is capable of supporting these strategies. A useful way of doing this is to use a TOWS matrix[32] as shown in Figure 3.6. This builds directly on the information in a SWOT exercise. Each box of the TOWS matrix can be used to identify options that address a different combination of the internal factors (strengths and weaknesses) and the external factors (opportunities and threats). For example, the top left-hand box prompts a consideration of options that use the strengths of the organisation to take advantage of opportunities in the business environment. An example for Pharmcare might be the re-training of the salesforce to deal with changes in pharmaceuticals buying. The bottom right-hand box prompts options that minimise weaknesses and also avoid threats; for Pharmcare this might include the need to develop their ICT systems to service better more informed patients. Quite likely this would also help take advantage of opportunities arising from changes in the buying structure of the industry (top right). The bottom left box suggests the need to use strengths to avoid threats, perhaps by building on the success of their health-care education department to also better service informed patients.

3.5 MANAGING STRATEGIC CAPABILITY

The previous section was concerned with diagnosing strategic capability. This section considers what managers might do to manage and improve resources and capabilities to the strategic benefit of their organisation.

One lesson that emerges from an understanding of the strategic importance of capabilities is that the basis of competitive advantage may lie in aspects of the organisation that are difficult to discern or be specific about. The first point is, then, to emphasise that, if managers are to manage the resources and capabilities of their organisation, the sort of analyses explained here, especially value chain analysis and activity systems mapping, are centrally important. If capabilities are not understood at these levels, there are dangers that managers may take the wrong course of action. For example, managers in an industrial cleaning company undertook an activity mapping exercise. It revealed that the way their van drivers dealt with collecting often filthy garments from industrial premises was especially valued by customers. This had developed through custom and practice, competitors did not do it and the managers themselves were not aware of it explicitly until they did the exercise. The irony was that they were just about to outsource the van delivery service! They were about to lose control of one of their bases of competitive advantage for the sake of cost reduction.

Assuming, then, that such analyses have been undertaken, what can managers do?

3.5.1 Managing activities for capability development[33]

There are different ways in which managers might develop strategic capabilities:

- *Internal capability development.* Could capabilities be added or upgraded so that they become more reinforcing of outcomes that deliver against critical success factors? This might be done, for example, by:

  - *Leveraging capabilities.*[34] Managers might identify strategic capabilities in one area of their organisation, perhaps customer service in one geographic business unit of a multinational, that are not present in other business units. They might then seek to extend this throughout all the business units. Whilst this seems straightforward, studies[35] find it is not. The capabilities of one part of an organisation might not be easily transferred to another because of the problems of managing change (see Chapter 14).

  - *Stretching capabilities.* Managers may see the opportunity to build new products or services out of existing capabilities. Indeed, building new businesses in this way is the basis of related diversification, as explained in Chapter 7.

- *External capability development.* Similarly, there may be ways of developing capabilities by looking externally. For example, this could be by developing new capabilities by acquisition or entering into alliances and joint ventures (see Chapter 10).

- *Ceasing activities.* Could current activities, not central to the delivery of value to customers, be done away with, outsourced or reduced in cost? If managers are aware of the capabilities central to bases of competitive advantage, they can retain these and focus on areas of cost reduction that are less significant.

- *Monitor outputs and benefits* when it is not possible to fully understand capabilities. There are organisations where managers may know that there are activities that have a positive impact on competitive advantage, but may not fully understand just how such positive impact arises. For example, the delivery of value may be dependent on highly specialised skills as in a cutting-edge hi-tech firm; or on complex linkages far down in the organisation. Here managers may have to be careful about disturbing the bases of such capabilities whilst, at the same time, ensuring that they *monitor the outputs and benefits* created for customers.[36]

3.5.2 Managing people for capability development

One of the lessons of this chapter is that the bases of competitive advantage often lie in the day-to-day activities that people undertake in organisations, so developing the ability of people to recognise the relevance of what they do in terms of how that contributes to the strategy of the organisation is important. More specifically:

KEY DEBATE

The resource-based view of competitive advantage: is it useful to managers?

The view that the resource-based view explains the superior performance of firms has been questioned.

The resource-based view (RBV) of strategy has become highly influential. Much academic research has been carried out on it and managers readily talk about the importance of building on strategic capabilities or core competences to gain competitive advantage. However, some academics have raised questions about the value of RBV.

Scott Newbert[1] undertook a systematic assessment of 166 research studies employing RBV. He concluded that only 53% actually provided empirical evidence to support the claim that it explains the superior performance of firms. Others, too, have raised questions about the explanatory value of RBV.

The critique

Richard Priem and John Butler[2] raise the first two bases of the critique:

1. *The risk of tautology.* The underlying explanation of RBV is that the resource characteristics (or capabilities) that lead to competitive advantage are those that are valuable and rare. Since competitive advantage is defined in terms of value and rarity this verges on tautology. To say that a business performs better than another because it has superior resources or is better at some things than other businesses is not helpful unless it is possible to be specific about what capabilities are important, why and how they can be managed.

2. *The lack of specificity.* However, there is typically little specific in what is written about RBV. 'Top management skills' or 'innovatory capacity' mean little without being specific about the activities and processes that they comprise. And there is relatively little research that identifies such specifics or how they can be managed. Priem and Butler suggest this is particularly so with regard to the argued importance of tacit knowledge in bestowing competitive advantage: 'This may be descriptively correct, but it is likely to be quite difficult for practitioners to effectively manipulate that which is inherently unknowable.'

3. *Stability versus change.* A third critique is that RBV may only hold in relatively stable conditions where 'the rules of the game' in an industry remain relatively fixed.[3] In more unpredictable environments the value of resources can diminish, emphasising, of course, the importance of dynamic capabilities.

The response

Jay Barney,[4] one of the main proponents of RBV, accepts that there is a need to understand more about how resources are used and how people behave in bestowing competitive advantage. However, he defends the managerial relevance of RBV because he believes it highlights that managers need to identify and develop the most critical capabilities of a firm.

In his earlier writing[5] Barney argued that an organisation's culture could be a source of sustainable advantage provided it was valuable, rare and difficult to imitate. In such circumstances he suggested managers should 'nurture these cultures'. However, he went on to argue that:

> If one firm is able to modify its culture, then it is likely that others can as well. In this case the advantages associated with the culture are imitable and thus only a source of normal economic performance. Only when it is not possible to manage a firm's culture in a planned way does that culture have the potential of generating expected sustained superior financial performance.

In other words, he argues that valuable sources of competitive advantage are the intangible assets and resources or competences embedded in a culture in such a way that not only can competitors not imitate them, but managers cannot readily manage them. Priem and Butler would no doubt argue that this makes their point: that RBV is not very helpful in providing practical help to managers.

References:
1. S.L. Newbert, 'Empirical research on the Resource-based View of the Firm: an Assessment and Suggestions for Future Research', *Strategic Management Journal*, 28, 121–46, 2007.
2. R. Priem and J.E. Butler, 'Is the resource-based view a useful perspective for strategic management research?', *Academy of Management Review*, vol. 26, no. 1 (2001), pp. 22–40.
3. J. Kraaijenbrink, J.-C. Spender and A.J. Groen. 'The resource-based view: A review and assessment of its critiques', *Journal of Management*, 36, 1, 349–72, 2010.
4. J.B. Barney, 'Is the resource based view a useful perspective for strategic management research? Yes', *Academy of Management Review*, vol. 26, no. 1 (2001), pp. 41–56.
5. J.B. Barney, 'Organizational culture: can it be a source of sustained competitive advantage?', *Academy of Management Review*, vol. 11, no. 3 (1986), pp. 656–65.

Questions

1 How specific would the identification of strategic capabilities need to be to permit them to be managed to achieve competitive advantage?

2 Do you agree that if it were possible to identify and manage such capabilities they would be imitated?

3 Is the RBV useful?

- *Targeted training and development* may be possible. Often companies design training and development programmes that are very general. For strategic purposes it may be important to target the development of skills and competences which can provide competitive advantage.

- *Staffing policies* might be employed to develop particular competences. For example, an oil company that sought to build its competitive advantage around the building of close customer relationships in markets for industrial oils did so by ensuring that senior field managers with an aptitude for this were promoted and sent to different parts of the world that needed to be developed in such ways.

- *Organisational learning* may be recognised as central, particularly in fast-changing conditions. Here successful firms may be those that have grown the *dynamic capabilities* to continually readjust and refine bases of competitive advantage. In effect their competence becomes that of learning and development.

- *Develop people's awareness* that what they do in their jobs can matter at the strategic level. It is a common complaint in organisations that 'no one values what I do'. Helping people see how their work relates to the bigger strategic picture can both enhance the likelihood that they will, indeed, contribute positively to helping achieve competitive success and increase their motivation to do so.

Much of the discussion in this chapter builds on research and the writing of scholars who take a resource-based view of strategy. They therefore emphasise the central importance of managing resources and capabilities for competitive advantage. The Key Debate summarises the arguments for and against the practical value of such an approach.

SUMMARY

- *The competitive advantage* of an organisation is likely to be based on the strategic *capabilities* it has that are valuable to customers and that its rivals do not have or have difficulty in obtaining. Strategic capabilities comprise both *resources and competences*.

- The concept of *dynamic capabilities* highlights that strategic capabilities need to change as the market and environmental context of an organisation changes.

- Sustainability of competitive advantage is likely to depend on an organisation's capabilities being of at least *threshold value* in a market but also being *valuable*, relatively *rare*, *inimitable and non-substitutable*.

- Ways of *diagnosing organisational capabilities* include:

  - *Benchmarking* as a means of understanding the relative performance of organisations.

  - Analysing an organisation's *value chain* and *value network* as a basis for understanding how value to a customer is created and can be developed.

  - *Activity mapping* as a means of identifying more detailed activities which underpin strategic capabilities.

  - *SWOT analysis* as a way of drawing together an understanding of strengths, weaknesses, opportunities and threats an organisation faces.

- Managers need to think about how and to what extent they can manage the *development of strategic capabilities* of their organisation by internal and external capability development and by the way they manage people in their organisation.

WORK ASSIGNMENTS

*✱ Denotes more advanced work assignments. * Refers to a case study in the Text and Cases edition.*

3.1 Using Tables 3.1 and 3.2 identify the resources and competences of an organisation with which you are familiar. You can answer this in relation to Dyson, Amazon* or Formula One* if you wish.

3.2✱ Undertake an analysis of the strategic capability of an organisation with which you are familiar in order to identify which capabilities, if any, meet the criteria of (a) value, (b) rarity, (c) inimitability and (d) non-substitutability (see section 3.3). You can answer this in relation to Dyson, Amazon* or Formula One* if you so wish.

3.3✱ For an industry or public service consider how the strategic capabilities that have been the basis of competitive advantage (or best value in the public sector) have changed over time. Why have these changes occurred? How did the relative strengths of different companies or service providers change over this period? Why?

3.4 Undertake a value chain or network analysis for an organisation of your choice (referring to Illustration 3.4 could be helpful). You can answer this in relation to a case study in the book such as Tesco* or Ryanair* if you wish.

3.5✱ For a benchmarking exercise for which you have access, make a critical assessment of the benefits and dangers of the approach that was taken.

Integrative assignment

3.6 Prepare a SWOT analysis for an organisation of your choice and in relation to competitors (see Illustration 3.6). Explain why you have chosen each of the factors you have included in the analysis, in particular their relationship to other analyses you have undertaken in Chapters 2 and 3. What are the conclusions you arrive at from your analysis and how would these inform an evaluation of strategy (see Chapter 11)?

VIDEO ASSIGNMENT

Visit **MyStrategyLab** and watch the *Maersk* case study.

1 What are the strategic capabilities that Maersk claim provide them with competitive advantage in the global freight market?

2 Drawing on VRIN, suggest on what bases might these be sustainable over time.

RECOMMENDED KEY READINGS

- For an understanding of the resource-based view of the firm, an early and much cited paper is by Jay Barney: 'Firm resources and sustained competitive advantage', *Journal of Management*, vol. 17 (1991), pp. 99–120. For a review of the development of RBV and evidence of its explanatory power see: Scott Newbert, 'Empirical research on the Resource Based View of the firm: an assessment and suggestions for future research', *Strategic Management Journal*, vol. 28 (2007), pp. 121–46.

- The concept of Dynamic Capabilities is reviewed in C.L. Wang and P.K. Ahmed, 'Dynamic Capabilities: a review and research agenda', *International Journal of Management Reviews*, vol. 9, no. 1 (2007), pp. 31–52

and by Veronique Ambrosini and Cliff Bowman, 'What are dynamic capabilities and are they a useful construct in strategic management?', *International Journal of Management Reviews*, vol. 11, no. 1 (2009), pp. 29–49.

- Michael Porter explains how mapping activity systems can be important in considering competitive strategy in his article 'What is strategy?' (*Harvard Business Review*, Nov–Dec 1996, pp. 61–78).

- For a critical discussion of the use and misuse of SWOT analysis see T. Hill and R. Westbrook, 'SWOT analysis: it's time for a product recall', *Long Range Planning*, vol. 30, no. 1 (1997), pp. 46–52.

REFERENCES

1. The concept of resource-based strategies was introduced by B. Wernerfelt, 'A resource-based view of the firm', *Strategic Management Journal*, vol. 5, no. 2, pp. 171–80, 1984. A much cited paper is by Jay Barney: 'Firm resources and sustained competitive advantage', *Journal of Management*, vol. 17 (1991), no. 1, pp. 99–120. There are now many books and papers that explain and summarise the approach: for example D. Hoopes, T. Madsen and G. Walker in the special issue of the *Strategic Management Journal*, 'Why is there a resource based view?' (vol. 24, no. 10, pp. 889–902, 2003) and J. Barney and D. Clark, *Resource-Based Theory: Creating and Sustaining Competitive Advantage*, Oxford University Press, 2007.

2. For summary papers on dynamic capabilities see C.L. Wang and P.K. Ahmed, 'Dynamic Capabilities: a review and research agenda', *International Journal of Management Reviews*, 9, 1, 31–52, 2007 and V. Ambrosini and C. Bowman, 'What are dynamic capabilities and are they a useful construct in strategic management?', *International Journal of Management Reviews*, 11, 1, 29–49, 2009. Also see C. Helfat, S. Finkelstein, W. Mitchell, M. Peteraf, H. Singh, D. Teece and S. Winter, *Dynamic Capabilities: Understanding Strategic Change in Organizations*, Blackwell Publishing, 2007.

3. David Teece has written about dynamic capabilities originally in D.J. Teece, G. Pisano and A. Shuen: 'Dynamic capabilities and strategic management', *Strategic Management Journal*, vol. 18 (1997), no. 7, pp. 509–34. More recently he has expanded his explanation in D. Teece, Explicating dynamic capabilities: the nature and micro-foundations of (sustainable) enterprise performance, *Strategic Management Journal*, 28, 1319–50, 2007, pp. 1320–1.

4. D. Leonard-Barton, 'Core capabilities and core rigidities: a paradox in managing new product development', *Strategic Management Journal*, vol. 13, pp. 111–25, 1992.

5. K.M. Eisenhardt and J.A. Martin, 'Dynamic capabilities: what are they?', *Strategic Management Journal*, vol. 21 (2000), no. 10/11, pp. 1105–21.

6. Gary Hamel and C.K. Prahalad were the academics who promoted the idea of core competences. For example, G. Hamel and C.K. Prahalad, 'The core competence of the corporation', *Harvard Business Review*, vol. 68, no. 3 (1990), pp. 79–91. The idea of driving strategy development from the resources and competences of an organisation is discussed in G. Hamel and C.K. Prahalad, 'Strategic intent', *Harvard Business Review*, vol. 67, no. 3 (1989), pp. 63–76; and G. Hamel and C.K. Prahalad, 'Strategy as stretch and leverage', *Harvard Business Review*, vol. 71, no. 2 (1993), pp. 75–84.

7. The VRIN criteria were originally introduced by Jay Barney in his 1991 paper (see 1 above).

8. For a discussion of the concept of value, see C. Bowman and V. Ambrosini, 'Identifying valuable resources', *European Management Journal*, 25, 4, 320–9, 2007.

9. 'Can Apple survive without Steve Jobs', *Sunday Times*, 18 January 2009.

10. This is borne out in a meta-study of research on RBV by S.L. Newbert, 'Empirical, research on the Resource Based View of the firm: an assessment and suggestions for future research, *Strategic Management Journal*, 28, 121–46, 2007.

11. The seminal paper on causal ambiguity is S. Lippman and R. Rumelt, 'Uncertain imitability: an analysis of interfirm differences in efficiency under competition', *Bell Journal of Economics*, vol. 13 (1982), pp. 418–38.

12. The distinction between and importance of characteristic and linkage ambiguity is explained by A.W. King and C.P. Zeithaml in 'Competencies and firm performance: examining the causal ambiguity paradox', *Strategic Management Journal*, vol. 22 (2001), no. 1, pp. 75–99.

13. For a fuller discussion of path dependency in the context of strategic capabilities, see D. Holbrook, W. Cohen, D. Hounshell and S. Klepper, 'The nature, sources and consequences of firm differences in the early history of the semiconductor industry', *Strategic Management Journal*, vol. 21, nos 10–11 (2000), pp. 1017–42.

14. The importance of non-substitutability and ways of identifying possible bases of substitution are discussed in M.A. Peteraf and M.E. Bergen, 'Scanning dynamic competitive landscapes: a market and resource based framework', *Strategic Management Journal*, vol. 24, no. 10 (2003), pp. 1027–42.

15. The importance of analysing and understanding knowledge is discussed in I. Nonaka and H. Takeuchi, *The Knowledge-creating Company*, Oxford University Press, 1995. There are also collections of articles on organisational knowledge: e.g. the Special Issue of the *Strategic Management Journal* edited by R. Grant and J.-C. Spender, vol. 17, 1996 and the *Harvard Business Review on Knowledge Management*, HBR Press, 1998. More recently Mark Easterby-Smith and Isabel Prieto have explored the relationships in: 'Dynamic capabilities and knowledge management: an integrative role for learning', *British Journal of Management*, 19, 235–49, 2008.

16. See I. Nonaka and H. Takeuchi, 15 above.

17. E.C. Wenger and W.M. Snyder, 'Communities of practice: the organisational frontier', *Harvard Business Review*, vol. 73 (Jan–Feb 2000), no. 3, pp. 201–7 and E. Wenger, *Communities of Practice: Learning, Meaning and Identity*, Cambridge University Press, 1999.

18. See R. Camp, *Benchmarking: the Search for Industry Best Practices that Lead to Superior Performance*, Quality Press, 2006.

19. See A. Murdoch, 'Lateral benchmarking, or what Formula One taught an airline', *Management Today*, November 1997, pp. 64–7. See also the Formula One case study in the case study section of this book (Text and Cases version only).

20. An extensive discussion of the value chain concept and its application can be found in M.E. Porter, *Competitive Advantage*, Free Press, 1985.

21. For an extended example of value chain analysis see 'Understanding and using value chain analysis' by Andrew Shepherd in *Exploring Techniques of Analysis and Evaluation in Strategic Management* edited by Veronique Ambrosini, Prentice Hall, 1998.

22. The importance of profit pools is discussed by O. Gadiesh and J.L. Gilbert in 'Profit pools: a fresh look at strategy', *Harvard Business Review*, vol. 76 (May–June 1998), no. 3, pp. 139–47.

23. H. Schultz and D. Yang Young, *Pour your Heart Into It*, Hyperion, 1997.

24. See M. Porter, 'What is Strategy?' (*Harvard Business Review*, Nov–Dec, 61–78, 1996) and N. Siggelkow, 'Evolution towards fit', *Administrative Science Quarterly*, 47, 1, 125–59, 2002.

25. We are grateful for this example based on the doctoral dissertation of Bjorn Haugstad, Strategy as the Intentional Structuration of Practice, Translation of Formal Strategies into Strategies in Practice, submitted to the Said Business School, University of Oxford in 2009.

26. The Institute of Public Policy Research, Shared Responsibilities, National Security Strategy for the UK, 2009.

27. 'Disaggregation' is a term used by D. Collis and C. Montgomery, 'Competing on resources', *Harvard Business Review*, July–August, 140–50, 2008.

28. A good example of such computer-based systems for analysing organisational capabilities can be found in a paper by C. Eden and F. Ackermann, 'Mapping distinctive competencies: a systemic approach', *Journal of the Operational Research Society*, vol. 51 (2000), no. 1, pp. 12–20.

29. For a more comprehensive account of the use of such network mapping, see V. Ambrosini, *Tacit and Ambiguous Resources as Sources of Competitive Advantage*, Palgrave Macmillan, 2003. Also see Chapter 6 of *Making Strategy* by F. Ackermann and C. Eden with I. Brown, Sage Publications, 2005.

30. The idea of SWOT as a common-sense checklist has been used for many years: for example, S. Tilles, 'Making strategy explicit', in I. Ansoff (ed.), *Business Strategy*, Penguin, 1968. See also T. Jacobs, J. Shepherd and G. Johnson's chapter on SWOT analysis in V. Ambrosini (ed.), *Exploring Techniques of Strategy Analysis and Evaluation*, Prentice Hall, 1998. For a critical discussion of the (mis)use of SWOT, see T. Hill and R. Westbrook, 'SWOT analysis: it's time for a product recall', *Long Range Planning*, vol. 30 (1997), no. 1, pp. 46–52.

31. For background reading on the pharmaceutical industry see, for example, 'The drug industry – from bench to bedside', *The Economist*, 4 November 2006, and *Science Business* by Gary Pisano, Harvard Business School Press, 2006.

32. See H. Weihrich, 'The TOWS matrix – a tool for situational analysis', *Long Range Planning*, April 1982, pp. 54–66.

33. For a fuller discussion of how managers may manage strategic capabilities, see C. Bowman and N. Collier, 'A contingency approach to resource-creation processes', *International Journal of Management Reviews*, 8, 4, 191–211, 2006.

34. Leveraging is a term used by D. Collis and C. Montgomery (see 27 above).

35. See C.A. Maritan and T.H. Brush, 'Heterogeneity and transferring practices: implementing flow practices in multiple plants', *Strategic Management Journal*, vol. 24 (2003), no. 10, pp. 945–60.

36. This observation is made by Veronique Ambrosini in her book (see 29 above).

'Inside Dyson': a distinctive company?

Jill Shepherd, Segal Graduate School of Business, Simon Fraser University, Vancouver, Canada

Dyson is a private company, famous for its distinctive vacuum cleaners. It is not listed on a stock market and James Dyson, its founder and master inventor, has accumulated a personal fortune of over £1bn (~€1.1bn; ~$1.5bn). He is the sole owner of the company and is one of the few people to appear on Top Rich lists who has made money from his own inventions.

In 2005 the profit of the company reached £100m despite selling fewer vacuum cleaners than competitor Hoover. In terms of value rather than units sold, Dyson sells more in the US than Hoover, a company it sued for patent infringement winning around $5 (~€3.5) million. It is a global company, distributing its products in 45 countries including competitive markets such as China, the USA and Japan, as well as in its home market of the UK.

The company is built upon innovative products that are marketed as robust, presented well in bright colours and often in advertisements featuring James Dyson himself. From bag-less vacuum cleaners to energy-efficient and time-efficient hand-dryers for public places, to desk fans with no blades; all of the products are distinctive. His latest idea involves space saving kitchen appliances and even whole kitchens. All elements of the kitchens will be cubes with controls sliding into the main body so that the cubes fit and stack together into bigger cubes.

It hasn't all been straightforward success though, Dyson was about to launch a vacuum that could pick up water and dust. Customers were suspicious that such '3 in 1' products would not work and were not at all positive about wetting their carpets no matter how attractive the product design. Similarly a purple and silver washing machine with two rotating drums did not sell well and was also withdrawn.

Sir James Dyson

Dyson promote a story of their own heritage that suggests that the way the company works today is a function of the early career development path of its

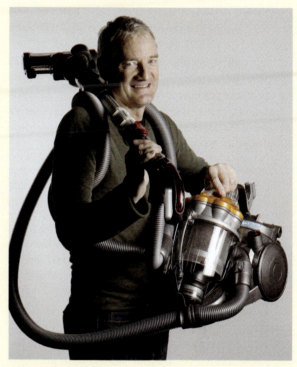

Source: Getty Images.

leader. Dyson studied in art schools, rebelling against his family's tradition of reading Classics at Cambridge University. At art school he sought to apply engineering to functional problems in a way that respected design as an art. His first commercially successful vacuum product used cyclone technology. But from the beginning, he had problems convincing manufacturers both that the technology could be transferred to vacuum cleaners and could be patented. His confident answer was to set up his own firm: adopting unconventional routes and taking risks are still embedded within the organisational culture of Dyson.

Though, by 2010, the company was run by CEO Martin McCourt, James Dyson's own image and personal brand remained central to the firm's promotion. Apart from featuring in many of their adverts, he was highly visible beyond corporate boundaries. He appears to enjoy promoting engineering and design. He finances yearly design awards, collaborated with fashion designer Issey Miyake in an engineering themed fashion show and attempted to fund a Dyson School of Design Innovation. This latter endeavour was abandoned when the UK government put too many hurdles in its way thus limiting Dyson's own independence.

Engineering and design

Investment in R&D at Dyson quadrupled between 2004 and 2009. Dyson HQ is in a rural part of the west of England and is home to 350 engineers and scientists as well as the usual company personnel. It is also linked to 20 specialist laboratories all close by. Their large testing facility in Malaysia operates continually with over 120 testing stations. The operation in the UK employs 1200 varied people: some experienced, some freshly qualified, some with 'way out' ideas. James Dyson has said:

> 'We want people who are creative and courageous – unconditioned fresh-thinkers. We don't strap people into a suit and plonk them behind a desk, we like to give people the chance to make a difference.'

Success revolves around engineering ideas that are fine-tuned, not always on computer screens, but in the hands of engineers who make 100s, even 1000s of prototypes. Special computerised technology helps the engineers develop prototypes but they also use plasticine, cardboard or whatever material they wish to make prototypes in an almost child-like fashion. The engineers will tell you that the journey from prototype to prototype is an iterative journey of failures that creates new ideas. In walkabouts and feedbacks, they are encouraged to fiddle, to 'take the road less travelled' and to be 'less than sensible'. The same engineers report that, whilst competitors may have good robust engineering, they are not as inventive in terms of initial ideas and do not have the persistence and patience to make wacky ideas work in robust terms.

There is a clear corporate-level commitment to product development with half of all profit being channelled into the creation of new ideas supported by their mantra of *thinking, testing, breaking, questioning*. It is product engineering that takes centre stage on the company website and generally in all company communications. This company is obvious in its desire to promote the idea that a Dyson product means new, different, a radical change: a Dyson product whether vacuum or washing machine *is* an innovation and the bright colours help these clever products stand out from the crowd. For example,

the Dyson air multiplier™ performs the same function as a conventional air fan but in a radically different way. Conventional fans cause buffering of the air as the blades interrupt its flow. The multiplier™ 'amplifies surrounding air, giving an uninterrupted stream of flow of smooth air'. When you look at its sleek design you wonder whether it is a function of the innovation in engineering or design or the blurring of the two. Either way, design is deeply embedded in engineering and of all the capabilities at Dyson engineering is king.

Unlike Apple, another design great, who designs then subcontracts all manufacturing, Dyson believe the combination of design engineering and manufacturing is crucial in developing the most inimitable competences that can be protected through patents. Dyson believes in patents to protect its differentiated products, but this does not mean competitors do not try to imitate. Within Dyson's vacuums there is 'patented Ball technology for improved manoeuvrability'. The Miele equivalent has 'unique swivel head technology'. Hoover USA has Wind Tunnel vacuums available in 'fresh colours'. Dyson's colours are usually bright and it does launch exclusive editions based on novel colours. Dyson's hand-blade hand dryer wipes water off your hands in seconds using less energy rather than evaporating water as in standard hand dryers. The competitor product from US specialists in hand drying, the Xlerator, also claims to dry hands in seconds and with far less energy than standard hand dryers. The Dyson desk fan has 11 patent separate applications and involved every discipline within the company.

Global working

James Dyson was heavily criticised in the UK press for taking the managerial decision to place the manufacturing part of his vacuum value chain in Malaysia and later that of his hand dryers in Nanjing in China. He needed, he said, to follow competitors to lower cost manufacturing as margins were being eaten away. One hundred jobs were lost in the UK in the first move and several hundred in the second. Later, with manufacturing costs down and profits up, more engineers were hired in the UK. James Dyson says the decision to move to Malaysia was not an easy one for him. It was not solely based on cost but also his belief that he needed to have a testing facility nearer to suppliers and those were all in the East. In contrast, Miele and Excel Dryer Corporation keep their manufacturing in their home countries.

Dyson and its competitors

Company	Location of headquarters	Product range	Manufacturing locations	Relative company size (1 largest, 5 smallest) based on approximate global turnover	Distribution	Distinctive capabilities?
Dyson	UK	Vacuums, fan, hand dryers, moving into integrated kitchens and robotic vacuums following the success of iRobots	Asia	4	Own online and through retail outlets	Engineering design
Electrolux	Sweden	Range of vacuums, washing machines, fridges and ovens and a robotic vacuum	Not known	2	Retail outlets	Emphasis on energy-saving products Brand licensing of over 50 brands
Hoover (Techtronic Floor Care Technology Limited)	USA and Hong Kong for (TTI)	Vacuums and for TTI Floor Care power tools, outdoor power equipment, floor care appliances, solar-powered lighting and electronic measuring products In USA Hoover range includes patented and trade-marked 'Wind Tunnel' with no loss of suction	Not known, possibly various around Asia	1	Vacuums sold through retail outlets and own online shop in the USA	Possibly the sheer scale of its global operations rather than any particular capability gives it the edge?
Hoover Limited	UK (Italy)	Vacuums and a wide range of domestic appliances			Hoovers sold in retail outlets and online accessories only	
Miele	Germany	Domestic appliances from microwaves to wine storage	Germany ('90% of value creation within Germany')	3	Only through stores including Miele stores, Miele specialists and Miele studios Online stores also	Engineering that results in highly reliable and robust products
Excel Dryer Corporation	USA	A range of hand dryers	USA (products very much advertised as 'Made in USA')	5	Can be bought direct or through licensed distributors Sees end users (e.g. restaurants), distributors, architects and government as customers	Transformation possibly, given the choice by new owner in 1997 to collaborate with a partner – Invent Resources – that produced the Xlerator product and changed the financial profile of the company

Dyson claims to be helping national competitiveness by pulling the UK up the value chain as global competition heats up. China claims contracts like Dyson's help pull China up the manufacturing value chain too towards ever more complex products of the highest quality. Dyson himself appears to view China as a major market. He has made choices to reflect that, such as launching his hand dryers there by offering them free to the Sofitel Hotel in Nanjing. As the costs of making things seem to be an ever decreasing part of the price a consumer pays, perhaps design and development are the future.

Dyson's secrecy of success

Undoubtedly a success story, it is a firm that prefers to keep its secret of success just that – secret. So much is evident, for example in their UK HQ. Access to the building and then subsequent areas is via thumb print and even then some areas are out of bounds. They have even developed their own sound-absorbing panels to ensure that conversations can be kept secret.

Postscript: In March 2010 James Dyson stood down as chairman, although he maintained his role as 'chief inventor'.

Questions

1 Using frameworks from the chapter, analyse the strategic capabilities of Dyson.

2 To what extent do you think any of the capabilities can be imitated by competitors?

3 Which of Dyson's distinctive capabilities may, over time, become threshold capabilities?

4 Bearing in mind your answers to questions 1 and 2, how crucial is Sir James Dyson to the future of of the company? What might be the effect of his completely leaving or selling the company?

4

STRATEGIC PURPOSE

Learning outcomes

After reading this chapter you should be able to:

● Consider appropriate ways to express the *strategic purpose* of an organisation in terms of *statements of purpose*, *values*, *vision*, *mission* or *objectives*.

● Identify the components of the *governance chain* of an organisation.

● Understand differences in *governance structures* and the advantages and disadvantages of these.

● Identify differences in the *corporate responsibility* stances taken by organisations and how *ethical issues* relate to strategic purpose.

● Undertake *stakeholder analysis* as a means of identifying the influence of different stakeholder groups in terms of their power and interest.

mystrategylab

MyStrategyLab is designed to help you make the most of your studies.

Visit **www.pearsoned.co.uk/mystrategylab** to discover a wide range of resources specific to this chapter, including:

• A personalised **Study plan** that will help you understand core concepts

• **Audio** and **video clips** that put the spotlight on strategy in the real world

• **Online glossaries** and **flashcards** that provide helpful reminders when you're looking for some quick revision.

(4.1) INTRODUCTION

In September 2008 Lehman Brothers, then the fourth largest investment bank in the United States, collapsed: the biggest banking collapse in history. The view of the financial press was that the failure was avoidable. In their view central to the problem was, not only a flawed strategy, but the failure of the Lehman board to be more responsible and proactive in monitoring and constraining CEO Dick Fuld's reckless pursuit of that strategy. It was a failure of both strategy and governance.

The previous two chapters have looked respectively at the influence of the environment and capabilities on an organisation's strategic position. These were important in the downfall of Lehman Brothers, but this case also shows the importance of being clear about what purposes drive the strategy of organisations, who influences such purposes and who monitors performance against them. These are the concerns of this chapter. An important concept here is that of **stakeholders**, **those individuals or groups that depend on an organisation to fulfil their own goals and on whom, in turn, the organisation depends**. An underlying question is whether the strategic purpose of the organisation should be determined in response to the expectations of a particular stakeholder, for example shareholders in the case of a commercial enterprise, or to broader stakeholder interests – at the extreme society and the social good. Figure 4.1 summarises the different influences on strategic purpose discussed in the chapter:

- The chapter begins in section 4.2 by developing the discussion in Chapter 1 about different ways in which organisations express *strategic purpose*, including statements of *values*, *vision*, *mission* and *objectives*.

- Section 4.3 considers *corporate governance* and the *regulatory framework* within which organisations operate. The concern is with the way in which formally constituted bodies

Figure 4.1 Influences on strategic purpose

such as investors or boards influence strategic purpose through the formalised processes of supervising executive decisions and actions. In turn this raises issues of *accountability*: who are strategists accountable to? Differences in the approach to corporate governance internationally are also discussed.

● Section 4.4 is concerned with issues of *social responsibility and ethics*. Here the question is which purposes an organisation *should* fulfil. How should managers respond to the expectations society has of their organisations, both in terms of *corporate responsibility* and in terms of the *behaviour of individuals* within organisations, not least themselves?

● In all this it is, then, important to understand *different stakeholder expectations* and their relative influence on strategic purpose. This requires an understanding of both the *power* and *interest* of different stakeholder groups. This is addressed through *stakeholder analysis* in section 4.5.

4.2 ORGANISATIONAL PURPOSE: VALUES, MISSION, VISION AND OBJECTIVES

It is executives who form a view on the purpose of their organisation. It can be that an explicit statement of such a purpose is expected of the organisation by one or more stakeholders; or that managers themselves decide such a statement is useful; or that a founding entrepreneur's initial purpose has an enduring legacy. The purpose of an organisation may be expressed in different ways.

4.2.1 Statements of mission, vision and value

Harvard University's Cynthia Montgomery[1] argues that defining and expressing a clear and motivating purpose for the organisation is at the core of a strategist's job. In the absence of such clarity, the strategy of an organisation is a mystery to those who work within the organisation and those who observe it from the outside. They end up having to interpret for themselves why the organisation is doing what it is doing. Montgomery's view is that the stated purpose of the organisation must address the question: what is the organisation there to do that makes a difference, and to whom? If the stakeholders of an organisation can relate to such a purpose it can be highly motivating. So Montgomery suggests that executives need to find ways of expressing strategic purpose in ways that are easy to grasp and that people can relate to. There are three ways in which executives typically attempt to do this:

KEY CONCEPT

Mission statement

● A **mission statement** aims **to provide employees and stakeholders with clarity about the overriding purpose of the organisation**, sometimes referred to in terms of the apparently simple but challenging question: 'What business are we in?' A mission statement should make this clear in terms of long-term purpose. The two linked questions managers need to ask are 'What would be lost if the organisation did not exist?' and 'How do we make a difference?' Though they do not use the term 'mission statement', Jim Collins and Jerry Porras[2] suggest this can best be addressed by managers starting with a descriptive statement of what the organisation does, then repeatedly delving deeper into the purpose of what the organisation is there for by asking 'why do we do this?' They use the example of managers in a gravel and asphalt company arriving at the conclusion that its mission is to make people's lives better by improving the quality of built structures.

● A **vision statement** is concerned with the desired future state of the organisation; an aspiration that will enthuse, gain commitment and stretch performance. So here the question is: 'What do we want to achieve?' Porras and Collins suggest managers can identify this by asking: 'If we were sitting here in twenty years what do we want to have created or achieved?' They cite the example of Henry Ford's original vision in the very early days of automobile production that the ownership of a car should be within the reach of everyone.

● **Statements of corporate values** communicate the underlying and enduring core 'principles' that guide an organisation's strategy and define the way that the organisation should operate.[3] So a question to ask is: 'Would these values change with circumstances?' And if the answer is 'yes' then they are not 'core' and not 'enduring'. An example is the importance of leading-edge research in some universities. Whatever the constraints on funding, such universities hold to the enduring centrality of this.

Illustration 4.1 shows examples of mission, vision and value statements. Many critics regard such statements as bland and too wide-ranging.[4] However, they have become widely adopted, arguably because if there is substantial disagreement within the organisation or with stakeholders as to its mission or vision, there can be real problems in resolving the strategic direction of the organisation. So they can be a useful means of focusing debate on the fundamentals of the organisation.

Collins and Porras claim that the long-run success of many US corporates – such as Disney, General Electric or 3M – can be attributed (at least in part) to their clarity on such statements of purpose.[5] There are, however, potential downsides to public statements of corporate purpose and values if an organisation demonstrably fails to live them out in practice. For example, Lehman Brothers' (see Illustration 4.2) 2007 annual report included twelve principles amongst which were 'doing the right thing', 'demonstrating a commitment to excellence', 'demonstrating smart risk management', 'acting always with ownership mentality' and, of course, 'maximizing shareholder value'.

4.2.2 Objectives

Whether or not organisations use mission, vision or value statements, they use objectives. **Objectives are statements of specific outcomes that are to be achieved** and are often expressed in financial terms. They could be the expression of desired sales or profit levels, rates of growth, dividend levels or share valuation.[6] Organisations may also have market-based objectives, many of which are quantified as targets – such as market share, customer service, repeat business and so on. Increasingly organisations are also setting objectives referred to as 'the triple bottom line', by which is meant not only economic objectives such as those above, but also environmental and social objectives to do with their corporate responsibility to wider society (see section 4.4.1 below).

There are three related issues that managers need to consider with regard to setting objectives.

● *Objectives and measurement.* Some managers argue that objectives are not helpful unless their achievement can be measured. Certainly there are times when specific quantified objectives are required, for example when urgent action is needed and it becomes essential for management to focus attention on a limited number of priority requirements – as in a

ILLUSTRATION 4.1

Mission, vision and values statements

Can well-crafted statements of mission, vision or values be an important means of motivating an organisation's stakeholders?

Whirpool

Vision

Every home . . . Everywhere . . . with Pride, Passion and Performance.

Our vision reinforces that every home is our domain, every customer and customer activity our opportunity. This vision fuels the passion that we have for our customers, pushing us to provide innovative solutions to uniquely meet their needs.

Pride . . . in our work and each other.

Passion . . . for creating unmatched customer loyalty for our brands.

Performance . . . that excites and rewards global investors with superior returns.

We bring this vision to life through the power of our unique global enterprise and our outstanding people . . . working together . . . everywhere.

Mission

Everyone, passionately creating loyal customers for life.

Our mission defines our focus and what we do differently to create value. We are a company of people captivated with creating loyal customers. From every job, across every contact, we will build unmatched customer loyalty . . . one customer at a time.

Values

Our values are constant and define the way that all Whirlpool Corporation employees are expected to behave and conduct business everywhere in the world.

Respect – We must trust one another as individuals and value the capabilities and contributions of each person.

Integrity – We must conduct all aspects of business honorably – ever mindful of the longtime Whirlpool Corporation belief that there is no right way to do a wrong thing.

Diversity and Inclusion – We must maintain the broad diversity of Whirlpool people and ideas. Diversity honors differences, while inclusion allows everyone to contribute. Together, we create value.

Teamwork – We must recognize that pride results in working together to unleash everyone's potential, achieving exceptional results.

Spirit of Winning – We must promote a Whirlpool culture that enables individuals and teams to reach and take pride in extraordinary results and further inspire the 'Spirit of Winning' in all of us.

Age Concern

Our mission

Our mission is to promote the well-being of all older people and to help make later life a fulfilling and enjoyable experience.

Principles

Values and principles underpin what we do, why we do it, and guide how we work to achieve our mission. Our underlying principles are:

- Ageism is unacceptable: we are against all forms of unfair discrimination, and challenge unfair treatment on grounds of age
- All people have the right to make decisions about their lives: we help older people to discover and exercise these rights
- People less able to help themselves should be offered support: we seek to support older people to live their lives with dignity
- Diversity is valued in all that we do: we recognise the diversity of older people and their different needs, choices, cultures and values
- It is only through working together that we can use our local, regional and national presence to the greatest effect.

Values

Our work is also guided by a set of values:

- Enabling: we enable older people to live independently and exercise choice.
- Influential: we draw strength from the voices of older people, and ensure that those voices are heard.
- Dynamic: we are innovative and driven by results and constantly deliver for older people.
- Caring: we are passionate about what we do and care about each individual.
- Expert: we are authoritative, trusted and quality-orientated.

Sources: Whirlpool and Age Concern websites 2010.

Questions

1 Which of these statements do you think are likely to motivate which stakeholders? Why?

2 Could any of them have been improved? How?

3 Identify other statements of mission, vision, purpose or values that you think are especially well crafted and explain why.

CORPORATE GOVERNANCE **123**

turnaround situation (see section 14.5.1). If the choice is between going out of business and surviving, there is no room for latitude through vaguely stated requirements. However, it may be that in other circumstances – for example, in trying to raise the aspirations of people in the organisation – more attention needs to be paid to qualitative statements of purpose such as mission or vision statements than to quantified objectives.

- *Identifying core objectives.*[7] Managers in most companies set objectives which are financial in nature because they recognise that unless adequate profits are made to satisfy shareholders and allow for reinvestment in the business, it will not survive. It may be, however, that there are other aspects of business performance upon which survival and prosperity of the business are based. For example, how the organisation is distinctive from its rivals, or how it is to achieve competitive advantage and sustain it. As Chapter 3 pointed out, this is likely to be on the basis of capabilities that are valued by customers and distinctive from competition. Identifying objectives that capture the bases of such competitive advantage and allow monitoring of performance against it become crucial too. For example, low-cost airlines such as Southwestern in the US set an objective on turnaround time for their aircraft because this is at the core of their distinctive low-cost advantage.

- *Objectives and control.* A recurring problem with objectives is that managers and employees 'lower down' in the hierarchy are unclear as to how their day-to-day work contributes to the achievement of a higher level of objectives. This could, in principle, be addressed by a 'cascade' of objectives – defining a set of detailed objectives at each level in the hierarchy. Many organisations attempt to do this. Here consideration needs to be given to a trade-off: how to achieve required levels of clarity on strategy without being over-restrictive in terms of the latitude people have,[8] an issue discussed in section 13.3.3).

Whatever statements of mission, vision, values are employed, or whatever the objectives that are set, it is important to understand who influences what they are. The rest of the chapter examines this.

4.3 CORPORATE GOVERNANCE[9]

Corporate governance is concerned with the structures and systems of control by which managers are held accountable to those who have a legitimate stake in an organisation.[10] These are the stakeholders that, in ownership and management terms, influence an organisation. Governance has become an increasingly important issue for organisations for three main reasons.

- *The separation of ownership and management control* of organisations (which is now the norm except with very small businesses) means that most organisations operate within a hierarchy, or chain, of governance. This chain represents those groups that influence an organisation through their involvement in either ownership or management of an organisation.

- *Corporate failures and scandals*, such as that of Enron in 2001 and Lehman Brothers and the Royal Bank of Scotland in 2008, have fuelled public debate about how different parties in the governance chain should interact and influence each other. Most notable here is the relationship between shareholders and the boards of businesses, but an equivalent issue in the public sector is the relationship between government or public funding bodies and public-sector organisations.

● *Increased accountability to wider stakeholder interests* has also been increasingly advocated; in particular the argument that corporations need to be more visibly accountable and/or responsive, not only to 'owners' and 'managers' in the governance chain but to wider social interest.

4.3.1 The governance chain

The **governance chain** shows the roles and relationships of different groups involved in the **governance of an organisation**. In a small family business, the governance chain is simple: there are family shareholders, a board with some family members and there are managers, some of whom may be family too. Here there are just three layers in the chain. However, even in such businesses there are variations, for example, in the extent of family involvement and influence.[11] In large businesses influence on governance can be complex. Figure 4.2 shows a governance chain for a typical large, publicly quoted organisation. Here the size of the organisation means there are extra layers of management internally, while being publicly quoted

Figure 4.2 The chain of corporate governance: typical reporting structures

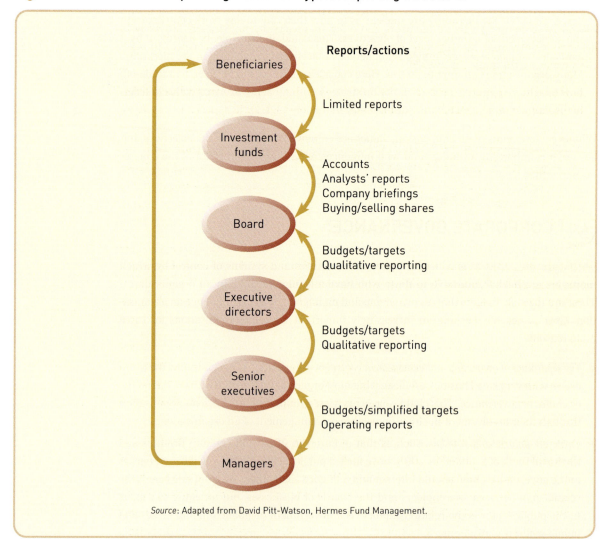

Source: Adapted from David Pitt-Watson, Hermes Fund Management.

introduces more investor layers too. Individual investors (the ultimate beneficiaries) often invest in public companies through investment funds, for example unit trusts or pension funds, which then invest in a range of companies on their behalf. Such funds are of growing importance. By 2010 they owned over 50 per cent of the equity of US corporations (19 per cent in 1970) and over 70 per cent in the UK (25 per cent in 1963), with similar growth elsewhere in Europe. Funds are typically controlled by trustees, with day-to-day investment activity undertaken by investment managers. So the ultimate beneficiaries may not even know in which companies they have a financial stake and have little power to influence the companies' boards directly.

The relationships in such governance chains can be understood in terms of the *principal–agent model.*[12] 'Principals' pay 'agents' to act on their behalf, just as homeowners employ estate agents to sell their homes. In Figure 4.2, the beneficiaries are the ultimate principals and fund trustees and investment managers are their agents in terms of achieving good returns on their investments. Further down the chain, company boards are principals too, with senior executives their agents in managing the company. There are many layers of agents between ultimate principals and the managers at the bottom, with the reporting mechanisms between each layer liable to be imperfect.

Principal–agent theory assumes that agents will not work diligently for principals unless incentives are carefully and appropriately aligned. However, it can be seen from Figure 4.2 that in large companies board members and other managers driving strategy are likely to be very remote from the ultimate beneficiaries of the company's performance. In such circumstances, the danger is twofold:

● *Self-interest.* Any agent in the chain may act out of self-interest. Managers will be striving for promotion and/or increased earnings, investment managers will be seeking to increase their bonuses, and so on.

● *Misalignment of incentives and control.* As influence passes down the governance chain, the expectations of one group are not passed on to the next appropriately. For example, ultimate beneficiaries may be mainly concerned with the long-term security of their pension fund, but the investment managers or the executives with whom they interact may place a greater emphasis on short-term growth.

The result may be that decisions are taken that are not in the best interests of the final beneficiary. This is just what has happened in the case of many of the corporate scandals of recent years, such as Lehman Brothers (see Illustration 4.2).

In this context, the governance chain helps highlight important issues that affect the management of strategy:

● *Responsibility to whom?* A fundamental question in large corporations is whether executives should regard themselves as *solely* responsible to shareholders, or as 'trustees of the assets of the corporation' acting on behalf of a wider range of stakeholders. (See the key debate at the end of the chapter.) Even in terms of formal governance structures this varies across the world, as section 4.3.3 shows.

● *Who are the shareholders?* If managers do see themselves as primarily responsible to shareholders, what does this mean in terms of the governance chain? As explained above, the final beneficiaries are far removed from the managers, so for many managers responsibility to them is notional. In practical terms, directors of a firm are likely to engage most frequently with institutional representatives of those shareholders – an investment manager or analyst from a pension fund or insurance company perhaps. Strategists within

ILLUSTRATION 4.2

The collapse of Lehman Brothers

Executive decisions may not always be in the best interest of shareholders; with disastrous results.

In 2008 Lehman Brothers was the fourth largest investment bank in the USA. Founded in the mid 1800s, its chief executive was Dick Fuld. Under his guidance the bank had been pursuing a strategy of rapid growth and, in common with other banks, up to 2008 this included the development of derivative products linked to the housing boom. The idea was to reduce their vulnerability to market fluctuations and allow them to take on higher lending risks through 'securitisation'.

The Times suggested that Lehman's strategy of investment on a huge scale in the US real estate market was 'in the hope of emulating the profitability of the big players in investment banking'. This involved: 'packaging debt into marketable instruments and selling them to investors . . . (so that) . . . risk could be diversified by spreading it across a wide investor base'. The problem was that such 'packages' included assets that were of dubious value. The result was that, when the housing boom ended and the value of housing plummeted, far from spreading risk, Lehman, together with many other banks that had followed similar strategies, found such products worthless. The banks, Lehman included, had mis-read the market and embarked on a strategy based on products that few people understood (many of the executives included). Moreover Lehman had intensi-fied its exposure in the housing market even after the onset of the credit crisis that had developed.

In September 2008 Lehman collapsed and filed for bankruptcy. The knock-on effect was felt the world over as other banks increasingly turned to govern-ments or new investors for funding to support them. *The Times* leader laid the problems of Lehman Brothers at the feet of Dick Fuld and his board:

> Mr Fuld has been the imperious chief executive of Lehmans . . . since 1994. A curious cross between Gordon Gekko and Tony Soprano, Mr Fuld was an unapologetic mogul of Wall Street: he put down his colleagues in public: he was good at straight talking but not so practised at straight-listening and ultimately he deluded himself and those around him that, having seen off a brush with bankruptcy in the late 1990s, he and his bank had taken the precautions necessary to weather any financial storm. At Lehman's annual general meeting last April (2008), he said: 'The worst of the impact on the financial services industry is behind us.' Two months later his bank revealed $2.8 (~€2.0) billion in quarterly losses . . . What happened to Lehman Brothers was avoidable. Mr Fuld could have ensured more prudent management of the bank. A board other than Lehman's compliant one might have supervised him more closely or ousted him. After the failure of Bear Stearns (another major financial services business) . . . it ought to have been the prime concern of the Lehmans board to anticipate and prevent a similar outcome.

The Times went on to suggest that, given the need for capital to survive, Lehman's board might have decided to sell the business or part of the business such as its fund management arm. Instead: 'Fuld and Lehman's board proved to have wholly unrealistic expectations of the genuine value of the bank . . . (and) . . . a catastrophic failure to understand the Lehman's business model or the nature of the finan-cial market place that had changed . . .'

Source: *The Times*, 16 September 2008, p. 2; © The Times/The Sun/ nisyndication.com.

Questions

1 Why might Fuld and the Lehman board have behaved the way they did?

2 What other mechanisms in the governance chain should (or could) have prevented what happened?

3 What changes in corporate governance are required to prevent similar occurrences?

a firm therefore face a difficult choice, even if they espouse primary responsibility to shareholders. Do they develop strategies they believe to be in the best interest of a highly fragmented group of unknown shareholders; or to meet the needs and aspirations of the investment managers? A similar problem exists for public-sector managers. They may see themselves as developing strategies in the public good, but they may face direct scrutiny from another body such as a government department or an agency appointed by the government. Is the strategy to be designed for the general public good, or to meet the scrutiny of the government department? For example, managers and doctors in the UK health service are dedicated to the well-being of their patients. But increasingly how they manage their services is governed by the targets placed upon them by a government department, which presumably also believes it is acting in the public good.

- *The role of institutional investors.* The role of institutional investors with regard to the strategy of firms differs according to governance structures around the world (see section 4.3.3). However, a common issue is the extent to which they do or should actively seek to influence strategy (see Illustration 4.3). Historically, in economies like those of the UK or US, investors have exerted their influence on firms through the buying and selling of shares rather than through an engagement with the company on strategic issues. The stock market becomes the judge of their actions through share price movements. There are signs, however, that investors are becoming more actively involved in the strategies of the firms in which they invest.[13] Such involvement varies a good deal[14] but has grown.

- *The role of boards.* Boards of directors typically consist of both executives and non-executive directors. The balance between these varies by type of organisation and by country. However, the principle is that the non-executive directors are there either to represent particular stakeholders, or to take a dispassionate view on the strategy and performance of the firm. The danger is that non-executive directors become too aligned with executives within the company. In the US and UK critics have pointed out that many non-executive directors are chosen on the basis of their previous association and links with senior executives within a firm, with the danger that this reduces the likelihood of their objectivity in performing their roles. There have been attempts to reduce these dangers with, for example, codes of conduct for the appointment of non-executive directors.

- *Scrutiny and control.* Given the concerns about governance that have grown in the last decade, there have been increasing attempts to build means of scrutinising and controlling the activities of 'agents' in the chain to safeguard the interests of the final beneficiaries. Figure 4.2 indicates the information typically available to each 'player' in the chain to judge the performance of others. There are increasing statutory requirements as well as voluntary codes placed upon boards to disclose information publicly and regulate their activities. Nonetheless managers have a great deal of discretion as to what information to provide to whom and what information to require of those who report to them. For example, how specific should a chief executive be in explaining future strategy to shareholders in public statements such as annual reports? What are the appropriate targets and measures to incentivise and control management within a firm? Should these primarily be concerned with the achievement of shareholder value? Or is more of a balanced scorecard approach appropriate to meet the needs of various stakeholders (see section 13.3.3)? Are the typical accountancy methods (such as return on capital employed) the most appropriate measures or should measures be specifically designed to fit the needs of particular strategies or particular stakeholder/shareholder expectations? There are no categoric answers to these

ILLUSTRATION 4.3

Investor interventions

To what extent and how should investors intervene in a company?

Piedmont and M&B

In 2010 M&B was the UK's largest owner of pubs, including Harvester, O'Neill's and All Bar One. It was a company that analysts saw as performing well in 2009. However in January 2010, Simon Laffin, then Chairman of M&B, was ousted by a group of shareholders headed by Joe Lewis who was reported to run Piedmont 'largely from a super yacht in the Caribbean'.

In autumn 2009 M&B had asked the takeover panel in the UK to investigate whether Piedmont was attempting to take over the company without a formal bid. This followed Piedmont's representatives on the Board blocking the appointment of two non-executive directors, Laffin taking over as Chairman and in turn ejecting the Piedmont directors from the Board. M&B management won backing from some big institutional investors such as Standard Life and Aviva on this who said it was wrong for a minority shareholder to be able to nominate so many Board members.

At the AGM in January 2010 Joe Lewis (with 23% shareholding through Piedmont), supported by Elpida, the investment vehicle of Irish racing tycoons John Magnier and J.P. Macmanus (with a 17.6% shareholding), proposed the removal of Simon Laffin from the Board. They secured the support of 66% of shareholders for this. Lewis expressed concerns about mismanagement, greed, high central overheads and pension provisions for departing directors at M&B: concerns which Laffin dismissed as 'complete nonsense'.

The new Chairman appointed was John Lovering, previously Chairman of Debenhams. In the knowledge that the recent feud had cost the group some £2 (~€2.2; ~$3) million he commented: 'Most observers think there should be more shareholder activism, and I agree with that . . . but there must be easier and less fractious ways of achieving these goals.'

The *Financial Times* commented: 'For Mr Lewis the next few months will test his supporters' contention that they are the exponents of sensible, engaged stewardship . . . (but) . . . there is one benefit of the damaging struggle over M&B: if any shareholders were asleep, they are wide awake now.'

Investor AB and Astra Zeneca

Investor AB, the Swedish investment group, is linked to the Wallenberg family and in 2009 held a 3.5% stake in Astra Zeneca. The Wallenberg policy is investment for the long term: they therefore have a strategic, not just a financial, interest in the firms in which they invest. In 2008 Boje Eckholm, the President and Chief Executive of Investor AB, questioned the long term viability of the business model of big pharmaceutical firms and in particular whether it discouraged the development of new medicines.

'You have to ask yourself: do you have economies of scale in R & D? . . . One of the fundamental ways that companies create value for shareholders is strong R & D. It raises the question: is big better? Maybe you have to split into smaller parts.'

His question, then, was whether farming out research to smaller organisations might make sense. This question came at a time when large pharmaceutical companies such as Astra Zeneca were grappling with rising research costs, intense competition from generic drugs and some high profile late stage failures in the research and development process of a promising new drug. Management at Astra Zeneca were reluctant to comment on Mr Eckholm's questions.

Sources: *Financial Times*, 29 January 2010 and the *Observer* Business Section, 24 January 2010, p. 3. *The Times*, 4 April 2008, p. 55.

Questions

1 Did the investors in the respective companies intervene in appropriate ways?

2 What is the role of the Chairman (or woman) in such circumstances?

3 In what ways should top management of companies behave in such circumstances?

questions. How managers answer them will depend on what they decide the strategic purpose of the organisation is, which itself will be influenced by their view on whom they see themselves responsible to.

The governance chain, then, typically operates imperfectly for at least five reasons: (i) a lack of clarity on who the end beneficiaries are; (ii) unequal division of power between the different 'players' in the chain; (iii) with different levels of access to information available to them; (iv) potentially agents in the chain pursuing their own self-interest; and (v) using measures and targets reflecting their own interests rather than those of end beneficiaries. In such circumstances it is not surprising that there are attempts to reform corporate governance and that governance structures are changing around the world.

4.3.2 Different governance structures

The governing body of an organisation is typically a board of directors. The primary statutory responsibility of a board is to ensure that an organisation fulfils the wishes and purposes of the formally recognised primary stakeholders. However, who these stakeholders are varies. In the private sector in some parts of the world it is shareholders, but in other parts of the world it is a broader or different stakeholder base. In the public sector, the governing body is accountable to the political arm of government – possibly through some intermediary such as a funding body. These differences lead to differences in how the purposes of an organisation are shaped and how strategies are developed as well as the role and composition of boards.

At the most general level there are two governance structures: the shareholder model and the stakeholder model.[15]

A shareholder model of governance

The shareholder model is epitomised by the economies of the US and UK. Here shareholding is relatively dispersed and shareholders have legitimate primacy in relation to the wealth generated by the corporations rather than, for example, the rights of other stakeholders such as employees, union representatives or banks. However, proponents argue that maximising shareholder value benefits other stakeholders too. At least in principle, the trading of shares provides a regulatory mechanism for maximising shareholder value. Dissatisfied shareholders may sell their shares, the result being a drop in share price and the threat of takeovers for underperforming firms. So the shareholder interest in a company is assumed to be largely financial.

There are arguments for and against the shareholder model. The *argued advantages* include:

- *Benefits for investors.* Relative to the stakeholder model the investor gets a higher rate of return. Shareholders can also reduce risk through diversifying their holdings in an equity market where shares can be readily traded. The system also provides for minority shareholding rights both through high disclosure of information required by companies but also in empowering them with voting rights (e.g. to appoint directors).

- *Benefits to the economy.* Since the system facilitates higher risk-taking by investors, there is a higher likelihood of the encouragement of economic growth and of entrepreneurship.

- *Benefits for management.* Arguably the separation of ownership and management makes strategic decisions more objectively related to the potentially different demands and constraints of financial, labour and customer markets. A diversified shareholding also means that no one shareholder is likely to control management decisions, provided the firm performs well.

The *argued disadvantages* include:

- *Disadvantages for investors*. Relatively dispersed shareholdings prevent close monitoring of management. This may result in the managers sacrificing shareholder value to pursue their own agendas. For example, CEOs may further their own egos and empires with mergers that add no value to shareholders.

- *Disadvantages for the economy*: *the risk of short-termism*. Lack of control of management may lead to them taking decisions to benefit their own careers (for example, to gain promotion). This, combined with the threat of takeovers, may encourage managers to focus on short-term gains at the expense of long-term projects.[16]

- *Corporate reputation and top management greed*. The lack of management control allows for the huge compensations the managers reward themselves in the form of salary, bonuses and stock options. In the USA CEOs have over 500 times more compensation than their lowest-paid employees.[17]

The stakeholder model of governance

An alternative model of governance is the stakeholder model. This is founded on the principle that wealth is created, captured and distributed by a variety of stakeholders. This may include shareholders but could include family holdings, other investors such as banks, as well as employees or their union representatives. As such, management needs to be responsive to multiple stakeholders who, themselves, may be formally represented on boards. Germany, Italy and Japan are often cited as examples of the stakeholder model.

In practice, under the stakeholder model one or two large groups of investors or *block holders* often come to dominate ownership. For example, in Germany nearly three-quarters of all the German listed companies have a majority owner – very different from the UK or USA for example. Majority ownership is also common in Italy and France. There is also concentrated ownership of firms in Japan, with a small group of shareholders owning a large percentage of the company and a system of cross-shareholding, where large companies own shares of other companies and banks finance the same subgroup.

There are *argued advantages* for the stakeholder model of governance:

- *Long-term horizons*. It is argued that the major investors – banks or other companies, for example – are likely to regard their investments as long-term, thus reducing the pressure for short-term results as against longer-term performance.

- *Advantages for stakeholders*. Apart from the argument that the wider interests of stakeholders are taken into account, it is also argued that employee influence is a deterrent to high-risk decisions and investments. The long-term perspective of majority shareholders will, likely, also be in the interest of other stakeholders.

- *Advantages for investors*. Perhaps ironically it is argued that it is block investments that provide economic benefits. Given investors' concern for the strategic direction of the company, there may be a closer level of monitoring of management, with investors having greater access to information from within the firm. Further, because power may reside with relatively few block investors, intervention is easier in case of management failure.

There are also *argued disadvantages* of the stakeholder model of governance:

- *Disadvantages for management*. Close monitoring could lead to interference, slowing down of decision processes and the loss of management objectivity when critical decisions have to be made.

Table 4.1 Benefits and disadvantages of governance systems

	Shareholder model	Stakeholder model
Benefits	For investors: • Higher rate of return • Reduced risk For the economy: • Encourages entrepreneurship • Encourages inward investment For management: • Independence	For investors: • Closer monitoring of management • Longer-term decision horizons For stakeholders: • Deterrent to high-risk decisions
Disadvantages	For investors: • Difficult to monitor management For the economy: • The risk of short-termism • And top management greed	For management: • Potential interference • Slower decision-making • Reduced independence For the economy: • Reduced financing opportunities for growth • Weak market for corporate control

- *Disadvantages for investors*. There is relatively weak representation of minority shareholders. It is the dominant shareholders that tend to have the major influence, not least because they may well have representatives on boards. Due to lack of financial pressure from shareholders, long-term investments may also be made on projects where the returns may be below market expectations.

- *Disadvantage for the economy*. There are fewer alternatives for raising finance, thus limiting the possibilities of growth and entrepreneurial activity. There is also a relatively weak market for corporate control. The dominance of ownership by large block holders and the relatively high debt financing rather than equity financing can mean that firms, even when performing poorly, may be protected from takeover.

These argued advantages and disadvantages are summarised in Table 4.1.

It is also worth noting that there are implications with regard to the financing of businesses. In the shareholder model, equity is the dominant form of long-term finance and commercial banks provide debt capital, so relationships with bankers are essentially contractual. There are significant implications. Managers need to limit gearing to a prudent level, so more equity is needed for major strategy developments. It also means that the company itself has a higher degree of influence over strategic decisions since the banks are not seeking a strategic involvement with the company. However, if strategies start to fail, the organisation can become increasingly dependent on the bank as a key stakeholder. This often happens in family-owned small businesses. In the extreme banks may exercise their power by withdrawing funds, even if this liquidates the company. In contrast, in some stakeholder systems (notably Japan and to a lesser extent Germany), banks often have significant equity stakes or are part of the same parent company. They are less likely to adopt an arm's-length relationship, more likely to seek active strategic involvement and less likely to withdraw funds in difficult times.

Three qualifications to the governance models explained above need to be made in relation to ownership:

- *Family-controlled firms* can be very large indeed – such as Wal-Mart and Mars. Here share ownership may be concentrated in family hands and it may be that the board is largely family-controlled.

- *State ownership*: many large corporations are either state-owned or owned by sovereign wealth funds that are, themselves, state-controlled. Such funds include, for example, the Abu Dhabi and Kuwait Investment Authorities, the China Investment Corporation and the Government of Singapore Investment Corporation. Firms with such ownership may nominally correspond to a stakeholder model of governance in that they have a dominant block shareholder and many of the advantages and disadvantages of the stakeholder system identified above may prevail.

- *Public services* have a wide variety of arrangements for governing bodies, but there are some commonalities. Governing bodies are often 'representational' of key stakeholders, in practice even if not by regulation. This particularly applies to the place of employees and unions on governing bodies. There has also been a move in many countries to increase the proportion of (so-called) independent members on governing bodies, the nearest equivalent to non-executive directors in the private sector.

4.3.3 Changes and reforms to governance structures

International pressures but also history may influence how governance models change and there is an active debate in many countries on the relative merits of the different governance systems. For example, in many respects historically and culturally the Netherlands is close to Germany and the Nordic countries and, as such, there are those who favour the stakeholder model. There are, however, also those who advocate the shareholder model, reflecting the strong links with the UK and US politically, culturally and economically.[18] In Japan, institutional and foreign investors are gaining influence, and deregulation and liberalisation are increasing the pressure to change governance structures. In Germany, too, there are pressures for change, with arguments being made that, if German companies are to remain globally competitive, employee representation on boards needs to be reviewed, not least to reduce costs and speed decision-making. In Sweden historically firms were privately owned or in the hands of family-controlled foundations, holding companies and investment companies, but in the last decade this has significantly reduced. In India there was a high level of state protectionism. However, since 1991 there has been radical change. India is still characterised by family firms, but with increasing separation of ownership and management and a move towards a shareholder model of governance.

Many governments have also been proactive in reforming aspects of corporate governance. Reforms have taken many forms.[19] There has been legislation on tightening accounting standards and increasing auditor independence from management; on the nature of internal financial controls and external disclosure of information; on the role and independence of non-executive directors; and in the US, on the requirement for shareholder approval of stock-based compensation plans for executives. Throughout Europe there has been an attempt to increase the power and ease of voting for shareholders.

4.3.4 How boards of directors influence strategy

A central governance issue is the role of boards of directors and of directors themselves. Since boards have the ultimate responsibility for the success or failure of an organisation as well as the benefits received by shareholders or wider stakeholders, they must be concerned with strategy.

Under the shareholder model there is typically a single-tier board structure, with a majority of non-executive directors and the role of driving the company forward as well as an oversight role on behalf of shareholders. The emphasis on outside directors is intended to bring greater independence to the primary role of the board, that of oversight on behalf of shareholders. However, as explained above, this is not without its problems since how non-executives are chosen has raised questions about their independence.

The stakeholder model can involve a two-tier board structure. For example, in Germany for firms of more than 500 employees there is a supervisory board (*Aufsichtsrat*) and a management board (*Vorstand*). The supervisory board is a forum where the interest of various groups is represented, including shareholders and employees but also typically bankers, lawyers and stock exchange experts. Strategic planning and operational control are vested with the management board, but major decisions like mergers and acquisitions require approval of the supervisory board. In other European countries, notably the Netherlands and France, two-tier boards also exist.

Two issues are, then, especially significant here:

- *Delegation*. Strategic management can be entirely delegated to management, with the board receiving and approving plans and decisions. Here the 'stewardship' role of the board requires processes that ensure that an organisation's strategy is not 'captured' by management at the expense of other stakeholders. The two-tier board system seeks to do this. It is less clear how this occurs in the single-board structure typical of the shareholder model; the Lehman case (Illustration 4.2) is an example of the dangers.

- *Engagement*. The board can engage in the strategic management process. This has practical problems concerning the time and knowledge level of non-executive directors in particular to perform their role this way. This problem can be especially pronounced in organisations such as charities or public bodies with governing boards or trustees of people committed to the mission of the organisation, keen to become involved but with limited operational understanding of it.

In the guidelines increasingly issued by governments[20] or advocated by commentators there are some common themes:

- Boards must be seen to *operate 'independently' of the management* of the company. So the role of non-executive directors is heightened.

- Boards must be *competent to scrutinise the activities of managers*. So the collective experience of the board, its training and the information available to it are crucially important.

- Directors must have the *time* to do their job properly. So limitations on the number of directorships that an individual can hold are also an important consideration.

- However, it is the *behaviour of boards* and their members that is likely to be most significant[21] whatever structural arrangements are put in place. For example, respect, trust, 'constructive friction' between board members, fluidity of roles, individual as well as collective responsibility, and the evaluation of individual director and collective board performance.

SOCIAL RESPONSIBILITY AND ETHICS[22]

Underlying the discussion of corporate governance is an issue highlighted in the introduction to this chapter. Is the purpose of an organisation and its strategy for the benefit of a primary stakeholder such as the shareholders of a company, or is it there for the benefit of a wider group of stakeholders? In turn this raises the question of societal expectations placed on organisations, how these impact on an organisation's purposes and, in turn, on its strategy. This section considers, first, *corporate social responsibility*: the role businesses and other organisations might take in society. Second, it considers the *ethics* of the behaviour and actions of people in relation to the strategy of their organisations.

4.4.1 Corporate social responsibility

The sheer size and global reach of many companies means that they are bound to have significant influence on society. Further, the widely publicised corporate scandals and failures of the last two decades have fuelled a concern about the role they play. The regulatory environment and the corporate governance arrangements for an organisation determine its minimum obligations towards its stakeholders. However, such legal and regulatory frameworks pay uneven attention to the rights of different stakeholders. For example, customers, suppliers or employees are *contractual stakeholders* in that they have a legal relationship with an organisation, whereas *community stakeholders* such as local communities and pressure groups do not have the equivalent protection of the law. **Corporate social responsibility** (CSR) **is the commitment by organisations to 'behave ethically and contribute to economic development while improving the quality of life of the workforce and their families as well as the local community and society at large'.**[23] CSR is therefore concerned with the ways in which an organisation exceeds its minimum obligations to stakeholders specified through regulation.

Different organisations take different stances on CSR which are reflected in how they manage such responsibilities. Table 4.2 outlines four stereotypes to illustrate these differences. They represent a progressively more inclusive 'list' of stakeholder interests and a greater breadth of criteria against which strategies and performance will be judged. The discussion that follows also explains what such stances typically involve in terms of the ways companies act.[24]

The laissez-faire view (literally 'let do' in French) represents an extreme stance. Proponents argue that the only responsibility of business is to make a profit and provide for the interests of shareholders.[25] It is for government to prescribe, through legislation and regulation, the constraints which society chooses to impose on businesses in their pursuit of economic efficiency. Organisations should meet these minimum obligations but no more. Expecting companies to exercise social duties beyond this can, in extreme cases, undermine the authority of government.

This stance may be taken by executives who are persuaded of it ideologically or by smaller businesses that do not have the resources to do other than minimally comply with regulations. Insofar as social good is pursued, this is justified in terms of improving profitability.[26] This might occur, for example, if social obligations were imposed as a requirement for gaining contracts (for example, if equal opportunities employment practices were required from suppliers to public-sector customers) or to defend their reputation. Responsibility for such actions is

Table 4.2 Corporate social responsibility stances

	Laissez-faire	Enlightened self-interest	Forum for stakeholder interaction	Shaper of society
Rationale	Legal compliance: make a profit, pay taxes and provide jobs	Sound business sense	Sustainability or triple bottom line	Social and market change
Leadership	Peripheral	Supportive	Champion	Visionary
Management	Middle-management responsibility	Systems to ensure good practice	Board-level issue; organisation-wide monitoring	Individual responsibility throughout the organisation
Mode	Defensive to outside pressures	Reactive to outside pressures	Proactive	Defining
Stakeholder relationships	Unilateral	Interactive	Partnership	Multi-organisation alliances

likely to be with middle managers or functional heads rather than with the chief executive, who is unlikely to see this role as part of his or her brief. Relationships with stakeholders are likely to be largely unilateral and one-way rather than interactive. The problem is that society increasingly expects more than this from large organisations and the evidence is that chief executives themselves are aware of this and agree organisations should play a more proactive role.[27]

Enlightened self-interest is tempered with recognition of the long-term financial benefit to the shareholder of well-managed relationships with other stakeholders. The justification for social action is that it makes good business sense. An organisation's reputation is important to its long-term financial success. Given that employees see it as important that their employer acts in a socially responsible manner, a more proactive stance on social issues also helps in recruiting and retaining staff. So, like any other form of investment or promotion expenditure, corporate philanthropy or welfare provision might be regarded as sensible expenditure.[28] The sponsorship of major sporting or arts events by companies is an example. The avoidance of 'shady' marketing practices is also necessary to prevent the need for yet more legislation in that area. Managers here would take the view that organisations not only have responsibility to their shareholders, but also a responsibility for *relationships with* other stakeholders (as against *responsibilities to* other stakeholders). So communication with stakeholder groups is likely to be more interactive than for laissez-faire-type organisations. They may well also set up systems and policies to ensure compliance with best practice (for example, ISO 14000 certification, the protection of human rights in overseas operations, etc.) and begin to monitor their social responsibility performance. Top management may also play more of a part, at least insofar as they support the firm taking a more proactive social role.

A *forum for stakeholder interaction*[29] explicitly incorporates multiple stakeholder interests and expectations rather than just shareholders as influences on organisational purposes and strategies. Here the argument is that the performance of an organisation should be measured in a more pluralistic way than just through the financial bottom line. Companies in this category might retain uneconomic units to preserve jobs, avoid manufacturing or selling 'anti-social' products and be prepared to bear reductions in profitability for the social good. Some financial service organisations have also chosen to offer socially responsible investment 'products' to investors. These include only holdings in organisations that meet high standards of social responsibility in their activities.

In such organisations responsibility for CSR may be elevated to board-level appointments and structures may be set up for monitoring social performance across its global operations. Targets, often through balanced scorecards, may be built into operational aspects of business and issues of social responsibility managed proactively and in a coordinated fashion. The expectation is that such a corporate stance will, in turn, be reflected in the ethical behaviour of individuals within the firm. Organisations in this category inevitably take longer over the development of new strategies as they are committed to wide consultation with stakeholders and with managing the difficult political trade-offs between conflicting stakeholders' expectations.

Shapers of society regard financial considerations as of secondary importance or a constraint. These are activists, seeking to change society and social norms. The firm may have been founded for this purpose, as in the case of Traidcraft UK, a public limited company established with the specific mission of fighting world poverty. Here the social role is the *raison d'être* of the business. Such organisations may see their strategic purpose as 'changing the rules of the game' through which they may benefit but by which they wish to assure that society benefits. In this role it is unlikely that they will be operating on their own: rather they are likely to be partnering with other organisations, commercial and otherwise, to achieve their purposes.

The extent to which this is a viable stance depends upon issues of regulation, corporate governance and accountability. It is easier for a privately owned organisation to operate in this way, since it is not accountable to external shareholders. Arguably the great historical achievements of the public services in transforming the quality of life for millions of people were largely because they were 'mission-driven' in this way, supported by a political framework in which they operated. However, in many countries there have been challenges to the legitimacy of this mission-driven stance of public services and demands for citizens (as taxpayers) to expect demonstrable best value from them. Charitable organisations face similar dilemmas. It is fundamental to their existence that they have zeal to improve the interests of particular groups in society, but they also need to remain financially viable, which can lead to them being seen as over-commercial and spending too much on administration or promotional activities.

Illustration 4.4 shows different examples of company activities that have significant social impacts and Table 4.3 provides some questions against which an organisation's actions on CSR can be assessed.

Managers' increasing sympathy with CSR is not solely for ethical reasons but because there is a belief that there are advantages to businesses in so doing and dangers if they do not.[30] Social responsibility is justified in terms of the 'triple bottom line' – social and environmental benefits as well as increased profits. Indeed it is argued that socially responsible strategies should be followed because they can provide a basis of gaining competitive advantage. The need is to seek 'win–win' situations to optimise the economic return on environmental investments.[31] Fighting the AIDS pandemic in Africa is not just a matter of 'good works' for a pharmaceutical company or an African mining company, it is central to their own

ILLUSTRATION 4.4

The social impact of business strategies

The activities of businesses can have significant impacts on societies. But what motivates such activities?

Social good or spotting the market trend?

In 2009 Pepsi Co launched a range of healthy snacks targeting 8–12-year-old schoolchildren. There were also plans to launch a children's porridge under the Quaker brand and to publish a health audit of its products. This followed Pepsi Co's decision 5 years earlier to stop promoting full-sugar Pepsi and focus on the diet and non-sugared alternatives, Pepsi Max and Diet Pepsi. The company also claimed to have reduced saturated fat in its Walkers Crisps by 70% by switching from palm oil to sunflower oil. Salman Amin, Pepsi Co's CEO in Britain, explained that, whilst it would take years: 'I think we will lick obesity as a social issue. . . . I'm a huge optimist.' Commentators also pointed out that Pepsi Co had, in the past, been good at spotting trends in food consumption and capitalising on them.[1]

Cheap medicines for the world's poor or a smart competitive move?

In early 2009 Andrew Witty, the Chief Executive of GlaxoSmithKlein (GSK) announced the decision to cut its prices in the 50 least developed countries in the world to no more than 25% of levels in the UK and the US prices on all medicines produced by GSK, re-invest 20% of any profits it made in the least developed countries into hospitals, clinics and staff and share knowledge about potential drugs currently protected by patents by making them available in a 'patent pool'. This followed repeated criticisms of drug companies for defending their patents, fighting off generic alternatives and refusing to drop prices for HIV drugs despite the HIV/AIDS crisis in Africa and Asia. Witty hoped it might 'stimulate a different behaviour' adding: 'maybe someone has to move before many people move.'

Whilst campaigners widely applauded the decisions there remained some concerns. Why shouldn't current HIV drugs be included in the patent pool?

And might the GSK decision undermine the generics industry already attempting to supply cheap drugs to poor countries? Indeed the *Guardian* (14/2/09) wrote 'GSK would love to undermine the Indian and Chinese generics companies, which sell copies of their drugs at rock bottom prices in Africa and Asian countries where patents do not apply.'[2]

Powering African homes – or cheap power for Europe?

In 2009 the World Bank announced its $80 (~€56) billion support to build the Grand Inga Dam in the Democratic Republic of Congo. This would feed electricity to South Africa, Egypt, Nigeria and other countries in Africa. At 40,000 MW it would have twice the generation capacity of the Three Gorges Dam in China. However the feasibility study also examined the possibility of extending supply to southern Europe. Critics argued it was a: 'flight of fancy that would only benefit huge Western multinationals and quite possibly feed African energy into European households' when less than 30% of Africans have access to electricity – in some African countries as low as 10%. Supporters, on the other hand, pointed out that it could bring electricity to 500 million African homes and that diverting power to Europe had the benefit of attracting additional financing, thus potentially aiding the local community.[3]

Sources: (1) The *Observer*, 23 August 2009, p. 3; (2) *Financial Times*, 4 March 2009, p. 4; (3) the *Observer* Media and Business, 23 August 2009, p. 1.

Questions

1 How would you categorise each of the decisions in terms of the stances on social responsibility in Table 4.2?

2 To what extent and how should the development of strategic options consider the impact on society?

Table 4.3 Some questions of corporate social responsibility

Should organisations be responsible for . . .

INTERNAL ASPECTS

Exployee welfare
. . . providing medical care, assistance with housing finance, extended sick leave, assistance for dependants, etc.?

Working conditions
. . . job security, enhancing working surroundings, social and sporting clubs, above-minimum safety standards, training and development, etc.?

Job design
. . . designing jobs to the increased satisfaction of workers rather than just for economic efficiency? This would include issues of work/life balance?

Intellectual property
. . . respecting the private knowledge of individuals and not claiming corporate ownership?

EXTERNAL ASPECTS

Environmental issues
. . . reducing pollution to below legal standards if competitors are not doing so?
. . . energy conservation?

Products
. . . dangers arising from the careless use of products by consumers?

Markets and marketing
. . . deciding not to sell in some markets?
. . . advertising standards?

Suppliers
. . . 'fair' terms of trade?
. . . blacklisting suppliers?

Employment
. . . positive discrimination in favour of minorities?
. . . maintaining jobs?

Community activity
. . . sponsoring local events and supporting local good works?

Human rights
. . . respecting human rights in relation to: child labour, workers' and union rights, oppressive political regimes? Both directly and in the choice of markets, suppliers and partners?

interests. Similarly, helping reduce carbon emissions provides a business opportunity for a car manufacturer.[32]

The evidence is equivocal as to whether there really are economic pay-offs to a proactive stance on CSR. There is a claim for the links of an enlightened self-interest approach to superior financial performance.[33] A more qualified view, however, is that a visible concern for CSR benefits performance most for firms where there are low levels of innovation or in industries where there are few other bases of differentiation between firms.[34]

4.4.2 The ethics of individuals and managers

Ethical issues have to be faced at the individual as well as corporate level and can pose difficult dilemmas for individuals and managers. For example, what is the responsibility of an individual who believes that the strategy of his or her organisation is unethical (for example, its trading practices) or is not adequately representing the legitimate interests of one or more stakeholder groups? Should that person leave the company on the grounds of a mismatch of values; or is *whistle-blowing* appropriate, such as divulging information to outside bodies, for example regulatory bodies or the press?

Given that strategy development can be an intensely political process with implications for the personal careers of those concerned, managers can find difficulties establishing and maintaining a position of integrity. There is also potential conflict between what strategies are in managers' own best interests and what strategies are in the longer-term interests of their organisation and the shareholders. Some organisations set down explicit guidelines they expect their employees to follow. Texas Instruments posed these questions:[35]

Is the action legal? . . . If no, stop immediately.

Does it comply with our values? . . . If it does not, stop.

If you do it would you feel bad? . . . Ask your own conscience if you can live with it.

How would this look in the newspaper? . . . Ask if this goes public tomorrow would you do it today?

If you know it's wrong . . . don't do it.

If you are not sure . . . ask; and keep asking until you get an answer.

Perhaps the biggest challenge for managers is to develop a high level of self-awareness of their own behaviour in relation to the issues raised above.[36] This can be difficult because it requires them to stand apart from often deep-rooted and taken-for-granted assumptions that are part of the culture of their organisation – a key theme of the next chapter.

4.5 STAKEHOLDER EXPECTATIONS[37]

It should be clear from the preceding sections that the decisions managers have to make about the purpose and strategy of their organisation are influenced by the expectations of stakeholders. This poses a challenge because there are likely to be many stakeholders, especially for a large organisation (see Figure 4.3), with different, perhaps conflicting, expectations. This means that managers need to take a view on (i) which stakeholders will have the greatest influence, therefore (ii) which expectations they need to pay most attention to and (iii) to what extent the expectations and influence of different stakeholders vary.

4.5.1 Stakeholder groups

External stakeholders can be usefully divided into four types in terms of the nature of their relationship with the organisation and how they might affect the success or failure of a strategy:[38]

- *Economic stakeholders*, including suppliers, competitors, distributors (whose influence can be identified using the five forces framework from Chapter 2 (Figure 2.2) and shareholders (whose influence can be considered in terms of the governance chain discussed in section 4.3.1).

Figure 4.3 Stakeholders of a large organisation

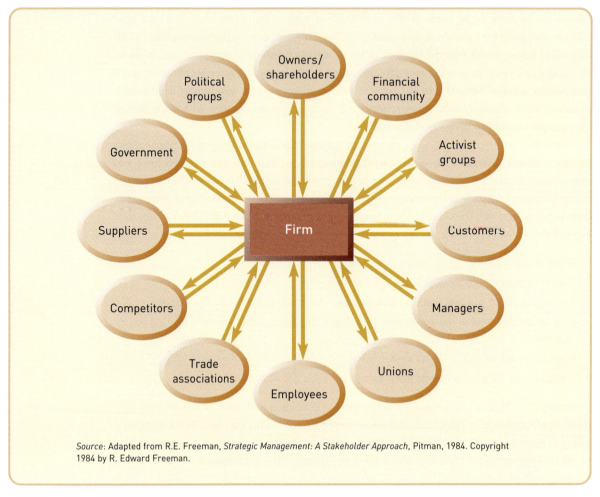

Source: Adapted from R.E. Freeman, *Strategic Management: A Stakeholder Approach*, Pitman, 1984. Copyright 1984 by R. Edward Freeman.

- *Social/political stakeholders*, such as policy makers, regulators and government agencies that may directly influence the strategy or the context in which strategy is developed.

- *Technological stakeholders*, such as key adopters, standards agencies and owners of competitive technologies that will influence the diffusion of new technologies and the adoption of industry standards.

- *Community stakeholders*, who are affected by what an organisation does; for example, those who live close to a factory or, indeed, wider society. These stakeholders have no formal relationship with the organisation but may, of course, take action (e.g. through lobbying or activism) to influence the organisation.

The influence of these different types of stakeholders is likely to vary in different situations. For example, the 'technological group' will be crucial for strategies of new product introduction whilst the 'social/political' group is usually particularly influential in the public-sector context or for companies operating in different countries with different political and legal systems.

There are also stakeholder groups internal to an organisation, which may be departments, geographical locations or different levels in the hierarchy. Individuals may belong to more than one stakeholder group and such groups may 'line up' differently depending on the issue or strategy in hand. Of course, external stakeholders may seek to influence an organisation's

Table 4.4 Some common conflicts of expectations

- In order to grow, short-term profitability, cash flow and pay levels may need to be sacrificed.
- 'Short-termism' may suit managerial career aspirations but preclude investment in long-term projects.
- When family businesses grow, the owners may lose control if they need to appoint professional managers.
- New developments may require additional funding through share issue or loans. In either case, financial independence may be sacrificed.
- Public ownership of shares will require more openness and accountability from the management.
- Cost efficiency through capital investment can mean job losses.
- Extending into mass markets may require a reduction in quality standards.
- In public services, a common conflict is between mass provision and specialist services (e.g. preventative dentistry or heart transplants).
- In large multinational organisations, conflict can result because of a division's responsibilities to the company and also to its host country.

strategy through their links with internal stakeholders. For example, customers may exert pressure on sales managers to represent their interests within the company.

Since the expectations of stakeholder groups will differ, it is normal for conflict to exist regarding the importance or desirability of aspects of strategy. In most situations, a compromise will need to be reached. The more companies globalise the more they add further complications as they operate in multiple arenas. For example, an overseas division is part of the parent company, which will likely have expectations about consistent global behaviour and performance, but is also part of a local community, which may well have different expectations. Table 4.4 shows some typical situations which give rise to conflicting stakeholder expectations. It may, however, also be possible in developing a strategy to look for compatible stakeholder expectations. For example, managers of the Cornish conservation tourist attraction, the Eden Project, looked for 'synergies around purpose' amongst different stakeholders to obtain support and funding for it. Both the European Union and the local economic development agency were interested in developing the economy of Cornwall, one of the poorest areas in the UK, and the Millennium Commission, a government-sponsored funding body, was interested in developing local iconic architecture.

The stakeholder concept is, then, valuable when trying to understand the political context within which strategy develops. Indeed, taking stakeholder expectations and influence into account is an important aspect of strategic choice, as will be seen in Chapter 11.

4.5.2 Stakeholder mapping[39]

There are different ways in which stakeholder mapping can be used to gain an understanding of stakeholder influence.[40] The approach to **stakeholder mapping** here **identifies stakeholder**

Figure 4.4 Stakeholder mapping: the power/interest matrix

Source: Adapted from A. Mendelow, *Proceedings of the Second International Conference on Information Systems*, Cambridge, MA, 1986.

expectations and power and helps in understanding political priorities. It underlines the importance of two issues:

● The *interest* each stakeholder has in imposing its expectations on the organisation's purposes and choice of strategies.

● The *power* each stakeholder has to influence strategy.

These two dimensions form the basis of the power/interest matrix shown as Figure 4.4. The matrix classifies stakeholders in relation to the power they hold and the extent to which they are likely to show interest in supporting or opposing a particular strategy. The matrix helps in thinking through stakeholder influences on the development of strategy. However, it must be emphasised that how managers handle relationships will depend on the governance structures under which they operate (see section 4.3) and the stance taken on corporate responsibility (section 4.4.1). For example, in some countries unions may be weak but in others they may be represented on supervisory boards; banks may take an 'arm's-length' relationship with regard to strategy in some countries, but be part of the governance structures in others. A laissez-faire type of business may only pay attention to stakeholders with the most powerful economic influence (for example, investors), whereas shapers of society might seek to engage with and influence the expectations and involvement of stakeholders who would not typically see themselves as influential.

In order to show the way in which the matrix may be used, take the example of a business where managers see themselves as formulating strategy by trying to ensure the compliance of stakeholders with their own assessment of strategic imperatives. In this context the matrix indicates the type of relationship that managers might typically establish with stakeholder groups in the different quadrants. Clearly, the acceptability of strategies to *key players* (segment D) is of major importance. It could be that these are major investors or particular individuals or agencies with a lot of power – for example, a major shareholder in a family firm or a government funding agency in a public-sector organisation. Often the most difficult issues relate to stakeholders in segment C. Although these might, in general, be relatively passive, a disastrous situation can arise when their level of interest is underrated and they reposition to segment D and frustrate the adoption of a new strategy. Institutional shareholders such as pension funds or insurance firms can fall into this category. They may show little interest unless share prices start to dip, but may then demand to be heard by senior management. Managers might choose to address the expectations of stakeholders in segment B, for example community groups, through information provision. It may be important not to alienate such stakeholders because they can be crucially important 'allies' in influencing the attitudes of more powerful stakeholders: for example, through lobbying.

Stakeholder mapping can also help in understanding the following issues:

- In *determining purpose and strategy*, which stakeholder expectations need to be most considered?
- Whether the *actual levels of interest and power* of stakeholders properly reflect the corporate governance framework within which the organisation is operating, as in the examples above (institutional investors, community groups).
- Who the key *blockers* and *facilitators* of a strategy are likely to be and the appropriate response.
- Whether *repositioning* of certain stakeholders is desirable and/or feasible: for example, to lessen the influence of a key player or, in certain instances, to ensure that there are more key players who will champion the strategy (this is often critical in the public-sector context).
- *Maintaining* the level of interest or power of some key stakeholders: for example, public 'endorsement' by powerful suppliers or customers may be critical to the success of a strategy. It may also be necessary to discourage some stakeholders from repositioning themselves. This is what is meant by *keep satisfied* in relation to stakeholders in segment C, and to a lesser extent *keep informed* for those in segment B.

All this can raise difficult ethical issues for managers in deciding the role they should play in the political activity surrounding stakeholder management. This takes the debate back to the considerations of governance and ethics discussed earlier in section 4.4. For example, are managers really the honest brokers who weigh the conflicting expectations of stakeholder groups? Or should they be answerable to one stakeholder – such as shareholders – and hence is their role to ensure the acceptability of their strategies to other stakeholders? Or are they, as many authors suggest, the real power themselves, constructing strategies to suit their own purposes and managing stakeholder expectations to ensure acceptance of these strategies?

Illustration 4.5 shows some of the practical issues of using stakeholder mapping to understand the political context surrounding a new strategy. The example relates to a German bank considering the centralisation of its corporate banking services in its headquarters in Frankfurt with the implication of the closure of its Toulouse office. The example illustrates two further issues.

- *Heterogeneity of stakeholder groups*, which typically contain a variety of subgroups with different expectations and power. In the illustration, *customers* are shown divided into those who are largely supportive of the strategy (customer X), those who are actively hostile (customer Y) and those who are indifferent (customer Z). So, when using stakeholder mapping, there is a balance to be struck between describing stakeholders too generically – hence hiding important issues of diversity – and too much subdivision, making the situation confusing and difficult to interpret.

ILLUSTRATION 4.5

Stakeholder mapping at Tallman GmbH

Stakeholder mapping can be a useful tool for determining the political priorities for specific strategic developments or changes.

Tallman GmbH was a German bank providing both retail and corporate banking services throughout Germany, Benelux and France. There were concerns about its loss in market share in the corporate sector which was serviced from two centres – Frankfurt (for Germany and Benelux) and Toulouse (for France). It was considering closing the Toulouse operation and servicing all corporate clients from Frankfurt. This would result in significant job losses in Toulouse, some of which would be replaced in Frankfurt alongside vastly improved IT systems.

Two power/interest maps were drawn up by the company officials to establish likely stakeholder reactions to the proposed closure of the Toulouse operation. Map A represents the likely situation and map B the preferred situation – where support for the proposal would be sufficient to proceed.

Referring to map A, it can be seen that, with the exception of customer X and IT supplier A, the stakeholders in box B are currently opposed to the closure of the Toulouse operation. If Tallman was to have any chance of convincing these stakeholders to change their stance to a more supportive one, the company must address their questions and, where possible, alleviate their fears. If such fears were overcome, these people might become important allies in influencing the more

Map A: The likely situation

A	B	Shareholder M (-) Toulouse office (-) Customer X (+) French minister (-) Marketing (-) IT supplier A (+)
C Customer Z German minister	**D** Customer Y (+) Frankfurt office (+) Corporate finance (+)	

Map B: The preferred situation

A French minister	B	Shareholder M (-) Toulouse office (-) Marketing (-) IT supplier A (+)
C Customer Z German minister	**D** Customer X (+) Customer Y (+) Frankfurt office (+) Corporate finance (+)	

- *The role and the individual* currently undertaking that role need to be distinguished. It is useful to know if a new individual in that role would shift the positioning. Serious misjudgements can be made if care is not paid to this point. In the example, it has been concluded that the German minister (segment C) is largely indifferent to the new development. However, a change of minister might change this situation. Although removing such uncertainties entirely is impossible, there are implications for political priorities. For example, permanent officials advising the minister need to be kept satisfied, since they will outlive individual ministers and provide a continuity which can diminish uncertainty. It is also possible, of course, that the German minister's level of interest will be raised by lobbying from her French counterpart. This would have implications for how the company handles the situation in France.

powerful stakeholders in boxes C and D. The supportive attitude of customer X could be usefully harnessed in this quest. Customer X was a multinational with operations throughout Europe. It had shown dissatisfaction with the inconsistent treatment that it received from Frankfurt and Toulouse.

The relationships Tallman had with the stakeholders in box C were the most difficult to manage since, whilst they were considered to be relatively passive, largely due to their indifference to the proposed strategy, a disastrous situation could arise if their level of interest was underrated. For example, if the German minister were replaced, her successor might be opposed to the strategy and actively seek to stop the changes. In this case they would shift to box D.

The acceptability of the proposed strategy to the current players in box D was a key consideration. Of particular concern was customer Y (a major French manufacturer who operated only in France – accounting for 20 per cent of Toulouse corporate banking income). Customer Y was opposed to the closure of the Toulouse operation and could have the power to prevent it from happening, for example by the withdrawal of its business. The company clearly needed to have open discussions with this stakeholder.

By comparing the position of stakeholders in map A and map B, and identifying any changes and mismatches, Tallman could establish a number of tactics to change the stance of certain stakeholders to a more positive one and to increase the power of certain stakeholders. For example, customer X could be encouraged to champion the proposed strategy and assist Tallman by providing media access, or even convincing customer Y that the change could be beneficial.

Tallman could also seek to dissuade or prevent powerful stakeholders from changing their stance to a negative one: for example, unless direct action were taken, lobbying from her French counterpart may well raise the German minister's level of interest. This would have implications for how the company handled the situation in France. Time could be spent talking the strategy through with the French minister and also customer Y to try to shift them away from opposition at least to neutrality, if not support.

Activity

To ensure that you are clear about how to undertake stakeholder mapping, produce your own complete analysis for Tallman GmbH against a different strategy, that is *to service all corporate clients from Toulouse*. Ensure that you go through the following steps:

1 Plot the most likely situation (map A) – remembering to be careful to *reassess* interest and power for each stakeholder in relation to this *new* strategy.

2 Map the preferred situation (map B).

3 Identify the mismatches – and hence the political priorities. Remember to include the need to *maintain* a stakeholder in its 'opening' position (if relevant).

4 Finish off by listing the actions you would propose to take and give a final view of the degree of political risk in pursuing this new strategy.

4.5.3 Power[41]

In considering stakeholder expectations the previous section highlighted the importance of power and how it is shared unequally between various stakeholders. For the purposes of this discussion, **power is the ability of individuals or groups to persuade, induce or coerce others into following certain courses of action.** As Table 4.5 shows, there are different sources of power. It is not only derived from people's hierarchical position within an organisation or formal corporate governance arrangements. It could be a function of the resources or know-how they control or the networks they have built up, for example.

The relative importance of these sources of power will vary over time. Indeed changes in the business environment can significantly shift the power balance between organisations and

Table 4.5 Sources and indicators of power

Sources of power	
Within organisations	**For external stakeholders**
• Hierarchy (formal power), e.g. autocratic decision-making • Influence (informal power), e.g. charismatic leadership • Control of strategic resources, e.g. strategic products • Possession of knowledge and skills, e.g. computer specialists • Control of the human environment, e.g. negotiating skills • Involvement in strategy implementation, e.g. by exercising discretion	• Control of strategic resources, e.g. materials, labour, money • Involvement in strategy implementation, e.g. distribution outlets, agents • Possession of knowledge or skills, e.g. subcontractors, partners • Through internal links, e.g. informal influence
Indicators of power	
Within organisations	**For external stakeholders**
• Status • Claim on resources • Representation • Symbols	• Status • Resource dependence • Negotiating arrangements • Symbols

their stakeholders. For example, consumers' knowledge of different companies' offerings through internet browsing has increased their power as they compare different offerings and reduce their traditional loyalty to a particular supplier. The distribution of power will also vary in relation to the strategy under consideration. For example, a corporate finance function will be more powerful in relation to developments requiring new capital or revenue commitments than in relation to ones which are largely self-financing or within the financial authority of separate divisions or subsidiaries.

Since there are a variety of different sources of power, it is useful to look for *indicators of power*, the visible signs that stakeholders have been able to exploit sources of power. These include: the *status* of the individual or group (such as job grade or reputation); the *claim on resources* (such as budget size); *representation* in powerful positions; and *symbols* of power (such as office size or use of titles and names). For external stakeholders a key indicator is *resource dependence*; for example, the relative size of shareholdings or loans, or the proportion of a company's business tied up with any one customer, or a similar dependence on suppliers. One way of assessing resource dependence is to consider the ease with which a supplier, financier or customer could switch or *be switched* at short notice.

An underlying theme in this chapter has been that strategists have to consider the overall strategic purpose of their organisations. However, a central question that arises is what stakeholder expectations they should respond to in so doing. The key debate provides three views on this in the context of publicly quoted large commercial organisations.

KEY DEBATE

Three views on the purpose of a business

Since there is no one categoric view of the overarching purpose of a business, stakeholders, including managers, have to decide.

Milton Friedman and profit maximisation

Milton Friedman,[1] the renowned economist, wrote:

> In a free enterprise, private property system, a corporate executive is an employee of the owners of the business. He has direct responsibility to his employers. That responsibility is to conduct the business in accordance with their desires, which generally will be to make as much money as possible while conforming to the basic rules of society. . . . What does it mean to say that the corporate executive has a 'social responsibility'? . . . If the statement is not pure rhetoric, it must mean that he is to act in some way that is not in the interests of his employers. . . . Insofar as his actions in accord with his 'social responsibility' reduce returns to stockholders, he is spending their money. Insofar as his actions raise the price to customers, he is spending the customers' money. Insofar as his actions lower the wages of some employees he is spending their money.

Milton Friedman's maxim was that 'the business of business is business', that the 'only social responsibility of business is to increase its profit'. Market mechanisms are then adequate in themselves. If customers are not satisfied, they take their business elsewhere. If employees are not satisfied they work elsewhere. It is the job of government to ensure that there is a free market to allow those conditions to take effect.

Charles Handy's stakeholder view

Citing the corporate scandals of the last decade, Charles Handy[2] argues that the driving for shareholder value linked to stock options for executives, especially in the USA, has resulted in the system 'creating value where none existed'. He accepts

> that there is, first, a clear and important need to meet the expectations of a company's theoretical owners: the shareholders. It would, however, be more accurate to call them investors, perhaps even gamblers. They have none of the pride or responsibility of ownership and are . . . only there for the money. . . . But to turn shareholders' needs into a purpose is to be guilty of a logical confusion. To mistake a necessary condition for a sufficient one. We need to eat to live; food is a necessary condition of life. But if we lived mainly to eat, making food a sufficient or sole purpose of life, we would become gross. The purpose of a business, in other words, is not to make a profit. It is to make a profit so that the business can do something more or better. That 'something' becomes the real justification for the business.

The new capitalists' argument: 'Society and share owners are becoming one and the same'

In their book *The New Capitalists*,[3] the authors also recognise that 'a corporation is the property of its stock owners and should serve their interests'. However, it is the 'millions of pension holders and other savers . . . [who] . . . own the world's giant corporations'. These 'new capitalists are likely to be highly diversified in their investments'. Investment funds, such as pension funds, are their representatives and 'hold a tiny share in hundreds, perhaps even thousands, of companies around the world'. They then argue:

> Imagine that all your savings were invested in one company. The success of that company alone would be your only interest. You would want it to survive, prosper and grow, even if that did damage to the economic system as a whole. But your perspective would change if you had investments in lots of companies. [Then] it is to your disadvantage that any business should seek to behave socially irresponsibly towards other businesses, the customers, employees or society generally. By so doing they will damage the interests of other firms in which you have an interest. The new capitalist has an interest in all the firms in which he or she is investing behaving responsibly: 'in creating rules that lead to the success of the economic system as a whole, even if, in particular circumstances, those rules may tie the hands of an individual company' . . . . managers of a business should quite properly 'concentrate single mindedly on the success of their own organisations . . . however they will not be serving their share owners' interest if they undertake activities that may be good for them individually, but damaging to the larger economic system.

References:
1. M. Friedman, 'The social responsibility of business is to increase its profits', *New York Times. Magazine*, 13 September (1970).
2. C. Handy, 'What's a business for?', *Harvard Business Review*, vol. 80, no. 12, December (2002), pp. 49–55.
3. S. Davies, J. Lukommik and D. Pitt-Watson, *The New Capitalists*, Harvard Business School Press, 2006.

Questions

1 Which view do you hold:
  (a) as a manager?   (b) as a shareholder?
2 What are the implications of the different views for managers' development of organisational strategy?

SUMMARY

- An important managerial task is to decide how the organisation should express its strategic purpose through statements of *mission, vision, values* or *objectives*.
- The purpose of an organisation will be influenced by the expectations of its *stakeholders*.
- The influence of some key stakeholders will be represented formally within the *governance structure* of an organisation. This can be represented in terms of a *governance chain*, showing the links between ultimate beneficiaries and the managers of an organisation.
- There are two generic governance structure systems: the *shareholder model* and the *stakeholder model*, though there are variations of these internationally.
- Organisations adopt different stances on *corporate social responsibility* depending on how they perceive their role in society. Individual managers may also be faced with ethical dilemmas relating to the purpose of their organisation or the actions it takes.
- Different stakeholders exercise different influence on organisational purpose and strategy, dependent on the extent of their power and interest. Managers can assess the influence of different stakeholder groups through *stakeholder analysis*.

VIDEO ASSIGNMENT

Visit **MyStrategyLab** and watch the *Eden* case study.

1 Write a statement of Eden's mission, vision and values.

2 Explain how Eden's management developed its strategy on the basis of aligning stakeholder interests.

WORK ASSIGNMENTS

✳ *Denotes more advanced work assignments. * Refers to a case study in the Text and Cases edition.*

4.1 Write mission and vision statements for an organisation of your choice and suggest what strategic objectives managers might set. Explain why you think these are appropriate.

4.2 * For an organisation of your choice, map out a governance chain that identifies the key players through to the beneficiaries of the organisation's good (or poor) performance. To what extent do you think managers are:

 (a) knowledgeable about the expectations of beneficiaries;
 (b) actively pursuing their interests;
 (c) keeping them informed?

4.3 What are your own views of the strengths and weaknesses of the stakeholder and shareholder models of governance?

4.4 Identify organisations that correspond to the overall stances on corporate social responsibility described in Table 4.2.

4.5 Identify the key corporate social responsibility issues which are of major concern in an industry or public service of your choice (refer to Table 4.3). Compare the approach of two or more organisations in that industry, and explain how this relates to their competitive standing.

4.6 Using Illustration 4.5 as a worked example, identify and map out the stakeholders for RED, Manchester United* or an organisation of your choice in relation to:

 (a) current strategies;
 (b) different future strategies of your choice.

What are the implications of your analysis for the strategy of the organisation?

Integrative assignment

4.7 Using specific examples suggest how changes in corporate governance and in expectations about corporate social responsibility may require organisations to develop new capabilities (Chapter 3) and influencing the choice of strategies they follow (Chapter 11).

RECOMMENDED KEY READINGS

- The case for the importance of clarity of strategic values and vision is especially strongly made by J. Collins and J. Porras, *Built to Last: Successful Habits of Visionary Companies*, Harper Business, 2002 (in particular see chapter 11).

- For books providing a fuller explanation of corporate governance: R. Monks and N. Minow (eds), *Corporate Governance*, 4th edition, Wiley-Blackwell, 2008; and J. Solomon, *Corporate Governance and Accountability*, 2nd edition, Wiley, 2007. For a provocative critique and proposals for the future of corporate governance linked to issues of social responsibility see S. Davies, J. Lukomnik and D. Pitt-Watson, *The New Capitalists*, Harvard Business School Press, 2006.

- For a review of different stances on corporate social responsibility see P. Mirvis and B. Googins, 'Stages of corporate citizenship', *California Management Review*, vol. 48, no. 2 (2006), pp. 104–26. Also see A.B. Carroll and K.M. Shabana, 'The business case for Corporate Social Responsibility', *International Journal of Management Reviews*, vol. 12, no. 1 (2010), pp. 85–105.

- For more about the stakeholder concept and analysis see K. Scholes's chapter in V. Ambrosini with G. Johnson and K. Scholes (eds), *Exploring Techniques of Analysis and Evaluation in Strategic Management*, Prentice Hall, 1998. Also J.M. Bryson, 'What to do when stakeholders matter: stakeholder identification and analysis techniques', *Public Management Review*, vol. 6, no. 1 (2004), pp. 21–53.

REFERENCES

1. Cynthia A. Montgomery, 'Putting leadership back into strategy', *Harvard Business Review*, Jan 2008, pp. 54–60.
2. J. Collins and J. Porras, 'Building your company's vision', *Harvard Business Review*, Sept-Oct, 1996, pp. 65–77.
3. P. Lencioni, 'Make your values mean something', *Harvard Business Review*, vol. 80, no. 7 (2002), pp. 113–17.
4. For example, see B. Bartkus, M. Glassman and B. McAfee, 'Mission statements: are they smoke and mirrors?', *Business Horizons*, vol. 43, no. 6 (2000), pp. 23–8; and B. Bartkus, M. Glassman and B. McAfee, 'Mission statement quality and financial performance', *European Management Journal*, vol. 24, no. 1 (2006), pp. 86–94.
5. See J. Collins and J. Porras, *Built to Last: Successful Habits of Visionary Companies*, Harper Business, 2002.
6. Communicating effectively with the investing community is essential, as discussed by A. Hutton, 'Four rules', *Harvard Business Review*, vol. 79, no. 5 (2001), pp. 125–32.
7. See Sayan Chatterjee, 'Core objectives: clarity in designing strategy', *California Management Review*, 47, 2, 2005, 33–49.
8. See A. Neely, 'Measuring performance in innovative firms', in R. Delbridge, L. Grattan and G. Johnson (eds), *The Exceptional Manager*, Oxford University Press, 2006, chapter 6.
9. Useful general references on corporate governance are: R. Monks and N. Minow (eds), *Corporate Governance*, 4th edition, Blackwell, 2008; and J. Solomon, *Corporate Governance and Accountability*, 2nd edition, Wiley, 2007. Also see Ruth Aguilera and Gregory Jackson, 'The cross-national diversity of corporate governance: dimensions and determinants', *Academy of Management Review*, vol. 28, no. 3 (2003), pp. 447–65.
10. This definition is based on, but adapted from, that in S. Jacoby, 'Corporate governance and society', *Challenge*, vol. 48, no. 4 (2005), pp. 69–87.
11. M.K. Fiegener, 'Locus of ownership and family involvement in small private firms', *Journal of Management Studies*, vol. 47, no. 2 (2010), pp. 296–321.
12. The principal–agent model is part of agency theory which developed within organisational economics but is now widely used in the management field as described here. Two useful references are: K. Eisenhardt, 'Agency theory: an assessment and review', *Academy of Management Review*, vol. 14, no. 1 (1989), pp. 57–74; J.-J. Laffont and D. Martimort, *The Theory of Incentives: The Principal–Agent Model*, Princeton University Press, 2002.
13. For a strong advocacy of this position see S. Davies, J. Lukomnik and D. Pitt-Watson, *The New Capitalists*, Harvard Business School Press, 2006.
14. For a typology and examples of ways in which investors engage with firms, see N. Amos and W. Oulton, 'Approaching and engaging with CR', *Corporate Responsibility Management*, vol. 2, no. 3 (2006), pp. 34–7.
15. Within this broad classification there are other models. For further explanation see, for example, A. Murphy and K. Topyan, 'Corporate governance: a critical survey of key concepts, issues, and recent reforms in the US', *Employee Responsibility and Rights Journal*, vol. 17, no. 2 (2005), pp. 75–89.
16. See J.A. McCahery, P. Moerland, T. Raijmakers and L. Renneboog, *Corporate Governance Regimes: Convergence and Diversity*, Oxford University Press, 2002.
17. See S. Jacoby (2005) (see reference 10).
18. We are grateful to Rob Pieters for this background to governance systems in the Netherlands.
19. For a discussion of corporate governance reforms in continental Europe see L. Anriques and P. Volpin, 'Corporate governance reforms in continental Europe', *Journal of Economic Perspectives*, vol. 21, no. 1 (2007), pp. 117–40.
20. In the USA: the Sarbanes–Oxley Act (2002). In the UK: D. Higgs, 'Review of the role and effectiveness of non-executive directors', UK Department of Trade and Industry, 2003.
21. See D. Norburn, B. Boyd, M. Fox and M. Muth, 'International corporate governance reform', *European Business Journal*, vol. 12, no. 3 (2000), pp. 116–33; J. Sonnenfeld, 'What makes great boards great', *Harvard Business Review*, vol. 80, no. 9 (2002), pp. 106–13.
22. Practising managers might wish to consult B. Kelley, *Ethics at Work*, Gower, 1999, which covers many of the issues in this section and includes the Institute of Management guidelines on ethical management. Also see M.T. Brown, *Corporate Integrity: Rethinking Organisational Ethics and Leadership*, Cambridge University Press, 2005.
23. This definition is based on that by the World Business Council for Sustainable Development.
24. Based on research undertaken at the Center for Corporate Citizenship at the Boston College, reported in P. Mirvis and B. Googins, 'Stages of corporate citizenship', *California Management Review*, vol. 48, no. 2 (2006), pp. 104–26.
25. Often quoted as a summary of Milton Friedman's argument is M. Friedman: 'The social responsibility of business is to increase its profits', *New York Times Magazine*, 13 September 1970.
26. See A. McWilliams and D. Seigel, 'Corporate social responsibility: a theory of the firm perspective', *Academy of Management Review*, vol. 26 (2001), pp. 117–27.
27. See *The State of Corporate Citizenship in the US: A View from Inside, 2003–2004*, Center for Corporate Citizenship, Boston College; also reported in Mirvis and Googins, reference 24.
28. See M. Porter and M. Kramer, 'The competitive advantage of corporate philanthropy', *Harvard Business Review*, vol. 80, no. 12 (2002), pp. 56–68.
29. H. Hummels, 'Organizing ethics: a stakeholder debate', *Journal of Business Ethics*, vol. 17, no. 13 (1998), pp. 1403–19.
30. D. Vogel, 'Is there a market for virtue? The business case for corporate social responsibility', *California Management Review*, vol. 47, no. 4 (2005), pp. 19–45.
31. S.A. Waddock and C. Bodwell, 'Managing responsibility: what can be learned from the quality movement', *California Management Review*, vol. 47, no. 1 (2004), pp. 25–37; and R. Orsato, 'Competitive environmental strategies: when

does it pay to be green?', *California Management Review*, vol. 48, no. 2 (2006), pp. 127–43.

32. These examples are given by Porter and Kramer, reference 28.

33. K. Schnietz and M. Epstein, 'Does a reputation for corporate social responsibility pay off?', *Social Issues in Management Conference Papers*, Academy of Management Proceedings, 2002. This paper shows that the Fortune 500 firms that were also in the Domini Social Index outperformed the others in terms of stock return.

34. Clyde E. Hull and Sandra Rothenberg, 'Firm performance: the interactions of corporate social performance with innovation and industry differentiation', *Strategic Management Journal*, vol. 29 (2008), pp. 781–9.

35. We are grateful to Angela Sutherland of Glasgow Caledonian University for this example.

36. M.R. Banaji, M.H. Bazerman and D. Chugh, 'How (UN)ethical are you?', *Harvard Business Review*, vol. 81, no. 12 (2003), pp. 56–64.

37. Early writings about stakeholders are still worthy of note. For example, the seminal work by R.M. Cyert and J.G. March, *A Behavioral Theory of the Firm*, Prentice Hall, 1964; and R.E. Freeman, *Strategic Management: A Stakeholder Approach*, Pitman, 1984. Also see J. Bryson, 'What to do when stakeholders matter: stakeholder identification and analysis techniques', *Public Management Review*, vol. 6, no. 1 (2004), pp. 21–53.

38. A fuller explanation of how these three groups interact with organisations can be found in J. Cummings and J. Doh, 'Identifying who matters: mapping key players in multiple environments', *California Management Review*, vol. 42, no. 2 (2000), pp. 83–104.

39. This approach to stakeholder mapping has been adapted from A. Mendelow, *Proceedings of the 2nd International Conference on Information Systems*, Cambridge, MA, 1991. See also K. Scholes's chapter, 'Stakeholder analysis', in V. Ambrosini with G. Johnson and K. Scholes (eds), *Exploring Techniques of Analysis and Evaluation in Strategic Management*, Prentice Hall, 1998. For a public-sector explanation, see K. Scholes, 'Stakeholder mapping: a practical tool for public sector managers', in G. Johnson and K. Scholes (eds), *Exploring Public Sector Strategy*, Financial Times Prentice Hall, 2001, chapter 9; and J. Bryson, 'What to do when stakeholders matter: stakeholder identification and analysis techniques', *Public Management Review*, vol. 6, no. 1 (2004), pp. 21–53.

40. For example, see Ronald K. Mitchell, Bradley R. Agle and Donna J. Wood, 'Toward a theory of stakeholder identification and salience: defining the principle of who and what really counts', *The Academy of Management Review*, vol. 22, no. 4 (1997), pp. 853–86, and Kalle Pajunen, 'Stakeholder influences in organizational survival', *Journal of Management Studies*, vol. 43, no. 6 (2006), pp. 1261–88.

41. D. Buchanan and R. Badham, *Power, Politics and Organisational Change: Winning the Turf Game*, Sage, 1999, provide a useful analysis of the relationship between power and strategy.

(RED)™

Phyl Johnson, Strategy Explorers

'We can shop to help end Aids in Africa' Oprah Winfrey

(RED)™ sometimes referred to as (Product)RED, was created in 2006 as a form of creative capitalism: an organisation that collaborates with some of the world's best known corporate brands but for a charitable purpose. (RED) is global organisation that administers and promotes an umbrella brand ((RED)™) that member corporations may use for their products and then pay back into the Global Fund to fight Aids, tuberculosis and malaria in Africa. Its set-up was funded by leading players in the world's corporate markets such as Bill Gates of Microsoft and the financier George Soros but was inspired and is led by U2 front-man Bono and US political activist Bobby Shriver. (See the (RED) manifesto.)

Rwanda was selected as the initial country to benefit from sales of the (RED)™ products but by 2010 they were active in Swaziland, Ghana and Lesotho. The early corporate members included American Express with a (RED)™ credit card, Apple with a (RED)™ iPod, Motorola with a (RED)™ phone and Gap with a series of (RED)™ T-shirts. Later, baby buggy manufacturer Bugaboo, Hallmark [greetings cards], Dell, Nike, Starbucks and Diptyque candles all joined the initiative.

The sole recipient of monies raised by the (RED)™ initiative is The Global Fund, which, since its start in 2002, rose to become the dominant funder of programmes to fight Aids, tuberculosis and malaria. It has been estimated that with more than 600 programmes running, The Global Fund has saved in excess of 4.5 million lives by providing Aids treatment for 2.3 million people, anti-tuberculosis treatment for 5.4 million people and the distribution of 88 million insecticide-treated bed nets for the prevention of malaria. The percentage that (RED)™ donates to this Global Fund is unclear.

Support for the (RED)™ campaign repeatedly comes from Microsoft's Bill Gates; writing in *Time Magazine*:[1]

It's a great thing: the companies make a difference while adding to their bottom line, consumers get to

THE (RED)™ MANIFESTO

ALL THINGS BEING EQUAL, THEY ARE NOT.

AS FIRST WORLD CONSUMERS, WE HAVE TREMENDOUS POWER. WHAT WE COLLECTIVELY CHOOSE TO BUY, OR NOT TO BUY, CAN CHANGE THE COURSE OF LIFE AND HISTORY ON THIS PLANET.

(RED) IS THAT SIMPLE AN IDEA. AND THAT POWERFUL. NOW, YOU HAVE A CHOICE. THERE ARE (RED) CREDIT CARDS, (RED) PHONES, (RED) SHOES, (RED) FASHION BRANDS. AND NO, THIS DOES NOT MEAN THEY ARE ALL RED IN COLOR, ALTHOUGH SOME ARE.

IF YOU BUY A (RED) PRODUCT OR SIGN UP FOR A (RED) SERVICE, AT NO COST TO YOU, A (RED) COMPANY WILL GIVE SOME OF ITS PROFITS TO BUY AND DISTRIBUTE ANTI-RETROVIRAL MEDICINE TO OUR BROTHERS AND SISTERS DYING OF AIDS IN AFRICA.

WE BELIEVE THAT WHEN CONSUMERS ARE OFFERED THIS CHOICE, AND THE PRODUCTS MEET THEIR NEEDS, THEY WILL CHOOSE (RED). AND WHEN THEY CHOOSE (RED) OVER NON-(RED), THEN MORE BRANDS WILL CHOOSE TO BECOME (RED) BECAUSE IT WILL MAKE GOOD BUSINESS SENSE TO DO SO. AND MORE LIVES WILL BE SAVED.

(RED) IS NOT A CHARITY. IT IS SIMPLY A BUSINESS MODEL. YOU BUY (RED) STUFF. WE GET THE MONEY, BUY THE PILLS AND DISTRIBUTE THEM. THEY TAKE THE PILLS, STAY ALIVE, AND CONTINUE TO TAKE CARE OF THEIR FAMILIES AND CONTRIBUTE SOCIALLY AND ECONOMICALLY IN THEIR COMMUNITIES.

IF THEY DON'T GET THE PILLS, THEY DIE. WE DON'T WANT THEM TO DIE. WE WANT TO GIVE THEM THE PILLS. AND WE CAN. AND YOU CAN. AND IT'S EASY.

ALL YOU HAVE TO DO IS UPGRADE YOUR CHOICE.

Source: http://www.joinred.com/manifesto.asp.

show their support for a good cause, and – most important – lives are saved.

In other articles he has acknowledged that governments also need to be more generous in the battle against life-threatening and preventable disease in Africa, but believes that as consumers, most people would want to *'associate themselves with saving lives'* and that Gap with their T-shirts or Armani with their sunglasses offer this opportunity through (RED).

Perhaps as a result of the fame of its leaders, in particular Bono who is highly active on behalf of (RED), it has maintained a high profile amongst the glitterati of world society. This is especially the case in the USA. Vocal supporters have included the US chat show host Oprah Winfrey, Hollywood star Scarlett Johansson and the music industry's Lady Gaga. All of these will offer interviews, talk-show time and concert appearances as either fund or awareness raising endeavours.

However, the international response to (RED) has not been universally positive. The moot point being that at its heart, is this endeavour about philanthropy or exploitation: should you use an illness to market a product?

Environmental arguments against (RED) focus on the downside of linking consumerism to charitable giving. Instead of supporting (RED)'s own phrase *Buying Red Saves Lives*, environmental groups make the argument: buy less and give money to charity instead; save the planet *and* its people.

Arguments against (RED) also come from other quarters and suggest that weak campaigns, as they see (RED) to be, dilute international will and skill to make a genuine difference to people's suffering. In an article published in the UK's leading medical journal *The Lancet*, a socio-political argument is made against (RED) as a mask or *'charitainment'* that hides the true complexity and seriousness of Africa's position in relation to the west. For instance, (RED) is about consumers making *connections* from the prosperous west to the third world of Africa. But there always have been socio-political *connections* between the west and Africa. At first it was slavery, then more complicated forms of economic relationships normally ending with African states coming off the worst, e.g. being crippled by debts to the international community that cleared countries of their health resources just at the time when the Aids epidemic began to take hold. The *Lancet* article argues that the (RED) initiative is fluff, window dressing that hides the real issue and distracts us from higher impact solutions such as major government sponsored and tax funded coordinated and sustained funding. In short, it allows western consumers to feel better about what is ultimately the maintenance of an unhealthy status quo.

Quite apart from challenges as to the purpose of (RED), questions have been raised as to its effectiveness as a business model, its governance and transparency of the percentages of sales donated to The Global Fund. A 2007 article in *Advertising Age*[2] claimed that the campaign had raised only $18m (~€12.6m) in a year despite a marketing outlay by companies involved in the scheme of $100 million. Whereas Bill Gates suggested in 2008 that between January 2007 and July 2008 (RED) had raised $100 million. Gap was the biggest spender on advertising in the 2007 period with a budget of $7.8 million. Critics ask, if the purpose of (RED) is to raise money then a crucial challenge is why not cut out the product and get Gap etc. to donate their 7.8 million direct to The Global Fund: why is (RED) needed and for whom does it really exist?

A spokeswoman for (RED) claimed that the *Ad Age* figure of 100 million was merely a 'phantom number pulled out of thin air'. Yet it refuses to go away, appearing in most commentaries that are critical of (RED).

However, an article in the *Independent*[3] went on to do its own mathematics: 'I believe the money raised in six months since the product range was launched is $25 million on an advertising investment of $40 million. As such, arguably this is a good rate of return on an advertising investment in the time available.' They went on to argue:

> What the (RED) initiative has set out to do – and with some success if $25 million in six months is half the profits (RED) products would have made – is create a stream of revenue for the fight against AIDS in Africa which will far exceed one-off payments from corporate philanthropy budgets. It looks set to create a major source of cash for the global fund, and one which is sustainable. It is an entirely new model for fund raising.

But wouldn't it be better if people simply gave the money that they spend on the products directly to charity? 'If only that were the choice. But most people wouldn't give the cost of a new iPod to the global fund.' They continued: 'The money (RED) has raised means that some 160,000 Africans will be put on life-saving anti-retrovirals in the coming months, orphans are being fed and kept in school in Swaziland and a national HIV treatment and prevention programme has begun in Rwanda.'

Moving the spotlight from the governance, purpose and model of (RED) and toward its collection of corporate collaborators does not simplify the issue. If the purpose of business is to be in business, then why would American Express for example donate 1% of its customers' spend on their (RED)™ credit cards to (RED) and ultimately The Global Fund? Does it make shareholder sense? Taking the example of Gap, on their website, their head of social responsibility states

> Acting in an ethical way is not only the right thing to do – it also unlocks new ways for us to do business better.

Hence they find themselves at the forefront of the (RED) campaign. *The Times*[4] newspaper offered a stinging critique of Gap's position.

> My problem here is with what this ((Red)™) does for the very idea of capitalism, for companies pursuing their real and entirely wholesome responsibility of making money. Free market capitalism, untrammelled by marketing people in alliance with special interest groups on a mission to save the world, has done more to alleviate poverty than any well-intentioned anti-poverty campaign in the history of the globe.

By concentrating on selling quality, low-priced goods, some of them made with labour that would otherwise lie idle (and dying) in the developing world, Gap saves lives. By helping to keep prices down and generating profits, Gap ploughs money back into the pockets of people in the US, the UK and elsewhere. This creates the demand for imports of products from the developing world, which keeps the poor of those countries from suffering even more than they do now.

In a complex world, we all operate in a division of labour. Companies make profits. It is what they are designed to do. It is what they do best. When they depart from that mission, they lead their employees and their shareholders down a long, slow route to perdition.

You think that is over the top? What is most troubling about campaigns such as (Product)RED is that they represent an accommodation with groups who think the business of capitalism is fundamentally evil. By appeasing people who regard globalisation as a process of exploitation, companies such as Gap are making the world much worse for all of us. They are implicitly acknowledging that their main business – selling things that people want for a profit – is inherently immoral and needs to be expiated by an occasional show of real goodness.

Rather than resisting it, they are nurturing and feeding an anti-business sentiment that will impoverish us all. What's more, this encroachment by companies is fundamentally undemocratic. Companies should not collude with interest groups and non-governmental organisations to decide on public priorities. That is for free people, through their elected governments, to do.

None of this is to say companies – or the people who run them – should not behave morally. They should observe not only the law, but the highest ethical standards, which means honesty, straight dealing and openness. It might even at times be in their corporate interests (i.e. longer-term profitability) to contribute to political or charitable causes – in those cases shareholders can and should vote on the appropriation of funds for such purposes.

Whether (RED) is good or bad for charity and business alike or a new path continues to be debated. Meanwhile, Bono and co. continue to sign up new corporate partners and generate new headlines, but all done in the glossiest magazines possible.

References:
1. *Time Magazine*, Thursday 31 July 2008.
2. Frazier, Mya, 'Costly Red Campaign reaps meager $18m', *Advertising Age*, 78, 10, 5 March 2007.
3. Vallely, P. 'The big question: does RED campaign help big Western brands more than Africa?', *Independent*, p. 50, 9 March 2007.
4. From Baker, Gerrard, 'Mind the Gap – With this attack on Globalization', *The Times*, 24 October 2006. © The Times/The Sun/nisyndication.com.

Source: (Product)RED website http://joinred.blogspot.com.

Questions

1 Drawing on the three perspectives in the Key Debate or the four stances in Table 4.2, what is the rationale of:
   (a) The founders of (Product)RED?
   (b) The Director of Social Responsibility for Gap?
   (c) The author of the article in *The Times*?
2 What views might shareholders of Gap have of (Product)RED?
3 In your view is (Product)RED an appropriate corporate activity?

5

CULTURE AND STRATEGY

Learning outcomes

After reading this chapter you should be able to:

● Identify organisations that have experienced *strategic drift* and the symptoms of strategic drift.

● Analyse how *history* influences the strategic position of organisations.

● Analyse the influence of an *organisation's culture* on its strategy using the *cultural web*.

● Recognise the importance of strategists questioning the *taken-for-granted aspects of a culture*.

(5.1) INTRODUCTION

Chapters 2, 3 and 4 have considered the important influences of the environment, organisational capabilities and stakeholder expectations on the development of strategy. Vital as these are to understand, there is a danger that managers fail to take into account other significant issues. One of these is the culture of the organisation. By 2010 Marks & Spencer had been wrestling with a strategic change for almost a decade; yet commentators still cited its cultural heritage of over a century as a major influence on its strategic direction. This highlights the danger of failing to take in how the past influences current and future strategy. Many organisations have long histories. The large Japanese Mitsui Group was founded in the 17th century; Daimler was founded in 19th century; managers in the UK retailer Sainsbury's still refer to the founding principles of the Sainsbury family in the 19th century. All these and many public-sector organisations – government departments, the police, universities, for example – are strongly influenced by their historical legacies that have become embedded in their cultures.

Figure 5.1 summarises the chapter structure. The chapter begins by explaining the phenomenon of *strategic drift* that highlights the importance of history and culture in relation to strategy development and identifies important challenges managers face in managing that development. The chapter then considers the two important and linked perspectives of *history and culture*. Section 5.3 examines the influence of the history of an organisation on its current and future strategy and goes on to consider how that history can be analysed. Section 5.4 then explains what is meant by culture and how cultural influences at the national, institutional and organisational levels influence current and future strategy. It then suggests how a culture can be analysed and its influence on strategy understood.

Historical and cultural perspectives can help an understanding of both opportunities and constraints that organisations face. The business environment (Chapter 2) cannot be

Figure 5.1 The influence of history and culture

understood without considering how it has developed over time. The capabilities of an organisation (Chapter 3), especially those that provide organisations with competitive advantage, may have built up over time in ways unique to that organisation. In so doing such capabilities may become part of the culture of an organisation – the taken-for-granted way of doing things, therefore difficult for other organisations to copy. However, they may also be difficult to change. The power and influence of different stakeholders (Chapter 4) are also likely to have historical origins that are important to understand. The theme of this chapter is, then, that understanding the strategic position of an organisation includes understanding that its culture sometimes has deep historical roots. Such an understanding also informs the evaluation of the feasibilty of a strategy (Chapter 11), helps explain how strategies develop (Chapter 12) and informs the challenges of strategic change (Chapter 14).

(5.2) STRATEGIC DRIFT

Historical studies of organisations have shown a pattern that is represented in Figure 5.2. **Strategic drift[1] is the tendency for strategies to develop incrementally on the basis of historical and cultural influences, but fail to keep pace with a changing environment**. An example of strategic drift is given in Illustration 5.1. The reasons and consequences of strategic drift are important to understand, not only because it is common, but also because it helps explain why organisations often seem to stagnate in their strategy development. Strategic drift also highlights some significant challenges for managers which, in turn, point to some important lessons.

5.2.1 Strategies change incrementally

Strategies of organisations most often change gradually. This is discussed more fully in Chapter 11. Here it is sufficient to summarise by explaining that there is a tendency for strategies to develop

Figure 5.2 Strategic drift

ILLUSTRATION 5.1
Motorola: Does history repeat itself?

The bases of a firm's success may persist over time but be the cause of strategic drift.

Founded in 1928, from the beginning, Motorola was known for its technological innovation. It introduced the 2-way walkie-talkie radio device widely used in the Second World War; and it marketed the first television for under $200 (€140). By the 1950s it had developed capabilities in printed circuit, ceramic substrate technology and electronic systems design. By the 1970s it was a leading producer of microprocessors and regarded as world leader in terms of technology.

By the mid 1980s Motorola was also the leading producer of cell phones using analogue technology. Indeed by the mid 1990s Motorola held over 60% of the US mobile telephone market and had experienced 27% year on year growth. At that time, however, these phones were bulky, expensive and targeted at business managers. In the mid 1990s digital technology was being developed. This overcame some of the shortcomings of analogue technology, reducing interference and allowing greater security, reduction in the size and weight of handsets, and more subscribers than analogue. It was technology supporting mass market development in a consumer market and demand grew rapidly.

Motorola claimed to be at the 'forefront of the development of digital technology'. However it chose to stay with analogue technology for many years, licensing its digital capabilities to Nokia and Eriksson. Indeed Motorola launched a new analogue phone, Star-TAC supported by an aggressive marketing campaign to promote it. This was despite the fact that wireless carrier customers were lobbying Motorola to develop digital phones.

By 1998 Motorola's market share had dropped to 34% and it was forced to lay off 20,000 people. Over the next decade, despite launching digital phones, Motorola faced an uphill battle to regain market share against competitors such as Eriksson and Nokia.

In 2005 Motorola launched its Razr V3 cell phone. Widely applauded for its technology and design, the initial selling price was $500. Motorola experienced initial success but by 2007 the price of a Razr had dropped to $30, Motorola's profits had plunged again, as had its share price; and once again it was planning to lay off workers. This was despite a market for more than 1 billion mobile phones per year.

What Motorola had overlooked was that the market had changed significantly. Consumers were replacing phones faster, typically every two years or less; in effect it was becoming a fashion market. Motorola on the other hand continued to focus on advancing technology in microchips, screen size and data speed. Moreover, just as in other fashion markets, competitors rapidly replicated the design benefits of the Razr.

By 2010 it was smartphones that were showing most growth in the market. Motorola's co-chief executive Sanjay Jha was confident in the development of the company's smartphone based on Google Inc's Android software. But some industry experts were worried that Motorola's sale of smartphones was relatively slow, together with continued decline in sales of their cheaper phones, their biggest selling product.

Even in Motorola's early days, critics suggested that the firm risked putting technology before market trends. The worry was that the same problem remained in 2010.

Sources: S. Finkelstein, 'Why smart executives fail: four case histories of how people learn the wrong lessons from history', *Business History*, 48, 2 (2006), pp. 153–70, and Brad Stone, *New York Times*, 3 February 2007.

Questions

1 Given that in the 1980s Motorola had the technology and knew the digital market was developing, give reasons why it persisted with analogue technology. (See Chapter 12 and the commentaries to help with this question.)

2 Update the illustration. Has Motorola learned its lessons?

on the basis of what the organisation has done in the past – especially if that has been successful.[2] For example, for many years UK retailer HMV had quite successfully developed its business by adapting to changing technology and tastes in the entertainment market. They had moved from vinyl to CDs; introduced DVDs and computer games when they arrived on the market; and increased the space allocation to them as demand increased. This is shown in phase 1 of the figure. In most successful businesses there are usually long periods of relative *continuity* during which established strategy remains largely unchanged or changes very *incrementally*. There are three main reasons for this:

- *Alignment with environmental change.* It could be that the environment, particularly the market, is changing gradually and the organisation is keeping in line with those changes by such incremental change. It would make no sense for the strategy to change dramatically when the market is not doing so.

- *The success of the past.* There may be a natural unwillingness by managers to change a strategy significantly if it has been successful in the past, especially if it is built on capabilities that have been shown to be the basis of competitive advantage (see Chapters 3 and 6) or of innovation (see Chapter 9). Managers quite understandably will argue that they should stick to what they know and do best.

- *Experimentation around a theme.* Managers may have learned how to build variations around their successful formula; in effect experimenting without moving too far from their capability base. (This is akin to what some writers have referred to as 'logical incrementalism'; see section 12.3.1).

This poses challenges for managers, however. For how long and to what extent can they rely on incremental change being sufficient? When should they make more fundamental strategic changes? And how can they detect when this is necessary?

5.2.2 The tendency towards strategic drift

HMV persisted in the conviction that there was a market for the sale of music and DVDs through specialist retail outlets. They continued to adjust their retail formats and extended product ranges in the search for a sustainable competitive position. They had difficulty, however, reconciling themselves to the need for more fundamental change to their business model given the shifts in the first decade of this century to the way in which people accessed music through the internet or bought through supermarkets.

Whilst an organisation's strategy may continue to change incrementally, the problem is that there do not need to be sudden or dramatic environmental changes for the strategy to become less aligned with the environment. Phase 2 of Figure 5.2 shows environmental change accelerating, but it is not sudden. For HMV it was not as if changes in buyer behaviour or the growth in supermarket sales of CDs and DVDs happened overnight. These changes took place over years. The problem that gives rise to strategic drift is that, as with many organisations, HMV's strategy was not keeping pace with these changes. There are at least five reasons for this:

- *Steady as you go.* Chapter 2 has provided ways to analyse the environment and such analyses may yield insights. But how are managers to be sure of the direction and significance of such changes? Or changes may be seen as temporary. Managers may be understandably wary of changing what they are likely to see as a winning strategy, on the basis of what might only be a fad in the market, or a temporary downturn in demand, especially if it is built on capabilities that have been the basis of competitive advantage. It may be easy to see major changes with hindsight, but it may not be so easy to see their significance as they are happening.

- *Building on the familiar.* Managers may see changes in the environment about which they are uncertain or which they do not entirely understand. In these circumstances they may try to minimise the extent to which they are faced with such uncertainty by looking for answers that are familiar, which they understand and which have served them well in the past. This will lead to a bias towards continued incremental strategic change.

- *Core rigidities.* As Chapter 3 explains, success in the past may well have been based on capabilities that are unique to an organisation and difficult for others to copy. However, the capabilities that have been bases of advantage can become difficult to change; in effect *core rigidities.*[3] There are two reasons. First, over time, the ways of doing things that have delivered past success may become taken for granted. This may well have been an advantage in the past because it was difficult for competitors to imitate them. However, taken-for-granted capabilities rarely get questioned and therefore tend to persist beyond their usefulness. Second, ways of doing things develop over time and become more and more embedded in organisational routines that reinforce and rely on each other and are difficult to unravel; this is discussed further in section 5.3.1 below.

- *Relationships become shackles.*[4] Success has probably been built on the basis of excellent relationships with customers, suppliers and employees. Maintaining these may very likely and quite rightly be seen as fundamental to the long-term health of the organisation. Yet these relationships may make it difficult to make fundamental changes to strategy that could entail changing routes to market or the customer base, developing products requiring different suppliers or changing the skill base of the organisation with the risk of disrupting relationships with the workforce.

- *Lagged performance effects.* The effects of such drift may not be easy to see in terms of the performance of the organisation. Financial performance may continue to hold up in the early stages of strategic drift. Customers may be loyal and the organisation, by becoming more efficient, cutting costs or simply trying harder, may continue to hold up its performance. So there may not be internal signals of the need for change or pressures from managers, or indeed external observers, to make major changes.

However, over time, if strategic drift continues, there will be symptoms that become evident: a downturn in financial performance, a loss in market share to competitors perhaps; a decline in the share price. Indeed such a downturn may happen quite rapidly once external observers, not least competitors and financial analysts, have identified that such drift has occurred. Even the most successful companies may drift in this way. Indeed, there is a tendency – which Danny Miller has called the Icarus Paradox[5] – for businesses to become victims of the very success of their past. They become captured by the formula that has delivered that success.

5.2.3 A period of flux

The next phase (phase 3) may be a period of *flux* triggered by the downturn in performance. Strategies may change but in no very clear direction. There may also be management changes, often at the very top as the organisation comes under pressure from its stakeholders to make changes, not least shareholders in the case of a public company. There may be internal rivalry as to which strategy to follow, quite likely based on differences of opinion as to whether future strategy should be based on historic capabilities or whether those capabilities are becoming redundant. Indeed, there have been highly publicised boardroom rows when this has happened. All this may result in a further deterioration of confidence in the organisation: perhaps a further drop in performance or share price, a difficulty in recruiting high-quality management, or a further loss of customers' loyalty.

5.2.4 Transformational change or death

As things get worse it is likely that the outcome (phase 4) will be one of three possibilities. (i) The organisation may die; in the case of a commercial organisation it may go into receivership for example. (ii) It may get taken over by another organisation. (iii) Or it may go through a period of *transformational change*. Such change could take form in multiple changes related to the organisation's strategy. For example, a change in products, markets or market focus, changes of capabilities on which the strategy is based, changes in the top management of the organisation and perhaps the way the organisation is structured.

Transformational change does not take place frequently in organisations and is usually the result of a major downturn in performance. Often it is transformational changes that are heralded as the success stories of top executives; this is where they most visibly make a difference. The problem is that, from the point of view of market position, shareholder wealth and jobs, it may be rather late. Competitive position may have been lost, shareholder value has probably already been destroyed and, very likely, many jobs will have been lost too. The time when 'making a difference' really matters most is in Phase 2 in Figure 5.2, when the organisation is beginning to drift. However, a study of 215 major UK firms identified just 28 that could be said to have avoided drift and consequent performance decline over the 20-year period 1983–2003 and only 6 of these had effected major transformational change.[6] The problem is that, very likely, such drift is not easy to see before performance suffers. So, to avoid the damaging effects of strategic drift, it is vital to take seriously the extent to which historical tendencies in strategy development tend to persist in the cultural fabric of organisations. The rest of this chapter focuses on this. The challenge is, then, how to manage change in such circumstances and this challenge is taken up in Chapter 14 on managing strategic change.

(5.3) WHY IS HISTORY IMPORTANT?

If the reasons for strategic drift are to be understood and addressed, the history of organisations needs to be taken seriously. There are also other reasons why understanding history can help in the management of strategy. First, it needs to borne in mind that managers may have spent many years in an organisation or in an industry such that the experience on which they base their decisions may be heavily influenced by that history (see the discussion on the 'Experience Lens' in the Commentary). It is therefore helpful if managers can 'stand apart' from that history so as to understand the influence it has on them and the extent to which the strategy they are seeking to develop is usefully informed by that history as distinct from being constrained by it. The discussion on the influence of organisational culture in section 5.4 below is relevant here.

Taking history seriously can also have at least four positive benefits:

1 *Avoiding recency bias.* There can be a tendency for managers to focus on the short term given the pressure of current events. Understanding the current situation in terms of the past can provide useful lessons. For example: have there been historical trends that may repeat themselves? How have competitors responded to strategic moves in the past? A historical perspective may also help managers see what gave rise to events that were seen as surprises in the past and learn from how their organisation dealt with them.

2 *'What if' questions.* History can also encourage managers to ask 'what if' questions. Asking what might have happened had there been other influences in the environment, different responses from customers or competitors or different initiatives or leadership within their organisation makes the present more evidently a product of circumstances. The current strategic position may then be seen as less fixed and possibilities for changes in the future more possible.

3 *History as legitimisation.* History can be used as a resource to *legitimise* future strategies or strategic change as shown in Illustration 5.2. Past changes may also be referred to as evidence of the organisational potential for making changes happen. Past successes in innovation or product or market development may be used as a basis for encouraging commitment to future changes.

4 *Innovation based on historic capabilities.* In the BMW museum in Munich there is a quote: 'Anyone who wants to design for the future has to leaf through the past'.[7] The museum may be about the history of BMW, but it is also about how the lessons of the past can give rise to new ideas and innovation. Indeed the Innovation and Technology Division of BMW is sited next to the museum and the archives of BMW. Innovation may build on historic capabilities in at least two ways. First, as technologies change, firms with experience and skills built over time that are most appropriate to those changes tend to innovate more than those that don't.[8] Or it could be that there are new combinations of knowledge as capabilities built up in adjacent technologies are adapted in innovative ways to new technological opportunities. For example, the development of lighting systems was derived from the way gas was distributed.[9] Similarly, successful firms that created the TV industry were previously radio manufacturers and it was they who exhibited greater innovation as the industry developed than the non-radio producers.[10] If managers seek to build future strategy on historic capabilities they do, however, need to ask themselves the extent to which the environment is changing in such a way that such capabilities will still be relevant. In other words if strategy is to evolve on the back of such capabilities, it can only do so if simultaneously the changes in markets, technologies and other aspects of the environment discussed in Chapter 2 are potentially converging with those capabilities. They need to develop a sensitivity, not only to the historic capabilities that matter but the relationship of these to an evolving environment.

5.3.1 Path dependency

A useful way of thinking of the role and influence of history is through the concept of *path dependency* and the associated notion of historical *lock-in*. **Path dependency is where early events and decisions establish 'policy paths' that have lasting effects on subsequent events and decisions.**[11] Organisational decisions are therefore historically conditioned. Path dependency's origins, its impact and how it can be understood are therefore important.

Examples often relate to technology. There are many instances where the technology we employ is better explained by path dependency than by the optimisation of such technology.

ILLUSTRATION 5.2

Building on Pringle's Scottish heritage

Managers may employ an organisation's history and heritage to support its strategy.

Pringle of Scotland are designers and manufacturers of luxury knitwear. They were founded in 1815 by Robert Pringle and grew to become a well recognised brand across the UK, USA and Japan. Pringle traded on a combination of its quality and highly recognisable plaids such as the iconic Argyle Pringle pattern. In the 1940s Pringle was favoured by the British Royal family and movie stars and saw their designs feature on a *Vogue* magazine front cover. A very traditional company, Pringle's knitwear had a strong connection with tartan and golf, two of Scotland's great exports [another being whisky]. Pringle's longest serving brand champion was UK golf champion Nick Faldo who promoted their sweaters from 1981 to 2001.

By the new millennium Pringle's fortunes were in decline and it was acquired in 2000 by the Hong Kong based Fang Brothers for just £6 (~€6.6, ~$9) million. They recruited a new CEO, Kim Winser from Marks and Spencer. She decided to reposition Pringle away from a staid, middle aged image towards a designer fashion brand. She recruited new young designers and moved the design function from Scotland to London. Nick Faldo was 'out' and super model Sophie Dahl was 'in' starring in a series of sexed-up ad campaigns. However, Winser decided to retain manufacturing in the long established Hawick mill in the Scottish Borders which she saw as a key part of the firm's heritage and the brand was re-launched as 'Pringle of Scotland': 'I have added Scotland to the name because in a lot of countries worldwide, it is definitely a bonus – people trust Scottish cashmere.'

But the new Pringle didn't attract the new trendy customers they hoped for and fortunes fell. The Fangs had invested more than £50m into the company since acquiring it, but losses continued. Given these losses the manufacturing base in Hawick in Scotland was eventually closed in 2006.

In 2008 Mary-Adair Macaire replaced Kim Winser. Macaire joined from Chanel and planned to reconnect further with the history of the brand. Her view was that to succeed Pringle had to make a clearer connection between their new collections, the work of former Gucci designer Clare Waight Keller, and its core product offer, such as cashmere twinsets. 'There has to be a connection, otherwise there is schizophrenia. . . . Here was a company that invented the twinset, yet didn't sell them in its stores.'

Her plan was to return to the old Hollywood glamour of Grace Kelly in a petite pastel twinset. She was quoted as saying; 'I'm not trying to turn Pringle into something that it wasn't already. I'm trying to revive its reputation and identity as a house that makes luxurious garments with a focus on knitwear and style.' Moreover, despite the closure of the factory, she still saw the Scottish heritage as vital: 'The Fangs tried hard to keep (the Hawick mill) going, but after eight years of investment, felt the funds could be better used elsewhere. We are actually producing more goods in Scotland now than when we had the factory.'

Between 2008 and 2010 the Fangs invested a further £18million, but the accounts reported a loss of £9.3million in the year to March 2009.

Questions

1 Why do you think successive CEOs of Pringle decided to employ the heritage of their businesses to support the strategy?

2 Identify other organisations that have employed their organisational histories to support their strategy.

3 What are the benefits and potential problems of legitimising a strategy on the basis of an organisation's history?

A famous one is the system used for typewriter keyboards in most English-speaking countries around the world: QWERTY. This originated in the 19th century because it was a layout that reduced the problem of the keys on mechanical typewriters getting tangled when sales people demonstrated the machine at maximum speed by typing the word 'typewriter'. There are more optimal layouts, but QWERTY has remained with us for over 150 years despite changes in typewriter technology and the eventual development of personal computers.[12] There are countless other examples ranging from technologies in nuclear power stations through to automobile engines.

Path dependency is not just about technology. It also relates to any form of behaviour that has its origins in the past and becomes entrenched. In an organisational context it could begin with a decision which, of itself, may or may not be especially significant and where consequential succeeding events are unforeseeable. If successful, this initial decision can lead to positive feedback in the form of self-reinforcing mechanisms. Within an organisation these could include the development of behavioural routines supported by hardware and technology that make up systems of selling, marketing, recruiting, accounting and so on;[13] and externally these could be reinforced by repeated usage of a product or service by networks of customers and suppliers who come to see it as the dominant or standard offering. The result could be '*lock-in*' around that product or service.

There are many examples in the business world of such patterns of development, both at an organisational level and beyond. Take the example of accounting systems. The lock-in of these has occurred at multiple levels involving networks comprising what people do, those with whom they interact within and outside their organisation, the skills, standards and systems in which they are trained and objects and technologies they generate or use. All these have developed over time and mutually reinforce each other, as Figure 5.3 shows. Rather like QWERTY, the 'rightness' or at least inevitability of such systems tends to be taken for granted. They also strongly influence decision-making, not least in relation to strategic analysis and strategic choice. Historic accounting systems also persist despite increasing numbers of experts, both in the accountancy profession and elsewhere,[14] who point to fundamental weaknesses in such systems, not least the failure of accounting systems to provide measures for many of the factors that account for the market value of firms.

Given such lock-in, path dependency has sometimes been described as like the 'furrows in a road' that become deeper and deeper as more and more traffic goes along. Once that happens the traffic has no option but to go along those furrows. Hence, for example, capabilities, once the bases of competitive advantage and success, become core rigidities leading to the phenomenon of strategic drift explained in section 5.2 above.

Path dependency is, then, a way of thinking about how historical events and decisions, within and around an organisation, have an effect on that organisation for good or ill in at least three ways:

- *Building strategy around the path-dependent capabilities* that may have developed within an organisation. This is at the root of much of the argument put forward for the building of competitive advantage discussed in Chapter 3 and further developed in Chapter 6. Indeed there is evidence that this is so. Path dependency has been shown to explain organisational strategies.[15] Firms tend to enter markets, focus on market segments and diversify in line with the previous path-dependent capabilities they have developed. In so doing they tend to focus on types of customers that they have serviced or capabilities on which their success has been based. This may be a basis for success but can also be dangerous as the Motorola example in Illustration 5.1 shows.

Figure 5.3 Path dependency and lock-in

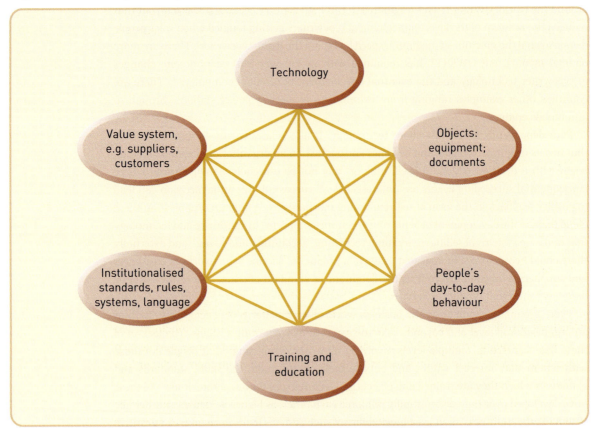

- *Path creation* suggests that some managers, whilst acknowledging the relevance and potential benefits of history, may actively seek to amend and deviate from path-dependent ways of doing things. In so doing, they may be sensitive enough to history to recognise what they can and cannot change. Going too far may be risky (see the discussion on 'legitimacy' in section 5.4.2 below), but setting in motion changes that are accepted as appropriate and beneficial by others in the network may be a way of achieving advantage. Arguably this is what new players in the insurance market such as the retailer Tesco have done. They have not tried to change basic principles of insurance provision; but they have significantly changed the way in which insurance is sold and distributed. In such circumstances managers need to see the past in relation to the future and ask what is relevant from the past that can help with the future and what the future demands but also does not require from the past.

- *Management style* may also have its roots in history. This may not only be in terms of the values of the founder, which indeed may have a strong influence, but also in the interplay between past ways of doing things and the lessons learned from the organisation's evolving environment.[16] Take Tesco as an example again. It is now one of the most successful international retailers. In its early days it was a family firm run by founder Jack Cohen, renowned for his authoritative and confrontational style. This gave rise to internal conflicts within the firm and between suppliers and Tesco. Things are different in Tesco now but the historic conflict has evolved into productive challenge and rivalry between managers and different parts of the firm that, arguably, have substantially contributed to its innovation and success.[17] Again, however, there is another side to these potential benefits. Just as capabilities that are path dependent and rooted in history may become entrenched, so might management style and this too may not be in line with the needs of a changing environment, giving rise to problems of change (see Chapter 14).

5.3.2 Historical analysis

How then might managers undertake a historical strategic analysis of their organisation? There are four ways this may be done.[18]

- *Chronological analysis.* At the most basic level this involves setting down a chronology of key events showing changes in the organisation's environment – especially its markets – how the organisation's strategy itself has changed and with what consequences – not least financial. Some firms have done this much more extensively by commissioning extensive corporate histories. These may sometimes be little more than public relations exercises, but the better ones are serious exercises in documenting history[19] and can help sensitise managers to the sort of questions raised above.

- *Cyclical influences.* Is there evidence of cyclical influences? Certainly these have been shown to exist in terms of economic cycles, but also in terms of cycles of industry activity, such as periods when there are many mergers and acquisitions. Understanding when these cycles might occur and how industry and market forces might change during such cycles can inform decisions on whether to build strategy in line with those cycles or in a counter-cyclical fashion.

- *Anchor points.* History may be regarded as continuous but historical events can also be significant for an organisation at particular points in time: these are sometimes known as 'anchor points'. They could be particularly significant events, either in terms of industry change or an organisation's strategic decisions. Or they might be policies laid down by a founder or by powerful senior executives. Or major successes or failures; or defining periods of time that have informed received wisdom or which managers have come to see as especially important. Such anchor points may be traced to many years ago in the organisation's history, yet may have profound effects on current organisational strategy and strategic thinking or exercise significant constraints on future strategy. This could, of course, be for the good: they may provide a very clear overall direction strategically that contributes to the sort of vision discussed in the previous chapter. They could, on the other hand, be a major barrier to challenging existing strategies or changing strategic direction. A famous example is Henry Ford's maxim 'You can have any color provided it's black', which set a trajectory for mass production and low variety in the car industry for decades. Currently government (and political opposition) health policy in the UK is constrained by the historical mantra that health provision should be 'free at point of delivery' when it clearly is not. Apple's 1984 advertising campaign marked its clear positioning against the domination of bland, standard products as then epitomised by IBM: the peak-time television ad featured a young female athlete hurling a sledgehammer at a TV image of an Orwellian Big Brother.

- *Historical narratives.* How do people in an organisation talk about and explain its history? In trying to understand the foundations of the strategy of an organisation a new chief executive or an external consultant will typically spend a good deal of time talking with people to try and understand the meaning and gain insights from their personal accounts of history.[20] What do they have to say about the way they see their organisation and its past, not least in terms of anchor points and origins of success? In turn, what are the implications for future strategy development? For example, historical accounts can be significant as the basis and legitimation of future strategy; indeed this is so even in a new firm where, for example, stories of its founding may play such a role. Does what people say suggest an organisation with the historic capabilities of relevance to particular markets and customers; one capable of innovation and change or one so rooted in past ways of doing things that there are risks of strategic drift?

History, then, is important in terms of how it influences current strategy for better or worse. As suggested here, there are ways in which history can be analysed. It is not always easy, however, to trace the links to the organisation as it currently exists. It is here that understanding the organisation's culture becomes important. The current culture of an organisation is, to a great extent, the legacy of its history; history becomes 'encapsulated in culture'.[21] So understanding an organisation's culture is one way of understanding the historical influences, which as we have seen, can be very powerful. The next section goes on to explain what culture is and how it can be analysed.

5.4 WHAT IS CULTURE AND WHY IS IT IMPORTANT?

There are many definitions of culture. In the Commentary on the Experience Lens it is defined as 'socially established structures of meaning'.[22] Edgar Schein defines *organisational culture* as the 'basic *assumptions and beliefs* that are shared by members of an organisation, that operate unconsciously and define in a basic taken-for-granted fashion an organisation's view of itself and its environment'.[23] Related to this are taken-for-granted *ways* '*we do things around here*'[24] that accumulate over time. So **organisational culture** is the **taken-for-granted assumptions and behaviours that make sense of people's organisational context** and therefore contributes to how groups of people respond and behave in relation to issues they face. It therefore has important influences on the development and change of organisational strategy.

KEY CONCEPT

Organisational culture

Different cultural contexts are likely to influence individuals, as Figure 5.4 shows. The sections that follow will identify the important factors and issues in terms of different cultural frames of reference and then show how culture can be analysed and characterised as a means of understanding its influences on both current and future organisational purposes and strategies. The Key Debate at the end of the chapter then raises some questions about the feasibility of undertaking such analysis.

5.4.1 National and regional cultures

Many writers, perhaps the most well known of whom is Geert Hofstede,[25] have shown how attitudes to work, authority, equality and other important factors differ from one country to another. Such differences have been shaped by powerful cultural forces concerned with history, religion and even climate over many centuries. Organisations that operate internationally need to understand and cope with such differences, which can manifest themselves in terms of different standards, values and expectations in the various countries in which they operate.[26] For example, Euro Disney's attempt to replicate the success of the Disney theme parks in the US was termed 'cultural imperialism' in the French media and has experienced difficulties. Wal-Mart failed to develop its retail presence in Germany because it failed to understand how German shopping

Figure 5.4 Cultural frames of reference

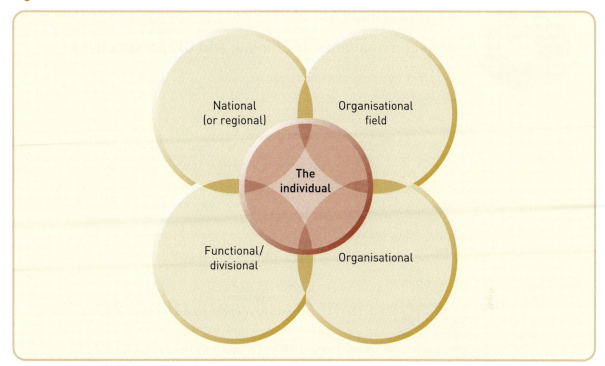

behaviour differed from US. Illustration 5.3 also shows how cultural differences underpin different conceptions of management between Chinese and Western managers.

Although they are not shown separately in Figure 5.4 (for reasons of simplification), it may also be important to understand *subnational* (usually regional) cultures. For example, attitudes to some aspects of employment and supplier relationships may differ at a regional level even in a relatively small and cohesive country like the UK, and quite markedly elsewhere in Europe (e.g. between northern and southern Italy). There may also be differences between urban and rural locations.

5.4.2 The organisational field[27]

The culture of an organisation is also shaped by 'work-based' groupings such as an industry (or sector), a profession or what is sometimes known as 'an organisational field'. An **organisational field is a community of organisations that interact more frequently with one another than with those outside the field and that have developed a shared meaning system.**[28] Such organisations may share a common technology, set of regulations or education and training. In turn this can mean that they tend to cohere around a **recipe:**[29] **a set of assumptions, norms and routines held in common within an organisational field about the appropriate purposes and strategies of field members**: in effect a 'shared wisdom'. For example, there are many organisations in the organisational field of 'justice', such as lawyers, police, courts, prisons and probation services. The roles of each are different and their detailed prescriptions as to how justice should be achieved differ. However, they are all committed to the principle that justice is a good thing which is worth striving for, they interact frequently on this issue, have developed shared ways of understanding and debating issues that arise and operate common routines or readily accommodate the routines of others in the field. Similar

ILLUSTRATION 5.3

Project management: Chinese and UK perspectives

A study of how project management is viewed in China and the UK surfaced significant different perspectives on management.

Project management can be important in the implementation of strategy and since the 1980s has become increasingly recognised in China as a useful management tool. Researchers have, however, found different conceptions of project management between managers in China and managers in the UK. These findings, in turn, inform an understanding of some underlying differences of the wider conception of management itself.

Relationship with the company

Chinese managers saw their personal career development as strongly linked to the company's development: none of those studied had changed their company since the start of their career in the construction industry. UK managers, on the other hand, were more individualistic and most had changed companies several times.

Team work

Both Chinese and UK managers placed a high value on team work, relationships with clients and with subcontractors but interpreted these differently. Chinese managers saw the team like a family where the team leader was like the father of the family and team members should support each other. So Chinese managers preferred to stay with their established teams and select new team members introduced to them by other members of the team. UK managers placed an emphasis on respect and trust but much more within the work context and with much less concern for how long people had worked in the team.

Relationship with clients

Chinese managers saw the client as: 'like your parents; you need to do whatever they instruct you . . . you need to do all you can to make them happy'. It was also important to build strong personal relationships with the client. UK managers saw the client as the provider of project funds, with a greater emphasis on contractual relationships: 'we deliver what the client wants, based on the contract'.

Relationship with subcontractors

For Chinese managers, subcontractors were like brothers and sisters of their project team family. They recognised

that there could be competition with subcontractors but saw the answer to this as the building of long-term relationships. UK managers also saw subcontractors as members of the project team but with an emphasis on their specialised techniques and skills. Again they preferred to keep a more impersonal, contractual distance.

Conflict resolution

Both groups of managers acknowledged that conflict with clients or subcontractors could be a possibility. For Chinese managers negotiation was the basis of conflict resolution. Failure to resolve problems which might end with a claim against a subcontractor was regarded as a loss of 'face' and reputation. Conflicts needed to be resolved amicably. Though they too preferred to settle things amicably, UK managers again emphasised contractual conditions. Claims on clients or contractual penalties on subcontractors were normal project management practice.

Attitudes to uncertainty

Both Chinese and UK managers accepted uncertainty as inherent in project management. However, Chinese managers found this more stressful and problematic than UK managers, who, rather, enjoyed the challenges that arose: 'I am very lucky in my job in that I have numerous different challenges every day and it's full of change.'

Source: Ping Chen and David Partington, An interpretive comparison of Chinese and Western conceptions of relationships in construction project management work, *International Journal of Project Management*, 22, 5, 397–406 (2004).

Questions

1 In what other aspects of managing strategy might the differences identified here be important?

2 If you are seeking to operate in a country with a very different culture, how would you set about trying to understand that culture and its underlying assumptions?

coherence around a recipe is common in other organisational fields; for example professional services such as accountancy (see Illustration 5.4) and many industries.

This links to the concept of path dependency discussed above. The different parties in an organisational field form a self-reinforcing network built on such assumptions and behaviours that, quite likely, will lead to behavioural lock-in. Indeed professions, or trade associations, often attempt to formalise an organisational field where the membership is exclusive and the behaviour of members is regulated. Such cultural influences can be advantageous – say to customers – in maintaining standards and consistency between individual providers. Managers can, however, become 'institutionalised' such that they do not see the opportunities or indeed threats from outside their organisational field and the recipes they inherit become difficult to change.

Just as previous chapters have shown the importance of environmental forces (Chapter 2), strategic capabilities (Chapter 3) and stakeholder expectations (Chapter 4), within an organisational field *legitimacy* is an important influence. **Legitimacy is concerned with meeting the expectations within an organisational field in terms of assumptions, behaviours and strategies.** Strategies can be shaped by the need for legitimacy in several ways. For example, through *regulation* (e.g. standards and codes of behaviour specified, perhaps by a professional body), *normative expectations* (what is socially expected), or simply that which is taken for granted as being appropriate (e.g. the *recipe*). Over time, there tends to develop a consensus within an organisational field about strategies that will be successful or acceptable – so strategies themselves become legitimised. By conforming to such norms, organisations may secure approval, support and public endorsement, thus increasing their legitimacy. Stepping outside that strategy may be risky because important stakeholders (such as customers or bankers) may not see such a move as legitimate. Therefore, organisations tend to mimic each other's strategies. There may be differences in strategies between organisations but within bounds of legitimacy.[30] This is shown in the discussion of strategy in Illustration 5.4. Of course, some fringe players may actually represent successful future strategies (e.g. internet providers of downloadable music), but *initially* this may not be seen – customers may remain loyal to established companies; investors and bankers may be reluctant to fund such ventures; and existing players in the market may dismiss what they see as aberrations.

Because recipes vary from one field to another, the transition of managers between sectors can prove difficult. For example, private-sector managers have been encouraged to join public services in an attempt to inject new ways of doing things into the public sector. Many have expressed difficulties in gaining acceptance of their ways of working and in adjusting their management style to the different traditions and expectations of their new organisation, for example in issues like consensus building as part of the decision-making process. Or, to take the example in Illustration 5.4, Michael Jones's different career background means he has some quite different views on strategy from his accountant colleagues.

5.4.3 Organisational culture

As the different definitions of culture provided at the beginning of this section suggest, culture can be conceived as consisting of different layers: the four proposed by Edgar Schein[31] are (see Figure 5.5):

- *Values* may be easy to identify in terms of those formally stated by an organisation since they are often explicit, perhaps written down (see section 4.2 in Chapter 4). For example,

ILLUSTRATION 5.4

Strategy debate in an accounting firm

The perceived legitimacy of a strategy may have different roots.

Edward Gray, the managing partner of QDG, one of the larger accountancy firms in the world, was discussing its global development with two of his senior partners. Global development had been the main issue at the firm's international committee in the US the previous week. Like most accountancy firms, QDG was organised along national lines. Its origins were in auditing but it now offered tax and financial advice, corporate recovery and information systems services. International co-operation was based on personal contacts of partners across the world. However, large clients were beginning to demand a 'seamless global service'. At the meeting was Alan Clark, with 20 years' experience as a partner and high reputation in the accountancy profession, and Michael Jones, new to QDG and unlike the others not an accountant, who headed up the information systems arm of QDG, having been recruited from a consultancy firm.

Gray: 'Unless we move towards a more global form of business, QDG could lose its position as one of the leading accountancy firms in the world. Our competitors are moving this way, so we have to. The issue is how?'

Clark was sympathetic but cautionary. He pointed out that clients were entering growing economies such as China. 'Governments there will insist on international standards of practice, but they have difficulties. For example, in China there is often no real concept of profit, let alone how to measure it. If there is to be a market economy, the need for the services we provide is high. There are however major problems, not least, the enormous number of people required. It is not possible to churn out experienced accountants overnight. Our professional standards would be compromised. The firm cannot be driven by market opportunity at the expense of standards. There is another issue. Our business is based on personal relationships and trust; this must not be compromised in the name of "global integration".'

Michael Jones suggested that the problem was more challenging: 'All our competitors are going global. They will be pitching for the same clients, offering the same services and the same standard of service. Where is the difference? To achieve any competitive advantage we need to do things differently and think beyond the obvious. For example why not a two-tier partnership, where smaller countries are non-equity partners. That would allow us to make decisions more quickly, allow us to enforce standards and give formal authority to senior partners looking after our major international clients.'

Alan Clark had expected this: 'This is not an opportunity to make money; it's about the development of proper systems for the economies of previously closed countries. We need to co-operate with other firms to make sure that there are compatible standards. This cannot be helped by changing a partnership structure that has served well for a hundred years.'

Gray: 'The view at last week's meeting was certainly that there is a need for a more internationally co-ordinated firm, with a more effective client management system, less reliance on who knows whom and more on drawing on the best of our people when we need them.'

Clark: 'I could equally argue that we have an unparalleled network of personal relationships throughout the world which we have been building for decades. That what we have to do is strengthen this using modern technology and modern communications.'

Edward Gray reconciled himself to a lengthy discussion.

Source: Adapted from the case study in G. Johnson and R. Greenwood, 'Institutional Theory and Strategic Management', in *Strategic Management: A Multiple-Perspective Approach*, edited by Mark Jenkins and V. Ambrosini, Palgrave, 2007.

Questions

1 What are the underlying assumptions of the arguments being advanced by the three partners?

2 What may be the origins of these assumptions?

3 How do the different views correspond to the discussions of strategic capabilities (Chapter 3) and competitive strategy (Chapter 6)?

Figure 5.5 Culture in four layers

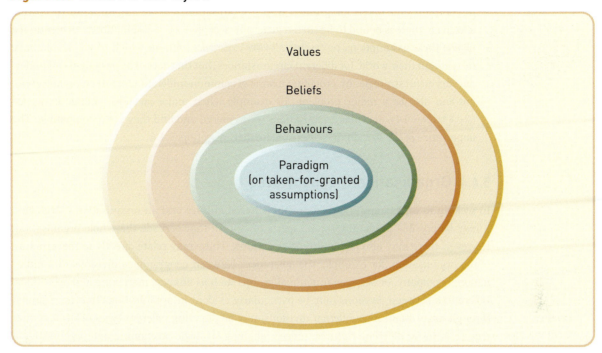

in the last decade, many banks espoused values of shareholder value creation, careful risk management and, of course, high levels of customer service. But they indulged in highly risky lending, resulting in the need for huge government financial support in 2009. Clearly the values that drove the strategies were different. It is therefore important to delve beneath espoused values to uncover underlying, perhaps taken-for-granted, values that can help explain the strategy actually being pursued by an organisation (see 5.4.7 below).

● *Beliefs* are more specific. They can typically be discerned in how people talk about issues the organisation faces; for example, a belief that the company should not trade with particular countries or, as with Michael Clark in Illustration 5.4, a belief in the rightness of accountancy systems and standards.

With regard to both values and beliefs it is important to remember that in relation to culture, the concern is with the collective rather than individuals' values and beliefs. Indeed it may be that individuals in organisations have values and beliefs that at times run counter to their organisation's, which can give rise to the sort of ethical tensions and problems discussed in section 4.4.2 of Chapter 4.

● *Behaviours* are the day-to-day way in which an organisation operates and can be seen by people both inside and often outside the organisation. This includes the work routines, how the organisation is structured and controlled and 'softer' issues around symbolic behaviours (see section 5.4.6 below). These behaviours may become the taken-for-granted 'ways we do things around here' that are potentially the bases for inimitable strategic capabilities (see section 3.3.3) but also significant barriers to achieving strategic change if that becomes necessary (see Chapter 14).

● *Taken-for-granted assumptions* are the core of an organisation's culture. They are the aspects of organisational life which people find difficult to identify and explain. In this book we refer to them as the 'organisational paradigm'. The **paradigm is the set of assumptions held in common and taken for granted in an organisation**. For an organisation to operate effectively there is bound to be such a generally accepted set of assumptions. As mentioned above, these assumptions represent *collective experience* without which people would have to 'reinvent their world' for different circumstances that they face. The paradigm can under-pin successful strategies by providing a basis of common understanding in an organisation, but can also be a major problem, for example when major strategic change is needed (see Chapter 14), or when organisations try to merge and find they are incompatible. The importance of the paradigm is discussed further in section 5.4.6.

5.4.4 Organisational subcultures

In seeking to understand the relationship between culture and an organisation's strategies, it may be possible to identify some aspects of culture that pervade the whole organisation. However, there may also be important *subcultures*. These may relate directly to the structure of the organisation: for example, the differences between geographical divisions in a multi-national company, or between functional groups such as finance, marketing and operations. Differences between divisions may be particularly evident in organisations that have grown through acquisition. Also different divisions may be pursuing different types of strategy that require or foster different cultures. Indeed, aligning strategic positioning and organisational culture is a critical feature of successful organisations. Differences between business functions can also relate to the different nature of work in different functions. For example, in an oil company like Shell or BP differences are likely between those functions engaged in 'upstream' exploration, where time horizons may be in decades, and those concerned with 'downstream' retailing, with much shorter market-driven time horizons. Arguably, this is one reason why both Shell and BP pay so much attention to trying to forge a corporate culture that crosses such functions.

5.4.5 Culture's influence on strategy

George Davis, the founder of clothing retailers Next and GIVe, who also established the highly successful Per Una brand in Marks & Spencer, sees culture as central to management: 'Culture is the thing that that makes us do things and stops us doing things.'[32] The taken-for-granted nature of culture is what makes it centrally important in relation to strategy and the manage-ment of strategy. There are three primary reasons for this.

- *Cultural 'glue'*. There are benefits in the taken-for-granted nature of culture. Josephine Rydberg-Dumont, president of IKEA, argues that, because all employees take as given the way the firm operates, it reduces the need for constant supervision. Moreover, since an aspect of the culture is to constantly question the status quo, it 'fuels' innovation. There are then benefits to the taken-for-granted aspect of culture.

- *Captured by culture*. Organisations can, however, be 'captured' by their culture. Managers, faced with a changing business environment, are more likely to attempt to deal with the situation by searching for what they can understand and cope with in terms of the existing culture. The result is likely to be the incremental strategic change with the risk of eventual strategic drift explained in section 5.2. Culture is, in effect, an unintended driver of strategy.

Figure 5.6 Culture's influence on strategy development

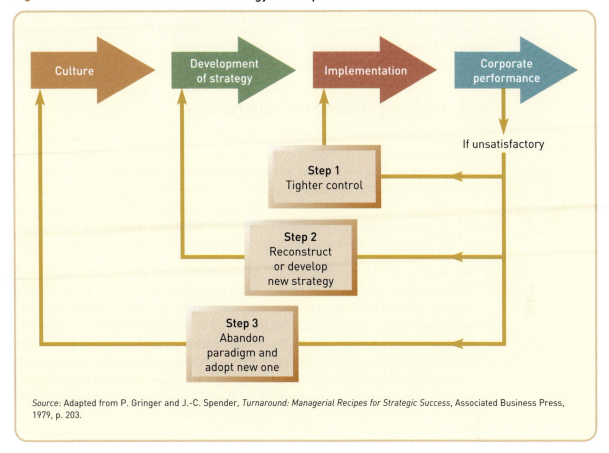

Source: Adapted from P. Gringer and J.-C. Spender, *Turnaround: Managerial Recipes for Strategic Success*, Associated Business Press, 1979, p. 203.

● *Managing culture*. Because it is difficult to observe, identify and control that which is taken for granted, it is also difficult to manage. This is why having a way to analyse culture so as to make it more evident is important – the subject of the next section. (However, see the key debate at the end of the chapter.)

The effect of culture on strategy is shown in Figure 5.6.[33] Faced with a stimulus for action, such as declining performance, managers first try to improve the implementation of existing strategy. This might be through trying to lower cost, improve efficiency, tighten controls or improve accepted way of doing things. If this is not effective, a change of strategy may occur, but a change in line with the existing culture. For example, managers may seek to extend the market for their business, but assume that it will be similar to their existing market, and therefore set about managing the new venture in much the same way as they have been used to. Alternatively, even where managers know intellectually that they need to change strategy, indeed know technologically how to do so, they find themselves constrained by path-dependent organisational routines and assumptions or political processes, as seems likely in Illustration 5.1. This often happens, for example, when there are attempts to change highly bureaucratic organisations to be customer-oriented. Even if people who accept the need to change a culture's emphasis on the importance of conforming to established rules, routines and reporting relationships, they do not readily do so. It is a fallacy to assume reasoned argument necessarily changes deeply embedded assumptions rooted in collective experience built up over long periods of time. Readers need only think of their own experience in trying to persuade others to rethink their religious beliefs, or indeed, allegiances to sports teams, to realise this. So it is with groups and organisations: people prefer the familiar and typically minimise uncertainty or ambiguity. They are likely to continue to do so until there is, perhaps, dramatic evidence of the redundancy of the culture, quite likely as the result of the organisation entering phases 3 or 4 of strategic drift (see Figure 5.2).

5.4.6 Analysing culture: the cultural web

KEY
CONCEPT
Cultural web

In order to understand the existing culture and its effects it is important to be able to analyse an organisation's culture. The cultural web[34] is a means of doing this (see Figure 5.7). The **cultural web shows the behavioural, physical and symbolic manifestations of a culture** that inform and are informed by the taken-for-granted assumptions, or paradigm, of an organisation. It is in effect the inner two ovals in Figure 5.5. The cultural web can be used to understand culture in any of the frames of reference discussed above but is most often used at the organisational and/or functional levels in Figure 5.4.[35] The elements of the cultural web are as follows:

- The *paradigm* is at the core of Figure 5.7. As previously defined it is the set of assumptions held in common and taken for granted in an organisation: in effect it is the *collective experience* applied to a situation to make sense of it and inform a likely course of action. The assumptions of the paradigm are, quite likely, very basic but may or may not align with the logic of a strategy. For example, it may seem self-evident that a newspaper business's core assumptions are about the centrality of news coverage and reporting. However, from a strategic point of view, increasingly newspapers' revenues are reliant on advertising income and the strategy may need to be directed to this. The paradigm of a charity may be

Figure 5.7 The cultural web of an organisation

about doing good works for the needy, but this cannot be achieved if it is not run effectively for the purpose of raising money. It is quite likely that, even if the rational view is to build a strategy around revenue generation for the newspaper or the charity, people in those organisations may still interpret issues and behave in line with its paradigm. So under-standing what the paradigm is and how it informs debate on strategy matters. The problem is that, since it is unlikely to be talked about, or even be something that people are conscious of, trying to identify it can be difficult; especially if you are part of that organisation. Outside observers may find it easier to identify simply by listening to what people say and watching what they do and emphasise; but this may not be so easy for insiders who are part of the culture. One way of 'insiders' getting to see the assumptions they take for granted is to focus initially on other aspects of the cultural web because these are to do with more visible manifestations of culture. Moreover these other aspects are likely to act to reinforce the assumptions within that paradigm.

- **Routines** are 'the way we do things around here' on a day-to-day basis. These may have a long history and may well be common across organisations (see section 5.3 above). At their best, these lubricate the working of the organisation, and may provide a basis for distinctive organisational capabilities. However, they can also represent a taken-for-grantedness about how things should happen which, again, can guide how people respond to issues and be difficult to change.

- The **rituals** of organisational life are particular **activities or special events that emphasise, highlight or reinforce what is important in the culture**. Examples include training pro-grammes, interview panels, promotion and assessment procedures, sales conferences and so on. An extreme example, of course, is the ritualistic training of army recruits to prepare them for the discipline required in conflict. However, rituals can also be informal activities such as drinks in the pub after work or gossiping around photocopying machines. A checklist of rituals is provided in Chapter 14 (see Table 14.2).

- The *stories*[36] told by members of an organisation to each other, to outsiders, to new recruits and so on, may act to embed the present in its organisational history and also flag up important events and personalities. They typically have to do with successes, disasters, heroes, villains and mavericks (who deviate from the norm). They can be a way of letting people know what is conventionally important in an organisation.

- **Symbols**[37] are objects, events, acts or people that convey, maintain or create meaning over and above their functional purpose. For example, offices and office layout, cars and job titles have a functional purpose, but are also typically signals about status and hierarchy. Particular people may come to represent specially important aspects of an organisation or historic turning points. The form of language used in an organisation can also be particu-larly revealing, especially with regard to customers or clients. For example, the head of a consumer protection agency in Australia described his clients as 'complainers'. In a major teaching hospital in the UK, consultants described patients as 'clinical material'. Whilst such examples might be amusing, they reveal an underlying assumption about customers (or patients) that might play a significant role in influencing the strategy of an organisation. Although symbols are shown separately in the cultural web, it should be remembered that many elements of the web are symbolic. So, routines, control and reward systems and structures are not only functional but also symbolic.

- **Power** was defined in Chapter 4 as **the ability of individuals or groups to persuade, induce or coerce others into following certain courses of action**. So *power structures* are distributions of power to groups of people in an organisation. The most powerful individuals or groups are likely to be closely associated with the paradigm. For example, in firms that experience strategic drift, it is not unusual to find powerful executives who have long association with long-established ways of doing things. In analysing power the guidance given in Chapter 4 (section 4.5.2) is useful.

- **Organisational structures are the roles, responsibilities and reporting relationships in organisations**. These are likely to reflect power structures and how they manifest themselves emphasises which roles and relationships really matter in an organisation. Formal hierarchical, mechanistic structures may emphasise that strategy is the province of top managers and everyone else is 'working to orders'. Structures with less emphasis on formal reporting relationships might indicate more participative strategy making. Highly devolved structures (as discussed in Chapter 13) may signify that collaboration is less important than competition and so on.

- **Control systems are the formal and informal ways of monitoring and supporting people within and around an organisation** and tend to emphasise what is seen to be important in the organisation. They include measurements and reward systems. For example, public-service organisations have often been accused of being concerned more with stewardship of funds than with quality of service. This is reflected in their control systems, which are more about accounting for spending rather than with quality of service. Individually based bonus schemes related to volume are likely to signal a culture of individuality, internal competition and an emphasis on sales volume rather than teamwork and an emphasis on quality.

Illustration 5.5 shows a cultural web drawn up by the partners of a medium-sized law firm as part of a strategic review. The key point to emerge was that the culture of the firm was dominated by their personalities and personal styles linked to an expectation of collective commitment and the need to 'fit in'. This was an issue for the firm as they faced a strategic choice of whether to try to sell their firm on to a much larger one or attempt to grow the firm with themselves at the helm. The problem for either choice was the dominance of these senior executives in the firm's culture: they were seen as 'the brotherhood; the heart of the firm'. If they were to sell the firm, they each would leave and so take away a significant element of the firm's formula for success. If they were to try to grow the firm, how would they duplicate themselves and develop the leadership potential of others to fill the expanding roles?

5.4.7 Undertaking cultural analysis

If an analysis of the culture of an organisation is to be undertaken, there are some important issues to bear in mind:

- *Questions to ask.* Figure 5.8 outlines some of the questions that might help build up an understanding of culture using the cultural web. However, analysing a culture is not straightforward, as the Key Debate at the end of the chapter explains.

- *Statements of cultural values.* As section 4.2 in Chapter 4 and 5.4.3 above explained, organisations may make public statements of their values, beliefs and purposes – for example, in annual reports, mission or values statements and business plans. There is a danger that these are seen as useful descriptions of the organisational culture. But this is likely to be at

ILLUSTRATION 5.5

The cultural web of a law firm

The cultural web can be used to identify the behaviours and taken-for-granted assumptions of an organisation.

This is an adapted version of a cultural web produced by partners and managers of a law firm.

Heroic commitment to the firm: if you don't fit, don't share the right principles, you exit

Unity, inclusivity and conformity

Stories
- Heroes
- Epic travel
- Commitment to the firm
- Wrong/bad people being sacked
- The salvation – our big money making deal

Symbols
- No one has offices
- All desks same size
- Being made a partner
- Dispersed share ownership
- Heading up major client accounts

Rituals/routines
- We celebrate long service to the firm
- We have routines that are about 'us leader, you follower'
- We don't really celebrate the success of the firm

Paradigm
- Almost a secret society element to it
- A brotherhood
- Like pioneers of our way of doing business
- Evangelising

Power
- The CEO and like minded senior executives
- Energy, drive, assertiveness
- Egotism
- Male

Rituals are about being the right kind of person.
'*We do leaving very well, Sinatra tours for long service.*'

Controls
- Lots of measurement
- Anxiety about control
- Overly anxious about monitoring

Structure
- Meetings; lots of them
- Absence of guiding principles
- Segmented structure

Power is the property of individuals, manifest in their visible energy.
'*Bursting into a room with an armful of papers is power, noise is power.*'

We are concerned about control, but paradoxically we love a crisis to rush in and solve

Meetings dominate the structure

Questions

1 How would you characterise the dominant culture here?

2 How do the various elements of the web inter-relate?

3 Draw up a cultural web for an organisation of your choice.

Figure 5.8 The cultural web: some useful questions

Stories
- What core beliefs do stories reflect?
- What stories are commonly told e.g. to newcomers?
- How do these reflect core assumptions and beliefs?
- What norms do the mavericks deviate from?

Symbols
- What objects, events or people do people in the organisation particularly identify with?
- What are these related to in the history of the organisation?
- What aspects of strategy are highlighted in publicity?

Routines and rituals
- Which routines are emphasised?
- Which are embedded in history?
- What behaviour do routines encourage?
- What are the key rituals?
- What assumptions and core beliefs do they reflect?
- What do training programmes emphasise?
- How easy are rituals/routines to change?

Power structures
- Where does power reside? Indicators include:
  (a) status
  (b) claim on resources
  (c) symbols of power
- Who 'makes things happen'?
- Who stops things happening?

(center diagram: Stories, Symbols, Routines and rituals, Paradigm, Power structures, Control systems, Organisational structures)

Control systems
- What is most closely monitored/controlled?
- Is emphasis on reward or punishment?
- Are controls rooted in history or current strategies?
- Are there many/few controls?

Organisational structures
- How formal/informal are the structures?
- Do structures encourage collaboration or competition?
- What types of power structure do they support?

Overall
- What do the answers to these questions suggest are the (few) fundamental assumptions that are the paradigm?
- How would you characterise the dominant culture?
- How easy is this to change?

best only partially true, and at worst misleading. This is not to suggest that there is any organised deception. It is simply that the statements of values and beliefs are often carefully considered and carefully crafted statements of the aspirations of a particular stakeholder (such as the CEO) rather than descriptions of the actual culture. For example, an outside observer of a police force might conclude from its public statements of purpose and priorities that it had a balanced approach to the various aspects of police work – catching criminals, crime prevention, community relations. However, a deeper probing might quickly reveal that (in cultural terms) there is the 'real' police work (catching criminals) and the 'lesser work' (crime prevention, community relations).

- *Pulling it together.* The detailed 'map' produced by the cultural web can be a rich source of information about an organisation's culture, but it is useful to be able to characterise the culture that the information conveys. Sometimes this is possible by means of graphic descriptors. For example, the managers who undertook a cultural analysis in the UK National Health Service (NHS) summed up their culture as 'The National Sickness Service'. Although this approach is rather crude and unscientific, it can be powerful in terms of organisational members seeing the organisation as it really is – which may not be immediately apparent from all of the detailed points in the cultural web. It can also help people to understand that culture drives strategies; for example, a 'national sickness service' would clearly prioritise strategies that are about developments in curing sick people above strategies of health promotion and prevention. So those favouring health promotion strategies need to understand that they are facing the need to change a culture and that in doing so they may not be able to assume that rational processes like planning and resource allocation will be enough (see Chapter 14).

If managers are to develop strategies that are different from those of the past, they need to be able to challenge, question and potentially change the organisational culture that under-pins the current strategy. In this context, the cultural analysis suggested in this chapter can inform aspects of strategic management discussed in other parts of this book.

- *Strategic capabilities.* As Chapter 3 makes clear, historically embedded capabilities are, very likely, part of the culture of the organisation. The cultural analysis of the organisa-tion therefore provides a complementary basis of analysis to an examination of strategic capabilities (see Chapter 3). In effect, such an analysis of capabilities should end up digging into the culture of the organisation, especially in terms of its routines, control systems and the everyday way in which the organisation runs, very likely on a 'taken-for-granted' basis.

- *Strategy development.* An understanding of organisational culture sensitises managers to the way in which historical and cultural influences will likely affect future strategy for good or ill. It therefore relates to the discussion on strategy development in Chapter 12.

- *Managing strategic change.* An analysis of the culture also provides a basis for the manage-ment of strategic change, since it provides a picture of the existing culture that can be set against a desired strategy so as to give insights as to what may constrain the development of that strategy or what needs to be changed in order to achieve it. This is discussed more extensively in Chapter 14 on managing strategic change.

- *Leadership and management style.* Chapter 14 also raises questions about leadership and management style. If one of the major requirements of a strategist is to be able to encourage the questioning of that which is taken for granted, the sort of analytical tools covered in this chapter and in this book can be an aid. However, it is also likely to require a management style – indeed a culture – that allows and encourages such questioning. If the leadership style is such as to discourage such questioning, it is unlikely that the lessons of history will be learned and more likely that the dictates of history will be followed.

- *Culture and experience.* There have been repeated references in this section to the role culture plays as a vehicle by which meaning is created in organisations. This is discussed more fully in the Commentary on the Experience Lens and provides a useful way in which many aspects of strategy can be considered (see the commentaries throughout the book).

KEY DEBATE

Understanding organisational culture

If organisational culture is so important an influence on strategy, then understanding just what it is and what its influences are is of key importance. But is this possible to do?

In this chapter, in particular section 5.4, it is argued that understanding an organisation's culture is important for the strategist and ways of doing this such as the cultural web are proposed. There are also a variety of other tools and techniques for analysing organisational cultures, such including survey instuments (for example see Kim Cameron and Robert Quinn, *Diagnosing and Changing Organizational Culture*, Jossey Bass, 2006) that are employed by managers and consultants.

However, in his book *Understanding Organizational Culture* Mats Alvesson suggests that there are dangers and problems in understanding organisational culture, in particular the temptation to simplify and trivialise what is meant by organisational culture. He suggests that managers often fall victim to 'seven sins':

Reifying culture: Seeing culture as an 'it'. So the need is to avoid the idea of 'culture' as something 'thing-like' that, for example, directly links to performance or can be readily managed. What really matters is the meaning shared by a collective and that is a more complex idea.

Essentializing culture: Describing culture in terms of a few essential traits, such as 'service minded, adaptable, personnel-oriented, open, individualistic, etc'. The danger again is a 'too strongly ordered and superficial view on culture'. The need is for a more careful interpretation of what culture means and recognition of variations within a culture.

Unifying culture: 'Equating cultural boundaries with formal or legal ones, as implied by terms such as corporate culture or national culture . . . Cultural orientations may not follow established social differentiation criteria.' Avoid treating organizations as homogeneous groups based on such categories.

Idealizing culture: Focusing on the levels of ideas, symbols and meanings 'in a social and material vacuum'. Such ideas are actually shaped and reshaped in the context of material reality and behaviours which themselves are 'loaded with meaning and symbolism and affect cultural patterns and processes'.

Consensualizing culture: Assuming that culture means a unity of shared values. 'Shared meanings do not

necessarily imply consensus and harmony . . . an organization may be characterized by shared ideas and beliefs about the significance of self interest, fierce internal competition and a view of corporate life as fairly harsh and jungle-like.'

Totalizing culture: Assuming that a culture can be captured 'once and for all' when 'it is the shared meanings on a specific topic that is of interest to pay attention to' such as core competences or the future of an industry.

Otherizing culture: The danger of contrasts, for example comparing one culture against another, which might be seen as superior or inferior. The danger of 'otherizing' is, again, that it tends to trivialize and prevent a more nuanced view of culture.

Alvesson concludes his warning against the seven sins by adding that there are 'sometimes pragmatic reasons . . . for simplifications and the expression of something accessible – which often leads to some of the sins above. . . . My point is, however, that the traps and temptations should be handled with great care. Caution should taken not to theorize culture in a way giving the seven sins privilege'.

Source: M. Alvesson, *Understanding Organizational Culture*, Sage, 2002, pp. 186–9.

Questions

1 Undertake a cultural analysis of an organisation. To what extent did you find yourself committing any of the 'seven sins'?

2 If, as Alvesson suggests, pragmatically some of the sins are difficult to avoid, how can managers avoid 'privileging' them?

3 Managers often talk about the need to 'manage organisational culture'. How feasible is this given the complex nature of organisational culture that Alvesson describes? (Reference to Chapter 14 may be helpful here.)

SUMMARY

- The history and culture of an organisation may contribute to its strategic capabilities, but may also give rise to strategic drift as its strategy develops incrementally on the basis of such influences and fails to keep pace with a changing environment.

- Historical, path-dependent processes play a significant part in the success or failure of an organisation and need to be understood by managers. There are historical analyses that can be conducted to help uncover these influences.

- Cultural and institutional influences both inform and constrain the strategic development of organisations.

- Organisational culture is the basic assumptions and beliefs that are shared by members of an organisation, that operate unconsciously and define in a basic taken-for-granted fashion an organisation's view of itself and its environment.

- An understanding of the culture of an organisation and its relationship to organisational strategy can be gained by using the cultural web.

WORK ASSIGNMENTS

✳ *Denotes more advanced work assignments. * Refers to a case study in the Text and Cases edition.*

5.1   Identify four organisations that, in your view, are in the different phases of strategic drift (see Figure 5.2). Justify your selection.

5.2✳   In the context of section 5.3, undertake a historical analysis of the strategy development of Club Med or an organisation of your choice and consider the question: 'Does history matter in managing strategy?'

5.3   Map out an organisational field (see section 5.4.2) within which an organisation of your choice operates. (As a basis for this you could for example use accountancy, an organisation operating in the public sector such as Cordia* or Formula One*.)

5.4   Identify (a) an organisation where its publicly stated values correspond with your experience of it and (b) one where they do not. Explain why (a) and (b) might be so.

5.5   Use the questions in Figure 5.8 to plot a cultural web for ClubMed, Cordia* or an organisation of your choice.

5.6✳   By using a number of the examples from above and taking into account the issues raised in the Key Debate, critically appraise the assertion that 'culture can only really be usefully analysed by the symptoms displayed in the way the organisation operates'. (You may wish to refer to Schein's book in the recommended key readings to assist you with this task.)

Integrative assignment

5.7✳   What is the relationship between competitive advantage, strategic capabilities, organisation culture, strategy development and the challenge of managing strategic change? (Refer to Chapters 3, 5, 6, 12 and 14.) Consider this in relation to a major change in strategy.

VIDEO ASSIGNMENT

Visit *MyStrategyLab* and watch the *IKEA* case study.

1 What does Josephine Rydburg-Dumont mean when she says: 'The importance of IKEA culture is, in a way, everything'?

2 What aspects of IKEA's cultural web can be identified from the video? What do you think the other aspects of the web might include?

RECOMMENDED KEY READINGS

- For a more thorough explanation of the phenomenon of strategic drift see Gerry Johnson, 'Rethinking incrementalism', *Strategic Management Journal*, vol. 9 (1988), pp. 75–91, and 'Managing strategic change – strategy, culture and action', *Long Range Planning*, vol. 25, no. 1 (1992), pp. 28–36. (These papers also explain the cultural web.) Also see Donald S. Sull: 'Why good companies go bad', *Harvard Business Review*, July/August 1999, pp. 42–52.

- For a historical perspective on strategy see: I. Greener, 'Theorizing path dependency: how does history come to matter in organizations?', *Management Decision*, vol. 40, no. 6 (2002), pp. 614–19; and Jorg Sydow, George Schraeyogg and Jochen Koch, 'Organisational path dependence: opening the black box', *Academy of Management Review*, vol. 34, no. 4 (2009), pp. 689–708.

- For a summary and illustrated explanation of institutional theory see Gerry Johnson and Royston Greenwood, 'Institutional theory and strategy', in *Strategic Management: A Multiple-Perspective Approach*, edited by Mark Jenkins and V. Ambrosini, Palgrave, 2007.

- For a comprehensive and critical explanation of organisational culture see Mats Alvesson, *Understanding Organizational Culture*, Sage, 2002.

REFERENCES

1. For an explanation of strategic drift see G. Johnson, 'Rethinking incrementalism', *Strategic Management Journal*, vol. 9, pp. 75–91, 1988 and 'Managing strategic change – strategy, culture and action', *Long Range Planning*, vol. 25, no. 1, pp. 28–36, 1992. Also see E. Romanelli and M.T. Tushman, 'Organizational transformation as punctuated equilibrium: an empirical test', *Academy of Management Journal*, vol. 7, no. 5, pp. 1141–66, 1994. They explain the tendency of strategies to develop very incrementally with periodic transformational change.

2. See D. Miller and P. Friesen, 'Momentum and revolution in organisational adaptation', *Academy of Management Journal*, vol. 23, no. 4, pp. 591–614, 1980.

3. See D. Leonard-Barton, 'Core capabilities and core rigidities: a paradox in managing new product development', *Strategic Management Journal*, vol. 13, pp. 111–25, 1992.

4. This is a term used by Donald S. Sull in accounting for the decline of high-performing firms (see 'Why good companies go bad', *Harvard Business Review*, July/August, 1999, pp. 42–52).

5. In *The Icarus Paradox* (D. Miller, Harper-Collins, 1990) Danny Miller makes a convincing case that organisations' success leads to a number of potentially pathological tendencies, not least of which are the tendencies to inflate the durability of bases of success and to build future strategies relatively uncritically. Hence the idea of the Icarus paradox, building on the Greek mythological character, Icarus, who successfully built himself wings to fly but then flew too close to the sun such that they melted.

6. This research, known as the Successful Strategic Transformers (SST) project, was in progress at the time of writing. It was part of the UK Advanced Institute of Management Research initiative. For an explanation of stage 1 of the research, on which these findings are based, see: G. Yip, T. Devinney and G. Johnson, 'Measuring long-term superior performance: the UK's long term superior performers 1984–2003', *Long Range Planning*, vol. 43, no. 3, 2009, pp. 390–413.

7. This quote by André Malroux and the story of the BMW museum was provided by the business historian Mary Rose.

8. See D. Holbrook, W. Cohen, D. Hounshell and S. Klepper, 'The nature, sources and consequences of firm differences in the early history of the semiconductor industry', *Strategic Management Journal*, vol. 21, no. 10–11, pp. 107–42, 2000.

9. Private correspondence with Mary Rose who suggests that: 'it links to Schumpeter and his notion of boundary crossing which may be between sectors, between technologies or informing the development and application of old technology with new knowledge'.

10. S. Klepper and K.L. Simons, 'Dominance by birthright: entry of prior radio producers and competitive ramifications in the US television receiver industry', *Strategic Management Journal*, vol. 21, no. 10–11, pp. 987–1016, 2000.

11. W.B. Arthur, Competing technologies, increasing returns and lock in by historical events', *Economic Journal*, vol. 99, pp. 116–31, 1989.

12. P.A. David, Clio and the economics of QWERTY, *Economic History*, 75 (2), 332–7, 1985.

13. For discussions of path dependency in an organisational context see: I. Greener, 'Theorizing path dependency: how does history come to matter in organizations?', *Management Decision*, 40 (6), 614–19, 2002 and Jorg Sydow, George Schraeyogg and Jochen Koch, 'Organisational path dependance: opening the black box', *Academy of Management Review*, 34 (4), 2009, 689–708.

14. The world's biggest accounting firms have called for radical reform; 'Big four in call for real time accounts', page 1, *Financial Times*, 8 Nov 2006.

15. Holbrook et al. (ref. 8 above).

16. See J.R. Kimberley and H. Bouchikhi, 'The dynamics of organizational development and change: how the past shapes the present and constrains the future', *Organization Science*, 6, 1, 9–18, 1995.

17. This example is also taken from stage 2 of the SST research project referred to in ref. 6 above. At the time of writing there are no published results from this stage of the research.

18. Also see D.J. Jeremy, 'Business history and strategy', in *The Handbook of Strategy and Management*, pp. 436–60, eds A. Pettigrew, H. Thomas and R. Whittington, Sage, 2002.

19. For good examples of corporate histories see G. Jones, *Renewing Unilever: Transformation and Tradition*, Oxford University Press, 2005; R. Fitzgerald, *Rowntrees and the Marketing Revolution, 1862–1969*, Cambridge University Press, 1995; T.R. Gourvish, *British Railways 1948–73*, Cambridge University Press, 1986.

20. Walsh and Ungson make the point that 'organisational memory' is stored in a number of ways but these include shared interpretations and individual recollections. See J.P. Walsh and G.R. Ungson, 'Organizational memory', *The Academy of Management Review*, vol. 16, no. 1, pp. 57–91, January 1991.

21. This quote is from S. Finkelstein, 'Why smart executives fail: four case histories of how people learn the wrong lessons from history', *Business History*, 48, 2, 153–70, 2006.

22. See Clifford Geertz, *The Interpretation of Culture*, Basic Books, 1973, p. 12 and see Mats Alvesson, *Understanding Organizational Culture*, Sage, 2002, p. 3.

23. This definition of culture is taken from E. Schein, *Organisational Culture and Leadership*, 2nd edition, Jossey-Bass, 1992, p. 6.

24. This is how Terrence Deal and Alan Kennedy define organisational culture in *Corporate Cultures: the Rites and Rituals of Corporate Life*, Addison-Wesley, 1982.

25. See G. Hofstede, *Culture's Consequences*, Sage, 2nd edn, 2001. For critiques of Hofstede's work, see B. McSweeney, 'Hofstede's model of national cultural differences and their consequences: a triumph of faith – a failure of analysis', *Human Relations*, vol. 55, no. 1, 89–118 (2002) and A.M. Soares, M. Farhangmeher and A.S. Shoham, 'Hofstede's dimensions of culture in international marketing studies', *Journal of Business Research*, 60, 3, 277–84, 2007.

26. On cross-cultural managerment also see R. Lewis, *When Cultures Collide: Managing Successfully across Cultures*, 2nd edition, Brealey, 2000, a practical guide for managers. It offers an insight into different national cultures, business conventions and leadership styles. Also S. Schneider and J.-L. Barsoux, *Managing across Cultures*, 2nd edition, Financial Times Prentice Hall, 2003. T. Jackson, 'Management ethics and corporate policy: a cross-cultural comparison', *Journal of Management Studies*, vol. 37, no. 3 (2000), pp. 349–70 looks at how national culture influences management ethics.

27. A useful review of research on this topic is: T. Dacin, J. Goodstein and R. Scott, 'Institutional theory and institutional change: introduction to the special research forum', *Academy of Management Journal*, vol. 45, no. 1 (2002), pp. 45–57. For a more general review see G. Johnson and R. Greenwood, 'Institutional theory and strategy', in *Strategic Management: a Multiple-Perspective Approach*, edited by Mark Jenkins and V. Ambrosini, Palgrave, 2007.

28. This definition is taken from W. Scott, *Institutions and Organizations*, Sage, 1995.

29. The term 'recipe' was introduced to refer to industries by J.-C. Spender, *Industry Recipes: the Nature and Sources of Management Judgement*, Blackwell, 1989. We have broadened its use by applying it to *organisational fields*. The fundamental idea that behaviours are driven by a collective set of norms and values remains unchanged.

30. D. Deephouse, 'To be different or to be the same? It's a question (and theory) of strategic balance', *Strategic Management Journal*, vol. 20, no. 2 (1999), pp. 147–66.

31. E. Schein (see reference 23) and A. Brown, *Organisational Culture*, Financial Times Prentice Hall, 1998, are useful in understanding the relationship between organisational culture and strategy. For a useful critique of the concept of organisational culture see M. Alvesson, *Understanding Organizational Culture*, Sage, 2002.

32. *Observer*, 7.2.10 Business section, p. 3.

33. Figure 5.4 is adapted from the original in P. Grinyer and J.-C. Spender, *Turnaround: Managerial Recipes for Strategic Success*, Associated British Press, p. 203, 1979.

34. A fuller explanation of the cultural web can be found in G. Johnson, *Strategic Change and the Management Process*, 1987, and G. Johnson, 'Managing strategic change: strategy, culture and action', *Long Range Planning*, vol. 25, Blackwell, no. 1 (1992), pp. 28–36.

35. A practical explanation of cultural web mapping can be found in G. Johnson, 'Mapping and re-mapping organisational culture', in V. Ambrosini with G. Johnson and K. Scholes (eds), *Exploring Techniques of Analysis and Evaluation in Strategic Management*, Prentice Hall, 1998.

36. See J. Martin and A.L. Wilkins, 'Organisational stories as symbols which control the organisation', in L.R. Pondy, P.J. Frost, G. Morgan and T.C. Dandridge (eds), *Organisational Symbolism*, JAI Press, 1983.

37. The significance of organisational symbolism is explained in G. Johnson, 'Managing strategic change: the role of symbolic action', *British Journal of Management*, vol. 1, no. 4 (1990), pp. 183–200.

Cultural turnaround at Club Med

Frédéric Fréry, ESCP Europe

In 2010, the repositioning of Club Med as an 'upscale, friendly and multicultural' tour operator was supposed to be achieved, through the complete renovation of its portfolio of vacation villages. However, the outcome of this strategy, implemented since the early 2000s, when Club Med had faced the loss of impetus of its historical model, was still unclear. Such a repositioning clearly clashed with Club Med's history and culture, generally associated with a relaxed atmosphere, rough and ready amenities and an open-minded lifestyle.

The 2009 results showed that, even if operating profits were finally up after several years of decrease, revenues were still declining. Club Med's Chairman and CEO Henri

Source: Shutterstock.

Giscard d'Estaing explained that the net loss (€58m; ~$81m) resulted from four elements: (1) the overall economic crisis, (2) the H1N1 flu virus and its impact on tourism, (3) the renovation cost of the villages, and (4) a 'limited number of property transactions, due to the mortgage crisis'. He also announced the opening of five new villages in China between 2010 and 2015. His promise was to 'deliver a new profitable Club Med for 2010'.

However, the break with Club Med's history and culture had to succeed: since 2004, this strategic turnaround had cost around €1bn.

Club Med's history: the years of growth

Club Med was founded after the Second World War by Gérard Blitz and Gilbert Trigano.

Coming from a Belgian diamond merchant family, Gérard Blitz was a world-class athlete in swimming and water-polo. In 1950, he spent some days of vacation in a tent village close to Calvi, Corsica. This gave him the idea to create a 'vacation camp' under the sun. He founded the Belgian association 'Club Méditerranée' in April 1950 and opened his first village on a desert beach on the island of Mallorca, Spain.

Blitz bought his tents from a French supplier, Gilbert Trigano. Apart from owning a family tent business, Trigano was a former resistance fighter and a reporter for the French Communist newspaper *L'Humanité*. Attracted by the vacation village concept, fascinated by

Figure 1 Club Med revenues (million euros)

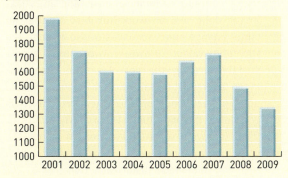

€1m is about $1.4m.

Figure 2 Club Med net profits (million euros)

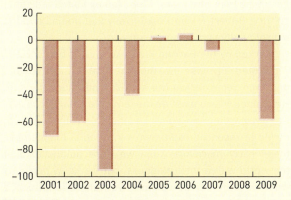

€1m is about $1.4m.

Blitz's personality, Trigano became the treasurer of the association in 1953, then president in 1963. The same year, Club Méditerranée was incorporated.

In 1955, Club Méditerranée opened a second tent village in Tahiti (Blitz's wife was of Tahitian origin). In 1956, a winter village was opened in Leysin, Switzerland, and in 1965, Club Méditerranée opened its first permanent village in Agadir, Morocco.

In 1966, in order to finance a vast international expansion plan in Northern Africa, Europe, America and Asia, the company was listed at the Paris stock exchange. During the next twenty years, dozens of villages opened, including two giant sailing ships, *Club Med 1* and *Club Med 2*.

First difficulties

In 1991, the year Blitz died, Operation Desert Storm strongly impacted the tourist industry and Club Med suffered heavy losses. In 1993, Gilbert Trigano was replaced as chairman and CEO by his son, Serge. In spite of his turnaround plan, Serge Trigano did not manage to put the situation right. In 1997, upset shareholders replaced him with an external manager, Philippe Bourguignon, the former CEO of EuroDisney.

Bourguignon's ambition was to 'transform a vacation villages company into a service company'. He implemented a growth strategy, both organic (new concepts such as a low-cost village for young people) and external (takeover of another tour operator and of a gym clubs chain). This ambitious expansion strategy came with a severe cost-cutting plan, a shift in human resource management (in the villages, many Club Med employees were replaced with local suppliers) and the implementation of a real IT infrastructure (many processes were still done manually). Club Med became profitable in 1998. In 1999, net profits grew by 48%. In 2000, revenues and profits soared again (+28% and +51% respectively). In three years, Club Med attracted more than 300,000 new customers. In 2001, when Gilbert Trigano died, Club Med had 127 villages, 24,200 employees and 1.8 million customers.

However, the terrorist attacks of 9/11 caused an immediate collapse of the tourist market. Bourguignon's volume strategy was no longer sustainable. Since he was disowned by Club Med's employees – who criticised his autocratic management and were used to Trigano's paternalism – he resigned from the chairmanship in 2002. He was replaced by the CEO he had recruited himself from Danone, Henri Giscard d'Estaing. Giscard d'Estaing was also the elder son of the former President of the French Republic.

The repositioning plan

When Giscard d'Estaing became chairman and CEO, Club Med was facing two external threats:

- The tourist industry was heavily affected by the terrorist threat.
- Thanks to the Internet, new low-cost entrants were rapidly expanding, and incumbents were offered vacation villages, similar to the Club Med concept, but at lower prices.

All this convinced Giscard d'Estaing to implement an upscale repositioning: the closing down of approximately 50 low-end villages, renovation of the existing infrastructure, opening of new prestigious establishments, a significant rise in services (all-includive package, open-bar policy, more comfortable rooms), but also a significant price rise. The number of villages decreased to 80 and a much more sophisticated advertising campaign was launched. Between 1998 and 2008, the proportion of high-end villages went from 18% to 47%, whereas low-end villages were disappearing. The clientele also evolved significantly: households with a high revenue accounted for 63% of customers in 2003, and 82% in 2005.

This repositioning was mainly financed by selling property, which reduced financial costs and amortisation, limited debt, and allowed Club Med to offer an acceptable balance sheet for investors to finance the renovation of its villages. However, two external events weakened this strategy: the market was still in a downturn (on top of terrorist threats, the 2004 tsunami in Asia also had an impact), and from 2007 the mortgage crisis brutally reduced the opportunity for property profits.

In 2010, analysts were still uncertain about the results of this profound strategic reorientation, which was disrupting Club Med's historical culture.

The roots of Club Med's culture

For more than fifty years, Club Med exhibited a distinct culture. Gilbert Trigano used to say that he had created a 'profoundly psychological industry'.

Marked by the Second World War, Blitz had created Club Med because he thought that all Europeans deserved vacations on the seaside and under the sun. He defined his concept as the 'antidote against civilisation'. According to Gilbert Trigano: 'More than Gérard, I tried to reconcile capitalism with utopia. I remember these early mornings when we were boldly building the world with a total madness, but we knew perfectly what we were doing: we knew we wanted to influence people's life and future.' Blitz was an idealist and

Trigano a pragmatist, but they agreed on 'gathering people hurt by modern society in a peaceful and soft place where they could regain their forces, an artificial environment to teach people to smile again'.

To do so, they built up a culture with rich symbols, rituals and myths. Villages were isolated from their local environment in order to break from day-to-day life. Amenities were limited: tents at first, then huts – often without electricity – with shared bathrooms. In this closed world, as of 1951, customers were named GMs (Gracious Members) and coordinators GOs (Gracious Organisers). On arrival, welcomed by GOs, GMs had to ban professional jargon and social origins. At the restaurant, there were only eight-people tables, in order to force GMs to make new acquaintances. As of 1956, Club Med banned money from the villages and implemented a payment system based on plastic pearl necklaces.

GOs were the keystone of the whole system. They were expected to maintain a permanent festive atmosphere through shows, village dances and sport competitions. During the first years, Blitz personally recruited them with his wife, Claudine. Gilbert Trigano insisted: 'Claudine informally played the role of head of personnel, which was a key role because everything relies on GOs. She and Gérard were the tutelary parents of the Club, they choose children in their image and maintain family relations with them.'

From an organisational point of view, the best GOs could become general managers of a village, in charge of all the operational aspects, from animation to hospitality and security. The best general managers – a job it was difficult to cope with after the age of 45, because it required an almost permanent night-and-day presence with GMs – could access administrative positions at Club Med headquarters in Paris, even if these coordinators were not necessarily good executives.

Under the trident logo (a reference to Poseidon and the Mediterranean Sea), Club Med generated a 'sea, sex and sun' alchemy which reached its apogee in the 1970s.

Towards a new culture

In the 1990s, this life in a community was no longer in line with social evolution. Loose morals were unacceptable for families. Villages were more and more considered as ghettos, without any contact with local cultures. Undue familiarity between GOs and GMs repelled some customers and the obligation to participate in all activities was seen as brigading.

As a consequence, as of 2002, after having asked Serge Trigano about Club Med's historical culture, Giscard d'Estaing attempted deep cultural change. An ambiance charter was produced. It highlighted the core values of the company: multicultural, pioneer, kindness, freedom, responsibility. It also spelled out inappropriate behaviours for GOs: cronyism, hasty judgement, individualism. As thick as a phone book, it also explained new procedures and limited 'vulgar' activities such as water games or roles played by a member of the opposite sex. A school village opened in Vittel in France, in order to train 10,000 employees (out of a total of 16,000). The goal was to reconsider relational behaviours, ways of dressing and attitudes. The organisation of the village was also modified. General managers – who used to supervise directly 15 services – were now assisted by two deputies (one in charge of hospitality, the other in charge of leisure).

A transformation in progress

This evolution was still in progress by 2010. Even if customer satisfaction had increased, the occupancy rate had not. Nothing indicated that shareholders would give Giscard d'Estaing enough time to complete Club Med's transformation: the share price plummeted from €54 in August 2007 to €13 in January 2010.

Even if Giscard d'Estaing maintained that his strategy was beginning to bear fruit, in mid-2009 he had had to react to the potential threat of a hostile takeover bid from external investors, who estimated that an upscale repositioning was inconsistent with Club Med's values and business model. An increase in capital dispelled this threat, but analysts were still cautious about the result of such a strategic and cultural turnaround.

Sources: clubmed.net; psychologies.com; *Les Echos*, 10 September 2007, 17 September 2007, 14 December 2009; *Challenges*, 11 December 2009; *Le Monde*, 16 December 2007; ESCP Europe monograph by J. de Florival and C. Hamard, 2007.

> ## Questions
>
> 1 Analyse Club Med's culture before 2000.
> 2 Explain the reasons for Club Med's success between the 1950s and the 1990s.
> 3 How do you explain Club Med's difficulties in the early 1990s?
> 4 Why did Bourguignon's plan fail? Do you think that Giscard d'Estaing's plan will be more successful?

COMMENTARY ON PART I

Part I of the book has discussed some of the main influences that managers in organisations have to take into account in developing the strategies of their organisations. The underlying theme here is that reconciling these different forces is problematic. Not only are there many of them, but also their effects are difficult to predict and they are likely to change, creating potentially high levels of uncertainty. The forces may also be in conflict with one another, or pulling in different directions. Understanding the strategic position of an organisation is therefore challenging for managers. In this Commentary the four strategy lenses introduced in the initial

Design lens

The concepts and analytic tools of strategy can be used to understand the complex and uncertain world managers face in developing strategy. So it makes sense to:

- Undertake rigorous and extensive analysis, drawing largely on principles of economics, to understand environmental forces, strategic capabilities and the power and influence of stakeholders.
- Integrate the insights from such analyses into a clear view of the strategic position of the organisation,
- Thus ensure that top management can take a rational approach to the development of future strategy by considering how the issues identified might be addressed by different strategic options.
- Involve managers in such analysis through systematic strategic planning.

Experience lens

The experience lens focuses attention on trying to understand why people make sense of influences on their organisations the way they do in terms of their individual or collective experience and how this shapes and constrains their responses. It highlights that such experience is *both* useful because it provides short cuts in sense making, and also dangerous because it becomes fixed and biases responses. It suggests that an uncertain future is likely to be understood in terms of past experience that acts as an 'uncertainty reduction mechanism'. It also warns that strategic capabilities (especially core competences) that have driven past success may become embedded in organisational culture, giving rise to strategic drift.

The experience lens suggests that it is important to:

- Understand the cultural influences on the organisations's strategic position.
- Encourage the questioning and challenging of that which is taken for granted.
- Surface the assumptions that managers have because it is likely to be such assumptions that drive strategic decisions.
- Use the frameworks of analysis described in Part I to challenge such taken-for-granted assumptions; e.g. by building scenarios to sensitise managers to possible futures.

THE STRATEGIC POSITION

Commentary are used to reconsider how managers can and do make sense of the strategic position they face. Note that:

- There is no suggestion here that one of these lenses is better than another, but they do provide different insights into the problems faced and the ways managers cope with the challenge.
- If you have *not* read the Commentary following Chapter 1 that explains the four lenses, you should now do so.

Variety lens

The variety lens highlights that new ideas and insights into the strategic position of an organisation are likely to arise by:

- The ambiguity and uncertainty of the future giving rise to different perspectives that can stimulate new ideas from within and around the organisation.
- Such ideas just as likely bubbling up from below as being originated at the top of an organisation.

So, if innovation is important, managers need to learn how to foster and harness the variety of views and ideas in an organisation by:

- Welcoming, being sensitive to and cultivating such variety rather than seeking to foster conformity and uniformity.
- Looking for ideas and views arising from anywhere in the organisation.
- Being wary of seeking to identify *the* strategic position of the organisation such as to foster conformity and a 'right way' of seeing things.

Discourse lens

The strategic position of an organisation is not so much a matter of objective 'fact' as that which is represented and privileged in the discourse of major stakeholders and powerful people, for example a CEO, senior managers, investors or government. What such stakeholders say shows how influential people seek to frame an explanation of the strategic position of an organisation. In this context, three points suggest there is a need to take a critical, even sceptical, view of discourse on strategy:

- Strategy discourse has as much to do with stakeholders (managers included) seeking to influence a situation as it has to do with objective fact. Nonetheless such discourse can have a very real influence on organisations' strategies.
- The concepts and tools associated with strategy can be employed by managers so that they can (a) look as though they have insights that give them a special place with regard to the destiny of the organisation and (b) justify a perspective on strategy that is in their own interest. In this sense strategy discourse is linked to power.
- People get locked into their ways of talking about strategy. It can be difficult to change this. In this sense dominant discourse can contribute to strategic drift.

PART II
STRATEGIC CHOICES

This part explains strategic choices in terms of:

- How organisations relate to competitors in terms of their competitive business strategies.

- How broad and diverse organisations should be in terms of their corporate portfolios.

- How far organisations should extend themselves internationally.

- How organisations are created and innovate.

- How organisations pursue strategies through organic development, acquisitions or strategic alliances.

INTRODUCTION TO PART II

This Part is concerned with the palette of strategic choices, or options, potentially available to an organisation for responding to the positioning issues discussed in Part I of the book. There are three overarching choices to be made as shown in Figure II.i. These are:

- Choices as to *how an organisation at a business level positions itself in relation to competitors*. This is a matter of deciding how to compete in a market. For example, should the business compete on the basis of cost or differentiation? Or is competitive advantage possible through being more flexible and fleet-of-foot than competitors? Or is a more cooperative approach to competitors appropriate? These *business strategy* questions are addressed in Chapter 6.

- Choices of *strategic direction*, in other words, which products, industries and markets to pursue. Should the organisation be very focused on just a few products and markets? Or should it be much broader in scope, perhaps very diversified both in terms of products (or services) and markets? Should it create new products or should it enter new countries? These questions relate to corporate strategy, addressed in Chapter 7, international strategy in Chapter 8 and innovation and entrepreneurial strategy, as discussed in Chapter 9.

- Choices about *methods by which to pursue strategies*. For any of these choices, should they be pursued independently by organic development, by acquisitions or by strategic alliances with other organisations? This is the theme of Chapter 10.

The discussion in these chapters provides frameworks and rationales for a wide range of strategic choices. But some words of warning are important here:

- *Strategic choices relate back to analysis of strategic position.* Part I of the book has provided ways in which strategists can identify forces at work in the business environment (Chapter 2), identify and build on strategic capabilities (Chapter 3), meet stakeholder expectations (Chapter 4) and build on the benefits, as well as be aware of the constraints, of their organisation's historical and cultural context (Chapter 5). Exploring these issues will provide the

Figure II.i Strategic choices

(6.1) INTRODUCTION

This chapter is about a fundamental strategic choice: what strategy should a business unit adopt in its market? Business strategy questions are fundamental both to stand-alone small businesses and to all the many business units that typically make up large diversified corporations. Thus a restaurant business has to decide a range of issues such as menus, décor and prices in the light of competition from other restaurants locally. Similarly, in a large diversified corporation such as Unilever or Nestlé, every business unit must decide how it should operate in its own particular market. For example, Unilever's ice-cream business has to decide how it will compete against Nestlé's ice-cream business on a range of dimensions including product features, pricing, branding and distribution channels. These kinds of *business* strategy issues are distinct from the question as to whether Unilever should own an ice-cream business in the first place: this is a matter of *corporate* strategy, the subject of Chapter 7.

Figure 6.1 shows the main themes that provide the structure for the rest of the chapter. Starting from a definition of *strategic business units (SBUs)*, the chapter has two main themes:

- *Generic competitive strategies*, including *cost leadership*, *differentiation* and *focus*, and considering the *strategy clock*. An important theme here will be how far these strategies are sustainable over time and here *strategic lock-in* is often important.

- *Interactive strategies*, building on the notion of generic strategies to consider interaction with competitors, especially in *hypercompetitive environments*, and including both *cooperative strategies* and *game theory*. Business strategy often involves avoiding counter-productive competition in favour of explicit or tacit cooperation.

Business strategy is not relevant just to the private business sector. Charities and public-sector organisations both cooperate and compete. Thus charities compete between each other for support from donors. Public-sector organisations also need to be 'competitive' against comparable organisations in order to satisfy their stakeholders and secure their funding. Schools compete in terms of examination results, while hospitals compete in terms of waiting times, treatment survival rates and so on. Although some of the detailed implications may vary

Figure 6.1 Business strategy

between sectors, wherever comparison is possible with other similar organisations, basic principles of business strategy are likely to be relevant. Very few organisations can afford to be demonstrably inferior to peers, and almost all have to make choices on key competitive variables such as costs, prices and quality.

(6.2) IDENTIFYING STRATEGIC BUSINESS UNITS

KEY CONCEPT

Strategic business unit (SBU)

The starting point for business strategy is identifying the relevant business unit. A **strategic business unit (SBU) supplies goods or services for a distinct domain of activity**. A small business focused on a single market, such as a restaurant or specialist retailer, would count as a strategic business unit. More commonly, though, SBUs refer to the distinct businesses within a large diversified corporation (sometimes these SBUs are called 'divisions' or 'profit centres'). For example, the Japanese entertainment group Namco Bandai is divided into four SBUS: Toys and Hobby (Power Rangers, Tamagotchi and similar), Game Contents (arcade games and similar), Visual and Music (animation and music publishing) and Amusement (theme parks). Typically within a large diversified corporation, each SBU will have responsibility for its own business strategy. In a large public-sector organisation, such as a local authority, individual schools might be considered too as SBUs, with their domain of activity being education in a geographical area.

Thus the SBU concept has three effects within large organisations. First, SBUs decentralise initiative to smaller units within the corporation as a whole. In Namco Bandai, Toys and Hobby can pursue its business strategy without continuously seeking permission from central headquarters for minor adjustments (see also section 7.6 on the role of the centre). Second, SBUs allow large corporations to vary their business strategies according to the different needs of the various external markets they serve. Namco Bandai does not have to impose the same business strategy (for example, a focus on low prices) across all its SBUs. Finally, the SBU concept encourages accountability. If managers determine the business strategy for their own SBU, then they can be held accountable for the success or failure of that strategy.

Identifying the right boundaries for SBUs is often complex.[1] Distinct markets can be defined at different levels of analysis: for example, Namco Bandai's Toys and Hobbies business could be further segmented by target age-group, distribution channel or geography. In many corporations, SBU boundaries change frequently as well: the computer company Dell is well known for reorganising its SBUs continuously, as market conditions change and units get too big. There are two basic criteria that can help in identifying appropriate SBUs:

- *Market-based criteria.* Different parts of an organisation might be regarded as the same SBU if they are targeting the same *customer types*, through the same sorts of *channels* and facing similar *competitors*. On the other hand, it would usually be sensible to distinguish a unit tailoring products or services to specific local needs from one that offers standardised products or services globally.

- *Capabilities-based criteria.* Parts of an organisation should only be regarded as the same SBU if they have similar strategic capabilities. Many traditional retailers or financial services companies operate their internet services as distinct SBUs. Even though they may be targeting very similar customers, the capabilities involved in the internet-based businesses are typically too different to the original physical stores or outlets to manage within the same unit.

(6.3) GENERIC COMPETITIVE STRATEGIES

This section introduces the competitive element of business strategy, with cooperation addressed particularly in section 6.4. **Competitive strategy is concerned with how a strategic business unit achieves competitive advantage in its domain of activity.** In turn, **competitive advantage is about how an SBU creates value for its users both greater than the costs of supplying them and superior to that of rival SBUs.** There are two important features of competitive advantage here. To be *competitive* at all, the SBU must ensure that users (customers or funders) see sufficient value that they are prepared to pay more than the costs of supply. To have an *advantage*, the SBU must be able to create greater value than competitors. In the absence of a competitive advantage, the SBU is always vulnerable to attack by competitors with better products or services or offering lower prices, and could be driven out of business.

Michael Porter[2] argues that there are two fundamental means of achieving competitive advantage. An SBU can have lower costs than its competitors. Or it can have products or services that are so exceptionally valuable to customers that it can charge higher prices than competitors. In defining competitive strategies, Porter adds a further dimension based on the scope of customers that the business chooses to serve. Businesses can choose to focus on narrow customer segments, for example a particular demographic group such as the youth market. Alternatively they can attempt to target a broad range of customers, across a range of characteristics such as age, wealth or geography.

Porter's distinctions define three 'generic' strategies: in other words, basic types of strategy that hold across many kinds of business situations. These three generic strategies are illustrated in Figure 6.2. In the top left-hand corner is a strategy of *cost leadership*, as exemplified in the British women's clothing market by retailers such as Matalan. Matalan seeks to use large economies of scale and tight cost discipline to serve a wide range of women with reasonably fashionable clothing at a good price. Monsoon's shops pursues a strategy of *differentiation*, offering

Figure 6.2 Three generic strategies

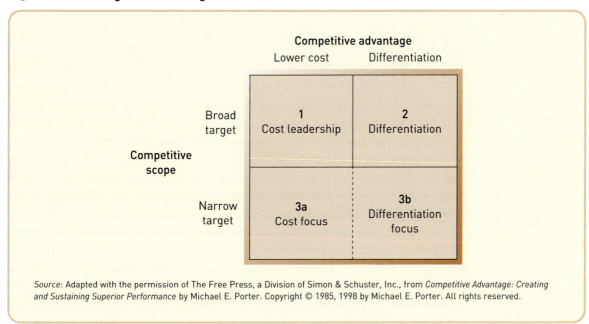

arty styles to women across a range of ages at significantly higher prices. The third generic strategy is *focus*, involving a narrow competitive scope. Porter distinguishes between cost focus and differentiation focus, but for him narrow scope is such a distinctive fundamental principle that these two are merely variations on the same basic theme of narrowness. For example, Evans targets only women needing larger-sized clothing, achieving a higher price for its distinctive products through a *differentiation focus* strategy. On the other hand, the clothing lines of the major supermarkets target shoppers who are simply looking for good-value standard clothing for their families, a *cost focus* strategy. The rest of this section discusses these three generic strategies in more detail.

6.3.1 Cost-leadership

Cost-leadership strategy involves becoming the lowest-cost organisation in a domain of activity. There are four key *cost drivers* that can help deliver cost leadership, as follows:

- *Input costs* are often very important, for example labour or raw materials. Many companies seek competitive advantage through locating their labour-intensive operations in countries with low labour costs. Examples might be service call-centres in India or manufacturing in China. Location close to raw material sources can also be advantageous, as for example the Brazilian steel producer CSN which benefits from its own local iron-ore facilities.

- *Economies of scale* refer to how increasing scale usually reduces the average costs of operation over a particular time period, perhaps a month or a year. Economies of scale are important wherever there are high fixed costs. Fixed costs are those costs necessary for at level of output: for example, a pharmaceutical manufacturer typically needs to do extensive R&D before it produces a single pill. Economies of scale come from spreading these fixed costs over high levels of output: the average cost due to an expensive R&D project halves when output increases from one million to two million units. Economies of scale in purchasing can also reduce input costs. The large airlines, for example, are able to negotiate steep discounts from aircraft manufacturers. For the cost-leader, it is important to reach the output level equivalent to the *minimum efficient scale*. Note, though, that *diseconomies of scale* are possible. Large volumes of output that require special overtime payments to workers or involve the neglect of equipment maintenance can soon become very expensive. As in Figure 6.3, therefore, the economies of scale curve is typically somewhat U-shaped, with the average cost per unit actually increasing beyond a certain point.

- *Experience*[3] can be a key source of cost efficiency. The *experience curve* implies that the cumulative experience gained by an organisation with each unit of output leads to reductions in unit costs (see Figure 6.3). There is no time limit: simply the more experience an organisation has in an activity, the more efficient it gets at doing it. The efficiencies are basically of two sorts. First, there are gains in labour productivity as staff simply learn to do things more cheaply over time (this is the specific *learning curve* effect). Second, costs are saved through more efficient designs or equipment as experience shows what works best. The experience curve has three important implications for business strategy. First, entry timing into a market is important: early entrants into a market will have experience that late entrants do not yet have and so will gain a cost advantage. Second, it is important to gain and hold market share, as companies with higher market share have more 'cumulative experience' simply because of their greater volumes. Finally, although the gains from experience are typically greatest at the start, as indicated by the steep initial curve in

Figure 6.3 Economies of scale and the experience curve

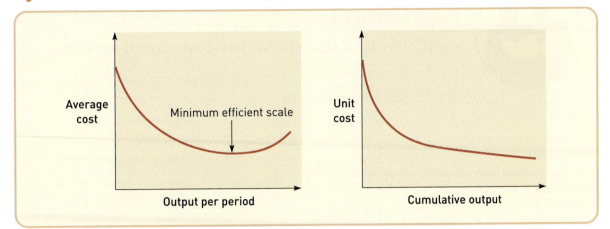

Figure 6.3, improvements normally continue over time. Opportunities for cost reduction are theoretically endless. Figure 6.3 compares the experience curve and economies of scale in order to underline the contrast here. Unlike scale, where diseconomies appear beyond a certain point, the experience curve implies at worst a flattening of the rate of cost reduction. Cost savings due to accumulated experience are continuously available.

- *Product/process design* also influences cost. Efficiency can be 'designed in' at the outset. For example, engineers can choose to build a product from cheap standard components rather than expensive specialised components. Organisations can choose to interact with customers exclusively through cheap web-based methods, rather than via telephone or stores. Organisations can also tailor their offerings in order to meet the most important customer needs, saving money by ignoring others: this, arguably, is the strategy of Barnet, the 'easyCouncil' (Illustration 6.1). In designing a product or service, it is important to recognise *whole-life costs*, in other words, the costs to the customer not just of purchase but of subsequent use and maintenance. In the photocopier market, for example, Canon eroded Xerox's advantage (which was built on service and a support network) by designing a copier that needed far less servicing.

Porter underlines two tough requirements for cost-based strategies. First of all, the principle of competitive advantage indicates that a business's cost structure needs to be *lowest* cost, i.e. lower than all competitors'. Having the second lowest cost structure implies a competitive disadvantage against somebody. Competitors with higher costs than the cost-leader are always at risk of being undercut on price, especially in market downturns. For businesses competing on a cost basis, cost leadership is always more secure than being second or third in terms of costs.

Porter's second requirement is that low cost should not be pursued in total disregard for quality. To sell its products or services, the cost-leader has to be able to meet market standards. For example, low-cost Chinese car producers seeking to export into Western markets not only need to offer cars that are cheap, but cars that meet acceptable norms in terms of style, service network, reliability, resale value and other important characteristics. Cost-leaders have two options here:

- *Parity* (in other words, equivalence) with competitors in product or service features valued by customers. Parity allows the cost-leader to charge the same prices as the average competitor in the marketplace, while translating its cost advantage wholly into extra profit (as

ILLUSTRATION 6.1

easyCouncils: a strategy for low-cost council services

The London Borough of Barnet has chosen a budget airline model for its services, on the lines of easyJet.

In 2008–09, with pressures on budgets increasing, Conservative Party-controlled councils in the United Kingdom were looking to save costs by adopting the low-cost model pioneered by airlines such as Ryanair and easyJet. Barnet, a borough council in North London with a population of over 300,000, is one of the pioneers.

The Conservative borough council is led by a former PwC management consultant, Mike Freer. In a context of falling central government subsidies, and wanting to save local taxes, the council is looking to cut costs by £15m (~€16.5; ~$22.5) a year. In 2008, the council launched a consultation process on radical reform called 'Future Shape'. In 2009, they declared their intention to adopt a budget airline model, which council officials dubbed 'easyCouncil'.

Mike Freer gave some examples. Just as budget airlines allow passengers to pay extra for priority boarding, in future householders will be able to pay extra to jump the queue in order to get faster responses on planning applications for new buildings or house extensions. Similarly, as airline passengers can choose whether to have a meal or not (and pay accordingly), users of adult social care will be allowed to choose their own options. Freer explained to the *Guardian*:

'In the past we would do things for our residents rather than letting them choose for themselves. We would tell them they need one hour help shopping, or one hour cleaning, meals-on-wheels, and they would get it, like it or not. Instead, we will assess what level of personal care they need, place a value on it and give them the budget. If they say, "Frankly, I'd like a weekend in Eastbourne [a holiday resort]", they can have it.'

Opposition Labour leader Alison Moore warned in the *Guardian*:

'There is a real danger of problems in the local community and that vulnerable people will lose out. People who are dependent on care services may find that they aren't there at the same quality as before.'

John Burgess, branch secretary of the main local government services trade union, commented:

'Democratically accountable public services are the best way to ensure quality services and value for money. Comparing public services to gimmicks used by a cheap airline company beggars belief.'

Barnet citizens differed on the new approach. 87-year-old Sarah Walker broke a bone in an accident, forcing her to spend three weeks in hospital. When she returned home, she was initially badly disabled and feared being sent to a local authority care home, from which she would never return. The council's new policy of avoiding expensive care homes and instead offering a burst of intensive help to ease the disabled into independence worked for her:

'I had three carers a day for the first week. One in the morning, one at lunchtime and one in the evening. They gave me the confidence to get back to doing things for myself. At the end of six weeks, I was managing quite well and I'm independent now. It would be a waste of money if they were sending someone once a week for ever more, so this was the right approach for me.'

On the other hand, 68-year-old Bill Kelly compared the Council's logic to electronic tagging in order to save the costs of prison for criminals: 'I can see Mr Freer giving us all ankle tags so they know where we are.'

Sources: R. Booth, 'Tory-Controlled Borough of Barnet adopts budget airline model', *Guardian*, 27 August 2009; J. Burgess, 'The budget airline model won't work for councils', *Guardian*, 2 September 2009.

Questions

1 What are the advantages and disadvantages of this approach to low-cost council services?

2 In what sense do borough councils 'compete'?

Figure 6.4 Costs, prices and profits for generic strategies

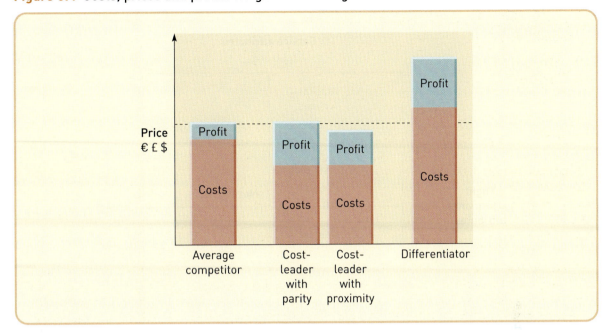

in the second column of Figure 6.4). The Brazilian steel producer CSN, with its cheap iron-ore sources, is able to charge the average price for its steel, and take the cost difference in greater profit.

● *Proximity* (closeness) to competitors in terms of features. Where a competitor is sufficiently close to competitors in terms of product or service features, customers may only require small cuts in prices to compensate for the slightly lower quality. As in the third column in Figure 6.4, the proximate cost-leader still earns better profits than the average competitor because its lower price eats up only a part of its cost advantage. This proximate cost-leadership strategy might be the option chosen initially by Chinese car manufacturers in export markets, for example.

6.3.2 Differentiation strategies

For Porter, the principal alternative to cost-leadership is differentiation.[4] **Differentiation involves uniqueness along some dimension that is sufficiently valued by customers to allow a price premium.** Relevant points of differentiation vary between markets. Within each market too, businesses may differentiate along different dimensions. Thus in clothing retail, competitors may differentiate by store size, locations or fashion. In cars, competitors may differentiate by safety, style or fuel efficiency. Where there are many alternative dimensions that are valued by customers, it is possible to have many different types of differentiation strategy in a market. Thus, even at the same top end of the car market, BMW and Mercedes differentiate in different ways, the first typically with a sportier image, the second with more conservative values. The strategy canvas provides one means of mapping these various kinds of differentiation (see section 2.4.3).

Managers can identify potential for differentiation by using perceptual mapping of their products or services against those of competitors. For example, Figure 6.5 maps customer perceptions of American airline companies along two bundles of attributes: flight performance

Figure 6.5 Mapping differentiation in the US airline industry

Source: Simplified from Figure 1, in D. Gursoy, M. Chen and H. Kim (2005), 'The US airlines relative positioning', *Tourism Management*, 26, 5, 57–67: p. 62.

attributes such as delays, and service attributes such as baggage problems or boarding complaints. Most of the larger airlines are quite closely bunched together. For example, US Air and Delta are not significantly differentiated from each other in terms of on-time flights, and they are perceived similarly in terms of service elements such as boarding, ticketing and reservations. One airline that does stand out as a differentiator is Southwest, which does well in terms of both flight delays and service. In the period studied, Southwest was also the most profitable of these airlines. It seems that Southwest was able to differentiate on attributes that were highly valued by its customers.

However, the attributes on which to differentiate need to be chosen carefully. Differentiation strategies require clarity about two key factors:

● *The strategic customer*. It is vital to identify clearly the strategic customer on whose needs the differentiation is based. This is not always straightforward, as discussed in section 2.4.2. For example, for a newspaper business, the strategic customers could be readers (who pay a purchase price), advertisers (who pay for advertising), or both. Finding a distinctive means of prioritising customers can be a valuable source of differentiation.

● *Key competitors*. It is very easy for a differentiator to draw the boundaries for comparison too tightly, concentrating on a particular niche. Thus specialist Italian clothing company Benetton originally had a strong position with its specialist knitwear shops. However, it lost ground because it did not recognise early enough that general retailers such as Marks & Spencers could also compete in the same product space of colourful pullovers and similar products.

There is an important condition for a successful differentiation strategy. Differentiation allows higher prices, but usually comes at a cost. To create a point of valuable differentiation typically involves additional investments, for example in R&D, branding or staff quality. The differentiator can expect that its costs will be higher than those of the average competitor. But, as in column 4 in Figure 6.4, the differentiator needs to ensure that the additional costs of differentiation do not exceed the gains in price. It is easy to pile on additional costs in ways that are not valued sufficiently by customers. The failures under British ownership of the luxury car companies Rolls-Royce and Bentley against top-end Mercedes cars are partly attributable to the expensive crafting of wood and leather interiors, the full cost of which even wealthy customers were not prepared to pay for. Just as cost-leaders should not neglect quality, so should differentiators attend closely to costs, especially in areas irrelevant to their sources of differentiation. As in Illustration 6.2, Volvo's differentiation strategy in the Indian bus market seems to have involved keeping an eye on costs as well.

6.3.3 Focus strategies

Porter distinguishes focus as the third generic strategy, based on competitive scope. A **focus strategy** targets a narrow segment of domain of activity and tailors its products or services to the needs of that specific segment to the exclusion of others. Focus strategies come in two variants, according to the underlying sources of competitive advantage, cost or differentiation. In air travel, Ryanair follows a *cost-focus strategy*, targeting price-conscious holiday travellers with no need for connecting flights. In the domestic detergent market, the Belgian company Ecover follows a *differentiation focus* strategy, gaining a price premium over rivals on account of its ecological cleaning products.

The focuser achieves competitive advantage by dedicating itself to serving its target segments better than others which are trying to cover a wider range of segments. Serving a broad range of segments can bring disadvantages in terms of coordination, compromise or inflexibility. Focus strategies are able to seek out the weak spots of broad cost-leaders and differentiators:

- *Cost focusers* identify areas where broader cost-based strategies fail because of the added costs of trying to satisfy a wide range of needs. For instance, in the United Kingdom food retail market, Iceland Foods has a cost-focused strategy concentrated on frozen and chilled foods, reducing costs against generalist discount food retailers such as Aldi which have all the complexity of fresh foods and groceries as well as their own frozen and chilled food ranges.

- *Differentiation focusers* look for specific needs that broader differentiators do not serve so well. Focus on one particular need helps to build specialist knowledge and technology, increases commitment to service and can improve brand recognition and customer loyalty. For example, ARM Holdings dominates the world market for mobile phone chips, despite being only a fraction of the size of the leading microprocessor manufacturers, AMD and Intel, which also make chips for a wide range of computers.

Successful focus strategies depend on at least one of three key factors:

- *Distinct segment needs*. Focus strategies depend on the distinctiveness of segment needs. If segment distinctiveness erodes, it becomes harder to defend the segment against broader competitors. For example, now that the boundaries are blurring between smartphones used by general consumers and smartphones used by business people, it has become easier for

ILLUSTRATION 6.2

Volvo's different Indian buses

Volvo has a strategy to sell buses at nearly four times the prevailing market price.

The Indian bus market has long been dominated by two home-players, subsidiaries of major Indian conglomerates: Tata Motors and Ashok Leyland. The two companies made simple coaches on a design that had hardly changed for decades. On top of a basic truck chassis, the two companies bolted a rudimentary coach body. Engines were a meagre 110–120 horse-power, and roared heartily as they hauled their loads up the steep mountain roads of India. Mounted at the front, the heat from the over-strained engines would pervade the whole bus. Air conditioning was a matter of open windows, through which the dust and noise of the Indian roads would pour. Suspension was old-fashioned, guaranteeing a shaky ride on pot-holed roads. Bags were typically slung on the top of the bus, where they were easily soiled and at high risk of theft. But at least the buses were cheap, selling to local bus companies at around Rs 1.2m (€15,000; $21,000).

In 1997, Swedish bus company Volvo decided to enter the market, with buses prices at Rs 4m, nearly four times as much as local products. Akash Passey, Volvo's first Indian employee, commissioned a consultancy company to evaluate prospects. The consultancy company recommended that Volvo should not even try. Passey told the *Financial Times*: 'My response was simple – I took the report and went to the nearest dustbin and threw it in'. Passey entered the market in 2001 with the high-priced luxury buses.

Passey used the time to develop a distinctive strategy. His basic product had superior features. Volvo's standard engines were 240–250 hp and mounted at the back, ensuring a faster and quieter ride. Air conditioning was standard of course. The positioning of the engine and the specific bus design of the chassis meant a more roomy interior, plus storage for bags internally. But Passey realised this would not be enough. He commented to the *Financial Times*: 'You had to do a lot of things to break the way business is done normally'.

Volvo offered post-sale maintenance services, increasing life expectancy of buses from three to ten years, and allowing bus operating companies to dispense with their own expensive maintenance workshops. Free training was given to drivers, so they drove more safely and took more care of their buses. The company advertised the benefits of the buses direct to customers in cinemas, rather than simply promoting them to the bus operators. To kick-start the market, Volvo supplied about 20 subsidised trial units to selected operators. Volvo trainees rode these buses, alerting the company immediately when something went wrong so Volvo could immediately send its engineers. Faster, smoother and more reliable travel allowed the bus operators to increase their ticket prices for the luxury Volvo buses by 35 per cent.

Business people and the middle classes were delighted with the new Volvo services. Speedier, more comfortable journeys allowed them to arrive fresh for meetings and potentially to save the costs of overnight stays. Tata and Ashok Leyland both now produce their own luxury buses, with Mercedes and Isuzu following Volvo into the market. None the less, the phrase 'taking a Volvo' has become synonymous with choosing a luxury bus service in India, rather as 'hoover' came to refer to any kind of vacuum cleaner.

In 2008, Volvo opened a new state-of-the-art bus factory in Bangalore. It is Volvo's most efficient bus factory worldwide, producing a fully-built bus in 20–25 days. Annual capacity is 1000 buses per year.

Source: J. Leahy, 'Volvo takes a lead in India', *Financial Times*, 31 August 2009.

Questions

1 Rank the elements of Passey's strategy for Volvo in order of importance. Could any have been dispensed with?

2 How sustainable is Volvo's luxury bus strategy?

Nokia and Apple to attack the traditional distinctive niche of Research in Motion (RIM) with its BlackBerry business phones.

- *Distinct segment value chains.* Focus strategies are strengthened if they have distinctive value chains that will be difficult or costly for rivals to construct. If the production processes and distribution channels are very similar, it is easy for a broad-based differentiator to push a specialised product through its own standardised value chain at a lower cost than a rival focuser. In detergents, Procter & Gamble cannot easily respond to Ecover because achieving the same ecological friendliness would involve transforming its purchasing and production processes.

- *Viable segment economics.* Segments can easily become too small to serve economically as demand or supply conditions change. For example, changing economies of scale and greater competition have eliminated from many smaller cities the traditional town-centre department stores, with their wider ranges of different kinds of goods from hardware to clothing.

6.3.4 'Stuck in the middle'?

Porter claims that managers face a crucial choice between the generic strategies of cost-leadership, differentiation and focus. According to him, it is unwise to blur this choice. As earlier, the lowest-cost competitor can always undercut the second lowest-cost competitor. For a company seeking advantage through low costs, therefore, it makes no sense to add extra costs by half-hearted efforts at differentiation. For a differentiator, it is self-defeating to make economies that jeopardise the basis for differentiation. For a focuser, it is dangerous to move outside the original specialised segment, because products or services tailored to one set of customers are likely to have inappropriate costs or features for the new target customers. This was a risk for RIM as it moved its BlackBerry business phones into the broader consumer market, for whom e-mail encryption was not so important. Porter's argument is that managers are generally best to choose which generic strategy they are pursuing and then stick rigorously to it. Otherwise there is a danger of being *stuck in the middle*, doing no strategy well.

Porter's warning about the danger of being stuck in the middle provides a useful discipline for managers. It is very easy for them to make incremental decisions that compromise the basic generic strategy. As profits accumulate, the successful cost-leader will be tempted to stop scrimping and saving. In hard times, a differentiator might easily cut back the R&D or advertising investments essential to its long-term differentiation advantage. Consistency with generic strategy provides a valuable check for managerial decision-making.

However, Porter's argument for pure generic strategies is controversial.[5] He himself acknowledges there are circumstances in which the strategies can be combined:[6]

- *Organisational separation.* It is possible for a company to create separate strategic business units each pursuing different generic strategies and with different cost structures. The challenge, however, is to prevent negative spill-overs from one SBU to another. For example, a company mostly pursuing differentiated strategies is liable to have high head-office costs that the low-cost SBUs will also have to bear. On the other hand, a cheap cost-leader might damage the brand-value of a sister SBU seeking differentiation. As illustrated by the failures of British Airways with its low-cost subsidiary Go, and Delta with its low-cost Song airline, in practice it can be very difficult to pursue different generic strategies within a single set of related businesses.

- *Technological or managerial innovation.* Sometimes technological innovations allow radical improvements in both cost and quality. Internet retailing reduces the costs of book-selling, at the same time as increasing product stock and, through online book reviews, improving advice. Managerial innovations are capable of such simultaneous improvements too. The Japanese car manufacturers' introduction of Total Quality Management led to reductions in production-line mistakes that both cut manufacturing costs and improved car reliability, a point of successful differentiation.

- *Competitive failures.* Where competitors are also stuck in the middle, there is less competitive pressure to remove competitive disadvantage. Equally, where a company dominates a particular market, competitive pressures for consistency with a single competitive strategy are reduced.

6.3.5 The Strategy Clock

The **Strategy Clock** provides another way of approaching the generic strategies (see Figure 6.6).[7] The Strategy Clock has two distinctive features. First, it is more market-focused than the generic strategies, being focused on prices to customers rather than costs to the organisation. Second, the circular design of the clock allows for more continuous choices than Michael Porter's sharp contrast between cost-leadership and differentiation: there is a full range of incremental adjustments that can be made between the 7 o'clock position at the bottom of the low-price strategy and the 2 o'clock position at the bottom of the differentiation

Figure 6.6 The Strategy Clock

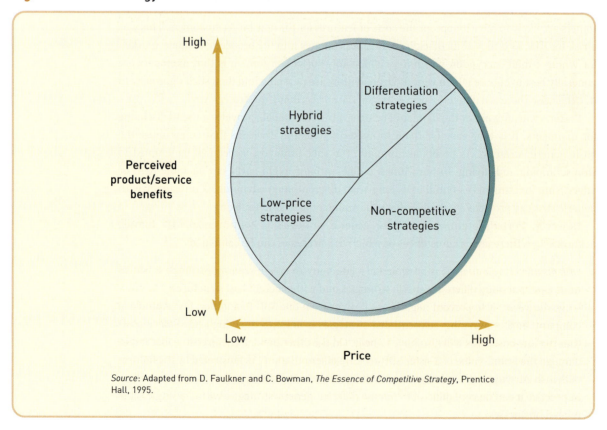

Source: Adapted from D. Faulkner and C. Bowman, *The Essence of Competitive Strategy*, Prentice Hall, 1995.

strategy. Organisations often travel around the clock, as they adjust their pricing and benefits over time.

The Strategy Clock identifies three zones of feasible strategies, and one zone likely to lead to ultimate failure:

● *The differentiation zone.* This zone contains a range of feasible strategies for building on high perceptions of product or service benefits amongst customers. Close to the 12 o'clock position is a strategy of *differentiation without price premium*. Differentiation without a price premium combines high perceived benefits and moderate prices, typically used to gain market share. If high benefits also entail relatively high costs, this moderate pricing strategy would only be sustainable in the short term. Once increased market share had been achieved, it might be logical to move to *differentiation with price premium* closer to a 1 or 2 o'clock position. Movement all the way towards the 2 o'clock position is likely to involve a focus strategy, in Michael Porter's terms. Such a *focused differentiation* strategy targets a niche where the higher prices and reduced benefits are sustainable, for instance because of a lack of competition in a particular geographical area.

● *The low-price zone.* This zone allows for different combinations of low prices and low perceived value. Close to the 9 o'clock position, a standard *low price* strategy would gain market share, by combining low prices with reasonable value (at parity with competitors). Again, if reasonable benefits are associated with higher costs, this position is unlikely to be sustainable for long. Either cuts in benefits or increases in prices would be desirable over time. A variation on the standard low price strategy is the *no frills* strategy, close to the 7 o'clock position. No frills strategies involve both low benefits and low prices, similar to low-cost airlines such as Ryanair (which even proposed to charge for use of its on-board toilets).

● *The hybrid strategy zone.* A distinctive feature of the Strategy Clock are the possibilities it allows between low-price and differentiation strategies.[8] Hybrid strategies involve both lower prices than differentiation strategies, and higher benefits than low-price strategies. Hybrid strategies are often used to make aggressive bids for increased market-share. They can also be an effective way of entering a new market, for instance overseas. Even in the case of innovations with high benefits, it can make sense to price low initially in order to gain experience curve efficiencies or lock-in through network effects (see section 6.3.6). Some companies sustain hybrid strategies over long periods of time: for example, furniture store IKEA, which uses scale advantages to combine relatively low prices with differentiated Swedish design.

● *Non-competitive strategies.* The final set of strategies occupy a zone of infeasible economics, with low benefits and high prices. Unless businesses have exceptional strategic lock-in, customers will quickly reject these combinations. Typically these strategies lead to failure.

The Strategy Clock's focus on price, and its scope for incremental adjustments in strategy, provide a more dynamic view on strategy than Porter's generic strategies. Instead of organisations being fairly fixed in terms of either a cost or a differentiation strategy, they can move around the clock. For example, an organisation might start with a *low price* strategy to gain market-share, later shift to a higher-priced *differentiation with premium* strategy in order to reap profits, and then move back to a *hybrid strategy* in order to defend itself from new entrants. However, Porter's generic strategies do remind managers that costs are critical. Unless an organisation has some secure cost advantage (such as economies of scale), a hybrid strategy of high perceived benefits and low prices is unlikely to be sustainable for long.

6.3.6 Lock-in and sustainable business strategies

Business strategies should ideally be sustainable over time. This may involve having competitive advantages that rivals cannot match. Thus, as in section 3.3, strategies are more likely to be sustained if underpinned by capabilities that combine all the VRIN characteristics of value, rarity, inimitability and non-substitutability. Another approach to sustaining business strategies is creating 'lock-in'.

Strategic lock-in is where users become dependent on a supplier and are unable to use another supplier without substantial switching costs.[9] Strategic lock-in is related to the concept of path dependency (see section 5.3.1) and essentially extends the principles of inimitability and non-substitutability. Under conditions of lock-in, imitators and substitutes are unable to attract customers. This is particularly valuable to differentiators. With customers securely locked in, it becomes possible to keep prices well above costs.

Lock-in can be achieved in two main ways:

- *Controlling complementary products or services.* Opportunities for lock-in to a particular product or service arise where other products or services are necessary for customers using it. This is often known as the 'razor and blade' strategy: once a customer has bought a particular kind of razor, they are obliged to buy compatible blades to use it. Apple originally applied a similar strategy when it used Digital Rights Management to ensure that music bought on its iTunes store could only be played on its own iPod players. To switch to a Sony player would mean losing access to all the iTunes music previously purchased.

- *Creating a proprietary industry standard.* Sometimes companies are so successful that they create an industry standard under their own control. Similar to the razor-and-blade effect, as customers invest in training and systems using that standard, it becomes more expensive to switch to another product or service. However, with industry standards, *network effects* also operate: as other members of the network also adopt the same standard, it becomes even more valuable to stay within it. Microsoft built this kind of proprietary standard with its Windows operating system, which holds more than 90 per cent of the market. For a business to switch to another operating system would mean retraining staff and translating files onto the new system, while perhaps creating communications problems with network members (such as customers or suppliers) who had stuck with Windows.

⓺․⓸ INTERACTIVE STRATEGIES

Generic strategies need to be chosen, and adjusted, in the light of competitors' strategies. If everybody else is chasing after cost leadership, then a differentiation strategy might be sensible. Thus business strategy choices *interact* with those of competitors. This section starts by considering business strategy in the light of competitor moves, especially in hypercompetition. It then addresses the option of cooperation and closes with game theory, which helps managers choose between competition and more cooperative strategies.

6.4.1 Interactive price and quality strategies

Richard D'Aveni depicts competitor interactions in terms of movements against the variables of price (the vertical axis) and perceived quality (the horizontal axis), similar to the Strategy Clock: see Figure 6.7.[10] Although D'Aveni applies his analysis to the very fast-moving environments

Figure 6.7 Interactive price and quality strategies

(i) Differentiator (D) improves quality

(ii) Mid-point business (M) counter-attacks on price

NB axes are not necessarily to linear scales.

Source: Adapted with the permission of The Free Press, a Division of Simon & Schuster, Inc., from *Hypercompetition: Managing the Dynamics of Strategic Manoeuvring* by Richard D'Aveni with Robert Gunther. Copyright © 1994 by Richard D'Aveni. All rights reserved.

he terms 'hypercompetitive' (see section 2.3.1), similar reasoning applies wherever competitors' moves are interdependent.

Figure 6.7 shows different organisations competing by emphasising either low prices or high quality or some mixture of the two. Graph i. starts with a 'first value line', describing various trade-offs in terms of price and perceived quality that are acceptable to customers. The cost-leading firm (here L) offers relatively poor perceived quality, but customers accept this because of the lower price. While the relative positions on the graph should not be taken exactly literally, in the car market this cost-leading position might describe some of Hyundai's products. The differentiator (D) has a higher price, but much better quality. This might be Mercedes. In between, there are a range of perfectly acceptable combinations, with the mid-point firm (M) offering a combination of reasonable prices and reasonable quality. This might be Ford. M's strategy is on the first value line and therefore entirely viable at this stage. On the other hand, firm U is uncompetitive, falling behind the value line. Its price is higher than M's, and its quality is worse. U's predicament is typical of the business that is 'stuck in the middle', in Porter's terms. U no longer offers acceptable value and must quickly move back onto the value line or fail.

In any market, competitors and their moves or counter-moves can be plotted against these two axes of price and perceived value. For example, in graph i of Figure 6.7, the differentiator (D) makes an aggressive move by substantially improving its perceived quality while holding its prices. This improvement in quality shifts customer expectations of quality right across the market. These changed expectations are reflected by the new, second value line (in green). With the second value line, even the cost-leader (L) may have to make some improvement to quality, or accept a small price cut. But the greatest threat is for the mid-point competitor, M. To catch up with the second value line, M must respond either by making a substantial improvement in quality while holding prices, or by slashing prices, or by some combination of the two.

However, mid-point competitor M also has the option of an aggressive counter-attack. Given the necessary capabilities, M might choose to push the value line still further outwards, wrong-footing differentiator D by creating a third value line that is even more demanding in terms of the price-perceived quality trade-off. The starting point in graph ii. of Figure 6.7 is all three competitors

L, M and D successfully reaching the second value line (uncompetitive U has disappeared). However, M's next move is to go beyond the second value line by making radical cuts in price while sustaining its new level of perceived quality. Again, customer expectations are changed and a third value line (in red) is established. Now it is differentiator D that is at most risk of being left behind, and it faces hard choices about how to respond in terms of price and quality.

Plotting moves and counter-moves in these terms underlines the dynamic and interactive nature of business strategy. Economically viable positions along the value line are always in danger of being superseded as competitors move either downwards in terms of price or outwards in terms of perceived quality. The generic strategies of cost-leadership and differentiation should not be seen as static positions, but as dynamic trajectories along the axes of price and quality. The movement towards more 'local' Starbucks stores demonstrates the need to be continually moving along the trajectory of differentiation (see Illustration 6.3).

A more detailed example of the sequence of decisions and possible options involved in competitive interaction is given in Figure 6.8.[11] This illustrates the situation of a business facing a

Figure 6.8 Responding to low-cost rivals

ILLUSTRATION 6.3

McCafés challenge Starbucks

Starbucks coffee chain is having to change its strategy in response to McDonald's.

In 2009, Starbucks was in trouble. With 16,000 outlets and operating in 49 countries, Starbucks was the world's largest coffee chain. But economic recession was taking its toll, with 2009 sales 5 per cent down on the previous year's. And fast-food chain McDonald's was pushing hard its cheap coffee concept, McCafés.

The McCafé concept had emerged in Australia in the 1990s. McCafés typically operate within or next to regular McDonald's outlets. They use high-quality coffee machines and sell different blends of coffee according to the tastes of local markets. The coffee is priced substantially lower than Starbucks' traditional prices. By 2009, nearly half of Germany's 1200 McDonald's restaurants operated a McCafé, and McCafés were spreading rapidly across Europe. The target was 1200 McCafés in Europe by the end of 2009, against Starbucks' 1300.

Starbucks' response to recession and competition was vigorous. Company founder and CEO Howard Schultz proclaimed:

> 'We are laser-focused on delivering the finest quality coffee and getting the customer experience right every time. We have . . . been putting our feet into the shoes of our customers and are responding directly to their needs. Our customers are telling us they want value and quality and we will deliver that in a way that is meaningful to them and authentic to Starbucks.'

The company announced a $500m ($700m) cost reduction programme, with investments in operational efficiencies and new technologies. Starbucks also entered the $17bn instant coffee market, launching its Starbucks Via™ Ready Brew coffee head-to-head against brands such as Nestlé and Maxwell House. In particular, it began to transform the format of its stores.

Traditionally, all Starbucks stores have been designed on the basis of a standard palette of colours and furniture, worldwide. Now, in Seattle – the very city where Starbucks had originally started – the company opened a new store without any of the usual branding. Named '15th Ave. Coffee and Tea', the new store was based on close study of local independent coffee stores. One local store-owner complained about Starbucks'

researchers: 'They spent the last 12 months in our store up on 15th [Avenue] with these obnoxious folders that said "Observation" '. The 15th Ave. Coffee and Tea store is a radical departure. Starbucks' logo is completely absent, and wine and beer are available. Table tops come from a landscaper's stone yard and the shop uses discarded theatre seats. Evenings offer live music and poetry readings.

In the United Kingdom, Starbucks' largest European market, the same thinking is being applied. Facing competition from companies like Costa Coffee, McDonald's and Wetherspoons, Darcy Willson-Rymer, Starbucks' local managing director, commented to the *Independent*: 'What we did was set the standard, then we allowed people to catch us up'. The UK's Starbucks chain is abandoning the old identikit format. Local artefacts, bolder colours, bigger community noticeboards and even second-hand furniture will all be used to create more individual stores. Carrot sticks and porridge are joining the usual high-calorie cakes and paninis. Willson-Rymer explained: 'In every store, there will be something that is locally relevant. The thing that needs to be the same in every store is the latte, the cappuccino, the product and the culture of coffee tastings and the knowledge.' He commented on past mistakes thus: 'The business is run 80 per cent heart and 20 per cent head, and we tried to flip it on its head. I don't know what the right proportion is, but I believe that the heart is back in the company.'

Sources: 'Starbucks tests new names for stores', *Seattle Times*, 16 July 2009; 'Starbuck chief admits: our shops are all wrong', *Independent*, 18 September 2009; 'McDonald's set to mug Starbucks in Europe', *Financial Times*, 26 May 2009.

Questions

1 Plot the moves of McDonald's and Starbucks on the axes of price and perceived quality, as in Figure 6.7.

2 What should be the response of a company with a similar original position as Starbucks (for example, Costa Coffee in the UK)?

low-price competitor, for example a high-cost Western manufacturer facing possible attack by cheap imports from Asia. There are three key decisions:

● *Threat assessment*. The first decision point is whether the threat is substantial or not. If there is a threat, the high-cost organisation should not automatically respond to a low-price competitor by trying to match prices: it is likely to lose a price war with its existing cost structure. The high-cost organisation needs a more sophisticated response.

● *Differentiation response*. If there are enough consumers who value them, the high-cost organisation can seek out new points of differentiation. For example, a Western manufacturer may exploit its closeness to local markets by improving service levels. At the same time, unnecessary costs should be stripped out. If increased differentiation is not possible, then more radical cost solutions should be sought.

● *Cost response*. Merger with other high-cost organisations may help reduce costs and match prices through economies of scale. If a low-cost business is synergistic with (in other words, has benefits for) the existing business, this can be an effective platform for an aggressive cost-based counter-attack. If there is neither scope for further differentiation nor synergy between the existing business and a possible new low-cost business, then the existing business must sooner or later be abandoned. For a Western manufacturer, one option might be to outsource all production to low-cost operators, simply applying its design and branding expertise. Another option would be to abandon manufacturing in favour of becoming a 'solutions provider', aggregating manufactured components from different suppliers and adding value through whole-systems design, consultantcy or service.

Equivalent decisions would have to be made, of course, by a low-price competitor facing a differentiator. When Apple entered the phone market with its expensive touchscreen iPhone, established handset manufacturers had first to decide whether Apple was a serious long-term threat, and then choose how far they should either match the iPhone's features or increase the price differential between their products and Apple's expensive ones.

6.4.2 Interactive strategies in hypercompetition

According to Richard D'Aveni, the kinds of move and counter-move outlined in the preceding section are a constant feature of hypercompetitive environments. As in section 2.3.1, hypercompetition describes markets with continuous disequilibrium and change, for example popular music or consumer electronics. In these conditions, it may no longer be possible to plan for sustainable positions of competitive advantage. Indeed, planning for long-term sustainability may actually destroy competitive advantage by slowing down response. Managers have to be able to act faster than their competitors.

Successful competitive interaction in hypercompetition demands speed and initiative rather than defensiveness. Richard D'Aveni highlights four key principles:

● *Cannibalise bases of success*: sustaining old advantages distracts from developing new advantages. An organisation has to be willing to cannibalise the basis of its own success.

● *Series of small moves rather than big moves*: smaller moves create more flexibility and give a series of temporary advantages. At the same time, smaller moves make it harder for competitors to detect and counter the overall strategic direction.

● *Be unpredictable*. If competitors can see a pattern they can predict the next competitive moves and quickly learn how to imitate or outflank an organisation. So surprise, unpredictability, even apparent irrationality can be important. Managers must learn ways of appearing to be unpredictable to the external world whilst, internally, thinking strategies through.

- *Mislead the competition.* Drawing on the lessons of game theory (see section 6.4.4), the organisation might signal particular moves, but then do something else (for example, talk about alliances, and then make an acquisition). Or the organisation might disguise initial success in a market, until ready to respond to competitor retaliation.[12]

6.4.3 Cooperative strategy

So far the emphasis has been on competition and competitive advantage. However, the competitive moves and counter-moves in section 6.4.1 make it clear that sometimes competition can escalate in a way that is dangerous to all competitors. It can be in the self-interest of organisations to restrain competition. Moreover, advantage may not always be achieved just by competing. Collaboration between some organisations in a market may give them advantage over other competitors in the same market, or potential new entrants. Collaboration can be explicit in terms of formal agreements to cooperate, or tacit in terms of informal mutual understandings between organisations. In short, business strategy has to include cooperative options as well as competitive ones.[13]

Figure 6.9 illustrates various kinds of benefits from cooperation between firms in terms of Michael Porter's five forces of buyers, suppliers, rivals, entrants and substitutes (section 2.3.1). Key benefits of cooperation are as follows:

- *Suppliers.* In Figure 6.9, cooperation between rivals A and B in an industry will increase their purchasing power against suppliers. Moreover, cooperation between rivals A and B may enable them to standardise requirements, enabling suppliers to make cost reductions to all parties' benefit. For example, two car manufacturers might agree on common component specifications, allowing their supplier to gain economies through production of the standardised part on a greater scale.

- *Buyers.* Conversely, cooperation between rivals A and B will increase their power as suppliers vis-à-vis buyers. It will be harder for buyers to shop around. Such *collusion* between rivals can help maintain or raise prices, as for example in the South African airline industry (see Illustration 6.4). On the other hand, buyers may benefit if their inputs are standardised, again enabling reductions in costs that all can share. For example, if food manufacturers supplying a retailer agree on common pallet sizes for deliveries, the retailer can manage its warehouses much more efficiently.

- *Rivals.* If cooperative rivals A and B are getting benefits with regard to both buyers and suppliers, other competitors without such agreements – in Figure 6.9, rival C – will be at a competitive disadvantage. Rival C will be in danger of being squeezed out of the industry.

- *Entrants.* Similarly, potential entrants will likely lack the advantages of the combined rivals A and B. Moreover, A and B can coordinate their retaliation strategies against any new entrant, for example by cutting prices by the same proportions in order to protect their own relative positions while undermining the competitiveness of the new entrant.

- *Substitutes.* Finally, the improved costs or efficiencies that come from cooperation between rivals A and B reduces the incentives for buyers to look to substitutes. Steel companies have cooperated on research to reduce the weight of steel used in cars, in order to discourage car manufacturers from switching to lighter substitutes such as aluminium or plastics.

Further kinds of cooperation will be considered under alliance strategy in section 10.4.

ILLUSTRATION 6.4

Cup-winners: competition and collusion in South Africa

Were South Africa's airlines cooperating to take advantage of the 2010 World Cup?

The 2010 Football World Cup was a great opportunity to put South Africa on the world tourism map. Up to three million international visitors were expected to visit the country during the month of June, many of whom might be encouraged to come back in the future. It was of course also a great opportunity for South African business. But in February 2010, the major domestic airlines were accused of exploiting the surge of demand by trying to fix prices together.

Domestic airline travel between matches would be important, as the World Cup involves 10 stadiums scattered around a large country. From Cape Town to Johannesburg is 880 miles, or 17 hours of hard driving. There are 2000 domestic flights a day.

The dominant player in both the domestic and international market is South African Airways (SAA), the national flag-carrier. Another major domestic player is Comair, which is part owned by British Airways, operator of many services between South Africa and Europe. However, many new airlines have entered the market in recent years. Significant low-cost airlines in South Africa are SA Express (founded 1994), SA Airlink (founded 1996), Kulula (founded 2001 by Comair), 1Time (founded 2004) and Mango (founded 2006). SA Airlink, SA Express and SAA had been part of a strategic alliance until 2006. Competition is a challenge for airlines: a half-full flight costs nearly as much as a full one, but of course earns half the money. It is not surprising then that SAA has made persistent losses in recent years.

The accusation of price-fixing had come in December 2009 from SAA itself, when the company offered cooperation with the competition authority in return for leniency. The accusation centred on a November e-mail sent by Comair's chief executive Erik Venter to SAA, 1Time, SA Airlink, Mango and SA Express regarding pricing strategy during the World Cup. The e-mail said: 'airlines have the option to either not provide any inventory [seats] for sale until such time [as they knew where matches would be played and when] or price all inventory at peak-time rates until such time as they have greater certainty'.

The *Sunday Times* reported the head of the competition authority as saying of Comair: 'they have set out a methodology to influence the pricing outcome'. CEO Venter riposted that the e-mail

'reflected textbook airline pricing principles that any commercial airline would implement, based on supply and demand and cost recovery . . . The email clearly states that Comair expects airline prices to fall once the airlines have implemented their extra capacity for the World Cup, and that the pricing is anticipated to average out at the level experienced over a typical South African peak holiday season.'

SAA and the other airlines had some history with regard to price-fixing. For example, in 2006, SAA, Kulula, SA Express and SA Airlink had been fined for agreeing a simultaneous standard increase in fuel surcharges. SAA had also been accused of offering travel agents inducements to recommend its flights to customers even when they knew cheaper flights were available. One low-cost competitor, Nationwide, had allegedly been driven out of business by this practice. The *Guardian* reported the England Football Supporters' Federation as warning:

'England's regular travellers are having to take a long and sober look at the costs involved in following the team. It would be a mistake for South Africa to regard the World Cup as a four-week opportunity to rip off fans.'

Sources: 'Airlines Investigated for Price-Fixing during World Cup', *Guardian*, 30 January 2010; 'Probes into Airlines to Proceed', *Sunday Times*, 31 January 2010; 'South African body probes claims of over-pricing', *BBC*, 15 February 2010.

Questions

1 What would be the advantages *and* the disadvantages of raising prices artificially during the World Cup?

2 Suggest three reasons why it may make sense that SAA raised the price-fixing accusation, rather than any other airline.

Figure 6.9 Cooperating with rivals

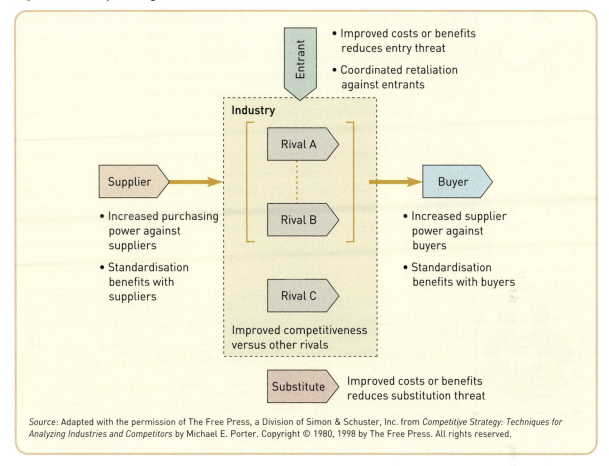

6.4.4 Game theory

Game theory provides important insights into competitor interaction.[14] The 'game' refers to the kinds of interactive moves two players make in a game of chess. **Game theory encourages an organisation to consider competitors' likely moves and the implications of these moves for its own strategy**. Game theorists are alert to two kinds of interaction in particular. First, game theorists consider how a *competitor response* to a strategic move might change the original assumptions behind that move: for example, challenging a competitor in one area might lead to a counter-attack in another. Second, game theorists are sensitive to the *strategic signals*, or messages, their moves might convey to competitors, for example with regard to how fiercely they seem willing to defend their position in a particular market. In the light of possible attacks and counter-attacks, game theorists often advise a more cooperative approach than head-to-head competition.

Game theory is particularly relevant where competitors are *interdependent*. Interdependence exists where the outcome of choices made by one competitor is dependent on the choices made by other competitors. For example, the success of price cuts by a retailer depends on the responses of its rivals: if rivals do not match the price cuts, then the price-cutter gains market-share; but if rivals follow the price cuts, nobody gains market-share and all players suffer from the lower prices. Anticipating competitor counter-moves is clearly vital to deciding whether to go forward with the price-cutting strategy.

There are two important guiding principles that arise from interdependence:

- *Get in the mind of the competitors.* Strategists need to put themselves in the position of competitors, take a view about what competitors are likely to do and choose their own strategy in this light. They need to understand their competitors' game-plan to plan their own.

- *Think forwards and reason backwards.* Strategists should choose their competitive moves on the basis of understanding the likely responses of competitors. Think forwards to what competitors might do in the future, and then reason backwards to what would be sensible to do in the light of this now.

Illustration 6.5 shows how these two principles can lead to exactly the opposite strategy to what would be chosen without regard for competitors.

The principles of getting in the mind of competitors and thinking forwards and reasoning backwards are also demonstrated by one of the most famous illustrations of game theory reasoning: the *prisoner's dilemma*. Game theorists identify many situations where organisations' strategic decisions are similar to the dilemma of two prisoners accused of serial crimes together

ILLUSTRATION 6.5

Innova and Dolla play a sequential game

Many competitive situations are 'sequential', where outcomes depend on the sequence of moves and counter-moves. In these situations, thinking forwards and reasoning backwards is crucial.

Innova and Dolla, competitors in the market for games consoles, face a decision on investment in research and development. Innova has highly innovative designers but is short of the finance required to invest heavily in rapid development of products. Dolla is strong financially but relatively weak in terms of its research and development. Thinking forwards then reasoning backwards can help Innova determine its move and when to make it.

The two companies know that high investment in R&D would shorten the development time, but they are also concerned about costs. Indeed, high levels of investment by both is the worst outcome. The expected pay-off is low for Innova because raising finance will be expensive for it; the expected pay-off is low for Dolla because, with equal investment, Innova has better chances of winning given its design capabilities.

Being short of funds, Innova particularly wants to keep its investment low. If Dolla were to invest low as well, Innova would expect a better pay-off because of its innovative capabilities. But Dolla knows that if it

goes for a low level of investment, it has no advantage over Innova's superior innovative capabilities. The likelihood therefore is that Dolla will counter Innova's low investment strategy with high investment.

Innova's situation can be seen as a series of sequential decisions, as in Figure 1. If Innova decides to invest low, it knows that Dolla is likely to respond high and gain the advantage simply by outspending its rival (pay-off C is 2:4). However, if Innova moves first and invests high, it places Dolla in a difficult position. If Dolla also invests high, it ends up with a low pay-off, as does Innova (pay-off A is just 1:1): they both have high expenses. In these circumstances, Dolla might well reject that strategy and economise by investing low. The resultant pay-off B (3:2) is better than pay-off A (1:1) for both parties, but particularly for Innova.

Working through these different game logics, Innova should realise that, despite its shortage of finance, it does not necessarily make sense to invest low. If it moves first and invests high, Dolla's own self-interest in responding low gives Innova both the and being interrogated in separate prison cells without the possibility of communicating with each other. The prisoners have to decide on the relative merits of: (i) loyally supporting each other by refusing to divulge any information to their interrogators; and (ii), seeking an advantage by betraying the other. If both stay silent, they might get away with most of their crimes and only suffer some lesser punishment, perhaps on just one or two offences. The interrogators, though, will tempt each of them to divulge full information by offering them their freedom if only they betray their fellow criminal. However, if both betray, then the judge is unlikely to be grateful for the confessions, and will punish them for all their crimes. The dilemma for each of the prisoners is how much to trust in their mutual loyalty: if they both refuse the temptation to divulge, they can both get away with the lesser punishment; on the other hand, if one is sure that the other will not betray, it makes even more sense to betray the loyal one as that allows the betrayer to go totally free. The two prisoners are clearly interdependent. But because they cannot communicate, they each have to get in the mind of the other, think forwards to what they might do, and then reason backwards in order to decide what their own strategy should be – stay silent or betray.

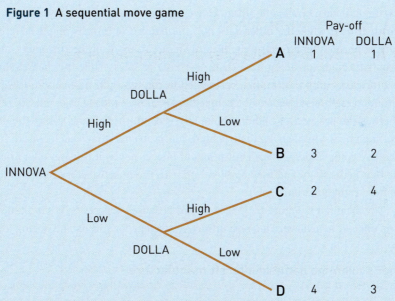

Figure 1 A sequential move game

Source: From *Thinking Strategically: The Competitive Edge in Business, Politics and Everyday Life* by Avinash K. Dixit and Barry J. Nalebuff. Copyright © 1991 by Avinash K. Dixit and Barry J. Natebuff. Used by permission of W.W. Norton & Company, Inc.

advantage of higher investment and that of superior designers. Of course, if there is some way of Innova signalling a decision to invest high whilst actually investing low, thus persuading Dolla to invest low too, then Innova achieves its most attractive outcome (pay-off D).

Question

Given the clear incentive to Innova to move first with a high investment strategy, what should Dolla do and what might be the sequence of decisions and pattern of outcomes then?

The prisoner's dilemma has its equivalence in business where there are two major players competing head-to-head against each other in a situation of tight interdependence. This is the position of Airbus and Boeing in the aircraft business, Sony and Microsoft in the games market, or British Airways and Virgin in transatlantic travel. It would be relevant to the strategic decisions of two such interdependent companies in a range of situations: for example, if one company was thinking about making a major investment in an innovative new product that the other company could match; if one company was pondering an attack on the home market of the other company; or if the two companies were contemplating making competing takeover bids for a third company. For two such competitors to communicate directly about their strategies in these situations would likely be judged illegal by the competition authorities. They therefore have to get into each other's minds, think forwards and reason backwards. How will the other company act or react, and in the light of that, what strategy is best?

The kind of situation two interdependent competitors could get into is represented in the prisoner's dilemma matrix of Figure 6.10. Suppose the two main aircraft manufacturers Airbus and Boeing were both under pricing pressure, perhaps because of falling demand. They each have to decide whether to announce radical price cuts or to hold their prices up. If both choose to hold their prices, neither gets an advantage over the other and they both get the returns represented in the top left-hand quadrant of Figure 6.10: for the sake of illustration, each might earn profits of €500m. However, if one competitor pursues the radical price cuts on their own while the other does not, the pattern of returns might be quite different: the radical price-cutter attracts a significantly larger share of airline customers and earns €700m profits through spreading fixed costs over greater sales, while the market-share-losing competitor earns only €100m (as represented in the top-right and bottom-left quadrants). This situation might tempt one of the competitors to choose radical price cuts for two reasons: first, there is the prospect of higher profits; but, second, there is the risk of the other competitor cutting prices while leaving them behind. The problem is that if each reasons in the same way, the two competitors will *both* cut prices at once. They will thus set off a price war in which neither gains share and they both end up with the unsatisfactory return of just €300m (the bottom-right quadrant).

The dilemma in Figure 6.10 is awkward because cooperation is simultaneously attractive and difficult to achieve. The most attractive strategy for Airbus and Boeing jointly is for them

Figure 6.10 Prisoner's dilemma game in aircraft manufacture

Hypothetical data constructed for illustration purposes only

both to hold their prices, yet in practice they are likely to cut prices because they must expect the other to do so anyway. A distinctive feature of game theory is that it frequently highlights the value of a more cooperative approach to competitor interaction, rather than aggressive competition. The cooperation need not be in the form of an explicit agreement: cooperation can be tacit, supported by the recognition of mutual self-interest in not attacking each other head-to-head. Game theory therefore encourages managers to consider how a 'game' can be transformed from lose–lose competition to win–win cooperation. There are four principles that can help here:

- *Ensure repetition*. The prisoner's dilemma above assumes just one interaction. The thinking forwards is quite limited. In many circumstances, though, it is easier to achieve tacit co-operation if the two players know that they will be making similar interdependent decisions over time. Ensuring repetition makes cooperation much more likely. In a repetitive game, starting with a cooperative approach, and only making more aggressive moves in *response* to the aggression of the other player, has been shown generally to help players maintain a mutually satisfactory position of tacit cooperation. In this approach, both Airbus and Boeing would start by holding their prices; if one cut its prices, the other would simply cut its prices for one period, hoping that the first would move back to the higher price-level; if the first company did move back to the higher prices, the second would follow. The idea is that in repeated interactions over time, players can learn from each other's moves and counter-moves the benefits of cooperation.

- *Signalling*. Another insight from game theory is that strategic moves are also signals to competitors. Strategists need to be aware of the messages that their moves convey and read the messages of their competitors' moves. If Airbus failed to punish a price cut of Boeing with its own price cut, then Boeing might decide that Airbus was not serious about the market and would continue its price-cutting strategy. Responding aggressively to an initial price cut may actually support long-term cooperation in a repeated game.

- *Deterrence*. As above, signalling can clearly be about deterring unwanted strategic moves by competitors. During the Cold War, game theorists attribute the lack of direct warfare between the United States and the Soviet Union to the fact that both possessed nuclear deterrents: if one country attacked the other, then the second country would retaliate with a nuclear attack. This was known as Mutually Assured Destruction (MAD), but it worked. In a similar vein, interdependent competitors have to demonstrate that the costs of an unwanted move will be very high. Two effective forms of deterrent would be maintaining extra capacity that could be used to flood the market, or holding a minor position in a com-petitor's key market that could easily be expanded. Even if these investments in deterrence are expensive, they may be worthwhile if they encourage cooperation.

- *Commitment*. It is important also to signal commitment. When the Roman invader Julius Caesar burnt his ships on the shores of England, the message was to his adversaries as much as his own invading army. The Ancient Britons knew that Caesar would fight to the death: they had strong incentives to negotiate a peace with him. Caesar's signal of commitment was credible because it was costly and irreversible. Similarly, if a company invests heavily in developing its brand in a market, or building up a portfolio of patents, then competitors will know that it is highly committed, and be less likely to attack head-on. Again, additional investments have a signalling value that can help cooperation long-term.

KEY DEBATE

To be different or the same?

Can differentiation strategies rebound, making an organisation seem dangerously eccentric rather than delivering competitive advantage?

This chapter has introduced the potential value of differentiation strategies, in which the organisation emphasises its uniqueness. This is consistent also with the argument of the resource-based view (Chapter 3) in favour of the distinctiveness and inimitability of an organisation's resources. But how far should an organisation push its uniqueness, especially if there is a danger of it beginning to be seen as simply eccentric?

McKinsey & Co. consultant Philipp Natterman makes a strong case for differentiation.[1] He tracks the relationship between profitability and differentiation (in terms of pricing and product features) over long periods in both the personal computer and mobile phone industries. He finds that as differentiation falls over time, so too do industry profit margins. Natterman blames management techniques such as benchmarking (Chapter 3), which tend to encourage convergence on industry 'best practices'. The trouble with best practices is that they easily become standard practices. There is no competitive advantage in following the herd.

However, 'institutional theorists' such as Paul DiMaggio and Walter Powell point to some advantages in herd-like behaviour.[2] They think of industries as 'organisational fields' in which all sorts of actors must interact – customers, suppliers, employees and regulators. The ability of these actors to interact effectively depends upon being legitimate in the eyes of other actors in the field. Over time, industries develop institutionalised norms of legitimate behaviour, which it makes sense for everybody to follow. It is easier for customers and suppliers to do business with organisations that are more or less the same as the others in the industry. It is reassuring to potential employees and industry regulators if organisations do not seem highly eccentric. Especially when there is high uncertainty about what drives performance – for example, in knowledge-based industries – it can be a lot better to be legitimate than different. To the extent that customers, suppliers, employees and regulators value conformity, then it is valuable in itself. Being a 'misfit' can be costly.

This institutionalist appreciation of conformity makes sense of a lot of strategic behaviour. For example, merger waves in some industries seem to be driven by bandwagons, in which organisations become panicked into making acquisitions simply for fear of being left behind. Likewise, many management initiatives, such as business process re-engineering, e-business or outsourcing, are the product of fads and fashions as much as hard objective analysis. The insight from institutionalist theory, however, is that following the fashion is not necessarily a bad thing.

Thus institutional theory and the resource-based view appear to have opposing perspectives on the value of differentiation. David Deephouse has investigated this apparent trade-off between differentiation and conformity in the American banking industry and found a curvilinear relationship between differentiation and financial performance.[3] Strong conformity led to inferior performance; moderate differentiation was associated with improved performance; extreme differentiation appeared to damage performance.

Deephouse concludes in favour of 'balance' between differentiation and conformity. He also suggests that the value of differentiation depends on the extent to which key actors in the industry – customers, suppliers, employees, and so on – have converged on institutionalised norms of appropriate strategy. It seems that strategies can be too differentiated, but that how much 'too differentiated' is depends on the kind of industry that one is in.

References:
1. P.M. Natterman, 'Best practice does not equal best strategy', *McKinsey Quarterly*, no. 2 (2000), pp. 22–31.
2. P. DiMaggio and W. Powell, 'The iron cage revisited: institutional isomorphism and collective rationality in organizational fields', *American Sociological Review*, vol. 48 (1983), pp. 147–60.
3. D. Deephouse, 'To be different or to be the same? It's a question (and theory) of strategic balance', *Strategic Management Journal*, vol. 20 (1999), pp. 147–66.

Questions

1 To what extent do (a) universities and (b) car manufacturers compete by being different or the same?

2 Considering the nature of their industries, and key players within them, why might these organisations adopt these approaches to conformity or differentiation?

SUMMARY

- Business strategy is concerned with seeking competitive advantage in markets at the *business* rather than *corporate* level.

- Business strategy needs to be considered and defined in terms of *strategic business units* (SBUs).

- Different *generic strategies* can be defined in terms of cost-leadership, differentiation and focus.

- Managers need to consider how business strategies can be sustained through strategic capabilities and/or the ability to achieve a '*lock-in*' position with buyers.

- In *hypercompetitive* conditions sustainable competitive advantage is difficult to achieve. Competitors need to be able to cannibalise, make small moves, be unpredictable and mislead their rivals.

- *Cooperative strategies* may offer alternatives to competitive strategies or may run in parallel.

- Game theory encourages managers to *get in the mind of competitors* and *think forwards and reason backwards*.

WORK ASSIGNMENTS

✴ *Denotes more advanced work assignments.* * *Refers to a case study in the Text and Case edition.*

6.1   What are the advantages and what are the disadvantages of applying principles of business strategy to public-sector or charity organisations? Illustrate your argument by reference to a public-sector organisation of your choice.

6.2   Using either Porter's generic strategies or the Strategy Clock, identify examples of organisations following strategies of differentiation, low cost or low price, and stuck-in-the-middle or hybrid. How successful are these strategies?

6.3✴ You have been appointed personal assistant to the chief executive of a major manufacturing firm, who has asked you to explain what is meant by 'differentiation' and why it is important. Write a brief report addressing these questions.

6.4✴ Choose an industry or sector which is becoming more and more competitive (for example, financial services or fashion retailing). How might the principles of hypercompetitive strategies apply to that industry?

6.5✴ Drawing on section 6.4 (on cooperative strategies) write a report for the chief executive of a business in a competitive market (for example, pharmaceuticals* or Formula One*) explaining when and in what ways cooperation rather than direct competition might make sense.

Integrative assignment

6.6✴ Applying game theory ideas from section 6.4.4 to issues of international strategy (Chapter 8), how might a domestic player discourage an overseas player from entering into its home market?

VIDEO ASSIGNMENT

Visit *MyStrategyLab* and watch the *Land Rover* case study.

1 Identify Land Rover's generic strategy, in terms of Porter's generic strategies or the Strategy Clock, or both.

2 Given its competition, how sustainable is Land Rover's strategy?

RECOMMENDED KEY READINGS

- The foundations of the discussions of generic competitive strategies are to be found in the writings of Michael Porter, which include *Competitive Strategy* (1980) and *Competitive Advantage* (1985), both published by Free Press. Both are recommended for readers who wish to understand the background to discussions in section 6.3 on competitive strategy and competitive advantage.

- Hypercompetition, and the strategies associated with it, are explained in Richard D'Aveni, *Hypercompetitive*

Rivalries: Competing in Highly Dynamic Environments, Free Press, 1995.

- There is much written on game theory but a good deal of it can be rather inaccessible to the lay reader. Exceptions are R. McCain, *Game Theory: a Non-technical Introduction to the Analysis of Strategy*, South Western, 2003, and A. Dixit and B. Nalebuff, *The Art of Strategy: a Game Theorist's Guide to Success in Business and Life*, Norton, 2008.

REFERENCES

1. For a detailed discussion as to how organisational structures might 'address' an organisation's mix of SBUs see M. Goold and A. Campbell, *Designing Effective Organizations: How to Create Structured Networks*, Jossey-Bass, 2002. Also K. Eisenhardt and S. Brown, 'Patching', *Harvard Business Review*, vol. 77, no. 3 (1999), p. 72.

2. This section draws heavily on M. Porter, *Competitive Advantage*, Free Press, 1985. For a more recent discussion of the generic strategies concept, see J. Parnell, 'Generic strategies after two decades: a reconceptualisation of competitive strategy', *Management Decision*, vol. 48, no. 8 (2006), pp. 1139–54.

3. P. Conley, *Experience Curves as a Planning Tool*, available as a pamphlet from the Boston Consulting Group. See also A.C. Hax and N.S. Majluf, in R.G. Dyson (ed.), *Strategic Planning: Models and Analytical Techniques*, Wiley, 1990.

4. B. Sharp and J. Dawes, 'What is differentiation and how does it work?', *Journal of Marketing Management*, vol. 17, nos 7/8 (2001), pp. 739–59, reviews the relationship between differentiation and profitability.

5. See, for example, D. Miller, 'The generic strategy trap', *Journal of Business Strategy*, vol. 13, no. 1 (1992), pp. 37–42; C.W.L. Hill, 'Differentiation versus low cost or differentiation and low cost: a contingency framework', *Academy of Management Review*, vol. 13, no. 3 (1998), pp. 401–12; and S. Thornhill and R. White, 'Strategic purity: a multi-industry evaluation of pure vs hybrid business strategies',

Strategic Management Journal, vol. 28, no. 5 (2007), pp. 553–61.

6. C. Markides and C. Charitou, 'Competing with dual business models: a contingency approach', *Academy of Management Executive*, vol. 18, no. 3 (2004), pp. 22–36.

7. See D. Faulkner and C. Bowman, *The Essence of Competitive Strategy*, Prentice Hall, 1995.

8. For empirical support for the benefits of a hybrid strategy, see E. Pertusa-Ortega, J. Molina-Azorín and E. Claver-Cortés, 'Competitive strategies and firm performance: a comparative analysis of pure, hybrid and "stuck-in-the-middle" strategies in Spanish firms', *British Journal of Management*, vol. 20, no. 4 (2008), pp. 508–23.

9. W.B. Arthur, 'Increasing returns and the new world of business', *Harvard Business Review*, July–August (1996), pp. 100–9. See also the concept of system lock-in in A. Hax and D. Wilde, 'The Delta Model – discovering new sources of profitability in a networked economy', *European Management Journal*, vol. 19, no. 4 (2001), pp. 379–91.

10. R. D'Aveni, *Hypercompetition: the Dynamics of Strategic Maneuvering*, Free Press, New York.

11. This analysis is based on N. Kumar, 'Strategies to fight low cost rivals', *Harvard Business Review*, vol. 84, no. 12 (2006), pp. 104–13.

12. For other examples of misleading signals see G. Stalk Jr, 'Curveball: strategies to fool the competition', *Harvard Business Review*, September (2006), pp. 115–22.

13. Useful books on collaborative strategies are Y. Doz and G. Hamel, *Alliance Advantage: The Art of Creating Value through Partnering*, Harvard Business School Press, 1998; *Creating Collaborative Advantage*, ed. Chris Huxham, Sage, 1996; and D. Faulkner, *Strategic Alliances: Cooperating to Compete*, McGraw-Hill, 1995.

14. For readings on game theory see B. Nalebuff and A. Brandenburger, *Co-opetition*, Profile Books, 1997; R. McCain, *Game Theory: A Non-technical Introduction to the Analysis of Strategy*, South Western, 2003; and, for a summary, S. Regan, 'Game theory perspective', in M. Jenkins and V. Ambrosini (eds), *Advanced Strategic Management: a Multi-Perspective Approach*, 2nd edition, Palgrave Macmillan, 2007, pp. 83–101. A recent practical example is in H. Lindstädt and J. Müller, 'Making game theory work for managers', *McKinsey Quarterly*, December (2009).

Madonna: the reigning queen of pop?

Phyl Johnson, Strategy Explorers

She's the highest-ever paid female singer, in 2009 had the highest-earning tour of any artist and is second only to the Beatles in her haul of 11 UK number one albums. But the music industry has always been the backdrop for one-hit wonders and brief careers. Pop-stars who have remained at the top for decades are very few. Madonna is one such phenomenon; the question is, after almost thirty years at the top, how much longer can it last?

Described by *Billboard Magazine* as the smartest business woman in show business, Madonna Louise Ciccone began her music career in 1983 with the hit single 'Holiday' and in 2008, enjoyed success with the album *Hard Candy* featuring the hit single '4 Minutes' with Justin Timberlake. In the meantime, she had consistent chart success with many singles and eighteen albums, multiple sell-out world tours, major roles in six films, picked up numerous music awards, was inducted into the Rock and Roll Hall of Fame and has been the style icon behind a range of products (Pepsi, Max Factor, Gap, H&M and Louis Vuitton), and become a worldwide bestselling children's author.

The foundation of Madonna's business success has been her ability to sustain her reign as the 'queen of pop'. Phil Quattro, the President of Warner Brothers, said 'she always manages to land on the cusp of what we call contemporary music. Every established artist faces the dilemma of maintaining their importance and relevance, Madonna never fails to be relevant'. Madonna's chameleon-like ability to change persona, change her music genre with it and yet still achieve major record sales has been the hallmark of her success and is seemingly not replicable by other male and female artists.

Madonna's early poppy style was targeted at young 'wannabe' girls. The image that she portrayed through hits such as 'Holiday' and 'Lucky Star' in 1983 was picked up by Macy's, the US-based department store. They produced a range of Madonna lookalike clothes that mothers were happy to purchase for their daughters. One year later in 1984, Madonna underwent her first image change and in doing so offered the first hint of the smart cookie behind the media image. In the video for her hit *Material Girl*, she deliberately mirrored the glamour-based, sexual pussycat image of Marilyn

Source: Rex Features/Lehtikuva OY.

Monroe whilst simultaneously mocking both the growing materialism of the late eighties and the men fawning after her. Media analysts Sam and Diana Kirschner commented that with this kind of packaging, Madonna allowed the record companies to keep hold of a saleable 'Marilyn image' for a new cohort of fans, but also allowed her original fan base of now growing up wannabe girls to take the more critical message from the music. The theme of courting controversy but staying marketable enough has been recurrent throughout her career.

Madonna's subsequent image changes were more dramatic. First she took on the Catholic Church in her 1989 video *Like a Prayer* where, as a red-dressed 'sinner', she kissed a black saint easily interpreted as a Jesus figure. Her image had become increasingly sexual whilst also holding on to a critical social theme: e.g. her pointed illustration of white-only imagery in the Catholic Church. At this point in her career, Madonna took full control of her image in the $60 (~€42) million deal with Time-Warner that created her record company Maverick. In 1991, she published a coffee-table soft porn book entitled *Sex* that exclusively featured pictures of herself in erotic poses. Her image and music also reflected this erotic theme. In her 'Girlie' tour, her singles 'Erotica' and 'Justify my Love' and her fly-on-the wall movie *In Bed with Madonna* she played out scenes of sadomasochistic and lesbian fantasies. Although allegedly a period of her career she would rather forget, Madonna more than survived it. In fact, she gained a whole new demographic of fans who not only respected her artistic courage but also did not miss the fact that Madonna was consistent in her message: her sexuality was her own and not in need of a male gaze.

Changing gear in 1996, Madonna finally took centre stage in the lead role in the film *Evita* which she had chased for over five years. She achieved the image transition from erotica to saint-like persona of Eva Peron and won critical acclaim to boot. Another vote of confidence from the 'establishment' came from Max Factor, who in 1999 signed her up to front their relaunch campaign which was crafted around a glamour theme. Proctor & Gamble (owners of the Max Factor make-up range) argued that they saw Madonna as 'the closest thing the 90s has to an old-style Hollywood star . . . she is a real woman'.

Madonna's album *Ray of Light* was released in 1998. Radio stations world-wide were desperate to get hold of the album which was billed as her most successful musical voyage to date. In a smart move, Madonna had teamed up with techno pioneer William Orbit to write and produce the album. It was a huge success, taking Madonna into the super-trendy techno sphere, not the natural environment for a pop-star from the early 80s. Madonna took up an 'earth mother / spiritual' image and spawned a trend for all things eastern in fashion and music. This phase may have produced more than just an image as it is the time in Madonna's life that locates the beginning of her continued faith in the Kabbalah tradition of eastern spiritual worship.

By 2001, her next persona was unveiled with the release of her album *Music*. Here her style had moved on again to 'acid rock'. With her marriage to her second husband, British movie director Guy Ritchie, the ultimate 'American Pie' had become a fully-fledged Brit babe earning the endearing nickname of 'Madge' in the British press.

By 2003 some commentators were suggesting that an interesting turn of events hinted that perhaps 'the cutting edge' Madonna, 'the fearless', was starting to think about being part of, rather than beating, the establishment. When she launched her new Che Guevara-inspired

image, instead of maximising the potential of this image in terms of its political and social symbolism during the second Gulf War, in April 2003 she withdrew her militaristic image and video for the album *American Life*. That action, timed with the publication of her children's book *The English Roses* based on the themes of compassion and friendship, sparked questions in the press around the theme 'has Madonna gone soft?'

By late 2003 she negotiated a glitzy high profile ad campaign for the Gap clothing retailer in which she danced around accompanied by rapper Missy Elliot to a retrospective re-mix of her eighties track 'Get into the Groove'. Here Madonna was keeping the 'thirty-somethings', who remembered the track from first time around, happy. They could purchase jeans for themselves and their newly teenage daughters whilst also purchasing the re-released CD (on sale in-store).

Late 2005 saw the release of the world record breaking, Grammy and Brit Award winning *Confessions on a Dance Floor* album which was marketed as her comeback album after her lowest selling *American Life*. Here Madonna focused on the high selling principle of re-mix, choosing samples of the gay-iconic disco favourites of Abba and Giorgio Moroder to be at the heart of her symbolic reinvention of herself from artist to DJ. The 'Confessions' world tour achieved the highest-selling peak of her career with the album breaking the world record for solo female artists when it debuted at number one in over 40 countries.

Throughout 2008 Madonna lived through a mixed period in her personal and professional lives. In the wake of her divorce from her second husband, she attracted large amounts of negative publicity for the adoption of her youngest children from Malawi. There was also mixed media reaction to the publicity shots for her *Hard Candy* album as Madonna was back to her erotic best: wearing thigh-high boots and little else but with her highly toned body used to full effect. At 51 years of age some commentators questioned: is this sexy or smutty; does Madonna need dignity? Either way, her image, undeniably sultry and alluring, was still hitting the high notes.

Crucially, in 2009, as the music world moved into a phase where its highest earners were not those with the most record sales but those with the best-selling tours, Madonna reigned supreme. Her world record breaking 'Sticky and Sweet' world tour topped *Billboard*'s money-makers chart with a reported $242 million in revenue. This level of revenue was $100 million ahead of her nearest competitor Bon Jovi and showed her razor-sharp appreciation that her records were simply advertisements for her tours. Madonna, along with all artists, had seen record sales falling, and with online

Table 1

Releases	Year	Image	Target audience
Lucky Star	1982	Trashy pop	Young wannabe girls, dovetailing from fading disco to emerging 'club scene'
Like a Virgin Like a Prayer	1984	Originally a Marilyn glamour image, then became a Saint & Sinner	More grown-up rebellious – fan base, more critical female audience and male worshippers
Vogue Erotica Bedtime Stories	1990 1992 1994	Erotic porn star, sadomasochistic, sexual control, more Minelli in *Cabaret* than Monroe	Peculiar mix of target audiences: gay club scene, 90s women taking control of their own lives, also pure male titillation
Something to Remember Evita	1995	Softer image, ballads preparing for glamour image of Evita film role	Broadest audience target, picking up potential film audiences as well as regular fan base. Most conventional image. Max Factor later used this mixture of Marilyn and Eva Peron to market their glamour image.
Ray of Light	1998	Earth mother, eastern mysticism, dance music fusion	Clubbing generation of the 90s, new cohort of fans plus original fan base of now 30-somethings desperately staying trendy
Music	2000	Acid rock, tongue-in-cheek Miss USA/cowgirl, cool Britannia	Managing to hit the changing club scene and 30-something Brits
American Life	2003	Militaristic image Che Guevara Anti-consumerism of American dream	Unclear audience reliant on existing base
Confessions on a Dance Floor	2005	Retro-80s disco imagery, high motion dance-pop sound	Strong gay-icon audience, pop-disco audience, danced-based audience
Hard Candy	2008	Pop, dance, electro-pop urban	Deliberate move toward a more urban R&B direction with collaborations with Justine Timberlake and Kayne West pulling in a new young audience
Celebration	2009	Queen of pop	Compilation of hits from her entire career targeted at enduring/touring fan base

music sales still relatively small, had realised that live music, endorsements and merchandising were her best revenue generating avenues going forward. She signed a new ten year record deal with Live Nation, the largest concert promotion company in the world, ensuring that she retains 90% of gross touring revenues as well as 50% of endorsements.

Sell-out tours crucially rely on a return and return again fan base. Madonna used the 2009 release of *Celebration* (her definitive collection of hit singles) to keep her fan base warm until her next world trek. But at 50 plus, how long can Madonna keep it up? A positive indicator is that The Eagles, Neil Diamond, The Police and Billy Joel all appeared in the tour-earning top 20 of 2008. A negative indicator is that they are all male and selling nostalgia rather than their own sexually-charged image: an ageing female image may well be harder to sell and Madonna, with no female benchmarks to measure up to, found herself in uncharted territory. Yet again Madonna pioneers and currently endures as one of the most influential celebrity women on the planet.

Sources: 'Bennett takes the reins at Maverick', *Billboard Magazine*, 7 August 1999; 'Warner Bros expects Madonna to light up international markets', *Billboard Magazine*, 21 February 1998; 'Maverick builds on early success', *Billboard Magazine*, 12 November 1994; Jardine, A. (1999) 'Max Factor strikes gold with Madonna', *Marketing*, vol. 29, pp. 14–15; Kirschner, S. and Kirschner, D. (1997) 'MTV, adolescence and Madonna: a discourse analysis', in *Perspectives on Psychology and the Media*, American Psychological Association, Washington, DC; 'Warner to buy out maverick co-founder', *Los Angeles Times*, 2 March 1999; 'Why Madonna is back in Vogue', *New Statesman*, 18 September 2000; 'Madonna and Microsoft', *Financial Times*, 28 November 2000; 'Power of Goodbye: Madonna's Split May Herald Record Industry's Death', *The Times Online*, 12 October 2007.

Questions

1 Describe and explain the strategy being followed by Madonna in terms of the explanation of competitive strategy given in Chapter 6.

2 Why has she experienced sustained success over three decades?

3 Can Madonna sustain her success?

7

CORPORATE STRATEGY AND DIVERSIFICATION

Learning objectives

After reading this chapter, you should be able to:

● Identify alternative strategy options, including *market penetration*, *product development*, *market development* and *diversification*.

● Distinguish between different diversification strategies (*related* and *conglomerate* diversification) and evaluate *diversification drivers*.

● Assess the relative benefits of *vertical integration* and *outsourcing*.

● Analyse the ways in which a *corporate parent* can add or destroy value for its portfolio of business units.

● Analyse *portfolios* of business units and judge which to invest in and which to divest.

PEARSON
mystrategylab

MyStrategyLab is designed to help you make the most of your studies.

Visit **www.pearsoned.co.uk/mystrategylab** to discover a wide range of resources specific to this chapter, including:

● A personalised **Study plan** that will help you understand core concepts

● **Audio** and **video clips** that put the spotlight on strategy in the real world

● **Online glossaries** and **flashcards** that provide helpful reminders when you're looking for some quick revision.

7.1 INTRODUCTION

Chapter 6 was concerned with choices at the level of single business or organisational units, for instance through pricing strategies or differentiation. This chapter is about choices of *products and markets* for an organisation to enter or exit (see the figure in the Part II introduction). Organisations often choose to enter many new product and market areas. For example, the Virgin Group started out in the music business, but is now highly diverse, operating in the holiday, cinema, retail, air-travel and rail markets. Sony began by making small radios, but now produces games, music and movies, as well as a host of electronic products. As organisations add new units, their strategies are no longer concerned just with the business-level, but with the *corporate-level* choices involved in having many different businesses or markets.

Figure 7.1 indicates the basic themes of this chapter. First of all, there are questions to do with the *scope*, or breadth, of the corporate whole. **Scope is concerned with how far an organisation should be diversified in terms of products and markets**. Here a basic framework is provided by Ansoff's two axes, indicating different diversification strategies according to novelty of products or markets. Another way of increasing the scope of an organisation is through *vertical integration*, where the organisation acts as an internal supplier or a customer to itself (as for example an oil company supplies its petrol to its own petrol stations). Here we also consider the possibility of *outsourcing*, where an organisation 'dis-integrates' by subcontracting an internal activity to an external supplier.

Scope raises the two other key themes of the chapter. First, given that an organisation has decided to operate in different areas of activity, what should be the role of the 'corporate-level' (head-office) executives that act as 'parents' to the individual business units that make up their organisation's portfolio? How do corporate-level activities, decisions and resources add value to the actual businesses? As will be seen in the Key Debate at the end of this chapter, there is considerable scepticism about the value-adding role of corporate-level strategy. The second theme is, within an overall diversification strategy, which specific business units should be included in the corporate *portfolio*, and how should they be managed financially? Here portfolio matrices help structure corporate-level choices about which businesses to invest in and which to divest.

Figure 7.1 Strategic directions and corporate-level strategy

This chapter is not just about large commercial businesses. Even small businesses may consist of a number of business units. For example, a local builder may be undertaking contract work for local government, work for industrial buyers and for local homeowners. Not only are these different market segments, but the mode of operation and capabilities required for competitive success are also likely to be different. Moreover, the owner of that business has to take decisions about the extent of investment and activity in each segment. Public-sector organisations such as local government or health services also provide different services, which correspond to business units in commercial organisations. Corporate-level strategy is highly relevant to the appropriate drawing of organisational boundaries in the public sector, and privatisation and outsourcing decisions can be considered as responses to the failure of public-sector organisations to add sufficient value by their parenting.

KEY CONCEPT

Strategy directions

7.2 STRATEGY DIRECTIONS

The Ansoff product/market growth matrix[1] provides a simple way of generating four basic directions for corporate strategy: see Figure 7.2 for an adapted version. An organisation typically starts in the zone around point A, the top left-hand corner of Figure 7.2. According to Ansoff, the organisation basically has a choice between *penetrating* still further within its existing sphere (staying in zone A) or increasing its diversity along the two axes of increasing novelty of markets or increasing novelty of products. **Diversification involves increasing the range of products or markets served by an organisation. Related diversification involves diversifying into products or services with relationships to the existing business.** Thus on Ansoff's axes the organisation has two related diversification strategies available: moving rightwards by *developing new products* for its existing markets (zone B) or moving downwards

Figure 7.2 Corporate strategy directions

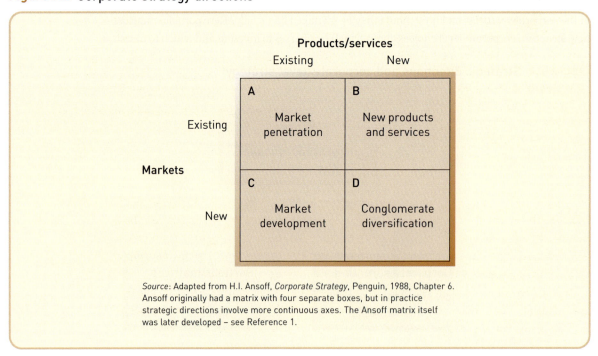

Source: Adapted from H.I. Ansoff, *Corporate Strategy*, Penguin, 1988, Chapter 6. Ansoff originally had a matrix with four separate boxes, but in practice strategic directions involve more continuous axes. The Ansoff matrix itself was later developed – see Reference 1.

ILLUSTRATION 7.1

Corporate strategy choices for Axel Springer

This German publishing company has many opportunities, and the money to pursue them.

In 2007, Mathias Döpfner, chairman and chief executive of Axel Springer publishers, had about €2bn ($2.8bn) to invest in new opportunities. The previous year, the competition authorities had prohibited his take-over of Germany's largest television broadcaster, ProSiebenSat.1 . . . Now Döpfner was looking for alternative directions.

Founded in 1946 by Axel Springer himself, by 2007 the company was already Germany's largest publisher of newspapers and magazines, with more than 10,000 employees and over 150 titles. Famous print titles included *Die Welt*, the *Berliner Morgenpost*, *Bild* and *Hörzu*. Outside Germany, Axel Springer was strongest in Eastern Europe. The company also had a scattering of mostly small investments in German radio and television companies. Axel Springer described its strategic objectives as market leadership in the German language core business, internationalisation and digitalisation of the core business.

Döpfner had opportunities for further penetration with his existing markets and products. Increased digitalisation of the core newspapers and magazines business was clearly important and would require substantial funding. There were also opportunities for the launch of new print magazine titles in the German market.

However, Döpfner was considering expanding also into new markets and new products. Such moves would likely involve acquisitions: 'it goes without saying', he told the *Financial Times*, 'that whenever a large international media company comes on to the market (i.e. is up for sale), we will examine it very closely – whether in print, TV or the online sector'. Döpfner mentioned several specific kinds of acquisition opportunity. For example, he was still interested in buying a large European television broadcaster, even if it would probably have to be outside Germany. He was also attracted by the possibility of buying under-valued assets in the old media (i.e. print), and turning them around in the style of a private-equity investor: 'I would love to buy businesses in need of restructuring, where we can add value by introducing our management and sector expertise'. However, Döpfner reassured his shareholders by affirming that he felt no need 'to do a big thing in order to do a big thing'.

Main source: *Financial Times Deutschland*, 2 April 2007.

Questions

1 Referring to Figure 7.2, classify the various strategic directions Mattias Döpfner is considering for Axel Springer.

2 Using the Ansoff axes, what other options could Döpfner pursue?

---

by bringing its existing products into *new markets* (zone C). In each case, the further along the two axes, the more diversified is the strategy. Alternatively, the organisation can move in both directions at once, following a *conglomerate diversification* strategy with altogether new markets and new products (zone D). Thus **conglomerate (unrelated) diversification** involves diversifying into products or services with no relationships to the existing businesses.

Ansoff's axes can be used effectively in brainstorming strategic options, checking that options in all four zones have been properly considered. This section will consider each of Ansoff's four main directions in some detail. Section 7.5 will examine the additional option of *vertical integration*.

7.2.1 Market penetration

For a simple, undiversified business, the most obvious strategic option is often increased penetration of its existing market, with its existing products. **Market penetration implies increasing share of current markets with the current product range**. This strategy builds on established strategic capabilities and does not require the organisation to venture into uncharted territory. The organisation's scope is exactly the same. Moreover, greater market share implies increased power vis-à-vis buyers and suppliers (in terms of Porter's five forces), greater economies of scale and experience curve benefits.

However, organisations seeking greater market penetration may face two constraints:

● *Retaliation from competitors*. In terms of the five forces (section 2.3.1), increasing market penetration is likely to exacerbate industry rivalry as other competitors in the market defend their share. Increased rivalry might involve price wars or expensive marketing battles, which may cost more than any market-share gains are actually worth. The dangers of provoking fierce retaliation are greater in low-growth markets, as any gains in volume will be much more at the expense of other players. Where retaliation is a danger, organisations seeking market penetration need strategic capabilities that give a clear competitive advantage. In low-growth or declining markets, it can be more effective simply to acquire competitors. Some companies have grown quickly in this way. For example, in the steel industry the Indian company LNM (Mittal) moved rapidly in the 2000s to become the largest steel producer in the world by acquiring struggling steel companies around the world. Acquisitions can actually reduce rivalry, by taking out independent players and controlling them under one umbrella.

● *Legal constraints*. Greater market penetration can raise concerns from official competition regulators concerning excessive market power. Most countries have regulators with the powers to restrain powerful companies or prevent mergers and acquisitions that would create such excessive power. In the United Kingdom, the Competition Commission can investigate any merger or acquisition that would account for more than 25 per cent of the national market, and either halt the deal or propose measures that would reduce market power. The European Commission has an overview of the whole European market and can similarly intervene. For example, when the German T-Mobile and French Orange companies proposed to merge their UK mobile phone operations in 2010, the European Commission insisted that the merged companies should divest a quarter of their combined share of the key mobile phone 1800 MHz spectrum.[2]

Market penetration may not be an option too where economic constraints are severe, for instance during a market downturn or public-sector funding crisis. Here organisations will need to consider the strategic option of *retrenchment*, withdrawal from marginal activities in order to concentrate on the most valuable segments and products within their existing business. However, where growth is still sought after, the Ansoff axes suggest further directions, as follows.

7.2.2 Product development

Product development is where organisations deliver modified or new products (or services) to existing markets. This can involve varying degrees of diversification along the rightward axis of Figure 7.2. For Sony, developing its Walkman products from the original tape-based product, through CDs and recently to MP3s involved little diversification: although the technologies differed, Sony was targeting the same customers and using very similar production processes and distribution channels. A more radical form of product development would be Axel Springer's move into the online media businesses: effectively the same consumer markets are involved as for its existing newspaper and magazine businesses, but the production technologies and distribution channels are radically different (see Illustration 7.1). This form of product diversification would typically be described as *related diversification*, as Axel Springer's online business would be related through similar customers to its existing newspaper and magazine customers.

Despite the potential for relatedness, product development can be an expensive and high-risk activity for at least two reasons:

- *New strategic capabilities*. Product development strategies typically involve mastering new processes or technologies that are unfamiliar to the organisation. For example, many banks entered online banking at the beginning of this century, but suffered many setbacks with technologies so radically different from their traditional high-street branch means of delivering banking services. Success frequently depended on a willingness to acquire new technological and marketing capabilities, often with the help of specialised information technology and e-commerce consultancy firms. Thus product development typically involves heavy investments and high risk of project failures.

- *Project management risk*. Even within fairly familiar domains, product development projects are typically subject to the risk of delays and increased costs due to project complexity and changing project specifications over time. An extreme example is Boeing's Dreamliner 787 plane: making innovative use of carbon-fibre composites, the Dreamliner had incurred two and a half years of delay by launch in 2010, and required $2.5bn (~€1.75bn) write-offs due to cancelled orders.

Strategies for product development are considered further in Chapter 9.

7.2.3 Market development

If product development is risky and expensive, an alternative strategy is market development. **Market development involves offering existing products to new markets.** Again, the degree of diversification varies along Figure 7.2's downward axis. Typically, of course, market development entails some product development as well, if only in terms of packaging or service. Nonetheless, market development remains a form of related diversification given its origins in similar products. Market development takes two basic forms:

- *New users*. Here an example would be aluminium, whose original users, packaging and cutlery manufacturers, are now supplemented by users in aerospace and automobiles.

- *New geographies*. The prime example of this is internationalisation, but the spread of a small retailer into new towns would also be a case.

In all cases, it is essential that market development strategies be based on products or services that meet the *critical success factors* of the new market (see section 2.4.3). Strategies based on simply off-loading traditional products or services in new markets are likely to fail. Moreover, market development faces similar problems to product development. In terms of strategic capabilities, market developers often lack the right marketing skills and brands to

ILLUSTRATION 7.2

Zodiac deflates: diversification and de-diversification

The Zodiac Group has managed a portfolio of related business for the best part of a century, with both diversification and de-diversification.

The Zodiac Group is probably best known for its Zodiac inflatable boats, used by Jacques Cousteau and seen in harbours around the world. But in 2007, Zodiac sold all its marine and leisure businesses and concentrated on aerospace.

The Zodiac company was founded in 1896 by Maurice Mallet just after his first hot-air balloon ascent. For 40 years, Zodiac manufactured only dirigible airships. In 1937, the German Zeppelin *Hindenburg* crashed near New York, which abruptly stopped the development of the market for airships. Because of the extinction of its traditional activity, Zodiac decided to leverage its technical expertise and moved from dirigible airships to inflatable boats. This diversification proved to be very successful: by 2004, over one million Zodiac rubber inflatables had sold worldwide.

However, because of increasing competition, especially from Italian manufacturers, Zodiac had been diversifying its business interests. In 1978, it took over Aerazur, a company specialising in parachutes, but also in life vests and inflatable life rafts. These products had strong market and technical synergies with rubber boats and their main customers were aircraft manufacturers. Zodiac confirmed this move to a new market in 1987 by the takeover of Air Cruisers, a manufacturer of inflatable escape slides for aeroplanes. As a consequence, Zodiac became a key supplier to Boeing, McDonnell Douglas and Airbus. Zodiac strengthened this position through the takeover of the two leading manufacturers of aeroplane seats: Sicma Aero Seats from France and Weber Aircraft from the USA. In 1997, Zodiac also took over, for €150m (~$210m), MAG Aerospace, the world leader for aircraft vacuum waste systems. In 1999, Zodiac took over Intertechnique, a leading player in active components for aircraft (fuel circulation, hydraulics, oxygen and life support, electrical power, flight-deck controls and displays, systems monitoring, etc.). By combining these competences with its traditional expertise in inflatable products, Zodiac launched a new business unit: airbags for the automobile industry.

In parallel to these diversifications, Zodiac strengthened its position in inflatable boats by the takeover of several competitors: Bombard-L'Angevinière in 1980, Sevylor in 1981, Hurricane and Metzeler in 1987. The company also developed a swimming-pool business. The first product line, back in 1981, was based on inflatable structure technology, and Zodiac later moved – again through takeovers – to rigid above-ground pools, modular in-ground pools, pool cleaners and water purification systems, inflatable beach gear and air mattresses.

However, by 2007, aircraft products accounted for 80 per cent of the total turnover of the group. Zodiac held a 40 per cent market share of the world market for some airline equipment: for instance, the electrical power systems of the new Airbus A380 and Boeing 787 were Zodiac products. Zodiac had even reached Mars: NASA Mars probes *Spirit* and *Opportunity* were equipped with Zodiac equipment, developed by its US subsidiary Pioneer Aerospace.

Chief Executive Jean-Louis Gérondeau explained the sale of the marine and leisure businesses thus: 'The proposed transaction . . . would allow the Zodiac Group . . . to reinforce its acquisition capabilities in the aerospace sector'. However, the sale was also a response to pressure from financial analysts, who considered Zodiac too diversified. The sale was rapidly followed in 2008 by three further acquisitions of aircraft cabin equipment companies: Driessen, Adder and TIA.

Source: Based on an illustration by Frédéric Fréry, ESCP Europe Business School.

Questions

1 Explain the ways in which relatedness informed Zodiac's diversification strategy over time.

2 What are the advantages and potential dangers of its decision to focus on the aircraft products market?

make progress in a market with unfamiliar customers. On the management side, the challenge is coordinating between different users and geographies, which might all have different needs. *International* market development strategy is considered in Chapter 8.

7.2.4 Conglomerate diversification

Conglomerate (or unrelated) diversification takes the organisation beyond both its existing markets and its existing products (i.e. zone D in Figure 7.2). In this sense, it radically increases the organisation's scope. Conglomerate diversification strategies are not trusted by many observers, because there are no obvious ways in which the businesses are better off for being together, while there is a clear cost in the managers at headquarters who control them. For this reason, conglomerate companies' share prices often suffer from what is called the 'conglomerate discount' – in other words, a lower valuation than the individual constituent businesses would have if stand-alone. In 2009, the French conglomerate Vivendi, with wide interests in mobile telephony and media, was trading at an estimated discount of 24 per cent on the value of its constituent assets. Naturally, shareholders were pressurising management to sell off its more highly valued parts on the open market.

However, it is important to recognise that the distinction between related and unrelated conglomerate diversification is often a matter of degree. Also relationships might turn out not to be so valuable as expected. Thus the large accounting firms have often struggled in translating their skills and client contacts developed in auditing into effective consulting practices. Similarly, relationships may change in importance over time, as the nature of technologies or customers change: see for example the decision by Zodiac to divest itself of its iconic boat business (Illustration 7.2).

(7.3) DIVERSIFICATION DRIVERS

Diversification might be chosen for a variety of reasons, some more value-creating than others.[3] Growth in organisational size is rarely a good enough reason for diversification on its own: growth must be profitable. Indeed, growth can often be merely a form of 'empire building', especially in the public sector. Diversification decisions need to be approached sceptically.

Four potentially value-creating drivers for diversification are as follows.

- *Exploiting economies of scope.* **Economies of scope refers to efficiency gains through applying the organisation's existing resources or competences to new markets or services.**[4] If an organisation has under-utilised resources or competences that it cannot effectively close or sell to other potential users, it is efficient to use these resources or competences by diversification into a new activity. In other words, there are economies to be gained by extending the scope of the organisation's activities. For example, many universities have large resources in terms of halls of residence, which they must have for their students but which are under-utilised out of term-time. These halls of residence are more efficiently used if the universities expand the scope of their activities into conferencing and tourism during vacation periods. Economies of scope may apply to both *tangible* resources, such as halls of residence, and *intangible* resources and competences, such as brands or staff skills.

- *Stretching corporate management competences ('dominant logics').* This is a special case of economies of scope, and refers to the potential for applying the skills of talented corporate-level managers (referred to as 'corporate parenting skills' in section 7.6) to new businesses. The **dominant logic is the set of corporate-level managerial competences applied across the portfolio of businesses**.[5] Corporate-level managers may have competences that can be applied even to businesses which do not share resources at the operating-unit level. Thus the French luxury-goods conglomerate LVMH includes a wide range of businesses – from champagne, through fashion and perfumes, to financial media – that share very few operational resources or business-level competences. However, LVMH creates value for these specialised companies by applying corporate-level competences in developing classic brands and nurturing highly creative people that are relevant to all its individual businesses. See also the discussion of dominant logic at Berkshire Hathaway in Illustration 7.4 later.

- *Exploiting superior internal processes*. Internal processes within a diversified corporation can often be more efficient than external processes in the open market. This is especially the case where external capital and labour markets do not yet work well, as in many developing economies. In these circumstances, well-managed conglomerates can make sense, even if their constituent businesses do not have operating relationships with each other. For example, China has many conglomerates because they are able to mobilise investment, develop managers and exploit networks in a way that stand-alone Chinese companies, relying on imperfect markets, cannot. For example, China's largest privately owned conglomerate, the Fosun Group, owns steel mills, pharmaceutical companies and China's largest retailer, Yuyuan Tourist Mart.[6]

- *Increasing market power*.[7] Being diversified in many businesses can increase power vis-à-vis competitors in at least two ways. First, having the same wide portfolio of products as a competitor increases the potential for *mutual forbearance*. The ability to retaliate across the whole range of the portfolio acts to discourage the competitor from making any aggressive moves at all. Two similarly diversified competitors are thus likely to forbear from competing aggressively with each other. Second, having a diversified range of businesses increases the power to *cross-subsidise* one business from the profits of the others. On the one hand, the ability to cross-subsidise can support aggressive bids to drive competitors out of a particular market. On the other hand, knowing this power to cross-subsidise a particular business, competitors without equivalent power will be reluctant to attack that business.

Where diversification creates value, it is described as 'synergistic'.[8] **Synergy refers to the benefits gained where activities or assets complement each other so that their combined effect is greater than the sum of the parts** (the famous 2 + 2 = 5 equation). Thus a film company and a music publisher would be synergistic if they were worth more together than separately. However, synergies are often harder to identify and more costly to extract in practice than managers like to admit.[9]

Indeed, some drivers for diversification involve negative synergies, in other words value destruction. Three potentially value-destroying diversification drivers are:

- *Responding to market decline* is one common but doubtful driver for diversification. Rather than let the managers of a declining business invest spare funds in a new business, conventional finance theory suggests it is usually best to let shareholders find new growth investment opportunities for themselves. For example, it is arguable that Microsoft's diversification into electronic games such as the Xbox – whose launch cost $500m (~€350m) in marketing alone – is a response to declining prospects in its core Windows operating systems business. But if future profits in the core business are likely to be low, shareholders might prefer Microsoft simply to hand back the surplus directly to them, rather than spending it on attacking strong companies such as Sony and Nintendo. If shareholders had wanted to invest in the games business, they could have invested in the original dominant companies themselves.

- *Spreading risk* across a range of markets is another common justification for diversification. Again, conventional finance theory is very sceptical about risk-spreading by diversification. Shareholders can easily spread their risk by taking small stakes in dozens of very different companies themselves. Diversification strategies, on the other hand, are likely to involve a limited range of fairly related markets. While managers might like the security of having more than one market, shareholders typically do not need each of the companies they invest in to be diversified as well – they would prefer managers to concentrate on managing their core business as well as they can. However, conventional finance theory does not apply to private businesses, where the owners have a large proportion of their assets tied up in their company: here it can make sense to diversify risk across a number of distinct activities, so that if one part is in trouble, the whole business is not pulled down.

- *Managerial ambition* can sometimes drive inappropriate diversification. It is argued that the managers of British banks such as Royal Bank of Scotland (at one point the fifth largest bank in the world) and HBOS (Britain's largest housing-lender) promoted strategies of excessive growth and diversification into new markets during the first decade of the 21st century. Such growth and diversification gave the managers short-term benefits in terms of managerial bonuses and prestige. But going beyond their areas of true expertise soon brought financial disaster, leading to the nationalisation of RBS and the takeover of HBOS by rival Lloyds bank.

(7.4) DIVERSIFICATION AND PERFORMANCE

Because most large corporations today are diversified, but also because diversification can sometimes be in management's self-interest, many scholars and policy-makers have been concerned to establish whether diversified companies really perform better than undiversified companies. After all, it would be deeply troubling if large corporations were diversifying simply to spread risk for managers, to save managerial jobs in declining businesses or to generate short-term growth, as in the case of RBS and HBOS.

Research studies of diversification have particularly focused on the relative benefits of related diversification and conglomerate or unrelated diversification. Researchers generally find that related or limited diversifiers outperform both firms that remain specialised and those which have unrelated or extensively diversified strategies.[10] In other words, the diversification–performance relationship tends to follow an inverted (or upside-down) U-shape, as in Figure 7.3. The implication is that some diversification is good – but not too much.

However, these performance studies produce statistical averages. Some related diversification strategies fail – as in the case of some accounting firms' ventures in consulting – while some conglomerates succeed – as in the case of LVMH. The case against unrelated diversification is not solid, and effective dominant logics or particular national contexts can play in its favour. The conclusion from the performance studies is that, although on average related diversification pays better than unrelated, any diversification strategy needs rigorous questioning on its particular merits.

Figure 7.3 Diversity and performance

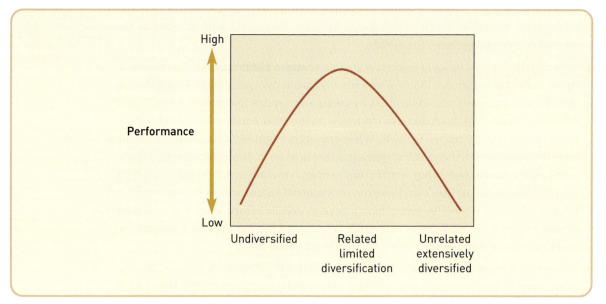

7.5 VERTICAL INTEGRATION

As well as diversification, another direction for corporate strategy can be vertical integration. **Vertical integration describes entering activities where the organisation is its own supplier or customer.** Thus it involves operating at another stage of the value network (see section 3.4.2). This section considers both vertical integration and vertical dis-integration, particularly in the form of outsourcing.

7.5.1 Forward and backward integration

Vertical integration can go in either of two directions:

- **Backward integration** refers to development into activities concerned with the inputs into the company's current business (i.e. they are further back in the value network). For example, the acquisition by a car manufacturer of a component supplier would be a backward integration move.

- **Forward integration** refers to development into activities concerned with the outputs of a company's current business (i.e. are further forward in the value network). For a car manufacturer, forward integration would be into car retail, repairs and servicing.

Thus vertical integration is like diversification in increasing corporate scope. The difference is that it brings together activities up and down the same value network, while diversification typically involves more or less different value networks. However, because realising synergies involves bringing together different value networks, diversification (especially related diversification) is sometimes also described as *horizontal integration*. For example, a company diversified in cars, trucks and buses could find benefits in integrating aspects of the various design or component-sourcing processes. The relationship between horizontal integration and vertical integration is depicted in Figure 7.4.

Figure 7.4 Diversification and integration options: car manufacturer example

Vertical integration is often favoured because it seems to 'capture' more of the profits in a value network. The car manufacturer gains the retailer's profits as well. However, it is important to be aware of two dangers. First, vertical integration involves investment. Expensive investments in activities that are less profitable than the original core business will be unattractive to shareholders because they are reducing their *average* or overall rate of return on investment. Second, even if there is a degree of relatedness through the value network, vertical integration is likely to involve quite different strategic capabilities. Thus car manufacturers who forwardly integrate into car service and repair have found that managing networks of small service outlets is very different to managing large manufacturing plants. Growing appreciation of both the risks of diluting overall returns on investment and the distinct capabilities involved at different stages of the value network has led many companies in recent years to vertically *dis*-integrate.

7.5.2 To integrate or to outsource?

As above, it is often proposed to replace vertically integrated operations by outsourcing or subcontracting. **Outsourcing is the process by which activities previously carried out internally are subcontracted to external suppliers.** Outsourcing can refer to the subcontracting of components in manufacturing, but is now particularly common for services such as information technology, customer call centres and human resource management. The argument for outsourcing to specialist suppliers is often based on strategic capabilities. Specialists in a particular activity are likely to have superior capabilities than an organisation for which that particular activity is not a central part of their business. A specialist IT contractor is usually better at IT than the IT department of a steel company.

However, Nobel prize-winning economist Oliver Williamson has argued that the decision to integrate or outsource involves more than just relative capabilities. His *transaction cost*

ILLUSTRATION 7.3

Deadly outsourcing? The Ministry of Defence under pressure

The UK's Ministry of Defence faces a dilemma over whether to outsource more of its support services, possibly at the expense of the safety of its own personnel.

Under pressure from budget cuts, and still committed to an expensive war in Afghanistan, in November 2009 the United Kingdom's Ministry of Defence (MoD) was planning to outsource more of its logistics and equipment support. This announcement came just one month after the publication of the official report on the 2006 Nimrod military aircraft crash, in which 14 personnel had died. The chairman of the inquiry, Charles Haddon-Cave, had castigated the MoD for 'lamentable' safety procedures. But he had also criticised two private-sector contractors, BAE Systems and Qinetiq, who had been involved in the safety checks for the doomed Nimrod aircraft. Haddon-Smith complained: 'there has been a shift in culture and priorities at the MoD towards business and financial targets at the expense of. . . . safety and airworthiness'.

But now the Ministry of Defence was launching its Defence Support Review (DSR), where it announced: 'past efficiencies have . . . been delivered from a range of increasingly innovative arrangements with industry. . . . The cost base has, and will continue to, migrate to industry.' The Defence Support Review claimed its recommendations could save £474m (~€521m; ~$711m) in the first four years of its plan, and up to £2.4bn over the subsequent six years. The BAE Systems contract for the support of Tornado fighter aircraft had already delivered savings of £1.3bn. The main MoD civil service union replied that it was '. . . concerned that the DSR is premature and will damage the MoD's ability to support the front-line'.

The Royal Air Force is the most committed of the three armed services to outsourcing support work to contractors. Minor repairs on aircraft are done in-theatre by RAF mechanics. However, more substantial maintenance is done by contractors such as BAE Systems, Rolls-Royce and Qinetiq at main operating bases distributed around the world. Contracts typically guarantee that aircraft will be available to fly a certain number of hours over an agreed period.

The Royal Navy relies on BAE Systems and Babcock for support of its submarine and surface fleets. It leases fishery protection vessels from BAE Systems as well. Availability contracts work less well for ships than for aircraft because there are fewer of them, making it harder to keep a contracted number of ships in service over an agreed period. The Army is the most reluctant to outsource repair and maintenance work, relying more on the in-house Defence Support Group. However, in 2008, it signed a contract with BAE Systems to sustain about 400 Panther command and liaison vehicles.

BAE Systems is the second largest defence contractor in the world, behind the American Lockheed-Martin. It makes and supports aircraft, missiles, ships, submarines and armoured vehicles. In 2009, BAE Systems employed over 30,000 people in the UK, about 10 per cent of all UK defence industry jobs. The 2006 Parliamentary Select Committee on Defence had established that about 5 per cent of all MoD defence contracts by value go to BAE Systems each year, while BAE Systems derived 28 per cent of their sales from the MoD. BAE Systems was effectively a monopoly supplier in the UK of air systems and aircraft support.

Sources: House of Commons Defence Committee, 7th Report, 2006; J. Lerner, 'MoD considers call for rise of outsourcing', *Financial Times,* 17 November 2009; 'Learning from the Nimrod Disaster', *Financial Times,* 30 October 2009.

Questions

1 Compare the arguments for defence outsourcing from strategic capabilities and transaction costs points of view.

2 If you were outsourcing aircraft maintenance, what might you be concerned about and how might you design the contract and the tendering process to reduce those concerns?

framework helps analyse the relative costs and benefits of managing ('transacting') activities internally or externally (see also the Key Debate at the end of this chapter).[11] In assessing whether to integrate or outsource an activity, he warns against underestimating the long-term costs of *opportunism* by external subcontractors (or indeed any other organisation in a market relationship). Subcontractors are liable over time to take advantage of their position, either to reduce their standards or to extract higher prices. Market relationships tend to fail in controlling subcontractor opportunism where:

- there are *few alternatives* to the subcontractor and it is hard to shop around;
- the product or service is *complex and changing*, and therefore impossible to specify fully in a legally binding contract;
- investments have been made in *specific assets*, which the subcontractor knows will have little value if they withhold their product or service.

Both capabilities and transaction cost reasoning have influenced the outsourcing decisions of the Ministry of Defence, see Illustration 7.3.

This transaction cost framework suggests that the costs of opportunism can outweigh the benefits of subcontracting to organisations with superior strategic capabilities. For example, mining companies in isolated parts of the Australian outback typically own and operate housing for their workers. The isolation creates specific assets (the housing is worth nothing if the mine closes down) and a lack of alternatives (the nearest town might be a hundred miles away). Consequently, there would be large risks to both partners if the mine subcontracted housing to an independent company specialising in worker accommodation, however strong its capabilities. Transaction cost economics therefore offers the following advice: if there are few alternative suppliers, if activities are complex and likely to change, and if there are significant investments in specific assets, then it is likely to be better to vertically integrate rather than outsource.

In sum, the decision to integrate or subcontract rests on the balance between two distinct factors:

- *Relative strategic capabilities*. Does the subcontractor have the potential to do the work significantly better?
- *Risk of opportunism*. Is the subcontractor likely to take advantage of the relationship over time?

VALUE CREATION AND THE CORPORATE PARENT

Given the doubt over diversification and integration strategies, it is clear that sometimes corporate parents are not adding value to their constituent businesses. Where there is no added value, it is usually best to divest the relevant businesses from the corporate portfolio. Thus when Carphone Warehouse recognised that its businesses would be more valuable separate rather than together, it decided in 2010 to break itself up entirely, creating a specialised retail business (including Best Buy, Europe's largest phone retailer) on the one hand, and a specialised home broadband service (TalkTalk) on the other. In the public sector too, units such as schools or hospitals are increasingly being given freedom from parenting authorities, because independence is seen as more effective. Some theorists even challenge the notion of corporate-level strategy altogether, the subject of the Key Debate at the end of this chapter.

This section examines how corporate parents can both add and destroy value, and considers three different parenting approaches that can be effective.

7.6.1 Value-adding and value-destroying activities of corporate parents[12]

Any corporate parent needs to demonstrate that they create more value than they cost. This applies to both commercial and public-sector organisations. For public-sector organisations, privatisation or outsourcing is likely to be the consequence of failure to demonstrate value. Companies whose shares are traded freely on the stock markets face a further challenge. They must demonstrate they create more value than any other rival corporate parent could create. Failure to do so is likely to lead to a hostile takeover or break-up. Rival companies that think they can create more value out of the business units can bid for the company's shares, on the expectation of either running the businesses better or selling them off to other potential parents. If the rival's bid is more attractive and credible than what the current parent can promise, shareholders will back them at the expense of incumbent management.

In this sense, competition takes place between different corporate parents for the right to own and control businesses. In the competitive market for the control of businesses, corporate parents must show that they have *parenting advantage*, on the same principle that business units must demonstrate competitive advantage. They must demonstrate that they are the best possible parent for the businesses they control. Parents therefore must have a very clear approach to how they create value. In practice, however, many of their activities can be value-destroying as well as value-creating.

Value-adding activities[13]

There are four main types of activity by which a corporate parent can add value.

- *Envisioning.* The corporate parent can provide a clear overall vision or *strategic intent* for its business units.[14] This vision should guide and motivate the business unit managers in order to maximise corporation-wide performance through commitment to a common purpose. The vision should also provide stakeholders with a *clear external image* about what the organisation as a whole is about: this can reassure shareholders about the rationale for having a diversified strategy in the first place. Finally, a clear vision provides a *discipline* on the corporate parent to stop it wandering into inappropriate activities or taking on unnecessary costs.

- *Coaching and facilitating.* The corporate parent can help business unit managers *develop strategic capabilities*, by coaching them to improve their skills and confidence. They can also facilitate cooperation and sharing across the business units, so improving the *synergies* from being within the same corporate organisation. Corporate-wide management courses are one effective means of achieving these objectives, as bringing managers across the business to learn strategy skills also provides an opportunity for them to build relationships between each other and see opportunities for cooperation.

- *Providing central services and resources.* The centre is obviously a provider of capital for *investment*. The centre can also provide central services such as treasury, tax and human resource advice, which if centralised can have *sufficient scale* to be efficient and to build up *relevant expertise*. Centralised services often have greater *leverage*: for example, combining the purchases of separate business units increases their bargaining power for shared inputs such as energy. This leverage can be helpful in *brokering* with external bodies, such as government regulators, or other companies in negotiating alliances. Finally, the centre can have an important role in managing expertise within the corporate whole, for instance by *transferring managers* across the business units or by creating shared *knowledge management* systems via corporate intranets.

- *Intervening*. Finally, the corporate parent can also intervene within its business units in order to ensure appropriate performance. The corporate parent should be able to closely *monitor* business unit performance and *improve performance* either by replacing weak managers or by assisting them in turning around their businesses. The parent can also *challenge and develop* the strategic ambitions of business units, so that satisfactorily performing businesses are encouraged to perform even better.

Value-destroying activities

However, there are also three broad ways in which the corporate parent can inadvertently destroy value:

- *Adding management costs*. Most simply, the staff and facilities of the corporate centre are expensive. The corporate centre typically has the best-paid managers and the most luxurious offices. It is the actual businesses that have to generate the revenues that pay for them. If their costs are greater than the value they create, then the corporate centre's managers are net value-destroying.

- *Adding bureaucratic complexity*. As well as these direct financial costs, there is the 'bureaucratic fog' created by an additional layer of management and the need to coordinate with sister businesses. These typically slow down managers' responses to issues and lead to compromises between the interests of individual businesses.

- *Obscuring financial performance*. One danger in a large diversified company is that the underperformance of weak businesses can be obscured. Weak businesses might be cross-subsidised by the stronger ones. Internally, the possibility of hiding weak performance diminishes the incentives for business unit managers to strive as hard as they can for their businesses: they have a parental safety-net. Externally, shareholders and financial analysts cannot easily judge the performance of individual units within the corporate whole. Diversified companies' share prices are often marked down, because shareholders prefer the 'pure plays' of stand-alone units, where weak performance cannot be hidden.[15]

These dangers suggest clear paths for corporate parents that wish to avoid value destruction. They should keep a close eye on centre costs, both financial and bureaucratic, ensuring that they are no more than required by their corporate strategy. They should also do all they can to promote financial transparency, so that business units remain under pressure to perform and shareholders are confident that there are no hidden disasters.

Overall, there are many ways in which corporate parents can add value. It is, of course, difficult to pursue them all and some are hard to mix with others. For example, a corporate parent that does a great deal of top-down intervening is less likely to be seen by its managers as a helpful coach and facilitator. Business unit managers will concentrate on maximising their own individual performance rather than looking out for ways to cooperate with other business unit managers for the greater good of the whole. For this reason, corporate parenting roles tend to fall into three main types, each coherent within itself but distinct from the others.[16] These three types of corporate parenting role are summarised in Figure 7.5.

ILLUSTRATION 7.4

Eating its own cooking: Berkshire Hathaway's parenting

A portfolio manager may seek to manage a highly diverse set of business units on behalf of its shareholders.

Berkshire Hathaway's chairman and CEO is Warren Buffett, one of the world's richest men – and also one of the most plain-spoken about how to run a business. With annual sales now over $100bn (€70bn), Buffet founded this conglomerate with a small textile business in the early 1960s. Berkshire Hathaway's businesses now are highly diverse. They include large insurance businesses (GEICO, General Re, NRG), manufacturers of carpets, building products, clothing and footwear, retail companies and NetJets, the private jet service. The company also has significant long-term minority stakes in businesses such as Coca-Cola and General Electric. Aged 79, Buffett remains highly active: in 2008, he took a 10 per cent stake in Goldman Sachs, the world's leading investment bank, and in 2009 he completed the purchase of BNSF, the second largest railway company in the United States. Since the mid-1960s, Berkshire has averaged a growth in book value of 20.3% each year.

The 2009 Berkshire Hathaway annual report explains how Buffet and his deputy chairman Charlie Munger run the business. With regard to shareholders, Buffet writes:

> Charlie Munger and I think of our shareholders as owner-partners, and of ourselves as managing partners. (Because of the size of our shareholdings we are also, for better or worse, controlling partners.) We do not view the company itself as the ultimate owner of our business assets but instead view the company as a conduit through which our shareholders own the assets. . . . In line with Berkshire's owner-orientation, most of our directors have a major portion of their net worth invested in the company. We eat our own cooking.

Berkshire has a clear 'dominant logic':

> Charlie and I avoid businesses whose futures we can't evaluate, no matter how exciting their products may be. In the past, it required no brilliance for people to foresee the fabulous growth that awaited such industries as autos (in 1910), aircraft (in 1930) and television sets (in 1950). But the future then also included competitive dynamics

that would decimate almost all of the companies entering those industries. Even the survivors tended to come away bleeding. Just because Charlie and I can clearly see dramatic growth ahead for an industry does not mean we can judge what its profit margins and returns on capital will be as a host of competitors battle for supremacy. At Berkshire we will stick with businesses whose profit picture for decades to come seems reasonably predictable. Even then, we will make plenty of mistakes.

Buffett also explains how they manage their subsidiary businesses:

> Charlie and I are the managing partners of Berkshire. But we subcontract all of the heavy lifting in this business to the managers of our subsidiaries. In fact, we delegate almost to the point of abdication: Though Berkshire has about 257,000 employees, only 21 of these are at headquarters. Charlie and I mainly attend to capital allocation and the care and feeding of our key managers. Most of these managers are happiest when they are left alone to run their businesses, and that is customarily just how we leave them. That puts them in charge of all operating decisions and of dispatching the excess cash they generate to headquarters. By sending it to us, they don't get diverted by the various enticements that would come their way were they responsible for deploying the cash their businesses throw off. Furthermore, Charlie and I are exposed to a much wider range of possibilities for investing these funds than any of our managers could find in his or her own industry.

Questions

1 In what ways does Berkshire Hathaway conform (and not conform) to the archetypal portfolio manager described in section 7.6.2?

2 Suggest some industries and businesses, or types of industries and businesses, that Warren Buffett is likely never to invest in.

Figure 7.5 Portfolio managers, synergy managers and parental developers

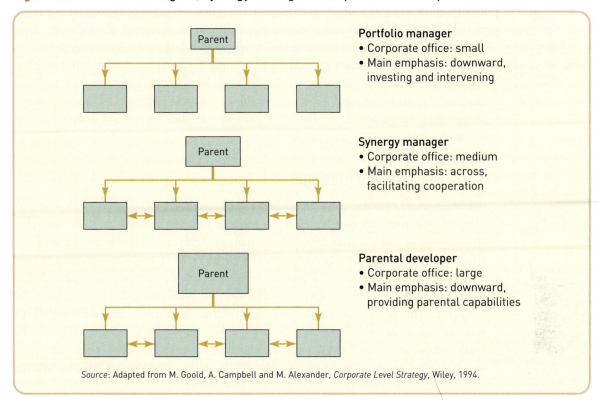

Portfolio manager
- Corporate office: small
- Main emphasis: downward, investing and intervening

Synergy manager
- Corporate office: medium
- Main emphasis: across, facilitating cooperation

Parental developer
- Corporate office: large
- Main emphasis: downward, providing parental capabilities

Source: Adapted from M. Goold, A. Campbell and M. Alexander, *Corporate Level Strategy*, Wiley, 1994.

7.6.2 The portfolio manager

The **portfolio manager** operates as an active investor in a way that shareholders in the stock market are either too dispersed or too inexpert to be able to do. In effect, the portfolio manager is acting as an agent on behalf of financial markets and shareholders with a view to extracting more value from the various businesses than they could achieve themselves. Its role is to identify and acquire under-valued assets or businesses and improve them. The portfolio manager might do this, for example, by acquiring another corporation, divesting low-performing businesses within it and intervening to improve the performance of those with potential. Such corporations may not be much concerned about the relatedness (see section 7.2) of the business units in their portfolio, typically adopting a conglomerate strategy. Their role is not to get closely involved in the routine management of the businesses, only to act over short periods of time to improve performance. In terms of the value-creating activities identified earlier, the portfolio manager concentrates on intervening and the provision (or withdrawal) of investment.

Portfolio managers seek to keep the cost of the centre low, for example by having a small corporate staff with few central services, leaving the business units alone so that their chief executives have a high degree of autonomy. They set clear financial targets for those chief executives, offering high rewards if they achieve them and likely loss of position if they do not. Such corporate parents can, of course, manage quite a large number of such businesses because they are not directly managing the everyday strategies of those businesses. Rather they are acting from above, setting financial targets, making central evaluations about the well-being and future prospects of such businesses, and investing, intervening or divesting accordingly.

Some argue that the days of the portfolio manager are gone. Improving financial markets mean that the scope for finding and investing cheaply in under-performing companies is much reduced. However, some portfolio managers remain and are successful. Private equity firms such as Apax Partners or Blackstone are a new way of operating a portfolio management style, typically investing in, improving and then divesting companies in loosely knit portfolios. For example, in 2010, Blackstone owned companies ranging from Hilton Hotels to the China BlueStar chemicals company, totalling more than 990,000 employees around the world. Illustration 7.4 includes a description of the portfolio parenting approach of Warren Buffet at Berkshire Hathaway.

7.6.3 The synergy manager

Obtaining synergy is often seen as the prime rationale for the corporate parent.[17] The **synergy manager is a corporate parent seeking to enhance value for business units by managing synergies across business units**. Synergies are likely to be particularly rich in the case of related diversification. In terms of value-creating activities, the focus is threefold: envisioning to build a common purpose; facilitating cooperation across businesses; and providing central services and resources. For example, at Apple, Steve Jobs's vision of his personal computers being the digital hub of the new digital lifestyle guides managers across the iMac computer, iPod, iPhone and iPad businesses to ensure seamless connections between the fast-developing offerings. The result is enhanced value through better customer experience. A metals company diversified into both steel and aluminium might centralise its energy procurement, gaining synergy benefits through increased bargaining power over suppliers.

However, achieving such synergistic benefits involves at least three challenges:

- *Excessive costs*. The benefits in sharing and cooperation need to outweigh the costs of undertaking such integration, both direct financial costs and opportunity costs. Managing synergistic relationships tends to involve expensive investments in management time.

- *Overcoming self-interest*. Managers in the business units have to want to cooperate. Especially where managers are rewarded largely according to the performance of their own particular business unit, they are likely to be unwilling to sacrifice their time and resources for the common good.

- *Illusory synergies*. It is easy to overestimate the value of skills or resources to other businesses. This is particularly common when the corporate centre needs to justify a new venture or the acquisition of a new company. Claimed synergies often prove illusory when managers actually have to put them into practice.

The failure of many companies to extract expected synergies from their businesses has led to growing scepticism about the notion of synergy. Synergistic benefits are not as easy to achieve as would appear. For example, in 2007 Daimler sold most of its stake in mass-market car manufacturer Chrysler after ten years of trying to extract synergies with its luxury Mercedes business. However, synergy continues to be a common theme in corporate-level strategy, as Illustration 7.2 on Zodiac exemplifies.

7.6.4 The parental developer[18]

The **parental developer seeks to employ its own central capabilities to add value to its businesses**. This is not so much about how the parent can develop benefits *across* business units or transfer capabilities between business units, as in the case of managing synergy. Rather parental developers focus on the resources or capabilities they have as parents which they can transfer *downwards* to enhance the potential of business units. For example, a parent could have a valuable brand or specialist skills in financial management or product development. If such parenting capabilities exist, corporate managers then need to identify a '*parenting opportunity*': a business which is not fulfilling its potential but which could be improved by applying the parenting capability, such as branding or product development. Such parenting opportunities are therefore more common in the case of related rather than unrelated diversified strategies and are likely to involve exchanges of managers and other resources across the businesses. Key value-creating activities for the parent will be the provision of central services and resources. For example, a consumer products company might offer substantial guidance on branding and distribution from the centre; a technology company might run a large central R&D laboratory.

There are two crucial challenges to managing a parental developer:

- *Parental focus.* Corporate parents need to be rigorous and focused in identifying their unique value-adding capabilities. They should always be asking what others can do better than them, and focus their energy and time on activities where they really do add value. Other central services should typically be outsourced to specialist companies that can do it better.

- *The 'crown jewel' problem.* Some diversified companies have business units in their portfolios which are performing well but to which the parent adds little value. These can become 'crown jewels', to which corporate parents become excessively attached. The logic of the parental development approach is if the centre cannot add value, it is just a cost and therefore destroying value. Parental developers should divest businesses they do not add value to, even profitable ones. Funds raised by selling a profitable business can be reinvested in businesses where the parent can add value.

(7.7) PORTFOLIO MATRICES

Section 7.6 discussed rationales for corporate parents of multi-business organisations. This section introduces models by which managers can determine financial investment and divestment within their portfolios of business. Each model gives more or less attention to one of three criteria:

- the *balance* of the portfolio, e.g. in relation to its markets and the needs of the corporation;

- the *attractiveness* of the business units in terms of how strong they are individually and how profitable their markets or industries are likely to be; and

- the '*fit*' that the business units have with each other in terms of potential synergies or the extent to which the corporate parent will be good at looking after them.

7.7.1 The BCG (or growth/share) matrix[19]

One of the most common and long-standing ways of conceiving of the balance of a portfolio of businesses is the Boston Consulting Group (BCG) matrix (see Figure 7.6). The **BCG matrix** uses **market share and market growth criteria for determining the attractiveness and balance of a business portfolio.** High market share and high growth are, of course, attractive. However, the

KEY CONCEPT

BCG matrix

Figure 7.6 The growth share (or BCG) matrix

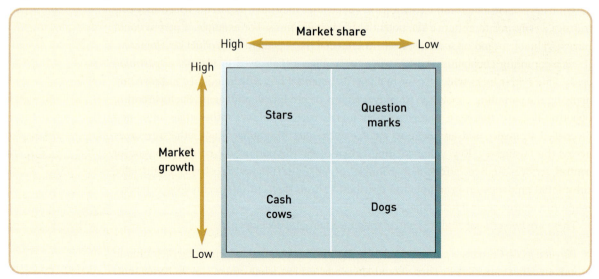

BCG matrix also warns that high growth demands heavy investment, for instance to expand capacity or develop brands. There needs to be a balance within the portfolio, so that there are some low-growth businesses that are making sufficient surplus to fund the investment needs of higher-growth businesses.

The growth/share axes of the BCG matrix define four sorts of business:

- A **star is a business unit within a portfolio which has a high market share in a growing market**. The business unit may be spending heavily to keep up with growth, but high market share should yield sufficient profits to make it more or less self-sufficient in terms of investment needs.

- A **question mark (or problem child) is a business unit within a portfolio that is in a growing market, but does not yet have high market share**. Developing question marks into stars, with high market share, takes heavy investment. Many question marks fail to develop, so the BCG advises corporate parents to nurture several at a time. It is important to make sure that some question marks develop into stars, as existing stars eventually become cash cows and cash cows may decline into dogs.

- A **cash cow is a business unit within a portfolio that has a high market share in a mature market**. However, because growth is low, investments needs are less, while high market share means that the business unit should be profitable. The cash cow should then be a cash provider, helping to fund investments in question marks.

- **Dogs are business units within a portfolio that have low share in static or declining markets** and are thus the worst of all combinations. They may be a cash drain and use up a disproportionate amount of managerial time and company resources. The BCG usually recommends divestment or closure.

The BCG matrix has several advantages. It provides a good way of visualising the different needs and potential of all the diverse businesses within the corporate portfolio. It warns corporate parents of the financial demands of what might otherwise look like a desirable portfolio of high-growth businesses. It also reminds corporate parents that stars are likely eventually to wane. Finally, it provides a useful discipline to business unit managers, underlining the fact

ILLUSTRATION 7.5

ITC's diverse portfolio: smelling sweeter

What was once the Imperial Tobacco Company of India now has a portfolio stretching from cigarettes to fragrances.

ITC is one of India's largest consumer good companies, with an increasingly diversified portfolio of products. Its chairman, Y.C. Deveshwar describes its strategy thus: 'It is ITC's endeavour to continuously explore opportunites for growth by synergising and blending its multiple core competences to create new epicentres of growth. The employees of ITC are inspired by the vision of growing ITC into one of India's premier institutions and are willing to go the extra mile to generate value for the economy, in the process creating growing value for the shareholders.'

ITC was founded in 1910 as the Imperial Tobacco Company of India, with brands such as Wills, Gold Cut and John Players. ITC now holds about two thirds of the market for cigarettes in India, with Philip Morris and BAT affiliated companies distant seconds with about 13 per cent each. However, cigarettes in India are highly discouraged by the Indian government, and increasingly heavily taxed.

ITC has a long diversification history. The company's original activities in the growth of leaf tobacco developed into a range of agricultural businesses within India, including edible oils, fruit pulp, spices and frozen foods. ITC had set up a packaging and printing business in the 1920s, originally to supply its cigarette business. By 2009, this was India's largest packaging solutions provider. In 1975, ITC had entered the hotel business, becoming the country's second largest operator with over 100 hotels by 2009, ranging from de luxe to economy. In 1979, the company also entered the paperboard industry, and three decades later was the country's largest producer, accounting for 29% of the market by value.

The early 21st century had seen many new diversification initiatives, especially in the booming Fast Moving Consumer Goods (FMCG) sector. Initially it started in the food business, with Kitchens-of-India ready-to-eat gourmet foods, the *Aashirvaad* wheat-flour business, Sunfeast biscuits and Bingo snacks. ITC's own agri-businesses were an important source of supply for these initiatives. *Aashirvaad* reached over 50 per cent Indian market share, while Sunfeast gained 12 per cent market share and Bingo 11 per cent by 2008. At the same time, ITC took advantage of the strong brand values of its Wills cigarettes to launch Wills Lifestyle, a range of upmarket clothing stores, with its own designs. In 2009, Wills Lifestyle was recognised as India's 'Most Admired Fashion Brand of the Year'. In 2005, ITC launched its personal care business, again using its cigarette brandnames: for example, 'Essenza Di Wills' (fragrances) and 'Fiama Di Wills' (hair and skin care).

ITC segmental sales and profits (Rs in Crores)

Segment	2005 sales	2005 profits	2009 sales	2009 profits
Cigarettes	10,002	2,288	15,115	4,184
Other FMCG	563	(195)	3,010	(483)
Hotels	577	141	1,014	316
Agribusiness	1,780	96.4	2,284	256
Paperboard, paper and packaging	1,565	280	1,719	509

5 Rs in Crores ~ US $1,000,000 ~€700,000. Profits are before interest and tax. Figures in brackets are losses.

Sources: ITC annual reports; M. Balaji, 2006, *ITC: Adding Shareholder Value through Diversifications*, IBSCDC; B. Gopal and S. Kora, 2009, *Indian Conglomerate ITC*, IBS Research Center.

Questions

1 How well does ITC's portfolio fit in terms of the BCG matrix?

2 Identify and evaluate the various synergies in ITC's business.

that the corporate parent ultimately owns the surplus resources they generate and can allocate them according to what is best for the corporate whole. Cash cows should not hoard their profits.

However, there are at least three potential problems with the BCG matrix:

- *Definitional vagueness.* It can be hard to decide what high and low growth or share mean in particular situations. Managers are often keen to define themselves as 'high-share' by defining their market in a particularly narrow way (for example, ignoring relevant international markets).

- *Capital market assumptions.* The notion that a corporate parent needs a balanced portfolio to finance investment from internal sources (cash cows) assumes that capital cannot be raised in external markets, for instance by issuing shares or raising loans. The notion of a balanced portfolio may be more relevant in countries where capital markets are under-developed or in private companies that wish to minimise dependence on external shareholders or banks.

- *Unkind to animals.* Both cash cows and dogs receive ungenerous treatment, the first being simply milked, the second terminated or cast out of the corporate home. This treatment can cause *motivation problems*, as managers in these units see little point in working hard for the sake of other businesses. There is also the danger of the *self-fulfilling prophecy*. Cash cows will become dogs even more quickly than the model expects if they are simply milked and denied adequate investment. Finally, the notion that a dog can be simply sold or closed down also assumes that there are *no ties to other business units* in the portfolio, whose performance might depend in part on keeping the dog alive. This portfolio approach to dogs works better for conglomerate strategies, where divestments or closures are unlikely to have knock-on effects on other parts of the portfolio.

7.7.2 The directional policy (GE–McKinsey) matrix

Another way to consider a portfolio of businesses is by means of the *directional policy matrix*[20] which categorises business units into those with good prospects and those with less good prospects. The matrix was originally developed by McKinsey & Co. consultants in order to help the American conglomerate General Electric manage its portfolio of business units. Specifically, the directional policy matrix positions business units according to (a) how attractive the relevant market is in which they are operating, and (b) the competitive strength of the SBU in that market. Attractiveness can be identified by PESTEL or five forces analyses; business unit strength can be defined by competitor analysis (for instance the strategy canvas): see section 2.4.3. Some analysts also choose to show graphically how large the market is for a given business unit's activity, and even the market share of that business unit, as shown in Figure 7.7. For example, managers in a firm with the portfolio shown in Figure 7.7 will be concerned that they have relatively low shares in the largest and most attractive market, whereas their greatest strength is in a market with only medium attractiveness and smaller markets with little long-term attractiveness.

The matrix also offers strategy guidelines given the positioning of the business units, as shown in Figure 7.8. It suggests that the businesses with the highest growth potential and the greatest strength are those in which to invest for growth. Those that are the weakest and in the least attractive markets should be divested or 'harvested' (i.e. used to yield as much cash as possible before divesting).

The directional policy matrix is more complex than the BCG matrix. However, it can have two advantages. First, unlike the simpler four-box BCG matrix, the nine cells of the directional

Figure 7.7 Directional policy (GE–McKinsey) matrix

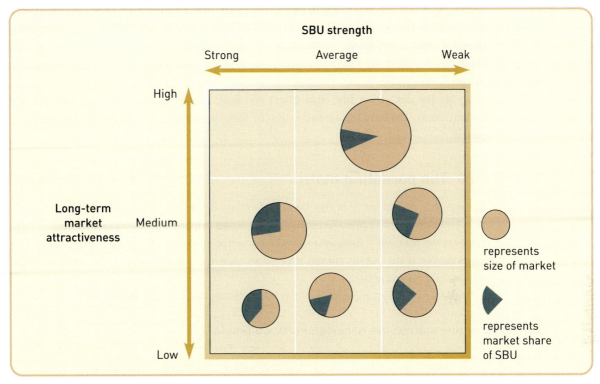

Figure 7.8 Strategy guidelines based on the directional policy matrix

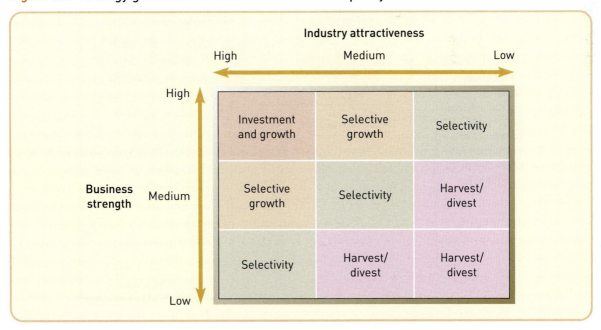

policy matrix acknowledge the possibility of a difficult middle ground. Here managers have to be carefully selective. In this sense, the directional policy matrix is less mechanistic than the BCG matrix, encouraging open debate on less clear-cut cases. Second, the two axes of the directional policy matrix are not based on single measures (i.e. market share and market growth).

Business strength can derive from many other factors than market share, and industry attractiveness does not just boil down to industry growth rates. On the other hand, the directional policy matrix shares some problems with the BCG matrix, particularly about vague definitions, capital market assumptions, motivation and self-fulfilling prophecy. Overall, however, the value of the matrix is to help managers invest in the businesses which are most likely to pay off.

So far the discussion has been about the logic of portfolios in terms of balance and attractiveness. The third logic is to do with 'fit' with the particular capabilities of the corporate parent.

7.7.3 The parenting matrix

The *parenting matrix* (or Ashridge Portfolio Display) developed by consultants Michael Goold and Andrew Campbell introduces parental fit as an important criterion for including businesses in the portfolio.[21] Businesses may be attractive in terms of the BCG or directional policy matrices, but if the parent cannot add value, then the parent ought to be cautious about acquiring or retaining them.

There are two key dimensions of fit in the parenting matrix (see Figure 7.9):

Figure 7.9 The parenting matrix: the Ashridge Portfolio Display

Source: Adapted from M. Goold, A. Campbell and M. Alexander, *Corporate Level Strategy*, Wiley, 1994

- *'Feel'*. This is a measure of the fit between each business unit's *critical success factors* (see section 2.4.3) and the capabilities (in terms of competences and resources) of the corporate parent. In other words, does the corporate parent have the necessary 'feel', or understanding, for the businesses it will parent?

- *'Benefit'*. This measures the fit between the *parenting opportunities*, or needs, of business units and the capabilities of the parent. Parenting opportunities are about the upside, areas in which good parenting can benefit the business (for instance, by bringing marketing expertise). For the benefit to be realised, of course, the parent must have the right capabilities to match the parenting opportunities.

The power of using these two dimensions of fit is as follows. It is easy to see that a corporate parent should avoid running businesses that it has no *feel* for. What is less clear is that parenting should be avoided if there is no *benefit*. This challenges the corporate parenting of even businesses for which the parent has high feel. Businesses for which a corporate parent has high feel but can add little benefit should either be run with a very light touch or be divested.

Figure 7.9 shows four kinds of business along these two dimensions of feel and benefit:

- *Heartland* business units are ones which the parent understands well and can continue to add value to. They should be at the core of future strategy.

- *Ballast* business units are ones the parent understands well but can do little for. They would probably be at least as successful as independent companies. If not divested, they should be spared as much corporate bureaucracy as possible.

- *Value-trap* business units are dangerous. They appear attractive because there are opportunities to add value (for instance, marketing could be improved). But they are deceptively attractive, because the parent's lack of feel will result in more harm than good (i.e. the parent lacks the right marketing skills). The parent will need to acquire new capabilities if it is to be able to move value-trap businesses into the heartland. It might be easier to divest to another corporate parent which could add value, and will pay well for the chance.

- *Alien* business units are clear misfits. They offer little opportunity to add value and the parent does not understand them anyway. Exit is definitely the best strategy.

This approach to considering corporate portfolios places the emphasis firmly on how the parent benefits the business units. It requires careful analysis of both parenting capabilities and business-unit parenting needs. The parenting matrix can therefore assist hard decisions where either high feel or high parenting opportunities tempt the corporate parent to acquire or retain businesses. Parents should concentrate on actual or potential heartland businesses, where there is both high feel and high benefit.

The concept of fit has equal relevance in the public-sector. The implication is that public-sector managers should control directly only those services and activities for which they have special managerial expertise. Other services should be outsourced or set up as independent agencies (see section 7.5).

KEY DEBATE

Why have corporate-level strategies anyway?

Do we really need diversified corporations?

The notion of corporate strategy assumes that corporations should own and control businesses in a range of markets or products. But 'transaction cost' economist Oliver Williamson believes that diversified corporations should only exist in the presence of 'market failures' (see also section 7.5.2). If markets worked well, there would be no need for business units to be coordinated through managerial structures. Business units could be independent, coordinating where necessary by simple transactions in the marketplace. The 'invisible hand' of the market could replace the 'visible hand' of managers at corporate headquarters. There would be no 'corporate strategy'.

Market failures favouring the diversified corporation occur for two reasons:

- *'Bounded rationality'*: people cannot know everything that is going on in the market, so perfectly rational market transactions are impossible. Information, for instance on quality and costs, can sometimes be better inside the corporate fold.
- *'Opportunism'*: independent businesses trading between each other may behave opportunistically, for example by cheating on delivery or quality promises. Cheating can sometimes be policed and punished more easily within a corporate hierarchy.

According to Williamson, activities should only be brought into the corporation when the 'transaction costs' of coping with bounded rationality (gaining information) and opportunism (guarding against cheats) are lower inside the corporate hierarchy than they would be if simply relying on transactions in the marketplace.

This comparison of the transaction costs of markets and hierarchies has powerful implications for trends in product diversification:

- Improving capital markets may reduce the relative information advantages of conglomerates in managing a set of unrelated businesses. As markets get better at capturing information there will be less need for conglomerates, something that may account for the recent decline in conglomerates in many economies.

- Improving protection of intellectual property rights may increase the incentives for corporations to license out their technologies to companies, rather than trying to do everything themselves. If the prospect of collecting royalties improves, there is less advantage for corporations keeping everything in-house.

Thus fewer market failures also means narrower product scope.

Williamson's 'transaction cost' view puts a heavy burden on corporations to justify themselves. Two justifications are possible. First, knowledge is hard to trade in the market. Buyers can only know the value of new knowledge once they have already bought it. Because they can trust each other, colleagues in sister business units within the same corporation are better at transferring knowledge than independent companies are in the open market. Second, corporations are not just about minimising the costs of information and cheating, but also about maximising the value of the combined resources. Bringing creative people together in a collective enterprise enhances knowledge exchange, innovation and motivation. Corporations are value creators as well as cost minimisers.

References:
1. O.E. Williamson, 'Strategy Research: Governance and Competence Perspectives', *Strategic Management Journal*, vol. 12, pp. 75–94 (1998).
2. B. Kogut and U. Zander, 'What Firms Do? Coordination, Identity and Learning', *Organization Science*, vol. 7, no. 5 (1996), 502–19.
3. S. Ghoshal, C. Bartlett and P. Moran, 'A New Manifesto for Management', *Sloan Management Review*, Spring (1999), pp. 9–20.

Question

Consider a diversified corporation such as Unilever (food, personal care and household): what kinds of hard-to-trade knowledge might it be able to transfer between product and country subsidiaries and is such knowledge likely to be of increasing or decreasing importance?

SUMMARY

- Many corporations comprise several, sometimes many, business units. Decisions and activities above the level of business units are the concern of what in this chapter is called the *corporate parent*.

- Organisational *scope* is often considered in terms of *related* and *unrelated* diversification.

- Corporate parents may seek to add value by adopting different parenting roles: the *portfolio manager*, the *synergy manager* or the *parental developer*.

- There are several portfolio models to help corporate parents manage their businesses, of which the most common are: the *BCG matrix*, the *directional policy matrix* and the *parenting matrix*.

- *Divestment* and *outsourcing* should be considered as well as diversification, particularly in the light of relative strategic capabilities and the transaction costs of *opportunism*.

WORK ASSIGNMENTS

✱ *Denotes more advanced work assignments.* * *Refers to a case study in the Text and Cases edition.*

7.1   Using the Ansoff axes (Figure 7.2), identify and explain corporate strategic directions for any one of these case organisations: CRH*, Ferrovial*, SAB Miller*.

7.2   Go to the website of any large multi-business organisation (for example, Google, Tata Group, Siemens) and assess the degree to which its corporate-level strategy is characterised by (a) related or unrelated diversification and (b) a coherent 'dominant logic' (see section 7.3).

7.3   For any large multi-business corporation (as in 7.2), explain how the corporate parent should best create value for its component businesses (as portfolio manager, synergy manager or parental developer: see section 7.6). Would all the businesses fit equally well?

7.4✱ For any large multi-business corporation (as in 7.2), plot the business units on a portfolio matrix (for example, the BCG matrix: section 7.7.1). Justify any assumptions about the relative positions of businesses on the relevant axes of the matrix. What managerial conclusions do you draw from this analysis?

Integrative assignment

7.5   Take a case of a recent merger or acquisition (see Chapter 10), and assess the extent to which it involved related or unrelated diversification (if either) and how far it was consistent with the company's existing dominant logic. Using share price information (see www.bigcharts.com or similar), assess shareholders' reaction to the merger or acquisition. How do you explain this reaction?

VIDEO ASSIGNMENT

Visit *MyStrategyLab* and watch the *Fridays* case study.

1 What are the benefits and disadvantages of Fridays' relationship with the supermarkets? Relatively how strong is Fridays vis-à-vis other competitors in this relationship?

2 Explain Fridays' diversification strategy in terms of the Ansoff axes and strategic relatedness (Chapter 7: Figure 7.2).

RECOMMENDED KEY READINGS

- An accessible discussion of corporate strategy is provided by A. Campbell and R. Park, *The Growth Gamble: When Leaders Should Bet on Big New Businesses*, Nicholas Brealey, 2005.

- M. Goold and K. Luchs, 'Why diversify: four decades of management thinking' in D. Faulkner and A. Campbell (eds), *The Oxford Handbook of Strategy*, vol. 2, Oxford

University Press, pp. 18–42, provides an authoritative overview of the diversification option over time.

- A summary of different portfolio analyses is provided in D. Faulkner, 'Portfolio matrices', in V. Ambrosini (ed.), *Exploring Techniques of Analysis and Evaluation in Strategic Management*, Prentice Hall, 1998.

REFERENCES

1. This figure is an extension of the product/market matrix: see I. Ansoff, *Corporate Strategy*, 1988, Chapter 6. The Ansoff matrix was later developed into the one shown below.

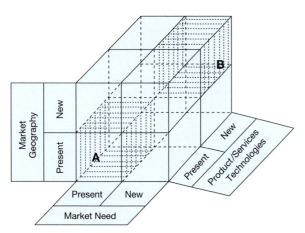

Source: H. Ansoff, *The New Corporate Strategy*, Wiley, 1988.

2. For the European Commission competition authority, http://ec.europa.eu/comm/competition; for the UK Competition Commission, see http://www.competition-commission.org.uk/.

3. For discussions of the challenge of sustained growth and diversification, see A. Campbell and R. Parks, *The Growth Gamble*, Nicholas Brearly (2005) and D. Laurie, Y. Doz and C. Sheer, 'Creating new growth platforms', *Harvard Business Review*, vol. 84, no. 5, (2006), 80–90.

4. On economies of scope, see D.J. Teece, 'Towards an economic theory of the multi-product firm', *Journal of Economic Behavior and Organization*, vol. 3 (1982), pp. 39–63.

5. See C.K. Prahalad and R. Bettis, 'The dominant logic: a new link between diversity and performance', *Strategic Management Journal*, vol. 6, no. 1 (1986), pp. 485–501; R. Bettis and C.K. Prahalad, 'The dominant logic: retrospective and extension', *Strategic Management Journal*, vol. 16, no. 1 (1995), pp. 5–15.

6. See C. Markides, 'Corporate strategy: the role of the centre' in A. Pettigrew, H. Thomas and R. Whittington (eds), *Handbook of Strategy and Management*, Sage, 2002. For a discussion of recent Chinese diversification patterns, see A. Delios, N. Zhou and W.W. Xu, 'Ownership structure and the diversification and performance of publicly-listed companies in China', *Business Horizons*, vol. 51, no. 6 (2008), pp. 802–21.

7. These benefits are often discussed in terms of 'multimarket' or 'multipoint' competition: see J. Anand, L. Mesquita and R. Vassolo, 'The dynamics of multimarket competition in exploration and exploitation activities', *Academy of Management Journal*, vol. 52, no. 4 (2009), pp. 802–21.

8. M. Goold and A. Campbell, 'Desperately seeking synergy', *Harvard Business Review*, vol. 76, no. 2 (1998), pp. 131–45.

9. A. Pehrson, 'Business relatedness and performance: a study of managerial perceptions', *Strategic Management Journal*, vol. 27, no. 3 (2006), pp. 265–82.

10. L.E. Palich, L.B. Cardinal and C. Miller, 'Curvilinearity in the diversification-performance linkage: an examination of over three decades of research', *Strategic Management*

Journal, vol. 21 (2000), pp. 155–74. The inverted-U relationship is the research consensus, but studies often disagree, particularly finding variations over time and across countries. For recent context-sensitive studies, see M. Mayer and R. Whittington, 'Diversification in context: a cross national and cross temporal extension', *Strategic Management Journal*, vol. 24 (2003), pp. 773–81 and A. Chakrabarti, K. Singh and I. Mahmood, 'Diversification and performance: evidence from East Asian firms', *Strategic Management Journal*, vol. 28 (2007), pp. 101–20.

11. For a discussion and cases on the relative guidance of transaction cost and capabilities thinking, see R. McIvor, 'How the transaction cost and resource-based theories of the firm inform outsourcing evaluation', *Journal of Operations Management*, vol. 27, no. 1 (2009), pp. 45–63. See also T. Holcomb and M. Hitt, 'Toward a model of strategic outsourcing', *Journal of Operations Management*, vol. 25, no. 2 (2007), pp. 464–81.

12. For a good discussion of corporate parenting roles, see Markides in reference 6 above. A recent empirical study of corporate headquarters is D. Collis, D. Young and M. Goold, 'The size, structure and performance of corporate headquarters', *Strategic Management Journal*, vol. 28, no. 4 (2007), pp. 383–406.

13. M. Goold, A. Campbell and M. Alexander, *Corporate Level Strategy*, Wiley, 1994, is concerned with both the value-adding and value-destroying capacity of corporate parents.

14. For a discussion of the role of a clarity of mission, see A. Campbell, M. Devine and D. Young, *A Sense of Mission*, Hutchinson Business, 1990.

15. E. Zuckerman, 'Focusing the corporate product: securities analysts and de-diversification', *Administrative Science Quarterly*, vol. 45, no. 3 (2000), pp. 591–619.

16. The first two rationales discussed here are based on M. Porter, 'From competitive advantage to corporate strategy', *Harvard Business Review*, vol. 65, no. 3 (1987), pp. 43–59.

17. See A. Campbell and K. Luchs, *Strategic Synergy*, Butterworth/Heinemann, 1992.

18. The logic of parental development is explained extensively in Goold, Campbell and Alexander (see reference 13 above).

19. For a more extensive discussion of the use of the growth share matrix see A.C. Hax and N.S. Majluf in R.G. Dyson (ed.), *Strategic Planning: Models and Analytical Techniques*, Wiley, 1990; and D. Faulkner, 'Portfolio matrices', in V. Ambrosini (ed.), *Exploring Techniques of Analysis and Evaluation in Strategic Management*, Prentice Hall, 1998; for source explanations of the BCG matrix see B.D. Henderson, *Henderson on Corporate Strategy*, Abt Books, 1979.

20. A. Hax and N. Majluf, 'The use of the industry attractiveness-business strength matrix in strategic planning', in R. Dyson (ed.), *Strategic Planning: Models and Analytical Techniques*, Wiley, 1990.

21. The discussion in this section draws on M. Goold, A. Campbell and M. Alexander, *Corporate Level Strategy*, Wiley, 1994, which provides an excellent basis for understanding issues of parenting.

Virgin: the global entrepreneur

John Treciokas

Introduction

Richard Branson founded Virgin in 1970 and has effectively used his personality to bring the Virgin brand to the attention of the consumer. Virgin's businesses are portrayed in an exciting light with a personal touch and this gives the Virgin brand a softer feel than other large multinational companies. The Virgin Group has grown over the last 40 years to become one of the largest private companies in the UK. Virgin currently has more than 200 branded companies worldwide, employing in the region of 50,000 employees in 29 countries with revenues in excess of £11 billion (approx. €12bn; $16 bn) in 2008.

The largest and most celebrated business, Virgin Atlantic celebrated 25 years of flying people across the Atlantic in 2009 with a striking advertising campaign which portrayed the excitement and fun of flying with, or working at, Virgin. Branson believes in the value of careful brand enhancement and the benefits of transferring this brand image across a diverse portfolio. Research has shown that the Virgin name is associated with words such as: 'fun', 'innovative', 'daring' and 'successful'.

However, does such a portfolio of businesses make strategic sense and will Virgin's conglomerate group of diverse companies survive after Richard Branson departs? These are the key questions facing the company in 2010, the start of a new decade.

Growth and strategy

Virgin began selling music records in 1970 when Branson was just twenty years old and its rapid growth led to an Oxford Street shop a year later. Further expansion into the music industry followed with the Virgin record label in 1973. From an early stage in the business Virgin courted controversy by signing the Sex Pistols, a 'punk rock group' whose rude and anti-establishment behaviour quickly brought them and Virgin high public exposure. Risk-taking and courting publicity epitomised Branson's philosophy from the outset.

Source: Steve Bell/Rex Features.

Virgin Atlantic was founded in 1984 and a year after Virgin Holidays began. These became the core of the Virgin group. In 1987 Virgin Records America was established: Branson commented, 'we were flying there a lot so it made sense to expand there too'. In 1988 Virgin Megastores (retail outlets with a huge selection of recorded music and related products) were opened in Glasgow and Paris, followed by numerous other British, European, American, Japanese and Pacific Basin cities. Virgin was becoming an international company.

Virgin at this stage of its existence was involved largely in two industries: travel/holidays and music. From the 1990s onwards there followed numerous acquisitions, divestments and joint ventures that resulted in a highly diversified group. Chief amongst these were:

- In 1992 the sale of Virgin Records to EMI for £510m, mainly to raise funds for Branson to invest further in his favourite business (Virgin Atlantic).
- The acquisition of the Our Price chain of shops in 1994, making Virgin Retail the UK's largest music retailer.
- The launch of a low-cost airline, Virgin Express in 1996.
- The acquisition in 1997 of the ailing West Coast rail franchise in the UK. Virgin Trains set about trying to improve its services and five years later introduced the tilting Pendolino trains, allowing faster services.

- The start of Branson's interest in the media business with the launch of Virgin One, a tabloid TV channel, in 1997.
- In 1999 the launch of Virgin Mobile, using other providers' networks via a joint venture with what is now T-mobile.
- The launch of a network of health clubs in 1999 and, in 2006, the acquisition of the Holmes Place health chain to give it a significant market share in the UK.
- The sale in 2000 Virgin of 49 per cent of Virgin Atlantic to Singapore Airlines – perhaps accepting that this was a risky and expensive business. Branson insisted, however, that Virgin would not lose its majority control in this core business.
- In 2008 Virgin Mobile in India was launched, in partnership with the Tata group. Tata Teleservices provided the network service, though it is marketed under the Virgin brand. The offering included music, entertainment and news on India's film industry, sports and stock market. The target market was the younger population – some 51 per cent of the 1.1 billion people in India are under 25 and two-thirds are under 35.
- In 2007, Virgin had tried a major move into the financial industry, with the attempted takeover of Northern Rock, a troubled British mortgage bank. The move was resisted by the press and some politicians – Branson has never quite been accepted by the establishment. However, at the beginning of 2010, Virgin continued this strategy with the purchase of a little-known private bank (Church House Trust) which enabled it to apply for a full banking licence and to offer its own mortgages and current accounts. Will this be the next major plank in the Virgin empire?

A move to merge several of its offerings occurred in 2006, when four Virgin companies combined to become one media company providing television, broadband, telephone and mobile phone services in partnership with NTL-Telewest. This company, trading as Virgin Media, had a total of nine million subscribers, giving it a strong position to compete with, and aggressively challenge, its major rival BSkyB. Virgin began to offer complete packages for the family, including a broad range of television packages, broadband at home and away, home telephone services and mobile phone services. This package often included free hardware to lock customers in for up to two years on a contract.

Since 2000 Virgin has also set up a rather futuristic attempt to launch a passenger service into suborbital space (Virgin Galactic) as well as more down to earth businesses like Virgin Comics and Virgin Healthcare.

Table 1 Other strategic developments: 1990–2010

1993	Virgin Radio commences broadcasting.
1994	Launch of Virgin Vodka and Virgin Cola.
1995	Launch of Virgin Direct, an investment product.
1996	Launch of Virgin Net, an internet service provider.
1997	Virgin Trains is founded to run a rail franchise in the UK.
1997	Virgin Cosmetics launches with four flagship stores.
1997	Virgin One commences operations in tabloid TV.
2000	Nine new companies are launched, including a new low-cost airline and mobile phone service, both in Australia.
2006	Virgin Express airline merged with SN Brussels Airline.
2006	Launch of airline in Nigeria.

The table also shows other strategic developments during this time.

Branson has also become increasingly interested in environmental issues, with the launch of the Virgin Earth Challenge. In 2007, he announced this challenge to produce practical designs that can remove large amounts of carbon dioxide from the atmosphere and offered a $25m (about €17.5m) prize. This initiative was part of a number of initiatives brought together by Branson under the banner of 'World Citizen'. These included 'People & Planet,' with the aim of ensuring that Virgin companies contribute to a sustainable society; Virgin Unite, a not-for-profit entrepreneurial foundation, with the aim of partnering to develop new ways to improve social and environmental issues; and the Virgin Green Fund to invest in companies in renewable energy and resource efficiency sectors in Europe and the US. Richard Branson also joined 'The Elders' – a group of leaders brought together by Nelson Mandela to promote peace and tackle humanitarian problems. It seems that Branson, like Microsoft's Bill Gates, was turning his attention to non-profit and CSR issues.

Corporate rationale

Branson's 2008 book, *Business Stripped Bare*, had the subtitle: 'the adventures of a global entrepreneur'. Virgin states on its own website that it is a 'leading branded venture capital organisation' and companies are part of a family rather than a hierarchy. It has minimal layers of management, no bureaucracy and a small global HQ.

Branson sees Virgin as adding value in three main ways in addition to the brand. These are: its public relations and marketing skills; its experience with 'green-field' start-ups; and its understanding of the opportunities presented by 'institutionalised' markets – by this he means those dominated by a few competitors who are not giving good value to customers because they have become inefficient, complacent or preoccupied with rivals.

The key criterion for whether Virgin backs a new venture is 'does an opportunity exist for restructuring a market and creating competitive advantage?' Each business is 'ring-fenced', so that lenders to one company have no rights over the assets of another and financial results are not consolidated. Virgin has a mix of privately owned and public-listed companies, as well as a mix of start-up small businesses and very large corporate ventures. Each may have very different strategic reasoning: some may be an attempt to keep Virgin in the public consciousness or possibly a method of training and developing managers. Some larger start-ups are serious strategic moves into new industries.

Increasingly large financial pockets and a proven track record in highly competitive industries have also enabled Virgin to enter into business opportunities with joint venture partners.

The future

Not all of Virgin's companies are successful and not all meet the standards of customer service that Virgin would like to see – both Virgin Media and Virgin Rail have had many customer complaints. None the less, Branson has created an image with the British public of a 'cheeky entrepreneur' who has battled the mighty 'monopoly' of British Airways and whose Virgin brand has grown into a business empire. The other lesser-known image – according to Branson-watcher and journalist Tom Bower – is one of a ruthless, crafty businessman always trying to get one over on his rivals.

It is difficult to discover the overall financial position of Virgin as it is made up of so many individual companies (many private) and there are no consolidated accounts. However, Bower states (2008) that the financial accounts show that the Virgin holding company lost £3.9m, even as its mainstay air-travel subsidiary made a profit of £123m. Sir Richard has argued that he pursues

growth, not profits, and builds companies for the long term. With the aviation industry in crisis in 2009/10 and Virgin's dependence on airlines, this must raise concerns for the future of the organisation.

Richard Branson does not mention his departure in interviews but states that the company has been carefully groomed to continue without him, and that the brand is now globally well known, thus implying that his publicity stunts are no longer required. However, can Virgin survive as an entity without Branson?

Notes

Some parts of this case are based on the previous cases on Virgin in earlier editions of this text, originally written by Urmilla Lawson and revised by Aidan McQuade.

References and sources
www.Virgin.com.
Bower, Tom *Branson*, Harper Perennial, 2008.
www.businessweek.com/November 2007.
www.reuters.com, 16 December 2009.
The Economist, 'Virgin rebirth', 12 September 2008.
The Economist, 'Toyota slips up', 12 December 2009.
Goff, Sharlene, *Financial Times*, 8 January 2010.

Questions

1 Describe Virgin's various diversification moves in terms of Ansoff's axes (Figure 7.2).

2 How does Virgin add value as a corporate parent? Is there anything more it should do to add value?

3 Assess whether moving further into the banking industry is the right strategic option for Virgin. Does the continued pursuit of this industry suggest a more careful hidden strategic plan that is not revealed to outsiders?

4 What would be the challenges faced by a successor to Richard Branson, and what might he or she do?

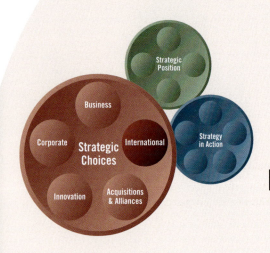

8

INTERNATIONAL STRATEGY

Learning outcomes

After reading this chapter, you should be able to:

- Assess the *internationalisation potential* of different markets.

- Identify sources of competitive advantage in international strategy, through both *global sourcing* and exploitation of *local factors*.

- Distinguish between four main types of international strategy.

- *Rank markets* for entry or expansion, taking into account attractiveness, cultural and other forms of distance and competitor retaliation threats.

- Assess the relative merits of different *market entry modes*, including joint ventures, licensing and foreign direct investment.

PEARSON mystrategylab

MyStrategyLab is designed to help you make the most of your studies.

Visit **www.pearsoned.co.uk/mystrategylab** to discover a wide range of resources specific to this chapter, including:

- A personalised **Study plan** that will help you understand core concepts
- **Audio** and **video clips** that put the spotlight on strategy in the real world
- **Online glossaries** and **flashcards** that provide helpful reminders when you're looking for some quick revision.

(8.1) INTRODUCTION

The last chapter introduced market development as a strategy, in relation to the Ansoff axes. This chapter focuses on a specific but important kind of market development, operating in different geographical markets. This is a challenge for all kinds of organisations nowadays. There are of course the large traditional multinationals such as Nestlé, Toyota and McDonald's. But recent years have seen the rise of emerging-country multinationals from Brazil, Russia, India and China. New small firms are increasingly 'born global', building international relationships right from the start. Public-sector organisations too are having to make choices about collaboration, outsourcing and even competition with overseas organisations. European Union legislation requires public-service organisations to accept tenders from non-national suppliers.

Figure 8.1 identifies five main themes of this chapter, with international strategy as the core. The themes are as follows:

- *Internationalisation drivers.* Drivers include market demand, the potential for cost advantages, government pressures and inducements and the need to respond to competitor moves. Given the risks and costs of international strategy, managers need to know that the drivers are strong to justify adopting an international strategy in the first place.

- *Geographical advantage.* In international competition, advantages might come from both geographic location of the original business and from the international configuration of their value network. Managers need to appraise these potential sources of competitive advantage carefully: if there are no competitive advantages, international strategy is liable to fail.

- *International strategy.* If drivers and advantages are sufficiently strong to merit an international strategy, then a range of strategic approaches are opened up, from the simplest export strategies to the most complex global strategies.

KEY CONCEPT

Four international strategies

Figure 8.1 International strategy framework

- *Market selection.* Having adopted the broad approach to international strategy, the question next is which country markets to prioritise and which to steer clear of. The issues here range from the economic to the cultural and political.

- *Entry mode.* Finally, once target countries are selected, managers have to determine how they should enter each particular market. Again, export is a simple place to start, but there are licensing, franchising, joint-venture and wholly owned subsidiary alternatives to consider as well.

The chapter takes a cautious view on international strategy. Despite the fashionable talk of increasing 'globalisation', there are many challenges and many pressures for localisation as well.[1] The chapter will therefore also consider the financial performance implications of growing internationalisation and the Key Debate at the end of this chapter considers the controversy around global, local and regional strategies.

The chapter distinguishes between international strategy and global strategy. **International strategy** **refers to a range of options for operating outside an organisation's country of origin**. Global strategy is only one kind of international strategy. **Global strategy** **involves high coordination of extensive activities dispersed geographically in many countries around the world**. This chapter keeps open alternative options to full global strategy.

(8.2) INTERNATIONALISATION DRIVERS

There are many general pressures increasing internationalisation. Barriers to international trade, investment and migration are all now much lower than they were a couple of decades ago. Better international legal frameworks means that it is less risky to deal with unfamiliar partners. Improvements in communications – from cheaper air travel to the internet – make movement and the spread of ideas much easier around the world. Not least, the success of new economic powerhouses such as the so-called BRICs – Brazil, Russia, India and China – is generating new opportunities and challenges for business internationally.[2]

However, not all these internationalisation trends are one-way. Nor do they hold for all industries. For example, migration is now becoming more difficult between some countries. Trade barriers still exist for some products, especially those relating to defence technologies. Many countries protect their leading companies from takeover by overseas rivals. Markets vary widely in the extent to which consumer needs are standardising – compare computer operating systems to the highly variable national tastes in chocolate. Some so-called multi-nationals are in fact concentrated in very particular markets, for example North America and Western Europe, or have a quite limited set of international links, for example supply or outsourcing arrangements with just one or two countries overseas. In short, managers need to beware 'global baloney', by which economic integration into a single homogenised and competitive world is wildly exaggerated (see the Key Debate at the end of this chapter). As in the Chinese retail market (Illustration 8.1), international drivers are usually a lot more complicated than that: Chinese markets are not only very different from Western ones, but vary widely within China itself.

Given internationalisation's complexity, international strategy should be underpinned by a careful assessment of trends in each particular market. Erasmus University's George Yip provides a framework for analysing 'drivers of globalisation'. In the terms of this chapter, these globalisation drivers can be thought of as 'internationalisation drivers' more generally. In this

ILLUSTRATION 8.1

Chinese retail: global or local?

Internationalisation is not a simple process, as supermarket chains Carrefour and Wal-Mart have found in China.

China is a magnet for ambitious Western supermarket chains. With an annual growth rate of 13 per cent a year, the Chinese market is predicted by Business Monitor International to grow in value by $1.2 (~€0.84) trn. between 2009 and 2014. 520 million people are expected to join the Chinese upper middle class by 2025.

Two leading Western companies in the Chinese retail market are French supermarket chain Carrefour and the world's largest retailer, the American Wal-Mart. The two companies have had very different strategies. French supermarket chain Carrefour was the first to enter the Chinese market in a substantial fashion, entering in 1995, after six years' experience in neighbouring Taiwan. Carrefour is following a decentralised strategy: except in Shanghai, where it has several stores, Carrefour allows its local store managers, scattered across the many different regions of China, to make their own purchasing and supply decisions. By 2009, Carrefour was the fifth largest retailer in China, though this meant only 0.6% overall market share. Wal-Mart was close behind with 0.5% share. Wal-Mart's initial approach had been based on its standard centralised purchasing and distribution strategy, supplying as much as it can from its new, state-of-the-art distribution centre in Shenzen. In 2009, however, Wal-Mart experimented with a smaller-scale local store format, which it intends to roll-out nationally. It is also integrating the Chinese operations of a budget Taiwanese retailer.

One early discovery for Wal-Mart was that Chinese consumers prefer frequent shopping trips, buying small quantities each time. While Wal-Mart assumed that Chinese consumers would drive to out-of-town stores and fill their cars with large frozen multi-packs on a once-a-week shop like Americans, in fact Chinese customers would break open the multi-packs to take just the smaller quantities they required. Now Wal-Mart supplies more of its frozen foods loose, offering customers a scoop so they can take exactly the amount they want. Wal-Mart also now allows trade unions into its stores, in marked contrast to its policy in the rest of the world.

Another discovery for Western retailers is the amount of regional variation in this vast and multi-ethnic country. In the north of China, soya sauces are important; in central China, chilli pepper sauces are required; in the south, it is oyster sauces that matter. For fruit, northerners must have dates; southerners want lychees. In the north, the cold means more demand for red meat and, because customers are wearing layers of clothing, wider store aisles. Northerners don't have much access to hot water, so they wash their hair less frequently, meaning that small sachets of shampoo sell better than large bottles. And, unlike other Chinese, apparently the citizens of Zhejiang province like their toilet paper as 'rough as sandpaper'.

The growth of companies such as Carrefour and Wal-Mart demonstrates that there is a substantial market for the Western retail model. Carrefour, for example, was a pioneer of 'private label' goods in China, while Wal-Mart brings logistical expertise. But progress has been slow and Chinese companies such as market-leader GOME have imitated. Wal-Mart has yet to make a profit in China; Carrefour finally is, but its 2–3% margins are significantly below the nearly 5% margins it enjoys in France. In 2008, Carrefour suffered from a Chinese boycott after a Parisian protest over Tibet associated with the Beijing Olympics and in 2009 Carrefour was obliged to deny that it was considering leaving China.

Sources: Financial Times, Wall Street Journal and Euromonitor (various).

Questions

1 What are the pros and cons of the different China strategies pursued by Carrefour and Wal-Mart?

2 What might be the dangers for a large Western retailer in staying out of the Chinese market?

Figure 8.2 Drivers of internationalisation

Source: Adapted from G. Yip, *Total Global Strategy II*, Financial Times Prentice Hall, 2003, Chapter 2.

www.pearsoned.co.uk/mystrategylab
KEY CONCEPT

Yip's globalisation framework

book, therefore, **Yip's globalisation framework sees international strategy potential as determined by market drivers, cost drivers, government drivers and competitive drivers** (see Figure 8.2).[3] In more detail, the four drivers are as follows:

● *Market drivers.* A critical facilitator of internationalisation is standardisation of market characteristics. There are three components underlying this driver. First, the presence of *similar customer needs and tastes*: for example, the fact that in most societies consumers have similar needs for easy credit has promoted the worldwide spread of a handful of credit card companies such as Visa. Second is the presence of *global customers*: for example, car component companies have become more international as their customers, such as Toyota or Ford, have internationalised, and required standardised components for all their factories around the world. Finally, *transferable marketing* promotes market globalisation: brands such as Coca-Cola are still successfully marketed in very similar ways across the world.

● *Cost drivers.* Costs can be reduced by operating internationally. Again, there are three main elements to cost drivers. First, increasing volume beyond what a national market might support can give *scale economies*, both on the production side and in purchasing of supplies. Companies from smaller countries such as the Netherlands and Switzerland tend therefore to become proportionately much more international than companies from the United States, which have a vast market at home. Scale economies are particularly important in industries with high product-development costs, as in the aircraft industry, where initial costs need to be spread over the large volumes of international markets. Second, internationalisation is promoted where it is possible to take advantage of variations in *country-specific differences*. Thus it makes sense to locate the manufacture of clothing in China or Africa, where labour is still considerably cheaper, but to keep design activities in cities such as New York, Paris, Milan or London, where fashion expertise is concentrated. The third element is *favourable logistics*, or the costs of moving products or services across borders relative to their final value. From this point of view, microchips are easy to source internationally, while bulky materials such as assembled furniture are harder.

- *Government drivers*. These can both facilitate and inhibit internationalisation. The relevant elements of policy are numerous, including tariff barriers, technical standards, subsidies to local firms, ownership restrictions, local content requirements, controls over technology transfer, intellectual property (patenting) regimes and currency and capital flow controls. No government allows complete economic openness and openness typically varies widely from industry to industry, with agriculture and high-tech industries related to defence likely to be particularly sensitive. Nevertheless, the World Trade Organization continues to push for greater openness and the European Union and the North American Free Trade Agreement have made significant improvements in their specific regions.[4]

- *Competitive drivers*. These relate specifically to globalisation as an integrated worldwide strategy rather than simpler international strategies. These have two elements. First, *interdependence* between country operations increases the pressure for global coordination. For example, a business with a plant in Mexico serving both the US and the Japanese markets has to coordinate carefully between the three locations: surging sales in one country, or a collapse in another, will have significant knock-on effects on the other countries. The second element relates directly to competitor strategy. The presence of *globalised competitors* increases the pressure to adopt a global strategy in response because competitors may use one country's profits to cross-subsidise their operations in another. A company with a loosely coordinated international strategy is vulnerable to globalised competitors, because it is unable to support country subsidiaries under attack from targeted, subsidised competition. The danger is of piecemeal withdrawal from countries under attack, and the gradual undermining of any overall economies of scale that the international player may have started with.[5]

The key insight from Yip's drivers framework is that the internationalisation potential of industries is variable. There are many different factors that can support or inhibit it, and an important step in determining an internationalisation strategy is a realistic assessment of the true scope for internationalisation in the particular industry. In the Chinese retail case (Illustration 8.1), it may be that the drivers for Western entry are as much competitive as market.

GEOGRAPHIC SOURCES OF ADVANTAGE

As is clear from the earlier discussion of cost drivers in international strategy, the geographical location of activities is a crucial source of potential advantage and one of the distinguishing features of international strategy relative to other diversification strategies. As INSEAD's Bruce Kogut has explained, an organisation can improve the configuration of its *value chain and network*[6] by taking advantage of country-specific differences (see section 3.4.2). There are two principal opportunities available: the exploitation of particular *locational advantages*, often in the company's home country, and sourcing advantages overseas via an *international value network*.

8.3.1 Locational advantage: Porter's Diamond[7]

As for any strategy, internationalisation needs to be based on strategic capabilities providing a sustainable competitive advantage. This competitive advantage has usually to be substantial. After all, a competitor entering a market from overseas typically starts with considerable *dis*advantages relative to existing home competitors, who will usually have superior market knowledge, established relationships with local customers, strong supply chains and the like. A foreign entrant must have significant competitive advantages to overcome such disadvantages. The example of the American giant retailer Wal-Mart provides an illustration: Wal-Mart has been successful in many Asian markets with relatively under-developed retail markets, but was forced to withdraw from Germany's more mature market after nearly a decade of failure in 2006. In Germany, unlike in most Asian markets, Wal-Mart had no significant competitive advantage over domestic retailers.

The sources of sustainable competitive advantage in general are considered in Chapters 3 and 6. However, the international context specifically raises the potential of locational sources of advantage. Countries, and regions within them, often become associated with specific types of enduring competitive advantage: for example, the Swiss in private banking, the northern Italians in leather and fur fashion goods, and the Taiwanese in laptop computers. Michael Porter has proposed a four-pointed 'diamond' to explain why some locations tend to produce firms with sustained competitive advantages in some industries more than others (see

Figure 8.3 Porter's Diamond – the determinants of national advantages

Porter's
Diamond

Figure 8.3). Specifically, **Porter's Diamond** suggests that locational advantages may stem from local factor conditions; local demand conditions; local related and supporting industries; and from local firm strategy structure and rivalry. These four interacting determinants of locational advantage work as follows:

- *Factor conditions.* These refer to the 'factors of production' that go into making a product or service (i.e. raw materials, land and labour). Factor condition advantages at a national level can translate into general competitive advantages for national firms in international markets. For example, the linguistic ability of the Swiss has provided a significant advantage to their banking industry. Cheap energy has traditionally provided an advantage for the North American aluminium industry.

- *Home demand conditions.* The nature of the domestic customers can become a source of competitive advantage. Dealing with sophisticated and demanding customers at home helps train a company to be effective overseas. For example, Japanese customers' high expectations of electrical and electronic equipment provided an impetus for those industries in Japan, leading to global dominance of those sectors. Sophisticated local customers in France and Italy have helped keep their local fashion industries at the leading edge for many decades.

- *Related and supporting industries.* Local 'clusters' of related and mutually supporting industries can be an important source of competitive advantage. These are often regionally based, making personal interaction easier. In northern Italy, for example, the leather footwear industry, the leatherworking machinery industry and the design services which underpin them group together in the same regional cluster to each other's mutual benefit. Silicon Valley forms a cluster of hardware, software, research and venture-capital organisations which together create a virtuous circle of high-technology enterprise.

- *Firm strategy, industry structure and rivalry.* The characteristic strategies, industry structures and rivalries in different countries can also be bases of advantage. German companies' strategy of investing in technical excellence gives them a characteristic advantage in engineering industries and creates large pools of expertise. A competitive local industry structure is also helpful: if too dominant in their home territory, local organisations can become complacent and lose advantage overseas. Some domestic rivalry can actually be an advantage, therefore. For example, the long-run success of the Japanese car companies is partly based on government policy sustaining several national players (unlike in the United Kingdom, where they were all merged into one) and the Swiss pharmaceuticals industry became strong in part because each company had to compete with several strong local rivals.

Porter's Diamond has been used by governments aiming to increase the competitive advantage of their local industries. The argument that rivalry can be positive has led to a major policy shift in many countries towards encouraging local competition rather than protecting home-based industries. Governments can also foster local industries by raising safety or environmental standards (i.e. creating sophisticated demand conditions) or encouraging cooperation between suppliers and buyers on a domestic level (i.e. building clusters of related and supporting industries in particular regions).

For individual organisations, however, the value of Porter's Diamond is to identify the extent to which they can build on home-based advantages to create competitive advantage in relation to others on a global front. For example, Dutch brewing companies – such as Heineken – had an advantage in early internationalisation due to the combination of sophisticated consumers and limited room to grow at home. Benetton, the Italian clothing company, has achieved global success by using its experience of working through a network of largely independent, often family-owned manufacturers to build its network of franchised retailers. Before embarking on an internationalisation strategy, managers should seek out sources of general locational advantage to underpin their company's individual sources of advantage.

8.3.2 The international value network

However, the sources of advantage need not be purely domestic. For international companies, advantage can be drawn from the international configuration of their *value network* (see section 3.4.2). Here the different skills, resources and costs of countries around the world can be systematically exploited in order to locate each element of the value chain in that country or region where it can be conducted most effectively and efficiently. This may be achieved both through foreign direct investments and joint ventures but also through **global sourcing**, i.e. **purchasing services and components from the most appropriate suppliers around the world, regardless of their location**. For example, in the UK, the National Health Service has been sourcing medical personnel from overseas to offset a shortfall in domestic skills and capacity.

Different locational advantages can be identified:

- *Cost advantages* include labour costs, transportation and communications costs and taxation and investment incentives. Labour costs are important. American and European firms, for example, are increasingly moving software programming tasks to India where a computer programmer costs an American firm about one-quarter of what it would pay for a worker with comparable skills in the USA. As wages in India have risen, Indian IT firms have already begun moving work to even more low-cost locations such as China, with some predicting that subsidiaries of Indian firms will come to control as much as 40 per cent of China's IT service exports.

- *Unique local capabilities* may allow an organisation to enhance its competitive advantage. For example, leading European pharmaceuticals company GSK has R&D laboratories in Boston and the Research Triangle in North Carolina in order to establish research collaborations with the leading universities and hospitals in those areas. Internationalisation, therefore, is increasingly not only about exploiting an organisation's existing capabilities in new national markets, but about developing strategic capabilities by drawing on capabilities found elsewhere in the world.

- *National market characteristics* can enable organisations to develop differentiated product offerings aimed at different market segments. American guitar-maker Gibson, for example, complements its US-made products with often similar, lower-cost alternatives produced in South Korea under the Epiphone brand. However, because of the American music tradition, Gibson's high-end guitars benefit from the reputation of still being 'made in the USA'.

Of course, one of the consequences of organisations trying to exploit the locational advantages available in different countries' organisations can be that they create complex networks of intra- and inter-organisational relationships. Boeing, for example, has developed a global web of R&D activities through its subsidiaries and partnerships with collaborating organisations (see Illustration 8.2).

ILLUSTRATION 8.2

Boeing's global nightmare

Boeing's decision to outsource production of its new Dreamliner aircraft turns into a logistical nightmare.

Work on Boeing's 787 Dreamliner aircraft began in 2003. Test flights did not begin until 2009, two years late. Airlines had cancelled orders and the company had had to pay compensation to customers for delivery delays. The company's CEO, Jim McNerney, admitted in 2009: 'We wouldn't do it exactly the same way. There's plenty of blame to go round. It's not just our suppliers' fault. It's equally our fault in many cases.'

Modern aircraft are tricky to develop. Boeing had experienced delays on its earlier 737 and 747 programmes, and more recently Airbus, the market leader, had significant problems with its giant A380 aircraft. But for Boeing the 787 was crucial to recapturing the lead from Airbus. Boeing was taking a radically different route to its European rival, going for a long-range 250–300, seat jet, by contrast to Airbus's flagship A380 with its potential 853 seats. The project was due to cost Boeing $10bn (~€7bn) in development and involve radically new technologies that would provide 20 per cent gains in fuel efficiency. Most radical of all, however, was the decision to subcontract 70 per cent of production to suppliers around the world.

The roll-call of 50 subcontractors was impressive. For example, in Japan, Mitsubishi would make the wings, Kawasaki would do the forward fuselage, while Fuji would take responsibility for the centre wing box. Sweden's Saab would make the cargo doors, while Italy's Alenia would produce the horizontal stabiliser and central fuselage. More suppliers came from France, Germany, South Korea and the United Kingdom. Back in the United States there were more than ten subcontractors, including such respected names as General Electric and Moog. Three 747 cargo planes, named 'Dreamlifters', were dedicated to transporting the various components from around the world to Boeing's assembly plant in the United States.

There were several potential advantages to this outsourcing. Boeing would get access to the tech-nological expertise of specialists around the world. These specialist subcontractors would supply some of the development funding. The fact that parts of the plane would be made in different countries was likely to help in the sale of aircraft to the respective national airlines. Costs of labour were likely to be lower outside the US and Boeing would have a smaller workforce of its own to manage during the inevitable downturns of the boom-and-bust aircraft industry.

But there were some unanticipated problems. Alenia found itself obliged to replant a 300-year-old olive grove before it could build its factory in southern Italy. Vought, an American supplier, in turn subcontracted some work to an Israeli company, who neglected to supply assembly instructions in English. Boeing had to send its engineers around the world to smooth out technical problems. Back in the United States, Boeing's own workers were unhappy to see so much work go overseas and imposed a 58-day strike during 2008.

Despite all these problems, the Dreamliner looks set for commercial success. Even after cancellations, its launch order book was for a record-breaking 892 aircraft, at $145m a piece. CEO Jim McNerney reflected none the less: 'we have learned a lot and have the scars to prove it'. He promised that Boeing would build later variants of the 787 more in-house.

Source: Flight International, 12 September 2008; *Financial Times*, 14 July 2008; *Reuters*, 22 September 2009.

Questions

1 What are the pros and cons of specifically *international* outsourcing?

2 Boeing will still subcontract some production work for later variants of the 787. What criteria should guide its choice of subcontractors?

(8.4) INTERNATIONAL STRATEGIES

Given the ability to obtain sources of international competitive advantage through home-based factors or international value networks, organisations still face difficult questions about what kinds of strategies to pursue in their markets. Here the key problem is typically the so-called global–local dilemma. **The global–local dilemma relates to the extent to which products and services may be standardised across national boundaries or need to be adapted to meet the requirements of specific national markets.** For some products and services – such as televisions – markets appear similar across the world, offering huge potential scale economies if design, production and delivery can be centralised. For other products and services – such as television programming – tastes still seem highly national-specific, drawing companies to decentralise operations and control as near as possible to the local market. This global–local dilemma can evoke a number of responses from companies pursuing international strategies, ranging from decentralisation to centralisation, with positions in between.

This section introduces four different kinds of international strategy, based on choices about the international *configuration* of the various activities an organisation has to carry out and the degree to which these activities are then *coordinated* internationally (see Figure 8.4). More precisely, configuration refers to the geographical dispersion or concentration of activities such as manufacturing and R&D, while coordination refers to the extent to which operations in different countries are managed in a decentralised way or a centrally coordinated way. The four basic international strategies are:[8]

● *Simple export.* This strategy involves a concentration of activities (particularly manufacturing) in one country, typically the country of the organisation's origin. At the same time, marketing of the exported product is very loosely coordinated overseas, perhaps handled by independent sales agents in different markets. Pricing, packaging, distribution and even branding policies may be determined locally. This strategy is typically chosen by organisations

Figure 8.4 Four international strategies

Source: Adapted 'Changing patterns of international competition', pp. 9–39, Figure 5 (Porter, M. 1987). Copyright © 1987, by The Regents of the University of California. Reprinted from the *California Management Review*, vol. 28, no. 2. By permission of The Regents.

with a strong locational advantage – as determined by the Porter Diamond, for example – but where the organisation either has insufficient managerial capabilities to coordinate marketing internationally or where coordinated marketing would add little value, for example in agricultural or raw material commodities.

- *Multidomestic*. This strategy is similarly loosely coordinated internationally, but involves a dispersion overseas of various activities, including manufacturing and sometimes product development. Instead of export, therefore, goods and services are produced locally in each national market. Each market is treated independently, with the needs of each local domestic market given priority – hence 'multidomestic'. Local adaptations can make the overall corporate portfolio increasingly diversified. This strategy is appropriate where there are few economies of scale and strong benefits to adapting to local needs. This multidomestic strategy is particularly attractive in professional services, where local relationships are critical, but it carries risks towards brand and reputation if national practices become too diverse.

- *Complex export*. This strategy still involves location of most activities in a single country, but builds on more coordinated marketing. Economies of scale can still be reaped in manufacturing and R&D, but branding and pricing opportunities are more systematically managed. The coordination demands are, of course, considerably more complex than in the simple export strategy. This is a common stage for companies from emerging economies, as they retain some locational advantages from their home country, but seek to build a stronger brand and network overseas with growing organisational maturity.

- *Global strategy*. This strategy describes the most mature international strategy, with highly coordinated activities dispersed geographically around the world. Using international value networks to the full, geographical location is chosen according to the specific locational advantage for each activity, so that product development, manufacturing, marketing and headquarters functions might all be located in different countries. For example, Detroit-based General Motors designed its Pontiac Le Mans at the firm's German subsidiary, Opel, with its high engineering skills; developed its advertising via a British agency with the creativity strengths of London; produced many of its more complex components in Japan, exploiting the sophisticated manufacturing and technological capabilities; and assembled the car in South Korea, a location where a lower-cost, yet skilled, labour force was available. All this, of course, required high investments and skill in coordination (see also the discussion of the transnational structure in section 13.2.4).

In practice, these four international strategies are not absolutely distinct. Managerial co-ordination and geographical concentration are matters of degree rather than sharp distinctions. Companies may often oscillate within and between the four strategies. Their choices, moreover, will be influenced by changes in the internationalisation drivers introduced earlier. Where, for example, tastes are highly standardised, companies will tend to favour complex export or global strategies. Where economies of scale are few, the logic is more in favour of multidomestic strategies.

(8.5) MARKET SELECTION AND ENTRY

Having decided on an international strategy built on significant sources of competitive advantage and supported by strong internationalisation drivers, managers need next to decide which countries to enter. Not all countries are equally attractive. To an extent, however, countries can initially be compared using standard environmental analysis techniques, for example along the dimensions identified in the PESTEL framework (see section 2.2.1) or according to the industry five forces (section 2.3). However, there are specific determinants of market attractiveness that need to be considered in internationalisation strategy, and they can be analysed under two main headings: the intrinsic characteristics of the market and the nature of the competition. A key point here is how initial estimates of country attractiveness can be modified by various measures of *distance* and the likelihood of competitor *retaliation*. The section concludes by considering different *entry modes* into national markets.

8.5.1 Market characteristics

At least four elements of the PESTEL framework are particularly important in comparing countries for entry:

- *Political*. Political environments vary widely between countries and can alter rapidly. Russia since the fall of Communism has seen frequent swings for and against private foreign enterprise. Governments can of course create significant opportunities for organisations. For example, the British government has traditionally promoted the financial services industry in the City of London by offering tax advantages to high-earning financiers from abroad and providing a 'light-touch' regulatory environment. It is important, however, to determine the level of *political risk* before entering a country. Carrefour, for example, found itself the subject of an unexpected consumer boycott in China because of political tensions surrounding Tibet (see Illustration 8.1).

- *Economic*. Key comparators in deciding entry are levels of Gross Domestic Product and disposable income which help in estimating the potential size of the market. Fast-growth economies obviously provide opportunities, and in developing economies such as China and India growth is translating into an even faster creation of a high-consumption middle class. However, companies must also be aware of the stability of a country's currency, which may affect its income stream. There can be considerable *currency risk*: thus British companies that relied on international subcontractors faced increased costs as the value of sterling fell during the economic crisis of 2009–10.

- *Social*. Social factors will clearly be important, for example the availability of a well-trained workforce or the size of demographic market segments – old or young – relevant to the strategy. Cultural variations need to be considered, for instance in defining tastes in the marketplace.

- *Legal*. Countries vary widely in their legal regime, determining the extent to which businesses can enforce contracts, protect intellectual property or avoid corruption. Similarly, policing will be important for the security of employees, a factor that in the past has deterred business in some South American countries.

A common procedure is to rank country markets against each other on criteria such as these and then to choose the countries for entry that offer the highest relative scores. However, Pankaj Ghemawat from Spain's IESE business school has pointed out that what matters is not just the attractiveness of different countries relative to each other, but also the compatibility of the countries with the internationalising firm itself.[9]

Thus Ghemawat underlines the importance of *match* between country and firm. For firms coming from any particular country, some countries are more 'distant' – or mismatched – than

ILLUSTRATION 8.3

Vale – a Brazilian giant in different cultures

Rapid overseas expansion brings this Brazilian multinational some contrasting experiences.

Until the late 1990s, Brazil's Vale mining company was a state-owned sleeping giant. 2001 brought the appointment as CEO of 42-year-old former investment banker Roger Agnelli, since when the company has transfomed itself into a dynamic conglomerate. Agnelli commented in 2010: 'Vale used to be fundamentally an iron-ore company. We used to operate essentially in Brazil. Now we are in 36 countries.' Vale is the world's largest producer of iron ore, the second largest producer of nickel and has a declared ambition of being one of the world's largest fertiliser producers. It has copper operations in South Africa, steel in California and coal in Australia.

Nevertheless, iron ore remains the driver of the business. The booming Chinese market has been a gift. Between 2001 and 2009, Vale's iron ore production increased from 122m tonnes to 300m tonnes, with China alone accounting for approaching half of all sales. In the recession year of 2009, iron ore was still profitable, while its non-ferrous and coal activities were by and large unprofitable. However, the nickel business in Canada and the coal business in Mozambique offer very contrasting insights into the challenges of Vale's new international businesses.

Vale's $17.6bn (~€12.3bn) takeover in 2006 of Inco, the world's largest nickel producer, was its first major overseas acquisition. Canada's largest national newspaper, the *Globe and Mail*, described Vale's arrival as 'The great Canadian mining disaster'. Many Canadians resented this takeover by what they regarded as a business from a developing country. The first top manager sent over by Vale spoke poor English. Of 29 senior Canadian managers in early 2007, three years later 23 had departed, mostly voluntarily. The Canadians regarded nickel, which requires underground mining and goes into many high-tech businesses, as technically much more complex than iron ore, a surface-mined basic commodity. According to the *Financial Times*, one Canadian manager said that iron ore was a high

school diploma business, nickel was a PhD business. At one tense meeting a Brazilian manager riposted: 'How come, if you're so smart, you didn't take *us* over?'. In July 2009, Inco's Canadian workers went on strike, remaining so into 2010.

A contrast so far has been Vale's experience in Mozambique. Like many Brazilian companies, Vale has been attracted to the two African countries of Angola and Mozambique because of the shared cultural and linguistic heritage of Portuese colonialism. About half the 3m black African slaves sent to Brazil between 1700 and 1850 came from Angola and in the 1820s, settlers in Angola and Mozambique applied to join the newly independent Brazil in a federation. Mozambique has some of the largest coal reserves in the world, but rudimentary infrastructure. Vale is working with Odebrecht, a Brazilian construction company, to develop not only the coal reserves, but to build a power station and the rail and port infrastructure necessary to get the coal to international markets. So vast is the task that Odebrecht has become Mozambique's largest single employer. Vale is planning £830m (€950m) of investment in Mozambique over the next couple of years. Agnelli is enthusiastic about long-term African prospects: 'The thing about Africa is that sooner or later it will become a reality . . . Africa is the future of the world's natural resources – along with South America.'

Sources: 'Vale's transformation', *Financial Times*, 25 February 2010; 'Brazil accelerates investment in Africa'. *Financial Times*, 9 February 2010; 'Heading in opposite directions', *Financial Times*, 11 February 2010.

Questions

1 Is there any downside to Vale's ties to the Chinese market, and what should Vale do to mitigate this?

2 Suggest three reasons for Vale's different reception in Canada and Mozambique.

others. For example, a Spanish company might be 'closer' to a South American market than an East Asian market and might therefore prefer that market even if it ranked lower on standard criteria of attractiveness. As well as a relative ranking of countries, therefore, each company has to add its assessment of countries in terms of closeness of match.

Ghemawat's 'CAGE framework' measures the match between countries and companies according to four dimensions of distance, reflected by the letters of the acronym. Thus the **CAGE framework** **emphasises the importance of cultural, administrative, geographical and economic distance**, as follows:

● *Cultural distance.* The distance dimension here relates to differences in language, ethnicity, religion and social norms. Cultural distance is not just a matter of similarity in consumer tastes, but extends to important compatibilities in terms of managerial behaviours. Here, for example, US firms might be closer to Canada than to Mexico, which Spanish firms might find relatively compatible. Figure 8.5 draws on the GLOBE survey of 17,000 managers from 62 different societal cultures around the world to contrast specifically the orientations of American and Chinese managers on some key cultural dimensions. According to this

Figure 8.5 International cross-cultural comparison

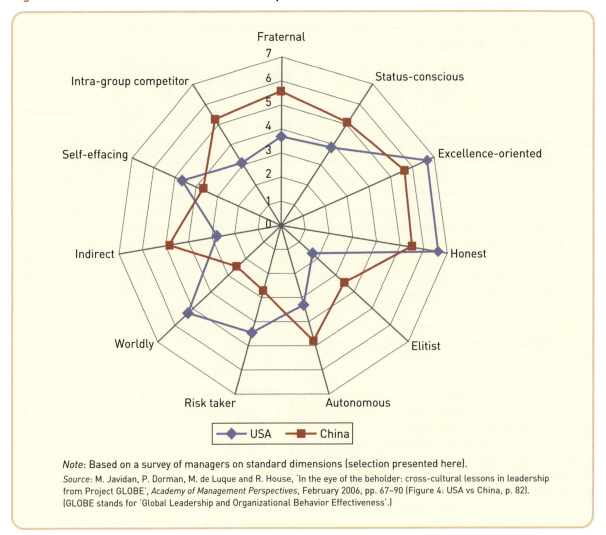

Note: Based on a survey of managers on standard dimensions (selection presented here).

Source: M. Javidan, P. Dorman, M. de Luque and R. House, 'In the eye of the beholder: cross-cultural lessons in leadership from Project GLOBE', *Academy of Management Perspectives*, February 2006, pp. 67–90 (Figure 4: USA vs China, p. 82). (GLOBE stands for 'Global Leadership and Organizational Behavior Effectiveness'.)

GLOBE survey, American managers appear to be typically more risk-taking, while Chinese managers are more autonomous.

- *Administrative and political distance.* Here distance is in terms of incompatible administrative, political or legal traditions. Colonial ties can diminish difference, so that the shared heritage of France and its former West African colonies creates certain understandings that go beyond linguistic advantages. See also, for example, the experience of the Brazilian Vale company in Mozambique, where shared Portuguese heritage made a difference (Illustration 8.3). Institutional weaknesses – for example slow or corrupt administration – can open up distance between countries. So too can political differences: Chinese companies are increasingly able to operate in parts of the world that American companies are finding harder, for example parts of the Middle East and Africa.

- *Geographical distance.* This is not just a matter of the kilometres separating one country from another, but involves other geographical characteristics of the country such as size, sea-access and the quality of communications infrastructure. For example, Wal-Mart's difficulties in Europe relate to the fact that its logistics systems were developed in the geographically enormous space of North America, and proved much less suitable for the smaller and denser countries of Europe. Transport infrastructure can shrink or exaggerate physical distance. France is much closer to large parts of Continental Europe than to the United Kingdom, because of the barrier presented by the English Channel and Britain's relatively poor road and rail infrastructure.

- *Economic.* The final element of the CAGE framework refers particularly to wealth distances. There are of course huge disparities in wealth internationally: around the world, there are 4–5 billion people in 2010 beneath the poverty threshold of income less than $2 a day.[10] Multinationals from rich countries are typically weak at serving such very poor consumers. However, these rich-country multinationals are losing out on large markets if they only concentrate on the wealthy elites overseas. University of Michigan academic C.K. Prahalad points out that the aggregated wealth of those at the 'base of the pyramid' in terms of income distribution is very substantial: simple mathematics means that those 4–5 billion below the poverty threshold represent a market of more than $2000bn per year. If rich-country multinationals can develop new capabilities to serve these numerically huge markets, they can bridge the economic distance, and thereby both significantly extend their presence in booming economies such as China and India and bring to these poor consumers the benefits that are claimed for Western goods. See Illustration 8.4 for examples of innovative base-of-the-pyramid strategies in India.

8.5.2 Competitive characteristics

Assessing the relative attractiveness of markets by PESTEL and CAGE analyses is only the first step. The second element relates to competition. Here, of course, Michael Porter's five forces framework can help (see section 2.3). For example, country markets with many existing competitors, powerful buyers (perhaps large retail chains such as in much of North America and Northern Europe) and low barriers to further new entrants from overseas would typically be unattractive. However, an additional consideration is the likelihood of retaliation from other competitors.

In the five forces framework, retaliation potential relates to rivalry, but managers can extend this by using insights directly from 'game theory' (see section 6.4.4). Here the likelihood and

ILLUSTRATION 8.4

Base of the Pyramid strategies

In India, Base of the Pyramid strategy means more than just low prices. Base of the Pyramid involves reshaping distribution channels, designing new products and forming partnerships.

Distribution channels

Procter & Gamble, the global consumer goods company, generates $20bn (~€14bn) worth of sales from developing markets. To reach poorer communities, however, it has to rely on tiny, crowded and often chaotic retail stores. Its strong brands and expensive packaging were often hidden from view underneath a ramshackle counter. Procter & Gamble has therefore hired a team of local sales agents in order to build ties with store owners, to educate them in the importance of display and to negotiate better shelf space for its products.

Product design

Nokia, the world's largest mobile phone company, has three R&D facilities in India. In order to serve markets where electricity is hard to find, they have produced a mobile phone that can operate for more than two weeks on a single charge – and which comes with a flashlight. Recognising that phones are often too costly on an individual basis, Nokia's phone allows friends and families to share a device by maintaining as many as five separate phone books and providing controls on how much any individual user can talk or spend.

Partnerships

Coca-Cola has developed an orange-flavoured fortified beverage called Vitingo, which will sell in 18 gram packets at Rs 2.50 (€0.04) each. The beverage has added nutrients (iron, vitamin C, folic acid and so on) to compensate for deficiencies in many poor people's diet, a problem called 'Hidden Hunger'. After a successful pilot project, during 2009 Coca-Cola is entering 30 Orissa districts in partnership with the local non-governmental organisation and micro-finance insitution BISWA.

Sources: The Economic Times, 11 January 2010; People and Strategy, 1 April 2009.

Questions

1 Can you imagine any risks or dangers that Western companies might face in pursuing Base of the Pyramid strategies?

2 Is there anything that Western companies might learn from Base of the Pyramid strategies in emerging markets that might be valuable in their home markets?

---

ferocity of potential competitor reactions are added to the simple calculation of relative country market attractiveness. As in Figure 8.6, country markets can be assessed according to three criteria:[11]

- *Market attractiveness* to the new entrant, based on PESTEL, CAGE and five forces analyses, for example. In Figure 8.6, countries A and B are the most attractive to the entrant.
- *Defender's reactiveness*, likely to be influenced by the market's attractiveness to the defender but also by the extent to which the defender is working with a globally integrated, rather than multidomestic, strategy. A defender will be more reactive if the markets are important to it and it has the managerial capabilities to coordinate its response. Here, the defender is highly reactive in countries A and D.

Figure 8.6 International competitor retaliation

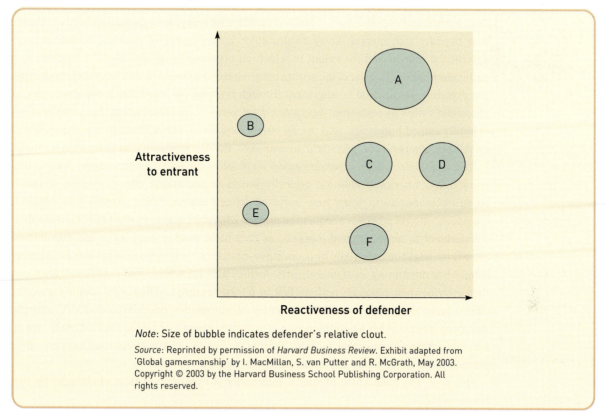

Note: Size of bubble indicates defender's relative clout.

Source: Reprinted by permission of *Harvard Business Review*. Exhibit adapted from
'Global gamesmanship' by I. MacMillan, S. van Putter and R. McGrath, May 2003.
Copyright © 2003 by the Harvard Business School Publishing Corporation. All
rights reserved.

- *Defender's clout*, i.e. the power that the defender is able to muster in order to fight back. Clout is typically a function of share in the particular market, but might be influenced by connections to other powerful local players, such as retailers or government. In Figure 8.6, clout is represented by the size of the bubbles, with the defender having most clout in countries A, C, D and F.

Choice of country to enter can be significantly modified by adding reactiveness and clout to calculations of attractiveness. Relying only on attractiveness, the top-ranked country to enter in Figure 8.6 is country A. Unfortunately, it is also one in which the defender is highly reactive, and the one in which it has most clout. Country B becomes a better international move than A. In turn, country C is a better prospect than country D, because, even though they are equally attractive, the defender is less reactive. One surprising result of taking defender reactiveness and clout into account is the re-evaluation of country E: although ranked fifth on simple attractiveness, it might rank overall second if competitor retaliation is allowed for.

This sort of analysis is particularly fruitful for considering the international moves of two interdependent competitors, such as Unilever and Procter & Gamble or British Airways and Singapore Airlines. In these cases the analysis is relevant to any aggressive strategic move, for instance the expansion of existing operations in a country as well as initial entry. Especially in the case of globally integrated competitors, moreover, the overall clout of the defender must be taken into account. The defender may choose to retaliate in other markets than the targeted one, counter-attacking wherever it has the clout to do damage to the aggressor. Naturally, too, this kind of analysis can be applied to interactions between diversified competitors as well as international ones: each bubble could represent different products or services.

8.5.3 Entry modes

Once a particular national market has been selected for entry, an organisation needs to choose how to enter that market. Entry modes differ in the degree of resource commitment to a particular market and the extent to which an organisation is operationally involved in a particular location. In order of increasing resource commitment, the four key entry mode types are: *exporting*; contractual arrangement through *licensing and franchising* to local partners, as McDonald's does to restaurant operators; *joint ventures*, in other words the establishment of jointly owned businesses; and *wholly owned subsidiaries*, either through the acquisition of established companies or 'greenfield' investments, the development of facilities from scratch.

The *staged international expansion* model emphasises the role of experience in determining entry mode. Internationalisation typically brings organisations into unfamiliar territory, requiring managers to learn new ways of doing business.[12] The **staged international expansion model proposes a sequential process whereby companies gradually increase their commitment to newly entered markets, as they build market knowledge and capabilities**. Thus firms might enter initially by licensing or exporting, thereby acquiring some local knowledge while minimising local investments. As they gain knowledge and confidence, firms can then increase their exposure, perhaps first by a joint venture and finally by creating a wholly owned subsidiary. An example is the entry of automobile manufacturer BMW into the American market. After a lengthy period of exporting from Germany to the USA, BMW set up a manufacturing plant in Spartanburg, South Carolina in order to strengthen its competitive position in the strategically important American market.

However, the gradualism of staged international expansion is now challenged by two phenomena:

- '*Born-global firms*', in other words new small firms that internationalise rapidly at early stages in their development.[13] New technologies now help small firms link up to international sources of expertise, supply and customers worldwide. For such firms, waiting till they have enough international experience is not an option: international strategy is a condition of existence. GNI, the mini-multinational in Illustration 8.5, illustrates this born-global process.

- *Emerging-country multinationals* also often move quickly through entry modes. Prominent examples are the Chinese white-goods multinational Haier, the Indian pharmaceuticals company Ranbaxy Laboratories and Mexico's Cemex cement company.[14] Such companies typically develop *unique capabilities* in their home market that then need to be rolled out quickly worldwide before competitors catch up. For example, Haier became skilled at very efficient production of simple white goods, providing a cost advantage that is transferable outside its Chinese manufacturing base. Haier now has factories in Italy and the United States, as well as the Philippines, Malaysia, Indonesia, Egypt, Nigeria and elsewhere round the world.

Where the demands and pace of international competition rule out more gradualist staged expansion, two fundamental principles can help guide choice of market entry mode:

- *The breadth of competitive advantage* in the target market. This determines whether entry into the market can be done relying upon the company's own capabilities, or whether it must draw on the capabilities of local partners, for instance to access distribution channels or to manufacture locally.

ILLUSTRATION 8.5

The mini-multinational

GNI, a biotechnology start-up, has fewer than one hundred employees, but operates in five countries in four continents.

Christopher Savoie is a US entrepreneur who originally studied medicine in Japan, becoming fluent in Japanese and adopting Japanese citizenship. In 2001, he founded GNI, a biotechnology company that by 2006 had raised ¥3bn (€20m; $14m) in investment funds, including a stake from famed global investment bank Goldman Sachs. The company already has operations in Tokyo and Fukuoka, Japan; in Shanghai, China; in Cambridge and London, UK; and in San Jose in California. There is also collaboration with a laboratory in Auckland, New Zealand. Savoie comments: 'We take the best in each country and put them together'.

GNI's strategy is to focus on Asian ailments that have been neglected by big Western pharmaceutical companies, for example stomach cancer and hepatitis. According to Savoie: 'Asia has been getting the short end of the stick. As a small company, we had to choose a niche, and we thought that half of humanity was an acceptable place to start.'

GNI's scientists work on umbilical cords, providing genetic tissue that has been virtually unaffected by the environment. However, Japanese parents traditionally keep their children's umbilical cords. GNI therefore works with the Rosie Maternity Hospital in Cambridge to source its basic genetic materials. On the other hand, GNI in Japan has ready access to supercomputers, and Japanese scientists have worked out the algorithms required to analyse the genetic codes. Japan also has been the main source of investment funds, where regulations on start-ups are relaxed. China comes in as an effective place to test treatments on patients. Regulatory advantages mean that trials can be carried out more quickly in China, moreover for one tenth of the cost of Japan. In 2005, GNI merged with Shanghai Genomics, a start-up run by two US-educated entrepreneurs. Meanwhile, in San Jose, there is a business development office seeking out relationships with the big American pharmaceutical giants.

Savoie describes the business model as essentially simple: 'We have a Chinese cost structure, Japanese supercomputers and, in Cambridge, access to ethical materials (umbilical cords) and top clinical scientists. This is a network we can use to take high-level science and turn it into molecules to compete with the big boys.'

Sources: D. Pilling, 'March of the Mini-Multinational', *Financial Times*, 4 May 2006; www.gene-networks.com.

Questions

1 Analyse GNI's value network in terms of cost advantages, unique capabilities and national characteristics.

2 What managerial challenges will GNI face as it grows?

- *Tradability*, in other words the ability to rely on trading relationships, rather than the firm's own presence. Tradability is determined by two factors: ease of transport from home country to target country, and the quality of legal protection in the target country. Legal protection refers for example to the ability to enforce contracts, to safeguard performance standards or to protect intellectual property such as patented technologies. Tradability is low where it is unsafe to trade through market-based contracts with local partners.

Other case-specific factors are liable to enter the calculation of appropriate entry mode as well, not least the availability of suitable local partners. Nonetheless, the two principles of

Figure 8.7 Modes of international market entry

competitive advantage and tradability do suggest the following broad guidelines for entry mode (Figure 8.7):

- *Export* is the baseline option, and is suitable where the product or services are easily transported from country to country and where the home-based competitive advantages are sufficiently broad to minimise reliance on local companies.

- *License or franchise* the product or service where competitive advantages are too narrow to go it alone, but the legal environment is such that licensees and franchisees can be relied on not to abuse their contracts, under-perform on standards or steal the intellectual property.

- *Joint ventures* work where competitive advantages are narrow, but local licensees or franchisees cannot be trusted with intellectual property or long-term performance. A joint venture involving shared ownership gives the foreign company more direct control and ensures that the local partner has an interest in maximising the value of the common enterprise rather than solely their own stand-alone interests.

- *Wholly owned subsidiary* is an attractive route where competitive advantages are sufficiently broad not to depend on local partners, but where nonetheless transport difficulties rule out simple export. Such wholly owned subsidiaries can be via new 'greenfield' investments (as for example many Japanese car companies have entered European markets) or via acquisition, where the integration of a local firm completes the breadth of competitive advantage required.

8.6 INTERNATIONALISATION AND PERFORMANCE

Just as for product and service diversity discussed in section 7.4 the relationship between internationalisation and performance has been extensively researched.[15] Some of the main findings from such research are these:

- *An inverted U-curve.* While the potential performance benefits of internationalisation are substantial, in that it allows firms to realise economies of scale and scope and benefit from the locational advantages available in countries around the globe, the combination of diverse locations and diverse business units also gives rise to high levels of organisational complexity. After a point, the costs of organisational complexity may exceed the benefits of internationalisations. Accordingly, theory and the balance of evidence suggest an inverted U-shaped relationship between internationalisation and performance (similar to the findings on product/service diversification shown in section 7.4), with moderate levels of internationalisation leading to the best results. However, Yip's recent research on large British companies suggests that managers may be getting better at internationalisation, with substantially internationalised firms actually seeing performance improving at the point where international sales are above about 40 per cent of total sales.[16] Experience and commitment to internationalisation may be able to deliver strong performance for highly internationalised firms.

- *Service-sector disadvantages.* A number of studies have suggested that, in contrast to firms in the manufacturing sector, internationalisation may not lead to improved performance for service-sector firms. There are three possible reasons for such an effect. First, the operations of foreign service firms in some sectors (such as accountants or banks) remain tightly regulated and restricted in many countries; second, due to the intangible nature of services, they are often more sensitive to cultural differences and require greater adaptation than manufactured products which may lead to higher initial learning costs; third, the services typically require a significant local presence and reduces the scope for the exploitation of economies of scale in production compared to manufacturing firms.[17]

- *Internationalisation and product diversity.* An important question to consider is the interaction between internationalisation and product/service diversification. Compared to single-business firms it has been suggested that product-diversified firms are likely to do better from international expansion because they have already developed the necessary skills and structures for managing internal diversity.[18] At the other end of the spectrum there is general consensus that firms that are highly diversified both in terms of product and international markets are likely to face excessive costs of coordination and control leading to poor performance. As many firms have not yet reached levels of internationalisation where negative effects outweigh possible gains and because of current scepticism with regard to the benefits of high levels of product diversification, many companies currently opt for reducing their product diversity whilst building their international scope. Unilever, for example, has been combining a strategy of growing internationalisation with de-diversification.

(8.7) ROLES IN AN INTERNATIONAL PORTFOLIO

Just as for product diversification, international strategies imply different relationships between subsidiary operations and the corporate centre. The complexity of the strategies followed by organisations such as General Electric or Unilever can result in highly differentiated networks of subsidiaries with a range of distinct strategic roles. Subsidiaries may play different roles according to the level of local resources and capabilities available to them and the strategic importance of their local environment (see Figure 8.8).[19]

Figure 8.8 Subsidiary roles in multinational firms

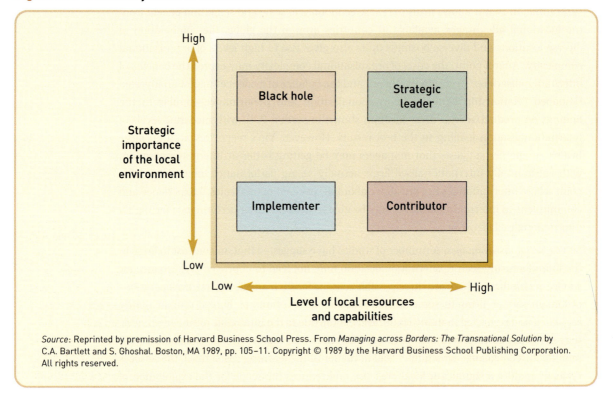

- *Strategic leaders* are subsidiaries that not only hold valuable resources and capabilities but are also located in countries that are crucial for competitive success because of, for example, the size of the local market or the accessibility of key technologies. Japanese and European subsidiaries in the United States often play this role.

- *Contributors* are subsidiaries located in countries of lesser strategic significance, but with sufficiently valuable internal capabilities to nevertheless play key roles in a multinational organisation's competitive success. The Australian subsidiary of the Swedish telecommunications firm Ericsson played such a role in developing specialised systems for the firm's mobile phone business.

- *Implementers*, though not contributing substantially to the enhancement of a firm's competitive advantage, are important in the sense that they help generate vital financial resources. In this sense, they are similar to the 'cash cows' of the Boston Consulting Group matrix. The danger is that they turn into the equivalent of 'dogs'.

- *Black holes* are subsidiaries located in countries that are crucial for competitive success but with low-level resources or capabilities. This is a position many subsidiaries of American and European firms found themselves in over long periods in Japan. They have some of the characteristics of 'question marks' in the Boston Consulting Group matrix, requiring heavy investment (like an astrophysicist's black hole, sucking matter in). Possibilities for overcoming this unattractive position include the development of alliances and the selective and targeted development of key resources and capabilities.[20]

These various subsidiary roles relate to how these subsidiaries are generally controlled and managed, and this is discussed in Chapter 13.

KEY DEBATE

Global, local or regional?

Debate rages over whether companies are really becoming more global, or whether local or indeed regional pressures remain strong.

Ted Levitt, Harvard Business School professor and former non-executive director of the international advertising firm Saatchi & Saatchi, has provocatively made the case for deep commitment to global strategies in all kinds of markets. He argues that modern communications technologies are creating homogeneous market needs, while manufacturing technologies are increasing the benefits of scale. Given the cost advantages of scale, and the diminishing importance of consumer differences, companies that commit to truly global strategies will be able to use low prices to sweep out all competitors still focused on local needs. He argues: 'The global company will seek to standardize its offering everywhere . . . Companies that do not adapt to the new global realities will become victims of those that do.' He cites Coca-Cola, Rolex, Sony and McDonald's as exemplars of the trend. Companies should not hanker over detailed differences left over from the past, but recognise the big picture of coming globalisation.

Levitt's sweeping argument brought a spirited response from American academics Gerry Wind and Susan Douglas, warning of 'the Myth of Globalization'. They challenge both the trend to homogenisation and the growing role of scale economies. Even apparently global companies adapt to country needs: for example Coca-Cola sells local products in Japan alongside its classic Coke, and its Dasani bottled water is a success in the United States, but a failure in Europe. As to scale, new flexible automation technologies may even be reducing economic order sizes, allowing short production runs adapted to local needs. Besides, as the world gets richer, consumers will be less price-sensitive and more ready to spend on indulging their local tastes. Wind and Douglas warn that blind confidence in the inevitability of globalisation will surely lead to business disappointment.

Between the two poles of global and local there is a third position: regional. Pankaj Ghemawat points out that most international trade is intra-regional.

European countries trade predominantly with each other. The trend towards intra-regional trade is actually growing, from about 40 per cent of all trade forty years ago to 55 per cent at the beginning of the 21st century. This is reflected in the nature of multi-national companies as well. Alan Rugman calculates that in the early years of the 21st century over 300 out of the world's largest corporations still have more than half their sales in their home region. An apparently global company like McDonald's is effectively bi-regional, with eighty per cent of its sales concentrated in North America and Europe. Established multinationals such as General Electric and Procter & Gamble have 60 per cent and 55 per cent of their sales respectively back home in North America.

Ted Levitt might be impatient with these empirical details. The essential issue for him is: where are things going in the future? Certainly there are still local differences in taste, but are these declining overall? Maybe there is a growth of intra-regional trade, but is this just the result of transitional events such as the creation of the North American Free Trade Association or the sucking-in of imports by China? We should not be distracted by temporary blips on the grand highway to global integration.

Sources: T. Levitt, 'The globalization of markets', *Harvard Business Review*, May–June (1983), pp. 92–102; Wind and Douglas, Columbia; P. Ghemawat, 'Regional strategies for global leadership', *Harvard Business Review*, December (2005), 98–108; A. Rugman, *The Regional Multinationals* (2005), Cambridge University Press.

Questions

1 Make a list of products and services which are getting more 'global' over time; then make a list of products and services which are still very 'local'.

2 How many countries in the world have you visited in your lifetime? How many countries had your parents visited by the same age?

SUMMARY

- Internationalisation potential in any particular market is determined by Yip's four drivers: market, cost, government and competitors' strategies.

- Sources of advantage in international strategy can be drawn from both global sourcing through the international value network and national sources of advantage, as captured in Porter's Diamond.

- There are four main types of international strategy, varying according to extent of coordination and geographical configuration: simple export, complex export, multidomestic and global.

- Market selection for international entry or expansion should be based on attractiveness, multidimensional measures of distance and expectations of competitor retaliation.

- Modes of entry into new markets include export, licensing and franchising, joint ventures and overseas subsidiaries.

- Internationalisation has an uncertain relationship to financial performance, with an inverted U-curve warning against over-internationalisation.

- Subsidiaries in an international firm can be managed by portfolio methods just like businesses in a diversified firm.

WORK ASSIGNMENTS

✳ *Denotes more advanced work assignments. * Refers to a case study in the Text and Case edition.*

8.1 Using Figure 8.2 (Yip's internationalisation drivers), compare two markets you are familiar with and analyse how strong each of the drivers is for increased international strategy.

8.2✳ Taking an industry you are familiar with that is strong in your home country (for example, fashion in France, cars in Germany), use the four determinants of Porter's Diamond (Figure 8.3) to explain that industry's national advantage.

8.3 Using the four international strategies of Figure 8.4, classify the international strategy of Tesco*, Ekomate* or any other multinational corporation with which you are familiar.

8.4✳ Using the CAGE framework (section 8.5.1), assess the relative 'distance' of the United States, China, India and France for a British company (or a company from a country of your choice).

8.5✳ Take any part of the public or not-for-profit sector (for example, education, health) and explain how far internationalisation has affected its management and consider how far it may do so in the future.

Integrative assignment

8.6 As in 8.3, use the four international strategies of Figure 8.4 to classify the international strategy of Tesco*, Ekomate* or any other multinational corporation with which you are familiar. Drawing on section 13.2, how does this corporation's organisational structure fit (or not fit) this strategy?

VIDEO ASSIGNMENT

Visit *MyStrategyLab* and watch the *Electrolux* case study.

1 Describe Electrolux's changing international strategy in terms of the four strategies of Figure 8.4. Why is it changing in this way?

2 What roles could a large subsidiary such as the Italian Zanussi play in the Electrolux international portfolio (see Figure 8.8.)?

RECOMMENDED KEY READINGS

- An eye-opening introduction to the detailed workings – and inefficiencies – of today's global economy today is P. Rivoli, *The Travels of a T-Shirt in the Global Economy: an Economist Examines the Markets, Power and Politics of World Trade*, Wiley, 2006. A more optimistic view is in T. Friedman, *The World Is Flat: the Globalized World in the Twenty-First Century*, Penguin, 2006.

- An invigorating perspective on international strategy is provided by G. Yip, *Total Global Strategy II*, Prentice Hall, 2003. A comprehensive general textbook is S. Segal-Horn and D. Faulkner, *Understanding Global Strategy*, Southwestern, 2010.

- A useful collection of academic articles on international business is in A. Rugman and T. Brewer (eds), *The Oxford Handbook of International Business*, Oxford University Press, 2003.

REFERENCES

1. For another cautious view, see M. Alexander and H. Korine, 'Why you shouldn't go global', *Harvard Business Review*, December (2008), pp. 70–7.

2. T. Friedman, *The World Is Flat: the Globalized World in the Twenty-First Century*, Penguin, 2006 and P. Rivoli, *The Travels of a T-Shirt in the Global Economy: an Economist Examines the Markets, Power and Politics of World Trade*, Wiley, 2006.

3. G. Yip, *Total Global Strategy II*, Prentice Hall, 2003.

4. Useful industry-specific data on trends in openness to trade and investment can be found at the World Trade Organization's site, www.wto.org.

5. G. Hamel and C.K. Prahalad, 'Do you really have a global strategy?', *Harvard Business Review*, vol. 63, no. 4 (1985), pp. 139–48.

6. B. Kogut, 'Designing global strategies: comparative and competitive value added changes', *Sloan Management Review*, vol. 27 (1985), pp. 15–28.

7. M. Porter, *The Competitive Advantage of Nations*, Macmillan, 1990.

8. This typology builds on the basic framework of M. Porter, 'Changing patterns of international competition', *California Management Review*, vol. 28, no. 2 (1987), pp. 9–39, but adapts its terms for the four strategies into more readily understandable terms: note particularly that here 'global' strategy is transposed to refer to the top left box, and the top right box is described as 'complex export'.

9. P. Ghemawat, 'Distance still matters', *Harvard Business Review*, September (2001), 137–47.

10. C.K. Prahalad and A. Hammond, 'Serving the world's poor, profitably', *Harvard Business Review*, September (2002), 48–55; Economist Intelligence Unit, 'From subsistence to sustainable: a bottom-up perspective on the role of business in poverty alleviation', 24 April 2009.

11. This framework is introduced in I. MacMillan, A. van Putten and R. McGrath, 'Global Gamesmanship', *Harvard Business Review*, vol. 81, no. 5 (2003), pp. 62–71.

12. For detailed discussions about the role of learning and experience in market entry see: M.F. Guillén, 'Experience, imitation, and the sequence of foreign entry: wholly owned and joint-venture manufacturing by South Korean firms and business groups in China, 1987–1995', *Journal of International Business Studies*, vol. 83 (2003), pp. 185–98; and M.K. Erramilli, 'The experience factor in foreign market entry modes by service firms', *Journal of International Business Studies*, vol. 22, no. 3 (1991), pp. 479–501.

13. G. Knights and T. Cavusil, 'A taxonomy of born-global firms', *Management International Review*, vol. 45, no. 3 (2005), pp. 15–35.

14. For analyses of emerging-country multinationals, see T. Khanna and K. Palepu, 'Emerging giants: building world-class companies in developing countries', *Harvard Business Review*, October (2006), pp. 60–9 and the special

issue on 'The internationalization of Chinese and Indian firms – trends, motivations and strategy', *Industrial and Corporate Change*, vol. 18, no. 2 (2009).

15. A useful review of the international dimension is: M. Hitt and R.E. Hoskisson, 'International diversification: effects on innovation and firm performance in product-diversified firms', *Academy of Management Journal*, vol. 40, no. 4 (1997), pp. 767–98.

16. For detailed results on British companies, see G. Yip, A. Rugman and A. Kudina, 'International success of British companies', *Long Range Planning*, vol. 39, no. 1 (2006), pp. 241–64.

17. See N. Capar and M. Kotabe, 'The relationship between international diversification and performance in service firms', *Journal of International Business Studies*, vol. 34 (2003), pp. 345–55; F.J. Contractor, S.K. Kundu and C. Hsu, 'A three-stage theory of international expansion: the link between multinationality and performance in the service sector', *Journal of International Business Studies*, vol. 34 (2003), pp. 5–18.

18. S.C. Chang and C.-F. Wang, 'The effect of product diversification strategies on the relationship between international diversification and firm performance', *Journal of World Business*, vol. 42, no. 1 (2007), pp. 61–79.

19. C.A. Bartlett and S. Ghosal, *Managing across Borders: the Transnational Solution*, The Harvard Business School Press, 1989, pp. 105–11; A.M. Rugman and A. Verbeke, 'Extending the theory of the multinational enterprise: internalization and strategic management perspectives', *Journal of International Business Studies*, vol. 34 (2003), pp. 125–37.

20. For a more far-reaching exploration of the role of subsidiaries in multinational corporations, see J. Birkinshaw, *Entrepreneurship and the Global Firm*, Sage, 2000.

CASE EXAMPLE

Lenovo computers: East meets West

Introduction

In May 2005, the world's thirteenth largest personal computer company, Lenovo, took over the world's third largest personal computer business, IBM's PC division. Lenovo, at that time based wholly in China, was paying $1.75bn (~€1.23bn) to control a business that operated all over the world and had effectively invented the personal computer industry back in 1981. Michael Dell, the creator of the world's largest PC company, commented simply: 'it won't work'.

Lenovo had been founded back in 1984 by Liu Chuanzhi, a 40-year-old researcher working for the Computer Institute of the Chinese Academy of Sciences. His early career had included disassembling captured American radar systems during the Vietnam War and planting rice during the Chinese Cultural Revolution. Liu Chuanzhi had started with $25,000 capital from the Computer Institute and promised his boss that he would build a business with revenues of $250,000. Working in the Computer Institute's old guardhouse, and borrowing its office facilities, one of Liu's first initiatives was reselling colour televisions. But real success started to come in 1987, when Lenovo was one of the first to package Chinese-character software with imported PCs.

Lenovo began to take off, with Liu using the support of his father, well placed in the Chinese government, to help import PCs cheaply through Hong Kong. During 1988, Lenovo placed its first job advertisement, and recruited 58 young people to join the company. Whilst the founding generation of Lenovo staff were in their forties, the new recruits were all in their twenties, as the Cultural Revolution had prevented any university graduation for a period of 10 years in China. Amongst the new recruits was Yang Yuanqing, who would be running Lenovo's PC business before he was 30, and later become Chairman of the new Lenovo–IBM venture at the age of 41. It was this new team which helped launch the production of the first Lenovo PC in 1990, and drove the company to a 30 per cent market share within China by 2005. The company had partially floated on the Hong Kong Stock Exchange in 1994.

Lenovo's Chairman, Yang Yuanqing
Source: Press Associated Images/Kin Cheung/AP.

The deal

Work on the IBM PC deal had begun in 2004, with Lenovo assisted by management consultancy McKinsey & Co. and investment banker Goldman Sachs. IBM wanted to dispose of its PC business, which had only 4 per cent market share in the USA and suffered low margins in a competitive market dominated by Dell and Hewlett-Packard. Higher-margin services and mainframe computers would be IBM's future. As well as Lenovo, IBM had private equity firm Texas Pacific Group in the bidding. Lenovo offered the better price, but Texas Pacific was persuaded enough to take a stake in the new group, while IBM took 13 per cent ownership. The government-owned Chinese Academy of Sciences still owned 27 per cent of the stock, the largest single shareholder.

The new Chairman, Yang Yuanqing, had a clear vision of what the company was to achieve, while recognising some of the challenges:

'In five years, I want this (Lenovo) to be a very famous PC brand, with maybe double the growth of the industry. I want to have a very healthy profit margin, and maybe some other businesses beyond PCs, worldwide. We are at the beginnings of this new company, so we can define some fundamentals about the culture. The three words I use to describe this are "trust, respect, compromise".'

He continued:

'As a global company maybe we have to sacrifice some speed, especially during our first phase. We need more communication. We need to take time to understand each other. But speed was in the genes of the old Lenovo. I hope it will be in the genes of the new Lenovo.'

IBM was not leaving its old business to sink or swim entirely on its own. Lenovo had the right to use the IBM brand for PCs for five years, including the valuable ThinkPad name. IBM's salesforce would be offered incentives to sell Lenovo PCs, just as they had had with IBM's own-brand machines. IBM Global Services was contracted to provide maintenance and support. IBM would have two non-voting observers on the Lenovo board. Moreover, Stephen Ward, the 51-year-old former head of IBM's PC division, was to become Lenovo's Chief Executive Officer.

Managing the new giant

Having an IBM CEO was not entirely a surprise. After all, the $13bn business was nearly 80 per cent ex-IBM and customers and employees had to be reassured of continuity. But there were some significant challenges for the new company to manage none the less.

Things had not started well. When the Chinese team first flew to New York to meet the IBM team, they had not been met at the airport as they had expected and was normal polite practice in China. Yang and Ward had disagreed about the location of the new headquarters, Yang wishing it to be shared between Beijing and near New York. Ward had prevailed, and Yang moved his family to the USA. The new organisation structure kept the old IBM business and the original Lenovo business as separate divisions. But still the new company needed considerable liaison with China, a 13-hour flight away, across 12 time zones. Tele-conferencing between the East Coast and China became a way of life, with the Americans calling typically at either 6.00 in the morning or 11.00 at night to catch their Chinese colleagues. Calls were always in English, with many Chinese less than fluent and body language impossible to observe.

The Chinese nature of the company was an issue for some constituencies. IBM had had a lot of government business, and populist members of the US Congress whipped up a scare campaign about Chinese computers entering sensitive domains. In Germany, labour laws allowed a voluntary transition of IBM employees to Lenovo, and many German workers chose not to transfer, leaving the company short-staffed. There was some discomfort amongst former IBM employees in Japan about Chinese ownership. Between the two dominant cultures, American and Chinese, there were considerable differences. Qiao Jian, Vice President for Human Resources, commented:

'Americans like to talk; Chinese people like to listen. At first we wondered why they kept talking when they had nothing to say. But we have learnt to be more direct when we have a problem, and the Americans are learning to listen.'

Cultural differences were not just national. Lenovo was a new and relatively simple company – basically one country, one product. Multinational giant IBM Corporation, founded in 1924, was far more complex. The Lenovo management team, mostly in their thirties, were much younger than IBM's, and the average age of the company as a whole was just 28. IBM was famous for its management processes and routines. Qiao Jian commented: 'IBM people set a time for a conference call and stick to it every week. But why have the call if there is nothing to report?' On the other hand, IBM people had a tendency for being late for meetings, something that was strictly discouraged within Lenovo.

Some results

At first, the response to the new Lenovo was positive. IBM customers stayed loyal and the stock price began to climb (see Figure 1). Remaining IBM executives recognised that at least they were part of a business committed to PCs, rather than the Cinderella in a much larger IBM empire. The fact that a Lenovo PC manufactured in China had a labour cost of just $3.00 offered a lot of opportunity.

However, market leader Dell responded to the new company with heavy price cuts, offering $100 savings on the average machine. With market share in the crucial American market beginning to slip, ex-IBM CEO Stephen Ward was replaced in December 2005 by William Amelio. This was a coup for Lenovo, as Amelio had been running Dell's Asia–Pacific region. As well as knowing Lenovo's competitor from the inside, Amelio, based for several years in Singapore, had a good understanding of Asian business:

Figure 1 Lenovo Group's stock price, 2001–2006, compared with NASDAQ index

Week of Jun 3, 2002: ■ LHL.F 0.42 ■ ^IXIC 1,535.48

© [type Function] Yahoo! Inc.

2002 Jul Oct 2003 Apr Jul Oct 2004 Apr Jul Oct 2005 Apr Jul Oct 2006 Apr Jul Oct2007

Source: http://finance.yahoo.com/echarts.

'In the five years I have been in Asia, one thing I have learned . . . is to have a lot more patience. I have to be someone who has a high sense of urgency and drive, but I have also learned how to temper that in the various cultures that I have dealt with in order to be more effective.'

Amelio started by addressing costs, removing 1,000 positions, or 10 per cent, from Lenovo's non-China workforce. He integrated the IBM business and the old Lenovo business into a single structure. The company launched a new range of Lenovo-branded PCs for small and medium-sized American businesses, a market traditionally ignored by IBM. To improve its reach in this segment, Lenovo expanded sales to big American retailers such as Office Depot. US market share began to recover, pushing beyond 4 per cent again. Lenovo began to consider entry into the Indian market.

Amelio's actions seemed to pay off. After a precipitous slide during the first half of 2006, the stock price turned up. But there was no disguising that the stock price in the autumn of 2006 was still below where

it was five years earlier, and that it continued to trail the hi-tech American NASDAQ index.

Sources: L. Zhijun, *The Lenovo Affair*, Wiley, Singapore, 2006; *Business Week*, 7 August (2006), 20 April (2006), 22 December (2005) and 9 May (2005); *Financial Times*, 8 November (2005), 9 November (2005) and 10 November (2005).

Questions

1 What national sources of competitive advantage might Lenovo draw from its Chinese base? What disadvantages derive from its Chinese base?

2 In the light of the CAGE framework and the MacMillan *et al.* competitor retaliation framework (Figure 8.6), comment on Lenovo's entry into the American market.

3 Now that Lenovo is international, what type of generic international strategy should it pursue – simple export, multidomestic, complex export or global?

9

INNOVATION AND ENTREPRENEURSHIP

Learning outcomes

After reading this chapter you should understand how to:

● Identify and respond to key *innovation dilemmas*, such as the relative emphases to place on technologies or markets, product or process innovations, open versus closed innovation, and the underlying business model.

● Anticipate and to some extent influence the *diffusion* (or spread) of innovations.

● Decide when being a *first-mover* or a *follower* is most appropriate in innovation, and how an incumbent organisation should respond to innovative challengers.

● Anticipate key issues facing entrepreneurs as they go through the *stages of growth*, from start-up to exit.

● Evaluate opportunities and choices facing *social entrepreneurs* as they create new ventures to address social problems.

Key terms

Business model p. 301

Diffusion p. 303

Disruptive innovation p. 309

Entrepreneurial life cycle p. 311

First-mover advantage p. 307

Innovation p. 296

Open innovation p. 300

Platform leadership p. 300

S-curve p. 304

Social entrepreneurs p. 315

Tipping point p. 304

PEARSON
mystrategylab

MyStrategyLab is designed to help you make the most of your studies.

Visit www.pearsoned.co.uk/mystrategylab to discover a wide range of resources specific to this chapter, including:

• A personalised **Study plan** that will help you understand core concepts

• **Audio** and **video clips** that put the spotlight on strategy in the real world

• **Online glossaries** and **flashcards** that provide helpful reminders when you're looking for some quick revision.

(9.1) INTRODUCTION

This chapter is about creating the new – both new products or services and new organisations. Such innovation and entrepreneurship are fundamental to today's economy. But they also pose hard choices. For example, should a company look always to be a pioneer in new technologies, or rather be a fast follower, as Apple typically is? How should a company react to radical innovations that threaten to destroy their existing revenues, as the Kodak film business had to with the rise of electronic cameras? How should entrepreneurs handle takeover bids from powerful rich companies: was social networking site MySpace right to sell out to media giant News Corporation (see Illustration 1.1)?

The chapter focuses particularly on the choices involved in innovation and entrepreneurship. Entrepreneurship is a fundamental organisational process. All businesses start with an act of entrepreneurship, and, in the form of 'social entrepreneurship', entrepreneurship is extending beyond purely commercial markets. Innovation is a key aspect of business-level strategy as introduced in Chapter 6, with implications for cost, price and sustainability. As such, it too is relevant in both public and private spheres. Promoting greater innovation and entrepreneurship is crucial to the improvement of public services.

The two main themes that link innovation and entrepreneurship are *timing* and *relationships* (see Figure 9.1). Timing decisions include when to be first-mover or fast second in innovation; when, and if, an innovation will reach its tipping point, the point where demand takes off; and, for an entrepreneurial new venture, when founders should finally exit their enterprise. The other theme is relationships. Creating innovations or new organisations is very rarely done alone. Successful innovation and entrepreneurship are typically done through relationships. These relationships come in many forms: sometimes relationships between organisations and their customers; sometimes relationships between big business and small start-ups; sometimes between business and 'social entrepreneurs'.

Figure 9.1 The innovation–entrepreneurship framework

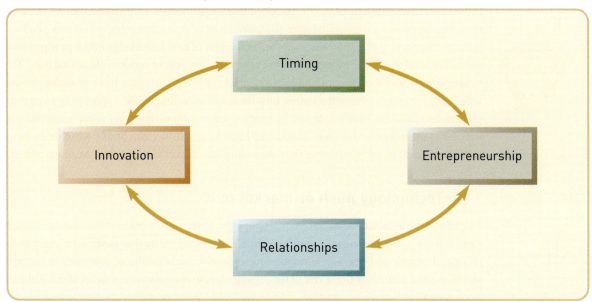

Within Figure 9.1's broad framework, this chapter will examine first innovation, then entrepreneurship:

● Section 9.2 starts with four fundamental *innovation dilemmas*: technology push as against market pull; product innovation rather than process innovation; open versus closed innovation; and, finally, technological as opposed to broader business model innovation. None of these are absolute 'either-or' dilemmas, but managers and entrepreneurs must choose where to concentrate their limited resources.

● Section 9.3 considers issues surrounding the *diffusion*, or spread, of innovations in the marketplace. Diffusion processes often follow *S-curve patterns*, raising further typical issues for decision, particularly with regard to tipping points and tripping points.

● Section 9.4 completes the discussion of innovation by considering choices with regard to timing. This includes *first-mover* advantages and disadvantages, the advantages of being '*fast second*' into a market, and the issue of how established *incumbents* should respond to innovative challengers.

● Section 9.5 addresses *entrepreneurship*. The section discusses typical choices facing entrepreneurs as their ventures progress through the uncertain *stages of growth*, from start-up to exit. It also examines the kinds of *relationships* that entrepreneurs may have to form, particularly with larger firms practising 'open innovation'.

● Section 9.6 finally introduces *social entrepreneurship*, by which individuals and small groups can launch innovative and flexible new initiatives that larger public agencies are often unable to pursue. Again, social entrepreneurs face choices with regard to relationships, particularly with big business.

The Key Debate at the end of this chapter brings entrepreneurship and innovation together again by considering the issue of whether small or large firms are better at innovation.

INNOVATION DILEMMAS

Innovation raises fundamental strategic dilemmas for strategists. Innovation is more complex than just invention. *Invention* involves the conversion of new knowledge into a new product, process or service. **Innovation involves the conversion of new knowledge into a new product, process or service *and* the putting of this new product, process or service into actual use**.[1] The strategic dilemmas stem from this more extended process. Strategists have to make choices with regard to four fundamental issues: how far to follow technological opportunity as against market demand; how much to invest in product innovation rather than process innovation; how far to open themselves up to innovative ideas from outside; and finally whether to focus on technological innovation rather than extending innovation to their whole business model.[2]

9.2.1 Technology push or market pull

People often see innovation as driven by technology. In the pure version of this *technology push* view, it is the new knowledge created by technologists or scientists that pushes the innovation process. Research and development laboratories produce new products, processes or services and then hand them over to the rest of the organisation to manufacture, market and distribute. According to this push perspective, managers should listen primarily to their scientists and technologists, let them follow their hunches and support them with ample resources. Generous R&D budgets are crucial to making innovation happen.

An alternative approach to innovation is *market pull*. Market pull reflects a view of innovation that goes beyond invention and sees the importance of actual use. The role of market pull has been promoted since MIT professor Eric von Hippel's discovery that in many sectors users, not producers, are common sources of important innovations.[3] In designing their innovation strategies, therefore, organisations should listen in the first place to users rather than their own scientists and technologists. Von Hippel refines this focus on users to point out that in many markets it is not ordinary users that are the source of innovation, but *lead-users*. In medical surgery, top surgeons often adapt existing surgical instruments in order to carry out new types of operation. In extreme sports such as snowboarding or windsurfing, it is leading sportspeople who make the improvements necessary for greater performance. In this view, then, it is the pull of users in the market that is responsible for innovation. Managers need to build close relationships with lead-users such as the best surgeons or sporting champions. Marketing and sales functions identify the lead-users of a field and then scientists and technologists translate their inventive ideas into commercial products, processes or services that the wider market can use.

There are merits to both the technology push and market pull views. Relying heavily on existing users can make companies too conservative, and vulnerable to disruptive technologies that uncover needs unforeseen by existing markets (see section 9.4.3). On the other hand, history is littered with examples of companies that have blindly pursued technological excellence without regard to real market needs. Technology push and market pull are best seen as extreme views, therefore, helping to focus attention on a fundamental choice: relatively how much to rely on science and technology as sources of innovation, rather than what people are actually doing in the marketplace. In practice, most organisations find a compromise between the two views, with the balance varying both between industries and over time. As at the skateboarding company Sole Technology, users may be key at start-up, but internally led innovation can become more important with growth (see Illustration 9.1). The key issue for managers is to be aware of the dilemma and to review their organisation's balance between the two extremes consciously rather than relying on habit or prejudice.

9.2.2 Product or process innovation

Just as managers must find a balance between technological push and market pull, so must they determine the relative emphasis to place on product or process innovation. *Product innovation* relates to the final product (or service) to be sold, especially with regard to its features; *process innovation* relates to the way in which this product is produced and distributed, especially with regard to improvements in cost or reliability. Some firms specialise more in product innovation, others more in process innovation. For example, in computers, Apple has generally concentrated its efforts on designing attractive product features (for instance the MacBook Air), while Dell has innovated in terms of efficient processes, for instance direct sales, modularity and build-to-order.

The relative importance of product innovation and process innovation typically changes as industries evolve over time. Usually the first stages of an industry are dominated by product innovation based on new features. Thus the early history of the automobile was dominated by competition as to whether cars should be fuelled by steam, electricity or petrol, have their engines at the front or at the rear, and have three wheels or four.[4] Industries eventually

ILLUSTRATION 9.1

Shoes for skateboarders

Innovation at Sole Technologies is driven by both users and technology.

After taking a degree in industrial software, Pierre André Senizergues started his career as a professional skateboarder in France. In less than twenty years, he created an action shoe and apparel business with $200m (~€140m) sales, and seven brands, including Etnies with its famous distinctive 'E' and the big snowboarding boot brand ThirtyTwo. He also created the first skateboard shoe research laboratory in the world.

Things had not started out so promisingly for Senizergues. In 1988 he signed to ride for the skateboard brand of a new French venture. The very next year he was forced to retire from professional skateboarding with back problems. Although he spoke poor English and had little business experience, he persuaded his employers to grant him the licence to sell its Etnies shoes in the United States. The first five years were very hard, but Senizergues introduced his own designs and from the mid-1990s Etnies began to take off. In 1996, Senizergues bought the Etnies brand from the French venture and incorporated it and other brands – including éS, Emerica and ThirtyTwo – under the Sole Technology umbrella. Growth over the next ten years ran at double digits per annum.

From the first, Senizergues had been able to use his expertise as a professional skateboarder in his designs. He told the *Financial Times*: 'In this market, you have to be authentic, you have to come from skateboarding.' For example, in the 1990s he had noticed that skateboarders were buying unsuitable low-top shoes for their looks, rather than high-top shoes with the proper performance characteristics. Senizergues responded by designing low-top shoes that had the necessary durability. His company has stayed close to its sports, sponsoring more than 100 athletes around the world. It listens closely to customers. The company's website has a design-your-own-shoe facility and it often releases potential specifications for its new products through blogs, in order to solicit feedback and ideas. The average age of Sole Technology's 400 employees is 28, with many still involved in action sports.

However, Senizergues has also built the world's first skateboarding research facility, the Sole Technology Institute. With 10,000 square feet, it reproduces typical skateboarding obstacles such as rails, stairs and ledges. Senizergues believes that it is time for skateboarding to do its own biomechanical research, instead of borrowing technologies developed in other sports. One of the outputs of the Sole Technology Institute has been the G202 gel-and-air technology. As the trend for girls' shoes moved towards slim silhouettes during 2006, this gel-and-air technology has allowed Sole Technology to keep right abreast of fashion.

Sources: Financial Times, 23 August 2006; Footwear News, 20 February 2006; www.soletechnology.com.

Questions

1 For what reasons is it important to be 'authentic' in the skateboarding shoe market?

2 If a big company like Nike or Adidas was looking to grow in this market, what would you advise them to do?

Figure 9.2 Product and process innovation

Source: Adapted from J. Abernathy and W. Utterback, 'A dynamic model of process and product innovation', *Omega*, vol. 3, no. 6 (1975), pp. 142–60.

coalesce around a *dominant design*, the standard configuration of basic features: after Henry Ford's 1908 Model T, cars generally became petrol-driven, with their engines at the front and four wheels. Once such a dominant design is established, innovation switches to process innovation, as competition shifts to producing the dominant design as efficiently as possible. Henry Ford's great process innovation was the moving assembly line, introduced in 1913. Finally, the cycle is liable to start again, as some significant innovation challenges the dominant design: in the case of cars recently, the emergence of electric power.[4]

Figure 9.2 provides a general model of the relationship between product and process innovation over time. The model has several strategic implications:

- *New developing industries* typically favour product innovation, as competition is still around defining the basic features of the product or service.

- *Maturing industries* typically favour process innovation, as competition shifts towards efficient production of a dominant design of product or service.

- *Small new entrants* typically have the greatest opportunity when dominant designs are either not yet established or beginning to collapse. Thus, in the early stages of the automobile industry, before Ford's Model T, there were more than one hundred mostly small competitors, each with their own combination of product features. The recent challenge to the petrol-based dominant design has provided opportunities to small companies such as the Californian start-up Tesla Motors, which had produced more than 1000 electric Roadsters by the beginning of 2010.

- *Large incumbent firms* typically have the advantage during periods of dominant design stability, when scale economies and the ability to roll out process innovations matter most. With the success of the Model T and the assembly line, by the 1930s there were just four large American automobile manufacturers, Ford, General Motors, Chrysler and American Motors, all producing very similar kinds of cars.

This sequence of product to process innovation is not always a neat one. In practice, product and process innovation are often pursued in tandem.[5] For example, each new generation of microprocessor also requires simultaneous process innovation in order to manufacture the new microprocessor with increasing precision. However, the model does help managers confront the issue of where to focus, whether more on product features or more on process efficiency. It also points to whether competitive advantage is likely to be with small new entrants or large incumbent firms. Other things being equal, small start-ups should time their entry for periods of instability in dominant design and focus on product rather than process innovation.

9.2.3 Open or closed innovation

The traditional approach to innovation has been to rely on the organisation's own internal resources – its laboratories and marketing departments. Innovation in this approach is secretive, anxious to protect intellectual property and avoid competitors free-riding on ideas. This 'closed' model of innovation contrasts with the newer 'open model' of innovation.[6] **Open innovation involves the deliberate import and export of knowledge by an organisation in order to accelerate and enhance its innovation**. The motivating idea of open innovation is that exchanging ideas openly is likely to produce better products more quickly than the internal, closed approach. Speedier and superior products are what are needed to keep ahead of the competition, not obsessive secrecy.

Open innovation is being widely adopted. For example, technology giant IBM has established a network of ten 'collaboratories' with other companies and universities, in countries ranging from Switzerland to Saudi Arabia. Last.fm, the online music service, hosts special 'hack days', when it invites its users for a day of free food, drink and work on developing new applications together. The American InnoCentive company has a network of 64 knowledge 'seekers', including giants Procter & Gamble, Eli Lilly and Dow Chemical, which set 'challenges' for which prizes of up to $1m are given for solutions: so far, more than 348 challenges have been solved with the participation of over 165,000 'solvers'.

Open innovation typically requires careful support of collaborators. In particular, dominant firms may need to exercise platform leadership. **Platform leadership refers to how large firms consciously nurture independent companies through successive waves of innovation around their basic technological 'platform'**.[7] Video games console companies such as Microsoft and Sony have to manage relationships with a host of large and small video games publishers in order to ensure that their consoles are supported by an attractive set of games, making full use of the latest technological possibilities. Similarly, mobile phone companies such as Nokia and Apple have to encourage and support the thousands of independent producers of 'apps' for their phones.

The balance between open and closed innovation depends on three key factors:

● *Competitive rivalry*. In highly rivalrous industries, partners are liable to behave opportunistically and steal advantages. Closed innovation is better where such rivalrous behaviours can be anticipated.

● *One-shot innovation*. Opportunistic behaviour is more likely where innovation involves a major shift in technology, likely to put winners substantially ahead and losers permanently behind. Open innovation works best where innovation is more continuous, so encouraging more reciprocal behaviour over time.

- *Tight-linked innovation.* Where technologies are complex and tightly interlinked, open innovation risks introducing damagingly inconsistent elements, with knock-on effects throughout the product range. Apple, with its smoothly integrated range of products from computers to phones, has therefore tended to prefer closed innovation in order to protect the quality of the user experience.

9.2.4 Technological or business-model innovation

Many successful innovations do not rely simply upon new science or technology, but involve reorganising into new combinations all the elements of a business. Here innovators are creating whole new *business models*, bringing customers, producers and suppliers together in new ways, with or without new technologies.[8] A **business model** describes **how an organisation manages incomes and costs through the structural arrangement of its activities**. For Ryanair, business-model innovation involved the generation of revenues via direct sales through the internet, thereby cutting out intermediary travel agents, while also using cheap secondary airports. Internet sales and cheaper airports were much more important than technological innovation. The internet technology itself was not Ryanair's creation and it had the same aeroplanes as most of its competitors. Thus it can be as effective to innovate in terms of business model as in technology.

Opportunities for business-model innovation can be analysed in terms of the value chain, value net or activity systems frameworks introduced in sections 3.4.2 and 3.4.3[9]. These frameworks point managers and entrepreneurs to two basic areas for potential innovation:

- *The product.* A new business model may redefine what the product or service is and how it is produced. In terms of the value chain specifically, this concerns technology development, procurement, inbound logistics, operations and procurement. For example, when Nucor pioneered electric-arc mini-mill technology in the steel industry, it was able to use scrap metal as its raw material rather than pure iron, employ non-unionised labour and outsource a lot of its product development to its equipment supplier Voest Alpine.

- *The selling.* A new business model may change the way in which the organisation generates its revenues, with implications for selling and distribution. In terms of the value chain, this concerns outbound logistics, marketing, sales and service. Nucor, for example, sold its cheap but low-quality steel at standard prices on the internet, by contrast to the traditional steel producers' reliance on elaborate negotiations with individual customers on prices and specifications.

The business model concept emphasises the fundamental features of how business activities are organised. In terms of business models, mature industries therefore often have a lot of standardisation. For example, most accounting firms are organised in similar ways, earning the majority of their income from audit and relying on a high ratio of junior staff to partners. Business strategy within an industry characterised by standardised business models is mostly about differentiation. Thus accounting firms might differentiate themselves within the same model by emphasising particular kinds of sectoral expertise or international networks.

However, the fundamental nature of business models means that business-model innovation tends to imply radical change. Business-model innovation is not just a matter of technology, but involves a wide range of the firm's activities. Thus the business model concept

ILLUSTRATION 9.2

Blockbuster's busted business model

Blockbuster's store rental model is challenged by new business models for movie and game distribution.

There are a lot of ways for people to see a movie nowadays. They can go to the cinema. They can buy a DVD from specialist retailers such as HMV or large supermarkets such as Tesco or Lidl. They can order a DVD online and receive it through the post. They can download movies via the internet. They can rent via a kiosk or vending machine. Or they can do it the old-fashioned way and rent it from a video store.

Blockbuster, of course, is famous for its stores: in 2010 it had 7000 stores in 18 countries around the world. The first Blockbuster store opened in 1985 in Texas. Soon Blockbuster was the world's largest movie rental company, and in 1994 was bought by media conglomerate Viacom for $7.6bn (~€5.3bn). Ten years later, as Blockbuster's growth stalled, Viacom spun it off as an independent company again, now valued at $7.5bn.

Blockbuster's business model had been an attractive one at first. Two decades ago, in a period of limited television channels, movie rental had given customers unheard-of choice of viewing. Blockbuster used its huge buying power to obtain the latest releases from the film studios at little cost. Blockbuster would give 40 per cent of the rental income to the studios and supply them with information on usage for market research purposes. Studios typically would hold back from releasing the movie to other rental companies or to retailers for an initial period, making Blockbuster the essential outlet for the latest hits. Blockbuster was able to leverage this business model into rapid growth, using a mixture of its own stores, franchising and acquisitions. It also extended the model to the rental of video games.

However, the market is now much more complex. For a start, television channels began to proliferate. In the United States, Netflix emerged in 1997, originally using a rental-by-mail model. By 2009, Netflix had mailed its two billionth DVD. In the United Kingdom, DVD mail-rental company Lovefilm

was founded in 2002, and by 2010 had 50 per cent of the national market, as well as a strong position in Scandinavia. The mail-rental model offers customers a far greater choice (Lovefilm has 70,000 titles, against the few hundred in a typical Blockbuster store) and needs only a few centralised distribution centres, as against a labour-intensive network of retail stores. Moreover, as internet capacity has improved, both Netflix and Lovefilm have also begun to stream movies straight to customers' computers. Another rental model was pioneered by 2003 start-up Redbox, which had established a network of 22,000 DVD vending machines across the United States by the end of 2009.

Blockbuster responded in several ways. In 2004, it launched its own on-line rental service, with customers able to return their DVDs simply through a local store. In 2009, Blockbuster launched its own vending machines in the United States. The company closed more than 1800 stores. It withdrew from some national markets altogether, for example Spain, Portugal, Ecuador and Peru. But still 2009 was a year of heavy financial losses. The Blockbuster shareprice, which had peaked at over $30 in 2002, had fallen to 41 cents in 2010.

Sources: Financial Times, 24 February 2010; The Times, 28 December 2009; The Express on Sunday, 28 February 2010.

Questions

1 Compare the pros and cons of the various business models for movie consumption.

2 What potential competitive advantages did Blockbuster have as a company as the new business models emerged in the last decade or so?

helps managers and entrepreneurs consider science and technology as just one part of the whole package that contributes to innovation. Innovation can be drawn from all parts of the value chain, not just technology development. Indeed, radical technological innovation often requires business-model innovation too. For example, in order to promote adoption of its innovative electric cars in France, Toyota has formed a partnership with electricity supplier EDF and local authorities to create networks of subsidised public charging points. Illustration 9.2 describes the radical repercussions of business-model innovation in the movie rental business.

(9.3) INNOVATION DIFFUSION

So far, this chapter has been concerned with sources and types of innovation, for example technology push or market pull. This section moves to the diffusion of innovations after they have been introduced.[10] **Diffusion is the process by which innovations spread amongst users.** Since innovation is typically expensive, its commercial attractiveness can hinge on the pace – extent and speed – at which the market adopts new products and services. This pace of diffusion is something managers can influence from both the supply and demand sides, and which they can also model using the S-curve.

9.3.1 The pace of diffusion

The pace of diffusion can vary widely according to the nature of the products concerned. It took 38 years for the television to reach 150 million units sold; it took just 7 years for Apple's iPod to reach the same number. The pace of diffusion is influenced by a combination of supply-side and demand-side factors, over which managers have considerable control. On the *supply side*, pace is determined by product features such as:

- *Degree of improvement* in performance above current products (from a customer's perspective) that provides incentive to change. For example, 3G mobile phones did not provide sufficient performance improvement to prompt rapid switch in many markets. Managers need to make sure innovation benefits sufficiently exceed costs.

- *Compatibility* with other factors, e.g. digital TV becomes more attractive as the broadcasting networks change more of their programmes to that format. Managers and entrepreneurs therefore need to ensure appropriate complementary products and services are in place.

- *Complexity*, either in the product itself or in the marketing methods being used to commercialise the product: unduly complex pricing structures, as with many financial service products such as pensions, discourage consumer adoption. Simple pricing structures typically accelerate adoptions.

- *Experimentation* – the ability to test products before commitment to a final decision – either directly or through the availability of information about the experience of other customers. Free initial trial periods are often used to encourage diffusion.

- *Relationship management*, in other words how easy it is to get information, place orders and receive support. Google's 2010 launch of its first phone, the Android Nexus One, was hampered because the company was not used to providing the access to help staff that mobile phone customers generally expect. Managers and entrepreneurs need to put in place an appropriate relationship management processes to assist new users.

On the *demand side*, three key factors tend to drive the pace of diffusion:

- *Market awareness.* Many potentially successful products have failed through lack of consumer awareness – particularly when the promotional effort of the innovator has been confined to 'push' promotion to its intermediaries (e.g. distributors).

- *Network effects* refer to the way that demand growth for some products accelerates as more people adopt the product or service. Once a critical mass of users have adopted, it becomes of much greater benefit, or even necessary, for others to adopt it too. Facebook enjoyed network effects as its usage raced to 150 million in just four years. Likewise, people use Microsoft PowerPoint because almost all their collaborators are likely to use it too (see also section 6.3.6).

- *Customer innovativeness.* The distribution of potential customers from early-adopter groups (keen to adopt first) through to laggards (typically indifferent to innovations). Innovations are often targeted initially at early-adopter groups – typically the young and the wealthy – in order to build the critical mass that will encourage more laggardly groups – the poorer and older – to join the bandwagon. Clothing fashion trends typically start with the wealthy and then are diffused to the wider population. Managers and entrepreneurs therefore need to target innovations initially at likely early-adopters.

9.3.2 The diffusion S-curve

The pace of diffusion is typically not steady. Successful innovations often diffuse according to a broad *S-curve* pattern.[11] The shape of the **S-curve reflects a process of initial slow adoption of innovation, followed by a rapid acceleration in diffusion, leading to a plateau representing the limit to demand** (Figure 9.3). The height of the S-curve shows the extent of diffusion; the shape of the S-curve shows the speed.

Diffusion rarely follows exactly this pattern, but nonetheless the S-curve can help managers and entrepreneurs anticipate upcoming issues. In particular, the S-curve points to four likely decision points:

- *Timing of the 'tipping point'.* Demand for a new product or service may initially be slow but then reaches a tipping point when it explodes onto a rapid upwards path of growth.[12] A **tipping point is where demand for a product or service suddenly takes off, with explosive growth**. Tipping points are particularly explosive where there are strong *network effects*: in other words, where the value of a product or service is increased the more people in a network use them. Being aware of a possible tipping point ahead can help managers plan investment in capacity and distribution. Companies can easily underestimate demand. In the mid-1980s, American companies predicted that by 2000 there would be 900,000 mobile phones worldwide. That year came, and 900,000 phones were sold every 19 hours. The Finnish company Nokia was able to seize worldwide leadership.[13] Failing to anticipate a tipping point leads to missed sales and easy opportunities for competitors.

- *Timing of the plateau.* The S-curve also alerts managers to a likely eventual slowdown in demand growth. Again, it is tempting to extrapolate existing growth rates forwards, especially when they are highly satisfactory. But heavy investment immediately before growth turns down is likely to leave firms with over-capacity and carrying extra costs in a period of industry shake-out.

Figure 9.3 The diffusion S-curve

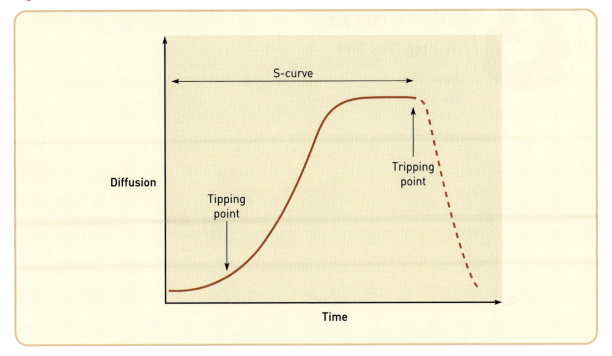

- *Extent of diffusion.* The S-curve does not necessarily lead to one hundred per cent diffusion amongst potential users. Most innovations fail to displace previous-generation products and services altogether. For example, in music, traditional turntables and LP discs are still preferred over CD and MP3 players by many disc jockeys and music connoisseurs. A critical issue for managers then is to estimate the final ceiling on diffusion, being careful not to assume that tipping point growth will necessarily take over the whole market.

- *Timing of the 'tripping point'.* The tripping point is the opposite of the tipping point, referring to when demand suddenly collapses.[14] Of course, decline is usually more gradual. However, the presence of network effects can lead to relatively few customer defections setting off a market landslide. Such landslides are very hard to reverse. This is what happened to social networking site Friendster, as American and European users defected to MySpace and Facebook. The tripping point concept warns managers all the time that a small dip in quarterly sales could presage a rapid collapse.

To summarise, the S-curve is a useful concept to help managers and entrepreneurs avoid simply extrapolating next year's sales from last year's sales. However, the tripping point also underlines the fact that innovations do not follow an inevitable process, and their diffusion patterns can be interrupted or reversed at any point. Most innovations, of course, do not even reach a tipping point, let alone a tripping point. The Segway Human Transporter, launched in 2001 as the environmentally friendly technology that would replace the car, sold 6,000 units in its first two years, despite launch production capacity of nearly 500,000 a year.

ILLUSTRATION 9.3

Twitter flies high

How long can the explosive growth of the microblogger Twitter continue? And what is its business model?

Alexa.com estimation of numbers using Twitter

The traffic data are based on the set of Alexa toolbar users, which may not be a representative sample of the global Internet population.

Source: Alexa.com.

Twitter was founded in 2006 by Jack Dorsey, Biz Stone and Evan Williams, all in their early 30s. The original idea for Twitter was conceived during a brainstorming day, and implemented in just two weeks. Biz Stone recalls a dialogue with Evan Williams: 'Early on someone said: "Twitter is fun, but it isn't useful". Ev said: "Neither is icecream".'

A lot of people soon began to think Twitter fun. A key moment was the Spring 2007 South by Southwest film and music festival in Austin, Texas. Twitter hired two large plasma screens streaming Twitter messages from festival-goers. During the event, Twitter usage went from 20,000 'tweets' (messages) per day to 60,000 per day. Then Barack Obama used Twitter publicly during the 2008 US presidential elections. By early 2010, Alexa.com was estimating that more than 6 per cent of global internet users were visiting twitter.com per day ('daily reach').

Twitter usage is free, so a persistent question as Twitter grows is about its business model – how it would earn revenues. Twitter raised $135m (~€94.5m) in venture capital during 2009, but was cautious about how to make the venture pay. Ev Williams said: 'We think Twitter will make money. I just think it will take some time to figure it out.' The founders rejected the use of advertising. However, they were considering

how they could get companies to pay for referrals from Twitter to their own websites. At the start of 2010, Biz Stone told the *Financial Times*: 'We need to build a business out of Twitter – that needs to start happening in 2010'.

Meanwhile, social networking site Facebook was developing Twitter-like features and new imitators were springing up. In Japan, for instance, start-up Ameba Now was gaining users by signing up Japanese celebrities, offering Japanese characters and supporting 'smiley' icons, something that Twitter lacks. Within three months of its December 2009 launch, Ameba Now had one million users, against Twitter's 4.7 million in Japan. Twitter also has a high wastage rate – only 40 per cent of those who sign on are retained as regular users.

Sources: *New York Times*, 25 March 2009; www.eweek.com, 20 October 2009; *Financial Times*, 1 January 2010 and 12 March 2010.

Questions

1 How should investors in Twitter interpret Alexa.com's daily reach data?

2 Propose three ways that Twitter could make money and consider their respective pros and cons.

9.4 INNOVATORS AND FOLLOWERS

A key choice for managers is whether to lead or to follow in innovation. The S-curve concept seems to promote leadership in innovation. First-movers get the easy sales of early fast growth and can establish a dominant position. There are plenty of examples of first-movers who have built enduring positions on the basis of innovation leadership: Coca-Cola in drinks and Hoover in vacuum cleaners are powerful century-old examples. On the other hand, many first-movers fail. Even Apple failed with its pioneering Personal Digital Assistant, the Newton, launched in 1993. Hewlett-Packard and Palm captured the PDA market nearly a decade later. This late-entry success is not unusual. Amazon entered the online bookselling market in 1995, four years after the real online pioneer, the Computer Literacy bookstore of Silicon Valley, California.

9.4.1 First-mover advantages and disadvantages

A **first-mover advantage** **exists where an organisation is better off than its competitors as a result of being first to market with a new product, process or service**. Fundamentally, the first-mover is a monopolist, theoretically able to charge customers high prices without fear of immediate undercutting by competitors. In practice, however, innovators often prefer to sacrifice profit margins for sales growth and, besides, monopoly is usually temporary. There are five potentially more robust first-mover advantages:[15]

KEY CONCEPT

First-mover advantage

- *Experience curve benefits* accrue to first-movers, as their rapid accumulation of experience with the innovation gives them greater expertise than late entrants still relatively unfamiliar with the new product, process or service (see section 6.3.1).
- *Scale benefits* are typically enjoyed by first-movers, as they establish earlier than competitors the volumes necessary for mass production and bulk purchasing, for example.
- *Pre-emption of scarce resources* is an opportunity for first-movers, as late movers will not have the same access to key raw materials, skilled labour or components, and will have to pay dearly for them.
- *Reputation* can be enhanced by being first, especially since consumers have little 'mind-space' to recognise new brands once a dominant brand has been established in the market.
- *Buyer switching costs* can be exploited by first-movers, by locking in their customers with privileged or sticky relationships that later challengers can only break with difficulty. Switching costs can be increased by establishing and exploiting a *technological standard* (see section 6.3.6).

Experience curve benefits, economies of scale and the pre-emption of scarce resources all confer cost advantages on first-movers. It is possible for them to retaliate against challengers with a price war. Superior reputation and customer lock-in provide a marketing advantage, allowing first-movers to charge high prices, which can then be reinvested in order to consolidate their position against late-entry competitors.

But the experience of Apple with its Newton shows that first-mover advantages are not necessarily overwhelming. Late movers have two principal potential advantages:[16]

- *Free-riding.* Late movers can imitate technological and other innovation at less expense than originally incurred by the pioneers. Research suggests that the costs of imitation are only 65 per cent of the cost of innovation.
- *Learning.* Late movers can observe what worked well and what did not work well for innovators. They may not make so many mistakes and be able to get it right first time.

9.4.2 First or second?

Given the potential advantages of late movers, managers and entrepreneurs face a hard choice between striving to be first or coming in later. London Business School's Costas Markides and Paul Geroski argue that the most appropriate response to innovation, especially radical innovation, is often not to be a first-mover, but to be a '*fast second*'.[17] A fast second strategy involves being one of the first to imitate the original innovator. Thus fast second companies may not literally be the second company into the market, but they dominate the second generation of competitors. For example, the French Bookeen company pioneered the e-book market in the early 2000s, but was followed by Sony's eReader in 2006 and Amazon's Kindle in 2007.

There are three contextual factors to consider in choosing between innovating and imitating:

- *Capacity for profit capture.* David Teece emphasises the importance of innovators being able to capture for themselves the profits of their innovations.[18] This depends on the ease with which followers can imitate. The likelihood of imitation depends on two primary factors. First, imitation is likely if the innovation is in itself *easy to replicate*: for example, if there is little tacit knowledge involved or if it is embedded in a product that is sold in the external marketplace (unlike many process technologies) and is therefore easy to 'reverse-engineer' (see section 3.3). Second, imitation is facilitated if *intellectual property rights* are weak, for example where patents are hard to define or impractical to defend.[19] It is unwise for companies to invest in first-moves if imitators are likely to be able quickly to seize their share of innovation profits.

- *Complementary assets.* Possession of the assets or resources necessary to scale up the production and marketing of the innovation is often critical.[20] Many small European bio-tech start-up companies face this constraint in the pharmaceuticals industry, where marketing and distribution channels in the United States, the world's largest market, are essential complementary assets, but are dominated by the big established pharmaceutical companies. Small European start-ups can find themselves obliged either to sell out to a larger company with the complementary marketing and distribution assets, or to license their innovation to them on disadvantageous terms. For organisations wishing to remain independent and to exploit their innovations themselves, there is little point in investing heavily to be first-mover in the absence of the necessary complementary assets.

- *Fast-moving arenas.* Where markets or technologies are moving very fast, and especially where both are highly dynamic, first-movers are unlikely to establish a durable advantage. The American electronics company Magnavox was the first to launch an electronic video game console in 1972, the Odyssey. But both the market and the technologies were evolving quickly. Magnavox only survived into the second generation of video game consoles, finally exiting in 1984. The seventh generation is now firmly dominated by Microsoft (entered in 2001), Sony (entered in 1994) and Nintendo (entered in 1983). In slower-moving markets and technologies, such as Coca-Cola's drinks arena, durable first-mover advantages are more probable. Managers and entrepreneurs need, therefore, to assess future market and technological dynamism in calculating the likely value of first-mover advantage.

9.4.3 The incumbent's response

For established companies in a market, innovation is often not so much an opportunity as a threat. Kodak's dominance of the photographic film market was made nearly worthless by the sudden rise of digital photography. Likewise, Blockbuster's network of video stores became redundant with the rise of internet film downloads (see Illustration 9.2).

As Harvard Business School's Clay Christensen has shown, the problem for incumbents can be twofold.[21] First, managers can become too attached to existing assets and skills. After all, these are what their careers have been built on. Second, relationships between incumbent organisations and their customers can become too close. Existing customers typically prefer incremental improvements to current technologies, and are unable to imagine completely new technologies. Incumbents are reluctant to 'cannibalise' their existing business by introducing something radically different. After all, as in Figure 9.4, incumbents usually have some scope for improving their existing technology, along the steady upwards trajectory described as Technology 1. Innovations on this trajectory are termed 'sustaining innovations', because they at least allow the existing technology to meet existing customer expectations.

The challenge for incumbents, however, is disruptive innovation. A **disruptive innovation creates substantial growth by offering a new performance trajectory that, even if initially inferior to the performance of existing technologies, has the potential to become markedly superior.** This superior performance can produce spectacular growth, either by creating new sets of customers or by undercutting the cost base of rival existing business models. Such disruptive innovation involves the shift from Technology 1 in Figure 9.4 to Technology 2. Disruptive innovations are hard for incumbents to respond to because their initial poor performance is likely to upset existing customer relationships and because they typically involve changing their whole business model. Thus, in the music industry, the major record companies were long content to keep on selling traditional CDs through retailers, marketing them through promotions and radio-plugging. They responded to MP3 online music simply by prosecuting operators such as Napster for breach of copyright and highlighting the relatively poor sound quality of peer-to-peer file sharing. However, the British band Arctic Monkeys, and its small independent record company Domino, radically disrupted the majors' marketing

Figure 9.4 Disruptive innovation

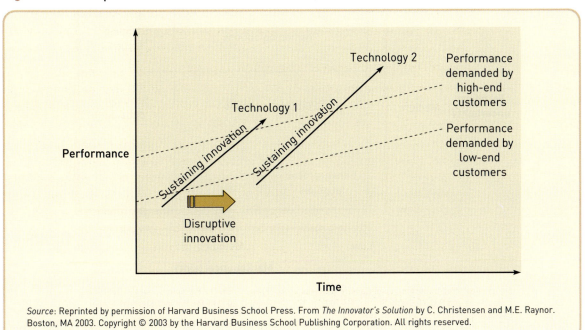

model by giving away MP3 tracks free over the internet in order to create an independent fan-base. In 2006, the Arctic Monkeys' debut CD ended up selling nearly 400,000 copies in its first week, a record for the top 20 United Kingdom album chart.

Incumbents can follow two policies to help keep them responsive to potentially disruptive innovations:

● *Develop a portfolio of real options.* Companies that are most challenged by disruptive innovations tend to be those built upon a single business model and with one main product or service. Columbia's Rita McGrath and Wharton's Ian MacMillan recommend that companies build portfolios of *real options* in order to maintain organisational dynamism.[22] Real options are limited investments that keep opportunities open for the future (for a more technical discussion, see section 11.3.2). Establishing an R&D team in a speculative new technology or acquiring a small start-up in a nascent market would both be examples of real options, each giving the potential to scale-up fast should the opportunity turn out to be substantial. McGrath and MacMillan's portfolio identifies three different kinds of options (Figure 9.5). Options where the market is broadly known, but the technologies are still uncertain, are *positioning options*: a company might want several of these, to ensure some position in an important market, by one technology or another. On the other hand, a company might have a strong technology, but be very uncertain about appropriate markets, in which case it would want to bet on several *scouting options* to explore which markets are actually best. Finally, a company would want some *stepping stone* options, very unlikely in themselves to work, but possibly leading to something more promising in the future. Even if they do not turn a profit, stepping stones should provide valuable learning opportunities. An important principle for options is: 'Fail fast, fail cheap, try again'.

Figure 9.5 Portfolio of innovation options

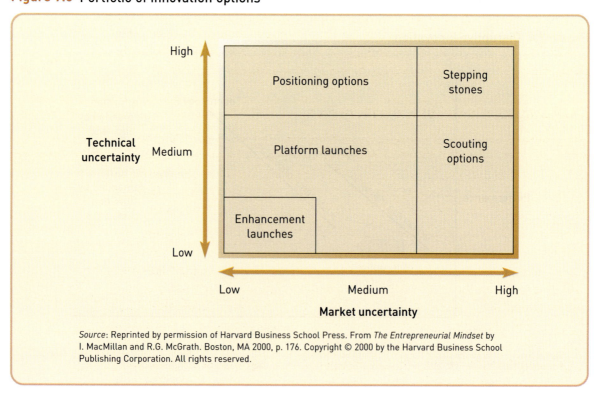

- *Develop new venture units*. New ventures, especially when undertaken from a real options perspective, may need protection from the usual systems and disciplines of a core business. It would make no sense to hold the managers of a real option strictly accountable for sales growth and profit margin: their primary objective is preparation and learning. For this reason, large incumbent organisations often set up innovative businesses as relatively autonomous 'new venture units', sometimes called new venture divisions, typically with managers hired specially from outside.[23] For example, in 2003 Delta Airlines, the American international airline dating from the 1920s, responded to the threat of low-cost airlines in its domestic markets by establishing Song Airlines as a stand-alone competitor. Song adopted the low-cost airline business model but also innovated with free personal entertainment systems at every seat, including audio MP3 selections, trivia games that could be played against other passengers and satellite television. In-flight safety instructions would be sung in different musical styles, by request. The risks of such autonomous venture units are twofold.[24] First, the new units may be denied resources that the core business could easily supply, such as branding or management information systems. Second, innovation becomes isolated from the core business: for the core organisation, innovation is something that somebody else does. Delta responded to the second risk threat by reabsorbing Song into its main operations, at the same time incorporating several of Song's innovations such as satellite television.

(9.5) ENTREPRENEURSHIP AND RELATIONSHIPS

Given the difficulties of large incumbent firms in fostering innovation, many would conclude that the best approach is to start up a new venture. Independent entrepreneurs such as James Dyson, the pioneer of bagless vacuum cleaners, and Larry Page and Sergey Brin of Google are exemplars of this entrepreneurial approach to innovation (see case examples for Chapters 3 and 12).[25] This section introduces some key issues for entrepreneurial innovators, and then points to a more complex set of relationships with large firms, raising further choices for entrepreneurs. It concludes by considering the opportunities of social entrepreneurship.

9.5.1 Stages of entrepreneurial growth

Entrepreneurial ventures are often seen as going through four stages of a life cycle: see Figure 9.6. The **entrepreneurial life cycle progresses through start-up, growth, maturity and exit**.[26] Of course, most ventures do not make it through all the stages – the estimated failure rate of new businesses in their first year is more than one fifth, with two thirds going out of business within six years.[27] However, each of these four stages raises key questions for entrepreneurs:

- *Start-up*. There are many challenges at this stage, but one key question with implications for both survival and growth are sources of capital. Loans from family and friends are common sources of funds, but these are typically limited and, given the new-business failure rate, likely to lead to embarrassment. Bank loans and credit cards can provide funding too, and there is often government funding especially for new technologies or economically disadvantaged social groups or geographical areas. *Venture capitalists* are specialised investors in new ventures, especially when there is some track-record. Venture capitalists usually insist on a seat on the venture's board of directors and may install their preferred managers. Venture capitalist backing has been shown to significantly increase the chances of a

Figure 9.6 Stages of entrepreneurial growth and typical challenges

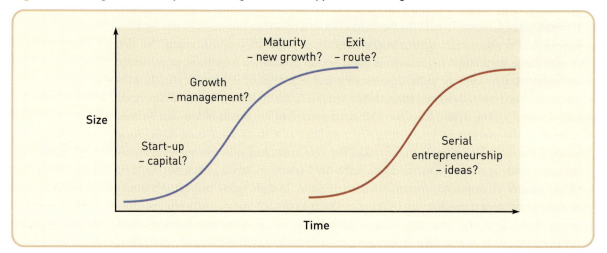

venture's success, but venture capitalists typically accept only about one in four hundred propositions put to them.[28]

● *Growth.* A key challenge for growth ventures is management. Entrepreneurs have to be ready to move from doing to managing. Typically this transition occurs as the venture grows beyond about twenty employees. Many entrepreneurs make poor managers: if they had wanted to be managers, they would probably be working in a large corporation in the first place. The choice entrepreneurs have to make is whether to rely on their own managerial skills or to bring in professional managers. In 2001, the youthful founders of Google, Larry Page and Sergey Brin, responded to pressure from their venture capitalists by recruiting 46-year-old Eric Schmidt, former Chief Executive of the large software company Novell, to run their company.

● *Maturity.* The challenge for entrepreneurs at this stage is retaining their enthusiasm and commitment and generating new growth. This is a period when entrepreneurship changes to *intrapreneurship*, the generation of new ventures from inside the organisation. An important option is usually *diversification* into new business areas, a topic dealt with in Chapter 7. Amazon.com in the United States has moved from book-selling to automotive parts, groceries and clothing. When generating new ventures at this stage, it is critical to recall the odds on success. Research suggests that many small high-tech firms fail to manage the transition to a second generation of technology, and that it is often better at this point simply to look for exit.[29]

● *Exit.* Exit refers to departure from the venture, either by the founding entrepreneurs, or by the original investors, or both. At the point of exit, entrepreneurs and venture capitalists will seek to release capital as a reward for their input and risk-taking. Entrepreneurs may consider three prime routes to exit. A simple *trade sale* of the venture to another company is a common route. Thus social networking site MySpace.com was bought by the News Corporation just two years after foundation (Illustration 1.1). Some entrepreneurs may sell to their own managers, in the form of a *management buy-out* (MBO). Another exit route for highly successful enterprises is an *initial public offering* (IPO), the sale of shares to the public, for instance on the American NASDAQ exchange. IPOs usually involve just a portion of the total shares available, and may thus allow entrepreneurs to continue in the business and provide funds for further growth. Google raised $1.67bn (~€1.17bn) with its 2004 IPO, selling only 7 per cent of its shares. It is often said that good entrepreneurs plan for their exit right from start-up, and certainly venture capitalists will insist on this.

ILLUSTRATION 9.4

Fatima's dignified gowns

A business administration degree is just the starting point for this entrepreneurial venture.

Fatima Ba-Alawi graduated in business administration from the University of Portsmouth in 2005. Less than one year later, seven National Health Service hospitals were trialling her innovative hospital gowns, with interest from private sector hospital operator Bupa too. Her new company, DCS Designs (Dignity, Comfort and Safety), had got off to a flying start.

Ba-Alawi had arrived in the United Kingdom in 1998, as a refugee from Somalia speaking no English. After studying for English GCSEs and A Levels, she says: 'I applied to the University of Portsmouth to read business administration because the idea of going into business always appealed to me'. She was keen to be have her own business after finding it 'deeply unpleasant working for somebody else at a fast food outlet as a teenager'.

It was while working in a local hospital as a care assistant that her business idea came to her. Conventional hospital gowns require patients to lift off the whole garment for medical examinations, which was undignified for wearers and awkward for carers. Ba-Alawi designed a new type of gown which provided extra coverage for the back and gave easy access points for examinations. The gowns also had an anti-microbial finish combating microbes such as the dangerous MRSA and C-Diff bugs. DCS gowns were more dignified, more comfortable and more safe.

While still studying, Ba-Alawi approached the University of Portsmouth's Centre for Enterprise for support. She won £500 (~€550; $750) in the University's Enterprise Challenge competition, which she used to fund an initial prototype and carry out some market research. The University's enterprise mentoring service provided her with one-to-one coaching,

which helped her develop her business plan. This business plan won a further University prize, worth £2000, which she used to fund a patent application and register her company, DCS Designs Ltd. She next put in a bid to the University's Student SEED Fund, gaining more support plus an office in the University's Centre for Enterprise and access to virtual office facilities. The SEED fund allowed Ba-Alawi to manufacture sample gowns and distribute them to hospitals, at the same time as launching the DCS Designs website, which had a facility for user feedback. The local Enterprise Hub also provided access to a local patent attorney to help protect her intellectual property.

Progress was slow, though. It was not until 2007 that DCS gained its first sales. NHS hospitals typically preferred to rent gowns, outsourcing the problems of laundering and repair. However, Ba-Alawi was recognised as an official 'Dignity Champion' by the Department of Health, and the company slowly progressed. In 2009, Ba-Alawi commented that her venture was 'a journey of sacrifices, sleepless nights and sometimes foodless nights! But it was worth it. . . . What pays is persistence, patience and perseverance.'

Sources: Financial Times, 12 April 2006; *Evening Standard*, 13 September 2005; *Independent*, 4 September 2008; http://www.sehta.co.uk/files/Fatima%20Ba-AlawiSellingtotheNHS.pdf.

Questions

1 What challenges would you anticipate for Ba-Alawi's DCS Designs company if it takes off? How should she deal with them?

2 What does your university or college do to support student entrepreneurship?

Entrepreneurs who have successfully exited a first venture often become *serial entrepreneurs*. Serial entrepreneurs are people who set up a succession of enterprises, investing the capital raised on exit from earlier ventures into new growing ventures. For example, British retailer George Davies set up first the Next fashion chain, then George, then Per Una and most recently GIVe. For serial entrepreneurs, the challenge often is no longer so much funding but good ideas.

9.5.2 Entrepreneurial relationships

For many, entrepreneurship is about independence, working for oneself. This pride in independence is reinforced by a common stereotype of entrepreneurs as heroic individuals, starting their businesses at night in a university laboratory, or in the spare room at home or in a local lock-up garage. William Hewlett and David Packard, founders of the famous computing and printer company, and Steve Jobs of Apple, are oft-quoted examples of the garage stereotype. But digging beneath the stereotype soon reveals a more complex story, in which relationships with large companies can be important right from the start. Often entrepreneurs have worked for large companies beforehand, and continue to use relationships afterwards.[30] While Hewlett came fairly directly out of Stanford University's laboratories, Packard worked at General Electric and Litton Industries. The Hewlett-Packard company used Litton Industries' foundries early on, and later used relationships at General Electric to recruit experienced managers. Steve Jobs worked for William Hewlett for a summer job aged 12, and later was the fortieth employee at video games company Atari.

Thus entrepreneurship often involves managing relationships with other companies, especially big companies. Three concepts are particularly influential here:

- *Corporate venturing.* Many large corporations, such as Intel, Nokia and Shell, have developed corporate venture units that invest externally in new ventures as safeguards against disruptive innovations and potential drivers of future growth.[31] Large corporations gain by increasing the range of ideas they are exposed to, by protecting early-stage ventures from internal bureaucracy and by spreading their risk. Entrepreneurs gain by accessing not just capital but also knowledge of large-company thinking in their domain and contacts with other members of the large company's network. It is crucial that both entrepreneurs and corporate venture capitalists continuously monitor the set of expectations behind the investment: is the investment more profit-driven in terms of expecting good financial returns or is it more strategic, in the sense of being about technological or market development? Shifting expectations on the part of the corporate venture capitalist can lead to the disruption of longer-term plans by the entrepreneurial new venture. In recent years, companies such as Siemens and Nokia have sold or diluted their stakes in some of their corporate venture units, and companies such as Ericsson and Diageo have had to close them down entirely.

- *Spin-offs (or spin-outs).* These in a sense go in the opposite direction to corporate venturing, involving the generation of small innovative units *from* larger organisations.[32] Companies such as Fairchild Semiconductor are famous for generating many successful spin-offs, including Intel, AMD and LSI Logic, typically as the result of internal disagreements over the appropriate direction for technological innovation. However, spin-off relationships can be more amicable, with the larger parent organisation offering the new venture seed capital and access to its marketing or technological resources. The spin-off gains the flexibility of being independent, while the parent retains a stake in any future success. Sometimes parents will seek to buy out the spin-off entrepreneurs, and reintegrate the venture into the original organisation.[33] For entrepreneurial spin-off companies, therefore, there are potential benefits to managing a constructive relationship with their original parent.

● *Ecosystems.* Following the 'open innovation' approach (section 9.2.3), high-technology companies such as Cisco, IBM and Intel often foster 'ecosystems' of smaller companies. These ecosystems are communities of connected suppliers, agents, distributors, franchisees, technology entrepreneurs and makers of complementary products.[34] Apple for example has created an ecosystem around its iPod, in which more than one hundred companies manufacture accessories and peripherals such as cases, speakers and docking units. Large firms get the benefits of increased customer satisfaction through the provision of complementary products. Ecosystem members get the benefit of a large and often lucrative market: iPod accessories get plenty of retail shelf space and superior margins. Small entrepreneurial firms wishing to participate in such ecosystems have to be skilled in managing relationships with powerful technological leaders.

9.5.3 Social entrepreneurship

Entrepreneurship is not just a matter for the private sector. The public sector has seen increasing calls for a more entrepreneurial approach to service creation and delivery. Recently too the notion of social entrepreneurship has become common. **Social entrepreneurs are individuals and groups who create independent organisations to mobilise ideas and resources to address social problems, typically earning revenues but on a not-for-profit basis**.[35] Independence and revenues generated in the market give social entrepreneurs the flexibility and dynamism to pursue social problems that pure public-sector organisations are often too bureaucratic, or too politically constrained, to tackle. Social entrepreneurs have pursued a wide range of initiatives, including small loans ('micro-credit') to peasants by the Grameen bank in Bangladesh, employment creation by the Mondragon cooperative in the Basque region of Spain, and fair trade by Traidcraft in the United Kingdom. This wide range of initiatives raises at least three key choices for social entrepreneurs.

● *Social mission.* For social entrepreneurs, the social mission is primary. The social mission can embrace two elements: end-objectives and operational processes. For example, the Grameen bank has the end-objective of reducing rural poverty, especially for women. The process is empowering poor people's own business initiatives by providing micro-credit at a scale and to people that conventional banks would ignore.

● *Organisational form.* Many social enterprises take on cooperative forms, involving their employees and other stakeholders on a democratic basis and thus building commitment and channels for ideas. This form of organisation raises the issue of which stakeholders to include, and which to exclude. Cooperatives can also be slow to take hard decisions. Social enterprises therefore sometimes take more hierarchical charity or company forms of organisation. Cafédirect, the fair-trade beverages company, even became a publicly listed company, paying its first dividend to shareholders in 2006.

● *Business model.* Social enterprises typically rely to a large extent on revenues earned in the marketplace, not just government subsidy or charitable donations. Housing associations collect rents, micro-credit organisations charge interest and fair-trade organisations sell produce. Social entrepreneurs are no different to other entrepreneurs, therefore, in having to design an efficient and effective business model. This business model might involve innovative changes in the value chain. Thus fair-trade organisations have often become much

ILLUSTRATION 9.5

Sociable rats in search of a model

Rats have proved they can detect landmines in Africa. The problem now is how to make them pay.

There are 70 countries around the world affected by landmines left behind from earlier wars. In 2008, these landmines caused 5,200 casualties worldwide. Large areas of land are too dangerous to use for agriculture. But traditional mine-detecting equipment or mine-detecting dogs are very expensive.

Belgian Bart Weetjens had an idea: use rats. Rats have a very sensitive sense of smell, well able to detect the TNT in landmines. As Weetjens told the *Boston Globe*: 'Rats are organized, sensitive, sociable and smart'. In 1998, Weetjens established APOPO as a social enterprise dedicated to developing the potential for rats in de-mining. In 2003, Weetjens began field-testing African giant pouched rats in Mozambique, a country with 3 million landmines. The following year, APOPO's first eleven rats passed their offical test on a real minefield and were ready for action.

The rats work on a Pavlovian basis: for each detected mine, they get a banana or some peanuts. Rats are cheap to train: $4000 (~€2800) per rat, compared to $40,000 for dogs. They are easier to house and transport than dogs, and also less susceptible to tropical diseases. Because they are lighter than dogs, they don't trip off landmines themselves. Finally, rats are more sociable than dogs: they will work with anyone who rewards them, while dogs are inflexible, only working with those to whom they have formed an attachment. A single rat can inspect 1,000 square feet in about 30 minutes, something that would take a human a whole day working with an electronic mine-detector.

Initial funding for APOPO's development phase had come from the University of Antwerp and the Belgian Directorate for International Co-operation. By 2008, more than half of its funding was coming from various government grants, over a third from philanthropic foundations and corporate gifts, some 6 per cent from technical and research institutes and about 5 per cent from APOPO's own fundraising. Principal amongst these fundraising initiatives is the 'Hero Rat' scheme. For €5 ($7) a month, supporters can adopt a rat, each with a name and picture on APOPO's website.

The problem for APOPO is securing its viability. Because grants are typically just to cover costs, APOPO has never made the kinds of profits necessary to build financial reserves. Now that the rats are a proven concept, research funding is harder to get. As yet, there is no secure business model.

In 2010, financial adviser Alvin Hall visited APOPO on behalf of the BBC. He advised Weetjens to increase the minimum donation for adopting a 'Hero Rat'. He also proposed the creation of an endowment fund, allowing large donations to give APOPO some permanent capital. Hall also encouraged APOPO to think about diversification ventures.

One promising avenue for diversification is tuberculosis (TB) detection. APOPO is running trials in Tanzania using the rats to detect TB in the saliva of sick patients. TB is responsible for 1.7 million deaths each year, mainly in poor countries. Apparently these sensitive rats can process as many saliva samples in a few minutes as a human lab technician can in a whole day. The rats have even detected TB in samples that had been missed by conventional tests. APOPO's 2010 mission statement reflects this widening role: 'to become the centre of excellence in detection rat technologies, to enhance the impact of life-saving actions'.

Sources: www.apopo.org; *Boston Globe*, 23 November 2008; www.bbc.co.uk, 5 March 2010.

Questions

1 What are the advantages and disadvantages of a social enterprise approach in this kind of domain?

2 What would be your advice to Bart Weetjens as he searches for a secure long-term business model?

more closely involved with their suppliers than commercial organisations, for example advising farmers on agriculture and providing education and infrastructure support to their communities. Illustration 9.5 shows how mine-clearing venture APOPO is struggling to find a viable business model.

Social entrepreneurs, just like other entrepreneurs, often have to forge relationships with large commercial companies. For example, a new social enterprise called Ten Senses established Bulgaria's first fair-trade shop with assistance from the multinational bank Citigroup and the oil company Royal Dutch Shell. Harvard Business School's Rosabeth Moss Kanter points out that the benefits to business of involvement with social enterprise can go beyond a feel-good factor and attractive publicity.[36] She shows that involvement in social enterprise can help develop new technologies and services, access new pools of potential employees, and create relationships with government and other agencies that can eventually turn into new markets. Kanter concludes that large corporations should develop clear strategies with regard to social entrepreneurship, not treat it as ad hoc charity.

SUMMARY

www.pearsoned.co.uk/mystrategylab
AUDIO SUMMARY

- Strategists face four fundamental dilemmas in innovation: the relative emphasis to put on technology push or market pull; whether to focus on product or process innovation; how much to rely on 'open innovation'; and finally how far to concentrate on technological innovation as opposed to broader business-model innovation.

- Innovations often diffuse into the marketplace according to an S-curve model in which slow start-up is followed by accelerating growth (the tipping point) and finally a flattening of demand. Managers should watch out for 'tripping points'.

- Managers have a choice between being first into the marketplace and entering later. Innovators can capture first-mover advantages. However, 'fast second' strategies are often more attractive.

- Established incumbents' businesses should beware disruptive innovations. Incumbents can stave off inertia by developing portfolios of real options and by organising autonomous new venture units.

- Entrepreneurs face characteristic dilemmas as their businesses go through the entrepreneurial life cycle of start-up, growth, maturity and exit. Entrepreneurs also have to choose how they relate to large firms, particularly as they may become involved in their ecosystems or strategies for open innovation.

- Social entrepreneurship offers a flexible way of addressing social problems, but raises issues about appropriate missions, organisational forms and business models.

KEY DEBATE

Are large firms better innovators than small firms?

The famous Austrian economist Joseph Schumpeter proposed that large firms are proportionately more innovative than small firms. This proposition is a controversial one. If true, it would discourage laboratory scientists and engineers from leaving their large firm employers to set up their own ventures. It would encourage large firms like Google and Cisco to keep on buying up small innovative firms and absorbing them into their own corporate strategies. It would make government policy makers more tolerant of huge, domineering firms like Microsoft who claim that their large scale is important to continued innovation in computer software.

Schumpeter's proposition for the advantages of large firms in innovation has several points in its favour:

- Large firms have greater and more diverse resources, helping them to bring together all the various necessary elements for innovation.
- Large firms may have a greater propensity for innovation risk, knowing that they can absorb the costs of innovation failure.
- Large firms have better incentives to innovate, because they are more likely to be able to capitalise on innovation, having all the required complementary assets (distribution channels and so on) to roll it out fast and under their control.

On the other hand, there are good reasons why small firms might be more innovative:

- Small firms are typically more cohesive, so that knowledge is more easily shared.
- Small firms are typically more flexible and less bureaucratic, so that they can innovate faster and more boldly.
- Small firms are more motivated to innovate simply to survive, while large firms can simply defend and exploit their dominance of existing markets.

There has been plenty of research on whether small or large firms are proportionately more innovative. Some researchers have focused on the input side, for example measuring whether large firms are more research intensive in terms of R&D expenditure as a percentage of sales. Other researchers have focused on the output side, for example counting whether large firms have proportionately greater numbers of patents for innovations. There is no final consensus on the overall patterns of innovation. However, recent research findings suggest that in general:

- Large firms are relatively less research intensive in high technology industries, for example electronics and software.
- Large firms are relatively more innovative in service industries than in manufacturing industries.

It seems that the research so far cannot provide any firm rules about whether large or small firms are better innovators in general. However, research scientists, acquisitive large firms and government policy makers need to consider carefully the specifics of particular industries.

References:
C. Camisón-Zornosa, R. Lapiedra-Alcani, M. Segarra-Ciprés and M. Boronat-Navarro, 'A Meta-Analysis of Innovation and Organizational Size', *Organization Studies*, vol. 25, no. 3 (2004), pp. 331–61.
C-Y Lee and T. Sung, 'Schumpeter's Legacy: a New Perspective on the Relationship between Firm Size and R&D', *Research Policy*, vol. 34 (2005), pp. 914–31.

Question

What kinds of managerial action might you consider if you were trying to increase the innovativeness of a large firm in a high technology manufacturing industry?

WORK ASSIGNMENTS

✴ Denotes more advanced work assignments. Refers to a case study in the Text and Cases edition.*

9.1✴ For a new product or service that you have recently experienced and enjoyed, investigate the strategy of the company responsible. With reference to the dilemmas of section 9.2, explain whether the innovation was more technology push or market pull, product or process driven, or technological or more broadly business model based.

9.2 Go to a web traffic site (such as alexa.com) and compare over time trends in terms of 'page views' or 'reach' for older sites (such as Amazon.com) and newer sites (such as spotify.com, or any that has more recently emerged). With reference to section 9.3, how do you explain these trends and how would you project them forward?

9.3✴ With regard to a new product or service that you have recently experienced and enjoyed (as in 9.1), investigate the strategic responses of 'incumbents' to this innovation. To what extent is the innovation disruptive for them (see section 9.4.3)?

9.4 With reference to the entrepreneurial life cycle, identify the position of either Dyson (Chapter 3), Google (Chapter 12), Web Reservations*, Ekomate* or Leax *. What managerial issues might this case company anticipate in the coming years?

9.5 Use the internet to identify a social entrepreneurial venture that interests you (via www.skollfoundation.org, for example), and, with regard to section 9.5.3, identify its social mission, its organisational form and its business model.

Integrative assignment

9.6 Consider a for-profit or social entrepreneurial idea that you or your friends or colleagues might have. Drawing on section 15.4.4, outline the elements of a strategic plan for this possible venture. What more information do you need to get?

RECOMMENDED KEY READINGS

- P. Trott, *Innovation Management and New Product Development*, 4th edition, Financial Times Prentice Hall, 2008, provides a comprehensive overview of innovation strategy issues. A lively and accessible survey of many innovation issues, together with a wealth of examples, is C. Markides and P. Geroski, *Fast Second: How Smart Companies Bypass Radical Innovation to Enter and Dominate New Markets*, Jossey-Bass, 2005.

- A good collection of accessible articles on specialised innovation topics by leading academics is J. Fagerberg, D. Mowery and R. Nelson (eds), *The Oxford Handbook of Innovation*, Oxford University Press, 2005. An equivalent collection on entrepreneurship is M. Casson, B. Yeung, A. Basu and N. Wadeson (eds), *The Oxford Handbook of Entrepreneurship*, Oxford University Press, 2006.

- P.A. Wickham, *Strategic Entrepreneurship*, 4th edition (2008) is becoming the standard European text with regard to entrepreneurial strategy.

- Social entrepreneurship is discussed usefully in A. Nicholls (ed.), *Social Entrepreneurship: New Paradigms of Sustainable Social Change*, Oxford University Press, 2006.

REFERENCES

1. This definition adapts, in order to include the public sector, the definition in P. Trott, *Innovation Management and New Product Development*, 3rd edition, Financial Times Prentice Hall, 2005.

2. A good discussion of the academic theories that underpin these dilemmas is in R. Rothwell, 'Successful industrial innovation: critical factors for the 1990s', *R&D Management*, vol. 22, no. 3 (1992), pp. 221–39.

3. J. Abernathy and W. Utterback, 'A dynamic model of process and product innovation', *Omega*, vol. 3, no. 6 (1975), pp. l42–60.

4. P. Anderson and M.L. Tushman, 'Technological discontinuities and dominant designs: a cyclical model of technological change', *Administrative Science Quarterly*, vol. 35 (1990), pp. 604–33.

5. J. Tang, 'Competition and innovation behaviour', *Research Policy*, vol. 35 (2006), pp. 68–82.

6. H. Chesbrough and M. Appleyard, 'Open innovation and strategy', *California Management Review*, vol. 50, no. 1 (2007), pp. 57–73; O. Gasman, E. Enkel and H. Chesbrough, 'The future of open innovation', *R&D Management*, vol. 38, no. 1 (2010), pp. 1–9.

7. A. Gawer and M. Cusumano, *Platform Leadership: How Intel, Microsoft and Cisco Drive Industry Innovation*, Harvard Business School Press (2002).

8. See the special issue on business models in *Long Range Planning*, 2010, especially D.J. Teece, 'Business models, business strategy and innovation', *Long Range Planning*, vol. 43, nos 3/4 (2010).

9. J. Magretta 'Why business models matter', *Harvard Business Review*, vol. 80, no. 5 (2002), pp. 86–92; H. Chesbrough, 'Business model innovation: it's not just about technology anymore', *Strategy & Leadership*, vol. 35, no. 6 (2007), pp. 12–17.

10. Innovation diffusion is discussed in the classic E. Rogers, *Diffusion of Innovations*, Free Press, 1995; C. Kim and R. Maubourgne, 'Knowing a winning idea when you see one', *Harvard Business Review*, vol. 78, no. 5 (2000), pp. 129–38; and J. Cummings and J. Doh, 'Identifying who matters: mapping key players in multiple environments', *California Management Review*, vol. 42, no. 2 (2000), pp. 83–104 (see especially pp. 91–7).

11. J. Nichols and S. Roslow, 'The S-curve: an aid to strategic marketing', *The Journal of Consumer Marketing*, vol. 3, no. 2 (1986), pp. 53–64 and F. Suarez and G. Lanzolla, 'The half-truth of first-mover advantage', *Harvard Business Review*, vol. 83, no. 4 (2005), pp. 121–7. This S-curve refers to innovation diffusion. However, the S-curve effect sometimes also refers to the diminishing performance increases available from a maturing technology: A. Sood and G. Tellis, 'Technological evolution and radical innovation', *Journal of Marketing*, vol. 69, no. 3 (2005), pp. 152–68.

12. M. Gladwell, *The Tipping Point*, Abacus, 2000. Tipping points are also important in public policy and can help anticipate emerging problems, for example crime waves and epidemics.

13. www.bbcnews.com. 12 January 2007.

14. S. Brown, 'The tripping point', *Marketing Research*, vol. 17, no. 1 (2005), pp. 8–13.

15. C. Markides and P. Geroski, *Fast Second: How Smart Companies Bypass Radical Innovation to Enter and Dominate New Markets*, Jossey-Bass, 2005; R. Kerin, P. Varadarajan and R. Peterson, 'First-mover advantage: a synthesis, conceptual framework and research propositions', *Journal of Marketing*, vol. 56, no. 4 (1992), pp. 33–47; and P.F. Suarez and G. Lanzolla, 'The half-truth of first-mover advantage', *Harvard Business Review*, vol. 83, no. 4 (2005), pp. 121–7.

16. F. Suarez and G. Lanzolla, 'The half-truth of first-mover advantage', *Harvard Business Review*, vol. 83, no. 4 (2005), pp. 121–7. See also S. Min, U. Manohar and W. Robinson, 'Market pioneer and early follower survival risks: a contingency analysis of really new versus incrementally new product-markets', *Journal of Marketing*, vol. 70, no. 1 (2006), pp. 15–33.

17. C. Markides and P. Geroski, *Fast Second: How Smart Companies Bypass Radical Innovation to Enter and Dominate New Markets*, Jossey-Bass, 2005.

18. David Teece, the academic authority in this area, refers to the capacity to capture profits as 'the appropriability regime': see D. Teece, *Managing Intellectual Capital*, Oxford University Press, 2000.

19 An excellent survey of intellectual property rights is in *The Economist Magazine*, Survey: Patents and Technology, 25 October 2005.

20. D. Teece, *Managing Intellectual Capital*, Oxford University Press, 2000.

21. See J. Bower and C. Christensen, 'Disruptive technologies: catching the wave', *Harvard Business Review*, vol. 73, no. 1 (1995), pp. 43–53 and C. Christensen and M.E. Raynor, *The Innovator's Solution*, Harvard Business School Press, 2003.

22. R.G. McGrath and I. MacMillan, *The Entrepreneurial Mindset*, Harvard Business School Press, 2000.

23. C. Christensen and M.E. Raynor, *The Innovator's Solution*, Harvard Business School Press, 2003.

24. V. Govindarajan and C. Trimble, 'Organizational DNA for strategic innovation', *California Management Review*, vol. 43, no. 3 (2005), pp. 47–75.

25. Excellent textbooks on strategic entrepreneurship include J.A. Timmons, *New Venture Creation: Entrepreneurship in the 21st Century*, 6th edition, Irwin (2004) and P.A. Wickham, *Strategic Entrepreneurship*, 4th edition (2008).

26. D. Flynn and A. Forman, 'Life cycles of new venture organizations: different factors affecting performance', *Journal of Developmental Entrepreneurship*, vol. 6, no. 1 (2001), pp. 41–58.

27. D. Flynn and A. Forman, 'Life cycles of new venture organizations: different factors affecting performance',

Journal of Developmental Entrepreneurship, vol. 6, no. 1 (2001), pp. 41–58.

28. D. Flynn and A. Forman, 'Life cycles of new venture organizations: different factors affecting performance', *Journal of Developmental Entrepreneurship*, vol. 6, no. 1 (2001), pp. 41–58.

29. For a detailed account of Cisco's policy of taking over high-technology firms, see D. Mayer and M. Kenney, 'Economic action does not take place in a vacuum: understanding Cisco's acquisition and development strategy', *Industry and Innovation*, vol. 11, no. 4 (2004), pp. 293–325.

30. P. Audia and C. Rider, 'A garage and an idea: what more does an entrepreneur need?', *California Management Review*, vol. 40, no. 1 (2005), pp. 6–28.

31. H. Chesbrough, 'Making sense of corporate venture capital', *Harvard Business Review*, vol. 80, no. 3 (2002), pp. 4–11; A. Campbell, J. Birkinshaw, A. Morrison and R. van Basten Batenburg, 'The future of corporate venturing', *MIT Sloan Management Review*, vol. 45, no. 1 (2003), pp. 33–41.

32. S. Klepper, 'Spinoffs: a review and synthesis', *European Management Review*, vol. 6 (2009), pp. 159–71.

33. A. Parhankangas and P. Arenius, 'From a corporate venture to an independent company: a base for a taxonomy for corporate spin-off firms', *Research Policy*, vol. 32 (2003), pp. 463–81.

34. B. Iyer, C.-H. Lee and N. Venkatraman, 'Managing in a "Small World Ecosystem"', *California Management Review*, 48, 3 (2006), 28–47.

35 A. Nicholls (ed.) *Social Entrepreneurship: New Paradigms of Sustainable Social Change*, Oxford University Press (2006); J. Austin, H. Stevenson and J. Wei-Skillern. 'Social and commercial entrepreneurship: same, different, or both?' *Entrepreneurship Theory and Practice*, 30, no. 1 (2006).

36 R. Moss Kanter, 'From spare change to real change', *Harvard Business Review*, May-June 1999.

Skype: innovators and entrepreneurs

Introduction

Niklas Zennström and Janus Friis have been a golden pair in the Internet business. For a period during the early 2000s, their Kazaa peer-to-peer file sharing business was the world's largest music sharing site. After selling that business to Sharman Networks, they moved quickly to establish Skype in 2003, which quickly became the dominant player in the world's VoIP (Voice over Internet Protocol) telephone market. Skype's free Internet-based VoIP service was an attractive alternative to the expensive traditional landline and mobile telephone services, gaining 60 million users by 2005. That same year, they sold Skype to eBay for $2.6bn (~€1.8bn) – an impressive figure for a business whose total revenues were just $60m and had still not turned a profit. The eBay deal, however, turned out not to be an unblemished success.

Two entrepreneurs

Zennström is the older of the two, aged 40 at the sale to eBay. He took a first degree in business and then an MSc in engineering and computer science from Uppsala University in Sweden. He then entered the telecommunications industry, spending nine years in Tele2, a fast-expanding European telecoms group. He met Friis in 1997, hiring him to manage a help-desk. Friis, a Dane, is 11 years younger and failed even to graduate from high school. But from the late 1990s the two worked closely together on a series of new ventures: as well as Kazaa and Skype, these included Altnet, claimed to be the world's first secure peer-to-peer wholesale network, Joltid, a company in traffic optimisation technologies, and the portal everyday.com.

The pair were committed to disruptive innovation. Zennström told the *Financial Times*: 'It's everyone's obligation to fight against monopolies and also companies that provide bad services.' Of the traditional landline and mobile telephone companies, he declares: 'They deserve to be challenged. They provide bad and expensive service.'

Co-founders of Skype – Niklas Zennström (left) and Janus Friis (right)

Source: Rex Features/Steve Forrest.

The Skype business model

Skype's software allows people to use the Internet to make free calls to other Skype users all over the world. Given the cost of traditional international calls, this was an exciting idea. Initial funding, however, was not easy to find as the music industry was still pursuing a lawsuit against the two founders regarding the illegal filesharing their earlier Kazaa venture appeared to facilitate. For fear of legal action, Zennström and Friis dared not even enter the USA. Most traditional venture capitalists gave the new venture a wide berth. Moreover, it was not easy to see how to make money out of free calls.

The business model is more complicated than that, of course. Most users have free calls, certainly. However, Skype has very low costs, as customers download the software off the Internet and it is the customers' computers and Internet connections that make the network. It costs nothing to keep connections open continuously. Marketing is cheap, because customers naturally invite others to join. Skype has no telephone help-desk, citing the overwhelming number of customers and the effectiveness of its standard Internet queries services. Skype makes its money from its ancillary services, such as SkypeOut, which allows customers to call traditional landline or mobile numbers for a fee, often very small.

Zennström explains the model: 'We want to make as little money as possible per user. We don't have any cost per user, but we want a lot of them.'

This overturns the traditional landline and mobile phone business model. Traditional telephone companies of both types face high costs of both marketing and capacity building. Customers are typically charged according to distance and by the minute. The traditional principle is to maximise revenues per customer, completely the opposite to Skype. Zennström summarised to *Business Week*:

When you're a phone company, you have marketing and customer-acquisition costs. When you have a customer, you have an operational cost of running the network. Then you have a cost for billing systems. That's an operator business model.

The business model of Skype is completely different. Skype has a software business model. We don't have any distribution or marketing costs for each user – our software is spread virally. And when we have a new user, we have zero cost for serving that user because they're using P2P (peer-to-peer) software and their own bandwidth. So we have zero costs of getting new users and zero costs of running traffic. Our costs are only business development and software development.

Comparing the positions of the two types of companies, he added: 'Something that is a great business model for us is probably a terrible model for them.'

As shown in the figure, Skype's service has been attracting snowballing usage. The tipping point came towards the end of 2004, and by March 2010 Skype was achieving more than 23 million users in a single day. Of course, this success raised an awkward paradox. If Skype became near universal, who would be left for people to call using the paid service of SkypeOut to access traditional phones?

eBay's move

Skype was always likely to be for sale. Zennström and Friis had sold Kazaa quickly and their initial funders would want a profitable early exit too. It was not surprising that rumours started during 2005 of possible acquisition from technology giants such as Google, Microsoft and Yahoo!. In the end, however, it was online auctioneer eBay who did the deal, slightly surprisingly as it was not seen as a communications company.

There are similarities in the underlying business models of the two companies. Both benefit from 'network effects', where value rises disproportionately fast with increasing members of the network. One more precise rationale from eBay's point of view was that

Skype Dialtone – Peak Number of Accounts Logged in during One Day

$Y = 24681x^2 - 183682x + 3E + 09$
$R^2 = 0.9889$

$Y = 9848x^2 - 4E + 08$
$R^2 = 0.988$

online ···· Linear (online) --- Raly (online)

Source: Phil Wolff, *Skype Journal*, 8 March 2010; reproduced with permission.

Skype connections could be placed directly on the eBay site, allowing customers potentially to phone sellers with a single click of the button. Also, sellers could place voice links directly on their eBay sites, so that customers could click directly to a message, paying eBay a fee every time they did. On the other hand, Skype would strengthen its links with eBay's subsidiary PayPal, which Skype already used for managing payments for its SkypeOut service.

For Zennström, however, one major attraction of eBay was that it looked likely to leave Skype more alone. Companies like Yahoo! and Microsoft tend to integrate their acquisitions closely into their existing operations, extinguishing autonomy. Zennström and Friis might be working with eBay for some time. The deal included an 'earn-out' arrangement which would push Skype's final sale price to over $4bn if they managed to meet revenue and profit targets over the coming years. Anyway, the two had an exciting vision for the future: to become the world's biggest and best platform for all communication – text, voice or video – from any Internet-connected device, whether a computer or a mobile phone.

eBay's role

eBay had a lot to offer an ambitious company like Skype. Founded only in 1995, it had reached revenues of $4.55bn and 11,600 employees in the space of 10 years. Zennström commented of Meg Whitman, eBay's Chief Executive since 1998: 'I think I can learn a lot of things from Meg. We want to see things through, but we also have some other ideas.' Skype would still have its own strategy, budgets, culture and brands. Zennström insisted to the *Financial Times*:

> One of the important things for us, but also one of the great things with eBay, is that we wanted to make sure that we could merge with a bigger company, but that Skype stays as one company. Meg said: 'Take advantage of the resources we have, but we are not going to tell you what to do because you're the best in the world to run your own business.'

The managerial demands of rapid growth were considerable. Staff quadrupled to 300 between 2005 and 2006, and included 30 nationalities scattered all over the world. eBay introduced five of its own senior managers to help, including a new president responsible for day-to-day operations, a chief financial officer and a new human resource director. But Skype was keen to preserve its own culture. According to Zennström, still the CEO, Skype's passionate, pioneering culture had to be both protected and nurtured: 'It's how you operate, how you behave. It starts when we are hiring people. They need to be really thrilled about Skype as a movement, rather than a place to work.'

eBay's exit

While Skype protected its culture, synergies were hard to find. Skype's sales in 2007 had reached $383m, but eBay users were not making the hoped-for use of Skype connections. Targets were missed. In October 2007, Zennström was obliged to step down as CEO and eBay wrote down the value of its investment by $1.4bn. In March 2008, after a 30 per cent slide in share price, Meg Whitman resigned as CEO of eBay. The new CEO, John Donahue, commented on Skype: 'If the synergies are strong, we'll keep it in our portfolio. If not, we'll reassess it.' In September 2009, eBay announced that it was selling 65 per cent of its interest to the Silver Lake group of investors for $2bn. However, it transpired that eBay had neglected to acquire the source-code for Skype software back in 2005. To buy off the threat of legal action and close the deal with Silver Lake, eBay was obliged to give Zennström and Friis 14 per cent of their company back.

Sources: 'Phone Service the "Zero Cost" Way', *Business Week online*, 7 January 2004; www.wikipedia.org; *The Economist*, 15 September 2005; *Financial Times*, 17 and 19 April 2006; *Financial Times*, 17 September 2009.

Questions
1 What are the advantages, and what are the possible limits, of Skype's business model?
2 What went wrong with eBay's acquisition of Skype?

10

MERGERS, ACQUISITIONS AND ALLIANCES

Learning outcomes

After reading this chapter you should be able to:

● Establish the potential role of *organic* (stand-alone) strategies.

● Identify key issues in the successful management of *mergers and acquisitions.*

● Identify the key issues in the successful management of *strategic alliances.*

● Determine the appropriate choices between *organic* development, *mergers and acquisitions* and *strategic alliances.*

● Compare *key success factors* in mergers, acquisitions and alliances.

PEARSON
mystrategylab

MyStrategyLab is designed to help you make the most of your studies.
Visit **www.pearsoned.co.uk/mystrategylab** to discover a wide range of resources specific to this chapter, including:

• A personalised **Study plan** that will help you understand core concepts

• **Audio** and **video clips** that put the spotlight on strategy in the real world

• **Online glossaries** and **flashcards** that provide helpful reminders when you're looking for some quick revision.

(10.1) INTRODUCTION

Mergers, acquisitions and alliances are often in the news. For example in 2009, Italian carmaker Fiat formed an alliance with the American Chrysler as part of its internationalisation strategy. In 2010, the American foods conglomerate Kraft acquired the British Cadbury confectionery company in pursuit of its diversification strategy. Acquisition by one company of another, complete merger between two companies, and strategic alliance between different companies are all very common methods for carrying out strategies.

This chapter therefore addresses mergers, acquisitions and alliances as key methods for pursuing strategic options. It will consider them alongside the principal alternative of 'organic' development, in other words the pursuit of a strategy relying on the company's own resources. Figure 10.1 shows how the main strategic options considered in the previous three chapters – diversification, internationalisation and innovation – can all be achieved through mergers and acquisitions, alliances and organic development. Of course, these three methods can also be used for many other strategies, for example consolidating markets or building scale advantages.

The chapter starts with organic development. Organic development is the default option: relying on the organisation's internal resources is the natural first option to consider. The chapter then introduces the two principal external options: first mergers and acquisitions (often abbreviated as M&A) and then strategic alliances. The final section systematically compares the two external options against the internal option of organic development. Given the frequent failures of acquisitions and alliances, the fundamental issue is when to acquire, when to ally or when is it better to 'do it yourself'? The final section also considers key success factors in M&A and alliances. The problematic success record of acquisitions in particular is the subject of the Key Debate at the end of this chapter.

Figure 10.1 Three strategy methods

(10.2) ORGANIC DEVELOPMENT

The default method for pursuing a strategy is to 'do it yourself', relying on internal capabilities. Thus **organic development is where a strategy is pursued by building on and developing an organisation's own capabilities**. For example, Amazon's entry into the e-books market with its Kindle product was principally organic, relying on its own subsidiary Lab126 and drawing on its expertise in book retailing, internet retail and software. For Amazon, this do-it-yourself (DIY) diversification method was preferable to allying with an existing e-book producer such as Sony or buying a relevant hi-tech start-up such as the French pioneer Bookeen.

There are four principal advantages to relying on organic development:

● *Knowledge and learning.* Using the organisation's existing capabilities to pursue a new strategy can enhance organisational knowledge and learning. Direct involvement in a new market or technology is likely to promote the acquisition and internalisation of deeper knowledge than a hands-off strategic alliance, for example.

● *Spreading investment over time.* Acquisitions typically require an immediate upfront payment for the target company. Organic development allows the spreading of investment over the whole time span of the strategy's development. This reduction of upfront commitment may make it easier to reverse or adjust a strategy if conditions change.

● *No availability constraints.* Organic development has the advantage of not being dependent on the availability of suitable acquisition targets or potential alliance partners. There are few acquisition opportunities for foreign companies wanting to enter the Japanese market, for example. Organic developers also do not have to wait until the perfectly matched acquisition target comes on to the market.

● *Strategic independence.* The independence provided by organic development means that the organisation does not need to make the same compromises as might be necessary if it made an alliance with a partner organisation. For example, partnership with a foreign collaborator is likely to involve constraints on marketing activity in their home market.

The reliance of organic development on internal capabilities can be limiting. It is not easy to use existing capabilities as the platform for major leaps in terms of innovation, diversification or internationalisation, for example. However, as in the example of Amazon's Kindle, organic development can sometimes be sufficiently radical to merit the term 'corporate entrepreneurship'. **Corporate entrepreneurship refers to radical change in the organisation's business, driven principally by the organisation's own capabilities.**[1] Bringing together the words 'entrepreneurship' and 'corporate' underlines the potential for significant change or novelty not only by external entrepreneurship (see also corporate venture units in section 9.5.2), but also by reliance on internal capabilities from within the corporate organisation. Thus for Amazon, the Kindle was a radical entrepreneurial step, taking it from retailing into the design of innovative consumer electronic products.

The concept of corporate entrepreneurship is valuable because it encourages an entrepreneurial attitude inside the firm. There are many examples of corporate entrepreneurship, such as the creation of low-cost airline Ryanair from inside the aircraft leasing company Guinness Peat. Often, however, organisations have to go beyond their own internal capabilities and look externally for methods to pursue their strategies. The main themes of this chapter, therefore, are first mergers and acquisitions and second strategic alliances.

(10.3) MERGERS AND ACQUISITIONS

Mergers and acquisitions (M&A) frequently grab the headlines, as they involve large sums of money and very public competitions for shareholder support. They can also provide a speedy means of achieving major strategic objectives. However, they can also lead to spectacular failures too. A famous case is that of the Royal Bank of Scotland, whose 2007 takeover of the Dutch ABN AMRO ended in commercial disaster and the bank's nationalisation by the British government.

10.3.1 Types of mergers and acquisitions

An **acquisition** involves one firm taking over the ownership ('equity') of another, hence the alternative term 'takeover'. Most acquisitions are ultimately *friendly*, where the acquirer and the target firm agree the terms together, and the target's management recommends acceptance to its shareholders. Sometimes acquisitions are *hostile*: here the would-be acquirer offers a price for the target firm's shares without the agreement of the target's management and the outcome is decided by which side wins the support of shareholders. Thus Cadbury's management initially rejected the hostile bid by Kraft, seeking more friendly alternative partners such as Hershey. On the other hand, **a merger is the combination of two previously separate organisations, typically as more or less equal partners.** For example, in 2009, the French Banque Populaire and Caisse d'Epargne merged to form a new bank called Groupe BPCE, which became the second largest in France. In practice, the terms 'merger' and 'acquisition' are often used interchangeably, hence the common shorthand M&A or just acquisitions.

Mergers and acquisitions can also happen in the public and non-profit sectors: for example, the Finnish government created the new Aalto University in 2010 by merging the Helsinki School of Economics, the Helsinki University of Art and Design and the Helsinki University of Technology. Even if the government is the ultimate owner of the organisations involved, as in this case, it can be appropriate to use the term 'merger' rather than simply 'reorganisation' (see Chapter 13). Publicly owned institutions frequently build up highly distinctive cultures or systems of their own, as if they were in fact independent organisations. Where there are major cultural or systems differences between organisations, the scale and depth of the managerial issues approximate to those that would be involved in a change of ownership. 'Merger' is therefore often used in such cases as that better reflects the scale of the task involved than simply 'reorganisation'.

Mergers and acquisitions are typically cyclical phenomena, involving high peaks and deep troughs. Thus 2007 was a record year for global mergers and acquisitions, involving a value of nearly $6.6bn (~€4.6bn), four times the amount of the previous trough in 2002. As the worldwide recession took hold, the value of global M&A in 2009 fell to $3.6bn (~€2.5bn).[2] These cycles are driven by over-optimism on the part of managers, shareholders and bankers during upturns, and by an exaggerated loss of confidence during downturns. This cyclical pattern should warn managers that M&A may have a strong fashion or bandwagon element. Especially in an upturn, managers should ask very carefully whether acquisitions are really justified. In an upturn too, the laws of supply and demand suggest that the price of target firms is very likely to be excessively high.

Global activity in mergers has traditionally been dominated by North America and Western Europe, whereas it has been much less common in other economies, for example Japan. Many national governance systems put barriers in the way of acquisitions, especially hostile acquisitions (see section 4.3.2). However, companies from fast-developing economies such as China and India have recently undertaken many large-scale acquisitions in order to access Western markets or technology, or to secure material resources needed for growth. For example, the Chinese computer company Lenovo bought IBM Computers and the Indian company Tata bought the car companies Jaguar and Land Rover in the United Kingdom and the Anglo-Dutch steel company Corus (see Illustration 10.2 later).

10.3.2 Motives for mergers and acquisitions

There are three broad types of motive for M&A: strategic, financial and managerial.[3]

Strategic motives for M&A

Strategic motives for M&A involve improving the actual business of the organisation in some way. These motives are often related to the reasons for diversification in general (see section 7.3). Strategic motives can be categorised in three main ways:[4]

- *Extension.* Mergers and acquisitions can be used to extend the reach of a firm in terms of geography, products or markets. Acquisitions can be speedy ways of extending international reach. Thus in 2010 the Chinese Geely car company bought the Swedish Volvo car company in order to build its global presence. Acquisitions can also be an effective way of extending into new markets, as in diversification (see Chapter 7).

- *Consolidation.* Mergers and acquisitions can be used to consolidate the competitors in an industry. Bringing together two competitors can have at least three beneficial effects. In the first place, it increases market power by reducing competition: this might enable the newly consolidated company to raise prices for customers. Second, the combination of two competitors can increase efficiency through reducing surplus capacity or sharing resources, for instance head-office facilities or distribution channels. Finally, the greater scale of the combined operations may increase production efficiency or increase bargaining power with suppliers, forcing them to reduce their prices.

- *Capabilities.* The third broad strategic motive for mergers and acquisitions is to increase a company's capabilities. High-tech companies such as Cisco and Microsoft regard acquisitions of entrepreneurial technology companies as a part of their R&D effort. Instead of researching a new technology from scratch, they allow entrepreneurial start-ups to prove the idea, and then take over these companies in order to incorporate the technological capability within their own portfolio (see section 9.5.2). Capabilities-driven acquisitions are often useful where industries are converging (see section 2.3.1). Thus the telephone company AT&T bought computer company NCR as it perceived industry convergence between telephony and computing.

Financial motives for M&A

Financial motives concern the optimal use of financial resources, rather than directly improving the actual businesses. There are three main financial motives:

- *Financial efficiency.* It is often efficient to bring together a company with a strong balance sheet (i.e. it has plenty of cash) with another company that has a weak balance sheet (i.e. it has high debt). The company with a weak balance sheet can save on interest payments by using the stronger company's assets to pay off its debt, and it can also get investment funds from the stronger company that it could not have accessed otherwise. The company with the strong balance sheet may be able to drive a good bargain in acquiring the weaker company. Also, a company with a booming share price can purchase other companies very efficiently by offering to pay the target company's shareholders with its own shares (equity), rather than paying with cash upfront.

- *Tax efficiency.* Sometimes there may be tax advantages from bringing together different companies. For example, one company may be operating in a low-taxation country, and profits from the other company in a higher-tax area can be transferred to be taxed there. Or a company that is making high profits may buy a company that has accumulated losses in order to reduce its own tax liability. Naturally, there are legal restrictions on this strategy.

- *Asset stripping or unbundling.* Some companies are effective at spotting other companies whose underlying assets are worth more than the price of the company as a whole. This makes it possible to buy such companies and then rapidly sell off ('unbundle') different business units to various buyers for a total price substantially in excess of what was originally paid for the whole. Although this is often dismissed as merely opportunistic profiteering ('asset stripping'), if the business units find better corporate parents through this unbundling process, there can be a real gain in economic effectiveness.

Managerial motives for M&A

As for diversification (see section 7.3), acquisitions may sometimes serve managers' interests better than shareholders' interests. 'Managerial' motives are so called, therefore, because they are self-serving rather than efficiency-driven. M&A may serve managerial self-interest for two types of reason:

- *Personal ambition.* There are three ways that acquisitions can satisfy the personal ambition of senior managers, regardless of the real value being created. First, senior managers' personal financial incentives may be tied to short-term growth targets or share-price targets that are more easily achieved by large and spectacular acquisitions than the more gradualist and lower-profile alternative of organic growth. Second, large acquisitions attract media attention, with opportunities to boost personal reputations through flattering media interviews and appearances. Here there is the so-called 'managerial hubris' (vanity) effect: managers who have been successful in earlier acquisitions become over-confident and embark on more and more acquisitions, each riskier and more expensive than the one before.[5] Finally, acquisitions provide opportunities to give friends and colleagues greater responsibility, helping to cement personal loyalty by developing individuals' careers.

- *Bandwagon effects.* As noted earlier, acquisitions are highly cyclical. In an upswing, there are three kinds of pressure on senior managers to join the acquisition bandwagon. First, when many other firms are making acquisitions, financial analysts and the business media may criticise more cautious managers for undue conservatism. Second, shareholders will fear that their company is being left behind, as they see opportunities for their business being snatched by rivals. Lastly, employees will worry that if their company is not acquiring, it will become the target of a hostile bid itself. For managers wanting a quiet life during a 'merger boom', the easiest strategy may be simply to join in. But the danger is of paying too much for an acquisition that the company does not really need in the first place.

In sum, there are bad reasons as well as good reasons for acquisitions and mergers. The average performance of acquisitions is unimpressive, with some suggesting that half of acquisitions fail (see Key Debate at the end of the chapter). It is therefore well worth asking sceptical questions of any M&A strategy. The converse can be true of course: there can be bad reasons for resisting a hostile takeover. Senior managers may resist being acquired because they fear losing their jobs, even if the price offered represents a good deal for their shareholders.

10.3.3 M&A processes

Acquisitions take time. First there is the search to identify an acquisition target with the best possible fit. Then there is the process of negotiating the right price. Finally managers will have to integrate the new and old businesses together, in order to realise the full value of their purchase. In other words, acquisition should be seen as a process over time. Each step in this process imposes different tasks on managers. This section will consider three key steps: target choice, valuation and integration.

Target choice in M&A

Here there are two main criteria to apply: strategic fit and organisation fit.[6]

- *Strategic fit* refers to the extent to which the target firm strengthens or complements the acquiring firm's strategy. Strategic fit will relate to the original strategic motives for the acquisition: extension, consolidation and capabilities. Managers need to assess strategic fit very carefully. The danger is that potential synergies (see section 7.3) in M&A are often exaggerated in order to justify high acquisition prices. Also, negative synergies ('contagion') between the companies involved are easily neglected.[7] An example of negative synergy was when the Bank of America bought the aggressive investment bank Merrill Lynch for $47bn (~€33bn) in 2008. Under its new owner, Merrill Lynch lost business because it was no longer allowed to advise on deals targeting the extensive list of corporations that were already lending clients of Bank of America. Consequently Merrill Lynch was a less valuable business with its new parent than when free to chase any deal it wanted.

- *Organisational fit* refers to the match between the management practices, cultural practices and staff characteristics between the target and the acquiring firms. Large mismatches between the two are likely to cause significant integration problems. The acquisition of Californian genetic engineering company Genentech by Swiss pharmaceutical company Roche raises many questions of organisational fit (see Illustration 10.1). International acquisitions are particularly liable to organisational misfits, because of cultural and language differences between countries.[8] A comparison of the two companies' cultural webs (section 5.4.6) might be helpful here.

Together, strategic and organisational fit determine the potential for the acquirer to add value, the parenting issue raised in section 7.6. Where there is a bad organisational fit, the acquirer is likely to destroy value through its corporate parenting regardless of how well the target fits strategically.

The two criteria of strategic and organisational fit can be used to create a screen according to which potential acquisition targets can be ruled in or ruled out. Note that, because the set of firms that meet the criteria *and* that are actually available for purchase is likely to be small, it is very tempting for managers to relax the criteria too far in order to build a large enough pool

ILLUSTRATION 10.1

Swiss in the Valley

Swiss pharmaceutical giant Roche faced strong resistance to its takeover of Californian biotech company Genentech.

Founded in 1896, by 2009 Swiss pharmaceutical company Roche had 80,000 employees worldwide, sales of $33.6bn (~€23.5bn) and a 56 per cent stake in the San Francisco biotechnology company Genentech. Genentech, however, was jealous of its autonomy, and regarded data on its experiments and trials as not Roche's property. Taking advantage of Genentech's fall in relative value because of a weak dollar, the Swiss company launched a bid for full control, at $89 a share, valuing the company at $44bn. Genentech's management refused the offer.

Genentech had been founded in 1976 by a young venture capitalist and an assistant professor at the San Francisco campus of the University of California. In 1977, the Silicon Valley start-up was the first in the world to express a human gene in bacteria, and in the following year it was the first to produce synthetic human insulin. Roche had bought its stake in the successful young company in 1990, but taken a hands-off approach. By 2009, Genentech was the second largest biotechnology company in the United States, with 11,000 employees. Many of these employees were top scientists, lured to the company by a combination of good salaries, stock options and a large amount of academic freedom. Genentech allowed its scientists to pursue their own research projects one day a week, and to publish articles in scientific journals. In 2008, Genentech had been awarded more patents in molecular biology than the U.S. government and the ten campuses of the University of California combined. *Science* magazine named Genentech as the best employer for scientists seven years in a row. In 2008, former biotech researcher Dr. Art Levinson, Genentech's CEO since 1995 and a supporter of the company's traditional Friday 'beer fests', had been voted by another magazine as America's 'nicest' CEO.

Roche was obliged to raise its bid, to $94 per share. Genentech's management reluctantly accepted. They had originally hoped for $112 per share, but the economic crisis of the time made that unrealistic. As shareholders themselves, however, Roche's bid had made the top management and many of Genentech's scientists very wealthy people.

Although now in full control of Genentech, the management challenges for Roche were substantial. Laurence Lasky, a Silicon Valley venture capitalist and former scientist at Genentech, commented of Roche: 'They're Swiss, and Genentech is a bunch of California cowboys'. Roche indeed had a different culture. Based in the staid town of Basel, it was still half-owned by descendants of the founding families. Its products are typically based upon chemical compounds, very different to Genentech's genetic engineering. Like many other 'big pharma' companies, moreover, the stream of new products from its research laboratories was drying up. Roche hoped to replenish its product portfolio by getting full access to Genentech's research, while also saving costs by merging its U.S. headquarters with that of Genentech in California.

Roche chairman Franz Humer, a Swiss lawyer, was none the less very positive, telling the *Wall Street Journal*: 'I am delighted that the intensive negotiations have led to a successful conclusion. . . . I have spoken with Art (Levinson) and he's extremely committed to make a success of the new company.' However, a close observer of Genentech remarked: 'the assets of Genentech walk out in tennis shoes every night, and you hope they walk back in next morning'.

Sources: San Francisco Chronicle, 13 March 2009, 17 August 2008; International Herald Tribune, 13 March 2009; Wall Street Journal, 17 March 2009.

Questions

1 Assess the strategic and organisational fits of Roche and Genentech

2 What must Roche do to ensure the success of this takeover?

of possible acquisitions. Strict strategic and organisational fit criteria are particularly liable to be forgotten after the failure of an initial acquisition bid. Once having committed publicly to an acquisition strategy, senior managers are susceptible to making ill-considered bids for other targets 'on the rebound'.

Valuation in M&A

Negotiating the right price for an acquisition target is absolutely critical. Offer the target too little, and the bid will be unsuccessful: senior managers will lose credibility and the company will have wasted a lot of management time. Pay too much, though, and the acquisition is unlikely ever to make a profit net of the original acquisition price.

Valuation methods include financial analysis techniques such as payback period, discounted cash flow and shareholder value analysis (see Chapter 11).[9] For acquisition of publicly quoted companies, there is the additional guide of the market value of the target company's shares. However, acquirers typically do not simply pay the current market value of the target, but have to pay a so-called *premium for control*. This premium is the additional amount that the acquirer has to pay to win total control compared to the ordinary valuation of the target's shares as an independent company. Depending on the state of the financial markets, this premium might involve paying at least 30 per cent more for the shares than normal. Especially where the target resists the initial bid, or other potential acquirers join in with their own bids, it is very easy for bid prices to escalate beyond the true economic value of the target.

It is therefore very important for the acquirer to be strictly disciplined with regard to the price that it will pay. Acquisitions are liable to the *winner's curse* – in order to win acceptance of the bid, the acquirer may pay so much that the original cost can never be earned back.[10] This winner's curse effect operated when the Royal Bank of Scotland's consortium competed with Barclays Bank to acquire the Dutch bank ABN AMRO: the Royal Bank of Scotland won, but the excessive price of €70bn (~$98bn) soon drove the victor into financial collapse and government ownership. The negative effects of paying too much can be worsened if the acquirer tries to justify the price by cutting back essential investments in order to improve immediate profits. In what is called the *vicious circle of overvaluation*, over-paying firms can easily undermine the original rationale of the acquisition by imposing savings on exactly the assets (e.g. brand-marketing, product R&D or key staff) that made up the strategic value of the target company in the first place.

Integration in M&A

The ability to extract value from an acquisition will depend critically on the approach to integrating the new business with the old. Integration is frequently challenging because of problems of organisational fit. For example, there might be strong cultural differences between the two organisations (see section 5.4) or they might have incompatible financial or information technology systems (see section 13.3). Illustration 10.2 describes some integration issues for British car company Jaguar-Land Rover after acquisition by Indian conglomerate Tata. Poor integration can cause acquisitions to fail. It is crucial to choose the correct approach to integration of merged or acquired companies.

INSEAD's Philippe Haspeslagh and David Jemison[11] argue that the most suitable approach to integration depends on two key criteria:

● *The extent of strategic interdependence*. Where there is high interdependence, the presumption is in favour of tight integration. If the acquisition is driven by the need to transfer capabilities

Figure 10.2 Acquisition integration matrix

Source: P. Haspeslagh and D. Jemison, *Managing Acquisitions*, Free Press, 1991.

(for example, technology) or to share resources (for example, distribution channels), the value can only be extracted through integrating the businesses thoroughly. Of course, some acquisitions take the form of unrelated or conglomerate diversification (see section 7.2). In unrelated acquisitions, the lack of strategic interdependence means there is little need for integration beyond financial systems.

- *The need for organisational autonomy.* The nature of the organisations involved might modify the logic of strategic interdependence, however. An acquired firm that has a very distinct culture, or is geographically distant, or is dominated by prima donna professionals or star performers might be better left only loosely or gradually integrated. Sometimes an acquisition can be made precisely because the distinctiveness of the acquired organisation is valuable to the acquirer:[12] in this case, of course, it is best to learn gradually from the distinct culture, rather than risk spoiling it by clumsy integration.

As in Figure 10.2, therefore, these two criteria drive three main approaches to integration, plus a fourth residual approach:

- *Absorption* is preferred where there is strong strategic interdependence and little need for organisational autonomy. Absorption implies rapid adjustment of the acquired company's old strategies to the needs of the new owner, and corresponding changes to the company's culture and systems.

- *Preservation* is appropriate where there is little interdependence and a high need for autonomy – as in a conglomerate, perhaps. Preservation allows old strategies, cultures and systems to continue much as before, with changes confined to the essential minimum such as the financial reporting procedures needed for control.

- *Symbiosis* is indicated where there is strong strategic interdependence, but a high need for autonomy – perhaps in a professional services organisation dependent on the creativity of its staff. Symbiosis implies that both acquired firm and acquiring firm learn the best qualities from the other. Symbiosis takes time and is the most complex of the integration approaches.

ILLUSTRATION 10.2

From Nano to Jaguar

In 2008, the Indian Tata group, makers of the ultra-cheap Nano car, bought two iconic British car brands, Jaguar and Land Rover. It had to integrate these in the most demanding times.

The Tata Group is the largest privately-owned company in India, with interests spanning from steel to hotels. Its chairman, Ratan Tata, has embarked on an internationalisation strategy that included the takeover of the Anglo-Dutch Corus steel company in 2007. In January 2008, Tata Motors, already producing a range of cars and SUVs, launched the revolutionary Nano, the world's cheapest car, selling for less than $2000 (~€1400). Two months later, Tata Motors acquired its first prestige marques, Jaguar and Land Rover, from the struggling Ford Motors for $2.3bn.

With 16,000 employees in the UK, based at three manufacturing sites and two design and engineering centres, the takeover caused alarm. Would Tata save money by closing sites? Might it transfer production to its low cost base in India? Ratan Tata was quick to reassure. On a personal visit to the company, he recalled that his father had bought a classic Jaguar more than half a century ago. He talked about reviving the revered British Daimler brand and returning Jaguar to racing. Jaguar-Land Rover then announced its intention to hire 600 more skilled staff to support a £700m project to develop environmentally-friendly cars. And Tata was well-placed to sell Jaguars and Land Rovers in the booming Indian market.

Jaguar-Land Rover still faced challenges. As a subsidiary of Ford, Jaguar-Land Rover had relied on Ford Credit to finance its operations and sales. Now Jaguar-Land Rover needed its own relationships with the banks. All its information technology was based on Ford systems. Jaguar-Land Rover CEO David Smith commented: 'We're pulling companies that were embedded in Ford back out again and switching our financing to other providers. And the IT is an absolute hydra. It's going to be the most difficult part.'

However, Tata did not insist on tight integration into the Indian parent. Oversight is provided by a three-man strategy board, meeting every two months and comprising Ratan Tata, the head of Tata Automotive and David Smith himself. Smith commented: 'Tata wants us to be autonomous – I've got all the executive authority I need. . . . We can make decisions quickly – that's what will be most different from life at Ford.' The Jaguar-Land Rover executive committee, directly responsible for the company's operations, had no Tata representatives. Nevertheless, Jaguar-Land Rover would be making use of Tata Motors' expertise in cost control and the Tata Consultancy Division's skills in information technology.

A year after the takeover, David Smith commented again: 'We are still learning how the relationship with Tata will work. It's clearly more personal and based on individual relationships.' Of Ratan Tata, who had been a passionately-involved champion of the Nano and had trained as an architect and engineer, David Smith remarked: '[He] is very interested in the business. The designers love him, because he's an architect and is not only quite capable of telling them what he thinks, he can say it in the right language too.'

By Spring 2009, relationships were being tested by the economic crisis. Jaguar-Land Rover's sales had fallen by more than 30 per cent and the company had plunged into losses. The British government was refusing a financial bail-out. What would Tata do now?

Sources: Management Today, 1 May 2009; Financial Times, 4 August 2008.

Questions

1 In the light of Haspeslagh and Jemison's matrix, assess Tata's initial approach to the integration of Jaguar-Land Rover

2 How might Tata's approach change in the economic crisis?

- *Holding* is the residual category where there is very little to gain by integration and it is envisaged that the acquisition will be 'held' temporarily before being sold to another company. It is best in these cases simply to leave the acquired unit largely alone.

Especially for the more active absorption and symbiosis forms of integration, the ultimate success of the acquisition will depend upon how well the integration process is managed. Here methods of managing strategic change explained in Chapter 14 will be relevant. However, because acquisitions often involve the loss of jobs, sudden career changes, management relocations and the cancellation of projects, it is argued that organisational justice is particularly important for successful integration.[13] **Organisational justice refers to the perceived fairness of managerial actions, in terms of distribution, procedure and information**. Thus:

- *Distributive justice* refers to the distribution of rewards and posts: for example, it will be seen as unfair in a merger between equals if the large majority of senior management posts go to one of the partners, and not the other.

- *Procedural justice* refers to the procedures by which decisions are made: for example, if integration decisions are made through appropriate committees or task forces with representation from both sides, then the perception of fair procedures is likely to be high.

- *Informational justice* is about how information is used and communicated in the integration: if decisions are explained well to all those involved, they are more likely to be accepted positively.

Kraft offended principles of both procedural and informational justice when it assured investors and employees before its 2010 takeover of Cadbury that it would keep open the Somerdale chocolate factory near Bristol, with its 400 workers. Within a month of completing the takeover, Kraft informed its workers that production would be transferred to Poland, causing political controversy and a loss of trust amongst all its newly acquired staff.

10.3.4 M&A strategy over time

M&A strategies evolve over time. First, mergers and acquisitions will rarely be one-off events for an organisation. Organisations often make many acquisitions as their strategy develops: in this sense, they become *serial acquirers*. Second, over time some acquired units are liable to lose their fit with an organisation's evolving strategy: these units become candidates for *divesture*. This subsection examines serial acquisitions and divesture in turn:

- *Serial acquirers* are companies that make multiple acquisitions, often in parallel. Working on simultaneous acquisitions is very demanding of managerial time and skills. However, repeating the acquisition process does provide an opportunity for acquiring companies to accumulate experience about how to do M&A better. Serial acquirers therefore often develop specialist teams for managing the acquisition process, from target selection through negotiation of a price and then integration. Specialist teams can build up expertise and procedures for dealing effectively with selection, negotiation and integration. IBM for example made 50 software acquisitions in the period 2002–8. In order to make these 50 acquisitions, the company had to assess around 500 different potential acquisition targets, choosing not to proceed in the vast majority of cases. But for those 50 that the company did finally buy, IBM had to establish 50 different integration teams, with 10 or more teams each working in parallel at any one time.[14]

● *Divesture* (or divestment) is the process of selling a business that no longer fits the corporate strategy.[15] This is obviously a central part of an 'asset stripping' strategy (see section 10.3.2), but ought to be on the agenda of every diversified corporation. The key determinant of divesture is whether the corporate parent has 'parenting advantage': in other words, the corporate parent can add more value to the business unit than other potential owners of the business (see section 7.4). A corporate parent that does not have parenting advantage should divest the business for the best price it can obtain. Corporate parents are often reluctant to divest businesses, seeing it as an admission of failure. However, a dynamic perspective on M&A would encourage managers to view divestures positively. Funds raised by the sale of an ill-fitting business can be used either to invest in retained businesses or to buy other businesses that fit the corporate strategy better. Obtaining a good price for the divested unit can recoup any losses it may have originally made. Sometimes, however, a less positive reason for divesture is pressure from competition authorities, which may force the sale of businesses to reduce companies' market power. For example, in 2007 the European Commission obliged Tui, the powerful German tour operator, to sell its Irish tour business Budget Travel in order to increase competition in the fast-consolidating European tourism industry.

Acquisitions, therefore, are an important method for pursuing strategies. However, they are not easy to carry out and they are sometimes adopted for misguided reasons. It is important to consider the alternative of strategic alliances.

(10.4) STRATEGIC ALLIANCES

KEY
CONCEPT

Strategic
alliances

Mergers and acquisitions bring together companies through complete changes in ownership. However, companies also often work together in strategic alliances that involve only partial changes in ownership, or no ownership changes at all. The companies remain distinct. Thus a **strategic alliance is where two or more organisations share resources and activities to pursue a strategy**. This is a common method in strategy: Andersen Consulting has estimated that the average large corporation is managing around 30 alliances.[16]

Alliance strategy challenges the traditional organisation-centred approach to strategy in at least two ways. First, practitioners of alliance strategy need to think about strategy in terms of the collective success of their networks as well as their individual organisations' self-interest.[17] **Collective strategy is about how the whole network of alliances of which an organisation is a member competes against rival networks of alliances.** Thus for Microsoft, competitive success for its Xbox games console relies heavily on the collective strength of its network of independent games developers such as Bungie Studios (makers of Halo), Bizarre Creations (Project Gotham Racing) and Team Ninja (Dead or Alive). Part of Microsoft's strategy must include having a stronger network of games developers than its rivals such as Sony and Nintendo. Collective strategy also challenges the individualistic approach to strategy by highlighting the importance of effective collaboration. Thus success involves collaborating as well as competing. **Collaborative advantage is about managing alliances better than competitors**.[18] Microsoft needs not only to have a stronger network than rivals such as Sony and Nintendo. If it wants to maximise the value of the Xbox, Microsoft must be better at working with its network in order to ensure that its members keep on producing the best games. The more effectively it collaborates, the more successful it will be. Illustration 10.3 describes Apple's approach to collective strategy and collaboration for the iPod.

ILLUSTRATION 10.3

Apple's iPod network

Does Apple manage its network of collaborators well?

By 2009, Apple had sold 200 million iPods. But this success was not Apple's alone. And Apple's relationship with its network of subcontractors and licensees was controversial.

When Apple had first launched the iPod in 2001, it needed help. The iPod combines different kinds of technologies in a uniquely small format. Apple relied substantially on external component suppliers. For example, the fifth generation iPod hard-drive – accounting for about half the total components costs – was sourced from Toshiba in Japan. The multimedia processor came from American Broadcom. The mobile memory came from the Korean Samsung. The lithium battery was Sony's. Assembly was carried out in Taiwan. The success of the iPod attracted a swarm of companies into the iPod accessory market, with companies such as Griffin from the United States and Logitech from Switzerland supplying attractive add-ons such as docking stations, cases and speakers.

Apple is at the heart, therefore, of a network spanning many companies across the world. However, the company has always been protective of its intellectual property. During the 1980s, Apple had tightly controlled the licensing of its Macintosh computer operating system, restricting independent companies from creating compatible software applications for the mass market. Meanwhile, Microsoft had opened up its operating systems, allowing a flood of independent applications that had helped give it dominance of the market.

Apple somewhat modified its strategy for the iPod. Initially the iPod was a completely closed system that worked only with the Macintosh and iTunes music warehouse. Gradually it allowed other audio file formats to be played on the system, but by 2009 Apple was still resisting Microsoft's WMA format. The company licensed none of its hardware, ensuring control of its production and maintenance of its premium pricing policy. It was impossible for any independent company to manufacture cheap iPods, in the way for instance Taiwanese manufacturers had produced cheap IBM/Microsoft-compatible personal computers during the 1980s. However, the company did license to accessory-producers the technology needed to access iPod ports. Apple benefited from royalties from its licensees, as well as the development of attractive complementary products. But the relationship with accessory-producers was arm's-length, with no information about new iPod products released ahead. A spokesman at accessory-producer Griffin commented: 'It's very much a hands-off relationship. We do not know what [new product] is coming down the pipe ahead of time.'

Apple's strategy seems to be paying off. Microsoft's rival music-player, the Zune, has been a comparative failure. However, Apple's position at the heart of a network can be seen another way: it is also surrounded by some powerful players. For example, Sony is a supplier of lithium batteries. Sony builds iPod accessories such as car adaptors and boomboxes. Sony Music supplies its artists, such as Leona Lewis and Michael Jackson, via the iTunes site. And finally, of course, Sony has its own MP3 music-player, the Walkman, plus its own media download site, mystore (see also Figure 2.3).

Sources: M. Cusumano, 'The Puzzle of Apple', *Communications of the ACM*, vol. 51, no. 9 (2008), pp. 22–4; G. Linden, K. Kraemer, and J. Dedrick, 'Who Captures Value in a Global Innovation Network? Apple's iPod', *Communications of the ACM,* vol. 52, no. 3 (2009), pp. 140–5; P. Taylor, 'iPod ecosystem offers rich pickings', *Financial Times*, 25 January 2006, p. 15.

Questions

1 What are pros and cons of Apple's tight control of licensing?

2 What are the pros and cons of maintaining a 'hands-off' relationship with accessory-producers such as Griffin?

10.4.1 Types of strategic alliance

In terms of ownership, there are two main kinds of strategic alliance:

- *Equity alliances* involve the creation of a new entity that is owned separately by the partners involved. The most common form of equity alliance is the *joint venture*, where two organisations remain independent but set up a new organisation jointly owned by the parents. For example, General Motors and Toyota have operated the NUMMI joint venture since 1984, producing cars from both companies in the same plant in California. A *consortium alliance* involves several partners setting up a venture together. For example, IBM, Hewlett-Packard, Toshiba and Samsung are partners in the Sematech research consortium, working together on the latest semiconductor technologies.

- *Non-equity alliances* are typically looser, without the commitment implied by ownership. Non-equity alliances are often based on contracts. One common form of contractual alliance is *franchising*, where one organisation (the franchisor) gives another organisation (the franchisee) the right to sell the franchisor's products or services in a particular location in return for a fee or royalty. Kall-Kwik printing, 7-Eleven convenience stores and McDonald's restaurants are examples of franchising. *Licensing* is a similar kind of contractual alliance, allowing partners to use intellectual property such as patents or brands in return for a fee. *Long-term subcontracting* agreements are another form of loose non-equity alliance, common in automobile supply. For example, the Canadian subcontractor Magna has long-term contracts to assemble the bodies and frames for car companies such as Ford, Honda and Mercedes.

The public and voluntary sectors often get involved in both equity and non-equity strategic alliances. Governments have increasingly encouraged the public sector to contract out the building and maintenance of capital projects such as hospitals and schools under long-term contracts. Individual public organisations often band together to form purchasing consortia as well. A good example of this is university libraries, which typically negotiate collectively for the purchase of journals and books from publishers. Voluntary organisations pool their resources in alliance too. For example, relief organisations in areas suffering from natural or man-made disasters typically have to cooperate in order to deliver the full range of services in difficult circumstances. Although public- and voluntary-sector organisations might often be seen as more naturally cooperative than private-sector organisations, many of the issues that follow apply to all three kinds of organisation.

10.4.2 Motives for alliances

The definition of strategic alliances puts the stress on sharing, of resources or activities. Although sharing is the key motivator for most alliances, there may be less obvious reasons as well. Four broad rationales for alliances can be identified, as summarised in Figure 10.3:

- *Scale alliances.* Here organisations combine in order to achieve necessary scale. The capabilities of each partner may be quite similar (as indicated by the similarity of the A and B organisations in Figure 10.3), but together they can achieve advantages that they could not easily manage on their own. Thus combining together can provide economies of scale in the production of *outputs* (products or services). Combining might also provide economies of scale in terms of *inputs*, for example by reducing purchasing costs of raw materials or

Figure 10.3 Strategic alliance motives

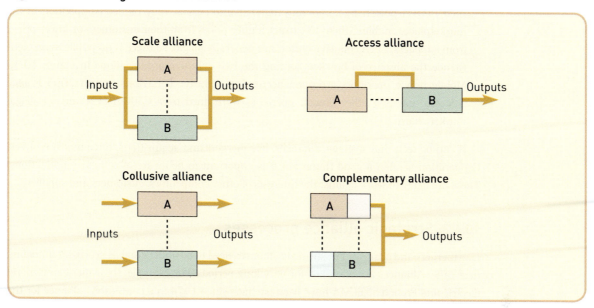

services. Thus health management organisations often combine together to negotiate better prices with pharmaceutical companies. Finally, combining allows the partners to *share risk* as well. Instead of organisations stretching themselves to find enough resources on their own, partnering can help each partner avoid committing so many resources of its own that failure would jeopardise the existence of the whole organisation.

- *Access alliances*. Organisations frequently ally in order to access the capabilities of another organisation that are required in order to produce or sell its products and services. For example, in countries such as China and India, a Western company (in Figure 10.3, organisation A) might need to partner with a local distributor (organisation B) in order to access effectively the national market for its products and services. Here organisation B is critical to organisation A's ability to sell. Access alliances can work in the opposite direction. Thus organisation B might seek a licensing alliance in order to access inputs from organisation A, for example technologies or brands. Here organisation A is critical to organisation B's ability to produce or market its products and services. Access can be about not only tangible resources such as distribution channels or products, but also about intangible resources such as knowledge.

- *Complementary alliances*. These can be seen as a form of access alliance, but involve organisations at similar points in the value network combining their distinctive resources so that they bolster each partner's particular gaps or weaknesses. Figure 10.3 shows an alliance where the strengths of organisation A (indicated by the darker shading) match the weaknesses of organisation B (indicated by the lighter shading); conversely, the strengths of organisation B match the weaknesses of organisation A. By partnering, the two organisations can bring together complementary strengths in order to overcome their individual weaknesses. An example of this is the General Motors–Toyota NUMMI alliance: here the complementarity lies in General Motors getting access to the Japanese car company's manufacturing expertise, while Toyota obtains the American car company's local marketing knowledge.

- *Collusive alliances.* Occasionally organisations secretly collude together in order to increase their market power. By combining together into cartels, they reduce competition in the marketplace, enabling them to extract higher prices from their customers or lower prices from suppliers. Such collusive cartels are generally illegal, so there is no public agreement (hence the absence of brackets joining the two collusive organisations in Figure 10.3). Mobile phone operators are often accused of collusive behaviour and in 2005 France Telecom and two other French operators were fined over €500m ($700m) for illegal market-sharing.

It can be seen that strategic alliances, like mergers and acquisitions, have mixed motives. Cooperation is often a good thing, but it is important to be aware of collusive motivations. These are likely to work against the interests of other competitors, customers and suppliers.

10.4.3 Strategic alliance processes

Like mergers and acquisitions, strategic alliances need to be understood as processes unfolding over time. Alliances are often last for very long periods. For example, the American General Electric and French SNECMA have been partners since 1974 in a continuous alliance for the development and production of small aero-engines. The needs and capabilities of the partners in a long-standing alliance such as this are bound to change over time. However, the absence of full ownership means that emerging differences cannot simply be reconciled by managerial authority; they have to be negotiated between independent partners. This lack of control by one side or the other means that the managerial processes in alliances are particularly demanding. The management challenges, moreover, will change over time.

The fact that neither partner is in control, while alliances must typically be managed over time, highlights the importance of two themes in the various stages of the alliance process:

- *Co-evolution.* Rather than thinking of strategic alliances as fixed at a particular point of time, they are better seen as co-evolutionary processes.[19] The concept of co-evolution underlines the way in which partners, strategies, capabilities and environments are constantly changing. As they change, they need realignment so that they can evolve in harmony. A co-evolutionary perspective on alliances therefore places the emphasis on flexibility and change. At completion, an alliance is unlikely to be the same as envisaged at the start.

- *Trust.* Given the probable co-evolutionary nature of alliances, and the lack of control of one partner over the other, trust becomes highly important to the success of alliances over time.[20] All future possibilities cannot be specified in the initial alliance contract. Each partner will have made investments that are vulnerable to the selfish behaviour of the other. This implies the need for partners to behave in a trustworthy fashion through the whole lifetime of the alliance. Trust in a relationship is something that has to be continuously earned. Trust is often particularly fragile in alliances between the public and private sectors, where the profit motive is suspect on one side, and sudden shifts in political agendas are feared on the other.

Oxfam's partnership principles explicitly address issues of co-evolution and trust: see Illustration 10.4.

The themes of trust and co-evolution surface in various ways at different stages in the lifespan of a strategic alliance. Figure 10.4 provides a simple stage model of strategic alliance

ILLUSTRATION 10.4

Oxfam's partnership principles: co-evolution and trust

Oxfam, an international non-governmental organisation dedicated to the overcoming of poverty, has developed principles that are relevant to private-sector alliances too.

Founded in 1942 as the Oxford Committee for Famine Relief, Oxfam was originally intended to help civilians in Nazi-occupied Europe suffering from starvation. By 2009, it was working against poverty in more than 70 countries, drawing on 3000 local partnerships. These partnerships vary in nature. In some, the local partner is essentially a sub-contractor, spending funds provided by Oxfam on an agreed programme. Other partnerships are more in the nature of joint ventures. For example, in Senegal, Oxfam has established and works with a network of six community agricultural organisations on a long-term basis to help small local farmers get access to markets for their rice.

Oxfam's reliance on local partners has led it to define five principles of partnership:

1. *Complementary purpose and added value.* Here Oxfam commits itself to partnerships that add value to its objectives of empowering and benefiting the poor. At the same time, it recognises that both sides have their own distinct capacities and resources and that each partner should be explicit about these different contributions and limitations.
2. *Mutual respect for values and beliefs.* By this Oxfam insists that partners should have common ground in terms of shared values and beliefs, while respecting differences.

3. *Clarity about roles, responsibilities and decision-making.* Oxfam believes that effective relationships rely upon good communication, reliability and agreed decision-processes. Partners should celebrate their successes and be committed to learning together from their failures.
4. *Transparency and accountability.* Oxfam recognises it should be accountable to its partners, but at the same time underlines that both it and its partners are ultimately accountable to the people and communities for whom they work.
5. *Commitment and flexibility.* Oxfam looks for long-term partnerships. Recognising that it may not be a permanent donor, it promises to be open about its funding plans and to help partners build their capacity to raise funds from other sources.

Source: www.oxfam.org/uk/resources.

Questions

1 How does Oxfam approach the issues of co-evolution and trust in its alliances?
2 To what extent do Oxfam's principles apply to private-sector business, and how might they be adapted to increase their relevance?

evolution. The amount of committed resources changes at each stage, but issues of trust and co-evolution recur throughout:

● *Courtship.* First there is the initial process of courting potential partners, where the main resource commitment is managerial time. This courtship process should not be rushed, as the willingness of both partners is required. Similar criteria apply to alliances at this stage as to acquisitions. Each partner has to see a strategic fit, according to the rationales in section 10.3.2. Equally, each partner has to see an organisational fit. Organisational fit can be considered as for acquisitions (section 10.3.4). However, because alliances do not entail the same degree of control as acquisitions, mutual trust between partners will need to be particularly strong right from the outset.

Figure 10.4 Alliance evolution

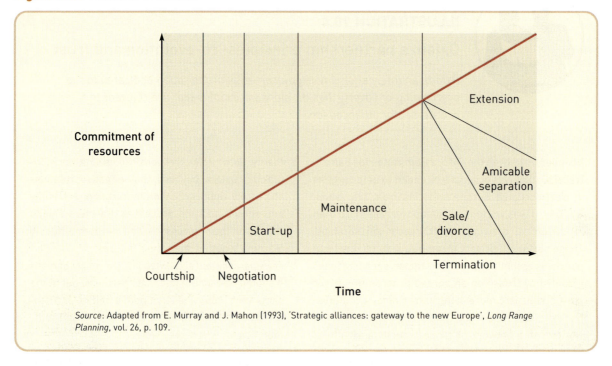

Source: Adapted from E. Murray and J. Mahon (1993), 'Strategic alliances: gateway to the new Europe', *Long Range Planning*, vol. 26, p. 109.

● *Negotiation.* Partners need of course to negotiate carefully their mutual roles at the outset. In equity alliances, the partners also have to negotiate the proportion of ownership each will have in the final joint venture. Again there is likely to be a significant commitment of managerial time at this stage, as it is important to get initial contracts clear and correct. In the case of the Areva–Siemens joint venture (Illustration 10.5), Siemens regretted the low share that it originally agreed. Although the negotiation of ownership proportions in a joint venture is similar to the valuation process in acquisitions, strategic alliance contracts generally involve a great deal more. Key behaviours required of each partner need to be specified upfront. However, a ruthless negotiation style can also damage trust going forward. Moreover, co-evolution implies the need to anticipate change. In an acquired unit, it is possible to make adjustments simply by managerial authority. In alliances, initial contracts may be considered binding even when starting conditions have changed. It is wise to include an option for renegotiating initial terms right at the outset.

● *Start-up.* Start-up is the next stage, with considerable investment of material and human resources normally involved. Trust is very important at this stage. First, the initial operation of the alliance puts the original alliance agreements to the test. Informal adjustments to working realities are likely to be required. Also, people from outside the original negotiation team are typically now obliged to work together on a day-to-day basis. They may not have the same understanding of the alliance as those who initiated it. Without the mutual trust to make adjustments and smooth misunderstandings, the alliance is liable to break up. This early period in an alliance's evolution is the one with the highest rate of failure.

● *Maintenance.* This refers to the ongoing operation of the strategic alliance, with increasing resources likely to be committed. The lesson of co-evolution is that alliance maintenance is not a simple matter of stability. Alliances have to be actively managed to allow for changing external circumstances. The internal dynamics of the partnership are likely to evolve as

ILLUSTRATION 10.5

Nuclear fission: Areva and Siemens break up

Co-evolution is not easy, as two leading French and German companies discover.

In 2001, Siemens, the German industrial conglomerate, and Areva, the French nuclear industry giant, merged their nuclear reactor businesses into a new joint venture called Areva NP. The joint venture was 34 per cent owned by Siemens, 66 per cent owned by Areva. As the German government had promised to exit nuclear power altogether for environmental reasons, Siemens no longer saw nuclear power as central to its strategy. The joint venture agreement gave the French a right-to-buy option for the Siemens minority stake.

In 2009, the new Siemens CEO, Peter Löscher, sent Areva's CEO Ann Lauvergeon a short email announcing that the Germans would be exercising their right to sell their stake to the French. The email took Madame Lauvergeon completely by surprise: 'It made me think of those men who abandon their wives by leaving a note on the kitchen table'. What had gone wrong in the eight years? Areva NP had been a success. It was the global leader in a market for nuclear reactors that was booming again. Rising oil prices and alarm over global warming made nuclear power increasingly attractive. By 2009, after many years of minimal construction, 51 plants were being built around the world, with 171 more planned. Areva NP was active not only in Europe but in the United States and China.

The recovery of the nuclear industry was in fact one source of the problem: with a new CEO, Siemens wanted back in. Siemens was frustrated by its lack of control as a minority shareholder, and by the slow decision-making in Areva NP generally. Moreover, it wanted to get a larger slice of the business than just the nuclear reactors – the big profits were elsewhere in the value chain, in fuel and recycling. Areva, the French parent company, already had a significant presence through the whole value chain.

During 2007, Siemens looked either to increase its stake in Areva NP to 50:50 or to take a direct stake in the French parent, Areva. But, more than 80 per cent

owned by the French government, Areva was not easily for sale. Moreover, Nicolas Sarkozy, then a senior French government minister and soon French President, told German Chancellor Angela Merkel that France could not tolerate a role for Siemens while the German government refused to back nuclear power in its own country. Siemens had to enrol Merkel's support to prevent Areva from exercising its right-to-buy option and forcing Siemens to sell.

In late 2008, Siemens began talks with the Russian nuclear power giant Rosatom. Rosatom had a presence through the whole value chain, including the highly profitable fuel business. With memories of the Soviet nuclear disaster at Chernobyl still live, Rosatom needed Siemens' high reputation for quality. In March 2009, Siemens and Rosatom announced a joint venture with the ambition of displacing Areva NP as world leader.

Ending the Areva NP joint venture was not simple, however. Siemens' strength was in hardware, but Areva owned the software that made it work. Areva was obliged to buy Siemens' stake (~€4bn; ~$5.6bn), but lacked the funds to do so. Also, the original joint venture agreement had included a non-compete clause in case of break-down. So far as Areva was concerned, Siemens' new joint venture put it in breach of the contract, and so not entitled to the full value of its stake. And the two companies were still working together on various nuclear power stations. Indeed, Areva and Siemens were being jointly sued for €2bn for cost and time over-runs on a project in Finland. It was going to be a messy divorce.

Sources: L'Expansion, 1 April 2009; Financial Times, 28 April 2009.

Question

In what respects did co-evolution break down in the Areva NP joint venture?

well as the partners build experience. Here again trust is extremely important. Gary Hamel has warned that alliances often become *competitions for competence*.[21] Because partners are interacting closely, they can begin to learn each other's particular competences. This learning can develop into a competition for competence, with the partner that learns the fastest becoming the more powerful. The more powerful partner may consequently be able to renegotiate the terms in its favour or even break up the alliance and go it alone. If on the other hand the partners wish to maintain their strategic alliance, trustworthy behaviour that does not threaten the other partner's competence is essential to maintaining the cooperative relationships necessary for the day-to-day working of the alliance.

- *Termination.* Eventually, there will be some kind of *termination* of the alliance. Often an alliance will have had an agreed time span or purpose right from the start, so termination is a matter of completion rather than failure. Here separation is amicable. Sometimes the alliance has been so successful that the partners will wish to extend the alliance by agreeing a new alliance between themselves, committing still more resources. Sometimes too the alliance will have been a success in another sense, with one partner wishing to buy the other's share in order to commit fully to a particular market, while the other partner is happy to sell. The sale of one half of a joint venture need not be a sign of failure. However, occasionally alliances end in bitter divorces, as when Areva threatened to take Siemens to court (see Illustration 10.5). Termination needs to be managed carefully, therefore. Co-evolution implies that mutual trust is likely to be valuable after the completion of any particular partnership. Partners may be engaged in several different joint projects at the same time. For example, Cisco and IBM are partners on multiple simultaneous projects in wireless communications, IT security, data centres and data storage. The partners may need to come together again for new projects in the future. Thus Nokia, Ericsson and Siemens have had mobile telephone technology joint projects since the mid-1990s. Maintaining mutual trust in the termination stage is vital if partners are to co-evolve through generations of multiple projects.

(10.5) COMPARING ACQUISITIONS, ALLIANCES AND ORGANIC DEVELOPMENT

It will be clear so far that all three methods of M&A, strategic alliances and organic development have their own advantages and disadvantages. There are also some similarities. This section first considers criteria for choosing between the three methods, and then draws together some key success factors for M&A and alliances.

10.5.1 Buy, ally or DIY?

Acquisitions and strategic alliances have high failure rates. As in the Key Debate at the end of this chapter, acquisitions are thought to fail about half the time. Acquisitions can go wrong because of excessive initial valuations, exaggerated expectations of strategic fit, underestimated problems of organisational fit and all the other issues pointed to in this chapter. But strategic alliances too have roughly 50 per cent failure rates.[22] Alliances also suffer from miscalculations in terms of strategic and organisational fit, but, given the lack of control on either side, have their own particular issues of trust and co-evolution as well. With these high failure rates, acquisitions and alliances need to be considered cautiously alongside the default option of organic development (Do-It-Yourself).

Figure 10.5 Buy, ally or DIY matrix

	Buy	Ally	DIY
High urgency	Fast	Fast	Slow
High uncertainty	Failures potentially saleable	Share losses and retain buy option	Failures likely unsaleable
Soft capabilities important	Culture and valuation problems	Culture and control problems	Cultural consistency
Highly modular capabilities	Problem of buying whole company	Ally just with relevant partner unit	Develop in new venture unit

The best approach will differ according to circumstances. Figure 10.5 presents a 'buy, ally or DIY' matrix summarising four key factors that can help in choosing between acquisitions, alliances and organic development:[23]

- *Urgency.* Acquisitions can be a relatively short-cut method for pursuing a strategy. It would probably take decades for Tata to build up on its own two international luxury car brands equivalent to Jaguar and Land Rover (Illustration 10.2). Tata's purchase of the two brands gave an immediate kick-start to its strategy. Alliances too may accelerate the strategy by accessing additional resources or skills, though usually less quickly than a simple acquisition. Typically organic development (DIY) is slowest: everything has to be made from scratch.

- *Uncertainty.* It is often better to choose the alliance route where there is high uncertainty in terms of the markets or technologies involved. On the upside, if the markets or technologies turn out to be a success, it might be possible to turn the alliance into a full acquisition, especially if a buy option has been included in the initial alliance contract. If the venture turns out a failure, then at least the loss is shared with the alliance partner. Acquisitions also have merit if things do not turn out well: acquired units can usually be resold, even if at a lower price than the original purchase. On the other hand, a failed organic development might have to be written off entirely, with no sale value, because the business unit involved has never been on the market beforehand.

- *Type of capabilities.* Acquisitions work best when the desired capabilities (resources or competences) are 'hard', for example physical investments in manufacturing facilities. Hard resources such as factories are easier to put a value on in the bidding process than 'soft' resources such as people or brands. Hard resources are also typically easier to control post-acquisition than people and skills. As with the Roche takeover of Genentech (see Illustration 10.1), acquisitions pose the risk of significant cultural problems. Sometimes too the acquiring company's own image can tarnish the brand image of the target company. Acquisition of soft resources and competences should be approached with great caution. Indeed, the DIY organic method is typically the most effective with sensitive soft capabilities such as people. Internal ventures are likely to be culturally consistent at least. Even alliances can involve culture clashes between people from the two sides, and it is harder to control an alliance partner than an acquired unit.

● *Modularity of capabilities.* If the sought-after capabilities are highly *modular*, in other words they are distributed in clearly distinct sections or divisions of the proposed partners, then an alliance tends to make sense. A joint venture linking just the relevant sections of each partner can be formed, leaving each to run the rest of its businesses independently. There is no need to buy the whole of the other organisation. An acquisition can be problematic if it means buying the whole company, not just the modules that the acquirer is interested in. The DIY organic method can also be effective under conditions of modularity, as the new business can be developed under the umbrella of a distinct 'new venture division' (see section 9.5.2), rather than embroiling the whole organisation.

Of course, the choice between the three options of buy, ally and DIY is not unconstrained. Frequently there are no suitable acquisition targets or alliance partners available. One problem for voluntary organisations and charities is that the changes of ownership involved in mergers and acquisitions are much harder to achieve than in the private sector, so that their options are likely to be restricted to alliances or organic development in any case. The key message of Figure 10.5 remains nonetheless: it is important to weigh up the available options systematically and to avoid favouring one or the other without careful analysis.

10.5.2 Key success factors

Figure 10.5 indicates that, despite high failure rates, M&A and strategic alliances can still be the best option in certain circumstances. The question then is how to manage M&A and alliances as effectively as possible. Figure 10.6 provides a summary checklist of key factors, stemming from the discussion so far in this chapter. Many of the factors are similar across both M&A and alliances, but there are differences as well.

Naturally, *strategic fit* is critical in both M&A and alliances. The target or the partner should suit the desired strategy. As in section 10.3.4, it is very easy to overestimate synergies – and neglect negative synergies – in alliances as well as M&A. However, *organisational fit* is vital as well, in both cases. In particular, cultural differences are hard to manage, especially where people resources are important. Because of the lack of control, organisational fit issues are liable to be even harder to manage in alliances than in acquisitions, where the ownership rights of the buyer at least provide some managerial authority. *Valuation* likewise is a crucial issue in both M&A and alliances, especially equity alliances. Acquisitions are liable to the 'winner's curse' (section 10.3.4) of excessive valuation, particularly where there have been bid battles between competitors. But even alliance partners need to assess their relative contributions accurately in order to ensure that they do not commit too many resources with too little return and too little control.

However, M&A and alliances each raise some very distinct issues to manage. At the start of the process, alliances rely on courtship between willing partners, whereas that need not be the same for M&A. Mergers do require mutual willingness of course, but, if negotiations go poorly,

Figure 10.6 Key success factors in mergers, acquisitions and alliances

	M&A	Alliances
Similar	Strategic fit Organisational fit Valuation	Strategic fit Organisational fit Valuation
Different	Hostile option Integration Divesture	Courtship Co-evolution Termination

there often remains the option of the *hostile takeover* bid. The process of a hostile bid is princi-pally about persuading shareholders rather than talking with the target's managers. In M&A, a crucial issue is the right approach to *integration*: absorption, preservation or symbiosis. In strategic alliances, the option to fully integrate the two partners into a single whole does not exist. Rather the task is the continued maintenance of a partnership between independent organisations which must *co-evolve*. Finally, *divesture* of acquired units and the *termination* of alliances tend to differ. Divestures are typically one-off transactions with purchasers, with few consequences for future relationships. On the other hand, the way in which alliances are terminated may have repercussions for important future relationships, as new projects and simultaneous projects often involve the same partners. In sum, it can be seen that the neces-sity for courtship, co-evolution and sensitive termination frequently makes the strategic alliance process a much more delicate one than simple acquisition.

SUMMARY

- There are three broad *methods* for pursuing strategy: *mergers and acquisitions*, *strategic alliances* and *organic development*.

- Organic development can be either continuous or radical. Radical organic development is termed *corporate entrepreneurship*.

- Acquisitions can be *hostile* or *friendly*. Motives for mergers and acquisitions can be *strategic*, *financial* or *managerial*.

- The acquisition process includes *target choice*, *valuation* and *integration*.

- Strategic alliances can be *equity* or *non-equity*. Key motives for strategic alliances include *scale*, *access*, *complementarity* and *collusion*.

- The strategic alliance process relies on *co-evolution* and *trust*.

- The choice between acquisition, alliance and organic methods is influenced by four key factors: *urgency*, *uncertainty*, *type of capabilities* and *modularity of capabilities*.

KEY DEBATE

Merger madness?

Mergers and acquisitions involve huge sums of money, but how wisely is it being spent?

This chapter has introduced the importance of mergers and acquisitions as a method of development, but also pointed to some challenges. There have been some spectacular failures. When in 2001 media company Time Warner merged with Internet company AOL, Time Warner shares were worth a total of $90bn (€63bn). Just under three years later, Time Warner investors' holdings in the merged company were worth only $36bn, a loss of over $50bn (in the same period, media companies' valuations had fallen on average 16 per cent).

Harvard Business School professor Michael Porter has been a prominent sceptic of mergers and acquisitions, noting that half of all acquired companies are sold off again within a few years.[1] The figure shows the aggregate dollar return (that is, the change in stock price associated with the acquisition announcement) of acquiring companies in the USA between 1996 and 2001.[2] In 2000, acquiring firms' shareholders lost, in all, more than $150bn. The authors of this study calculate that in the whole period of 1991 to 2001, acquiring firms' shareholders lost more than $7 for every $100 spent on acquisitions.

One interpretation of these large losses is that mergers and acquisitions represent a reckless waste of money by managers who are careless of investors' interests. Indeed there is evidence that CEOs suffer the consequences, over half being replaced within a relatively short time period.[3] It might be appropriate therefore to make mergers and acquisitions more difficult by legislating to help target companies resist or refuse hostile bids. If the law restricted hostile bids, wasteful acquisitions could be cut.

There are drawbacks to restricting mergers and acquisitions, however.[4] Even if acquiring companies often fail to make money for their shareholders, they can improve the profitability of the system as a whole in at least two ways:

● The threat of being taken over if they do not satisfy their shareholders helps keep managers focused on performance. The financial press reports just such threats regularly.
● Mergers and acquisitions can be an effective way of restructuring stagnant firms and industries. The absence of hostile takeovers in Japan is often blamed for the slow restructuring of Japanese industry since the early 1990s.

Aggregate dollar return (US $billion)

References:
1. M. Porter, 'From competitive advantage to corporate strategy', *Harvard Business Review*, May–June (1987), pp. 43–60.
2. S.B. Moeller, F.P. Schlingemann and R.M. Stulz, 'Wealth destruction on a massive scale? A study of acquiring firm returns in the recent merger wave', *Journal of Finance*, vol. 60, no. 2 (2005), pp. 757–82.
3. K.M. Lehn and M. Zhao, 'CEO turnover after acquisitions: are bad bidders fired?', *Journal of Finance*, vol. LXI, no. 4 (2006), pp. 1759–810.
4. 'Hostile bids are back again: who should rejoice?', *The Economist*, 21 February 2004.

Questions

1 For a recent large merger or acquisition, track the share prices of the companies involved (using www.bigcharts.com, for instance), for several weeks both before and after the announcement. What do the share price movements suggest about the merits of the deal?

2 Identify a hostile takeover threat from press reports. What action did the company's management do to resist the takeover?

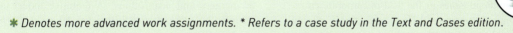

WORK ASSIGNMENTS

✱ *Denotes more advanced work assignments.* * *Refers to a case study in the Text and Cases edition.*

10.1 Write a short (about ten lines) statement to a chief executive who has asked you to advise whether or not the company should develop through M&A. Write a similar statement to a chief executive of a hospital who is considering possible mergers with other hospitals.

10.2✱ For a recently announced acquisition, track the share prices (using www.bigcharts.com for example) of both the acquiring firm and the target firm in the period surrounding the bid? What do you conclude from the behaviour of the share prices about how investors regard the bid. Which company's investors are likely to benefit more?

10.3✱ Compare the M&A integration processes in the case studies Ferrovial* and Mergers in Education*. What do you conclude about effective and less effective practice?

10.4✱ Critically evaluate the proposition that alliance strategy is ethically superior to competitive strategy because it involves cooperation and the mutual creation of value.

10.5 Explain why family-owned companies might prefer organic development to either alliance or acquisitions.

Integrative assignment

10.6✱ Systematically compare the advantages of corporate entrepreneurship with independent entrepreneurship (section 9.5). What are the skills and personality characteristics the independent entrepreneurs and corporate entrepreneurs need most, and how do they differ between the two types of entrepreneur?

VIDEO ASSIGNMENT

Visit *MyStrategyLab* and watch the *Prêt-à-Manger* case study.

1 Assess the motives for McDonald's acquisition of a stake in Prêt-à-Manger (section 10.3.3) and assess the strategic and organisational fit (section 10.3.4).

2 In terms of the Haspeslagh and Jemison integration model (section 10.3.4), how *did* McDonald's approach integration and how *should* it have approached integration?

RECOMMENDED KEY READINGS

- A comprehensive book on mergers and acquisitions is: P. Gaughan, *Mergers, Acquisitions and Corporate Restructurings*, 4th edition, Wiley, 2007. For some alternative perspectives, see the collection by D. Angwin (ed.), *Mergers and Acquisitions*, Blackwell, 2007.

- A useful book on strategic alliances is J. Child, D. Faulkner and S. Tallman, *Cooperative Strategy: Managing Alliances, Networks and Joint Ventures*, Oxford University Press, 2005.

REFERENCES

1. P. Sharma and J. Chrisman, 'Towards a reconciliation of the definitional issues in the field of corporate entrepreneurship', *Entrepreneurial Theory and Practice*, Spring 1998, pp. 11–27; D. Garvin and L. Levesque, 'Meeting the challenge of corporate entrepreneurship', *Harvard Business Review*, October 2006, pp. 102–12.

2. Zephyr *Annual Global M&A Report 2009*, Bureau van Dijk, 2010.

3. R. Schoenberg, 'Mergers and acquisitions', in D.O. Faulkner and A. Campbell (eds), *The Oxford Handbook of Strategy: Vol. II*, Oxford University Press, 2005.

4. This adapts J. Bower, 'Not all M&As are alike – and that matters', *Harvard Business Review*, March 2001, pp. 93–101.

5. M. Hayward and D. Hambrick, 'Explaining the premiums paid for large acquisitions: evidence of CEO hubris', *Administrative Science Quarterly*, vol. 42 (1997), pp. 103–27.

6. This builds on D. Jemison and S. Sitkin, 'Corporate acquisitions: a process perspective', *Academy of Management Review*, vol. 11, no. 1 (1986), pp. 145–63.

7. J.M. Shaver, 'A paradox of synergy: contagion and capacity effects in mergers and acquisitions', *Academy of Management Review*, vol. 31, no. 4 (2006), pp. 962–78.

8. See J. Child, D. Faulkner and R. Pitkethly, *The Management of International Acquisitions*, Oxford University Press, 2001.

9. A useful discussion of valuation methods in acquisitions is in Chapter 9 of D. Sadlter, D. Smith and A. Campbell, *Smarter Acquisitions*, Prentice Hall, 2008.

10. N. Varaiya and K. Ferris, 'Overpaying in corporate takeovers: the winner's curse', *Financial Analysts Journal*, vol. 43, no. 3 (1987), pp. 64–70.

11. P. Haspeslagh and D. Jemison, *Managing Acquisitions: Creating Value through Corporate Renewal*, Free Press, 1991; P. Puranam, H. Singh and S. Chaudhuri, 'Integrating acquired capabilities: when structural integration is (un)necessary', *Organization Science*, vol. 20, no. 2 (2009), pp. 313–28.

12. G. Stahl and A. Voigt, 'Do cultural differences matter in mergers and acquisitions? A tentative model and examination', *Organization Science*, vol. 19, no. 1 (2008), pp. 160–78.

13. K. Ellis, T. Reus and B. Lamont, 'The effects of procedural and informational justice in the integration of related acquisitions', *Strategic Management Journal*, vol. 30 (2009), pp. 137–61.

14. R. Uhlaner and A. West, 'Running a winning M&A shop', *McKinsey Quarterly*, March 2008, pp. 106–12.

15. L. Dranikoff, T. Koller and A. Schneider, 'Divesture: strategy's missing link', *Harvard Business Review*, May 2002, pp. 75–83 and M. Brauer, 'What have we acquired and what should we acquire in divesture research? A review and research agenda', *Journal of Management*, vol. 32, no. 6 (2006), pp. 751–85.

16. Andersen Consulting, *Dispelling the Myths of Strategic Alliances*, 1999.

17. R. Bresser, 'Matching collective and competitive strategies', *Strategic Management Journal*, vol. 9, no. 4 (1988), pp. 375–85.

18. J. Dyer, *Collaborative Advantage*, Oxford University Press, 2000.

19. A. Inkpen and S. Curral, 'The coevolution of trust, control, and learning in joint ventures', *Organization Science*, vol. 15, no. 5 (2004), pp. 586–99; R. ul-Huq, *Alliances and Co-evolution in the Banking Sector*, Palgrave, 2005.

20. A. Arino and J. de la Torre, 'Relational quality: managing trust in corporate alliances', *California Management Review*, vol. 44, no. 1 (2001), pp. 109–31.

21. G. Hamel, *Alliance Advantage: the Art of Creating Value through Partnering*, Harvard Business School Press, 1998.

22. Andersen Consulting, *Dispelling the Myths of Strategic Alliances*, 1999.

23. This draws on J. Dyer, P. Kale and H. Singh, 'When to ally and when to acquire?', *Harvard Business Review*, vol. 82, no 7/8 (2004), pp. 108–15, and X. Yin and M. Shanley, 'Industry determinants of the merger versus alliance decision', *Academy of Management Review*, vol. 31, no. 2 (2008), pp. 473–91.

Final Fantasy captures Lara Croft: acquisitions and alliances in electronic games

During 2009, Japanese games maker Square Enix launched a series of radical strategic initiatives. Famous for its role-playing games such as the *Final Fantasy* series, Square Enix established strategic alliances with the strategy games developers Double Helix and Gas Powered Games in the United States and Wargaming.net in the United Kingdom. Most radically, it also acquired the British Eidos Group, famous for the Lara Croft games. Square Enix President Yōichi Wada commented: 'Our goal is to become one of the top ten players in the world's media and entertainment industry. Since the games market is global, both our contact with our customers and our game development must become global too'.

Source: iStockphoto.

The Japanese games industry

Square Enix's strategic moves came at a challenging time for the Japanese games industry. The Japanese had enjoyed two decades of domination built on the worldwide success of Japanese consoles such as the Sony PlayStation. But the growing success of Microsoft's Xbox gave an opportunity to American games developers to return to the console market. Indeed, American games developers found that their development skills were more transferable in the new cross-over markets, where games needed to be developed for PCs, consoles and mobile phones alike. Moreover, the Americans had the advantage of proximity to Hollywood, bringing in new creative talent and offering opportunities for film tie-ins. At the same time, Japan's ageing population was shrinking the market for traditional electronic games.

Square Enix's Yōichi Wada recognised the predicament of the Japanese industry vis-à-vis the Americans:

> In the last five to ten years, the Japanese games industry has become a closed environment, with no new people coming in, no new ideas, almost xenophobic . . . The lag with the US is very clear. The US games industry was not good in the past but it has now attracted people from the computer industry and from Hollywood, which has led to strong growth.[1]

At the same time, the basic economics of the games industry are changing, with rising costs due to growing technological sophistication. A typical modern game can cost from $3,000,000 (about €2,000,000) to over $20,000,000 to develop.[2] Games generally take from one to three years to develop. Yet only one in twenty games is estimated ever to make a profit. In other words, the risks are very high and the necessary scale to compete is rising.

Square Enix's strategy

Square Enix itself is the creation of a merger. Square had been founded in 1983, and in 1987 launched the first of its famous *Final Fantasy* role-playing game series. Enix had been founded in 1975, and launched its role-playing *Dragon Quest* series in 1986. The two companies merged in 2003, after the financial failure of Square's film-venture, *Final Fantasy: the Spirit Within*. Yōichi Wada, President of Square, became the president of the new merged company.

Square Enix's strategy is based on the idea of 'polymorphic content'. Its various franchises (*Final Fantasy*, *Dragon Quest* and so on) are developed for all possible hardware or media rather than any single gaming platform. Square Enix games can be played on consoles, PCs, mobile phones or online, and spin-offs include TV series, films, comics and novels. In 2005,

Square Enix bought the Japanese arcade-game company Taito Corporation, famous for its *Space Invaders* game. *Space Invaders* versions have appeared on PlayStation, Xbox and Wii consoles, as well as PCs.

By 2008, Yōichi Wada was presiding over a company that was increasingly diversified, with sales of ¥136bn (about €1 bn) and just over 3,000 employees. However, it was still overwhelmingly Japanese (85 per cent of sales at home) and lacked scale by comparison with competitors such as Electronic Arts and Activision, respectively four and three times as large. On the plus side, Square Enix was reportedly cash rich, with a 'war-chest' available for acquisitions of about ¥40bn (about €300m).[3] During the summer of 2008, Square Enix made a friendly bid for the Japanese game developer Tecmo, whose fighting games *Ninja Garden* and *Dead or Alive* were popular in North America and Europe. Tecmo rejected the bid. Wada began to look overseas.

Lara Croft falls

Eidos is a British games company best-known for the action-adventure games series, *Tomb Raider*, starring the extraordinary Lara Croft. However, during 2008, disappointing sales for *Tomb Raider: Underworld* drove its share-price down from £5 (~€5.5; ~$7.5) to around 30 pence. Eidos' founder and chief executive, Jane Cavanagh, was forced to resign. The company declared losses of £136m (about €149m), on sales of £119m (down from £179m two years earlier). In April 2009, Square Enix bought the company for £84m (about €92.4m), a premium of 129% over Eidos' current market value. Given the declining success of the *Tomb Raider* franchise, many speculated that Square Enix had overpaid for its first overseas acquisition.

The acquisition of Eidos did offer Square Enix global reach, however. About one third of Eidos' sales were in the United States and 40 per cent in Europe, excluding the United Kingdom. Eidos also brought Square Enix its first studios outside Japan, with studios in the United Kingdom, Denmark, Hungary, the United States, Canada and China. Yōichi Wada commented: 'It is significant that we have opened a window for creative talents worldwide.'

Wada chose to keep Phil Rogers, the new Eidos chief executive, in place, along with the rest of his management team. Wada described a new Group structure, in which Square Enix, the arcade business Taito and Eidos would each be stand-alone divisions: 'Our aim is to implement a hybrid management structure which avoids the extremes of being either too global or too local'.[4] He continued: 'The Group's management and administration departments will be integrated, while our product and service delivery will be established locally in each territory to maximise our business opportunities through better understanding of local customers' tastes and commercial practices.' Wada also recognised the new strength that Eidos brought in action-adventure games, by contrast with Square Enix's traditional core of role-playing games. He declared his commitment both to sharing technologies across the businesses and to sustaining particular strengths: 'While promoting shared technology and expertise amongst our studios, we will also develop products which reflect the unique identity of each studio, regardless of locality.' Wada also commented on the nature of the skilled games developers he was acquiring: 'It is always difficult to manage creatives anywhere in the world. We want to cherish the Eidos studio culture but change it where it is necessary.'[5]

One thing that Square Enix was quick to do was to end the Eidos distribution agreement with Warner Bros for its products in the United States. Square Enix regarded itself as strong enough to do that itself.

Strategic alliances

At the same time as acquiring Eidos, Square Enix cemented three significant strategic alliances. In the United Kingdom, Square Enix tied up with the strategy game developer Wargaming.net (famous for the *Massive Assault* series) in order to produce the World War II game *Order of War*. This would enter the market at the end of 2009 as Square Enix's first global product release. In the United States, Square Enix formed partnerships with Gas Powered Games (producer of the *Supreme Commander* strategy game) and with Double Helix (producer of the *Front Mission* strategy series). Together with the Eidos acquisition, these partnerships significantly extended Square Enix's range beyond its traditional core in role-playing games. They also extended the company's geographical reach. Yōichi Wada commented: 'We see great opportunities in North American and European markets, both of which are expected to be maintaining sustainable growth over these coming years. Therefore it is crucial that we create alliances with proven developers such as Gas Powered Games in order to serve these significant markets better by providing products and services in tune with customer tastes.'[6]

All three of these new partners were relatively small (around 100 employees each), privately-owned and had their origins as start-ups during the 1990s. To take one example, Gas Powered Games had been founded in 1998 by Chris Taylor and colleagues from the games developer Cavedog Entertainment. Chris Taylor had spent his whole career in games, with his first game *Hardball II* released in 1989. In an interview, Chris Taylor explained his motivation for setting up his own company, Gas Powered Games:

> I had that dream really from the day I first walked into my first full time job as a games programmer. I wanted to be the guy running the company. . . . We've created our own original IPs (intellectual properties) consistently. Some are great, some are not so great, but the fact is you have to keep throwing darts at the board. You have to keep trying to make great stuff, and you can't do that if you're inside of a large megalithic corporation to the same degree . . .[7]

Chris Taylor described how Square Enix, traditionally a role-playing company, and Gas Powered Games, more a strategy game developer, were working together on their first venture, *Supreme Commander 2*:

> One of the things that we took as a cue from Square Enix was the way they embrace character and story. We were all into that, so that was easy. When we asked them, 'How should we develop our game to work with their philosophy?', they said, 'Don't do that because we want you to do what you do. You make games for the Western market, and we're interested in making games for the Western market.' So if we changed, we would be missing the point. Which was terrific, because that meant we could do what we loved to do, make great RTS (real-time strategy) games . . . and if we tried to change them in any way, we'd be moving away from the goal.[8]

A games enthusiast's view

In the space of a few months, Square Enix had transformed its profile. From its base in Japanese-style role-playing games, it was developing a significant presence in strategy and action adventure. It had studios across the world. Its various games titles were big across Asia, Europe and America. Games enthusiast Randy commented on a gamers' website:

> Square Enix publishing a western-developed game? Is the far-reaching JRPG (Japanese role-playing game) developer dumping the androgynous boy-heroes and shovel-wide swords for WWII fatigues and M1 Carbines? No, not entirely. But they *are* bringing Wargaming.net into the fold to do it for them. First, Square Enix buys out the house that Lara Croft built, and now they're into real-time strategy war games. *Nothing in this life makes sense anymore.*[9]

References:
1. M. Palmer, 'Square Enix views Eidos as a jump to next level', *Financial Times*, 28 April 2009.
2. 'Cost of making games set to soar', www.bbcnews.co.uk, 17 November 2005.
3. 'Square Enix needs to show growth scenario to market', *Nikkei*, 9 October 2007.
4. Joint interview with Yoichi Wada and Phil Rogers, www.square-enix.com, 26 May 2009.
5. M. Palmer, 'Square Enix views Eidos as a jump to next level', *Financial Times*, 28 April 2009.
6. 'Square Enix and Gas Powered Games announce strategic partnership', *Newswire Association*, 12 November 2008.
7. P. Elliott, 'Foot on the gas', *gamesindustry.biz*, 19 August 2008.
8. X. de Matos, 'Interview: Chris Taylor on Supreme Commander 2', *joystiq.com*, 9 June 2009.
9. Randy, 'Square Enix tries hand at WWI RTS with Order of War', *Gaming Nexus*, 17 April 2009. Italics in original.

Questions

1 Explain why Square Enix chose alliances in some cases and acquisitions in others.
2 How should Square Enix manage its Eidos acquisition in order to maximise value creation, and how might that management approach change over time?
3 What are the strengths and weaknesses of the alliance strategy, and what problems might Square Enix anticipate over time?

COMMENTARY ON PART II

In Part II of the book the central concern is the strategic choices available to organisations. The chapters offer a range of such strategic choices, their rationales and evidence as to why some seem more effective than others. But this raises three linked questions on which the four lenses provide differing insights:

- How do such options get generated?
- What form are they likely to take?
- How should they be dealt with or addressed?

Design lens

High value is placed on extensive information search and analysis of the wide range of factors, both internal and external, that might influence future strategy. So it can be expected that an extensive range of strategic options will be available for managers to consider. These should be justified in terms of an objective assessment of the extent to which they address the strategic issues facing the organisation, in particular how they:

- Meet the goals and objectives of the organisation;
- Address key opportunities and threats arising from the organisation's changing environment and its strategic capabilities;
- Might achieve competitive advantage.

Indeed it is important that managers provide such a convincing rationale since it is unlikely that strategic options will be considered unless they are supported in this way.

Experience lens

Strategy develops incrementally based on past strategy, past experience and the culture of the organisation within a political context. So those strategic options considered are heavily influenced by such factors. Indeed managers may have ready-made solutions on the basis of past experience and search for opportunities and circumstances to put them into effect. The strategies of successful organisations are also likely to be mimicked by others. So managers in different organisations tend to consider similar strategic options. The result is that the strategic options that surface are not likely to be innovative but, rather, build on current strategy.

Analytic tools do not give rise to the strategies under consideration. They may, however, be used as a way of checking why a strategy might be worth considering; or convincing other managers and stakeholders that they should be.

Managers faced with assessing strategic options should seek to understand their origins in terms of the history of organisations, the expectations and biases of managers and other stakeholders who influence strategy development. Challenging the experience bases of such options may not be straightforward. Objective analysis of the viability of strategic options may be disregarded or not taken seriously. It may be important to emphasise more the surfacing and challenging of managers' assumptions underlying the options they advance.

STRATEGIC CHOICES

Note that:

- There is no suggestion here that one of these lenses is better than another, but they do provide different insights into the problems faced and the ways managers cope with the challenge.

- If you have *not* read the Commentary following Chapter 1 which explains the four lenses, you should now do so.

Variety lens

The emphasis here is on the variety of potential ideas throughout an organisation. Given such variety, it is possible that innovative strategic options could originate from anywhere in the organisation rather than be planned from the top. However, the options that do develop are likely to be ill-formed and only partially address the strategic issues facing the organisation.

Managers looking to generate strategic options will:

- Help create an organisational context that encourages open exchange of information, experimentation and trial and error behaviour and discourages a reliance on established ways of doing things;
- Actively seek and encourage ideas and suggestions from people at all levels in the organisation;
- Be prepared to entertain innovative and partially formed ideas rather than rely on well-formed strategic options articulated from the top of the organisation;
- Discern patterns in such ideas and synthesise them into coherent strategies.

Discourse lens

Strategic options surfaced will be based on the discourse of which managers are part or which is in their self-interest. So:

- Strategic options that are favoured or gain most support are likely to be those that fit within the generally accepted discourse on strategy that prevails inside an organisation or in its organisational field/industry; or strategy discourse which is currently fashionable.
- The use of the language of strategy in the advocacy of a strategic option may be one way in which a manager may seek to gain political influence or legitimacy within an organisation.

Managers should therefore exercise a healthy scepticism in relation to the strategic options being advanced. They should understand that *how* a strategy is talked about can be seen as an important influence on *which* strategies are advocated and favoured and which are not. Moreover they should be concerned to probe the personal motivations and self-interest of those advancing them.

PART III

STRATEGY IN ACTION

This part explains:

- Criteria and techniques that can be used to evaluate possible strategic options.

- How strategies develop in organisations; in particular, the processes that may give rise to intended strategies or to emergent strategies.

- The way in which organisational structures and systems of control are important in organising for strategic success.

- The leadership and management of strategic change.

- Who strategists are and what they do in practice.

INTRODUCTION TO PART III

The first two Parts of the book have been concerned with how a strategist can think through the strategic position of an organisation and the strategic choices available to it. In this Part of the book the focus moves to strategy in action. It is concerned with how a strategy actually takes shape in an organisation and what strategists actually do.

The next chapter explains ways in which the strategic choices explained in Part II can be evaluated. In particular it suggests three criteria that can be applied. *Suitability* asks whether a strategy addresses the key issues relating to the opportunities and constraints an organisation faces. *Acceptability* asks whether a strategy meets the expectations of stakeholders. And *feasibility* invites an explicit consideration of whether a strategy could work in practice. In each case tools and techniques of evaluation are provided, explained and illustrated.

Chapter 12 examines two broadly different explanations *of how strategies actually develop* in organisations. Do strategies come about in organisations by first being conceived analytically and then implemented? In other words, do strategies develop on the basis of deliberate intent? Or is strategy more emergent, for example on the basis of people's experience or as a result of responses to competitive action? Or are elements of both explanations evident in organisations? And what are the implications of these different explanations for managing strategy?

Chapter 13 considers the relationship between strategy and how an organisation functions in terms of people working with each other within different *structures and systems*. These may be formally established by management or may be more informal relationships; but they will all affect the organisation's ability to deliver its strategy. The chapter considers how successful organising requires these various elements to work together in order to create mutually reinforcing *configurations* of structures and systems that are matched to an organisation's strategies.

The development of a new strategy may also require significant change for an organisation and this is the theme of Chapter 14. The *leadership of strategic change* is examined, first by acknowledging that managing change is not the same in all organisations; that the change context matters. The chapter then examines different approaches to managing change, including styles of managing change and the variety of levers employed to manage strategic change. The chapter concludes by revisiting the importance of context to consider how different levers might be employed in different change contexts.

This Part of the book then concludes by discussing *what strategists themselves actually do*. It examines three issues in the practice of strategy. First, who are included in strategy-making activities, often not just top management but middle managers, consultants and planners too. Second, the kinds of activities strategists are involved in, from selling strategic issues to communicating chosen strategies. Third, the kinds of methodologies that strategists use, including strategy workshops, projects, hypothesis testing and business planning.

11

EVALUATING STRATEGIES

Learning outcomes

After reading this chapter you should be able to:

● Employ three *success criteria* for evaluating strategic options:

– *Suitability*: whether a strategy addresses the key issues relating to the *opportunities and constraints* an organisation faces.

– *Acceptability:* whether a strategy meets the *expectations* of stakeholders.

– *Feasibility:* whether a strategy could *work in practice*.

● For each of these use a range of different *techniques for evaluating strategic options*, both financial and non-financial.

PEARSON mystrategylab

MyStrategyLab is designed to help you make the most of your studies.

Visit **www.pearsoned.co.uk/mystrategylab** to discover a wide range of resources specific to this chapter, including:

• A personalised **Study plan** that will help you understand core concepts

• **Audio** and **video clips** that put the spotlight on strategy in the real world

• **Online glossaries** and **flashcards** that provide helpful reminders when you're looking for some quick revision.

(11.1) INTRODUCTION

Part II of the book introduced an array of strategic options and choices. The strategist has therefore to decide between these options; to decide what the organisation is actually going to do. This can be a challenge. It is not unusual for managers in a business – or indeed a group of students analysing a case study – to generate a long list of options. How is a decision to be made between them? This chapter and the next explain different ways in which this may occur. In this chapter the focus is on systematic criteria and techniques that can be used to evaluate strategic options against those criteria. It provides tools that managers can use to approach such decisions from a rational design perspective (see the Commentary following Chapter 1). This begs the question, of course, as to how such choices are made in practice; that is the focus of Chapter 12 which follows.

This chapter is structured around three key evaluation criteria (see Table 11.1), summarised by the acronym **SAF**e. They are:

- *Suitability*, which is concerned with assessing which proposed strategies address the key issues relating to the *opportunities and constraints* an organisation faces. To what extent and how does it take advantage of opportunities, build on strengths or overcome threats and weaknesses that may have been identified in understanding the strategic position of the organisation?

- *Acceptability*, which is concerned with whether the expected *performance outcomes* of a proposed strategy meets the *expectations of stakeholders*.

- *Feasibility* is concerned with whether a strategy could *work in practice*; therefore whether an organisation has or can obtain the capabilities to deliver a strategy.

SAFe can be used to assess the viability of strategic options. In effect the criteria pose the question as to why some strategies might succeed better than others. The chapter is therefore about moving towards making a strategy happen. In the rest of the chapter each of the criteria

Table 11.1 The SAFe criteria and techniques of evaluation

Suitability	• Does a proposed strategy address the *key opportunities and constraints* an organisation faces?
Acceptability	• Does a proposed strategy meet the *expectations of stakeholders*? • Is the level of risk acceptable? • Is the likely return acceptable? • Will stakeholders accept the strategy?
Feasibility	• Would a proposed strategy *work in practice?* • Can the strategy be financed? • Do people and their skills exist or can they be obtained? • Can the required resources be obtained and integrated?

is introduced, followed by explanations, with illustrations, of techniques of evaluation and key questions appropriate to each of them.

SUITABILITY

Part I explained how the strategic position of an organisation can be understood in terms of key drivers and expected changes in its *environment* and its *strategic capabilities* in the context of *historical* and *cultural influences*. These factors provide opportunities but also place constraints on the future direction of an organisation. **Suitability** **is concerned with assessing which proposed strategies address the *key opportunities and constraints* an organisation faces** through an understanding of the strategic position of an organisation: it is therefore concerned with the overall *rationale* of a strategy. At the most basic level, the need is to assess the extent to which a proposed strategy:

- Exploits the opportunities in the environment and avoids the threats;
- Capitalises on the organisation's strength and strategic capabilities and avoids or remedies the weaknesses.

So the concepts and frameworks already discussed in Chapters 2 to 5 can be especially helpful in understanding suitability. Some examples are shown in Table 11.2. However, there is an

Table 11.2 Suitability of strategic options in relation to strategic position

Concept	Figure/Table/ Illustration	Helps with understanding	Suitable strategies address (examples)
PESTEL	Ill. 2.1	Key environmental drivers Changes in industry structure	Industry cycles Industry convergence Major environmental changes
Scenarios	Ill. 2.2	Extent of uncertainty/risk Extent to which strategic options are mutually exclusive	Need for contingency plans or 'low-cost probes'
Five forces	Fig. 2.2 Ill. 2.3	Industry attractiveness Competitive forces	Reducing competitive intensity Development of barriers to new entrants
Strategic groups	Fig. 2.8	Attractiveness of groups Mobility barriers Strategic spaces	Need to reposition to a more attractive group or to an available strategic space
Strategic capabilities	Figs 3.2, 3.5 Ill. 3.5	Industry threshold standards Bases of competitive advantage	Eliminating weaknesses Exploiting strengths
Value chain	Figs 3.5, 3.6	Opportunities for vertical integration or outsourcing	Extent of vertical integration or possible outsourcing
Cultural web	Fig. 5.5 Ill. 5.4	The links between organisational culture and the current strategy	The strategic options most aligned with the prevailing culture

Table 11.3 Some examples of suitability

Strategic option	Why this option might be suitable in terms of:	
	Environment	Capability
Directions		
Retrenchment	Withdraw from declining markets Maintain market share	Identify and focus on established strengths
Market penetration	Gain market share for advantage	Exploit superior resources and capabilities
Product development	Exploit knowledge of customer needs	Exploit R&D
Market development	Current markets saturated New opportunities for: geographical spread, entering new segments or new uses	Exploit current products and capabilities
Diversification	Current markets saturated or declining	Exploit strategic capabilities in new arenas
Methods		
Organic development	Partners or acquisitions not available or not suitable	Building on own capabilities Learning and competence development
Merger/acquisition	Speed Supply/demand P/E ratios	Acquire capabilities Scale economies
Joint development	Speed Industry norm Required for market entry	Complementary capabilities Learning from partners

important point to bear in mind. It is likely that a great many issues will have been raised if the concepts and tools discussed in Part I have been employed. It is therefore important that the really important issues are identified from amongst all these. Indeed a major skill of a strategist is to be able to discern these *key strategic issues*. Evaluating the suitability of a strategy is very difficult unless the key strategic issues have been clearly sorted out from the less important issues.

The discussions about possible strategic choices in Part II were concerned not only with understanding what choices might be 'available' to organisations but also providing reasons why each might be considered. So the examples in those sections also illustrate why strategies might be regarded as *suitable*. Table 11.3 summarises these points from earlier sections and provides examples of reasons why strategies might be regarded as suitable. There are, however, also a number of screening techniques that can be used to assess the suitability of proposed strategies by reviewing their relative merits against key opportunities and constraints.

11.2.1 Ranking

Here possible strategies are assessed against key factors relating to the strategic position of the organisation and a score (or ranking) established for each option. Illustration 11.1 gives an

ILLUSTRATION 11.1

Ranking options for SRR Consulting

Ranking can usefully provide an initial view of the suitability of strategic oprions by comparing strategic options against the key strategic factors from the SWOT analysis.

Simon and Ruth were both IT specialists who returned to their companies after completing their MBAs. Raj, a friend of theirs, had been an IT consultant who did the same MBA course a year later. His MBA project looked at the feasibility of setting up an IT consultancy partnership with Simon and Ruth. SRR was established in 2008. Their strategy was initially to build on 'outsourcing' the IT needs of the organisations they worked for. Raj had worked on IT assignments for business start-ups for a consultancy: 'It was not big business for them and they were delighted to have me operate as an associate; in effect outsourcing that work'. Simon worked for a medium-sized local engineering business and Ruth for a retailer with a small chain of local shops. As Simon explained: 'Neither of our employers really needed IT specialists full-time: an outsourced facility made good economic sense.'

Ruth continued: 'Our first year went well. We provided a good service to our previous employers together with developing business with some other contacts. We are both the owners and the consultants of SRR and our overheads are pretty low so we have made a reasonable living. Our problem now is, where from here? We are keen to grow the business, not just because we would like a higher income, but because with our rather limited client base we are vulnerable. We have built on our IT expertise and the sectors we know, but we have reached something of a ceiling with regard to our personal contacts. We can see a number of possible options. There is an opportunity on the management development aspects of IT; how can IT be used to aid better management? Most of our clients don't understand this. Our problem is that we are not trainers so we would need to develop those skills or hire someone who has them. Another option is to actively go out and develop new contacts. The problems here are that it means branching out into sectors unfamiliar to us and that will take our time – which won't be fee earning – so it would reduce our income at least in the short term. Linked to this is the possibility of going for much bigger clients. This might get us bigger fees, perhaps, but it would quite possibly mean competition with some big competitors. In the last year our business has also been very local. We could stick with the same sectors we know but broaden the geographic area. The problem there, of course, is we are not known. Finally we have been approached by another IT consultancy about the possibility of a merger. They operate in complementary sectors and do have training capabilities, but it is bigger than us and I don't know if we are ready to lose our own identity yet.'

Simon, Ruth and Raj had begun a ranking exercise to look at these options as shown below.

Questions

1 Are there other options or factors that you think Simon, Ruth and Raj should consider?

2 How could you improve the ranking analysis?

3 Consider the most favoured options in terms of acceptability and feasibility criteria.

Ranking exercise

Strategic options	Key strategic factors								
	Fit with technical competences	Fit with sector know how	Builds on our known reputation	Increases non fee earning management time	Reached our 'contact ceiling'	Builds on client need	Higher fee income	Increased competition	Ranking
1. Develop new contacts	✓	✗	✓	✗	✓	?	?	?	3–2 (B)
2. Develop bigger clients	✓	?	✗	✗	✓	✗	✓	✗	3–3 (C)
3. Geographic market development	✓	✓	✓	✗	✓	✓	✗	✗	5–3 (B)
4. Develop IT training	✗	✓	✓	✗	✓	✓	✓	✓	6–2 (A)
5. Merger	✓	✓	?	✓	✓	?	?	✓	5–0 (A)

✓ = favourable; ✗ = unfavourable; ? = uncertain or irrelevant.
A = most suitable; B = possible; C = unsuitable.

example. One of the advantages of this approach is that it forces a debate about the implications and impacts of specific key factors on specific strategic proposals. It therefore helps overcome a potential danger in strategy evaluation; namely that managers are likely to interpret the impact of particular factors, or have preferences for proposed strategies, in terms of their own subjectivity.

More sophisticated approaches to ranking can assign weightings to factors in recognition that some will be of more importance in the evaluation than others. It should, however, be remembered that assigning numbers, of itself, is not a basis of evaluation; any scoring or weighting is only a reflection of the quality of the analysis and debate that goes into the scoring.

A similar approach can be adopted in relation to examining proposed strategies in terms of the responses of competitors. Section 6.4.4 on game theory emphasised that the viability of a strategy should take into account the likely response of competitors to any strategy an organisation might consider. Ranking can be used for this purpose. In effect the key factors become the key competitors. Each proposed strategy is then considered in terms of the likely responses of each competitor to that strategy. Suitability is then assessed in terms of which proposed strategy would be most likely to be effective in competitive terms.

11.2.2 Screening through scenarios

Here strategic options are considered against a range of future scenarios (see section 2.2.2 and Illustration 2.2). This is especially useful where a high degree of uncertainty exists. Suitable options are ones that make sense in terms of the various scenarios. As a result of such analysis it may be that several strategic options need to be 'kept open', perhaps in the form of contingency plans, developed as 'low-cost probes' or further evaluated in terms of their feasibility (see 11.4 below). Or it could be that an option being considered is found to be suitable in different scenarios. Indeed a criterion of strategy evaluation for Shell is that a chosen strategy needs to be suitable in terms of a range of different crude oil prices.

One of the other advantages of screening through scenarios is that, as managers screen the possible strategies in terms of the different scenarios, they come to see which would be most suitable in different environmental contexts. This can then sensitise managers to the need for changes in strategy, or changes in strategic emphasis, given changes in the environment.

11.2.3 Screening for bases of competitive advantage

One of the key issues in evaluating a strategy is whether it is likely to provide a basis of competitive advantage. Quite possibly the factors relating to this may have been built into the ranking exercises explained above. However, if they have not, then it may be sensible to consider this question specifically. Table 11.4 provides a basis for doing this.

As Chapters 3 and 6 explained, the likely bases of competitive advantage reside in the strategic capabilities of an organisation. Screening for bases of competitive advantage therefore requires the following steps:

- An identification of the key strategic capabilities underpinning a proposed strategy.
- The screening of these strategic capabilities in terms of their suitability to deliver either:
  (a) Cost leadership or
  (b) Differentiation benefits as valued by the customer.

  It is these two critical requirements, as explained in Chapter 6, that are the bedrock upon which competitive strategies might be built.

Table 11.4 Assessing bases of competitive advantage

Strategic capabilities underpinning the proposed strategy	Contribution to cost leadership differentiation	Perceived value to customers	Rarity	Inimitability	Non-substitutability

- Screening each of the strategic capabilities against the VRIN criteria explained in Chapter 3 (section 3.3) upon which sustainability of competitive advantage is based:

    V value; the potential to achieve competitive advantage in a market, though this has to bear in mind the need to achieve this at a cost that allows an organisation to realise acceptable levels of return (see 11.3.2 below).

    R rarity; the extent to which the strategic capability is distinctive or unique to the organisation and, very important, cannot readily be obtained or acquired by a competitor.

    I inimitability; how difficult it would be for competitors to imitate the strategic capability.

    N non-substitutability in terms of products or services or competences.

Such an analysis may well reveal that very few strategic capabilities are difficult to imitate in isolation. As section 3.4.3 on activity systems made clear, however, it is likely that it is not a generic capability that matters, but rather the linkages between the activities that make up the capability. So care has to be taken in this analysis to ensure that these linkages are identified and taken into consideration. Moreover it is important to remember the important point made in the discussion of inimitability in section 3.3.3. Difficulty of imitation is likely to be because strategic capabilities are complex (not least because of such linkages), causally ambiguous or embedded in an organisation's culture. So, again, care needs to be taken that the bases of strategic capability are well understood through disaggregation rather than expressed in overly abstract terms (see section 3.4.3).

11.2.4 Decision trees

Decision trees can also be used to assess strategic options against a list of key factors. Here options are 'eliminated' and preferred options emerge by progressively introducing requirements which must be met (such as growth, investment or diversity). Illustration 11.2 provides an example.

ILLUSTRATION 11.2

A strategic decision tree for a law firm

Decision trees evaluate future options by progressively eliminating others as additional criteria are introduced to the evaluation.

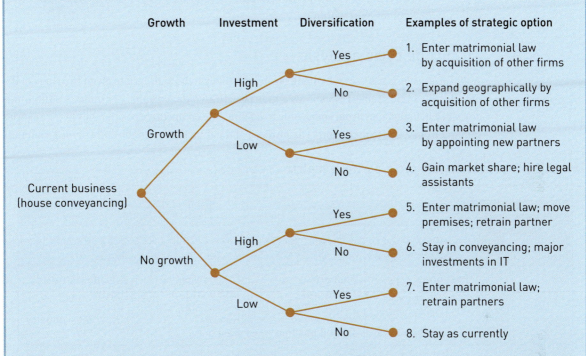

Growth	Investment	Diversification	Examples of strategic option
	High	Yes	1. Enter matrimonial law by acquisition of other firms
Growth		No	2. Expand geographically by acquisition of other firms
	Low	Yes	3. Enter matrimonial law by appointing new partners
		No	4. Gain market share; hire legal assistants
	High	Yes	5. Enter matrimonial law; move premises; retrain partner
No growth		No	6. Stay in conveyancing; major investments in IT
	Low	Yes	7. Enter matrimonial law; retrain partners
		No	8. Stay as currently

Current business (house conveyancing)

A law firm had most of its work related to house conveyancing (the legal aspects of buying property) where profits had been significantly squeezed. Therefore, it wanted to consider a range of new strategies for the future. Using a strategic decision tree it was able to eliminate certain options by identifying a few key criteria which future developments would incorporate, such as growth, investment (in premises, IT systems or acquisitions), and diversification (for example, into matrimonial law which, in turn, often brings house conveyancing work as families 'reshape').

Analysis of the decision tree reveals that if the partners of the firm wish growth to be an important aspect of future strategies, options 1–4 are ranked more highly than options 5–8. At the second step, the need for low-investment strategies would rank options 3 and 4 above 1 and 2, and so on.

The partners were aware that this technique has limitations in that the choice at each branch of the tree can tend to be simplistic. Answering 'yes' or 'no' to diversification does not allow for the wide variety of alternatives which might exist between these two extremes, for example *adapting the 'style' of the conveyancing service* (this could be an important variant of options 6 or 8). Nevertheless, as a starting point for evaluation, the decision tree provided a useful framework.

Questions

1 Try reversing the sequence of the three parameters (to diversification, investment and growth) and redraw the decision tree. Do the same eight options still emerge?

2 Add a fourth parameter to the decision tree. This new parameter is development by *internal methods* or by *acquisition*. List your 16 options in the right hand column.

The end point of the decision tree is a number of discrete development opportunities. The elimination process is achieved by identifying a few key elements or criteria which possible strategies need to achieve. In Illustration 11.2 these are growth, investment and diversification. As the illustration shows, choosing growth as an important requirement of a future strategy ranks options 1–4 more highly than 5–8. At the second step, the need for low investment strategies would rank options 3 and 4 above 1 and 2; and so on. The danger here is that the choice at each branch on the tree can tend to be simplistic. For example, as the illustration points out, answering 'yes' or 'no' to diversification does not allow for the wide variety of options which might exist within it.

11.2.5 Life cycle analysis

A *life cycle analysis* assesses whether a strategy is likely to be appropriate given the stage of the industry life cycle. Table 11.5 shows a matrix with two dimensions. The market situation is described in four stages, from embryonic to ageing. The competitive position has five categories ranging from weak to dominant. The purpose of the matrix is to establish the appropriateness

Table 11.5 The industry life cycle/portfolio matrix

Competitive position	Stages of industry maturity			
	Embryonic/ Developing	Growth	Mature	Ageing/Decline
Dominant	Fast grow Start up	Fast grow Attain cost leadership Renew Defend position	Defend position Attain cost leadership Renew Fast grow	Defend position Focus Renew Grow with industry
Strong	Start up Differentiate Fast grow	Fast grow Catch up Attain cost leadership Differentiate	Attain cost leadership Renew, focus Differentiate Grow with industry	Find niche Hold niche Hang in Grow with industry Harvest
Favourable	Start up Differentiate Focus Fast grow	Differentiate, focus Catch up Grow with industry	Harvest, hang in Find niche, hold niche Renew, turnaround Differentiate, focus Grow with industry	Retrench Turnaround
Tenable	Start up Grow with industry Focus	Harvest, catch up Hold niche, hang in Find niche Turnaround Focus Grow with industry	Harvest Turnaround Find niche Retrench	Divest Retrench
Weak	Find niche Catch up Grow with industry	Turnaround Retrench	Withdraw Divest	Withdraw

Source: Arthur D. Little.

of particular strategies in relation to these two dimensions. The consultancy firm Arthur D. Little suggests a number of criteria for establishing where an organisation is positioned on the matrix and what types of strategy are most likely to be suitable:

- **Position within the life cycle** can be determined in relation to market growth rate, growth potential, breadth of product lines, numbers of competitors, spread of market share between competitors, customer loyalty, entry barriers and technology. It is the balance of these factors which determines the life-cycle stage. For example, an embryonic industry is characterised by rapid growth, changes in technology, fragmented market shares and pursuit of new customers: an ageing industry by falling demand, declining number of competitors and, often, a narrow product line.

- **Competitive position** within its industry can be determined as follows:

  - A *dominant* position is rare in the private sector unless there is a quasi-monopoly position. In the public sector there is a legalised monopoly status (though this is becoming rarer).

  - *Strong* organisations are those that can follow strategies of their own choice without too much concern for competition.

  - A *favourable* position is where no single competitor stands out, but leaders are better placed (as, for example, in clothing retailing).

  - A *tenable* position is that which can be maintained by specialisation or focus.

  - *Weak* competitors are ones which are too small to survive independently in the long run.

Whilst this matrix is of use in providing guidance and raising questions in the evaluation of possible strategies, the danger is that it is taken over-literally: it does not, of itself, provide directive answers.

ACCEPTABILITY

Acceptability is concerned with **whether the expected performance outcomes of a proposed strategy meet the expectations of stakeholders**. These can be of three types, the '3 Rs': *risk*, *return* and *stakeholder reactions*. It is sensible to use more than one approach in assessing the acceptability of a strategy.

11.3.1 Risk

The first R is the *risk* an organisation faces in pursuing a strategy. **Risk concerns the extent to which the outcomes of a strategy can be predicted**. For example, risk can be high for organisations with major long-term programmes of innovation, where high levels of uncertainty exist about key issues in the environment, or about market behaviour, or where there are high levels of public concern about new developments – such as genetically modified crops.[1] Formal risk assessments are often incorporated into business plans as well as the investment appraisals of major projects. Importantly, risks other than ones with immediate financial impact are included, such as 'risk to corporate or brand image' or 'risk of missing an opportunity'. Developing a good understanding of an organisation's strategic position (Part I of this book) is at the core of good risk assessment. However, the following tools can also be helpful in a risk assessment.

Sensitivity analysis[2]

Sometimes referred to as *what-if* analysis, sensitivity analysis allows each of the important assumptions underlying a particular strategy to be questioned and challenged. In particular, it tests how sensitive the predicted performance or outcome (e.g. profit) is to each of these assumptions. For example, the key assumptions underlying a strategy might be that market demand will grow by 5 per cent a year, or that a new product will achieve a given sales and contribution level, or that certain expensive machines will operate at 90 per cent loading. Sensitivity analysis asks what would be the effect on performance (for example, profitability) of variations on these assumptions. For example, if market demand grew at only 1 per cent, or by as much as 10 per cent, would either of these extremes alter the decision to pursue that strategy? This can help develop a clearer picture of the risks of making particular strategic decisions and the degree of confidence managers might have in a given decision. Illustration 11.3 shows how sensitivity analysis can be used.

ILLUSTRATION 11.3

Sensitivity analysis

Sensitivity analysis is a useful technique for assessing the extent to which the success of a preferred strategy is dependent on the key assumptions which underlie that strategy.

In 2009 the Dunsmore Chemical Company was a single-product company trading in a mature and relatively stable market. It was intended to use this established situation as a 'cash cow' to generate funds for a new venture with a related product. Estimates had shown that the company would need to generate some £4m (~€4.4m; ~$6m) cash (at 2009 values) between 2010 and 2015 for this new venture to be possible.

Although the expected performance of the company was for a cash flow of £9.5m over that period (the *base case*), management were concerned to assess the likely impact of three key factors:

- Possible increases in *production costs* (labour, overheads and materials), which might be as much as 3 per cent p.a. in real terms.
- *Capacity-fill*, which might be reduced by as much as 25 per cent due to ageing plant and uncertain labour relations.
- *Price levels*, which might be affected by the threatened entry of a new major competitor. This could

(a) Sensitivity of cash flow to changes in real production costs

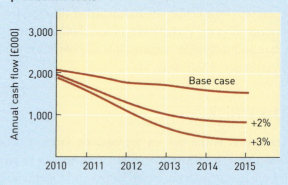

squeeze prices by as much as 3 per cent p.a. in real terms.

It was decided to use sensitivity analysis to assess the possible impact of each of these factors on the company's ability to generate £4m. The results are shown in the graphs.

Financial ratios[3]

The projection of how key financial ratios might change if a strategy were adopted can provide useful insights into risk. At the broadest level, an assessment of how the *capital structure* of the company would change is a good general measure of risk. For example, strategies that would require an increase in long-term debt will increase the gearing (or 'leverage') of the company and, hence, its financial risk. This is not because high long-term debt is the risk in itself, but because of the mandatory interest payments that go with it: if performance dips, these interest payments still have to be paid.

A consideration of the likely impact of a proposed strategy on an organisation's *liquidity* is also important in assessing risk. Indeed many businesses fail, not because they are inherently unprofitable, but because of a lack of cash liquidity and an inability to raise capital. For example, a small retailer eager to grow quickly may be tempted to fund the required shop-fitting costs by delaying payments to suppliers and increasing bank overdraft. Attractive as this may be to

(b) Sensitivity of cash flow to changes in plant utilistion

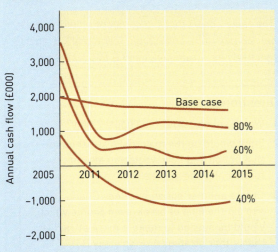

(c) Sensitivity of cash flow to reductions in real price

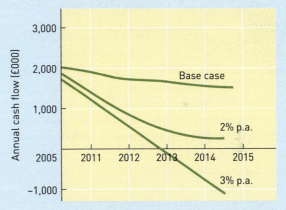

the extent to which they could protect price levels if such competition emerged. They therefore developed an aggressive marketing strategy to deter potential entrants.

From this analysis, management concluded that their target of £4m would be achieved with *capacity utilisation* as low as 60 per cent, which was certainly going to be achieved. Increased *production costs* of 3 per cent p.a. would still allow the company to achieve the £4m target over the period. In contrast, *price* squeezes of 3 per cent p.a. would result in a shortfall of £2m.

Management concluded from this analysis that the key factor which should affect their thinking on this matter was the likely impact of new competition and

Questions

What should the company do if its marketing campaigns fail to stop real price erosion:

1 Push to achieve more sales volume/ capacity fill?

2 Reduce unit costs of production?

3 Something else?

improve short-term cash flow, it could mean that the survival of the business becomes dependent on the likelihood of either creditors or the bank demanding payments from the company – an issue that clearly requires careful assessment.

Break-even analysis

Break-even analysis[4] is a simple and widely used approach which allows variations in assumptions about key variables in a strategy to be examined. It demonstrates at what point in terms of revenue the business will recover its fixed and variable costs and therefore break even. It can therefore be used to assess the risks associated with different price and cost structures of strategies as shown in Illustration 11.4.

ILLUSTRATION 11.4

Using break-even analysis to examine strategic options

Break-even analysis can be a simple way of quantifying some of the key factors which would determine the success or failure of a strategy.

A manufacturing company was considering the launch of a new consumer durable product into a market segment where most products were sold to wholesalers which supplied the retail trade. The total market was worth about €4.8.m (or $6.6m) (at manufacturers' prices) – about 630,000 units. The market leader had about 30 per cent market share in a competitive market where retailers were increasing their buying power. The company wished to evaluate the relative merits of a high-price/high-quality product sold to wholesalers (strategy A) or an own-brand product sold directly to retailers (strategy B).

The table summarises the market and cost structure for the market leader and these alternative strategies.

The table shows that the company would require about 22 per cent and 13 per cent market share respectively for strategies A and B to break even.

Questions

1 Which option would you choose? Why?

2 What would be the main risks attached to that option and how would you attempt to minimise these risks?

3 Create another option (strategy C) and explain the kind of break-even profile which would be needed to make it more attractive than either strategy A or strategy B.

Market and cost structure	Market leader	Strategy A	Strategy B
Price to retailer	€10.00	€12.00	€8.00
Price to wholesaler	€7.00	€8.40	–
Total variable costs (TVC)	€3.50	€4.00	€3.10
Contribution to profit per unit sold (= Price sold-TVC)	€3.50	€4.40	€4.90
Fixed costs (FC)	€500,000	€500,000	€500,000
Break-even point: no. of units to sell (= FC/Contribution to profit)	142,857	136,363	81,633
Total market size (units)	630,000	630,000	630,000
Break-even point: market share (= Break-even point units/Mkt size)	22.6%	21.6%	13.0%
Actual market share	30.0%	–	–

11.3.2 Return

The second R is **returns**. These are **the financial benefits which stakeholders are expected to receive from a strategy**. In the private sector typically these are shareholders and lenders; in the public sector the equivalent is funders, typically government departments. Measures of return are a common way of assessing proposed new ventures or major projects within businesses. So an assessment of financial and non-financial returns likely to accrue from specific strategic options could be a key criterion of acceptability of a strategy – at least to some stakeholders. There are different approaches to understanding return. This section looks briefly at three of these. It is important to remember that there are no absolute standards as to what constitutes good or poor return. It will differ between industries and countries and between different stakeholders. So it is important to establish what return is seen as acceptable by which stakeholders. Views also differ as to which measures give the best assessment of return, as will be seen below.

Financial analysis[5]

Traditional financial analyses are used extensively in assessing the acceptability of different strategic options. However, there are three considerations to be borne in mind when carrying out a financial analysis for the purpose of strategy evaluation:

- *The problem of uncertainty.* Be wary of the apparent thoroughness of the various approaches to financial analysis. Most were developed for the purposes of investment appraisal. Therefore, they focus on discrete projects where the additional cash inflows and outflows can be predicted with relative certainty: for example, a retailer opening a new store has a good idea about likely turnover based on previous experience of similar stores in similar areas. Such assumptions are not necessarily valid in many strategic contexts because the outcomes are much less certain. It is as strategy implementation proceeds (with the associated cash-flow consequences) that outcomes become clearer (see the discussion of 'real options' below).

- *The problem of specificity.* Financial appraisals tend to focus on direct *tangible* costs and benefits rather than the strategy more broadly. However, it is often not easy to identify such costs and benefits, or the cash flows specific to a proposed strategy, since it may not be possible to isolate them from other ongoing business activities. Moreover such costs and benefits may have spillover effects. For example, a new product may look unprofitable as a single project. But it may make strategic sense by enhancing the market acceptability of other products in a company's portfolio.

- *Assumptions.* Financial analysis is only as good as the assumptions built into the analysis. If assumptions about sales levels or costs are misguided, for example, then the value of the analysis is reduced, even misleading. This is one reason why sensitivity testing based on variations of assumptions is important.

Three commonly used bases of financial analysis (see Figure 11.1) are:

- Forecasting the *return on capital employed (ROCE)* for a specific time period after a new strategy is in place. For example, a ROCE of 15 per cent by year 3. This, then, is a profit measure of return and is shown in Figure 11.1(a). The ROCE (typically profit before interest and tax – PBIT, divided by capital employed) is a measure of the earning power of the resources used in implementing a particular strategic option. Its weakness is that it does not focus on cash flow or the timing of cash flows (see the explanation of DCF below).

Figure 11.1 Assessing profitability

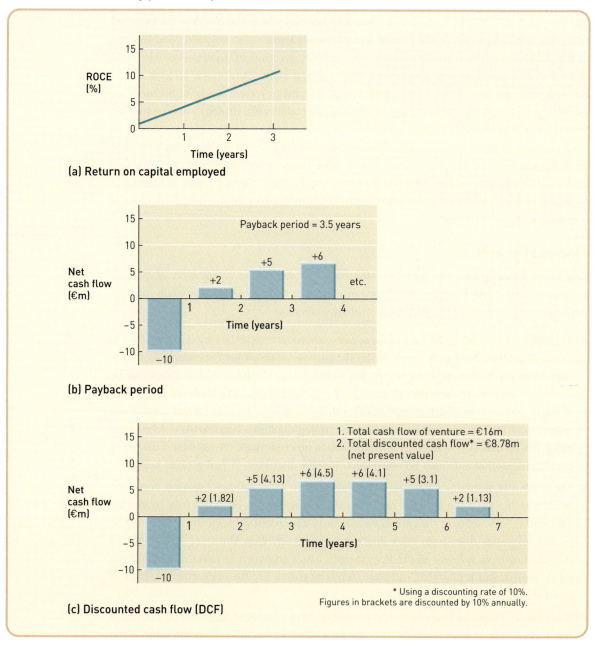

(a) Return on capital employed

(b) Payback period

(c) Discounted cash flow (DCF)

- Estimating the *payback period* is a cash flow measure. This is the length of time it takes before the cumulative cash flows for a strategic option become positive. In the example in Figure 11.1(b) the payback period is three and a half years. This measure has the virtue of simplicity and is most often used where the difficulty of forecasting is high and therefore risk is high. In such circumstances this measure can be used to select projects or strategies that have the quickest payback. Payback is often used in combination with DCF (see below), for example by setting criteria such as a payback period of, say, three years together with a positive NPV. Of course acceptable payback periods vary from industry to industry. A venture capitalist investing in the turnaround of an existing business may expect a fast return, whereas public infrastructure projects such as road building may be assessed over payback periods exceeding 50 years.

- Calculating *discounted cash flows (DCF)*. This is a widely used investment appraisal technique using common cash-flow forecasting techniques with the purpose of identifying which proposed projects are likely to achieve the best cumulative cash flow. The resulting measure is the net present value (or NPV) of the project, one of the most widely used criteria for assessing the financial viability of a project. Whilst on the face of it the project with the best NPV should be selected, given that a DCF is only as valid as the assumptions built into it, (a) sensitivity testing of assumptions is important and (b) it may be more prudent to regard any project with a positive NPV as worthy of further consideration and evaluation.

Taking the example of DCF in Figure 11.1(c), once the cash inflows and outflows have been assessed for each of the years of a strategic option they are discounted by an appropriate cost of capital hurdle. This reflects the fact that cash generated early is more valuable than cash generated later. The discount rate is also set at a level that reflects the riskiness of the strategy under consideration (i.e. a higher rate the greater the risk). In the example, the cost of capital or discounting rate of 10 per cent (after tax) reflects the rate of return required by those providing finance for the venture – shareholders and/or lenders. The 10 per cent cost of capital shown here *includes* an allowance for inflation of about 3–4 per cent. It is referred to as the 'money cost of capital'. By contrast, the 'real' cost of capital is 6–7 per cent *after* allowing for or *excluding* inflation.

The projected after-tax cash flow of £2m (~€2.2m; ~$3m) at the start of year 2 is equivalent to receiving £1.82m (~€2.00m; ~$2.73m) now – £2m multiplied by 0.91 or 1/1.10. £1.82m is called the *present value* of receiving £2m at the start of year 2 at a cost of capital of 10 per cent. Similarly, the after-tax cash flow of £5m (~€5.5m; ~$7.5m) at the start of year 3 has a present value of £4.13m (~€4.54m; ~$6.20m) – £5m multiplied by 1/1.10 squared. The *net present value (NPV)* of the venture, as a whole, is calculated by adding up all the annual present values over the venture's anticipated life. In the example, this is 7 years. The NPV works out at £8.78m (~€9.66m; ~$13.17m). Allowing for the time value of money, the £8.78m is the extra value that the strategic initiative will generate during its entire lifetime. However, it would be sensible to undertake a sensitivity analysis, for example by assuming different levels of sales volume increases, or different costs of capital in order to establish what resulting NPV measures would be and at what point NPV falls below zero. For example, in Figure 11.1(c) a cost of capital or discounting rate of about 32 per cent would produce a zero NPV. Such sensitivity testing is, then, a way in which DCF can be used to assess risk.

The key debate at the end of the chapter discusses how the use of DCF is regarded differently in different countries.

Shareholder value analysis

Shareholder value analysis[6] (SVA) poses the question: which proposed strategies would increase or decrease shareholder value? From a shareholder's point of view, what matters is the cash-generating capability of the business since this determines (a) the ability to pay dividends in the short term and (b) for a business to reinvest for the future, which, in turn, should enable a future flow of dividend payments. In the public sector the equivalent issue is the need to deliver best-value services within financial limits, though it is often difficult to identify clearly what is meant by 'value' in this context.

Table 11.6 Measures of shareholder value

(a) Total shareholder return (TSR)	(b) Economic profit or economic value added (EVA)
Given • Opening share price, £1 • Closing share price, £1.20 • Dividend per share received during financial year, 5p Then • Increase in share price (20p) plus dividend received (5p) = 25p TSR is • 25p divided by opening share price of £1 expressed as a percentage = 25%	Given • Operating profit after tax, £10m • Capital employed, £100m • Cost of capital, 8% Then • The capital or financing charge required to produce the operating profit after tax is the capital employed of £100m × the cost of capital of 8% = (£8m) EVA is • Operating profit (after tax) of £10m less the cost of the capital, £8m = £2m

Managing for shareholder value is, then, concerned with maximising shareholders' return in terms of dividends plus stock appreciation. There are several measures of shareholder value, but two are common. One is external to the company. The other is internal:

● The external measure is referred to as *total shareholder return (TSR)*. In any financial year, it is equal to the increase in the price of a share plus the dividends received per share actually received in that year. This is then divided by the share price at the start of the financial year. A simple example is given as Table 11.6(a).

● The internal measure is called *economic profit* or *economic value added (EVA)*. If the operating profit (after tax) is greater than the cost of the capital required to produce that profit then EVA is positive. An example is given as Table 11.6(b). Quite likely in the early stage of a new venture EVA is negative but the aim is to achieve a growing and positive EVA.

From the point of view of evaluating business strategies, the central question becomes which proposed strategy would maximise shareholders' returns? There are *key value drivers* which have the most influence on the cash generation capability. So, in evaluating proposed strategies, it is important to consider their effects on these value drivers. Some of these are relatively obvious; for example minimising *costs* and maximising *sales growth*, which improves cash flow and may help achieve economies of scale. Others are less obvious:[7]

● *Capital expenditure* can be a major cash outflow that could reduce shareholder value. So, on the face of it, keeping capital expenditure low improves shareholder value. However, doing so can mean that there is a reduced ability to grow a business for the long term. So the emphasis needs to be on how capital expenditure contributes to improving revenues or reducing costs elsewhere. How does the capital expenditure for a proposed strategy *enhance product features* leading to increased sales and/or better prices; or *reduce costs* (for example, through increased labour productivity) or *decrease working capital* (for example, through stock reduction by streamlining production or distribution)?

- *Cost of capital.* It is important that the cash flows generated from a given strategy should exceed the cost of capital. A major limitation of traditional accounting measures such as operating profit (profit before interest and taxation) is that they may ignore the cost of capital and therefore give misleading signals about whether value is created or destroyed. In turn, this can give misleading views about the acceptability of proposed strategies. The cost of capital therefore needs to be taken into account in evaluating a proposed strategy.

- *The management of working capital* such as stock, debtors and creditors will increase or decrease shareholder value. What is the effect of different proposed strategies on levels of working capital?

- *Maintaining and extending competitive advantage over time* can be a significant contributor to shareholder value since margins are particularly sensitive to high levels of competitive rivalry.

Although shareholder value analysis has helped address some of the shortcomings of traditional financial analyses, it has been criticised for over-emphasising short-term returns.[8] Nevertheless, the idea of valuing a strategy may serve to give greater realism and clarity to otherwise vague claims for strategic benefits. Perhaps the major lesson, however, is that firms that most successfully employ SVA do so within an overall approach to managing for value throughout the firm rather than merely as a technique for purposes of analysis.[9]

Cost–benefit[10]

Profit measures may be too narrow an interpretation of return, particularly where intangible benefits are an important consideration. This is usually so for major public infrastructure projects for example, such as the siting of an airport or a sewer construction project (see Illustration 11.5) or in organisations with long-term programmes of innovation (e.g. pharmaceuticals or aerospace). The *cost–benefit* concept suggests, however, that a money value can be put on all the costs and benefits of a strategy, including tangible and intangible returns to people and organisations other than the one 'sponsoring' the project or strategy.

Although in practice monetary valuation is often difficult, it can be done and, despite the difficulties, cost–benefit analysis is useful provided its limitations are understood. Its major benefit is in forcing managers to be explicit about the various factors that influence strategic choice. So, even if people disagree on the value that should be assigned to particular costs or benefits, at least they can argue their case on common ground and compare the merits of the various arguments.

Real options[11]

The previous approaches assume a reasonable degree of clarity about the outcomes of a strategic option. There are, however, situations where precise costs and benefits of strategies only become clear as implementation proceeds. For example, product development in a pharmaceuticals company may take many years. Its early stages in the laboratory are likely to be relatively low-cost. It is only later, if a viable product is developed, that costs become clear and still later, when launched, that demand becomes clear. In these circumstances the traditional DCF approach discussed above will tend to undervalue a 'project' because it does not take into account the value of options that could be opened up by the particular project.[12] For example, the development of a drug may not eventually lead to a viable product and the project may

ILLUSTRATION 11.5

Sewerage construction project

Investment in items of infrastructure – such as sewers – often requires a careful consideration of the wider costs and benefits of the project.

The UK's privatised water companies were monopolies supplying water and disposing of sewage. One of their priorities was investment in new sewerage systems to meet the increasing standards required by law. They frequently used cost–benefit analysis to assess projects. The figures below are from an actual analysis.

Cost/Benefit	£m*	£m*
Multiplier/linkage benefits		0.9
Flood prevention		2.5
Reduced traffic disruption		7.2
Amenity benefits		4.6
Investment benefit		23.6
Encouragement of visitors		4.0
Total benefits		42.8
Costs		
Construction cost	18.2	
Less: Unskilled labour cost	(4.7)	
Opportunity cost of construction	(13.5)	
Present value of net benefits (NPV)	29.3	

* (£1m is about €1.1m or $1.5m)

Note: Figures discounted at a *real* discount rate of 5% over 40 years.

Benefits

Benefits result mainly from reduced use of rivers as overflow sewers. There are also economic benefits resulting from construction. The following benefits are quantified in the table:

- The multiplier benefit to the local economy of increased spending by those employed on the project.
- The linkage benefit to the local economy of purchases from local firms, including the multiplier effect of such spending.
- Reduced risk of flooding from overflows or old sewers collapsing – flood probabilities can be quantified using historical records, and the cost of

flood damage by detailed assessment of the property vulnerable to damage.
- Reduced traffic disruption from flooding and road closures for repairs to old sewers – statistics on the costs of delays to users, traffic flows on roads affected and past closure frequency can be used to quantify savings.
- Increased amenity value of rivers (for example, for boating and fishing) can be measured by surveys asking visitors what the value is to them or by looking at the effect on demand of charges imposed elsewhere.
- Increased rental values and take-up of space can be measured by consultation with developers and observed effects elsewhere.
- Increased visitor numbers to riverside facilities resulting from reduced pollution.

Construction cost

This is net of the cost of unskilled labour. Use of unskilled labour is not a burden on the economy, and its cost must be deducted to arrive at opportunity cost.

Net benefits

Once the difficult task of quantifying costs and benefits is complete, standard discounting techniques can be used to calculate net present value and internal rate of return, and analysis can then proceed as for conventional projects.

Source: G. Owen, formerly of Sheffield Business School.

Questions

1 What do you feel about the appropriateness of the listed benefits?

2 How easy or difficult is it to assign money values to these benefits?

have to be closed down. There could, however, be other outcomes of value: the research could create valuable new knowledge or provide a 'platform' from which other products or process improvements spring; or perhaps be a basis for a licensing arrangement or even the sale of know-how to another company. So a strategy should be seen as a *series* of 'real' options (i.e. choices of direction at points in time as the strategy takes shape) which should be evaluated as such. Illustration 11.6 provides an example. A real options approach to evaluation therefore typically increases the expected value of a project because it adds the expected value of possible future options opened up by that project. There are four main benefits of this approach:

- *Bringing strategic and financial evaluation closer together.* Arguably it provides a clearer understanding of both strategic and financial return and risk of a strategy by examining each step (option) separately.

- *Valuing emerging options.* In taking such an approach, it allows a value to be placed on options that might be opened up by an initial strategic decision.

- *Coping with uncertainty.* Advocates of a real options approach argue it overcomes, or provides an alternative to, profitability analyses that require managers to make assumptions about future conditions that may well not be realistic. As such it can be linked into ways of analysing uncertain futures such as scenario analysis (see section 2.2). For example, applying a real options approach might well have two effects. First, to defer decisions as far as possible because (secondly) the passage of time will clarify expected returns – even to the extent that apparently unfavourable strategies might prove viable at a later date.

- *Offsetting conservatism.* One problem with financial analyses such as DCF is that the hurdle rates set to reflect risk and uncertainty mean that ambitious but uncertain projects (and strategies) tend not to receive support. The real options approach, on the other hand, tends to value higher more ambitious strategies. There have, therefore, been calls to employ real options together with more traditional financial evaluation such as DCF. In effect DCF provides the cautionary view and real options the more optimistic view.

It must, however, be stressed that a real options approach is only useful where a strategy is, or can be structured, in the form of options; for example, where there are stages, as in pharmaceutical development, such that each stage gives the possibility of abandoning or deferring going forward. So it would not be suited, for example, to a project where major capital outlay was required at the beginning.

11.3.3 Reaction of stakeholders

The third R is the likely *reaction* of stakeholders to a proposed strategy. Section 4.5.2 and Illustration 4.5 showed how *stakeholder mapping* can be used to understand the political context and consider the political agenda in an organisation. It also showed how stakeholder mapping can be used to consider the likely reactions of stakeholders to new strategies and thus evaluate the acceptability of a strategy. There are many situations where stakeholder reactions could be crucial. For example:

- *Owners*' (e.g. shareholders, family owners, the state) financial expectations have to be taken into account and the extent to which these are met will influence the acceptability of a strategy. A proposed strategy might also call for the financial restructuring of a business, for example an issue of new shares, which could be unacceptable, for example to a powerful group of shareholders, since it dilutes their voting power.

ILLUSTRATION 11.6

Real options evaluation for developing premium beers in India

A real options approach can be used to evaluate proposed projects with multiple options.

A brewer of premium beers had been exporting its products to India for many years. They were considering an investment in brewing capacity in India. Although it was envisaged that, initially, this would take the form of brewing standard products locally and distributing through existing distributors, there were other ideas being discussed, though these were all contingent on the building of the brewery. Management took a real options approach to evaluating the project as set out in the figure below.

The evaluation of the proposal to build the brewery considered three options; to invest now, at a later date, or not invest at all. However, the building of the brewery opened other options. One of these was to cease operating through existing third party distributors and open up their own distribution network. Again, there were alternatives here. Should they invest in this immediately after the brewery was built, at a later date or not invest in it at all and continue through their current distibutors? The investment in the brewery, especially if better distribution systems were to be developed, in turn opened up other options. Currently being discussed, for example, was whether there existed a market opportunity to develop and produce beers tailored more specifically to the Indian market. Again, should there be investment in this soon after the building of the brewery, at a later date, or not at all? It was also recognised that other options might emerge if the project went forward.

The board used a real options approach, not least because they needed to factor in the potential added value of the options opened up by the brewery.

They would employ DCF to evaluate the brewery project. However, they would also evaluate the other options assuming the brewery was built. In each of these evaluation exercises DCF would also be used, adjusting the cost of capital to the perceived risk of the options. This would give them an indication of NPV for each of those options. The possible positive NPVs of the subsequent options could then be taken into account in assessing the attractiveness of the initial brewery project.

They also recognised that, if they invested in the brewery so as to further develop their presence in India, greater clarity on both costs and market opportunities would emerge as the project progressed. So it would make sense to revisit the evaluation of the other options at later stages as such information became available.

> ### Question
>
> What are the advantages of the real options approach to this evaluation over other approaches (a) to building the brewery; and (b) to other ideas being considered?

| Initial investment in brewery | Development of distribution capability | Product diversification |

- *Bankers* and other providers of interest-bearing loans are concerned about the *risk* attached to their loans and the competence with which this is managed. It is likely they will manage this risk through taking securities against it. Nonetheless a good track record in managing that risk could be regarded (in itself) as a reason for bankers to invest further with some companies and not others. The extent to which a proposed strategy could affect the capital structure of the company could also be important. For example, would it increase the gearing ratio (of debt to equity), which determines how sensitive the solvency of the company is to changes in its profit position? Interest cover is a similar measure that relates interest payments to profit. They will also be concerned with the *liquidity* of the company, because a deteriorating liquidity position may require correction through additional loans and an increased risk profile. So the question needs to be asked: how will the proposed strategy affect liquidity?

- *Regulators* are important stakeholders in industries such as telecommunications, financial services, pharmaceuticals and power. They may have what amounts to decision-making powers over aspects of an organisation's strategy, such as price or geographic expansion.

- *Employees and unions* may resist strategic moves such as relocation, outsourcing or *divestment* if they see them as likely to result in job *losses*.

- *The local community* will be concerned about jobs but also with the *social cost* of an organisation's strategies, such as pollution or marketing – an issue of growing concern. Matters of business ethics and social responsibility were discussed in section 4.4.

- *Customers* may also object to a strategy. Their sanction is to cease buying from the company, perhaps switching to a competitor. For example, a new business model, such as marketing online, might run the risk of a backlash from existing retail channels, which could jeopardise the success of the strategy.

Overall, there is a need to be conscious of the impact on the various stakeholders of the strategic options being considered. Managers also need to understand how the capability to meet the varied expectations of stakeholders could enable the success of some strategies whilst limiting the ability of an organisation to succeed with other strategies.

FEASIBILITY

Feasibility is **concerned with whether a strategy could *work in practice***: therefore whether an organisation has the capabilities to deliver a strategy. An assessment of feasibility is likely to require two key questions to be addressed: (a) do the resources and competences currently exist to implement a strategy effectively? And (b) if not, can they be obtained? These questions can be applied to any resource area that has a bearing on the viability of a proposed strategy. Here the focus is on three areas, however: finance, people (and their skills) and the importance of resource integration.

11.4.1 Financial feasibility

A central issue in considering a proposed strategy is the funding required for it so the *cash flow analysis and forecasting*[13] required for evaluating the acceptability of possible strategies is also relevant here. The need is to identify the cash required for a strategy, the cash generated by following the strategy and the timing of any new funding requirements. This then informs consideration of the likely sources for obtaining funds.

Table 11.7 Financial strategy and the business life cycle

Life cycle phase	Funding requirement	Cost of capital	Business risk	Likely funding source(s)	Dividends
Development/launch	High	High	High	Equity (venture capital)	Zero
Growth	High	Low/medium	High	Debentures and equity (growth investors)	Nominal
Maturity	Low/medium	Medium	Medium	Debt, equity and retained earnings	High
Decline	Low/negative	Medium/high	Low	Debt	High

Managers need to be familiar with different sources of funds as well as the advantages and drawbacks of these. This is well explained in standard financial texts.[14] This is not only a matter of the feasibility of a strategy, but also its acceptability to different stakeholders, not least those providing the funds. So the discussion in section 11.3 is relevant here too. Decisions on which funding sources to use will also be influenced by the current financial situation of the organisation such as ownership (e.g. whether the business is privately held or publicly quoted) and by the overall corporate goals and strategic priorities of the organisation. For example, there will be different financial needs if a business is seeking rapid growth by acquisition compared with if it is seeking to consolidate its past performance.

A useful way of considering funding is in terms of which financial strategies might be needed for different 'phases' of the development and life cycle of a business – see Table 11.7. In turn this raises the question as to whether such sources of finance are available and, if not, whether the proposed strategy is both feasible and acceptable.

- *Emerging and new-launch businesses*[15] are high-risk businesses. They are at the beginning of their life cycle and are not yet established in their markets; moreover, they are likely to require substantial investment. A stand-alone business in this situation might, for example, seek to finance such growth from specialists in this kind of investment, such as venture capitalists who, themselves, seek to offset risk by having a portfolio of such investments. Schemes for private investors (so-called 'business angels') have also become popular. Such sources of funds are, however, likely to be high-cost since the funders are aware of the high business risk.

- *Growth businesses* may remain in a volatile and highly competitive market position. The degree of business risk may therefore remain high, as will the cost of capital in such circumstances. However, if a business in this phase has begun to establish itself in its markets, perhaps as a market leader in a growing market, then the cost of capital may be lower. In either case, since the main attractions to investors here are the product or business concept and the prospect of future earnings, equity capital is likely to be appropriate, perhaps by public flotation.

- *Mature businesses* are those operating in mature markets and the likelihood is that funding requirements will decline. If such a business has achieved a strong competitive position with a high market share, it should be generating regular and substantial surpluses. Here the business risk is lower and the opportunity for retained earnings is high. In these circumstances, if funding is required, it may make sense to raise this through debt capital as well as equity, since reliable returns can be used to service such debt. Provided increased debt (*gearing* or *leverage*) does not lead to an unacceptable level of risk, this cheaper debt funding will in fact increase the residual profits achieved by a company in these circumstances.

- *Declining businesses* are likely to find it difficult to attract equity finance. However, borrowing may be possible if secured against residual assets in the business. At this stage, it is likely that the emphasis in the business will be on cost cutting, and it could well be that the cash flows from such businesses are quite strong. These businesses may provide relatively low-risk investments.

This life-cycle framework does not, however, always hold. There are exceptions. For example, a company seeking to develop *new and innovative businesses* on a regular basis might, in effect, be acting as its own venture capitalist, accepting high risk at the business level and seeking to offset such risk by 'cash cows' in its portfolio (see section 7.7.1). Or some companies may need to sell off businesses as they mature to raise capital for further investment in new ventures. Public-sector managers know about the need to balance the financial risk of services too. They need a steady core to their service where budgets are certain to be met, hence reducing the financial risk of the more speculative aspects of their service.

11.4.2 People and skills

Chapter 3 showed how organisations that achieve sustainable competitive advantage may do so on the basis of competences that are embedded in the skills, knowledge and experience of people in that organisation. Indeed, ultimately the success of a strategy will likely depend on how it is delivered by people in the organisation. These could be managers but they could also be more junior people in the organisation who are nonetheless critical to a strategy, for example as the front-line contact with customers. Three questions arise: do people in the organisation currently have the competences to deliver a proposed strategy? Are the systems to support those people fit for the strategy? If not, can the competences be obtained or developed?

The first step here is the same as suggested in sections 11.2.1–3 for the screening for competitive advantage. The need is to identify the key strategic capabilities underpinning a proposed strategy, but specifically in terms of the people and skills required. The second step is to determine if these exist in the organisation. It could be, of course, that the proposed strategy is built on the argument that they do. If so, how realistic is this? Or it could be that the assumption is that these can be obtained or developed. Again, is this realistic?

Many of the issues of feasibility in relation to the structures and systems to support such competence development and people are addressed in Chapter 13 on organising and Chapter 14 on managing strategic change. Other critical questions that need to be considered include:[16]

- *Work organisation.* Will changes in work content and priority-setting significantly alter the orientation of people's jobs? Will managers need to think differently about the tasks that need to be done? What are the critical criteria for effectiveness needed? Are these different from current requirements?

- *Rewards.* How will people need to be incentivised? Will people's career aspirations be affected? How will any significant shifts in power, influence and credibility need to be rewarded and recognised?

- *Relationships.* Will interactions between key people need to change? What are the consequences for the levels of trust, task competence and values-congruence? Will conflict and political rivalry be likely?

- *Training and development.* Are current training and mentoring systems appropriate? It may be necessary to take into account the balance between the need to ensure the successful delivery of strategy in the short term and the required future development of people's capabilities.

- *People.* Given these issues, will different people be required than currently and at what levels in the organisation?

11.4.3 Integrating resources

The success of a strategy is likely to depend on the management of many resource areas; not only people and finance, but also physical resources, such as buildings, information, technology and the resources provided by suppliers and partners. It is possible, but not likely, that a proposed strategy builds only on existing resources. It is more likely that additional resources will be required. The feasibility of a strategy therefore needs be considered in terms of the ability to obtain and integrate such resources – both inside the organisation and in the wider value network. Serious problems can result from the failure to think through the need for such integration. This is especially the case where a strategy involves the complex integration of diverse resources. For example, as Illustration 11.7 shows, the highly publicised chaos at the opening of BA's Terminal 5 at Heathrow in 2008 was not the result of a single problem, but of a failure to integrate the many different resources, systems and competences required to ensure its effectiveness.

 EVALUATION CRITERIA: FOUR QUALIFICATIONS

There are four qualifications that need to be made to this chapter's discussion of evaluation criteria:

- *Conflicting conclusions and management judgement.* Conflicting conclusions can arise from the application of the criteria of suitability, acceptability and feasibility. A proposed strategy might look eminently suitable but not be acceptable to major stakeholders, for example. It is therefore important to remember that the criteria discussed here are useful in helping think through strategic options but are not a replacement for management judgement. Managers faced with a strategy they see as suitable, but which key stakeholders object to, have to rely on their own judgement on the best course of action, but this should be better informed through the analysis and evaluation they have undertaken.

- *Consistency between the different elements of a strategy.* It should be clear from the chapters in Part II that there are several elements of a strategy, so an important question is whether the component parts work together as a 'package'. So *competitive strategy* (such as low cost or differentiation), strategy *direction* (such as product development or diversification) and

ILLUSTRATION 11. 7

Chaos at Heathrow Terminal Five

Thinking through the integration of the elements of a strategy is fundamental to effective strategy implementation.

With an investment of over £4.3 (€4.7; $6.4) billion, the new state of the art Terminal 5 (T5) was a key element of British Airways' strategy to consolidate its international and domestic flights in a showpiece hub at the world's busiest international airport, Heathrow. It opened on 27th March 2008. It was perhaps the worst 'grand opening' of all time. The first day ended with a malfunctioning baggage handling system, resultant travel chaos, passengers stranded, baggage lost and appalling headlines for the airport operator BAA and for BA. It was followed by the resignation of five key executives from these organisations.

This malfunction of the state-of-the-art auto-mated baggage handling system, designed to process 12,000 bags an hour, certainly had a knock-on impact. However, other seemingly more mundane issues also contributed to the problems. Many staff found difficulty locating the staff car parks, reporting unclear road signs and misdirection. Overflow car parks were not open so staff were driving round in circles trying to find a place to park. This led to queues of staff trying to get to 'airside' [restricted access] work stations. One experienced check-in operator commented 'It took an hour for people to get to the right place. The place is so enormous; we don't know where we are going, we've been given no maps, no numbers to ring.'

At 04.00 hrs check-in desks were still closed, so passengers began to queue. When the desks finally opened the rush to the desks created chaos. By 06.00 hrs, passengers on inbound flights were kept waiting to collect their bags and 300 passengers were back-logged waiting to board flights. As the morning continued so did the length of the wait [over $2\frac{1}{2}$ hours] to collect baggage from inbound flights. The cause was a clogged underground baggage con-veyer, exacerbated by staff's failure to remove bags quickly enough. By the afternoon, flights were being cancelled but there seemed little understanding of how to process stranded passengers. Finally at 16.30 all check-in was suspended.

Later Willie Walsh [CEO of BA] admitted that many issues contributed to the overall failure.

'There were problems in the car parks, airport areas, computer glitches and the baggage system. In isolation, they would not have had the impact they did, but in combination they led to service disruption. We never took control during the day.'

In fact there had been extensive trials, including twenty fully loaded baggage system tests. However, Jamie Bowden, an aviation analyst and former BA customer services manager, commented:

'Many areas of BA had told managers month after month they were not ready or did not feel confident to move in [to T5] but there was a general feeling of hubris – "Don't worry it'll be alright on the day".'

One eye witness who had attempted to travel on a BA domestic flight from T5 that day reported that many elements and many organisations were part of the unpreparedness.

'The new fancy lifts from the rail link weren't working. Then I was confronted with chaos in departures, BAA staff who were unable to direct me and BA staff who could tell me nothing of the likely departure time, if at all, of my flight. I chose to leave and tried to call home but the payphones weren't connected. I found no one from BAA who could direct me to an exit and eventually a BA person sent me through passport control with no passport. Finally when I tried to leave on a coach, the coach company's computerised ticketing wasn't working. All round chaos: not just BA.'

Sources: C. Buckley, Heathrow's Managing Director Quits after Fiasco at Terminal 5, *The Times*, 14th May 2008; K. Done, Long Haul to restore BA's Reputation, *Financial Times*, 29th March 2008; T. Webb, Walsh Hits Heavy Turbulence, *The Observer*, 20th April 2008; What Did Go Wrong at Terminal 5? BBC News Website, 30th March 2008; What Went Wrong at Heathrow's T5? BBC News website, 7th May 2008.

Questions

1 Identify the key resources and activities that would have contributed to an effective 'grand opening'.

2 Suggest why the chaos occurred.

KEY DEBATE

What is the best approach to strategic investment decisions?

There are differences around the world in the bases and types of analyses used for strategic investment decisions (SIDs). Research has particularly highlighted the difference between the bases of SIDs in the USA and UK where shareholder models of governance prevail and countries where stakeholder models prevail such as Japan and, traditionally, Germany (see section 4.3.2). The differences highlighted are these:

● In the US and UK there is an emphasis on financial bases of appraisal. This goes hand in hand with the widespread use of DCF as a financial basis of evaluation. In a set of studies carried out over a ten year period,[1] 100% of managers in firms questioned in the USA reported using the DCF approach. The comparable figure in the UK was 50% of firms, though this had dropped from 84% in 1986. The widespread use of DCF also went hand in hand with expected internal rates of return for proposed projects. This focus on financial analysis was argued to be associated with the need to meet the expectations of the financial markets and, in particular, the pressures for short term results due to the relatively arm's-length relationships with institutional investors in the US and UK.

● In Japan and Germany there was an emphasis on broader bases of strategic appraisal and the importance of achieving long term viable and secure market positioning. Here, the popularity of DCF was markedly less; in Germany (28%) and Japan (18%). Other methods of analysis such as *Payback* and *Return on Capital Employed* [ROCE] were more widely applied and rates of return expectations were lower, more flexible or, as in Japan, not much emphasised. All this may be because of firms' closer relationships with financial institutions (eg banks) or the higher incidence of family ownership (as in Germany) encouraging a longer term perspective, reducing the threat of acquisition pressure and for short term results. Perhaps because of the emphasis on a broader strategic approach, there was also less of a

concern with more sophisticated methods of financial appraisal.

The evidence of explanations lying in the governance systems seems to be borne out in Germany where changes are occurring. Here family ownership of firms remains common. In these firms, there appears to have been little change in the SID analysis over time. The preference is for measures of payback and ROCE at lower levels of target return and longer time frames: 5/7 years as opposed to 2/3 years in the USA and UK. But in the publicly owned corporations in Germany there has been a shift towards the USA/UK approach.

Others[2] have argued that there really should be no conflict between a financial and a strategic orientation: that good financial analysis complements rather than contradicts good strategy analysis, providing that, built into any financial analysis, are assumptions about markets and bases of sustainable competitive advantage. So the role of financial analysis should be to highlight rather than mask such key issues.

References:
1. C. Carr and C. Tomkins, Context, Culture and the Role of the Finance Function in Strategic Decisions: A comparative Analysis of Britain, Germany, the USA and Japan, *Management Accounting Research*, 9, 213–239, 1998; C. Carr, Are German, Japanese and Anglo-Saxon Strategic Decision Styles Still Divergent in the Context of Globalization? *Journal of Management Studies*, vol. 42, no. 6, pp. 1155–1188, September 2005.
2. P. Barwise, P. Marsh and R. Wensley, Must finance and strategy clash, *Harvard Business Review*, September–October 1989.

Question

1 What are the arguments for the evaluation of strategic options being based on an emphasis: i) on financial bases of evaluation; ii) broader strategic bases of evaluation?

2 What approaches to the evaluation of strategic options would *you* propose, and why?

*method*s of pursuing strategies (such as organic development, acquisition or alliances) need to be considered as a whole and be consistent. There are dangers if they are not. For example, suppose an organisation wishes to develop a differentiation strategy by building on its capabilities developed over many years to develop new products or services within a market it knows well. There may be dangers in looking to develop those new products through acquiring other businesses which might have very different capabilities that are incompatible with the strengths of the business.

●	*The implementation and development of strategies* may throw up issues that might make organisations reconsider whether particular strategic options are, in fact, feasible or uncover factors that change views on the suitability or acceptability of a strategy. This may lead to a reshaping, or even abandoning, of strategic options. It therefore needs to be recognised that, in practice, strategy evaluation may take place through implementation, or at least partial implementation. This is another reason why experimentation, low-cost probes and real options evaluation may make sense.

●	*Strategy development in practice.* More generally, it should not be assumed that the careful and systematic evaluation of strategy is necessarily the norm in organisations. Strategies may develop in other ways. This is the subject of Chapter 12 which follows. The final chapter (15) also explains what managers actually do in managing strategic issues.

SUMMARY

●	Proposed strategies may be evaluated using the three SAFe criteria:

  ●	*Suitability* is concerned with assessing which proposed strategies address the *key opportunities and constraints* an organisation faces. It is about the *rationale* of a strategy.

  ●	The *acceptability* of a strategy relates to three issues: the level of *risk* of a strategy, the expected *return* from a strategy and the likely *reaction of stakeholders*.

  ●	*Feasibility* is concerned with whether an organisation has or can obtain the capabilities to deliver a strategy.

VIDEO ASSIGNMENT

Visit **MyStrategyLab** and watch the *Inamo* case study.

In setting up Inamo, in terms of the SAFe criteria:

1	On what bases might the founders have judged the project to be 'suitable'?

2	What aspects of 'feasibility' would they need to consider? In particular, consider the need to *integrate* the different aspects of the Inamo business model.

WORK ASSIGNMENTS

* Denotes more advanced work assignments. * Denotes case study in the Text and Case edition.

11.1   Undertake a ranking analysis of the choices available to easySolution, Marks & Spencer (C)*, or an organisation of your choice similar to that shown in Illustration 11.1.

11.2   Using the criteria of suitability, acceptability and feasibility undertake an evaluation of the strategic options that might exist for easySolution, Aids Alliance* or an organisation of your choice.

11.3   Undertake a risk assessment to inform the evaluation of strategic options for an organisation of your choice.

11.4   Write an executive report on how sources of funding need to be related to the nature of an industry and the types of strategies that an organisation is pursuing.

11.5   Suggest how managers could have better considered and managed the integration between the various resources required for a successful opening of Heathrow Terminal 5 (see Illustration 11.7).

11.6* Using examples from your answer to previous assignments, make a critical appraisal of the statement that 'Strategic choice is, in the end, a highly subjective matter. It is dangerous to believe that, in reality, analytical techniques will ever change this situation.' Refer to the commentary at the end of Part II of the book.

Integrative assignment

11.7* Explain how the SAFe criteria might differ between public- and private-sector organisations. Show how this relates to both the nature of the business environment (Chapter 2) and the expectations of stakeholders (Chapter 4).

RECOMMENDED KEY READINGS

- A companion book which explores techniques of strategy evaluation more fully is V. Ambrosini with G. Johnson and K. Scholes (eds), *Exploring Techniques of Analysis and Evaluation in Strategic Management*, Prentice Hall, 1998.

- Readers may wish to consult one or more standard texts on finance. For example: G. Arnold, *Corporate Financial Management*, 4th edition, Financial Times Prentice Hall,

2009; P. Atrill, *Financial Management for Decision Makers*, 4th edition, Financial Times Prentice Hall, 2006.

- A classic paper that considers the relationship between financial approaches to evaluation and 'strategic' approaches is P. Barwise, P. Marsh and R. Wensley, 'Must finance and strategy clash?', *Harvard Business Review*, September–October 1989.

REFERENCES

1. L. Levidow and S. Carr, 'UK: precautionary commercialisation', *Journal of Risk Research*, vol. 3, no. 3 (2000), pp. 261–70.

2. For those readers interested in the details of sensitivity analysis see: A. Satelli, K. Chan and M. Scott (eds), *Sensitivity Analysis*, Wiley, 2000. For a more detailed exploration of different approaches see A.G. Hadigheh and T. Terlaky. 'Sensitivity analysis in linear optimization: invariant support set intervals', *European Journal of Operational Research*, vol. 169, no. 3 (2006), pp. 1158–76.

3. See C. Walsh, *Master the Management Metrics That Drive and Control Your Business*, Financial Times Prentice Hall, 4th edition, 2005.

4. Break-even analysis is covered in most standard accountancy texts. See, for example, G. Arnold, *Corporate Financial Management*, 4th edition, Financial Times Prentice Hall, 2009.

5. Most standard finance and accounting texts explain in more detail the financial analyses summarised here. For example see G. Arnold (reference 4 above), Chapter 4.

6. The main proponent of shareholder value analysis is A. Rappaport, *Creating Shareholder Value: the New Standard for Business Performance*, 2nd edition, Free Press, 1998. See also R. Mill's chapter, 'Understanding and using shareholder value analysis', Chapter 15 in V. Ambrosini with G. Johnson and K. Scholes (eds), *Exploring Techniques of Analysis and Evaluation in Strategic Management*, Prentice Hall, 1998.

7. S. Williams, 'Delivering strategic business value', *Strategic Finance*, vol. 86, no. 2 (2004), pp. 41–8.

8. A. Kennedy, *The End of Shareholder Value*, Perseus Publishing, 2000.

9. This point is made clear in a research study reported by P. Haspeslagh, T. Noda and F. Boulos, 'It's not just about the numbers', *Harvard Business Review*, July–August, pp. 65–73, 2001.

10. A 'classic' explanation of cost–benefit analysis is J.L. King, 'Cost–benefit analysis for decision-making', *Journal of Systems Management*, vol. 31, no. 5 (1980), pp. 24–39. A detailed example in the water industry can be found in: N. Poew, 'Water companies' service performance and environmental trade-off', *Journal of Environmental Planning and Management*, vol. 45, no. 3 (2002), pp. 363–79.

11. Real options evaluation can get lost in the mathematics, so readers wishing to gain more detail of how real options analysis works can consult one of the following: T. Copeland, 'The real options approach to capital allocation', *Strategic Finance*, vol. 83, no. 4 (2001), pp. 33–7; T. Copeland and V. Antikarov, *Real Options: a Practitioner's Guide*, Texere Publishing, 2001; L. Trigeorgis, *Managerial Flexibility and Strategy in Resource Allocation*, MIT Press, 2002; P. Boer, *The Real Options Solution: Finding Total Value in a High Risk World*, Wiley, 2002. Also see M.M. Kayali, 'Real options as a tool for making strategic investment decisions', *Journal of American Academy of Business*, vol. 8, no. 1 (2006), pp. 282–7; C. Krychowski and B.V. Quelin, 'Real options and strategic investment decisions: Can they be of use to scholars?', *Academy of Management Perspectives*, vol. 24, no. 2 (2010), pp. 65–78.

12. T. Luehrman, 'Strategy as a portfolio of real options', *Harvard Business Review*, vol. 76, no. 5 (1998), pp. 89–99.

13. See G. Arnold on funds flow analysis (ref. 4 above), Chapter 3, p. 108.

14. See: P. Atrill, *Financial Management for Decision Makers*, 4th edition, Financial Times Prentice Hall, 2006, Chapters 6 and 7; G. Arnold (ref. 4 above), Part IV.

15. There has been much research and publication around the funding of this start-up phase. For example: D. Champion, 'A stealthier way to raise money', *Harvard Business Review*, vol. 78, no. 5 (2000), pp. 18–19; Q. Mills, 'Who's to blame for the bubble?', *Harvard Business Review*, vol. 79, no. 5 (2001), pp. 22–3; H. Van Auken, 'Financing small technology-based companies: the relationship between familiarity with capital and ability to price and negotiate investment', *Journal of Small Business Management*, vol. 39, no. 3 (2001), pp. 240–58; M. Van Osnabrugge and R. Robinson, 'The influence of a venture capitalist's source of funds', *Venture Capital*, vol. 3, no. 1 (2001), pp. 25–39.

16. These issues are based on those identified by C. Marsh, P. Sparrow, M. Hird, S. Balain and A. Hesketh (2009) 'Integrated organization design: the new strategic priority for HR directors', in P.R. Sparrow, A. Hesketh, C. Cooper, and M. Hird (eds) *Leading HR*, London: Palgrave Macmillan.

EasySolution

The business idea

One thing always annoyed Camilla Oxley as she worked on her biochemistry doctorate at the University of Oxford. Each day she wasted about 20 minutes manually preparing the 'buffer solutions' in which she would carry out her experiments. She calculated that this repetitive and tedious task would consume about 500 hours across her whole time as a doctoral student.

Buffer solutions, though, were absolutely critical to her research work – and that carried out by about 150,000 laboratory research groups in the United Kingdom and United States alone. Buffer solutions involve creating varying mixes of liquid chemicals which must have an exact pH (acid-alkali balance) at a particular temperature. The mixes must be absolutely accurate for the reliability of the experiment. A bad mix could lead to the discarding of chemicals worth up to £100 (~€110; ~$150) or so a litre. Because of the tedium of daily preparation, researchers have been known to create large stocks of buffer solutions which deteriorated over time and so jeopardised the reliability of many weeks of experimental work.

Camilla believed that the tedious process of buffer solution preparation should be automated in a machine. After all, computers were helping to automate other parts of the experimental process. The average number of experiments carried out per day by researchers had trebled in recent years. Manual buffer solution preparation was becoming a bottle-neck.

Camilla mentioned her automation idea to fellow biochemistry doctoral student Jochen Klingelhoefer. Jochen had a background in electrical engineering and technical consulting and was also involved in Oxford University's entrepreneurial community. He knew that the University's business idea competition, Idea Idol, was coming up in March 2009. Camilla and he teamed together to prepare a two-minute 'elevator pitch' for a machine for the automated preparation of buffer solutions, called EasySolution. Against more than one hundred initial competitors, EasySolution emerged as winners of Idea Idol 2009.

Camilla Oxley preparing a buffer solution
Source: Richard Whittington.

After success at Idea Idol, everything began to snowball for EasySolution. The prize was worth £7,500, plus £2,000 worth of free advice from a local law firm. EasySolution's success had also attracted the attention of two Saïd Business School MBA students: Ville Lehtonen, with an MSc in computer sciences and experience in product management, business-to-business sales and private equity; and Andrew Hunt, a graduate in classical languages and with a prize-winning background in marketing. With Ville as Chief Executive Officer, Jochen as Chief Technology Officer, Andrew as Director for Business Development and Camilla as Chief Science Officer, the four formed an equally-owned new company, LabMinds Ltd, in order to take EasySolution to market.

The business plan

The four started work on a business plan for the new company, eventually to be presented to a group of 'business angels' (early-stage investors) in September 2009. A survey of 200 potential users in the University of Oxford, plus discussions with product development companies, helped to refine the original product idea.

Table 1 Product prices and costs

	Sale	Maintenance
Revenue	£9,990	£1,500
Production Cost	−£3,000	–
Delivery	−£750	–
Service	–	−£300
Replacement	–	−£120
VAT (15%)	−£814	−£141
Commission (20%)	−£1,085	−£188
Gross Profit	£4,341	£751
Profit Margin	43.5%	50.1%

EasySolution was now defined as a machine that could make exact mixes of solutions with precise pH values at particular temperatures, according to commands delivered via internet, intranet or touch-screen. Creation of solutions would take one minute, and exact contents, time of creation and name of creator would be recorded in a log entry accessible to the laboratory manager. The proposed price of a machine was £9,990 (about €11,000), just below the level at which complex purchasing procedures are typically triggered in university laboratories. There would also be a maintenance charge of 15% for the machine, in line with rates paid for comparable laboratory devices (see Table 1). The only similar machines were typically much larger: for example, the American scientific products giant Millipore manufactured systems capable of producing solutions of 100 litres upwards, against the 1 litre or so for EasySolution. The only substitute was the purchase of standard buffer solutions from large scientific supplies companies, but these were typically expensive (£20 upwards) and required ordering well in advance.

The business plan proposed development of the core EasySolution machine in five key phases (see Table 2). The first phase would be devoted to a feasibility study funded by the founding team itself, friends and family

and hopefully grants from various government schemes supporting new businesses. The feasibility study, development and prototyping would be carried out by specialist companies DC Allen and Design Technology International Ltd. Development work would continue into phase 2, before production and launch of the core EasySolution product in phase 3. Phase 4 represents the continued growth of the company, leading towards eventual exit. Exit was expected to be in the form of either sale to an established large pharmaceutical or scientific equipment company or an initial public offering (IPO) to investors at large. The business plan pointed to the success of earlier start-ups in the specialised scientific products market, such as Harvard Bioscience and PerkinElmer, in achieving exit valuations based on net profit multiples of between 14 and 17.

Table 3 summarises the financial forecasts presented to investors. As above, the first year would be mostly concerned with development and investment. Sales were only expected to take off in year two (phase 3), with 350 units sold. By year three, machine sales were expected to reach £15m, with significant additional revenues from maintenance worth £1.65m. Production and maintenance were to be outsourced to specialised companies. After production, delivery and maintenance costs, LabMinds expected a gross profit of more than £7m in year 3.

Net profits in Table 3 came after significant operating (OPEX) and capital (CAPEX) expenditures. Operating expenditures planned in the first year included modest salaries for the management team, office charges, travel and marketing. In the second year, OPEX was expected to rise significantly, with the hiring of a Finance Director, an office manager, a software team and the building of a professional sales team for the United States as well as the United Kingdom. Capital expenditures were

Table 2 LabMinds' proposed development stages

Phase 1 (Month 1)	Development company DC Allen runs a feasibility study to identify not only the best way to create the whole system (based on the product specification by LabMinds), but also the easiest ways to get around core patents. The 2 core patents (likely described in product description) will be filed in this phase. Financing need: Roughly £30,000
Phase 2 (Months 2–7)	Proof of principles created on a level where the system can be demonstrated to potential customers to support pre-sales efforts. The official goal is to be able to create any solution at any temperature and pH combination, and being able to prove the sterility of the machine. Financing need: Roughly £150,000
Phase 3 (Months 8–19)	Prepare production. All the certifications necessary (nature of the product and the target market requires a rather wide range) will be acquired during this period. In parallel everything is being set up for mass production and the aesthetic aspects of the product are being finished. Financing need: Roughly £500,000
Phase 4 (Unknown)	Day-to-day operations with sales and marketing clearly being in their element now. Financing need: Roughly £1,000,000 mainly to fuel the marketing and sales efforts
Phase 5	Exit

Table 3 LabMinds' Revenue, Profit and Investment Forecasts

(000's)	Year 1	Year 2	Year 3
Unit Sales	0	350	1500
Sales Revenue		£3,496	£14,985
Maint Revenue		£263	£1,650
Gross Profit		£1,653	£7,345
OPEX	−£211	−£1,166	−£2,000
CAPEX	−£432	−£271	−£500
Net Profit	−£643	£216	£4,845
Investment	£650	£1,000	
Government	£270	£126	
Debt Financing	£25	£200	
Founding Capital	£10		

more front-loaded. Plans in the first year included more than £400,000 for payment to the product development companies DC Allen and Design Technology International Ltd, and a further £21,000 to create a family of patents intended to protect LabMinds' intellectual property. The business plan predicted continuing capital expenditures on product development and patents for the second year, though at a lower rate. CAPEX was expected to rise again in Year 3 with the development of further complementary machines.

Funding for the early years was expected to come from various sources. The founders themselves would put in an initial £15,000 and would raise convertible loans for a further £25,000 (a convertible loan gives the lender the option of converting the debt to equity). Various government support schemes were expected to contribute significantly, and a consultant was to be retained to assist in making grant applications. The most important source of funds, however, would be business angels and similar investors, with two rounds of investment in the first year and a third substantial

one (£1m) in the second. The investors in the first two rounds were expected to acquire about 40–50 per cent of the equity, and the investor in the third and largest round would receive just under 10 per cent of the equity. By the end of the second year, other employees and advisors were expected to hold a further 10 per cent or so of the equity. The business plan envisaged that at this point the original four founders would still own 25–35 per cent of a company valued at around £10m.

Investors were being offered access to a potentially huge market. The LabMinds team estimated the potential total market for EasySolution machines at about £1.0bn annually in the United Kingdom and the United States alone. Annual maintenance revenues for this market could reach £150m. But laboratories were not the only potential market. The business plan also pointed out that the basic technology could find other applications, for example in coffee-making or the preparation of cocktails for bars. LabMinds had a lot of upside.

Questions

1 Imagine that you are a potential investor hearing a short pitch from the EasySolution team based on the 2009 business plan. Using the SAFe framework, what questions would you raise with the team under:

(a) Suitability?

(b) Acceptability?

(c) Feasibility?

2 If you were interested in investing in EasySolutions, which round of investment would you prefer to participate in? Why?

12

STRATEGY DEVELOPMENT PROCESSES

Learning outcomes

After reading this chapter you should be able to:

● Explain what is meant by *intended* and *emergent* strategy development.

● Identify intended processes of strategy development in organisations including: the role *of strategic leadership*, *strategic planning systems* and *externally imposed strategy*.

● Identify processes that give rise to emergent strategy development such as: *logical incrementalism*, *political processes*, *the influence of prior decisions* and *organisational systems*.

● Explain some of the challenges managers face in strategy development including: managing *multiple strategy processes*, strategy development in *different contexts* and *managing intended* and *emergent strategy*.

Key terms

Emergent strategy p. 404

Intended strategy p. 398

Learning organisation p. 406

Logical incrementalism p. 405

Political view of strategy development p. 406

Strategic planning p. 400

(12.1) INTRODUCTION

We are familiar with successful strategies: Google's dominance of the internet; Ryanair becoming one of the most profitable airlines in the world; Apple's development of the iPhone; Zara's entrance into the UK fashion market. We know about failed strategies: Lehman Brothers and the Royal Bank of Scotland in banking; Woolworths in UK retailing; high-profile, once successful car manufacturers. Parts I and II of the book addressed how strategists might understand the strategic position of their organisation and what strategic choices are available. Chapter 11 explained different ways in which strategies can be evaluated. However, none of this directly addresses the question that is the theme of this chapter: *how do strategies actually develop?* (Chapter 15 then examines in more detail which people get involved in these processes and what they actually do in developing strategies.)

Figure 12.1 summarises the structure of this chapter. It is organised around two views of strategy development: strategy as intended and strategy as emergent. The *intended strategy* explanation is that strategies come about as the result of the deliberations of top management. This is sometimes known as the *rational/analytic view* of strategy development, or, as in the commentary sections of this book, *a design view* of strategy development. The second view is that of *emergent strategy*: that strategies do not develop on the basis of a grand plan but tend to emerge in organisations over time. The discussion in the commentaries of the experience, Variety and Discourse Lenses relates to this explanation. As the chapter will show, these two views are not mutually exclusive.

● The next section (12.2) of the chapter discusses intended strategy. First, there is an explanation of how strategies may be the outcome of *leadership*, *'command'* or *vision* of individuals.

Figure 12.1 Strategy development process

This is followed by a discussion of what formal *planning systems* in organisations might look like and the role they play. The section concludes with a discussion of how strategies might be deliberately *imposed* on organisations from the outside.

- The next section of the chapter (12.3) then switches to explanations of how strategies might emerge in organisations. The common feature of the different explanations here is that they do not see strategy-making as a distinct and separate organisational activity, but rather see strategies developing out of more day-to-day and routine aspects of organisations. The section offers four explanations of how this might occur: *logical incrementalism*, the influence of *political processes* in organisations, the effects of *prior decisions* on future strategy and finally how strategies could be the *outcome of organisational systems*.

- The final section of the chapter (12.4) raises some *implications for managing strategy development* including:

  - The likelihood that different explanations of strategy development should not be seen as independent or mutually exclusive. Rather that *multiple processes of strategy development* may all be seen within organisations.

  - How different approaches to strategy development may be more or less well suited to *different contexts*.

  - The implications for *managing intended strategy and emergent strategy development processes*.

INTENDED STRATEGY DEVELOPMENT

KEY CONCEPT

Intended strategy

Intended strategy is deliberately formulated or planned by managers. This may be the result of *strategic leadership, strategic planning* or sometimes the *external imposition* of strategy deliberately formulated elsewhere. Its development may also be associated with the use of the sort of tools, techniques and frameworks for strategic analysis and evaluation explained in this book.

12.2.1 Strategic leadership: the role of vision and command

An organisation's strategy may be influenced by strategic leaders: individuals (or perhaps a small group of individuals) whose personality, position or reputation gives them dominance over the strategy development process. They are therefore personally identified with and central to the strategy of their organisation. Such an individual could be central because he or she is the owner or founder of the organisation. This is often the case in small businesses and family businesses. It may also be that an individual still remains central after a business becomes very large: such is the case with Richard Branson at Virgin or Ratan Tata of the Tata Corporation. Or it could be that an individual chief executive has made major strategic changes and, as such, personifies the success of the organisation's strategy, as was the case with Michael O'Leary at Ryanair. Illustration 12.1 provides examples of strategic leaders' views on how they influence the strategy of their organisations.

In any of these circumstances, strategy may be – or may be seen to be – the deliberate intention of that leader. This may manifest itself in different ways.

- *Strategic leadership as command.* The strategy of an organisation might be dictated by an individual. This is, perhaps, most evident in owner-managed small firms, where that individual

ILLUSTRATION 12.1

CEO influence on strategy development

Different CEOs place different emphases on their influence on strategy in different circumstances.

Take a hard look at what the future might hold.
When Michael Jackson arrived at AutoNation. . . . the auto industry was selling as many as 17 million units a year, but its high fixed costs made him face what would happen if the economic environment changed. At his first management meeting he therefore announced his desire to find a business model that would let AutoNation break even if the auto industry sold only 10 million units. . . . 'Everybody looked at me like I had 6 heads', he recalls.

> 'Eventually we came to the conclusion that amongst other things it would take a credit crisis to get volumes that low, because in our business nothing moves without credit. So we got out of the finance and leasing business. . . . Without the limitation on risk we put in place, we would be in deep serious trouble at the moment.' (2009 when the credit crisis was at its height)[1]

Put strategy centre stage.
Bill Nuti, Chairman and CEO of NCR:

> 'The world moves at a pace that requires strategy to be front and centre all of the time. . . . there are too many variables that come into play in a normal cycle, let alone this one (the credit crisis of 2009) that can rapidly change the course of your company, so I bring strategy up at every single meeting.'[1]

The courage to take decisions and back your judgement.
Edward Breen of Tyco International stresses the importance of decisiveness, often with imperfect information:

> 'A lot of CEOs are slow to react and their problems get away from them. . . . you have to get as much data as quickly as possible. But you will never get all of it – so you need to make decisions quickly.'[1]

Sanjiv Ahuja, Chief Executive, Orange Group:

> 'You, as a leader, are supposed to make some decisions that are necessarily not going to be very popular. And that is OK; but stand up and be counted for those

decisions. Sometimes those decisions are where you bet your job, but that's OK; stand up and be counted for those.'[2]

Howard Lester, Chairman and CEO, Williams-Sonoma:

> 'Great leaders have a strength of conviction. You have the responsibility to really think through what you are doing. You ask a lot of opinions; it's not as if you go hide from everybody because you have made up your mind. But I think my point of view has always been that if I have an opinion and people can't argue me out of it, then I must be right. And I have to have the strength of that conviction and the courage to stick to it.'[2]

Communicate and be clear about the mission.
Terry Lundgren, Chairman, President and CEO of Macy's:

> 'The only way to address uncertainty is to communicate and communicate. When you think you've just about got to everybody, then communicate some more.'[1]

Domenico De Sole, former President and CEO, Gucci Group:

> 'What I say to everybody is that the mission should be clear and repeated all the time. It is important for a CEO to keep repeating the same basic principle and make sure that everybody at every level of the organisation shares the mission, shares the dream and understands what needs to be done.'[2]

References:
1. D. Carey, M. Patsalos-Fox and M. Useem, 'Leadership lessons for hard times', *McKinsey Quarterley*, July 2009.
2. *Leading by Example*, Harvard Business School Press, 2007.

Questions

1 Do you agree with all the views of the CEOs? If not, why not?

2 What else would you emphasise as an important contribution CEOs make to strategy development?

is in direct control of all aspects of the business. Danny Miller and Isabel Le Breton-Miller suggest there are advantages and disadvantages here. On the plus side it can mean speed of strategy adaptation and 'sharp, innovative, unorthodox strategies that are difficult for other companies to imitate'. The downside can, however, be 'hubris, excessive risk taking, quirky, irrelevant strategies'.[1]

- *Strategic leadership as vision.* It could be that a strategic leader determines or is associated with an overall vision, mission, or strategic intent (see section 4.2) that motivates others, helps create the shared beliefs within which people can work together effectively and shapes more detailed strategy developed by others in an organisation. Some writers see this as *the* role of the strategic leader.[2] For example, CEO of Tesco Sir Terry Leahy is recognised as driving and sustaining the need to regard customers as *the* primary stakeholder in the firm and the associated explicit core purpose: 'to create value for customers to earn their lifetime loyalty'.

- *Strategic leadership as decision-making.* It is likely that, whichever strategy development processes exist, there will be many different views and, perhaps, much but incomplete evidence to support those views. One of the key roles of leaders is to have the ability to weigh such different views, interpret data, have the confidence to take timely decisions and the authority to get others to buy into those decisions.

- *Strategic leadership as symbolic.* A strategic leader might, in effect, embody the strategy of the organisation whether or not he or she directly manages the organisation. Richard Branson no longer runs Virgin on a day-to-day basis; but he is seen as the embodiment of the Virgin strategy (see the Chapter 7 case example) and is frequently the public face of the company.

12.2.2 Strategic planning systems

A second way in which intended strategies develop is through formalised **strategic planning** systems.[3] These **take the form of systematised, step-by-step, procedures to develop an organisation's** strategy. For example, in a study of strategic planning systems of major oil companies, Rob Grant[4] noted the following stages in the cycle for a large corporation:

- *Initial guidelines.* The cycle's starting point is usually a set of guidelines or assumptions about the external environment (e.g. price levels and supply and demand conditions) and the overall priorities, guidelines and expectations of the corporate centre.

- *Business-level planning.* In the light of these guidelines, business units or divisions draw up strategic plans to present to the corporate centre. Corporate centre executives then discuss those plans with the business managers usually in face-to-face meetings. On the basis of these discussions the businesses revise their plans for further discussion.

- *Corporate-level planning.* The corporate plan results from the aggregation of the business plans. This coordination may be undertaken by a corporate planning department that, in effect, has a coordination role. The corporate board then has to approve the corporate plan.

- *Financial and strategic targets* are then likely to be extracted to provide a basis for performance monitoring of businesses and key strategic priorities on the basis of the plan.

Grant found that some of the companies he studied were much more formal and regularised than others (e.g. the French Elf Aquitaine and Italian ENI), with greater reliance on written reports and formal presentations, more fixed planning cycles, less flexibility and more specific objectives and targets relating to the formal plans. Where there was more informality or flexibility (e.g. BP, Texaco and Exxon), companies placed greater emphasis on more general financial targets. Central corporate planning departments also played different roles. In some organisations they acted primarily as coordinators of business plans. In others they were more like internal consultants, helping business unit managers to formulate their plans. Illustration 12.2 is a schematic representation of how strategic planning takes form in a large multinational drinks company.

Formalised strategic planning systems may play a role in how future organisational strategy is determined but this may not always be so. For example, the decisions about competitive

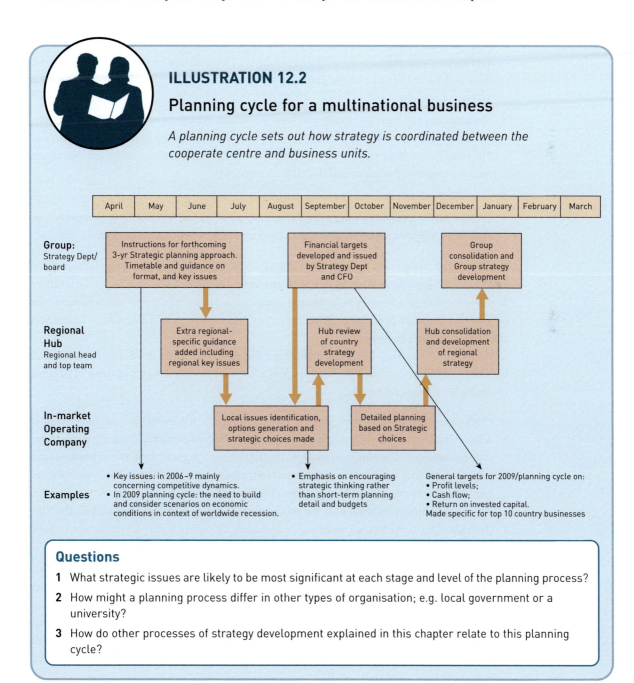

ILLUSTRATION 12.2

Planning cycle for a multinational business

A planning cycle sets out how strategy is coordinated between the cooperate centre and business units.

	April	May	June	July	August	September	October	November	December	January	February	March

Group: Strategy Dept/board — Instructions for forthcoming 3-yr Strategic planning approach. Timetable and guidance on format, and key issues — Financial targets developed and issued by Strategy Dept and CFO — Group consolidation and Group strategy development

Regional Hub Regional head and top team — Extra regional-specific guidance added including regional key issues — Hub review of country strategy development — Hub consolidation and development of regional strategy

In-market Operating Company — Local issues identification, options generation and strategic choices made — Detailed planning based on Strategic choices

Examples
- Key issues: in 2006–9 mainly concerning competitive dynamics.
- In 2009 planning cycle: the need to build and consider scenarios on economic conditions in context of worldwide recession.

- Emphasis on encouraging strategic thinking rather than short-term planning detail and budgets

General targets for 2009/planning cycle on:
- Profit levels;
- Cash flow;
- Return on invested capital.
Made specific for top 10 country businesses

Questions

1 What strategic issues are likely to be most significant at each stage and level of the planning process?

2 How might a planning process differ in other types of organisation; e.g. local government or a university?

3 How do other processes of strategy development explained in this chapter relate to this planning cycle?

strategy in a business-level strategic plan will quite likely be taken in management meetings in that business. There the processes associated with strategy development may correspond to any of those explained in this chapter and elsewhere in the book (e.g. see Chapter 15 and the Commentaries). However, such decisions may *then* be built into the formal plan.

A strategic planning system may therefore play several roles within an organisation. Typically four are emphasised:

- *Formulating* strategy by providing means by which managers can understand strategic issues, for example by establishing overall *objectives*, encouraging the use of *analytic tools* such as those explained in this book and by *encouraging a longer-term view* of strategy than might otherwise occur. Planning horizons and associated objectives and bases of analysis vary, of course. In a fast-moving consumer goods company, 3- to 5-year plans may be appropriate. In companies which have to take very long-term views on capital investment, such as those in the oil industry, planning horizons can be as long as 15 years (in Exxon) or 20 years (in Shell).

- *Learning*: Rita McGrath and Ian MacMillan[5] argue that managers can benefit from planning if they see it as a means of learning rather than a means of 'getting the right answers'. They emphasise 'discovery-driven' planning which emphasises the need for *questioning and challenging* received wisdom and the taken-for-granted.

- *Co-ordinating* business-level strategies within an overall corporate strategy.

- *Communicating* intended strategy throughout an organisation and *providing agreed objectives or strategic milestones* against which performance and progress can be reviewed.

However, it should also be recognised that a planning system may also play a *psychological role*. By *involving people* in strategy development it can help to create *ownership* of the strategy. It can also provide a *sense of security* and logic, not least among senior management who believe they *should* be proactively determining the future strategy and exercising control over the destiny of the organisation.

Henry Mintzberg has, however, challenged the extent to which planning provides such benefits.[6] Arguably there are five main dangers in the way in which formal systems of strategic planning have been employed:

- *Confusing strategy with the strategic plan.* Managers may see themselves as managing strategy when what they are doing is going through the processes of planning. Strategy is, of course, not the same as 'the plan': strategy is the long-term direction that the organisation is following, not just a written document. Linked to this may be a confusion between *budgetary processes* and strategic planning processes. The two may come to be seen as the same so that strategic planning gets reduced to the production of financial forecasts rather than thinking through of the sort of issues discussed in this book. Of course it may be important to build the output of strategic planning into the budgetary process; but they are not the same.

- *Detachment from reality.* The managers responsible for the implementation of strategies, usually line managers, may be so busy with the day-to-day operations of the business that they cede responsibility for strategic issues to specialists *or* consultants. However, these rarely have power in the organisation to make things happen. The result can be that strategic planning becomes an intellectual exercise removed from the reality of operations. Specialist strategic planners may also come to believe that centrally planned strategy determines what goes on in an organisation. In fact it is what people do and the experience they draw on to do it that are likely to play a much more significant role (see section 12.3 and the Experience Lens in the Commentary). If formal planning systems are to be useful, those responsible for them need to draw on such experience and involve people throughout the organisation if planning is to avoid being removed from organisational reality.

- *Paralysis by analysis.* Strategic planning can also become over-detailed in its approach, concentrating on extensive analysis that, whilst technically sound, misses the major strategic issues facing the organisation. For example, it is not unusual to find companies with huge amounts of information on their markets, but with little clarity about the strategic importance of that information. The result can be *information overload* with no clear outcome.

- *Lack of ownership.* The strategy resulting from deliberations of a corporate planning department, or a senior management team, may not be owned more widely in the organisation. In one extreme instance, a colleague discussing a company's strategy with its planning director was told that a strategic plan existed, but found it was locked in the drawer of the executive's desk. Only the planner and a few senior executives were permitted to see it! There is also a danger that the process of strategic planning may be so cumbersome that individuals or groups might contribute to only part of it and *not understand the whole.* The result can be that the business-level strategy does not correspond to the intended corporate strategy. This is particularly problematic in very large firms.

- *Dampening of innovation.* Highly formalised and rigid systems of planning, especially if linked to very tight and detailed mechanisms of control, can contribute to an inflexible, hierarchical organisation with a resultant stifling of ideas and dampening of innovative capacity.

Table 12.1 summarises these potential benefits and potential dangers.

The evidence of the extent to which the pursuit of such systemised planning results in organisations performing better than others is equivocal[7] – not least because it is difficult to isolate formal planning as the dominant or determining effect on performance. However, there is some evidence that planning may be beneficial if it is designed to work in conjunction with bottom-up emergent processes of strategy development, approximating to the 'logical incremental' processes explained in section 12.3.1 below.[8] It may also be especially beneficial in dynamic environments, where decentralised authority for strategic decisions is required

Table 12.1 The potential benefits and dangers of strategic planning

Benefits	Dangers
• Helping determine and direct strategy	• Confusing strategy with the strategic plan
• Help understand strategic issues	• Detachment from reality
• Coordinating business-level strategies	• Paralysis by analysis
• A means of implementing an agreed strategy	• Lack of ownership
• Involving people and creating ownership of a strategy	• Dampening of innovation

(see Chapter 13) but where there is a need for co-ordination of strategies arising from such decentralisation.[9]

There has been a decline in the use of formal corporate planning departments[10] and a shift to business unit managers taking responsibility for strategy development and planning (see Chapter 15). Strategic planning is becoming more project-based and flexible.[11] In this respect the emphasised role for strategic planning has become less as a vehicle for top-down development of intended strategy and more of a vehicle for the co-ordination of strategy emerging from below.

12.2.3 Externally imposed strategy

The third way in which intended strategies manifest themselves is in situations where managers face what they see as the imposition of strategy by powerful external stakeholders. Strategies being imposed in such ways may have been determined elsewhere, perhaps through systematic strategic planning; or they may have developed in a more emergent fashion (see section 12.3 below). However, to the managers of the organisation having it imposed on them, it is experienced as an 'intended strategy'.

For example, government may dictate a particular strategic direction as in the public sector, or where it exercises extensive regulatory powers in an industry. Or it may choose to deregulate or privatise a sector or organisation currently in the public sector. In the UK public sector a more direct interventionist approach began to be used in the early 2000s. So-called special measures were employed for schools or hospitals deemed to be under-performing badly, with specialist managers being sent in to turn round the ailing organisations and impose a new strategic direction. Businesses in the private sector may also be subject to such imposed strategic direction, or significant constraints on their choices. A multinational corporation seeking to develop businesses in some parts of the world may be subject to governmental requirements to do this in certain ways, perhaps through joint ventures or local alliances. An operating business within a multidivisional organisation may also regard the overall corporate strategic direction of its parent as akin to imposed strategy. Venture capitalists may impose strategies on the businesses they acquire.[12]

(12.3) EMERGENT STRATEGY DEVELOPMENT

Although strategy development is often associated with top-management intentionality, an alternative explanation is that of **emergent strategy**: that **strategies emerge on the basis of a series of decisions, a pattern in which becomes clear over time**. This explains an organisation's strategy, not as a 'grand plan', but as a developing 'pattern in a stream of decisions'.[13] These cumulative decisions may subsequently be more formally described, for example in annual reports and strategic plans, and be seen as the intentional strategy of the organisation. It will not, however, have been the plan that developed the strategy; it will be the emerging strategy that informed the plan.

There are different explanations of emergent strategy[14] and this section summarises these. As Figure 12.2 shows, the different explanations can be thought of in terms of a continuum according to how deliberately managed the processes are. The explanations are: logical incrementalism, strategy as the outcome of political processes, as adaptation from prior decisions and finally as the outcome of organisational systems and routines.

Figure 12.2 A continuum of emergent strategy development processes

12.3.1 Logical incrementalism

The first explanation of how strategies may emerge is that of *logical incrementalism*. This explanation, in effect, bridges intentionally and emergence in that it explains how management may deliberately cultivate a bottom-up, experimental basis for strategies to emerge. **Logical incrementalism** is the development of strategy by experimentation and learning 'from partial commitments rather than through global formulations of total strategies'.[15] It was a term coined by James Quinn in his study of how strategies developed in multinational businesses.[16] There are four main characteristics of strategy development in this way.

● *Environmental uncertainty*. Managers realise that they cannot do away with the uncertainty of their environment by relying on analyses of historical data or predicting how it will change. Rather, they try to be sensitive to environmental signals by encouraging constant environmental scanning throughout the organisation.

● *General goals*. There may be a reluctance to specify precise objectives too early, as this might stifle ideas and prevent innovation and experimentation. So more general rather than specific goals may be preferred, with managers trying to move towards them incrementally.

● *Experimentation*. Managers seek to develop a strong, secure, but flexible, core business. They then build on the experience gained in that business to inform decisions both about its development and experimentation with 'side-bet' ventures. Commitment to strategic options may therefore be tentative in the early stages of strategy development. Such experiments are not the sole responsibility of top management. They emerge from what Quinn describes as '*subsystems*' in the organisation. By this he means the groups of people involved in, for example, product development, product positioning, diversification, external relations, and so on.

● *Coordinating emergent strategies*. Top managers may then utilise a mix of formal and informal processes to draw together an emerging pattern of strategies from these subsystems. These may then be formed into coherent statements of strategy for stakeholders (e.g. shareholders, financial commentators, the media) who need to understand the organisation's strategy.

Quinn argued that, despite its emergent nature, logical incrementalism can be 'a conscious, purposeful, proactive, executive practice' to improve information available for decisions and build people's psychological identification with the development of strategy. Logical incrementalism therefore suggests that strategy development can be deliberate and intended, whilst relying on organisational subsystems to sense what is happening in the environment and to try out ideas through experimentataion. It is a view of strategy development similar to the descriptions that managers themselves often give of how strategies come about in their organisations as Illustration 12.3 shows.

Arguably, developing strategies in such a way has considerable benefits. Continual testing and gradual strategy implementation provides improved quality of information for decision-making, and enables the better sequencing of the elements of major decisions. Since change will be gradual, the possibility of creating and developing a commitment to change throughout the organisation is increased. Because the different parts, or 'subsystems', of the organisation are in a continual state of interplay, the managers of each can learn from each other about the feasibility of a course of action. Such processes also take account of the political nature of organisational life, since smaller changes are less likely to face the same degree of resistance as major changes. Moreover, the formulation of strategy in this way means that the implications of the strategy are continually being tested out. This continual readjustment makes sense if the environment is considered as a continually changing influence on the organisation.

Given logical incrementalism's emphasis on learning, it is a view of strategy development which corresponds to the '**learning organisation**'[17] – an organisation **that is capable of continual regeneration from the variety of knowledge, experience and skills within a culture that encourages questioning and challenge**. Proponents of the learning organisation argue that formal structures and systems of organisations typically stifle organisational knowledge and creativity. They, too, argue that the aim of top management should be to facilitate rather than direct strategy development by building pluralistic organisations, where conflicting ideas and views are surfaced and become the basis of debate; where knowledge is readily shared and experimentation is the norm such that ideas are tried out in action.

As with logical incrementalism the learning organisation sees organisations as social networks,[18] where the emphasis is not so much on hierarchies as on different interest groups that need to cooperate and learn from each other. It also sees strategy development occurring on the basis of ideas bubbling up from below and being moulded at the top rather than being directed from the top. In these respects there are similarities to the Variety Lens discussed in the Commentaries.

12.3.2 Strategy as the outcome of political processes

The second explanation of how strategies may emerge is that they are the outcome of the bargaining and power politics that go on between executives or between coalitions within the organisation and major stakeholders. Managers may well have different views on issues and how they should be addressed; they are therefore likely to seek to position themselves such that their views prevail. They may also seek to pursue strategies or control resources to enhance their political status. For example, Motorola's inability to move fast enough from analogue to digital technology for mobile phones and its consequent loss of market dominance (see Illustration 5.1 in Chapter 5) was substantially the result of divisional 'warring tribes' across the company seeking to preserve their own interests.[19] The **political view of strategy**

ILLUSTRATION 12.3

An incrementalist view of strategic management

Managers often see their job as managing adaptively: continually changing strategy to keep in line with the environment, whilst maintaining efficiency and keeping stakeholders happy.

● 'You know there is a simple analogy you can make. To move forward when you walk, you create an imbalance, you lean forward and you don't know what is going to happen. Fortunately, you put a foot ahead of you and you recover your balance. Well, that's what we're doing all the time, so it is never comfortable.'[1]

● 'I begin wide-ranging discussions with people inside and outside the corporation. From these a pattern eventually emerges. It's like fitting together a jigsaw puzzle. At first the vague outline of an approach appears like the sail of a ship in a puzzle. Then suddenly the rest of the puzzle becomes quite clear. You wonder why you didn't see it all along.'[2]

● 'We haven't stood still in the past and I can't see with our present set-up that we shall stand still in the future; but what I really mean is that it is a path of evolution rather than revolution. Some companies get a successful formula and stick to that rigidly because that is what they know – for example, [Company X] did not really adapt to change, so they had to take what was a revolution. We hopefully have changed gradually and that's what I think we should do. We are always looking for fresh openings without going off at a tangent.'[3]

● 'In our business you cannot know the future; it's changing so fast. That's why I employ some of the best brains in the industry. Their job is to keep at the forefront of what's happening and, through what they are working on, to help create that future. I don't give them a strategic plan to work to; my job is to discern a strategy from what they tell me and what they are doing. Of course they don't always agree

– why would they, they can't *know* the future either – which means there's a good deal of debate, a good deal of trial and error and a good deal of judgement involved.'[4]

● 'The analogy of a chess game is useful in this context. The objective of chess is clear: to gain victory by capturing your opponent's king. Most players begin with a strategic move, that assumes a countermove by the opponent. If the countermove materialises, then the next move follows automatically, based on a previous winning strategy. However, the beauty of chess is the unpredictability of one's opponent's moves. To attempt to predict the outcome of chess is impossible, and therefore players limit themselves to working on possibilities and probabilities of moves that are not too far ahead.'[5]

References:
1. Quotes from interviews conducted by A. Bailey as part of a research project sponsored by the Economic and Social Research Council (Grant No.: R000235100).
2. Extract from J.B. Quinn, *Strategies for Change*, Irwin, 1980.
3. Extracts from G. Johnson, *Strategic Change and the Management Process*, Blackwell, 1987.
4. CEO of a hi-tech business in an interview with a co-author.
5. From a manager on an MBA course.

Questions

1 With reference to these explanations of strategy development, what are the main advantages of developing strategies incrementally?

2 Is incremental strategy development bound to result in strategic drift (see section 5.2)? How might this be avoided?

development[20] is, then, that **strategies develop as the outcome of bargaining and negotiation among powerful interest groups** (or stakeholders). This is the world of boardroom battles often portrayed in film and TV dramas. Illustration 12.4 shows how the differences of views on strategy between its founder and different company directors at the budget airline easyJet played out over 2008 and 2009.

A political perspective on strategic management suggests that the rational and analytic processes often associated with developing strategy (see section 12.2.2 above and the Design Lens in the Commentary) may not be as objective and dispassionate as they appear. Objectives may reflect the ambitions of powerful people. Information used in strategic debate is not always politically neutral. A manager or coalition may exercise power over another because they control important sources of information. Powerful individuals and groups may also strongly influence which issues get prioritised.[21] In such circumstances it is bargaining and negotiation that give rise to strategy rather than careful analysis and deliberate intent.

None of this should be surprising. In approaching strategic problems, people are likely to be differently influenced by at least:

- *Personal experience* from their roles within the organisation.
- *Competition for resources and influence* between the different subsystems in the organisation and powerful people within them who are likely to be interested in preserving or enhancing their positions.[22]
- *The relative influence of stakeholders* on different parts of the organisation. For example, a finance department may be especially sensitive to the influence of financial institutions whilst a sales or marketing department will be strongly influenced by customers.[23]
- *Different access to information* given their roles and functional affiliations.

In such circumstances there are two reasons to expect strategy development to build gradually on the current strategy. First, if different views prevail and different parties exercise their political muscle, compromise may be inevitable. Second, it is quite possible that it is from the pursuit of the current strategy that power has been gained by those wielding it. Indeed it may be very threatening to their power if significant changes in strategy were to occur. It is likely that a search for a compromise solution accommodating different power bases will end up with a strategy which is an adaptation of what has gone before. So, often organisational politics are seen as constraining strategy development.

There are, however, more positive ways of seeing political processes. The conflict and tensions that manifest themselves in political activity, arising as they do from different expectations or interests, can be the source of new ideas (see the discussion on the Variety Lens in the Commentaries and on 'ambidexterity' in section 12.4.1) or challenges to old ways of doing things.[24] New ideas may be supported or opposed by different 'champions' who will battle over what is the best idea or the best way forward. Arguably, if such conflict and tensions did not exist, neither would innovation. The productive management of such tensions may be a learned competence or dynamic capability (see section 3.2.2) in some organisations that provides them with a basis for competitive advantage. Further, as section 14.4.5 shows, the exercise of power may be important in the management of strategic change.

All of this suggests that political activity has to be taken seriously as an influence on strategy development. Whatever thinking goes into a strategy will need to go hand in hand with activity to address the political processes at work. This is addressed in other parts of this book, in particular sections 4.5.2–3 and 14.4.5 as well as in the Commentaries.

ILLUSTRATION 12.4

Boardroom battles at easyJet

Political processes in organisations can influence the development of strategy.

Sir Stelios Haji-Ioannou founded easyJet in 1995 and was Chairman between 2000 and 2003. He resigned from this position in 2003 saying he wanted to 'concentrate on new ventures' but that he intended to 'remain a significant share holder of this company for a very long time'. His influence took centre stage in autumn 2008 when a private boardroom spat became public, took a subsequent 12 months to resolve, saw a change of 3 senior directors and ended with Sir Stelios getting 50% of his own way.

In 2007, the easyJet share price was flying high at 630p (~€6.9 ~$9.5), but, by autumn 2008 it had nose-dived to 266p per share. Perhaps worried about his investment, perhaps keen to re-extend his influence, Sir Stelios increased his shareholding in the company by taking on the voting rights of the shares held by his sister. He then made his concerns about the growth plans of Andrew Harrison [the CEO at the time] public by writing to Sir Colin Chandler, who was then Chairman, demanding changes to the board of directors as well as the scaling down of growth plans. In particular his objection was to plans to place a £3.4bn (~€3.7bn; ~$5.1bn) order with Airbus.

Press reports at the time claimed that at least two of the non-executive directors of easyJet had threatened to resign if Sir Stelios forced his way back to the helm of the company. In fact, it was the Finance Director who decided to leave for a position elsewhere in the FTSE 100 and in May 2009 Sir Colin Chandler also stepped down earlier than expected amid whispers of his simply being fed-up with the row on the plans for expansion between Stelios and the management team.

During this period, Sir Stelios had attempted to tone down the perception of the disagreement describing it as 'a debate not a dispute' and claiming he was simply exercising his right to protect his investment. Other key figures saw it differently. Sir David Michels, the senior independent non-executive director and widely respected corporate figure, said that the stress of running the company was not helped by a dominant [38%] shareholder: 'it is a company with one large shareholder and that always produces particular pressures. On top of that the shareholder is a very public and on the whole respected figure.'

Sir Stelios had always retained the right, with a shareholding of over 25%, to appoint two non-executive directors and more importantly make himself chairman. The threat of this action and confusion at the rationale for his objection, not only to the plans for growth, but also his suggested alternative [a pay-out to shareholders] left analysts wary of the stock.

As 2009 drew to a close it appeared the matter was reaching a resolution. With a new Chairman [Sir Michael Rake] in place since June 2009 Sir Stelios finally relented and approved a scaled down version of the expansion plans. But the final casualty was CEO Andrew Harrison. At end of the year he announced his plans to step down in the summer of 2010 and seek 'new challenges'. His replacement was Carolyn McCall who joined the board in July 2010. The following week she announced a review of the growth strategy. In the same week Sir Stelios called for an emergency general meeting of shareholders.

Sources: Mark Kleinman, 'easyJet Directors Threaten to Take Off'. *Daily Telegraph*, 15 November 2008; R. Lea, 'O'Leary Faces Lawsuit over Attack on easyJet Founder', *The Times*, 13 February 2010; Lauren Mills, 'Stelios Plays Down his Clash with Directors'. *Daily Mail*, 15 November 2008; Dan Milmo, 'easyJet Entrepreneur Stelios wins Boardroom Battle after Chairman Quits Early'. *Guardian*, 7 April 2009; Dominic O'Connell, 'Stelios Grabs Controls at easyJet', *Sunday Times*, 16 November 2008.

Questions

1 Do you consider the reported events at easyJet exceptional? Can you identify other examples?

2 The influence of Sir Stelios resides in his being the founder of easyJet and a major shareholder. What bases of political influence would executives draw on in disagreements a) with shareholders and b) between themselves?

12.3.3 Strategy informed by prior decisions

The third explanation of how strategies may emerge is as the product of prior decisions which inform or constrain strategy development. In many ways this is to be expected. It would be strange and, arguably, dysfunctional for an organisation to change its strategy fundamentally very often. So one way of explaining emergent strategy is that managers deliberately seek to maintain a continuity of strategy. There are, however, also explanations that suggest that such continuity may be much less deliberate; that it could be the outcome of path dependency or of organisational culture.

Emergent strategy as managed continuity

The strategy of an organisation may develop on the basis of a series of strategic moves each of which makes sense in terms of previous moves. Figure 12.3 illustrates this. A business may start with a new product idea. Its initial success may give rise to product development and product extensions building on this initial success. This may be followed by launches of the product into new markets. An acquisition might follow in the belief that this is synergistic with the current product offering. Over time the company may then become more acquisitive, perhaps seeking to diversify into related products. In this way each strategic move is informed by the rationale of the previous strategic move, such that over time the overall strategic approach of the organisation becomes more and more established. It is common to find management justifying successive strategic moves in this way.

Path-dependent strategy development

There is, however, a less deliberate explanation of such continuity. Path dependency was explained in Chapter 5 (section 5.3). Path dependency is where early events and decisions

Figure 12.3 Strategic direction from prior decisions

establish 'policy paths' that have lasting effects on subsequent events and decisions.[25] It therefore explains strategic decisions as historically conditioned. It also adds a degree of potential perversity to the pattern of continuity. The same decision sequence shown in the sort of incremental progression explained in Figure 12.3 may hold even if the opening move (in this case a product launch) is not especially successful. For example, a company may develop a product based on technology to which it is wedded and on the basis of which there is some initial success in the market. However, even if the initial success does not continue, further product development and product extensions may take place, perhaps because the company has invested large amounts of capital in the technology. Mixed success with these new products may then encourage the business to acquire another company in a related area in an attempt to strengthen the initial product range. Experience with this acquisition gives the business confidence to make further acquisitions in more diversified product areas. Thus the business ends up as a widely diversified company when it originally sought only to launch a single new product. In effect the company pursues a strategy in which they reinforce sub-optimal prior strategic decisions: they 'dig the hole deeper'.

Organisation culture and strategy development

The influence of culture on strategy was also explained in Chapter 5 (section 5.4). Here the emphasis is on strategy development as the outcome of the taken-for-granted assumptions, routines and behaviours in organisations. This taken-for-grantedness works to define, or at least guide, how people view their organisation and its environment. It also tends to constrain what is seen as appropriate behaviour and activity.[26] It is very likely, then, that decisions about future strategy will be within the bounds of the culture and that a pattern of continuity will be the outcome, subsequently post-rationalised by managers. Examples of this are given in Chapter 5 together with the potential problems that can arise. Not least amongst these is that such culturally bounded strategy development can lead to strategic drift (see section 5.2 of Chapter 5).

12.3.4 Strategy as the product of organisational systems

The fourth explanation of how strategies may emerge is on the basis of an organisation's systems. Rather than seeing strategy development as about foresight and anticipation taking form in directive plans from the top of the organisation, strategy development can be seen as the outcome of managers at much lower levels making sense of and dealing with problems and opportunities by applying established ways of doing things. In so doing they are likely to be heavily influenced by the systems and routines with which they are familiar in their particular context. Two useful explanations have developed as to how this occurs: the resource allocation process[27] (RAP) explanation of strategy development and the attention-based view[28] (ABV) of strategy development. Both emphasise that established ways of allocating resources in organisations will tend to play a significant part in what sort of solutions to problems are advocated and those to which resources are allocated.

A classic example of how the resource allocation process can influence strategy is Robert Burgelman's study[29] of how Intel became a microprocessor company in the 1980s. This is explained in Illustration 12.5. There are two main insights that this explanation of strategy development offers, shown graphically in Figure 12.4.

● *Organisational systems as a basis for making sense of issues.* Managers are likely to make sense of issues they face on the basis of the systems and routines with which they are familiar and

Figure 12.4 Strategy development as the product of structures, systems and routines

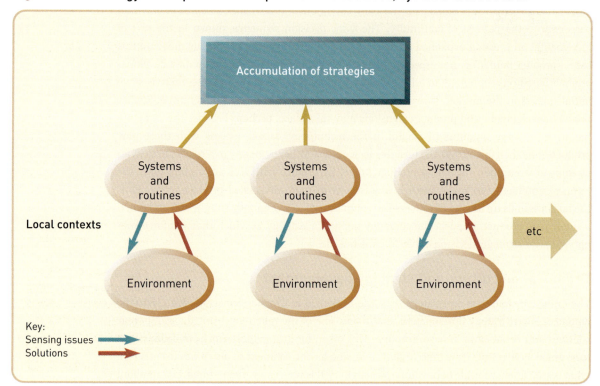

which directly affect them. For example, a finance director will be primarily concerned with the financial systems of the organisation or an operations director with operations. Managers within a business unit will be primarily concerned with the systems relating to that business; managers at the corporate level with systems at that level. Reward systems for company directors based on year-on-year earnings growth can encourage a focus on short-term rather than long-term strategies. Overhead allocation routines can exaggerate the profitability of some products or services and therefore encourage their perceived significance and development at the expense of others. Targets set by government for those managing public services can result in a focus on some issues at the expense of others. Vertical reporting relationships in hierarchies will focus managers' attention on issues within their part of the organisation as distinct from cooperating on wider issues across the wider organisation.

Whereas top-down explanations of strategy development assume that managers' focus of attention will readily cohere around clearly identified overarching 'strategic issues', this explanation emphasises that (a) it may not be analysis of an organisation's overall strategic position so much as local systems that surface issues that get attended to; and (b) such issues are likely to be locally defined.

● *Organisational systems provide bases of solutions to strategic issues.* Systems and routines also provide solutions that managers can draw on when faced with problems. However, responses may differ depending on the context the managers are in and the associated systems and routines. A common example is the way in which different responses emerge as a result of a downturn in company performance. Marketing managers, seeing this as a downturn in the market, may originate solutions which are to do with sales promotion and

ILLUSTRATION 12.5

The development of the microprocessor business at Intel

Resource allocation systems rather than management's intention may drive strategy development.

Between 1968 and 1985 Intel specialised in integrated circuit memory products. By the early 1980s it had two main product areas. DRAM (Dynamic Random Access Memory) had been the basis of the firm's growth and top management remained committed to R&D investment in it. However, given increased competition, DRAMs had lost market share. EPROM (Erasable Programmable Read Only Memory) had become Intel's most profitable product. There was also the emerging business in microprocessors. Microprocessors, however, involved different processes, with an emphasis on chip design rather than manufacturing processes as in the other product areas.

By the end of the 1980s, however, it was the microprocessor business that emerged as the basis of Intel's future growth and identity. This did not happen because of top management's planned direction. They remained committed to the memory business. However, in a company in which there had been an ethos of top-down financial rigour, a resource allocation rule had been created by the first Finance Director designed to maintain Intel as a technological leading-edge company. It stipulated that manufacturing capacity was allocated in proportion to the profit margins achieved in the different product sectors.

The emphasis within the DRAM group was on finding sophisticated technical solutions to DRAM's problems; it was, however, innovation in markets where innovation was no longer commerically viable. DRAM managers nonetheless continued to fight to have manufacturing capacity assigned purely to DRAM, proposing that capacity be allocated on the basis of manufacturing cost. Senior management refused, however, to change the basis of resource allocation.

By the early 1980s DRAMs amounted to only 5 per cent of Intel's revenue, down from 90 per cent. Since DRAM profits were also declining and microprocessor profits were increasing, over time DRAM lost manufacturing capacity within Intel to the microprocessor area. Once this decision was made to keep the resource allocation rule, the strategic freedom left to corporate managers to recover the founding businesses to which they were very attached diminished as market share fell beyond what could be deemed worthwhile recovering. DRAM managers had to compete internally with the technological prowess of the other product areas where morale and excitement were at high levels and innovation was happening in an increasingly dynamic market. And as microprocessors became more and more profitable, the business received increased funding, with manufacturing capacity and investment increasingly allocated away from memory towards them, providing it with the basis for future growth. Eventually corporate managers realised that Intel would never be a player in the 64K DRAM memory game, despite having been the creator of the business. In 1985, top management came to realise they had to withdraw from the DRAM market.

Lingering resistance to the exit continued. Manufacturing personnel ignored implications of exiting from DRAM by trying to show they could compete in the marketplace externally, by explaining failure in terms of the strong dollar against the Japanese yen and battling with poor morale. Eventually Andy Grove, CEO from 1987, took the executive decision to withdraw from EPROM too, leaving no doubt that microprocessors now represented Intel's future strategic direction. The subsequent exit from EPROM was rapidly executed. Staff associated with EPROM left and set up their own start-up.

Source: Based on the case study on Intel by Jill Shepherd (Segal Graduate School of Business, Simon Fraser University, Canada) in 8th edition of *Exploring Corporate Strategy*.

Questions

1 What other examples can you think of where resource allocation processes strongly influence strategy development?

2 What role should top management play in relation to resource allocation processes in organisations?

advertising to generate more sales, research and development managers may see it as a need for product innovation and accountants may see it as a need for tighter controls and cost cutting. Each is drawing on the context in which they find themselves and the associated systems and routines for dealing with such problems.

This explanation highlights two potential problems of strategy development. First, since managers in different contexts have different foci of attention, they may well define issues differently and respond in different ways. Examples were given above in relation to different management functions. Another example is between the business unit and the corporate centre of an organisation. Managers in the business unit, close to a market, may pay attention to routines and systems to do with competitors and customers whereas senior corporate executives may be concerned with balancing resource allocation across businesses, with systems relating to financial markets and with government regulation. There is evidence to suggest that this is one reason why middle-management concerns about changes in markets may go unheeded.[30]

Second, this explanation emphasises that it may not be top-down strategic intent that drives the strategy of an organisation so much as the accumulation of local decisions strongly influenced by local context. These may then be post-rationalised into an apparently coherent strategy. It also helps explain why the strategy development is likely to be a political process (section 12.3.2) since there may be different perceptions of strategic issues and different views on solutions.

12.4 IMPLICATIONS AND CHALLENGES FOR MANAGING STRATEGY DEVELOPMENT

The discussion of different strategy development processes in sections 12.2 and 12.3 has implications for how managers manage the strategy development process.

12.4.1 Multiple strategy development processes

The processes explained above are not discrete or mutually exclusive. It is likely that there will be multiple processes at work in any organisation and the effective management of strategy development needs to take this into account. Indeed, a number of observers of strategy development have suggested that organisations manifest processes that are, in effect, 'planned emergence' with top-down overall intent taking into account and building on bottom-up emergence of strategy.

Even if there is a dominant mode of strategy development in an organisation other processes will, then, be evident too. For example, if a planning system exists in a large organisation, there will also undoubtedly be political activity; indeed the planning system itself may be used for negotiating purposes. It has to be recognised, therefore, that there is *no one right way* in which strategies are developed. The challenge is for managers to recognise the potential benefits of different processes of strategy development so as to build organisations capable of adapting and innovating within a changing environment yet achieving the benefits of more formal processes of planning and analysis to help this where necesssary.[31] There are, however, some useful insights from research that can guide a consideration of appropriate strategy development processes.

Organisational ambidexterity

Multiple strategy processes may need to exist because the strategic needs of organisations require it. For example, an organisation may seek to *exploit* the capabilities that it has built up over time in order to build and sustain competitive advantage. It may seek to do so by top management being fairly directive about the strategy to be followed and coordinating and controlling this through a *planning* system. It will also, very likely, mean that there will be *incremental* development of strategy since strategy will be built on established ways of doing things. The risk, however, is that there may not be enough *exploration* of bases of new capabilities and bases of innovation. If such exploration is to take place there is likely to be a greater need for *organisational learning* (see section 12.3.1) to be more in evidence. The conclusion is that in some organisations there may be a need for both exploitation and exploration – what has become known as '*organisational ambidexterity*'. However, this may be problematic because the different processes associated with exploitation and exploration require different management styles, organisational systems and cultural contexts. In relation to the processes explained in this chapter and elsewhere in the book there are, however, suggestions as to how this might be possible.

- *Structural ambidexterity.* Many organisations have maintained the main core of the business devoted to exploitation with tighter control and careful planning but created separate units or temporary, perhaps project-based, teams for exploration[32] (see section 13.2.5). These separate units devoted to exploration, very likely much smaller in size, may be less tightly controlled[33] with much more emphasis on learning and processes to encourage new ideas.

- *Diversity rather than conformity.* Contradictory behaviours may be beneficial, so there may be benefits from diversity of views in line with the concept of *organisational learning* and with the inevitable consequence of political activity. Such diversity might be on the basis of managers with different experience that gives rise to useful debate. Stanford Univerity's Robert Burgelman argues that somewhere in an organisation, quite likely close to the market and therefore perhaps at junior levels, there will be those who are dissatisfied with the prevailing strategy or think it is inadequate in the face of what they perceive to be changing industry circumstances. He argues[34] that senior executives need to distinguish between dissonant 'noise' in the organisation and such 'strategic signalling', value 'constructive confrontation' and channel it into a 'searing intellectual debate' until a clearer strategic pattern emerges.

- *The role of leadership.* In turn this has implications for leadership roles in organisations. Leaders need to encourage and value different views and potentially contradictory behaviours rather than demanding uniformity.[35] This may well mean running with new ideas and experiments to establish just what makes sense and what does not. However, they also need to have the authority, legitimacy and recognition to stop such experiments when it becomes clear that they are not worthwhile pursuing and make decisions about the direction that is to be followed which, once taken, are followed by everyone in the organisation – including those who have previously dissented.

- *Tight and loose systems.* All this suggests that there needs to be a balance between systems of strategy development that can exploit existing capabilities – perhaps employing the disciplines of strategic planning – and 'looser' systems that encourage new ideas and experimentation. This might, in turn, be linked to the idea that there needs to be some overall common 'glue', perhaps in the form of a clear *strategic intent* in terms of mission and values such that different units in the organisation may be allowed to express how such mission is achieved in their different ways.

Perceptions of strategy development

It is also likely that processes of strategy development will be seen differently by different people. For example, senior executives tend to see strategy development more in terms of intended, rational, analytic planned processes, whereas middle managers see strategy development more as the result of cultural and political processes. Managers in public-sector organisations tend to see strategy as externally imposed more than managers in commercial businesses, largely because their organisations are answerable to government bodies.[36] People who work in family businesses tend to see more evidence of the influence of powerful individuals, who may be the owners of the businesses. The chapter's Key Debate shows very different accounts of the strategy development for a highly successful strategy.

12.4.2 Strategy development and organisational context

Processes of strategy development are likely to differ according to context. Therefore different ways of thinking about strategy development and different processes for managing strategy may make sense in different circumstances. At the risk of over-generalisation there are three major contextual influences. The first two can be considered together.

Organisational characteristics and the nature of the environment

Organisations differ in their characteristics and exist in different environments. The combination of these two contextual dimensions is likely to affect strategy development processes.

First, in terms of the *characteristics of the organisation*, is it *small or large?* In a small organisation individual and fairly detailed direction of strategy may be possible by a chief executive but this may be more difficult in a larger organisation. If the organisation is large, is it also *complex?* Some large organisations, for example, nonetheless operate in a single industry or with a core business model: a major retailer such as Wal-Mart for example. Others are more complex in that they are more diverse, perhaps including many different business units; for example a highly diversified conglomerate such as GE. Or they may comprise diverse and specialised technologies as in universities or a local government with many different services. In such circumstances top management needs to recognise that the possibility of planning detailed strategies from the top is limited, arguably dangerous, since specialists lower down in the organisation know more about the environment in which the organisation operates than they do.

Second, what is the *nature of the environment?*[37]

- *In stable environments* historic tendencies are capable of being understood and are likely to influence the future nature of the environment.
- In relatively *dynamic and uncertain* environments history is less a predictor, so managers need to seek to take a view of the future rather more than the past.
- *Complex* environments are difficult to comprehend; and here complexity is likely to go hand in hand with dynamic change. For example, high-tech industries may be in this category.

Figure 12.5 shows strategy processes are likely to differ according to these organisational characteristics and different environments.[38] For example:

Figure 12.5 Strategy development contexts

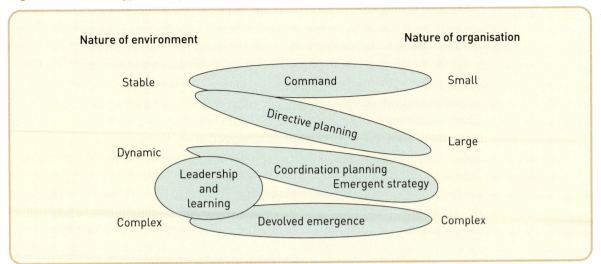

- The *command* mode of strategy is likely to be found most in small organisations in relatively stable environments. A strategic leader – perhaps an owner of a small firm – may be able to draw on extensive experience of how to compete in an industry, use that experience to direct strategy and manage the implementation of that strategy in a fairly hands-on manner given the size of the organisation.

- *Directive planning* in which top management determines and drives strategy is most likely in large stable organisations that are not too complex. Here managers are likely to understand their business units well and, if environmental change does occur, it may be predictable; so it could make sense to analyse the environment extensively on a historical basis as a means of trying to forecast likely future conditions. Examples might include major retailers, raw material suppliers or mass manufacturing. It may also be possible to identify some predictors of environmental influences. For example, in some public services, demographic data such as birth rates might be used as lead indicators to determine the required provision of schooling, health care or social services. There are, however, two problems here. First, competitors in the same sort of environment may all end up following the same strategies; and this could be a recipe for high degrees of competition and low profits (see Chapter 6). Second, environmental conditions may change. Many organisations have found increasingly dynamic and/or complex conditions. When this happens it could be that they find difficulties in adjusting to those changed conditions because their strategy development processes are not suited to them.

- *'Co-ordination planning'*: Where organisations face more turbulent or complex situations there is an important role for planning but it is likely to differ from top-down directive planning.[39] It may play the role of promoting strategic thinking throughout the organisation. For example, a role of strategic planning in many large conglomerates is to provide business units with guideline key assumptions about the future environment together with overall objectives that are to be met. They will then act to integrate the strategies that emerge from those business units.

- *Emergent strategy* processes are also more likely in complex organisations where the environment is also more complex. Professional services such as accountancy and health services are examples. Here specialist units may be dealing with particular markets or needs. In such circumstances it is likely that there will be devolved power of decision-making since top managers at the centre of the organisation cannot expect to understand markets or technologies such that they can take directive decisions at such levels. Strategies will be more likely to emerge from operating units. Top management's role may be more to do with setting overall strategic direction and co-ordinating and shaping emerging strategy from below.

- *Leadership and learning:* The situation of dynamic or complex environments therefore poses an additional challenge. Not only is co-ordination necessary, but it is likely that some stimulus from the top will be needed to galvanise change or to empower and legitimise new ideas from the bottom. So leadership may play an important role here both in establishing clarity of an overall mission or vision and in encouraging organisational learning and development. Further, in terms of the impact new leaders such as CEOs have on organisations, there seems to be evidence that this may vary according to how dynamic the environment is. Whilst the influence of new CEOs in relatively stable environments may be long-lasting, in fast-changing environments their influence may be much more short-lived.[40]

Life cycle effects

The third contextual influence on strategy development processes is how organisations develop over time. For example:

- *Life cycle stages.* In the early stage of an organisation's development, very likely strategy development will be heavily influenced by the founder; as such it is likely to be a 'command' style of management. As organisations develop, especially in new industries there is likely to be a reliance on managers' experience and drawing lessons from what other organisations do, with relatively low use of more rational search mechanisms. As organisations and industries mature, however, they may use more analytic approaches to strategy development.[41]

- *Strategic inflection points.* Burgelman and Grove[42] argue that all organisations face what they call 'strategic inflection points' where there are shifts in fundamental industry dynamics which management needs to recognise and act upon. The problem management faces is how to do this when they are busily working to maximise their competitive advantage and returns in the prevailing industry structure. This is where managers need to take seriously the 'dissonance' that exists in their organisations. So this relates to the challenge of organisational ambidexterity and the strategy development processes required for this (see above).

12.4.3 Managing intended and emergent strategy

This chapter has drawn a distinction between intended and emergent strategy. It has also made the point that the different processes of strategy development are not mutually exclusive; organisations have multiple processes. A problem that managers face, then, is that it is not unusual for organisations to have an intended strategy, perhaps the result of a strategic planning process, but to be following a different strategy in reality. We all experience this as customers of organisations that have stated strategies quite different from what we experience – government agencies that are there purportedly to serve our interests but act as bureaucratic officialdom, companies that claim they offer excellent customer service but operate call centres that frustrate customers and fail to solve problems, universities that claim excellence of teaching but are more concerned with their staff's research, or vice versa. Drawing on the explanations provided in this chapter, Figure 12.6 shows how realised strategy may come to be different from intended strategy.

- *Intended strategy* is the strategy deliberately formulated or planned by senior executives, as explained in section 1.2 and represented by route 1 in Figure 12.6. It may well be expressed in a formal document. It may also be accompanied by mechanisms designed to implement the intentions – project plans or objectives and targets, for example. However, intention and plans are not action; what an organisation actually does can be influenced by other processes.

- *Emergent strategy* is that which emerges on the basis of a series of decisions, a pattern which becomes clear over time. How this happens is explained in section 12.3.3 in terms of the influences of learning, political processes, prior decisions and organisational systems and is represented by route 2 in Figure 12.6.

- *Realised strategy* is what the organisation is actually doing in practice (3 in Figure 12.6). This may have come about as a result of the intended strategy, but it may have come about as the outcome of emergent strategy processes. In truth the likelihood is that it will be a combination of the two: both intended and emergent processes are likely to influence what actually happens.

- *Unrealised strategy* (route 4) is the aspects of the intended strategy that do not come about in practice. There are several reasons for this: the environment changes and managers decide that the strategy, as planned, should not be put into effect; the plans prove to be unworkable or unacceptabel in practice; or the emergent strategy comes to dominate. (Also see the discussion of the drawbacks of planning systems in section 12.2.2 above.)

There are at least four important implications here for strategists:

- *Awareness.* First, and most fundamental, have managers taken steps to check if the intended strategy is actually being realised? It should not be assumed that top management of organisations is always close enough to customers or gets sufficient feedback so as to understand

Figure 12.6 Strategy development routes

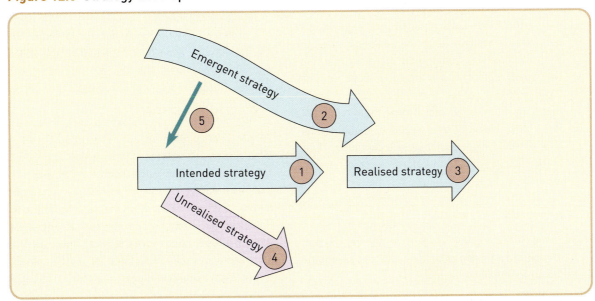

the extent of difference between what is intended as the strategy and what is actually happening.

- *The role of strategic planning.* As has been pointed out, strategic planning might not perform the role of formulating strategies so much as the useful role of co-ordinating the strategies that emerge within the organisation; this is route 5 in Figure 12.6. This may be useful because it may be important that there is a formal explanation of the strategy for the stakeholders of the organisation. However, the danger is that this does little more than pull together 'received wisdom' built up over the years such that the plan merely post-rationalises where the organisation has come from. If strategic planning systems are to be employed managers need to learn two key lessons:

  - They are not a substitute for other processes of strategy development. These other processes need to be managed too (see below).

KEY DEBATE

Honda and the US motorcycle market in the 1960s

There are different explanations of how successful strategies develop.

In 1984, Richard Pascale published a paper which described the success Honda had experienced with the launch of its motorcycles in the US market in the 1960s. It was a paper that has generated discussion about strategy development processes ever since. First he gave explanations provided by the Boston Consulting Group (BCG):

'The success of the Japanese manufacturers originated with the growth of their domestic market during the 1950s. This resulted in a highly competitive cost position which the Japanese used as a springboard for penetration of world markets with small motorcycles in the early 1960s. . . . The basic philosophy of the Japanese manufacturers is that high volumes per model provide the potential for high productivity as a result of using capital intensive and highly automated techniques. Their market strategies are therefore directed towards developing these high model volumes, hence the careful attention that we have observed them giving to growth and market share.'

Thus the BCG's account is a rational one based upon the deliberate intention of building of a cost advantage based on volume.

Pascale's second version of events was based on interviews with the Japanese executives who launched the motorcycles in the USA:

'In truth, we had no strategy other than the idea of seeing if we could sell something in the United States. It was a new frontier, a new challenge, and it fitted the 'success against all odds' culture that Mr. Honda had cultivated. We did not discuss profits or deadlines for breakeven. . . . We knew our products . . . were good but not far superior. Mr. Honda was especially confident of the 250cc and 305cc machines. The shape of the handlebar on these larger machines looked like the eyebrow of Buddha, which he felt was a strong selling point. . . . We configured our start-up inventory with 25 per cent of each of our four products – the 50cc Supercub and the 125cc, 250cc and 305cc machines. In dollar value terms, of course, the inventory was heavily weighted toward the larger bikes. . . . We were entirely in the dark the first year. Following Mr. Honda's and our own instincts, we had not attempted to move the 50cc Supercubs. . . . They seemed wholly unsuitable for the US market where everything was bigger and more luxurious.

- There needs to be realistic expectations of the role of strategic planning. For example, is its primary role one of co-ordination of emergent strategies; or is the expectation that it will contribute proactively to the development of strategy by, for example, encouraging the challenge of received wisdom and ways of doing things? If it is the latter, then the role of the strategic planner becomes one of internal consultancy as well as analyst and co-ordinator.

- *Managing emergent strategy.* The processes of strategy development that give rise to emergent strategy may be rooted in organisational routines and culture, but they are not unmanageable. Indeed, this is as much about managing strategy as is strategic planning. Resource allocation processes can be changed; political processes can be analysed and managed (see section 4.5 on stakeholder analysis in Chapter 4); challenge to the norms and routines of organisation culture can be encouraged. A clear mission or vision can help

...We used the Honda 50s ourselves to ride around Los Angeles on errands. They attracted a lot of attention. But we still hesitated to push the 50cc bikes out of fear they might harm our image in a heavily macho market. But when the larger bikes started breaking, we had no choice. And surprisingly, the retailers who wanted to sell them weren't motorcycle dealers, they were sporting goods stores.'

Two very different accounts, yet they describe the same market success. Since the publication of the paper, many writers on strategy have hotly debated what these accounts actually represent. For example, Henry Mintzberg observed: 'the conception of a novel strategy is a creative process (of synthesis), to which there are no formal techniques (analysis)'. He argued any formal planning was in the implementation of the strategy: 'strategy had to be conceived informally before it could be programmed formally'. He went on to add, 'While we run around being "rational", they use their common sense . . . they came to America prepared to *learn*.'

Michael Goold, the author of the original BCG report, defended it on the grounds that

'its purpose was to discern what lay behind and accounted for Honda's success in a way that would help others to think through what strategies would be likely to work. It tries to discern patterns in Honda's strategic decisions and actions and to use these patterns in identifying what works well and badly.'

Richard Rumelt concluded that

'the "design school" is right about the reality of forces like scaled economies, accumulated experience and accumulative development of core competences over time . . . but my own experience is that coherent strategy based upon analyses and understandings of these forces is much more often imputed than actually observed.'

And Pascale himself concluded that the serendipitous nature of Honda's strategy showed the importance of learning; that the real lessons in developing strategies were the importance of an organisation's agility and that this resides in its culture, rather than its analyses.

Source: This case example is based on R.T. Pascale, 'Perspectives on strategy: the real story behind Honda's success', *California Management Review*, vol. 26, no. 3 (Spring 1984), pp. 47–72; and H. Mintzberg, R.T. Pascale, M. Goold and R.P. Rumelt, 'The Honda effect revisited', *California Management Review*, vol. 38, no. 4 (1996), pp. 78–116.

Questions

1 Are the different accounts mutually exclusive?

2 Which of the different explanations of strategy development explained in the chapter do you discern in the Honda story?

3 Do you think Honda would have been more or less successful if it had adopted a more formalised strategic planning approach to the launch?

direct the bottom-up strategy development and strategic planning systems can help co-ordinate the outcomes of such processes.

● *The challenge of strategic drift.* A major strategic challenge facing managers was identified in Chapter 5 as the risk of strategic drift (see section 5.2): the tendency for strategies to develop incrementally on the basis of historical and cultural influences, but fail to keep pace with a changing environment. The discussion in section 12.3 of this chapter suggests that such a pattern may be a natural outcome of the influence of organisational culture, individual and collective experience, political processes and prior decisions. This further highlights that strategy development processes in organisations need to encourage people to have the capacity and willingness to challenge and change their core assumptions and ways of doing things.

SUMMARY

This chapter has dealt with different ways in which strategy development occurs in organisations. The main lessons of the chapter are:

● It is important to distinguish between *intended* strategy – the desired strategic direction deliberately planned by managers – and *emergent strategy* which may develop in a less deliberate way from the behaviours and activities inherent within an organisation.

● Most often the process of strategy development is described in terms of intended strategy as a result of *planning systems* carried out objectively and dispassionately. There are benefits and disbenefits of formal strategic planning systems. However, there is evidence to show that such formal systems are not an adequate explanation of strategy development as it occurs in practice.

● Intended strategy may also come about on the basis of central *command, the vision of strategic leaders* or the *imposition of strategies* by external stakeholders.

● Strategies may emerge from within organisations. This may be explained in terms of:

  ● How organisations may proactively try to cope through processes of *logical incrementalism and organisational learning.*

  ● The outcome of the bargaining associated with *political activity* resulting in a negotiated strategy.

  ● Strategy development on the basis of *prior decisions, path dependency* and the taken-for-granted elements of *organisational culture* that favour certain strategies.

  ● Strategies developing because *organisational systems* favour some strategy projects over others.

● In *managing strategy development processes*, managers face challenges including*:*

  ● *Multiple processes of strategy development* are likely to be needed if organisations are to achieve both the benefits of the *exploitation* of existing capabilities and the *exploration* for new ideas and capabilities (*organisational ambidexterity*).

  ● Recognising that *different processes of strategy development may be needed at different times and in different contexts.*

  ● Managing the processes that may give rise to *emergent strategy.*

WORK ASSIGNMENTS

✴ *Denotes more advanced work assignments. * Refers to a case study in the Text and Cases edition.*

12.1   Read the annual report of a company with which you are familiar as a customer (for example, a retailer or transport company). Identify the main characteristics of the intended strategy as explained in the annual report, and the characteristics of the realised strategy as you perceive it as a customer.

12.2   Using the different explanations in sections 12.2 and 12.3, characterise how strategies have developed in different organisations (for example, Google, Cordia* or RACC*).

12.3✴ Planning systems exist in many different organisations. What role should planning play in a public-sector organisation such as local government or the National Health Service and a multinational corporation such as SABMiller*?

12.4✴ Incremental patterns of strategy development are common in organisations, and managers see advantages in this. However, there are also risks of strategic drift. Using the different explanations in sections 12.2 and 12.3, suggest how such drift might be avoided.

12.5   Suggest why different approaches to strategy development might be appropriate in different organisations such as a university, a fashion retailer, a diversified multinational corporation and a high-technology company.

Integrative assignment

12.6✴ Assume you were asked to advise a chief executive of a long-established, historically successful multinational business with highly experienced managers that is experiencing declining profits and falling market share. What might you expect to be the causes of the problems? What processes of strategy development would you propose to address them?

RECOMMENDED KEY READINGS

● A much quoted paper that describes different patterns of strategy development is H. Mintzberg and J.A. Waters, 'Of strategies, deliberate and emergent', *Strategic Management Journal*, vol. 6, no. 3 (1985), pp. 257–72.

● The changing role of strategic planning in the oil industry is explained by Rob Grant; see 'Strategic planning in a turbulent environment: evidence from the oil majors', *Strategic Management Journal*, vol. 24 (2003), pp. 491–517. Also see M. Mankins, 'Stop making plans, start making decisions', *Harvard Business Review*, January 2006, pp. 77–84.

● A fascinating case study of the effects of resource allocation routines on the developing strategy of Intel

is provided by Robert Burgelman in 'Fading memories: a process theory of strategic business exit in dynamic environments', *Administrative Science Quarterly*, vol. 39 (1994), pp. 34–56.

● J. Brews and M.R. Hunt, 'Learning to plan and planning to learn: resolving the planning school/learning school debate', *Strategic Management Journal*, vol. 20 (1999), pp. 889–913.

● Insights into the importance of multiple processes of strategy development can be found in S.L. Hart, 'An integrative framework for strategy-making processes', *Academy of Management Review*, vol. 17, no. 2 (1992), pp. 327–51.

REFERENCES

1. The role of a command style in small businesses is discussed in D. Miller and I. Le Breton-Miller, 'Management insights from great and struggling family businesses', *Long Range Planning*, vol. 38 (2005), pp. 517–30. The quotes here are from p. 519.

2. For example see W. Bennis and B. Nanus, *The Strategies for Taking Charge*, Harper and Row, 1985 and J. Collins and J. Porras, *Built to Last: Successful Habits of Visionary Companies*, Harper Business, 2002.

3. In the 1970s and 1980s there were many books written on formal strategic planning approaches to strategy development. They are less common now but, for example, see N. Lake, *The Strategic Planning Workbook*, Kogan Page, 2nd edn (2006); J.M. Bryson, *Strategic Planning For Public and Nonprofit Organizations: a Guide to Strengthening and Sustaining Organizational Achievement*, 3rd edn, Jossey-Bass, 2005; and S. Haines, *The Systems Thinking Approach to Strategic Planning and Management*, St. Lucie Press, 2000.

4. R. Grant, 'Strategic planning in a turbulent environment: evidence from the oil majors', *Strategic Management Journal*, vol. 24 (2003), pp. 491–517.

5. R.G. McGrath and I.C. MacMillan, *Discovery-driven Growth*, Harvard Business School Press, 2009.

6. Many of these dangers are drawn from H. Mintzberg, *The Rise and Fall of Strategic Planning*, Prentice Hall, 1994.

7. Studies on the relationship between formal planning and financial performance are largely inconclusive. Some studies have shown benefits in particular contexts. For example, it is argued there are benefits to entrepreneurs setting up new ventures; see F. Delmar and S. Shane, 'Does business planning facilitate the development of new ventures?', *Strategic Management Journal*, vol. 24 (2003), pp. 1165–85. And other studies actually show the benefits of strategic analysis and strategic thinking, rather than the benefits of formal planning systems; e.g. see C.C. Miller and L.B. Cardinal, 'Strategic planning and firm performance: a synthesis of more than two decades of research', *Academy of Management Journal*, vol. 37, no. 6 (1994), pp. 1649–65.

8. P.J. Brews and M.R. Hunt, 'Learning to plan and planning to learn: resolving the planning school/learning school debate', *Strategic Management Journal*, vol. 20 (1999), pp. 889–913.

9. T.J. Andersen, 'Integrating decentralized strategy making and strategic planning processes in dynamic environments', *Journal of Management Studies*, vol. 41, no. 8 (2004), pp. 1271–99. Also M. Ketokivi and X. Castaner, 'Strategic planning as an integrative device'. *Administrative Science Quarterly*, vol. 49 (2004), pp. 337–65.

10. See reference 4 above.

11. See M. Mankins, 'Stop making plans, start making decisions', *Harvard Business Review*, January 2006, pp. 77–84.

12. See B. King, 'Strategizing at leading venture capital firms: of planning, opportunism and deliberate emergence', *Long Range Planning*, vol. 41 (2008), pp. 345–66.

13. H. Mintzberg and J.A. Waters, 'Of strategies, deliberate and emergent', *Strategic Management Journal*, vol. 6, no. 3 (1985), pp. 257–72.

14. See S. Elbanna, 'Strategic decision making: process perspectives', *International Journal of Management Reviews*, vol. 8, no. 1 (2006), pp. 1–20, for a useful explanation of differences between deliberate, intended strategy development and explanations of emergent and incremental strategy development.

15. See J.B. Quinn, *Strategies for Change*, Irwin, 1980. See also J.B. Quinn, 'Strategic change: logical incrementalism' in J.B. Quinn and H. Mintzberg, *The Strategy Process*, 4th edn, 2003, Prentice Hall.

16. See J.B. Quinn, *Strategies for Change*, reference 15, p. 58.

17. The concept of the learning organisation is explained in P. Senge, *The Fifth Discipline: the Art and Practice of the Learning Organization*, Doubleday/Century, 1990. Also M. Crossan, H.W. Lane and R.E. White, 'An organizational learning framework: from intuition to institution', *Academy of Management Review*, vol. 24, no. 3 (1999), pp. 522–37.

18. The concept of the organisation as a set of social networks is discussed by, for example, M.S. Granovetter, 'The strength of weak ties', *American Journal of Sociology*, vol. 78, no. 6 (1973), pp. 1360–80, and G.R. Carroll and A.C. Teo, 'On the social networks of managers', *Academy of Management Journal*, vol. 39, no. 2 (1996), pp. 421–40.

19. See S. Finkelstein, 'Why smart executives fail: four case histories of how people learn the wrong lessons from history', *Business History*, vol. 48, no. 2 (2006), pp. 153–70.

20. For political perspectives on management, see: J.R. DeLuca, *Political Savvy: Systematic Approaches to Leadership behind the Scenes*, Evergreen Business Group, 2nd edn (1999) and G.J. Miller, *Managerial Dilemmas: the Political Economy of Hierarchy*, Cambridge University Press, 2006.

21. For a discussion and an explanatory model of this political perspective, see V.K. Narayanan and L. Fahey, 'The micro politics of strategy formulation', *Academy of Management Review*, vol. 7, no. 1 (1982), pp. 25–34.

22. For an example of how different political coalitions can influence see S. Maitlis and T. Lawrence, 'Orchestral manoeuvres in the dark: understanding failure in organizational strategizing, *Journal of Management Studies*, vol. 40, no. 1 (2003), pp. 109–40.

23. This is sometimes referred to as a 'resource dependency view' of strategy development; for the original argument see J. Pfeffer and G.R. Salancik, *The External Control of Organizations: a Resource Dependence Perspective*, Harper and Row, 1978.

24. This is the argument advanced by J.M. Bartunek, D. Kolb and R. Lewicki, 'Bringing conflict out from behind the scenes: private, informal, and nonrational dimensions of conflict in organizations', in D. Kolb and J. Bartunek (eds), *Hidden Conflict in Organizations: Uncovering Behind the Scenes Disputes*, Sage, 1992.

25. W.B. Arthur, 'Competing technologies, increasing returns and lock in by historical events', *Economic Journal*, vol. 99 (1989), pp. 116–31.

26. Two of the early extensive case studies showing how cultural and political processes give rise to the emergence of strategies are A. Pettigrew, *The Awakening Giant*, Blackwell, 1985; and G. Johnson, *Strategic Change and the Management Process*, Blackwell, 1987.

27. The RAP explanation is sometimes known as the Bower–Burgelman explanation of strategy development after two US professors – Joe Bower and Robert Burgelman. Their original studies are J.L. Bower, *Managing the Resource Allocation Process: a Study of Corporate Planning and Investment*, Irwin, 1972; and R.A. Burgelman, 'A model of the interaction of strategic behavior, corporate context and the concept of strategy', *Academy of Management Review*, vol. 81, no. 1, pp. 61–70; and 'A process model of internal corporate venturing in the diversified major firm', *Administrative Science Quarterly*, vol. 28, pp. 223–44 both in 1983. Also see J.L. Bower and C.G. Gilbert, 'A revised model of the resource allocation process', in *From Resource Allocation to Strategy*, eds J.L. Bower and C.G. Gilbert, pp. 439–55, Oxford University Press, 2005.

28. William Ocasio, 'Towards an attention-based view of the firm', *Strategic Management Journal*, vol. 18 (Summer Special Issue, 1997), pp. 187–206.

29. The Intel case is also written up by Robert Burgelman, see *Strategy as Destiny: How Strategy Making Shapes a Company's Future*, Free Press, 2002. Also see Burgelman, 'Fading memories: a process theory of strategic business exit in dynamic environments', *Administrative Science Quarterly*, vol. 39 (1994), pp. 34–56.

30. J.S. McMullen, D.A. Shepherd and H. Patzelt, 'Managerial (in)attention to competitive threats', *Journal of Management Studies*, vol. 46, no. 2 (2009), pp. 157–80.

31. This idea of a balance between analytic rigour and intuition and imagination is the theme of G. Szulanski and K. Amin, 'Learning to make strategy: balancing discipline and imagination', *Long Range Planning*, vol. 34 (2001), pp. 537–56.

32. M.L. Tushman, and C.A. O'Reilly, 'Ambidextrous organizations: managing evolutionary and revolutionary change', *California Management Review*, vol. 38, no. 4 (1996), pp. 8–30.

33. R. Duncan, 'Characteristics of organisational environments and perceived environmental uncertainty', *Administrative Science Quarterly*, vol. 17, no. 3 (1972), pp. 313–27.

34. Robert Burgelman and Andrew Grove, 'Strategic dissonance', *California Management Review*, vol. 38, no. 2 (1996), pp. 8–28.

35. R.A. Burgelman and A.S. Grove, 'Let chaos reign, then rein in chaos – repeatedly: managing strategic dynamics for corporate longevity', *Strategic Management Journal*, vol. 28 (2007), pp. 965–79.

36. For a discussion of the differences between strategy development in the public and private sectors, see N. Collier, F. Fishwick and G. Johnson, 'The processes of strategy development in the public sector' in *Exploring Public Sector Strategy*, G. Johnson and K. Scholes (eds), Pearson Education, 2001.

37. See R. Duncan (reference 33).

38. See, for example, S. Hart and C. Banbury, 'How strategy making processes can make a difference', *Strategic Management Journal*, vol. 15, no. 4 (1994), pp. 251–69.

39. See reference 9.

40. A.D. Henderson, D. Miller and D.C. Hambrick, 'How quickly do CEOs become obsolete? Industry dynamism, CEO tenure and company perormance', *Strategic Management Journal*, vol. 27 (2006), pp. 447–60.

41. G. Gavetti and J.W. Rivkin, 'On the origin of strategy: action and cognition over time', *Organization Science*, vol. 18, no. 3 (2007), pp. 420–39.

42. See reference 35.

Google: who drives the strategy?

Phyl Johnson, Strategy Explorers

From an idea to a verb in less than 15 years: 'to Google – to search the Internet'

If you are in need of the answer to a question and close to a computer what do you do: Google it. With the exception of 'Hoover' it is hard to think of another example of an organisation whose product's name has become so synonymous with the activity of the product that it becomes a commonly used verb. Google has achieved this in just a few years, growing at an eye-watering pace to its current internationally dominant position in internet search. It has to be one of the most successful strategies ever; so how did they do it?

Unsurprisingly, Google has attracted the attention of analysts, researchers and other organisations trying to uncover their formula for success. Moreover, their business model has taken over from GE and IBM before it as the model to learn and replicate. At the heart of this hugely successful enterprise is a famously unstructured style of operating and a CEO who claims their strategy is based on trial and error: can this really be the case?

> 'Google is unusual because it's really organized from the bottom up. . . . It often feels at Google people are pretty much doing what they think best and they tolerate having us around. . . . We don't really have a five-year plan. . . . We really focus on what's new, what's exciting and how can you win quickly with your new idea.' Eric Schmidt, Google CEO[1]

About Google

Google started life as the brainchild of Larry Page and Sergey Brin when they were students at the IT power-house Stanford University in the USA. Google was born from coursework the pair undertook in 1998 to improve internet search engine results. After University and when Page and Brin launched their own search engine product, it gained followers and users very quickly, attracted financial backing and enabled them to launch their IPO* in the USA stock market in 2004, so making Google a publicly owned corporation.

Source: Press Association Images/Mark Lennihan/AP.

From the beginning Google has been different. Page and Brin insisted that their IPO follow a very unusual route: instead of using investment banks as dictators of their initial share price, they launched a kind of open IPO. In this auction, buyers decided on the fair price for a share and not the investment banks. A quirky route to market that some saw as arrogant and established a theme for Google: breaking the mould. This continued as Google set up its governance structure with a two-tier board of directors, common in some European countries (e.g. Germany) but extremely rare in the USA. The advantage of the two-tier system for founders Page and Brin was the additional distance it places between them and their shareholders and the increased managerial freedom it offered to them to run their company their way. Page confirmed this by penning an open letter to shareholders claiming that Google was not a conventional company and that they did not intend to become one.

Running the company the Google way involved another curious and unlikely twist in 2001. Page and Brin recruited successful CEO Eric Schmidt from Novell Inc and, between the three of them, they shared power at the top. Schmidt dealt with administration and the company's investors and had the most traditional CEO role. Page was centrally concerned with the social structure of Google whilst Brin took a lead in the area of ethics. There have been very few successful triumvirates in history and many epic failures. Either politics and confusion create rifts in which three become

---

* IPO: Initial Public Offering of shares in a company to the public to buy, often referred to as the flotation of a company on a stock market.

two and two become one; or the three power holders become overly consensual. But against the odds it went well for Google.

With 132 million customers and a network of 1 million computers worldwide, Google is without a doubt the dominant player in internet search with 67.5% market share, way ahead of Yahoo [8.4%].[2] But they are also widely diversified thanks to their highly acquisitive approach to business. Their other areas of operation include Blogging, Radio & TV Advertising, Online Payment Services, Social Networks and Mobile Phone Operating Systems. Their guiding principle in acquisition seems to be: if they can't innovate something in-house, buy it. In this way Google were buying a product, technical expertise and usually a fan base of early adopters. This is in contrast to Apple, for example, who seek to innovate in-house. In the period between 2001 and 2009 they acquired some 50 companies. Many of these were small starts-ups but others were already established with a significant enough band of internet followers to be attractive, the most famous of which was YouTube in 2001 for $1.65 (~€1.15) billion.

In 2010, Google was still expanding at a startling rate,* and following twin tracks in its operation, those of search tools and productivity tools. Their aim to retain their position as the *King of Search* but always follow the same mantra was delivered on multiple YouTube broadcasts by the senior Google executives: *'To organize the world's information'*.

The disorganisation organisation

In many ways, life inside the Googleplex [Google's HQ] is the image of a disorganised organisation where it can be difficult to work out who is responsible for what. An example of this was Google's failure to renew its own domain name in the German market in 2007 as well as an instance when no legal representative for the company appeared at a Belgian law suit.

Google famously launch half-finished products into the market and don't control information flow about their products by advertising: in fact they don't advertise at all. With regard to product development their approach is to launch a part-finished [*beta*] product, let Google fanatics find it, toy with it, essentially error-check and de-bug it. This may be a good use of end users but also a significant release of control.

The legacy of Google's rapid growth is an organisation with less structuring than would be expected for

its size and breadth of operation. Control of workflow, quality and to a large extent the nature of projects that are under way is down to employees and not management. Google is a famously light-managed organisation. They have a 1:20 ratio of employees to managers. This is half the number of managers that would be the case in the average US organisation [1:10] and considerably less than some European countries [France 1:7.5].

Engineers work in small autonomous teams and the work they produce is quality assured using peer review and not classical supervision. So there is the potential for these small work teams, with their freedom for self-initiated project work, to create a situation of project proliferation in which a large percentage of activity may not be contributing to the strategic direction the leadership wish the firm to take. Moreover, engineers at Google are allowed to allocate 20% of their work time to personal projects that interest them as a means to stimulate innovation and create new knowledge as well as potential products. However, some commentators suggest that reports from inside Google estimate many engineers spend more like 30% of their time on labour of their own choice – a lot of opportunity for new ideas but also for chaos.

This form of highly organic organisation [sometimes referred to as an ecosystem] is more familiar in much smaller organisations, under the 300 employee level and in creative industries such as advertising agencies. But for an organisation the size of Google [more than 16,000 employees] the disorganisation and anti-bureaucratic approach is something that they pride themselves on.

> 'Google is run by its culture and not by me. . . . It's much easier to have an employee base in which case everybody is doing exactly what they want every day. They're much easier to manage because they never have any problems. They're always excited, they're always working on whatever they care about. . . . But it's a very different model than the traditional, hierarchical model where there's the CEO statement and this is the strategy and this is what you will do, and it's very very measured. We put up with a certain amount of chaos from that.' Eric Schmidt: CEO[3]

The rigid organisation

Irrespective of the image that Google has as an organisation that sees the benefits in releasing managerial control and rigid hold over strategic direction, there are some significant areas of rigidity built into the system.

One key area is that of recruitment. With an extremely highly rated employment brand, Google can afford to be choosy. Close to 100 talented applicants

---

* An example of their pace in growth being employee numbers, from 1,628 employees in 2003 to 19,604 in 2008.

chase each job at the Googleplex. The pay is competitive but not way ahead of the competition. However, perks, including free meals, a swimming pool and massages, all help attract employees. So too does the 20% of free time engineers can spend on their own interests. In return Google have rigid recruitment criteria and processes and are unashamedly elitist.

Engineers must have either a Masters or Doctorate from a leading University and they must pass through a series of assessment tests and interviews. The criteria for these are derived in a highly scientific manner; after all Google measure *everything.* The end product of this is that Google actually recruit against a psychometric profile* of *googleness* and can therefore hire and retain a fairly predictable employee population: much easier to manage.

Their laissez-faire attitude toward the management of employees can be read as control as well as freedom. Peer review is a famously stringent form of performance management. Amongst professionals, reputation is key and if someone is being reviewed by peers the pattern is toward harder and higher quality work. The way peer reviews are carried out and indeed the way many processes within Google are followed is formulaic and rigid. For example, work teams are kept small and limited to a maximum of six. Projects to be worked on must be limited, deadlines are short [no longer than six weeks] and as ever in Google there is measurement.

'Everyone who meets Sergy Brin notices his aptitude as a mathematician. Math is everywhere at Google: in pricing policy, in discussions among engineers, in decisions about whether to develop a new product, in the development of those products in recruiting, and in evaluating employee performance. Google measures and analyzes everything.' Girard (2009 pp. 97–98]

'We're very analytical. We measure everything, and we systematized every aspect of what's happening in the company. For example, we introduced a spreadsheet product this week. I've already received hourly updates on the number of people who came in to apply to use the spreadsheet, the number of people using it, the size of the spreadsheet.' Eric Schmidt[4]

* Personality type.

Google's internal technical platform is a major part of its success. They have the capacity to record and analyse vast aspects of data from their user and customer groups. In addition, there is an in-house intranet called 'Moma' that tracks huge amounts of data in real time. Google is all about information, capturing it, tracking it and applying it all in a systematic and organised manner. The technology itself is the strategy and the strategy is the technology.

As Google continues to travel at a high velocity into the future, on some level major decisions have been and remain to be made. Who decided to buy YouTube and make the other acquisitions? Who do the shareholders hold responsible for strategic success and failure? In early 2010, Google back-tracked on a deal they had made with China to allow some content to be censored by the Chinese authorities. However, after a security breach into its gmail system, Google reversed course. Who made these decisions? Moreover, as information capture about users and the personalisation of search engines to those users becomes more advanced, so does the hunger of organisations and perhaps even governments for that information. The triumvirate who run Google find themselves with some big strategic thinking to do around decisions that will have huge ramifications around the Google world.

Primary source: Girard B. (2009) *The Google Way: How one company is revolutionizing management as we know it.* No Starch Press, San Francisco, CA.

References:
1. Interview by Nicholas Carlson with Google CEO Eric Schmidt: 'We Don't Really Have A Five-Year Plan' *Washington Post Leadership series* 20 May 2009.
2. Cited in Web Ultimatum shakes the great firewall of China to its foundations *The Times*, 14 January 2010.
3. As above.
4. Quoted on p. 97 of Girard (2009).

Questions

1 What influences strategy development in Google?

2 What are the strengths and weaknesses of their approach?

3 Is the Google approach transferable to other organisations?

13

ORGANISING FOR SUCCESS

Learning outcomes

After reading this chapter you should be able to:

- Identify *key challenges in organising* for success, including ensuring control, managing knowledge, coping with change and responding to internationalisation.

- Analyse main organisation *structural types* in terms of their strengths and weaknesses.

- Recognise key issues in designing organisational *control systems* (such as planning and performance targeting systems).

- Recognise how the three strands of strategy, structure and systems should reinforce each other in *organisational configurations* and the managerial dilemmas involved.

PEARSON

mystrategylab™

MyStrategyLab is designed to help you make the most of your studies.

Visit **www.pearsoned.co.uk/mystrategylab** to discover a wide range of resources specific to this chapter, including:

- A personalised **Study plan** that will help you understand core concepts
- **Audio** and **video clips** that put the spotlight on strategy in the real world
- **Online glossaries** and **flashcards** that provide helpful reminders when you're looking for some quick revision.

(13.1) INTRODUCTION

Strategies only happen because people do things. To take one end of the scale: if American multinational retailer Wal-Mart wants to achieve its strategy, it needs to get its 2.1 million employees pointing in the right direction. To take the other end of the scale: even a football team has to ensure that all its members will play the right kind of game. Thus strategies require organisation and this involves both structures and systems. If the organisation does not support the strategy, then even the cleverest strategy will fail because of poor implementation.

This chapter examines organising for successful strategy implementation. It focuses particularly on two key elements of organisational 'design': organisational structures and organisational systems. **Structures give people formally defined roles, responsibilities and lines of reporting with regard to strategy.** **Systems support and control people as they carry out structurally defined roles and responsibilities.**

Figure 13.1 expresses the interdependency between strategy, structure and systems. In the ideal organisational design, all three should support each other in a circular process of mutual reinforcement. This chapter captures the importance of mutual reinforcement between elements with the concept of 'configuration', explained in section 13.4. However, the chapter will also underline how difficult it sometimes can be to configure the organisation in order to support strategy. In particular, the Key Debate at the end of the chapter questions the extent to which formal organisational structures can be simply reshaped to align with strategy. Sometimes the organisational elements of structure and systems can get out of synchrony with the strategy, fatally undermining it or even redefining its direction. In Figure 13.1, it is worth noticing that structure and systems not only flow *from* strategy but also feed *into* it.

This chapter addresses the following topics therefore:

- *Structures*, in other words the formal roles, responsibilities and lines of reporting in organisations. The chapter considers the main types of structures, including functional, multidivisional, matrix, project and transnational structures.

Figure 13.1 Organisational configurations: strategy, structure and systems

- *Systems*, what supports and controls people within and around an organisation. These systems include formal mechanisms such as performance targeting and planning, and more informal ones such as cultural and market systems.

- *Configurations*, the mutually supporting elements that make up an organisation's design. As well as strategy, structure and systems, these elements can include staff, style, skills and superordinate goals, as encapsulated in the *McKinsey 7-S framework*.

(13.2) STRUCTURAL TYPES

Managers often describe their organisation by drawing an organisation chart, mapping out its formal structure. These structural charts define the 'levels' and roles in an organisation. They are important to managers because they describe who is responsible for what. But formal structures matter in at least two more ways. First, structural reporting lines shape patterns of communication and knowledge exchange: in many organisations people tend not to talk much to people much higher or lower in the hierarchy, or in different parts of the organisation. Second, the kinds of structural positions at the top suggest the kinds of skills required to move up the organisation: a structure with functional specialists such as marketing or production at the top indicates the importance to success of specialised functional disciplines rather than general business experience. In short, formal structures can reveal a great deal about the role of knowledge and skills in an organisation. Structures can therefore be hotly debated (see Illustration 13.1).

This section reviews five basic structural types: functional, multidivisional, matrix, transnational and project.[1] Broadly, the first two of these tend to emphasise one structural dimension over another, either functional specialisms or business units. The three that follow tend to mix structural dimensions more evenly, for instance trying to give product and geographical units equal weight. However, none of these structures is a universal solution to the challenges of organising. Rather, the right structure depends on the particular kinds of challenges each organisation faces. Researchers propose a wide number of important challenges (sometimes called 'contingencies') shaping organisational structure, including organisational size, extent of diversification and type of technology.[2] This implies that the first step in organisation design is deciding what the key challenges facing the organisation actually are. Section 13.2.6 will particularly focus on how the five structural types fit both the traditional challenge of control and the three new challenges of change, knowledge and internationalisation.

13.2.1 The functional structure

Even a small entrepreneurial start-up, once it involves more than one person, needs to divide up responsibilities between different people. The **functional structure divides responsibilities according to the organisation's primary specialist roles such as production, research and sales**. Figure 13.2 represents a typical organisation chart for such a functional organisation. This kind of structure is particularly relevant to small or start-up organisations, or larger organisations that have retained narrow, rather than diverse, product ranges. Functional structures may also be used within a multidivisional structure (see below), where the divisions themselves may split themselves up according to functional departments (as in Figure 13.2).

Figure 13.2 also summarises the potential advantages and disadvantages of a functional structure. There are advantages in that it gives senior managers direct hands-on involvement

ILLUSTRATION 13.1

Volkswagen: a case of disputed centralisation

A new chief executive introduces a more centralised structure over this multi-brand giant.

Figure 1 Volkswagen, November 2006 (simplified)

Figure 2 Volkswagen, January 2007 (simplified)

In 2007, following the Porsche car company's building up of a controlling stake and the installation of a new chief executive, German car manufacturer Volkswagen announced a major reorganisation. For the previous few years, Volkswagen had been organised as two groups of brands under the main Volkswagen and Audi labels (see Fig. 1), with technical and marketing expertise clustered around particular brands within these. Now the company was to be reorganised into two main groups, a mass-market group (VW, Skoda, SEAT) and a more luxury market group (Audi, Bentley, Bugatti and Lamborghini). Volkswagen also had a large stake in truck company Scania. The company would be more centralised, with new corporate responsibilities for production, sales, distribution and R&D (see Fig. 2). The new CEO, Martin Winterkorn, would also act as head of R&D and be directly responsible for the VW group of brands.

The stated aim of this more centralised structure was to increase synergies between the various brands. More centralised R&D would help ensure the sharing of engines and components, and centralisation of production would assist the optimisation of factory usage across the company. The departing head of the Volkswagen group took another view. He asserted that, in order to ensure cross-functional integration and motivation, expertise needed to identify closely with particular brands. According to him, the new structure mimicked the centralised Porsche structure, but Porsche was a much smaller company with just one main brand. Porsche's spokespersons responded by recalling that Porsche was the most profitable car company in the world, while Volkswagen was one of the least.

Questions

1 Which type of structure did the old decentralised structure resemble most and which type of structure is Volkswagen moving closer to?

2 What pros and cons can you see in the new Volkswagen structure?

Figure 13.2 A functional structure

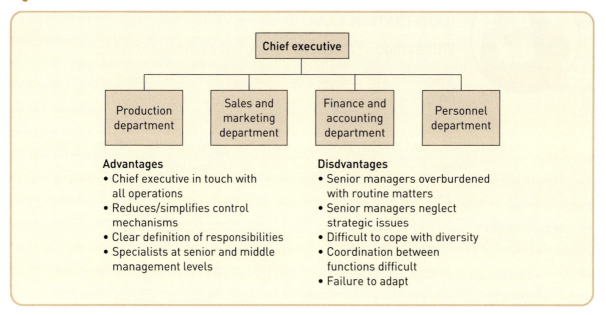

in operations and allows greater operational control from the top. The functional structure provides a clear definition of roles and tasks, increasing accountability. Functional departments also provide concentrations of expertise, thus fostering knowledge development in areas of functional specialism.

However, there are disadvantages, particularly as organisations become larger or more diverse. Perhaps the major concern in a fast-moving world is that senior managers focus too much on their functional responsibilities, becoming overburdened with routine operations and too concerned with narrow functional interests. As a result, they find it hard either to take a strategic view of the organisation as a whole or to coordinate separate functions quickly. Thus functional organisations can be inflexible, poor at adapting to change. Separate functional departments tend also to be inward-looking – so-called 'functional silos' – making it difficult to integrate the knowledge of different functional specialists. Finally, because they are centralised around particular functions, functional structures are not good at coping with product or geographical diversity. For example, a central marketing department may try to impose a uniform approach to advertising regardless of the diverse needs of the organisation's various business units around the world.

13.2.2 The multidivisional structure

A **multidivisional structure is built up of separate divisions on the basis of products, services or geographical areas** (see Figure 13.3). Divisionalisation often comes about as an attempt to overcome the problems that functional structures have in dealing with the diversity mentioned above.[3] Each division can respond to the specific requirements of its product/market strategy, using its own set of functional departments. A similar situation exists in many public services, where the organisation is structured around *service departments* such as recreation, social services and education.

There are several potential advantages to divisional structures. As self-standing business units, it is possible to control divisions from a distance by monitoring business performance

Figure 13.3 A multidivisional structure

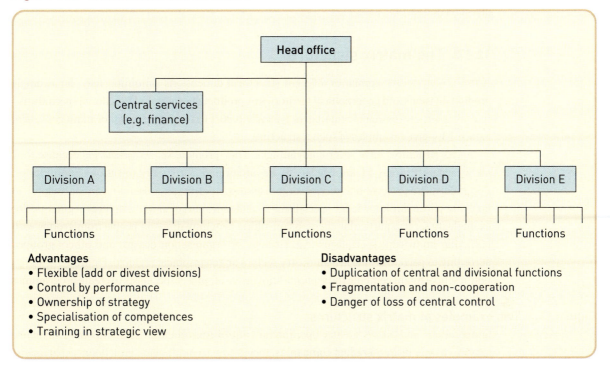

Advantages
- Flexible (add or divest divisions)
- Control by performance
- Ownership of strategy
- Specialisation of competences
- Training in strategic view

Disadvantages
- Duplication of central and divisional functions
- Fragmentation and non-cooperation
- Danger of loss of central control

(see section 13.3.3). Having divisions also provides flexibility because organisations can add, close or merge divisions as circumstances change. Divisional managers have greater personal ownership for their own divisional strategies. Geographical divisions – for example, a European division or a North American division – offer a means of managing internationally (see section 13.2.4). There can be benefits of specialisation within a division, allowing competences to develop with a clearer focus on a particular product group, technology or customer group. Management responsibility for a whole divisional business is good training in taking a strategic view for managers expecting to go on to a main board position.

However, divisional structures can also have disadvantages of three main types. First, divisions can become so self-sufficient that they are *de facto* independent businesses, but duplicating the functions and costs of the corporate centre of the company. In such cases of *de facto* independence, it may make more sense to split the company into independent businesses, and de-mergers of this type are now common. Second, divisionalisation tends to get in the way of cooperation and knowledge-sharing between business units: divisions can quite literally divide. Expertise is fragmented and divisional performance targets provide poor incentives to collaborate with other divisions. Finally, divisions may become too autonomous, especially where joint ventures and partnership dilute ownership. Here, divisions pursue their own strategies almost regardless of the needs of the corporate parent. In these cases, multidivisionals become *holding companies*, where the corporate centre effectively 'holds' the various businesses in a largely financial sense, exercising little control and adding little value. Figure 13.3 summarises these potential advantages and disadvantages of a multidivisional structure.

Large and complex multidivisional companies often have a second tier of *subdivisions* within their main divisions. Treating smaller strategic business units as subdivisions within a large division reduces the number of units that the corporate centre has to deal with directly. Subdivisions can also help complex organisations respond to contradictory pressures. For example, an organisation could have geographical subdivisions within a set of global product divisions (see section 13.2.4).

13.2.3 The matrix structure

A **matrix structure** combines different structural dimensions simultaneously, for example product divisions and geographical territories or product divisions and functional specialisms.[4] In matrix structures, middle managers typically report to two or three senior managers each. Figure 13.4 gives examples of such a structure.

Matrix structures have several advantages. They promote *knowledge-sharing* because they allow separate areas of knowledge to be integrated across organisational boundaries. Particularly in professional service organisations, matrix organisation can be helpful in applying particular knowledge specialisms to different market or geographical segments. For example, to serve a particular client, a consulting firm may draw on people from groups with particular knowledge specialisms (e.g. strategy or organisation design) and others grouped according to particular markets (industry sectors or geographical regions). Figure 13.4 shows how a school might combine the separate knowledge of subject specialists to create programmes

Figure 13.4 Two examples of matrix structures

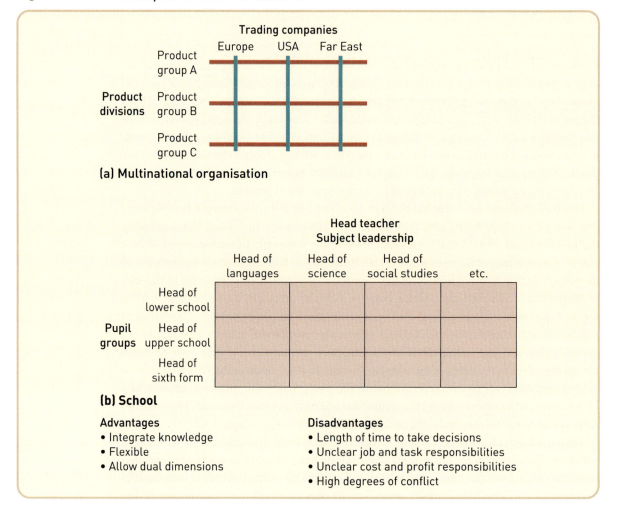

(a) Multinational organisation

(b) School

Advantages
- Integrate knowledge
- Flexible
- Allow dual dimensions

Disadvantages
- Length of time to take decisions
- Unclear job and task responsibilities
- Unclear cost and profit responsibilities
- High degrees of conflict

of study tailored differently to various age groups. Matrix organisations are *flexible*, because they allow different dimensions of the organisation to be mixed together. They are particularly attractive to organisations operating globally, because of the possible mix between local and global dimensions. For example, a global company may prefer geographically defined divisions as the operating units for local marketing (because of their specialist local knowledge of customers). But at the same time it may still want global product units responsible for the worldwide coordination of product development and manufacturing, taking advantage of economies of scale and specialisation. This combination of dimensions is the approach of American multinational Procter & Gamble, for instance (see Illustration 13.2).

However, because a matrix structure replaces single lines of authority with multiple cross-matrix relationships, this often brings problems. In particular, it will typically take *longer to reach decisions* because of bargaining between the managers of different dimensions. There may also be *conflict* because staff find themselves responsible to managers from two structural dimensions. In short, matrix organisations are hard to control.

As with any structure, but particularly with the matrix structure, the critical issue in practice is the way it actually works (i.e. behaviours and relationships). The key ingredient in a successful matrix structure can be senior managers good at sustaining collaborative relationships (across the matrix) and coping with the messiness and ambiguity which that can bring. It is for this reason that Chris Bartlett and Sumantra Ghoshal describe the matrix as involving a 'state of mind' as much as a formal structure (see also Illustration 13.2).[5]

13.2.4 Multinational/transnational structures

Operating internationally adds an extra dimension to the structural challenge. As in Figure 13.5, there are essentially four structural designs available for multinationals. Three are simple extensions of the principles of the multidivisional structure (section 13.2.2), so are dealt with briefly. The fourth, the transnational structure, is more complex and will be explained at more length.

The three simpler multinational structures are as follows:

- *International divisions.* An international division is a stand-alone division added alongside the structure of the main home-based business. This is often the kind of structure adopted by corporations with large domestic markets (such as in the United States or China), where an initial entry into overseas markets is relatively small-scale and does not require structural change to the original, much bigger, home businesses. For example, a Chinese car, truck and motorbike manufacturer might have separate divisions for each of its product areas in its home market of China, but run its overseas businesses in a separate 'international division' combining all three product areas together. The international division is typically run from headquarters, but not integrated with the domestic business. As in Figure 13.5, the international division structure is centralised but not highly coordinated.

- *Local subsidiaries.* These subsidiaries typically have most of the functions required to operate on their own in their particular local market, for example design, production and marketing. They are thus a form of geographic divisional structure. They have high local responsiveness and are loosely coordinated. A local subsidiary structure is very common in professional services such as law, accounting and advertising, where there are few economies of scale and responsiveness to local regulations, relationships or tastes is very important. This structure fits the multidomestic strategy introduced in Chapter 8.

ILLUSTRATION 13.2

Procter & Gamble's evolving matrix

Having replaced its multidivisional structure in 1987, P&G has constantly revised its matrix, and shown how it is not only a structure but also a 'state of mind'.

In 2010, Procter and Gamble (P&G), the giant American consumer products company, declared of its matrix organisational structure: 'We have made P&G's structure an important part of our capacity to grow. It combines the global scale of a $79 (~€55) billion global company with a local focus to win with consumers and retail customers in each country where P&G products are sold.' The 2010 matrix is summarised alongside. Apparently simple, this structure was the outcome of nearly a quarter of a century of revisions, one of which had cost the Chief Executive his job.

P&G first experimented with a matrix structure in 1987. On top of the existing product divisions in the American market, P&G overlaid a strengthened second axis of central corporate functions. These corporate functions gave functional managers in the divisions access to specialised expertise. For example, divisional sales executives still had a primary ('solid-line') relationship with their divisional top managers, but now had a secondary ('dotted-line') relationship with the central Vice President of Sales overseeing all the American divisions. In the following few years, P&G's central functions extended their responsibilities globally, and central 'category' presidents' took responsibility for innovation in product areas worldwide. By 1995, P&G had created four profit-responsible regions across the world (North America, Latin America, Europe/Middle East/African and Asia). P&G now had a global matrix, with global functions and global categories cross-cutting the four regions.

Declining growth in the late 1990s prompted a major revision of P&G's matrix structure, with the establishment of Global Business Units (with profit responsibility for products worldwide), Market Development Organisations (tasked with sales growth in local markets), plus centralised Global Business Services and Corporate Functions managing internal business processes and providing specialised expertise. This new structure was launched by a new Chief Executive, the aggressive Durk Jager. Management layers were simultaneously reduced from 13 to 7, and 15,000 people were laid off. Jager was a man who said of himself: 'I break kneecaps. I make heads roll'. But performance collapsed in the first year of the new structure, and it was soon Jager that was fired.

Adapted from: http://www.pg.com/en_US/company/global_structure_operations/corporate_structure.shtml.

In 2000, Alan Lafley took over as Chief Executive. He retained P&G's basic matrix of Global Business Units, Market Development Organizations, Global Business Services and Corporate Functions. But, described as like 'a nerdy college professor', Lafley brought a gentler style. In 2010, Lafley was still at the top of P&G, now as Chairman, with a decade of solid success behind him.

Sources: P&G.com; M. Piskorski and A. Spadini, Procter & Gamble: Organization 2005 (A), Harvard Business School Case no, 707–516; R. Degen (2009), 'Designing Matrix Organizations that Work', International School of Management working paper no. 33, Paris.

Questions

1 Compare the balance of power between categories and regions in the 1995 structure to that between Global Business Units and Market Development Organizations in the post-2000 structure. What implications would this shift have for strategy?

2 How does this case illustrate the claim that a matrix is 'a state of mind', not just a formal structure?

● *Global product divisions.* This kind of structure is often used where economies of scale are very important. Organising the design, production and marketing on the basis of global divisions rather than local subsidiaries typically maximises cost efficiency. To return to the Chinese car, truck and motorbike manufacturer, there would be just three divisions each responsible for their particular product area across the whole world, China included. There would be very little scope for adaptation to local tastes or regulations in particular markets. In global product divisions, local responsiveness would typically be very low. This structure fits the global strategy introduced in Chapter 8.

The international division, local subsidiary and global product division structures all have their particular advantages, whether it is managing relative size, maximising local responsiveness or achieving economies of scale. The fourth structure, however, tries to integrate the advantages of the local subsidiary structure with those of the global product divisional structure.

In terms of Figure 13.5, the **transnational structure combines local responsiveness with high global coordination.**[6] According to Bartlett and Ghoshal, transnational structures are similar to matrices but distinguish themselves by their focus on knowledge-sharing, specialisation and network management, as follows:

● *Knowledge-sharing.* While each national or regional business has a good deal of autonomy, in the transnational they should see themselves as sources of ideas and capabilities for the whole corporation. Thus a good idea that has been developed locally is offered for adoption by other national or regional units around the world.

● *Specialisation.* National (or regional) units specialise in areas of expertise in order to achieve greater scale economies on behalf of the whole corporation. Thus a national unit that has particular competences in manufacturing a particular product, for example, may be given responsibility for manufacturing that product on behalf of other units across the world.

Figure 13.5 Multinational structures

● *Network management*. The corporate centre has the role of managing this global network of specialisms and knowledge. It does so first by establishing the specialist role of each business unit, then sustaining the systems and relationships required to make the network of business units operate in an integrated and effective manner.

The success of a transnational corporation is dependent on the ability *simultaneously* to achieve global competences, local responsiveness and organisation-wide innovation and learning. This requires clarity as to boundaries, relationships and the roles that the various managers need to perform. For example:

● *Global business managers* have the overriding responsibility to further the company's global competitiveness, which will cross both national and functional boundaries. They must be the *product/market strategists*, the *architects* of the business resources and competences, the *drivers of product innovation* and the *coordinators* of transnational transactions.

● *Country or area managers* have potentially a dual responsibility to other parts of the transnational. First, they must act as a *sensor* of local needs and feed these back to those responsible internationally for new products or services. Second, they should seek to *build* unique competences: that is, country managers should seek to become centres of excellence, allowing them to be *contributors* to the company as a whole, in manufacturing or research and development, for instance.

● *Functional managers* such as finance or IT have responsibility for setting standards and ensuring worldwide innovation and learning across the various parts of the organisation. This requires the skill to recognise and spread best practice across the organisation. So they must be able to *scan* the organisation for best practice, *cross-pollinate* this best practice and be the *champions* of innovations.

● *Corporate (head office) managers* integrate these other roles and responsibilities. Not only are they the *leaders*, but they are also the *talent spotters* among business, country and functional managers, facilitating the interplay between them. For example, they must foster the processes of innovation and knowledge creation. They are responsible for the *development* of a strong management centre in the organisation.

Theoretically the transnational combines the best of local decentralisation with the best of global centralisation. However, the transnational can be very demanding of managers in terms of willingness to work not just at their national business units but for the good of the transnational as a whole. Diffuse responsibilities also make for similar complexities and control problems to those of the matrix organisation.[7]

13.2.5 Project-based structures[8]

Many organisations rely heavily on project teams with a finite lifespan. A **project-based structure is one where teams are created, undertake the work (e.g. internal or external contracts) and are then dissolved.**[9] This can be particularly appropriate for organisations that deliver large and expensive goods or services (civil engineering, information systems, films) or those delivering time-limited events (conferences, sporting events or consulting engagements). The organisation structure is a constantly changing collection of project teams created, steered and glued together loosely by a small corporate group. Many organisations use such teams in a more ad hoc way to complement the 'main' structure. For example, *task forces* are set up to make progress on new elements of strategy or to provide momentum where the regular structure of the organisation is not effective.

The project-based structure can be highly flexible, with projects being set up and dissolved as required. Because project teams should have clear tasks to achieve within a defined period, accountability and control are good. As project team members will typically be drawn from different departments within the firm, projects can be effective at knowledge exchange. Projects can also draw on members internationally and, because project lifespans are typically short, project teams may be more willing to work temporarily around the world. There are disadvantages, however. Without strong programme management providing overarching strategic control, organisations are prone to proliferate projects in an ill-coordinated fashion. The constant breaking up of project teams can also hinder the accumulation of knowledge over time or within specialisms.

Overall, project-based structures have been growing in importance because of their inherent flexibility. Such flexibility can be vital in a fast-moving world where individual knowledge and competences need to be redeployed and integrated quickly and in novel ways.

13.2.6 Choosing structures

From the discussion so far, it should be clear that functional, multidivisional, matrix, transnational and project structures each have their own advantages and disadvantages. Organisational designers, therefore, have to choose structures according to the particular strategic challenges (or 'contingencies') they face. Here the various structures are considered in the light of four general challenges that have become particularly important for many contemporary organisations in recent years:

- The need for *control* in a world where organisations are increasingly large, complex and under scrutiny. One extreme of complexity is the American retailer Wal-Mart, which in 2010 had 2.1 million employees. Control is also important because investors, regulators and pressure groups typically watch closely to see that organisations actually deliver on the strategic promises they make.

- The *speed of change* and the increased levels of *uncertainty* in the business environment, as discussed in Chapter 2. As a result, organisations need to have flexible designs and be skilled at reorganising.

- The growing importance of *knowledge creation* and *knowledge-sharing* as a fundamental ingredient of strategic success, as discussed in Chapter 3. Organisational designs should both foster concentrations of expertise and encourage people to share their knowledge.

- The rise of *internationalisation*, as discussed in Chapter 8. Organising for a international context has many challenges: communicating across wider geography, coordinating more diversity and building relationships across diverse cultures are some examples. Wal-Mart operates in Japan, China, India, Latin America and the UK (as ASDA), as well as the United States. Internationalisation also brings greater recognition of different kinds of organising around the world.

Table 13.1 summarises how the five basic structures – functional, multidivisional, matrix, transnational and project – meet these challenges of control, change, knowledge and internationalisation faced by many contemporary organisations. No structure scores high across all four challenges. Organisational designers therefore face trade-offs and choices. If they seek

Table 13.1 Comparison of structures

Challenge	Functional	Multidivisional	Matrix	Transnational	Project
Control	***	**	*	**	**
Change	*	**	***	***	***
Knowledge	**	*	***	***	**
Internationalisation	*	**	***	***	**

* Stars indicate typical capacities to cope with each challenge, with three stars indicating high, two indicating medium and one indicating poor.

control, but are less concerned for flexibility in response to change or global reach, then they might prefer a functional structure. If they want to foster knowledge and flexibility on a global scale, then they might consider a matrix or transnational structure. In other words, structural choice depends on the particular strategic challenges the organisation faces. The difficult trade-offs involved are illustrated by the debate around Volkswagen's structure (Illustration 13.1) and the evolving nature of Procter & Gamble's structure (Illustration 13.2).

In reality, few organisations adopt a structure that is just like one of the pure structural types discussed above. Structures often blend different types into hybrid structures (see section 13.4.1 below), tailor-made to the particular mix of challenges facing the organisation. While Table 13.1 considers general challenges for contemporary organisations, Goold and Campbell provide *nine design tests* against which to check specific tailor-made structural solutions.[10] The first four tests stress fit with the key objectives and constraints of the organisation:

- *The Market-Advantage Test*. This test of fit with market strategy is fundamental, following Alfred Chandler's classic principle that 'structure follows strategy'.[11] For example, if coordination between two steps in a production process is important to market advantage, then they should probably be placed in the same structural unit.

- *The Parenting Advantage Test*. The structural design should fit the 'parenting' role of the corporate centre (see Chapter 7). For example, if the corporate centre aims to add value as a synergy manager, then it should design a structure that places important integrative specialisms, such as marketing or research, at the centre.

- *The People Test*. The structural design must fit the people available. It is dangerous to switch completely from a functional structure to a multidivisional structure if, as is likely, the organisation lacks managers with competence in running decentralised business units.

- *The Feasibility Test*. This is a catch-all category, indicating that the structure must fit legal, stakeholder, trade union or similar constraints. For example, after scandals involving biased research, investment banks are now required by financial regulators to separate their research and analysis departments from their deal-making departments.

Goold and Campbell then propose five more tests based on good general organisational design principles, as follows:

- *The Specialised Cultures Test*. This test reflects the value of bringing together specialists so that they can develop their expertise in close collaboration with each other. A structure scores poorly if it breaks up important specialist cultures.

- *The Difficult Links Test*. This test asks whether a proposed structure will set up links between parts of the organisations that are important but bound to be strained. For example, extreme decentralisation to profit-accountable business units is likely to strain relationships with a central research and development department. Unless compensating mechanisms are put in place, this kind of structure is likely to fail.

- *The Redundant Hierarchy Test*. Any structural design should be checked in case it has too many layers of management, causing undue blockages and expense. Delayering in response to redundant hierarchies has been an important structural trend in recent years.

- *The Accountability Test*. This test stresses the importance of clear lines of accountability, ensuring the control and commitment of managers throughout the structure. Because of their dual lines of reporting, matrix structures are often accused of lacking clear accountability.

- *The Flexibility Test*. While not all organisations will face the same general rise in environmental velocity as referred to with regard to Table 13.1, a final important test is whether the design will be sufficiently flexible to accommodate possible changes in the future. Here Kathleen Eisenhardt argues for structural 'modularity' (i.e. standardisation) in order to allow easy 'patching' (i.e. transfer) of one part of the organisation to another part of the organisation, as market needs change.[12] For example, if strategic business units are similar in structural size and internal management systems throughout a large organisation, it becomes easy to switch them between divisions as new opportunities for collaboration between units become apparent.

Goold and Campbell's nine tests provide a rigorous screen for effective structures. But even if the structural design passes these tests, the structure still needs to be matched to the other key element of an organisation's configuration, its systems. Systems too will have to reinforce strategy and structure.

(13.3) SYSTEMS

Structure is a key ingredient of organising for success. But structures can only work if they are supported by formal and informal organisational systems.[13] Systems give control over the organisation. If structures are like the bones in a body, systems are the muscles that control how things move. Illustration 13.3 on the changing structures and systems of the World Health Organization demonstrates the linkages between structures and systems.

Systems as means of control can be subdivided in two ways. First, systems tend to emphasise either control over inputs or control over outputs. Input control systems concern themselves with the *resources* consumed in the strategy, especially financial resources and human commitment. Output control systems focus on ensuring satisfactory *results*, for example the meeting of targets or achieving market competitiveness. The second subdivision is between direct and indirect controls. Direct controls involve *close supervision* or monitoring. Indirect controls are more *hands-off*, setting up the conditions whereby desired behaviours are achieved semi-automatically. How the five systems we shall consider emphasise input or output controls and direct or indirect control is summarised in Table 13.2.

Organisations normally use a blend of these control systems, but some will dominate over others according to the strategic challenges. As for structures, these challenges include change, knowledge and internationalisation and different systems cope with some of these

ILLUSTRATION 13.3

The World Health Organization's structure comes under pressure

New strategic challenges are shifting the organisation towards centralisation.

2009 was a testing year for the World Health Organization (WHO). The swine flu virus (H1N1), orginating in Mexico in April, swept quickly around the world. In June, the WHO Director-General Dr Margaret Chan declared: 'The world is moving into the early days of its first influenza pandemic of the 21st Century'. It looked like the worst pandemic since the 1968 Hong Kong flu killed an estimated one million people worldwide. Hundreds of millions of people rushed to be vaccinated.

As the coordinator of health policy for the United Nations, the WHO has a staff of 8000 health and other experts. About 1800 work at headquarters in Geneva. The remainder are spread around six regional offices (Africa, Europe, South-East Asia, Americas, East Mediterranean and West Pacific) and 147 country offices. WHO projects range from children's medicine, through leprosy eradication to dealing with HIV/AIDS.

Traditionally the WHO has been decentralised. Regional offices, typically with around 100 professional staff plus support staff, would lead in dealing with the characteristic health problems of their region. They also managed administrative, personnel, medical supply and field security services within their regions. However, criticisms of inefficiency from member states and the apparent rising threat of pandemics (worldwide disease outbreaks) were creating pressures for change. While there had been famous pandemics in history (for example, the Black Death), since the Hong Kong flu of 1968 there had been the emergence of HIV/AIDs in the 1980s, the SARS scare of 2003, the Avian flu scare of 2004–07 and then the H1N1 crisis of 2009.

Dr Margaret Chan had been director of health in Hong Kong since the 1990s, dealing with SARS and early outbreaks of Avian flu. In 2004 she had become an Assistant Director-General of the WHO. One of her first acts on arriving in Geneva was to set up a Strategic Health Operations Centre, a nerve centre for monitoring disease outbreaks across the world. In 2006, Chan became Director-General of the whole of WHO. She launched a further set of managerial reforms.

Principal amongst these reforms was the creation in 2008 of a global service centre, based in Kuala Lumpur. This global service centre provides administrative services and support to all staff in WHO offices worldwide in respect of human resources, payroll, procurement and accounts payable. Most of the previous posts carrying out these functions in Geneva, the regional offices and country offices were suppressed. A second important reform was the creation of a global management system, launched in 2009. This is based on an Enterprise Resource Management system produced by the American company Oracle, and brings together all existing WHO systems in the areas of finance, human resources, travel, programme planning and procurement.

By December, 2009, the H1N1 pandemic had claimed 10,000 lives across 208 countries. This was less than feared, and some accused the WHO of exaggerating the original threat. Margaret Chan told *The Canadian Press* in an interview: 'I can understand all these suspicions and conspiracy thinking, but I must emphasize that there is no basis for that. . . . All the measures that I put in place in Hong Kong in 1997 (an early outbreak of avian flu) became the gold standard. The aggressive approach by WHO . . . to put SARS back in the box is paying dividends. . . . I think we must remain prudent and observe the evolution of the (H1N1) pandemic in the course of the next six to 12 months before crying victory.'

Sources: www.who.int; *The Canadian Press*, 28 December 2009; 'A World Health Organization Primer' (www.medscape.com).

Questions

1 How is the strategy of the WHO changing and with what consequences for its structure and systems?

2 What barriers and threats can be envisaged to the direction of the WHO's structural and system reforms?

Table 13.2 Types of control systems

	Input	Output
Direct	Direct supervision; Planning systems	Performance targeting
Indirect	Cultural systems	Internal markets

better than others. As we shall see, input measures tend to require that the controllers have high levels of knowledge of what the controlled are supposed to do. In many knowledge-intensive organisations, especially those generating innovation and change, controllers rarely have a good understanding of what their expert employees are doing, and tend to rely more on output controls. At least they can know when a unit has made its revenue or profitability targets. Direct control relies heavily on the physical presence of management, although now surveillance through information technology can substitute. For this reason, international organisations may make use of indirect controls for their geographically dispersed subsidiaries. On the other hand, direct control systems can be very effective for small organisations on a single site.

13.3.1 Direct supervision

Direct supervision is the direct control of strategic decisions by one or a few individuals, typically focused on the effort put into the business by employees. It is a dominant process in small organisations. It can also exist in larger organisations where little change is occurring and if the complexity of the business is not too great for a small number of managers to control the strategy *in detail* from the centre. This is often found in family businesses and in parts of the public sector with a history of 'hands-on' political involvement (often where a single political party has dominated for a long period).

Direct supervision requires that the controllers thoroughly understand what is entailed by the jobs they supervise. They must be able to correct errors, but not cramp innovative experiments. Direct supervision is easiest on a single site, although long-distance monitoring (for instance, of trading strategies in banking) is now possible through electronic means. Direct supervision can also be effective during a *crisis*, when autocratic control through direct supervision may be necessary to achieve quick results. Turnaround managers are often autocratic in style. Quite often, especially in the public sector, there are expectations of direct supervision that go far beyond the controllers' actual competence.

13.3.2 Cultural systems

Organisations typically have distinctive cultures which express basic assumptions and beliefs held by organisation members and define taken-for-granted ways of doing things (see Chapter 5). Despite their taken-for-granted, semi-conscious nature, organisational cultures can seem a tempting means of managerial control. Managers may therefore try to influence organisational culture through various deliberate mechanisms in order to achieve the kinds of employee behaviour required by their strategy.[14] Such **cultural systems** aim to standardise **norms of behaviour within an organisation in line with particular objectives**. Cultural systems exercise an *indirect* form of control, because of not requiring direct supervision: it becomes a matter of willing conformity or *self*-control by employees. Control is exerted on the *input* of employees, as the culture defines the norms of appropriate effort and initiative that employees will put into their jobs.

Three key cultural systems are:

- *Recruitment*. Here cultural conformity may be attempted by the selection of appropriate staff in the first place. Employers look to find people who will 'fit'. Thus some employers may favour recruiting people who have already shown themselves to be 'team-players' through sport or other activities.

- *Socialisation*. Here employee behaviours are shaped by social processes once they are at work. It often starts with the integration of new staff through training, induction and mentoring programmes. It typically continues with further training throughout a career. Symbols can also play a role in socialisation, for example the symbolic example of leaders' behaviours or the influence of office décor, dress codes or language.

- *Reward*. Appropriate behaviour can be encouraged through pay, promotion or symbolic processes (for example, public praise). The desire to achieve the same rewards as successful people in the organisation will typically encourage imitative behaviour.

It is important to recognise that organisations' cultures are not fully under formal management control. Sometimes aspects of organisational culture may persistently contradict managerial intentions, as with peer-group pressure not to respond to organisational strategies. Cynicism and 'going through the motions' are common in some organisations. Sometimes the culture of an organisation may even drive its strategy (see Chapter 5). On the other hand, some cultures can bring about desired results, even without deliberate management intervention. For example, workers often form spontaneous and informal 'communities of practice', in which expert practitioners inside or even outside the organisation share their knowledge to generate innovative solutions to problems on their own initiative.[15] Examples of these informal communities of practice range from the Xerox photocopying engineers who would exchange information about problems and solutions over breakfast gatherings at the start of the day, to the programmer networks which support the development of Linux 'freeware' internationally over the internet.

13.3.3 Performance targeting systems

Performance targets focus on the *outputs* of an organisation (or part of an organisation), such as product quality, revenues or profits. These targets are often known as key performance indicators (KPIs). The performance of an organisation is judged, either internally or externally, on its ability to meet these targets. However, within specified boundaries, the organisation remains free on how targets should be achieved. This approach can be particularly appropriate in certain situations:

- *Within large businesses*, corporate centres may choose performance targets to control their business units without getting involved in the details of how they achieve them. These targets are often cascaded down the organisation as specific targets for sub-units, functions and even individuals.

- In *regulated markets*, such as privatised utilities in the UK and elsewhere, government-appointed regulators increasingly exercise control through agreed *performance indicators* (PIs), such as service or quality levels, as a means of ensuring 'competitive' performance.[16]

● In *the public services*, where control of resource inputs was the dominant approach historically, governments are attempting to move control processes towards outputs (such as quality of service) and, more importantly, towards outcomes (for example, patient mortality rates in health care).

Many managers find it difficult to develop a useful set of targets. There are at least three potential problems with targets:[17]

● *Inappropriate measures* of performance are quite common. For example, managers often prefer indicators that are easily measured or choose measures based on inadequate understanding of real needs on the ground. The result is a focus on the required measures rather than the factors that might be essential to long-term success. In the private sector, focus on short-term profit measures is common, at the expense of investment in the long-run prosperity of the business. To take a public-sector case, inappropriate 'national indicators' appeared to be a problem with child protection services in Illustration 13.4.

● *Inappropriate target levels* are a common problem. Managers are liable to give their superiors pessimistic forecasts so that targets are set at undemanding levels, which can then be easily met. On the other hand, superiors may over-compensate for their managers' pessimism, and end up setting excessively demanding targets. Unrealistically ambitious targets can either demotivate employees who see no hope of achieving them regardless of their effort, or encourage risky or dishonest behaviours in order to achieve the otherwise impossible.

● *Excessive internal competition* can be a result of targets focused on individual or sub-unit performance. Although an organisation by definition should be more than the sum of its parts, if individuals or sub-units are being rewarded on their performance in isolation, they will have little incentive to collaborate with the other parts of the organisation. The struggle to meet individualistic targets will reduce the exchange of information and the sharing of resources.

These acknowledged difficulties with targets have led to the development of two techniques designed to encourage a more balanced approach to target-setting. The most fundamental has been the development of the balanced scorecard approach.[18] **Balanced scorecards set performance targets according to a range of perspectives, not only financial**. Thus balanced scorecards typically combine four specific perspectives: the *financial perspective*, which might include profit margins or cash flow; the *customer perspective*, which sets targets important to customers, such as delivery times or service levels; the *internal perspective*, with targets relating to operational effectiveness such as the development of IT systems or reductions in waste levels; and finally the future-oriented *innovation and learning perspective*, which targets activities that will be important to the long-run performance of the organisation, for example investment in training or research. Attending to targets relevant to all four perspectives helps ensure that managers do not focus on one set of targets (e.g. financial) at the expense of others, while also keeping an eye to the future through innovation and learning.

A second more balanced approach to target-setting is strategy mapping, developing the balanced scorecard idea. **Strategy maps link different performance targets into a mutually supportive causal chain supporting strategic objectives**. Figure 13.6 shows an extract of a strategy map for a delivery company based on the four perspectives of finance, customers, internal processes, and innovation and learning. In this map, investments in well-trained and motivated drivers under the heading of 'innovation and learning' lead to on-time deliveries under the heading of 'internal processes', and thence to satisfied customers and finally to

KEY CONCEPT

Balanced scorecards

ILLUSTRATION 13.4

Structure, systems and saving children's lives

Changing structures and systems is not a quick fix in protecting children from parental abuse and neglect.

England and Wales have a problem: the homicide of children by their own parents. In the period 1998 to 2008, an average of about 40 children were killed by their parents annually. In 2008, about 200,000 children were living in households with a known high risk of domestic abuse and violence.

The death of nine-year-old Victoria Climbié in 2000 at the hands of her great aunt and boyfriend prompted a major reform of child protection services in England and Wales. Victoria Climbié's death had come after nine months of regular warning signs to the local social, police and medical services. The lack of coordination in picking up signs of abuse between these agencies was seen as a major weakness. One result was the merger of local education and children's social services into *unified children's services departments*. Another was to create '*common assessment frameworks*' (CAFs), a way for all agencies (from police to doctors) to record their dealing with a particular child on a standardised form accessible to all. A system of *national indicators* for measuring child protection was also introduced.

The homicide rate drifted down after the implementation of the reforms between 2003 and 2005, but then started to climb back towards the average, with 43 homicides in 2007–08. The 2007 death by neglect and abuse of 17-month-old 'Baby P' – in the same local authority area as Victoria Climbié and again after months of warning signs to police, medical and social work services – prompted a further review of services. The review found that under 10 per cent of local authorities had adopted the national indicators for child protection: local authorities complained that the targets were focused excessively on proper process and timescales, rather than meaningful outcomes. None the less, the review basically confirmed the new structure and systems, while urging more effective implementation through better training of social workers, revised indicators, more resources, centralised computer support and improved communications between agencies.

On the ground, however, there was considerable dissatisfaction with the post-Climbié reforms. 81 per cent of professionals in one poll claimed that the merger between educational and social services was not working (www.publicservice.co.uk). Most of the merged departments were headed by former directors of education, with little understanding of the social work for which they were responsible. Social workers complained about excessive form filling in order to demonstrate correct procedures. A boy told the review: 'It seems like they have to do all this form filling – their bosses' bosses make them do it – but it makes them forget about us'. An academic commentator estimated that social workers were now spending 80 per cent of their time in front of computers rather than with clients. The common assessment framework (CAF) form is eight pages long. One school head reported to the *Guardian* newspaper: 'You can no longer pick up the phone to the agencies for advice or referral without hearing "Where is the CAF?"'.

Speaking to the *Guardian*, Maggie Atkinson, director for learning and children in the town of Gateshead, urged patience: 'Bringing services together into one department creates a different culture, not immediately, but over a period of time. This change in culture is only really beginning to be embedded in local services and to put it into reverse would be a wasted opportunity. It doesn't matter whether the director comes from education or social services. What you need to do the job is broad shoulders, effective management and a very strong team around you.'

Sources: L. Lightfoot, 'A marriage on the rocks', *Guardian*, 17 March 2009; 'The Protection of Children in England: a Progress Report', *Every Child Matters*, March 2009.

Questions

1 List the advantages and disadvantages of the new structure and systems for children's services.

2 What kinds of actions and initiatives might be appropriate in terms of the cultural systems of children's services?

Figure 13.6 A strategy map

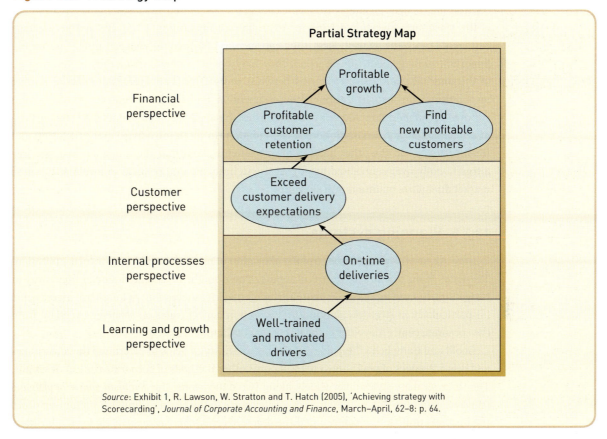

Partial Strategy Map

Source: Exhibit 1, R. Lawson, W. Stratton and T. Hatch (2005), 'Achieving strategy with Scorecarding', *Journal of Corporate Accounting and Finance*, March–April, 62–8: p. 64.

profitable growth. The causal chain between the various targets underlines the need for balance between them: each depends on the others for achievement. Thus strategy maps help in reducing the problem of partial measures referred to above; the problems of inappropriate target levels and internal competition are not so easily resolved.

13.3.4 Market systems

Market disciplines (or *internal markets*) can be brought inside organisations to control activities internally.[19] **Market systems typically involve some formalised system of 'contracting' for resources or inputs from other parts of an organisation and for supplying outputs to other parts of an organisation**. Control focuses on outputs, for example revenues earned in successful competition for internal contracts. The control is indirect: rather than accepting detailed performance targets determined externally, units have simply to earn their keep in competitive internal markets.

Internal markets can be used in a variety of ways. There might be *competitive bidding*, perhaps through the creation of an internal investment bank at the corporate centre to support new initiatives. Also, a customer–supplier relationship may be established between a central service department, such as training or IT, and the operating units. Typically these internal markets are subject to considerable regulation. For example, the corporate centre might set rules for *transfer prices* between internal business units to prevent exploitative contract pricing, or insist on *service-level agreements* to ensure appropriate service by an essential internal supplier, such as IT, for the various units that depend on it.

Internal markets work well where complexity or rapid change makes detailed direct or input controls impractical. Arguably this is the case in the specialised and fast-moving environment of the Macquarie investment bank in Australia (see Illustration 13.5). But market systems can create problems as well. First, they can increase bargaining between units, consuming important management time. Second, they may create a new bureaucracy monitoring all of the internal transfers of resources between units. Third, an overzealous use of market mechanisms can lead to dysfunctional competition and legalistic contracting, destroying cultures of collaboration and relationships. These have all been complaints made against the internal markets and semi-autonomous Foundation Hospitals introduced in the UK's National Health Service. On the other hand, their proponents claim that these market processes free a traditionally over-centralised health service to innovate and respond to local needs, while market disciplines maintain overall control.

13.3.5 Planning systems

Planning systems **plan and control the allocation of resources and monitor their utilization.** The focus is on the direct control of inputs. These might be simple financial inputs (as in budgeting), human inputs (as in planning for managerial succession) or long-term investments (as particularly in strategic planning). This section concentrates on strategic oversight from the corporate centre, developing the discussion in Chapter 12.

Goold and Campbell's[20] typology of three *strategy styles* helps to determine the advantages and disadvantages of planning systems against other methods of corporate central oversight. The three strategy styles differ widely along two dimensions: the *dominant source of planning influence*, either top-down (from the corporate centre to the business units) or bottom-up (from the business units to the centre); and the *degree of performance accountability* for the business units, either tight or reasonably relaxed. As in Figure 13.7, the three strategy styles align themselves on these two dimensions thus:

Figure 13.7 **Strategy styles**

Source: Adapted from M. Goold and A. Campbell, *Strategies and Styles*, Blackwell, 1989, Figure 3.1, p. 39.

ILLUSTRATION 13.5

Controlling investment bankers

Known as the 'Millionaire Factory', Macquarie's entrepreneurial bankers are pursuing deals all over the world. Now there is a new CEO.

Sydney-based Macquarie Bank is Australia's largest investment bank and its most successful division, the Infrastructure Group, is the largest operator of toll roads in the world. Its funds own Copenhagen Airport and the Thames Water company and during 2006 it launched an audacious and ultimately unsuccessful bid for the London Stock Exchange. Despite this set-back, 2006 was another record year for Macquarie. Its total staff has risen from under 5000 in 2003 to just less than 10,000 in 2007; its international staff rose from less than a thousand to 3200 in the same period.

The long-standing chief executive, Allan Moss, joined Macquarie in 1977, when it was still a sub-sidiary of British merchant bank Hill Samuel with about 50 employees. A Harvard MBA (he graduated in the top 5%), Moss became chief executive in 1993 and listed the bank on the Australian Stock Exchange in 1995. According to the *Financial Times*, Moss has an image of a 'bumbling professor', spilling coffee and tripping over telephone cords. He does not travel overseas much, preferring to stay in Sydney, and he works short hours by investment banker standards, 8.30 a.m. to 7.30 p.m.

Moss describes the bank's culture as one of 'freedom within boundaries'. For him, Macquarie is a federation of businesses in which entrepreneurs can thrive: 'we provide the infrastructure, the capital, the brand and a controlled framework – and the staff provide the ideas'. The culture is very competitive internally, with colleagues pitching for 'mandates' (the responsibility for a bit of business) against each other. One former banker observed: 'Walking into Macquarie is like walking into a Turkish bazaar. Everyone has the same rug and they're all competing to sell the same rug.' In fact, though, the internal competition produces highly innovative ideas – for example, the proposal that the bank should provide financing for patients' operations, including cosmetic surgery such as breast implants. The rule-of-thumb guiding promotion to one of the coveted – and lucrative – 250 executive directorships has been generating an annual profit personally of $5m (Australian; ~€3.5m or ~US$4.5m). The company receives 70,000 un-solicited CVs from would-be Macquarie bankers every year. All hires go through the same distinctive and rigorous psychological testing process.

Of course, some doubt whether Macquarie's successful run can go on for ever. The *Financial Times* quoted one close observer of Macquarie: 'I am starting to detect some hubris at the bank. It has done so well it is inevitable. Allan [Moss] is loyal to those he trusts and only time will tell whether he is trusting his lieutenants a bit too much.' In 2008, Moss retired. His successor as CEO, Nicholas Moore, announced: 'I have been here for 22 years and have grown up with this organisation. I have seen the culture and organisation work year in, year out. I think we have a winning formula.'

The new CEO had to deal with the banking crisis. Macquarie's shares slid from $66 Aus in May 2008 to less than $16 at the bottom of the crisis in March 2009. By early 2010 Macquarie was back at $55, but the gloss had certainly come off the millionaires' factory by then.

Sources: Financial Times, 17 December 2005, 28 May 2008; Sydney Morning Herald, 19 August 2006.

Questions

1 In this account, what control systems are particularly important to Macquarie?
2 What threats are there to these systems?

- The *strategic planning* style is the archetypal planning system, hence its name. In the Goold and Campbell sense, the strategic planning style combines both a strong planning influence on strategic direction from the corporate centre with relatively relaxed performance accountability for the business units. The logic is that if the centre sets the strategic direction, business unit managers should not be held strictly accountable for disappointing results that might be due to an inappropriate plan in the first place. In the strategic planning style, the centre focuses on inputs in terms of allocating resources necessary to achieve the strategic plan, while exercising a high degree of direct control over how the plan is executed by the businesses.

- The *financial control* style involves very little central planning. The business units each set their own strategic plans, probably after some negotiation with the corporate centre, and are then held strictly accountable for the results against these plans. This style differs from the strategic planning style in that control is against financial outputs, similar to a performance targeting system. If the businesses devised the plans, then they should take full responsibility for success or failure. Business unit managers in the financial control style have a lot of autonomy and typically receive high bonus payments for success. But failure may easily lead to dismissal. The financial planning style fits with the portfolio manager or restructurer roles of the corporate centre referred to in Chapter 7.

- The *strategic control* style is in the middle, with a more consensual development of the strategic plan between the corporate centre and the business units and moderate levels of business unit accountability. Under the strategic control style, the centre will typically act as coach to its business unit managers, helping them to see and seize opportunities in a supportive manner. This style often relies on strong cultural systems to foster trust and mutual understanding. Thus the strategic control style is often associated with the synergy manager or parental developer roles of the corporate centre discussed in Chapter 7.

Thus the three strategy styles vary with regard to their reliance on, and application of, planning systems. The direct control of inputs characteristic of the strategic planning style is only appropriate in certain circumstances. In particular, it makes sense where there are large, risky and long-range investments to be allocated: for example, an oil company typically has to take the decision to invest in the ten-year development of an oilfield at the corporate centre, rather than risk delegating it to business units whose resources and time-horizons may be limited. On the other hand, the financial control style is suitable where investments are small, relatively frequent and well understood, as typically in a mature, non-capital-intensive business. The strategic control style is suitable where there are opportunities for collaborating across businesses and there is a need to nurture new ones.

The strategic planning style (not the practice of strategic planning in general) has become less common in the private sector in recent years. The style is seen as too rigid to adapt to changing circumstances and too top-down to reflect real business circumstances on the ground. However, it is important to recognise the internal consistency of all three styles, including strategic planning. Each achieves logical combinations of accountability and strategic influence. Problems occur when organisations construct systems of planning and accountability that depart substantially from the diagonal line in Figure 13.7. Too far below the line (the 'south-west' corner) implies an excessively relaxed combination of weak direction from the centre and low accountability for the businesses. Too far above the diagonal line (the 'north-east' corner) implies a harsh combination of strong direction from the centre and strict accountability in the businesses. In the 'north-east' corner, business managers are held accountable even for mistakes that may have their origins in the centre's own plans.

(13.4) CONFIGURATIONS

The introduction of this chapter introduced the concept of configurations. **Configurations are the set of organisational design elements that interlink together in order to support the intended strategy**. Figure 13.1 focused on the mutually supporting elements of strategy, structure and systems. This section begins by extending these three elements with the McKinsey 7-S framework and finishes by considering likely tensions or dilemmas amongst the elements of organisational design and some methods for managing them.

13.4.1 The McKinsey 7-S framework

The McKinsey & Co consulting company has developed a framework for assessing the degree to which the various elements of an organisation's design fit together in a mutually supporting manner. **The McKinsey 7-S framework highlights the importance of fit between strategy, structure, systems, staff, style, skills and superordinate goals.**[21] Together these seven elements can serve as a checklist in any organisational design exercise: see Figure 13.8.

This chapter has already addressed strategy, structure and systems. This section will comment on the remaining four elements of the 7-S framework, as follows:

Figure 13.8 The McKinsey 7 Ss

Source: R. Waterman, T. Peters and J. Phillips, 'Structure is not organization', *Business Horizons*, June 1980, pp. 14–26: p. 18.

- *Style* here refers to the leadership style of top managers in an organisation. Leadership styles may be collaborative, participative, directive or coercive, for instance (see Chapter 14). Managers' behavioural style can influence the culture of the whole organisation (see Chapter 5). The style should fit other aspects of the 7-S framework: for example, a highly directive or coercive style is not likely to fit a matrix organisation structure, as in the case of Durk Jager at Procter & Gamble (see Illustration 13.2).

- *Staff* is about the kinds of people in the organisation and how they are developed. This relates to systems of recruitment, socialisation and reward (section 13.3.2). A key criterion for the feasibility of any strategy is: does the organisation have the people to match (see section 11.4.2)? A common constraint on structural change is the availability of the right people to head new departments and divisions (the 'People Test': see 13.2.6).

- *Skills* relates to staff, but in the 7-S framework refers more broadly to capabilities in general (see Chapter 3). The concept of capabilities here raises not only staff skills but also issues to do with how these skills are embedded in and captured by the organisation as a whole. For example, how do the organisation's training schemes, information technology and reward systems transform the talents of individuals into the organisational capabilities required by the strategy?

- *Superordinate goals* refers to the overarching goals or purpose of the organisation as a whole, in other words the mission, vision and objectives that form the organisational purpose (see Chapter 4). Superordinate goals are placed at the centre of the 7-S framework: all other elements should support these.

The McKinsey 7-S framework highlights at least three aspects of organising. First, organising involves a lot more than just getting the organisational structure right; there are many other elements to attend to. Second, the 7-S framework emphasises fit between all these elements: everything from structure to skills needs to be connected together. Third, if managers change one element of the 7-S, the concept of fit suggests they are likely to have to change all the other elements as well in order to keep them all appropriately aligned to each other. Changing one element in isolation is liable to make things worse until overall fit is restored.

13.4.2 Configuration dilemmas

Although the concept of configurations and the 7-S framework emphasise the importance of mutual fit between elements, in practice this is often hard to achieve. Managing typically involves trade-offs and tensions between different desirable states. Seeking perfect solutions on one element of the configuration may very well oblige compromises on another element. Given that many of these tensions are very hard to escape, this section briefly considers various ways in which they can at least be managed.

Figure 13.9 summarises five key dilemmas in organising. First, formal hierarchies are often necessary to ensure control and action, but they can sit uneasily with the informal networks that foster knowledge exchange and innovation. Second, vertical accountability promotes maximum performance by subordinates, but it can easily lead managers to maximise their own self-interest, at the expense of horizontal relationships. Third, empowering employees lower down the organisation gives scope for potentially valuable initiatives and experiments, but over the long term can lead to incoherence. Fourth, while centralisation might be needed for standardisation of products and processes, this can be at the cost of the initiative and flexibility fostered by decentralisation. Finally, adopting best practice on a particular element

Figure 13.9 Some dilemmas in organising for success

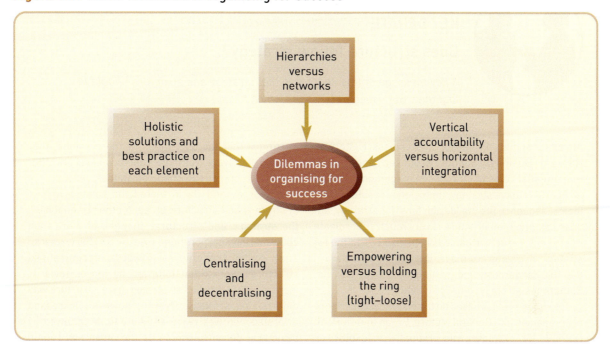

of the organisation, for instance financial controls, may actually be damaging if it does not fit with the needs of the organisation as a whole.

Managers should recognise that any organisational design is likely to face dilemmas of these kinds and that it is hard to optimise on all dimensions. However, they may be able to manage these dilemmas in three ways:

- By *subdividing* the organisation, so that the one part of the organisation is organised optimally according to one side of these dilemmas, while the rest responds to the other. Thus, for example, IBM created its revolutionary personal computer in a specialised new-venture division, kept separate from the traditional mainframe activities which were dominated by principles of hierarchy and vertical accountability highly antagonistic to radical innovation.[22]

- By *combining* different organising principles at the same time. Thus organisation design expert Jay Galbraith argues for the potential of 'hybrid structures': for instance, a 'front–back' structure combines centralised functional specialisms in manufacturing and research at the 'back', while customer-facing units at the front are organised in a more decentralised way around particular market segments, such as industry or geography.[23]

- By *reorganising* frequently so that no one side of the dilemma can become too entrenched. The rate of major reorganisation for large UK companies increased from once every four years to once every three years in the last decade.[24] Given this pace of reorganising, many organisations are like pendulums, constantly swinging between centralisation and devolution, for example, without resting long on one side or the other.[25]

A final dilemma arising from the interconnectedness of configurations is which element drives the others. The extent to which strategic elements drive structural elements is the subject of the Key Debate.

KEY DEBATE

Does structure follow strategy?

A key message of this chapter is that strategy and structure should fit together. But which determines which?

Alfred Chandler, Professor of Business History at Harvard Business School, proposed one of the fundamental rules of strategic management: 'unless structure follows strategy, inefficiency results'.[1] This logical sequence fits the 'design lens' for strategy, but does assume that structure is very much subordinate to strategy: structure can easily be fixed once the big strategic decisions are made. But some authors warn that this dangerously underestimates structure's role. Sometimes strategy follows structure.

Chandler's rule is based on the historical experience of companies like General Motors, Exxon and DuPont. DuPont, for example, was originally an explosives company. During the First World War, however, the company anticipated the peace by deliberately diversifying out of explosives into new civil markets such as plastics and paints. Yet the end of the war plunged DuPont into crisis. All its new businesses were loss-making; only explosives still made money. The problem was not the diversification strategy, but the structure that DuPont used to manage the new civil businesses. DuPont had retained its old functional structure, so that responsibilities for the production and marketing of all the new businesses were still centralised on single functional heads. They could not cope with the increased diversity. The solution was not to abandon the diversification strategy; rather it was to adopt a new structure with decentralised divisions for each of the separate businesses. DuPont thrives today with a variant of this multidivisional structure.

Hall and Saias accept the importance of strategy for structure but warn that the causality can go the other way.[2] An organisation's existing structure very much determines the kinds of strategic opportunities that its management will see and want to grasp. For instance, it is easy for a company with a decentralised multidivisional structure to make acquisitions and divestments: all it has to do is add or subtract divisions, with few ramifications for the rest of the business. On the other hand, it can be very hard for the top managers of a decentralised multidivisional organisation to see opportunities for innovation and knowledge-sharing within the operations of the divisions: they are too far away from the real business. In other words, structures can shape strategies.

Amburgey and Dacin tested the relative impact of strategy and structure on each other by analysing the strategic and structural changes of more than 200 American corporations over nearly thirty years.[3] They found that moves towards decentralised structures were often followed by moves towards increasingly diversified strategies: here, structure was determining strategy. Overall, however, increased diversification was twice as likely to be followed by structural decentralisation as the other way round. In other words, structure does follow strategy, but only most of the time.

Henry Mintzberg concludes that 'structure follows strategy as the left foot follows the right'.[4] In other words, strategy and structure are related reciprocally rather than just one way. Mintzberg warns that a simple 'design' approach to strategy and structure can be misleading. Structure is not always easy to fix after the big strategic decisions have been made. Strategists should check to see that their existing structures are not constraining the kinds of strategies that they consider.

References:
1. A. Chandler, *Strategy and Structure: Chapters in the History of American Enterprise*, MIT Press, 1962, p. 314.
2. D.J. Hall and M.A. Saias, 'Strategy follows structure!', *Strategic Management Journal*, vol. 1, no. 2 (1980), pp. 149–63.
3. T. Amburgey and T. Dacin, 'As the left foot follows the right? The dynamics of strategic and structural change', *Academy of Management Journal*, vol. 37, no. 6 (1994), pp. 1427–52.
4. H. Mintzberg, 'The Design School: reconsidering the basic premises of strategic management', *Strategic Management Journal*, vol. 11 (1990), pp. 171–95.

Question

Hall and Saias suggest that organisational structures can influence the kinds of strategies that management teams will pursue. What kinds of organisations might be particularly susceptible to structural constraints on their strategies?

SUMMARY

- Successful organising means responding to the key challenges facing the organisation. This chapter has stressed control, change, knowledge and internationalisation.

- There are many *structural types* (e.g. functional, divisional, matrix, transnational and project). Each structural type has its own strengths and weaknesses and responds differently to the challenges of control, change, knowledge and internationalisation.

- There is a range of different organisational *systems* to facilitate and control strategy. These systems can focus on either inputs or outputs and be direct or indirect.

- The separate organisational elements, summarised in the *McKinsey 7-S framework*, should come together to form a coherent *reinforcing configuration*. But these reinforcing cycles also raise tough dilemmas that can be managed by *subdividing*, *combining* and *reorganising*.

WORK ASSIGNMENTS

✱ *Denotes more advanced work assignments. * Refers to a case study in the Text and Cases edition.*

13.1 Go to the website of a large organisation you are familiar with and find its organisational chart (not all organisations provide these). Why is the organisation structured like this?

13.2 Referring to section 13.2.2 on the multidivisional structure, consider the advantages and disadvantages of creating divisions along different lines – such as product, geography or technology – with respect to a large organisation you are familiar with or a case organisation such as CRH*, SABMiller* or Sony*.

13.3✱ Referring to Figure 13.6, write a short executive brief explaining how strategy maps could be a useful management system to monitor and control the performance of organisational units. Be sure to analyse both advantages and disadvantages of this approach.

13.4 As a middle manager with responsibility for a small business unit, which 'strategy style' (section 13.3.5) would you prefer to work within? In what sort of circumstances or corporate organisation would this style not work so well for you?

Integrative Assignment

13.5 Take a recent merger or acquisition (see Chapter 10), ideally one involving two organisations of roughly equal size, and analyse how the deal has changed the acquiring or merged company's organisational structure. What do you conclude from the extent or lack of structural change for the new company going forward?

RECOMMENDED KEY READINGS

- The best single coverage of this chapter's issues is in R. Daft, *Understanding the Theory and Design of Organizations*, South-Western, 2009.

- For a collection of relevant articles, see the special issue 'Learning to design organizations', R. Dunbar and W. Starbuck (eds), *Organization Science*, vol. 17, no. 2 (2006).

- M. Goold and A. Campbell, *Designing Effective Organizations*, Jossey-Bass, 2002, provides a practical guide to organisational design issues.

REFERENCES

1. A good review of new and old structural types can be found in G. Friesen, 'Organisation design for the 21st century', *Consulting to Management – C2M*, vol. 16, no. 3 (2005), pp. 32–51.

2. The view that organisations should fit their structures to key challenges ('contingencies') is associated with the long tradition of research on contingency theory: see L. Donaldson, *The Contingency Theory of Organizations*, Sage, 2001, or R. Whittington, 'Organizational structure', in *The Oxford Handbook of Strategy*, Volume II, Oxford University Press, 2003, Chapter 28, for summaries.

3. This view of divisionalisation as a response to diversity was originally put forward by A.D. Chandler, *Strategy and Structure*, MIT Press, 1962. See R. Whittington and M. Mayer, *The European Corporation: Strategy, Structure and Social Science*, Oxford University Press, 2000, for a summary of Chandler's argument and the success of divisional organisations in contemporary Europe.

4. For a review of current experience with matrix structures, see S. Thomas and L. D'Annunzio, 'Challenges and strategies of matrix organisations: top-level and mid-level managers' perspectives', *Human Resource Planning*, vol. 28, no. 1 (2005), pp. 39–48, and J. Galbraith, *Designing Matrix Structures that Actually Work*, Jossey-Bass, 2009.

5. See C. Bartlett and S. Ghoshal, 'Matrix management: not a structure, more a frame of mind', *Harvard Business Review*, vol. 68, no. 4 (1990), pp. 138–45.

6. C. Bartlett and S. Ghoshal, *Managing across Borders*, 2nd edition, Harvard Business School Press, 2008.

7. Recent research finds that transnational structures generally perform better than either centralised or decentralised structures: see J.-N. Garbe and N. Richter, 'Causal analysis of the internationalization and performance relationship based on neural networks', *Journal of International Management*, vol. 15, no. 4 (2009), pp. 413–31.

8. The classic article on project-based organisations is by R. DeFillippi and M. Arthur, 'Paradox in project-based enterprise: the case of film-making', *California Management Review*, vol. 40, no. 2 (1998), pp. 125–45. For some difficulties, see M. Bresnen, A. Goussevskaia and J. Swann, 'Organisational routines, situated learning and processes of change in project-based organizations', *Project Management Journal*, vol. 36, no. 3 (2005), pp. 27–42.

9. For a discussion of more permanent team structures, see Thomas Mullern, 'Integrating the team-based structure in the business process: the case of Saab training systems', in A. Pettigrew and E. Fenton (eds), *The Innovating Organization*, Sage, 2000.

10. M. Goold and A. Campbell, *Designing Effective Organizations*, Jossey-Bass, 2002. See also M. Goold and A. Campbell, 'Do you have a well-designed organization?', *Harvard Business Review*, vol. 80, no. 3 (2002), pp. 117–224.

11. A.D. Chandler, *Strategy and Structure: Chapters in the History of American Enterprise*, MIT Press, 1962.

12. This practice of 'patching' parts of the organisation on to each other according to changing market needs is described in K. Eisenhardt and S. Brown, 'Patching: restitching business portfolios in dynamic markets', *Harvard Business Review*, vol. 25, no. 3 (1999), pp. 72–80.

13. The point has been argued by E. Fenton and A. Pettigrew, 'Theoretical perspectives on new forms of organizing', in A. Pettigrew and E. Fenton (eds), *The Innovating Organization*, Sage, 2000, Chapter 1.

14. C. Casey, 'Come, join our family: discipline and integration in corporate organizational culture, *Human Relations*, vol. 52, no. 2 (1999), pp. 155–79; for an account of the socialisation of graduate trainees, see A.D. Brown and C. Coupland, 'Sounds of silence: graduate trainees, hegemony and resistance', *Organization Studies*, vol. 26, no. 7 (2005), pp. 1049–70.

15. E.C. Wenger and W.M. Snyder, 'Communities of practice: the organized frontier', *Harvard Business Review*, vol. 78, no. 1 (2000), pp. 139–46.

16. D. Helm and T. Jenkinson, *Competition in Regulated Industries*, Clarendon Press, 1999, provides a number of in-depth case studies of competitive implications of deregulation.

17. The value of goals and performance targets has been debated vigorously: see L. Ordonez, M. Schweitzer, A Galinksy and M. Bazerman, 'Goals gone wild: the systematic side effects of overprescribing goal setting', *Academy of Management Perspectives*, vol. 23, no. 1 (2009), pp. 6–16 and E. Locke and G. Latham, 'Has goal setting gone wild?', *Academy of Management Perspectives*, vol. 23, no. 1 (2009), pp. 17–23.

18. See R. Kaplan and D. Norton, 'Having trouble with your strategy? Then map it', *Harvard Business Review*, vol. 78, no. 5 (2000), pp. 167–76 and R. Kaplan and D. Norton, *Alignment: How to Apply the Balanced Scorecard to Strategy*, Harvard Business School Press, 2006.

19. Companies like Royal Dutch Shell have been experimenting with internal markets to stimulate innovation. See Gary Hamel, 'Bringing Silicon Valley inside', *Harvard Business Review*, vol. 77, no. 5 (1999), pp. 70–84. For a discussion of internal market challenges, see A. Vining, 'Internal market failure', *Journal of Management Studies*, vol. 40, no. 2 (2003), pp. 431–57.

20. M. Goold and A. Campbell, *Strategies and Styles*, Blackwell, 1987.

21. R. Waterman, T. Peters and J. Phillips, 'Structure is not organization', *Business Horizons*, June 1980, pp. 14–26.

22. R.A. Burgelman, 'Managing the new venture division: implications for strategic management', *Strategic Management Journal*, vol. 6, no. 1 (1985), pp. 39–54.

23. J. Galbraith, 'Organizing to deliver solutions', *Organisational Dynamics*, vol. 31, no. 2 (2002), pp. 194–207.

24. R. Whittington and M. Mayer, *Organising for Success: A Report on Knowledge*, CIPD, 2002.

25. For an analysis of this process at a leading pharmaceutical firm, see S. Karim and W. Mitchell, 'Innovating through acquisition and internal development: a quarter-century of boundary evolution at Johnson & Johnson', *Long Range Planning*, vol. 37, no. 6 (2004), pp. 525–38.

Hurricane Katrina: human-made disaster?

Introduction

Early on Monday morning, 29 August 2005, Hurricane Katrina struck the southern American state of Louisiana, rushing quickly inland to the city of New Orleans. With wind speeds at 125 miles per hour (200 km/h), the levees (dykes) protecting the city collapsed in several places. Over the next few days, the world watched in horror as New Orleans and the surrounding areas struggled with chaos. Hurricane Katrina claimed 1,836 lives and left vivid images of bodies floating in the streets, families stranded on rooftops and 25,000 hungry and thirsty people trapped for days in the notorious Superdome. Six months after the hurricane, more than half of New Orleans' population had still not returned to the city.

Ultimately, of course, the destruction wrought by Hurricane Katrina had natural causes. But there is every sign that the damage and suffering were significantly increased by organisational failures. The disaster of Hurricane Katrina was partly a consequence of organisational design.

A new organisation

The government organisation ultimately responsible for coordinating the response to Katrina was the US Department of Homeland Security. This itself was a recent creation, a reaction to the terrorist attacks of September 11, 2001. One finding from investigations into the circumstances surrounding 9/11 was the difficulty of coordinating all the information regarding terrorist threats. For example, before the attacks, a flight training school had alerted local authorities about a student who only seemed interested in learning how to fly civil airliners, not about how to take off or land. But the information had not been passed on to the Federal Bureau of Investigations (FBI): the student went on to be one of the terrorist hijackers involved in 9/11.

The US government responded to 9/11 by placing terrorism as the highest priority. It believed that one way of improving coordination in response to potential terror threats was by centralising relevant government

Source: Reuters/Robert Galbraith.

departments. Nine days after the 9/11 attack, President Bush appointed Pennsylvania Governor and decorated Vietnam veteran Tom Ridge to create and head a new department. The White House vetoed some of Tom Ridge's more radical proposals, so that both the Justice Department and the FBI remained independent. However, finally 22 departments were swept together in 2002 to create the new Department for Homeland Security (see Figure 1 for an organisational chart).

Involving more than 180,000 employees, this was the biggest reorganisation of the US government since the creation of the Pentagon in 1947. Amongst the major agencies that were gathered together under Tom Ridge's command were Customs, Immigration, Narcotics, the Coast Guard, the Secret Service and, most important here, the Federal Emergency Management Agency (FEMA). All were to unite in the fight against terrorism. As the head of the US Customs Service said: 'Terrorism is our highest priority, bar none. Ninety eight per cent of my attention . . . has been devoted to that one issue.' Tom Ridge anticipated turf battles between the newly amalgamated agencies but declared: 'The only turf we should be worried about protecting is the turf we stand on.'

FEMA, however, resisted the reorganisation. Responsible for responding to natural disasters such as hurricanes or earthquakes, FEMA had since 1993 been represented directly inside the President's Cabinet.

Figure 1 Department of Homeland Security organisation chart

Source: http://www.dhs.gov/xabout/structure/editorial_0644.shtm.

Merger within the new Department of Homeland Security relegated FEMA to a mere internal division, with no direct Cabinet-level representation. FEMA's then head protested to the President's chief of staff: 'I told him it was a big mistake. The fact that FEMA could report to the President, any President – Democrat, Republican or independent – was what made the agency effective.' In the wake of 9/11, of course, this sounded like special pleading.

Within the new organisation, response to natural disasters had a low priority. In 2004, the Department drew up a list of 15 planning scenarios, doomsday events that could cause major fatalities. Twelve of these involved shadowy international terrorist groups, with plots involving mustard gas, sarin, nuclear weapons and anthrax, amongst other imaginative possibilities. One planning scenario did raise the threat of a hurricane flooding a nameless southern city and causing more than a thousand deaths. But terror attacks held the attention and these attracted the budgets.

Resources for protection against natural disasters began to get squeezed. Tom Ridge retired and was replaced by a new Secretary for Homeland Security,

Michael Chertoff, a former judge. Various FEMA functions were stripped off and reallocated to other parts of the reorganisation. FEMA lost $80m (~€56m) from its $550m operating budget. It struggled to get resources for rehearsing a response to a New Orleans hurricane scenario, and when it did do so, funds were denied for a follow-up. Between 2000 and 2005, the budget for the New Orleans Engineering Corps, responsible for the levees protecting the city, was cut by 44 per cent. Meanwhile, the Ohio Fire Service was able to get funds for bulletproof vests to protect their dogs in the event of terrorist attack.

Testing the new organisation

Hurricane Katrina gave several days' notice, forming over the Bahamas on 23 August and sweeping over Florida two days later. Early on Saturday morning, 27 August, a FEMA watch officer posted a warning of a severe hurricane threat to the New Orleans area, capable of causing thousands of fatalities. Michael Chertoff was at home that day, working on immigration issues. On Saturday night, New Orleans Mayor Ray Nagin ordered an evacuation of the city's 400,000 citizens. But, with no certainty that the hurricane would actually hit, and with what force, not everybody wanted to leave their homes for fear of looting. Moreover, many had no means of transport, including tragically many old people who were to be trapped without power in their nursing homes. When the hurricane struck on the Monday morning, 60,000 people were still in New Orleans.

The city was not ready. FEMA's planning for the state of Louisiana as a whole had called for 69 truck-loads of water, 69 truckloads of ice and 34 truckloads of food to be in place. It planned for 400 buses and 800 drivers to ferry people to shelters. On the Sunday, FEMA had just 30 truckloads of water, 17 truckloads of ice and 15 truckloads of meals. FEMA had no buses in the state at all.

FEMA had got one officer into the city on the Sunday, but was otherwise not represented locally. When the flooding started, communications broke down. The various services had different communications systems, and the batteries on mobile devices soon ran down, with no power available to recharge. FEMA's high-tech communications wagon only reached New Orleans on the Friday (long after the world's journalists) and in the meantime Mayor Nagin's team had broken into an Office Depot store in order to steal functioning communications equipment. The sole FEMA officer on the ground had to bully his way onto one of the few helicopters available to confirm the broken levees on the first day. The Department of Homeland Security operations centre in Washington, guarding against panic responses, insisted on verification by a second source before passing the message up the chain, but no second source was available. Secretary Chertoff briefed President Bush about immigration issues on Monday morning, and made no mention of the hurricane.

The Department of Homeland Security struggled to cope over the following days. Michael Brown, FEMA's Head, flew to nearby Baton Rouge, but suffered from poor communications and found himself increasingly bypassed by Department Head Michael Chertoff in Washington. The evacuation of the Superdome only began on the Friday, after the instigation of food rationing, and the Washington operations centre overlooked 20,000 refugees at the New Orleans Convention Center for several days, thinking it the same building as the Superdome. Aircraft were delayed because of the lack of air marshals required by anti-terrorist regulations. The Department of Homeland Security insisted that all evacuees would have to be security screened before being allowed on planes, and then took eight hours to fly in security staff. A large consignment of food packs from the United Kingdom was turned away because of fears of Mad Cow Disease.

At a Thursday press conference in Washington, Michael Chertoff praised 'the genius of the people at FEMA' in their response to the disaster. 'I think it is a source of tremendous pride to me to work with the people who've pulled off this really exceptional response.' But television reports direct from New Orleans contradicted this picture every hour. The failure of FEMA, and of local agencies, was becoming very apparent. Facing heavy criticism, FEMA's head, Michael Brown, resigned on 13 September. Michael Chertoff kept his job.

Sources: C. Cooper and R. Block, *Disaster: Hurricane Katrina and the Failure of Homeland Security*, Times Books, 2006; and I. Daaddler and I. Destler, 'Advisors, Czars and Councils', *The National Interest*, 1 July (2002).

Questions

1 What was the 'strategy' of the Department of Homeland Security in the period immediately before Hurricane Katrina?

2 In the light of this strategy, what, if any, changes should be made to the Department's organisational structure after Hurricane Katrina?

3 Who was responsible for the organisational failures surrounding the response to Hurricane Katrina?

14

LEADERSHIP AND STRATEGIC CHANGE

Learning outcomes

After reading this chapter you should be able to:

● Identify *types* of required strategic change.

● Analyse how *organisational context* might affect the design of strategic change programmes.

● Undertake a *forcefield analysis* to identify forces blocking and facilitating change.

● Identify and assess the different styles of leading and managing strategic change.

● Assess the value of different *levers* for strategic change.

● Identify the pitfalls and problems of *managing change programmes*.

(14.1) INTRODUCTION

Davit Brandon took over as CEO of Domino's Pizza after a period of little change. He introduced himself to his management team as follows: 'If you are the kind of people and type of organisation that loves change, that believes change is good, change is exciting and embracing change is something that you really want to get good at and want to do, then you are going to love me. If you are the kind of person who wants things always to be the way they have been and you want to sit around and talk about the good old days, then I am not your guy, because truthfully I am here to create better days and that is going to require change'.[1] Harvard's John Kotter makes this distinction: 'Management is about coping with complexity . . . without good management complex enterprises tend to become chaotic . . . Leadership, by contrast is about coping with change'.[2] Clearly David Brandon saw himself as a leader of change.

Strategic change is inherent in much of this part of the book. Chapter 11 posed questions about the feasibility of strategies; could they work in practice? Chapter 12 provided different explanations of how strategies develop. Chapter 13 addressed issues to do with organising

Figure 14.1 Key elements in managing strategic change

to deliver strategies. These considerations are all important in managing strategic change. However, central to strategic change is ensuring that people make a strategy happen. This chapter is about how managers can lead people to effect strategic change. This leadership role is most often associated with chief executives, but, in fact, it may occur at different levels in organisations: other senior managers and middle managers too may take leadership roles in change.

Figure 14.1 provides a structure for the chapter. Section 14.2 begins by explaining important issues that need to be considered in *diagnosing the context* an organisation faces when embarking on strategic change, in terms of the *types of change* required, the variety of *contextual factors* that need to be taken into account, and the *forces blocking or facilitating change*. Section 14.3 discusses the management of strategic change in terms of the roles played by *leaders of strategic change*. It then goes on to explain how *styles of change leadership* need to align with the context of change. Section 14.4 then reviews *levers for change*, including the need to build a compelling *case for change*, to *challenge the taken for granted*, change organisational *routines*, *systems and symbols*, the role of *political activity*, and more specific *change tactics*. Section 14.5 draws all this together by considering what overall lessons can be drawn about *managing change programmes.*

In doing this the chapter builds on four key premises:

- *Strategy matters*. What has been written in Parts I and II of the book should be seen as an essential precursor in identifying the need for and direction of strategic change. So it is important to be clear about:

  - Why strategic change is needed (discussed in Chapters 2 to 5).

  - The bases of the strategy in terms of strategic purpose, perhaps encapsulated in a statement of vision or mission (section 4.2) and bases of competitive advantage (Chapter 6).

  - What the strategy is in terms of strategy directions and methods (Chapters 7 to 10).

- *Context matters*. The approach taken to managing strategic change needs to be *context-dependent*. There is, therefore, no 'one right way' of managing strategic change. Managers need to consider how to balance different approaches according to the circumstances they face.

- *Inertia* and *resistance* to change are likely. Managers report that the major problem in managing change is the tendency of people to hold on to existing ways of doing things. Much of Chapter 5 and the discussion of the Experience Lens in the Commentary on Chapter 1 explain why this is so.

- *Leadership matters*. This does not mean that leadership of change is always and exclusively from the top of an organisation – though such leadership does matter. Leadership of change needs to happen at different levels in an organisation.

Strategic
change
context

(14.2) DIAGNOSING THE CHANGE CONTEXT

How change is managed will depend on the magnitude of the challenge faced in trying to effect strategic change. It is therefore useful to consider the *type* of change required, the wider *context* in which change is to occur, the specific *blockages* to change that exist and forces that exist to *facilitate* the change process.

Figure 14.2 Types of change

Source: Adapted from J. Balogun and V. Hope Hailey, *Exploring Strategic Change*, 3rd edition, Prentice Hall, 2007.

14.2.1 Types of strategic change

Types of strategic change

As shown in Chapter 5 (section 5.2.1) and 12 (section 12.3), strategy development is often *incremental* in nature. It builds on rather than fundamentally changes prior strategy. More fundamental change is less common. Balogun and Hope Hailey[3] develop this insight further to identify four types of strategic change (see Figure 14.2), and these have implications for how change might be managed.

The axes in Figure 14.2 are concerned with (a) the extent of change and (b) the nature of change. In terms of the *extent* of change, the question is whether change can occur in line with the current business model and within the current culture as a *realignment* of strategy? Or does it require significant culture change; in effect more *transformational* change? The nature of change is concerned with the speed at which it happens. Arguably, it is beneficial for change in an organisation to be *incremental* since this allows time to build on the skills, routines and beliefs of those in the organisation. However, if an organisation faces crisis or needs to change direction fast a '*big bang*' approach to change might be needed on occasion. Combining these two axes suggests four types of strategic change:

1 *Adaptation* is change that can be accommodated within the current culture and occur incrementally. It is the most common form of change in organisations.

2 *Reconstruction* is change that may be rapid and involve a good deal of upheaval in an organisation, but which does not fundamentally change the culture. It could be a *turnaround* situation where there is need for major structural changes or a major cost-cutting programme to deal with a decline in financial performance or difficult or changing market conditions. How this might be managed is discussed further in section 14.5.1 in this chapter.

3 *Revolution* is change that requires rapid and major strategic as well as culture change. This could be in circumstances where the strategy has been so bounded by the existing

culture that, even when environmental or competitive pressures might require fundamental change, the organisation has failed to respond. This might have occurred over many years (see the discussion of strategic drift in section 5.2) and resulted in circumstances where pressures for change are extreme – for example, a takeover threatens the continued existence of a firm. How this might be managed is discussed further in section 14.5.2.

4 *Evolution* is change in strategy that requires culture change, but over time. In some respects this is the most challenging type of strategic change since, for many in an organisation, there may be no pressing need for change. How this might be managed is discussed in section 14.5.3.

Many of the tools of analysis in Part I of the book can help identify the type of change required. For example, does the change require a substantial reconfiguration of the value chain (section 3.4.2), significant changes in the activities underpinning strategic capabilities (section 3.4.3) or major cultural change (section 5.4.6)? Care does, however, need to be taken in considering the significance of new strategies on required change. For example, a business may launch new products without requiring fundamental changes in the assumptions and beliefs of the organisation. On the other hand, some changes in strategy, even if they do not take the form of dramatic product changes, may require fundamental changes in core assumptions in the organisation. For example, the shift from a production focus for a manufacturer to a customer-led, service ethos may not entail product changes, but will very likely require significant culture change.

14.2.2 The importance of context

Leading change in a small entrepreneurial business, where a motivated team is driving change, would be quite different from trying to do so in a major corporation, or perhaps a long-established public-sector organisation, with set routines, formal structures and perhaps a great deal of resistance to change. So it is dangerous to assume that leading change effectively in one context is the same as in another. Moreover, an assumption that approaches to change are readily transferable between contexts may be risky. For example, many government departments in different parts of the world have sought to import change management practices from consultancies or by recruiting managers from commercial enterprises but have often found this problematic.[4] Illustration 14.1 gives an example of the contextual issues faced in trying to manage change in the UK Ministry of Defence (MOD).[5]

Approaches to leading change therefore need to be differ according to context.[6] Balogun and Hope Hailey's 'Change Kaleidoscope' builds on this point to identify contextual features to take into account in designing change programmes. Figure 14.3 summarises these.

Here are some examples of how the contextual features shown in Figure 14.3 might require different approaches to change:

● The *time* available for change could differ dramatically. A business may face immediate decline in turnover or profits from rapid changes in its markets. This is a quite different context for change compared with a business where the management may see the need for change coming in the future, perhaps years away, and have time to plan it carefully as a staged incremental process.

● The *scope* of change might differ either in terms of the *breadth* of change across an organisation or the *depth* of culture change required. The scope of change in an organisation such as

Figure 14.3 The Change Kaleidoscope

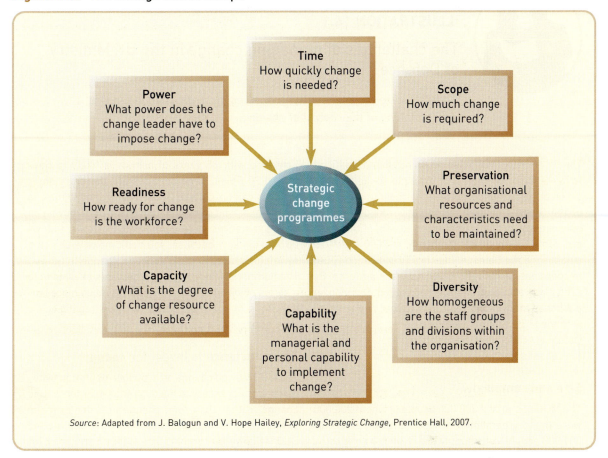

Source: Adapted from J. Balogun and V. Hope Hailey, *Exploring Strategic Change*, Prentice Hall, 2007.

the MOD in Illustration 14.1 is wholly different in terms of both breadth and depth than, for example, adaptive change in a successful small business and would be likely to be a much bigger challenge.

- *Preservation* of some aspects of an organisation may be needed: in particular capabilities on which changes need to be based. Suppose, for example, that a computer software business needs to become more formally organised because of its successful growth. This could well upset technical experts who have been used to a great deal of independence and ready access to senior management when it could be vital to preserve their expertise and motivation.

- A *diversity* of experience, views and opinions within an organisation may help the change process. However, if an organisation has followed a strategy for many decades, such continuity may have led to a very homogeneous way of seeing the world, which could hamper change. So gauging the nature and extent of diversity is important.

- Is there *capability* or experience of managing change in the organisation? There may be managers who have experience of leading change in the past, or a workforce that has been used to and has accepted past changes, whilst people in another organisation may have little experience of change.

- *Capacity* for change in terms of available resources will also be significant: change can be costly, not only in financial terms, but also in terms of management time.

ILLUSTRATION 14.1

The challenges of managing change in the UK Ministry of Defence

Understanding the challenge of managing strategic change requires an understanding of the context of change.

The UK Ministry of Defence (MOD) has found it difficult to make major changes. For example, in 2004, of the seven principles underpinning the recommendations of the Smart Procurement Initiative begun in 1998 only one was properly implemented and, of the other six, some hardly at all. Or, again, in 2000 the MOD established the Defence Logistics Organisation (DLO) to coordinate across the army, navy and air force. By 2005 it was accepted that this had stalled. Drawing on published studies and their own experience working with the MOD, Derrick Neal and Trevor Taylor, of the Defence Academy at Shrivenham, explain some of the reasons that existed in 2005.

Size and complexity

The MOD comprised 300,000 people of whom 200,000 were military personnel. It also relied on a further 300,000 people in its supply chain. Moreover it comprised many parts so: 'Change initiated in one part of the system runs into resistance and difficulty from arrangements elsewhere, or has implications for other parts of the system that were not foreseen by the original change initiators.' It is also difficult to change all the systems simultaneously.

Empowerment

The MOD cannot decide overall defence strategy since that is decided by politicians. However, there is significant autonomy within the MOD. There were 13 top-level budget holders (TLBs), within each of which there was then further delegation of responsibility. The result was some 36 defence agencies and below them 120 'integrated project teams'. When the MOD centre tries to generate change, locally empowered leaders often produce their own version of change programmes. In 2003 it was found that there were 150 uncoordinated change initiatives under way within the DLO.

Personnel systems

The MOD employs both military staff and civilian staff. Military staff expect to move locations frequently.

Someone with 35 years of service is likely to have moved 20 times. Time horizons are therefore short within a 'can do' culture. Those who wished to make a quick impact did so by initiating change but moving on before initiatives were completed. However, follow-up was unlikely because 'you don't make your name by implementing another officer's change initiative'. The number of 'fast-track' civil servants likely to hold a series of jobs in quick succession is much more limited; most are not expected to move regularly. So time horizons are different for them.

The reluctance to invest for change

The MOD viewed change as a 'budget-neutral activity': that it was necessary to make savings in order to fund change, rather than fund change in order to make savings. For example, it was only after the stalled DLO initiative that the MOD recognised the need for investment in that change programme and obtained funding from the Treasury to try and address it.

The lack of urgency

There was no feeling of crisis. Paradoxically, for people who often find themselves at serious risk, they see the institutions that surround them as secure and fixed. The only signal of required change was from the Treasury's financial initiatives, which may be seen as a threat.

Source: Based on D. Neal and T. Taylor, 'Spinning on dimes: the challenges of introducing transformational change into the UK Ministry of Defence', *Strategic Change*, vol. 15 (2006), pp. 15–22.

Questions

1 Use the checklist of the Change Kaleidoscope in section 14.2.2 to identify the range of contextual issues that need to be taken into account in influencing change in the MOD.

2 What approach to change should be adopted to improve the MOD's ability to manage change?

- What is the *readiness* for change? Is there a felt need for change across the organisation, widespread resistance, or pockets or levels of resistance in some parts of the organisation and readiness in others?
- Who has the *power* to effect change? Often it is assumed that the chief executive has such power, but in the face of resistance from below, or perhaps resistance from external stakeholders, this may not be the case. It may also be that the chief executive supposes that others in the organisation have the power to effect change when they do not, or do not see themselves having it.

This consideration of context needs to be borne in mind throughout the rest of this chapter. It also raises an important overarching question: *is one-off change possible?* Does the organisation in question have the capacity, capability, readiness and power structures to achieve the scope of change required? For example, in a study of attempts to manage change in hospitals[7] it was found that their governance and organisational structures prevented any clear authority to manage change. This, combined with the resource constraints under which they laboured, meant that major one-off change initiatives were not likely to succeed. In such circumstances, it may be that the context needs to be changed before the strategic change itself can occur. For example, it could be that new managers with experience of leading change need to be introduced to enhance the capability and readiness for change and get the organisation to a point where it is ready to embark on a more significant strategic change programme. Or it may need to be recognised that change has to be managed in stages. The researchers in the hospital study reported above found that change tended to take place by one initiative making limited progress, then stalling, followed by a later one making further advances.

14.2.3 Forcefield analysis

A **forcefield analysis** provides an initial view of change problems that need to be tackled by identifying forces for and against change. It allows some key questions to be asked:

- What aspects of the current situation would block change, and how can these be overcome?
- What aspects of the current situation might aid change in the desired direction, and how might these be reinforced?
- What needs to be introduced or developed to aid change?

A forcefield analysis can be informed by many of the concepts and frameworks already introduced in the book. As explained above, for example, the Change Kaleidoscope can inform a forcefield analysis. But so too, for example, can the following:

- *Mapping activity systems* (section 3.4.3) can provide insights into aspects of the organisation that have provided the basis for an organisation's historical success. These may be a basis upon which future change might be built; or, again, may have taken form in ways of doing things that have ceased to be advantageous but are very difficult to change.
- *Stakeholder mapping* (section 4.5.2) can provide insight into the power of different stakeholders to promote change or to resist change.
- *The culture web* (see section 5.4.6) is a means of diagnosing organisational culture and therefore an understanding of the symbolic, routinised as well as structural and systemic factors that may be taken for granted and can act for or against change. It can also be used to envisage what the culture of an organisation would need to look like to deliver future strategy.[8]

ILLUSTRATION 14.2

A forcefield analysis for the UK Forestry Commission

A forcefield analysis can be used to identify aspects of the organisation that might aid change, blockages to change and what needs to be developed to aid change.

In the late 1990s the Forestry Commission in the UK was wrestling with significant strategic challenges. The collapse in world timber prices meant that alternative sources of income were needed. Additionally, the government's policy was to develop an emphasis on forestry for leisure and social inclusion, not just the production of timber. However, what emerged from a cultural web analysis was that the organisation's current culture raised problems over moving to such a future.

Foresters saw themselves as *the* forestry experts, which translated into an attitude of 'FC knows best', a tendency to see the forests as 'theirs' and the public as a 'nuisance', getting in the way of efficient timber production. There was also an ingrained public sector ethos – a sense of contributing to society rather than working for commercial gain. The command and control style of management had also led to a deference to senior management and there was the bureaucracy of a public sector organisation. It also took at least 50 years to grow trees: linked to this was a deep sense of tradition making the organisation conservative and slow to change.

Forcefield analysis was then used to consider what changes in culture would be needed if the Forestry Commission were to put more emphasis on 'forests for the community'. As well as identifying many barriers to change that needed to be removed, the forcefield analysis identified aspects of the culture that might facilitate change. These included the powerful support for change of the 'Director General', the commitment of employees to the organisation, the ethos of hard work and the potential flexibility, together with a desire from within the organisation to change the command and control culture. It was also possible to identify what might be added to this: for example, widespread participation in the change programme could help achieve ownership of future vision; and increased diversity of personnel together with a more inclusive management style with more listening and less telling could promote more innovation and commitment.

Source: Adapted from The Forestry Commission case study by Anne McCann.

Pushing	Resisting
• Hard work ethic that delivers results • Commitment of employees • Juggling priorities/potential flexibility • Forestry know-how • Encouragement/support of change from the top	• Traditional structure/ways of working • Bureaucracy • Departmental silos • Homogeneous workforce • Conservative/risk averse/slow to change • Command and control management style • Deference to senior staff • Past experience of change was that nothing really changed
Additional • Encouragement to work in new ways • Increased diversity of staff • Clear articulation of a vision for the future • Participation in the change process • Skills development	

Questions

1 What might be some of the problems in managing changes indicated by the forcefield analysis?

2 Undertake a forcefield analysis for an organisation of your choice.

- *The 7-S framework* (section 13.4.1) can highlight aspects of the infrastructure of an organisation that may act to promote or block change.

As well as helping to identify the current forces acting for and against change, each of these frameworks can also be used to help think through what might be needed as additional forces to promote change. Illustration 14.2 shows how a forcefield analysis was used in the UK's Forestry Commission's strategic change programme.

 ## 14.3 LEADING STRATEGIC CHANGE

This section of the chapter is concerned with the role people play in leading strategic change and how they do it. It begins by explaining how *leadership change roles* may exist in different parts and at different levels in an organisation. It then goes on to consider the different *styles of strategic leadership* that might be adopted and how these need to be aligned with different contexts of change.

14.3.1 Strategic leadership roles

Leadership **is the process of influencing an organisation (or group within an organisation) in its efforts towards achieving an aim or goal.**[9] Without effective leadership of strategic change the risk is that people in an organisation are unclear about its purpose or lack motivation to deliver it. Strategic leadership is therefore central to strategic change. There are three key roles that are especially significant in terms of leading strategic change:

- *Envisioning future strategy.*[10] The effective strategic leader needs to ensure there exists a clear and compelling vision of the future and communicate clearly a strategy to achieve that both internally and to external stakeholders. In the absence of top management doing this, those who attempt to lead change elsewhere in an organisation are likely to construct such a vision themselves. This may be well intentioned but can lead to confusion, highlighting the importance of overall clarity on the purpose of strategic change.

- *Aligning* the organisation to deliver that strategy.[11] This involves ensuring that people in the organisation are committed to the strategy, motivated to make the changes needed and empowered to deliver those changes. There is, then, a need for leaders to build and foster relationships of trust and respect across the organisation.[12] It may, however, also be necessary to change the management of the organisation to ensure such commitment, which is a reason that top teams often change as a precursor to or during strategic change.

- *Embodying change.* A strategic leader will be seen by others, not least those within the organisation, but also other stakeholders and outside observers, as intimately associated with a future strategy and a strategic change programme. A strategic leader is, then, symbolically highly significant in the change process and needs to be a role model for future strategy (see section 14.4.4 below on symbolic levers for change).

Whilst there is often an emphasis on individuals at the top of an organisation, the leadership of change also involves others in and around the organisation.

Middle managers

A top-down approach to managing strategy and strategic change sees middle managers as implementers of top-management strategic plans. Here their role is to ensure that resources are allocated and controlled appropriately and to monitor the performance and behaviour of staff. However, middle managers have multiple roles in relation to the management of strategy.[13] In the context of managing strategic change there are three other roles they play:

- *'Sense making'* of strategy. Top management may set down a strategic direction; but how it is explained and made sense of in specific contexts (e.g. a region of a multinational or a functional department) may, intentionally or not, be left to middle managers. If misinterpretation of that intended strategy is to be avoided, it is therefore vital that middle managers understand and feel an ownership of it. They are therefore a crucial *relevance bridge* between top management and members of the organisation at lower levels, in effect translating a change initiative into a message that is locally relevant. A number of researchers have made the point that, in this role, how they make sense of top-down strategy and how they talk about and explain it to others becomes critically important.[14] In this sense they can play a *local leadership* role.

- *Reinterpretation and adjustment* of strategic responses as events unfold (e.g. in terms of relationships with customers, suppliers, the workforce and so on); this is a vital role for which middle managers are uniquely qualified because they are in day-to-day contact with such aspects of the organisation and its environment.

- *Advisers* to more senior management on what are likely to be blockages and requirements for change.

When it comes to strategic change, middle managers are therefore in a key 'mediating' role between those trying to direct from the top and the operating level. The Key Debate at the end of the chapter takes this into account and considers strategic change in relation to a top-down perspective, but also in relation to some of the roles played by middle managers.

Newcomers and outsiders

Whilst managers in the organisation have important roles to play, 'outsiders' can also play an important role in strategic change. These could include:

- A *new chief executive* from outside the organisation may be introduced into a business to enhance the capability for change or to bring a fresh perspective, not bound by the constraints of the past, or the embedded routines that can prevent strategic change. This is especially so in turnaround situations (see 14.5.1 below).

- *New management* from outside the organisation can also increase the diversity of ideas, help break down cultural barriers to change and increase the experience of and capability for change. However, their successful influence is likely to depend on how much explicit *visible backing* they have from the chief executive. Without such backing they may be seen as lacking authority and influence.

- *Consultants* are often used to help formulate strategy or to plan the change process. They are also increasingly used as facilitators of change processes: for example, in a coordinating capacity, as project planners for change programmes, as facilitators of project teams working on change, or of strategy workshops used to develop strategy and plan means of strategic change. The value of consultants is threefold. First, they do not inherit the cultural baggage of the organisation and can therefore bring a dispassionate view to the process. Second, as a result, they may ask questions and undertake analyses which challenge taken-for-granted ways of seeing or doing things. Third, they signal symbolically the importance of a change process, not least because their fees may be of a very high order.

- *Other stakeholders* may be key influencers of change. For example, government, investors, customers, suppliers and business analysts all have the potential to act as change agents on organisations.

14.3.2 Styles of strategic leadership

There is no one best style of strategic leadership. Moreover there is evidence[15] that **successful strategic leaders are able to adjust their style of leadership to the context they face**. This has become known as '**situational leadership**'. Here this is explained, first by reviewing different generic approaches to managing change, next by considering more specific styles of leading change, then by considering how these may need to differ by context.

Theory E and theory O

On the basis of many years' study of corporate change programmes, Michael Beer and Nitin Nohria observe that, broadly, there are two approaches to managing change which they describe as 'Theory E and Theory O'.[16]

- *Theory E* is change based on the pursuit of economic value and is typically associated with the top-down, programmatic use of the 'hard' levers of change. The emphasis is on changes of structures and systems, financial incentives, often associated with portfolio changes, downsizing and consequent job layoffs.

- *Theory O* is change based on the development of organisational capability. The emphasis here is on culture change, learning and participation in change programmes and experimentation.

However, Beer and Nohria argue that, stark as these alternatives seem to be, a combination of the two approaches may not only be required, but be beneficial. This might involve, for example:

- *Sequencing change* to start with theory E approaches and move on to theory O approaches.

- *Embracing both approaches* simultaneously and being explicit about it to people in the organisation and external stakeholders.

- *Combining direction from the top with participation from below*. By so doing the benefits of both clarity of overall strategic direction and potential upward spontaneity can be achieved.

- *Using incentives to reinforce change* rather than to drive change.

Styles of change leadership

Within these two generic approaches to change there are several styles of change leadership: Table 14.1 summarises these.[17]

- **Education involves persuading others of the need for and means of strategic change**. Four phases of this style of change leadership have been advocated:[18]

  - Convince employees that change is imperative and why the new direction is the right one. Again this emphasises the necessity for clarity of future vision and strategy.

  - Since change is likely to be interpreted differently throughout the organisation,[19] frame the changes in ways relevant to the different groups and functions that have to enact the change and gather feedback on how this is understood and communicated within those groups.

Table 14.1 Styles of leading change

Style	Description	Advantages	Disadvantages
Education	Use small group briefings to discuss things with people and explain things to them. The aim is to gain support for change by generating understanding and commitment. This is likely to be accompanied by delegation of responsibility for change.	Spreads support for change. Also ensures a wide base of understanding.	Takes a long time. If radical change is needed, fact-based argument and logic may not be enough to convince others of need for change. Easy to voice support, then walk away and do nothing.
Collaboration	Widespread involvement of the employees on decisions about both what and how to change.	Spreads not only support but ownership of change by increasing levels of involvement.	Time-consuming. Little control over decisions made.
Participation	Strategic leaders retain overall coordination and authority but delegate elements of the change process.	Again, spreads ownership and support of change, but within a more controlled framework. Easier to shape decisions.	Can be perceived as manipulation.
Direction	Change leaders make the majority of decisions about what to change and how. Use of authority to direct change.	Less time-consuming. Provides a clear change direction and focus.	Potentially less support and commitment, and therefore proposed changes may be resisted.
Coercion	Use of power to impose change.	Allows for prompt action.	Unlikely to achieve buy-in without a crisis.

Source: Adapted from J. Balogun and V. Hope Hailey, *Exploring Strategic Change*, 3rd edn, 2008.

- Ensure ongoing communication of the progress of change.
- Reinforce behavioural guidelines in line with the change and reward the achievement of change goals.

However, there are problems here. The assumption that reasoned argument in a top-down fashion will overcome perhaps years of embedded assumptions about what 'really matters' may be optimistic. There may be apparent acceptance of change without its actually being delivered. Such an approach to change can also take a long time and can also be costly, for example in terms of training and management time.

- **Collaboration** in the change process is the involvement of those affected by strategic change in setting the change agenda; for example, in the identification of strategic issues, the strategic decision-making process, the setting of priorities, the planning of strategic change or the drawing up of action plans. Such involvement can foster a more positive attitude to change; people may see the constraints the organisation faces as less significant[20] and feel increased ownership of, and commitment to, a decision or change process. It may therefore be a way of building readiness and capability for change. However, there are potential problems here too. People may come up with change solutions that are not in line with, or do not achieve the expectations of, top management or key stakeholders. For example, there is the risk that solutions will be found from within the existing culture or that the agenda for change will be negotiated and may therefore be a compromise. In either case there is the risk of perpetuating the status quo or merely an adaptation of it. A strategic change leader who takes this approach may, therefore, need to retain the ability to intervene in the process, but this runs the risk of demotivating employees who have been involved in the change process.

- **Participation** **retains the coordination of and authority over processes of change by a strategic leader who delegates *elements* of the change process.** For example, particular stages of change, such as ideas generation, data collection, detailed planning, the development of rationales for change or the identification of critical success factors, may be delegated to project teams or task forces. Such teams may not take full responsibility for the change process, but become involved in it and see their work building towards it. The responsibility for the change is retained by the strategic leader who ensures the monitoring of progress and that change is seen to occur. An advantage is that it involves members of the organisation, not only in originating ideas, but also in the *partial implementation* of solutions, helping build commitment to the change. It may also be that the retention of the agenda and means of change by the strategic leader reduces the possibility of a negotiated compromise and means that more radical change can be achieved. The potential problem is that employees may see this approach as manipulation and become disenchanted and demotivated.

- **Direction** **involves the use of personal managerial authority to establish a clear strategy and how change will occur**. It is top-down management of strategic change where change 'solutions' and the means of change are 'sold' to others who are tasked with implementing them. The need here is for both clarity of strategic vision and the specifics of a change programme in terms of critical success factors and priorities. The approach may be needed if there is a need for fast change or control over the change agenda (for example to meet the expectations of dominant external stakeholders). The danger is that it can result in explicit resistance to change or people going along with the rhetoric of change whilst passively resisting it. It is also worth noting that even where top management people see themselves adopting participative styles, their subordinates may perceive this as directive and, indeed, may welcome such direction if they see major change as needed.[21]

- **Coercion** is direction in its most extreme form. It **is the imposition of change or the issuing of edicts about change**. This is the explicit use of power and may be necessary if the organisation is facing a crisis, for example.

Illustration 14.3 provides examples of different strategic leadership styles.

Different styles for different contexts

Clearly different styles of change are likely to suit different managers' personality types. However, since strategic leaders with the greatest *capability* to manage change have the ability to adopt different styles in different circumstances, it is useful to consider the appropriateness of different styles to different contexts.

- *Time and scope.* Education or collaboration may be most appropriate for incremental change within organisations, but where transformational change is required, more centralised control or directive approaches may be more appropriate.

- *Capability and readiness for change.* Research on leadership has shown that leadership styles need to differ according to the ability and willingness of employees to change. Translating

ILLUSTRATION 14.3

Leadership styles for managing change

Successful top executives have different leadership styles.

Don't noodle

Terry Lundgren, CEO of Federated Department Stores:

'I have always been a pretty good listener, and I am quick to admit that I do not have all the answers. So I am going to listen. But shortly after I listen, the second piece is to pull the trigger. I have all the input, and here is what we are going to do. People need closure on a decision. If you listen and then noodle on it, people get confused, and that's not effective leadership.'[1]

The promised land

James Strachan, former Chairman of the Audit Commission UK, reporting what a CEO had told him:

'All you have to do is to figure out precisely where you want to go and you need to be able to paint that "promised land" in technicolour. Second you need to ask whether you have got the right people around you, particularly at the top: if not change them tomorrow – literally tomorrow. Third you delegate; but you do so without actually absolving yourself of all responsibility. You still own the ultimate responsibility – the buck stops with you – but you significantly delegate to people to enable them to bring out the best in themselves. Last you praise their success to high heaven.'[2]

He then added:

'The lesson about change for me is that in times of change there is a lot of turbulence, confusion, worry and concern. This is all natural. So people naturally gravitate towards a leadership that tries to take this confusion and describe it in simple terms about why we are doing this, what the "promised land" that we are going to get to is and why all this agony is worthwhile. In terms of change it is simplicity and conviction that rule.'

Coach but don't coddle

Allan G. Laffley, CEO of Procter & Gamble:

'My approach to leadership is to raise aspiration and then achieve great execution . . . communicate priorities clearly, simply and frequently . . . to a large degree our division leaders must define their own future. I play the role of coach; but coaching doesn't mean coddling. I expect our managers to make choices . . . to help managers make these strategic choices leaders must sometimes challenge deeply held assumptions. . . . Being a role model is vital . . . I know that I must be ready for moments of truth that alert the organization to my commitment.'[3]

Be dedicated and collegiate

Sir Terry Leahy of Tesco has overseen one of the biggest retail transformations in the world. Yet he is

'disarmingly ordinary. . . . His speech is serious and straightforward. He's no showman . . . He talks only about Tesco; . . . it's like meeting a religious leader faithfully reciting a creed. . . . His co-workers respect him for his decision-making but he doesn't make his moves on a whim. . . . Everything is analysed, taken apart, discussed and put back together. . . . He's gathered around him senior managers who've been with him and the group for years. He's in charge but he's also collegiate.'[4]

He also likes to talk and listen to people in the stores:

'What makes Leahy different is the extraordinary degree to which he chats with junior staff and absorbs their views and the attention he pays to customers.'

References:
1. Interview by Matthew Boyle, in *Fortune*, 12 December 2005, vol. 152, no. 12, pp. 126–7.
2. *Lessons Learned: Straight Talk from the World's Top Business Leaders: Managing Change*, Harvard Business School Press, 2007.
3. *Leadership Excellence*, November 2006, vol. 23, no. 11, pp. 9–10.
4. Chris Blackhurst, 'Sir Terry Leahy', *Management Today*, February 2004, p. 32. Reproduced from *Management Today* magazine with the permission of the copyright owner, Haymarket Business Publications Limited.

Questions

1 How would you describe each of the styles illustrated here in terms of those explained in section 14.3.2?

2 What might be the benefits and problems of each of the leadership styles? In what circumstances?

3 Only some stakeholders are specifically mentioned in the examples. Does this mean that the style should be the same towards all stakeholders of the organisation? If not, how would they differ?

Figure 14.4 Styles of change leadership according to organisational capability and readiness

High

Capability

| Participation | Collaboration |
| Direction | Education/ coaching |

Low

Low ← → High

Readiness

these findings into aspects of the Change Kaleidoscope it is likely that styles of change leadership will need to differ according to the extent of capability and readiness for strategic change in the organisation (see Figure 14.4). Where there is low readiness and capability for change, then direction may be the most appropriate style. Where there is high readiness but low capability then education, training and coaching may be appropriate. Where capability is high but readiness is low, involving people in the change process whilst retaining overall central control (participation) may make sense. Where both readiness and capability are high, then collaboration may be possible and top management may be able to delegate much of the change agenda.

● *Power.* In organisations with *hierarchical power structures* a directive style may be common and it may be difficult to break away from it, not least because people expect it. On the other hand, in 'flatter' power structures, a more networked or learning organisation described elsewhere in this book, e.g. section 12.3.1), it is likely that collaboration and participation will be common, indeed desirable.

● *Styles of managing change are not mutually exclusive.* For example, clear direction on overall vision might aid a more collaborative approach to more detailed strategy development. Education and communication may be appropriate for some stakeholders, such as financial institutions; participation may be appropriate for groups in parts of the organisation where it is necessary to build *capability and readiness*; whereas if there are parts of the organisation where change has to happen fast, *timing* may demand a more directive style.

 14.4 LEVERS FOR MANAGING STRATEGIC CHANGE

Some levers for change have already been discussed elsewhere in the book. The importance of clarity of a strategic vision was discussed in section 5.2 together with the importance of other goals and objectives. The effects of changes in organisational structure and control systems of organisations were addressed in Chapter 13. This section of the chapter examines other possible change levers. In so doing it is worth noting that many of these correspond to the elements of the cultural web (section 5.4.6). The implication is that the forces that act to embed and protect current ways of doing things might also provide bases for change.

14.4.1 A compelling case for change

Whichever style of management is adopted a convincing case for change has to be presented. McKinsey & Co, the consultants,[22] argue that too often the case for change is made in terms of top management's perception of what is important: for example meeting expectations of shareholders or beating competition. When most managers and employees are asked what motivates them, on the other hand, there are many more factors that motivate: the impact on society, on customers, on the local working team, or on employees' personal well-being. A compelling case for change needs to speak to these different bases of motivation, not just to top-management perceptions of change needs. It may, of course, be difficult for top management to understand and relate to these different needs: so it may make sense to involve employees, themselves, in the creation of stories of change that, in effect, 'translate' corporate imperatives of change into local motivating messages. It is also important that the case for change does not just focus on the understanding of why change is needed, but the action required todeliver it.

14.4.2 Challenging the taken-for-granted

A major challenge in achieving strategic change can be the need to change often long-standing mindsets or taken-for-granted assumptions – the paradigm (see section 5.4.6). There are different views on how this might be achieved.

One view is that sufficient evidence, perhaps in the form of careful strategic analysis, will itself serve to challenge and therefore change the paradigm. However, where long-standing assumptions have persisted, they can be very resistant to change. People find ways of questioning, reconfiguring and reinterpreting such analysis to bring it in line with the existing paradigm. It may take much persistence to overcome this. Others argue that encouraging people to question and challenge each other's assumptions and received wisdom by making them explicit is valuable.[23] Scenario planning (see section 2.2.2) is similarly advocated as a way of overcoming individual biases and cultural assumptions by getting people to see possible different futures and the implications for their organisations.[24]

Others argue that senior managers in particular can be too far removed from the realities of their organisations and need to be brought face-to-face with them. They may rarely speak to customers directly or experience themselves the services offered by their own firms. A senior executive of a rail company explained that in the past senior executives in the organisation had always travelled first class or by chauffeur-driven car. Hardly any of them had ever travelled in a crowded railway carriage. He introduced a policy that all senior executives should travel economy class wherever possible.

14.4.3 Changing operational processes and routines

In the end, strategies are delivered through day-to-day processes and routines of the operations of the organisation. These might be formalised and codified or they might be less formal 'ways we do things around here' which tend to persist over time and guide people's behaviour. As has been seen in the discussion in Chapter 3, it may be that such routines can be the basis of its core competences and therefore its competitive advantage. However, they can also be serious blockages to change. The relationship between strategic change and day-to-day processes and routines is therefore important to consider in at least four respects:

- *Planning operational change*. The planning of the implementation of an intended strategy requires the identification of the key changes in the routines required to deliver that strategy. In effect, strategic change needs to be considered in terms of the re-engineering of organisational processes.[25] For example, in Shell Lubricants until 2002 seven people were involved in different aspects of order processing routines. In the search for improved efficiency and customer service, one person was given overall responsibility for an order, with the consequent reduction in order time of 75 per cent, reduction in order processing costs of 45 per cent and vastly improved customer satisfaction.[26]

- *Challenging operational assumptions*. Changing organisational processes and routines may also have the effect of challenging the often taken-for-granted assumptions under-pinning them. In turn this may have the effect of getting people to question and challenge deep-rooted beliefs and assumptions in the organisation. Richard Pascale argues: 'It is easier to act your way into a better way of thinking than to think your way into a better way of acting';[27] in other words, it is easier to change behaviour and by so doing change taken-for-granted assumptions than to try to change taken-for-granted assumptions as a way of changing behaviour. If this is so, the style of change employed (see section 14.3.2 above) needs to take this into account: it suggests that education and communication to persuade people to change may be less powerful than involving people in the activities of changing.

- *Operation-led change*. Operational change may not simply be the outcome of planned strategic change; it could be that opportunities for operational change can stimulate innovation and new strategic thinking. Michael Hammer[28] argues that managers do not consider changes at the operational level sufficiently radically. Typically they benchmark best practice against industry standards rather than looking for best practice wherever it can be found (see section 3.4.1). He gives the example of Taco Bell in the US, which saved costs and improved the quality of its offering by re-examining its operational processes in terms of best practice in manufacturing instead of fast-food operations.

- *Bottom-up changes to routines*. Even when changes in routines are not planned from the top, people do change them and this may result in wider strategic change. Research[29] shows that this can occur proactively through managers deliberately '*bending* the rules of the game'. This could give rise to resistance, but persistent bending may eventually achieve enough support from different stakeholders such that new routines become acceptable. When sufficient questioning of the status quo is achieved, those seeking change may actively *subvert* existing ways of doing things so as to make clear a funda-mental change from the past. This could, for example, be an approach adopted by middle managers in seeking to carry with them both people who work for them and more senior managers, both of whom may be resistant to change. It is an incremental, experimental process that is, however, likely to suffer setbacks and require persistence and political acumen.

The overall lesson is that changes in routines may appear to be mundane, but they can have significant impact. Illustration 14.4 gives some examples of changes in routines linked to strategic change.

ILLUSTRATION 14.4

Changes in routines and symbols

Changes in organisational routines and symbols can be a powerful signal of and stimulus for change.

Changes in routines

- A drug can only be promoted on launch on the basis of claims substantiated by clinical data, so how pharmaceutical firms conduct clinical trials is strategically important. The traditional approach has been to base extensive data collection on a scientific research protocol and then to write a report explaining why all this data had been collected: a highly time-consuming and costly process. Some firms changed their procedures to ensure that scientific tests addressed regulatory and medical need. They created ideal claims statements and drafted the report they would need. Only then did they create research protocols and data collection forms, specifying the data required from the trials to support the claims.

- In a retail business with an espoused strategy of customer care, the chief executive, on visiting stores, tended to ignore staff and customers alike: he seemed to be interested only in the financial information in the store manager's office. He was unaware of this until it was pointed out; his change in behaviour afterwards, insisting on talking to staff and customers on his visits, became a 'story' which spread around the company, substantially supporting the strategic direction of the firms.

Language that challenges and questions

- A chief executive facing a crisis addressed his board: 'I suggest we think of ourselves like bulls facing a choice: the abattoir or the bull ring. I've made up my mind: what about you?'

- When the new management team (Gordon Bethune as Chief Executive and Greg Brenneman as Chief Operating Officer) took over ailing Continental Airlines they chose their language carefully. The future winning orientation was made clear consistently. The overall strategy was referred to as the 'Go forward plan', the marketing plan was 'Fly to win' and the financial plan 'Fund the future'. It was language reinforced in how Brenneman explained the determination to succeed: 'Did you know there are no rear view mirrors on an airplane? The runway behind is irrelevant.'[1]

Symbols of change

- In a textile firm the workforce was instructed to take machinery associated with 'old ways of doing things' into the yard at the rear of the factory and smash it up.

- The head nurse of a recovery unit for patients who had been severely ill decided that, if nurses wore everyday clothes rather than nurses' uniforms, it would signal to patients that they were on the road to recovery and a normal life; and to nurses that they were concerned with rehabilitation. However, the decision had other implications for the nurses too. It blurred the status distinction between nurses and other non-professional members of staff. Nurses preferred to wear their uniforms. Whilst they recognised that uniforms signalled a medically fragile role of patients, they reinforced their separate and professional status as acute care workers.[2]

References:
1. J.M. Higgins and C. McCallaster, 'If you want strategic change don't forget your cultural artefacts', *Journal of Change Management*, vol. 4, no. 1 (2004), pp. 63–73.
2. M.G. Pratt and E. Rafaeli, 'Organisational dress as a symbol of multi-layered social idealities', *Academy of Management Journal*, vol. 40, no. 4 (1997), pp. 862–98.

Questions

For an organisation with which you are familiar:

1 Identify at least five important routines, symbols or rituals in the organisation.

2 In what way could they be changed to support a different strategy? Be explicit as to how the symbols might relate to the new strategy.

3 Why are these potential levers for change often ignored by change agents?

14.4.4 Symbolic changes[30]

Change levers are not always of an overt, formal nature: they may also be symbolic in nature. **Symbols are objects, events, acts or people which express more than their intrinsic content.** They may be everyday things which are nevertheless especially meaningful in the context of a particular situation or organisation. (In this sense the organisational processes and routines discussed above are also symbolic in nature.) Changing symbols can help reshape beliefs and expectations because meaning becomes apparent in the day-to-day experiences people have of organisations, such as the symbols that surround them (e.g. office layout and décor), the type of language and technology used and organisational rituals. Consider some examples.

- Many *rituals*[31] of organisations are concerned with effecting or consolidating change. Table 14.2 identifies and gives examples of such rituals and suggests what role they might play in change processes.[32] New rituals can be introduced or old rituals done away with as ways of signalling or reinforcing change.

- Changes in *physical aspects* of the work environment are powerful symbols of change. Typical here is a change of location for the head office, relocation of personnel, changes in dress or uniforms, and alterations to offices or office space.

- The *behaviour of managers*, particularly strategic leaders, is perhaps the most powerful symbol in relation to change. So, having made pronouncements about the need for change, it is vital that the visible behaviour of change agents be in line with such change.

- The *language* used by change agents is also important.[33] Either consciously or unconsciously, language and metaphor may be employed to galvanise change. Of course, there is also the danger that strategic leaders do not realise this and, whilst espousing change, use language that signals adherence to the status quo, or personal reluctance to change.

Illustration 14.4 also gives some examples of such symbolic signalling of change. However, there is an important qualification to the idea that the manipulation of symbols can be a useful lever for managing change. The significance and meaning of symbols are dependent on how they are interpreted. Since their use may not be interpreted as intended (see the nursing

Table 14.2 Organisational rituals and change

Types of ritual	Role	Examples in managing change
Rites of passage	Signify a change of status or role	Induction to new roles Training programmes
Rites of enhancement	Recognise effort benefiting organisation Similarly motivate others	Awards ceremonies Promotions
Rites of renewal	Reassure that something is being done Focus attention on issues	Appointment of consultant Project teams and workshops
Rites of integration	Encourage shared commitment Reassert rightness of norms	Celebrations of achievement or new ways of doing things
Rites of conflict reduction	Reduce conflict and aggression	Negotiating committees
Rites of challenge	'Throwing down the gauntlet'	New CEO setting challenging goals

example in Illustration 14.4), whilst they may be a powerful lever for change, their impact is difficult to predict.

14.4.5 Power and political systems[34]

Section 4.5 explained the importance of understanding the political context in and around the organisation. There is also a need to consider strategic change within this political context. This can be important because it may be necessary to build a political context for change. To effect change powerful support may be required from individuals or groups or a reconfiguration of *power structures* may be necessary, especially if transformational change is required. Table 14.3 shows some of the mechanisms associated with managing change from a political perspective.

- *Acquiring resources* or being identified with important resource areas or areas of expertise. In particular the ability to withdraw or allocate such resources can be a valuable tool in overcoming resistance or persuading others to accept change or build readiness for change.
- *Association with powerful stakeholder groups* (elites), or their supporters, can help build a power base or help overcome resistance to change. Or a manager facing resistance to change may seek out and win over someone highly respected from within the very group resistant to change. It may also be necessary to *remove individuals or groups* resistant to change. Who these are can vary – from powerful individuals in senior positions to whole layers of resistance, perhaps executives in a threatened function or service.

Table 14.3 Political mechanisms in organisations

Activity areas	Mechanisms			Problems
	Resources	**Elites**	**Building alliances**	
Building the power base	Control of resources Acquisition of/identification with expertise Acquisition of additional resources	Sponsorship by an elite Association with an elite	Identification of change supporters Alliance building Team building	Time required for building Perceived duality of ideals Perceived as threat by existing elites
Overcoming resistance	Withdrawal of resources Use of 'counter-intelligence'	Breakdown or division of elites Association with change agent Association with respected outsider	Foster momentum for change Sponsorship/reward of change agents	Striking from too low a power base Potentially destructive: need for rapid rebuilding
Achieving compliance	Giving resources	Removal of resistant elites Need for visible 'change hero'	Partial implementation and collaboration Implantation of 'disciples' Support for 'young Turks'	Converting the body of the organisation Slipping back

- *Building alliances* and *networks* of contacts and sympathisers may be important in overcoming the resistance of more powerful groups. Attempting to convert the whole organisation to an acceptance of change is difficult. There may, however, be parts of the organisation, or individuals, more sympathetic to change than others with whom support for change can be built. Marginalisation of those resistant to change may also be possible. However, the danger is that powerful groups in the organisation may regard the building of support coalitions, or acts of marginalisation, as a threat to their own power, leading to further resistance to change. An analysis of power and interest using the stakeholder mapping (section 4.5.1) can, therefore, be useful to identify bases of alliance and likely resistance.

However, the political aspects of change management are also potentially hazardous. Table 14.3 also summarises some of the problems. In overcoming resistance, the major problem may simply be the lack of power to undertake such activity. Trying to break down the status quo may become so destructive and take so long that the organisation cannot recover from it. If the process needs to take place, its replacement by some new set of beliefs and the implementation of a new strategy is vital and needs to be speedy. Further, as already identified, in implementing change, gaining the commitment of a few senior executives at the top of an organisation is one thing; it is quite another to convert the body of the organisation to an acceptance of significant change.

14.4.6 Change tactics

There are also more specific tactics of change which might be employed to facilitate the change process.

Timing

The importance of timing is often neglected in thinking about strategic change. But choosing the right time tactically to promote change is vital. For example:

- *Building on actual or perceived crisis* is especially useful the greater the degree of change needed. If there is a higher perceived risk in maintaining the status quo than in changing it, people are more likely to change. Indeed, it is said that some chief executives seek to elevate problems to achieve perceived crisis in order to galvanise change. For example, a threatened takeover may be used as a catalyst for strategic change.

- *Windows of opportunity* in change processes may exist. The arrival of a new chief executive, the introduction of a new, highly successful product, or the arrival of a major competitive threat on the scene may provide opportunities to make more significant changes than might normally be possible. Since change will be regarded nervously, it may also be important to choose the time for promoting such change to avoid unnecessary fear and nervousness. For example, if there is a need for the removal of executives, this may be best done before rather than during the change programme. In such a way, the change programme can be seen as a potential improvement for the future rather than as the cause of such losses.

- *The symbolic signalling of time frames* may be important. In particular, conflicting messages about the timing of change should be avoided. For example, if rapid change is required, the maintenance of procedures or focus on issues that that signal long time horizons may be counter-productive.

Visible short-term wins

A strategic change programme will require many detailed actions and tasks. It is important that some are seen to be successful quickly. Identifying some 'low-hanging fruit' – changes that may not be big but can be made easily and yield a quick payoff – can be useful. This could take the form, for example, of a retail chain introducing a new product range and demonstrating its success in the market or the breaking down of a long-established routine and the demonstration of a better way of doing things. In themselves, these may not be especially significant aspects of a new strategy, but they may be visible indicators of a new approach associated with that strategy. The demonstration of such wins can therefore galvanise commitment to the wider strategy.

One reason given for the inability to change is that resources are not available to do so. This may be overcome if it is possible to identify '*hot spots*' on which to focus resources and effort. For example, William Bratton, famously responsible for the Zero Tolerance policy of the New York Police Department, began by focusing resource and effort on narcotics-related crimes. Though associated with 50–70 per cent of all crimes he found they only had 5 per cent of the resources allocated by NYPD to tackle them. Success in this field led to the roll-out of his policies into other areas and to gaining the resources to do so.[35]

 ## 14.5 MANAGING STRATEGIC CHANGE PROGRAMMES

There are, then, a variety of change levers that change agents may use. Indeed, most successful change initiatives rely on multiple levers for change.[36] So choosing the appropriate levers, rather than following a set formula for managing strategic change, is important. This will depend on the change context and the skills and styles of those managing change. For example, to take the extremes, if the need is to overcome resistance to achieve fast results, then the emphasis may have to be on changing elements of the strategy itself from the top and achieving behavioural compliance to a change programme. On the other hand, if there is a need and the time to 'win hearts and minds' then there will need to be a focus on changing people's values and a much greater emphasis on their involvement in changing the culture. Illustration 14.5 shows these differences.

This section first revisits three types of change identified in section 14.2.1 to consider which levers managers use in which contexts. It concludes by summarising evidence as to why change programmes fail and the lessons that can be learned from that.

14.5.1 Turnaround strategy

There are circumstances where the emphasis has to be on rapid reconstruction, in the absence of which a business could face closure, enter terminal decline or be taken over. This is commonly referred to as a **turnaround strategy**, **where the emphasis is on speed of change and rapid cost reduction and/or revenue generation** and managers need to prioritise the things that give quick and significant improvements. Typically it is a situation where a directive approach to change (see section 14.3.2) is required. Some of the main elements of turnaround strategies are as follows:[37]

- *Crisis stabilisation*. The aim is to regain control over the deteriorating position. This requires a short-term focus on cost reduction and/or revenue increase, typically involving some of

ILLUSTRATION 14.5

Change programmes at IBM and Pace

Change programmes need to be tailored to context.

Values-based change at IBM

Sam Palmisano took over as CEO of IBM in 2002. His predecessor Lou Gerstner had made major changes but, as Palmisano explained: 'Then there was "a burning platform"'. In 2002 there was a need for a continuation of change but 'instead of galvanizing people through fear of failure, you have to galvanize them through hope and aspiration'. Palmisano believed it was impossible to do this in a company as complex as IBM by relying on structures and control systems. It had to be through values.

In July 2003 over a three-day period over 50,000 employees took part in an intranet discussion on company values: the 'ValuesJam'. Much of what was posted was highly critical. IBM talked a lot about trust but spent endless time auditing people; no one questioned the views of senior executives; mistakes were not tolerated or seen as part of learning. It was uncomfortable and some senior executives wanted to pull the plug on the exercise. But Palmisano insisted it continue and joined in, posting his personal views and acknowledging problems.

In many respects the values that emerged extended what IBM already espoused: 'dedication to every client's success', 'innovation that matters – for our company and the world', 'trust and personal responsibility in all relationships'. However they were not being enacted. So the next step was to identify where the values were not being delivered. This was also rolled out to an online jam again (see Illustration 15.2), identifying examples of processes and routines contrary to the values.

Palmisano then instigated changes in control systems to bring them in line with the values. This included changes to the incentive scheme for managing directors of IBM businesses, through to providing funds to line managers to use at their discretion to generate business or develop client relationships. Price setting was also made more client-friendly, especially for products and services crossing IBM businesses, involving significant reworking of the IBM pricing routines.[1]

Turnaround at Pace

Pace manufactures products for the digital TV markets: in particular set-top boxes for customers such as BSkyB and Canal+. When Neil Gaydon took over as Chief Executive in 2006 the company was facing bankruptcy with a loss of £15m (~€16.5m; ~$22.5m) on sales of £175m and a bank facility that had just been withdrawn. By 2010 the company was reporting profits of £69.9m on revenues of over £1 billion.

Gaydon broadened the customer base. At the turn of the century 90% of revenue came from just two customers. By 2010 Pace had more than 100 customers worldwide. In addition he focused on key areas of market development; in particular on high definition television and on pay-TV operations which have a higher price level and offer better margins.

However he also introduced a major reorganisation of the company. He significantly pruned management and organised the company into small teams focused on particular customers. Each team was given a lot of freedom, controlled its own profit and loss account and bonuses were linked to the teams' performance, incentivising everyone to get results. Pace, notorious for late deliveries and over-runs on R&D costs, significantly improved its reliability and cost control.

Reference:
1. Based on Paul Hemp, 'Leading change when business is good', *Harvard Business Review*, vol. 82, no. 12 (2004), pp. 60–70.

Questions

1 Compare the different approaches of Palmisano and Gaydon. Why were they different?

2 How do they compare to that of John Howie and Craig Lockhart at Faslane (see the case example).

3 Which levers for change described in the chapter are evident in each case? Which others might have been used and why?

Table 14.4 Turnaround: revenue generation and cost reduction steps

Increasing revenue	Reducing costs
• Ensuring marketing mix tailored to key market segments • Review pricing strategy to maximise revenue • Focus organisational activities on needs of target market sector customers • Exploit additional opportunities for revenue creation related to target market • Invest funds from reduction of costs in new growth areas	• Reduce labour costs and reduce costs of senior management • Focus on productivity improvement • Reduce marketing costs not focused on target market • Tighten financial controls • Tight control on cash expenses • Establish competitive bidding for suppliers; defer creditor payments; speed up debtor payments • Reduce inventory • Eliminate non-profitable products/services

the steps identified in Table 14.4. There is nothing novel about these steps: many of them are good management practice. The differences are the speed at which they are carried out and the focus of managerial attention on them. The most successful turnaround strategies also focus on reducing direct operational costs and on productivity gains. Less effective approaches pay less attention to these and more on the reduction of overheads.[38]

However, too often turnarounds are seen as no more than cost-cutting exercises when a wider alignment between causes of decline and solutions may be important. For example, where the business decline is principally a result of changes in the external environment it may be folly to expect that cost-cutting alone can lead to renewed growth. Other elements of turnaround strategies are therefore important.

- *Management changes.* Changes in management may be required, especially at the top. This usually includes the introduction of a new chairman or chief executive, as well as changes to the board, especially in marketing, sales and finance, for three main reasons. First, because the old management may well be the ones that were in charge when the problems developed and be seen as the cause of them by key stakeholders. Second, because it may be necessary to bring in management with experience of turnaround management. Third, because, if new management come from outside the organisation, they may bring different approaches to the way the organisation has operated in the past.

- *Gaining stakeholder support.* Poor quality of information may have been provided to key stakeholders. In a turnaround situation it is vital that key stakeholders, perhaps the bank or key shareholder groups, and employees are kept clearly informed of the situation and improvements as they are being made.[39] It is also likely that a clear assessment of the power of different stakeholder groups (see section 4.5.1) will become vitally important in managing turnaround.

- *Clarifying the target market(s) and core products.* Central to turnaround success is ensuring clarity on the target market or market segments most likely to generate cash and grow profits. A successful turnaround strategy involves getting closer to customers and improving the flow of marketing information, especially to senior levels of management, so as to focus revenue-generating activities on key market segments. Of course, a reason for the poor performance of the organisation could be that it had this wrong in the first place. Clarifying the target market also provides the opportunity to discontinue or outsource products and services that are not targeted on those markets, eating up management time for little return or not making sufficient financial contribution.

- *Financial restructuring.* The financial structure of the organisation may need to be changed. This typically involves changing the existing capital structure, raising additional finance or renegotiating agreements with creditors, especially banks.

All of this requires the ability of management to prioritise those things that give quick and significant improvements.

14.5.2 Managing revolutionary strategic change

Revolutionary change differs from turnaround (or reconstruction) in two ways that make managing change especially challenging. First, the need is not only for fast change but also cultural change. Second, it may be that the need for change is not as evident to people in the organisation as in a turnaround situation; or that they see reasons to deny the need for change. This situation may have come about as a result of many years of relative decline in a market, with people wedded to products or processes no longer valued by customers – the problem of strategic drift. Or it could be that the problems of the organisation are visible and understood by its members, but that people cannot see a way forward. Managing change in such circumstances is likely to involve:

- *Clear strategic direction.* In these circumstances the need for the articulation of a clear strategic direction and decisive action in line with that direction is critical. So this is the type of change where individual CEOs who are seen to provide such direction are often credited with making a major difference. They may well also become the symbol of such change within an organisation and externally.

- *Combining rational and symbolic levers.* Very likely some of the hard decisions outlined above for turnaround will be taken: for example, portfolio changes, greater market focus, top management changes and perhaps financial restructuring. However, often these are also employed to send major symbolic messages of change. Most common here is the replacement of very senior executives or, perhaps, major changes in board structure signalling both internally and externally the significance of change at the very top. Similarly, the introduction of new managers, often at a senior level, may make sense in gaining the benefits of a fresh perspective, but also signals the significance of change. Consultants may also be used to provide a dispassionate analysis of the need for change but also to signal how meaningful the change process is.

- *Multiple styles of change management.* Whilst a *directive style* of change management is likely to be evident, this may need to be accompanied by other styles. It may be supported by determined efforts to *educate* about the need for change and the use of *participation* to involve people in aspects of change in which they have specific expertise or to overcome their resistance to change.

- *Working with the existing culture.* It may be possible to work with elements of the existing culture rather than attempt wholesale culture change.[40] This involves identifying those aspects of culture that can be built upon and developed and those that have to be changed – in effect a forcefield approach (see section 14.2.3). For example, as Illustration 5.2 showed, when Mary-Adair Macaire became CEO at the struggling Scottish knitwear firm, Pringle, in 2009 she built a change programme that emphasised its past reputation and identity for quality and stylish knitwear and the pride employees took in that.

- *Monitoring change.* Revolutionary change is likely to require the setting and monitoring of unambiguous targets that people have to achieve. Often these will be linked to overall financial targets and in turn to improved returns to shareholders.

14.5.3 Managing evolutionary strategic change

Managing change as evolution involves transformational change, but incrementally. It can be thought of in two ways. The first is in terms of the creation of an organisation capable of continual change, akin to a learning organisation (section 12.3.1) or one that has achieved organisational ambidexterity (section 12.4.1). Insights into how this might be achieved are also explained in the Variety Lens in the Commentaries. Trying to achieve this in practice is a significant challenge for management, not least because it requires:

- *Empowering the organisation.* Rather than top-down management, there is the need here for people throughout the organisation to accept the responsibility for contributing strategic ideas, for innovating, and for accepting change as inevitable and desirable. Clearly, then, there is a need for a high level of involvement in the change agenda.

- *A clear strategic vision.* It is the responsibility of top management to create the context within which new ideas can bubble up from below around a coherent view of long-term goals. This requires them to provide very clear guidelines – vision, mission or 'simple rules' – around which those ideas can cohere. In so doing, they need to find the balance between the clarity of such vision that allows people to see how they can contribute to future strategy whilst avoiding specifying that strategy in such detail as to constrain people's enthusiasm to contribute and innovate.

- *Continual change and a commitment to experimentation* with regard to organisational processes throughout the organisation.

A second way of conceiving of strategic change as evolution is in terms of the movement from one strategy to a changed strategy but over perhaps many years. Here the principles that might guide managers are these:

- *Stages of transition.* Identifying interim stages in the change process is important. For example, in terms of the change context (see section 14.2.2) there may be insufficient readiness or an insufficient capacity to make major changes initially. It will therefore be important to establish these conditions before other major moves are taken.

- *Irreversible changes.* It may be possible to identify changes that can be made that, whilst not necessarily having immediate major impact, will have long-term and irreversible impacts. For example, a law firm or accountancy firm that wishes to manage an evolutionary approach to strategic change might legitimately see this as dependent on the skills and focus of its partners. Changing the criteria for appointment of partners to achieve this might be one way of doing this. The time horizons for the effects of such changes to take effect would be many years but, once made, the effects would be difficult to reverse.

- *Sustained top management commitment* will be required. The danger is that the momentum for change falters because people do not perceive consistent commitment to it from the top.

- *Winning hearts and minds.* Culture change is likely to be required in any transformational change. This may be more problematic than for revolutionary change because people may simply not recognise that there are problems with regard to the status quo. The need is for multiple levers for change to be used consistently: education and participation as styles of managing change to allow people to see the need for change and contribute to what that change should be; the signalling of the meaning of change in ways that people throughout the organisation understand both rationally and emotionally; and levers that signal and achieve improved economic performance.

14.5.4 Why change programmes fail

Research into why change programmes fail can also provide lessons on the pitfalls to avoid. This section summarises seven of the main failings.[41]

- *Death by planning.* The emphasis is put on planning the change programme rather than delivering it. There is a continuous stream of proposals and reports, each one requiring agreement amongst managers affected by the changes. Sub-committees, project teams and working groups may be set up to examine problems and achieve buy-in. The result can be 'analysis paralysis' and a discourse about change rather than the delivery of change. This may also be linked to the politicisation of the change programme where meetings about change become forums for debate and political game-playing.

- *Loss of focus.* Change is often not a one-off process; it might require an ongoing series of initiatives, maybe over years. However, the risk is that these initiatives are seen by employees as 'change rituals' signifying very little. There is also the risk that the original intention of the change programme becomes eroded by other events taking place; for example, a redundancy programme.

- *Reinterpretation.* The attempted change becomes reinterpreted according to the old culture. For example, an engineering company's intended strategy of adding value in ways that customers valued was interpreted by the engineers within the firm as providing high levels of technical specification which they, not customers, determined.

- *Disconnectedness.* People affected by change may not see the change programme connecting to their reality. Senior executives, as proponents of the change, might not be seen to be credible in terms of understanding the realities of change on the ground. Or perhaps new systems and initiatives introduced are seen as out of line with the intentions of the intended change.

- *Behavioural compliance.* There is the danger that people appear to comply with the changes being pursued in the change programme without actually 'buying into' them. Change agents may think they see change occurring, when all they see is superficial compliance.

- *Misreading scrutiny and resistance.* Those promoting change in the organisation are likely to face either resistance to the change programme or critical scrutiny of it. Often the response to this is to see such behaviour as negative and destructive. It can, on the other hand, be seen as ways in which 'change recipients' in the organisation are engaging with the changes likely to affect them. They are likely to question change and evaluate it in terms of its significance for them. Even if resistance occurs, this is a way of keeping the agenda for

KEY DEBATE

The management of change from top to bottom

Strategic change has always been seen as the responsibility of top management: but to what extent can top managers manage change?

John Kotter, one of the world's foremost authorities on leadership and change, argues that problems of strategic change arise because top executives fail to take the necessary steps to manage such changes. These include:

- Establishing a sense of urgency on the basis of market threats or opprortunities.
- Forming a powerful coalition of stakeholders for change.
- Creating and communicating a clear vision and strategy to direct the change and ensuring that the behaviour of the guiding coalition is in line with the vision.
- Removing obstacles to change, changing systems that undermine the vision and encouraging non-traditional ideas and activities.
- Creating short-term wins.
- Consolidating improvements but also continuing the process of change.

However, Julia Balogun studied a top management change initiative from the point of view of how middle managers interpreted it. She found that, whilst top managers believed they were being clear about the intended strategy, change actually took place by middle managers making sense of change initiatives in terms of their own *mental models* in relation to their *local responsibilities and conditions*, through discussion with their peers and on the basis of rumour. Top managers were inevitably too far removed from these dynamics and could not be expected to understand them in detail or manage them in specific ways. She argues that 'Senior managers can initiate and influence direction of change but not direct change'. They can:

- Monitor how people respond to change initiatives.
- Engage as much as possible with how people make sense of change and work with their reality, responding to their issues and interpretations.
- Live the changes they want others to adopt, especially avoiding inconsistencies between their actions, words and deeds.
- Focus on creating the understanding of higher-level principles rather than the details.

Hari Tsoukas and Robert Chia go further. They argue that change is an inherent property of organisations. Hierarchy and management control dampen that inherent change.

'Change programmes trigger ongoing change: they provide the discursive resources for making certain things possible, although what exactly will happen remains uncertain when a change programme is initiated. It must first be experienced before the possibilities it opens up are appreciated and taken up (if they are taken up). Change programmes are . . . locally adapted, improvised and elaborated. . . . If this is accepted what is, then, the meaning of "planned change"? . . . Change has been taken to mean that which occurs as a consequence of deliberate managerial action. In the view put forward here such a definition is limited. Although managers certainly aim at achieving established ways of thinking and acting through implementing particular plans, nonetheless, change in organizations occurs without necessarily intentional managerial action as a result of individuals trying to accommodate new experience and realize new possibilities. In the view suggested here, an excessive preoccupation with planned change risks failing to recognize the always already changing texture of organizations' (pp. 578–579).

References:
J. Kotter, 'Leading change: why transformation efforts fail', *Harvard Business Review*, March–April (1995), pp. 59–67.
J. Balogun and G. Johnson, 'Organizational restructuring and middle manager sensemaking', *Academy of Management Journal*, vol. 47, no. 4 (2004), pp. 523–49.
J. Balogun, 'Managing change: steering a course between intended strategies and unanticipated outcomes', *Long Range Planning*, vol. 39 (2006), pp. 29–49.
H. Tsoukas and R. Chia, 'On organizational becoming: rethinking organizational change', *Organization Science*, vol. 13, no. 5 (2002), pp. 567–82.

Questions

1 What are the problems associated with top-down or bottom-up views of change management?

2 If you were a senior executive which approach would you take and in what circumstances?

3 Are the different views irreconcilable? (You will find the perspectives on the management of strategy in the commentaries useful background reading.)

change on the table. Moreover, resistance that is explicit is more capable of being addressed than that which is passive or covert. So those managing the change programme need to see scrutiny and resistance as a basis for engaging others in the change programme.

● *Broken agreements and violation of trust.* The need for a clear message about the need for and direction of change has been emphasised in this chapter. However, if senior management fail to provide honest assessments of the situation or provide undertakings to employees on which they subsequently renege, then they will lose the trust and respect of employees and, very likely, ensure heightened resistance to change.

Many of the problems and challenges of managing strategic change are reflected in the Key Debate for this chapter.

SUMMARY

www.pearsoned.co.uk/mystrategylab

A recurrent theme in this chapter has been that approaches, styles and means of change need to be tailored to the context of that change. Bearing in mind this general point, this chapter has emphasised the following:

● There are different *types of strategic change* which can be thought of in terms of the *extent* of culture change required and its *nature* – whether it can be achieved through incremental change or requires urgent action (the 'big bang' approach). Different approaches and means of managing change are likely to be required for these different types of change.

● It is also important to diagnose wider aspects of organisational context summarised in the Change Kaleidoscope. These include the *resources and skills that need to be preserved*, the degree of *homogeneity or diversity* in the organisation, the *capability, capacity and readiness* for change and the *power* to make change happen.

● *Forcefield analysis* is a useful means of identifying blockages to change and potential levers for change.

● *Situational leadership* suggests that strategic leaders need to adopt different *styles* of managing strategic change according to different contexts and in relation to the involvement and interest of different groups.

● *Levers for managing strategic change* need to be considered in terms of the type of change and context of change. Such levers include building a *compelling case for change, challenging the taken-for-granted*, the need to change *operational processes, routines* and *symbols*, the importance of *political processes*, and other change *tactics*.

WORK ASSIGNMENTS

✱ *Denotes more advanced work assignments. * Refers to a case study in the Text and Cases edition.*

14.1 Drawing on section 14.2.2 assess the key contextual dimensions of an organisation (such as for the case example on Faslane) and consider how they should influence the design of a programme of strategic change.

14.2 Use a forcefield analysis to identify blockages and facilitators of change for an organisation (such as one for which you have considered the need for a change in strategic direction in a previous assignment). Identify what aspects of the changes suggested by this analysis can be managed as part of a change programme and how.

14.3 Compare and contrast the different styles of managing change of leaders you have read about in the press or in this book (for example, John Howie and Craig Lockhart at Faslane, Fergus Chambers at Cordia* or Stuart Rose at Marks & Spencer*).

14.4✱ In the context of managing strategic change in a large corporation or public-sector organisation, to what extent, and why, do you agree with Richard Pascale's argument that it is easier to act ourselves into a better way of thinking than it is to think ourselves into a better way of acting? (References 30 to 36 will be useful here.)

14.5✱ There are a number of books by renowned senior executives who have led major changes in their organisation. Read one of these and note the levers and mechanisms for change they employed, using the approaches outlined in this chapter as a checklist. How effective do you think these were in the context that the change leader faced, and could other mechanisms have been used?

Integrative assignment

14.6✱ What would be the key issues for the corporate parent of a diversified organisation with a multidomestic international strategy (see Chapter 8) wishing to change to a more related portfolio? Consider this in terms of (a) the strategic capabilities that the parent might require (Chapters 3 and 7), (b) the implications for organising and controlling its subsidiaries (Chapter 13), (c) the likely blockages to such change and (d) how these might be overcome (Chapter 14).

RECOMMENDED KEY READINGS

- J. Balogun and V. Hope Hailey, *Exploring Strategic Change*, Prentice Hall, 3rd edition, 2008, builds on and extends many of the ideas in this chapter. In particular, it emphasises the importance of tailoring change programmes to organisational context and discusses more fully many of the change levers reviewed in this chapter.

- The paper by John Kotter, 'Leading change: why transformation efforts fail', *Harvard Business Review*, March–April 1995, pp. 59–67 (also see the Key Debate) provides a useful view of what a change programme might look like. An alternative but complementary perspective is provided by Julia Balogun, 'Managing change: steering a course between intended strategies

and unanticipated outcomes', *Long Range Planning*, vol. 39 (2006), pp. 29–49.

- For an understanding of different approaches to managing change: M. Beer and N. Nohria, 'Cracking the code of change', *Harvard Business Review*, vol. 78, no. 3 (May–June 2000), pp. 133–41.

- The study of change programmes by L.C. Harris and E. Ogbonna, 'The unintended consequences of culture interventions: a study of unexpected outcomes', *British Journal of Management*, vol. 13, no. 1 (2002), pp. 31–49 provides a valuable insight into the problems of managing change in organisations.

REFERENCES

1. *Lessons Learned: Straight Talk from the World's Top Business Leaders: Managing Change*, Harvard Business School Press, 2007, p. 25.

2. J. Kotter, 'What leaders really do', *Harvard Business Review*, December 2001, pp. 85–96.

3. *Exploring Strategic Change* by J. Balogun and V. Hope Hailey, 3rd edition, Prentice Hall, 2008, is a sister text to this book; this part of the chapter draws on their Chapter 3 on the context of strategic change.

4. For a discussion of the problems of importing change programmes from the private sector to the public sector, see F. Ostroff, 'Change management in government', *Harvard Business Review*, vol. 84, no. 5 (May 2006), pp. 141–7.

5. Based on D. Neal and T. Taylor, 'Spinning on dimes: the challenges of introducing transformational change into the UK Ministry of Defence', *Strategic Change*, vol. 15 (2006), pp. 15–22.

6. For an interesting example of how different contexts affect receptivity to change, see J. Newton, J. Graham, K. McLoughlin and A. Moore, 'Receptivity to change in a general medical practice', *British Journal of Management*, vol. 14, no. 2 (2003), pp. 143–53.

7. See J.-L. Denis, L. Lamothe and A. Langley, 'The dynamics of collective change leadership and strategic change in pluralistic organizations', *The Academy of Management Journal*, vol. 44, no. 4 (2001), pp. 809–37.

8. Approaches to how to use the cultural web for the purposes outlined here are dealt with in detail in the chapter, 'Mapping and re-mapping organisational culture', in V. Ambrosini with G. Johnson and K. Scholes (eds), *Exploring Techniques of Analysis and Evaluation in Strategic Management*, Prentice Hall, 1998, and the similar chapter in G. Johnson and K. Scholes (eds), *Exploring Public Sector Strategy*, Prentice Hall, 2000.

9. This definition of leadership is based on that offered by R.M. Stodgill, 'Leadership, membership and organization', *Psychological Bulletin*, vol. 47 (1950), pp. 1–14. For a more recent and more comprehensive discussion of leadership, see G.A. Yukl, *Leadership in Organizations*, 6th edition, Prentice Hall, 2005.

10. See D. Ulrich, N. Smallwood and K. Sweetman, *Leadership Code: the Five Things Great Leaders Do*, Harvard Business School Press, 1999.

11. This is emphasised by John Kotter (reference 2).

12. The importance of relationship building was one of the findings of the research of Paul Hersey and Ken Blanchard (*Management of Organizational Behavior: Utilizing Human Resources*, Prentice Hall, 1988).

13. See S. Floyd and W. Wooldridge, *The Strategic Middle Manager: How to Create and Sustain Competitive Advantage*, Jossey-Bass, 1996.

14. See for example J. Balogun and G. Johnson: 'Organizational restructuring and middle manager sensemaking', *Academy of Management Journal*, August 2004; J. Balogun, 'Managing change: steering a course between intended strategies and unanticipated outcomes', *Long Range Planning*, vol. 39 (2006), pp. 29–49; J. Sillence and F. Mueller, 'Switching strategic perspective: the reframing of accounts of responsibility', *Organization Studies*, vol. 28, no. 2 (2007), pp. 155–76.

15. The discussion on different approaches of strategic leaders and evidence for the effectiveness of the adoption of different approaches can be found in D. Goleman, 'Leadership that gets results', *Harvard Business Review*, vol. 78, no. 2 (March–April 2000), pp. 78–90, and C.M. Farkas and S. Wetlaufer, 'The ways chief executive officers lead', *Harvard Business Review*, vol. 74, no. 3 (May–June 1996), pp. 110–12.

16. See M. Beer and N. Nohria, 'Cracking the code of change', *Harvard Business Review*, vol. 78, no. 3 (May–June 2000), pp. 133–41.

17. Different authors explain change styles in different ways. This section is based on the typologies used by J. Balogun and V. Hope Haley (see 3 above, section 2.4, pp. 31–6) and D. Dunphy and D. Stace, 'The strategic management of corporate change', *Human Relations*, vol. 46, no. 8 (1993), pp. 905–20. For an alternative framework see R. Caldwell, 'Models of change agency: a fourfold classification', *British Journal of Management*, vol. 14, no. 2 (2003), pp. 131–42.

18. For example D.A. Garvin and M.A. Roberto, 'Change through persuasion', *Harvard Business Review*, February 2005, pp. 104–12.

19. See Balogun and Johnson (reference 14).

20. For evidence of the effects of involvement in the strategy development process see: N. Collier, F. Fishwick and S.W. Floyd, 'Managerial involvement and perceptions of strategy process', *Long Range Planning*, vol. 37, no. 1 (2004), pp. 67–83.

21. Evidence for this is provided by D. Dunphy and D. Stace (reference 17 above) and see also Collier, Fishwick and Floyd (reference 20 above).

22. See Carolyn Aiken and Scott Keller, 'The irrational side of change management', *The McKinsey Quarterly*, no. 2, 2009, 101–9.

23. For an example of this approach see J.M. Mezias, P. Grinyer and W.D. Guth, 'Changing collective cognition: a process model for strategic change', *Long Range Planning*, vol. 34, no. 1 (2001), pp. 71–95. Also for a systematic approach to strategy making and change based on such surfacing, see F. Ackermann and C. Eden with I. Brown, *The Practice of Making Strategy*, Sage, 2005.

24. For a discussion of the psychological context, thinking flaws, and the impact that these have for managers as they consider the future, see K. van der Heijden, R. Bradfield, G. Burt, G. Cairns and G. Wright, *The Sixth Sense: Accelerating Organizational Learning with Scenarios*, Wiley, 2002, chapter 2.

25. See M. Hammer and J. Champy, *Reengineering the Corporation: A Manifesto for Business Revolution*, HarperCollins, 2004.

26. This example is given by Michael Hammer in 'Deep change: how operational innovation can transform your

company', *Harvard Business Review*, vol. 82, no. 4 (April 2004), pp. 84–93.

27. This quote is on page 135 of R. Pascale, M. Millemann and L. Gioja, 'Changing the way we change', *Harvard Business Review*, vol. 75, no. 6 (November–December 1997), pp. 126–39.

28. See 26 above.

29. See Gerry Johnson, Stuart Smith and Brian Codling, 'Institutional change and strategic agency: an empirical analysis of managers' experimentation with routines in strategic decision-making', in *The Cambridge Handbook of Strategy as Practice*, edited by D. Golsorkhi, L. Rouleau, D. Seidl and E. Vaara, 2010.

30. For a fuller discussion of this theme, see G. Johnson, 'Managing strategic change: the role of symbolic action', *British Journal of Management*, vol. 1, no. 4 (1990), pp. 183–200. Also see J.M. Higgins and C. McCallaster, 'If you want strategic change don't forget your cultural artefacts', *Journal of Change Management*, vol. 4, no. 1 (2004), pp. 63–73.

31. For a discussion of the role of rituals in change, see D. Sims, S. Fineman and Y. Gabriel, *Organizing and Organizations: an Introduction*, Sage, 1993.

32. See H.M. Trice and J.M. Beyer, 'Studying organisational cultures through rites and ceremonials', *Academy of Management Review*, vol. 9, no. 4 (1984), pp. 653–69; H.M. Trice and J.M. Beyer, 'Using six organisational rites to change culture', in R.H. Kilman, M.J. Saxton, R. Serpa and associates (eds), *Gaining Control of the Corporate Culture*, Jossey-Bass, 1985.

33. See C. Hardy, I. Palmer and N. Phillips, 'Discourse as a strategic resource', *Human Relations*, vol. 53, no. 9 (2000), p. 1231.

34. This discussion is based on observations of the role of political activities in organisations by, in particular, H. Mintzberg, *Power in and around Organizations*, Prentice Hall, 1983, and J. Pfeffer, *Power in Organizations*, Pitman, 1981. However, perhaps the most interesting book on political management remains Niccolo Machiavelli's sixteenth-century work, *The Prince* (available in Penguin Books, 2003). It is also the basis of a management book by Gerald Griffin, *Machiavelli on Management: Playing and Winning the Corporate Power Game*, Praeger, 1991.

35. For a fuller discussion of this approach by Bratton and other change agents, see W.C. Kim and R. Mauborgne, 'Tipping point leadership', *Harvard Business Review*, vol. 81, no. 4 (April 2003), pp. 60–9.

36. For a review of research that makes this point see: D. Buchanan, L. Fitzgerald, D. Ketley, R. Gallop, J.L. Jones, S.S. Lamont, A. Neath and E. Whitby, 'No going back: a review of the literature on sustaining organizational change', *International Journal of Management Reviews*, vol. 7, no. 3 (2005), pp. 189–205.

37. Turnaround strategy is more extensively explained in D. Lovett and S. Slatter, *Corporate Turnaround*, Penguin Books, 1999, and P. Grinyer, D. Mayes and P. McKiernan, 'The sharpbenders: achieving a sustained improvement in performance', *Long Range Planning*, vol. 23, no. 1 (1990), pp. 116–25. Also see V.L. Barker and I.M. Duhaime, 'Strategic change in the turnaround process: theory and empirical evidence', *Strategic Management Journal*, vol. 18, no. 1 (1997), pp. 13–38.

38. See the 'Sharpbenders' study (reference 37 above).

39. See K. Pajunen, 'Stakeholder influences in organizational survival', *Journal of Management Studies*, vol. 43, no. 6 (2006), pp. 1261–88.

40. The value of working with aspects of the existing culture is a finding from the research of S. Finkelstein, C. Harvey and T. Lawton, documented in *Breakout Strategy*, McGraw-Hill, 2007.

41. The observations and examples here are largely based on L.C. Harris and E. Ogbonna, 'The unintended consequences of culture interventions: a study of unexpected outcomes', *British Journal of Management*, vol. 13, no. 1 (2002), pp. 31–49; J.D. Ford, L.W. Ford and A.D. Amelio, 'Resistance to change: the rest of the story', *Academy of Management Review*, vol. 23 (2008), pp. 362–77; and D.A. Garvin and M.A. Roberto (18 above).

Managing change at Faslane

Thirty miles west of Glasgow is HM Naval Base Clyde (Faslane), the home of the UK's nuclear submarines that carry the Trident weapon system. It is a Ministry of Defence (MOD) installation, but managed by private sector Babcock Marine, part of Babcock International.

The Babcock Marine office overlooks Gareloch on which the naval base is situated and where the ships and the 148-metre-long Trident submarines are maintained. As well as the base's offices there is also accommodation for the sailors, all within a heavily guarded barbed wire perimeter fence. Over the peninsula is Coulport, also part of the base, where nuclear warheads are processed and loaded onto submarines.

John Howie was the Babcock Marine Managing Director from 2002 to 2006.

John, how did Babcock Marine get involved at Faslane?

Faslane had been run entirely by the MOD and the Royal Navy. By 2000 the MOD had decided they needed to significantly reduce the cost and improve operational effectiveness of their naval bases and that in-house MOD management would find that difficult given the restrictions they operated under as part of a wider civil service. So they established partnering arrangements with industrial firms. In 2002 we signed a contract initially for a five-year period to deliver £76 (~€83; ~$114) million of cost savings without affecting the service provided to the Navy. A percentage of that saving would come to us as profit; the bulk would go to the customer as cost reduction. Our profit was entirely a share of the savings, so no cost reduction, no profit; but the contract made sure we couldn't do that by prejudicing service levels.

Over 1,700 civil service posts and nearly 300 Royal Navy personnel and civil servants were seconded to us. In addition there remained 1,000 other civil servants on site, security personnel, police and the MOD Guard Service, Royal Marines, together with the sailors, ships and the submarines. The population of Faslane and Coulport is about 7,500 people.

What was it like when you arrived?

The customer support ethos didn't feel right. Despite being a naval base, the staff saw buildings and infra-

Source: Babcock Faslane.

structure facilities as more important than supporting the Navy. The focus was from the waterfront inward rather than looking outwards to the ships and submarines. I think that was because the people who looked after the site were often civilians who had been here much longer than the Navy people who looked after ships and submarines and generally moved on after 2–3 years. The civilians had built up empires. So the challenge was to become focused on delivering services to the customer, the Navy.

Moreover a public sector manager who's got wide-ranging responsibilities and a fairly large budget has no incentive to reduce costs. They don't share in any benefits and were brought up in a system where, if they hadn't spent their budget, next year it would be cut. So we believed that a big opportunity might come from changing the mindset: to see their job as to deliver with the minimum possible spend.

Another difficulty is that every significant decision of a civil servant could be questioned by an elected politician. That makes people naturally conservative. You also end up with lots of layers in the organisation; lots of people with limited autonomy who focus on doing things within their own control. It's procedural; a 'handle turning' exercise.

With political accountability it's also important to demonstrate an audit path for the decision you made. So speedy decision making is secondary to being able to demonstrate why you made the decision.

What of the management here before Babcock?

The commodore in charge when this process started was willing to change in a way some of his predecessors hadn't been. He'd come to the same conclusion about the need to change from infrastructure focus to naval focus. He saw partnering as the opportunity to better manage the people. The commodore's management team were a mix of people who either believed change was necessary and were willing to give partnering a try or people who were likely to be personally disadvantaged by partnering and were less supportive.

What of the workforce?

There was a perception that because of the base's role supporting the nuclear deterrent, they were ring-fenced from radical changes. Their view was that the base was doing a good job so why would you want to change that? There was no perception of a need to save money. They'd also been through a whole raft of MOD change, not least large-scale outsourcing programmes. There was the feeling of flavour-of-the-month change pro-grammes. So the backdrop was a workforce forcibly transferred to a private company and fearful of what change would mean.

So how did you set about change?

We brought in people from Babcock who had lived through similar changes. What they didn't necessarily understand was how to run a naval base, but the MOD transferred people to us who knew how to do that. Our job was to manage them differently.

The initial aim was to get visibility about how money was being spent whilst focusing on things that matter to the customer. We looked carefully at structures and processes to figure out how they operated and ask how that could be done differently. For example, there was a process that required any change to be documented and passed through a series of review points. After all, in a nuclear naval base you have to be sure that changing something fundamental to safety can be done without unacceptable risk. At each stage of that process people were given 14 days to review it; and of course everyone looked at it on day thirteen. So the overall process took about 56 days. It also became clear that a number of the review points weren't adding value; it was: 'I'm letting you look at this because you might be interested', not because involvement was critical. By taking those stages out you free up people's bureaucratic burden. You also don't give them 14 days to review it; you give them two days. Now that 56-day process is six days; a simple example of process re-engineering.

All that sounds very mechanistic

It's not like that. We are an organisation that doesn't own any physical assets other than the people who walk through the gate every day. So change is very much about people. And with 2,000 people you get access to a whole raft of ideas and change initiatives that we would never have thought of because we had never worked in this environment. So part of it was about removing shackles from people to come up with their own change ideas. But culturally that's a challenge, when for many there's no incentive to come up with a change when it might mean that people next to you get made redundant.

So how do you do it?

We had a management structure that wasn't right to deliver change. We had seven layers in it. It's now (2006) down to a maximum of four layers. We've reappointed all the jobs. We asked other companies which had been through large-scale changes: 'what should we learn from what you did?' The answer was: 'Implement the management structural changes early'. People tried to launch transformational change with the existing team, got two or three years into it, realised it wasn't working, and then changed the structure. We are doing it the other way round. We implemented all the low-level changes upfront because they're easy. That allowed us to deliver £14 million of saving in the first year against a target of £3 million. But once you get into more transformational change – about trying to deliver a strategy of being the best, most profitable organisation supporting the UK submarine fleet – we needed different skill sets. So we've changed the structure. The management team we had was about 250; it's now about half of that.

The problem is that as we get away from the changes which are relatively mechanistic we get into changes that are much more complex in nature.

It also seems a difficult political situation

The first thing is to understand who you need to have as allies, such as the Naval Base Commander. Our success was intertwined. I have a parent company to satisfy, whilst the Commodore has to manage the relationships with the wider MOD and the Navy Board. Beyond that you have to look at the wider stakeholders. If the commanding officers of the ships and submarines were saying 'we're getting a bad service' we'd have struggled. Or if the security people thought we weren't interested in national security. Another key stakeholder was the local community. We did a lot of work upfront with two local councils because the base represents 9.5% of employment in the area and we've reduced by about 400 full-time equivalent posts. Some of those have been naval posts rather than local people. And 98 reductions have been voluntary redundancies. Fairly quickly the meetings with the councils stopped because they became comfortable we were doing things the right way.

So, what has been achieved?

Year 1 the target was £3 million of savings; we delivered £14 million. Year 2 the target was £12 million; we delivered £16 million. By the end of Year 5 we had delivered around £100 million against our £76 million target; that's over 20% reduction in annual running costs. By the end of Year 10 we should have saved £280 million; that's 38.2%. And the Navy's view was that the service they received was better, attitude better, communication better, responsiveness better. So we have delivered both cost reductions and service improvement.

Craig Lockhart, part of the original Babcock management team, succeeded John Howie in 2006. He takes up the story in 2009.

'We are in our second year of having a performance scorecard. We started to measure outputs. Everyone down to team leaders have become acutely aware that business performance is not something to be hidden. It has to be transparent. However, it wasn't just about measurement. Business planning had been top-down. As our journey developed we appreciated that it was a hearts and minds issue: that we had to get the entire workforce aligned around common objectives. We held "the event in the tent" sessions and nearly 3,000 people went through day-long discussions where we allowed them to challenge and express their views about the transformation of Naval Base Clyde.'

'They got to ask real questions and started to see that they got real answers. If there was bad news we would tell them it was bad news. If it was good news we would tell them it's good news but it was always honest news. So, we started to get the trust of the workforce. Now we've got the trade unions talking about "our company". We followed it up with blank business plans. We said, "We've given you the broad headings, the broad objectives from a company point of view, but what's important is where do you think you fit in". They were tasked to generate their own team, their own departmental business plans.'

'By 2009 we were also producing a joint business plan with the customer. It's not a Babcock Marine business plan or an MOD business plan. It's a plan on behalf of Clyde. And by the end of the year the Commodore and his team of directors will co-locate with us. We will be working together.'

In April 2010, Craig was able to announce* that Faslane would become the home base, not just for nuclear submarines but for the entire UK submarines fleet. Together with the associated submarines and nulear training schools, it could mean up to 2000 more jobs at the base by 2014.

* *Source: Helensburgh Advertiser, 29 April 2010.*

Questions

1 In relation to sections 14.2.1 and 14.5, what is the type of change being pursued at Faslane?

2 Describe the change styles of John Howie and Craig Lockhart.

3 What levers of change are being used (see section 14.4)? What others could be used and why?

4 Assess the effectiveness of the change programme.

15

THE PRACTICE OF STRATEGY

Learning outcomes

After reading this chapter you should be able to:

● Identify *key people involved in strategising*, including top management, strategy consultants, strategic planners and middle managers.

● Assess which people should be included in addressing different strategic issues.

● Evaluate different approaches to strategising activity, including *analysis*, *issue-selling*, *decision-making structures* and *communicating*.

● Recognise key elements in various methodologies commonly used in strategising, including *strategy workshops*, *projects*, *hypothesis testing* and writing *business cases* and *strategic plans*.

PEARSON mystrategylab

MyStrategyLab is designed to help you make the most of your studies.

Visit **www.pearsoned.co.uk/mystrategylab** to discover a wide range of resources specific to this chapter, including:

● A personalised **Study plan** that will help you understand core concepts

● **Audio** and **video clips** that put the spotlight on strategy in the real world

● **Online glossaries** and **flashcards** that provide helpful reminders when you're looking for some quick revision.

(15.1) INTRODUCTION

If you were to be appointed as a strategic planner, or became a managing director of a business, what would you actually do to develop a strategy? This final chapter examines how managers actually practise strategy, using the theoretical concepts, tools and techniques introduced earlier in the book. Whereas Chapter 12 introduced the overall organisational process of strategy development, this chapter is about what managers do *inside* the process. The aim is to examine the practicalities of strategy-making for top managers, strategic planning specialists, strategy consultants or managers lower down the organisation.

The chapter has three sections as shown in Figure 15.1:

- *The strategists.* The chapter starts by looking at the various people involved in making strategy. It does not assume that strategy is made just by top management. As pointed out in Chapter 12, strategy is often emergent, and involves people from all over the organisation and often from outside. The Key Debate at the end of the chapter addresses the controversial involvement of external strategy consultants. Readers can ask themselves how they fit into this set of strategists, or how they might in the future.

- *Strategising activities.* The chapter continues by considering the kinds of work and activity that strategists carry out in their strategy-making. This includes, not just the strategy analysis that has been central to a large part of this book, but also the managing of strategic issues over time, the realities of strategic decision-making and the critical task of communicating strategic decisions throughout the organisation.

- *Strategising methodologiess.* The final section covers some of the practical methodologies that managers use to carry out their strategising activities. This includes strategy workshops for formulating or communicating strategy; strategy projects and strategy consulting teams; hypothesis testing to guide strategy work; and the writing of strategic plans and business cases.

Figure 15.1 The pyramid of strategy practice

Figure 15.1 integrates these three sections in a *pyramid of practice*.[1] The pyramid highlights three questions that run through this chapter: *who* to include in strategy-making; *what* to do in carrying out strategising activity; and *which* strategising methodologies to use in organising this strategising activity. Placing strategists at the top of the pyramid emphasises the role of managerial discretion and skill in strategy-making. It is the strategists who choose and enact both the strategising activity and the strategy methodologies that are at the base of the pyramid. Strategists' choices and skill with regard to activity and methodologies can make a real difference to final outcomes. The rest of the chapter seeks to guide practising strategists through the key choices they may have to make in action.

 ## THE STRATEGISTS

This section introduces the different types of people involved in strategy. It starts at the top-management level, but includes strategic planners, consultants and middle managers. One key issue is how middle managers can increase their influence in strategy-making.

15.2.1 Top managers and directors

The conventional view is that strategy is the business of top management. This view suggests that top management is clearly separated from operational responsibilities, so that it can focus on overall strategy.[2] If top managers are directly involved in operations such as sales or service delivery, they are liable to get distracted from long-term issues by day-to-day responsibilities and to represent the interests of their departments or business units rather than the interests of their organisation as a whole. In the private sector at least, top managers' job titles underline this strategic responsibility: company directors set direction, managers manage.

In reality, the top management role involves much more than setting direction. Also, different roles are played by different members, whether *Chief Executive Officer*, the *Top Management Team* or *Non-Executive Directors*:

- The *Chief Executive Officer* is often seen as the 'chief strategist', ultimately responsible for all strategic decisions. Chief Executives of large companies typically spend about one-third of their time on strategy.[3] Michael Porter stresses the value of a clear strategic leader, somebody capable of setting a disciplined approach to what fits and what does not fit the overall strategy.[4] In this view, the Chief Executive Officer (or Managing Director or equivalent top individual) owns the strategy and is accountable for its success or failure. The clarity of this individual responsibility can no doubt focus attention. However, there are dangers. First, centralising responsibility on the Chief Executive Officer can lead to excessive personalisation. Organisations respond to setbacks simply by changing their Chief Executive Officer, rather than examining deeply the internal sources of failure. Second, successful Chief Executives can become over-confident, seeing themselves as corporate heroes and launching strategic initiatives of ever-increasing ambition.[5] The over-confidence of heroic leaders often leads to spectacular failures. Jim Collins's research on 'great' American companies that outperformed their rivals over the long term found that their Chief Executive Officers were typically modest, steady and long-serving.[6]

- The *top management team*, often an organisation's executive directors, also shares responsibility for strategy. They can bring additional experience and insight to the Chief Executive

Officer. In theory, they should be able to challenge the Chief Executive Officer and increase strategic debate. In practice, the top management team is often constrained in at least three ways. First, except in the largest companies, top managers often carry operational responsibilities that either distract them or bias their strategic thinking: for example, in a business the marketing director will have ongoing concerns about marketing, the production director about production, and so on. In the public sector the top management team will also, very likely, be heads of operating departments. Second, top managers are also frequently appointed by the Chief Executive Officer; consequently, they may lack the independence for real challenge. Finally, top management teams, especially where their members have similar backgrounds and face strong leadership, often suffer from '*groupthink*', the tendency to build strong consensus amongst team members and avoid internal questioning or conflict.[7] Top management teams can minimise groupthink by fostering diversity in membership (for example, differences in age, career tracks and sex), by ensuring openness to outside views, for example those of non-executive directors, and by promoting internal debate and questioning.

- *Non-executive directors* have no executive management responsibility within the organisation, and so in theory should be able to offer an external and objective view on strategy. Although this varies according to national corporate governance systems (see section 4.3.2), in a public company the chairman of the board is typically non-executive. The chairman will normally be consulted closely by the Chief Executive Officer on strategy, as he or she will have a key role in liaising with investors. However, the ability of the chairman and other non-executives to contribute substantially to strategy can be limited. Non-executives are typically part-time appointments. The predominant role for non-executive directors in strategy, therefore, is consultative, reviewing and challenging strategy proposals that come from the top management executive team. A key role for them also is to ensure that the organisation has a rigorous system in place for the making and renewing of strategy. It is therefore important that non-executives are authoritative and experienced individuals, that they have independence from the top management executive team and that they are fully briefed before board meetings.

Top management capability in making strategy should not simply be assumed. Managers are often promoted to strategic roles for their success in dealing with operations or their professional skill in a particular functional specialism. These kinds of experience do not necessarily provide the skills needed for the tasks involved in making strategy. There are at least three important qualities senior managers need if they are to contribute effectively to high-level strategy-making:

- *Mastery of analytical concepts and techniques*, as introduced in this book, cannot be assumed. Sometimes an executive education course can help improve understanding of strategy concepts and techniques.

- *Social and influencing skills* are necessary if analysis is to be understood and accepted by senior colleagues. Again, senior managers are not equally effective in strategic discussions, but there are now many professional coaches who can help.

- *Group acceptance as a player* in strategic discussions. Boards and senior executive teams are social groups like any other, where members have to win respect. Clear and significant success in one's own particular sphere of responsibility is normally a precondition for being respected as a contributor to wider discussions of the organisation's strategy.

15.2.2 Strategic planners

Strategic planners, sometimes known as strategy directors, corporate development managers or similar, **are managers with a formal responsibility for coordinating the strategy process** (see Chapter 12). Although small companies very rarely have full-time strategic planners, they are common in large companies and increasingly widespread in the public and not-for-profit sectors. As in Illustration 15.1, organisations frequently advertise for strategic planning jobs. Here, the personal specifications give a clear picture of the types of role a typical strategic planner might be expected to play. In a large corporation a strategic planner would not only be working on a three-year strategic plan, but investigating acquisition targets, monitoring competitors and helping territory senior managers (country managers) with their own plans. In this the role is not just about analysis in the back office. Strategic planning is also about communications, team work and influencing skills.

Although the job in Illustration 15.1 is being advertised externally, strategic planners are often drawn from inside their own organisations. Internal strategic planners are likely to have an advantage in the important non-analytical parts of the job. As internal recruits, they bring to the planning role an understanding of the business, networks with key people in the organisation and credibility with internal audiences. Moreover, an internal appointment to a strategic planning role can serve as a developmental stage for managers on track for top management roles. Participating in strategy provides promising managers with exposure to senior management and gives them a view of the organisation as a whole.

Strategic planners do not take strategic decisions themselves. However, they typically have at least three important tasks:[8]

- *Information and analysis*. Strategic planners have the time, skills and resources to provide information and analysis for key decision-makers. This might be in response to some 'trigger' event – such as a possible merger – or as part of a regular planning cycle. A background of good information and analysis can leave an organisation much better prepared to respond quickly and confidently even to unexpected events as they occur. Strategic planners can also package this information and analysis in formats that ensure clear communication of strategic decisions.

- *Managers of the strategy process*. Both for the headquarters and for business units, strategic planners can assist and guide other managers through their strategic planning cycles (see Illustration 12.2 in Chapter 12). This will involve acting as a bridge between the corporate centre and the businesses by clarifying corporate expectations and guidelines. It could also involve helping business-level managers develop strategy by providing templates, analytical techniques and strategy training. This bridging role is important in achieving alignment of corporate-level and business-level strategies. Researchers[9] point out that this alignment is often lacking; that 60 per cent of organisations do not link financial budgets to corporate strategic priorities; and that the measures of performance of 70 per cent of middle managers and more than 90 per cent of front-line employees have no link to the success or failure of strategy implementation.

- *Special projects*. Strategic planners can be a useful resource to support top management on special projects, such as acquisitions or organisational change. Here strategy planners will typically work on project teams with middle managers from within the organisation and often with external consultants. Project management skills are likely to be important.

In addition to these tasks, they typically work closely with the CEO, discussing and helping refine his or her strategic thinking. Indeed, many strategic planners are physically located

ILLUSTRATION 15.1

Wanted: Team member for strategy unit

The following advertisement appeared on the UK Cabinet Office website. It gives an insight into the kind of work such strategic planners do and the skills and background required.

Job Description for a Team Member: Band A

About the Strategy Unit

The PMSU (Prime Minister's Strategy Unit) has three main roles:

- to carry out strategy reviews and provide policy advice in accordance with the Prime Minister's policy priorities;
- to support Government Departments in developing effective strategies and policies – including helping them to build their strategic capability; and
- to identify and effectively disseminate thinking on emerging issues and challenges facing the UK e.g. through occasional strategic audits.

Post holders will be members of small teams set up to address issues where innovative approaches and fresh thinking are necessary to ensure the achievement of the Government's objectives. Teams will be drawn from both inside and outside the Civil Service and work intensively on an issue, for periods ranging from 3–4 weeks to 3–4 months or longer depending on the task.

Candidates will need to have first rate policy or strategy experience, strong interpersonal skills, and the ability to write clearly and compellingly. Outstanding analytical and problem solving skills are absolutely essential to the role.

Essential competences for the SU

Strategic Thinking
1. Knowledge and understanding of government priorities
2. Knowledge of the wider policy environment, including political or institutional restraints
3. Ability to derive clear goals and strategies from a complex brief

Analysis and Use of Evidence
1. Knows and deploys a range of analytical tools
2. Uses a variety of tools in collecting and analysing evidence
3. Works in partnership with a wide range of analytical experts to achieve project goals
4. Ability to understand complex statistical data
5. Understands what constitutes good evidence

People Management
1. Able to develop individuals for high performance
2. Champions equality and diversity, and promotes best practice
3. Able to give good feedback that people can act on

Programme and Project Management
1. Can work with a team to develop a project plan
2. Anticipates, manages and monitors programme/project risks
3. Ensures effective communications with stakeholders

Specialist Professional Skills

Essential
1. Good quality qualifications or training in economics, social policy, operational research or similar
2. Excellent quantitative and qualitative analytical skills
3. Sector knowledge – an understanding of social policy is an advantage

Desirable
1. Experience in working in a think-tank or high profile management consultancy role or policy or analytical arm of a government department.

Source: from Extracts from Strategy Unit Job Description for a Team Member: Band A from http://www.cabinetoffice.gov.uk/strategy/jobs/band_a.asp. Crown Copyright material is reproduced with permission under the terms of the Click-Use Licence.

Questions

1 What would be the attractions of this job for you? What would be the disadvantages?

2 What relevant skills and experience do you already have, and what skills and experience would you still need to acquire before you were able to apply for this job?

close to the CEO. In doing all this, they may have relatively few resources – perhaps a small team of support staff – and little formal power, but their closeness to the CEO is likely to mean that managers throughout an organisation are likely to use them to sound out ideas.[10]

15.2.3 Middle managers

As in section 15.2.1, a good deal of conventional management theory excludes middle managers from strategy-making. Middle managers are seen as lacking an appropriately objective and long-term perspective, being too involved in operations.[11] In this view, middle managers' role is limited to strategy implementation. This is, of course, a vital role. However, there is increasing middle management involvement in strategy-making for at least three reasons.[12] First, many organisations are decentralising their organisational structures to increase accountability and responsiveness in fast-moving and competitive environments. As a result, strategic responsibilities are being thrust down the organisational hierarchy. Second, the rise of business education means that middle managers are now better trained and more confident in the strategy domain than they used to be. These higher-calibre middle managers are both more able and more eager to participate in strategy. Third, the shift away from a traditional manufacturing economy to one based more on professional services (such as design, consulting or finance) means that often the key sources of competitive advantage are no longer resources such as capital, which can be handed out from the headquarters, but the knowledge of people actually involved in the operations of the business. Middle managers at operational level can understand and influence these knowledge-based sources of competitive advantage much more effectively than remote top managers.

In this context, there are at least four roles they have in relation to the management of strategy:[13]

- *Information source.* Their knowledge and experience of the realities of the organisation and its market is likely to be greater than that of many top managers. So middle managers are a potential source of information about changes in the strategic position of the organisation.

- *'Sense making'* of strategy. Top management may set down a strategic direction; but how it is explained and made sense of in specific contexts (e.g. a region of a multinational or a functional department) may, intentionally or not, be left to middle managers.[14] They are therefore a crucial *relevance bridge* between top management and members of the organisation at lower levels, in effect translating strategy into a message that is locally relevant. If misinterpretation of that intended strategy is to be avoided, it is therefore vital that middle managers understand and feel an ownership of it. (See also the Key Debate in Chapter 11.)

- *Reinterpretation and adjustment* of strategic responses as events unfold (e.g. in terms of relationships with customers, suppliers, the workforce and so on); this is a vital role for which middle managers are uniquely qualified because of their day-to-day contact with such aspects of the organisation and its environment.

- *Champions of ideas.* Given their closeness to markets and operations middle managers may not only provide information but champion new ideas that can be the foundation of new strategies.

Middle managers may also increase their influence on strategy when they have:

- *Key organisational positions.* Middle managers responsible for larger departments, business units or strategically important parts of the organisation have influence because they are likely to have critical knowledge.[15] Also, managers with outward-facing roles (for example, in marketing) tend to have greater strategic influence than managers with inward-facing roles (such as quality or operations).[16]

- *Access to organisational networks.* Middle managers may not have hierarchical power, but can increase their influence by using their internal organisational networks. Drawing together information from network members can help provide an integrated perspective on what is happening in the organisation as a whole, something that otherwise can be difficult to get when occupying a specialised position in the middle of an organisation. Mobilising networks to raise issues and support proposals can also give more influence than any single middle manager can achieve on their own.[17] Strategically influential middle managers are therefore typically good networkers.

- *Access to the organisation's 'strategic conversation'.* Strategy-making does not just happen in isolated, formal episodes, but is part of an ongoing strategic conversation amongst respected managers.[18] To participate in these strategic conversations middle managers should: maximise opportunities to mix formally and informally with top managers; become at ease with the particular language used to discuss strategy in their organisation; familiarise themselves carefully with the key strategic issues; and develop their own personal contribution to these strategic issues.

In the public sector elected politicians have traditionally been responsible for policy and public officials supposed to do the implementation. However, three trends similar to those in the corporate world are challenging this division of roles. First, the rising importance of *specialised expertise* has shifted influence to public officials who may have made their careers in particular areas, while politicians are typically generalists. Second, public sector reform in many countries has led to increased *externalisation of functions* to quasi-independent 'agencies' or 'QUANGOs' (quasi-autonomous non-governmental organisations) which, within certain constraints, can make decisions on their own. Third, the same reform processes have changed *internal structures* within public organisations, with decentralisation of units and more 'executive' responsibility granted to public officials. All this is supported by the discourse of 'New Public Management', which encourages officials to be more enterprising and accountable. In short, strategy is increasingly part of the work of public officials too.[19]

15.2.4 Strategy consultants

External consultants are often used in the development of strategy. Leading consultancy firms that focus on strategy include Bain, the Boston Consulting Group, Monitor and McKinsey & Co.[20] Most of the large general consultancy firms also have operations that provide services in strategy development and analysis. There are also smaller 'boutique' consultancy firms and individual consultants who specialise in strategy.

Consultants may play different roles in strategy development in organisations:[21]

- *Analysing, prioritising and generating options.* Strategic issues may have been identified by executives, but there may be so many of them, or disagreement about them, that the organisation faces a lack of clarity on how to go forward. Consultants may analyse such issues afresh and bring an external perspective to help prioritise them or generate options for executives to consider. This may, of course, involve challenging executives' preconceptions about their views of strategic issues.

- *Transferring knowledge.* Consultants are the carriers of knowledge and perceived best practice within and between their clients.

- *Promoting strategic decisions.* In doing this, consultants may substantially influence the decisions that organisations eventually take. A number of major consultancies have been criticised in the past for undue influence on the decisions made by their client organisation, leading to major problems. For example, McKinsey & Co. was heavily associated with Enron's controversial 'asset-lite' business model, and was also the proponent of Swissair's failed 'Hunter' strategy of strategic alliances.[22]

- *Implementing strategic change.* Consultants play a significant role in project planning, coaching and training often associated with strategic change. This is an area that has seen considerable growth, not least because consultants were criticised for leaving organisations with consultancy reports recommending strategies, but taking little responsibility for actually making these happen.

The value of strategy consultants is often controversial (see the Key Debate at the end of this chapter). For example, in the UK government departments have increasingly been criticised for spending too much on consultants. The consultancy spend by nineteen UK central government departments was reported to be over £873 million (~€960m; ~$1309m) in 2008–09.[23] But consultants are often blamed for failures when it is the client's poor management of the consulting process that is ultimately at fault. Many organisations select their consultants unsystematically, give poor initial project briefs and fail to act on and learn from projects at the end. There are three key measures that client organisations can undertake to improve outcomes in strategy consulting:[24]

- *Professionalise purchasing of consulting services.* Instead of hiring consulting firms on the basis of personal relationships with key executives, as is often the case, professionalised purchasing can help ensure clear project briefs, a wide search for consulting suppliers, appropriate pricing, complementarity between different consulting projects and proper review at project-end. The German engineering company Siemens has professionalised its consultancy purchasing, for example, establishing a shortlist of just ten preferred management consulting suppliers.

- *Develop supervisory skills* in order to manage portfolios of consulting projects. The German railway company Deutsche Bahn and automobile giant DaimlerChrysler both have central project offices that control and coordinate all consulting projects throughout their companies. As well as being involved in the initial purchasing decision, these offices can impose systematic governance structures on projects, with clear responsibilities and reporting processes, as well as review and formal assessment at project-end.

- *Partner effectively* with consultants to improve both effectiveness in carrying out the project and knowledge transfer at the end of it. Where possible, project teams should include a mix of consultants and managers from the client organisation, who can provide inside information, guide on internal politics and, sometimes, enhance credibility and receptiveness. As partners in the project, client managers retain knowledge and experience when the consultants have gone and can help in the implementation of recommendations.

15.2.5 Who to include in strategy development?

There is a potentially wide range of people to involve in any strategic issue: as well as the Chief Executive and the top management team, non-executive directors, strategic planners,

Figure 15.2 The access/execution paradox

strategic consultants and middle managers. This raises questions about who should be included in addressing particular strategic issues. The paradox of strategy inclusion is that those with the most access to the CEO on strategy are often strategic planners and strategy consultants who have little responsibility for strategy implementation and little knowledge of business on the ground (see Figure 15.2). The middle managers who have both the knowledge and the implementation responsibility can have least access to the CEO in strategy discussions, either because they are too busy with operational realities or because they are seen as biased. Strategy is not necessarily being made by the most appropriate people.

There is no general rule about inclusion or exclusion in strategy-making, but there are criteria that can guide managers about whom to include according to the nature of the strategic issues in hand. Research by McKinsey & Co. indicates that the people involved should vary according to the nature of the issue (see Figure 15.3[25]). For example, issues that are urgent and could involve major changes to strategy (such as a merger or acquisition opportunity) are best approached by small special project teams, consisting of senior managers and perhaps planners and consultants. Issues which may be important but are not urgent (such as deciding on key competitors) can benefit from more prolonged and open strategic conversations, both formal and informal. Urgent issues that do not involve major change (such as responding to competitor threats) require only limited participation. Issues that may involve major changes but require idea generation over time (such as the search for global opportunities) might benefit from more open participation, though this might be organised more formally through a series of planned events, such as conferences bringing together large groups of managers in particular geographical regions.

Illustration 15.2 shows two approaches to achieving productive inclusion in strategy-making at IBM, with its 'strategy jam' and the International Trade Centre's value chain mapping in Uganda. The public sector also often uses the internet for public consultations and discussion forums with regard to controversial policy issues: see for example www.communities.gov.uk/.

ILLUSTRATION 15.2

Jamming and mapping

Participation in strategy making can be important in global businesses and developing enterprises alike.

Jamming at IBM[1]

IBM has developed a $3m (~€2.1m) information technology platform that allows its 300,000 employees to participate in global debates about strategic issues (see Illustration 14.5). These debates are called 'jams' after the structured improvisation ('jamming') used in jazz music. Jams typically combine off-site face-to-face brain-storming sessions with 'threaded' discussions, theme-based forums and electronic idea-ratings organised through the corporate intranet site. All IBM employees have equal access to the jam sessions. IBM manager Mike Malloney explained: 'It's like jazz collaboration, with people building on other people's ideas in a structured format. Jams are a blend of technology and a kind of grassroots discussion of ideas.'

IBM has used jams to address managerial roles, post-merger integration, organisational barriers to innovation and revenue growth (informally dubbed the 'logjam') and the development of a new values statement (the 'ValuesJam'). The ValuesJam took place over three days, generating 2.3 million page views and over a million words of input. Tens of thousands of employee ideas were refined into 65 key ideas, using online voting and IBM's proprietary natural language analytical software ('jamalyzer'). A small team then set to work on refining these further into three overarching values based on innovation, the customer and trust. Chief Executive Sam Palmisano commented on the ValuesJam:

> 'Yes, the electronic argument was hot and contentious and messy. . . . We had done three or four big online jams before . . . Even so, none of those could have prepared us for the emotions unleashed by this topic.'

Mapping in Uganda[2]

The International Trade Centre (ITC) in Geneva (www.intracen.org) is responsible for helping enterprises improve exports. In many developing countries where it operates there is little reliable published information available, development activities can be fragmented and people tend to be reticent unknown individuals. The Ugandan fish processing and exporting

sector provides one example of how these difficulties can be overcome.

ITC worked alongside the Uganda Export Promotion Board to facilitate meetings of stakeholders from all stages of the fish value network on a strategy for export growth. Stakeholders included enterprise owners, community leaders, government and development agencies, services providers such as transport, inspections, customs, banks, freight forwarders and packagers. Meeting in Kampala, they collaborated on a series of exercises to identify market opportunities, diagnose sector performance issues and organise development activity implementation.

They mapped the core stages of their value chains on large wall sheets from target markets back to sources of supply. Sector-wide issues and market requirements were broken down into value chain stage components and illustrated on these maps. The process surfaced tacit information and 'market realities' and stimulated new ideas for value addition, cost cutting and diversification (see Illustration 3.4). It also helped participants see 'the big picture opportunities', understand their mutual dependency and participate in the design of solutions, agree on the priorities to raise sector performance and who should implement which parts of the strategy and how.

Source: (1) S.J. Palmisano, 'Leading change when business is good', *Harvard Business Review*, December (2004), pp. 60–70; PR Newswire, 30 November (2005); (2) Ian Sayers, Senior Advisor for the Private Sector, Division of Trade Support Services, the International Trade Centre, Geneva.

Questions

1 Why was it important at IBM and in the Ugandan fishing industry to obtain wide input on strategic issues? What strategic issues would not require the same kind of input?

2 If you were a smaller company, without the information technology resources of IBM or the help of government agencies as in Uganda, how might you be able to get employee input into strategy development?

Figure 15.3 Who to include in strategy making?

A good deal of this book is concerned with strategy analysis, and indeed analysis can be an important input into strategy-making. However, as suggested in Chapter 12, strategy is often not the outcome of rational analysis. Analysis is frequently done in an ad hoc and incomplete fashion and not always followed through. Or the analysis activity itself may serve other functions than a simple input into subsequent decisions. Research shows that managers typically use a 'strategy toolkit' of between one and nine tools, with just four being the most common number of tools cited.[26] SWOT (strengths, weaknesses, opportunities and threats) analysis is the most widely used tool in strategy, but even this simple tool is typically used in a way far from the technical ideal. One study found frequent deviations from textbook recommendations, by both managers and consultants.[27] For example, in practice SWOT analyses tend to produce unmanageably long lists of factors (strengths, weaknesses, opportunities and threats), often

(15.3) STRATEGISING

The previous section introduced the key strategists; this section concentrates on what people do in strategising. The section starts with strategy analysis, then issue-selling, decision-making and communications about the chosen strategy. In practice, of course, these activities rarely follow this logical sequence; or they may not happen at all. As Chapter 12 made clear, strategies do not always come about in such ways and strategic decisions are often made without formal analysis and evaluation. So the section ends with a reminder about the often 'messy' nature of strategy development.

15.3.1 Strategy analysis

well over 50 or so. The result is these factors are rarely probed or refined, little substantive analysis is done to investigate them and they are often not followed up systematically in subsequent strategic discussions. (See the discussion on SWOT in section 3.4.4.)

Advocates of the extensive use of strategy tools would argue that their greater use would help ensure strategy development is better informed and managerial bias and ingrained assumptions challenged. Criticism of poor analysis may, however, sometimes be misplaced. There are both *cost* and *purpose* issues to consider. First of all, analysis is costly in terms of both resources and time. There are of course the costs of gathering information, particularly if using consultants. But with regard to time there is also the risk of '*paralysis by analysis*', where managers spend too long perfecting their analyses and not enough time taking decisions and acting upon them.[28] Managers have to judge how much analysis they really need. Second, with regard to purpose, analysis is not always simply about providing the necessary information for good strategic decisions anyway. Ann Langley has shown that the purposes of analysis can be quite different.[29] Setting up a project to analyse an issue thoroughly may even be a deliberate form of *procrastination*, aimed at putting off a decision. Analysis can also be *symbolic*, for example to rationalise a decision after it has already effectively been made. Managers may be asked to analyse an issue in order to get their *buy-in* to decisions that they might otherwise resist. Analyses can also be *political*, to forward the agenda of a particular manager or part of the organisation.

The different purposes of strategy analysis have two key implications for managers:

- *Design the analysis according to the real purpose*. The range and quality of people involved, the time and budget allowed, and the subsequent communication of analysis results should all depend on underlying purpose, whether informational, political or symbolic. For example, prestigious strategy consulting firms are often useful for political and symbolic analyses. Involving a wide group of middle managers in the analysis may help with subsequent buy-in.

- *Invest appropriately in technical quality*. For many projects, improving the quality of the technical analysis will make a valuable addition to subsequent strategic decisions. On other occasions, insisting on technical perfection can be counter-productive. For example, a SWOT analysis that raises lots of issues may be a useful means of allowing managers to vent their own personal frustrations, before getting on with the real strategy work. It may sometimes be better to leave these issues on the table, rather than probing, challenging or even deleting them in a way that could unnecessarily alienate these managers for the following stages.

15.3.2 Strategic issue-selling

Organisations typically face many strategic issues at any point in time. But in complex organisations these issues may not be appreciated to the same extent, or may not even be recognised at all, by those involved in developing strategy. Some issues will be filtered out in the organisational hierarchy; others will be sidelined by more urgent pressures. Moreover, senior managers will rarely have sufficient time and resources to deal with all the issues that do actually reach them. So strategic issues compete for attention. What get top management attention are not necessarily the most important issues.[30]

Strategic issue-selling is the process of gaining the attention and support of top management and other important stakeholders for strategic issues. Managers need to consider at least four aspects in seeking attention and support for their issues:

Figure 15.4 Formal channels for issue-selling

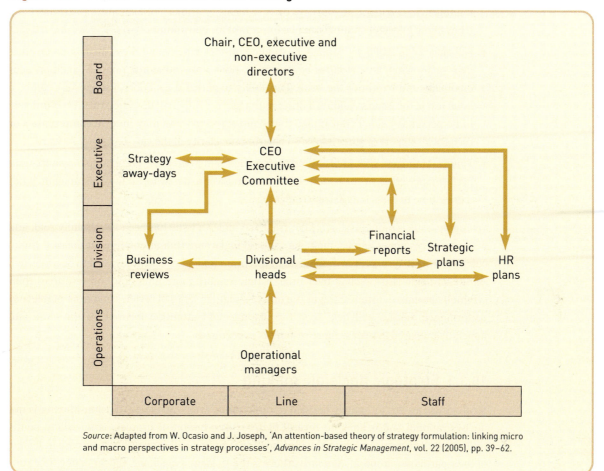

Source: Adapted from W. Ocasio and J. Joseph, 'An attention-based theory of strategy formulation: linking micro and macro perspectives in strategy processes', *Advances in Strategic Management*, vol. 22 (2005), pp. 39–62.

- *Issue packaging.* Care should be taken with how issues are packaged or framed. Clearly the strategic importance of the issue needs to be underlined, particularly by linking it to *critical strategic goals* or *performance metrics* for the organisation. Generally clarity and succinctness win over complexity and length. It also usually helps if the issue is packaged with *potential solutions*. An issue can easily be put aside as too difficult to address if no ways forward are offered at the same time.

- *Formal and informal channels.* Managers need to balance formal and informal channels of influence. Figure 15.4 indicates some *formal channels* for selling issues in a multidivisional organisation (based on General Electric). Here formal channels are split between corporate, line and staff. On the corporate side, they include the annual business reviews that the CEO carries out with each divisional head, plus the annual strategy retreats (or workshops) of the top executive team. The line channel involves the regular line interaction of operational managers, divisional heads and the CEO and other executive directors. Finally, there are the various reporting systems to staff functions, including finance, human resources and strategic planning. Formal channels are of course not just for upwards influence, but typically two-way: for example, strategic plans often iterate between divisions and corporate headquarters until a mutually satisfactory position is reached. Moreover, formal channels are rarely enough to sell strategic issues. *Informal channels* can, however, be very important and often decisive in some organisations. Informal channels might include ad hoc conversations with influential managers in corridors, on journeys or over meals or drinks. For example, Illustration 15.3 shows how informal channels can be important for consultants.[31]

- *Sell alone or in coalitions.* Managers should consider whether to press their issue on their own or to assemble a *coalition of supporters*, preferably influential ones. A coalition adds credibility and weight to the issue. The ability to gather a coalition of supporters can be a good test of the issue's validity: if other managers are unpersuaded, then the CEO is unlikely to be persuaded either. But notice that enlisting supporters may involve compromises or reciprocal support of other issues, so blurring the clarity of the case being put forward.

- *Timing.* Managers should also time their issue-selling carefully. For example a short-term performance crisis, or the period before the handover to a new top management team, is not a good time to press long-term strategic issues.

Selling an issue is only the start, of course. Even after an issue has been successfully sold, and actions and resources agreed, managers should make sure that attention is *sustained*.[32] Initial commitments in terms of top management attention and other resources need to be protected. As the strategic issue evolves over time, it may require more attention and resources than originally promised. Establishing at the outset a regular series of reviews and a set of relevant performance metrics will help keep top management attention focused on the issue and hopefully prepared to release more resources as required.

15.3.3 Strategic decision-making

Strategic issues are ultimately decided upon in many ways. Strategic decision-making is not always rational and is liable to several biases.[33] The notion of strategic issue-selling points to the so-called *champion's bias*: the likelihood that people will exaggerate their case in favour of their particular proposal. Similarly, there is the *sunflower syndrome*, the tendency (like sunflowers following the sun) to follow the lead of the most senior person in the decision-making process, or to try to anticipate their view even before they have expressed it. Decision-makers often hold exaggerated opinions of their competence, leading to over-optimistic decisions, especially where there are few data available. At the same time, they can be risk-averse, being unduly deterred by substantial downsides, even when the chances of such downsides are very slight.

Just putting decisions in the hands of a team of managers, therefore, does not on its own guarantee rigorous and effective decision-making. Katherine Eisenhardt's research on strategic decision-making in fast-moving environments suggests four helpful guidelines for managers:[34]

- *Build multiple, simultaneous alternatives.* Having several alternatives on the table at the same time helps to encourage critical debate. This can help counter phenomena such as the champion's bias and the sunflower syndrome. It is also faster than taking proposals sequentially, where alternatives are only sought out after a previous proposal has been examined and rejected. Examining multiple, simultaneous alternatives is a practice adopted by Barclays Bank, for example, where the rule is that proposals should never be presented in isolation, but always alongside at least two other alternatives.[35]

- *Track real-time information.* Eisenhardt's research found that fast decision-makers do not cut back on the amount of information; they use a different type of information – real-time

ILLUSTRATION 15.3

Dinner with the consultants

Consultants operate through both formal and informal channels to influence strategic thinking.

Locco* was a major European automotive component manufacturer. In the mid 1990s, it began to experience declining profits. The CEO therefore invited consultants to undertake a strategic review of the firm. This consultancy team included a partner, a senior consultant and a junior consultant. Their recommendations led to changes in Locco's product and market strategy.

Like all other consultancy assignments the consultants undertook extensive analysis of industry data and company data. However in addition to this more formal work, there was more informal engagement between the consultants and the management, including three dinners held during the period of the project.

At home with the CEO

At the beginning of the assignment the CEO invited the partner and senior consultant to meet senior managers at his home for dinner 'to get together in a more informal way . . . to get to know each other better . . . and . . . learn more about the history of our company', but also to establish trust between the managers and the consultants.

Others saw it differently. For example the marketing and sales manager viewed it as an attempt by the CEO to influence the outcome of the project: '(he) likes to do this. While dining in his home you can hardly oppose his views'. The consulting partner was somewhat wary, fearing a hidden agenda but nonetheless seeing it as an opportunity to 'break the ice' as well as gaining political insight and understanding of the management dynamics.

Over dinner discussion was largely between the CEO and the consultants with the CEO setting out some concerns about the project, not least the danger of cost cutting leading to a loss of jobs. As they mingled over after dinner drinks other sensitive issues were raised by other managers.

At the castle

In the third week of the project the consultant invited the CEO to a restaurant in a converted castle. He saw this as an opportunity to get to know the CEO better, to gain his agreement to the consultants' approach to the project, but also to gain a clearer understanding of the politics amongst the senior management and establish more insight into the CEO's perceived problems of Locco.

Over the meal the consultant established that there were two management 'camps' with different views of strategy. The consultant also took the opportunity to influence and gain the CEO's approval for the agenda for the next management meeting.

At the pizzeria

Some weeks later the senior consultant invited middle managers who he saw as 'good implementers' for pizza and beer at an Italian restaurant to 'exchange information and get opinions on some of our analyses, see how some of the middle managers react . . .'. Some of those who attended were sceptical about the meeting but went along. Senior managers were not invited.

At the dinner the consultant discussed his initial analysis, particularly on strategic competences. He also raised some issues to do with the political dynamics within the senior management team. The consultant regarded the dinner as a success both in terms of establishing a rapport but also in establishing that 'some (of the managers) know exactly why the company has a problem . . . they already have some ideas for solutions . . . but their voices are not heard'. The managers who attended were, on the whole, also positive about the dinner, many regarding it as 'good fun' though others who were not there felt threatened by their absence.

* A pseudonym used by the researchers.

Adapted from A. Sturdy, M. Schwarz and A. Spicer, 'Guess who's coming to dinner? Structures and uses of liminality in strategic management consultancy', *Human Relations*, vol. 59, no. 7, pp. 929–60 (2006).

Questions

1 Why are informal settings such as dinners useful?

2 Could the consultants have influenced the agenda in more formal ways ? How?

3 If you had been one of the managers at the Italian restaurant, what would your views of the meeting been?

information. These managers prefer immediate information from current operations, rather than statistical trends and forecasts. They tend to spend a lot of time in face-to-face meetings, 'managing by wandering around' and reviewing the most up-to-date indicators, such as weekly and even daily measures of sales, cash, stocks or work-in-progress. In fast-moving environments especially, a quick decision may be better than a delayed decision, and trend data are liable to be rapidly outdated anyway.

● *Seek the views of trusted advisers.* Experienced managers can provide fast feedback on what is likely to work or not based on extensive knowledge from their past. They can also ask tough questions given what they have seen before. The instincts of experienced managers are faster, and often both more reliable and more credible, than lengthy analysis undertaken by junior managers or consultants. Older middle managers whose careers have plateaued can also be good people to listen to, especially to identify risks and problems: not only do they have the experience, but they usually have less self-interest at stake.

● *Aim for consensus, but not at any cost.* Fast decision-makers seek consensus amongst the decision-making team, but do not insist on it. Consensus can be too slow and often leads to mediocre choices based on the lowest common denominator. Fast decision-makers recognise that debates cannot always be resolved to everybody's satisfaction. Eisenhardt's advice is that the Chief Executive or some other senior person should have the courage at a certain point simply to decide. Having had the chance to voice their position, the responsibility of other managers is to accept that decision and to get on with implementation.

However, it is easy to exaggerate both the importance and the effectiveness of decision-making. Many decisions are not followed through with actions. Many strategies are emergent rather than consciously decided (see Chapter 12).

Two widely held views about decision-making have been implicitly challenged so far. First, *intuition* is not always a bad thing.[36] Immersion in real-time information or the long experience of older middle managers can provide a strong 'gut feel' for what should be done. This gut feel can provide the basis for inspired hunches where there are few reliable data to be analysed anyway, for instance in the creation of radically new markets or products. Such intuition can also be beneficial, especially in the idea generation stage of problem solving and in circumstances where fast decisions are needed. Higher levels of intuition are also found more amongst entrepreneurs than the population of managers generally and seem to be related to an orientation towards intentions of organisational growth.[37] Table 15.1 provides suggested guidelines as to how managers might harness and develop their intuitive capabilities.

Second, constructive *conflict* in decision-making teams can be positively useful.[38] Conflict can expose champion's biases. It can challenge optimistic self-assessments of managerial competence. Conflict is fostered by having diverse managerial teams, with members prepared to be devil's advocates, challenging assumptions or easy consensus. But productive conflict needs careful management. Table 15.2 uses the idea of games with rules to summarise ways in which this might be done (also see the discussion on 'organisational ambidexterity' in section 12.4.1).

15.3.4 Communicating the strategy

Deciding strategy is only one step: strategic decisions need to be communicated. Managers have to consider which stakeholders to inform (see Chapter 4) and how they should tailor their messages to each. Shareholders, key customers and employees are likely to be particularly

Table 15.1 Guidelines for developing intuitive capabilities

1. Open up the closet	To what extent do you: experience intuition; trust your feelings; count on intuitive judgements; suppress hunches; covertly rely upon gut feel?
2. Don't mix up your I's!	Instinct, insight and intuition are not synonymous; practise distinguishing between your instincts, your insights, and your intuitions.
3. Elicit good feedback	Seek feedback on your intuitive judgements; build confidence in your gut feel; create a learning environment in which you can develop better intuitive awareness.
4. Get a feel for your batting average	Benchmark your intuitions; get a sense for how reliable your hunches are; ask yourself how your intuitive judgement might be improved.
5. Use imagery	Use imagery rather than words; literally visualise potential future scenarios that take your gut feelings into account.
6. Play devil's advocate	Test out intuitive judgements; raise objections to them; generate counter-arguments; probe how robust gut feel is when challenged.
7. Capture and validate your intuitions	Create the inner state to give your intuitive mind the freedom to roam; capture your creative intuitions; log them before they are censored by rational analysis.

Source: E. Sadler-Smith and E. Shefy, 'The intuitive executive: understanding and applying "gut feel" in decision making', *Academy of Management Executive*, vol. 18, no. 4, pp. 76–91 (2004).

Table 15.2 Managing conflict

Rulebook	• Establish clear behavioural boundaries. • Encourage dissenting voices. • Keep debate professional, not emotional.
Referees	• Ensure the leader is (a) open to differing views, (b) enforces the rules.
Playing field	• Ensure each side of the debate has a chance to win. • Be clear on the basis of resolution (e.g. decision from the top or consensus).
Gaps to exploit	• Does each group have a specific objective to champion?
Relationships	• Ensure individuals (a) deliver on their commitments, (b) behave with integrity. • Ensure leaders throughout the organisation further test perspectives up and down the hierarchy.
Energy levels	• Ensure sufficient tension to promote useful debate, but monitor this. • Do leaders understand what people really care about?
Outcomes	• Ensure leader gives bad news without damaging relationships. • Ensure dignity in losing and risk-taking rewarded.

Source: Reprinted by permission of *Harvard Business Review*. Exhibit from 'How to pick a good fight' by S.A. Joni and D. Beyer, December 2009, pp. 48–57. Copyright © 2009 by the Harvard Business School Publishing Corporation. All rights reserved.

central, all with different needs. For every new strategy, there should be a communications strategy to match. It is also important to remember that communication is a two-way process. Harvard's Michael Beer and Russell A. Eisenstat[39] argue that effective communication needs to involve *both* advocacy of a strategy by senior management and inquiry about the concerns of influential internal and external stakeholders. In the absence of the former, there is lack of clarity, confusion and frustration. In the absence of the latter, concerns will surface in any case, but in ways that actively or passively undermine the new strategy.

As a minimum, effective employee communications are needed to ensure that the strategy is understood. In the absence of this there are two likely consequences:

- *Strategic intent will be reinterpreted.* As the Key Debate in Chapter 12 showed, it is inevitable that people in the organisation will interpret intended strategy in terms of their local context and operational responsibilities.[40] The more such reinterpretation occurs, the more unlikely it is the intended strategy will be implemented.

- *Established routines will continue.* Old habits die hard; so top management may underestimate the need to make very clear what behaviours are expected to deliver a strategy. Of course, effective communication is only one way in which change can be managed; the wider lessons of managing strategic change in this regard need to be taken into account (see Chapter 14).

One example of an organisation seeking high understanding of strategy by all employees is the Volvo Group, where the target is that 90 per cent of employees will be aware of the company's strategic goals, tested by an annual attitude survey.[41]

In shaping a communications strategy for employees, four elements need to be considered in particular:[42]

- *Focus.* Communications should be focused on the key issues that the strategy addresses and the key components of the strategy. If top management cannot show they are clear on these, then it cannot be expected that others will be. If possible it also helps to avoid unnecessary detail or complex language. CEO Jack Welch's famous statement that General Electric should be 'either Number One or Number Two' in all its markets is remembered because of this clear focus on the importance of being a dominant player wherever the company competed.

- *Media.* Choosing appropriate media to convey the new strategy is important.[43] Mass media such as e-mails, voicemails, company newsletters, videos, intranets and senior manager blogs can ensure that all staff receive the same message promptly, helping to avoid damaging uncertainty and rumour-mongering. However, face-to-face communications are important too in order to demonstrate the personal commitment of managers and allow for interaction with concerned staff. So, for example, senior managers may undertake *roadshows*, carrying their message directly to various groups of employees with conferences or workshops at different sites. They may also institute *cascades*, whereby each level of managers is tasked to convey the strategy message directly to the staff reporting to them, who in turn are required to convey the message to their staff, and so on through the organisation. Of course, if this is to be effective, it is essential that the key issues and components of the strategy are clear. Such roadshows and cascades may, of course, also raise new issues and should therefore be part of a two-way communication process.

- *Employee engagement.* If a two-way process of communication is to be achieved, it needs to involve multiple levels of management. Indeed, it is often helpful to engage employees more widely in the communication strategy, so that they can see what it means for them personally and how their role will change. Interchanges through roadshows and cascades can help, but some organisations use imaginative means to create more active engagement. For example, one British public-sector organisation invited all its staff to a day's conference introducing its new strategy, at which employees were invited to pin a photograph of themselves on a 'pledge wall', together with a hand-written promise to change at least one aspect of their work to fit the new strategy.[44] However, employee engagement also means listening to employees. For example, in 2010 Toyota had to recall 5.6 million vehicles in the US alone due to safety defects, so damaging its reputation for reliability. Toyota's top management had apparently ignored warnings of potential problems by its own long-serving factory workers. In 2006 they had sent a two-page memo to the company's president warning that the focus on lowering cost and increasing speed of production was threatening safety standards.[45]

- *Impact.* Communications should be impactful, with powerful and memorable words and visuals. A strong 'story-line' can help by encapsulating the journey ahead and imagined new futures for the organisation and its customers. One struggling medical centre in New Mexico communicated its new strategy, and inspired its staff, with a story-line representing the organisation as 'The Raiders of the Lost Art', conveying a simultaneous sense of courage in adversity and recovery of old values.[46]

15.3.5 The messiness of everyday strategising

There is a danger of seeing strategising as part of a neat, linear process driven by management rationality. Chapter 12 made it clear that this is not always so; that there are multiple processes at work that contribute to the development of strategy. There may be careful analysis and design of strategy communications, but these go hand in hand with more everyday practices. Senior executives do meet over lunch or coffee and discuss strategic issues. Managers spend most of their time in face-to-face, telephone and increasingly e-mail discussion with other managers. A large proportion of face-to-face contact is in meetings. Some of these may be formally designated as strategy meetings; but in others that are not, issues with strategic implications will arise and be discussed. As sections 12.3.2 and 12.3.4 explained, in such settings, strategic issues and solutions may arise on the basis of organisational politics and as the product of organisational systems. In such circumstances, centrally important to managers is their political acumen within their network of contacts, their ability to use persuasive language[47] and also their ability to build coherent narratives of strategy from the often fragmented discussions that take place and views that get aired.[48]

 ## STRATEGY METHODOLOGIES

Strategists may use a range of methodologies to organise and guide their strategising activity. The methodologies introduced here are not analytical concepts or techniques such as in most of the rest of the book, but approaches to managing the strategising process. These could include strategy workshops (or 'away-days') and strategy projects. Projects may be driven by hypothesis-testing techniques. Finally, strategising output typically has to fit the format of a business case or strategic plan. This section introduces key issues in each of these methodologies.

15.4.1 Strategy workshops

Strategy workshops (sometimes called strategy away-days or off-sites) are a common methodology for making strategy.[49] These workshops usually **involve groups of executives working intensively for one or two days, often away from the office, on organisational strategy**. Such executives are typically senior managers in the organisation, although workshops can also be a valuable mechanism for involving a wider group of managers. Workshops are used typically to formulate or reconsider strategy, but also to review the progress of current strategy, address strategy implementation issues and to communicate strategic decisions to a larger audience. Workshops can be either ad hoc or part of the regular strategic planning process, and they may be stand-alone or designed as a series of events. As well as facilitating strategy-making, workshops can have additional roles in team-building and the personal development of individual participant. Illustration 15.4 shows how they can contribute to strategy development as well as how they can go wrong.

Strategy workshops can be a valuable part of an organisation's strategy-making activity. Research suggests, however, that their form can influence the nature of participants' debate of strategy and its likely success;[50] so their design matters. First, whatever the purpose of the workshop is, clarity of that purpose is strongly correlated with perceived success.[51] Given this, if the purpose is to *question existing strategy or develop new strategy* successful workshops are likely to involve:

- *Strategy concepts and tools* likely to promote questioning of the current strategy.

- *A specialist facilitator to* guide participants in the use of such tools and concepts, free managers to concentrate on the discussion, help keep the discussion focused on the strategic issues and ensure participants contribute equally to discussion.

- *The visible support of the workshop sponsor* (perhaps the CEO) for the questioning and the facilitator. In the absence of this the workshop is unlikely to succeed.[52]

- *The diminishing of everyday functional and hierarchical roles.* This may be aided by a distinctive off-site location to signal how different from everyday routine the workshop is, help detach participants from day-to-day operational issues and symbolically affirm the occasion is not subject to the usual norms of executive team discussion. Ice-breaking and other apparently playful exercises – sometimes called 'serious play'– at the beginning of a workshop can help generate creativity and a willingness to challenge orthodoxies.[53]

On the other hand, workshops with the purpose of *reviewing the progress of current strategy* are likely to be successful if they have a more operational agenda and if participants maintain functional and hierarchical roles.

Workshops are, however, prone to at least two problems. First, if the purpose is to encourage questioning, there is the danger that the structure of the workshop, or the absence of support of the workshop sponsor, fails to do this, such that participants simply draw on their existing preconceptions. Especially when reduced to a routine part of the strategic planning cycle, and involving the usual group of senior managers, workshops may not be able to produce new ideas that significantly challenge the status quo.[54] Second, workshops can become detached from subsequent action. Precisely because they are separated from the ordinary routines of the organisation, it can be difficult to translate workshop ideas and enthusiasm back into the workplace.

ILLUSTRATION 15.4

A tale of two workshops

How strategy workshops are designed is a significant influence on their success.

Given the growth of the business the directors of Hotelco* decided to hold two two-day workshops to re-think the organisational structure needed for the company's future strategic direction. Both workshops were facilitated by an external consultant.

Workshop 1

The first workshop was held in a luxury rural hotel in the South of England far away from Hotelco's modest offices. This was not just to 'get away from the office', but also because: 'It freed up the mind . . . It was a great experience'.

Together with one of the directors, the facilitator had organised the agenda. The 'command style' of the CEO was replaced by a participative approach orchestrated by the facilitator: 'He made it a more level playing field'. He had interviewed staff about the core values of the business and provided a report to the directors as a basis for the discussion: 'Does everyone know what Hotelco stands for?'

The directors became genuinely engaged with the discussion: 'It focused our minds. It made us all understand the things we were good at and . . . the things we were weak at and what we needed to do.' They regarded the workshop as a success, concluding that a change was needed from an authoritarian, command management style to a more structured and devolved approach to management, with responsibility being passed to middle levels, so freeing up the top team to focus more on strategy.

This outcome was not, however, carried forward. On their return to the office, the directors came to the conclusion that what was agreed during the workshop was unrealistic, that they were 'carried away with the process'. The result was significant back-tracking but without a clear consensus on a revised structure for the business.

Workshop 2

The second two-day workshop, two months later, was for the top team and their seven direct reports

and used the same facilitator. It took place in one of the group's own hotels. Again the workshop began with a discussion of the interviews on Hotelco's values. One of the directors then made a presentation raising the idea of an operational board. However, in discussion it emerged that the directors were not uniformly committed to this – especially the CEO. Eventually, as the facilitator explained:

> 'I had to sit the four directors in another room and say: look, until you sort this out; you're just going to create problems. . . . The four directors got into a heated argument and forgot about the other seven.'

This was not, however, how the directors saw it. Their view was that the facilitator was seeking to impose a solution rather than facilitate discussion.

With the directors in one room and the direct reports in another, the comments of each group were transmitted between rooms by the facilitator. It was a situation that satisfied no one. In the afternoon the CEO intervened, replacing the idea of a seven person 'operational board' with an intermediary level of three 'divisional directors'.

No one was content with the workshop. One of the seven who was not to be a divisional director commented: 'I didn't know where I sat any more. I felt my job had been devalued.' A director also recognised: 'We left these people feeling really deflated.'

* Hotelco is a pseudonym for a small UK hotel group.

Questions

1 Evaluate the design of the two workshops in terms of the guidelines in section 15.4.1.

2 If you were a facilitator, how would you have organised the workshops differently?

3 What benefits (or disadvantages) might such workshops have in comparison with other approaches to strategy development for such an organisation?

In designing workshops that will be closely connected to subsequent action, managers should consider:

- *Identifying agreed actions* to be taken. Time should be set aside at the end of the workshop for a review of workshop outputs and agreement on necessary actions to follow up. However this, of itself, may well not make a sufficiently powerful bridge to operational realities.
- *Establishing project groups.* Workshops can build on the cohesion built around particular issues by commissioning groups of managers to work together on specific tasks arising from the workshop and report on progress to senior management.
- *Nesting of workshops.* Especially if a workshop has expected participants to question current strategy and develop radical new ideas, it may be useful to have a series of workshops, each of which gradually becomes more and more grounded in operational realities.
- *Making visible commitment by the top management.* The chief executive or other senior manager needs to signal commitment to the outcomes of the workshop not only by their statements but by their actual behaviours.

15.4.2 Strategy projects

Both strategy-making and strategy implementation are often organised in the form of projects or task forces.[55] **Strategy projects involve teams of people assigned to work on particular strategic issues over a defined period of time.** Projects can be instituted in order to explore problems or opportunities as part of the strategy development process. Or they might be instituted to implement agreed elements of a strategy, for example an organisational restructuring or the negotiation of a joint venture. Translating a strategic plan or workshop outcomes into a set of projects is a good means of ensuring that intentions are translated into action. They can also include a wider group of managers in strategy activity.

Strategy projects should be managed like any other project. In particular they need:[56]

- *A clear brief or mandate.* The project's objectives should be agreed and carefully managed. These objectives are the measure of the project's success. 'Scope creep', by which additional objectives are added as the project goes on, is a common danger.
- *Top management commitment.* The continuing commitment of top management, especially the top management 'client' or 'sponsor', needs to be maintained. Top management agendas are frequently shifting, so communications should be regular.
- *Milestones and reviews.* The project should have from the outset clear milestones with an agreed schedule of intermediate achievements. These allow project review and adjustment where necessary, as well as a measure of ongoing success.
- *Appropriate resources.* The key resource is usually people. The right mix of skills needs to be in place, including project management skills, and effort should be invested in 'team-building' at the outset. Strategy projects are often part-time commitments for managers, who have to continue with their 'day jobs'. Attention needs to be paid to managing the balance between managers' ordinary responsibilities and project duties: the first can easily derail the second.

Projects can easily proliferate and compete. Programme managers should manage overlaps and redundancies, merging or ending projects that no longer have a distinct purpose because of changing circumstances. Senior management should have careful oversight of the whole portfolio, and again be ready to merge and end projects or even programmes, in order to prevent the 'initiative fatigue' that is often the result of project proliferation.

15.4.3 Hypothesis testing

Strategy project teams are typically under pressure to deliver solutions to complex problems under tight time constraints. **Hypothesis testing is a methodology used particularly in strategy projects for setting priorities in investigating issues and options** and is widely used by strategy consulting firms and members of strategy project teams.

Hypothesis testing in strategy is adapted from the hypothesis testing procedures of science.[57] It starts with a proposition about how things are (*the descriptive hypothesis*), and then seeks to test it with real-world data. For example, a descriptive hypothesis in strategy could be that being large-scale in a particular industry is essential to profitability. To test it, a strategy project team would begin by gathering data on the size of organisations in the industry and correlate these with the organisations' profitability. Confirmation of this initial descriptive hypothesis (i.e. small organisations are relatively unprofitable) would then lead to several *prescriptive hypotheses* about what a particular organisation should do. For a small-scale organisation in the industry, prescriptive hypotheses would centre on how to increase scale: one prescriptive hypothesis in this case would be that acquisitions were a good means to achieve the necessary scale; another would be that alliances were the right way. These prescriptive hypotheses might then become the subjects of further data testing.

This kind of hypothesis testing is ultimately about setting practical priorities in strategy work. Hypothesis testing in business therefore differs from strict scientific procedure (see Illustration 15.5). The aim finally is to concentrate attention on a very limited set of promising hypotheses, not on the full set of all possibilities. Data are gathered in order to support favoured hypotheses, whereas in science the objective is formally to try to refute hypotheses. Business hypothesis testing aims to find a robust and satisfactory solution within time and resource constraints, not to find some ultimate scientific truth. Selecting the right hypotheses can be helped by applying *Quick and Dirty Testing* (QDT). Quick and Dirty Testing relies on the project team's existing experience and easily accessed data in order to speedily reject unpromising hypotheses, before too much time is wasted on them.

15.4.4 Business cases and strategic plans

Strategising activities, such as workshops or projects, are typically oriented towards creating an output in the form of a *business case* or *strategic plan*. Keeping this end goal in mind provides a structure for the strategising work: what needs to be produced shapes the strategising activities. A **business case** usually **provides the data and argument in support of a particular strategy proposal, e.g. investment in new equipment.** A **strategic plan** **provides the data and argument in support of a strategy for the whole organisation.** It is therefore likely to be more comprehensive, taking an overall view of the organisation's direction over a substantial period of time. Many organisations have a standard template for making business cases or proposing a strategic plan, and where these exist, it is wise to work with that format. Where there is no standard template, it is worth investigating recent successful business cases or plans within the organisation, and borrowing features from them.

A project team intending to make a business case should aim to meet the following criteria:[58]

ILLUSTRATION 15.5

Hypothesis testing at a bank

This outline of a consulting engagement for a large, diversified bank shows how the hypothesis testing process can shape a strategy project.

1 Defining the problem/question

The consultants' first step is to define the problem. As usual, the strategic problem has to do with the existence of a gap between what the client wants (here a certain level of profitability for a particular product) and what it has (declining profitability). In short, the consultants' problem is that the bank's profitability for this product is below target levels.

2 Develop a set of competing descriptive hypotheses about problem causes

The consultants gather some preliminary data and draw on their own experience to generate some possible descriptive hypotheses about the causes of the problem. Thus they know that some large national competitors are already exiting from this type of product; that profitability varies dramatically across competitors involved in this product; and that some specialised new entrants have taken significant market share. Three possible hypotheses emerge: that the industry structure is basically unattractive; that the bank lacks the right strategic capabilities; that the bank is targeting the wrong customer segments. The consultants use quick and dirty testing to reject the first two hypotheses: after all, some competitors are making profits and the bank has strong capabilities from long presence in this product area. Accordingly, the starting descriptive hypothesis is that the bank is targeting unprofitable customer segments.

3 Testing the starting descriptive hypothesis

The consultants next design a study to collect the data needed to support the descriptive hypothesis. They carry out a market segmentation analysis by customer group by doing interviews with customers across different geographies and income levels. They analyse the kinds of service different segments require and the fees they might pay. The consultants find that their data supports their starting hypothesis: the bank's branches are concentrated in locations which prosperous customers willing to pay higher fees for this product do not use. (Had they not been able to confirm their hypothesis, the consultants would

have returned to the other two competing hypotheses, step 2.)

4 Develop prescriptive hypotheses

The consultants then develop prescriptive hypotheses about actions necessary to attract more profitable customer segments. One prescriptive hypothesis is that a better portfolio of branch locations will enhance profitability. The consultants carry out data gathering and analysis to support this hypothesis, for example comparing the profitability of branches in different kinds of locations. They find that the few branches that happen to be in the right locations do have higher profitability with this product.

5 Make recommendations to the client

The consultants prepare a set of preliminary recommendations based on the descriptive hypothesis and validated prescriptive hypotheses: one of these is that the branch locations need changing. These recommendations are checked for acceptability and feasability with key managers within the bank and adjusted according to feedback. Then the consultants make their formal presentation of final recommendations.

Source: Jeanne Liedtka, Darden School of Management, University of Virginia.

Questions

1 Select an important strategic issue facing an organisation that you are familiar with (or an organisation that is publicly in trouble or a case study organisation). Try generating a few descriptive hypotheses that address this issue. Use quick and dirty testing to select an initial descriptive hypothesis.

2 What data should you gather to confirm this descriptive hypothesis and how would you collect it? Should the descriptive hypothesis be confirmed, what possible prescriptive hypotheses follow?

- *Focus on strategic needs.* The team should identify the organisation's overall strategy and relate its case closely to that, not just to any particular departmental needs. A business case should not look as if it is just an HR department or IT department project, for example. The focus should be on a few key issues, with clear priority normally given to those that are both strategically important and relatively easy to address.

- *Supported by key data.* The team will need to assemble appropriate data, with financial data demonstrating appropriate returns on any investment typically essential. However, qualitative data should not be neglected – for example, striking quotations from interviews with employees or key customers, or recent mini-cases of successes or failures in the organisation or at competitors. Some strategic benefits simply cannot be quantified, but are not the less important for that: information on competitor moves can be persuasive here. The team should provide background information on the rigour and extent of the research behind the data.

- *Provide a clear rationale.* Analysis and data are not enough; make it clear *why* the proposals are being made. The reasons for the choice of recommendations therefore need to be explicit. Many specific evaluation techniques that can be useful in a business cases are explained in Chapter 11.

- *Demonstrate solutions and actions.* As suggested earlier, issues attached to solutions tend to get the most attention. The team should show how what is proposed will be acted on, and who will be responsible. Possible barriers should be clearly identified. Also recognise alternative scenarios, especially downside risk. Implementation feasibility is critical.

- *Provide clear progress measures.* When seeking significant investments over time, it is reassuring to offer clear measures to allow regular progress monitoring. Proposing review mechanisms also adds credibility to the business case.

Strategic plans have similar characteristics in terms of focus, data, actions and progress measures. Strategic plans are, however, more comprehensive, and they may be used for entrepreneurial start-ups, business units within a large organisation, or for an organisation as a whole. Again formats vary. However, a typical strategic plan has the following elements, which together should set a strategy team's working agenda:[59]

- *Mission, goals and objectives statement.* This is the point of the whole strategy, and the critical starting place. While it is the starting place, in practice a strategy team might iterate back to this in the light of other elements of the strategic plan. It is worth checking back with earlier statements that the organisation may have made to ensure consistency. Section 4.2 provides more guidance on mission, goals and objectives.

- *Environmental analysis.* This should cover the key issues identified in terms of the whole of the environment, both macro trends and more focused issues to do with customers, suppliers and competitors. The team should not stop at the analysis, but draw clear strategic implications. (See Chapter 2.)

- *Capability analysis.* This should include a clear identification of the key strengths and weaknesses of the organisation and its products relative to its competitors and include a clear statement of competitive advantage. (See Chapter 3.)

- *Proposed strategy.* This should be clearly related to the environmental and organisational analyses and support the mission, goals and objectives. It should also make clear options that have been considered and why the proposed strategy is preferred. Particularly useful here are Chapters 6 to 11.

KEY DEBATE

What good are strategy consultants?

Strategy consultants are frequent participants in strategy making, and typically bring good analytical and project management skills. Why are they so controversial then?

There is no shortage of books criticising strategy consultants. Titles such as *Con Tricks*, *Dangerous Company* and *Rip Off!* provide the flavour. And there have been some spectacular failures. As in section 15.2.4, McKinsey & Co. took a good deal of blame for the strategic mistakes of Enron and Swissair.

The accusations made against strategy consultants are at least three-fold. First, they rely too much on inexperienced young staff fresh out of business school, who typically have the slimmest understanding of how client organisations and their markets really work. Second, they are accused of handing over strategy recommendations, and then walking away from implementation. Third, they are perceived as expensive, overpaid individually and always trying to sell on unnecessary extra projects. Clients end up paying for more advice than they really need, much of it unrealistic and unimplementable.

These accusations may be unfair. Most large strategy consulting firms are now organised on industry lines, so building up expertise in particular areas, and they increasingly recruit experienced managers from these industries. Most consultants also prefer to work in joint client–advisor teams, so that clients are involved in generating the recommendations that they will have to implement. Some consultancies, such as Bain, make a point of getting closely involved in implementation too. Finally, consultants are in a competitive market and their clients are typically sophisticated buyers, not easily fooled into buying advice they do not need: the fact that strategy consulting business increased in Europe from €3bn (~$4.2bn) in 1996 to €8bn in 2004 suggests there is plenty of real demand.

There are some successes too. Bain claims that, since 1980, its clients' stock prices have on average outperformed the Standard & Poor's 500 large American companies index by four to one (www.bain.com). Some great corporate managers have originated in strategy consulting: Lou Gerstner, who turned around IBM, and Meg Whitman, leader of eBay, both started as McKinsey & Co. strategy consultants. And one of the world's most influential management books ever, *The Concept of the Corporation*, came from Peter Drucker's consulting assignment with General Motors during World War II.

There are clues to managing strategy consultants in the criticisms, however: for example, make sure to hire consultants with relevant experience; connect analysis to implementation; and keep a close eye on expenditure. James O'Shea and Charles Madigan close their book with a provocative quotation from Machiavelli's *The Prince*: 'Here is an infallible rule: a prince who is not himself wise cannot be wisely advised. . . . Good advice depends on the shrewdness of the prince who seeks it, and not the shrewdness of the prince on good advice.'

Sources: The European Federation of Management Consultancy Associations (www.feaco.org); J. O'Shea and C. Madigan, *Dangerous Company: Consulting Powerhouses and the Businesss they Save and Ruin*, Penguin, 1998; C.D. McKenna, *The World's Newest Profession: Management Consulting in the Twentieth Century*, Cambridge University Press, 2006.

Questions

1 What measures can a strategy consultant take to reassure a potential client of his or her effectiveness?

2 Are there any reasons to suspect that some people might want to exaggerate criticisms of strategy consultants' conduct?

- *Resources*. The team will need to provide a detailed analysis of the resources required, with options for acquiring them. Critical resources are financial, so the plan should include income statements, cash flows and balance sheets over the period of the plan. Other important resources might be human, particularly managers or people with particular skills. A clear and realistic timetable for implementation is also needed.

- *Key changes*. What does the plan envisage are the key changes required in structures, systems and culture and how are these to be managed? Chapters 13 and 14 are most relevant here.

SUMMARY

- The practice of strategy involves critical choices about *who to involve* in strategy, *what to do* in strategising activity, and *which strategising methodologies* to use in order to guide this activity.

- Chief executive officers, senior managers, non-executive directors, strategic planners, strategy consultants and middle managers are all involved in strategising. Their degree of appropriate involvement should depend on the nature of the strategic issues.

- Strategising activity can involves *analysing*, *issue-selling*, *decision-making* and *communicating*. Managers should not expect these activities to be fully rational or logical and can valuably appeal to the non-rational characteristics of the people they work with.

- Practical methodologies to guide strategising activity include *strategy workshops*, *strategy projects*, *hypothesis testing*, and creating *business cases* and *strategic plans*.

WORK ASSIGNMENTS

✳ *Denotes more advanced work assignments. * Refers to a case study in the Text and Cases edition.*

15.1 Go to the careers or recruitment web page of one of the big strategy consultants (such as www.bain.com, www.bcg.com, www.mckinsey.com). What does this tell you about the nature of strategy consulting work? Would you like this work?

15.2 Go to the website of a large organisation (private or public-sector) and assess the way it communicates its strategy to its audiences. With reference to section 15.3.4, how focused is the communication; how impactful is it; and how likely is it to engage employees?

15.3 If you had to design a strategy workshop, suggest who the participants in the workshop should be and what roles they should play in (a) the case where an organisation has to re-examine its fundamental strategy in the face of increased competitive threat; (b) the case where an organisation needs to gain commitment to a long-term, comprehensive programme of strategic change.

15.4✳ For any case study in the book, imagine yourself in the position of a strategy consultant and propose an initial descriptive hypothesis (section 15.4.3) and define the kinds of data that you would need to test it. What kinds of people would you want in your strategy project team (see sections 15.2.5 and 15.4.2)?

15.5✳ Go to a business plan archive (such as the University of Maryland's www.businessplanarchive.org or use a Google search). Select a business plan of interest to you and, in the light of section 15.4.4, assess its good points and its bad points.

Integrative assignment

15.6✳ For an organisation with which you are familiar, or one of the case organisations, write a strategic plan (for simplicity, you might choose to focus on an undiversified business or a business unit within a larger corporation). Where data are missing, make reasonable assumptions or propose ways of filling the gaps. Comment on whether and how you would provide different versions of this strategic plan for (a) investors; (b) employees.

RECOMMENDED KEY READINGS

- For an overview of top management involvement in strategy, see P. Stiles and B. Taylor, *Boards at Work: How Directors View their Roles and Responsibilities*, Oxford University Press, 2001. For an overview of the middle management role, see S. Floyd and B. Wooldridge, *Building Strategy from the Middle*, Sage, 2000.

- For an explanation of the role of strategic planners, see D. Angwin, S. Paroutis and S. Mitson, 'Connecting up strategy; are senior strategy directors a missing link?', *California Management Review*, vol. 51, no. 3 (2009), pp. 74–94.

- *Strategy as Practice*, by Gerry Johnson, Ann Langley, Leif Melin and Richard Whittington (Cambridge University Press, 2007) provides examples of academic studies of strategy practice, as do three journal special issues: the 'Micro strategy and strategizing', *Journal of Management Studies*, vol. 40, no. 1 (2003); 'Strategizing: the challenges of a practice perspective', *Human Relations*, vol. 60, no. 1 (2007); and R. Whittington and L. Cailluet, 'The crafts of strategy', *Long Range Planning* (Special Issue, June 2008).

- A practical guide to strategising methodologies is provided by E. Rasiel and P.N. Friga (2001), *The McKinsey Mind*, which has much more general relevance than that particular consulting firm.

REFERENCES

1. A theoretical basis for this pyramid can be found in R. Whittington, 'Completing the practice turn in strategy research', *Organization Studies*, vol. 27, no. 5 (2006), pp. 613–34 and P. Jarzabkowski, J. Balogun and D. Seidl, 'Strategizing: the challenges of a practice perspective', *Human Relations*, vol. 60, no. 1 (2007), pp. 5–27.

2. The classic statement is A. Chandler, *Strategy and Structure: Chapters in the History of American Enterprise*, MIT Press, 1962.

3. S. Kaplan and E. Beinhocker, 'The real value of strategic planning', *MIT Sloan Management Review*, Winter 2003, pp. 71–6.

4. M.E. Porter, 'What is strategy?', *Harvard Business Review*, November–December 1996, pp. 61–78.

5. M. Haywood and D. Hambrick, 'Explaining the premium paid for large acquisitions: evidence of CEO hubris', *Administrative Science Quarterly*, vol. 42, no. 1 (1977), pp. 103–28.

6. J. Collins, *Good to Great*, Random House, 2001.

7. I. Janis, *Victims of Groupthink: a Psychological Study of Foreign-Policy Decisions and Fiascoes*, Houghton Mifflin, 1972; R.S. Baron, 'So right it's wrong: groupthink and the ubiquitous nature of polarized group decision making', in Mark P. Zanna (ed.), *Advances in Experimental Social Psychology*, vol. 37, pp. 219–53, Elsevier Academic Press, 2005.

8. E. Beinhocker and S. Kaplan, 'Tired of strategic planning?', *McKinsey Quarterly*, special edition on Risk and Resilience (2002), pp. 49–57; S. Kaplan and E. Beinhocker, 'The real value of strategic planning', *MIT Sloan Management Review*, Winter 2003, pp. 71–6.

9. R.S. Kaplan and D.P. Norton, 'The office of strategy management', *Harvard Business Review*, October 2005, pp. 72–80.

10. D. Angwin, S. Paroutis and S. Mitson, 'Connecting up strategy; are senior strategy directors a missing link?', *California Management Review*, vol. 51, no. 3 (2009), pp. 74–94.

11. See A. Chandler (reference 2).

12. G. Johnson, L. Melin and R. Whittington, 'Micro-strategy and strategising: towards an activity-based view', *Journal of Management Studies*, vol. 40, no. 1 (2003), pp. 3–22.

13. S. Floyd and W. Wooldridge, *The Strategic Middle Manager: How to Create and Sustain Competitive Advantage*, Jossey-Bass, 1996 and S. Mantere, 'Role expectations and middle manager strategic agency', *Journal of Management Studies*, vol. 45, no. 2 (2008), pp. 294–316.

14. See for example J. Balogun and G. Johnson: 'Organizational restructuring and middle manager sensemaking', *Academy of Management Journal*, August 2004; J. Balogun, 'Managing change: steering a course between intended strategies and unanticipated outcomes', *Long Range Planning*, vol. 39 (2006), pp. 29–49.

15. A. Watson and B. Wooldridge, 'Business unit manager influence on corporate-level strategy formulation', *Journal of Managerial Issues*, vol. 18, no. 2 (2005), pp. 147–61.

16. S. Floyd and B. Wooldridge, 'Middle management's strategic influence and organizational performance', *Journal of Management Studies*, vol. 34, no. 3 (1997), pp. 465–85.

17. S. Mantere 'Strategic practices as enablers and disablers of championing activity', *Strategic Organization*, vol. 3, no. 2 (2005), pp. 157–84.

18. F. Westley, 'Middle managers and strategy: micro-dynamics of inclusion', *Strategic Management Journal*, vol. 11 (1990), pp. 337–51.

19. See D. Moyniham, 'Ambiguity in policy lessons: the agentification experience', *Public Administration*, vol. 84, no. 4 (2006), pp. 1029–50 and L.S. Oakes, B. Townley and D.J. Cooper, 'Business planning as pedagogy: language and control in a changing institutional field', *Administrative Science Quarterly*, vol. 43, no. 2 (1997), pp. 257–92.

20. The websites of the leading strategy consultants are useful sources of information on strategy consulting and strategy in general, as well as strategy consulting careers: see www.mckinsey.com; www.bcg.com; www.bain.com; www.monitor.com.

21. For theoretical discussion of advisers in strategy, see L. Arendt, R. Priem and H. Ndofor, 'A CEO-adviser model of strategic decision-making', *Journal of Management*, vol. 31, no. 5 (2005), pp. 680–99.

22. C.D. McKenna, *The World's Newest Profession*, Cambridge University Press, 2006; R. Whittington, P. Jarzabkowski, M. Mayer, E. Mounoud, J. Nahapiet and L. Rouleau, 'Taking strategy seriously: responsibility and reform for an important social practice', *Journal of Management Inquiry*, vol. 12, no. 4 (2003), pp. 396–409.

23. 'Whitehall spending on consultants rises', *Daily Telegraph*, 22 February 2010.

24. S. Appelbaum, 'Critical success factors in the client-consulting relationship', *Journal of the American Academy of Business* (March 2004), pp. 184–91; M. Mohe, 'Generic strategies for managing consultants: insights from client companies in Germany', *Journal of Change Management*, vol. 5, no. 3 (2005), pp. 357–65.

25. E. Beinhocker and S. Kaplan (reference 8) Figure 2, p. 56.

26. P. Jarzabkowski, M. Giulietti and B. Oliveira, 'Building a strategy toolkit: lessons from business', AIM Executive briefing, 2009. Also see G. Hodgkinson, R. Whittington, G. Johnson and M. Schwarz, 'The role of strategy workshops in strategy development processes: formality, communication, coordination and inclusion', *Long Range Planning*, vol. 30 (2006), pp. 479–96.

27. T. Hill and R. Westbrook, 'SWOT analysis: it's time for a product recall', *Long Range Planning*, vol. 30, no. 1 (1997), pp. 46–52.

28. A. Langley, 'Between paralysis by analysis and extinction by instinct', *Sloan Management Review*, vol. 36, no. 3 (1995), pp. 63–76.

29. A. Langley, 'In search of rationality: the purposes behind the use of formal analysis in organisations', *Administrative Science Quarterly*, vol. 34 (1989), pp. 598–631.

30. This draws on the attention-based view of the firm: see W. Ocasio and J. Joseph, 'An attention-based theory of strategy formulation: linking micro and macro perspectives in strategy processes', *Advances in Strategic Management*, vol. 22 (2005), pp. 39–62.

31. For an insightful analysis of the role of mealtimes and other informal moments to influence strategy, see A. Sturdy, M. Schwarz and A. Spicer, 'Guess who's coming to dinner? Structures and the use of liminality in strategic management consultancy', *Human Relations*, vol. 10, no. 7 (2006), pp. 929–60.

32. B. Yakis and R. Whittington, 'Sustaining strategic issues: five longitudinal cases in human resource management', paper to the *Academy of Management*, Philadelphia, 2007.

33. D. Lovallo and O. Siboney, 'Distortions and deceptions in strategic decisions', *McKinsey Quarterly*, no. 1 (2006). A good review of decision-making biases is in G. Hodgkinson and P. Sparrow, *The Competent Organization*, Open University Press, 2002.

34. K.M. Eisenhardt, 'Speed and strategic choice: how managers accelerate decision making', *California Management Review*, Spring 1990, pp. 39–54.

35. M. Mankins, 'Stop wasting valuable time', *Harvard Business Review*, September 2004, pp. 58–65.

36. C. Miller and R.D. Ireland, 'Intuition in strategic decision-making: friend or foe in the fast-paced 21 century?', *Academy of Management Executive*, vol. 21, no. 1 (2005), pp. 19–30.

37. G.P. Hodgkinson, E. Sadler-Smith, L.A. Burke, G. Claxton and P.R. Sparrow, 'Intuition in organizations: implications for strategic management', *Long Range Planning*, vol. 42, no. 3 (2009), pp. 277–97.

38. K.M. Eisenhardt, J. Kahwajy and L.J. Bourgeois, 'Conflict and strategic choice: how top teams disagree', *California Management Review*, vol. 39, no. 2 (1997), pp. 42–62. Also R.A. Burgelman and A.S. Grove, 'Let chaos reign, then rein in chaos – repeatedly: managing strategic dynamics for corporate longevity', *Strategic Management Journal*, vol. 28 (2007), pp. 965–79.

39. M. Beer and R.A. Eisenstat, 'How to have an honest conversation', *Harvard Business Review*, vol. 82, no. 2 (2004), pp. 82–9.

40. See J. Balogun and G. Johnson (reference 14).

41. C. Nordblom, 'Involving middle managers in strategy at Volvo Group', *Strategic Communication Management*, vol. 10, no. 2 (2006), pp. 24–8.

42. This builds on M. Thatcher, 'Breathing life into business strategy', *Strategic Communication Management*, vol. 10, no. 2 (2006), pp. 14–18. Also Beer and Eisenstat (see reference 39 above).

43. R.H. Lengel and R.L. Daft, 'The selection of communication media as an executive skill', *Academy of Management Executive*, vol. 2, no. 3 (1988), pp. 225–32.

44. R. Whittington, E. Molloy, M. Mayer and A. Smith, 'Practices of strategizing/organizing: broadening strategy work and skills', *Long Range Planning*, vol. 39 (2006), pp. 615–29.

45. 'The Toyota way is famous. In reality it is to ignore warnings from within the firm', *The Times*, 12 March 2010, p. 55.

46. G. Adamson, J. Pine, T. van Steenhoven and J. Kroupa, 'How story-telling can drive strategic change', *Strategy and Leadership*, vol. 34, no. 1 (2006), pp. 36–41.

47. See D. Samra-Fredericks, 'Strategizing as lived experience and strategists' everyday efforts to shape strategic direction', *Journal of Management Studies*, vol 42, no. 1 (2003), pp. 1413–42.

48. J.D. Ford, 'Organizational change as shifting conversations', *Journal of Strategic Change*, vol. 12, no. 6 (1999), pp. 480–500.

49. For a survey of strategy workshops in practice, see G. Hodgkinson, R. Whittington, G. Johnson and M. Schwarz, 'The role of strategy workshops in strategy development processes: formality, communication, coordination and inclusion', *Long Range Planning*, vol. 30 (2006) pp. 479–96.

50. This is based on research by G. Johnson, S. Prashantham, S. Floyd and N. Bourque, 'The ritualization of strategy workshops', *Organization Studies*, forthcoming.

51. G. Hodgkinson et al. (see reference 49).

52. For a discussion of a failed strategy workshop from different points of view, see G. Hodgkinson and G. Wright, 'Confronting strategic inertia in a top management team: learning from failure', *Organization Studies*, vol. 23, no. 6 (2002), pp. 949–78 and R. Whittington, 'Completing the practice turn in strategy research', *Organization Studies*, vol. 27, no. 5 (2006), pp. 613–34.

53. L. Heracleous and C. Jacobs, 'The serious business of play', *MIT Quarterly*, Fall 2005, pp. 19–20.

54. C. Bowman, 'Strategy workshops and top-team commitment to strategic change', *Journal of Managerial Psychology*, vol. 10, no. 8 (1995), pp. 4–12; B. Frisch and L. Chandler, 'Off-sites that work', *Harvard Business Review*, vol. 84, no. 6 (2006), pp. 117–26.

55. P. Morris and A. Jamieson, 'Moving from corporate strategy to project strategy', *Project Management Journal*, vol. 36, no. 4 (2005), pp. 5–18. A comparative study of strategy project development teams is in F. Blackler, N. Crump and S. McDonald, 'Organizing processes in complex activity networks', *Organization*, vol. 72, no. 2 (2000), pp. 277–300.

56. H. Sirkin, P. Keenan and A. Jackson, 'The hard side of change management', *Harvard Business Review*, October 2005, pp. 109–18; J. Kenny, 'Effective project management for strategic innovation and change in an organizational context', *Project Management Journal*, vol. 34, no. 1 (2003), pp. 43–53.

57. This section draws on E. Rasiel and P.N. Friga, *The McKinsey Mind*, McGraw-Hill, 2001, H. Courtney, *20/20 Foresight: Crafting Strategy in an Uncertain World*, 2001, and unpublished material from J. Liedtka, University of Virginia.

58. J. Walker, 'Is your business case compelling?', *Human Resource Planning*, vol. 25, no. 1 (2002), pp. 12–15; M. Pratt, 'Seven steps to a business case', *Computer World*, 10 October 2005, pp. 35–6.

59. Useful books on writing a business plan include: C. Barrow, P. Barrow and R. Brown, *The Business Plan Workbook*, Kogan Page, 2008 and A.R. DeThomas and S.A. Derammelaan, *Writing a Convincing Business Plan*, Barron's Business Library, 2008.

CASE EXAMPLE

Ray Ozzie, software strategist

During 2005 and 2006, Ray Ozzie took an increasingly important strategic role at the computer software giant Microsoft, finally emerging as the company's Chief Software Architect. At the centre of Ozzie's new strategy was the endeavour to 'webify' Microsoft, widely perceived to have fallen behind Internet upstarts such as Google and Yahoo!. Developing this new strategy involved more than formulating a bold and challenging new vision for Microsoft. Ozzie faced difficult decisions even in the sheer practicalities of strategy making. Thus Ozzie had to design a top management strategy retreat; he had to find a way of maintaining the momentum after that retreat; and finally, he had to decide how best to communicate the key themes of the emerging new strategy.

Ozzie was regarded by many experts as a software genius. In 1984 he had founded Iris Associates, which five years later launched, under contract for the Lotus Development Corporation, the first commercial e-mail and collaboration software for major corporations, Lotus Notes. Lotus Development Corporation bought Iris for $84m (~€59m) in 1994, and the next year computer giant IBM in turn bought Lotus. Three years later, Ozzie left IBM to found Groove Networks, another collaboration software company. In March 2005, Microsoft bought Groove Networks in order to integrate its collaboration features into the next generation of its Office products. Ozzie joined Microsoft as a new employee.

What Microsoft paid for Groove Networks was undisclosed, but it certainly made Ozzie an even wealthier man. In other respects, however, Ozzie's position was not so comfortable. Ozzie's starting position was as only one of three chief technology officers at Microsoft, a company with 70,000 employees. Initially he would be commuting weekly from his home in Boston on the East Coast to the Microsoft headquarters in Redmond on the West Coast. Besides, Groove Networks had been Ozzie's own show, and much smaller, with just 200 employees. As Ozzie said in an interview with MSNBC: 'The great thing about a small company is that you can put a lot of effort into one thing – but you can have limited impact. In a larger

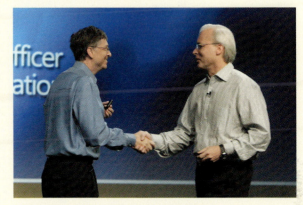

Bill Gates (left) and Ray Ozzie (right)
Source: Press Associated Images/Jeff Chiu/AP.

role, I'll probably have less focused impact, across a broader range of things.'

The company that Ozzie was joining did indeed operate across a broad range of products. It was responsible for the near universal Microsoft Windows operating system; for the equally pervasive Microsoft Office range of products; for the Xbox games business; for the MSN Internet portal; and for MSNBC cable television. Total turnover was $40bn and the company had $35bn cash reserves. The company was still dominated by Bill Gates, who had founded it in 1975 and boasted in 2005 that he had worked every single day in the intervening 30 years. In 2005, Gates was still the company's Chief Software Architect.

But by 2005 the company was apparently stagnating. Turnover and profits were still climbing, but the stock price had been stuck for several years. From a peak of nearly $60 a share, Microsoft had been fluctuating around $25 (see the figure). Microsoft's core business model relied on selling proprietary software direct either to users or to computer manufacturers for pre-installation on machines. This model was being challenged by free open-source software (such as Linux) and web-based companies whose software was free off the Internet and supported by advertising (such as Google or Yahoo!). Microsoft was widely perceived as yesterday's company.

Microsoft corporation
Price history – MSFT (9/11/1996–9/8/2206)

Source: www.msnbc.com.

The first strategy retreat

Ozzie was not going into Microsoft blind. As a *Fortune* article describes, even before being hired, Ozzie had attended the March retreat of the company's top 110 or so executives, including Bill Gates. The two-day retreat was organised by Microsoft's CEO, Steve Ballmer, and took place at the luxurious Semiahmoo Resort, over-looking the Pacific and with a spa and two golf courses. According to *Fortune*, the retreat kicked off with a team-building exercise in which the executives broke into groups of six or seven. Each group was given a bag of parts for a battery-powered Mars rover. The goal: build the rover quickly, but with the fewest parts. Bill Gates's team won. On the second day, groups were assigned to breakout sessions in order to brainstorm various strategic issues. Gates, Ozzie and several other top technologists were put in a group tasked with defining Microsoft's 'core' – the set of things Microsoft does uniquely well that could be used across all Microsoft's product lines. Ozzie recalled the breakout session: 'It was the first time I had a chance as an insider to see how people within the company relate to Bill.' When the group went into its appointed conference room, he told *Fortune*, 'they tended to just naturally fall with Bill at one end and other people around the sides. In some ways they were being deferential, and in some ways he was just one of the gang in a really lively peer discussion.'

The nature of Microsoft's core emerged as the key strategic issue from Semiahmoo. Ballmer, however, seemed unable to push the issue forward. The group of executives he had asked to arrange a larger event to develop the issue refused to organise it. They argued it was premature and likely to cause undue alarm to involve more people at that stage. The momentum from Semiahmoo seemed to have evaporated, until Ballmer turned to Ozzie to ask him to take forward the concept of the strategic core. Soon after, Ballmer asked Ozzie to take the lead with another top management retreat, to take place in June. As Ozzie commented to *Fortune*: 'I had more than a bit of anxiety, given I had never worked with these folks before'.

The second strategy retreat

Ozzie worked closely with Gates, Ballmer and some other senior executives to design this second retreat. It would take place over one day at Robinswood House, a small hotel based on a nineteenth-century pioneer lodge close to Microsoft's headquarters. Just 15 senior executives were to attend; Gates was not invited. The Robinswood facilities were cramped and somewhat basic, with everybody sitting elbow to elbow in a small room. The room was cold and the food attracted complaints. Everybody had been circulated before the meeting with a 51-page memo from Ozzie with his diagnosis of the strategic challenge facing Microsoft.

Ozzie kicked off the retreat by restating the strategic challenge to Microsoft. *Fortune* reports that Ozzie maintained his usual genial and non-confrontational style, but no punches were pulled about Microsoft's past mistakes. Ozzie recalled how the group of senior managers then went through a 'cathartic exercise of venting about every negative thing' in the company's technical and organisational strategy of recent years. 'It was story after story after story.' For 14 hours, the senior Microsoft executives worked continuously debating the future of the company. The group's conclusion was that Microsoft needed major change. At the end of the debate, Ballmer demanded of his colleagues: 'If there are any concerns, you've got to say them now.' There was no dissent.

The follow-up

This time Ballmer and Ozzie worked hard to ensure follow-through. A series of weekly half-day meetings were scheduled for the executives who had been at the retreat, with strong pressure for attendance. Ozzie set the agenda for the meetings and for eight weeks the executives debated specific aspects of the new strategy in a conference room right next door to Ballmer's office. There was a good deal of controversy still, but progress was made. In mid-September, Ballmer announced a set of major organisational changes and promotions. Most significant was the merger of Windows and MSN to create a new Platform Products and Services group within Microsoft, firmly based on the web. Significant too was Ozzie's promotion to chief technology officer for Microsoft as a whole, and the movement of his office and staff to the high-security top-floor suite where Gates and Ballmer had their offices too.

The web strategy moved forward. In late October Bill Gates and Ray Ozzie each released important internal memos (soon leaked to the Internet). The Gates memo was dated Sunday 30 October, subject Internet Services Software and e-mailed to all Microsoft Executive Staff and Direct Reports and the Distinguished Engineers group. Gates recalled his memo of 10 years earlier, entitled the 'Internet Tidal Wave', which had launched a revolution within Microsoft to catch up with the first-generation Internet challenge. He then introduced the new issue of Internet software (or web-based) services. He attached Ozzie's own memo on which he commented: 'I feel sure we will look back on [this] as being as critical as the Internet Tidal Wave. Ray outlines the great things we and our partners can do using the Internet Services approach. The next sea change is upon us.'

Ozzie's own attached memo dated from the Friday before and was addressed to Executive Staff and Direct Reports. It was 5,000 words long, with the subject line 'The Internet Services Disruption'. The memo started positively, by asserting that Microsoft was in the midst of its most important new product phase in its history, referring to the launch of the Xbox 360 and many other products. But it continued quickly to remind readers that the company was innovating at a time of great turbulence and change. This was not unprecedented, however. The memo continued by recalling that the company had needed to review its core strategy and direction roughly every five years throughout its history.

Ozzie recalled three previous changes, including the Internet Tidal Wave, on a five-year cycle going back to 1990. He then proposed the existence of a new business model, Internet-based software supported by advertising. He insisted that everybody should reflect on the environmental change, on the company's strengths and weaknesses and on its leadership responsibilities. He warned that if his fellow employees did not reflect and respond quickly and decisively, the company as it stood was seriously at risk. He repeatedly used the word 'we' to underline the common challenge.

The final parts of Ozzie's memo were particularly significant. Invoking 'Bill' Gates and 'Steve' Ballmer by their first names, he insisted that the senior leadership was absolutely committed to the vision outlined in the memo. As evidence, he cited the recent reorganisation of the company into three divisions, including the creation of the new Platform Products and Services group. Ozzie also carefully outlined what he called 'Next Steps'. Here he specified a timetable by which division presidents would be assigning individual managers as 'scenario owners' to take forward various initiatives, to work together with Ozzie, to consult within Microsoft and finally to develop concrete new plans. Ozzie provided the address for an internal blog that he would keep, which would provide relevant documents and his own thoughts as they continued to develop. He also promised to experiment with various other ways to allow Microsoft employees to engage with him directly in the strategic conversation.

On 1 November, Bill Gates and Ray Ozzie jointly unveiled the new strategy to a press conference in San Francisco. In June 2006, Gates announced that he would be retiring from a full-time role in Microsoft, easing out over two years. Ozzie took over Gates's role as the company's Chief Software Architect. He had meanwhile bought himself an apartment near the Microsoft headquarters, overlooking Seattle harbour. His wife started commuting to him.

Main sources: D. Kirkpatrick and J.L. Yang, 'Microsoft's new brain', *Fortune*, 15 May (2006), pp. 52–63; 'Bill Gates: Internet Software Services', at http://blogs.zdnet.com/web2explorer/?page_id=53; 'Ray Ozzie: the Internet Services Disruption', at http://www.scripting.com/disruption/ozzie/TheInternetServicesDisruptio.htm; 'Microsoft to buy Groove Networks', MSNBC, 10 March (2005).

Questions

1 Why was the Semiahmoo retreat not successful in creating sustained momentum around the issue of Microsoft's 'core'?

2 Why was Ozzie more successful in creating follow-on action after the Robinswood retreat?

3 Comment on Ozzie's communications strategy with regard to the Internet Services Disruption.

COMMENTARY ON PART III

This Part of the book was concerned with strategy in action. A central question is what role managers can play to ensure that a strategy is pursued effectively. In Chapter 1 the overall model for this book was introduced in section 1.2. The point was made that managing strategy should not necessarily be seen as a linear process: that the activities and challenges raised in different parts of this book interact and inform each other. However, by necessity, the book is presented in a linear fashion and strategic management is often discussed in terms of strategy formulation followed by strategy implementation.

Design lens

Building on the notion that thinking precedes organisational action, managing strategy is, indeed, seen as a linear process. So managers should:

- Systematically evaluate the relative merits of strategic options so as to select the optimum strategy in terms of the economic benefit to the organisation.
- Persuade managerial colleagues, other people throughout the organisation and external stakeholders to accept the logic of the strategy by employing the evidence of high-quality objective analysis.
- Implement that strategy through project planning to ensure appropriate resourcing, timing and sequencing.
- And establishing an appropriate organisational structure and set of control systems to monitor the progress of strategy implementation.

Experience lens

The idea of implementation of strategy following strategy formulation is misleading. Rather:

- Strategies typically develop from what the organisation is doing and the issues that people perceive on the basis of their experience and culture; current strategy therefore informs and moulds future strategy. In effect 'strategy follows structure'.
- Moreover, political processes of bargaining and negotiation play an important role in what strategies are chosen and pursued. So the strategy followed is likely to be political compromise.

The implication is that significant strategic change is likely to be resisted because of cultural inertia or if it threatens the political status quo.

Managers therefore face a choice:

- Accept the likelihood of a strategy based on incremental change from the status quo and have low expectations of change.
- If they believe a more radical change of strategy is required, challenge and change to the underlying assumptions and political structures that preserve the status quo are needed. Whilst analytic persuausion might play a role in this, it is likely that it will be necessary to employ means of cultural change and overcome political blockages to change.

STRATEGY IN ACTION

In this commentary the strategy lenses are used to explore this key issue further. Does it make sense to manage strategy as a process of formulation followed by implementation of strategy? Note that:

- There is no suggestion here that one of these lenses is better than another, but they do provide different insights into the problems faced and the ways managers cope with the challenge.
- If you have *not* read the Commentary following Chapter 1, which explains the four lenses, you should now do so.

Variety lens

Strategies emerge as patterns of order from the ideas that bubble up from within and around an organisation. Managers are one, but not the only, mechanism by which strategies get selected. This also occurs by new ideas attracting 'positive feedback' from inside and outside the organisation (e.g. customers in the market); and by their becoming embedded in organisational routines. So, again, the neat division between strategy formulation and strategy implementation is misleading.

If a strategy is to be pursued effectively, but also allow new ideas to continue to arise, managers have three roles to play:

- It is top managers' role to identify the potential of new ideas and mould these into a coherent strategy that people inside and outside the organisation can understand.
- They need to translate this strategy into a few key guiding principles or 'simple rules' that ensure the coherence of strategy but within which there is sufficient latitude to permit people to experiment and try out new ideas. Extensive and cumbersome controls and overly tight structural boundaries should be avoided.
- Given the variety of different experience and ideas that exist in organisations, managers should assume that there will be potential but variable readiness for change. The bases for this may well differ across the organisation, as will ideas about how a change of strategy should be enacted. So managers need to be prepared to work with such variation rather than assume or insist on uniformity.

Discourse lens

Strategy and its management are essentially about discourse – written and spoken. Its use, deliberately or not, is central to which strategies are followed and how they take effect. This raises the question of the role of such discourse. It needs to be recognised that:

- Discourse that is appropriate to the needs of stakeholders can have a powerful effect on getting strategies accepted and put into effect. Managers seeking to persuade others of the 'rightness' of a strategy need to tailor strategic messages with stakeholders' expectations and identities in mind.
- Given that power of language, especially in framing and motivating change, managers should pay particular attention to the language they use to present and justify change and motivate people to follow a strategy.
- In the selection of a strategy managers may also employ the language of strategy to justify its benefits and to signal its inevitable success. Those interested in establishing if there is substance to such claims need to be prepared to question and challenge below the surface of such language.

CASE STUDIES

Co-edited by Steve Pyle

Thames Valley University

GUIDE TO USING THE CASE STUDIES

The main text of this book includes 87 short *illustrations*, 15 *key debates* and 15 *case examples* which have been chosen to enlarge specific issues in the text and/or provide practical examples of how business and public sector organisations are managing strategic issues. The *case studies* which follow allow the reader to extend this linking of theory and practice further by analysing the strategic issues of specific organisations in much greater depth and proposing 'solutions' to some of the problems or difficulties identified. There are also over 33 *classic cases* on the Companion Website. These are a selection of cases from recent editions of the book which remain relevant for teaching.

The case studies are intended to serve as a basis for class discussion and not as an illustration of either good or bad management practice. They have been chosen (or specifically written) to provide readers with a core of cases which, together, cover most of the main issues in the text. As such, they should provide a useful backbone to a programme of study but could sensibly be supplemented by other material. We have provided a mixture of longer and shorter cases to increase the flexibility for teachers. Combined with the *illustrations* and the short *case examples* at the end of each chapter (in both versions of the book) this increases the reader's and tutor's choice. For example, when deciding on material for Chapter 2, the case example, *Global Forces and the Western European Brewing Industry*, tests the reader's understanding of the main issues influencing the competitive position of a number of organisations in the same industry with a relatively short case. For a case that permits a more comprehensive industry analysis *The Pharmaceutical Industry* could be used. However, if the purpose is more focused, for example to illustrate the use of 'five forces' analysis, the *European Tour Operators* case study or Illustration 2.3 on *The Steel Industry* could be used.

Some cases are written entirely from published sources but most have been prepared in cooperation with and approval of the management of the organisation concerned. We would nonetheless also encourage readers and tutors to take every opportunity to explore *live* strategic issues in both their own organisation and others.

The following brief points of guidance should prove useful in selecting and using the case studies provided:

- The summary table that follows indicates the main focus of each of the chosen case studies – together with important subsidiary foci (where appropriate). In general, the sequence of cases is intended to mirror the chapter sequence. However, this should not be taken too literally because, of course, many of these cases cover a variety of issues. The 'classification' provided is therefore for guidance only. We expect readers to seek their own lessons from cases, and tutors to use cases in whichever way and sequence best fits the purpose of their programmes.

- In the commentary after chapter one we introduce the concept of 'strategy lenses'. Where there are cases that lend themselves to exploration through different lenses, this is indicated as a secondary focus for those cases.

- Where cases have been chosen to illustrate the issues of strategic choice and strategy in action covered later in the book, it will normally be a prerequisite that some type of analysis of the strategic position is undertaken, using the case material. So care needs to be taken to balance the time taken on such strategic analysis so as to allow the time required to analyse the main issues for which the case has been chosen.

- Where the text and cases are being used as the framework for a strategy programme (as we hope they will), it is important that students undertake additional reading from other sources and that their 'practical' work is supplemented by other material as mentioned above. Frequently company websites can be used to provide additional information, especially the latest financial figures.

- The cases do not have questions attached (although suggested questions are provided in the instructor's manual) in order to allow programme leaders to use the case in the most appropriate way for their own purposes. However the cases are written in such a way as to suggest the key issues they raise.

GUIDE TO THE MAIN FOCUS OF CASES IN THE BOOK

PAGE NUMBER IN THE BOOK	CASES	Introduction to strategy	Strategy lenses	The environment	Strategic capability	Strategic purpose	Culture and strategy	Business level strategy	Directions and corporate level strategy	International strategy	Innovation and entrepreneurship	Mergers, acquisitions and alliances	Strategy evaluation	Strategy development	Organising for success	Managing strategic change	The practice of management	Public sector/not-for-profit mgt	Small business strategy
542	**The LEGO Group:** working with strategy	●●	●																
547	**The global pharmaceutical industry:** swallowing a bitter pill			●●						●									
557	**Vodafone:** developing a total communications strategy in the UK market			●●				●											
565	**European Tour Operators:** confronting competition in the tourism industry			●●						●									
569	**Evolution and revolution in the Hi-Fi sector**		●	●●				●											●
573	**Amazon.com© 2007–early 2009**				●●				●										
586	**The Formula 1 constructors**				●●			●											
595	**Web Reservations International:** challenging industry norms				●●					●									●
601	**Manchester United FC:** continuing success but at what cost?		●			●●													
605	**Hermes Fund Management, Total and Premier Oil:** the responsibility and accountability of business		●			●●													
609	**From small town pharmacy to a multinational corporation:** Pierre Fabre, culture as a competitive advantage		●			●	●●												
613	**Cordia LLP:** service reform in the public sector		●				●●							●	●	●		●●	
618	**Ryanair:** the low fares airline – future destinations?			●	●			●●		●									
630	**Will we still love IKEA?**		●					●●		●									
635	**CRH plc:** successful corporate-level strategy in a challenging environment								●●	●		●							
643	**SABMiller**		●						●●	●									
650	**Marks and Spencer plc:** where next for the icon of British retailing?		●					●	●●								●		

Key: ●● = major focus   ● = important subsidiary focus

Page	CASES	Introduction to strategy	Strategy lenses	The environment	Strategic capability	Strategic purpose	Culture and strategy	Business level strategy	Directions and corporate level strategy	International strategy	Innovation and entrepreneurship	Mergers, acquisitions and alliances	Strategy evaluation	Strategy development	Organising for success	Managing strategic change	The Practice of management	Public sector/not-for-profit mgt	Small business strategy
658	**Tesco:** from domestic operator to multinational giant		●							●●		●							
665	**Ekomate Systems and the Indian software industry:** leveraging network relationships for international growth									●●		●							●
669	**Sustaining the magic at Bang & Olufsen**						●	●		●●		●		●		●			
672	**Cordys:** innovation in business process management										●●								
677	**iPod to iPad:** innovation and entrepreneurship at Apple		●								●●								
681	**Grupo Ferrovial and the acquisition of Amey plc**								●			●●							
687	**Who runs education now?** Mergers and de-mergers in the public sector											●●			●			●●	
692	**Severstal**			●								●●							
697	**Queensland Rail:** QR Ltd (QR)											●●						●●	
701	**The Changan–Ford joint venture:** same bed but different dreams?		●			●						●●							
705	**TNK-BP:** from Russia without love – a joint venture that almost fell apart					●						●●							
709	**International HIV/AIDS Alliance**					●						●●	●●	●				●	
717	**Doman Synthetic Fibres plc (B)**				●								●●						
724	**Sony Corporation:** restructuring continues, problems remain															●●			
728	**LEAX:** managing through a crisis				●									●		●			
732	**Design and development of strategy processes at RACC**		●											●				●●	
736	**Consulting in MacFarlane Solutions**		●															●●	●
739	**NHS Direct:** managing in difficult times					●							●	●●				●●	

Key: ●● = major focus ● = important subsidiary focus

GUIDE TO THE CLASSIC CASES ON THE COMPANION WEBSITE*

CASES	Introduction to strategy	The environment	Strategic capability	Strategic purpose	Culture and strategy	Business level strategy	Directions and corporate level strategy	International strategy	Innovation and entrepreneurship	Mergers, acquisitions and alliances	Strategy evaluation	Strategy development processes	Organising for success	Managing strategic change	The practice of management	Public sector/not-for-profit management	Small business strategy
Ministry of Sound: rapid growth but a questionable future	●																●
Electrolux	●																
Airline industry post-9/11: reshaping strategies and planning for the future in the wake of global shock		●															
Amazon (A): long-term planning of a successful dot.com			●														
Amazon (B): latest developments in a successful dot.com			●														
eBay			●														
Sheffield Theatres: strategy formulation for a wide audience of public and commercial stakeholders				●												●	
Eurotunnel: clash of cultures threatens to derail Anglo–French rail link				●	●												
Iona				●												●	
Salvation Army: strategic challenges for a global not-for-profit organisation with a mission				●				●								●	
Marks and Spencer (A): can new initiatives and new management reverse a decline?					●												
BMW: driving organic growth through market development in the automotive industry		●				●											
Thorntons: a variety of strategies in the manufacture and retail of chocolates						●											
VSM: the development of global competitive strategy in a declining market						●											
News Corporation: corporate logic and corporate management in a worldwide media business							●										
Wimm-Bill-Dann: where from here for a high-growth diversified Russian conglomerate?							●				●						
Barclaycard: a market leader's strategic options for maintaining market dominance							●				●						

* Classic cases are available at **www.pearsoned.co.uk/mystrategylab.**

CASES	Introduction to strategy	The environment	Strategic capability	Strategic purpose	Culture and strategy	Business level strategy	Directions and corporate level strategy	International strategy	Innovation and entrepreneurship	Mergers, acquisitions and alliances	Strategy evaluation	Strategy development processes	Organising for success	Managing strategic change	The practice of management	Public sector/not-for-profit management	Small business strategy
Royal Bank of Scotland: corporate level strategy as seen by the chairman							●										
Coopers Creek: developments in domestic and international collaboration for a New Zealand winery			●					●									●
Eden Project (A): inspiration, innovation and entrepreneurship to create a new 'wonder of the world'									●								
Eden Project (B): latest developments in a successful tourist attraction									●								
Police Mergers: are mergers the best way forward in tackling major crime?										●							
GSK: the wisdom of mergers for a global phatmaceutical giant										●							
Alliance Boots: a major merger in the pharmaceutical distribution and retailing sector										●							
Ericsson: innovation from the periphery – the development of mobile telephone systems												●					
Direct & Care: strategy development in the multi-stakeholder context of public sector services												●				●	
Intel												●					
Arts Council: changes in structure and responsibilities in funding the arts in the UK													●			●	
BBC: structural changes to deliver a better service													●			●	
Sony (A): a diverse high-tech multinational responds to change with repeated reorganisations													●				
Sony (B): more structural changes at the high-tech multinational													●				
Marks and Spencer (B): turnaround at the high street legend														●			
Forestry Commission: from forestry management to service provider: the challenge of managing change				●										●			
UNHCR: managing change in a global not-for-profit organisations				●										●		●	

The LEGO Group: working with strategy

Anders Bille Jensen

The LEGO Group has historically been a successful family led, innovative and high growth company in the global toy industry. Then it experienced a period of poor performance and strategic uncertainty. The company improved its situation in 2008 and again in 2009. Developing the company requires ongoing efforts which involve many aspects of strategic management.

• • •

In its annual report for 2009 the LEGO Group announced sales of 11,661 million DKK[1] ($\approx$ £1397m $\approx$ $2134m $\approx$ €1566m) and operating profits of 3002 million DKK ($\approx$ £360m $\approx$ $549m $\approx$ €403m) (Figures 1 and 2). This was an impressive increase of 22 per cent in sales (over 2008) and an even more impressive increase of over 50 per cent in profits. Even though 2008 had been a good year for the LEGO Group with sales 19 per cent up, the performance in 2009 was even better. What made this particularly encouraging was that the global toy market was stagnant or even declining. It looked as if the LEGO Group in 2010 could be back on a healthy growth track after a turbulent period.

The creation and international expansion of the LEGO Group

LEGO was founded in 1932 in the village of Billund, Denmark, by Ole Kirk Christiansen and remained a family run firm for most of its history. The company manufactured stepladders, ironing boards, stools and wooden toys. The wooden toys quickly became the best selling item. In 1934 the company changed its name to LEGO – a conjunction of the Danish words 'LEg GOdt' ('play well').

In 1949 the company started producing early versions of the well known LEGO plastic bricks. However, plastic was then a new material and the public was hesitant to accept it – preferring more traditional wooden toys. In 1958 the current interlocking principle with studs and tubes was invented and patented. The tightly gripping pieces made it possible to build more stable and bigger constructions

———
[1] DKK1 $\approx$ £0.12 $\approx$ $0.18 $\approx$ €0.13 as at 1 June 2010.

Source: Getty Images/Dorling Kindersley.

than before. The same year Ole died and his son, Godtfred, took over the company. As a junior Vice President, Godtfred had in fact been one of the main driving forces behind the growth of the company for years.

The LEGO bricks gained in popularity and the basic bricks were supplemented with figures and technical features, such as small electronic engines, which extended the playing opportunities. The first LEGOLAND theme park was established in 1968 in Billund. The LEGO Group began to grow on an international scale and the number of employees increased from just 65 in 1950 to 1000 in 1970.

In 1978, Godtfred's son, Kjeld, took over as CEO after graduating from business school and gaining experience in the Swiss subsidiary. Godtfred continued serving on the board and remained passionate about the development of the company and its products until his death in 1995.

This case study was prepared by Anders Bille Jensen, University of Southern Denmark. It is intended as a basic for class discussion and not as an illustration of good or bad practice. © Anders Bille Jensen 2010. Not to be reproduced or quoted without permission. LEGO and the LEGO logo are trademarks of The LEGO Group. Thanks to the LEGO Group for contributing to this case.

Figure 1 Sales history

Figure 2 Profit history

Figure 3 Number of employees

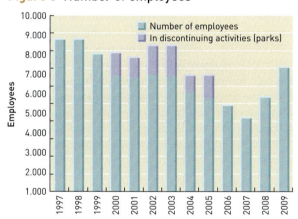

Figure 4 Gearing (equity ratio)

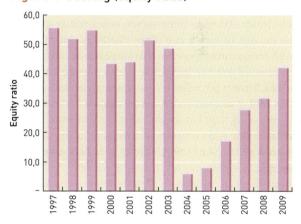

In the 1970s and 1980s the environment became more hostile. The oil crisis caused the world economy to slow down. The LEGO Group dealt with these challenges successfully by introducing innovative products (e.g. LEGO TECHNIC, and new play themes like LEGO Castle, LEGO Space and LEGO Cowboys). They also entered new markets in the US, South America and Asia. In 1985 the company employed 5000 people (3000 in Billund). The strong development continued into the early 1990s. It received numerous prizes, including the 1996 IMD 'Distinguished Family Business Award'. Success had been built on a combination of effective leadership, innovative products and international growth. Above all the LEGO brand had become established as unique and iconic.

A new strategy (1995–98)

Kjeld Christiansen wanted the company to continue its impressive growth. But how was this to be achieved?[i]

As a starting point the LEGO brand held a strong position in its markets. But it also faced strong competition from the traditional and much bigger toy manufacturers Mattel and Hasbro. New competitors such as Sony, Nintendo, Activision and Visual Arts were entering the scene with increasingly more advanced electronic games. Market research showed that children seem to mature earlier thus demanding more from the toys they are using at a younger age. This meant that the age span during which children play with LEGO products might get shorter unless the company developed new, more exciting products.

A key question was should the company focus on the traditional brick or should it use its brand as a platform to innovate in new areas?

Some ambitious objectives were set in 1995 to guide future strategic developments:

● the brand should become the best known global brand among families with children by 2005;
● sales should be increased by 100–200 per cent over the coming 10 years;
● 3–4 new LEGOLAND parks should be built in different countries;

● the brand should be expanded into dominating children's rooms by entering into alliances with partners in related areas such as films, clothing and games.

At the same time a new and more decentralised management style was introduced. The idea was to strengthen the management of the organisation, making it less dependent on Kjeld. Over the next few years, a number of senior and long serving managers left as they disagreed with the new management style and/or with the new strategy. New management and specialists were hired to support the new strategy.

Results for 1995, 1996 and 1997 remained profitable but on a downward trend. In 1998 the LEGO Group had its first ever deficit.[2]

Crisis and unsustainable turnaround attempts (1999–2003)

Kjeld realised that the company was in unfamiliar territory. He decided to hire a new Chief Operating Officer (COO) with turnaround experience. The long term objectives were maintained but the immediate problems were addressed with a 'Fitness' programme (essentially a restructuring and cost cutting programme). As a result a total of 1000 people were laid off. 1999 concluded with the successful launch of LEGO *Star Wars* products (building on the phenomenal success of the film) and LEGOLAND in California being opened. The company returned to profitability but it was short lived. In 2000 sales declined once again and this resulted in a loss close to 1 billion DKK. In 2001 the company was back in profit again and in 2002 things were looking up with the opening of LEGOLAND in Germany and there was another year of profits. In 2003 the LEGO group announced the 'Sustainable Growth' programme which included a new distribution strategy by setting up LEGO's own dedicated shops in the US. However, 2003 turned out to be disastrous. Weak sales (down 25 per cent) and a deficit close to 1 billion DKK. These were turbulent years, with the LEGO Group's fortunes fluctuating from year to year in unpredictable fashion and apparent inconsistency in strategic responses (see Figures 1–4).

The LEGO Group's explanations at the time for these fluctuations were:

● the rapidly changing environment;
● difficulties in financial control and logistics;
● longer lead times needed for running in new activities such as the new LEGOLAND parks.

The public, however, began to be more critical about the development of the LEGO Group – the company experienced a sharp drop in image surveys – from a solid 1st or 2nd position to 7–8th position for the most admired companies in Denmark.[ii]

The turning point (2004)

At the beginning of 2004 Kjeld took on more involvement and responsibility for strategy and the COO left the company. Kjeld admitted that serious mistakes had been made and the company needed to get back on track.[iii]

Kjeld identified a combination of internal and external factors responsible for the problems. There had been too few and too weak product launches. After the spectacular success in 2002 with Harry Potter and *Star Wars*, production capacity had been expanded but in 2003 there were no new movies that could drive LEGO sales. In an attempt to expand in the small children's segment the famous and strong name of LEGO DUPLO had been changed into LEGO EXPLORER but consumers did not welcome this change and sales were down. On the retail side 2003 started with too high inventories in the shops, which had to be sold before the shops could buy new LEGO supplies. Added to this, competitors were more active and the exchange rate of the US$ had weakened against the Danish Krone (DKK).

What were the solutions to these challenges?

Getting back on track (2005–09)

The main strategic developments since 2004 can be summarised as follows:

Organisation, management and expectations

One of the basic challenges for the LEGO Group was to set some kind of new, stable direction for the organisation after many layoffs, shifting priorities and changes at senior management level.[3] By reinforcing his CEO responsibility Kjeld sent a signal that the family was behind the company. Heavy write-offs on LEGOLAND parks and other assets were an attempt to mark a new beginning. Kjeld also set a modest objective for sales initially – official expectations for 2004 were set at the 1998 level. Later, in October 2004, Kjeld handed over the CEO position to Jørgen Vig Knudstorp ('Jørgen'), then a 35-year-old executive Vice President. His relatively young age and his background caused some discussion in the press. Would he be able to handle the task or would he fail?[iv]

---

[2] The LEGO Group is actually a group of privately owned companies. Financial figures have not been reported consistently and exact comparisons year to year are not possible.

---

[3] A conservative estimate is that more than 75 per cent of the top senior management group was replaced within a few years, leaving only a weak 'corporate memory' of LEGO Group's culture and experience.

Focus on core business and improving the capital structure

The heavy financial losses had also resulted in a weaker capital structure which limited the investment options for the future (Figure 4). It was briefly discussed whether the company should be sold, but this would be the worst option Kjeld could think of. Instead he decided to support the company with a loan, simplified the corporate structure and he agreed to sell the LEGOLAND parks after realising that this business was significantly different from the rest. The divestment took place in 2005. The buyer was the Merlin Entertainments Group which also own a number of other leisure businesses, including for example Madame Tussauds. Kjeld's family have recently increased their share to 34 per cent in the set-up but the business is run separately from the LEGO Group.

Focus on distribution

A major part of LEGO sales take place via big retailers and some of the major retail customers were putting significant pressure on the company due to their own problems – Wal-Mart wanted both more innovation and shorter delivery times. KMART went bankrupt. As most toys, including LEGO products, are seasonal and sold around Christmas, forecasting is important but also difficult and sometimes based on the personal experience of key employees. With many new people in key positions the LEGO Group had a problem with 'corporate memory' and learned the hard way that high stock levels in the retail sector can block the introduction of new products and lead to retailers demanding discounts. For this reason the LEGO Group has put a lot of effort into getting closer to retailers in order to understand their sales to end costumers.

Focus on cost and the supply chain

Most toys are produced in China resulting in very low cost. But the LEGO Group had most of its production in high cost countries. This was a concern for management. Could the LEGO Group compete?

As a first step in cutting costs the whole procurement process was reviewed and the number of suppliers was cut significantly. Cost reductions were significant – more than DKK 1 billion annually in savings.[v]

The next step was outsourcing. An outsourcing agreement with Flextronics meant that only 20 per cent of the products were to be manufactured in Billund and the rest manufactured in cheaper locations (e.g. Eastern Europe) and managed by Flextronics. This would have led to layoffs in Denmark. However, by 2008 the LEGO Group changed its philosophy about its supply chain.[vi] LEGO sales are highly seasonal – with more than half related to Christmas. This means that the order horizon is rather short. Consequently flexibility – the ability to react to short term changes in the

demand situation – is a priority over cost in a number of situations. As a result, Flextronics and the LEGO Group have agreed to end the cooperation – the LEGO Group felt that they could manage their own global manufacturing operations more effectively themselves. The layoffs were cancelled.

Innovation – and end users

The LEGO Group is blessed with enthusiastic users[4] – the bricks appeal to people all over the world and the principle is timeless. But the concept has to be updated all the time, reflecting classic play themes such as fire stations and pirates as well as themes which are topical due to blockbuster movies or other driving forces (e.g. the Harry Potter phenomenon). Thus, new concepts and products based on the LEGO bricks are paramount in keeping the LEGO Group alive and growing. As it is very difficult to predict what will turn out to be a success, innovation requires many experiments and tests. Says Jørgen: 'Only 1 in 50 of the original ideas ever becomes a real product.' The LEGO Group has been very successful at inviting users to participate in product development – users know what would interest them and the company recognises the importance of customer responsiveness.

Playing in the digital and 'new media' age

The LEGO Group has developed a new digital strategy. Part of this strategy is to develop an online multiplayer game – called LEGO Universe. Players can build, create and play together via the internet. The launch, however, was postponed a couple of times while the LEGO Group worked on the right balance between the 'old' and the 'new' business and how they should work together. The game was set to launch in 2010.

Cooperation with licensing partners in the movie and gaming industry opens up new growth paths for the LEGO Group. In 2009 the LEGO Group and Warner Bros announced that they would make a LEGO movie. Other filmmakers have had this idea before but the LEGO Group had rejected earlier initiatives for brand reasons. The film will probably be an action adventure in a LEGO world. The LEGO Group is thus following the strategy of Mattel and Hasbro which already have similar agreements to promote their toy brands and figures in movies.

A decisive moment – and growth record in 2008 and 2009[vii]

In 2008 and into 2009 the financial crisis was escalating on a global scale. The Board decided boldly that the LEGO

---

[4] It has been estimated that approximately 1.5 per cent of the content on Youtube.com is related to LEGO products. Users make videos of their models and show them on the net.

Group could accommodate more risk and production was increased to prepare for 2009 onwards and new equipment was ordered. The decision proved to be right and the LEGO Group had a very successful 2008 and 2009 – the biggest growth rate since 1981.

The LEGO Group has now shown steady progress since 2005. The structural changes in the company can be seen from the fact that the profit in 2008 was more than triple that of 2002 – with the same sales level. Both sales and profit improved again in 2009.

'Under Construction': defining the future strategy

The strength of the recovery came earlier and was stronger than expected. Jørgen is proud of the results and his people. But he is also aware that the borderline between success and failure is sharp. The challenge is to maintain long term planning whilst coping with short term fluctuations; however, he now has the luxury that he can work with a longer time horizon and more financial security.

On a 10 year horizon he foresees an average growth of 7 per cent per year. Compared with the latest results this may seem to be modest growth. Even so it means that production will have to be more than doubled and this requires significant investments in equipment, people, product development and marketing. From a marketing point of view there is a whole range of opportunities as the LEGO Group is currently the 5th biggest global toy company with a market share of approx 4.8 per cent (see Table 1).

The LEGO Group has developed a new understanding of its roots – and this leaves one clear priority. As Jørgen explains:

> The LEGO brick will continue to be our foundation. In some markets we don't have a huge presence yet, and there our goal is to increase market share by raising awareness and attracting new audiences to our products. Whereas in other markets, for example Germany, we already have a high market share so to increase that we need to cater for new target groups. An example of that is our brand new concept LEGO Games which are board games that involve the whole family and not only the boys.

This is an example of the 'obviously LEGO, but never seen before' principle. You recognise all the elements – the

Table 1 Ranking of top global toy companies*

1. Mattel
2. Bandai-Namco
3. Hasbro
4. Tomy-Takara
5. The LEGO Group
6. MGA Entertainment
7. Crayola-Hallmark
8. Jakks Pacific
9. Vtech
10. Spinmaster

Selected results
12. Playmobil
14. MEGA
50. Knex

* Based on estimated global turnover (2008) – retail sales to consumers.

Source: LEGO Group based on NPD figures.

board, the dice etc. But you have never seen a buildable and changeable board and buildable and changeable dice before.

The recovery began with a three-page strategy memo in 2004 and this proved to be the starting point for the successful development in the period up to 2009. Sitting in his office – filled with LEGO models and sketches made by his children – Jørgen now needs to find the right strategy for the continued success of the LEGO Group. What would you advise him to do?

Sources:
The case has been written based on multiple sources including a general review of literature, TV/radio interviews, internet searches and, not at least, interviews with key people at The LEGO Group. The company is extensively followed by a broad range of media and events are reported simultaneously in many media at the same time.

Financial figures and many facts are based on material from the company's homepage, including annual reports, press releases and historical facts.

References:
[i] An analysis of some of the challenges facing the LEGO Group in the 1990s can be found in *Ugebrevet Mandag Morgen*, no. 13, 1 April 1996, pp. 17–28.
[ii] This development can, for instance, be seen in the annual surveys in *Børsen/Berlingskes Nyhedsmagasiner* or similar.
[iii] See e.g. Berlingskes Nyhedsmagasin, 25 September 2000, p. 25.
[iv] Jørgen has given many interviews. In *Berlingske Nyhedsmagasiner*, 27 October 2006, there is an overview of his background and thoughts after two years of turbulent experience as CEO.
[v] See e.g. *Jyllands-Posten*, 2 March 2005.
[vi] See e.g. *Jyllands-Posten*, 2 February, 16 May and 2 July 2008.
[vii] Some of these events and thoughts about the future are summarised in *Børsen Magasiner*, 30 September 2009, pp. 27–33.

The global pharmaceutical industry: swallowing a bitter pill

Sarah Holland

The case describes the evolution of the pharmaceutical industry and its unusual strategic environment. Attention is drawn to environmental pressures from regulators and payers. Key forces driving the industry are discussed, including addressing unmet medical needs, the importance of innovation and time to market, and globalisation. The case illustrates how an increasingly hostile environment, combined with a decline in R&D productivity, led to waves of job losses, and sparked a fresh round of consolidation in the industry. On the global level, the historical supremacy of the US was being challenged with the highest market growth rates recorded in emerging markets. The case is designed to facilitate teaching of analysis frameworks including PESTEL, Porter's five forces, the concept of the 'strategic customer' and industry critical success factors. It may also be used for stakeholder analysis and as a basis for discussion of social responsibility.

● ● ●

A CEO's dilemma

On 23 September 2008, Pfizer CEO Jeff Kindler took to the stage at the World Business Forum to be interviewed by Fox News anchor Liz Clayman. Pfizer was the world's number 1 pharmaceutical company with $13 billion[1] (€9.5bn or £8.6bn) in annual revenues from its block-buster cholesterol-lowering drug Lipitor. Contributing almost a third of company turnover, Lipitor faced patent expiry with dramatic loss of sales value in 2011. A key drug intended to replace it had failed in late-stage clinical testing and investors were losing confidence. Clayman wanted to know how Kindler planned to keep Pfizer afloat. Acknowledging that no one drug could replace Lipitor, Kindler described Pfizer's broad pipeline of new drugs and 'very strong balance sheet and significant amount of cash'. Kindler faced the legacy of the blockbuster business model, and his company was focused on conventional medicines at a time of increased regulatory scrutiny and declining R&D productivity. Something needed to change, but what?

Industry evolution

As described in Box 1, the pharmaceutical industry is characterised by a highly risky and lengthy research and development (R&D) process, intense competition for *intellectual property*,[2] stringent government regulation and powerful purchaser pressures. How has this unusual picture come about?

The origins of the modern pharmaceutical industry can be traced to the late nineteenth century, when dyestuffs were found to have antiseptic properties. Penicillin was a major discovery, and R&D became firmly established within the sector. The market developed some unusual characteristics. Decision making was in the hands of medical practitioners whereas patients (the final consumers) and payers (governments or insurance companies) had little knowledge or influence. Consequently, medical practitioners were insensitive to price but susceptible to the efforts of sales representatives.

Two important developments occurred in the 1970s. Firstly, the thalidomide tragedy (an anti-emetic for morning sickness that caused birth defects) led to much tighter regulatory controls on clinical trials. Secondly, legislation was enacted to set a fixed period on patent protection – typically 20 years from initial filing. On patent expiry, rivals could launch *generic* medicines with exactly the same active ingredients as the original brand, at a lower price. The dramatic impact of generic entry is illustrated by

---

[1] $1 = €0.73 or £0.66.

[2] Terms given in **bold italic** are defined in the Glossary at the end of the case.

BOX 1   The drug development process

The pharmaceutical industry has long new product lead times, with discovery to marketing authorisation typically taking almost 12 years (Figure 1). New product development can be divided into distinct research and development phases. The research phase produces a *new chemical entity* (*NCE*) with the desired characteristics to be an effective drug. Development encompasses all of the formulation, toxicology and clinical trial work necessary to meet stringent regulatory requirements for marketing approval.

During all of these phases 'attrition' occurs, as promising agents fail particular hurdles, so most R&D projects never result in a marketed drug. Late-stage failures are particularly costly and not uncommon – in 2005–06 AstraZeneca lost three Phase 3 drugs, Pfizer and BMS one each. Of those that reach the market, 80 per cent fail to recoup their R&D investment. The cost of developing a new drug is estimated at over $1 billion. When the costs of all the projects that do not reach fruition are considered, it becomes clear that pharmaceutical R&D is a very high stakes game.

Given the enormous risks and considerable investment involved, it is not surprising that pharmaceutical companies compete fiercely to establish and retain *intellectual property* rights. Only by securing a patent that can be defended against imitators can the value of all this R&D be recouped.

The industry is subjected to rigorous regulatory scrutiny. Government agencies such as the *Food and Drug Administration* (*FDA*) in the USA thoroughly examine all of the data to support the purity, stability, safety, efficacy and tolerability of a new agent. The time taken is governed by legislation and typically averages 12 months. Obtaining marketing approval is no longer the end of the road in many countries, as further hurdles must be overcome in demonstrating the value of the new drug to justify price and/or reimbursement to cost-conscious payers.

Figure 1 Creating new pharmaceuticals

	Discovery/Preclinical Testing	Clinical Trials				FDA	Phase IV
		Phase I	Phase II	Phase III			
Years	6.5	1.5	2	3.5		1.5	
Test Population	Laboratory and animal studies	20 to 100 healthy volunteers	100 to 500 patient volunteers	1,000 to 5,000 patient volunteers	File IND at FDA	Review process/ approval	Additional post-marketing testing required by FDA
Purpose	Assess safety, biological activity and formulations	Determine safety and dosage	Evaluate effectiveness, look for side effects	Confirm effectiveness, monitor adverse reactions from long-term use	File NDA/BLA at FDA	Review process/ approval	Additional post-marketing testing required by FDA
Success Rate	5,000 compounds evaluated	5 enter trials				1 approved	

It takes 10–15 years on average for an experimental drug to travel from the lab to patients.

Source: PhRMA, Medicines in Development – Biotechnology – 2006 Report, p. 51.

Allegra, a treatment for hay fever, which lost 84 per cent of US sales in just 12 weeks following patent expiry. Generics had a major impact on the industry, driving innovation and a race to market, since the time during which R&D costs could be recouped was drastically curtailed.

The pharmaceutical industry is unusual since in many countries it is subject to a 'monopsony' – there is effectively only one powerful purchaser, the government. From the 1980s on, governments around the world focused on pharmaceuticals as a politically easy target in efforts to control rising healthcare expenditure. Many introduced price or reimbursement controls. The industry lacked the public or political support to resist these changes.

Business environment

Ageing populations create pressure on healthcare systems, since 'over-65s' consume four times as much healthcare per head as younger people. Combined with an epidemic of chronic disease linked to obesity, this created an unsustainable situation. Universal coverage systems (such as in Spain and the UK) were slow or unable to introduce the latest treatments, while the insurance-funded system in the US could afford the latest innovations but were unable to share the benefits with an increasing part of the population. A 2008 report estimated that 46 million Americans, over 15 per cent of the population, lacked health insurance.[i]

In response to these pressures, payers used a variety of methods to control pharmaceutical spending (see Table 1). Some put the emphasis on the manufacturer and distributor, others on the prescriber and patient. Controls were designed to reward genuine advances – price and/or reimbursement levels were based on perceived innovation and superior effectiveness.

In countries with supply-side controls, negotiating price or reimbursement could take up to a year. In those with demand-side controls, market penetration was delayed while negotiating with bodies such as the **National Institute for Clinical Excellence** (**NICE**) in the UK. NICE typified a general trend towards **evidence-based medicine**, where payers expected objective evidence of effectiveness to justify funding new therapies, often in comparison to existing drugs. The impact of NICE decisions reverberated well beyond the UK, as countries collaborated internationally on value assessments. Where new drugs were approved for funding, this was increasingly in the context of formal patient selection and treatment guidelines, so their use was carefully controlled and individual prescribers had limited decision-making power.

Switching to generics is one way to cut drug expenditure. Many countries experimented with 'e-prescribing' where physicians were presented with recommended options, influencing their decisions. Payers were increasingly effective in establishing generic drugs as first-line treatment for common ailments such as osteoporosis, asthma, dyslipidemia and depression, with patented drugs only used if those failed. In volume terms, generic drugs were growing and patented drugs were in decline – so sales growth for patented drugs relied on securing ever higher prices for innovation.

The industry adopted a number of strategic responses to these challenges. A common response was to conduct pharmacoeconomic evaluations to demonstrate the added value offered by a new drug from improved efficacy, safety, tolerability or ease of use. For example, a study of the cost of diabetes – the fastest-growing chronic disease in the world – found that 60 per cent was driven by hospitalisations, 27 per cent was medicines, and correct outpatient treatment could avoid much of the hospital costs. Some companies introduced **disease management initiatives**, which involved understanding the goals of the healthcare system in addressing a specific disease. The firm offered a broad-based service to improve disease outcomes, positioning its products as one part of the solution. A later innovation was the 'pay for performance' deal, for example UK reimbursement of the cancer drug Velcade was linked to disease response.

Government price controls created another challenge for the industry in the form of 'parallel trade'. The principle of free movement of goods across the Single European Market meant that distributors were free to source drugs in low-price markets and ship them to high-price markets, pocketing the difference. EU parallel trade was estimated at €4.7 billion by 2008, with the highest penetration in Denmark where it accounted for 15 per cent of pharmacy sales.

Parallel trade was prevalent in Asia and raised concern in the US due to price differentials with Canada. Canada had stringent and inflexible pricing and reimbursement criteria. In contrast, historically the US had no formal price controls and price increases were customary. Over time, this led to a wide disparity in prices (Lipitor was nearly twice the price in the US), which exposed the industry to sensationalist newspaper headlines and consumer backlash.

Table 1 Methods used to control pharmaceutical spending

Controls on suppliers	Mixed effect	Controls to influence demand
• Negotiated prices	• Partial reimbursement at price negotiated with manufacturer	• Patient co-payments*
• Average pricing		• Treatment guidelines
• Reference pricing	• Generic substitution	• Indicative or fixed budgets
• Positive and negative lists		• Incentives to prescribe or dispense generics or parallel imports
• Constraints on wholesalers and pharmacists		• Transfer from prescription-only to OTC
• Imposed price cuts		

* Where the patient pays some of the drug cost.

BOX 2 — Biologics – the future or the past?

Biopharmaceuticals or 'biologics' are large molecules that behave like natural substances, such as therapeutic proteins and monoclonal antibodies. The discovery and design of biologics entails optimising specificity, affinity, and making the molecules as close to human substances as possible to avoid provoking an immune response. Biologics are produced through large scale fermentation in very costly plants. It is not yet possible to deliver biologics orally, so they are given by injection and used to treat specialist conditions such as cancer and rheumatoid arthritis. Biologics are much more specific in their action than small molecules, avoiding unexpected 'off-target' side effects, and reducing failures in late-stage development. Because of their benefits and use in high unmet need diseases, biologics generally secure much higher prices than small molecules.

Initially associated with small biotech start-ups, biologics became mainstream – contributing $80bn in 2008 with projected sales growth three times that of small molecules. Companies that invested early in biologics benefited from this rapid growth. Other companies noted this success and many acquired biologics capabilities.

In addition to lower attrition and superior pricing, biologics were thought to be at less risk from generic threat. The sophisticated capabilities required to develop and manufacture a complex *biosimilar* product took substantial investment, acting as a barrier to entry. Furthermore, regulators were slow to clarify the requirements for approval of biosimilars. However top generics companies clearly saw the potential. Sandoz led the way with human growth hormone and erythropoietin in the EU, while Dr Reddy's launched cancer drug Reditux in India. Chinese companies piled into the field with 20 versions of G-CSF[3] on the Chinese market. In a remarkable shift, even Merck planned to launch biosimilars.

Perhaps the research-based industry should instead focus on the next major patient-focused innovation. For example, stem cell therapies appear to offer significant potential in tissue regeneration, with remarkable claims being made in fields such as multiple sclerosis, diabetes and heart disease. Many issues and challenges remain and completely new capabilities are needed, but this type of complex multifaceted approach might better exploit industry capabilities and deliver real advances for patients.

Industry sectors

Prescription-only or *ethical* drugs contribute about 85 per cent of the $750bn global pharmaceutical market by value and 50 per cent by volume. Ethical products divide into conventional pharmaceuticals and more complex *biopharmaceutical* agents and vaccines (see Box 2). The other 15 per cent of the market comprises *over the counter* (OTC) medicines, which may be purchased without prescription. Both ethical and OTC medicines may be patented or *generic*.

The typical cost structure at ethical pharmaceutical companies comprises manufacturing of goods (25 per cent), research and development (16–24 per cent), administration (10 per cent), and sales and marketing (25 per cent). The key strategic capabilities at these companies are R&D and sales and marketing. Pressure on margins created an incentive to restructure manufacturing, rationalising the number of production sites and often outsourcing to China or India.

Manufacturing and distribution efficiency was key for generics manufacturers. In the 1990s, US generics prices collapsed, accompanied by a shakeout to determine cost leadership. The speed and aggression of generic attacks on branded products increased sharply. Economies of scale, including finance to support complex patent disputes, proved decisive and the sector consolidated. The top 10 generics companies soon accounted for nearly half the global market. Acquisition remained a preferred strategy to increase geographical footprint, gain economies of scale and access new technologies, with 62 *M&A* transactions from 2006 to 2008. Given the number of blockbusters facing patent expiry and markets with untapped potential (e.g. Italy, Spain, France, Japan), not surprisingly growth in generics outstripped the overall market. Future growth will be driven by growth in *biosimilars* (see Box 2).

A new type of industry player appeared in the 1980s – small biotechnology start-ups backed by venture capital to exploit the myriad opportunities created by molecular

---

[3] Granulocyte colony stimulating factor, used to boost white blood cell count during cancer chemotherapy.

biology and genetic engineering. Initially, *biotechs* were associated with biopharmaceutical agents, e.g. recombinant insulin, the industry's first product, launched in 1982. Biotechs now pursue a huge variety of core capabilities creating a global, extraordinarily diverse and innovative sector, clustered together in locations such as San Francisco and Boston. Because of the very long product development cycle, most biotechs take years to reach profitability, if at all, and in 2008 revenues of $95bn were concentrated in a tiny subgroup of highly profitable firms. The global credit squeeze had a dramatic effect on the sector: biotech *IPOs* became very rare, and access to venture and debt funding dried up. By 2009, over half of public biotechs had less than a year's cash left. To conserve cash, companies restructured to cut jobs and programmes, sought grant funding and chased deals with cash-rich pharma companies. Many were set to disappear through merger or acquisition.

Over the counter (OTC) medicines are bought by the consumer without a prescription. The global OTC market was estimated at $104 billion in 2008 with the top 10 manufacturers accounting for more than half of volume. Switching medicines from prescription-only to OTC was costly for pharma companies both to secure approval and to undertake consumer-oriented marketing. However, consumer brand loyalty then provided defence against generic competition and prolonged the product life cycle.

A final important category of medicine is vaccines, which were re-emerging as a key revenue generator. Prophylactic vaccines often provide lifelong protection against serious diseases, preventing at least 3 million deaths annually worldwide and saving an estimated $7–20 healthcare dollars for every dollar spent on vaccines. This nearly $20 billion market is highly concentrated: just five global players account for over 85 per cent market share. Their vaccine sales grew at 32 per cent per year between 2004 and 2007 as they launched high priced vaccines for new applications such as human papilloma virus (HPV). Entry barriers are high, with specialised skills required in manufacturing, conducting large and complex clinical trials and managing surveillance programmes. Vaccines have higher development success rates and lower risk of generic entry than conventional medicines, and offer blockbuster sales potential. Novartis, AstraZeneca and Pfizer all entered the sector through acquisitions in 2006–09.

BOX 3

US dominance under threat?

A number of factors have contributed to industry globalisation. Chief is the international convergence of medical science and practice under the influence of modern communications technology and increased travel and information exchange. Well-funded US universities and hospitals generally lead their fields, while US scientific congresses provide the most prestigious platforms for new discoveries.

Leading corporations have globalised, and are present in all significant markets. Production sites have a global mandate and are selected by worldwide screening. R&D is sourced from the best place worldwide, which often means the US. Between 1990 and 2008, R&D investment in the US grew 5.6 times, in Europe only 3.5 times. In 2008, leading industry players originated predominantly from the US and Europe, with only Teva from Israel and Takeda from Japan in the top rank. Strong US market growth gave US companies a springboard in achieving global ambitions, and in 2008 they occupied 5 of the top 10 slots (Table 2).

Biotechnology companies are 'born global' – from their inception they draw upon a global pool of collaborators and investors, rather than growing from small domestic beginnings. Here once again the US dominates: publicly traded biotechs employ over four times more people in the US than the EU, with a similar ratio for R&D spend.

In the longer term, US scientific and medical dominance may be under threat from Asia. The Chinese government has declared its intention to become a leader in the field and is pouring money into new universities and science parks. Routine chemistry and toxicology are already often outsourced to Chinese start-ups, but as US returnees seek more innovative projects this will extend up the value chain. India accounts for about 30 per cent of global generics, but has similar ambitions to become a major source of R&D and is already an important location for cost-effective clinical trials. From 2001 to 2008 the number of US clinical trials dropped 30 per cent, while in India the number registered with the FDA jumped from 46 to 493. Companies are also establishing R&D sites – from 2001 to 2006, 18 sites closed in the EU while 14 new sites opened in Asia.

Key markets

The majority of global pharmaceutical sales originate in the US, Japan, EU, China and Brazil, with 10 key countries contributing over 80 per cent of the global market. Pharmaceutical market growth is strongly aligned with GDP growth. The US is by far the largest market by volume and value: $291 billion in 2008 – nearly 40 per cent of global sales. Historically the fastest growing key market, the US contribution to global growth fell from over 50 per cent to 9 per cent in just two years from 2006 to 2008, the consequence of generic impact, fewer new products and reduced consumer demand. Nevertheless, the US remained critical to success: for drugs launched after 2004, two-thirds of sales were from the US compared with just a quarter from the EU.

Following regulatory changes in 1997, *direct-to-consumer* (*DTC*) advertising transformed the US marketplace and fuelled rapid growth. However, companies' costs for providing drug benefits to employees were increasing up to 20 per cent annually, causing the CEO of General Motors to declare that 'the cost of health care in the U.S. is making American businesses extremely uncompetitive versus our global counterparts'.[ii] *Managed Care Organisations (MCOs)* asked consumers for increasing co-pays and implemented other cost-control measures. Medicare reforms extended drug coverage for the elderly, but also made the government overnight the largest direct purchaser of medicines, creating new pricing leverage. All these pressures combined with recession caused unprecedented market contraction in 2009. Further turmoil was predicted in the US operating environment due to the uncertain impact of President Obama's proposed healthcare reforms. If successful, they would at last extend healthcare coverage to all Americans, potentially expanding the market. The industry was set to contribute around $80bn to the cost of the reforms and anticipated continued pricing pressures.

Japan has the second largest market for pharmaceuticals, with sales of $77 billion in 2008. The Japanese operating environment was historically very different from the US and EU. This divergence occurred at all levels, from medical practice, healthcare delivery and funding, to regulatory requirements, the lack of generics, distribution, and the accepted approach to sales and marketing. Not surprisingly, domestic companies dominated the market. The industry experienced significant turbulence in the 1990s. Economic recession caused tax revenues to fall, while the cost of treating the world's most rapidly ageing population rose. This resulted in unprecedented price cuts, changes to healthcare funding and the introduction of stringent price controls, limiting market growth to an average below 3 per cent from 1994 to 2008.

The European pharmaceutical market, which contributed 32 per cent of global sales in 2008, was highly fragmented and driven by governments' forever changing cost containment plans, resulting in a lack of predictability for companies' operational planning. The UK market was projected to fall out of the top 10 by 2013, illustrating the strong impact of NICE decisions on reimbursement and access. The annual growth rate of the European market was expected to be constrained to 3–6 per cent per year from 2008 to 2013. EU expansion provided opportunities for growth, but also new challenges from generics and low-priced parallel imports.

For industry players to maintain growth they had to either capture a disproportionate share of established markets, or focus on accessing those still in their growth phase. A new world order was apparent, with Brazil, Russia, India, China, Mexico, South Korea and Turkey predicted to contribute almost half of market growth from 2009 to 2013. By 2013 these markets were expected to overtake the EU, with China positioned as the third largest market globally. In addition to the high net worth individuals who could afford the most innovative treatments, their middle class populations were growing more rapidly than at any time in history. 'We should be finding ways of innovating down that pyramid' commented Abbas Hussein, GSK's president of emerging markets.[iii] Indeed, this offered a lifeline to companies focused on primary care, if they could adapt to the countries' varied needs and environments. Success seemed most probable for generics offering the reassurance of a known brand and reliable manufacturer, so-called *branded generics*. GlaxoSmithKline experimented with differential pricing within and across countries, acquired branded generics businesses from BristolMyersSquibb (BMS) and AstraZeneca, and established a strategic alliance to commercialise Dr Reddy's portfolio of generics.

Innovation

Pharmaceutical companies' key contribution to medical progress is the crucial ability to turn fundamental research findings into proven innovative treatments that are widely available and accessible.[iv] Companies with consistently high levels of R&D spending and productivity became industry leaders. For this reason, stock market valuations place as much importance on the R&D *pipeline* (i.e. the products in development) as on the currently marketed products.

The holy grail of pharmaceutical R&D used to be the *blockbuster*. Blockbuster drugs were genuine advances that achieved rapid, deep market penetration. Because of their superlative market performance, blockbusters determined the fortunes of individual companies. Glaxo went from being a small player to a top tier global company on the strength of a single drug – Zantac for stomach ulcers. A blockbuster was typically a long term therapy for a common disease that offered a step change in efficacy or tolerability, marketed globally with annual sales exceeding $1 billion.

While blockbusters made immense contributions to company fortunes, they were few and far between. Andrew Witty, the CEO of GlaxoSmithKline, likened the hunt for them to 'finding a needle in a haystack right when you need it'.[v] Focusing on blockbusters exposed an already high-stakes industry to even greater levels of risk. This was dramatically brought home in September 2004 when the cardiovascular safety risks of Vioxx emerged, and Merck withdrew the brand from the market. Merck lost $2.5bn in sales, a quarter of its stock market value, and faced the prospect of numerous liability suits. Blockbusters also exacerbated the impact of patent expiries. The top 15 companies were projected to lose $70 billion in sales from 2009 to 2013 due to generic erosion, with $17 billion to be borne by Pfizer alone.

Unfortunately, R&D productivity was in decline and development times were lengthening. The number of trials and number of patients required for each new drug application increased enormously. The average cost to develop a new drug exceeded $1 billion and had grown at double the rate of inflation for 20 years. Despite increasing R&D spend from 11 per cent of annual sales to 20 per cent or more, the industry was struggling to replace the value lost through patent expiries. Attrition rates across all phases of development increased as regulators became ever more safety conscious, mirrored by a steady decline in annual numbers of **new chemical entities (NCEs)** launched each year from 1998 to 2008. By 2009 spiralling R&D investment had become unsustainable and the brakes were being applied hard, with projected growth down to 2 per cent per year.

Lilly CEO John Lechleiter expressed a need to 'reinvent innovation . . . at a time when the world desperately needs more new medicines, we're taking too long, spending too much and producing far too little'. In response to these challenges, companies endeavoured to be both creative and efficient. They narrowed their areas of therapeutic focus, exiting whole areas, seeing depth of expertise as key to success. Lilly created a special unit to do rapid, small clinical tests that would quickly and cheaply shake out molecules that were not going to make it. Recognising that the fastest growing brands were biopharmaceuticals, many companies acquired biologics capabilities. All sought external innovation through licensing deals and acquisitions, although with few real 'jewels' available the cost of deals spiralled. Some reorganised their R&D to create smaller and more nimble units: GlaxoSmithKline's research centres competed for funding like internal biotechs.

To better manage some of the tremendous risks involved, companies started moving towards a more network-based approach to innovation. Merck, Pfizer, Lilly, Johnson & Johnson and PureTech Ventures created Enlight Biosciences to support new technologies to reduce the risk of drug development. Companies, foundations and regulators working on Alzheimer's disease pooled data and resources to create a shared understanding of the disease and how best to monitor it. AstraZeneca and BMS collaborated to develop late-stage diabetes drugs together, sharing cost, risk and reward.

Sales and marketing

Sales and marketing capability became an important source of competitive advantage. A company that developed a strong global franchise with its customers could maximise return on its in-house products and was in a good position to attract the best in-licensing candidates.

The traditional focus of drug marketing was the personal *detail* in which a sales representative (rep) discussed the merits of a drug in a face-to-face meeting with a doctor and often handed over free samples. Promotion was subject to industry self-regulation. For example, in the UK, reps had to pass an examination testing medical knowledge. In some countries, government regulatory agencies checked that promotional claims were consistent with the data.

There were important differences in the marketing of 'primary care' and 'specialist' products. Office-based practitioners generally prescribed primary care products, whereas treatment with specialist products was typically initiated in hospitals. Sales volume, marketing spend and skills required differed for the two segments. Product-led muscle marketing was the name of the game in the primary care sector, while specialist products involved more cost-effective targeted relationship marketing.

The term 'high compression marketing' was coined to describe global launches of primary care brands. This involved near-simultaneous worldwide launches, global branding and heavy investment in promotion. The aim was to create a rapid take-off curve that maximised return by creating higher peak year sales earlier in the product lifecycle. The archetype was the launch of Celebrex in 1999, which netted $1 billion sales in the first nine months.

In the US an important marketing tool was DTC advertising, where spending reached $4.8 billion by 2008. DTC was costly because of the vast target audience and expensive television advertising, but profitable. Well-informed patients asked for drugs by brand name, creating a powerful 'pull' strategy. It also required new marketing skills – both Pfizer and Novartis employed consumer marketers. Drug advertising became much more visible and, combined with high profile safety alerts, helped fuel a backlash against the industry.

Sales-force size, or 'share of voice', was historically a key competitive attribute. The more sales reps companies deployed, the higher their sales. Numbers in the US tripled from 1995 to 2002, reaching around 90,000. However, doctors had less time to see reps, with calls averaging less than five minutes. More reps selling fewer drugs meant productivity declined sharply. Eventually, Pfizer called a halt to the 'arms race', downsizing in 2005. Over 500,000 sales reps were let go across the industry between 2006 and 2008.

With pipelines shifting to high unmet need diseases treated by specialists, the era of lavish launches and massive sales forces was over. Selling was becoming a more complex process with multiple stakeholders interested in cost-effectiveness as well as clinical arguments, requiring new skills. A few companies built strategies around specific customer groups, aiming to satisfy their needs on multiple dimensions. In other words, they developed a franchise. The broad-based approach of Baxter in renal dialysis and Novo Nordisk in diabetes care, utilising a web of alliances to address multiple customer needs, made them formidable competitors. Some commentators foresaw a more collaborative, network-based approach in sales and marketing as well as R&D.

Corporate social responsibility

During the twentieth century average life expectancy in developed countries increased by over 20 years. Much of this improvement can be attributed to pharmaceutical innovation. Few other industries have done as much for the well-being of mankind. So how did an industry that has delivered such benefits acquire such a tarnished image and become an easy target for unpredictable government intervention?

One problem is that pharmaceuticals have one of the characteristics of what economists describe as a 'public good' – i.e. expensive to produce but inexpensive to reproduce. The manufacturing cost of drugs is often tiny compared with the amortised cost of R&D that led to the discovery. Setting prices that attempt to recoup R&D therefore looks like corporate greed in comparison with the very low prices that can be charged for generics.

Some companies damaged the industry's overall reputation. In January 2009, Eli Lilly paid a record $1.4bn fine for off-label promotion of the antipsychotic drug Zyprexa, the largest amount paid by a single defendant in the history of the United States Department of Justice. Even more seriously, companies were accused of putting profits before patient safety. After the withdrawal of Vioxx, Merck was accused of ignoring problems during product development, and publishing misleading scientific results. The lack of trust from patients and politicians spilled over onto the FDA, which was perceived as too closely aligned with the industry. Renewed legislation defining the role and funding of the FDA emphasised safety. The FDA was empowered to demand Risk Evaluation and Mitigation Strategies (REMS) – costly additional programmes implemented after product approval to monitor and ensure drug safety. By the end of 2008, one-third of new drug approvals involved REMS.

The industry also faced condemnation of its response to the enormous unmet need in developing countries. Although effective drugs and vaccines existed for many diseases affecting millions, often their cost was beyond the means of the people who needed them. It was argued that companies could reallocate some R&D efforts in favour of tropical diseases, sell low-priced essential drugs and provide technology transfer. Inept responses to these demands did not help the industry's public image.

Industry consolidation

The pharmaceutical industry remains relatively fragmented, with very large numbers of domestic and regional players. By contrast, it has consolidated at the global level, with the top 10 companies holding 43 per cent of the market by 2008. Table 2 shows how the industry response to slowing revenues and declining productivity was a wave of mergers and acquisitions. Mergers resulted in the formation of Novartis, Sanofi-Aventis, AstraZeneca and GlaxoSmithKline, while Pfizer acquired Monsanto (Warner-Lambert), then Pharmacia. Even Merck, which had doggedly followed an organic growth strategy, finally announced a merger with Schering-Plough in March 2009.

One rationale for mergers and acquisitions was to combine a company with a strong pipeline but weak sales and marketing with its converse. The acquisition of Warner-Lambert gave Pfizer full marketing rights to Lipitor, which Pfizer built into the world's best-selling drug. Another rationale was to acquire global commercial reach. Pfizer's acquisition of Pharmacia took the company from number 4 in Europe and number 3 in Japan to number 1 globally. More recent moves were precipitated by falling revenue and the attraction of eliminating duplicated costs. Turning necessity into opportunity, companies seized the chance to access growth segments. Returning to Jeff Kindler's dilemma, his solution was to merge with Wyeth. Within a month of closing the deal on 16 October 2009, Pfizer announced a 35 per cent reduction in R&D square footage with six site closures. Importantly, Wyeth offered capabilities in biologics and vaccines – both of which Pfizer lacked.

Table 2 Leading global pharmaceutical companies, 2005 and 2008

2005		2008			
Company	Total sales ($bn)	Company	Total sales ($bn)	Share of global market (%)	Sales growth (2007–08, %)
Pfizer[1,3] (US)	45.9	Pfizer (US)	43.4	6.0	−2.7
GlaxoSmithKline[2] (UK)	35.3	GlaxoSmithKline (UK)	36.5	5.0	−3.7
Sanofi-Aventis[4] (Fr)	30.9	Novartis (CH)	36.2	5.0	5.2
Novartis (CH)	29.6	Sanofi-Aventis (Fr)	35.6	4.9	5.3
Johnson & Johnson (US)	27.2	AstraZeneca (UK)	32.5	4.5	8.0
AstraZeneca (UK)	24.7	Roche (CH)	30.3	4.2	9.8
Merck & Co (US)	23.9	Johnson & Johnson (US)	29.4	4.1	1.0
Roche (CH)	20.1	Merck & Co (US)	26.2	3.6	−4.0
Abbott (US)	14.8	Abbott (US)	19.5	2.7	10.8
Bristol-Myers Squibb (US)	14.7	Lilly (US)	19.1	2.7	10.3

Notes:

	Created	Originating companies	
1	2000	Warner-Lambert (US)	Pfizer (US)
2	2000	Glaxo Wellcome (UK)	SmithKline Beecham (UK)
3	2003	Pfizer (US)	Pharmacia (US)
4	2004	Sanofi (France)	Aventis (France)

Another key argument for critical mass was to leverage investment in 'technology platforms'. With a larger R&D programme, more projects could benefit from the new capability and help amortise its cost. But there was little evidence that mergers enhanced R&D productivity. Some argued that mergers actually reduced productivity – more management layers resulted in greater bureaucracy, less freedom to innovate and reduced research output, supported by analyses showing lower output from merged companies.[vi] The success of biotechs in drug discovery suggested creativity was greater in small R&D organisations. Although individually a much less reliable source of new drugs than large companies, collectively they produced more, for less.

Where next?

At the start of 2010, global pharmaceutical companies were pursuing a variety of strategies. A few were well positioned to benefit from the growth in generics, e.g. Novartis (Sandoz) – but was this the right focus for a high-margin, innovation-based industry? A few owned vaccine businesses (GSK, Merck, Sanofi-Aventis, Novartis) or had just acquired them (Pfizer, AstraZeneca). Others had made belated moves into biopharmaceuticals (AstraZeneca, Merck). A few players such as J&J emphasised consumer health and OTC products. Others were busy acquiring greater presence in key emerging markets. Most retained unaffordable cost bases.[vii]

An intriguing response to environmental change was adopted by Roche, which positioned itself as operating a 'personalised healthcare' business model. Roche was the global leader in diagnostics and the strategic vision was to

offer value through targeting treatments to patients that would benefit most.[viii] This concept appealed to regulators and payers, who endorsed the linkage of high-priced cancer drugs such as Amgen's Vectibix with diagnostic tests to identify patients who would not respond. Investing in discovery and development of tests added further to cost and complexity, but offered the chance to build unique competencies.

A small minority questioned the whole business model. Observing the higher multiples earned by Roche and Abbott, some companies were considering diversification into medical devices, veterinary products or nutraceuticals. Procter & Gamble actually closed internal discovery efforts in 2006. The company argued that in-house efforts could not hope to keep pace with, nor offer the choice and impact of external innovation. By February 2009 P&G was reportedly trying to sell its pharmaceutical business altogether. Chief Executive AG Lafley commented that 'today, Pharma companies trade at multiples at or below consumer products'.

Summary

The industry was facing its toughest outlook yet with both big pharma and biotech sectors starting to shrink. The industry had made a tremendous contribution to human well-being, yet was vilified in the media and targeted by governments in their efforts to curb spiralling healthcare costs. R&D costs had risen sharply, but productivity was down and the product life cycle had shortened. Product approval, pricing/reimbursement and promotion were subject to increasingly onerous regulation, yet free trade allowed wholesalers to extract a large chunk from the value chain. Exciting opportunities remained – large emerging markets, scientific advances, personalised healthcare, more educated consumers and of course unmet medical need. However, the blockbuster paradigm had failed and industry consolidation was driven by the need to cut costs to survive. The industry more than ever needed to get a handle on the slippery business of scientific creativity and provide its critics with indisputable evidence of its value by offering a true step change in outcomes for patients.

References:
[i] 'Income, Poverty, and Health Insurance Coverage in the United States: 2007', US Census Bureau (August 2008).
[ii] *The Washington Post*, 11 February 2005.
[iii] *Scrip News*, 25 November 2009.
[iv] 'The Truth about Drug Innovation: Thirty-five Summary Case Histories on Private Sector contributions to pharmaceutical science', Manhattan Institute for Policy Research, June 2008, www.manhattan-institute.org/html/mpr_06.htm.
[v] 'Andrew Witty's prescription for GlaxoSmithKline', *The Economist*, 14 August 2008.
[vi] 'Lessons from 60 years of pharmaceutical innovation', *Nature Reviews Drug Discovery*, 8 (December 2009), pp. 959–68; doi:10.1038/nrd2961.
[vii] From the analyst's couch: Pharmaceutical industry financial performance, *Nature Reviews Drug Discovery*, 8 (December 2009), pp. 927–8 | doi:10.1038/nrd3049.
[viii] 'Are we approaching the post-blockbuster era? Pharmacodiagnostics and rational drug development', *Expert Reviews Molecular Diagnostics*, 8(6) (2008), pp. 689–95.

APPENDIX Glossary

big pharma A group term for large globalised pharmaceutical companies.

biologic, or biopharmaceutical Large molecules that behave like natural substances, such as therapeutic proteins and monoclonal antibodies.

biosimilar Molecules designed to mimic the therapeutic effects of an original biologic agent – similar in molecular structure but not identical.

biotech Shorthand for biotechnology, biotech companies typically discover and develop products, which may be diagnostics, therapeutics or vaccines. However, some biotechs simply provide services to other companies.

blockbuster A drug that is marketed globally and has annual sales exceeding $1bn.

branded generics Branded generics are original brands that have lost patent protection and are priced similarly to identical generic medicines, but offer the reassurance that they are produced by an established manufacturer.

detail/detailing Detailing refers to a sales call in which a pharmaceutical sales representative ('rep') discusses the merits of a drug in a face-to-face meeting with a doctor and may provide free samples.

direct-to-consumer (DTC) DTC advertising involves communication of promotional messages directly to consumers via print, radio, television and the internet.

disease management initiatives These involve understanding the goals of the healthcare system in addressing a specific disease. The firm then aligns itself with the healthcare providers, to offer an integrated service that improves eventual disease outcomes, positioning its products as one part of the solution.

ethical Ethical medicines can only be obtained with a prescription from a qualified medical practitioner.

evidence-based medicine Basing medical decisions, and decisions to fund therapy, on objective evidence of effectiveness.

Food and Drug Administration (FDA) The FDA is responsible for approving drugs for marketing in the US and regulating the US pharmaceutical market.

generic medicine A generic medicine contains exactly the same active ingredients as the original brand, but is typically launched at less than 60 per cent of the price. Generics manufacturers cannot use the original manufacturer's brand name. Drugs are known by both a brand and a 'generic' name, for example 'Viagra' is a Pfizer brand name; the generic name is 'sildenafil'. Generic names refer to the active ingredients and are independent of manufacturer.

intellectual property Proprietary knowledge that can be defended against imitation using patent law.

IPO Initial public offering – launch of a company on the stockmarket.

M&A Mergers and acquisitions.

Managed Care Organisation (MCO) MCOs operate within the US healthcare market and act as an interface between patients and healthcare providers such as hospitals. MCOs provide defined healthcare benefits for client populations in return for regular premiums, which may be paid by individuals or their employers.

market exclusivity Period during which a first-in-class drug is the only product of its type on the market and faces no class competition.

National Institute for Clinical Effectiveness (NICE) A government-funded organisation in the UK that aims to provide evidence-based guidelines on the optimal and most cost-effective use of drugs and other medical interventions.

new chemical entity (NCE) A completely new molecule launched as a medical treatment for the first time.

over-the-counter (OTC) medicines OTC medicines can be purchased by consumers without a prescription.

pipeline Drugs that are in development but have not yet reached the market.

Vodafone: developing a total communications strategy in the UK market

Roger A. Strang

• • •

We will be the communications leader in an increasingly connected world.

Vodafone website, 2009

In 2009, Vodafone, the world's largest mobile telephone operator by revenue, was under increasing pressure to develop a strategy to ensure leadership in the rapidly growing market for high-speed internet services in its UK home market. The challenge for the company was that the development of new technologies for voice, data and video transmission was blurring the boundaries among traditional industries and forcing reconsideration of what was required for a strategy of 'total communications'.

This growth in demand for new services had attracted the interest not only of Vodafone's traditional competitors in the telephone industry, but also from other communications companies such as Virgin Media (the largest cable operator in the UK) and Sky Broadcasting which was the UK's largest provider of satellite-based television. Other new competitors included the largest UK retailer of mobile phones and services, Carphone Warehouse and suppliers such as Apple (iTunes) and Nokia (Ovi) which had been investing heavily in digital content. Google was also increasingly involved in the communications field with a new, open, mobile operating system, Android and investments in mobile search and advertising.

In addition to changes in competition, Vodafone and other operators faced rapid changes in technology with the growth of IP (internet protocol allowing voice, data and video to be digitised for high-speed distribution over multiple networks), the emergence of new broadcasting technology such as Wi-MAX (extended Wi-Fi), and the continued upgrading of speeds over fixed and mobile networks. The UK was also switching to digital television and operators were offering services such as 'on demand'

Source: Alamy Images/Rob Wilkinson.

viewing and digital video recording which were challenging traditional business models.

There had also been significant regulatory changes in the UK communications industry which had been a global leader in opening up communications markets to competition across the full range of services. These changes included privatising the national telephone company, BT, and forcing it to allow access to its network at competitive rates; issuing licenses for additional mobile operators (and allowing 'virtual' operators or MVNOs which could lease network capacity without the capital cost of building their own); and supporting competition in television and internet services. Ofcom (Office of Communications) was the UK regulator charged with ensuring competition and delivery of basic services. Consumers had benefited greatly from these technological and regulatory changes with real costs falling 34 per cent between 2003 and 2008 and rapid growth in the number of competitors as well as the range and quality of hardware and services provided.

In the light of these technical and regulatory changes, many of the competitors in the market were building their strategies around a perceived consumer need for 'converged' services. This meant providing multiple services ranging up to the 'quad play' offered by Virgin Media (fixed line telephony, mobile telephony, television and broadband internet). In 2009, most of the companies offered at least three of these services (a 'triple play') which varied depending on the nature of their networks and their willingness to invest or partner. Vodafone was unique among the major competitors in focusing largely on mobile services and this was a concern to both shareholders and managers within the company. Management's challenge was to decide which if any of the other services they should provide and, if so, should the services be provided by their own networks (built or acquired) or through partnerships?

The UK market

In 2009, the UK market was still in the grip of the global financial crisis. This crisis had begun to have a devastating impact in 2008 and the UK government, like most developed countries, invested heavily to save the large banks, protect depositors and stimulate economic activity. The UK economy was expected to recover more slowly than other countries because of the significant role of financial services in the economy and other factors.

The longer-term outlook was more positive. Immigration and increasing birth rates meant that the population (61 million) was expected to grow 4 per cent over the next five years. There would be public spending constraints to reduce the debt incurred in fighting the recession but it was hoped that these would be offset by growing private sector activity. Personal disposable income grew 8 per cent from 2002 to 2007 and some forecasters looked for this growth to resume some time in the future. The 2012 Olympics were to be held in London and this was expected to stimulate growth in investment and tourism.

Fixed line telephone

The UK fixed line telephone market was declining although at a slower rate than in other European countries. Ofcom reported that the number of lines had dropped from 34.9 million in 2003 to 33 million in 2009. Call minutes on fixed lines had decreased 15 per cent from 167 billion to 138 billion over the same period. By 2009 only 55 per cent of UK voice minutes originated from fixed line phones and mobile originated calls were expected to exceed fixed line minutes in 2010. Trends in revenue from voice and other

Table 1 UK communications industry: revenues and trends

	2006	2007 £B	2008
FIXED LINE			
Voice	9.5	9.3	9.0
Data (residential internet)	3.3	3.4	3.4
Corporate data services	3.1	3.2	3.3
Total	15.9	15.9	15.7
MOBILE			
Voice	10.6	11.3	11.5
Messaging	2.6	2.9	2.9
Data	0.6	0.8	0.9
Total	13.8	15.0	15.3
TELEVISION			
Subscriptions	3.8	4.1	4.3
Advertising	3.5	3.6	3.5
Licence fee and other	3.4	3.4	3.4
Total	10.6	11.1	11.2

Source: Compiled from figures on OfCom website.

services are given in Table 1. Ofcom research found that 12 per cent of UK households were 'mobile only' in early 2009 compared to an EU average of 24 per cent.

As in most countries, the UK fixed line network had been developed by the government, which subsequently privatised the service as British Telecom or BT. In order to encourage competition the regulator required BT to offer other operators wholesale service through their network at competitive terms. This eventually forced BT to set up a separate division, Openreach, to provide network voice and internet services to other operators as well as to other divisions of BT. Ofcom went further and in 2002 introduced a process called local loop unbundling (LLU) which required BT to allow other operators to install their own equipment in BT local exchanges to provide voice and broadband internet services to their own nearby customers. This meant that operators could provide these services without the cost of building and maintaining a national network.

After further price cuts and operating changes were imposed on BT in 2004 and 2005, LLU became an attractive option for other operators which rapidly expanded their services. Operators using LLU have significant upfront costs for buying and installing network equipment but after that they have low monthly line rental charges which in 2009 were £1.30[1] (€1.43 or $1.94) for DSL broadband and £7.20 (€7.94 or $10.79) for broadband and voice. Since these upfront costs were included in the wholesale rates, there were economies of scale for larger operators which used LLU.

The low incremental costs of providing voice services meant that many operators were able to provide bundles of

---

[1] The exchange rate used is £1 = €1.10 and £1 = $1.50.

fixed line voice and broadband, including 'free' broadband with voice services. This encouraged the adoption of fixed broadband services with one-third of connections in 2008 coming from LLU lines. By the end of 2008, 35 per cent of BT's exchanges had been unbundled and 85 per cent of UK consumers (primarily in urban areas) had a choice of fixed voice provider. The result was that in 2009, BT's share of fixed line voice minutes fell below 50 per cent with strong competition from Virgin Media, TalkTalk (a service offered by retailer, Carphone Warehouse), Orange and Sky.

In terms of cross-ownership, BT fixed line subscribers were equally likely to have mobile phones from the four largest operators but less likely to be a Virgin Mobile subscriber. Similarly they were more likely to subscribe to BT partner Sky TV than to Virgin Media. Virgin Media subscribers were also equally likely to subscribe to one of the four major mobile operators but more likely to subscribe to Virgin Mobile and very much more likely to subscribe to Virgin TV.

Mobile telephone

Ofcom reported that at the end of 2008 there were 76.8 million mobile subscriptions in the UK, up 3 million from the previous year and 24 million from 2003. With 61 million population this gave a penetration rate of over 120 per cent, similar to other developed markets in Europe. Mobile voice minutes had exceeded 100 billion and represented over 45 per cent of total call minutes. Mobile revenues in 2008 were estimated at £15.3 billion, up 58 per cent from 2003. Average monthly revenue per subscriber was £17, down 2 per cent from the previous year due to increasing price competition and regulatory pressure to reduce certain industry charges.

There were five major network operators in the UK in 2009 and more than 100 virtual network operators (MVNOs) which lease network services and resell them under their own brand. Ofcom estimated that O$_2$ continued to be the market leader in 2008 with 28 per cent share of revenues including the fees paid by the Tesco Mobile MVNO. Vodafone was next with 26 per cent followed by Orange (owned by France Telecom, 22 per cent), T-Mobile (carrier of the Virgin Mobile MVNO and owned by Deutsch Telekom, 17 per cent) and 3UK (owned by Hutchison Whampoa, 8 per cent). The market share of MVNOs continued to grow, reaching 12.7 per cent of subscribers at the end of 2008. Virgin Mobile was the largest with 6.2 per cent of subscribers, followed by Tesco Mobile with 2.6 per cent.

Wireless operator margins in the UK were up to 10 points lower than in other European countries because of the strong competition. The profit pressure was leading to industry consolidation, with the merger of Orange and T-Mobile agreed for 2010. In early 2009 Vodafone and O$_2$ announced a major network sharing agreement covering five European countries including the UK. This meant that while they would continue to manage their own networks, they would share ownership of the masts, towers and sites.

The large wireless operators purchase handsets under global contracts with the major suppliers (Nokia had 40 per cent of the UK handset market followed by Samsung at 21 per cent) and discount retail prices heavily to attract new subscribers. In recent years operators have been able to negotiate with suppliers to introduce their own branded handsets. Mobile handset sales in the UK declined in 2009 for the first time. UK wireless operators have also followed their low-cost competitors to offer SIM-only plans which allow consumers to use their current handsets and pay a significantly lower monthly tariff. These plans were 22 per cent of new subscriptions in the first half of 2009 and a major factor in the first annual decrease in overall UK handset sales.

Although overall handset sales were down 3 per cent compared with 2008, sales of smartphones (iPhone, Blackberry and their competitors) were up 26 per cent and reached 16 per cent of the market. Apple had entered the UK market with the iPhone in late 2007 under an exclusive arrangement with O$_2$. Demand for the iPhone meant that Apple became the first handset supplier to negotiate a share of the operator's ongoing revenue, although this was later renegotiated. The iPhone was very successful in the UK, with over 2 million sold in the first year. The exclusive arrangement ended in late 2009 when Orange began selling the iPhone with Vodafone scheduled to follow in 2010. Less than 15 per cent of all mobile phone owners used internet services but 80 per cent of iPhone users accessed the internet, 75 per cent accessed email and 56 per cent linked to social networking sites.

Average churn (customers switching) rates in the market had been over 20 per cent annually helped by the introduction of number portability in 2007 and competitive tactics such as subsidising handsets for new subscribers. Some operators, notably O$_2$, had tried to reduce churn by providing a superior customer experience but the biggest impact came from switching post-paid customers to longer contracts. By 2009 most contracts were 18 months with 24 months becoming more common. The low tariff of the SIM-only plans had increased the proportion of contract (post-paid) subscribers to 39 per cent in 2009 but most UK mobile users were still on prepaid plans. Contract users were preferred by operators since they were more loyal, their usage rates were four times higher and, despite continuing price declines, they paid an estimated 11 pence per minute compared with 8 pence for prepaid.

Television

Television in the UK is dominated by the five 'public service broadcast' channels; BBC 1, BBC 2, ITV 1, Channel 4 and Five. The BBC channels together with their additional

Table 2 Television market shares and trends
(Audience share in multichannel homes in %)

	2006	2007	2008
BBC (all channels)	30.6	31.2	31.8
ITV	22.0	22.3	22.6
Channel 4	11.2	11.2	11.7
BSkyB	8.7	7.6	6.8
Five	5.1	5.6	5.9
UKTV	4.0	3.9	3.9
Virgin Media	2.6	2.7	2.6
All Other	15.8	15.5	14.9

Source: Bureau of Advertising Research.

channels and radio services are supported by an annual licence fee paid by all UK residents with a TV set in their homes. ITV and the two other channels also provide additional 'portfolio' channels and are supported by advertising. Television services are also provided by what Ofcom defines as 'multichannel operators' led by BSkyB, UKTV, Viacom and Virgin which are largely supported by a mix of subscription and advertising. Altogether Ofcom reports that there were 495 channels at the end of 2008 compared with 470 channels a year earlier. They noted that new channel licence applications in 2008 were 77, the lowest total since 1998. As noted in Table 1, subscription revenue continued to increase in 2008 but advertising revenue declined due primarily to the economic recession but also to the growth in online advertising.

Market shares for the major operators are given in Table 2. The five public service channels had lost share of viewers for their primary channels but the gain in viewers for their portfolio of channels (generally more specialised) increased their overall audience share. The BBC's iPlayer, which allows on-demand viewing by storing 30 days of programming, also strengthened their position. BSkyB was the worst hit of the multichannel operators, with audience share down 11 per cent in 2008 compared with 2007 and 43 per cent since 2003.

Overall the TV operators spent £5 billion for content in 2008, up 2 per cent over 2007. The largest portion was £1.2 billion for sports and films, also up 2 per cent. Sports was one of the few forms of content that many viewers wanted to watch in real time and the cost of broadcast rights to English Premier League football had escalated each time the contract was up for bid. This meant that the successful 2007 bidders were again the pay television operators, primarily Sky. Sky's partner, Setanta, had the remainder of the games but in 2009 the company was forced into bankruptcy by the recession. EU regulators were concerned that there was a trend towards major sports leagues not being available on free-to-air television and were discussing regulatory changes. The difficulty was that the leagues themselves had become very dependent on the broadcast rights income.

In early 2009 there were estimated to be 26 million UK homes with TV, a slight increase over the previous year. The process of switching to digital TV was well under way in the UK and is expected to be completed by 2012. In early 2009 it was estimated that almost 90 per cent of UK households could receive digital terrestrial TV (DTT) signals which require a special aerial and either a set-top box or a specially equipped TV. Using this DTT platform, the Freeview package of more than 50 TV and 20 radio channels is received by over 12 million UK households and this had helped the public service broadcasters build share for their digital channels. HD (High Definition) TV was introduced in 2008 and 2.3 million households had HD-ready equipment in 2009.

In 2008 there were almost 9 million homes equipped to receive satellite broadcasts and 3.5 million homes with cable connections (both up 4 per cent over the previous year). Most of the homes receiving satellite signals were Sky subscribers and most of the cable homes were customers of Virgin Media. Cable was potentially available to 49 per cent of the 24 million UK households and IPTV (Internet Protocol TV or TV broadcast using the same digital 'packets' that are used for the internet) was available to 39 per cent of households but penetration rates were relatively low.

Broadband

Fixed broadband internet service was available in 65 per cent of UK households in 2009, an increase of 12 per cent over the previous year. Most homes and small businesses (13.5 million) are served by their existing phone lines using DSL technology with 3.7 million cable customers representing the balance. One analyst, Forrester, predicted that the number of households with broadband would grow to 22.5 million by 2012 with most of the growth in DSL despite it being slower and less reliable. Cable was expected to grow to 4 million while 'other' (WiMAX and Fibre To The Home) was expected to increase from 200,000 to 1.1 million. Most customers accessed the internet through computers, which were in 74 per cent of UK households in 2009.

Wireless (mobile) broadband is provided by all major operators through 3G cards for laptops and has become increasingly competitive, with many packages for less than £20 per month. Demand for these was growing rapidly, with 263,000 new customers reported for May 2009 alone. Most of these subscribers (75 per cent) also had a fixed line broadband subscription so saw the mobile service as complementary. There were over 12,000 WiFi hotspots in the UK in early 2008. The largest operator of these was The Cloud with 7000, followed by BT Openzone (2323) and T-Mobile (1260).

As noted earlier, the rapid growth of broadband in the UK had been helped by local loop unbundling. The economics of this encouraged consolidation among the 700 ISPs and by 2009 the five largest providers had 91 per cent of all connections. In 2009 the leader was BT with 26 per cent of the retail connections, followed by TalkTalk (part of Carphone Warehouse) which had recently acquired Tiscali to give it a 25 per cent share. Virgin Media had 23 per cent and was followed by BSkyB with 12 per cent and Orange Home with 5 per cent.

Although broadband customer churn was lower than fixed and mobile it was still over 1 per cent per month, with the major complaint being the difference between claimed and actual speed. Most subscribers were offered 'up to 10 Mbps' (megabits per second) but an Ofcom study in mid-2009 found that the average speed across all fixed line broadband providers was 4 Mbps, with significantly lower speeds in the evenings due to the limited ability of DSL to cope with higher usage levels. The study found that Virgin's cable network delivered an average of 8 Mbps in its lowest speed service ('up to 10 Mbps'). Virgin introduced 50 Mbps service across its network in 2009 and had successfully tested up to 200 Mbps.

In 2008, BT announced plans to invest £1.5 billion in a fibre-based superfast network which could be available to 40 per cent of UK homes and businesses by 2012. This was expected to deliver speeds of 'up to' 40 Mbps and potentially 100 Mbps where there were fibre connections into the home (FTTH). This connection was expensive (over £500 per home) so was not expected to be widely implemented although it was a cornerstone of the strategy of one major US telecommunications operator.

Mobile internet services used the operators' 2G and 3G networks and were generally slower at 3 Mbps with up to 7 Mbps possible on networks equipped with the latest technology. They were also subject to variation due to network capacity, location, load and other factors. Future technologies would have higher speeds but were not expected to match those of cable and fibre.

Bundled services

In 2009 Ofcom estimated that there were 13 operators providing multiple communications services defined as any combination of two or more services (e.g. fixed line and dial-up broadband). Excluding mobile services they reported that 46 per cent of UK consumers purchased some form of bundled services in early 2009, up 7 points from the previous year. Of these 46 per cent of consumers brought the 'double play' of fixed voice and broadband from a single supplier while 34 per cent brought the 'triple play' by adding in TV. In a related study, Ofcom noted that the internet was becoming the vehicle for accessing traditional media with 20 per cent of adults using it to listen to the radio and 17 per cent using it to watch TV. Comparative pricing of bundles are given in Table 3.

Table 3 Lowest cost broadband options: major suppliers

(July 2009)

	Broadband Fixed Voice	Broadband Fixed Voice Mobile	Broadband Fixed Voice TV	Broadband Fixed Voice Mobile TV
BSkyB			£26.50	
BT	£26.90		£25.92	
O₂	£23.48	£28.38		
Orange Home	£21.04	£29.84		
TalkTalk	£17.74			
Virgin Media	£24.47	£36.21	£24.47	£36.21
Vodafone	£35.00	£35.00		

Source: Pure Pricing UK Broadband, Bundling and Convergence Update, July 2009. Note promotion offers excluded. Services offered may differ among operators.

Competitor strategies

The two other large wireless operators, **O₂** and **Orange,** had both moved aggressively into the fixed line voice and broadband market by investing in LLU. Orange had set up Orange Home via an early acquisition and by 2009 had close to 1 million subscribers or over 5 per cent of the market. O₂ had entered the market in 2006 with the acquisition of Be, an internet service provider. They began investing in LLU in 2007 and by 2009 they were in exchanges reaching over 60 per cent of the UK population and had over 500,000 subscribers. O₂ UK is a subsidiary of Telefonica, originally the Spanish national telecommunications operator but by 2009 a major multinational company with over 260 million subscribers to its wireless, fixed line, internet and pay TV services. Telefonica sees itself as 'one of the world's leading integrated operators in the telecommunications sector'.

BT's 2008 annual report recorded the company's strategy as follows:

We aim to be a global leader in converged communications services. Convergence – bringing fixed-line and mobile technologies, IT and communications, networks and services – is the core of what we offer our customers. At BT we call this 'unified communications'.

However, a new CEO and a major write-off (£700 million) in its Global Services consulting business appeared to have tempered its ambitions by 2009 although the company retained the strap line, 'Bringing it all together'. BT was the dominant player in providing both fixed line voice and broadband services in the UK. Its core advantage was its national fixed line network which had been built during the previous five years and which was to be upgraded again.

By early 2009 BT supported most fixed line voice services in the UK and over 14 million DSL broadband lines representing over 5 million of its own retail customers, almost 6 million LLU customers and almost 4 million wholesale customers. BT also offered mobile services through its own

MVNO which was hosted by Vodafone. Its IPTV service BT Vision offers more than 200,000 customers 'Television on Your Terms' with no monthly subscription, access to a range of television and radio channels as well as on-demand and pay-per-view services which are delivered over BT's network using IPTV technology.

BSkyB or Sky is a publicly traded UK company but it is 39 per cent owned by News Corp., the global media group. Since 1988 it has offered pay TV services over satellite, eventually including a package of 25 of its own channels covering sports, news, entertainment, gambling and special interests which it offers along with many others. In 2006, in partnership with BT, it began offering fixed line voice (Sky Talk) and broadband (Sky Broadband). By mid-2009 Sky reported 9.4 million television subscribers, 1.8 million telephone subscribers and 2.2 million broadband.

The Sky annual report noted that 16 per cent of its subscribers purchased a bundle of all three services, an increase from 11 per cent the previous year. Average monthly revenue per user increased from £36 to £39 and the annualised churn rate stayed flat at 9.9 per cent. Sky offered a limited on-demand package but more than half of the TV subscriptions included a digital video recorder to allow subscribers to 'control their viewing'. Sky relied on attracting viewers by securing rights to sports, first-run movies and popular TV series but in 2009 the company was coming under pressure from Ofcom to wholesale more of its channels to other operators.

Carphone Warehouse announced in 2009 that it would split its business into two separate entities in 2010. The retail and distribution business was owned 50 per cent by the US retailer Best Buy and operated 2400 retail outlets across nine European countries as well as Best Buy Europe. TalkTalk was its communications business which in 2009 had 4.1 million broadband customers and an additional 1.1 million fixed voice and dial-up subscribers. TalkTalk had grown with aggressive marketing including 'free' broadband with voice services and acquisitions including AOL UK in 2006 and Tiscali in 2009. The Tiscali acquisition cost £236 million and added 1.4 million subscribers. The company estimated annual savings of £40–50 million particularly from migrating the 50 per cent of Tiscali customers who were not served by LLU lines onto the fully unbundled TalkTalk network. By September 2009, TalkTalk had unbundled 1714 BT exchanges covering 81 per cent of the UK population.

In 2008 **Virgin Media** noted in its annual report that the company provided, 'the first "quad-play" offering of television, broadband, fixed line telephone and mobile telephone services in the UK together with the most advanced TV on demand features available in the UK market'. Virgin Media was formed in 2007 when the former NTL rebranded as part of the 2006 acquisition of the UK's leading MVNO, Virgin Mobile. The company is organised in three areas: cable including television, broadband and fixed line voice (77 per cent revenue, 37 per cent gross margin), mobile (14 per cent revenue, 44 per cent gross margin) and content including its own TV channels as well as its joint venture with the BBC, UKTV (9 per cent revenue, 44 per cent gross margin). Overall revenues in 2009 were expected to be £5 billion with a net loss due to acquisition-related writeoffs.

In 2009, Virgin's cable network passed 12.6 million UK households of which 3.7 million were TV subscribers, 3.8 million broadband and 4.1 million telephone. An additional 225,000 subscribers were served by LLU lines under the Virgin National brand. Virgin's fibre network linked to exchanges much closer to customers than the BT network and the final connection was made by coaxial cable supplemented by copper wires for voice communications. This allowed the company to deliver much higher broadband speeds than any other competitor and to provide a higher quality on-demand television service. In 2009 cable subscribers were continuing to move to bundled services with 60 per cent taking all three services and 25 per cent taking two. The average annual revenue per cable subscriber was £570 in 2009 and the annual churn was 15 per cent. Virgin noted that broadband customers were more profitable than television customers and that triple play customers were not only more profitable but also more loyal.

Vodafone strategy

Vodafone began as Racal Telecom, a division of Racal Electronics and completed the first UK mobile call in 1985. It adopted the name Vodafone Group plc when it became an independent public company in 1991. Beginning in the mid-1990s Vodafone began an aggressive strategy of growth through acquisitions and by September 2009 the company operated in 25 countries (with partner networks in 43 more) and had 323 million customers. The company described itself as 'the world's leading telecommunications company' noting that it had operations throughout Europe, the Middle East, Africa, Asia, the Americas and Australasia. The group primarily focused on mobile telephones but in 2007 began to acquire or lease fixed line capacity in a number of European countries.

Vodafone's recent growth in developing markets had been enthusiastically led by CEO Arun Sarin but in July 2008 he was succeeded by Vittorio Colao, who came in with a strong reputation as a cost cutter. Early in 2009 he announced a change in corporate strategy to focus on four objectives:

1 Drive *operational performance* through value enhancement ('maximising the value of our existing customer relationships, not just the revenue') and cost reduction.

2 Pursue growth opportunities in *total communications*. This involved expansion in mobile data services, growth in enterprise (business) customers including medium, small and home offices and broadband. In this last area the company announced, 'We will adopt a market-by-market approach focused on the service, rather than the technology. It will be targeted at enterprise and high value consumers as a priority.'

3 Execution in *emerging markets* including expanding delivery of mobile services and selective expansion into new markets.

4 Strengthen *capital discipline* including a goal of generating £5–6 billion in free cash flow annually with the investment priorities of support for existing business and expansion of mobile data, entertainment and broadband.

Vodafone Group revenues for the fiscal year ending 31 March 2009 were £41 billion, up from £35.5 billion the previous year. However, net profit fell from £6.8 billion to £3.1 billion due to a one-time impairment charge of £5.9 billion to write down the value of earlier acquisitions, principally in Spain and Turkey. The company annual report noted that overall organic growth (growth from existing businesses) in revenue was actually slightly negative although adjusted operating profit showed organic growth of 2 per cent on the year. Free cash flow was £5.7 billion and capital expenditures totalled £6.0 billion for the year. Interim results through September 2009 showed revenue growth of 9 per cent (organic growth of −3 per cent), EBITDA[2] up 2.4 per cent and free cash flow up 29 per cent.

Vodafone UK faced a number of challenges in 2009. It had lost the leadership in the UK mobile telephone market to O_2 and with the announced merger of Orange and T-Mobile it would drop to third. Churn rates in 2008 had reached 35 per cent (17 per cent for contract and 48 per cent for prepaid) but were coming down in 2009. Vodafone had a stronger position with high value consumers, as shown by a higher proportion of contract customers (41 per cent) than the market and an ARPU (Average Revenue Per User per month) of £22 (£41 contract and £8 for prepaid) which was significantly above the UK average of £17. Vodafone had invested heavily in marketing in all its markets and its brand was well known with its strap line, 'Make the most of now'. In the UK the company was active in sports sponsorship, including Formula 1 racing and England cricket.

Vodafone UK also had the largest share of 3G subscribers and was the leader in marketing 3G 'dongles' or cards for laptop connections with an increase of 50 per cent in 2008 to a total of 3.56 million. Its 3G network offered speeds of up to 7 Mbps and the company hoped to be able to offer up to 14 Mbps within a year. Vodafone targeted business travellers with its Passport service offering home country voice rates when roaming in Europe and mobile data services for a fee of £10 per day.

Vodafone did offer fixed voice and broadband using wholesale services from BT but its prices were high and it had few subscribers. The priority was to partner with leading internet companies to provide products and services that integrate the mobile and PC environments and 'enables consumers to use their mobiles to replicate fixed line activities'. The company sought to be more competitive against fixed line competitors by offering fixed line prices when customers call from within or near their home (Vodafone at Home).

Vodafone UK was headed by Gary Laurence who had been appointed CEO in September 2008 as the fifth CEO in five years. He had previously been CEO of Vodafone Netherlands and before that held a number of marketing positions in Vodafone corporate. He had joined the company in 2000 when the internet service provider he headed, Vizzavi, was acquired by Vodafone. As he reviewed the situation, he could see three major options: to continue the current course of focusing solely on mobile voice and data; to look for a partner to provide a stronger broadband offering; or to invest in the company's own broadband network through LLU directly or through an acquisition.

Vodafone was already the leader in mobile internet in the UK so the mobile focus strategy had proven to be effective in the short run. Vodafone was also investing in upgrading its network to provide faster speeds and was already working with its suppliers on technologies for the next generation of wireless (4G). In 2009 no standards had been approved for 4G and it would take several years to deploy but it was expected to offer transmission speeds of up to 20 Mbps and more. This was certainly adequate for most current applications including video viewing but would it be sufficient for new applications and would it appeal to consumers used to higher speeds and greater reliability from faster fixed networks?

Table 4 **Operating results, Vodafone UK and Europe** (fiscal year ending 31 March (£m))

	UK		Europe	
	2009	2008	2009	2008
Revenue	5,392	5,424	29,634	26,081
Service revenue	4,912	4,952	27,886	24,430
Organic growth	(1.1%)		(1.7%)	
EBITDA	1,219	1,431	10,422	9,690
EBITDA margin	22.6%	26.4%	35.2%	37.2%
Operating profit (adj)	235	431	6,631	6,206

Source: Vodafone 2009 Annual Report

---

[2] Earnings Before Interest, Taxes, Depreciation and Amortisation.

A partnership would allow Vodafone to gain access to a network with less capital investment than building or acquiring a network. A logical partner would be BT with which Vodafone already had a relationship where it leased fixed line services and in turn hosted BT's MVNO. The two companies had also recently announced a partnership to provide services to corporations. Vodafone also had a joint venture with O_2 to manage its mobile network so perhaps this could be extended to the fixed line network. In any partnership there would be questions of control, branding and the ability to secure a competitive advantage using a shared network.

Building or acquiring its own network would involve considerable capital expense but it would allow Vodafone to integrate horizontally to provide a full range of voice and data services under its control and with its established brand. The building costs could be reduced by unbundling exchanges on a regional basis where Vodafone was strongest. Many of these would be the same exchanges that BT was planning to link with its new high-speed network. Although there had been consolidation among internet service providers, there were some smaller operators that could be acquired. Based on the recent price for Tiscali, the cost would be £150–200 per subscriber.

CASE STUDY

European Tour Operators: confronting competition in the tourism industry

Eric Viardot

European tour operators have managed to achieve a strong position in the tourism industry. Most notably the two biggest ones, TUI Travel and Thomas Cook have a large market share. However, in the latter part of the decade (2007–10) the industry has experienced a downturn because of the turbulent environment which has created new threats and modified the competitive forces.

• • •

The tourism industry since 2000

At the end of 2008, the tourism industry was a major industry. Worldwide it generated US$5474 billion (€4023bn or £3665bn) of economic activity, represented 9.4 per cent of total world GDP and provided 219.8 million jobs (7.6 per cent) of total employment.[i]

The second half of the twentieth century had seen a constant growth of the tourism industry. If the business had slowed in 2001–03 following terrorist attacks in New York, Djerba and Bali, it had bounced back. In 2007, for the first time ever, the number of international tourist arrivals recorded worldwide exceeded 900 million, according to the World Tourism Organisation (UNWTO), a specialised agency of the United Nations (UN) for tourism policy, as illustrated in Figure 1.

However, the global economic crisis starting in September 2008 and getting worse throughout 2009 had brought the business to a halt, with a general slowdown of activities, massive unemployment, and a major credit crunch for consumers.

Figure 1 International tourist arrivals

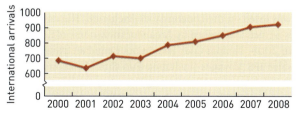

Source: UNWTO, June 2009.

Competition: a continuing consolidation in the European tourism industry

Over the 10 years from 1998 to 2008, the competitive landscape of the tour operator industry changed dramatically as the market experienced a continuing concentration of the players.

The trend had been accelerated in 2007 with the acquisition of MyTravel, the number 3 European Tour Operator by Thomas Cook, the number 2, on February 2007. One month later TUI announced its acquisition and merger with First Choice, the fifth biggest tour operator and number 2 in the UK.

Those two moves radically decreased the number of players and in 2008 the combined revenues of the two biggest tour operators were three times higher than the three following competitors, while in 2005 it was less than twice as high (see Table 1).

TUI Travel Plc

In 2009, TUI Travel Plc was the biggest tour operator in Europe. A tour operator (also named tour wholesaler) offered packaged or 'all inclusive' prepaid and preplanned holidays to its customers, usually through travel agents. It was a pre-assembly of basic travel components sold for a fixed price. A standard package was composed of air transportation (outbound and return), hotel accommodation, transfers from the airport to the hotel and back, as well as optional items such as insurance, meals, excursions, etc.

The flights (usually charters) left and returned on given dates; the duration of the stay was fixed. This type of

---

Table 1 Tour operators market share (MS) and revenues in Europe in 2005 and 2008

	MS 2008 (%)	Revenues 2008 (€bn)		MS 2005 (%)	Revenues 2005 (€bn)
TUI	18.6	15.6	TUI	21	16.0
Thomas Cook	13.9	11.7	Thomas Cook	13	7.8
REWE	5.1	4.3	MyTravel	8	4.8
Kuoni	3.4	2.8	REWE	8	4.8
Club Med	2.1	1.7	First Choice	6	3.6
			Kuoni	4	2.4
Total market		84.0	Club Med	4	2.4
			Iberostar	4	2.4
			Altour	2	1.2
			Hotelplan	2	1.2
			Total market		60.0

Sources: TUI LTC Annual Reports.

vacation offered security and good value for the vacationer as tour operators were able to get very good prices compared to a Do-It-Yourself holiday. Indeed, tour operators had managed to industrialise and standardise the process of holiday-making, turning it into a mass-market business.

With more than 30 million customers representing a turnover of more than €16 billion, TUI Travel Plc was, in 2008, the market leader in tourism in Europe. The company, listed on the London Stock market, has achieved this position through an aggressive acquisition strategy led originally by the TUI group, a German company whose top management decided to exit the mining industry in the mid-1990s and to enter the tourism business, a growth service business.

In 2008, TUI Travel Plc had 50,000 employees with over US$11 billion in fixed assets. It owned about 4000 travel agencies in 20 countries with a very strong presence in Germany, Great Britain and the Netherlands as well as in Belgium (under the various brands of TUI ReiseCenter, FIRST Reisebüro, Hapag-Lloyd Reisebüro, TUI TravelCenter, First Choice, 2wentys, Sunsstart, Lunn Poly, etc.).

TUI Travel Plc also owned 80 tour operators active in 20 European markets. Some of its most famous brands were TUI, Nouvelles Frontières 1-2-Fly, Gebeco, Robinson, Thomson, Fritidsresor, Star Tour, Jetair, and Gulet. Those tour operators were selling not only fully packaged tours but also individual travel components (flights, car rental, hotel accommodation, etc.). In 2005, across Europe, call centres and online bookings combined accounted for 25 per cent of sales. It had doubled to 30 per cent pure online bookings in 2008.

In addition, TUI Travel Plc owned more than 160 aircraft with control of various airlines such as Arkefly, Britannia, Corsairfly Hapagfly, Jetairfly and Thomsonfly. TUI was also present in the low cost airline market with Hapag-Lloyd-Express in Germany and Thomsonfly.com in the UK. The airlines ran as independent entities with

responsibility for results at a local level whilst the fleet operations, maintenance and purchasing were centralised and managed by the TUI Airline Management team in Hanover.

In 2008, TUI Travel Plc was Europe's largest holiday hotelier with 297 hotels and some 83,728 beds. This made it number 12 in the rankings of the biggest hotel chains around the world.[ii] The group also owned 37 incoming agencies with more than 5000 staff and tour guides who were taking care of customers in more than 70 countries. They organised the transportation between airport and hotel, provided local excursions, offered assistance for car rentals, etc. TUI Travel Plc was also present in cruise activity with four cruise liners belonging to Hapag-Lloyd Cruises.

The main shareholders were TUI AG (51.7 per cent), AllianceBernstein Investments LP (6.3 per cent), Marathon Asset Mgt (3.1 per cent), Legal & General Inv. Mgt (2.2 per cent), Barclays Global Investors (2.2 per cent), Standard Life Investments (1.7 per cent).

Thomas Cook

The German company Thomas Cook AG was created in 2002 when German retailer Karstadt Quelle and Deutsche Lufthansa set up a 50–50 joint venture for the purchase of Thomas Cook Holdings, the famous British tour company founded in 1841.

In June 2007, following competition authority clearance, Thomas Cook merged with its British competitor MyTravel, another integrated international group. MyTravel Group was very strong in the UK where it made more than 66 per cent of its revenues. MyTravel Group was also an integrated international group. It was selling travel and tour services (including air travel, hotels, retail travel services and tour operators, but no longer cruises) from about 1000 travel outlets in Europe, North America, and the UK under more than 100 brands. The company had undergone reorganisation after experiencing a continuing decrease in revenues.

The new group was called Thomas Cook Group Plc and was listed on the London Stock Exchange. The new group is 51 per cent owned by Arcandor (new name of Karstadt). In 2008, Thomas Cook bought out Canadian travel wholesaler IFS Voyages (including Fun Sun Vacations, Intair, Exotik Tours, and Boomerang Tours).

In 2008, Thomas Cook operated in 21 countries. It had a fleet of 93 aircraft, a network of more than 3400 owned or franchised travel offices, and interests in 86 hotels and resort properties. It was selling travel tours and charter flights to more than 22.3 million customers and had about 31,000 employees. It primarily operates under the Thomas Cook Airtours, Condor, Direct Holidays, Neckermann,

Sunquest and Ving brands. In 2008 total sales amounted to £8.8 billion.

ReweTouristik, from Germany was the third largest travel group. It was primarily offering package holidays under the brands ADAC Reisen, Dertour, ITS, Jahn Reisen, Meier's Weltreisen and Tjaereborg. It was operating more than 1300 travel agencies, and was claiming to have the biggest managed travel distribution network in Germany. It was also running 54 hotel complexes, and had a stake in the LTU holiday airline.

The indirect competition

Tour operators no longer compete exclusively among themselves but face competition from online channels as well as some suppliers (notably airlines) providing both the transportation and accommodation for holiday makers as a package. In 2008, 72 per cent of internet bookings in Europe were through supplier and tour operator websites and 28 per cent through online agencies. In 2005, the split was 66 per cent to 34 per cent, and in 2002, it was 54 per cent to 46 per cent.

Though the European market was different, it seemed that it was heading in the same direction as the US market. There the online market penetration was almost three times bigger than in Europe with 32 per cent penetration rate against 11 per cent in Europe. Furthermore the majority of the online bookings were dominated by some major online travel agencies (OLTAs) such as Expedia, Travelocity and Priceline.com. Over the past decade, these online operators had taken market share from traditional tour operators with a compound annual growth rate (CAGR) of more than 50 per cent, while tour operators were going downhill with a CAGR of −5.3 per cent (see Figure 2).

Furthermore, the OLTAs had increased their package business from effectively zero in 1999 to more than US$6 billion in 2008, representing 17 per cent of their total gross bookings.

Figure 2 US packaged travel market by tour operators and online travel agency packages (OTA), 2000–10 ($bn)

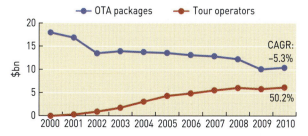

Source: PhoCusWright, Inc., 'The US Packaged Travel Landscape 2006–2010'.

Figure 3 US and UK total travel market and packaged travel share 2008 ($bn)

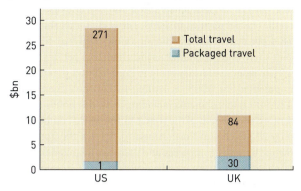

Source: adapted from PhoCusWright, Inc., 'The US Packaged Travel Landscape 2006–2010'.

Naturally, the tour operator market was more developed in Europe than in the US. Actually, though, the two travel markets were more or less equal in size – the tour operator market represented only 7 per cent of the market (US$18 billion) while it was estimated that in Europe it was about 25 per cent of the total market, including some countries such as the UK where tour operators represented 35 per cent of the total market (see Figure 3).

There were a number of structural reasons for this difference. First, Europeans take more vacations than Americans. Secondly, US travellers tend to be more independent and prefer booking individual components over pre-set packaged tours. Lastly, the climate of Northern Europe makes for the success of 1–2 week winter breaks to sunnier destinations such as Southern Mediterranean countries; this annual rite is very similar to the Canadian market.

Also the American tour operator market was less concentrated than in Europe, as 90 per cent of tour operators did less than US$100 million in total gross bookings, and 74 per cent made under US$10 million. The small tour operators catered to the lower and middle segments of the vacation market. They were making their revenues with low margins on the high volume of sales of relatively simple packages to low cost vacation destinations (e.g. Florida, Las Vegas, the Caribbean, and Mexico).

The European tour operators were also directly competing with some of the largest industry suppliers, mostly the transportation companies (mainly airlines) and the lodging industry (mainly hotel groups).

Regarding the airline suppliers which transport holiday makers, TUI was competing directly with some low cost airlines in Europe with its two brands ThomsonFly and Hapag Lloyd Express while Thomas Cook was competing with the charter airlines. The low cost airlines (LCA) are the most dynamic segment of the airline industry in Europe.

During the last 10 years LCAs have constantly improved their market share, gaining mostly on traditional airlines (e.g. Air France, Lufthansa, Iberia and BA) and also a little on the charter airlines. In 2008, The LCA market share was 18.4 per cent while traditional airlines still had 55.7 per cent share and the charter airlines had 25.9 per cent.

The lodging industry is big in Europe but it is extremely fragmented. In 2008, according to Eurostat, there were 422,000 establishments including 200,000 hotels (representing 45 per cent of the rooms in the world compared to only 27 per cent in North America). Most of the hotels are owned by small companies and there are a limited number of chains which are mostly American. TUI is competing directly with those chains and ranked number 11 in 2009 (see Table 2).

Table 2 The largest hotel chains in the world

Rank	Corporate chain	Rooms	Hotels
1	InterContinental Hotels Group	556,246	3,741
2	Wyndham Hotel Group	543,234	6,473
3	Marriott International	513,832	2,832
4	Hilton Hotels Corp.	501,478	2,935
5	Accor	486,512	4,121
6	Choice Hotels International	435,000	5,376
7	Best Western International	315,401	4,164
8	Starwood Hotels Worldwide	265,600	871
9	Carlson Hospitality Worldwide	145,331	945
10	Global Hyatt Corp.	140,416	749
11	TUI AG/TUI Hotels and Resorts	82,111	279
12	Sol Meliá SA	80,856	407

Source: hotelsmag.com.

Business perspective for the future

In November 2008, TUI Travel made the decision to cut summer capacity by 27 per cent to British travellers in 2009 as it anticipated a sharp decline in consumer confidence, an increase of unemployment in the UK and a sustained weakness of the pound against the euro. A few weeks before, its main competitor, Thomas Cook, had announced it would take out 15 per cent of its capacity. The reduction in capacity could have been even more drastic if another competitor, XL Leisure Group, the third largest tour operator in the UK, had not collapsed in September 2008.

Table 3 International tourist arrivals by (sub) regions

	Full year				Share
	2000	2005	2007	2008*	2008*
	(million)				(%)
World	684	804	904	922	100
Europe	*392.5*	*441.6*	*487.3*	*487.9*	*52.9*
Northern Europe	43.7	52.8	58.1	57.0	6.2
Western Europe	139.7	142.6	154.9	153.2	16.6
Central/Eastern Europe	69.4	87.5	96.5	98.9	10.7
Southern/Mediter. Eu.	139.8	158.7	177.9	178.9	19.4
Asia and the Pacific	*110.1*	*153.6*	*191.9*	*154.1*	*20.0*
North-East Asia	58.3	85.9	100.9	101.0	11.0
South-East Asia	36.1	48.5	59.7	61.6	6.7
Oceania	9.6	11.0	11.2	11.1	1.2
South Asia	6.1	8.1	10.1	10.4	1.1
Americas	*128.2*	*133.3*	*142.9*	*147.2*	*16.0*
North America	91.5	89.9	95.3	97.8	10.6
Caribbean	17.1	18.8	19.8	20.3	2.2
Central America	4.3	6.3	7.8	8.3	0.9
South America	15.3	18.3	20.0	20.8	2.3
Africa	*27.9*	*37.3*	*45.1*	*47.0*	*5.1*
North Africa	10.2	13.9	15.3	17.2	1.9
Subsaharan Africa	17.6	23.4	25.8	29.7	3.2
Middle East	*24.9*	*37.9*	*47.0*	*55.6*	*6.0*

Source: UNWTO, World Tourism Barometer, June 2009.

Overall a decline of 5–6 per cent of the tourism activity was forecast for 2009 with different outcomes from one region to another. While Africa experienced a 3 per cent growth and South America was flat (+0.2 per cent), there was a strong decline in arrivals in the Middle East (−18 per cent) and Europe (−10 per cent) at the same time as Asia and Pacific were down by 6 per cent and North America by almost 7 per cent. More details can be found in Table 3.

Once again the industry had to adapt. Nevertheless, in the longer term, the expansion of tourism seemed to be a mega-trend shaping the future of the world economy and activity. UNWTO was still forecasting that the 1.0 billion arrivals mark would be passed in 2010 and by 2020 there would be 1.6 billion international tourist arrivals.

References:
[i] WTTC, www.wttc.org/eng/Tourism_Research/Tourism_Economic_Research Tourism.
[ii] *Hotels Magazine*, 25 June 2009, www.hotelsmag.com/article/CA6667503.html.

Evolution and revolution in the Hi-Fi sector

Robert MacIntosh

This case study explores the ways in which technological changes can impact on the strategy of individual firms and whole sectors. Focusing on the music industry, the case examines the impact of digital distribution and reproduction of music on firms that manufacture high quality listening equipment.

● ● ●

Introduction

'Music is spiritual. The music business is not.'

Van Morrison

Music has the power to change our mood, to mark the significant events in our lives, to shape our culture and to allow successive generations to delineate a sonic gap between them and their parents. Yet music is also a global business and one which is changing before our very eyes. In our increasingly wireless and digital world, music can accompany you wherever you go. In the home, in the car, on your phone or on your PC – music has become omnipresent.

As the technology changes in this industry sector, business models have begun to change bringing new entrants and new forms of competition. As consumers, we face a dizzying array of listening devices that might suit our needs and these products are available through a range of distribution networks from online retailers to supermarkets, and electrical stores to specialist hi-fi retailers or dealers. At the upper end of the market, specialist hi-fi retailers serve what is sometimes known as the 'audiophile' market. Audiophiles are those who demand exceptionally high levels of clarity and sonic performance from hi-fi equipment. A rule of thumb which is often quoted is that if your hi-fi is worth more than your car, then you qualify as an audiophile. Specialist manufacturers such as Linn, Meridian, Naim and others produce sound systems which can cost upwards of £100,000 (€111,000 or $151,000). Entry level systems from such firms typically start between £1000 (€1106 or $1513) and £2000 (€2212 or $3026).[1] Here the business model is simple. Specialist manufacturers distribute their products through specialist retailers

or franchised dealerships where consumers are offered the chance to audition products and can receive advice on which speakers, cables, sources and amplifiers might make the best system at a given budget. Specialist magazines review such products and consumers expect outstanding results given the cost of the purchase.

In the early 1970s there was a dominant logic in the hi-fi industry: better sound meant bigger and better speakers. Ivor Tiefenbrun was a music fan who felt that this mindset was all wrong. The journey from recorded music to sound in your sitting room can be described as a chain with three main links: the source of the signal, the amplifier(s) and the speakers. Using precision engineered components, Tiefenbrun developed a turntable with a suspended sub-chassis, the LP12, to ensure that the first link in the chain (i.e. the source) was of the highest quality. The firm he founded, Linn HiFi, revolutionised the industry and continues to offer high quality sound and vision systems today. As we entered the twenty-first century, however, a dramatic shift took place toward digital sources of music, first in the form of CDs and later in other soft formats such as MP3.[2] This shift had two consequences. First, it brought a range of new competitors into the music industry, most notably Apple. Second, it has reopened the debate about the importance of sources in hi-fi systems. This case study examines the strategy of one firm (AVI), as it struggles to capitalise on the revolution that is taking place in the world of high fidelity music.

---

[1] Exchange Rates used in the case are £1 = €1.106 and £1 = $1.513.

[2] The label MP3 refers to one particular technology for compressing and storing digital music. Despite the fact that the best-selling digital music device, the iPod, uses a different storage and compression technique developed by Apple, MP3 has become the most commonly used way of referring to such devices. An analogy might be the misattribution of the brand Hoover to describe the generic category of products that are vacuum cleaners.

Table 1 Worldwide sales figures

	2003	2004	2005	2006	2007	2008
Home audio/ home cinema – retail volumes ('000 units)	154,004	156,643	157,417	158,967	161,325	165,164
Home audio/ home cinema – retail value (US$ m)	28,862	31,127	30,203	30,192	30,288	31,686

Source: Euromonitor International.

The Hi-Fi industry

Quantifying the market size for specialist hi-fi equipment is not a straightforward exercise, especially as hi-fi begins to converge with TV, computing and mobile telephony. A cursory examination of standard industry data and market reports shows that it is difficult to extract data on the specialist niche from the broader data set.

In total, the global market for audio and video products in 2008 is around $31 billion. However, this data covers every type of platform, component and budget. To make some progress, some simple assumptions might help. If, for example, one assumes that 1 per cent of all audio and video related sales represent the specialist hi-fi sector, the global market for such products equates to somewhere in the region of $300 million annually. The figures in Table 1 show that the market for all audio and video products is growing slowly (the period 2007–08 saw growth of around 4 per cent) but this pattern of overall growth masks diverging experiences in different product categories. Sales of traditional hi-fi products such as separate CD players, amplifiers and speakers have been steady or in decline. This has been offset by sharp growth in the emerging areas of home cinema systems, and computer-based installations of hi-fi systems.

According to industry analysts, 'the trend towards downsizing and multifunctionality is only likely to deepen within [the consumer electronics] sector in the medium term'.[i] It is also worth noting that data on the hi-fi industry is not yet available for the post-credit crunch period. Analysts do however point to a 19 per cent reduction in the consumer confidence index and predict that 'sales of expensive in-home audio/video products will be hit hardest',[ii] not least because access to consumer credit has been constricted by the banking crisis.

The computing revolution

'The iPod is the most beautiful invention in music since the guitar.'
Bono

In 2001, the computing firm Apple launched a new product which would change the music business forever.

When Steve Jobs, Apple's CEO, introduced the iPod to the world he was very clear that Apple was changing the rules of the game. At the press launch he argued that music was a great arena for Apple to use its particular skills. He declared that 'there were a few niche players, like Creative, and a few larger companies which haven't had a hit yet with digital music, like Sony'.[3] However, Jobs figured that Apple could not only 'find the recipe in digital music' but that 'the Apple brand was going to be fantastic' in this new territory because people trusted Apple for new technology that worked well. The iPod was not the first portable, digital media player but it has been by far the most successful, capturing over 70 per cent of the market according to the company's own market analysis. Jonathon Ive, Apple's influential designer, believes that 'innovating is in Apple's DNA' and that core to the Apple brand is the idea that the technology works so well that you do not really need an instruction manual.[iii] The iPod outsells its rivals despite higher purchase prices partly because it exudes cool.

Computing technology brought new dimensions to music consumption. It was possible to carry your entire music library around in your pocket, and with successive generations of iPods you were soon able to carry photos and movies too. The slick and desirable physical product was matched by a clever tie-in to the iTunes store, which if anything has been more successful than the iPod itself. There are now over 100 million iTunes accounts registered and the site was expected to sell its 10 billionth tune by the end of 2009. Hence Apple controls not only the hardware but the distribution channel, spawning 'the iPod economy' for a range of complementary products including cases, speaker docks, chargers and car kits – not bad for a firm with no history in the music business. Traditional hi-fi firms are somewhat suspicious of the quality of the music reproduced by these new devices, citing the impact of compression of the original source signals during the digitising process. The view is held that such compression does irreparable damage to the sound and limits the extent to which it can be considered as truly high fidelity.

Evolving into a new competitive landscape

Ashley James and Martin Grindrod are both passionate about engineering excellence, good design and music. The company they run together, AVI, was founded in 1989 and is based in Gloucestershire, England. Though small, the firm has ambitions to become global by thinking strategically about the new competitive landscape facing hi-fi firms and music lovers alike. AVI began by making hi-fi components much like other specialist retailers. Yet

---

[3] Footage of the iPod product launch can be found on YouTube.

Ashley James believes that the company's latest product range is a radical breakthrough. Many specialist hi-fi manufacturers made CD players which relied on laser assemblies made by Philips. These laser assemblies read the data off the spinning disc and are the starting point of reproducing the recorded sound. In 1997 Philips changed the design of this key component which led to reduced reliability of CD players for many firms, including AVI. It was, says James, the first inkling that something was beginning to change. 'The reliability issues caused by the new lasers were the beginning of the end of the traditional hi-fi business. By 2006, we noticed that people had stopped buying CD players.' With the core business under threat, James felt the need to think differently.

In the meantime, AVI had noticed the new products offered by Apple. In 2003 James bought his first iPod to see what all the fuss was about. Out of curiosity he tried using the iPod as a source with AVI's own high quality speakers. He recalls that the results were underwhelming. However, conversations he had had with a contact from the IT industry came back to him. The point that was being made was that iTunes was rather better as a source than iPods themselves. This line of thought led James to wonder whether anything could be done to improve the quality of the sound to levels typically associated with good hi-fi. Using a Macintosh computer rather than his new iPod, and hooking the digital source up to AVI's own DAC[4] (digital to analogue convertor), suddenly things sounded very different. This was the genesis of both a new product range and a whole new business model for AVI.

In product terms, AVI developed a new range of active speakers which incorporated high quality digital to analogue signal processors as part of an integrated and computer-based music system. This meant that music listeners would benefit from all the convenience of computerised music and being able to browse libraries, create playlists, etc. The contentious issue remained that of the source signal. In simple terms, to compress music into small file sizes for use on portable devices you need to digitise by sampling at a particular rate. Apple's iTunes began with a standard rate of 128 kilobytes per second (kbps) but has recently switched to 256 kbps as hard disks get bigger and the bandwidth available from internet service providers increases. A heated debate exists about the consequences of sampling rates. Traditionalists argue that the damage to the sound by such compression is irreversible. Others argue that audiophiles who bemoan the horrors of compressed music are 'listening with their eyes ... playing

vulnerable passages again and again to identify problems when they should be listening to the music'.[iv] AVI decided that iTunes represented a source that was more than good enough for most purposes.

Customers who tried the new product loved it. AVI's website contains glowing tributes from both long term hi-fi fanatics and newcomers, claiming that AVI's Apple-based solution 'transformed the way in which we listen to music'.[v] There remained a significant problem, which James puts in blunt terms. 'Basically, we're none too popular with the hi-fi fraternity because we've come up with a product that suggests that you don't need a hi-fi.' Most of AVI's competitors still sold separate components which could be mixed and matched to make up a hi-fi system. AVI's new product idea was a single integrated system which, though still expensive, would be markedly cheaper than many of the other specialist hi-fi manufacturers that the company would compete against. AVI struggled hard to get traditional hi-fi retailers and distributors to stock the product and met with limited success in trying to get influential magazines to review the kit. Then James had another creative thought, why not side-step the traditional distribution process too? In a market where luxury, expensive products are the norm, was there space for a lower cost strategy? AVI began to drive costs down, selling direct over the internet and through electrical retail stores that would bundle an AVI system up with the sale of large screen TVs and cinema systems. 'Not going through traditional hi-fi shops increased our business five fold. We couldn't believe it', says James. Though AVI remains passionate about high quality sound, it no longer competes in the very upper echelons of the market in pricing terms.

This still left AVI as a very small player in a large market. How could a small, UK-based firm get noticed and compete? 'Our end game in distributing was always to try and attract the attention of a Chinese manufacturer so that we could achieve global scale through partnership', says James. It's early days, but AVI has signed an agreement with the Hailun Piano Company, the fourth largest manufacturer of pianos in China. Orders have been placed that represent a significant jump in volume for AVI and the medium term plan is to migrate production to China by formalising the partnership with Hailun.

Continuing to change

'I taught them everything they know, just not everything I know.'

James Brown

---

[4] Sound stored in digital form (as bits and bytes) needs to be converted into analogue form in order to drive a loudspeaker or headphones. This process is performed by a DAC.

AVI is now positioned to take advantage of the booming digital music environment. For the firm, this has involved technological moves in terms of new products as well as strategic moves in terms of distribution models, partnerships and sources of competitiveness. The challenges continue to evolve however. iTunes dominates the online music business but competitors are eyeing the economic opportunities. Amazon, Tesco and others now offer online music stores. Mobile telephone firms offer 'all you can listen to' business models for a fixed monthly fee and Spotify has changed the competitive terrain again by introducing a free music player where users can listen to, but do not own the music. Then there is piracy to think about. In demographic terms, today's teenagers are tomorrow's hi-fi customers but they have grown up in an environment where it is considered unusual or perhaps unnecessary to pay for music.

Conclusion

The global market of home audio-visual equipment represents a huge opportunity for firms. The convergence of differing technologies, sectors and skill sets means that it is also an industry in flux. Firms offering hi-fi equipment face significant choices about how to respond to this changing environment. For incumbent firms, the choice may be between remaining within an established niche with loyal customers but declining sales or developing new products or services to capitalise on the growth opportunities that exist. This case describes the way in which one incumbent firm, AVI, effected a radical change in its product offering, supply networks and business model. For those that are new to the industry, there are a different set of challenges involved in leveraging their existing skills and experience in ways which might establish competitive advantage in a new arena.

References:

[i] Euromonitor International, 'Doing more with less: Why many consumers are downsizing to gadgets that are smaller, cheaper or multifunctional – Research from C&C', Euromonitor, Global Market Information Database, 24 April 2009.

[ii] Euromonitor International, 'Global consumer electronics: Trends, developments and insights', Euromonitor, Global Market Information Database.

[iii] Interviewed in *Engineering and Technology*, vol. 4, no. 12 (September 2009), pp. 60–2.

[iv] Article on AVI Ltd's website: www.avihifi.co.uk.

[v] Customer testimonial taken from AVI Ltd's website: www.avihifi.co.uk.

Useful links:
www.avihifi.co.uk; www.linn.co.uk; www.meridian-audio.com; www.naim-audio.com.

Amazon.com© 2007–early 2009

Gary J. Stockport

This case study is concerned with the continual roll-out of Amazon's global strategy through the development of resources and strategic capabilities. It is about global dominance through the development and use of technology and acquisitions and alliances to offer an increasing array of products and services and continually enhancing customer experience. The case discusses the widening of Amazon's business through serving three distinct and different groups of customers. The case highlights a number of potentially disruptive technologies including Kindle and cloud computing.

• • •

Introduction

By 2008, Amazon.com had a market capitalisation of some US$29.4 billion[1] (£19.3bn or €21.4bn) (see Appendix 6) and employed around 20,700 employees. It was a truly global company and it had established websites in Canada, the UK, Germany, France, Japan and China and 47 per cent of consolidated sales were outside its home country (see Appendix 2). The company sold everything from books to jewellery to digital music and it had recently established itself as a major player in cloud computing with the development and provision of services in 'the cloud'.

Amazon had faced many challenges over the years. It had 'weathered' significant challenges such as the technology bubble 'bursting' during April 2000 as well as deteriorating shareholder sentiment at various times. The organisation had survived and overcame all these challenges, and even within the 'eye' of the recent global financial crisis, Amazon continued to make strategic investment decisions for the longer term. CEO Jeff Bezos pointed out: 'When we plant a seed, it tends to take 5 to 7 years before it has a meaningful impact on the economics of the company.'

As 2009 rolled on, some strategic issues that Bezos had himself identified and needed to consider included the following:

_____
[1] $1 ≈ £0.66 ≈ €0.73.

- How might depressed consumer sentiment in the global financial crisis affect its growth?
- Is the continued heavy investment in technology and innovation the right strategy for building and maintaining Amazon's sustainable competitive advantage?
- What is the optimal balance between catering for the needs of Amazon's different customer groups? As Amazon developed from being just an online retailer to a web services provider for sellers and now moving into providing web technology infrastructure development, it may face challenges in trying to reconcile its vision of being 'customer-centric' through having to consider which group(s) of customers should take priority.
- Generally, is Amazon's business model the right model looking ahead five years or more?

The founder – Jeff Bezos

At the age of 14, Jeff Bezos, the stepson of a petroleum engineer, admitted to wanting to become an astronaut or a physicist, or something that would allow him to use cutting edge technology. During his high school years he founded his first venture, the DREAM Institute, which was a summer school programme aimed at stimulating creative thinking in youngsters.

By the age of 30, Jeff Bezos, the Princeton 'summa cum laude' graduate with a Bachelor degree in Electrical

This case study is an update of a number of case studies written about Amazon.com and published in earlier editions of this textbook.

This version of the case was written by Professor Gary J. Stockport and MBA students Tricia Ong, Celina Chien, Eun-Ah Lee, Wentao (Mark) Wa, Mary Ngusaru and Michael Yoo: Business School, The University of Western Australia. It is intended as a basis for class discussion and not as an illustration of good or bad practice. © Gary J. Stockport 2010. Not to be reproduced or quoted without permission.

Engineering and Computer Science, was the youngest Senior Vice President of D.E. Shaw, running a Wall Street hedge fund. Whilst working at Shaw, Bezos came up with the statistic that the electronic world, known as the World Wide Web, would grow at an incredible rate of 2300 per cent monthly. Bezos, stunned by these growth figures, felt driven to act quickly, saying: 'I decided that when I was eighty, I wouldn't regret quitting a Wall Street job when I was thirty, but when I was eighty I might really regret this great opportunity.'

After quitting his job, Bezos drove his wife, MacKenzie, and their dog across the US in a Chevy Blazer that his stepfather had donated, arriving in Seattle on 5 July 1994. Bezos had already chosen books as his preferred product due to their low price point and the size of the global market, estimated at over US$80 billion at the time. He believed web-based technology would provide customers with a much larger range of titles at their fingertips as well as enable better organisation and presentation of the millions of books.

Seattle was a logical choice to locate the business as it was close to Ingram Books, the largest US book distributor. It also had access to a large supply of computer software talent. Furthermore, the State of Washington had a more favourable sales tax climate. Over the next 12 months, whilst operating from the garage of his rented home, Bezos, his wife, and three others established relationships with shippers and wholesalers, developed the software and tried to raise money. The business went 'live' with an online store in July 1995.

Early growth

Bezos believed the power of the internet lay in continuous communication and word of mouth, which made branding even more important. As a result, he chose to name his site after the world's largest river, believing Amazon would become the biggest bookshop in the world. Bezos pointed out: 'A brand for a company is like a reputation for a person. You earn reputation by trying to do hard things well.'

In 1995, Amazon had no significant online rivals and although Barnes and Noble had a 14 per cent market share of traditional retail bookstores, it had no online presence. Once launched, it took less than a year for Amazon to be recognised as the web's largest and best online bookstore with over 1 million titles. During this early growth period, Bezos did a lot of the manual work himself such as loading and unloading packages in the back of his Chevy Blazer and delivering them to the Post Office. Unable to raise critical funds needed to grow the business from his existing contacts in New York's money market, Bezos relied on private investment of $1.2 million and

Silicon Valley funding for a further $8 million. During 1997, an initial public offering (IPO) comprising 3 million shares raised $50 million and enabled an aggressive expansion of the business.

Vision

The vision behind Amazon has progressively changed since it started in 1995. What began as the goal to become the world's biggest and best online bookstore developed into a store where customers could buy 'anything with a capital A'. It also wanted to become the world's most 'customer-centric' company. Bezos added:

> Our goal is to be Earth's most customer-centric company. I will leave it to others to say if we've achieved that. But why? The answer is three things. The first is that customer-centric means figuring out what your customers want by asking them, then figuring out how to give it to them, and then giving it to them. That's the traditional meaning of customer-centric, and we're focused on it. The second is innovating on behalf of customers, figuring out what they don't know they want and giving it to them. The third meaning, unique to the internet, is the idea of personalisation: redecorating the store for each and every individual customer. If we have 10.7 million customers . . . then we should have 10.7 million stores.

Defining the business

The core of what defined Amazon, as reflected in the 1997 Letter to Shareholders, has remained over the years. This letter contained a series of core commitments such as their emphasis on longer term market leadership. Extracts from it are reproduced opposite.

From originally serving just website retail customers, Amazon in 2009 served three distinct groups of customers:

- *Consumer customers*: through its retail websites, Amazon provided a wide range of merchandise, low prices, and convenience to its consumers;
- *Seller customers*: sellers that sold their products either on Amazon's websites or on their own brand websites and fulfilled their orders using Amazon's fulfilment facilities;
- *Developer customers*: customers that used Amazon web services which provided access to Amazon's technology infrastructure that enabled them to create virtually any type of business. See Appendix 3 for a more detailed analysis defining Amazon's business.

Central to Amazon's strategy was growth. Figure 1 shows Amazon's approach of achieving growth through

1997 LETTER TO SHAREHOLDERS

(From the 6th Paragraph)

Because of our emphasis on the long term, we may make decisions and weigh tradeoffs differently than some companies. Accordingly, we want to share with you our fundamental management and decision-making approach so that you, our shareholders, may confirm that it is consistent with your investment philosophy:

- We will continue to focus relentlessly on our customers
- We will continue to make investment decisions in light of long-term market leadership
- We will continue to measure our programs and the effectiveness of our investments analytically, to jettison those that do no provide acceptable returns, and to step up our investment in those that work best. We will continue to learn from both our successes and our failures.
- We will make bold rather than timid investment decisions where we see a sufficient probability of gaining market leadership advantages. Some of these investments will pay off, others will not, and we will have learned another valuable lesson in either case.
- When forced to choose between optimising the appearance of our GAAP accounting and maximising the present value of future cash flows, we'll take the cash flows.

Source: Extract of 1997 letter to Shareholders reprinted in the 2002 and subsequent Annual Reports.

Figure 1 Amazon's Strategy

Source: Originally drawn by Jeff Bezos in 2005.

being 'customer-centric' and continually improving the customer experience by offering lower prices and wider selection. This in turn fed back to the increasing use of Amazon's websites (traffic) by customers and sellers, which again fed back to growing resources for innovation for improved customer experience, and so the 'virtuous' cycle continued. Amazon's brand mantra was to relentlessly serve the customer by shaping the customer experience. Its corporate logo had continually evolved over the past 10 years to match Amazon's shifting business offerings.

Amazon had built a three pillar strategy to guide and reach Bezos' vision. These pillars were selection, price and convenience, with its foundation on innovation.

- *Selection*: Amazon offered the widest selection of products, from its vast selection of retail products to Amazon's software and Cloud Computing offerings;
- *Price*: Amazon was committed to price leadership and to consistently and continuously offer this with no sacrifice to quality. For example, Amazon offered free shipping offers to customers along with a guarantee of on-time delivery;
- *Convenience*: Amazon continually strived to 'please' its customers. For example, Amazon dedicated many resources to understanding what its customers wanted by offering customer review and feedback forms on all of its products.

These three pillars were supported by Amazon's continual commitment to innovation and investing in the future. Bezos concluded: 'There's more to innovation ahead of us than innovation behind us.' Underpinning innovation was the emphasis upon technology.

Fulfilment

Although Amazon was commonly regarded as an online business, products had to be physically shipped to customers. Amazon's many fulfilment centres were typically strategically located in a number of cities in North America, Europe and Asia, often near airports. In total, they comprised some 19.7 million square feet of properties all over the world (see Appendix 4). In 2008, Amazon.com opened a new 600,000 square feet fulfilment centre in Hazleton, PA to serve Amazon's Northeast customers. Another new facility in Goodyear, Arizona of more than 500,000 square feet was also opened.

During 2008, Amazon launched 'Frustration-Free Packaging', a new initiative designed to make it easier for customers to take products from their packages. Frustration-Free Packaging was launched in the US with 19 bestselling products from leading manufacturers including Fisher-Price, Mattel, Microsoft and electronics manufacturer Transcend. Amazon intended to expand this initiative across its international sites during 2009.

Staff

Amazon had always taken a strategic approach to recruiting. As mentioned earlier, it located in Seattle as there was a large supply of computer software talent available. Over the years, it had continually strengthened its management team. For example, during 1997 Richard Dalzell, a former Wal-Mart Vice President joined as Chief Information Officer (CIO). He brought expertise in merchandising and logistics systems, supply chain systems, international retailing and merchandising systems, and commercial decision support and data mining systems. Other senior managers had been recruited from a variety of companies such as AlliedSignal, Apple, Black and Decker, Delta Airlines and Microsoft.

More generally, Amazon recruited 'tightly' around their need to service the customer. Bezos added:

> Companies get skills-focused, instead of customer-needs focused. When [companies] think about extending their business into some new area, the first question is 'why should we do that – we don't have any skills in that area.' That approach puts a finite lifetime on a company, because the world changes and what used to be cutting-edge skills have turned into something your customers may not need anymore. A much more stable strategy is to start with 'what do my customers need?' Then do an inventory of the gaps in your skills.

Culturally, Bezos ensured that his company was never satisfied with the status quo and never too comfortable and he emphasised: 'I ask our people to wake up afraid and terrified (about the customer) every morning.' He also pointed out: 'customers are the folks who have the money. Our competitors are never going to send us money!'

Technology, technology, technology

Despite the progressive change in their vision, Bezos' typical response about the main difference between conventional retail and his business was:

> The three most important things in retail are location, location, location. The three most important things for our consumer business are technology, technology, technology. That's what takes the place of real estate in our business.

Amazon believed the continual investment in technological innovation helped Amazon to achieve two complementary goals. Firstly, it improved efficiency, ultimately lowering operating costs and enabling the company to offer lower prices to customers. Secondly, heavy investment in research and development enabled Amazon to find new ways to improve customer experience. With its advanced technology, Amazon had no need to segment customers based upon the more traditional marketing methods such as demographic or human behaviour. Customer search patterns and purchasing behaviour were tracked almost instantaneously as soon as a customer accessed the website. Furthermore, Amazon's website made intelligent recommendations of what other customers purchased after a new customer found a product they were interested in. In many ways, Amazon had built the ultimate virtual salesperson right at the customer's fingertips, by leveraging off information from millions of customer transactions and online window-shoppers. This competency was very powerful and other organisations had failed to produce similar market data on such a large scale. Bezos concluded by claiming that:

> by building new technologies ourselves we get to offer a better customer experience for millions of people. Does this give us an advantage? Absolutely [but] you have to continue to innovate. This is something that has to be refreshed every day, every week and every year.

Amazon's continual emphasis upon technology led to a number of major outcomes between 2007 to early 2009 including Kindle, improving Amazon Web Services, offering digital content and enhancing accessibility.

Kindle

Amazon developed and marketed an innovative wireless electronic reading device called Amazon Kindle under the Amazon brand. This device was unveiled in the final quarter of 2007 and enabled customers to download books, magazines, newspapers and blogs. Amazon Whispernet, Kindle's wireless delivery system, used a nationwide (US) high speed data network and Kindle users could easily gain access to the Kindle Store where over 90,000 books were available. There were no additional charges for wireless access or service commitments for customers so this was a truly convenient 'value add' for Amazon's book shoppers. Kindle supported a 'ready-to-use' function and as it did not require any set-up or software installation users were able to use Kindle immediately. Kindle users could also store their personal documents in various formats such as DOC, HTML and JPEG.

By June 2008, Kindle had become the top selling product among Amazon's vast selection of consumer electronics products and the 'most wished for' electronics item by

Amazon customers. Amazon had increased the number of book titles available to Kindle from 90,000 to 190,000 with more books being added every day. Amazon built relationships with partners such as Simon & Schuster, Inc. and Christian Publishers, making even more titles available and further 'fuelling' interest in this revolutionary product.

During early 2009, Amazon launched Kindle 2, an improved version of the original product with longer battery life and a new 'Text-to-Speech' feature. Amazon was a major player in the professionally narrated audiobooks business through its subsidiaries Audible and Brilliance, and the 'Text-to-Speech' feature would be likely to introduce new customers to the convenience of listening to books and thereby expand the professionally narrated audiobooks industry. Amazon further enhanced Kindle for iPhone and iPod touch in March 2009, which allowed customers to enjoy over 240,000 books.

Amazon Web Services

The most disruptive technological innovations released by Amazon between 2007 and early 2009 were through Amazon Web Services (AWS). AWS products were examples of Cloud Computing, a model whereby IT vendors host hardware and software in their own data centres and make them accessible via the internet. The trend in Cloud Computing has been compared to the development of the electricity network more than a century ago, whereby companies stopped having to produce their own power and instead plugged into a national electric grid. In the same way, individuals and organisations can now connect to a 'cloud' of computing resources to fuel their information and processing needs on the internet. The benefit of this approach was that companies with access to huge economies of scale can sell their hardware or software processing power to users on a 'pay as you use' basis far cheaper than a user could individually. If the internet community could facilitate this disruptive technology, personal computers as we know them today may become obsolete and products such as Kindle or 'dumb terminals' could take their place.

A number of big technology names had already embraced the Cloud Computing revolution, including Google, IBM and Sun Systems. However, Amazon's EC2 was commonly regarded as being the most popular and more commercialised than any of its competitor's offerings. Products that AWS released included AWS Premium Support, Amazon Mechanical Turk, Amazon EBS, Amazon CloudFront and Public Data Sets on AWS.

AWS Premium Support provided IT customers with fast, one-on-one technical assistance and released new features that enabled developers to build even more powerful and fault resilient applications on the internet. These new capabilities were amongst the top requests from developers.

During the third quarter of 2008, Amazon Mechanical Turk launched a new set of web-based tools that made it easier for businesses to outsource work to an on-demand workforce to businesses worldwide. These web tools allowed customers to utilise the internet to outsource thousands of tasks, manage a virtual workforce and easily download work results. This technology opened up the service to a wider range of customers because it no longer required clients to have programming skills. With these new web-based tools, any business could submit work that required human intelligence to a workforce of hundreds of thousands of workers from over 100 countries in just a few minutes. This enabled businesses to get important work done quickly and inexpensively.

In the same quarter (third quarter of 2008), Amazon's innovative AWS division launched the Amazon Elastic Block Store (Amazon EBS), a new and improved storage feature for EC2 that provided unlimited storage potential to clients using the Amazon EC2 service.

The last quarter of 2008 was a busy and productive one for AWS. EC2 was upgraded for compatibility with Microsoft products such as Microsoft Windows Server and Microsoft SQL Server, and provided even greater flexibility for deploying solutions in the AWS 'cloud'.

AWS also launched Amazon CloudFront, a high-performance, self-service, pay-as-you-go method of distributing data over the internet at high data transfer speeds. Adam Selipsky, Vice President of Product Management and Developer Relations at AWS claimed:

> Our customers asked us for a way to globally distribute their most frequently accessed content with all the benefits that AWS provides: low, pay-as-you-go pricing, high performance and reliability.[i]

AWS also introduced Public Data Sets on AWS, which enabled developers and researchers to cost-effectively create, share and consume large sets of data free of charge. AWS had been working to lower the barriers to entry for fellow scientists for the past five years, and Public Data Sets on AWS would provide virtually free resources to researchers. By increasing the number of people with access to important and useful data, and making it easy to compute on that data with cost-efficient services such as Amazon EC2, AWS hoped to fuel innovation and further accelerate the pace of new discoveries.

AWS was voted the fifth most influential biztech product of 2008 by ZD Net. Peter De Santis, General Manager of EC2 concluded: 'For over 2 years, we've focused on delivering a cost-effective, web scale infrastructure to developers, giving them complete flexibility in the kinds of solutions they deliver.'

Digital contents

Another significant expansion for Amazon between 2007 and early 2009 was in its digital content offerings. During 2007, Amazon launched a MP3 Music Store, a digital music downloads store. All MP3 contents on the Amazon MP3 store were offered without Digital Rights Management (DRM) software, so customers could listen to these MP3s without any restrictions. EMI music, one of the major music providers, joined this launch and the Warner Music Group had become another supplier by the end of 2007. This DRM-free partnership with major music providers helped Amazon establish its strategic position as the world's largest selection of DRM-free MP3.

From early 2008, Amazon made DRM-free MP3 music downloads from Sony Music Entertainment available to customers on Amazon MP3. Consequently, Amazon MP3 became the only retailer to offer customers DRM-free MP3s from all the major music labels, as well as over 33,000 independent labels. It also announced in January 2008 an international roll-out of Amazon MP3, where every song was playable on virtually any digital music capable device, including the PC, Mac®, iPod®, iPhone™ and BlackBerry®. Later in the year, Amazon launched a New Artists Store featuring comprehensive artist content, including full album discographies, CDs, DRM-free MP3 and vinyl catalogue selection along with community features such as artist images, biographies and related products.

In September 2008, Amazon's subsidiary IMDb.com announced that users could watch over 6000 full length feature films and TV episodes for free on IMDb.com. This included new stores devoted to customers' favourite TV series and children's programming. It rolled-out a German version in November, www.imdb.de, specifically to help German-speaking movie and TV lovers easily find information for their favourite films and TV shows.

Accessibility

Many technology developments were aimed at enhancing customer accessibility. For example, during early 2008, Amazon launched a new feature, Amazon Currency Converter, on its website allowing international customers to pay for their purchases in the currency of their payment card, instead of US dollars. This enabled international customers to purchase eligible items from its website with greater ease and certainty.

Along similar lines, Amazon launched 'Bill Me Later's' next generation payments service for its customers to complete purchases instantly online without using a credit card. With its flexible financing programmes Bill Me Later, Inc. was a leader in the digital payments industry. Its network included hundreds of top-tier merchants including Borders, Bluefly, Continental Airlines, eLUXURY, Fujitsu, JetBlue, Toshiba, Toys 'Я' Us, US Airways, Walmart.com and Zappos.

In April 2008, Amazon.com launched Amazon TextBuyIt, a new service that allowed customers to use text messages to find and buy products sold on Amazon.com. With the addition of TextBuyIt to Amazon's existing mobile offering, including its mobile site and mobile iPhone site, customers could now shop virtually anywhere using either text message or their mobile device's web browser.

In order to expand Amazon's IT offering to its developer clients, Amazon Payments announced early in 2009 the general availability of Amazon Flexible Payments Service (Amazon FPS). This effectively allowed developers to accept payments from Amazon's millions of customers and enabled developers to monetise their innovations quickly.

Market and product and service expansion

Amazon's emphasis on technology and innovation enabled it to quickly roll out its activities across the world (see Appendix 5). During 2007, it launched a number of new sites that served customers with specific needs. In early 2007, Amazon launched Endless.com which focused on shoe and handbag items. It provided free overnight shipping, 'a 110 per cent price guarantee' on its products and convenient navigation and search functions for over 250 brands and 15,000 styles of shoes and handbags. Endless.com operated '24-hour-a-day customer service phone support', which enhanced and facilitated the customer shopping experience. By mid-2007, it had added over 50 new brands to its existing selection.

Amazon launched two music stores, Classical Music Blowout Store and Go Indie Music Store. According to Thomas May, Amazon's senior music editor, there were a decreasing number of bricks-and-mortar music stores and increasing demand for the selection of classical music offered on Amazon. Go Indie Music Store provided music buyers with hundreds of titles from more than 30 independent music labels.

Amazon All Business Centre was introduced as a new category store, providing one-stop shopping for start-up businesses as well as growing businesses. This store offered various solutions targeted at entrepreneurs' needs and some of the key offerings were customer forums, laptops, software solutions, furniture and stationery. The store also provided customers with services such as Amazon Web Services, Fulfilment and Amazon Corporate Accounts.

Amazon continuously expanded globally via its international network. After the initial success of Amazon Jewellery, Amazon launched its Jewellery & Watches Store in the UK, Germany, France and Japan. Amazon's jewellery business had remarkable growth in the second quarter of 2007, 260 per cent in diamond sales, 169 per cent in coloured gemstones and 107 per cent in sterling silver sales. The success attracted various brands, such as Crislu, Elle, Miss Sixty, Nautica and Technomarine.

During 2008, Amazon launched its Office Supplies Store, a single shopping destination that offered competitive prices on products for the classroom, home office, small office, corporate office 'and everything in-between'. This new store included a selection of more than 500,000 products from thousands of manufacturers, including both well known and hard to find brands such as Avery, Hammermill and Raymond Geddes.

Amazon also diversified into auto parts, launching its Motorcycle Store as a single shopping destination for motorcycle and parts, accessories and protective gear. The store showcased a selection of more than 300,000 products from over 500 manufacturers, including top brands like Alpine Stars, Fox Racing, Harley Davidson, Suzuki and Tour Master.

During August 2008, Amazon unveiled the Software en Espanol Store, a new category store featuring essential Spanish language and bilingual software products. With content primarily in English accompanied by some Spanish information, the store featured an extensive selection of business and office software as well as educational offerings and software for children. The Amazon Software en Espanol Store was designed to be the destination for Hispanic consumers and to help meet the needs of the nearly 1.6 million Hispanic-owned businesses in the US.

Amazon 'kicked off' 2009 with the launch of Amazon's Inauguration Store, which offered customers everything considered necessary to attend an event, host an inauguration party or watch the milestone occasion from home. Another launch included Amazon's PC Casual Game Download Store which offered over 600 game titles to compete with PC game portals such as Yahoo Games.

Acquistions and alliances

Over the 2007 to early 2009 period, strategically aligned acquisitions and alliances remained a key way for Amazon to pursue technology development, applications and extend products or services. These alliances benefited Amazon's partners through, for example, access to capital, management expertise and Amazon's huge customer database. Some examples of acquisitions included:

In June 2008, the company acquired Fabric.com, a leading online store that offered custom measured and cut fabrics, as well as patterns, sewing tools and accessories. This acquisition enabled Fabric.com to further expand its selection of fabrics and accessories while enabling Amazon.com to offer its customers a wider variety of products in the sewing, craft and hobby segment.

In October 2008, Amazon acquired Reflexive Entertainment, a PC casual game distributor and developer. Reflexive's CEO Lars Brubaker announced its acquisition with the expectation that Reflexive would serve a broader range of customers via Amazon's distribution channel.

Amazon.com also completed its acquisition of AbeBooks, an online marketplace for books, with over 110 million primarily used, rare and out-of-print books listed for sale by thousands of independent booksellers from around the world. AbeBooks added millions of customers to Amazon's existing consumer base and expanded its geographic reach with AbeBook's global websites (AbeBooks.com, AbeBooks.ca, AbeBooks.co.uk, AbeBooks.de, AbeBooks.fr, AbeBooks.it and Iberlibro.com). AbeBooks.com also had affiliates in Germany and the US.

Competitors

Based on Amazon's Annual Report (2009a), it was possible to identify six different types of competitors. Firstly, there were physical-world retailers, publishers, vendors, distributors, manufacturers and producers of Amazon's products. Examples included Wal-Mart and Barnes & Noble. Secondly, there were other online e-commerce and mobile e-commerce sites, including sites that sold or distributed digital content. A major player, eBay, had achieved less than half of Amazon's sales, but earned much higher net income and net profit margin (see Appendix 1). John Donahoe, CEO of eBay, recently announced that it would focus on the 'secondary market . . . as a part of its effort to transform its core marketplace business' (Morrison, 2009). Thirdly, there were indirect competitors including media companies, web portals, comparison shopping websites and web search engines. Fourthly, there were companies that provided e-commerce services, including website development, fulfilment and customer services. Fifthly, there were companies that provided infrastructure web services or other information storage or computing services or products. As Amazon entered into the web infrastructure industry, two new competitors were Apple and Google. Finally, there were companies that designed, manufactured, marketed or sold digital media devices. Again, Apple and Google were competitors within this category. Appendix 6 provides a comparison of some competitor's revenue.

Key financials

Appendix 2 presents sales and income as allocated to North America and International Segments 2001–08.

Capital expenditure and cash

In line with Amazon's mission to become the 'Earth's most customer-centric company for its three primary customer sets: consumers, sellers and developers' (Amazon.com, 2009a), Amazon continued to invest heavily in technology innovation. Bezos pointed out:

> We transform much of customer experience – such as unmatched selection, extensive product information, personalized recommendations, and other new software features – into largely a fixed expense. With customer experience costs largely fixed, our costs as a percentage of sales can shrink rapidly as we grow our business.

This commitment to invest heavily in technology innovation was reflected in the high rate of year-on-year growth in technology and content operating expenses and cost of internal-use software and website development (see Appendix 7). During 2008, US$1033 million was spent on the development and enhancement of various areas of technology and content, including seller platforms, web services, digital initiatives as well as technology infrastructure. In 2008, Amazon had also capitalised US$187 million of internal-use software and website development cost. This amount represented an increase of 45 per cent from its 2007 level ($129m).

Another stated strategic financial focus for Amazon was on 'Long term, sustainable growth in free cash flow' (Amazon.com, 2009a). Typically, Amazon offered short

credit terms to its customers and enjoyed longer payment terms from suppliers, the value difference being approximately 26 days. This operational advantage enabled Amazon to use funds collected from customers as a source of working capital. As a consequence of this, and in conjunction with other cash management initiatives, Amazon was able to maintain a strong cash flow position and fund its continuous investment in technology innovation. Amazon's long term debt data also indicated that it was relying less on long term debt to fund its innovation and operations activities (see Appendix 7).

Share price

Since listing in 1997, Amazon had yet to pay dividends to shareholders. Investors had therefore to rely upon share price fluctuations for investor return. Figure 2 shows Amazon's share price relative to the market index.

Doubts about Amazon's plan to continue its massive spending to build its new Web Services technology and capacity combined with investors' frustration with the apparent lack of payoff in Amazon's earlier investment resulted in its stock price falling close to 50 per cent from 2004 to 2006 (Sage, 2006). Consequently, during 2007, Amazon was forced to invest in its technology and market expansion at a slower rate in order to subdue shareholder

Figure 2 Amazon share price 2006–9 relative to market index DJI and IXIC

Source: Yahoo! Finance.

anxiety. However, this slowdown of investment in innovation did not last long, 'I believe you have to be willing to be misunderstood if you're going to innovate', Bezos said when an interviewer remarked that he was able to ignore criticism from Wall Street, the press, and others about Amazon's investments in innovation (Burrows, 2008). Accordingly, in 2008, investment and expenses on investment rebounded to pre-2007 levels and was supported by shareholder sentiment due to positive returns being delivered to the market.

2009 and beyond – mixed opinions

During 2008, Amazon warned that the global financial crisis would amplify the strategic and financial risks it faced and would be likely to make general trading conditions far more challenging during 2009. However, analysts were divided about whether Amazon would be able to 'weather the storm' better than its peers. For example, a senior analyst at Sanford C. Bernstein predicted that Amazon would continue to outperform its competition.

Amazon's ability to maintain strong cash flow whilst reducing its reliance on borrowed funds for day-to-day operations has seen it gain favourable commentary from the share market. In addition, Amazon's recent announcement

of its plans to redeem US$335 million of the outstanding principal on its convertible subordinated notes due by the end of March 2009 further confirmed the strength of its cash position and was well received by the market (Kelleher, 2009).[vi]

However, other analysts were keen to point out that as Amazon's survival had been reliant on sales growth, a significant reduction in the sales growth rate would have a considerable impact on Amazon's cash flow and future ability to invest in technology innovation. Symptoms of decreasing consumer demand were reflected in Amazon's 2008 December quarter revenue, which had only grown by 18 per cent in comparison to 40 per cent in the last quarter of 2007.

Amazon's international sales contribution, currently at 47 per cent, was expected to increase to 50 per cent of its consolidated sales in the near future (Amazon.com, 2009a). Whilst this would spread the risk of a slow-down in North American markets, it would also increase Amazon's exposure to foreign exchange risk, which amounted to a loss of US$320 million in fourth quarter in 2008 alone. Clearly, there was much for Bezos to consider.

Reference:
[i] Phil Muncaster, 'Amazon Cloud Front takes off', Vnunet.com, 2008.

APPENDIX 1 Peer comparison 2008

Dow Jones Industry: Etailing (B2C)

Rank	Company name	Sales USD m	Employees	Market cap USD m	Net income USD m	Net profit margin
1	Amazon.com, Inc.	19,166.00	20,700	29,413.66	645.00	3.41%
2	eBay, Inc.	8,541.26	16,200	15,305.78	1,779.47	20.83%
3	Priceline.com Incorporated	1,884.81	1,780	3,210.43	193.47	10.46%
4	Ticketmaster Entertainment, Inc.	1,240.48	3,600	229.99	169.35	13.45%
5	Overstock.com, Inc.	834.37	1,036	216.05	−12.66	−1.52%
6	Value Vision Media, Inc.	781.55	869	11.78	22.45	2.87%
7	United Fuel & Energy Corporation	446.04	420	8.51	−5.21	−1.17%
8	Rue du Commerce SA	408.90	246	39.69	3.75	0.92%
9	Digital River, Inc.	394.23	1,335	1,081.42	63.60	16.13%
10	DeNA Co., Ltd.	321.77	446	1,513.08	73.32	23.96%

Source: Reuters, Factiva (exhibited in Dow Jones Company Report for Amazon.com. Inc.).

APPENDIX 2 Sales and income as allocated to segments, 2001–08

	Calendar years ended 31 December ($m)							
	2008	2007	2006	2005	2004	2003	2002	2001
North America								
Net sales	$10,228	$8,095	$5,869	$4,711	$3,847	$3,259	$2,761	$2,461
Cost of sales	7,733	6,064	4,344	3,444	2,823	2,392	2,020	1,802
Gross profit	2,495	2,031	1,525	1,267	1,024	867	741	659
Direct segment operating expenses (1)	2,050	1,631	1,295	971	703	583	562	600
Segment operating income (loss)	445	400	230	296	321	284	179	59
International								
Net sales	8,938	6,740	4,842	3,779	3,074	2,005	1,172	662
Cost of sales	7,163	5,418	3,911	3,007	2,496	1,614	921	522
Gross profit	1,775	1,322	931	772	578	391	251	140
Direct segment operating expenses (1)	1,127	873	661	502	409	313	250	243
Segment operating income (loss)	648	449	270	270	169	78	1	−103
Consolidated								
Net sales	19,166	14,835	10,711	8,490	6,921	5,264	3,933	3,123
Cost of sales	14,896	11,482	8,255	6,451	5,319	4,006	2,941	2,324
Gross profit	4,270	3,353	2,456	2,039	1,602	1,258	992	799
Direct segment operating expenses	3,177	2,504	1,956	1,473	1,112	896	812	843
Segment operating income (loss)	1,093	849	500	566	490	362	180	−44
Stock-based compensation	−275	−185	−101	−87	−58	−88	−69	−5
Other operating income (expense)	24	−9	−10	−47	8	−3	−47	−363
Income (loss) from operations	842	655	389	432	440	271	64	−412
Total non-operating income (expense), net	59	5	−12	−4	−85	−232	−215	−144
Benefit (provision) for income taxes	−247	−184	−187	−95	233	−4	1	–
Cumulative effect of change in accounting principle	−9	–	–	26	–	–	1	−11
Net income (loss)	$645	$476	$190	$359	$588	$35	−$149	−$567
Segment highlights:								
Y/Y net sales growth:								
North America	26%	38%	25%	22%	18%	18%	12%	3%
International	33	39	28	23	53	71	77	74
Consolidated	29	39	26	23	31	34	26	13
Y/Y gross profit growth:								
North America	23%	33%	20%	24%	18%	17%	13%	14%
International	34	42	21	33	48	55	78	83
Consolidated	27	37	20	27	27	27	24	22
Y/Y segment operating income growth:								
North America	11%	74%	−22%	−8%	13%	58%	212%	N/A
International	44	66	0	59	116	7,700	−101	−29
Consolidated	29	68	−12	16	35	101	−509	−86
Net sales mix:								
North America	53%	55%	55%	55%	56%	62%	70%	79%
International	47	45	45	45	44	38	30	21
Gross Margin:								
North America	24.4%	25.1%	26.0%	26.9%	26.6%	26.6%	26.8%	26.8%
International	19.9	19.6	19.2	20.4	18.8	19.5	21.4	21.1
Consolidated	22.3	22.6	22.9	24.0	23.1	23.9	25.2	25.6

Sources: Compiled from various sources.

APPENDIX 3 Defining the business

As mentioned in the main body of the case study, from originally serving just website retail customers, Amazon in 2009 served three distinct groups of customers:

- *Consumer customers*: through their retail websites, Amazon provided a wide range of merchandise, low prices, and convenience to their consumers.
- *Seller customers*: sellers that sold their products either on Amazon's websites or on their own brand websites and fulfilled their orders using Amazon's fulfilment facilities.
- *Developer customers*: customers that used Amazon Web Services (AWS) which provided access to Amazon's technology infrastructure that enabled them to create virtually any type of business. These services include:

  - Amazon Simple Storage Service (Amazon S3)
  - Amazon Elastic Compute Cloud (Amazon EC2)
  - Amazon Simple Queue Service (Amazon SQS)
  - Amazon SimpleDB
  - Amazon Flexible Payments Service (Amazon FPS)
  - Amazon Mechanical Turk.

Amazon's retail offerings included:

- Browsing
- Searching
- Review and content
- Recommendations and personalisation
- One-click technology
- Secure credit card payment
- Availability and fulfilment
- Kindle and Accessibility
- Digital contents

There were two principal operation divisions for Amazon's retail sites:

- North America division operated www.amazon.com, www.amazon.ca, www.shopbop.com, and www.endless.com
- International division operated www.amazon.co.uk, www.amazon.de, www.amazon.co.jp, www.amazon.fr, www.amazon.cn, and www.joyo.cn

The principal retail segments under these sites included:

- *Media*: books, movies, music, digital downloads, software, video games;
- *Electronic and other general merchandise (EGM)*: electronics and computers, devices, home and garden, toys, children and baby, grocery, apparel, shoes and jewellery, health and beauty, sports and outdoors, auto and industrial, and tools;
- *'Other'*: Amazon Enterprise Solutions, Amazon Web Services, co-branded credit card, miscellaneous marketing, and others.

Amazon divided the company into three functional areas:

- *Product development*: Departments within this area included editorial, marketing, product feasibility, pricing, website design and site navigation, e-commerce solutions and Kindle;
- *Technology content and development*: Software and technical production along with databases, information technology systems and engineering and computer science;
- *Supply chain and distribution*: Distribution centres, business-to-business client relationship management, and supply chain management.

APPENDIX 4 Fulfilment and warehousing

Fulfilment centres were located in the following cities, often near airports.

North America:
- Arizona: Phoenix, Goodyear
- Delaware: New Castle
- Indiana: Whitestown, Munster
- Kansas: Coffeyville
- Kentucky: Campbellsville, Hebron (near CVG), Lexington, and Louisville
- Nevada: Fernley and Red Rock (near 4SD)
- New Hampshire: Nashua
- Pennsylvania: Carlisle, Chambersburg, Hazleton, and Lewisberry
- Texas: Dallas/Fort Worth
- Ontario, Canada: Mississauga (a Canada Post facility)

Europe:
- Amazon.co.uk warehouse: Glenrothes
- Bedfordshire, England: Marston Gate
- Inverclyde, Scotland: Gourock
- Fife, Scotland: Glenrothes
- Neath Port Talbot, Wales: Crymlyn Burrows near Jersey Marine
- Loiret, France: Orléans-Boigny
- Loiret, France: Orléans-Saran
- Hesse, Germany: Bad Hersfeld
- Saxony, Germany: Leipzig

Asia:
- Chiba, Japan
- Guangzhou, China
- Suzhou, China
- Beijing, China

Source: 'Amazon' from *Wikipedia*. This appendix uses material from *Wikipedia* article 'Amazon.com' and is available under the Creative Commons Attribution-ShareAlike License, http://creativecommons.org/licenses/by-sa/3.0//.

APPENDIX 5 Chronology of retail product globally rolled out across Amazon's websites

Global Selection

Product categories	US	UK	Germany	France	Japan	China	Canada
Physical media	'95	'98	'98	'00	'00	'04	'02
Electronics	'99	'01	'01	'05	'03	'04	**'08**
Toys	'99	'01	'04	'07	'04	'04	
Baby	'99	'07	'07	'07	'07	'06	
Tools and hardware	'99	'04	'04				
Home and garden	'00	'04	'04	'07	'03		
Apparel and accessories	'02	**'08**	**'08**		'07		
Sports and outdoors	'03	'07	'06		'05	'06	
Jewelry and watches	'03	'07	'07	'07	'07	'06	
Health and personal care	'03	**'08**	'07		'06	'06	
Beauty	'04	**'08**	**'08**		**'08**	'06	
Shoes	'05	'07	'07		'07		
Dry goods	'06						
Auto parts and accessories	'06		**'08**				
Digital media	'07	**'08**					
Office supplies	**'08**						
Fabric	**'08**						
Motorcycle and ATV parts and accessories	**'08**						

Source: Adopted from Morgan Stanley Technology Conference, 4 March 2009.

APPENDIX 6 Competitor's revenue comparison

Revenue (US$,000)	2000	2001	2002	2003	2004	2005	2006	2007	2008
Amazon	2,761,983	3,122,433	3,932,936	5,263,699	6,921,124	8,490,000	10,711,000	14,835,000	19,166,000
eBay	431,424	748,821	1,214,100	2,165,096	3,271,309	4,552,401	5,969,741	7,672,329	8,541,261
Barnes and Noble	3,468,043	4,375,804	4,870,390	5,269,335	5,951,015	4,873,595	5,139,618	5,286,674	5,121,804
Yahoo!	1,110,178	717,422	953,067	1,625,097	3,574,517	5,257,668	6,425,679	6,969,274	7,208,502
Apple	7,983,000	5,363,000	5,742,000	6,207,000	8,279,000	13,931,000	19,315,000	24,006,000	32,479,000
Wal-Mart	166,809,000	193,295,000	219,812,000	246,525,000	258,681,000	287,989,000	348,368,000	378,476,000	405,607,000
Google		86,426	439,508	1,465,934	3,189,223	6,138,560	10,604,917	16,593,986	21,795,550

Source for 2006–08: Dow Jones Factiva (Originally from Reuters).

Source for 2000–05: Adopted from Amazon.com (B) – from 2004 to 2006 by Stockport, 2007 (Originally from Mergent and Amazon annual reports).

APPENDIX 7 Technology expense, technology cost capitalised, free cash flows and long term debt 2001–08

(in millions)	Calendar Years Ended December 31							
Technology and Content	2008	2007	2006	2005	2004	2003	2002	2001
Operating Expenses								
Value	$1033	$818	$662	$451	$283	$257	$216	$242
Y/Y Operating expenses growth:	26%	23%	47%	59%	10%	2%	−11%	N/A
Internal-Use Software and Website Development Cost Capitalised								
Value	$187	$129	$123	$90	$44	$83	$92	N/A
Y/Y Capitalised Cost Growth:	45%	5%	37%	105%	−47%	−10%	N/A	N/A
Free Cash Flow								
Value	$1364	$1181	$486	$529	$477	$347	$135	−$170
Y/Y Free cash Flow Growth:	15%	143%	−8%	11%	37%	157%	179%	N/A
Long Term Debt								
Value	$409	$1282	$1247	$1521	$1855	$1945	$2277	N/A
Y/Y Free cash Flow Growth:	−68%	3%	−18%	−18%	−5%	−15%	N/A	N/A

Source: Amazon.com.

The Formula 1 constructors

Mark Jenkins

This case describes four periods of dominance by particular firms in a highly competitive technological context. Formula 1 (F1) motorsport is the pinnacle of automotive technology. Highly specialised constructors design and build single seat racing cars (and sometimes engines) to compete for annual championships which bring huge financial and reputational rewards. These four eras explore the stories of three contrasting companies each within a different competitive time period in terms of how they both created and lost the basis for sustained competitive advantage.

• • •

'Between two and four on a Sunday afternoon this is a sport. All the rest of the time it's commerce.'

Frank Williams, Managing Director, Williams F1

In 1945 the Fédération Internationale de l'Automobile (FIA) established Formula A as the premier level of motorsport. In the years that followed Formula A became referred to as Formula One (F1) and a drivers' world championship was introduced in 1950. By the mid-1960s F1 had moved from being a basis for car manufacturers to promote and test their products, to a highly specialist business where purpose built cars were developed through leading edge technology.

F1 had become a TV sporting event which enjoyed the third highest audience in the world, surpassed only by the Olympics and World Cup Soccer.

There have been between 10 and 14 race car manufacturers or constructors competing in F1 at any one time. In 2008 the top three teams were Ferrari, McLaren and BMW, all medium sized businesses turning over between $300 million (€220m or £200m) and $400 million (€293m or £268m) per annum. For the first three years of their entry into F1 in 2002 Toyota are estimated to have committed $1 billion on capital and running costs of which only one-fifth will have come from sponsorship. The top teams would typically have their own testing and development equipment, which would include wind-tunnels and other facilities. The larger teams would employ between 450 and 800 people in their F1 operations, a quarter of whom travel around the world attending Grand Prix every two to three weeks throughout the F1 season (March to November). Labour costs account for around

Source: Corbis/Michael Kim.

25 per cent of the budget. All the teams would have highly qualified technical staff which would include race engineers (who work with the driver to set up the car), designers, aerodynamicists, composite experts (to work with specialised carbon-composite materials) and systems specialists.

In addition to sponsorship, revenue is provided by prize money generated by winning championship points. The prize money is a way of dividing up the royalties earned from media coverage and other revenues negotiated on behalf of the teams by the Commercial Rights Holder: Bernie Ecclestone's Formula One Group (FOG). In 2009 around 15 per cent of Ferrari's budget was estimated to come from prize money.

The Formula 1 Constructors provide a unique context to consider the competitive advantage of different multi-million pound organisations over time. The pace of change and the basis of advantage are constantly changing, shown by the fact that since the start of the world championships, only two constructors have won the championship consecutively more than four times (McLaren 1988–91; Ferrari

---

Table 7.1 Summary of world champions

Year	Driver	Car/Engine	Constructors' Cup
1950	Giuseppe Farina	Alfa Romeo	
1951	Juan Manuel Fangio	Alfa Romeo	
1952	Alberto Ascari	Ferrari	
1953	Alberto Ascari	Ferrari	
1954	Juan Manuel Fangio	Maserati	
1955	Juan Manuel Fangio	Mercedes-Benz	
1956	Juan Manuel Fangio	Lancia-Ferrari	
1957	Juan Manuel Fangio	Maserati	
1958	Mike Hawthorn	Ferrari	Vanwall
1959	Jack Brabham	Cooper/Climax	Cooper/Climax
1960	Jack Brabham	Cooper/Climax	Cooper/Climax
1961	Phil Hill	Ferrari	Ferrari
1962	Graham Hill	BRM	BRM
1963	Jim Clark	Lotus/Climax	Lotus/Climax
1964	John Surtees	Ferrari	Ferrari
1965	Jim Clark	Lotus/Climax	Lotus/Climax
1966	Jack Brabham	Brabham/Repco	Brabham/Repco
1967	Denny Hulme	Brabham/Repco	Brabham/Repco
1968	Graham Hill	Lotus/Ford	Lotus/Ford
1969	Jackie Stewart	Matra/Ford	Matra/Ford
1970	Jochen Rindt	Lotus/Ford	Lotus/Ford
1971	Jackie Stewart	Tyrrell/Ford	Tyrrell/Ford
1972	Emerson Fittipaldi	Lotus/Ford	Lotus/Ford
1973	Jackie Stewart	Tyrrell/Ford	Lotus/Ford
1974	Emerson Fittipaldi	McLaren/Ford	McLaren/Ford
1975	Niki Lauda	Ferrari	Ferrari
1976	James Hunt	McLaren/Ford	Ferrari
1977	Niki Lauda	Ferrari	Ferrari
1978	Mario Andretti	Lotus/Ford	Lotus/Ford
1979	Jody Scheckter	Ferrari	Ferrari
1980	Alan Jones	Williams/Ford	Williams/Ford
1981	Nelson Piquet	Brabham/Ford	Williams/Ford
1982	Keke Rosberg	Williams/Ford	Ferrari
1983	Nelson Piquet	Brabham/BMW	Ferrari
1984	Niki Lauda	McLaren/Porsche	McLaren/Porsche
1985	Alain Prost	McLaren/Porsche	McLaren/Porsche
1986	Alain Prost	McLaren/Porsche	Williams/Honda
1987	Nelson Piquet	Williams/Honda	Williams/Honda
1988	Ayrton Senna	McLaren/Honda	McLaren/Honda
1989	Alain Prost	McLaren/Honda	McLaren/Honda
1990	Ayrton Senna	McLaren/Honda	McLaren/Honda
1991	Ayrton Senna	McLaren/Honda	McLaren/Honda
1992	Nigel Mansell	Williams/Renault	Williams/Renault
1993	Alain Prost	Williams/Renault	Williams/Renault
1994	Michael Schumacher	Benetton/Ford	Williams/Renault
1995	Michael Schumacher	Benetton/Renault	Benetton/Renault
1996	Damon Hill	Williams/Renault	Williams/Renault
1997	Jacques Villeneuve	Williams/Renault	Williams/Renault
1998	Mika Hakkinen	McLaren/Mercedes	McLaren/Mercedes
1999	Mika Hakkinen	McLaren/Mercedes	Ferrari
2000	Michael Schumacher	Ferrari	Ferrari
2001	Michael Schumacher	Ferrari	Ferrari
2002	Michael Schumacher	Ferrari	Ferrari
2003	Michael Schumacher	Ferrari	Ferrari
2004	Michael Schumacher	Ferrari	Ferrari
2005	Fernando Alonso	Renault	Renault
2006	Fernando Alonso	Renault	Renault
2007	Kimi Raikonen	Ferrari	Ferrari
2008	Lewis Hamilton	McLaren	Ferrari
2009	Jenson Button	Brawn	Brawn

Note: Constructors' championship is based on the cumulative points gained by a team during the season. Currently each team is limited to entering two cars and drivers per race.

1999–2004) and only Ferrari (1975–77) and Williams (1992–94) have also won for three consecutive years (Table 1). The remainder of the case considers each of these periods of competitive dominance in chronological order.

Ferrari and its renaissance in the mid-1970s

The period 1975–77 saw a renaissance for the Ferrari team. Its previous F1 World Championship had been won in 1964, one of the few reminders of the glorious 1950s and early 1960s when the bright red cars of Ferrari dominated motor racing. Ferrari is the oldest of all the Grand Prix teams still racing. This heritage gives the team a special place in the hearts of all motor racing enthusiasts. Founded by Enzo Ferrari, an ex-driver and manager of the Alfa Romeo racing team, it and other Italian marques such as Maserati and Alfa dominated the sport during the 1950s. Ferraris have taken part in more than 780 grand prix (the next highest is McLaren with 658) and, despite the variable nature of the team's performance, drivers continue to view a contract with Ferrari as something very special. Perhaps this is why world champions such as Alain Prost, Nigel Mansell and Michael Schumacher have been attracted to the team at times when their cars have been far from the fastest or most reliable.

While the majority of constructors were British specialists who buy in components such as engines and gearboxes, Ferrari has always done everything itself. All the major components are made at its Maranello factory, which enjoys the most up-to-date facilities. While other constructors will paint their cars whatever colour required by their flagship sponsor, Ferraris always have been and, one assumes always will be, bright red, the national colour of Italy, a throwback from the time when F1 cars were colour coded by country of origin. The cars have, until recently, very little evidence of sponsorship; it has always been the Ferrari emblem – a black prancing horse – which has the most prominent position. The Italian public see Ferrari as a national icon, as observed by Niki Lauda:

> The Italians love you when you win and hate you when you lose and whatever you do, win, lose or simply break wind everyone in Italy wants to know about it!

The influence of Enzo Ferrari, or *Il Commendatore* as he was frequently known, was pervasive and the myths and stories surrounding him still permeate the team. It was legendary that Ferrari himself hardly ever attended a race and very rarely left the Maranello factory where his beloved cars were made. He relied on the media and his advisors for information which often created a highly political atmosphere. Ferrari's first love was motor racing, and this was despite having created a very successful range of road-going cars which he saw primarily as the source of funding for

his racing. The merger between Fiat and Ferrari in 1969 provided Ferrari with a huge cash injection. Ferrari had sold 40 per cent of the company to Fiat and allowed Fiat to build the road cars. However, Enzo, who was then 71, would retain control of the racing operation in order to concentrate on his first love, motor racing at the highest level: Formula One.

Ferrari has always built its own engines using a large technical team dedicated to the task of engine design and development. In 1971 the company opened its own test track at Fiorano, literally a few hundred yards from the Maranello factory. At the time it was the most advanced and sophisticated test circuit in the world, enabling the cars to be constantly tested and developed between the track and the factory. This effectively gave Ferrari its own grand prix circuit. All the competitors were obliged to hire a circuit such as Silverstone in the UK and transport their cars and equipment for a two or three day test. Ferrari himself attended most of the tests and would make sure he was kept informed as to exactly what was being tested and why. Enzo himself had always declared his love for the distinctive sound and power of a Ferrari engine as indicated by former Ferrari driver, Nigel Mansell: 'Enzo Ferrari believed that the engine was the most important part of the race car. Colin [Chapman – head of Lotus] believed it was the chassis.'

The early 1970s began shakily for Ferrari. The new ownership and influence from Fiat meant increased resources, but also increased pressure for results. At this time F1 was dominated by the Ford DFV engine. Built by Cosworth Engineering near Northampton and funded by the Ford Motor Company, the DFV was F1's first purpose built engine; it was light, powerful and relatively inexpensive. In 1968 the engines were available for £7500 each and were fully capable of winning a Grand Prix. This enabled the British constructors, who specialised in chassis design, to become increasingly competitive. In 1971 and 1973 every Grand Prix was won by a car using a DFV engine.

In 1971 the Ferraris were very fast, but not reliable. It got worse in 1972 and 1973 with cars only finishing every other race and rarely in the points. Enzo himself had been suffering poor health and the team seemed unable to turn around despite having the huge resources of Fiat at its disposal. However, through 1974 things began to change. Mauro Forghieri had been recalled to Ferrari in 1973 as technical director. He had been responsible for some of the more successful Ferraris of the 1960s, but had fallen from grace and spent the later part of the 1960s working on 'special projects'.

In addition to the arrival of Forghieri, a new team boss was also appointed. At 25 years old, a qualified lawyer with connections to the Agnelli family which owned Fiat, Luca di Montezemolo was an unlikely right-hand man for *Il Commendatore*. However, he was given a relatively free hand by Ferrari and brought much needed management discipline to the team. Whilst there had always been a huge supply of talent at Ferrari, particularly in the design and development of engines, it had not always reached its collective potential. Enzo's autocratic style of 'divide and rule' had created much confusion and rivalry within the team. Montezemolo defined strict areas of responsibility in order to reduce the amount of interference and internal politics. This created a situation where the various technical teams (chassis and suspension; engine; gearbox) concentrated on, and were fully accountable for, their own areas. Montezemolo was also instrumental in the recruitment of driver Niki Lauda.

In 1974 Lauda and the design team had embarked upon an exhaustive testing and development programme at the Fiorano test track. The new car, the 312B, was very fast; however, there were still reliability problems and although Lauda was leading the championship at the British Grand Prix, the lead was lost through technical problems. In 1975 the fruits of Forghieri's creative ideas and the intensive testing at Fiorano were exemplified in the new 312T which featured a wide, low body with a powerful 12-cylinder engine and a revolutionary transverse (sideways mounted) gearbox ('flat 12') which improved the balance of the car, making it handle extremely well. Lauda, with the support of team-mate Regazzoni, was able to easily secure both the drivers' and constructors' world championships. The Ferraris dominated the 1975 season. With their elegant handling and the power advantage of the engine, they were in a class of their own. Because the majority of the competition all had the same engine and gearbox combination (Ford DFV and Hewland gearbox), they were unable to respond to a chassis/gearbox/engine combination which was unique to Ferrari.

1976 continued in much the same vein, with Lauda and Regazzoni winning the early races. Montezemolo had been promoted to head up Fiat's entire motorsport operation and Daniele Audetto was moved from managing the rally team to Sporting Director at Ferrari. However, things were not to go as smoothly as in 1975. At the German Grand Prix, Lauda lost control of the car in the wet conditions and crashed in flames. He was rescued by four other drivers, but not before suffering severe burns and inhaling toxic fumes. His life was in the balance for some weeks while the Grand Prix series continued with James Hunt (McLaren) reducing Lauda's lead in the championship. Miraculously Lauda recovered from his injuries and although still badly scarred, he returned to race for Ferrari. He and Hunt went into the last Grand Prix of 1976 (Japan) with Lauda leading by three points. There was heavy rain and Lauda pulled out of the race leaving the drivers' championship to Hunt, although Ferrari still collected the constructors' championship. On paper it was a good year, but Ferrari should have

dominated 1976 as it had 1975. Audetto who, perhaps not surprisingly, had been unable to live up to the role created by Montezemolo and had failed to develop a strong relationship with Lauda, returned to the world of rallying. Ferrari entered 1977 in a state of disarray.

In 1977 Ferrari was still the team to beat, although the testing and development lost through Lauda's six week convalescence had undermined the crushing dominance which the team had earlier shown. The competition were beginning to find ways of catching up. The Brabham team moved away from the Ford DFV and used an Alfa Romeo 'flat 12' similar to the Ferrari engine. Tyrrell launched the revolutionary P34 six wheeled car which seemed to be the only car able to stay with the Ferrari. Ferrari itself was not standing still and launched the 312T2 in 1976 which was a significant development on the original 312T. Ferrari won the 1977 drivers' and constructors' championship, but this was the end of the partnership with Niki Lauda; the relationship had never been the same since the Nurburgring accident. Lauda left to join Brabham. Lauda was not perhaps the fastest racer on the track, but he was always able to develop a car and build relationships with the design team which enabled Ferrari to translate the drivers' senses into reliable technical solutions.

The unprecedented run of Ferrari success continued in 1978 with the 312T3 car. In 1979 South African Jody Scheckter won the drivers' championship in a Ferrari, with the team also taking the constructors' championship. Ferrari's greatest moment was when drivers Scheckter and Villeneuve finished first and second at the Italian Grand Prix at Monza.

However, 1979 was the last time that Ferrari was to win a drivers' world championship for 21 years. 1980 was a disaster for Ferrari: the 312T5 car, although a significant development from the 312T4, was outclassed by the competition. New innovations in aerodynamics brought the 'ground effect' revolution, pioneered by Lotus and quickly adopted by Williams and Brabham. Here the underside of the car featured two 'venturi', or channels, either side of the driver. These were aerodynamically designed to create a low pressure area under the car which sucked the car to the track allowing faster cornering. Sliding strips of material or 'skirts' were used to create a seal for the air flowing under the car. Ferrari's engine was one of the most powerful, but it was a 'flat 12' meaning that the cylinders were horizontal to the ground creating a low and wide barrier which gave no opportunity to create the ground effect achieved with the slimmer V8 DFV engines. In 1978 Alfa Romeo had launched a V12 engine to replace its flat 12 for this very reason. No such initiative had been taken at Ferrari which was concentrating on a longer term project to develop a V6 turbocharged engine. The lowest point came in the Canadian Grand Prix when the reigning world champion, Jody Scheckter, failed to qualify his Ferrari for the race, a bit like Italy failing to qualify for the soccer World Cup. Once again the full wrath of the Italian press descended on the team.

McLaren and Honda domination in the late 1980s

The period from 1988 to 1991 was unusual in the hyper-competitive world of F1, where the pace of change is rarely matched in any other competitive environment. This period was notable because of the dominance of one constructor. In one year the McLaren team won 15 of the 16 races. Such dominance had not been seen before and will almost certainly never be seen again.

Founded by New Zealander and F1 driver Bruce McLaren in 1966, the McLaren team had its first victory in the Belgian Grand Prix of 1968. Tragically McLaren himself was killed two years later while testing. Lawyer and family friend Teddy Mayer took over as team principal. The team continued to develop and in 1974 secured a long term sponsorship from Philip Morris to promote the Marlboro brand of cigarettes. This was a partnership that was to last until 1996, probably the most enduring relationship between a constructor and a 'flagship' sponsor. In September 1980 Ron Dennis became joint team principal with Mayer, a position which he took over solely in 1982, when Mayer was 'encouraged' by Philip Morris to take a less active role in the management of McLaren.

Dennis had been a mechanic for the highly successful Cooper team in 1966, but left to set up his own Formula Two (a smaller, less expensive formula) team in 1971. By the end of the 1970s he had built a reputation for professionalism and immaculate presentation. His Project Four company brought in designer John Barnard who had some radical ideas about using carbon fibre, rather than metal, as the basis for a race car chassis. These ideas were to provide the basis for the MP4 car. Both Dennis and Barnard were perfectionists, with Dennis' obsession with immaculate presentation and attention to detail complemented by Barnard's uncompromising quest for technical excellence.

In 1986 John Barnard left to join the struggling Ferrari team. The partnership between Dennis and Barnard had been stormy, but a huge amount had been achieved through the energy of these two individuals: Dennis providing the managerial and commercial acumen and Barnard highly innovative design skills. To replace Barnard, Brabham designer Gordon Murray was brought into the team, perhaps best known for developing the innovative 'fan car' for Brabham in 1978. Murray, like Barnard, was at the leading edge of F1 car design.

A further factor in McLaren's success had been its relationship with engine suppliers. In the mid-1980s turbo charging became the key technology and in 1983 it used a

Porsche turbo engine which was funded by the electronics company TAG. However, the emerging force in engine development was Honda which had re-entered F1 in 1983 in partnership with Williams. Importantly the engines were supported by a significant commitment from Honda in both people and resources. Honda used the relationship as an opportunity to develop some of its most talented engineers and to transfer F1 design and development capabilities to its production car programme. In the mid-1980s the Williams/Honda partnership was very successful, but following Frank Williams' road accident in 1986, Honda began to have doubts about the future of the Williams team and agreed to move to supply both McLaren and Lotus for the 1987 season.

Half way through 1987 McLaren announced that it had recruited two of the top drivers in F1 to their team for the 1988 season: Alain Prost and Ayrton Senna. This was unusual as most teams tended to have a clear hierarchy, with a lead driver being supported by a 'number two' who was regarded as either less skilful and/or less experienced than the lead driver. However, McLaren appeared to feel that it would be able to deal with the potential problems that such a structure could cause.

Prost and Senna were real contrasts. Senna was fast, determined and ruthless. Prost was fast too, but a great tactician and adept at team politics, making sure that the whole team was behind him. It was rumoured that a key reason for Honda moving to McLaren was that it now had Alain Prost.

In 1988 the Honda powered MP4 car was without question the fastest and most reliable car on the circuit. This meant that effectively the only real competition for Prost and Senna was each other. This competition between two highly committed and talented drivers resulted in one of the most enduring and bitter feuds the sport has ever known. In 1990 the acrimony with Senna culminated in Prost moving to Ferrari.

Ron Dennis and his professional management style was synonymous with the success of McLaren, indicating that the era of the 'one man band' Formula One constructor was past. His record since taking over in 1982 has been impressive. Eddie Jordan, principal of the Jordan team held him in high regard:

> He's won that many Grand Prix, he's won that many championships, he's been on pole that many times and he's got the best drivers. Everyone hates him; but they only hate him because he's the best.

Dennis' negotiating and marketing abilities were legendary throughout Formula One. McLaren also created its own marketing consultancy operation where the smaller teams engaged it to find sponsors. In 1991 *Management Week* had Ron Dennis on the front cover with the question:

THE FORMULA 1 CONSTRUCTORS 591

'Is Ron Dennis Britain's best manager?' Dennis likens the management of McLaren to that of a game of chess: 'you've got to get all the elements right, the overall package, the budget, the designer, the engine, the drivers, the organisation'. Dennis is renowned for being hyper-competitive and once chastised a driver who was delighted with finishing second with the comment – 'remember, you're only the first of the losers'. Dennis' ambitions went beyond F1 and in 1988 he began a project to build a road-going car, the McLaren F1. In many ways this mirrored the development of Ferrari who had made the progression from producing dedicated race cars to also develop road-going cars. The McLaren F1 was launched in 1994 and with a price tag of £634,000 and a top speed of 231 mph became the most expensive and fastest road-going car in the world.

The McLaren–Honda combination had dominated F1 from 1988 through to 1991, and it was difficult to see what more could be achieved. In September 1992 Honda confirmed that it was pulling out of F1 racing. It had been hugely successful and achieved all of its objectives; it was now time to stand back from F1 and find some new challenges. Dennis had been told about Honda's thinking in late 1991, but it appeared that he had not taken it seriously enough and the team had no real engine alternatives. This meant it lost valuable winter development time as it tried to find a new engine supplier. In 1993 the team competed with 'off the shelf' Ford engines available to anyone who had the cash to buy them. Senna's skills still gave McLaren five victories, despite having a less than competitive car. However, at the end of 1993 Senna left the McLaren team to move to Williams, which he saw as having the superior car and engine combination. Former world champion and adviser to Ferrari, Niki Lauda, saw this as the terminal blow: 'Senna was a leader. He told them exactly what was wrong with the car. Hakkinen [Senna's replacement] is not in a position to do that, so the reaction time is much longer. Senna motivated the designers.'

The mid-1990s was a particularly difficult period for McLaren. Having tried Peugeot engines in 1994 the company moved to Mercedes in 1995. Mercedes had been considering a major commitment to F1 and in 1995 it concluded a deal which involved taking equity stakes in McLaren (40 per cent) and also in specialist engine builder Ilmor Engineering based near Northampton (which it subsequently purchased) which was to build the Mercedes engines used in F1.

Williams and the technological revolution: the mid-1990s

During the period 1992–94 Williams cars won 27 out of 48 races, they secured the F1 constructors' title for all three years and the world championship for drivers was won in a Williams in 1992 (Nigel Mansell) and 1993 (Alain Prost).

Like many of the founders of Formula One constructors, Frank Williams began as a driver, perhaps not of the same standing as Bruce McLaren or Jack Brabham, but nonetheless someone who lived and breathed motor racing. His desire to remain in the sport led him to develop a business buying and selling racing cars and spare parts and in 1968 Frank Williams (Racing Cars) Ltd was formed. A series of triumphs, tragedies and near bankruptcies led to the establishment of Williams Grand Prix Engineering in 1977 when Frank Williams teamed up with technical director Patrick Head. Frank Williams' approach and style owes a lot to the difficult years in the 1970s when he survived on his wits and very little else, including at one time operating from a public telephone box near the workshop when the phones were disconnected as he had not paid the bill. His style could be described as autocratic, entrepreneurial and certainly frugal, despite the multi-million-pound funding he managed to extract from the likes of Canon, R.J. Reynolds and Rothmans. Williams saw his role as providing the resources for the best car to be built. His long-standing relationship with Head was pivotal to the team and brought together a blend of entrepreneurial energy and technical excellence needed to succeed in F1.

The first car from this new alliance was the FW06, designed by Patrick Head and with support from Saudi Airlines. The team enjoyed success in 1980/81 by winning the constructors' championship both years and with Alan Jones winning the drivers' title in 1980. Jones was a forthright Australian who knew what he wanted and was not afraid to voice his opinions. His approach to working with the team was very influential and coloured Frank Williams' view of drivers: 'I took a very masculine attitude towards drivers and assumed that they should behave – or should be treated – like Alan.'

Further success occurred in 1986/87 with Nelson Piquet winning the drivers' title in 1987 and Williams the constructors' title in both years. This was despite the road accident in 1986 which left Frank Williams tetraplegic and confined to a wheelchair. However, 1988 was Williams' worst season; with Honda having switched to supplying McLaren the company was forced to suddenly switch to uncompetitive Judd V10 engines. Williams did not win a single race, McLaren won 15 out of the 16 Grand Prix of 1988 and a disillusioned Nigel Mansell left and went to Ferrari. Frank Williams had to search frantically for a new engine deal, which he found in 1990 with Renault. This relationship became a far-reaching and durable one, with Renault putting human and financial resources into the project with Williams. The company also sought to develop the relationship further and extended its activities with Renault by running its team of saloon cars for the British

Touring Car Championship, and also provided engineering input and the Williams name for a special edition of the Renault Clio.

In 1990 a lack of driver talent meant that the team was only able to win two races. In 1991 Nigel Mansell was persuaded to return from retirement by Frank Williams and narrowly missed taking the 1991 title, but in 1992 the team dominated the circuits, effectively winning the championship by the middle of the season. Nigel Mansell went into the record books by winning the first five consecutive races of the season. However, deterioration in the relationship between Williams and Mansell led to the driver's retirement from F1 at the end of the year.

In a sport where personnel change teams frequently, the stable relationship between Williams and Head provided enviable continuity compared with the rest of the field. Head's designs had often been functional rather than innovative, but he had always been able to take a good idea and develop it further. These have included ground effect (originally developed by Lotus), carbon-composite monocoque (McLaren), semi-automatic gearbox (Ferrari), and active suspension (Lotus). The car development process was always a top priority at Williams and Head was supported by many junior designers who then went on to be highly influential in Formula One, such as Neil Oatley (McLaren), Adrian Newey (McLaren and Red Bull), Frank Dernie (Ligier, Lotus and Arrows) and Ross Brawn (Benetton, Ferrari and Brawn).

This focus on developing the car and engine combination sometimes meant that the driver took second place in the Williams philosophy, despite the fact that a good test driver, who could help the technicians define and solve problems, was essential to the development process. There had been a number of high profile disputes with drivers which had, in part, been attributable to Frank Williams' 'masculine' approach to dealing with drivers. In 1992 Nigel Mansell left when he felt his 'number one' driver position was threatened by the recruitment of Alain Prost for 1993 (although Prost himself left the following year for the same reason regarding the hiring of Ayrton Senna). A similar situation arose when the 1996 world champion, Damon Hill, was not retained for the 1997 season and was replaced with Heinz-Harald Frentzen. In an interview with the *Sunday Times* Patrick Head set out the reasons for the decision not to hold on to Hill:

We are an engineering company and that is what we focus on. Ferrari are probably the only team where you can say the driver is of paramount importance and that is because [Michael] Schumacher is three-quarters of a second a lap quicker than anyone else.

This emphasis on the driver being only part of the equation was not lost on Paul Stewart, who was concentrating on developing the Stewart Grand Prix entry to F1 in 1996:

If you look at the Williams team, they rely on a solid framework, their organisation, their engine, their car design is all amalgamated into something that gives a platform for everyone to work on. They don't believe putting millions into a driver is going to make all the difference.

Williams' emphatic dominance in the 1992 season was due to a number of factors: the development of the powerful and reliable Renault engine was perfectly complemented by the FW15 chassis which incorporated Patrick Head's development of some of the innovations of the early 1990s, namely semi-automatic gearboxes, drive-by-wire technology and Williams' own active suspension system. As summarised by a senior manager at Williams F1:

I think we actually were better able to exploit the technology that was available and led that technology revolution. We were better able to exploit it to the full, before the others caught up . . . it wasn't just one thing but a combination of ten things, each one giving you another 200/300th of a second, if you add them up you a get a couple of seconds of advantage.

However, in 1993 the Benetton team made a great deal of progress, with both the gearbox and suspension innovations largely attributed to the development skills of their new driver, Michael Schumacher. Williams' technical lead coupled with the tactical race skills of Alain Prost, supported by promoted test driver Damon Hill (due to Mansell's sudden exit), secured the 1993 world championship and constructors' championship for Williams F1.

1994 was a disastrous year, but not for reasons of performance as Williams won the constructors' championship for the third successive year (this was always the declared primary objective, with the drivers' championship very much a secondary aim). Frank Williams had, for some time, regarded Brazilian Ayrton Senna as the best driver around and, now with the obvious performance advantage of the FW15 chassis and the Renault V10 engine, Senna was keen to move to Williams, which he did, partnered by Damon Hill for the 1994 season. Tragically at the San Marino Grand Prix at Imola on 1 May 1994 Senna was killed in an accident, an event which devastated not only the Williams team but the sport as a whole.

In 1995 the Benetton team had eclipsed the Williams domination. Benetton had developed a car using many of the technological innovations used by Williams (with the help of ex-Williams designer, Ross Brawn). In addition Renault's ambitions to match Honda's previous domination of the sport as an engine supplier from 1986 to 1991 led the company to supply Benetton with Renault engines as well as Williams. 1995 was the year of Benetton and Michael Schumacher, breaking the three year domination of the

Williams team. However, in 1996 Schumacher moved to the then uncompetitive Ferrari team for £27 million, putting him in third place in the Forbes chart of sports top earners. This left the way clear for Williams to dominate the season, with Benetton failing to fill the gap left by Schumacher.

Ferrari: the return to glory: 1999–2004

Ferrari was struggling in the mid-1980s. A key problem was that new developments in aerodynamics and the use of composite materials had emerged from the UK's motorsport valley.[1] Ferrari had traditionally focused on the engine as its competitive advantage, which made perfect sense given that, unlike most of the competition which outsourced their engines from suppliers such as Cosworth, Ferrari designed and manufactured its own engines. However, it appeared that these new technologies were effectively substituting superior engine power with enhanced grip due to aerodynamic downforce and improved chassis rigidity.

In 1986 British designer John Barnard was recruited to the top technical role, but was not prepared to move to Italy. Surprisingly Enzo Ferrari allowed him to establish a design and development facility near Guildford in Surrey that became known as the Ferrari 'GTO' or Guildford Technical Office. It seemed that rather than being a unique and distinctively Italian F1 team, Ferrari was now prepared to imitate the British constructors whom Enzo had once, rather contemptuously, referred to as the '*Garagistes*'. The concept of the GTO was that it would concentrate on the design of the following year's car, whereas in Maranello they would focus on building and racing the current car. However, the fact that Barnard was defining the technical direction of Ferrari meant that he became increasingly involved in activities at both sites.

Enzo Ferrari's death in 1988 created a vacuum which was filled by executives from the Fiat organisation. It was written into the contract that on Enzo's death Fiat's original stake would be increased to 90 per cent. This greater investment led to attempts to run Ferrari as a formal subsidiary of the Fiat group. Barnard became frustrated with the interference and politics of the situation and left to join Benetton in 1989. In 1992 Fiat appointed Luca di Montezemolo as CEO with a mandate to take Ferrari back to the top. Montezemolo, who had been team manager for Ferrari during the mid-1970s, had subsequently taken on a range of high profile management roles including running Italy's hosting of the Soccer World Cup in 1990. One of his first actions was to re-appoint John Barnard as technical director and re-establish GTO. He was quoted

in *The Times* as follows: 'In Italy we are cut away from the Silicon Valley of Formula One that has sprung up in England.' With an Englishman heading up design, he followed this up with the appointment of a Frenchman, Jean Todt, to handle the overall management of the team. Both appointments were clear signals to all involved in Ferrari that things were going to change. Todt had no experience in F1 but had been in motorsport management for many years and had led a successful rally and sportscar programme at Peugeot.

The physical separation between design and development in Guildford and the racing operation in Maranello led to problems and Barnard and Ferrari parted company in 1996, this time for good. At the end of 1996 Ferrari recruited double world champion Michael Schumacher from the Benetton team and followed this by recruiting two further individuals from Benetton: Rory Byrne, who had overall responsibility for designing the car, and Ross Brawn, who managed the entire technical operation. With Barnard and his UK operation gone, Byrne and Brawn faced the task of building up a new design department in Maranello of around 50 people. One of the most important tasks for the new team was to take advantage of the fact that Ferrari made its own engines, by integrating the design of the engine, chassis and aerodynamics as early in the process as possible. Ferrari's historic emphasis on the engine was replaced by a focus on integration, summarised by Ross Brawn: 'it's not an engine, it's not an aero-package, it's not a chassis. It's a Ferrari'.

At this time Ferrari also entered into a long term partnership with Shell to provide both financial and technical support to the team, a departure for Ferrari which had previously always worked with Italian petroleum giant Agip. In these kinds of arrangements Ferrari led a trend away from selling space on cars to long term commercial and technological arrangements, with coordinated marketing strategies for commercial partners to maximise the benefits of their investments.

This rejuvenated team provided the basis for Michael Schumacher's dominance of F1. In 1999 Ferrari won its first constructors' championship for 12 years. In 2000 Ferrari secured both championships and it was at this point that the team felt it had truly returned to the glory of the mid-1970s, it having been 21 years since its last drivers' world championship. In 2002 Schumacher and Ferrari were so dominant that a series of regulation changes were introduced to try and make the racing more competitive.

Schumacher's talent as a driver and a motivator of the team (he learnt Japanese to converse with an engine technician recruited from Honda) was critical, but another key aspect in Ferrari's advantage for 2002 had been its relationship with Bridgestone tyres where it designed and developed its compounds specifically for Michael Schumacher

---

[1] A region in Warwickshire, England, which is home to a cluster of leading F1 and Motorsport Companies.

and Ferrari. Despite stronger competition from Williams, McLaren and Renault in 2003, Ferrari won both drivers' and constructors' titles and repeated the feat again in 2004, giving it a record-breaking sixth consecutive constructors' title and Michael Schumacher a seventh world championship, breaking Juan Fangio's record which had stood since 1957.

However, for 2005 and 2006 the competition became much stronger and despite being competitive Ferrari lost the drivers' and constructors' titles to Renault F1 team (formerly Benetton). Renault benefited from the rising talent of Fernando Alonso, who proved himself a match for Schumacher in both driving and team motivation. In 2005 changes in the regulations meant that tyres were required to last for the whole race, which often benefited the Michelin technology used by Renault and left Ferrari struggling towards the end of the race on its Bridgestone tyres. In 2006 a more drastic change to the regulations meant that the constructors had to shift from 3.5 litre V10 engines to smaller V8s, with engine design to be frozen for three years from 2007. In many ways an engine change should have benefited Ferrari, but the team struggled to get the performance in the early part of the season. Towards the end of the 2006 season Michael Schumacher announced his intention to retire at the end of the year, Jean Todt was promoted to CEO, highly experienced engine director Paolo Martinelli moved to a job with Fiat and Ross Brawn announced he was taking a sabbatical in 2007.

The changing face of Formula One

New regulation changes in 2009 introduced Kinetic Energy Recovery systems (KERs) to Formula One. These systems made the F1 cars hybrids, with energy generated during braking being stored and then used to provide a power boost, controlled by the driver, for overtaking. Most of the teams regarded this as an unnecessary expense and many decided not to use the system. However, towards the end of 2009 both Ferrari and McLaren were demonstrating the advantage of KERS and other teams re-introduced the systems, which in most cases used advanced battery technology.

It was expected that the new regulations introduced for 2009 would increase the spread of performance between the teams, but in fact the opposite occurred, with the gap between the first five cars reducing to 0.33 seconds at the Australian Grand Prix. As F1 had now moved to a single tyre supplier (Bridgestone) there was no competitive advantage in the tyres; however, it became clear that cars and drivers who were kinder to their tyres would be able to generate faster times than those who tended to be more aggressive and thereby increase the wear rate and reduce the performance of the tyres.

Regulations were also introduced to try to find ways of reducing costs through a ban on testing, wind tunnel usage and temporary shut-down of factories. In finalising a new agreement from 2009 to 2012 the teams have agreed to reduce costs to the level of early 1990s. In 1992 Frank Williams' team employed 190 people (it also won the world championship that year), whereas in 2008 it employed 540, so as a rough proxy Williams is looking at a 65 per cent reduction in infrastructure from 2008 levels. All of this suggests that the F1 teams need to find new and more cost effective ways of creating competitive advantage. They will have to generate greater performance with fewer resources. One of the biggest costs in the development of an F1 car involves the use of wind tunnels, specialist facilities designed to simulate the aerodynamic characteristics of the car on the track. Many of the teams are investing heavily in Computation Fluid Dynamics (CFD) technology which allows the aerodynamic properties of a design to be simulated by computer, potentially removing the need for these expensive and energy-consuming facilities.

For 2010, at the instigation of the FIA, a number of new entrants will appear: Virgin Racing, Hispania Racing Team and Lotus Racing are not directly affiliated to car manufacturers. They will be set up on the basis of the new low-cost operations which the current teams are attempting to move towards. They will use Cosworth engines and will be attempting to build cars which are as competitive as the leading teams but on a fraction of the budget.

Looking at the Formula One constructors raises some important questions around the challenge of sustaining successful performance in a highly competitive context. How are these teams able to sustain success after they have dominated the championships? What are the different ways in which this can be achieved in different organisations? And how does the basis for success shift over time? These four cases illustrate some of the challenges which organisations face in attempting to both create and sustain competitive advantage.

Web Reservations International: challenging industry norms

James A. Cunningham and William Golden

This case describes the market growth of Web Reservations International, an Irish SME company, which is a market leader in the budget, youth and independent travel (BYIT) market through its online reservation system and business model. The case covers the development of the company from inception through organic growth and its recent acquisitions which have enabled it to adapt and extend the business model and enter new international markets.

• • •

The world of independent travelling offers great expectations, new life experiences and opportunities to make new friends. For the independent traveller hostels provide low cost accommodation and are used as key staging bases to explore new countries and continents. In addition to accommodation hostels can provide a range of services including bar, bike hire, common room, free airport pick-up, guest kitchens, internal access, luggage storage and travel information desk.

Tom Kennedy owned the Avalon House Hostel in Dublin, Ireland. In the mid-1990s, in an effort to make the business more efficient, he contracted Ray Nolan, an IT specialist, a self-taught computer programmer and owner of Raven Computing, to develop a software program which would allow his hostel to manage the check-in and checkout process. Following the successful installation of the software at Avalon House Hostel Nolan resold the reservations management system as *Backpack* to a number of hostels.

In 1999 Ray Nolan and Tom Kennedy founded privately owned Web Reservations International (WRI) and created an online reservation site for hostel bookings – www.hostelworld.com. The company's revenue grew by 1436 per cent from 2000 to 2002 compared to the industry average of 269 per cent for the top 50 technology companies in Ireland. By 2010 WRI employed over 100 people and was the biggest global provider of confirmed online reservations for the budget accommodation sector. Through its hostelworld.com division WRI offers confirmed online reservations for over 24,000 hostels and budget hotels in over 180 countries. WRI provides online confirmed reservations to over 24,000 accommodation providers, directly and through more than 3500 global affiliate partners. Turnover in 2003 was €7 million (£6.34m or $9.55m), with a profit of €1.8 million (£1.63m or $2.46m) on the basis of having handled bookings worth about €70 million (£63.39m or $95.54m).[1] By 2005, turnover reached €28.5 million (£25.82m or $38.86m) and pre-tax profit rose to €12.5 million (£11.32m or $17.05m).

Budget youth and independent travel (BYIT) market

Increasingly, the trend among travellers is to bypass traditional channels to organise holiday and business travel. According to the UNWTO worldwide receipts from international tourism reached $944 billion in 2008 up $87 billion on 2007 receipts. The first four months of 2009 showed a decline of 22 million tourist arrivals (247 million) in comparison to the same time period in 2008. This decline in tourism arrivals lead to revised forecasts ranging from −6 per cent to −4 per cent for 2009. However, long term forecasts suggest that international arrivals will reach 1.6 billion by 2020, with the three most prominent receiving regions being Europe, East Asia and the Pacific

---

[1] Exchange rates used in the case study are £1 = €1.106 and £1 = $1.513.

and the Americas. Over 51 per cent of visits in 2007 were for leisure, recreation and holidays, the purpose of 27 per cent visits was for visiting friends and family and 15 per cent of travel was for business and professional reasons, with air accounting for 47 per cent of the means of travel and road accounting for 42 per cent.[i]

The proportion of international tourists who are young travellers (15–24 year olds) grew from 14.6 per cent in 1980 to 20 per cent in 2001 and now represents over 20 per cent of all international visitors.[ii] The BYIT market comprises of students, youths, backpackers and independent travellers. They are typically web savvy, value conscious and tend to take extended vacations and set the travel trends for the business travellers of the future. These travellers' spend per trip has increased by 40 per cent since 2002, with 80 per cent using the internet to search for information to research their trip before travelling, and online bookings have increased to 50 per cent in 2007 from 10 per cent in 2002.[iii] Despite the deepening international economic crisis, only 16 per cent of budget travellers changed their plans. User rating and reviews were deemed the most important factors in choosing their accommodation.[iv] Within the independent accommodation category, a new segment has opened up, termed 'flashpackers', who are travellers in their thirties who previously backpacked and have caught the 'travel bug' again.

Online travel companies, because of the low prices, low commission and margins and the high cost of traditional booking systems, had neglected the BYIT sector. These traditional booking systems, called Global Distribution Systems (GDS), provide pre-internet travel booking systems. However, the high cost of installing and using GDS systems makes them unsuitable for both BYIT product providers and travel companies. In comparison, WRI's online booking system provides a web only, low-cost booking system, effectively becoming the GDS of the BYIT sector.

Traditionally, the value of the market was vastly underestimated as the value of hostel bookings ranged from €10 to €20 with a number of people sharing a room. The entire market has changed in many ways, making the internet an obvious tool for reaching this global market. No longer does the BYIT market consist of poor students checking out the cheapest possible holidays. Nowadays, hostellers and budget travellers are often older people or families, with hostels now offering single and family rooms to cater to this market, in addition to multi-bed dormitories. Hostellers and backpackers carry credit cards and typically go online daily in internet cafes, avail themselves of WiFi facilities or use their mobile phones, making online booking easy. Moreover, they demand a more structured travel experience, seeking outdoor adventure or cultural activities

and tours. WRI's online reservation system and websites cater for this demand. In addition, they spend plenty of money in restaurants rather than cooking in a communal hostel kitchen. Reflecting on these market changes, Kennedy, a co-founder of WRI, notes

> A few years ago, a hostel would have been full of people cooking their pasta or lentils, and they would all arrive by bike. Now everyone arrives by taxi from the ferry or airport and they all head into town for dinner.

The changes in the BYIT market coupled with the successful redevelopment of the *Backpack Online* software and the hostelworld.com and other related websites afforded WRI a dominant position in this market. Both Nolan and Kennedy realised that, while it was time-consuming and labour-intensive for an individual hostel to deal with e-mails and booking software, an automated booking service for hundreds or thousands of hostels could be the basis of a solid business. As Nolan states: 'Budget tourism was totally bypassed by technology until we came along . . . It was not serviced online before we existed. We created the industry.' In the early 1990s hostels generally ran their own individual websites, with no credit card booking facilities. By 2003, WRI had built relationships with 5000 hostels and was selling rooms on their behalf through an integrated internet reservation system. This grew to over 12,000 hostels by 2006 and to 24,000 hostels and budget hotels, guest houses, apartments and campsites by 2010.

The product and websites

A core product offered to hostels is *Backpack Online* (BPO) – a management system for youth hostels and budget accommodation. BPO is the first comprehensive browser based on a property management system (PMS) developed specifically for the hostel and budget accomodation sector. It integrates fully with WRI websites which allows hostel owners to upload availability and download bookings. In addition, the software provides a complete bed management system, with functionality which includes the ability to browse for availability, search for guests, review pending arrivals and set room accommodation allocations. Financial functionality is also included, which allows the viewing and printing of invoices, letters and vouchers and the generation of over 40 different reports that assist in the management of the property centre. These reports include end of shift payment analysis, bookings by booking source, income analysis and stock analysis.

WRI's main site – www.hostelworld.com – allows visitors to choose a destination or hostel, select an arrival date and the duration of their stay and quotes prices in

Figure 1 Hostelworld.com reservation details

Source: http://www.hostelworld.com.

whichever currency they wish to use, making the booking procedure extremely straightforward. Once a hostel has been selected, detailed information is available on the hostel's location, photographs of the exterior and interior, currency converter, room reviews, videos (as available) and all other relevant information for the chosen accommodation (see Figure 1). As well as the booking facility, WRI provides downloadable guides, podcasts and videos to the various continents, countries and cities where hostels are located. City guides provide lists of pubs, clubs and attractions with an interactive map to locate each one, and contain information on transport, weather, opening hours, public holidays, tourist offices etc. In essence, WRI websites provide all the information travellers need to know before booking accommodation. Since 2006 WRI has continued to improve the information content offered to users and the site content is available in 23 different languages. Information includes travel videos, podcasts, customised city guides and travel features. One of the significant developments on the web since 2006 has been the growth of social networking sites. WRI has responded to this significant trend by creating 'myworld', which allows users to connect with other travellers, upload travel photos, view bookings, change and cancel bookings, review hostels and store key personal data such as their credit card details. It has built an active community on relevant social networks, including Facebook and Twitter.

Hostelworld.com is aimed at the backpacker and student market. However, this is not the company's only site. WRI has several other key brands – hostels.com, trav.com and a newly launched bedandbreakfastworld.com.

Hostels.com has a listing of over 31,000 hostels worldwide and provides backpackers with all the resources they need in planning and booking a trip. In addition to booking hostels, backpackers can purchase activities, tours, transport tickets and travel insurance, and the website provides comprehensive information about travelling, destinations and activities.

Trav.com is targeted at value accommodation for the independent traveller and features 20,000 properties ranging from hotels, bed and breakfasts and holiday apartments to campsites. The customer promise of trav.com is no hidden taxes and service charges, guaranteed low prices and independent properties that are not available on other websites in addition to half a million reviews of properties.

The company developed and launched bedandbreakfastworld.com in 2010 with the largest inventory of online bookable B&B and guesthouse properties in Europe.

WRI owns individual domains in order to ensure that anybody searching for a hostel will ultimately land on a WRI site. The success of this strategy can be seen in the fact that sites controlled by WRI dominate any Google search for hostel accommodation in any major town or city in the world. WRI uses search engine optimisation and presents the same information in different formats depending on the website. Since 2006 WRI has developed content and social networking capabilities as a means to ensuring continued web dominance. User Generated Content (UGC) is a core component of its online marketing strategy. It has developed its own ratings system for hostels and has the largest database of reviews for budget accomodation with over 3 million reviews.

In pursing its dominance of the BYIT market WRI licenses its reservation technology to a wide range of affiliate travel websites (see Table 1). The number of affiliates using WRI's online booking technology reached 3500 in 2010.

Table 1 Sample of WRI websites and affiliate licences

Flagship websites	Affiliate licences
www.hostelworld.com	www.aerolineas.com.ar
www.hostels.com	www.busabout.com
www.trav.com	www.lonelyplanet.com
www.bedandbreakfastworld.com	www.routard.com
	www.ryanair.com
	www.travellerspoint.com
	www.travelportleisure.com
	www.tripadvisor.com
	www.visitbritain.com
	www.wizzair.com

WRI also provides a facility for tour/activity providers which allows them to advertise their offerings and allows customers to book them online. The WRI reservation system is being used by customers to book not just their hostel rooms, but also other elements of their holiday. Such activities may include city tours, bungee jumping, rafting, abseiling, or skydiving. These operate on the same model as its hotel booking model. The company has extended its travel services by concluding partnerships with other service providers such as travel insurance, flight booking, travel guides that offer exclusive promotions and special offers to their customers.

The revenue model

WRI's model is simple: it handles hostel bookings through a huge network of websites, and makes its money by holding onto the deposit paid for the accommodation (Nolan, 2004).

When using WRI's websites travellers are told immediately if a hostel has availability, available beds can then be booked and reserved right away by paying a 10 per cent deposit and small booking fee by credit card, debit card, paypal, etc. WRI offers the rooms at the lowest available price that the hostel charges, making its money by keeping the 10 per cent charge and the fee. The margins may be very small on a typical €10 hostel bed, but with 24,000 hostels in over 180 countries WRI operates on volume. Together with international coverage, as Nolan (2003) describes: 'Because we have hostels in both the southern and the northern hemispheres, we don't have a slow season.' Central to this is WRI's ability to keep the cost base low. The business is entirely web based, including customer service. This has enabled the company to reduce the cost of making €1 revenue from €2.56 to €0.45.

The revenue model that WRI has developed is designed to ensure that all parties – end customer, property owner and the partner – in the distribution chain gain from their interactions with WRI. The global scale WRI has reached, coupled with the revenue and business model, means that budget property operators have a greater audience reach through WRI's affiliate programme while keeping complete control over their own operations. The WRI business model offers greater choice, products, increases in booking and revenue and WRI provides a dedicated account manager for each property supported by a multilingual customer services team. The core business model focus of WRI 'is that WRI allow properties and partners the opportunity to grow their business with lower cost and more transparency.'

Competition

We see Travelocity and Expedia as our peers. We are not afraid of them. They are huge billion dollar companies but our technology is every bit as good as theirs. In fact, our booking process is probably simpler (Nolan, April 2003).

The competition for WRI breaks into two segments: competitors that compete in the accommodation booking market and online reservation competitors that offer hostel and budget accommodation.

General accommodation booking companies

Expedia, Travelocity and Orbitz were the three top ranked online travel agencies by US visitors in April 2005 (Nielsen/NetRatings Netview and MegaView Travel, 2005) and continue to be the leading players in the US market. Expedia (www.expedia.com) is a wholly owned subsidiary of IAC/InterActiveCorp listed on the NASDAQ and its focus is to be:

one of the world's leading online travel companies with the mission of becoming the largest and most profitable seller of travel in the world, by helping everyone everywhere plan and purchase everything in travel. Expedia's brands and businesses work together to share best practices and leverage geographic reach, scalable business models, and customer-related synergies.[vi]

Expedia continues to develop its Expert Searching and Pricing (ESP) technology which provides one of the most comprehensive flight options available online. ESP also allows customers to dynamically build complete trips that combine flights, special rate accommodation, transportation, and destination activities. Expedia operates Classic Custom Vacations, a leading distributor of premier vacation packages to destinations such as Hawaii, Mexico, Europe and the Caribbean.

In addition, it operates a corporate travel agency and, through other subsidiaries such as Travelscape, it cross-sells to third parties on a private label basis. Its other well known international brands include Hotels.com, Hotwire.com, TripAdvisor and Egencia. Expedia's directory has more than 80,000 hotel properties and 4 million rooms, in addition to discounted fares on over 450 airlines. The gross bookings for Expedia in the second quarter of 2009 were $5623 million, a revenue margin of 13.69 per cent and a 26 per cent room/night growth despite a gross booking decrease of 5 per cent for the quarter. The company has won many industry awards for its quality and user experiences, marketing materials, PR, technology (an average transaction speed of 19.54 seconds), superior offers, service, and security. In 2009 the US Travel Association named TripAdvisor the Innovator of the Year.

Hostel accommodation booking companies

Websites that compete directly with WRI include hostelbookers, hostelsclub and hostelmania.com. Hostelbookers (www.hostelbookers.com) is privately owned and based in the UK.

Hostelmania (www.hostelmania.com), founded by three backpackers in 2004, operates from offices in Spain, Gibraltar and the UK. Its marketing focus is centred on making worldwide hostel reservations easy. It operates a revenue model similar to WRI's. The core of hostelmania is 'to provide a simple way to book decent quality, inexpensive accommodation online, to minimise the hassles of travelling for you, and leave you with more time to enjoy yourself when you arrive at your destination'.[vii]

Market expansion and growth

> Half of this is in the technology, and half of it is in the unbelievable brand we have put behind it. It is outrageous what we have done. (Nolan, 2006)

Nolan and Kennedy since the foundation of the business were keen to become a dominant player in the BYIT market through organic growth and acquisitions. Hostels.com has been in operation since 1994 and had a well-established brand name in the market, listing over 6000 hostels worldwide at the time. Hostels.com received numerous industry awards (Yahoo Internet Life, CNET EZ Connect) and had over 10 million page requests per month for a variety of services including hostel accommodation, rail and airline tickets, car hire and travel guidebooks.

In a bold strategic move WRI acquired hostels.com in January 2003. It was a key player in the BIYT market and was a good fit with WRI in relation to market and product fit. Further acquisitions followed, which included WRI acquiring Hostels of Europe which provided marketing support and operated a website featuring 450 hostels throughout Europe in early 2004. In March 2005 it acquired WorldRes, a US hotel booking business which provided the company with access to independent and chain hotel contacts. In tandem with these acquisitions, Summit Partners (www.summitpartners.com), a leading private equity and venture capital firm, bought an equity stake in WRI for an undisclosed figure.

In February 2008 WRI announced that its Chief Operations Officer Feargal Mooney was taking over from Ray Nolan. Mooney previously held positions in operational finance with internet security company Baltimore Technologies and as a financial analyst with pharmaceutical firm Pfizer Inc. in New York. In addition the company announced the appointment of Fintan Drury as its new non-executive Chairman. He succeeded Paddy Holahan who had been Chairman of WRI since 2002. The company divested worldres to focus its efforts on the independent, budget accommodation segment of the market. In November 2009, the company announced that it had been acquired by the private equity firm Hellman and Friedman LLC for an undisclosed amount.

Future challenge

The main challenge is how can WRI maintain its dominant position in the BYIT market and broaden its global footprint while maintaning its unparalleled level of operating efficiency. The economic global crisis has impacted on the global travel industry and has put pressure on operating margins within the industry.

On the technology front, backpackers are more technologically savvy according to a WRI survey, with 95 per cent carrying a combination of laptops, mobile phones, iPods and digital cameras. WRI going live on the Apple iPhone in March 2008 illustrates the need for the continual investment at the customer interface. This is further evidenced by the launch of its hostelworld i-phone app in January 2010 which has been a resounding success with over 100,000 downloads in its first 6 months and is showcased on Apple's iPhone backpacker advert. Leveraging the knowledge and experience of travellers is another important aspect of maintaining and developing WRI, particularly as travellers are demanding more information about properties before making bookings. In response to this, WRI has developed video footage for the top 200 properties and has also enabled properties to upload their own property videos. Allowing travellers to do so will follow. This will enhance the social networking capability built into their websites and will become a significant factor in driving traffic in addition to developing the brands of WRI.

Despite the economic difficulties Mooney sees opportunities for future growth for WRI:

> Of course the economy is one the minds of hostel owners throughout the world . . . the hostel industry is well suited to thrive in this kind of climate. We collectively offer value when it is needed most. WRI is focused on being the fastest growing online provider of great value accomodation and we will continue to develop and use innovative technology to inspire independent travellers wherever they come from and are travelling to.

References:

i World Tourism Organisation, Tourism Highlights 2008 Edition, www.unwto.org.

ii See WYSE Travel Confederation, www.wysetc.org/Docs/PR_UNWTOPartnership.pdf.

iii See WYSE Travel Confederation, www.wysetc.org/Docs/New_HorizonsII_Press_Release.pdf.

iv WRI Press Release, 6 March 2009.

v http://investors.expediainc.com/phoenix.zhtml?c=190013&p=irol-irhome.

vi www.hostelmania.com/Application/about-us.aspx.

Manchester United FC: continuing success but at what cost?

Steve Pyle

This case describes the continuing dominance of Manchester United in English professional football despite the ongoing controversies around the huge debt held by the club. The case invites the reader to consider a number of issues including ownership structures, governance and the expectations of different stakeholders.

● ● ●

Introduction

Manchester United is the most celebrated and successful football club in the UK (although Liverpool supporters may dispute this), having won the English premier league for the eighteenth time in 2009. Within Europe they are the third biggest club behind only Real Madrid and Barcelona in terms of turnover and have done consistently well in the European Champions league – winning in 2008 and reaching the final in 2009. Yet despite success on the football field, the financial position of the club remains precarious. In the year to June 2009 MUFC increased revenues to a record level of £278.5 million[1] (≈ €307m or $422.5m) and increased profits (before interest and taxation) to £91.3 million (up 13.6 per cent) and yet the overall position is much less rosy. This 2009 profit was almost all due to the profit on the sale of players amounting to £80.7 million (most of this being due to Cristiano Ronaldo – who was sold to Real Madrid).

Red Football Limited (the parent company of MUFC owned by the Glazer family) reported a profit of only £6.4 million due to interest payments of £68.5 million paid on the enormous debt incurred to purchase the club. In January 2010 the accumulated debt stood at £716.5 million. The average fan – and MUFC has millions of self-professed supporters across the globe – probably has little interest in the finances as long as the trophies keep rolling in and the club signs top players playing exciting football. However, some fans do not like the way the club is run (or its American owners) and business commentators have raised concerns about the large and growing debt, most of which is secured against the assets of the club. Harry Philip

_____
[1] £1 ≈ €1.10 or $1.50

(financial analyst at Hermes Sports Partners) says: 'The turnover is spectacular but that debt is a ticking time bomb that they have to pay off'.[i]

Moreover many fans are unhappy about the way English premier league football clubs are developing into multinational businesses with global brands, aggressive marketing and foreign owners (some of dubious reputation). Some clubs (most notably Chelsea and Manchester City) have been spending vast sums and incurring huge debts that are not justified by the clubs' turnover but which are guaranteed by billionaire owners. However, as observers point out, these tycoons can easily get bored and withdraw funding from football, leaving the clubs with problems.

Can MUFC continue to thrive and satisfy all its stakeholders? Success in football is not guaranteed; if performances on the field slipped would MUFC be a sustainable business?

Manchester United FC – the growth of a brand

The basis of Manchester United's business success and global brand is rooted in the club's history and traditions. Initially Manchester United was just one of many English football clubs representing its locality and achieved limited success in the first 70 years of its existence. In the 1950s the manager at the time Matt (later Sir Matt) Busby built a brilliant and dynamic young team that won the league and became the first English club to enter the European Cup competition. Tragically this team was devastated in 1958 by the plane crash at Munich which resulted in the deaths of many of the best players. Instead of this breaking its spirit, the club bounced back and in so doing attracted thousands of admirers and well-wishers who started to follow the club. Busby continued to develop young and exciting teams, culminating in winning the European Cup for the first time in 1968 with three world class superstars – Bobby Charlton, Denis Law and the incomparable George Best. Manchester United became the best supported club in the country and its fame began spreading overseas.

For many years the club had been run as a private limited company with majority control in the hands of the Edwards family (firstly under the Chairmanship of Louis Edwards and later his son Martin). In 1989 Martin Edwards tried to sell the club for £10 million but the deal fell through. This seemed like a lot of money at the time but over the next 30 years the valuation of the club rocketed as the value of an iconic football brand name was realised and the growing commercialisation of football became more apparent with each passing year. When live televised matches became the norm in the 1980s and 1990s it was realised that big football clubs could be very valuable assets.

Life as a public limited company

Martin Edwards, as Chairman of the club, focused on the strategic problem of raising funds for ground improvements and sustaining playing success by attracting top players. In 1991 the club was floated on the London Stock Exchange with a valuation of £40 million. As a public limited company (plc) the club was able to raise further capital by share issues in 1994 and 1997 – it also enabled Martin Edwards to accumulate £71 million in share sales and in 2002 he stepped down as chairman. Sir Roy Gardner took over as Chairman – a smart move that ensured MUFC was taken seriously in the City of London by appointing a well respected and experienced businessman. Sir Roy was chief executive of Centrica, formerly British Gas and a non-executive director of Laporte, the chemicals giant.

At the time of the flotation in 1991, very few football clubs had the ownership structure of a plc and it was a controversial move. The manager Alex (later Sir Alex) Ferguson was quoted as saying: 'when the plc started there were grave doubts about it – I had them myself – but I think the supporters came round'.[ii]

What probably brought the supporters round was the continuing success of the team which had clearly now replaced Liverpool as the number one team in the country. In May 1997 Peter Kenyon was recruited from the sportswear company 'Umbro' for his marketing and branding experience. Later, as chief executive, he helped to build the club's global business interests. MUFC's sales of replica kits and all manner of club-related gifts continued to expand quickly and its merchandising success became the benchmark for the industry. Increasingly Manchester United became a well known brand across the world, particularly in South East Asia – the club made a point of playing pre-season games in SE Asia to help maintain its support in this region.

In 2003 Peter Kenyon was lured away by a huge financial package from rivals Chelsea, bankrolled by Russian billionaire Roman Abramovich; Kenyon's position at MUFC was successfully filled by his deputy, David Gill, whose financial expertise had been instrumental in the success of the plc.

Clean sheets or balance sheets

A public limited company has a different set of purposes and priorities compared to other forms of ownership structures common among football clubs. Shareholders demand profits and although some shares were held by supporters, the vast majority were owned by financial institutions which were looking for a return on their investment. MUFC as a plc was at the forefront of the revolution that was changing football from a traditional working class sport into a multinational business. Clubs had now become a critical element in the media industry's battles (Sky TV had massively increased the value of football on TV when it won the right to screen live games in 1992). Clubs were also getting a lot more income from major sponsors – Manchester United's deal with AON Corporation was believed to be worth a record £80 million over four years from 2010/11 to 2014/15. Some genuine football supporters began to feel alienated by the club's values and global aspirations – should a football club be striving for profits? The range of stakeholders that needed to be satisfied had become considerably wider – as is evident from the club's 1999 annual report: 'We have to ensure that shareholders, loyal supporters, customers and key commercial partners alike benefit from our performance.'[iii]

Inevitably not everyone was satisfied but Manchester United continued being a very successful club on and off the field. In the 14 years that MUFC was a plc (1991–2005) it dominated English football (winning the premier league title eight times and the FA cup four times) and the profits were rolling in. Everyone seemed to be benefiting from the success but there was an undercurrent of dissatisfaction among some supporters and resentment from other clubs. When MUFC decided not to enter the FA cup 1999–2000 in order to compete in the FIFA world club championship, many saw this as putting profit before tradition and the wishes of the fans.

Nevertheless, the plc years were extremely successful – the club's finances advanced rapidly and it was this success that attracted financial predators.

The Glazer takeover – a return to private ownership

One of the disadvantages of plc status is the risk of a takeover bid. Manchester United was a cash-rich club and the potential to exploit the brand attracted predatory interest. Earlier, in 1999, Sky TV had launched a £623 million takeover bid that was only blocked after reference to the (then) Monopolies and Mergers Commission on the grounds of public interest.

In the early 2000s Malcolm Glazer (a billionaire with diverse business interests in the USA) began to build a shareholding stake in MUFC. Glazer had no real knowledge of (or interest in) football at that time but he had successfully acquired Tampa Bay Buccaneers – an American football team – and thought he could be successful in England with a sports club. Glazer saw the potential of such a strong brand and believed that he might be able to market it successfully in the USA and globally. Under Stock Exchange rules, for Glazer to gain overall control, de-list MUFC from the London Stock Exchange and move the club back into private ownership he would have to acquire a 75 per cent ownership stake. A further 15 per cent stake would legally force any remaining shareholders to sell and thus give Glazer absolute control.

A group called 'Shareholders United' rallied support among small shareholders (mostly supporters of the club) and tried in vain to build a big enough share to block the takeover. Throughout the takeover battle a significant number of fans bitterly opposed the acquisition and initially the opposition was shared by the Board of Directors and even the manager, Alex Ferguson. For example David Gill, the CEO, cautioned against the acquisition saying: 'The Board continues to believe that Glazer's business plan assumptions are aggressive and could be damaging'.[iv]

Shareholders United and a pressure group called the Independent Manchester United Supporters Association (IMUSA) campaigned tirelessly and lobbied the FA, UEFA, FIFA and the British Government to intervene to block the takeover, but unlike 1999 this was unsuccessful. Some militant supporters even took direct action, including vandalising directors' cars and damaging merchandise in the club shop. One group of disillusioned fans founded a new independent football club (called FC United) and this small club has survived and prospered in minor league football – but it is no real threat to the giant that MUFC has become. As Glazer kept increasing the price he offered for the shares the Board was forced to accept that at £3 per share this represented a fair valuation and, although the plc Board never actually recommended the offer, they no longer actively opposed it and Glazer was able to make the necessary deals. Glazer steadily built his stake – after all, financial institutions will almost always sell at the right price. The crucial deal took place in March 2005 when Glazer acquired a 28.7 per cent stake held by J.P. McManus and John Magnier (two Irish millionaires who were speculative investors out to make a quick profit). By May 2005 Glazer had increased his stake to the critical 75 per cent level. He was therefore able

CS Table 9.1 The financing deal

Costs:	£m
Bought shares	790
Advisors' fees	22
	812

Financed by:	£m
Banks' preference shares	265
Loans from US hedge funds	275
Personal contribution	272
	812

to de-list the club from the Stock Exchange and soon after he bought out a sufficient number of the remaining shareholders to compulsorily purchase all the remaining shares. When the final takeover was complete the valuation of MUFC was estimated at £800 million ($1.5bn at the then prevailing exchange rate – see Table 1).

The Glazer years

Immediately after the takeover was complete the Glazer family began to pursue policies to dampen hostility. They pledged funds for transfers and quickly offered new contracts to Sir Alex Ferguson and David Gill to ensure continuity. They assured fans that they were long term investors not just in it for a quick profit. Malcolm Glazer was by this time an old and frail man (he turned 80 in May 2008) and appointed his sons (Joel, Ave and Bryan) to the Board to oversee the business.

During the takeover many fans were worried that ticket prices would soar in order to pay the increased costs of the borrowing undertaken by the Glazers to finance the takeover. This fear turned out to be somewhat misplaced. Ticket prices have gone up but they are still cheaper than many premiership clubs – notably Chelsea and Arsenal. The stadium is full for almost every match and there is a long waiting list for season tickets.

Manchester United continued to invest heavily in the stadium and its facilities – the developments completed in 2006 took ground capacity up to 75,691, making it by far the largest club ground in England. This means that the average attendances (and thus the match day revenues) were higher than key rivals – in 2007/08 Manchester United had an average league match attendance of 75,304 compared to its next biggest rival Arsenal whose average attendance was 60,040. The Manchester United superstore is still by far the most lucrative club shop in the country and sponsorships together with commercial income (most importantly broadcasting fees) ensure that the revenues continue to rise. This has enabled the club to service the interest payments on the debts.

On the playing side, success has continued unabated despite the massive investments made by Chelsea, Arsenal,

Liverpool and Manchester City. Manchester United completed a hat trick of league titles in 2009 and reached the European Champions League final in both 2008 and 2009 – beating Chelsea in 2008 and losing to Barcelona in 2009. Star players have continued to be signed, many for big fees (e.g. Owen Hargreaves, Dimitar Berbatov, Michael Carrick and Michael Owen). From the perspective of 2009, the fortunes of the club looked good, but how long could it last?

Alternative ownership structures

There are alternatives to the debt-financed pattern of ownership that is now happening in the English premier league. In Germany all professional clubs are required to have at least 51 per cent ownership by the members. In Spain the two richest clubs (Real Madrid and Barcelona) are owned and operated by the members – many thousands in number (called 'socios') – who elect a President to oversee the affairs of the club. This model does exist in England but only at relatively lower levels of the football pyramid – for example Brentford FC in the third tier and AFC Wimbledon in the fifth tier. Some clubs are lucky enough to have rich benefactors who provide funding at zero cost – for example Blackburn Rovers is supported by the legacy of Jack Walker (a lifetime supporter who left substantial funds to the club when he died). Chelsea is backed by the billionaire support of Roman Abramovich who has converted his loans to the club into equity so that they are secure as long as Abramovich retains his support. A further possibility would be for clubs to be supported by large firms which use the club as part of a promotion strategy and to support the local club in the communities where they are located – for example Philips supports PSV Eindhoven and Bayer supports Bayer Leverkusen. It is also possible for local government bodies to support clubs financially and in other ways (provision of stadia) but this too is not common at senior levels of football.

A sustainable future?

Despite the success on and off the field, the financial structure of MUFC remained a cause for concern. Commentators have speculated about the fate of the club if debts continue to rise. In 2010 the Glazers converted £500 million of debt into bonds which do not mature until 2017. This provides some security but the bonds still require annual interest payments of £45 million and are thus a continuing burden on the financial position of the club. In addition the Glazer family has further debts (taken out at high interest rates) and held by US hedge funds which are unlikely to be patient

in the event of any default on repayment. Whilst the revenue continues to roll in MUFC can service its debts but any falling away in performance can spell rapid collapse in football as almost all the revenue streams are strongly co-related with playing success. This happened to Leeds United in the period from 2001 to 2007 when it collapsed from a top 4 premier league club to the third tier of English football playing against the likes of Yeovil and Hartlepool rather than Manchester United or Chelsea. Such a fate may seem unlikely for MUFC but the club did get relegated after Sir Matt Busby retired – could history repeat itself if Sir Alex retires?

Michael Platini, the President of UEFA, expressed the concerns of many when he said:

> The goal is not to win titles but to make money to pay off debts. Look at Chelsea and Manchester United. FIFA and UEFA owe it to themselves to fight this. I am very concerned by clubs being bought by foreigners. I don't see why Americans come to invest in these clubs if not to turn them into 'products'. It's a never ending gold rush.[v]

Manchester United has defended itself against this by arguing that its debt is under control and its immense revenue streams allow it to service the debt. It also points out that compared to most clubs its players' salaries are a much lower percentage of turnover – it can afford to pay huge salaries whereas others cannot. Nonetheless, many fans are unimpressed and in 2010 another campaign launched by very wealthy supporters (nicknamed the 'Red Knights') began to plan for a takeover bid. However, in a privately owned company such a bid would have no chance of success unless, and until, the Glazer family decides it is time to sell out. Nonetheless the campaign was building up a head of steam in early 2010 and there is likely to be a price at which the Glazer family might say 'enough is enough' and decide to sell. However, would new owners be any better? That may depend on how any such deal is financed – the last thing the fans want is to replace one set of unpopular owners with another set of unpopular owners!

The key question remains – is the business model of MUFC sustainable and is the fundamental purpose of a football club consistent with this business model?

References:
[i] As quoted by the BBC at news.bbc.co.uk on 9 April 2009.
[ii] As quoted on the MUFC website at www.manutd.com on 22 November 2004.
[iii] MUFC plc Annual Report 1999.
[iv] MUFC Board Statement as quoted at www.joinmust.org on 26 July 2005.
[v] As quoted by the Times Online at www.timesonline.co.uk on 7 June 2008.

Hermes Fund Management, Total and Premier Oil: the responsibility and accountability of business

David Pitt-Watson and Gerry Johnson

This case raises two key questions: Is it the responsibility of institutional shareholders to intervene in the strategies being followed by companies in which they invest? If so, in which circumstances and how?

• • •

Déjà vu?

It seemed like a simple decision, but the issues it raised were surprisingly controversial. It was 2008, and the staff of Hermes Equity Ownership Service (EOS) were gathered for the weekly meeting. Natacha Dimitrijevic raised an issue which had come to her desk. Total, the giant French oil company, was inviting selected shareholders to look at some of the initiatives it was taking in promoting corporate responsibility. How should Hermes respond?

Historically, Total had never had a great reputation for Corporate Social Responsibility (CSR). Its environmental record, for example, had been tarnished by, among other things, its involvement in a large oil spill a decade ago, which had devastated the French coast and was only now being decided by the courts. Whilst its European competitors, BP and Shell, laid claim to addressing CRS issues, Total had a public reputation as a laggard. It therefore came as a surprise, to many a pleasant surprise, to discover that it was now taking CSR issues seriously.

But the invitation to shareholders which Hermes had received was not to visit any operation. It was to visit Total's operations in Burma/Myanmar.

'I really don't see how we can do that', said David Pitt-Watson, founder of Hermes EOS, and in 2009 its senior advisor.

First, it will be hugely controversial for anyone to visit that country. Second we have history in this one. We were the ones who persuaded Premier Oil to disinvest from Burma; we can't condone others operating there. In fact we should consider a serious engagement to persuade Total to get out of the country.

The regime in Burma had, for many years, been a military dictatorship. Its elected leader, Aung San Suu Kyi, was under house arrest. There was no free press. Widespread human rights abuses had been reported, including some associated with the building of oil and gas pipelines. Internationally, politicians had been vocal in demanding that companies think very carefully about whether they wished to maintain operations in Burma. However, most had fallen short of passing laws to enforce this.

'But there is a difference here' said Natacha:

This is Total making an improvement to their operations. Total has made a competitive advantage of operating in troubled regions. And we can't possibly persuade them to get out, even if it is the right thing to do: we only have a small shareholding. And in any case, there is little evidence that companies withdrawing their investment brings about positive change. In fact the assets are sold to those with fewer scruples.

Yet some eight years previously Hermes had worked with Premier Oil, the other leading Western investor in Burma/ Myanmar. That had resulted in Premier's disinvestment of its Burmese operations to Petronas, the Malaysian company, and a number of other changes to its governance, strategy and financial performance, all of which had proved positive. 'Surely', thought David, 'Total was similar. Surely, for consistency, Hermes should not only refuse to go on a controversial trip to Burma, they should also seek to persuade Total that they should disinvest.'

But Natacha also had made some good points; Total was larger, Hermes' shareholding smaller, it was a French company with good financial performance and underlying government support. It would be very costly and time-consuming for shareholders to put proper pressure on the company. Moreover, many believed, like Milton Freidman, that the prime duty of a company was to make profits. If so, that was what Total was doing. Its business model was

---

based on its skills to access and exploit oil and gas reserves in technically or politically difficult areas, mostly in non-OECD countries. For Total to leave Burma/Myanmar could be strategically problematic and potentially undermine the company's relations with other host governments. Set against these reasons for staying in Burma was the financial risk to Total if there was a change of regime, or sanctions imposed by the UN or the EU.

David and others had worked hard at Hermes, developing a strategy of fund management that made it distinctive from its peers. Hermes aimed to be a responsible owner of the companies whose shares it held on behalf of its clients. Whatever else Hermes said or did, it needed to have a view about whether Total was acting properly. And if it did intervene, it needed to be careful this was not some ill-thought-through initiative which was not in Hermes' clients' interests.

All this caused David to reflect on the Hermes approach which he had helped develop over 10 years. And, more specifically, on the Hermes engagement with Premier, resulting in its withdrawal from Burma/Myanmar in 2003 and the positive response of the share price that had seemed not only to be a step forward for the company, but also a vindication of Hermes' approach to Fund Management. Was Total really so different? Or might it have been wrong to pursue the case with Premier Oil in the first place? And in any case, what could and should a shareholder do?

Hermes and its investment philosophy

Hermes is the principal manager for the BT Pension Scheme and manages investment on behalf of other pension plans. It is one of Britain's most influential fund managers with around £40 billion[1] (€44bn or $60bn) under management, just under 1 per cent in the shares of most British companies, and about 0.3 per cent of those in continental European companies. It is one of the few large pension fund managers *not* owned by a bank or other large financial institution, and hence believes it offers a service which is independent of the conflicts of interest experienced in most large financial institutions. For many years it had taken a lead in promoting better management and governance and in intervening where there were continuing problems with company performance.

The central foundation of Hermes' approach was the observation that most investment managers do not try to influence the performance of the companies in which they invest; particularly on longer term issues. Like any company, their aim is to maximise the returns to its own shareholders. They did this in the main by buying shares they believed to

be cheap, and selling them when they seemed expensive – a process described by Warren Buffet, the leading American investment manager, as 'gin rummy behaviour (discard your least promising business at each turn)'.

Hermes philosophy was based on the belief that companies with engaged and active owners were likely to be worth more than those allowed to behave without any such constraint. This philosophy applied to all Hermes' equity holdings through its 'Equity Ownership Service'. Hermes was therefore passionate about governance; ensuring that the board of a company has the right mix of entrepreneurship, expertise and independence to maximise the company's value.

But such a philosophy had its downside. If shareholders seek to micro-manage companies, they can create chaos, especially given that most public companies have thousands of shareholders. Hermes believed, however, that, if shareholders do not take seriously their role as owners, as 'good stewards' on behalf of their clients, company boards have no one to whom they can be accountable. Like Adam Smith the company believed that this would create 'negligence and profusion' as company management would work for themselves rather than their shareholders.

For Hermes, successful stewardship involved using its vote in approving the board of directors, but also intervening in companies which were failing to resolve crucial issues, such as board structure, strategic direction, capital structure and corporate governance. David commented:

> Hermes' philosophy is different from most funds. It seeks to *create value* for our clients in the companies in which it invests, not just trying to pick winners. I wonder, was it in our clients' interest for Premier Oil to have been in Burma/Myanmar, and for Total to be there today? And being pragmatic, should we be devoting resources to this?

Premier Oil

He reflected on Hermes' engagement with Premier:

> Premier had problems beyond those of its trading in Burma/Myanmar. On the governance side, the fundamental issue was that the company was dominated by two major shareholders, Amerada Hess, a US company, and Petronas, the Malaysian National Oil Company, each of which held 25 per cent of the shares. Not content with the control and influence they wielded as such major shareholders, each of them also had two non-executive directors (NEDs) on the board. Hermes also deemed two other NEDs to be non-independent.
>
> We believed these board problems were reflected in a failure by the company to address some of the

---

[1] The exchange rate used is £1 = Euro 1.10 and £1 = $1.50.

problems it faced. It was in a strategic hole. It was not large enough to compete in production and downstream work with the emerging super-major oil companies, but not as lightweight and fleet-of-foot as it needed to be to fully exploit the exploration opportunities opened up by the super-major's focus on larger scale fields.

It had also allowed itself to become exposed to major ethical and reputational risks as a result of being the lead investor in the Yetagun gas field in Burma/Myanmar. Yes, it had done positive work in Burma/Myanmar, including building schools, funding teachers, AIDS education and environmental remediation. But this country was ruled by a military dictatorship which had refused to accept the results of democratic elections in 1990, where summary arrest, forced labour and torture were widely reported, and which had therefore become a pariah state.

We were also concerned that the board had not publicly stated how it was effectively managing the risks associated with its presence in Burma/Myanmar, or that the board, as it was constituted, could give shareholders the reassurance that they needed in that regard.

Premier's share price had dramatically underperformed the market for several years. That came as no surprise to us. There was no clear strategy, a restrictive capital structure and the involvement in Burma/Myanmar was not being managed. There was also the danger that the two large shareholders would steer the company in a direction which might not be in the interests of other investors. Why would potential shareholders buy the stock? And what fund manager would want to explain to its clients why it had invested in a pariah company?

With the combination of these issues, Premier Oil seemed a natural choice for Hermes' intervention. We wrote to the chairman of Premier, Sir David John, requesting a meeting to discuss the full range of the company's concerns.

Hermes had also been approached by two separate groups asking it to engage on the social, ethical and environmental issues raised by Premier. The first group was Hermes' clients, principally led by trade union pension fund trustees. Trade unions are often client trustee representatives, as well as having a particular interest in workers' rights. The second group was NGOs which were focusing on disinvestment from Myanmar/Burma including Amnesty International and the Burma Campaign Group. They had called a meeting of fund managers to propose a resolution to Premier's AGM criticising the company. The other fund managers who turned up at that meeting all had strong ethical investment mandates, however, so none had substantial shareholdings in Premier Oil.

It was after that meeting that Hermes decided to step up its engagement with Premier Oil. But we would not support a shareholder resolution criticising the company until all other avenues for discussion with the company had been exhausted.

The meeting also provided us with the opportunity to make contact with some of the NGOs active in Burma/Myanmar and among the Burmese people. So we began regular discussions with the Burma Campaign UK, explaining the different courses of action which the company might take. We also held regular discussions with other interested institutional investors. As part of this due diligence, we also accessed publicly and privately other sources of insight, such as the UK government, academics, consultants, brokers and journalists to give as rounded a view on Premier as possible. As you can imagine, such a process is costly of time, resources and effort.

Hermes' engagement with Premier Oil

Crucial to Hermes' approach was its desire to work with companies. It had done this with Premier but could it be done with Total? David explained what had been involved in the case of Premier Oil:

It began with a meeting with Sir David John, Premier Oil's chairman, in January 2001. It was clear to us that Sir David understood our concerns. They had already added a new, fully independent NED and Sir David gave assurances that further developments on the governance side were in train. He was also willing to discuss the strategic and ethical concerns and agreed to meet representatives of the Burma Campaign UK. In March 2001, Premier Oil also added another fully independent NED. Then at the May AGM, Sir David publicly acknowledged that the presence of two shareholders, each with 25 per cent of the company, was a burden on the company's share price. Later that year the company also began to clarify its strategic position by selling assets in Indonesia and restructuring its position in Pakistan.

Throughout this time we also liaised with pension funds in the United States which were engaged with Amerada Hess over their shareholding in Premier, and hence their involvement in Myanmar/Burma.

The first year of Hermes' engagement had, then, brought some progress but had failed fully to address Premier's fundamental problems. David continued:

We again met Sir David and Charles Jamieson, the CEO, in early 2002. They explained that since 1999 they had proposed a number of solutions to the company's strategic impasse, but each had been barred by one or other of the major shareholders. They were, however, confident that these shareholders now had a different attitude and that a resolution in the interests of all investors could be achieved – though it might take time. We offered to lend Hermes' support in the negotiations, should that prove valuable, and to call on our contacts at global institutions and share with them the concerns that certain of the directors of Premier had not proved themselves to be the friends of minority investors.

The company's preliminary results announcement in March 2002 highlighted the discussions with alliance partners on restructuring processes and committed the company to finding a solution before the end of the year. As a means to that end, in September, Premier Oil said that it was to 'swap assets for shares', with Petronas taking the Burma/Myanmar operation and a share of Premier's Indonesian activities, and Amerada a further segment of the Indonesian interest (in which Premier retained a stake). This was in return for cancelling their 25 per cent shareholdings, and losing their right to appoint NEDs – as well as a substantial cash payment from Petronas. Thus the shareholding and governance issues were resolved in one step, and the cash was to be used to cut Premier's debt burden dramatically. By the same action, Premier reduced its oil and gas production activities and focused on 'fleet-of-foot' exploration. And finally it had withdrawn from Myanmar in a way which was fully acceptable to shareholders accountable on their reputation, NGOs, and to the UK government.

The share price of Premier Oil rose 10 per cent on the announcement. Indeed, news of Premier's change in direction had been anticipated by the market for many months. As a result, Premier Oil's share price doubled (relative to the oil and gas sector) during the period of Hermes' engagement, netting an excess return to Hermes' clients of over £1 million, and more than 50 times that sum to other minority shareholders.

In David's view: 'Premier Oil became established as a strong independent E&P company with a real opportunity to continue to add value for its shareholders.'

The Total solution?

David believed that the engagement with Premier Oil ended well. But was this evidence for future action, in particular with regard to Total?

Hermes engaged robustly with Premier and found a sympathetic ear from its Chairman. But what if the board had objected to Hermes' point of view, as there was every indication Total might do? The central question seems to be how to balance Hermes' rights and responsibilities as the agent of pension funds with what it is proper, and possible, for a minority shareholder to achieve.

How should we respond to Total's invitation to see their Burmese operations? Total were convinced we would be impressed by how they were dealing with CSR issues, including support following the floods which had devastated part of the country. But trips to Myanmar/Burma, particularly those which would have been choreographed by the government, were controversial. It therefore surprised us to learn that some of the fund managers who, only a few years previously, had supported the aggressive motion condemning Premier Oil were prepared to go on the journey Total had organised.

But the trip was not the fundamental issue. The larger question was the responsibility of business. In the case of Premier Oil, Hermes had been addressing significant governance, strategic and financial issues as well as those of social responsibility; that was not so in the case of Total. Whilst Hermes had been pressing for some governance improvements, and more recently strongly challenging the company's strategic investment in Canadian oil sands, overall the company was well managed. This was about Total's involvement in Myanmar/Burma. Despite providing Hermes with an external audit of the local social and economic programme and a review of the financials of the Yadana project, Total's mitigation work and transparency was not fully convincing. And even if it was benefiting the population living along the pipeline, which NGOs still contested, the project was still a significant source of funding for the junta in power. But would it be right to try to push Total to disinvest? After all, their operation was not only legal; like Premier Oil, it was aiming to contribute to social development in Myanmar/Burma. Shouldn't we be pleased by Total's adoption of a more public commitment to social responsibility. Shouldn't they be congratulated on their adoption of better practice, not immediately pilloried for their involvement in Burma? And if Total withdrew, wouldn't shareholders lose out? And there were many other companies which vied for Hermes' attention.

David returned to his desk to check his emails. One was an invitation to speak at a conference about corporate responsibility, and the shareholder's responsibility in promoting it. He would share a platform with the Chair of Total. What, thought David, should he say at that conference?

From small town pharmacy to a multinational corporation: Pierre Fabre, culture as a competitive advantage

Ludovic Cailluet

The case deals with the development of a pharmaceutical and dermo-cosmetics company owned and controlled by its founder. Pierre Fabre Laboratories has made an extensive use of its culture to build a competitive advantage. The company's history pervades strategic options (selective distribution through pharmacists, manufacturing and R&D localisation), its choice of product development path (natural substances), organisational capabilities (innovation) and management style ('humanistic'). The history and culture of the company are explored as driving forces of its strategic development.

• • •

Background

'It is not really a legend . . . he did start off from the back-store behind the main square at Castres . . . and from there he built the Group to what we see today.'

Pierre Fabre, a pharmacist born in 1926, founded the company bearing his name on the eve of the 1960s. The venture has turned into a respected multinational pharmaceutical group pioneering new products in skincare and cosmetics with major brands such as Avène, Klorane and Ducray. While thriving internationally, the company has remained firmly rooted to the culture, values and very land of its place of origin. In 2009, with 9800 employees, the Pierre Fabre Group remains the second largest independent pharmaceutical company in France. Its growth rests on three divisions: pharmacy (oncology, central nervous system, cardio-vascular system, immunology and dermatology); family medication (OTC); and dermo-cosmetics. In 2008, it had a turnover of €1.75 billion (£1.59bn or $2.39bn) compared to €508 million in 1990 (see Figure 1) of which 50 per cent came from overseas operations. About 45 per cent of the Pierre Fabre Laboratories employees live and work in the French South-West. Over the years, the group has also established several other major plants elsewhere in France and abroad with 53 subsidiaries and sales offices. Still, the heart of the enterprise and its headquarters remain firmly in Castres, a quiet town of 42,000 inhabitants in South-West France.

Source: Thinkstock.

The sustained growth of the past three decades has raised several management issues within the company. The Group has grown and has had to adapt its managerial practices to suit its size, its strong international flavour and diversification. In doing so, the central dilemma faced by the Pierre Fabre Group has been how to bring about this transformation while maintaining its core values and culture, which are felt to remain key to its success, its identity and vital to the Group's cohesion. As the company

This case study originated from a research project conducted in 2003–2006 by Ludovic Cailluet and Eric Jolivet of Toulouse University, and Matthias Kipping of Pompeu Fabra University, in collaboration with Ombline de Saint-Exupéry. It is intended as a basis for class discussion and not as an illustration of good or bad practice.

Figure 1 Turnover of the Pierre Fabre Group 1989–2008

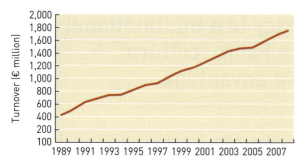

grows towards geographically and culturally distant lands, it has become increasingly more difficult to preserve and transmit this unique heritage.

In 2005, Mr Pierre Fabre decided to transfer 10 per cent of his shares to the company's employees via an employee stock purchase plan. By the end of 2007, 96 per cent of French employees, aided by bonuses, had opted for this scheme. The six largest European subsidiaries were offered the same plan in 2008 and their staff subscribed at the same rate.

Pierre Fabre donated 45 per cent of his shares to the non-profit Pierre Fabre Foundation in 2008 while announcing a restructuring of the Group's management. PFP, an intermediary holding company, was created with an entirely new board of external directors. Jean-Pierre Garnier, the former CEO of pharmaceutical giant GSK and a seasoned international executive, was hired to become the CEO of the group under Pierre Fabre as chairman. In its constitution, however, PFP has 'the obligation to ensure the company's continued independence, the diversity of its activities and its regional implantation'.

From pharmacy to manufacturing

'What we have achieved goes against all logic.'

Pierre Fabre

Pierre Fabre grew up in Castres in a well known local family of textile entrepreneurs. In 1944 he went to earn his PhD in pharmacy in Toulouse and in 1949 used family money to acquire a pharmacy in Castres (even though he was not yet of legal age to do so). His parents would continue to have a strong influence on him all through the first few decades of growth of his enterprise.

After having explored and exhausted all the avenues for growth in his pharmacy, Pierre Fabre moved towards the manufacture of drugs by setting up a semi-industrial laboratory in 1950. The turning point came with the introduction in 1961 of *Cyclo 3®*, a venotonic derived from a plant, which grew abundantly in the region. While

its beneficial effects were well known, Pierre Fabre was the first to turn it into a convenient formulation in phial and gel form. Unlike many pharmacist-entrepreneurs of the 1950s, Pierre Fabre invested all his profits into the development of the business.

Keeping an eye on the market: the Pierre Fabre 'way'
The entry into dermo-cosmetics via the acquisition of the *Klorane* laboratories in 1965 was the result of some shrewd market reading and analysis in a period when the dermo-cosmetic category was almost non-existent. *Klorane*, a small company, was known since World War I for its skincare products designed to treat the victims of chemical warfare agents. Pierre Fabre acquired the company and relocated it to Castres. He then re-invented the *Klorane* brand of shampoos and soaps while introducing a new range for babies using vegetable compounds. The innovation extended to the business side, with direct marketing targeted at young mothers. By 1967, some 20,000 sample sachets per month were being dispatched to maternity wards. Following the same pattern, the Group acquired various brands in the subsequent decade that were completely revamped according to the credo of selective distribution.

Right from the beginning, all the products were distributed exclusively in pharmacies, which in France up until today are independent shops owned by graduates in pharmacy. This was done with the help of dedicated marketing teams and sales representatives who constituted one of the pillars of the enterprise, on a par with the research division.

The company based its success from its early days on the 'magic triangle', linking the trio of client/patient, prescriber (physicians and specialists) and pharmacist. It has provided the medical legitimacy to justify premium pricing.

Intuition and creativity
Pierre Fabre himself is often described as a creative mind who more often than not has preferred to follow his instinct rather than any deliberate strategy based purely on financial considerations. He has also often followed his personal preferences and turned these into business opportunities. He was from very early on, for instance, interested by the curative properties of thermal spring waters and plant extraction. From that vision, the company has built two successful brands: Avène and Galenic. The former is a range of skincare products especially suited to sensitive skin. It was developed after the acquisition of a fledgling spa north of Montpellier. Using the unique properties of the Avène spring water, it has became the leading brand of the group in terms of sales in less than 20 years and a major international success. The success of Galenic (Elancyl) has been based on a unique integrated

system to procure plant ingredients, through long term partnerships with farmers, for the manufacturing of cosmetics: termed the 'phytofilière'.

Innovation and research

Given the size of the enterprise, the research output of the Pierre Fabre Laboratories has been truly remarkable. While the actual amount spent on R&D (€180 million) seems modest when compared with the big pharmaceutical companies, it still represents a sizeable one-third of the drug division's entire turnover for 2007.

The discovery and elaboration of the anti-cancer drug *Navelbine* was a major breakthrough for its research and development division. It was a scientific and technological 'tour de force' made possible by working closely with public research laboratories (CNRS) which helped discover the drug. It was subsequently developed by the *Laboratoires Pierre Fabre* and was a major commercial success for the company's oncology division.

The Canceropôle, a major cancer research centre and hospital scheduled to open in 2010 in Toulouse, represented a key milestone for the enterprise. It was in line with the Group's long-standing tradition of public–private partnerships and would offer company researchers the opportunity to work more closely with scientists and technicians from university and public research laboratories.

Since the end of the 1960s a clear link has also been forged between pharmaceutical research (drug elaboration) and dermo-cosmetic development. This helped to raise the quality of the formulations in both areas. Soon, the Pierre Fabre Laboratories began to be widely known for expertise in the development of galenic formulations and new methods of application with benefits for the comfort of the patients (e.g. oral instead of intravenous). A great source of pride for the entire Group was the certification in the 1990s by the US Food and Drug Administration (FDA) of two of its drug factories. Very rarely achieved in Europe, the FDA label has allowed the laboratories to offer production services to many other pharmaceutical companies, yielding additional revenues.

Regional anchorage and aesthetics

Right from the beginning, Pierre Fabre was very attached to his regional roots. In the late 1960s he made a clear choice of setting up his enterprise close to his ancestral home instead of going to some regional metropolis such as Montpellier or Toulouse. Though these big cities offered substantial advantages in terms of infrastructure and were steeped in rich medical and academic traditions, the entrepreneur chose family and personal ties, including political ones, over logistic considerations. The fact of being 'here' was seen as an advantage, the territorial rooting as a badge of honour and the guarantee of excellent access to regional decision makers. For a long time, recruitment remained strongly parochial, biased towards the local workforce. Pierre Fabre believed this reinforced the feeling of 'belonging', of cohesion, and promoted a sense of 'social peace'. Consequently, employees, especially in production and R&D units, remained very stable, with a large number of spouses and children also working for the Group.

Nevertheless, the enterprise very quickly learnt to recruit a diverse range of managers and executives, with the notable exception, until very recently, of the almost complete absence of foreign managers. The Group has, however, set internationalisation of the managers as one of the objectives to be attained in the near future.

The fact that the Group's headquarters were located at Castres sometimes made it difficult for the recruitment of high-level personnel: 'There is no question that the location is a handicap . . . [Some] do not wish to leave Paris . . . they cannot adapt themselves to the life of a small town where everybody knows what is going on.' But gradually this inconvenience turned into an attraction for many executives looking for a more sedate lifestyle. The efforts of the human resource department also did much in this regard:

> There exist completely different cultures . . . There are those who come from the Tarn area, to whom Pierre Fabre is everything . . . And then there are those from outside, who have come from Paris or elsewhere, who have known other companies before . . . and who will perhaps know others in the future. They do not at all have the same emotional bond with Pierre Fabre, but what is interesting is to have people of both kinds. This enterprise has never been shy of mixing teams, of intermingling persons of all ages for example.

Pierre Fabre's commitment to the region did not end with the hiring of local manpower. The company bought and restored several grand family estates in and around Castres. This includes 'Le Carla' mansion, where the founder's office is located, and 'La Michonne' and 'Théron Périé', which house the corporate headquarters and the Pierre Fabre Foundation respectively. A visit to the building and the immaculately kept park leaves a lasting impression:

> At Carla, it feels as though we have been received at (Pierre Fabre's) house', 'I meet the spouses of many employees who miss not having been to Carla . . . I have often invited people to Carla just to give them an opportunity to be there' (A PF executive).

The combination of local roots and the seriousness of a pharmacy company provides sales forces with a very specific and rich narrative. The fact that the company uses natural active components extracted from plants widely completes a strong story to tell to clients, partners and distributors. This is particularly true outside France in places where the name of Pierre Fabre is virtually unknown. This is becoming increasingly important in the context of popular interest in sustainable development and green issues. It is reinforced by a deliberate policy of organising hundreds of visits to the company's headquarters for partners, beauty consultants, doctors and pharmacists from all over the world.

Being a Pierre Fabre manager

Evidently, the success of such an enterprise owes much to its employees. The first characteristic most often cited by the managers themselves is the attention and care given to the individual: 'here we are not just a number'. The integration process for instance is very well crafted, with attention to spouses in the case of relocation. There are many examples of managers who have been able to retain their jobs, sometimes on a part-time basis, while they were fighting against cancer. This quality is visible at the top of the hierarchy and percolates down to the grass-roots of the Pierre Fabre Group. An academic study conducted through questionnaires in 2008 on the individual values of Pierre Fabre employees concluded that a strong sense of community was one of the characteristics of the company. This is often not what prevails in the industry.

At the same time, belonging to a 'family' also entails greater commitment and greater sacrifice. The company expects a high degree of availability, which can include – for managers – holidays and weekends: *There is a culture of perpetual availability for the evenings, for dinners with clients, etc. This includes everybody, irrespective of seniority or posting.'*

Attention to detail and autonomy

From Pierre Fabre's pharmacy days, the enterprise retained its rigour and strictness regarding production, quality control and attention to detail. This mentality also pervades its managerial style. At the same time, most managers recognise that they have great autonomy when it comes to making important decisions. They are encouraged, to some extent, to be entrepreneurs.

All managers are required to be an 'expert' in their domain. Their grasp of the subject is constantly tested and great stress is laid on prompt and rigorous implementation. Preparing for a meeting is extremely important. But having figures and details at one's fingertips is not enough. Force of conviction and a 'go-get-it' attitude are also highly valued. The annual 'senior staff meetings' and the 'marketing seminars' are intense periods when the product managers and group leaders defend their projects in front of executives often including the founder of the company.

Managers who have known other companies in the pharmaceutical sector, especially the larger, international ones, have been struck by the rapidity of the decision-making process at Pierre Fabre.

I have been with the real heavy-weights [companies], surrounded by financiers and cut off from on-the-ground realities . . . my aim [in coming here] was to get back to the vibrant atmosphere of a smaller enterprise (in terms of the global pharmaceutical giants) . . . When one asks for funds . . . one does not have to go through the entire process of going to the 'board', the assessments, the processing delays etc. Here, things move much more quickly in terms of decision making and action. On the other hand, in terms of value for the shareholder . . . the pressure is quite different.

Cordia LLP: service reform in the public sector

David Potter and Gerry Johnson

Throughout the world governments – central and local – are wrestling with how to manage increasingly pressured budgets, increase efficiency and improve quality of services. Glasgow City Council in Scotland has made structural changes to its services that are amongst the most radical in local government. Cordia is the result of one such change. Previously Cordia was a Council department. In 2009 Direct and Care became a Limited Liability Partnership (LLP) with the remit to develop its services as a business operating at 'arm's length' from the Council. But what would be involved in developing and implementing a strategy to deliver the benefits of such a change?

● ● ●

Introduction

Direct and Care Services (DACS) was a department of Glasgow City Council. It provided school catering, home care services and facilities management to other departments of the council and more prestigious catering services to public and private sector customers through Encore Hospitality Services. The department had been led by Fergus Chambers as Executive Director. Changes were triggered when, in 2008, Glasgow City Council settled an equal pay dispute which resulted in manual pay rates for DACS employees increasing by an average of 20 per cent. Fergus explained:

> Our predominantly female workers were graded at the same level as the predominantly male workers in other Council departments. But in many of those departments the male manual staff got bonuses and therefore we were open to pay disputes; we were not equal pay proof. We had to compensate staff over the last 5 years. We also had to develop a new pay and grading structure for the future. I have to 'break even' over a 3 year rolling period, so the Council decided that if we did not improve upon our competitive position they may have to consider other models for some of the services we offered. The favoured solution was a limited liability partnership (LLP). That means that as an LLP we would start on day one with a clean bill of health financially and it would give us a chance to improve efficiency over time. It would give us breathing space. We would not have to face an immediate competitive position. So we were established as an LLP.
>
> 99.9 per cent of the LLP is owned by the Council: the balance is owned by a company that is also owned

Source: Brendan Murphy, Cordia.

> by the Council and we still have politicians on the Board. So the Council still controls the strategic direction. The overall beneficiary is, of course, also the Council. If we generate profits they will either be re-invested or given back to the Council. But as a LLP we can trade as an independent company. We are no longer bound by Council rules and regulations.

In 2009 the department and all 9000 employees were transferred from the Council to Cordia (LLP). Fergus was appointed as Managing Director of the new business.

Organisational structure and culture

The new business inherited disparate service divisions from its former status as a council department. In 2009 these remained unaltered as Fergus held the view that the classic division of labour by service type was the most efficient way to organise the affairs of the LLP. Also he did not want to fundamentally alter management arrangements

---

Figure 1 Cordia's organisational structure

at such an early stage. The organisational structure for Cordia (LLP) is shown in Figure 1.

Under this structure, Cordia (LLP) has three operational service arms: Encore Hospitality Services, Facilities Management and Care Services, each of which has very different cultures. Fergus explained:

> Encore operates in the visitor attraction catering, university and event catering sectors. The division employs approximately 400 staff. It is regarded as the 'sexier' part of the business as we deliver banqueting and public catering services in some of Scotland's most prestigious venues. Encore is very commercially orientated. It has an aggressive business plan that expects it to double its turnover over the first three years of the LLP; from £12 million[1] (€13.27m or $18.08m) per annum to £24 million (€26.54m or $36.16m) per annum. If this happens Encore will be the largest operator in its sector in Scotland. To a large extent Encore management and staff identify with Encore as their employer more than they identify with Cordia.

> In the Facilities Management division the culture is very task orientated and functional. The managers and staff are all long time employees with an average of 22 years' service in this sector. The janitorial sector is largely unionised, unlike Encore which has very low trade union representation.

> The division employs 2500 staff and operates within 29 secondary schools and 230 primary schools throughout Glasgow. It also operates within children's homes. Staff are employed on 'term time' and therefore work only when the pupils are at school. The school meal division is an award winning business model ('Fuel Zone') and

has been recognised as leading change in school meals throughout the UK. It is facing increasingly difficult trading, however, as pupils are rejecting the menu offering and healthy eating policies are driving large parts of the pupil population in secondary schools towards private sector cafés and snack shops located around the schools.

> Care Services is the largest business division and the largest home care provider in Scotland. This is the 'sentimental service' with a very powerful sense of community purpose. The managers and staff strongly believe that their primary purpose is to serve their clients who receive their care services. Staff were historically employed by the Council's Department of Social Work in Glasgow and have developed a value system akin to their former employer. The historical emphasis is on caring for the client – the elderly – not on running the service as a business. Cordia senior management is striving to change this culture towards one that balances care duties with business management. The change goal is to maximise care standards whilst reducing cost.

> So a key issue for Cordia is how to develop a commercial orientation throughout the organisation and given the cultural differences between service divisions this is not a straightforward exercise.

Traditionally Cordia as a former council department was also built on a cultural assumption that jobs were virtually guaranteed for life. However, as Fergus explained, this was changing:

> The council has experienced considerable reorganisation over the preceding 10 years. The continuous policy year on year of trawling for early retirement or voluntary redundancies; the development of private public sector partnerships; the development of a shared service centre and the subsequent centralisation of support services;

---
[1] Exchange rates used in this case are £1 = €1.106 and £1 = $1.513.

the business re-engineering of the Council's ICT systems to reduce labour inputs; and finally the emergence of Cordia have all shaken to its core the assumption that jobs are guaranteed for life. Management is slowly accepting the idea that the market will determine job security. A key issue, however, is how to develop an understanding on the part of all employees, including management, that it will be Cordia's competitive position and the standard of their work in terms of productivity and quality which will determine whether Cordia retains its contracts or not.

Cordia: a strategic brand

Cordia was developed as a brand identity to demarcate the business from its former identity as a council department. As Fergus explains:

> We have people who have been in the public sector for 30 or 40 years. Most of them probably still see themselves employed by the Council. We needed a new organisational identity that all our staff could relate to in a positive way. This new identity we felt was best served by a bespoke brand that symbolically tapped into the very essence of what we thought our core competency was. We are in the relationship management business and I have always placed great emphasis on managing relationships between staff, suppliers, elected Council members and clients in a very cordial manner. So the idea of branding the new business as "Cordia" which is rooted in our culture of good relations amongst all stakeholders made sense to both me and my management team. The new brand will also provide a visual break from the past and will legitimise our change agenda; it will provide a banner for all staff to relate to positively.

In this context Fergus explained the underlying competitive position of Cordia's operations:

> Another purpose behind establishing Cordia was to improve the competitive position of the organisation and to bring in new business to produce profit streams. The industry competition in relation to Encore and to Facility Management is very strong in Scotland. There are mature providers which could compete with both Encore and for our school meals and cleaning and janitorial services. This is not the case with regard to Care Services. In Scotland this is a very immature market and most home care contracts are managed in-house via social work departments. This is starting to change. In England the situation is the total opposite with mature providers dominating all three sectors that we operate within. So we need to improve our competitive position with benchmarks as the market leaders in the various industry sectors we currently operate within.

Cultural change 'the Cordia way'

To support the emergence of the desired new culture and to cement the Cordia brand senior management in consultation with their staff drew up a set of company values shown in Table 1.

It was, however, recognised that the changes needed would involve a significant shift in the attitudes and behaviours of both management and staff. A cultural change programme called 'The Cordia Way' was therefore also launched to help develop a commercial culture throughout the business. This would involve all staff and management interpreting Cordia as 'the business' rather that as 'Direct and Care Services' or 'the department' or 'the Council'. This cultural change programme was designed and led by David Potter, Head of Commercial Strategy for Cordia who explained:

> The key issue was how to advance an understanding of the requirement of cultural change throughout the general management team (800 managers). The legacy of the former Council department was a collective perception that the organisation was not a business; that it was a Council department which delivered services within budget. In contrast to an independent business the council set operating budgets for each department once a year. These budgets did not include profit returns so, for example, return on capital employed was not a key consideration of management. The objectives of such a council department were to a) maintain service delivery standards that did not aggravate stakeholders and b) operate within budget and c) where possible add value to services without exceeding budget. The performance

Table 1 Company values

- **We are proud to serve our customers** – we provide high quality and value for money services that are important to people
- **We believe in team work** – when we combine our skills and knowledge we are stronger
- **We respect the opinion of others** – our success depends on everyone being able to communicate, listen, share and make a contribution
- **We value relationships** – they help define who we are and they secure our future
- **We are passionate and confident** – about achieving our goals and aspirations
- **We are eager to learn and improve** – developing our skills will help us grow
- **We are open, flexible and embrace change** – an approachable style helps discover new ways of doing things better and faster
- **We encourage innovation** – it inspires us to develop new ideas and motivates us

of the department was reported to council each month and as long as there were no overspends then performance was deemed satisfactory. This system established organisation-wide routines that bred a perception that we were not in charge of our own destinies. Short term thinking prevailed and both jobs and services were considered to be safe from external forces such as competition or changing market trends. This produced a potent internal focus towards everything we did as a Council department.

The Cordia Way involves six 20 week phases. In each phase there are 13 change leaders who head up teams of 8–10 managers. The teams work on a change project of their own choice, the objective being to improve the efficiency of the organisation as a business. Once this is developed they present it to the Cordia board for consideration to be implemented. Each change leader is democratically selected by the change team. We have successfully completed our pilot stage and 13 projects are currently under way. We have now successfully launched phase two of the Cordia Way.'

The metamorphosis of Cordia

By the end of 2009 Fergus faced a dilemma in terms of how he should structure his organisation. He recognised the success that the current structure had brought to the business, but also acknowledged that this might not be the best model for the challenges and changes that lay ahead:

'There are different views. Should our organisational structure reflect a more flexible commercial and fluid design? Cordia is changing into something quite different from Direct and Care. However, what this is to be has yet to be defined. For example it could be considered as any one of the following:

- As an extension of the council under the legal identity of an LLP. This identity would be supported by the fact that the LLP is, in an organisational sense, an extension of the Council. It is related to by the Leader and the Chief Executive of the Council as part of the "Council Family".
- As a former council department with a brand makeover. If service continues to be delivered in the same ways, terms and conditions remain the same and change is driven by council mandates rather from within the management team, then many will perceive Cordia in such terms.
- As a company the management of which are responsible for its commercial development. This depends on the discretion and authority allocated to the senior management team through its Board. The more they can influence real change then the

more Cordia will be perceived as a company with a management team driving its strategic and operational journey.

- As a set of distinct business divisions that serve the council. If the current organisational structure within Cordia remains intact then, arguably, it will be difficult to dislodge the idea of the historic role of Direct and Care as a former council department; i.e. a loose set of service divisions established to manage the delivery of council services.
- As a set of distinct business divisions which serve the open market. The only way this perception can be crafted with legitimacy is if Cordia can win considerable new business unrelated to the Council.

Fergus continued:

Currently £24 million of business can be considered as private work and £130 million Council work. For example through Encore, EquiU (our living aids business) Training and Development and ICT programming solutions, Cordia is starting to win contracts outside the Council. This has been aided by the appointment of a Business Development Manager and an assertion that, in the case of the training centre, its primary purpose is to build a business not just to deliver training. In the first year of trading Cordia has won circa £4.2 million in new business. But this represents just 1.5 per cent of the business Cordia manages on behalf of the Council. This ratio has to change.

Fergus believed he needed new business to flow through Cordia. However, he recognised the need not to lose sight of managing and developing existing business and in particular the need to leverage more value out of what had historically been produced from trading activities throughout the operation.

Managers recognise that the bases of existing revenue have to be contained by continuing existing services and that management effort needs to be on reducing cost and improving the quality of those services.

Fergus Chambers summarised the overall situation:

If costs don't come down and quality does not steadily improve, the organisation may be allowed to wither on the vine. Elements of Cordia's business could be parcelled out to the private sector. Or some of the services could splinter off into smaller community-driven arm's-length organisations. The undermining of the credibility of the council as a provider or agent of the provision of services to local people through critical media exposure could also influence whether Cordia fails or succeeds.

The public sector in Scotland, as elsewhere, is facing financial crisis with aggressive budget cuts being demanded as a result. Savings will have to come from increased productivity gained through service reforms. The cost of the local authority pension scheme is also now widely recognised as being difficult to sustain in the future. There are also emerging arguments to freeze pay rates for at least four years.

These perceived threats have to be dealt with as Cordia moves towards a market orientation based on a determined policy to reduce costs, increase productivity, and invest in management and organisational development techniques. That's the challenge. The core strategy for Cordia needs to be fully understood.

It is one that both contains and protects existing business whilst reducing cost and improving the quality of services. This strategy includes the pursuit of lucrative new business, the profits of which will be used to reduce the net cost to the main client groups for essential services such as home care. The strategy needs to be articulated and understood by all employed throughout the business. It should guide all organisational activities. Finally, there is an urgent requirement for the underlying culture of Cordia to complement the overarching business strategy. This is the purpose of the Cordia Way.

Ryanair: the low fares airline – future destinations?

Eleanor O'Higgins

The case focuses on the analysis of the airline industry environment, the internal resources/capabilities of Ryanair and the concept of sustainable competitive advantage. The case illustrates how a strategy that is grounded in the efficient deployment of assets/resources/competencies, whilst adding perceived value to customers, delivers a sustainable strategic advantage. The case also illustrates the difficulties and obstacles that stand in the way of achieving and retaining such advantage through changing circumstances.

• • •

There is only one thing in the world worse than being talked about, and that is not being talked about.

This is a quote from a novel by Oscar Wilde but it could be the mantra of budget airline Ryanair, Europe's largest carrier by passenger numbers and market capitalisation in 2009. The airline is often controversial, whether it was by annoying the Queen of Spain by using her picture without permission, or announcing plans to charge passengers to use toilets on its flights, or engaging in high-profile battles with the European Commission. Ryanair also made news with its achievements, winning international awards, like Best Managed Airline, or receiving a 2009 *FT-ArcelorMittal Boldness in Business* Award. This Award announcement said that Ryanair had 'changed the airline business outside North America – driving the way the industry operates through its pricing, the destinations it flies to and the passenger numbers it carries'.[i] Ryanair had been the budget airline pioneer in Europe, rigorously following a low-cost strategy. It had enjoyed remarkable growth, and in the

Source: Reuters/Yves Herman.

five years to 2009 was the most profitable airline in the world, according to *Air Transport* magazine.

Despite this apparent success, Ryanair faced issues. The most pressing, shared by all airlines, was an industry that was 'structurally sick' and 'in intensive care',[ii] with plunging demand in the global economic recession and uncertainty about oil prices. What strategy should Ryanair use to weather this storm? Would the crisis produce a long term change in industry structure? Could Ryanair take advantage of the situation as it had in the past, by growing when others were cutting back? A predicament of its own making was Ryanair's 29.8 per cent shareholding in Aer Lingus, the Irish national carrier, following an abortive takeover attempt. Aer Lingus' flagging share price had necessitated drastic write-downs, which had dragged Ryanair into its first ever losses in 2009.

Overview of Ryanair

In 2009, Ryanair had 33 bases and over 850 routes across 26 countries, connecting 147 destinations. It operated a fleet of 199 new Boeing 737–800 aircraft with firm orders for a further 112. It employed over 7000 people and was expected to carry approximately 67 million passengers in 2010.

Ryanair was founded in 1985 by the Tony Ryan family to provide scheduled passenger services between Ireland and the UK, as an alternative to the state monopoly airline, Aer Lingus. Initially, Ryanair was a full service conventional airline, with two classes of seating, leasing three different types of aircraft. Despite growth in passenger volumes, by the end of 1990 the company had faced many problems, disposing of five chief executives, and accumulating losses of IR£20 million. Its fight to survive in the early 1990s saw the airline transform itself to become Europe's first low fares, no frills carrier, built on the model of Southwest Airlines, the successful Texas-based operator. A new management team, led by Michael O'Leary, at first a reluctant recruit, was appointed. Ryanair was floated on the Dublin Stock Exchange in 1997 and is quoted on the Dublin and London Stock exchanges and also on the NASDAQ since 2002.

Mixed fortunes

Mixed results

Ryanair designated itself as the 'World's Favourite Airline' on the basis that in 2009, IATA ranked it as the world's largest international airline by passenger numbers. It was now the sixth largest airline in the world (when the large US carriers' domestic traffic is included). Over the next five years, Ryanair intended to grow to become the second largest airline in the world, ranked only behind its role model Southwest.

Releasing Ryanair's Q3 2009 results in January 2010, Michael O'Leary observed, 'The environment is, from Ryanair's perspective, great, because it is awful. We're doing remarkably well because this is the time when the lowest cost producer wins.'[iii] For the quarter, the company reported a much smaller net loss than expected of €10.9 million (£9.9m or $15m), instead of an earlier forecast loss of €35 million, with better than expected yields, falling 12 per cent rather than the forecast 20 per cent. Profits guidance for the full year improved to €275 million rather than the original €200 million forecast.

The airline had cut lossmaking routes in the UK and Ireland, replacing them with more profitable ones in France, Germany and Spain. Operating costs per passenger were cut by 4 per cent, despite a 3 per cent increase in average flight distance. Ryanair planned to open 146 new routes in 2010 and to increase market share thanks to the demise of several carriers.[iv]

These results and expectations for 2010 followed on full-year 2009 results (see Table 1), when Ryanair plunged to a €180 million loss, as its €144 million operating profit was eradicated by a €222 million write-down of its Aer Lingus shares and an accelerated €51.6 million depreciation charge. Excluding these exceptional charges, underlying profits fell 78 per cent from €480.9 million to €105 million. This was due largely to a surge in fuel prices as Ryanair failed to hedge when oil prices rose to $147 a barrel in July 2008. Then, bowing to shareholder pressure to cover against rocketing prices, it locked in fuel costs at $124 a barrel for 80 per cent of its consumption during the third quarter – just as oil prices crashed to a low of $33 a barrel during that period. Passenger numbers rose 15 per cent from 50.9 million to 58.5 million. Average fares fell 8 per cent to €40 and were forecast to decline steeply by a further 15 to 20 per cent to about €32 in fiscal 2010. (Ryanair's financial data are given in Tables 1a and 1b, and operating data are given in Table 1c.)

The airline contended that it could offer the lowest fares by cutting costs to levels that rivals could not achieve. It was planning to recruit 1200 new employees to service its new aircraft, but the number of passengers per employee was still expected to rise thanks to economies of scale from new routes and a decline in airport charges by directing traffic toward airports offering bargain deals. Having been caught short in its fuel hedging for 2008/09, Ryanair took advantage of the low oil price to hedge 90 per cent of its fuel costs during 2009/10, locking in a full year fuel cost saving of about €460 million.

Ancillary revenues

Ryanair provides various ancillary services connected with its airline service, including in-flight beverage, food and merchandise sales. It also distributes accommodation, travel insurance and car rentals through its website. This enables Ryanair to increase sales, while reducing unit costs. In 2009, Ryanair's website ranked 12th by number of visits for e-tailers in the UK (after EasyJet, which ranked 11th). Ancillary services accounted for 20.3 per cent of Ryanair's total operating revenues in 2009, compared to 18.0 per cent in 2008. In fact, ancillary revenues had climbed by 22 per cent, considerably faster than passenger revenues at 5 per cent, generating €10.20 per passenger and with higher margins.

Other ancillary revenue initiatives were introduced, such as onboard and online gambling, and a trial in-flight mobile phone service in 2009. A poll of *Financial Times* readers had produced a 72 per cent negative response to the question, 'Should mobile phones be allowed on aircraft?'[v] However, Michael O'Leary declared 'If you want a quiet flight, use another airline. Ryanair is noisy, full and we are always trying to sell you something.'[vi] Not all ancillary service initiatives were successful. In 2005, Ryanair pulled an in-flight entertainment system when passengers had resisted paying €8 to rent a games and entertainment console.

Ryanair was the first airline to introduce charges for check-in luggage. Virtually all budget airlines have followed suit, as they have with other Ryanair initiatives. It has continued to find ways of charging passengers for services once considered intrinsic to an airline ticket. Passengers were charged extra for checking in at the airport rather than online (which also incurs a charge), although those with hold luggage did not have the option of checking in online. While avoiding pre-assigned seats, an extra charge procures 'priority boarding'. Interestingly, Aer Lingus and BA have taken up a similar idea by enabling passengers to pre-book seats online for an extra charge.

Table 1a Ryanair consolidated income statement

	Year end 31 March 2009 (€ 000)	Year end 31 March 2008 (€ 000)	Year end 31 March 2007 (€ 000)
Operating revenues			
Scheduled revenues	2,343,868	2,225,692	1,874,791
Ancillary revenues	598,097	488,130	362,104
Total operating revenues – continuing operations	2,941,965	2,713,822	2,236,895
Operating expenses			
Staff costs	(309,296)	(285,343)	(226,580)
Depreciation	(256,117)	(175,949)	(143,503)
Fuel and oil	(1,257,062)	(791,327)	(693,331)
Maintenance, materials and repairs	(66,811)	(56,709)	(42,046)
Marketing and distribution costs	(12,753)	(17,168)	(23,795)
Aircraft rentals	(78,209)	(72,670)	(58,183)
Route charges	(286,559)	(259,280)	(199,240)
Airport and handling charges	(443,387)	(396,326)	(273,613)
Other	(139,140)	(121,970)	(104,859)
Total operating expenses	**(2,849,334)**	**(2,176,742)**	**(1,765,150)**
Operating profit – continuing operations	92,631	537,080	471,745
Other income/(expenses)			
Finance income	75,522	83,957	62,983
Finance expense	(130,544)	(97,088)	(82,876)
Foreign exchange gain/(losses)	4,441	(5,606)	(906)
Loss on impairment of available-for-sale financial asset	(222,537)	(91,569)	–
Gain on disposal of property, plant and equipment	–	12,153	91
Total other income/(expenses)	**(273,118)**	**(98,153)**	**(20,708)**
(Loss)/profit before tax	(180,487)	438,927	451,037
Tax on (loss)/profit on ordinary activities	11,314	(48,219)	(15,437)
(Loss)/profit for the year – all attributable to equity holders of parent	**(169,173)**	**390,708**	**435,600**
Basic earnings per ordinary share (Euro cents)	(11.44)	25.84	28.20
Diluted earnings per ordinary share (Euro cents)	(11.44)	25.62	27.97
Number of ordinary shares (in 000s)	1,478,472	1,512,012	1,544,457
Number of diluted shares (in 000s)	1,478,472	1,524,935	1,557,503

Source: Ryanair Annual Report 2009.

Some of Ryanair's revenue-generating ideas have provoked controversy – and publicity. One of the most talked about was its intention to charge passengers £1 to use the lavatory onboard, by installing a coin slot on its aircraft. While it has not implemented this concept (it may contravene security rules), the idea generated much publicity. Another idea mooted by Ryanair was a 'fat tax' for overweight passengers. In an online poll of over 30,000 respondents, the fat tax idea was approved by one in three. However, the airline later announced that it would not implement the surcharge because it could not collect it without disrupting its 25-minute turnarounds and online check-in process. The same online poll, supposedly to generate ideas for additional revenue, also gained 25 per cent approval for a €1 levy to use onboard toilet paper with Michael O'Leary's face on it.

Investor perspectives

Since its flotation in 1996, Ryanair has never declared or paid dividends on its shares. For the foreseeable future, Ryanair planned to retain any earnings to fund the business operations, including the acquisition of additional aircraft required for its planned entry into new markets, expansion of its existing services, and for routine replacements of its current fleet. The no-dividend policy, combined with its healthy cash position, has caused the company to seek alternative ways of improving the liquidity and marketability of its stock, through a series of share buy-backs of the equivalent of about 1.2 per cent of the issued share capital between 2006 and 2009. When a deal to place an aircraft order with Boeing foundered, Ryanair announced that it would probably substitute the capital it would have spent to undertake a mixture of share

Table 1b Ryanair consolidated balance sheet

	31 March 2009	31 March 2008
Non-current assets		
Property, plant and equipment	3,644,824	3,582,126
Intangible assets	46,841	46,841
Available-for-sale financial assets	93,150	311,462
Derivative financial instruments	59,970	–
Total non-current assets	3,844,785	3,940,429
Current assets		
Inventories	2,075	1,997
Other assets	91,053	169,580
Current tax	–	1,585
Trade receivables	41,791	34,178
Derivative financial instruments	129,962	10,228
Restricted cash	291,601	292,431
Financial assets: cash > 3 months	403,401	406,274
Cash and cash equivalents	1,583,194	1,470,849
Total current assets	2,543,077	2,387,122
Total assets	6,387,862	6,327,551
Current liabilities		
Trade payables	132,671	129,289
Accrued expenses and other liabilities	905,715	919,349
Current maturities of debt	202,941	366,801
Current tax	425	–
Derivative financial instruments	137,439	141,711
Total current liabilities	1,379,191	1,557,150
Non-current liabilities		
Provisions	71,964	44,810
Derivative financial instruments	54,074	75,685
Deferred tax	155,524	148,088
Other creditors	106,549	99,930
Non-current maturities of debt	2,195,499	1,899,694
Total non-current liabilities	2,583,610	2,268,207
Shareholders' equity		
Issued share capital	9,354	9,465
Share premium account	617,426	615,815
Capital redemption reserve	493	378
Retained earnings	1,777,727	2,000,422
Other reserves	20,061	(123,886)
Shareholders' equity	2,425,061	2,502,194
Total liabilities and shareholders' equity	6,387,862	6,327,551

Source: Ryanair Annual Report 2009.

buybacks and special dividends to shareholders after 2012, causing a 7.5 per cent rise in its share price.

Ryanair shares reached a high of €6.30 in April 2007 and plummeted to €1.97 in October 2008, as global equity markets reeled. In early 2010, the shares were trading in the €3.30 to €3.60 range, with an expected medium term target of €4.20, based on expected earnings and a PE ratio of 13. In mid-2009, its rival easyJet shares had a PE ratio of 29. Ryanair had often underperformed other budget airline peers on its PE ratio.

Ryanair's operations

Michael O'Leary said;

> Any fool can sell low air fares and lose money. The difficult bit is to sell the lowest airfares and make profits. If you don't make profits, you can't lower your air fares or reward your people or invest in new aircraft or take on the really big airlines like BA (British Airways) and Lufthansa.'[vii]

Table 1c Ryanair selected operating data

	2009	2008	2007	2006
Average yield per revenue passenger mile ('RPM') (€)	0.060	0.065	0.070	0.070
Average yield per available seat miles ('ASM') (€)	0.050	0.054	0.059	0.058
Average fuel cost per US gallon (€)	2.351	1.674	1.826	1.479
Cost per ASM (CASM) (€)	0.058	0.051	0.054	0.052
Break-even load factor	98%	79%	77%	75%
Operating margin	5%	20%	21%	22%
Total break-even load factor[a]	79%	67%	66%	65%
Average booked passenger fare (€)	40.02	43.70	44.10	41.23
Ancillary revenue per booked passenger (€)	10.21	9.58	8.52	7.45

Other data:

	2009	2008	2007	2006
Revenue passengers booked	58,565,663	50,931,723	42,509,112	34,768,813
Revenue passenger miles	39,202 m	34,452 m	26,943 m	20,342 m
Available seat miles	47,102 m	41,342 m	32,043 m	24,282 m
Booked passenger load factor	81%	82%	82%	83%
Average length of passenger haul (miles)	654	662	621	585
Sectors flown	380,915	330,598	272,889	227,316
Number of airports served	143	147	123	111
Average daily flight hour utilisation (hours)	9.59	9.87	9.77	9.60
Employees at period end	6,616	5,920	4,462	3,453
Employees per aircraft	36	36	34	35
Booked passengers per employee	8,852	8,603	9,527	10,069

[a] Total break-even load factor is calculated on the basis of total costs and revenues, including the costs and revenues from all ancillary services.

Source: Ryanair Annual Report 2009.

Certainly, Ryanair has stuck closely to the low-cost/low-fares model. Ever decreasing costs is its theme, as it constantly adapts its model to the European arena and changing conditions. In this respect, Ryanair differs in its application of the Southwest Airlines budget airline prototype, and its main European rival, easyJet, as the latter two are not as frill-cutting. One observer described the difference between easyJet and Ryanair as: 'easyJet, you understand is classy cheap, rather than just plain cheap.'[viii]

The Ryanair fleet

Ryanair continued its fleet commonality policy, using Boeing 737 planes to keep staff training and aircraft maintenance costs as low as possible, with an expected fleet of over 300 by 2012. Over the years, it has purchased newer, more environmentally friendly aircraft, reducing the average age of its aircraft to 2.4 years, the youngest fleet in Europe. The newer aircraft produce 50 per cent less emissions, 45 per cent less fuel burn and 45 per cent lower noise emissions per seat. Winglet modification provided better performance and a 2 per cent reduction in fuel consumption, a saving which the company believed could be even further improved. Despite larger seat capacity, new aircraft do not require more crew. In 2009, in aircraft buying mode, Ryanair sought to repeat its 2002 coup when it placed aircraft orders at the bottom of the market.

However, in December 2009 a plan to purchase 200 jets from Boeing was cancelled when negotiations over price collapsed: 'Eventually you lose interest dealing with a bunch of idiots who can't make a decision', declared Michael O'Leary when the deal fell through.[ix]

Notwithstanding strict adherence to Boeing 737 planes, in an attempt to extract ever greater discounts from Boeing, Ryanair invited Airbus, the European aircraft manufacturer, to enter into preliminary bidding for a multimillion-dollar order for 200-plus short-haul aircraft. However, Airbus rebuffed the Ryanair invitation, declaring this sales campaign would be too expensive and time-consuming.

Staff costs and productivity

Ryanair's 2009 employee count of 6369 people, comprising over 25 different nationalities, had almost doubled over the previous three years. This was accounted for almost entirely by flight and cabin crew to service expansion. Ryanair's 2009 Annual Report claimed that its average pay, including commissions to cabin crew for on-board sales, was €45,333, higher than almost all other major European airlines. Most of the company's pilots concluded negotiations with Ryanair to move them to new roster patterns with substantial pay increases of up to €10,000 per captain. Cabin crew also negotiated a new five-year pay agreement with the company, earning them significant pay increases, claimed Ryanair. By tailoring rosters, the carrier maximised productivity and time off for crew members, complying with EU regulations which impose a ceiling on pilot flying hours to prevent dangerous fatigue. Its passenger-per-employee ratio of 9195 was the highest in the industry.

Passenger service costs

Ryanair pioneered cost-cutting/yield-enhancing measures for passenger check-in and luggage handling. One was priority boarding and web-based check-in. Over half of its passengers use this, thus saving on check-in staff, airport facilities and time. Charging for check-in bags encouraged passengers to travel with fewer bags or even zero check-in luggage, thus saving on costs and enhancing speed. Before Ryanair began to charge for checked-in bags, 80 per cent of passengers were travelling with checked-in luggage; two years later this had fallen to 30 per cent. From October 2009, it adopted a 100 per cent web check-in policy, enabling a reduction in staff numbers, calculated to save €50 million per year. Ryanair claims that:

> passengers love web check-in. Never again will they have to arrive early at an airport to waste time in a useless check-in queue. As more passengers travel with carry-on luggage only, they are delighted to discover that they will never again waste valuable time at arrival baggage carousels either. These measures allow Ryanair to save our passengers valuable time, as well as lots of money.[x]

A natural next step announced by Ryanair was a move to 100 per cent carry-on luggage. Additional bags would be brought by passengers to the boarding gate, where they would be placed in the hold, and returned to them as they deplane on arrival. These efficiencies would allow more efficient airport terminals to be developed without expensive check-in desks, baggage halls, or computerised baggage systems, 'and enable Ryanair to make flying even cheaper, easier and much more fun again', claimed the company.[xi] The feasibility of the proposals to require passengers to carry hold baggage through security to the aircraft was yet to be tested.

Airport charges and route policy

Consistent with the budget airline model, Ryanair's routes were point-to-point only. It reduced airport charges by avoiding congested main airports, choosing secondary and regional destinations, eager to increase passenger through-put. Usually these airports are significantly further from the city centres they serve than the main airports, 'from nowhere to nowhere' in the words of Sir Stelios Haji-Ioannou, founder of easyJet, Ryanair's biggest competitor.[xii] It uses Frankfurt Hahn, 123 kilometres from Frankfurt; Torp, 100 kilometres from Oslo; and Charleroi, 60 kilometres from Brussels. In December 2003, the Advertising Standards

Authority rebuked Ryanair, and upheld a misleading advertising complaint against it for attaching 'Lyon' to its advertisements for flights to St Etienne. A passenger had turned up at Lyon Airport, only to discover that her flight was leaving from St Etienne, 75 kilometres away.

Ryanair continued to protest at charges and conditions at some airports, especially Stansted and Dublin, two of its main hubs. It opposed vehemently the British Airport Authority (BAA)[1] monopoly plans to build a '£4bn gold plated Taj Mahal at Stansted which we believe could be built for £1bn'. The airline was:

> deeply concerned by continued understaffing of security at Stansted which led to repeated passenger and flight delays . . . management of Stansted security is inept, and BAA has again proven that it is incapable of providing adequate or appropriate security services at Stansted. This shambles again highlights that BAA is an inefficient, incompetent airport monopoly.[xiii]

When BAA appealed its break-up, ordered by the UK Competition Commission in 2009, Ryanair secured the right to intervene in the appeal in support of the Commission.

In July 2009, Michael O'Leary made a high-profile announcement that Ryanair would cut winter capacity at Stansted by 40 per cent, because of Stansted's rejection of Ryanair's demand for cuts in airport charges and the UK government's plan to raise departure duty from £10 to £11 per passenger. In protest at rising charges at Dublin Airport from January 2010 and a €10 per passenger tourist tax in Ireland, Ryanair was also intending to reduce its Dublin traffic by 20 per cent.

However, both BAA and some observers derided Ryanair's threats to cut traffic by 40 per cent at Stansted. 'Michael O'Leary's ability to spin a tale has reached a new level this week. Along with the gullibility of parts of the media in accepting it. Hook, line and sinker.'[xiv] This was based on the contention that the airline should have compared its projected winter capacity of 24 aircraft at Stansted, not with its summer capacity of 40, but with its previous winter capacity of 28. Thus, the reduction would be only 14 per cent, not 40 per cent.

Marketing strategy

Following the introduction of its internet-based reservations and ticketing service, enabling passengers to make reservations and purchase tickets directly through the website, Ryanair's reliance on travel agents has been eliminated. It has promoted its website heavily through newspaper, radio and television advertising. As a result, internet bookings account for 99 per cent of all reservations.

---

[1] BAA is owned by Spanish company Ferrovial.

Ryanair minimises its marketing and advertising costs, relying on free publicity, by its own admission, 'through controversial and topical advertising, press conferences and publicity stunts'. Other marketing activities include distribution of advertising and promotional material and cooperative advertising campaigns with other travel-related entities, and local tourist boards.

As referred to earlier, one of Ryanair's publicity stunts was its unauthorised use of a photograph of Spanish Queen Sofia after she took a £13 flight from Santander in Northern Spain to London. When it incurred the Queen's displeasure, Ryanair apologised and promised to donate €5000 to a charity of her choice. In another instance of controversy over using pictures of the rich and famous, in 2008 Ryanair was forced to pay a fine of €60,000 to President Sarkozy of France and his Italian bride Carla Bruni for using their images with the slogan, 'With Ryanair, all my family can come to my wedding'.

So, what about Aer Lingus?

According to a commentator in the *Financial Times* 'Ryanair's bid for Aer Lingus was a *folie de grandeur*'.[xv] Even Michael O'Leary admitted 'it was a stupid investment. At the time, it was the right strategy to go for one combined airline but it has now proven to be a disaster.'[xvi]

During 2007, in a shock bid, Ryanair had acquired a 25.2 per cent stake in Aer Lingus, only a week after the flotation of the national carrier. It subsequently increased its interest to 29.8 per cent, at a total aggregate cost of €407.2 million. By July 2009, the investment had been written down to €79.7 million. At the time of the initial bid Ryanair declared its intention to retain the Aer Lingus brand and:

> up-grade their dated long-haul product, and reduce their short-haul fares by 2.5 per cent per year for a minimum of 4 years . . . one strong Irish airline group will be rewarding for consumers and will enable both to vigorously compete with the mega carriers in Europe . . . there are significant opportunities, by combining the purchasing power of Ryanair and Aer Lingus, to substantially reduce its operating costs, increase efficiencies, and pass these savings on in the form of lower fares to Aer Lingus consumers.[xvii]

It had been an achievement for the Irish government finally to have floated Aer Lingus after several false starts over a number of years. Aer Lingus and its board firmly rejected the Ryanair approach, stating that it had acted in 'a hostile, anticompetitive manner designed to eliminate a rival at a derisory price'. A combined Ryanair–Aer Lingus operation would account for 80 per cent of all flights between Ireland and other European countries. Affirming that his company was fundamentally opposed to a merger with Ryanair, even if it raised its price, then Aer Lingus Chief Executive Dermot Mannion stated:

> I cannot conceive of the circumstances where the Aer Lingus management and Ryanair would be able to work harmoniously together . . . this is simply a reflection of the fact that these organisations have been competing head to head, without fear or favour, for 20 years. It would be like merging Manchester United and Liverpool football clubs.[xviii,2]

In fact, the bid was opposed by a loose alliance representing almost 47 per cent of Aer Lingus shares. This included the Irish government, which still retained a 25.4 per cent holding, two investment funds operated on behalf of Aer Lingus pilots accounting for about 4 per cent of shares, and Irish telecom tycoon Denis O'Brien, who bought 2.1 per cent of shares deliberately to complicate Ryanair's move. A critical 12.6 per cent of the shareholding was controlled by the Aer Lingus employee share ownership trust (ESOT), which had the right to appoint two directors, and has a stake in future profits. Its members rejected the Ryanair offer by a 97 per cent majority vote.

Having abandoned this bid due to the shareholder opposition and a blocking decision by the European Commission on competition grounds, Ryanair renewed its bid in December 2008, with an offer of €1.40 per share, a premium of approximately 25 per cent over the closing price. It proposed to keep Aer Lingus as a separate company maintaining the Aer Lingus brand, to double Aer Lingus' short-haul fleet from 33 to 66 aircraft and to create 1000 associated new jobs over a five-year period. It claimed that if the offer was accepted, the Irish government would receive over €180 million and the ESOT members and other employees who owned 18 per cent of Aer Lingus would receive over €137 million in cash. However, in January 2009, when the offer was rejected by Aer Lingus management and by the ESOT and other parties, Ryanair decided to withdraw it.

Aer Lingus' fortunes continued to deteriorate, announcing losses for 2008 and projecting even worse for 2009. In July of that year its shares were trading at less than €0.50. In April, its CEO Dermot Mannion resigned after controversy over a potential secret pay-off deal in the event of a hostile takeover. While Ryanair did not have a seat on the board, it continued to denigrate Aer Lingus, forecasting 'a bleak future as a loss-making, subscale, regional airline, which has a high cost base and declining traffic numbers'.[xix] Meanwhile, the two airlines continued to compete vigorously, especially within the Irish market.

---

2 Manchester United and Liverpool have a longstanding legendary rivalry in English football.

In July 2009, Aer Lingus appointed a CEO to replace Dermot Mannion. This was Christoph Mueller, known as an 'axe man', former CEO of Sabena Airlines before it went bust in 2001. Mr Mueller had already crossed swords with Ryanair when it compared its fares to those of Sabena in advertisements that were alleged to be misleading, offensive and defamatory. When Ryanair lost a court case over the matter, and was ordered to publish an apology in Belgian newspapers and on its website, it used the apology to continue its publicity about its relatively lower fares.

Risks and challenges

In addition to the fallout from its foray into Aer Lingus, Ryanair faced various challenges in 2009, some specifc to itself and some general to the aviation industry.

Sharp economic downturn

The recession of 2008/09 created unfavourable economic conditions such as high unemployment rates and restricted credit markets, with reduced spending by leisure and business passengers alike. This constrained Ryanair's scope to raise fares, putting downward pressure on yields. Continued recession could restrict the company's planned passenger volume growth.

Growth and reducing yields

Growth plans by Ryanair entailed investment in new aircraft and routes. If growth in passenger traffic did not keep pace with its planned fleet expansion, overcapacity could result. Related pressures were additional marketing costs and reduced yields from lower fares to promote additional routes, especially to airports new to the Ryanair system. In its drive for growth, Ryanair was likely to encounter increased competition, putting even more downward pressure on yields, as airlines struggled to fill vacant seats to cover fixed costs.

Industrial relations

In the light of the recession and financial losses, Ryanair negotiated with all employee groups and secured a pay freeze for 2008/09 and 2009/10. It also planned to make 250 people redundant at Dublin Airport.

Ryanair came under fire for refusing to recognise unions and allegedly providing poor working conditions (for example, to reduce the company's electricity bill, staff are banned from charging their own mobile phones at work). It conducts collective bargaining with employees on pay, work practices and conditions of employment through internal elected Employee Representation Committees. However, there was pressure from the British Airline Pilots Association (BALPA) to enlist Ryanair pilots based in Britain.

In July 2006, the Irish High Court ruled that Ryanair had bullied pilots to accept new contracts, where pilots would have to pay €15,000 for re-training on new aircraft if they left the airline, or if the company were forced to negotiate with unions during the following five years. Some Ryanair managers were judged to have given false evidence in court. Meanwhile, Ryanair was contesting the claims of some pilots for victimisation under the new contracts. By 2009, only 11 of the 64 pilots who had lodged the claim remained with the company and still had claims.

Ryanair was ordered to pay 'well in excess' of €1 million in legal costs after a court refused the airline access to the names and addresses of pilots who posted critical comments about the company on a site hosted by the British and Irish pilots' unions. Michael O'Leary claimed anonymous pilots were using a website to intimidate and harass foreign-based pilots to dissuade them from working for the company. Nonetheless, Ryanair appeared to have no problems recruiting crew, including pilots, to meet its needs.

Input costs

Fuel

Perhaps the greatest concern is fuel prices. Jet fuel prices are subject to wide fluctuations, increases in demand and disruptions in supply-factors which Ryanair can neither predict nor control. In such unpredictable circumstances, even hedging is a risk. The situation is compounded by exchange rate uncertainties, although a decline of the US dollar against the euro and sterling worked in Ryanair's favour, as fuel prices are denominated in dollars. Conversely, a weak euro against the dollar works against Ryanair. Ryanair's declaration of 'no fuel surcharges ever' and its reliance on low fares limit its capacity to pass on increased fuel costs.

Airport charges and government taxes

Ryanair is especially sensitive to airports which raise charges, like Stansted and Dublin. Indirectly, it is also vulnerable to extra taxes and charges, such as the €10 tourist tax imposed by the Irish government.

Passenger compensation

On 17 February 2005, a new EU regulation came into effect, providing for standardised and immediate assistance for air passengers at EU airports for delays, cancellations and denied boarding. It was expected that the compensation costs would amount to a sector-wide bill of €200 million annually.

Passengers affected by cancellations must be offered a refund or rerouting and free care and assistance while waiting for their rerouted flight – specifically, meals, refreshments, and hotel accommodation where an overnight stay is necessary. Financial compensation is payable, unless the airline can prove unavoidable exceptional circumstances, like political instability, weather conditions, security and safety risks, or strikes. For Ryanair, the typical compensation cost would fall into the €250 category, based on the average distance of its flights. Passengers subject to long delays would also be entitled to similar assistance. However, four years after its introduction the new regulation was largely ignored and had no material impact on Ryanair, despite the emergence of online 'advisors' to help passengers make claims when their flights have been cancelled or delayed.

Environmental concerns

Aviation fuel has been exempt from carbon taxes, but the EU has established an Emissions Trading Scheme to encompass the aviation industry commencing in 2012. Ryanair was predicted to be the fourth most adversely affected airline in the world with a shortfall of 2.8 tonnes in CO_2 allowances, equivalent to €40 million in extra costs. This is despite its young fleet of fuel-efficient, minimal pollution aircraft. Ryanair has contended that any environmental taxation scheme should be to the benefit of more efficient carriers. Airlines with low load factors that generate high fuel consumption and emissions per passenger, and those offering connecting rather than point-to-point flights, should be penalised.

Sundry legal actions

Ryanair has been in litigation with the EU about alleged receipt of state aid at certain airports. An EU ruling in 2004 held that Ryanair had received illegal state aid from publicly owned Charleroi Airport, its Brussels base. Ryanair was ordered to repay €4 million. The Belgian authorities were claiming back a further €2.3 million in the Irish courts for its reimbursement to Ryanair of start-up costs at Charleroi. On appeal, the original EU decision was overturned in December 2008, Ryanair was refunded its €4 million and the Belgian authorities withdrew their claim. Nonetheless, the EU launched further investigations into allegations of illegal aid, subsidising Ryanair at publicly owned airports, such as Lubeck and Frankfurt Hahn in Germany, and Shannon in Ireland. Other legal challenges were launched against Ryanair by competitors. On another front Ryanair was vigorously opposing French government attempts to protect Air France–KLM by forcing easyJet and Ryanair to move their French-based staff from British employment contracts to more expensive French ones.

Often, Ryanair took the initiative on alleged illegal aid to rivals. For example, it filed a complaint with the EU Commission accusing Air France–KLM of attempting to block competition after the French airline filed a case alleging that Marseille was acting illegally by offering Ryanair discount airlines cut-price fees at its second, no-frills terminal. That complaint came a month after Ryanair called on the Commission to investigate allegations that Air France had received almost €1 billion in illegal state aid, benefiting unfairly from up to 50 per cent discounted landing and passenger charges on flights within France. Adverse rulings on these airport cases could curtail Ryanair's growth, if it was prevented from striking advantageous deals with publicly owned airports and was confined to the fewer privately owned airports across Europe.

On another front, Ryanair was being sued by BAA for its refusal to pay increased landing charges at Stansted. In other legal cases Ryanair has been accused of misleading passengers on its website by exaggerating price differentials with its competitors.[xx]

Customer services and perceptions

In 2003, Ryanair published a Passenger Charter, which includes doctrines on low fares, customer redress and punctuality. Its annual report offers figures claiming superiority over competitors with respect to punctuality, completed flights and fewest bags lost per 1000 passengers.

However, its Skytrax 2 star rating is among the worst for budget airlines. In Europe, only bmibaby and Wizzair achieve as low a rating. There have been suggestions that Ryanair's 'obsessive focus on the bottom line may have dented its public image. In an infamous incident, it charged a disabled man £18 (€25) to use a wheelchair'.[xxi] In response to protests over the charge, Ryanair imposed a 50-cent wheelchair levy on every passenger ticket. Campaigners for the disabled accused Ryanair of profiteering, declaring that the levy should be no more than 3 cents. It was the only major airline in Europe to impose such charges.

There was growing attention to extra charges continually being imposed by Ryanair on passengers, many on unavoidable services, such as check-in. In some instances, these extra charges make Ryanair more expensive than BA.[xxii] Examples were a family of four travelling to Ibiza from London with three bags for a two-week holiday costing £1157 with Ryanair compared to £913 with BA and £634 with easyJet. A single passenger travelling to Venice from London for a week at Christmas with one bag would pay a total £139 on Ryanair compared to £89 on BA and £121 on easyJet.

Ryanair features on many consumer complaint interactive websites, and some blogs have been established specifically to disparage the airline. In a blog entitled '20 reasons never to fly Ryanair', extra charges for booking fees, baggage overweight and low weight limits, premium rate helplines, and the fact that 'you are always being flogged stuff' were enumerated.[xxiii] When the *Irish Times* put Ryanair customers' gripes to its head of communications, Stephen McNamara, his response was to dismiss them as ' "subjective and inaccurate rubbish" and even implied they had been made up to further some anti-Ryanair agenda'.[xxiv] Among the complaints were:

> Customers want to be treated like a human being, to get to their desired destination (not 50/60 miles away) . . . to be allowed to bring luggage without persecution . . . a complete and utter lack of communication when flights run late . . . I'm sick of that miserable booking charge/service charge/admin charge system.

So, why are so many people willing to put up with an airline that, in the words of *The Economist*, 'has become a byword for appalling customer service, misleading advertising claims and jeering rudeness'?[xxv] Ryanair has responded to such comments, declaring that, in effect, customers vote with their feet by choosing Ryanair for its four tenets of customer service – low fares, a good on-time record, few cancellations and few lost bags. 'If you want anything more – go away', warns Michael O'Leary.[xxvi] The *Financial Times* aerospace correspondent observed that Ryanair still offered relative value compared to rail alternatives, at least on a journey from London to Scotland, even when Ryanair extras are factored in.

Other risks and challenges

As listed in its own report, Ryanair faced other risks – prices and availability of new aircraft, threats of terrorist attacks, dependence on key personnel (especially Michael O'Leary) and on external service providers and its internet website and the continued acceptance of budget carriers with respect to safety. Tied in with the latter are potential rises in insurance costs.

Ryanair's competitive space

Globally, the airline industry lost $11 billion in 2009, on top of $8.5 billion in 2008, with European airlines contributing $1 billion of that loss. Of the large European carriers, only Lufthansa was expecting to make a profit. BA, Air France–KLM and Scandinavian Air Systems (SAS) experienced severe losses, due to declining traffic from long-haul business class passengers. The woes of these legacy carriers were compounded by huge pension fund deficits.

Some industry analysts considered the economic recession of 2009 could offer an opportunity for budget carriers, as passengers who continued to travel were expected to trade down. By mid-2009, budget airlines accounted for over 35 per cent of scheduled intra-European traffic. Ryanair was the clear market share leader, with easyJet another dominant force (Table 2). The two were often compared and contrasted, since both operated mainly out of the UK and served the same markets. One issue was whether easyJet's use of primary airports would be better

than Ryanair at capturing the traffic trading down from network carriers.

Other budget carriers, of diverse size and growth ambitions, trajectories and regional emphases varied in different levels of services to passengers and use of main versus secondary airports. The comparison with the US budget airline market in Table 2 indicates that penetration in Europe is less than in the US, which suggests scope for growth in the sector in Europe. It also raises the question as to whether the extent of dominance enjoyed by Southwest offers a model for Ryanair to assert itself further. Another possible development trajectory for Ryanair was to follow up on its announcement in 2007 to offer €10 transatlantic flights, an idea which had not taken flight and appeared to have been shelved as of 2009.

Leading Ryanair into the future

'It is good to have someone like Michael O'Leary around. He scares people to death.' This praise of Ryanair's CEO came from none other than his fellow Irishman, Willie Walsh, CEO of BA.[xxvii] He has been described as 'at turns, arrogant and rude, then charming, affable and humorous, has terrorised rivals and regulators for more than a decade. And so far, they have waited in vain for him to trip up or his enthusiasm to wane.'[xxviii] In fact, Michael O'Leary has been pronouncing his intention to depart from the airline 'in two years' time'. He has declared that he would sever all links with the airline, refusing to 'move upstairs' as chairman. ' "You don't need a doddery oldie hanging around the place", he proclaimed.'[xxix]

O'Leary stays in budget hotels, always flies Ryanair, startling fellow passengers by taking their boarding passes at the gate and by boarding the plane last where he invariably gets a middle seat. He does not sit in an executive lounge, has no BlackBerry and does not use email.

In 2009, Michael O'Leary held 4.06 per cent of Ryanair's share capital, having sold 5 million shares at €3.75. Although O'Leary consistently praised his management team, Ryanair was inextricably identified with him. He was credited with single-handedly transforming European air transport. In 2001, O'Leary received the European Businessman of the Year Award from *Fortune* magazine; in 2004, the *Financial Times* named him as one of 25 European 'business stars' who have made a difference. The newspaper described him as personifying 'the brash new Irish business elite' and possessing 'a head for numbers, a shrewd marketing brain and a ruthless competitive streak'.[xxx]

Present and former staff have praised O'Leary's leadership style. 'Michael's genius is his ability to motivate and energise people. There is an incredible energy in that place. People work incredibly hard and get a lot out of it. They operate a very lean operation. It is without peer' said Tim

Table 2 Budget airlines sundry data – Europe and US (2008/09)

European market position				US market position	
Airline	Pax (m)[1]	Rating[3]	Airports[4]	Airline	Pax (m)[2]
Aigle Azur	1.46		26	AirTran	24.6
Air Berlin	28.6	4	126	Allegiant Air	3.9
Belle Air	0.46		24	American Trans Air (ATA)	0.4
Bmibaby	3.87	2	32	Frontier Airlines	10.1
Brussels Airlines	5.4	3	62	GoJet Airlines	1.5
Clickair[5]	6.3	3	40	Horizon Airlines (Alaska Air)	6.5
easyJet	44.6	3	110	Island Air Hawaii	0.5
FlyBe	7.5	3	65	JetBlue Airways	20.5
Germanwings	7.6	3	70	Midwest Airline Inc.	3.0
Jet2.com	3.5	3	51	Shuttle America Corp.	3.5
Meridiana	1.9	3	30	Southwest Airlines	101.9
Monarch Airlines	3.9		21	Spirit Airlines	5.5
Myair.com[5]	1.5		27	Sun County Airlines	1.3
Niki Airline	2.1	3	33	USA 3000 Airlines	0.8
Norwegian	9.1	3	85	Virgin America	2.5
Ryanair	57.7	2	140		
Sky Europe[5]	3.6	3	30		
Sterling[5]	3.8		39		
Sverigeflyg	0.5		15		
transavia.com	5.5	3	88		
TUIfly	10.5		75		
Vueling Airlines	5.9	3	45		
Windjet	2.7		28		
Wizz Air	5.9	3	58		

[1] *Sources*: European Low Fares Airlines Association (ELFAA), Company reports.

[2] *Sources*: CIA, Bureau of Transportation Statistics.

[3] Skytrax star rating from 1 to 5 – not all airlines rated.

[4] Number of airports served; *Sources*: European Low Fares Airlines Association (ELFAA), Company reports.

[5] These airlines have ceased operations.

Total passengers (pax)

European budget airlines   223.9
Ryanair as % of Total – 26%

Key Population Data
Population EU 27 (m) 500

Key Population Ratios
Budget ratio to EU 27 population 0.45

Total pax US budget airlines   186.4
Southwest as % of Total – 55%

Key Population Data
Population US (m) 307

Key Population Ratios
Budget ratio to US population 0.61

Jeans, a former sales and marketing director of Ryanair, currently CEO of a small low-cost rival, MyTravelLite.[xxxi]

O'Leary's publicity seeking antics are legendary. These included his 'declaration of war' on easyJet when, wearing an army uniform, he drove a tank to easyJet's headquarters at Luton Airport. In another stunt, when Ryanair opened its hub at Milan Bergamo he flew there aboard a jet bearing the slogan 'Arrivederci Alitalia'. He has also dressed up as St Patrick and as the Pope to promote ticket offers.

O'Leary's outspokenness has made him a figure of public debate. 'He is called everything from "arrogant pig" to "messiah"'.[xxxii] His avowed enemies include trade unions, politicians who impose airport taxes (he called UK Prime Minister Gordon Brown a 'twit' and a 'Scottish miser'[xxxiii]), environmentalists, bloggers who rant about poor service, travel agents, reporters who expect free seats,

regulators and the EU Commission, and airport owners like BAA, whom he once called 'overcharging rapists'.[xxxiv] An EU Commissioner, Philippe Busquin, denounced Michael O'Leary as 'irritating . . . and insists he is not the only Commissioner who is allergic to the mere mention of the name of Ryanair's arrogant chief'.[xxxv]

An *Irish Times* columnist, John McManus, suggested that 'maybe it's time for Ryanair to jettison O'Leary', asserting that O'Leary has become a caricature of himself. Perhaps the last words should go to Michael O'Leary himself: 'We could make a mistake and I could get hung', he said. He reiterated a point he had often made before:

It is okay doing the cheeky chappie, running around Europe, thumbing your nose, but I am not Herb Kelleher (the legendary founder of the original budget airline, Southwest Airlines). He was a genius and I am not.[xxxvi]

So, how do these comments (and the Aer Lingus bid) fit with Michael O'Leary's declaration to part company with Ryanair? Would he really go, and if so, what would happen to Ryanair and its ambitions? No one really knows the answer to these questions, but it is O'Leary's propensity to surprise his admirers and detractors alike.

References:

[i] 'The FT ArcelorMittal Boldness in Business Awards', *Financial Times* supplement, 20 March 2009, p. 25.

[ii] K. Done, 'Airline industry in intensive care', *Financial Times*, 25 March 2009, p. 22.

[iii] P. Clark, 'Upbeat Ryanair rides out the storm', *Financial Times*, 2 February 2009, p. 20.

[iv] K. Done, 'Ryanair sees opportunities in rivals' distress', *Financial Times*, 28 July 2009, p. 15.

[v] *Financial Times*, 9 September 2006, p. 16.

[vi] K. Done and T. Braithwaite, 'Ryanair to allow mobile phone calls next year', *Financial Times*, 31 August 2006, p. 1.

[vii] Ryanair Annual Report, 2001.

[viii] J. Guthrie, 'Sir Stelios beknighted as suits prove bolder risk takers', *Financial Times*, 30 July 2009, p. 16.

[ix] P. Clark, 'O'Leary in attack on Boeing', *Financial Times*, 19 December 2009, p. 1.

[x] Ryanair Annual Report 2009.

[xi] Ibid.

[xii] S. Lyall, 'No apologies from the boss of a no-frills airline', *The New York Times*, 1 August 2009 (The Saturday Profile).

[xiii] Ryanair 2007 half yearly results.

[xiv] B. Groom, 'Hot air from Ryanair', *Financial Times*, 23 July 2009, p. 16.

[xv] LEX, Ryanair, *Financial Times*, 3 June 2009, p. 16.

[xvi] L. Noonan, 'O'Leary admits stake in Aer Lingus was stupid disaster', *Irish Independent*, 6 March 2009.

[xvii] Statement from Ryanair's half yearly results presentation, 6 November 2006.

[xviii] S. Pogatchnik, 'Aer Lingus rejects Ryanair takeover offer', *Business Week* online, 3 November 2006.

[xix] Ryanair Full Year Results 2009.

[xx] Ryanair press release, 29 May 2009.

[xxi] D. Milmo, 'Ryanair – the world's least favourite airline', *Guardian*, 26 October 2006.

[xxii] R. Waite and S. Swinford, 'Ryanair more expensive than BA on some flights', *Sunday Times*, 9 August 2009.

[xxiii] Money Central – *Times Online* – 'WBLG: Twenty reasons never to fly Ryanair', 20 March 2009.

[xxiv] C. Pope, 'Pricewatch Daily', *Irish Times*, 14 August 2009, p. 11.

[xxv] Lyall, 'No apologies from the boss of a no-frills airline'.

[xxvi] Ibid.

[xxvii] K. Done, 'O'Leary shows it is not yet the end for budget air travel'. *Financial Times*, 2 August 2008, p. 11.

[xxviii] 'The FT ArcelorMittal Boldness in Business Awards', *Financial Times* supplement, 20 March 2009, p. 21.

[xxix] D. Dalby, 'I'm going for good, O'Leary tells Ryanair', *Sunday Times*, 20 November 2005.

[xxx] B. Groom, 'Leaders of the new Europe: Business stars chart a course for the profits of the future', *Financial Times*, 20 April 2004.

[xxxi] G. Bowley, 'How low can you go?' *Financial Times Magazine*, No. 9, 21 June 2003.

[xxxii] Ibid.

[xxxiii] Lyall, 'No apologies from the boss of a no-frills airline'.

[xxxiv] Ibid.

[xxxv] S. Creaton, 'Turbulent times for Ryanair's high-flier', *Irish Times*, 31 January 2004.

[xxxvi] Bowley, 'How low can you go?'

Will we still love IKEA?

Kevan Scholes

IKEA revolutionised the furniture market in many countries by making 'flat pack' furniture chic. But how did the company manage to stave off competition both from cheaper competitors and from traditionally built furniture? Importantly, is this a sustainable competitive model during or following a global recession?

● ● ●

'Despite my best efforts, IKEA's growth has faltered. Flat sales may look pretty respectable given the collapse in furniture markets around the world. Yet IKEA should be benefiting from trading down, the elimination of smaller rivals and new store openings'.

This was Anders Dahlvig, then President and CEO of the IKEA Group speaking to *The Times* in June 2009[i] reflecting on the challenges of the global recession. He was head of the world's biggest furnishings retailer with sales of £20.6 billion (€22.7 bn/$30.8 bn) in 2009 – more than three times the sales of 10 years earlier. But he had recently slashed 5000 jobs (out of a workforce of 120,000) and the company sales grew only 1.4 per cent in the year ending August 2009 despite 15 new store openings. The sector had experienced some spectacular failures in that year – for example, the closure in November 2008 of MFI, one of IKEA's largest rivals in the UK with 111 stores (compared with IKEA's 17 – much bigger – stores[1]).

The home furnishings market[ii]

By 2009 home furnishings was a huge market worldwide with retail sales in 2007 in excess of $US600 billion in items such as furniture, household textiles and floor coverings. More than 50 per cent of these sales were in furniture stores (including IKEA). IKEA had about 2.5 per cent of world sales through its 250+ stores in 24 countries and sales in excess of €20 billion (more details of IKEA's operations are summarised in Figures 1–4). Table 1 compares the geographical spread of the market and IKEA sales by region. Table 2 shows the date of each country's first IKEA stores.

---

[1] See *The Times* article referenced below in the text for more details of the UK competitors.

Source: Press Association Images/Heribert Proepper/AP.

IKEA's closest rivals were US companies led by Bed, Bath and Beyond (with about 1 per cent share).

IKEA's competitors

Home furnishings was a highly fragmented market with competition occurring locally rather than globally. In each region that IKEA had stores it would typically face competitors of several types:

● Multinational furniture retailers (like IKEA) all of whom were considerably smaller than IKEA. These included the Danish company Jysk (turnover ~ €1bn).

Table 1 The geographical spread of the market and of IKEA sales by region

	Europe	Americas	Asia/Pacific
% of global market (2007)	52	29	19
% of IKEA sales (2008)	82	15	3

Table 2 Countries' first stores

1958	**Sweden** – Älmhult	1989	**Italy** – Milan (Carugate)
1963	**Norway** – Oslo (Nesbru)	1990	**Hungary** – Budapest
1969	**Denmark** – Copenhagen (Ballerup)	1991	**Poland** – Platan
1973	**Switzerland** – Zürich (Spreitenbach)	1991	**Czech Republic** – Prague (Zlicin)
1974	**Germany** – Munich (Eching)	1991	**United Arab Emirates** – Dubai
1975	**Australia** – Artamon	1992	**Slovakia** – Bratislava
1976	**Canada** – Vancouver (Richmond)	1994	**Taiwan** – Taipei
1977	**Austria** – Vienna (Vösendorf)	1996	**Finland** – Esbo
1978	**Netherlands** – Rotterdam (Sliedrecht)	1996	**Malaysia** – Kuala Lumpur
1978	**Singapore** – Singapore	1998	**China** – Shanghai
1980	**Spain** – Gran Canaria (Las Palmas)	2000	**Russia** – Moscow (Chimki)
1981	**Iceland** – Reykjavik	2001	**Israel** – Netanya
1981	**France** – Paris (Bobigny)	2001	**Greece** – Thessaloniki
1983	**Saudi Arabia** – Jeddah	2004	**Portugal** – Lisbon
1984	**Belgium** – Brussels (Zaventem and Ternat)	2005	**Turkey** – Istanbul
1984	**Kuwait** – Kuwait City	2006	**Japan** – Tokyo (Funabashi)
1985	**United States** – Philadelphia	2007	**Romania** – Bucharest
1987	**United Kingdom** – Manchester (Warrington)	2009	**Ireland** – Dublin
1988	**Hong Kong** – Hong Kong (Shatin)		

Source: IKEA website: www.ikea.com.

- Companies specialising in just part of the furniture product range and operating in several countries – such as Alno from Germany in kitchens.
- Multi-branch retail furniture outlets whose sales were mainly in one country (such as MFI before its closure), and DFS in the UK. The USA market was dominated by such players (e.g. Bed, Bath & Beyond Inc., with revenues of some $US7bn).
- Non-specialist companies which carried furniture as part of a wider product range. In the UK the largest operator was the Home Retail Group whose subsidiary Argos offered some 18,500 general merchandise products through its network of 700 stores and online sales. Despite this more generalist offering Argos was number one in UK furniture retailing. General DIY companies such as Kingfisher (through B&Q in the UK and Castorama in France) were attempting to capture more of the bottom end of the furniture market.
- Small and/or specialised retailers and/or manufacturers. These accounted for some 90% of the market in Europe.

Figures 1–4 give some facts and figures about IKEA.

The IKEA formula for success

In June 2008, to mark the 50th anniversary of the launch of IKEA in Sweden, *The Times* ran an article[iii] looking at why many people seemed to love IKEA. This required a look at the origins of the company and how the founding values had shaped its development:

In the 50 years since IKEA launched, and the 21 years since the first British store opened its doors, the Swedish lifestyle giant has made itself an often derided yet essential part of the culture. We journey beyond the Billy bookcases to discover what makes its global flat-packed heart beat strong. . . . In the [company] museum, Juni Wannberg, with the company since 1984, tells me that story.

Ingvar Kamprad, the founder, grew up on a farm outside Älmhult. Älmhult is in the Småland region, and Smålanders are famed throughout the country for their informality, entrepreneurial spirit (Brio, the toymaker, also started here) and thrift. Especially their thrift: the IKEA catalogue is shot here, using employees as models. A lot of advertising is also done in-house. Managers fly economy and sometimes have to share hotel rooms. And, as any visitor to IKEA will know, staffing levels are hardly generous.

It's hard country, rocky, with poor soil. A century ago, many Smålanders left for America. Those who stayed had to graft. Kamprad's grandfather ran the general store, while his father was full of business ideas. 'What a great combination for a little guy!' enthuses Wannberg. Indeed so: Ingvar was an uncommonly enterprising boy. His aunt sent him bulk quantities of matches from Stockholm that he broke up and sold to locals at a profit. He launched the catalogue as a single-sheet mail order flyer (last year 191 million copies in 27 languages were produced, one of the biggest print runs in the world). Then he opted to concentrate on furniture, took on the established cartels by buying direct from small producers, brought in Danish designers, discovered flat-pack (by accident) and steadily expanded through the Fifties and Sixties.

. . . Kamprad got into low-cost supply very early, doing a deal in Communist Poland in the late Fifties.

Figure 1 IKEA's turnover, 1954–2009

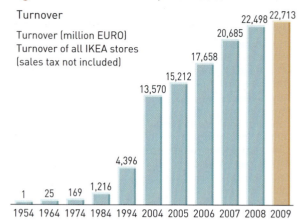

Turnover

Turnover (million EURO)
Turnover of all IKEA stores
(sales tax not included)

Figure 2 IKEA catalogues, 1954–2009

Catalogues

Catalogues (in millions).
The IKEA catalogue was
printed in 56 editions
and 27 languages

Figure 3 IKEA visits, 1954–2009

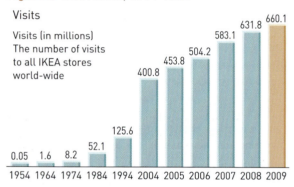

Visits

Visits (in millions)
The number of visits
to all IKEA stores
world-wide

Figure 4 IKEA stores, 1954–2009

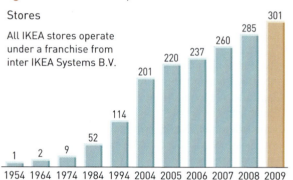

Stores

All IKEA stores operate
under a franchise from
inter IKEA Systems B.V.

The Poles, apparently, warmed to Kamprad's informality and his ability to drink. Poland is still IKEA's second biggest supplier, the biggest being China, which accounts for more than a fifth of procurement. The chain's purchasing power is such that it is estimated to make an extraordinary 18 per cent profit on sales, this despite passing on a large chunk of its cost savings to the customer. IKEA does not have any shareholders. Its ownership is shrouded in a series of foundations and trusts, but it remains a private company under, no one doubts, the control of the Kamprad family. The founder himself, now 82 and living in Switzerland, comes to Älmhult every Christmas to make a speech.

. . . [Meanwhile in London 2009] I don't suppose you'd guess Peter Högsted was in charge of 10,000 employees and a chunk of one of the world's best-known and most successful companies. He wears an open-necked shirt and jeans, he swears occasionally, and his office, perched on top of a multistorey car park on a retail estate in Wembley, North London, looks more like a Portakabin than the headquarters of a multinational. But then the hallmarks of this company are, firstly, a fanatical devotion to cost-cutting and, as part

of that devotion, an informal structure. 'It's a very well-regarded, very well-run operation,' says Richard Hyman, an independent retail consultant.

Högsted doesn't even have the whole Portakabin, merely a desk in the open-plan layout like everyone else. And yet this 39-year-old Dane is the managing director of IKEA UK, which this year celebrates its coming of age in Britain. 'Furniture retailing in this country traditionally was not great,' says Hyman. 'IKEA has changed that. It puts fashion in the product, it made good Scandinavian design accessible to lots of people.'

. . . Before IKEA, there was Habitat, but Habitat was never cheap, and consequently it never had more than a sliver, about 1 per cent, of the market. IKEA has about 7.5 per cent, second only to Argos. For a chain with a mere 17 stores [in the UK], albeit very large stores, IKEA has woven itself into the fabric of British culture, become part of the furniture if you will, remarkably quickly. Like Boots and Smiths in the 20th century, IKEA has become, like Borders, like Gap, one of those places where, in the 21st century, almost everyone shops at some stage.

Given its prices, IKEA has effectively removed personal wealth as a factor for most people in buying home furnishings. This makes IKEA more egalitarian, albeit a great deal less ubiquitous, than Starbucks. £1.50 for a cup of coffee is a lot. £150 for a sofa is not. And if you want a sofa, you do not want to wait three months, let alone until you inherit your parents'.

... IKEA is a retailing institution in Sweden, like Marks & Spencer is here, but I don't know if we can talk about cultural dominance in the UK when we have Argos with 700 stores or DFS with 300,' says Högsted. Perhaps not dominance (the £18 billion a year furniture market is the most fragmented in retailing, with fully 50 per cent of Britons still buying at their local high street shop), but for the young, for the full range of the middle class, for those aspiring to join the middle class, a trip to IKEA has become a modern ritual. Forty-five million customers will enter a British IKEA this year, close on a million a week, more than go to church, more than go to football.

We know that our core customers are 25–50,' says Högsted, '80 per cent are female, a majority have kids.' In terms of social class, 'Bs and C1s are the core', but IKEA also attracts a lot of what Högsted calls 'smart As'. They will leave the core furniture items, but they like our kitchens and they will go for kitchenware and tableware and textiles [all to be found in the cleverly demarcated Market Place]. Our customers know what is for me and what isn't. We are not for the rich, we are for the smart. If you want to use your furniture to display that you are rich, you will not shop at IKEA, but if you are smart it is OK.

... The world over, as people secure the essentials and become wealthier, they tend to spend their spare cash in predictable ways. Clothing and electronic items come first, but once they're togged up and plugged in, people spend on furniture and interior design. Sweden is a richer country than the UK. The money Britons became accustomed to spending on their homes in the Eighties and Nineties, the Swedes were spending in the Sixties, the Germans were spending in the Seventies, some Russians, and some Chinese, are spending now. And, with 231 stores in 24 countries serving 522 million customers, many of them are spending it in IKEA.

A richer country, Sweden, and also a colder, darker one. For good reasons, the home is historically important to the Swedes. They spend a lot of time in it. 'In Sweden,' says Anna Efverlund, an IKEA designer since 1980, the woman who came up with the brightly coloured plastic coat hanger so many of us use, 'it is rude not to ask if you can look around when you go into someone else's home.' Such social mores could only thrive in a far less class-ridden society than Britain used to be.

With a local market willing and able to spend, it is no accident that IKEA started in Sweden, near the small town of Älmhult, to be exact. Getting off the train from Malmö, countless logs from the northern forests passing in the opposite direction, I saw soon enough that Älmhult is a company town. Visitors stay in the IKEA Hotel and Restaurant on Ikeagatan, surrounded by visiting IKEA 'co-workers' talking about how great it is to work for IKEA. In the hotel basement are the IKEA archive and the IKEA museum. 'IKEA is part of the Swedish soul,' says Görel Karlsson, my guide.

Opposite is the world's first IKEA store, opened in 1958. This place must have looked like a spaceship back then; now, it looks like every other IKEA I've ever seen: a big blue and yellow shed with flags outside. Indeed, the single worst thing about IKEA, worse than the mystifying self-assembly instructions, is the external appearance of its stores. 'There is a terrible pathos,' says design guru Stephen Bayley, 'about IKEA's idealism for good design for everyone and the brute, corrupting ugliness of its presence wherever it goes.' That may be harsh and yet, although IKEA says cheap and beautiful need not conflict, when they do, cheap always wins. If a designer is asked to produce a chair to sell at £10 and comes up with a wonderful £12 chair, she either redesigns it or it doesn't get produced.

Of Älmhult's population of 9,000, 3,500 work directly for IKEA. It is not the headquarters – that is in the Netherlands for tax purposes – but it is, insiders say, 'the heart of IKEA'. Indeed, in the curious way co-workers have of echoing each other, they all use that same phrase. No surprise: managers from around the world come to Älmhult to learn the essentials of the IKEA story. IKEA is very big on its story.

Back in London, I meet Olivia Szdjnaa, 24, Tania Hamilton, 20, and Melissa Hurring, 25, all on the first rungs of the IKEA management ladder. Their youth is no accident. The average age of IKEA store managers is 32, and it is very big on harnessing the energy and enthusiasm of youth, an enthusiasm that can verge on passion, even idealism. IKEA's training internally and advertising externally assiduously maintains its status as an oppositional brand, an outsider, a cult. Its propaganda uses radical, sometimes leftist imagery: polo players contrasted unfavourably with kids playing football; a silver salver of caviar under the words 'for the few' up against a page full of hot dogs, 'for the many'.

These three young women talk in glowing terms of their employer: the Christmas gifts, the social outings, the lack of a hierarchy, the opportunity to switch jobs. IKEA has been called a 'Marmite'[2] brand (you love it or

---

[2] Marmite is a savoury spread made from yeast extract – similar to Vegemite in other countries. Consumers seem to either love it or hate it.

hate it), yet while plenty of people moan about wobbly tables, the firm does not incur the opprobrium directed at other global multiples. Indeed, in a customer satisfaction survey carried out by Verdict research, IKEA came third in the retail sector after Waitrose and John Lewis. Part of the reason for this popularity is that IKEA's staff are such zealous ambassadors for their employer.

Szdjnaa, Hamilton, Hurring and I drive to Ealing in West London. We are going to see Boyd Chung, a 32-year-old Malaysian IT consultant, as part of the firm's market research into how we use our homes and what products we want in them. 'What are you happy with?' they ask Chung. 'Nothing,' he says, gesturing helplessly around a flat overflowing with books, magazines, filing, electronic kit. It strikes me that a big part of IKEA's success is simply that we have much more stuff than we did 20 years ago, and need somewhere to put it all.

It rapidly emerges that Chung wants to be told what to do. One of the reasons he likes IKEA, he says, and I heard this time and again, is 'it is easy to navigate'. The IKEA pathway, the line of bossy blue arrows that forces you through the whole store, is much vilified. If you hate IKEA, even if you don't hate the queues and the self-assembly, you certainly hate the line. And yet direction is precisely what many customers want. 'My wife and I go there once or twice a month, for recreation, window-shopping, inspiration, and to see solutions to our problems,' says Chung. 'My friends here and in Malaysia all go to IKEA.'

Chung and his friends are part of an expanding global middle class, meritocrats defined by mobility and pragmatism, people with similar taste, regardless of race, religion or country of origin. The IKEA fan in Milton Keynes probably has as much, if not more, in common with the IKEA fan in Moscow or Monterey, than with her own compatriot who goes to MFI. What sells well in one country sells well in another; what flops in one place tends to flop everywhere. The average spend per store visit ($85 in 2005) is the same in Russia as it is in Sweden.

One-size-fits-all is the essence of the IKEA business model. To benefit from economies of scale, you can't be tweaking products to suit local tastes. Stephen Bayley bemoans this homogeneity: 'Products should have national characteristics, that's what people love.' But is it? Peter Högsted, sitting up there in his spare, functional HQ in Wembley, thinks not. 'There is this thesis that we are all so different,' he says, 'but we are not.'

The future

Commenting on the company's annual results in September 2009 Mikael Ohisson, IKEA's new chief executive (replacing Anders Dahlvig) talked about the challenge ahead:

> It has been a challenging year in which we have had to adapt to changed market conditions. We know that many of our customers have less money to spend and our low-price concept is therefore more relevant than ever.[iv]

References:
[i] 'Is IKEA's business model coming apart'?, David Wighton, *The Times*, 24 June 2009.
[ii] Data in this section comes from the IKEA website and from the DataMonitor report on Global Home Furnishings Retail-Industry Profile (Reference Code: 0199–2243 Publication date: April 2008).
[iii] From Robert Crampton, 'Why we love IKEA', *The Times*, 7 June 2008, © the Times/The Sun/nisyndication.com.
[iv] 'Sweden's IKEA builds record sales', BBC website: www.bbc.co.uk, 17 September 2009.

CRH plc: successful corporate-level strategy in a challenging environment

Mike Moroney

Even with a small corporate headquarters in a challenging environment, it is clear that corporate-level strategy can generate substantial value-added. Less well understood are the mechanisms of delivering these benefits at this level of strategy. These issues are explored in this case study on CRH (an international building materials company based in Ireland), which is an exemplar of corporate-level management.

● ● ●

In March 2010, CRH (one of the top four building materials companies in the world) announced financial results for 2009, against the backdrop of the worst global recession since the 1930s and a severe sector downturn. Unsurprisingly, the Group recorded its second successive annual decline in earnings, representing a total fall of almost two-thirds since the cyclical peak in 2007. At the same time, there were also encouraging signs for Chief Executive and former Finance Director Myles Lee and his management team. 2009 was CRH's 26th consecutive year of dividend growth, the underlying decline in profitability slowed markedly in the second half of the year, the yield from cost savings implemented during the downturn was €1.65 billion[1] annually and net debt fell to €3.7 billion (2008: €6.1 billion) reflecting strong operating cash flow and proceeds from the March 2009 rights issue, which raised €1.24 billion net of expenses. Such developments: 'have strengthened the Group operationally and position CRH well to respond to upside developments and to avail itself of value-enhancing acquisition opportunities as these arise across our markets.'[i]

The building materials industry

The industry involves the manufacture and distribution ('merchanting' and DIY) of primary materials (such as cement, aggregates, asphalt, ready-mixed concrete and asphalt products), 'heavyside' building products (for example, concrete products, road vaults and bricks) and

'lightside' building products (e.g., plumbing, heating, electrical and lighting products). The sectors served are new construction work (residential, industrial, commercial and public works) and repair, maintenance and improvement (RMI). In general, building materials and products are standard, similar across markets and largely stable over time. Production processes are also standard. Technology is non-proprietary and, for some products, relatively unsophisticated.

Characteristics

Building materials is a cyclical, commodity business, characterised in most markets by maturity and fragmentation. Cyclicality reflects the considerable capital investment involved, long lead times and 'lumpy' additions to capacity. Industry cycles are longer in duration and larger in amplitude than general economic cycles. However, their timing varies between countries. Building materials and products are largely commodities, with little difference between suppliers, who compete mainly on the basis of price. The construction sector is mature in the Western world, reflecting relatively stable economic activity and populations. Average growth in construction activity is less than half the rate of economic growth, while RMI accounts for upwards of half total output. By contrast, in newly emerging areas of the world (Asia, Eastern Europe, Latin America) and in Western countries at an earlier stage of economic development (such as Ireland, Finland and Portugal), construction is robust. On the other hand, cyclicality in such markets is more pronounced.

Traditionally, the building materials industry has been highly fragmented. Production is often linked to

---

[1] €1.65bn ≈ £1.48bn ≈ $2.23bn as at March 2010.

the location of reserves, of varying value, leading to a proliferation of facilities and low barriers to entry. In addition, building materials and products are, by and large, characterised by a high weight to value ratio. As a result, high transport costs rapidly outweigh scale economies and determine the radius of economic activity and competition, which in many cases can be 150 kilometres or less. Markets tend to be local in nature due to differences in building regulations, construction practices and product standards. Success is often determined by micro-market factors like locality, quality, reliability of service and price.[ii] As a result, the industry had developed as a large number of small and medium sized firms, often family owned and run.

Structural trends

Since the mid-1990s, a number of structural trends had emerged, in part prompted by sustained low levels of activity. In certain markets (particularly primary materials, 'heavyside' products and merchanting), supply side concentration and significant corporate activity had occurred, resulting in the disappearance of a number of previously well-known industry names. At the same time, a number of large, international building materials companies had emerged over time, typically using the base of a strong local market position and/or product competence as a springboard to expand into other regions and areas of activity. There was also evidence that local differences between geographic markets were eroding. This was driven by institutional factors (harmonisation of building regulations, product standards and tendering procedures), convergence in building practices across markets, consolidation of customers and homogenisation of their needs. Nonetheless, the underlying logic of fragmentation continued to prevail in many countries, in particular the US. Products and distribution were less concentrated than primary materials. Also, construction markets globally remained fragmented: the top five producers supplied only one-fifth of cement, and one-twentieth of aggregates, demand.[iii]

Sector outlook

Commencing with a decline in US housing in the first half of 2006, and exacerbated by the credit crunch, crisis in financial markets and severe global economic recession, by 2009 the construction and building materials industries were in the grip of a deep downturn from which no segment or region was immune. Substantial falls in peak-to-trough earnings were forecast for the building materials sector,[iv] matching the worst of past cycles. Bottom of cycle earnings were not expected until 2010, with 2013 seen as mid-cycle.[v] However, there were some positive signals.[vi] Fiscal stimulus packages were estimated to provide US$1 trillion in infrastructure funding globally. Building materials companies were implementing cost savings averaging 3 per cent of sales

(over 9 per cent in the case of CRH). In the first half of 2009, the sector completed €6.3 billion in equity funding and refinancing raised €12 billion in debt, largely removing balance sheet risk. Finally, there was evidence of renewed corporate merger and acquisition deals. There were also signs of a softening in acquisition multiples (of operating profits) from the double digit levels approaching 20 times in major deals in 2007, which had been fuelled by excessive leverage.[vii]

Profile of CRH

Headquartered in Dublin, Ireland, CRH had cyclical trough revenues of over €17 billion per annum and employed more than 80,000 people in over 3500 locations in 35 countries. The Group enjoyed a major presence in mature markets in Europe and North America and a growing foothold in emerging regions, including Eastern Europe and Latin America. CRH's prominence had been recognised by receiving many industry awards over the years for corporate governance,[viii] financial reporting, investor relations, and excellence/innovation in environmental and safety practices.

History, growth and development

CRH was formed in 1970 following the merger of two Irish companies Cement Limited and Roadstone Limited (an Irish building materials company). Since then, the Group has undergone major growth through three major phases of development (see below). In general, change has been evolutionary, involving a managed, learning process of building, augmenting and layering competences.

Organic market penetration in Ireland (from 1970)

During the 1970s, Irish construction enjoyed a boom on the back of a modernising economy. The newly merged CRH capitalised on this favourable environment through its vertically integrated and leading positions in virtually all domestic markets for 'heavyside' building materials and products.

Acquisition-led overseas expansion (from the late 1970s)

In the late 1970s, with a view to spreading risks and opportunities more broadly, CRH made a strategic decision to invest in familiar business sectors overseas, through add-on acquisitions of medium-sized, often family-owned, businesses. Early expansion in the UK and the Netherlands was followed by further acquisitions in mainland Europe. In 1977, Don Godson (later Chief Executive, 1994–2000) went to the US with 'a telephone and a cheque book'. By 2009, the Americas accounted for around half Group turnover and profits. CRH's presence in emerging regions gathered pace from the mid-1990s. The Group also expanded in a limited, but highly rewarding, way into new product areas, including merchanting and DIY, security fencing, clay brick products and glass fabrication (in the US).

Product focus, larger acquisitions (from the late 1990s)

During the 1990s, CRH's previous regional structure evolved into a more product-based organisation, to bring greater focus to business development and sharing best practice. At the same time, anticipating greater industry consolidation, the Group began to supplement traditional mid-size deals with larger acquisitions.

Strategy

CRH strategic vision is to 'be a responsible international leader in building materials delivering superior performance and growth'.[ix] The Group's strategy is 'to seek new geographic platforms in its core businesses and to take advantage of complementary product opportunities in order to achieve strategic balance and to establish multiple platforms from which to deliver performance and growth'.[x] Growth is achieved:

- through investing in new capacity;
- from developing new products and markets;
- by acquiring and growing mid-sized companies, augmented from time to time with larger deals.[xi]

Products and markets

CRH's core businesses included primary materials, 'heavyside' building products and specialist distribution (through builders' merchants and DIY stores). There were two notable characteristics of CRH's product/market portfolio. The first was leadership. Reflecting industry fragmentation, the Group focused on securing and maintaining leading positions in local or regional markets and in product segments or niches. Also unique was CRH's deliberately broad-based geographic, product and segment exposure (see Figure 1), which smoothed the effects of varying economic conditions and provided greater opportunities for growth. (CRH consistently outperformed peers, even during the industry downturns of the early 1980s, 1990s and 2000s.)

Management and organisation

Unlike its peers, CRH operated a federal structure, comprising a small central headquarters and four regionally focused product divisions (see Figure 2). To capitalise on local market knowledge, a high degree of individual responsibility was devolved to operational managers, within Group guidelines and controls. According to Jack Golden, Human Resources (HR) Director, 'while the local operating units have operational autonomy, they do not have independence'.

Figure 1 Broad-based exposure, International and Balanced (2009 data)

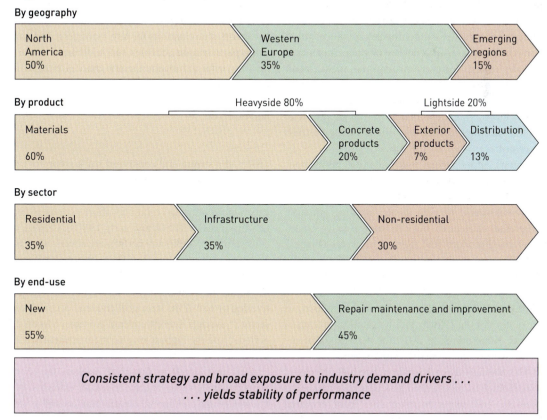

Source: CRH.

Figure 2 Group organisation (2010)

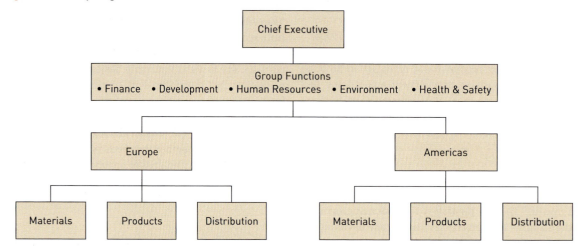

Source: CRH.

CRH adopted a rigorous approach to project evaluation, approval and review. The twin requirements of performance and growth were continually reinforced, with entities having to earn the right to grow. Planning was formalised and interactive, centring on the rolling five-year strategic plan, year one of which constituted the budget. Stretch targets were established for financial and operational output measures. Performance measurement was timely, formal and rigorous. This allowed early critical review of underperformance, to identify reasons, provide assistance, put in place corrective measures and enable senior management to draw broader lessons. However, ongoing cross-subsidisation was not contemplated. If necessary, CRH implemented a management change to support recovery of performance to satisfactory levels. This could include a strategic review to consider the most appropriate disposition for the business going forward.

Continuous improvement was relentless, as demonstrated by ongoing programmes of benchmarking and best practice. In addition, products and processes were continually re-engineered to yield greater returns, primarily through greater efficiencies (but also from selective expansion into related products and regional markets). Ongoing development investment (consistently well in excess of the level of depreciation[xii]) incorporated new plant, capacity extensions and major upgrades.

Over time, CRH's pool of managers had increased, as a result of continuing growth and a relentless stream of acquisitions. Nonetheless, in 2010 the core group of key corporate, group and operational managers numbered around 400. Managers were drawn from internally developed operating managers, experienced finance and development professionals, and owner-entrepreneurs from acquired companies, providing a healthy mix and depth of skills.

Notwithstanding the strong pace of growth, CRH's management was characterised by experience, stability and continuity. In 40 years, there had been only six Chief Executives, all of whom (like a majority of senior managers) were Irish. Having joined the Group, few managers left. There were several reasons for this constancy. Continuing success was clearly a factor, reinforced by CRH's market-driven, performance-related remuneration policy aimed at creating shareholder value. (This comprised variable compensation, share options for key managers, and employee share participation schemes.) In addition, a range of formal and informal mechanisms promoted integration (see below). Finally, low turnover, rotation and promotion from within resulted in a wealth of in-house industry knowledge and expertise.

Finances

CRH had a strong and consistent track record of financial performance. 2009 represented the 26th consecutive year of dividend increase, while the Group had previously experienced only two relatively short periods of declining EPS (in the early 1980s and early 1990s). CRH's level and consistency of financial performance was also superior to its peers internationally. From the mid-1980s to the cyclical peak of 2007, CRH had enjoyed an average Return on Equity of 16.5 per cent.[xiii] Its financial strength was attested by one of the strongest dividend cover ratios in the sector,[xiv] average interest cover of 9.5 times (over a 22-year period)[xv] and the highest long-term investment grade credit rating among its peers.[xvi]

CRH was noted in financial markets for its finance function, which was characterised by extensive business knowledge and operational contribution, as well as diligence, conservatism and prudence. (The function frequently brought in supplementary expertise on secondment.) Two hallmarks of CRH's financial management were a strong focus on return on capital and cash generation. Operations were required to earn 15 per cent Return on Net Assets (RONA) on an ongoing basis. Newly acquired businesses often found such financial rigour challenging. A cash generative mentality (generating around €700 million per annum in free cash flow[xvii]) pervaded all operations and was central to the Group's evaluation and control processes. Cash earnings were consistently around two-thirds higher than reported EPS (2.5 times in 2009), a major factor enabling CRH to fund its acquisition-led expansion overseas without compromising its financial principles. In the challenging environment of 2008/09, CRH severely curtailed its development spend (capital expenditure and acquisitions) and put in place annualised cost savings of €1.65 billion.

Overall, finance was an important component of CRH's strategy across sector cycles. Its contribution was evident in tight performance management, strong cash generation, a low Group tax charge, prudent financial governance and strategically timed fund-raisings to underpin development activity. (Since its previous equity funding in 2001, which raised €1.1 billion, CRH had invested €5 billion in capital expenditure and spent €11.5 billion on acquisitions.[xviii]) Favourable end of 2009 ratios for net debt to EBITDA[2] (2.1 times) and EBITDA/net interest (6.1 times) were testimony to the Group's financial flexibility and firepower at the trough of the cycle.

Corporate-level strategy at CRH

Consistent with its federalist philosophy, CRH's corporate headquarters was small, with a limited range of central functions. Fewer than 100 people were employed in Dublin. Including support staff in the four Divisions, around 200 people were engaged in headquarters-type activities. Traditionally, finance and business development were the only central functions. Of late, internal audit had grown in line with external compliance requirements. The Group development team also acted as a catalyst for renewal on cross-divisional deals, strategic planning and opportunities in emerging regions.

Notwithstanding small size and limited scope, corporate headquarters played a central role in driving the development and integration of CRH, in particular its strategy of acquisition-led expansion, through a variety of mechanisms.

Formal mechanisms

CRH's strategic stance was explicit, enduring and continually reinforced. Over time, the broad thrusts of the

Group's strategy had become progressively more articulated and refined under successive Chief Executives. Strategy was reinforced by rigorous measurement, evaluation and control processes, and by the value-added business contribution and advice of the finance function, ensuring early intervention and appropriate corrective measures.

CRH operated a Group-wide management development system to develop the critical experience base of managers, particularly when they were mobile, in their 20s and 30s. Over time, this system had become more formal and structured because, unlike in the past, managers were unlikely to get the requisite exposure to a wide range of CRH's operations unsystematically. A key element was the management database, on which the core 400 managers in the Group had recently been formally profiled.

There were a variety of formal development programmes for managers, many of which involved inputs and presentations on strategy from senior management, including the Chief Executive. A Management Seminar was held annually in Dublin in late March in advance of CRH plc's Annual General Meeting (AGM) in May. This event provided an opportunity for 150 senior managers to discuss strategy, based on a dedicated theme. Careful selection ensured that around 40 per cent of participating managers each year were first-time attendees. The Development Forum was run annually for a cross-section of experienced and relatively new development personnel, and was a very valuable training and best practice sharing/development activity. A Leadership Development Programme (LDP 1) was run in each Division in the winter. (As building materials is weather dependent, winter is downtime in many regions of the Group.) Aiming to give a periscope view, this programme covered strategy, personal development and networking. This was followed two years later by LDP 2, which was Group-wide.

The Business Leadership Programme (BLP) involved the four Divisions and Corporate headquarters, with the aim of preparing experienced managers for senior leadership roles. (It was supplemented by other programmes for developing specific competences, for example, negotiating skills for operating companies.) BLP involved four sessions over 12 months, with work-based assignments between sessions, and covered psychometric testing, mentor support and individually tailored development plans. The annual Euroforum with employees was initially established as a Section 13 agreement in response to the EU Information and Consultation Directive. Over time, a HR forum was established in conjunction with the Euroforum to tackle issues proactively, such as developing future HR competences for the Group.

At Division level, integrated product management had become progressively strengthened over time, especially in the US. Coordinated divisionally, ongoing best practice

---

[2] Earnings Before Interest, Tax, Depreciation and Amortisation.

activities involved meetings by small teams of experts at local, regional and international levels facilitated by technical advisors. These resulted in highly innovative ideas and exchanges of products, which '*push forward the frontiers of excellence and "sharing the learning" . . . we all have to continually get smarter in what we do, reducing costs and offering better quality and service to our customers*'.[xix] There were around seven best practice programmes in each of the four product-based divisions. Best practice was supplemented by benchmarking exercises and the development of common systems platforms (the latter particularly in the US).

Finally, communications and coaching opportunities were exploited to the full. CRH's excellence in external relations was mirrored internally, utilising communications technologies. The use of e-mail and bulletin boards was common, while regular editions of the internal news magazine *Contact* were read avidly by managers and employees alike. All formal integrative mechanisms involved de facto coaching, both team and individual. Such forums were used as opportunities to restate key messages, from reinforcing the 'right to grow' mantra at strategic level, to the minutiae of operational best practice.

Informal mechanisms

Notwithstanding the foregoing, 'the culture of performance and achievement which pervades CRH is its key strength'.[xx] This restless culture was nurtured and sustained constantly. CRH continually reinforced its core values in formal statements of strategy, in external and internal communications and through corporate folklore. (Managers in Poland referred to 'RONA the bitch'!) More subtle mechanisms also existed, including leading by example and clear norms of acceptable behaviour (such as the ethos of 'owning up' in financial reporting).

Strong informal networks existed among managers, even between far-flung regions of the Group's activities. These emerged from frequent manager rotation within and between Divisions, and from management development programmes, benchmarking and best practice activities (which provided ready forums for interaction). In addition, a social dimension accompanied formal events (involving dinner and, occasionally, golf). This contributed to a family atmosphere, such as that exhibited at the annual get-together of senior managers at CRH's AGM in Dublin each May. The AGM itself was an important ceremonial occasion, and served as an induction for new managers, all of whom attended in their first year in the Group.

Other informal mechanisms underpinned integration. Hierarchy and job descriptions were highly flexible. Harry Sheridan, former long-serving Finance Director, also held operational responsibility for the emerging region of Latin America in the 1990s. HR Director Jack Golden was involved in a wide range of Group issues pertaining to France, based on his previous experience as country manager there for another multinational. At operational level, informal mentoring, hands-on assistance and individual coaching were common within and across entities.

Acquisitions

Acquisitions were the most visible aspect of corporate-level strategy, consistently equalling 20 per cent of capital employed annually.[xxi] From 1978 to 2008, CRH completed around 750 deals, spending over €16.7 billion, almost 95 per cent in the period since 1995. The Group's acquisition performance was extolled widely. A leading global investment bank commented: 'CRH has the best track record of its peer group . . . of growing returns through acquisitions'.[xxii] It was estimated that historically acquisitions accounted for 70 per cent of CRH's profit growth (with organic growth contributing one-quarter, and currency movements the remainder).[xxiii]

Traditionally, CRH's acquisitions were add-on in nature (three to four deals per month with an average cost of €15 million[xiv]). However, in the period since 1995, over half of expenditure had been on larger deals, of which the Materials businesses accounted for the majority. By end of 2006, the Group had completed 34 such purchases, with no single deal amounting to more than 10 per cent of its capital base (see Figure 3). In general, CRH made acquisitions on very favourable terms: purchase prices represented a relatively low multiple of seven times operating profits[xxv] (although multiples for larger deals were somewhat higher). In part, this reflected 'the Group's commitment to completing transactions only at prices that will contribute to long-term value creation for its shareholders'.[xxvi] Moreover, CRH was adept at generating superior returns from deals. From an estimated level of 10 per cent on purchase, in general RONA rose to 12 per cent within the first year and to the benchmark level of 15 per cent within two to three years.[xxvii] Finally, as a result of its strong financial position, CRH had considerable 'fire-power'[xxviii] to finance a continuing high level of acquisition spend.

The acquisition process

Rigorous, comprehensive and inclusive, CRH's acquisition strategy was singular in conception and execution and had 'proven very difficult to replicate'.[xxix] Much of the time, all levels of management were consumed in acquisitions. For the initial identification phase, CRH had 14 development teams spread across the Group seeking opportunities and maintaining contact with an extensive database of potential targets accumulated over 30 years. At any one time, a considerable number of acquisitions were under active consideration, ensuring a steady flow of deals. Each purchase gave rise to further opportunities, in other product lines (occasionally new ones) and in other geographic areas.

Figure 3 CRH acquisitions 1991–2008

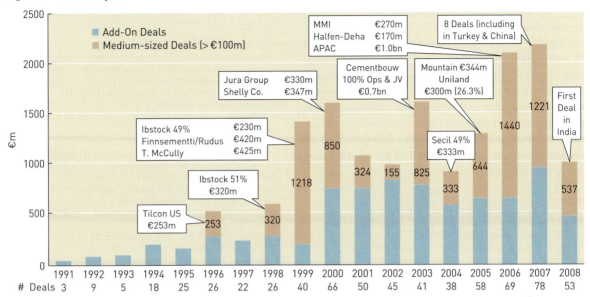

Courtship involved a patient and often long approach of familiarisation and coaching. CRH took time to assess suitability and strategic fit, and to know management and their evolving needs. Much effort was spent appraising the target of CRH's strategy, management, values and expectations, including up-front clarity on post-acquisition priorities. It was not unusual for CRH to walk away from a deal, on the grounds of timing, price or compatibility. Sometimes, acquisitions were completed at a later date.

To aid negotiation, CRH had codified in a classified, proprietary document the best practice, knowledge and processes involved in making an acquisition, gleaned from many years of experience. This was full of collected wisdom, including recommended letters of introduction, follow-up procedures and practical advice on deal-making. An experienced operational manager guided each acquisition team. At the appropriate time, a senior-level 'ambassador' was introduced to close the deal.

Before completion, each deal underwent rigorous evaluation, including qualitative operational review, due diligence, strict cash flow testing and Board approval. Traditionally, CRH's acquisitions shared many common characteristics:

- Medium-sized, privately owned, often family-run businesses;
- Geographic/product market leaders, with potential to enhance existing Group operations or fill a gap;
- Careful structuring of deals, often involving initial stakes with options to increase in new regions/product areas;
- Retention of owner-managers to ensure continuity and maintain human capital.

Post-acquisition integration to boost returns was rapid and well practised. Group financial, Management Information Systems and control systems were implemented immediately. Revenue and cost synergies were captured, often followed over time by targeted capital investment. Benchmarking and best practice programmes were also put in place. For a period, newly acquired entities operated under the guidance of a related existing CRH business, while the 'right to grow' mantra was exhorted informally through the hierarchy. After three years, a formal 'look back' review was carried out.

Although similar in principle, the acquisition process for larger deals was somewhat different. Higher-level (Corporate/Division) involvement and greater public availability of information on targets facilitated truncated courtship and rapid completion. While for the most part CRH engaged in negotiated deals, tendered bids were not uncommon and the Group did not rule out hostile or disputed acquisitions. Integration was assessed on a case-by-case basis. In a new region or product area, experienced CRH managers might be brought in to run the business for a period, with the situation determining the skills and experience required.

Outlook

As 2010 unfolded, CRH signalled a cautious outlook. The start of the year had been affected by prolonged severe weather in Europe and North America. Moreover, construction output was forecast to decline or be flat in the Group's major markets, with the shining exception of Poland. As against this, the Group was strong operationally and financially and well positioned to exploit the prospective sector upturn and emerging opportunities, including consolidation. At the same time, the stock market looked to the Group for a 'benchmark level' of acquisition spending of €1 billion annually.[xxx] Myles Lee and the CRH management team could look to the future with the confidence born out of outstanding business success and robust financial health. But high shareholder expectations and the demands of a hostile industry environment bred constant vigilance. Specifically, could the corporate strategy and funded acquisition model that had served the Group so well over the years be sustained?

References:

[i] CRH plc announcement of 2009 results, 2 March 2010.
[ii] Bank of America-Merrill Lynch, 'Cement handbook: Time for more selective stock picking', 22 June 2009, p. 14.
[iii] JP Morgan, 'Building materials', 10 September 2008, p. 22.
[iv] JP Morgan, 'Building materials: Sector overview', 22 April 2009, p. 27.
[v] UBS, 'European building materials: Significant upside to mid-cycle valuations', 13 July 2009, p. 2
[vi] Ibid., pp. 15, 18 and 29.
[vii] JP Morgan, 'Building materials: Sector overview', pp. 31–3.
[viii] UBS, 'European building materials: Significant upside to mid-cycle valuations', p. 7.
[ix] CRH Rights Issue Prospectus, March 2009, p. 52.
[x] Ibid., p. 21.
[xi] www.crh.com/chrcorp/about/characteristics/.
[xii] Goodbody Stockbrokers, 'CRH: Material upside', 28 June 2007, p. 16.
[xiii] Goodbody Stockbrokers, 'CRH: Revised forecasts but valuation rock bottom', 16 November 2007, p. 16.
[xiv] Goodbody Stockbrokers, 'CRH: Material upside', p. 20.
[xv] JP Morgan, 'Building materials', p. 271.
[xvi] UBS, 'European building materials: Significant upside to mid-cycle valuations', p. 31.
[xvii] JP Morgan, 'Building materials', p. 257.
[xviii] CRH Rights Issue Prospectus, March 2009, pp. 21 and 22.
[xix] CRH (2005), 'Contact', internal *CRH Magazine*, no. 14, p. 7.
[xx] CRH Annual Report 2005, Chairman's Statement, p. 7.
[xxi] Goodbody Stockbrokers, 'CRH: Material upside', p. 12.
[xxii] Goldman Sachs, 'CRH', 18 October 2005, p. 3.
[xxiii] Goodbody Stockbrokers, 'CRH: Still to play its "Trump Card"', 13 July 2005, p. 7.
[xxiv] Goodbody Stockbrokers, 'CRH: Material upside', p. 13.
[xxv] CRH Rights Issue Prospectus, March 2009, p. 22.
[xxvi] CRH Annual Report 2005, Chairman's Statement, p. 6.
[xxvii] Goodbody Stockbrokers, 'CRH: Still to play its "Trump Card"', p. 10.
[xxviii] Goodbody Stockbrokers, 'CRH: Material upside', p. 14.
[xxix] Merrill Lynch, 'Adding value or hot air?', 25 October 2005, p. 12.
[xxx] JP Morgan, 'Building materials', p. 256.

CASE STUDY

SABMiller

Gerry Johnson

South African Breweries grew on the basis of its strength in developing markets, first in Africa and then in other parts of the world. Following pressure from their investors to acquire a brewery in a developed market, SAB acquired Miller in 2002 to form SABMiller and became the second largest brewer by volume in the world. This case study explains how the company's strategy has developed and the challenges it faces.

●   ●   ●

Introduction

In 2009, 10 years after their listing on the London stock exchange, the Chairman of SABMiller, Meyer Khan, could boast that in that time the company had moved from 88th to 17th in the FTSE 100 and had increased its market capitalisation from US$5.5 billion (≈ £3.6bn ≈ €4.1bn) to US$22.4 billion (≈ £14.8bn ≈ €16.6bn).[1] In 2009 SABMiller was the second largest brewer by volume in the world following its acquisitions of the American brewer Miller in 2002 and in 2005 Grupo Empresarial Bavaria, South America's second largest brewer. Its brand portfolio included international brands Pilsner Urquell, Peroni Nastro Azzurro, Miller Genuine Draft and Grolsch along with local country brands such as Aguila, Castle Lager, Miller Lite, Snow and Tyskie.

However, SABMiller faced the challenge of dramatic industry consolidation. In the early 1990s the five largest brewing companies accounted for 17 per cent of global beer sales. By 2009 they accounted for 45 per cent. Moreover, three of SABMiller's main global competitors, Anheuser Busch, Interbrew and Ambev, had merged to claim market leadership with a consolidated 25 per cent global market share.

As it approached 2010 the company set out four strategic priorities as summarised in Table 1. This summary of strategy can be seen as a synthesis of the learning the company has developed over its history, first weathering the political crises of twentieth-century South African history, then building its operations in emerging and mature markets, where it gained a reputation as 'a turnaround specialist'.

---

[1] $1 = £0.66 = €0.74.

Source: SABMiller plc.

Background

Originally South African Breweries (SAB), the company is older than the state of South Africa itself and faced the challenge of doing business amidst the upheaval that the country experienced during the twentieth century, including the 'apartheid' regime from 1948 to 1994 and the worldwide opposition to this. A central feature of this was the campaign for economic sanctions on South Africa, aiming to restrict international business from investing in or trading with South Africa and restricting South African business from trading with international markets. In 1950 SAB moved its head office from London to Johannesburg. Southern Africa became the focus of its business expansion during the subsequent four decades.

In this time SAB responded to business restrictions by focusing on dominating domestic beer production through acquisition of competitors and rationalisation of

---

This case was originally prepared by Aidan McQuade, and subsequently updated by Gerry Johnson. The authors are grateful for the cooperation of SABMiller in its preparation. It is intended as a basis for class discussion and not as an illustration of good or bad practice.

Table 1 SABMiller's strategic priorities

1. Creating a balanced and attractive global spread of businesses	'Our acquisitions in recent years have given us a wide geographical spread with good exposure to emerging markets without being over-reliant on any single region. This allows us to capture new growth in developing markets and "value" growth as consumers around the world trade up from economy to mainstream and premium brands. We also look to identify and exploit opportunities for growth within our existing business portfolio. This can involve a range of activities, from entering into local joint ventures or partnerships, to buying or building breweries, to acquiring local brands to help shape a full, local, brand portfolio.'
2. Developing strong, relevant brand portfolios in the local market	'Our aim is to develop an attractive brand portfolio that meets consumers' needs in each of our markets. In many markets, growth is fastest at the top end, as shown by the increasing popularity of our international premium brands. Another rising consumer trend is the shift towards fragmentation. Affluent consumers are varying their choices and becoming more interested in speciality brands, craft beers, foreign imports and other subdivisions of the premium segment. And a third trend is the growing importance of female consumers.'
3. Constantly raising the performance of local businesses	'In order to raise our performance, we need to become more efficient, especially in our manufacturing processes. Efficiency is part of our day-to-day management and the rise in commodity costs compels us to do whatever we can to counteract the squeeze on our margins. All SABMiller operations strive to improve our products' route to market, to remove costs and to ensure that the right products reach the right outlets in the right condition.'
4. Leveraging our global scale	'As a global organisation we are constantly seeking to use the benefits of our scale while recognising that beer is essentially a local business and that local managers are in the best position to identify and exploit local opportunities. Our aim is to generate maximum value and advantage from our size without becoming overcentralised and losing our relevance and responsiveness in each market.'

production and distribution facilities. It also expanded its product portfolio, obtaining control of Stellenbosch Farmers' Winery in 1960 and in the course of the rest of that decade obtaining licences to brew Guinness, Amstel and Carling Black Label locally. Further expansions followed within the beverage sector, principally through acquisition, leading to SAB controlling an estimated 99 per cent of the market in South Africa by 1979, as well as commanding positions in Swaziland, Lesotho, Rhodesia (now Zimbabwe) and Botswana. In 1978 they also diversified into hotels and gambling by acquiring the Sun City casino resort.

By 1990 the process for establishing a multiracial democracy in South Africa was under way. This change in the political system eased SAB's expansion through the rest of Africa, which became a central strategic focus of the 1990s. By 2000 SAB's market dominance in southern Africa provided a serious deterrent to potential competitors, but there remained little space for it to expand there, particularly in alcoholic beverages.

Emerging onto the global market

In 1993 SAB had also made its first acquisition outside Africa, Hungary's largest brewery, Dreher, describing it as a 'beach-head move' into central Europe. So began a strategy explained in the 1998 annual report:

SAB's international focus has been on countries in which it believes it could use its expertise, which has been gained over 100 years in South Africa, to develop beer markets in emerging economies.

The strategy of developing brewing capabilities in underdeveloped beer markets continued through the 1990s. SAB established operations in China in 1994, forming a joint venture, China Resources Snow Breweries, with China Resources Enterprise Ltd, thus adding China's biggest beer brand, Snow, to its portfolio. There followed further acquisitions in Eastern Europe. In Poland this included the acquisition of a majority stake in Lech in 1995 followed by the acquisition of Tyskie in 1996. These two companies were merged in 1999. 1998 saw SAB's entry into Russia by establishing a 'greenfield' brewery in Kaluga, near Moscow. And there were acquisitions in Romania, Slovakia, and the Czech Republic.

SAB's strategy was more fully spelled out in the 2000 report:

In the less developed world, Africa and Asia and much of Europe, brewing remained highly fragmented, with beer drinkers supplied by breweries which were never more than small-scale and localised, often producing low-quality beer . . . This fragmentation presented the opportunity for SAB from the mid-1990s to create a profitable and fast-expanding business in emerging markets with huge potential. This opportunity involves, generally, taking a share in a brewery with a local partner and, while retaining the brand because drinkers tend to have fierce attachments to their local brew, transforming the business. This starts with upgrading quality and consistency to create a beer for which people are prepared to pay more and which can give us a healthy profit margin. Then comes improvement to marketing and distribution. Next we improve productivity and capacity. In each country we have begun by acquiring an initial local stronghold from which we can advance into regions beyond the brewery's original catchment area. We then build critical mass in the region and progress, over time, to a national basis. This is often achieved by acquiring further brewing businesses and focusing the brand portfolio. An optimum brand portfolio gives us a better overall marketing proposition, increases total sales and delivers economies of scale in production and distribution.

This process demands, on one level, great political sensitivity in dealing with governments, partners, local communities and our workforce and, on another level, the deployment of expert operational management skills learnt in South Africa . . . Our management structure is de-centralised, reflecting the local nature of beer branding and distribution.

Our businesses do not all advance at the same speed, nor have the same potential. It is characteristic of emerging markets that growth can be variable, and we are accustomed to temporary setbacks. However, the spread of our international businesses provides a 'portfolio effect', thereby reducing the impact of setbacks in one or two individual countries.

Challenges for the twenty-first century

By 2001 the focus on emerging markets led to SAB becoming the world's fifth largest brewer by volume, with breweries in 24 countries across the globe. However, analysts noted a problem. SAB's portfolio meant that it earned most of its profits in 'soft' currencies. A loss of confidence or devaluation of currencies in emerging markets could hurt SAB badly. The situation was exacerbated with a slump in the value of the South African rand in 2001 and there were fears it could be further affected by the devastating impact of the HIV/AIDS pandemic on the workforce, which, aside from the human cost, caused a decrease in productivity through the debilitating effects of the illness. Many commentators believed that for a brewery of its size SAB lacked, and needed to have, a major brand in developed markets.

In 1999 SAB decided on a listing on the London Stock Exchange (LSE), justifying it in terms of 'giving the group greater access to world capital markets and providing it with financial resources and flexibility' so as to 'enhance the ability of SAB to take advantage of increasing consolidation in the international brewing industry and to compete with

other international brewers for development opportunities throughout the world'.

The listing had its initial problems. SAB's share price lost over 15 per cent relative to the FTSE 100 in the year to the end of November 2000. Analysts argued, again, that this was because of the failure to make a major acquisition of a first-world (developed country) brand and its over-reliance on its developing markets.

SABMiller

In 2002 SAB succeeded in acquiring a major brand in a developed market: Miller Brewing Company, the second largest brewery in the USA. SAB paid Philip Morris Co. US\$3.6 billion in stock and assumed US\$2 billion of Miller's debt. The 2003 annual report explained that this gave 'the group access, through a national player, to a growing beer market within the world's largest profit pool, and at the same time diversifying the currency and geographic risk of the group'.

SAB became SABMiller following the acquisition and the second largest brewery by volume in the world. However, the acquisition brought with it its own problems. James Williamson, an analyst at SG Securities in London, commented:

> They didn't buy it because they thought it was a strong growth business. They bought it because they needed a mature cash cow. Unfortunately it's been losing more market share than expected.

Indeed, following the first full year of SABMiller operating Miller, its US market share had dropped from 19.6 per cent to 18.7 per cent and by September 2003 the share price of the company had dropped from 530 pence on the day of acquisition of Miller, to 456.5 pence.

SABMiller appointed Norman Adami, previously Head of its South Africa Beer business, as Head of Miller, and introduced the traditional SAB system of performance management that rewards strong performers and focuses on improving weaker performers. This was a considerable change from Miller's previous system of performance rating which routinely rated all staff at the highest level. SABMiller also announced that there would be a rationalisation of Miller's product portfolio from 50 brands to 11 or 12, meaning that market share would go down before it could go up again.

Continued acquisitions and international development

There followed a series of acquisitions. In 2003 the group made its first significant acquisition in Western Europe when it acquired Italy's Birra Peroni and subsequently developed

Table 2 Main acquisitions, joint ventures and brewery investments 2001–09

2001	A majority stake in the Sichuan Blue Sword Breweries Group in China.
2005	Buyout of joint venture partner in India, Shaw Wallace & Company.
2006	Acquisition of the Foster's business and brand in India and in South Vietnam. Joint venture with Vinamilk to establish a brewery in Vietnam. SABMiller and Coca-Cola Amatil form Pacific Beverages Pty Ltd, a joint venture to market, sell and distribute SABMiller brands in Australia.
2007	10-year partnership with Foster's Group to brew Foster's lager in the US. $170 million invested in a new brewery in Moscow. Pacific Beverages buys Australian premium brewer Bluetongue Brewery.
2008	Acquisition of Grolsch. Acquired the Vladpivo brewery in Vladivostock (Russia) and Sarmat brewery in the Ukraine.
2009	Acquisition of Bere Azuga, Romania. Acquired the remaining 50% interest in the Vietnamese business and remaining 28% in the Polish business. Acquired three further breweries in China. Investment in new plant in Juba (South Sudan), Russia, Tanzania, Mozambique and Angola.

the premium brand Peroni Nastro Azzuro as a premium global brand.

In 2005 there followed a merger with Grupo Empresarial Bavaria, the second largest brewer in South America, consolidating SABMiller as the world number two brewer and making Latin America the second largest source of profits after South Africa. Reviewing the Latin American operations at that time the CEO confirmed that SABMiller saw these markets as offering 'exciting prospects for growth' and added:

> Although the Bavaria businesses are well managed and profitable, we plan to create further value by applying SABMiller's operating practices and management skills. The best opportunities lie in brand portfolio development, creating good relationships with distributors and retailers, and improving merchandising at the point of sale.

Table 2 summarises the other main acquisitions, joint ventures and plant investments in the decade. Amongst these the Group saw Grolsch as another brand that could be developed internationally, though the acquisition may have been prompted by Heineken taking back the rights to Amstel in South Africa. SAB had been brewing Amstel there for 20 years as a premium northern European beer. Since this meant that South African breweries lost 10 per cent of their business, they argued the need for a replacement. Additionally, SABMiller was looking for a northern European brand with heritage: hence Grolsch. Grolsch was not only a replacement for Amstel in the South African portfolio, but filled a larger gap in SABMiller's international brand portfolio.

2008 also saw the establishment of a joint venture between Molson Coors, itself a merger of Molson Canada and Coors from the US, and the SABMiller business in the

US. The argued benefits of this included scale advantages and productivity improvements of US$500 million in the face of increasing cost pressures, improved logistics across the North American market and a complementarity of brands to compete more effectively against the dominance in the US of Anheuser Busch. Commentators saw the main target being attempted market share gain in the profitable light beer category which accounted for 40 per cent of total US beer sales and where the joint venture brands could claim a 47.5 per cent volume share of that category in US supermarkets. But they also pointed to the tendency for consumer preferences in terms of beer brands to move very slowly and Trevor Sterling (of Burnstein Reasearch) commented:

> Although Miller Coors appears to be trying to nibble Bud Light from two directions, it would be hard to convince consumers there was much difference between Miller Light and Coors Light which are priced at similar levels.

The 2009 annual report showed a drop in profits for the year (see financial summary in the appendix). However, CEO Graham Mackay stated via Bloomberg:

> Nothing is stopping us from the right acquisition . . . There is money available even if we have to raise capital. We think our shareholders would agree with it if it was the right acquisition.

He added, however, that:

> The right acquisition means something very different in an emerging market where a brewer can capitalise on growing volumes, than it does in the developed world where cost cuts and selling more premium beer is key.

Commentators noted that SABMiller's stock was the best performer amongst the world's biggest brewers and pointed to possible acquisition targets such as Dos Equis Brewer Fomento Economico Mexicano (Mexico) and Turkey's EFES Breweries International.

Where from here?

After over 100 years, SABMiller had emerged onto the world market at a time when it appeared that the twenty-first century might prove as turbulent as the twentieth century had been in South Africa. Many on those on the board had long experience of managing the Group; indeed most of the operating directors had grown with the firm from its South African past. However, deliberations as to the strategic priorities and strategic needs of the business varied.

Graham Mackay believed there that there would be a continuing shift both towards global beer brands and towards consumer preference for premium beers. There would also be further consolidation in the industry and in that context SABMiller would consider buying assets in both developed countries and emerging markets. However given 'the fact that most of the brewing industry is held in private family or foundation or other hands . . . it is very difficult to predict when assets will become available'. Moreover, he did not see the need for the Group to be bigger at any price: it was already large enough to use purchasing power to force down ingredient prices. In the meantime capital expenditure would be maintained in areas where growth was steady, including Africa and China, and eased off where it was less evident, such as Eastern Europe.

Analysts such as Simon Hales of Evolution Securities Ltd also saw further industry consolidation as likely and therefore further acquisitions as a possibility but, with regard to SABMiller, commented: 'They have to be very careful how they play their hand. SAB's big deal record hasn't been great.' This is a reference to the Miller acquisition, which he argued took longer than expected to repay the cost of capital.

The question facing SABMiller was: how could the Group continue to sustain its historical growth rate and performance going forward? The opportunities for acquisitions were shrinking: large transformational deals were fewer and with lower prospects of high financial returns. The competitive landscape had also radically changed. ABInbev had become the world's largest brewer, larger than the next two – SABMiller and Heineken – combined, and seemed to be focused on the Americas. The other global brewers were increasingly looking for growth from emerging markets as beer growth seemed to be slowing in more developed consumer markets. Heineken was pursuing growth in Africa and Carlsberg was investing heavily in Russia. Japanese brewers were becoming increasingly active in the Asian market. The added complication of the economic recession at the end of the decade had also impacted on all beer markets, albeit with different degrees of severity. SABMiller had always performed well given its emerging market footprint which had protected it from the declining beer volumes in the more mature markets such as Western Europe. By 2010 the company was looking to drive organic growth across its portfolio of countries. How would the portfolio of countries that SABMiller had built up through its acquisitions and joint ventures help it weather both the financial storm and the competitive challenges? Did this require a change in the strategy of the company in terms of the emphasis on the 'local vs. global' brands in its portfolio? Could there be yet another 'market changing' deal that can be shaped to win the battle in beer?

APPENDIX Five-year financial review

For the years ended 31 March

	2009 US$m	2008[1] US$m	2007 US$m	2006 US$m	2005 US$m
Income statements					
Group revenue	25,302	23,828	20,645	17,081	14,543
Revenue	18,703	21,410	18,620	15,307	12,901
Operating profit	3,148	3,448	3,027	2,575	2,547
Net finance costs	(706)	(456)	(428)	(299)	(143)
Share of associates' and joint ventures' post-tax results	516	272	205	177	148
Taxation	(801)	(976)	(921)	(779)	(823)
Minority interests	(276)	(265)	(234)	(234)	(208)
Profit for the year	1,881	2,023	1,649	1,440	1,521
Adjusted earnings	2,065	2,147	1,796	1,497	1,224
Balance sheets					
Non-current assets	28,159	31,947	25,683	24,286	12,869
Current assets	3,460	4,135	3,053	2,829	2,778
Total assets	31,619	36,082	28,736	27,115	15,647
Derivative financial instruments	(142)	(531)	(209)	(178)	–
Borrowings	(9,618)	(9,658)	(7,231)	(7,602)	(3,340)
Other liabilities and provisions	(5,746)	(7,649)	(6,295)	(5,750)	(3,552)
Total liabilities	(15,506)	(17,838)	(13,735)	(13,530)	(6,892)
Net assets	16,113	18,244	15,001	13,585	8,755
Total shareholders' equity	15,375	17,545	14,406	13,043	8,077
Minority interests in equity	738	699	595	542	678
Total equity	16,113	18,244	15,001	13,585	8,755
Cash flow statements					
EBITDA	4,164	4,518	4,031	3,348	2,736
Net working capital movements	(493)	(242)	(13)	(57)	56
Net cash generated from operations	3,671	4,276	4,018	3,291	2,792
Net interest paid (net of dividends received)	(116)	(410)	(385)	(248)	(79)
Tax paid	(766)	(969)	(801)	(869)	(625)
Net cash inflow from operating activities	2,789	2,897	2,832	2,174	2,088
Net capital expenditure	(2,072)	(1,927)	(1,351)	(984)	(738)
Net investments in subsidiaries, joint ventures and associates	(555)	(1,439)	(429)	(2,644)	(897)
Net other investments	(10)	5	(2)	(2)	456
Net cash inflow/(outflow) before financing and dividends	152	(464)	1,050	(1,456)	909
Net cash inflow/(outflow) from financing	620	1,240	(455)	1,733	(271)
Dividends paid	(877)	(769)	(681)	(520)	(412)
Effect of exchange rates	26	(113)	(18)	11	(56)
(Decrease)/increase in cash and cash equivalents	(79)	(106)	(104)	(232)	170
Per share information (US cents per share)					
Basic earnings per share	125.2	134.9	110.2	105.0	125.5
Diluted earnings per share	124.7	134.2	109.5	104.3	121.2
Adjusted basic earnings per share	137.5	143.1	120.0	109.1	101.0
Net asset value per share[2]	969.8	1,108.3	912.0	828.0	599.9
Total number of shares in issue (millions)	1,585.4	1,583.1	1,579.6	1,575.2	1,346.5

[1] Restated for the adjustments made to the provisional fair values relating to the Grolsch acquisition.
[2] Net asset value per share is calculated by expressing shareholders' funds as a percentage of the closing number of shares in issue.

	2009 US$m	2008[1] US$m	2007 US$m	2006 US$m	2005 US$m
Other operating and financial statistics					
Return on equity (%)[3]	13.4	12.2	12.5	11.5	15.2
EBITA margin (%)	16.3	17.4	17.4	17.2	16.4
EBITDA margin (%)	22.3	21.1	21.6	21.9	21.2
EBITDA interest cover (times)	6.6	9.2	9.2	11.4	19.1
Total borrowings to total assets (%)	30.4	26.8	25.2	28.0	21.3
Cash flow to total borrowings (%)	38.2	44.3	55.6	43.3	83.6
Revenue per employee (US$000's)	272.5	309.8	278.1	284.7	315.5
Average monthly number of employees	68,635	69,116	66,949	53,772	40,892
For the years ended 31 March					
Group revenue					
Primary segmental analysis					
Latin America	5,495	5,251	4,392	2,165	521
Europe	6,145	5,248	4,078	3,258	2,909
North America	5,227	5,120	4,887	4,912	4,892
Africa and Asia	4,132	3,367	2,674	2,221	1,937
South Africa:					
– Beverages	3,955	4,446	4,274	4,204	3,995
– Hotels and Gaming	348	396	340	321	289
	25,302	23,828	20,645	17,081	14,543
Operating profit (excluding share of associates and joint ventures)					
Primary segmental analysis					
Latin America	1,057	953	810	387	90
Europe	900	947	730	567	482
North America	230	462	366	454	487
Africa and Asia	352	330	272	257	249
South Africa: Beverages	704	962	1,043	1,011	906
Corporate	(97)	(94)	(101)	(86)	(82)
Group operating profit – before exceptional items	3,146	3,560	3,120	2,590	2,132
Exceptional credit/(charge)					
Latin America	45	(61)	(64)	(11)	–
Europe	(452)	–	(24)	–	(51)
North America	409	(51)	–	–	111
Africa and Asia	–	–	–	–	103
South Africa: Beverages	–	–	–	–	–
Corporate	–	–	(5)	(4)	252
	2	(112)	(93)	(15)	415
Group operating profit – after exceptional items	3,148	3,448	3,027	2,575	2,547
EBITA					
Primary segmental analysis					
Latin America	1,173	1,071	915	436	90
Europe	944	952	733	569	482
North America	581	477	375	454	487
Africa and Asia	642	568	467	422	383
South Africa:					
– Beverages	764	1,026	1,102	1,062	956
– Hotels and Gaming	122	141	100	84	73
Corporate	(97)	(94)	(101)	(86)	(82)
Group	4,129	4,141	3,591	2,941	2,389

[3] This is calculated by expressing adjusted earnings as a percentage of total shareholders' equity.

Source: www.sabmiller.com/files/reports/ar2009/2009_annual_report.pdf Five-year financial review, continued.

Marks and Spencer plc: where next for the icon of British retailing?

Phyl Johnson and Nardine Collier

In 2010, Marks and Spencer plc was the largest clothing retailer in the UK, it had 885 stores in 40 territories, 600 in the UK and boasted that one in three British women were wearing one of their Marks & Spencer bras. But still the analysts worried about the sustainability of the giant of UK retailing's recovery. In 2010 the new CEO took over and was faced with issues associated with reassessing the competitive strategy and the continuing challenges of strategic change.

● ● ●

In 2009, late into their 125th year of trading, the board of Marks and Spencer plc ended their search for a new CEO. The search had attracted a significant amount of media interest with many high profile names being suggested as potential external candidates as well as attention focused on at least two senior internal directors as the ultimate successor to Sir Stuart Rose: the man who turned around Marks and Spencer plc from near failure in the 1990s.

The board chose 50-year-old Dutchman Marc Bolland, previously the CEO of UK supermarket chain Morrisons. His appointment, announced on 18 November 2009, was greeted with a positive response from the media and share-holders alike.

Bolland, the successor to Sir Stuart, had ahead of him a significant challenge, to secure the future of the UK's largest retailer and the most famous name in the shopping malls. Marks and Spencer plc had long been the leading retailer in the UK, the organisation to which all commentators and analysts turn to when reporting whether the high street is having a good or bad season of sales and an organisation that was historically known and loved by the British people. But at the end of 2009 and early into 2010 commentators remained restless, investors nervous and there were several question marks about the future of this firm that needed to be resolved.

In 2009, despite delivering reasonable results through the 2008/09 recession period and in the previous year having topped the £1 billion[1] marker in pre-tax profits for the first time in a decade, Marks and Spencer plc still

Source: Getty Images.

retained something of the wounded giant about it. The company's reputation had suffered great injury when, in 1998, it was the first British retailer to make profits of £1 billion and yet within the year it was issuing profit warnings. This was a catastrophic and self-inflicted crash from its premier position. The company limped through a period of turbulent change punctuated by aggressive takeover bids but then, with Sir Stuart's appointment as CEO in 2004, finally saw its results regain health and return to the £1 billion profit level.

In July 2009, Sir Stuart Rose, the man who saved Marks and Spencer plc, announced his intention to stand down as CEO in 2010. This triggered speculation and debate as to just what he had done as CEO; what he had done well, in what he had failed and what legacy he was leaving his

_____
[1] £1 billion ≈ €1.1 billion or $1.5 billion as at 1 June 2010.

successor Marc Bolland. *Where next for Marks and Spencer plc?*

The Old History and Greenbury Era

Michael Marks began his penny market stalls in the late 1880s and soon partnered with Tom Spencer, a cashier of Marks' supplier. From this beginning Marks and Spencer plc grew steadily. Simon Marks took over the running of Marks and Spencer plc from his father, turning the penny bazaars into stores, establishing a simple pricing policy and introducing the 'St Michael' logo as a sign of quality. There was a feeling of camaraderie and a close-knit family atmosphere within the stores, with staff employed whom the managers believed would 'fit in' and become part of the family. Staff were also treated better and paid more than in other companies. The family nature of this firm dominated top management as well: until the late 1970s, the board was made up of family members only.

Simon Marks was renowned for his personal, top-down and autocratic management style as well as his infamous attention to detail. This manifested itself in the way Marks dealt with suppliers. He always used the same UK-based suppliers and meticulously ensured that goods were exactly to specification; a relationship designed to build reliance on Marks and Spencer plc within the supplier grouping and ensure high and consistent quality for the customer.

Marks and Spencer plc was hugely successful in terms of its delivery of this high quality and highly reliable brand to its customers, this in turn earning outstanding reward in terms of profit and market share. So historically, Marks and Spencer plc was run using a tried, tested and trusted recipe; a way of doing business. This was embedded in a set of fundamental principles, namely to:

1 Offer customers high-quality, well designed and attractive merchandise at reasonable prices under the brand name 'St Michael'
2 Encourage suppliers to use the most modern and efficient production techniques
3 Work with suppliers to ensure the highest standards of quality control
4 Provide friendly, helpful service and greater shopping comfort and convenience to customers
5 Improve the efficiency of the business, by simplifying operating procedures
6 Foster good human relations with customers, suppliers and staff and in the communities in which M&S trade.

Confident and comfortable at the top of the tree, Marks and Spencer plc was able to luxuriate in doing business in the way it chose. The company opted to have specialist buyers operating from a central buying office from which goods were allocated to the stores. The store managers followed central direction on merchandising, layout, store design and training. Every Marks and Spencer plc store was identical in the procedures it followed. This led to (and continuously re-created) a consistency of image and guarantee of Marks and Spencer plc standards. However, it also meant store managers were severely restricted in how they could respond to the local needs of customers and that the gaze of store managers was toward head office and not to the stores next door to them in the high street. Marks and Spencer plc seemed to operate in a world of its own.

Successive chief executives were renowned for their attention to detail in terms of supplier control, merchandise and store layout; and it seemed to work. Another recipe that Marks and Spencer plc seemed to follow was for CEOs to have considerable power by their being appointed as both Chair and CEO. This was the case for Sir Richard Greenbury, Chair and CEO from 1988 to 1999, who was famous for having strong opinions and being committed to the recipe of the past:

> We followed absolutely and totally the principles of the business with which I was imbued . . . I ran the business with the aid of my colleagues based upon the very long standing, and proven ways of running it.[i]

But perhaps most damagingly, given the power he held, he appeared to be allergic to bad news. On one occasion Greenbury had decided that to control costs there would be fewer full-time sales assistants. Although this led to an inability in stores to meet the service levels required by Marks and Spencer plc, when Greenbury visited, all available employees were brought in so that it appeared the stores were giving levels of service that, at other times, they were not. It also meant there was little disagreement with directives from the top, so policies and decisions remained unchallenged even when executives or store managers were concerned about negative effects. Customer satisfaction surveys that showed decreasing satisfaction throughout the late 1990s were kept from Greenbury by senior executives who felt he might be annoyed by the results.

But during Greenbury's tenure, Marks and Spencer plc held more than twice the market share of any other retailer and so, during the long years of growth, there were few changes to its methods of operation or strategies. Its reputation for good quality clothing was built on basics, the essentials which every customer needed and would outlast the current fashion and trends seen in other high street retailers. All assistants carried tape measures to assure a good fit and, as products remained in the store year round, exchanges and refunds were not problematic. As such, as late as the 1990s Marks and Spencer plc had no fitting rooms, took no credit cards, rarely held sales and ignored the loyalty card schemes sweeping British retailing. Until the late 1990s, its customers worked around these inconveniences and helped the firm to its record breaking year of trading in 1997–98 when its pre-tax profit topped the £1 billion mark. A financial result it took Marks and Spencer plc 10 long years and three CEOs to repeat.

The Marks and Spencer plc recipe catastrophically failed in 1998; share prices plummeted and this serious jolt led to many years of turbulence that Sir Stuart Rose later referred to as lost years. Marks and Spencer plc was forced to wake up to its contemporary marketplace on several fronts at once. First, its allegiance to British suppliers simply became too costly and Marks and Spencer plc was slow to follow its rivals' lead into sourcing cheaper goods from low-cost countries. Second, its customers had been departing to competitors and in Marks & Spencer womenswear it found itself squeezed by Next, Oasis and Gap from the upper end and George at Asda and Matalan from the lower end. Third, Marks and Spencer plc's home-bred bureaucracy and strongly embedded way of doing business meant that change, however badly needed, would come slowly. Marks and Spencer plc had lost touch with the marketplace and the results showed it, with a 23 per cent decline in profit in the first half of 1998 that snowballed to an over 50 per cent reduction by the year end and a startling tumble of more than 80 per cent in 1998–2001.

The 'in-betweeners': no one seemed to fit

The highly visible results failure led to an equally visible boardroom battle to replace Sir Richard Greenbury who left his post in 1999. In the end, Peter Salsbury, whom the media labelled Greenbury's preferred internal candidate, beat Keith Oates (Greenbury's own deputy) to the post. He did not last long. His track record inside Marks and Spencer plc had been relatively narrow, having only worked in the poorly performing womenswear division. Compounding this, he inherited a horrendous trading position at Christmas 1999 where badly planned refurbishments disrupted the already poor trading position and the £192 million purchase of 19 Littlewoods stores drained profits (both of which contributed to a profits warning early in his tenure in January 1999).

In 2000, the incoming Chairman, Luc Vandevelde, ensured Salsbury left the board of Marks and Spencer plc along with an unprecedented seven other directors. Vandevelde holding the position of Chairman took the unusual step to appoint himself as both CEO and Chair during a period when his board was under significant restructuring. He held both positions until 2004 and during that time executed what he described as the turnaround of Marks and Spencer plc. He appointed a new head of UK Retail, Roger Holmes (aged 40), whom he eventually promoted to CEO in 2003. As head of UK retailing, though, he immediately sought to segment the Marks

and Spencer plc customers using the store within a store concept. Perhaps the most widely witnessed and most successful innovation at this time was the Per Una joint venture that brought designer George Davies into the Marks and Spencer plc fold. Davies already had mega brands to his name in UK retailing (Next and George at Asda), Per Una was to be his third. One month after the launch of Per Una, Marks and Spencer plc reported its first sales increase for three years, a trend that continued beyond the 2008 results and even survived Davies' departure in 2004.

The Vandevelde era of 2000–2004 made important changes to the Marks & Spencer offering but also left the company open to a prolonged aggressive takeover attempt from Philip Green of the Arcadia group – more of which later. Vandevelde and Holmes together launched the Simply Food concept and began the opening of the stand-alone Marks & Spencer food stores in 2003. In addition they announced the intention to open 'Simply' food convenience stores in collaboration with BP service stations. They also introduced a loyalty card scheme that was combined with a credit card called '&More' where customers could earn Marks & Spencer vouchers to spend in store. Positive results continued through 2002 and 2003 as did Marks and Spencer plc's ability to attract more retail talent into its directorship. It was also at this time that Vandevelde promoted a serious commitment to Corporate Social Responsibility (CSR), leading the company to its first CSR review reporting its activity.

However, commentators began to turn against the Vandevelde/Holmes duo as they perceived the turnaround of Marks and Spencer plc to be slowing down. The end of year results in 2004 reported a failure to deliver market share gains, a slowdown in the sales in clothing and food and an over-reliance on Per Una with a rejection of other elements of the Marks & Spencer womenswear offering. Holmes made a series of admissions highlighting an inability to capture the influential 30–55-year-old womenswear market beyond Per Una and a mirrored degree of poor results and insufficient innovation in the Marks & Spencer Food ranges. Holmes, seen as the weak point by City investors, came under pressure.

In May 2004 Philip Green launched his £7 billion takeover bid. The Marks and Spencer plc board (in particular Lord Paul Myners) reacted quickly. Vandevelde, Homes, five executive directors and two non-executive directors were removed in the bid to win shareholder confidence. The deal that fought off Green also saw the commitment to buy the Per Una business from George Davies (catapulting him into the UK's mega rich list with a £125 million deal), the sale of the financial services business to HSBC Bank Plc for £762 million (but keeping 50 per cent of profits until 2014), the closure of the Lifestyle Stores opened by Holmes and, perhaps most importantly, the appointment of Stuart Rose as CEO.[1]

Rose fought off Green's repeated takeover attempts throughout the summer of 2004 starting at £7 billion moving up to £9.1 billion. A key turning point was the Rose commitment to deliver a 450p future share price to rival the 400p Green had offered and the leading Marks and Spencer plc investor (Brandes who owned 7.07 per cent of stock) had accepted. He presented an 11-point strategic review and, in late December 2005, it delivered: the shares hit a six-year high at 504p.

Sir Stuart saves the day

Lord Myners announced his interim period of Chairmanship would end in June 2006 and in this way he assured shareholders that due space would be awarded to the new team of Rose and incumbent Chairman Lord Burns to lead Marks and Spencer plc forward and away from the turbulence of 2004.

The appointment of Stuart Rose was seen as inspired and a real coup for the Marks and Spencer plc board. Rose, who had sold the Arcadia group to Philip Green and netted £25 million for himself in the process, was seen as a positive appointment by investors. His past experiences at Burtons Menswear, Evans & Principles (womenswear), Argos, Booker Cash and Carry and Arcadia characterised him as an experienced shopkeeper who could revitalise fatigued retailers and had a record of delivering shareholder value.

During the period when the Rose/Myners team fought off the Philip Green takeover bid, Rose was careful to project his understanding of the need for major change to city investors:

> We live in a tough, commercial world . . . The business definitely suffered a little from the A-word, arrogance, in the mid to late-90s. It looked out the window and found the world had passed it by.[ii]

However, he simultaneously followed a strategy of underpromising and overdelivering in terms of expectation setting. Specifically he repeatedly informed investors and commentators that he did not expect to see results from his 11-point strategic plan until well after spring 2005 when the first of his initiatives would be hitting the stores. He made a particular issue of delaying his use of the 'R word': recovery. Although tempted into it as results began to improve, he refused to express confidence and continued to project humility and his appreciation of the task ahead. Investors said they would give him until December 2005 for recovery.

His 11-point strategic plan to achieve turnaround revolved around five core values designed to win back Marks and Spencer plc's core customers: quality, value, service, innovation and trust.

- Shelving Per Una Due (designed for teens and twenties) as it was not targeted at natural Marks & Spencer customers
- Acquiring Per Una from Davies for £125 million (with Davies remaining as CEO for two years to retain brand direction)
- Cancelling more than 500 food products
- Developing supply chain and sourcing efficiency, to reduce the stock overhang
- Stopping waste and unnecessary administration costs
- Improving core services
- Returning £2.3 billion to shareholders (through buying back 635 million shares)
- Moving to out-of-town retail centres
- Restructuring and redundancy
- Changing employee mentality
- Closing or upgrading stores, which he likened to hospitals.

Popular with employees, Rose's initiatives very soon earned the very telling internal commentary the 'the grown-ups are back in charge'.[iii] So for some of the employees at least, the old Marks and Spencer plc was back.

By the end of 2004, Rose had hired Kate Bostock to run the crucial womenswear area of the business and immediately signalled the weight of this by appointing her to the main board of directors, one of the few female executive directors to sit on the board of a FTSE 100 company.

Trading through the early part of 2005 remained difficult for Marks and Spencer plc. The new ranges were described as drab, unappealing and confusing in comparison to the vibrant Per Una range. Gradually, as Rose and Bostock's changes started to take effect and staff had been taken through a £10 million training initiative to create a 'can-do' attitude, results began to change. Twiggy and supermodel Erin O'Connor were the first of many stars to be used by Marks and Spencer plc's new Executive Director of Marketing (Steven Sharp) to promote the crucial new collection of womenswear. In October 2005 they reported the first sales increase since 2003. The share price rose above the 400p barrier and the clothing ranges were heralded as practical and stylish. Rapid turn-around of new clothing lines in particular was helping to attract customers into the stores for repeat visits.

Moving into 2005 with its first growth in clothing for more than two years under its belt, Marks and Spencer plc continued to perform well and in February 2006 commentators declared the position a full recovery. Marks and Spencer plc was back to the position of outperforming a

---

[1] Stuart Rose was later knighted in 2008.

falling market, had over 15 million customers per week and was rated as one of the best performers in the FTSE. In April 2006 Marks and Spencer plc got the news it had been waiting for, its recovery had hit the sales at Next: back to beating its rivals. The newly refurbished stores, the advertising campaigns and fast-moving clothing stock had all contributed to Rose delivering six months ahead of target. In spite of this, he remained wary of the R word:

> We are pleased with the progress . . . but there remains much to do . . . I like to over-deliver and under-promise and recovery is a big word. Ask me in January 2007 and I'll probably be happy to use the R-word if we're still making progress . . . It's like going into a garden that's not been tended for five years . . . you've got to do all the weeding, aerate the soil, re-landscape, plant, and it's not until you sit down a couple of years later you think 'Oh, its looking quite good!' And that's what we're doing, we're gardening.[iv]

In mid-2006 Lord Myners stepped down as planned and made way for the appointment of Lord Burns as the new Chair for the Marks and Spencer plc board. Elsewhere, innovation continued throughout 2006 across several fronts. First, Steven Sharp continued to see high impact results with his TV adverts. In Marks & Spencer food he continued to use popular Irish actress Dervla Kirwan's sultry voiceover to let customers know that this was not just food, it was Marks & Spencer food. In clothing he used the concept of a Hollywood Christmas starring amongst others Hollywood A-lister Antonio Banderas and the iconic Bond theme tune singer Shirley Bassey to deliver a feature length advert to promote the evening collection. Second, following the launch of the 'Look Behind the Label' campaign in 2006 to promote a fair-trade agenda, Marks and Spencer plc consolidated its corporate social responsibility position with its 'Plan A' initiative (January 2007) to work toward the environmental sustainability of the business. The five-year plan, with a considerable budgetary commitment, ranged from supply chain auditing, carbon neutrality, 25 per cent reduction in packaging and the promotion of healthy living. Thirdly, the process of store modernisation continued during this period; for instance, by Christmas 2006 35 per cent of stores were modernised. All of this showing in terms of increases in market share in clothing from 10.4 per cent to 11.1 per cent and in food from 4.1 per cent to an all-time high of 4.3 per cent and an overall increase in sales of over 9 per cent.

In March 2007, the new Marks and Spencer plc website (M&S Direct) was launched. Working alongside the hugely successful internet retailer Amazon, the aim was to fully utilise all sales avenues. In Marks and Spencer plc stores, footfall was up to 21 million visitors per week and the changes that Rose and his executive team had designed were delivering the hopedfor results. The Marks & Spencer brand, now firmly consolidated under the Your M&S logo, seemed to be back as a statement of quality and value for the British consumer. Throughout 2007 smaller innovations along the theme of 'Plan A' continued to be fed into the business. A 'wash at 30 degrees' campaign was introduced on all clothing, fat levels were reduced in over 500 products and in April 2007 Marks and Spencer plc became the first UK retailer to offer schoolwear made from recycled materials. Both profit and sales continued to show steady (5 per cent +) growth.

Innovations along the CSR theme continued into 2008, famously introducing a 5p charge for carrier bags as well as the removal of all artificial colouring from all food and drink and the opening of two eco-factories in Sri Lanka to produce Autograph and Per Una lingerie.

However, by far the biggest change in 2008 was the return to an old familiar formula when, in April, Stuart Rose decided that he was to take on the joint role of CEO and Chair of the board of directors. This move, controversial as it was in breach of the advice of the combined code for corporate governance followed voluntarily by most FTSE 100 companies, was immediately unpopular with investors. The belief was that Rose now held too much power and that this combined role had been highly dangerous for Marks and Spencer plc in the past and could be so again.

However, the overall results for 2008 matched the economic climate: poor. In July Marks and Spencer plc issued a profit warning. In the third quarter, the UK's swift slide into recession had had a significant impact on sales and by September Marks and Spencer plc saw its worst quarterly sales since 2005 with a 6 per cent fall in like-for-like sales, with food falling marginally less than clothing and homeware. Rose announced a curtailment of capital expenditure, seeing not only his famed refurbishment programme grind to a halt but a scaling back of investment across the board: this being in direct contradiction to his promise less than a year earlier. These measures were all designed to ensure the board would not have to recommend a cut in dividend. But by 2009 that is precisely what happened and investors saw a 20.9 per cent cut in dividend.

After the first quarter of 2009, the drop in sales had started to slow down and proved to be less severe than the group had expected. Analysts had predicted a 5.5 per cent fall in Marks & Spencer food but they were able to report a 3.7 per cent fall. This news prompted mid-year growth in the share price. September saw a positive boost for Marks & Spencer food when figures showed it to be the most improved food retailer in the UK in terms of customer loyalty over the past decade. Sitting second only to Asda in the 2009 data, Marks and Spencer plc had overtaken Waitrose, its direct premium rival. Inspection of the figures revealed that Marks and Spencer plc overtook Tesco and Sainsbury's as far back as 2002 in the Vandevelde era, leading some critics to question the extent of Rose's own impact on Marks & Spencer food. By the end of 2009 and over the Christmas trading period the share price performed well and stayed above the 400p level only to tumble back down to 329p by late February 2010.

2009 was generally a difficult year for relations between the Marks and Spencer plc board and its investors. In the first half of the year, Rose and his Marketing Director (Stephen Sharp) were both forced to give up a £1 million package of bonus in shares in order to appease shareholders. The non-executive director (Louise Patten) who had signed off on the bonuses came under fire at the AGM with a motion to block her reappointment. Rose had already been forced to sell his stake in the business of another of his non-executives (Martha Lane-Fox), with this level of involvement being considered inappropriate. But the primary issue that occupied investors was Rose's position as joint Chair and CEO. He survived a much publicised shareholder revolt at the July AGM but the size of the vote (over 40 per cent voting against Rose's reappointment as Chair) was seen as a clear signal of the need for investors to be reassured about the future.

Finally, in July 2009, Rose ended one line of uncertainty and began another by announcing his intention to stand down as CEO in 2010 but not as Chair until 2011. In the period between July and November 2009 speculation was rife with regard to the succession which was THE primary topic of debate around Marks and Spencer plc.

Could it be an internal? Maybe John Dixon – head of E-Commerce – who had been invited to sit on the main board of Marks and Spencer plc or one of his nearest rivals, Kate Bostock (womenswear) or Ian Dyson (Finance Director). Various names were being dropped into media articles throughout the autumn of 2009 as potential external candidates for the CEO role, with most CEOs of successful UK retailers being mentioned: Sainsbury's, Asda, HMV, Mothercare, WH Smith. The suggestion was that although Marks and Spencer plc would prefer an internal candidate, industry observers strongly favoured an external appointment – largely a response to Stuart Rose's plan to stay on as Chair until the summer of 2011. So in many ways Marc Bolland's appointment both as an external appointment and a retailer with a track record suited the market. Bolland had, during his tenure at Morrisons, put an extra half million customers into the store and almost doubled net profits.

Irrespective of the Bolland appointment, Rose and the Marks and Spencer plc board looked set to remain the same for the medium term. Although he and the board stated that Rose had not ruled out leaving before his planned date of July 2011, investors speculated that there was a risk of egotism keeping him in post longer and therefore creating an almost impossible leadership task for Marc Bolland, the incoming CEO, from May 2010.

Where next?

In spite of its success, with its shares outperforming the UK general retail index by 19 per cent in 2009, Marks and Spencer plc (in particular Rose) continued to attract negative publicity almost exclusively linked to Rose's succession. The summer's shareholder rebellion rumbled on with commentators hinting at trouble ahead for a new CEO with the powerful and confident Rose remaining in the role of Chair.

Even with Bolland's new role as incoming CEO confirmed, debate continued as to the legacy that Rose's successor would face. The arch critic of Sir Stuart, Tony Shiret of Credit Suisse, continued to argue that Marks and Spencer plc is not the completely changed and transformed offering that it projected itself to be. Throughout 2009 he repeatedly commented in the press that Marks and Spencer plc was still failing to be a hit with the mid-age range demographic and that two-thirds of its customers were still 55 years + and that not much has changed. In a scathing 104-page research note he argued that, except for cost savings, Marks and Spencer plc had made little financial progress since Rose took over in 2004. He called for change to be more far-reaching. His primary point being Marks and Spencer plc could not sustain a position where it is not attracting 30-year-old women into its stores and that Rose, whilst tidying up Marks and Spencer plc, has not changed it radically enough to avoid the same old debates circling around for the next four or five years.

In an interesting turn of events that perhaps gave a nod of prescience to Shiret, a dangerous challenge in the 30-year demographic was launched in October 2009 by old Marks & Spencer saviour George Davies (the designer of the Per Una collection) who launched his new range of stores (GIVe) in 25 towns across the UK. The GIVe stores presented M&S with new and direct competition and were widely tipped to deliver to Davies the fourth mega brand of his career (Next, George at Asda, Per Una and GIVe). Early results in 2010 indicated he had hit the right notes for the 30+ market yet again. But he too made less than complimentary comments about the culture at Marks and Spencer plc: 'The biggest challenge for anybody coming into M&S is to free it from its constipated culture.'[v] Davies claimed that Rose had had some impact but not gone far enough, saying that he had been sprinkling laxative around during his six years but Bolland still had the primary issue to resolve.

Considering Shiret's concern about Marks and Spencer plc's reliance on the 55+ demographic it was not surprising to see Marks and Spencer plc end 2009 by choosing a team

(Joanna Lumley, Stephen Fry and John Sergeant) with a combined age of 180 years to head up its Christmas advertising campaign for 2009. It remained to be seen who had it right, Shiret or Marks and Spencer plc, and what kind of a board the new CEO would inherit: Rose or no Rose, that was the question.

Not long before Bolland took up his post as CEO on 1 May 2010, the shareholders expressed their frustration with the Marks and Spencer plc board yet again. The board, without shareholder consultation, had agreed to Bolland's negotiation of an impressive golden-hello deal which at £7.5 million in cash as well as shares was described by commentators as excessive and a bad start for Bolland's tenure at Marks and Spencer plc.[vi] Sir Stuart stood by his man, not only arguing that this was the right price for the right man but also 'He will have absolute control over the business from the day he starts'.[vii] It is hard not to raise an eyebrow and wonder just how tough Bolland will need to be through his period at the helm of the UK's most famous retailer.

References:
[i] Radio 4, August 2000.
[ii] *Irish Times*, 19 June 2004.
[iii] J. Bevan *The Rise and Fall of Marks & Spencer . . . and how it Rose again.* Profile Books, 2007.
[iv] *Financial Times*, 12 April 2006.
[v] 'Next, George, Per Una . . . now as fashion wizard has new designs on women', *Observer*, 7 February 2010.
[vi] 'Incoming Chief negotiates £15m "golden hello" for joining M&S', *The Financial Times*, 2 February 2010.
[vii] '£15m hello to M&S: What new boss can expect in pay and perks for his first year', *Daily Mail*, 2 February 2010.

APPENDIX 1

		2009 52 weeks	2008 52 weeks	2007 52 weeks	2006 52 weeks	2005 52 weeks
Gross margin	Gross profit/Revenue	37.2%	38.6%	38.9%	38.3%	34.7%
Net margin	Operating profit/Revenue	9.6%	13.4%	12.2%	10.9%	8.0%
Net margin excluding property disposals and exceptional items		8.5%	12.1%	12.2%	11.0%	8.7%
Profitability	Profit before tax/Revenue	7.8%	12.5%	10.9%	9.6%	6.7%
Profitability excluding property disposals and exceptional items		6.7%	11.2%	11.2%	9.6%	7.4%
Basic earnings per share	Basic earnings/ Weighted average ordinary shares in issue	32.3p	49.2p	39.1p	31.3p	17.6p
Earnings per share adjusted for property disposals and exceptional items		28.0p	43.6p	40.4p	31.4p	19.2p
Dividend per share declared in respect of the year		17.8p	22.5p	18.3p	14.0p	12.1p
Dividend cover	Profit attributable to shareholders/ Dividend payable	1.8x	2.3x	2.1x	2.2x	2.9x
Return on equity	Profit attributable to shareholders/ Average equity shareholders' funds	25.2%	45.6%	46.3%	50.0%	35.1%
Retail gearing	Retail debt + net post-retiremen liability/ Retail debt + net post-retirement liability + retail shareholders' funds	60.9%	64.0%	59.1%	68.8%	76.2%
Retail fixed charge cover	Operating profit before depreciation and operating lease charges/Fixed charges	3.5x	5.3x	5.9x	4.9x	4.1x
Net debt (£m)		2,490.8	3,077.7	1,949.5	1,729.3	2,147.7
Capital expenditure (£m)		652.0	1,054.5	792.4	337.7	229.4

APPENDIX 2 Marks and Spencer plc share price (p), September 2005–March 2010

Source: www.marksandspencer.com.

Tesco: from domestic operator to multinational giant

Michelle Lowe and Neil Wrigley

This case considers the emergence of Tesco plc as one of the world's leading multinational retailers. In a remarkable 10-year period, Tesco has transformed itself from a purely domestic operator to a multinational giant – with subsidiaries in Europe, Asia and North America – and in 2009 had 64 per cent of its operating space outside the UK. Examining market entry into Asia in more detail, the case compares 'success' in Thailand and South Korea with 'failure' in Taiwan. It also considers 'a high risk gamble' in Tesco's entry into the US market, long considered to be a graveyard of overambitious expansion by UK retailers.

· · ·

Introduction

In April 2009, Tesco, the UK's largest retailer and private sector employer of labour, announced annual sales for 2008/09 of almost £60 billion (€66bn or $90.2bn) together with profits of £3 billion (€3.3bn or $4.5bn). After a dramatic decade-long transformation from purely domestic operator to multinational giant, Tesco now had a remarkable 64 per cent of its operating space outside the UK,

Source: Getty Images.

was developing increasingly strong businesses across 11 Asian and European markets, had a rapidly expanding 'start-up' subsidiary operating in the western USA, and had announced its entry into the Indian market. Moreover, as signalled in both the title of its Annual Report (*Value Travels*) and the prominence given in that report to its international profile, the firm was publicly expressing its confidence that it had mastered the art of international expansion, so long a weakness of UK retailing. Tesco's emergence as the world's third largest retailer, operating 2025 stores and employing 183,600 staff outside the UK by 2008/09, represents one of the most successful examples of strategic diversification by any UK company and offers insight into the role of the 'corporate strategist', the CEO.

International expansion – from the UK to Central Europe, Asia and North America

In the early 1990s Tesco was the UK's second largest food retailer, lagging behind the market leader Sainsbury's in

terms of sales density, turnover growth and profitability. Over the next decade it managed a remarkable transformation – repositioning itself from its discount roots into a mass market customer-focused retailer serving all segments of the UK market. By judicious acquisition of some smaller rivals, and by innovative and flexible store development programmes which by the mid-2000s had transformed it into a genuine multi-format operator with 72 per cent of its UK stores in smaller convenience/supermarket formats of less than 15,000 square feet, it first captured market leadership in the UK then progressively accelerated its lead over closest rivals Sainsbury's and Asda/Wal-Mart. By 2007, on a conservative definition of the UK grocery market, its share was 27.6 per cent – almost twice as large as Asda/Wal-Mart and Sainsbury's with 14.1 per cent and 13.8 per cent respectively. Simultaneously, as that gap first emerged in the late 1990s and then widened, Tesco, as the increasingly dominant market leader, faced growing regulatory pressure relating to both market-competition conditions and land-use planning restrictions. It also experienced increasingly adverse media scrutiny and orchestrated campaigns to 'rein in' its visibly growing power. In response to the latter it moved quickly to embrace agendas of community responsiveness, urban regeneration, sustainable development, and ethical/responsible sourcing to address what the UK Government's Department for Environment, Food and Rural Affairs described as 'rising consumer expectations regarding the social responsibilities

This case was prepared by Michelle Lowe, Professor of Retail Management, University of Survey and Lead Innovation Fellow AIM and Neil Wrigley, Professor of Geography, University of Southampton and Editor of *Journal of Economic Geography*. It is intended as a basis for class discussion and not as an illustration of good or bad practice. © Michelle Lowe and Neil Wrigley. Not to be reproduced or quoted without permission.

Table 1 Tesco's international operations

Region	Country	Year of entry	Store numbers 2008/9	Employees 2008/9	Regional % of operating space 2008/9
Europe	Hungary	1994	149	21,356	
	Poland	1995	319	23,569	
	Czech Rep	1996	113	12,677	
	Slovakia	1996	70	8,286	30
	Rep Ireland	1997*	116	13,764	
	Turkey	2003	96	7,025	
Asia	Thailand	1998	571	38,166	
	S. Korea	1999	242	20,626	
	Taiwan	2000	Exited market 2005		
	Malaysia	2002	29	9,872	33
	Japan	2003	135	4,007	
	China	2004	70	19,452	
	India		Announced entry 2008		
North America	USA	2007	115	2,581	1

* Re-entry in 1997 following unsuccessful entry in 1980s.

Source: Figures derived from Tesco Annual Report, 2009.

of supermarkets'. In response to regulatory pressures, Tesco progressively refocused its operations and capital investment in an attempt to secure long-term growth – diversifying into non-food products and retail services (personal finance, telecoms, online shopping channels) and, most significantly, expanding out of its home market via one of the most comprehensive and sustained international diversifications ever attempted by a UK company.

After commencing the first stage of international expansion in Europe – entering the emerging post-Soviet consumer markets of Central Europe in the mid-1990s (see Table 1) – Tesco launched the next stage of its strategy in 1998. Following Terry Leahy's appointment as CEO in 1997, it committed to an Asian expansion programme, initially entering Thailand and South Korea. The growth potential of the Asian markets had been extensively researched by the firm for a number of years. However, the immediate catalysts for entry were the rapid liberalisation of previous restrictions on retail FDI across East Asia, and opportunities to make strategic majority-share acquisitions of fledgling but potentially market leading retail businesses at discounted prices, which resulted from the Asian economic crisis of 1997/98. Tesco's subsequent expansion in Asia was dramatic. Just 10 years later it had 1047 stores, accounting for 33 per cent of the firm's global operating space, in the region (see Table 1). South Korea now provided Tesco with its second largest market by sales after the UK. Significantly, Tesco had signalled its commitment to develop businesses in two of the world's key twenty-first century economies, China and India. In China it was rapidly building the scale of its operation following entry in 2004, and in India it had successfully negotiated a partnership arrangement for entering a market in which ownership of retail businesses by international operators was still strictly regulated.

On the other side of the world, Tesco had taken the potentially transformational, but high risk decision to enter the USA – the world's largest consumer market. Building on Leahy's strategic vision of the market opportunity to develop dense networks of a new breed of convenience-oriented, smaller-format stores served by a short-lead-time integrated food preparation/distribution system, Tesco had announced entry into the western USA in 2006. By the end of 2008, a year after opening its first store, it had already rolled out a chain of 115 stores together with a 675,000 square feet distribution centre with capacity to serve over 500 stores in Southern California, Arizona and Nevada.

As a result of this international expansion, by the mid-2000s Tesco had moved into the elite group of multinational retailers. As Table 2 shows, by 2006/07 there were 15 retailers generating sales outside their home markets of over $11 billion per annum (see Appendix for summaries of the key firms). For a variety of reasons – including the higher development costs (and associated sales densities) required in the tightly regulated UK market, and the relative 'immaturity' of a higher proportion of its international space – Tesco's international sales growth inevitably lagged behind the increase in its international operating space. Nevertheless, at more than $20 billion those sales were sufficient to rank the firm within the top 10 multinational retailers (Table 2). By 2008/09 Tesco's international sales had increased by a further 60 per cent, propelling it into a top five position in the ranking. Additionally, those international sales and also operating profits (if US start-up losses are excluded) were slowly but progressively moving into closer alignment with the proportion of international operating space (Table 3). In turn, that reflected rates of growth in the international

Table 2 Leading multinational retailers ranked by sales outside home market 2006/7

Rank	Name of company	Country of origin	International sales 2006/7 (US$m)	International sales % of total, 2006/7	No. of countries of operation
1	Wal-Mart	US	77,100	22	14
2	Carrefour	France	54,758	52	20
3	Ahold	Netherlands	49,562	82	5
4	Metro	Germany	45,125	56	30
5	Auchan	France	24,204	50	11
6	Aldi	Germany	23,476	47	14
7	Lidl & Schwarz	Germany	23,103	46	22
8	IKEA	Sweden	21,882	92	34
9	Tesco	UK	21,678	26	12
10	Delhaize	Belgium	19,914	77	8
11	Rewe	Germany	17,445	32	14
12	Tengelmann	Germany	15,989	46	15
13	Seven & I	Japan	14,144	34	4
14	Pinault	France	13,283	55	30
15	Costco	US	11,793	20	8

Source: N.M. Coe and N. Wrigley (2009) *'The Globalisation of Retailing'*, volume 1, p. xviii. Cheltenham: Edward Elgar.

Table 3 Tesco's international operating space, sales and operating profits as a percentage of the firm's global totals

	2001/2	2003/4	2005/6	2007/8	2008/9	2010/12 Est
International operating space (%)	42.1	49.7	55.9	61.3	64.6	–
International sales* (%)	15.3	19.6	24.0	26.3	29.7	35.2**
International operating profit (%)						
excluding US start-up losses	8.1	16.4	21.4	24.9	25.6	–
(including US start-up losses)	–	–	–	(22.5)	(20.3)	–

* ex-VAT.

Source: Figures calculated by authors from statistics available in Tesco Annual Reports and Financial Statements, except **Bank of America/Merrill Lynch estimate 8 December 2009.

subsidiaries which continued to exceed those achievable in Tesco's 'mature' and highly regulated home market.

Success in Asia – Thailand and South Korea

At the point of market entry into Thailand and South Korea in 1998/99, Tesco acquired majority stakes in two retail chains (Lotus in Thailand and Homeplus in South Korea) together having fewer than 20 stores or development sites and operating in markets still dominated by traditional forms of retailing. Whilst the growth potential for 'modern' retail across Asia was considerable, that potential was simultaneously attracting many of Tesco's major European and North American competitors – including Wal-Mart, Carrefour, Ahold, Casino and Delhaize. Nevertheless, a decade later Tesco had successfully turned foothold acquisitions into positions of market leadership (Thailand) or potential market leadership (South Korea), had developed extensive multi-format store networks (exceeding 800 stores), and had outperformed its multinational rivals to the extent that Wal-Mart and Carrefour had been forced to exit South Korea leaving Tesco as the dominant international retailer in both countries. Some of the key dimensions of Tesco's

success in those markets related to its mode of market entry, its determined efforts to build market scale, and its adaptive responses to growing pressures across East Asia for tighter regulation of the expansion of multinational retailers.

The Asian economic crisis of 1997/98 left major domestic conglomerates urgently seeking cash injections. As a result, Tesco was able to enter both markets via majority-share partnerships in the non-core retail businesses of the leading conglomerates: the CP Group in Thailand and Samsung in South Korea. Initially Tesco's share of the partnerships was 75 per cent in Thailand and 81 per cent in South Korea. However, subsequent capital injections by Tesco into the expansion of the chains rapidly reduced CP Group's share to zero, and Samsung's share first to 11 per cent and then in two subsequent stages to 1 per cent. Despite this rapid dilution of the local partners' share of the businesses, the partnerships offered Tesco knowledge of local business/regulatory conditions and consumer culture, plus the ability to build upon the 'local' appeal and customer image of the acquired chain – particularly in South Korea where retention of the Samsung name (Samsung-Tesco) proved to be essential.

In both countries, Tesco has made substantial and continuous post-entry capital investment to build scale and accrue market leadership advantages. In Thailand the investment has been pumped entirely into organic expansion and has required store development programmes of considerable flexibility. In South Korea, 'within market' acquisitions – 36 ex-Carrefour 'Homever' hypermarkets for £950 million in 2008 and 12 Aram Market hypermarkets in 2005 – have been used to enhance its market position and to keep pace (as the country's second ranked operator) with the domestic market leader E-Mart. Tesco's ability to finance those acquisitions (outbidding its rivals when necessary) and to sustain a substantial annual capital expenditure programme has rested on the firm's steadily growing profitability. That is to say, on the 'free cash flow' for investment generated from both its domestic and international operations and the ability to raise capital at advantageous rates which that profitability ensures.

Capital investment in both countries has occurred against a background of pressures (felt across many parts of East Asia) to tighten regulation and rein in expansion of the multinational retailers. Those pressures have ranged from attempts to re-impose restrictions on ownership and control, through efforts to protect existing retail structures via land-use zoning, to regulation of store-opening hours, retail formats, and 'below cost' selling. In Thailand, as development of large-format hypermarkets became more difficult, Tesco transferred its UK-developed small-store operating skills and began infilling its hypermarket framework with dense networks of small-format (Express) convenience stores, first in metropolitan Bangkok, subsequently in other leading cities. Those stores also had the additional benefit of being unrestricted by opening hours' regulation introduced to limit trading hours of larger-format stores. Additionally, it developed a novel low-build-cost 'Value' store format – essentially a stripped-down small hypermarket embedded within a local vendor market – to provide an entry vehicle for development in low-income rural 'up country' towns where expansion using conventional large-format hypermarkets was politically unfeasible. Finally, it invested considerable effort in working with local communities to counter mounting regulatory pressures – explaining the value of the benefits (employment, supply chain modernisation, infrastructure investment, skills training, export gateway opportunities) it offered to the Thai economy, and stressing the potential coexistence of 'traditional' and 'modern' components of the retail system.

Failure in Asia – Taiwan

Tesco entered Taiwan in 2000, developed six stores, and exited the market in 2005. In simple terms, several of the elements which had been key drivers of Tesco's success in Thailand and South Korea were absent in Taiwan. In particular, Tesco entered the market in which one of its major multinational retail competitors, Carrefour, had been operating for more than a decade and had built a strong and, in practice, unassailable market dominance. Moreover, unlike Thailand and South Korea and Tesco's subsequent Asian market entries into Malaysia and China, Tesco was unable to find a suitable local partner and was therefore obliged to attempt an entry based on *de nuovo* expansion. However, not only had many of the potentially most attractive sites for expansion already been developed by Carrefour, or were held under future development option, but also the highly complex Chinese land ownership system proved to be a difficult arena in which to transfer Tesco's skills in market/site location analysis and property acquisition/development.

As a result, despite determined efforts, Tesco was never able to develop the market scale necessary to support the substantial infrastructure investment required for the type of central distribution systems which so vitally underpinned its operations in Thailand and South Korea, With a market share of barely 3 per cent it became increasingly clear both to the firm and to industry analysts that there was little realistic opportunity of achieving a market penetration level in Taiwan where the subsidiary would become self-reinforcing in terms of profits.

The asset swap market exit solution

In late 2005 Tesco announced an innovative strategic divestment solution to its problems in Taiwan. The solution involved a cross-region swap of retail assets with its rival Carrefour, whereby each firm would simultaneously secure scale and benefit from strengthened market positions in different countries. It was agreed that in Taiwan Tesco's six stores and two development sites would be transferred to Carrefour whilst, in exchange, in Central Europe Carrefour would transfer 11 stores in the Czech Republic and four stores in Slovakia to Tesco. The deal clearly had competition and consumer welfare implications as it enhanced the dominance of the market leader in each country. Ultimately it was approved in Taiwan and the Czech Republic but in Slovakia was blocked by the Anti-Monopoly Office. Nevertheless, the Slovakian element of the swap was relatively small, and Tesco was able to exit its only unsuccessful Asian operation, learn valuable lessons for other Asian market entries, and simultaneously to strengthen its market position in Central Europe. Relative failure had been transformed into modest success by an agile and innovative strategic divestment.

A high risk gamble in the USA

In February 2006, after a year of intensive but closely guarded market research by a CEO-selected team of managers despatched to Los Angeles, and building on more than a decade of in-depth investigation of the potential and characteristics of the market, Tesco announced its intention to commit £1.25 billion over five years to enter the western USA. The entry vehicle was to be a chain of 'convenience' focused neighbourhood stores, later to be called Fresh & Easy Neighborhood Markets. The decision represented a significant shift in Tesco's previous 'emerging market'-focused internationalisation strategy. As the CEO of Fresh & Easy was to stress, the US represented: 'the first mature, well-served market, that we have opened into, so actually [Fresh & Easy] is not filling a vacuum and has to earn its place'.[i] It was also, very clearly, a high risk decision as the US market had a long record of proving to be the 'graveyard' of overambitious expansion by UK retailers. As a result, the entry announcement generated widespread scepticism of Tesco's ability to succeed where so many others had failed. Indeed, even sympathetic analysts questioned Tesco's ability to achieve the targets (e.g. store productivity) implicitly set for the US venture. The consensus view in Credit Suisse's (2007) terms was: 'it may be fresh, but it won't be easy'.[ii]

Tesco's decision to enter the US also represented an important reversal of its previous view of the likelihood of success in the market. Indeed, it had consistently resisted many opportunities to enter the USA via acquisition of regional food retailer chains of conventional large-format supermarkets – not least because of their track record of low profitability and the threat posed to them by the decade-long supercentre-driven transformation of Wal-Mart from purely general merchandise to US food retail market leader. The change in Tesco's assessment related to its growing skills in small format store operation, its belief in the competitive potential of dense networks of 'convenience'-focused neighbourhood stores providing an innovative retail offer, and evidence that the Wal-Mart threat could be countered in the type of urban markets Tesco had targeted for its US expansion.

Tesco's small format retail skills had developed in the UK as a competitive response to tightening regulation – both planning regulation which made large format out-of-centre stores become increasingly difficult to develop and competition regulation which blocked large-scale acquisitions but offered an opportunity for growth by acquisition in the convenience store market. In part, however, those skills had been developed *proactively* to gain competitive advantage in a rapidly expanding 'convenience culture' market. By the mid-2000s, the result was that Tesco had 700 Express convenience stores in the UK, supplemented by a range of other smaller format stores, e.g. 15,000-square-feet urban 'Metro' stores and, additionally, had begun to export the Express format to its international subsidiaries. Growing confidence in its ability to operate small formats

profitably offered Tesco the opportunity to explore a US market entry focused around 'convenience'. Additionally, it recognised that the model of dense networks of 10,000 square feet of high visibility corner-location stores successfully used by US drug retailers (chemists) such as Walgreens could be used to structure a chain of smaller format food stores on a mutually reinforcing network logic.

In terms of retail offer, Tesco recognised that opportunities existed to exploit the extensive experience of UK food retailers in chilled prepared-meals development and operation of the cool-chain distribution/logistics systems required by those products. US food retailers, and in turn the US food manufacturing industry, had traditionally offered few of these products to customers and the specialist distribution/logistics and quality control/traceability systems necessary to support extensive retail offers of that type were underdeveloped. As a result opportunities existed to develop a chain focused on offering high quality but affordable fresh and chilled prepared meal products, served by a short lead time responsive distribution system, supplying higher levels of own label products than typical amongst US food retailers.

In respect of the threat posed by Wal-Mart, Tesco recognised that impact to have been particularly strong on the weaker US regional supermarket chains – driving significant consolidation of those chains. Additionally, it recognised the traditional supermarket sector was essentially being squeezed between the Wal-Mart-led supercentre operators and a new group of discount retailers operating smaller format stores and achieving much higher levels of profitability than the supermarket chains. In particular the stores of the Albrecht family – Aldi on the east coast and Trader Joe's in the west – provided Tesco with evidence that the threat of Wal-Mart could be accommodated. The innovative Trader Joe's in particular offered a model of what was possible in the metro markets of the western USA, operating with exceptionally high sales densities and profitability. Moreover, it was exactly those urban markets which, as a result of escalating community resistance, Wal-Mart was finding it most difficult to enter with its huge supercentres.

Dimensions of Tesco's market entry and expansion

In November 2007, Tesco opened its first Fresh & Easy stores in Southern California. They averaged 10,000 square feet and carried a tightly edited range of 3,500 SKUs[1] with a focus on fresh and chilled prepared-meal products. Served by a 'short lead time' integrated food preparation/distribution system, they were based around entirely

---

[1] SKU = Stock Keeping Unit, i.e. a unique identifier for each distinct product.

self-scanning checkouts. Described by Fresh & Easy's CEO as 'designed to be as fresh as Whole Foods, with the value of Wal-Mart, the convenience of Walgreens, and a product range of Trader Joe's',[iii] the stores were rapidly rolled out in Southern California, Phoenix and Las Vegas, and a year later exactly 100 had opened.

Significant features of Tesco's US experience include:

1 *Attempts to engage with an online consumer culture.* In contrast to its previous international market entries, Tesco has proactively adopted digital/viral marketing techniques to address the challenge of defining, launching and embedding the Fresh & Easy brand. Determined efforts have been made by the firm to use blog and text-messaging based communication with online communities of customers and potential customers. Although occasionally these efforts have rebounded on the firm, Tesco has continued to explore these methods and to transfer learning into its wider international operations.

2 *Establishing brand visibility and maximising development opportunities via investment in underserved communities.* An important component of Tesco's entry into Los Angeles has been its commitment to develop stores in low income/deprived and ethnically segregated communities – visibly underserved by its major US competitors. Transferring the development-coalition and community-specific retail operating skills gained since the late 1990s in opening 'urban regeneration partnership' stores in deprived areas of many UK cities, Tesco quickly developed stores in Compton, South Central and similar areas of Los Angeles. Its continuing commitment to investment in underserved communities has, on the one hand, gained strong local community support and increasing national recognition, leading to a more rapid establishment of brand identity than might otherwise have been expected. On the other hand it has provided a rallying point for a variety of groups (notably retail labour unions strongly opposed to Tesco's decision to operate its US stores on a non-unionised basis) antagonistic to its market entry.

3 *Integrated food production/distribution supported by follower-suppliers.* To ensure reliable availability of high quality prepared food products critical to its vision of the Fresh & Easy brand in a context where it had concerns about prevailing quality/traceability standards of local third-party production, Tesco has been obliged to take the unusual step of managing its own food preparation. It has developed an 80,000 square feet 'food preparation' facility alongside its distribution centre (DC) in Riverside, and has been supported by the simultaneous move to California of two of its leading UK suppliers – Nature's Way Foods and 2 Sisters Food Group. These companies have jointly invested $170 million in processing plants adjacent to Tesco's DC and feed into the DC both shelf-ready packaged produce and also 40 per cent of the prepared meat, poultry, fruit and vegetable ingredients used in the food preparation facility.

4 *A surprisingly muted initial competitive response.* Entry of one of the world's largest retailers into the home market of the global leader (Wal-Mart), and into cities highly contested by leading US domestic operators, could be predicted to produce a fierce competitive response. Given the inability to protect the 'front region' innovations underlying its US chain, Tesco essentially had to attempt to lay down store networks as rapidly as possible before drawing that anticipated response. Within a year of Fresh & Easy's launch Wal-Mart had begun to trial a chain of small format stores closely modelled in terms of size, SKUs and neighbourhood orientation on the Tesco stores. However, by late 2009 those 'Marketside' stores remained confined to just four locations in Phoenix. Although scaling up of the trial was anticipated, Tesco had been given unexpected time to continue developing its store network density and to respond to 'front region' innovations (ranging, signage, store atmospherics) in the prototype Marketside stores.

5 *The reputational gamble of the CEO.* One of the defining characteristics of Leahy's strategic realignment of Tesco as a multinational operator had been his ability to engineer that transformation largely under the radar of hostile public scrutiny and retain financial market support for the strategy. That was never likely to be possible with an entry into the USA. Despite the relatively modest scale of the £1.25 billion five-year US investment (compared to annual international capital expenditure in 2008/09 of £2.1 billion) the firm, and its CEO in particular, was acutely aware of both the reputational risks and potentially transformational consequences of the US venture in the case of either success or failure.

> We've carefully balanced the risks. If it fails it's embarrassing. It might show up in my career [but] it'll cost an amount of money that is easily affordable by Tesco – call it £1 billion if you like. If it succeeds then it's transformational.[iv]

Leahy has, in effect, been required to publicly place his considerable 'reputational equity' on the line and has found it necessary to repeatedly signal strategic 'commitment' to the US venture.

Success or failure in the USA – the jury remains out

By late 2009 Tesco had opened more than 130 stores in the USA. In the face of a global economic crisis with origins in the sub-prime US housing market, the growth of some of the previously fast expanding western US markets targeted by Tesco had been decimated. The pace of Fresh & Easy's store openings had been slowed and the operations of the chain had been subject to a period of intense reappraisal. Start-up losses were running at a higher level than planned, and the UK media was eagerly seeking opportunities to announce a rare lapse in Tesco's seemingly unstoppable global expansion. Long term sceptics amongst the equity analysts continued to argue that Tesco was likely to 'head for the exit' and quit the US, writing off £1 billion of investment in the process.

On the other hand, economic recovery was beginning to emerge in the USA, the recession had provided opportunities for Tesco to build its store networks and acquire future development sites with limited competition, the core positioning of the 'brand' described by US Retailing Today (November 2007) as occupying: 'the white space where the combination of good food, good value, convenience and environmental sensitivity that matters to the emerging American consumer converge' retained its logic, and who would be prepared to bet against Leahy's reputational commitment to the venture.

References:
[i] Mason, T., *The Times*, 17 November 2007.
[ii] Exstein, M., *et al.* (2007) 'It may be fresh but it won't be easy', *Credit Suisse Equity Research*, 14 February.
[iii] *Financial Times*, 1 December 2007.
[iv] Leahy, T. (2007) 'Fresh but far from easy', *The Economist*, 21 June. (Available at www.economist.com.)

APPENDIX Tesco's leading multinational retail rivals

Wal-Mart: The world's largest industrial corporation in terms of sales ($379 billion in 2008/09) and the leading multinational retailer. Wal-Mart operates outside its US base in 14 international markets, including Argentina, Brazil, Canada, China, Japan, Mexico, the UK, and announced entry into India via a joint venture in 2006. Although widely viewed as essentially a large-format, 'big box' retailer, Wal-Mart has increasingly become a multi-format retailer in parts (particularly Latin America) of its international portfolio. Has enjoyed mixed fortunes internationally. Highly successful in Mexico and Canada, it strengthened its position elsewhere in South and Central America with acquisitions from Ahold. Less successful in parts of Asia and Europe (with the exception of its Asda chain in the UK) it was forced to exit Germany and South Korea having failed to achieve market scale.

Carrefour: The world's second largest retailer (but with annual sales in 2008/09 approximately one-third of Wal-Mart), this French firm was the pioneer retail multinational. In the late 1980s it entered emerging markets in East Asia (notably Taiwan) and South America (Brazil and Argentina) achieving 'first-mover' advantages and substantial profits. By the late 1990s, after its merger with French rival Promodes, it had operations in over 30 countries across Asia, South America and elsewhere in Europe. During the 2000s it has divested operations in several markets in which it had failed to achieve scale, but remains a widely dispersed retail multinational operating both large-format hypermarkets, supermarkets, and also small-format 'discount' stores under the Dia fascia.

Royal Ahold: Leading Dutch retailer which by the late 1990s/early 2000s had an extensive international presence in the USA, Latin America, East Asia, Scandinavia and Southern/Eastern Europe, promoting itself as a distinctive global operator. Its aggressive growth strategy and tolerance of high financial leverage lost the confidence of financial markets and in 2003 Ahold was the focus of a major corporate financial scandal. Subsequently Ahold was forced to sell many of its operations in Latin America, Asia and Europe to protect its 'core' retail chains (Stop & Shop, Giant and Albert Hein) in the USA and the Netherlands.

Metro: Second largest European retailer, this German firm has stores in over 30 countries across Asia Central, Eastern and Southern Europe, with foothold positions in North Africa. Distinctively in many markets, it operates solely via a bulk purchase 'cash & carry' format – under either the Metro or Makro fascias. The cash & carry (self-service warehouse) format, which is targeted towards registered business customers only and in which Metro is the global leader, has frequently allowed it to enter markets (e.g. India in 2003) as a 'wholesaler' where regulation restricts FDI by conventional retailers.

Aldi: German retail group, privately owned by the Albrecht family and divided into two divisions, Aldi Nord and Aldi Sud, together operating over 8000 smaller format 'hard discount' stores in 20 countries across Europe, the USA and Australia. In the USA an Albrecht family trust also owns the innovative Trader Joe's chain concentrated in Southern California which provided a model of the possibilities for Tesco's US subsidiary.

Ekomate Systems and the Indian software industry: leveraging network relationships for international growth

Shameen Prashantham

This short case study looks at the role of network relationships in the internationalisation of a small entrepreneurial software firm based in Bangalore, India. Small entrepreneurial firms face major challenges in achieving international growth given their resource scarcity. Network relationships (e.g. with customers and strategic partners) can help these firms to overcome some of their difficulties. This case describes how networks have influenced international growth in Ekomate Systems, a software firm led by an ambitious entrepreneur. However, it also shows that developing and leveraging network relationships is neither straightforward nor easy. A subtext of the case is the emergence of internationally minded entrepreneurial small firms from rising economies such as India (and China) which tap into, among others, co-ethnic or diaspora networks.

● ● ●

Origins of Ekomate

Ekomate Systems was founded in 1996 by Tom Thomas upon his return to his hometown of Bangalore after obtaining an MSc in computer engineering at the University of Texas in Austin. The son of an entrepreneur, Thomas felt that starting a business would be considerably more remunerative than employment. Moreover, he had gained some work experience in Intel, while in the US, and was acutely aware of the great potential of the internet. He was therefore keen to start a company that would enable client companies to get on the Web. The Ekomate website describes its offering as follows:

> Ekomate uses the offshore development model to help its clients get their IT work done, maintaining international quality at reasonable costs, thereby resulting in tremendous cost advantages to its clients. Ekomate follows ISO compliant processes for software development.

The Bangalore software industry[i]

In founding Ekomate, Thomas was riding on the crest of what would prove to be a substantial wave – the development of the Indian software industry. With Bangalore as its focal point, the Indian software industry has attracted several international companies from high cost advanced

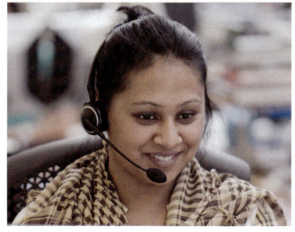

Source: Corbis/Helen King.

economies to outsource, at least partially, their software development needs. Regional shares of Indian exports are approximately two-thirds to North America, a quarter to Europe and the rest to other markets including Asia Pacific. It has been suggested that Bangalore's software industry emerged quite by accident, facilitated by historical factors. In the years following Independence (1947), a strategic decision was taken by the Indian government to locate certain key defence laboratories away from the nation's capital of New Delhi owing to its proximity to potentially hostile neighbours. Bangalore, a distant city with an established military presence from the days of British rule, was chosen as the location of such vital public sector undertakings as Hindustan Aeronautical Limited. These organisations attracted technical personnel from around the country and from the prestigious Bangalore-based Indian Institute of Science. The resultant pool of talent was arguably the forerunner to the supply of software professionals now available in Bangalore. Numerous engineering colleges have since been established in India where over 150,000 English-speaking engineering and science graduates are produced every year.

Ekomate's initial internationalisation (1996–2002)

For the first couple of years Ekomate's clientele was solely domestic. However, it had always been Thomas' ambition to attract international business, especially from the US. Not only was the US without doubt the leading market for Indian software development outsourcing, Thomas also had useful connections there through his Master's education in Texas and his stint at Intel. So he had been sending out feelers to former classmates and other contacts, seeking potential clients. These informal efforts paid off in 1998 when he secured his first US contract.

Subsequent business deals followed from the US, many of which were the consequence of connections with persons of Indian origin who are often referred to as Non-Resident Indians (NRIs). Thomas narrates various anecdotes that illustrate the benefits of information, advice and opportunities[ii] obtained through these connections with fellow Indians working in the US information technology industry. Often, it would be a case of a US-based former classmate or family friend referring Ekomate to prospective clients. Thomas notes of NRIs that:

> definitely for someone coming from India, or someone having an Indian perspective, it's very easy for them to talk to us. For us NRIs have been a powerful source of business. They know our working conditions. If you say Republic Day is a holiday or some other day is a holiday, they'll know why [chuckles]. It is difficult to explain to an American client how many holidays we have in India or why we have to work on Saturdays . . . NRIs just need the trust factor [that] this guy will not screw up, they'll deliver when they say; otherwise it is their neck on the line there.

For a young, growing company, the string of business contracts – including unsolicited business from a British client – provided sustenance and excitement. By 2002, fully 90 per cent of Ekomate's revenues were accounted for by international business. From a standing start in 1996,

the company had grown to a size of about 20 employees. The US remained the largest market. Ekomate wanted to maintain the strong focus on international markets. By that stage, Thomas saw international growth as being synonymous with the growth of his firm. In early 2002 he observed, 'If I have only Indian customers, then I cannot make payroll'. The international clients that Ekomate serves tend to be software SMEs that outsource some or all of their software programming to Ekomate. Thomas sought to continue his focus on working with software companies abroad rather than directly with end users:

> Our clients are basically small to medium firms – IT firms, essentially. We have one of their tech people interact with us and we develop software to their specifications. We have seen that working with the end-user is very difficult, as a small firm. We cannot afford to send people there and get specs.

In the light of the slowing US economy, compounded by the 9/11 terrorist attacks, by 2002 Thomas felt it imperative to diversify Ekomate's portfolio of markets so as not to be overly reliant on the US. Ekomate dabbled with a few other markets as well. These initial inroads did not, however, lead to further success, in large part because Thomas did not have the same level of network relationships in these other markets as compared to the US. Consequently, Ekomate struggled to consolidate on the initial business obtained from or contacts made in these markets. Much more promising, however, was the British market and Thomas turned his attention there in the ensuing years. He talked of his target markets in the following way:

> Definitely the US market is key because they adopt technology very fast. And all the trends are being driven from there. Followed closely by Europe, I would say – especially the UK because it is English-speaking and easier to break into.

Ekomate's subsequent internationalisation (2002 onwards)

Prompted by a mentor, having successfully applied for ISO accreditation for Ekomate's software processes by mid-2005, Thomas began to *actively* seek additional international business with a view to achieving further growth[iii] and thereby stability for Ekomate. Thomas' attention shifted to the UK. However, this time he decided not to rely purely on happenstance or serendipity. Given that he lacked the same level of network relationships as compared to the US, Thomas decided to look for useful connections to the UK on his doorstep, as it were. He began to engage with the India-based representatives of British trade organisations. This brought him into contact with the India manager for Scottish Development International which promotes trade to and from Scotland. As a result, he found himself on the guest list when a delegation of Scottish software firms visited Bangalore later that year. Thomas observed that:

> We definitely realised that just looking at the US alone is not a good strategy, so we're looking at parallel markets in Europe. So we've successfully built good relationships with trade organisation representatives of different countries. I have a good relationship with the Scotland country manager . . . The point is just to get exposed so that whenever Scottish companies visit India we are invited for events, we know what they are looking for.

Based on prior positive experiences in dealing with fellow Indians in the US, Thomas' strategy for the UK in general and Scotland in particular was to partner with a non-resident Indian business based in Scotland. The local partner would provide the frontend interface with the client while Ekomate would provide the backend software programming. In 2004, an Indian contact in Scotland introduced Thomas to a prospective partner with whom he forged a short-lived relationship (terminated owing to a personal crisis for the latter). However, some other contacts made on that visit led to another Scottish partnership being formed in November 2006. This Scottish company had set up a new web development business which entered into a relationship with Ekomate for outsourced software development in a new area of web development (open source content management systems). It was envisaged that Ekomate would be the backend engine for this type of software development for the Scottish firm. Ekomate relied on the expertise of an external consultant to drive this project, as it did not have the required expertise in house. But things did not go to plan. It became apparent that there had been a mismatch between the Scottish client's expectations and Ekomate's understanding of the requirement. Both the client and Ekomate realised that a major contributor to the difficulties had been faulty project management at the Scottish end. Yet by now sufficient damage had been done.

The foray into Scotland marked an important turning point in Ekomate's internationalisation trajectory. Having begun its initial internationalisation primarily in the US, which is both the largest market for IT services and the country where CEO Tom Thomas had the most connections, Ekomate began to explore less obvious international markets and, by April 2007, it became clear to Thomas that he simply had to start looking beyond the UK as well. He began to explore continental European markets. He involved himself with the Indo-Italian Chamber of Commerce in Bangalore, and became the Regional Member of the Board of Directors. Thomas' involvement in the Indo-Italian Chamber of Commerce began to yield useful networking opportunities. By mid-2008, following the opportunity to participate as one of two IT firms in an Italian trade fair, Ekomate had secured its first Italian client and appointed a local representative. Later that year, Thomas took advantage of an invitation to join a delegation to Sicily in December 2008; further Italian business relationships are in the process of being set up as a consequence. Thomas does acknowledge that there are linguistic barriers in Italy and these pose a challenge as Ekomate ponders how to consolidate its position in that market. But Thomas remains convinced that there is untapped market potential in Italy for a smaller Indian IT firm such as Ekomate given the stiff competition from more established Indian players in markets such as the US.

Corresponding to these new developments in relation to the international markets Ekomate was now targeting, Thomas found himself cultivating relationships less and less with non-resident Indians. He had to move beyond his comfort zone to engage with new contacts who did not have a shared ethnic heritage. In the pursuit of an expanded network of relationships, Thomas had to put in considerable effort, as evident from the following update he once provided of a travel schedule that was rather typical for him:

> I am planning a trip to New Zealand shortly to explore some relationships. Tomorrow I am meeting Finland trade officials to find a good date for a trip next year. I was recently in London for an outsourcing event.

Such networking efforts were on display in April 2009 when Thomas visited New Zealand and met several firms with the idea of finding a New Zealand partner to work with. Through the introduction of an associate in Bangalore, Thomas has been able to identify a Wellington-based firm as Ekomate's IT partner for New Zealand. Also, on this trip, Thomas re-established contact with New Zealand Trade and Enterprise, which help in making trade linkages. Efforts are now being made to secure a project from this region with one manager at Ekomate being assigned the task of researching the New Zealand software industry further. A dialogue had begun with prospective clients in the areas of open source and content management. However, in the time since the trip to New Zealand, the recession has made its presence felt there and the new projects are taking time to materialise. This is one of the reasons that Thomas put off a visit to a 'matchmaking' event in the UK held by UK Trade and Investment in November 2009, as he felt that the recession in the UK is still not over and buyers are not yet awarding new projects.

Subsequently, there was a positive turn of events in relation to Ekomate's client in Scotland. A newly appointed

Technical Director with considerable experience in software development visited the Ekomate offices in Bangalore in February 2010 where a new model of collaboration was worked out. In this cost-plus model, the client would have full involvement in selecting the technical resources for the project. There would also be a lot of back-and-forth training and interaction between the client in Scotland and Ekomate in Bangalore, such as sending the resources to Scotland. This is a radical departure from Ekomate's earlier methods of collaboration with other clients. Already an initial team of three people have started working in this mode, and Thomas and the Scottish client are very positive that this relationship will grow from strength to strength. The failure of the earlier project has not prevented the Scottish client and Ekomate from evolving this new mode of collaboration, as the bond of trust between the Scottish client's Managing Director and Thomas has become very strong.

As Thomas reflects over Ekomate's internationalisation journey, he emphasises that although network relationships do not always yield business opportunities that directly translate into revenues, they constitute an important source of learning about how to internationalise effectively. The following comment he made about one mentoring relationship in particular reflects his more general approach to learning through network relationships:

> my mentor cannot go out and get business for us; we have to do it. He has specifically taught me how to fish, if I can use that analogy; if he gives me fish then I will eat the fish, and tomorrow I will be hungry again. But if I know how to fish – which I am learning – then the process will be more long-lasting or sustaining.

Future directions

While the business development efforts in relatively new markets somewhat off the beaten track like Scotland, Italy and New Zealand are at a nascent stage, Ekomate has continued to obtain repeat business from clients elsewhere in the UK and in the US. The resultant growth has seen Ekomate's headcount almost double since 2002. Going forward, Ekomate is consciously targeting what Thomas describes as 'sustaining work' – software projects that were likely to lead to continuous repeat business (e.g. maintenance service contracts) as opposed to merely one-off contracts to build some software for a client. One of Thomas' main dilemmas, however, has been the choice between focusing on a few core areas of competence and diversifying the portfolio of technologies on the basis of client needs. With a view to keeping customer loyalty, he has chosen the latter option. Furthermore, Ekomate is in the process of diversifying into information technology-enabled services commonly referred to as business process outsourcing, with a view to further augmenting international revenues. Thomas summarises the future challenges of the company:

> How can Ekomate survive as a differentiated IT provider? How do we conserve every drop of cash flow, given the challenging economic climate globally? Should we focus on Microsoft development platform projects (where Ekomate has strengths) or should we explore other types of work (such as open source development), or work in specific areas such as manufacturing, aerospace and defence instead of being a generic IT services provider? If we look at these new areas, then how do we build up these capabilities in-house rather than rely on external consultants? Should we be looking at bringing out some new software product (as opposed to continuing purely as a software services firm)? How do we diversify into other areas of offshoring such as large-scale non-voice business process outsourcing (BPO)? Can we employ the underprivileged strata of society, and thereby work with a social mission? Can we look at opportunities in the Indian marketplace itself, such as e-governance projects where funds are plentiful, given that India is one of the economies still growing globally? How do we compete against the bigger Indian IT players in a flat world?

References:
[i] For a more detailed discussion see S. Prashantham, *The Internationalization of Small Firms: A Strategic Entrepreneurship Perspective*. London: Routledge, 2008.
[ii] S. Prashantham and C. Dhanaraj, 'The dynamic influence of social capital on the international growth of new ventures', *Journal of Management Studies*, in press.
[iii] For a conceptual discussion of this phase of internationalisation see S. Prashantham and S. Young, 'Post-entry speed of international new ventures', *Entrepreneurship Theory & Practice*, in press.

Sustaining the magic at Bang & Olufsen

Thomas Gulløv Longhi and Frank Brandt Kristensen

In the past, Bang & Olufsen (B&O) has managed to adapt to changing market conditions mainly by launching new products with the best available technology and a unique design. In 2007, B&O faced a dramatic downturn due to the global financial crisis and at the same time experienced a paradigm shift in the market with the main drivers based on digital and networked technology. New management, installed in 2008, changed the structure and introduced a new strategic plan, improving efficiency and enhanced product development whilst retaining the focus on B&O's core competence of unique design. This case explores the sustainability of the new strategy in a technology-driven market with major competitors which develop their own technology, often dictating the technology standards of the market.

• • •

Bang & Olufsen (B&O) was founded in 1925 in Struer, Denmark and it is considered to be one of the most important Danish design icons and an important part of Danish industrial legacy. B&O is a well-known global brand with a strong focus on design and high-tech solutions in televisions, music systems, speakers and multimedia products. The company dominates the high-end luxury segment where customers expect exclusive design, quality, and new technological solutions. In 2008, B&O was listed in the Top 20 Cool Brands as number 4 below Aston Martin, iPhone and Apple.

However, between 2007 and 2009, B&O lost 20 per cent of its turnover and the main markets of Germany, Denmark and Great Britain suffered in particular. The main reason for this can be explained by a lack of new successful product launches combined with the economic implications of the financial crises that emerged in 2008. Normally, new products launched within the previous 12 months correspond to approximately 25 per cent of turnover. Since 2007, new products have only contributed 10–16 per cent to turnover.

Technological transition in the market for consumer electronics

The market for consumer electronics is changing due to new technology. A transition from physical and broadcast media to digitally stored and network-based technology is taking place. Hence, the market has become more dynamic

due to the rivalry between dominant designs and standards in this new technological era. As a small manufacturer in the electronics industry, B&O is dependent on key suppliers of this new technology. Their expertise and competences in design, loudspeakers, TV screens and the ability to integrate all video and audio systems into one unit have until recently secured B&O a leading position in the luxury segment. However, in the last decade the product life-cycles within consumer electronics have been shortened significantly due to a rise in new technologies, such as HD protocols for televisions. The speed and the range of new product launches in the market have been a challenge for B&O, and the company has had problems meeting this technical development and thereby also consumer demand and expectations.

New management in B&O

In August 2008, Karl Kristian (nicknamed Kalle) Hvidt Nielsen was appointed as the new CEO of the company. He had come from a successful six-year appointment as CEO of Brüel & Kjær (a Danish manufacturer of microphones and electronics). Kalle Hvidt Nielsen has a technical background in engineering, but his time at Brüel & Kjær had given him the reputation of an international commercially oriented manager with a focus on internal profitability. With Kalle Hvidt Nielsen as CEO, Brüel & Kjær was transformed from being a technically oriented company into a commercially and service oriented company with a strong international focus. Shortly after Kalle Hvidt Nielsen was appointed new CEO for B&O, the company announced a new turnaround strategy with a focus on profitability and centred on the product range. This new strategy, named 'Pole Position', is a metaphor chosen from Formula One motor racing. By using the term 'Pole Position', the new strategy is meant to signal a clear goal, a sense of urgency, teamwork and clear tasks for each team member of the organisation. The vision for B&O is to develop exclusive audio and video products differentiating on design, quality, innovation and user friendliness, for which the following initiatives have been taken:

1 Focus on product development in fewer product categories. Primarily audio and video products.
2 Focus on one technological digital platform for each category. Enabling the company to reduce the time and cost for new product launches.
3 Focus on one global sales organisation to support the 800 authorised concept stores worldwide and the 400 Shop-in-Shops.
4 Adjust the cost structure in accordance with market conditions.

Changes in product development

At B&O, the main products have always been audio and video products. According to the new strategy, related product categories such as mobile phones, MP3 players, and standalone products like DVD2 will not be developed further. Consequently, the 'Pole Position' strategy of Kalle Hvidt Nielsen has led to the termination of a range of products and product categories in order to focus on the main areas of audio and video.

B&O has further initiated the development of one basic technological digital platform for all the products in the different product domains. In the past, the technology was developed separately for each new product with respect to the design specifications. The design was thus the primary agent, and the technical solution was made to fit the design. There was a constant need to update the many different technologies, which was both costly and challenging when combining and integrating different technologies. The new technological platforms would be based on one standardised platform – 'the hardware' – with different kinds of microchips, circuit boards and special software components. This new architectural system would be owned by B&O and enable the company to find strategic partners with in-depth knowledge in special technical areas such as a software protocol for HD. The ability to combine insourced specialised technology with B&O's own technology would ensure that the company would always be in line with the newest technology. In the future

the goal is to decrease the number of strategic partners by 30 per cent and to establish longstanding relations with key partners thereby securing B&O access to new and specialised technology. The company expects the new technological platform to be fully integrated in its product domains within two years. Having developed standardised platforms for each of the product domains, B&O is expected to develop new products both more quickly and more cost efficiently. The effects of this technological change are expected to show improved results from 2010 onwards.

Market segment for TV and video systems

B&O has for many years been considered the leading high-end television manufacturer. The market for televisions has seen considerable growth primarily due to the introduction of new technology, bigger flat screens, high definition and the change from analogue to digital TV. According to Futuresource Consulting, by the end of 2008 every household in Western Europe had on average 1.8 TVs of which 31 per cent were flat screen TVs. The positive development in the market for flat screen TV is expected to continue due to the poularity of bigger screens and new digital high definition solutions. However, the flat shape of the new televisions has made it difficult for B&O to differentiate on design, and has therefore increased the competition in the different segments of the TV market.

Historically, the strength of B&O has been in what the company describes as product 'magic'. Magic can be seen as unexpected functions or features that give the product the sense of quality that similar products do not have. Especially within televisions, B&O has held a dominant position combining superior image and sound quality with exclusive designs, as seen in its BeoVision 1 TV (2000–2005) (Figure 1).

By combining a beautiful and innovative design with superior image and sound, the B&O televisions have been

Figure 1 BeoVision 1

Table 1 Products in the market for 40 inch16:9 LED/LCD televisions

TV manufacturer	Type	Screen	Resolution	Price[1]
Bang & Olufsen	BeoVision 10	40 inch 16:9 LED	1920 × 1080	£6000
Samsung	UE40B8000	40 inch 16:9 LED	1920 × 1080	£1300
Sharp	LC40LE700E	40 inch 16:9 LED	1920 × 1080	£1300
Sony	KDL-40ZX1	40 inch 16:9 LED	1920 × 1080	£1900
Loewe	Individual	40 inch 16:9 LCD	1920 × 1080	£2800

[1] £6000 ≈ €6615 ≈ $9103.

considered in a class of their own. However, when the LCD technology and the HD standard were developed and became a part of the positioning and competition in the market, B&O's dominant market position began to weaken. In terms of the technological advantage, most television producers could now present LCD televisions with the same or even better image quality than B&O and where traditional televisions required a lot of space at the rear, the new LCD and LED screens were all flat. Since B&O had lost its competitive advantage in terms of both the design element and picture quality, the question therefore remained whether or not B&O would be able to respond to this new market situation. In October 2009, the first response came from B&O as the BeoVision 10 was introduced – a new 40-inch LED television which was the first television to follow the new B&O strategy.

With very little possibility of designing a new 'television sculpture' as had happened with BeoVision 1, the idea of BeoVision 10 was to create a 'broadcast painting' for the living room. Where other LCD and LED screens more or less follow the standard 16:9 format, the new BeoVision 10 instead follows a square design (Figure 2). This had enabled B&O to include more loudspeakers and a better

sound quality than with standard LCD screens. However, besides the aluminum casing and the wall brackets on the side of the TV the question is whether BeoVision 10 has the competitive advantage that justifies the relatively high product price (Table 1).

In the television market, prices and profit margins have been under pressure due to many television producers attempting to gain market share and at the same time introduce new technologies. To achieve economies of scale, more manufacturers such as Sony and Toshiba focus only on LCD technology while others, due to lack of profitability, have withdrawn from the market.

The production of electronic products is mainly based in Asia, Sony and Panasonic in Japan dominating the industry. With the increasing commercial success of digital technology, new players such as Samsung and LG from South Korea and producers in China have entered the market with a strong position due to lower production costs.

Besides the price and the production cost, B&O is also under pressure (technology, design and price) from the big volume segment, dominated by Samsung, Sony, Panasonic, LG and Philips (together holding more than 50 per cent of the market). Other competitors are the German Loewe (Sharp holds 29 per cent of the shares), Sharp (market leader in LCD in the Japanese market) and more traditional players such as Toshiba, Hitachi and JVC all of whom today only have a marginal position in the television market (Table 2).

Figure 2 BeoVision 10

Table 2 Technology and market shares in the global TV market, 2007

Technology	%	Market shares	%
CRT-TV	18	Samsung	16
Plasma	15	Sony	12
LCD	64	Panasonic	9
Other	3	LG	9
		Philips	8
		Others	46

Source: DisplaySearch.

Cordys: innovation in business process management

D. Jan Eppink

Cordys is an innovative developer of business process management software and is headquartered in the Netherlands. Founded in 2001, its first products were introduced in the market in 2006. Cordys has to deal with formidable competitors. The case describes the history of Cordys, its philosophy and its approach to the market. It ends with a consideration of some strategic options for the future.

• • •

Introduction

In August 2009 Jan Baan, founder, Chairman and CEO of Cordys was looking back on the growth of the company since its start in October 2001, and wondering what choices might be ahead. Some quotes from an interview for this case shed light on his perception of the role of the entrepreneur.

> Successful entrepreneurship is built on vision and the ability to translate that vision into real customer benefits. But it's also about seizing opportunities that cross your path.

> I started as an entrepreneur more than 30 years ago when I founded Baan in 1978. Once you are an entrepreneur you expect to be one throughout your life. Innovation at Baan ended after 20 years; they went the M&A way so I made a fresh start with Cordys. I expect to do a lot in the next 10 years.

> The transition from innovative start up to a successful software company requires strong leadership, especially in the areas of sales, marketing and operations.

History: from Baan to Cordys

Jan Baan started his first company, 'Baan', in 1978. He had been an administrator in several smaller firms in the Netherlands, where he noticed that there was a need for better financial management and tools to support managers in general. He also noted that the many suppliers of software preferred to develop client-specific and made-to-measure solutions. This made the software more expensive than would be the case with more standardised software.

Moreover, clients were often locked in by their choice of hardware. This led to his firm adopting Unix as a programming language, since this made the user companies more independent of the computer company. The company also began developing software that is now known as ERP solutions (see the appendix for a definition of technical terms). These products were sold in the home country but also abroad. In 1981 the first subsidiary in the USA was opened. By the turn of the decade the Baan company sold its software as an OEM to such companies as HP, IBM and ASK. In April 1993 the US-based venture capitalist firm General Atlantic Partners bought a third of the company for US$21 million (€15.26m or £13.87m).[1] At that time Baan had a turnover of US$63 million, which grew to US$684 million in 1997. In 1994 Jan Baan and his brother Paul set up the Oikonomos Foundation, a charity to run projects in developing countries. They transferred a large part of their shares in Baan Company to Vanenburg, the investment company of the Oikonomos Foundation. In May 1995 Baan Company was quoted on the NASDAQ and the Amsterdam Stock Exchange. The price of the shares doubled in the two months after the IPO. In the spring of 1998 the company decided to restate its earnings over the first quarter in view of changed SEC rules regarding revenue recognition. This led to questions in the financial press. In July 1998 Jan Baan decided to leave the company. Eventually, in the summer of 2000, Baan Company was sold to Invensys, a UK-based conglomerate.

Oikonomos sold part of its shares of Baan Company with the first IPO and again on two later occasions. Oikonomos

_____

[1] $1 ≈ £0.66 ≈ €0.725.

Table 1 Investments (in €m)

2001	28.2
2002	11.2
2003	14.0
2004	26.6
2005	33.0
2006	30.0
2007	60.0
2008	30.0

Source: www.cordys.com and Cordys presentations.

invested part of the money it received for the shares in Top Tier and WebEx, two innovative software companies. Top Tier was sold to SAP in March 2001, which netted Oikonomos some US$200 million. Part of the proceeds were used to finance the start-up of Cordys in autumn 2001. The shares of WebEx were also sold when Cisco acquired WebEx in 2007 for $3.2 billion. Around the middle of 2007, Argonaut Private Equity[2] decided to invest $67 million in Cordys. All these funds helped finance the start-up of Cordys and then the further development of its products (Table 1).

Foundations of the Cordys philosophy

Two different and apparently irreconcilable observations led to the start of Cordys. The first is that companies have to adapt very quickly to what is happening in their industry. This is especially the case if the online channel is a major part of the business strategy. To succeed, an agile consumer-driven innovation is required, which has a direct impact on critical business processes. The second is that often these processes are embedded in complex IT systems that are infrequently replaced, if at all (ten years on average).

Replacing or adapting such systems is complex, expensive and time-consuming. To take advantage of new developments in the market requires reaction times of days or even hours.

The speed of innovation manifests itself in what is now called 'the cloud' (see appendix). Cordys has chosen, as the only supplier so far, a strategy that aims at combining the best of both worlds for its customers. The Cordys Business Operations Platform was developed from scratch to do exactly what today's companies need: make business processes more agile and flexible and lower IT costs drastically. The platform bridges the gap between the existing inflexible

---

[2] Argonaut Private Equity is a US-based venture capital company that invests in and helps build emerging market leaders. It has more than $2 billion under management, provided by a single entrepreneur. Its investments vary from $1 to $200 million and cover all continents.

but stable business software and hardware (for instance from Oracle, SAP, IBM, and HP) and the dynamic world of the internet where a lot of innovation is going on to which companies have to adapt.

Jan Baan remarked in an interview for this case:

> You can do everything for the first time today without Bill Gates' Microsoft but with competitors such as Google. You are no longer forced to use Microsoft like everyone did till some years ago. It's the same with Larry Ellison's data base. In the new world order, Microsoft and Oracle are still giants but they are not core to everything today. You have alternatives.

Product development

Product development was helped by some specific circumstances. One was that Jan Baan had an overall idea of the kind of software that would be needed in a future in which internet speed would increase dramatically as well as having the necessary agility. When Top Tier was sold to SAP in spring 2001, one of the conditions Jan Baan as CEO of Vanenburg imposed was that Theodore van Dongen, now Cordys' Chief Technology Officer, and his development team would transfer from Top Tier to Cordys. With this, an enormous source of knowledge and creativity became quickly available. Furthermore, from time to time former Baan developers approached Cordys to find out if they could work there. The takeover by Invensys and the further integration of Baan was not welcomed by quite a few of them. Furthermore, Jan Baan was one of the first to involve engineers from India in software development in the late 1980s. These contacts he used to set up Cordys India, which now has some 400 people involved in software development.

The value proposition

Compared with traditional software, Cordys' software has a number of advantages. First of all, the 'time to value' can be measured in days rather than months or even longer. Upgrades are done automatically, which makes superfluous the often painful and risky process of manual upgrading. If the traditional software is custom designed there may be additional problems with getting updates, since these may have to be custom developed. Users pay a subscription per year, so there is no longer any need to sign contracts for expensive multi-year software licences as with traditional software. Moreover the software is easy to customise and use, since this was specifically demanded of the developers. The software was also developed as an integrated whole, rather than a product in which modules of acquired software had to be integrated. If a client company decides to choose cloud computing, rather than on-premise

Table 2 Revenues (in €m)

2006	5.0
2007	10.0
2008	20.0
2009	40.0 (estimate)

Source: www.cordys.com and Cordys presentations.

computing, there is no need for complex infrastructure. Finally, security and compliance with internal or external regulations is centralised, rather than fragmented. Fundamentally this boils down to lower costs and greater flexibility and speed of implementation.

Going to market

Cordys began selling its products in 2006, after more than four years of investing in product development. Sales in the beginning were aimed at further developing the product and knowing customers intimately rather than at maximising revenue. After 2006 sales started to increase at a high rate. Revenue for 2008 was around €20 million, with an estimate for 2009 of €40 million. In July 2009 the company announced that in the second quarter of the year licence revenue had increased by 200 per cent compared to Q2 of 2008. Q2 of 2009 showed a increase of 100 per cent compared to Q1 of 2009 (Table 2).

Cordys sells its software through three distribution channels. The first is through its own sales organisation. The company has four subunits: Cordys America with three offices, Cordys Europe with three national offices, Cordys Asia (excluding China) with offices in Hyderabad and Mumbai in India, and Cordys China with offices in Beijing and Shanghai. Another distribution channel is its partner network with companies such as Accenture and Capgemini (see Table 3). These companies have their own client base interested in the products, as well as a highly qualified workforce that can implement the products, often in co-operation with employees from Cordys. The third channel was opened in May 2009: Google Business Solutions Market Place. By buying a $95 a year licence to use Cordys

Table 3 Some major customers by geographic area

Americas	Comcast, Lockheed Martin, New York Stock Exchange, The World Bank, US Xpress
EMEA	ABB, ABN Amro Verzekeringen, AXA, Deutsche Kreditbank, Fortis Insurance, KPN, RWE/Essent, Siemens healthcare
ASIAPAC	Aegon Religare, China Mobile, China Post Logistics, Philips Electronics, Tata Motors

Some major partners
Accenture, Atos Origin, Capgemini, Cognizant, CSC, HP, Infosys, Logica, Ordina, Satyam, Teamsum, WIPRO

Source: www.cordys.com and Cordys presentations.

Process Factory, Google Apps users can build and run their own process flows in the cloud. Moreover, they can include unstructured collaboration into a structured workflow. Users can also build their own situational applications for such activities as travel approval, expense reports, new hire setup, budget approval, and payment requests.

Cordys has identified a number of vertical markets as its main targets. All of these have in common a very high level of IT expenses per employee. Banking and Insurance have the highest expenses in this respect: well over $24,000 per year. Utilities are also great spenders with $17,000, followed by Media with a little over $15,500 per year. Given the potential for reduction of IT-related expenses, companies in these industries have the most to win by adopting the Cordys approach.

Market acceptance was not immediate, even though the advantages of Cordys' approach was clear. Mark de Simone, Chief Sales and Business Development Officer, observed:

> One of the most formidable barriers to entry which Cordys faced in its first years of existence was 'inertia'. Even when all the tests from financial to technology, from ease of use to business sponsorship were passed, the last defence was always linked to the apparent cost of change. We often reminded our customers of the simplicity of the Web and how the world of transactions had changed overnight and that Cordys was heralding to interactions the same simplicity that the Web had heralded to transactions. Regardless of the huge logic of adoption, the fear of change and the career-changing impact for managers was always the toughest psychological barrier we had to overcome.

Variety of players in the industry

There are many different kinds of players in the industry. One group is the *web specialists*, for instance, Google and Salesforce.com (see appendix). These two companies have shown enormous growth over the last few years. Google's turnover increased from $1466 million in the fiscal year (FY) 2003 to $21,795 million in 2008. Salesforce.com's revenues for FY 2004 were $96 million and grew to $1076 for the fiscal year that ended on 31 January 2009. Another group of players are the *back office specialists*, such as SAP and Oracle. These are the suppliers of many of the now existing legacy systems and therefore have a large installed base. Total revenue for SAP increased from €7025 million in FY 2003 to €11,567 in FY 2008. Oracle's total revenues increased from $9672 million in FY 2002 to $23,252 in 2009.[3] In 2007 Cisco, a supplier of networking equipment (routers, switches etc.), acquired WebEx, a

---

[3] Please note that Oracle's fiscal year ends 31 May.

company that supplies web conferencing and collaboration solutions. Phil Wainewright[4] hints at the possibility that Cisco aims at positioning the WebEx application portfolio as a competitor to the likes of Google Apps, Salesforce.com, and Microsoft Online Services. He is, however, quite sceptical about the chances. Cisco System's turnover has not grown as fast as that of the companies mentioned above. Turnover in FY 2002 for Cisco was $18.9 billion with an increase to $39.5 in FY 2008, followed by a decline to $36.1 billion in 2009.[5] This development might put pressure on the company to find new sources of revenue and profit.

The web specialists and the back office specialists were not happy with the value proposition of the new entrant. On their actions Mark de Simone remarked:

> Cordys challenged the entire industry model on a number of fronts by defining a dramatically faster and lower cost way to design and modify enterprise and value-chain processes. The reaction from established competitors with vested interests in the status quo was immediate. Firstly they attacked on the architecture front by leveraging the "dogma" of the last 10 years of application development. In other words, it did not matter whether this new way was dramatically more productive, but it created confusion and complexity for the IT organisations to deal with the innovation. By playing the card of the traditional IT manager to whom the business had delegated the technical decisions, the competitors played the card of protecting the people whose past professional lives they had helped develop to the detriment of a radically better business model.

And also:

> Even competitors like Salesforce.com which created a new online model for deploying traditional CRM applications and disrupted the Oracle model, found itself on a defensive approach when asked to integrate multiple applications to its core CRM one and needed to reinvent a couple of integration mechanisms which largely failed. The message about Cordys coming all the way from the top was that our technology was not good, while probably, one could have faulted our go-to-market but not our technology. Salesforce.com had become a defender as opposed to an aggressor. We were the new Barbarians attacking Rome.

The future

Several strategic options might be considered in the months ahead. As far as business-level strategy is concerned, it would be crucial to see how competitors, older or new, would react to the market entry of the Cordys software. Might a hypercompetitive environment be in the making? As far as strategic directions are concerned, possibilities for market development might be further analysed. Cordys already operates in major developed and developing markets; would further enlargement of geographic scope be a possibility? In his book *The Way to Market Leadership* Jan Baan[6] mentioned that an ideal scenario would be for Cordys to become a good cash cow for the Oikonomos Foundation. Could that mean that eventually there could be a sale of Cordys or an IPO as with Baan Company?

---

[4] http://blogs.zdnet.com/SAAS?p=804.
[5] Cisco System's fiscal year ends end of July.

[6] Jan Baan (2005) *The Way to Market Leadership: My Life as an entrepreneur*. Putten, Vanenburg Group.

APPENDIX Technical terms

Enterprise Resource Planning (ERP software) Planning of business processes goes back a very long time. F.W. Taylor wrote about it as early as 1903 in his book *Shop Management*. This only had to do with planning of production processes in manufacturing plants. This kind of planning was all done by hand. In the 1970s this kind of planning eventually evolved into Material Requirements Planning (MRP) where clients' orders were translated into materials to be used (and purchased) and production plans. Still this was mostly done by hand. In the 1980s MRP was expanded to include other business processes, such as inventory control, human resources planning, financial planning, and accounting. Later this became known as Enterprise Resource Planning. The drop in costs of computers and computing power helped in the growth of ERP software. Developers of ERP software are, for instance, SAP, Oracle, Peoplesoft and Baan Company.

Cloud computing Many years ago John Cage of Sun Microsystems was the first to coin the phrase: 'the network is the computer'. By that he meant that in future a person could do a lot of 'computing' on other computers than his or her own. Since the speed of the internet has increased dramatically, this now has become possible. A person can email using software, computers, and databases owned and operated, for instance, by Google. The only thing one needs to do that is a web browser. For companies it is now possible to use business software and data bases that run on computers owned by a specialist company. New software enables companies in a supply chain to link their operations to increase productivity. This whole set of inter-linked computers, software and services offered is often called 'the cloud'. The cloud makes new business models possible. For instance, a company does not need to own hardware and software, but need only pay for the use of it. Because of the cloud, cost structures for users can change from one with high up-front costs and limited variable costs, to one with low initial investments but with costs that vary with use.

Web specialists and back office specialists A web specialist is a company that focuses on the web interface between the user of a service on the internet and the company that offers that service. This interface includes for instance navigation possibilities offered by the portal. Web specialists are for instance WebEx and Top Tier. A back office specialist is a company that specialises in software to run operations in a company. These operations are invisible for the user, for instance the handling of claims in an insurance company. The web specialist will develop the software for the interface with the customers that have a claim to settle, whereas the back office specialist develops the software for processing the claim including payment to the client. Examples of back office specialists are Oracle and SAP.

iPod to iPad: innovation and entrepreneurship at Apple

John Ashcroft

In 2001, Apple developed the concept of the digital hub – with the Apple Mac at the centre of a wide range of digital software and hardware for the consumer market. The succession of product developments by 2010 included the iPod, the iTouch, the iPhone and the iPad. By 2010, Apple had sold 250 million iPods, offering 140,000 applications from an iTunes store that had generated 3 billion downloads. Apple had become 'the largest mobile devices company in the world'. The case explores the importance of innovation and intrapreneurship at Apple as the roots of corporate success.

● ● ●

Introduction

In September 2009, Apple Inc. announced profits of $7.5 billion[1] ($\approx$ €5.4bn $\approx$ £4.9bn) on sales of $36.5 billion ($\approx$ €26.51bn $\approx$ £24.16bn). The company had sold over 200 million iPods, a product launched just eight years earlier. The company also announced it has sold over 2 billion applications for the iPhone, a product launched just two years earlier. The Apple success story since 2001 is staggering and the iPod is considered to be key in the transformation of Apple's fortunes.

In 2001, the year of the iPod launch, the company was experiencing some difficulty. 2001 was a critical year for Apple Inc. Sales had fallen to under $6 billion and the company announced losses of almost $350 million. The US economy was heading towards recession, with growth slowing. Apple sales had fallen from $8 billion in 2000 to $5.7 billion. Operating income had turned from a profit of $522 million to a loss of $344 million. Sales in the USA and Europe had fallen by 30 per cent, in Japan they had fallen by almost 50 per cent. Gross margins fell from 27 per cent to 23 per cent.

Desktop computer sales had been hammered, unit sales of the PowerMac had fallen by 35 per cent and those of the iMac by 45 per cent. Portable sales volumes were static and revenues were down by 8 per cent. Software service and other revenues had fallen by 13 per cent. The company was heavily dependent on the business and creative professional market. Over 76 per cent of sales were in the industrial and commercial sector. Consumer exposure was limited to the student/education market at some 15 per cent of revenues.

The high-end 'advanced' consumer market, the AB premium sector, accounted for the balance. The profit-generating Power Mac was at the wrong end of the product

Steve Jobs
Source: Getty Images/Bloomberg.

---

[1] $1 $\approx$ €0.73 $\approx$ £0.66

---

lifecycle curve. The iMac was dated. It had never really looked cool. The product range needed a revamp or better still a new product altogether.

Should Apple develop further into the consumer market? A consumer electronics product perhaps? Earlier experience with the Newton PDA (personal digital assistant) platform, the Apple Message Pad in the 1980s and the Apple Pippin games console in the 1990s was not a good omen. None of these consumer electronics products had been successful. In 2000, Apple considered video cameras, digital cameras, DVD players and music. After analysing the alternatives the company chose music. The iPod, 'One thousand songs in your pocket', was launched in 2001. So how and why did Apple develop this strategy?

The digital hub strategy

By 2001, Apple had developed the concept of the digital hub, a concept which envisaged the Apple Mac at the centre of a wide range of digital software for the consumer market. As the 2001 Financial Report declared:

> The Company believes that personal computing is entering a new era in which the personal computer will function for both professionals and consumers as the digital hub for advanced new digital devices such as digital music players, personal digital assistants, digital still and movie cameras, CD and DVD players, and other electronic devices. The attributes of the personal computer, including its ability to run complex applications, possess a high-quality user interface, contain large and relatively inexpensive storage, and easily connect to the Internet in multiple ways and at varying speeds, can individually add value to these devices and interconnect them as well. Apple is the only company in the PC industry that designs and manufactures the entire personal computer – from the hardware and operating system to sophisticated applications, and ties it all together with Apple's innovative industrial design, intuitive ease-of-use, and built-in networking, graphics, and multimedia capabilities – uniquely positioning the Company to offer digital hub products and solutions.

Apple had produced a unique stable of software products to facilitate this objective: iDVD, iMovie, iTunes and iPhoto. The organisation well understood the 'unique position' Apple enjoyed in the ability to design and manufacture the complete suite of hardware and software with internet connectivity. (The iTunes store was a major component of the iPod success which was to follow in 2003.)

The Apple recipe for success

In its filing to the SEC in 2001, Apple's Annual Report outlined the Key Success Factors (KSFs) in the computer and consumer electronics market: relative price performance, product quality, reliability, design innovation, software availability, product features, marketing and distribution capacity, service and support, corporate reputation, internet connectivity and constant development. The list is not so much a checklist but a tick list of Apple's capability.

In terms of constant development, 'Kaizen', the Apple campus address is '1 infinite loop, Cupertino, USA'. The address is a mantra for constant product development, smaller, simpler, less expensive devices, an infinite loop of product progression.

Market segmentation

In 2001, Apple identified four key segments within the market: Business, Creative Professionals, Education, and 'high-end' consumers. Apple's core product strengths were in the areas of CAD (Computer Aided Design) and DTP (Desktop Publishing). Apple and Quark Express were the core products for a high number of publishing solutions, including newspapers and magazines. In 2000, 75 per cent of sales were to the traditional business and professional markets. By 2009, the situation had reversed, with 60 per cent of sales in the consumer markets of education, students and the broader consumer market. The search for a consumer product in 2001 was the cause of this dramatic turnaround.

The search for a consumer product

Apple wanted to enter the market for consumer digital devices. Digital cameras and camcorders were well developed with big players in the game. Apple would face tough competition. On the other hand, the market for Digital MP3 players was relatively underdeveloped with no big players involved and significant design flaws in the products on offer. Apple chose music, or more specifically music on the move, because the market potential was huge and no one had 'got the recipe right'. In addition, as Apple's founder and chief executive Steve Jobs explained at the iPod launch, 'why music, because we all love music and it's always great to do something we love'.

Launch of the iPod

'Music on the move' had been pioneered by Sony with the Walkman and the Discman but the digital age beckoned. Consumers had music stored on computers. Updating the collections online was possible but the launch of Napster in 1999 and the subsequent legal challenge confused consumers about the legality of it all. Travelling with a large music library was only possible with a box of CD favourites. At the time of the iPod launch the most expensive MP3 players with flash memory were selling for around $249. The Rio 600 with 64MB of flash memory retailed at $199.

Price was no barrier to Apple. By tradition the company tended to follow a premium price entry model. Initial sales volumes and supply chain capability could be tested before adjustment of the market price followed.

The MP3 player offered the technical solution to digital music on the move. Hard drive players offered greater capacity up to 100MB but at a price. Data transfer was slow and early products were difficult to use and poorly designed. The chip for the players had been developed in 1997 but takeup of the product was shunned by the major manufacturers. Early players in the market were Saehan, Pontis and Diamond Rio. In 1999, some 23 other companies launched into the MP3 market. With the exception of Sony, Samsung and Thompson/RCA, all were small and medium-sized entrepreneurial firms and industry newcomers, many relying on sales through the internet.

By 2000, the US market was valued at $80 million, rising by 25 per cent to $100 million in 2001. Volumes had increased from 510,000 units to over 700,000 units. The market was fragmented, with as many as 50 manufacturers largely dependent on internet sales. The largest market shares were held by Diamond Rio and Pontis but both were financially vulnerable. (Pontis ceased production in 2002 and Diamond Rio filed for bankruptcy in the following year.) The large industry manufacturers such as Sony, Samsung and Thomson RCA were not big players. It was potentially a huge market but, according to Jobs, 'No one had found the recipe' for success.

Key success factors in the market were design, size, capacity, battery life, software and download facility. The Diamond Rio PMP 300 MP3 player had a capacity of 32MB with an additional storage slot capacity. Retailing for $200, it had the capacity to play 12 songs and an approximately 10-hour battery life. The product was not without design flaws and was vulnerable to performance problems. For Apple, the KSF mantra was outlined annually in the Annual Report. The market was attractive in terms of size and growth potential. Since the market was fragmented and had no major players, relative market and financial strengths could be brought into play. Tony Fadell, a former employee of Philips, had ideas for a brand new MP3 player; smaller in size, with large capacity, hard drive based, with a download content access and delivery system to legally obtain music.

Apple seized the opportunity to hire Fadell. He was given a budget and a development team and a one year to market timetable. Apple developed all three components in-house: the music store, the player and the software on the computer. They all worked together seamlessly. Steve Jobs had hands-on experience with the product design team at every stage. Design ethos – from out to in.

At Apple, engineering is reversed into design. Apple employees talk of 'deep collaboration' or 'cross-pollination' or 'concurrent engineering'. Products do not pass from team to team. There are not discrete sequential development stages. It is simultaneous and organic. Products are worked on in parallel by all departments at once, in endless rounds of interdisciplinary design review meetings.

The first iPod was launched with a 5GB Toshiba hard drive, a capacity for 1000 tunes and a price tag of $399 in October 2001, later followed by a 10GB version. The product was launched in Europe one month later: '1000 tunes in your pocket'.

In April 2003, the iTunes Music Store opened. Access to music and downloads became even easier. It was a unique blend of hardware, software and content availability.

Apple's iPod has experienced phenomenal growth since 2001. Like the Mac, the iPod largely created a new market rather than displacing an existing one. In 2002, Apple had 33 per cent of the hard drive market. A year later, it had 64 per cent of that market. Apple more than doubled sales, while the rest of the market failed to grow at all.

In 2004, Apple had 82 per cent of the hard drive market with sales of 2 million in the winter quarter. Other competitors were selling less than half a million units combined. Apple was not eating into other players' sales, it was greatly expanding the entire market for hard drive audio players.

By 2008, Apple was selling over 50 million units a year worldwide, with a dominant 75 per cent of the US market. The iTunes Music Store accounts for 87 per cent of all legal digital music sales in the USA. The success of the iPod has had a significant knock-on effect on the Apple core business as more consumers have experience of the great Apple product line.

Brand development and product extension

Apple had always relied on a programme of constant improvement in the product offer: smaller, simpler, more features, less expensive. By 2006 the iPod was into a fifth generation and the product family was widened with the appearance of the iPod Shuffle and the iPod Nano. In 2007, the iPod Touch appeared. The extended product offer was aimed to swamp the market map in terms of price segmentation and capacity.

The Nano was a flash-based product released in January 2005 costing $99 for a 512MB version. The solid state Nano appeared in February, available in 2GB and 4GB versions. In October 2005, the fifth generation iPod appeared, available in 30GB and 60GB with video play capacity. An 80GB version was to follow. The Shuffle appeared around the same time. Apple introduced two versions of the 'iPod Shuffle', priced at just $99 or $149, and respectively holding about 120 and 240 songs based on 512MB or 1GB of memory.

Based on flash memory, the new player was aimed at a low-end segment of the market that had been largely untapped by Apple to date.

By the time the Microsoft Zune arrived, Apple had created and dominated a new market empire, defended by a product range extended in price, range and quality. From the $99 Shuffle to the top-end video iPods with 80GB and video play capability priced at $399, the array was extensive.

In 2009 the iPod Nano complete with video camera appeared. The digital hub strategy continued to be developed and enhanced: music, photos, video.

The iTouch and iPhone

By 2007, the iPod product offer was comprehensive but maybe lacking internet connectivity and mobile connection. It was time to introduce the iPhone. The first iPhone was launched in 2007 but almost before you could fill the address book, the iPhone 3G was on the way. Launched in 2008, the improved 3G performance followed the Apple Kaizen mantra: 'Constant improvement – one infinite loop'. In 2009, the company launched the iPhone 3GS complete with camera and video camera. More features, much faster and with the new iPhone 3.0 software, it was the digital hub strategy incarnate: mobile, internet, music, camera, video.

The iPhone 2G only supported WiFi, GSM and Bluetooth. Slow speeds meant surfing the internet was quite limited. The iPhone 3G introduced third generation speeds to the original flagship model, and it also supported WiFi, GSM and Bluetooth. This made for a better experience, surfing, watching videos and downloading data onto the phone from the internet.

In 2007, iPhone sales were worth $123 million. In the first full year of sales, 2008, revenues were $1.8 billion; in 2009 revenues increased to $6.5 billion. The company had sold over 30 million phones since launch.

The iPhone had captured some 25 per cent of the US smartphone market, challenging the RIM BlackBerry and pushing Nokia into a furious programme of product development.

Where next for Apple? The games console

By the end of 2009, some analysts and pundits were arguing the next product for Apple should be the Games console, but was this the right strategy?

The Nintendo Wii, MS Xbox 360 and Sony PS3 dominate the market. Lifetime console shipment numbers for the US were 20.7 million for the Wii, 15.5 million for the Xbox 360 and 7.9 million for the PS3. Respective market shares were 47 per cent, 35 per cent and 18 per cent.

It is a big market. By 2012, the market is forecast to increase to a value of $25 billion and sales of 100 million units.

Apple has a strong brand franchise, a clear route to market and thousands of applications available for the iPhone and the iTouch. But this is not the MP3 market at the turn of the millennium. Three big players with strong technology operate in a market where shares swing with technology advances and latest product introductions.

Similar KSFs apply and the Kaizen ethic is apparent but the investment is huge. Rumours abounded that Apple was recruiting game executives and a raft of gaming-related patents. On the other hand, Apple is adept at misinformation and misdirection. The console was unlikely to be the next big Apple move.

Where next for Apple? The Apple tablet computer

In January 2010, Apple launched the iPad in a further extension of the digital hub strategy. The iPad is a computer with no physical keyboard but a touch screen device offering internet connectivity on the move with WiFi and 3G capability. Initially launched in the USA, the iPad offered a 10-inch touch screen and retailed for around $500 for the basic model. The iPad enables users to read newspapers, books and magazines, play music, read emails, store photos and watch videos with the ability to download content from the iTunes store.

In 2010, Apple also launched the iBookstore with the capability to download e-books and the opportunity to use the iPad as an e-book reader.

In terms of pricing, traditionally Apple would enter a new product with a premium price tag, developing volume and segment penetration before relaxing the price constraint. For the iPad the pricing strategy was geared to getting the product into the hands of as many people as possible 'right from the start'. Magnanimous marketing, perhaps or maybe with a strategic eye on the competition from the Sony e-reader and Amazon Kindle book readers.

References:

Jim Carlton, *Apple the Inside Story of Intrigue, Egomania and Business Blunders*, Times Books, 1997.

Michael Malone, *Infinite Loop: How Apple, the World's most Insanely Great Computer Company, Went Insane*, Currency/Doubleday, 1999.

Owen Linzmayer, *Apple Confidential 2.0: The Real Story of Apple Computer, Inc.*, No Starch Press, 1999.

John Sculley, *Odyssey: Pepsi to Apple, A Journey of Adventure, Ideas and the Future*, Harpercollins, 1987.

Steve Wozniak, *iWoz: Computer Geek to Cult iCon. Getting to the Core of Apple's Inventor*, W.W. Norton, 2006.

CASE STUDY

Grupo Ferrovial and the acquisition of Amey plc

Eric Cassells

This case follows the events leading to the rapid deterioration of Amey PLC's business in the UK in 2002, its acquisition in a distress sale by Grupo Ferrovial, the subsequent recovery of Amey's business, and its integration into Ferrovial Servicios. Amey and Ferrovial were following parallel strategies of diversification away from construction towards the growing services businesses of facilities management, infrastructure maintenance and operations, and the acquisition of Amey in early 2003 was intended as a decisive step in the internationalisation of Ferrovial's portfolio. The recovery of Amey's business in subsequent years records both turnaround and change management strategies, whilst aspects of Ferrovial's approach to corporate strategy and governance are also discussed.

● ● ●

On 29 May 2003 Grupo Ferrovial took full control of Amey plc after a recommended bid of 32 UK pence (€0.44 or $0.53) per share, valuing Amey at £84 million (€128m or $139m). This price reflected Amey's weakened position after an often successful, but uncontrolled rapid diversification and growth strategy had left it at the mercy of its bankers. Amey and Ferrovial had both been established construction sector companies in their respective national markets (UK and Spain), before both moving to diversify and spread risk in the infrastructure maintenance and facilities management sectors in the 1990s. Both had achieved some success – Amey in the emerging and fast-moving market for public sector 'Private Finance Initiative' service contracts in the UK, and Ferrovial principally within the Spanish national market.

If the acquisition was a lifeline to an Amey group struggling to maintain its cash resources and ability to finance itself, for Ferrovial it was a critical first step in an aggressive strategy of international acquisition and diversification which would see it become a global leader in integrated construction and services. It was also an acquisition whose success would have to be measured in the creation of shareholder value.

'Spain is too small' – how Ferrovial came to acquire Amey

Ferrovial was founded in 1952 by Rafael del Pino (father of the current group Chairman), with an initial focus on

---
Exchange rate in May 2003 £ = €1.39 = $1.65.

railway maintenance. Evolving into construction, Ferrovial made a decisive move into road construction in the mid-1960s. Ferrovial launched its shares with an IPO (Initial Public Offering) on 5 May 1999, with the del Pino family continuing to control approximately 60 per cent of the group thereafter. What followed the IPO was a period of rapid international expansion and diversification, capped by the acquisition in June 2006 of British Airports Authority, the largest independent airport operator globally.

As a company focusing primarily on construction within the Spanish national market, Ferrovial's business in the early 1990s was cash generative, but operating on relatively low margins within the competitive Spanish construction industry. Diversification and the drive for growth led Ferrovial into the services and facilities management sector ('services' hereafter) and into infrastructure investment, becoming a leading builder and operator of express toll roads in Spain.

The services sector offered Ferrovial a degree of risk diversification, characterised by higher margins and a longer cash cycle. Services contracts typically required heavy initial outlays of cash, but with more predictable positive cash flows over a longer contract life.

By the late 1990s, however, Ferrovial corporate management had come to the conclusion – as had many large Spanish companies – that 'Spain is too small'. The services sector was concentrated and dominated by three or four major competitors, and prospects for growth and profits were restricted. The goal was to find bigger markets where Ferrovial could lever its services expertise profitably.

This case was prepared by Eric Cassells of the Economics and International Business department at Oxford Brookes University Business School. It is intended as a basis for class discussion and not as an illustration of good or bad practice. The author would like to gratefully acknowledge the participation and contribution of Gillian Duggan, Mel Ewell, Steve Helliwell, José Leo, Iñigo Meirás, Andy Milner, Andrew Nelson, Alfonso Perez, and Chris Webster in the study. ©Eric Cassells, 2010. Not to be reproduced or quoted without permission.

Whilst many peer organisations in Spain chose to expand in the Spanish-speaking markets of Latin America,[i] Ferrovial's corporate managers looked elsewhere. Initially that meant more developed markets. The markets in the major developed European economies were researched for opportunities. Most of this research pointed to the United Kingdom as the most fertile market for expansion for three reasons:

1 It was perceived as the most 'open' of the European economies, with a history of foreign companies being encouraged to acquire or take stakes in British companies.

2 The UK had effectively pioneered the rapid growth of the services sector, through influential initiatives in the mass privatisation of public services and government-owned corporations and agencies, Private Finance Initiatives (PFI)[1] which sought to introduce private capital into the provision of public services, and Public Private Partnerships (PPP) which encouraged commercial companies to enter into joint ventures to build public infrastructure and run related services.

3 UK customers had become sophisticated as this market grew, with services provision contracts becoming more demanding. The market was no longer solely price driven, and the ability to demonstrate capabilities, expertise and a track record of delivery had become important.

The United Kingdom was therefore identified as the most favourable market for Ferrovial's first major international foray, and a period of researching potential target acquisitions started. Amongst the candidates examined were Serco (deemed 'too big'), Interserve, Jarvis and Amey. The last two had been identified as key potential targets because of their focus on facilities management and infrastructure maintenance services, but initial informal discussions between chief executives had been rejected by both target companies. In late 2002, however, the corporate finance division of PricewaterhouseCoopers in London

approached Ferrovial with a 'unique acquisition opportunity'. That unique opportunity turned out to be Amey plc – a major quoted UK services and facilities management company in financial distress.

Amey plc – 'too many good ideas'

When Steve Helliwell started at Amey in 1987, he joined a construction company with 400 employees. Amey was part of the large Hanson group of companies, and Steve watched as five of the Amey team led a management buyout from Hanson in 1989, and subsequently floated the company on the London Stock Exchange in 1994. With a reputation for strong financial controls, the company management decided to diversify into infrastructure and services management, winning early success with the UK's Ministry of Defence, the Highways Agency (winning the UK's first ever area road network management contract), and in the privatisation of British Rail in 1996.

This early success emboldened the company and a strategy to abandon construction in favour of infrastructure management and maintenance services coincided with the arrival of a new CEO in 1997.

Amey's new CEO, Brian Staples, has been described as an 'ideas man'. He set extremely ambitious stretch targets for Amey under the 'Project 100' initiative. Staples' goal was that Amey should be quoted within the primary UK FTSE stock market listing of the top 100 companies, with a market capitalisation of at least £1 billion. Thus began a period pursuing rapid growth targets, with all significant UK PFI contracts covering infrastructure management being bid for, and an aggressive programme of 'exotic' diversifications away from the core services business. The diversification strategy included setting up a business unit to develop information technology services (specifically customer information systems for railway stations), a common enough initiative during the years of the 'dot.com' boom which typically saw the value of technology stocks being massively upgraded (temporarily) on the markets.

With typical pragmatism, Iñigo Meirás (now CEO of Ferrovial) credits Staples as a 'visionary', but argues that 'the limits to growth were not seen'. Specifically:

1 The cost of bidding for public sector PFI contracts was not fully understood, with Amey incurring a cost of £40 million in 2002.[ii] Worse, industry accounting norms at this time allowed for the capitalisation of these bidding costs with no negative impact on the company's high reported profits and incentive schemes.

2 Limited planning had been made as to how the investment in a portfolio of these cash-hungry contracts was to be financed when they were successful – and Amey was nothing if not successful in bidding.

---

[1] The Public Finance Initiative (PFI) was increasingly used in the United Kingdom in the 1990s and 2000s as a means for government to access private sector investment capital to finance capital intensive public sector infrastructure projects and services. In return for providing the capital to fund the project or services, private sector companies were, typically, awarded associated construction, operations services, facilities management and maintenance contracts, often over a long time period. These contracts could cover a range of sectors such as transportation infrastructure, hospital construction and maintenance, and services for the military. The initiatives were part of a range of policies intended to provide funds for projects that might not otherwise have been completed, to instil private finance disciplines within public sector projects, and to reduce the size of government indebtedness recorded in the PSBR (Public Sector Borrowing Requirement).

3 The diversifications were similarly resource intensive in terms of cash and in terms of specialist capabilities which Amey had no experience of, and involved a level of business complexity that Amey was unfamiliar with.

Financial discipline had declined and Amey was 'throwing money at projects'. By 2002, these cash pressures had built up and come to a head relatively suddenly. Amey retreated from bidding on a number of then current contracts. Critically, Amey's high-profile success in winning a 33.33 per cent stake in the Tube Lines venture to operate and maintain a number of London Underground train lines was put at risk as it became clear that Amey could not finance its forward commitments.

Amey – from growth to survival

In January 2003 Mel Ewell found himself (as acting CEO of Amey) leading the directors in presenting a survival plan to their bankers, on which rested their ability to borrow the funds to pay the salaries of their employees that month. Ewell says that he feared the company had become a 'dead man walking'.

Ewell had arrived at Amey in late 2001 as Operations Director, having worked in the industry for a number of years. He knew he was joining a company that was known for 'energy, drive and optimism', one which had experienced six or seven years of success, and which had watched its valuation climb in a bull market. Ewell became concerned over the need for financial transparency in relation to the company's commitments arising from bidding for new contracts. He described Amey's outlook as one of 'having too many pigeons flying by'.

According to Andrew Nelson (now CFO of Amey), 2002 turned out to be the 'crunch year' for Amey. As early as April 2002, Amey was forced to make an announcement that the annual results would be off-target. In fact, the cash pressures at Amey had been building up and 2002 saw the first attempt to rein in spending with a target to cut overheads by 10 per cent. In the face of continued spending on more and many new contracts, and on diversification into technology provision, such a modest initiative was doomed to failure. The core services business remained successful and the contracts continued to generate cash. This cash, however, was being diverted into funding the technology business and the high level of bidding activity, which left Steve Helliwell (now in a role as Services Director) desperately trying to ensure his suppliers were paid and the workforce motivated. In the words of Chris Webster (now COO at Amey), Amey was quite suddenly seen as 'flaky' by trusted partners.

Early 2002 also saw Amey's Finance Director resign, and a successor was appointed by the third quarter of the year. Worse was to follow, however, as the replacement lasted less than 30 days before resigning in turn. Almost inevitably this became the signal for the bankers to turn their attention to Amey, and start exerting their influence. Events accelerated.

Having established that Amey was technically in default on its borrowings, the company was placed on 'special support' by its bankers, and an interim finance director from chartered accountants Deloitte was appointed to reassure the banks over Amey's financial discipline. Amey's perilous position quickly became obvious to investors:

- The level of payments made to suppliers was restricted by the banks, further straining these crucial operating relationships.
- In order to raise cash, Amey's most valuable asset (the portfolio of PFI contracts) was put up for sale (the deal to sell the portfolio to Laing Construction was closed in March 2003).
- In November 2002, CEO Brian Staples was told to find a buyer to rescue Amey.
- Unable to fund the valuable 33.33 per cent stake in Tube Lines, Amey's joint venture partners were required to use their own cash to close the deal on Amey's behalf, allowing Amey the option of buying back the stake within six months.
- On 31 December 2002, Brian Staples stood down as CEO, allowing Mel Ewell to step into the role.

In January 2003, Mel Ewell and his fellow directors found themselves persuading the banks to keep funding Amey, so that salaries and wage liabilities could be met. A 'siege mentality' had taken hold.

Due diligence – 'Amey was a car that broke down on the way to the garage, and what it needed most was petrol'

Amey survived January 2003. The banks continued to provide funds, based on the reintroduction of strict financial controls and the plan for recovery presented to them. Perhaps just as critical to Amey's survival was the announcement that – in a statement of faith despite Amey's troubles – the UK Highways Agency was awarding Amey a critical contract to manage and maintain highways across North West England, the largest such award to date.

Meanwhile Ferrovial had begun a period of two months of intensive study with PricewaterhouseCoopers to better understand the nature of Amey's financial problems, before a first formal meeting was held with Brian Staples (still CEO of Amey at the time) in December 2002. Staples discouraged Ferrovial from bidding.

Events accelerated further to overtake Staples, however. The banks supporting Amey were already heavily involved in its management, having arranged for an interim Chief Financial Officer to be appointed to control the finances and protect their interests. The next month, Brian Staples had stepped aside and Mel Ewell stepped up to be CEO (initially on an interim basis).

Ferrovial's due diligence study (led by Iñigo Meirás and Santiago Olivares) now continued with Amey's cooperation. Prior to formalising the bid for Amey, the bid risk logic was laid out:

1 Amey's problems stemmed principally from a series of strategic decisions and lack of financial control that arose from its aggressive pursuit of diversification and growth.

2 There were no significant problems identified in Amey's core 'services' operations. Indeed, these were cash generative, with an attractive base of loyal clients and a strong portfolio of service contracts. Once severed from the portfolio of 'exotic' diversifications made previously, these core operations could quickly underpin the future of Amey in services once more.

3 Ferrovial's acquisition strategy would be to quickly separate the healthy operations from the financial problems, and deal with the latter.

Crucially, Amey also held a 33.33 per cent interest in Tube Lines, a joint venture with Jarvis and Bechtel to provide infrastructure maintenance and services for Transport for London on a significant part of the London Underground, including the Northern, Jubilee and Piccadilly lines. Funding this stake had become a crucial problem for Amey, and had attracted the attention of the controversial left-wing Mayor of London, Ken Livingstone, who sought to portray these problems as an inevitable consequence of the privatisation of government services. For Ferrovial, however, access to this stake in Tube Lines was a valuable asset. Although Amey was regarded as a good business in its own right, this stake was a 'jewel in the crown'. In the words of Iñigo Meirás, Tube Lines was '60 per cent of the decision to invest in Amey'.

On 16 April 2003, Ferrovial's offer of 32 pence (£0.32) per share for the full share capital of Amey PLC was recommended by Amey's board of directors. Amey directors were disappointed at the offer price, but admired Ferrovial's negotiation approach. On 29 May 2003, Ferrovial took full control for a total cost of £85 million, with ensuing capital commitments of £148 million required to recapitalise Amey. Amey's history as an independent company ended. The future, however, seemed more secure.

Recovery and integration

Ferrovial had been impressed by the recovery plan put forward by Amey to its bankers, and had approved of the financial disciplines reintroduced by the interim Financial Director. In line with the bid logic, that Ferrovial was buying a strong business with financial problems, Mel Ewell was confirmed as CEO of Amey.

Ferrovial was transparent about the changes it wanted, however. The company set about protecting its interest by ensuring ongoing strong financial controls, performance discipline and adequate control over Amey's governance by making a limited number of key appointments. Santiago Olivares (Chief Operating Officer of Servicios) was appointed to Amey's board, joining the legal General Counsel, Carol Hui. Initially Santiago spent four days a week in Oxford as the companies came together. The other key appointment was the full-time Finance Director of Amey, and Jose Léo was to spend three years of his life working as part of the Amey board. It may have helped that Amey's senior management saw the Ferrovial team as 'smart people', with 'charm', very focused, and having done 'a lot of homework'. It may also have helped that Amey's people felt they were 'not swamped' by Ferrovial managers. All other senior appointments in Amey were made locally under Mel Ewell.

A 12 month objective for turning around the business was identified, and a programme for recovery was put in place to include:

- Re-installation of strong financial discipline, concentrating on closing ongoing bids, and rationing of bids to prioritise key opportunities. A bidding cost cap of £10 million per annum was imposed (by 2005 the external cost of such bidding had been brought down to £8 million).[iii]
- Enhancing the focus of the services operating business on delivering targeted key performance indicators.
- Rebuilding Amey's balance sheet through an issue of equity, and restructuring the bank debt, which in turn provided the resources to buy in the option to participate in the Tube Lines venture.
- Rebuilding the PFI portfolio (sold under bank instructions in April 2003).
- Focusing the business on the core services propositions, specifically the strengths in three areas: roads and highways infrastructure, support services and facilities management, and the Tube Lines investment in the London Underground.
- Closing the remaining construction risks and the exotic diversifications, and terminating non-performing contracts and deals (the latter eliminating over £25 million of potential liabilities).
- Reducing headcount by 15 per cent in 2003, slimming down corporate headquarters (Amey had 950 staff in its headquarters at acquisition, reduced to 500 five years later).

- Moving from expensive London premises to Oxford and rationalising its own property (£3 million of projected savings).
- Rationalising information technology provision (accounting for a saving of over £10 million).
- Confirming a new board of directors, and building a unified management team.

A major challenge for the senior management team during this period was the need to communicate the new strategic direction to customers, suppliers and staff. Mel Ewell is described by Jose Léo as a 'communications animal', and effort was put in by the board to assuring customers and suppliers that financial stability was rapidly being re-established. The Amey brand was well recognised in the market, and it was important to ensure all brand attributes turned positive again.

Additionally, Gillian Duggan was hired as Human Resources Director with a remit to build a culture focused on the values of the operating business. People were seen as key to performance in the services sector, and morale needed to be re-established. The values identified by Amey staff included a focus on safety in operations and a strong customer orientation. The launch of a new core values statement added a focus on performance and on profit, to create a simple balanced scorecard structure.

An additional area where a change in attitudes and behaviours was targeted related to management expectations of incentives from having been part of a quoted UK plc (through share options, etc.), to becoming a subsidiary of a previously little known (in the UK) Spanish group. For Jose Léo, now working full time as Finance Director at Amey, the sense that Amey's management identified themselves as 'part of the Ferrovial family' was a key milestone in the integration of the two companies.

Integration and growth

In March 2004, Amey was able to put together a refinancing facility without recourse to Ferrovial guarantees. Having turned the business around to focus on core activities, the board were able to agree a five year business plan with Ferrovial, largely building on the direction set under the original turnaround strategy. By May 2004, Amey's financial accounts were sufficiently positive for Ferrovial to approve the acquisition of a further one-third stake in Tube Lines from its partner Jarvis, making Amey the majority stakeholder in the venture.

By July 2005, Ferrovial was able to make a presentation to investors demonstrating the turnaround in Amey's fortunes. From recording an exceptional loss of £248 million in 2003, the 2004 profit showed £28 million, returning

an EBITDA[2] ratio of 10 per cent. £33 million of cash was generated by Amey in the same year. By most measures, the acquisition was calculated to create additional shareholder value using an economic value added approach with analysts' recommendations valuing Amey as part of Ferrovial in 2009 in the region of €1 billion (from a capital commitment on acquisition of £233 million).

In the view of Inigo Meiras, 'integration takes between 3 to 5 years', and over this timeframe there were a number of benefits claimed for the transaction. The benefits claimed for Amey are perhaps more obvious, with the discipline typical of construction companies, lost in their rapid transformation into a services company, reinstated once more. This financial discipline was mirrored by a new rigour in the way Amey approached the investments needed in the contract bidding process and to finance the commitments from those contracts. And all of this needed to be embedded in the core values promoted in Amey's culture programme. In addition to these benefits, two-way best practice synergies are claimed, with Ferrovial seen as a more sophisticated Facilities Manager, and Amey a repository of expertise on road maintenance.

In all of this, Ferrovial describes itself as 'facilitator' for Amey, creating an outline framework for the company's entrepreneurialism and creativity to develop the business. In Mel Ewell's view, some of that creativity has been transferred to Ferrovial, along with Amey's specific expertise in bidding on PFI and PPP contracts in the sophisticated UK market. Jose Léo also claims that the emphasis on communication shown in the Amey turn-around is 'alien to a traditional Spanish company', and has influenced Ferrovial's people practices. Léo moved to become CFO at British Airports Authority after three years at Amey, and for himself he claims to have become a 'UK CFO'. When asked what that means, he explains: 'even finance managers must communicate with their team'.

At a corporate level, Amey was an important first major step in Ferrovial's international strategy. Amongst the benefits claimed were:

- A rapid increase in the scale of Ferrovial's 'Servicios' business (Amey represented 40 per cent of the Servicios business in 2008), and in the balance of revenues and profits being generated outside Spain and Portugal, earning Ferrovial a reputation amongst international investors.
- Confidence to pursue a string of international acquisitions, including Webber in Texas and the global airport services company Swissport, leading to a presence in 49 countries with 106,000 employees by 2009.

---

[2] Earnings Before Interest, Taxes, Depreciation and Amortisation.

- The confidence to bid for control of the UK's politically sensitive British Airports Authority, operator of all major London airports (including Heathrow) and a number of UK regional airports.
- The cooperation of Amey in providing a proving ground for a stream of promising corporate managers seeking international exposure.

By 2006, perceptual studies carried out for Ferrovial by the consultancy firm Análisis e Investigación indicated that key stakeholders saw Ferrovial as highly focused on its multinational diversification and expansion strategy. Ferrovial's share price (€22.95 at IPO) grew to a maximum of €82.75 in April 2007, before slipping back in the global recession to €30.42 in December 2009. In the period from its IPO in 1999 to December 2009, however, its shares outperformed the IBEX 35 by approximately 260 per cent, and dividends per share increased tenfold by Financial Year 2008.

Corporate connections

Ferrovial Servicios (of which Amey is part) has grown significantly since the acquisition. Both companies describe their recent history as a 'journey from construction to integrated infrastructure management'. For Amey that meant a growth strategy where it divested itself of its construction business (and the property risk that went with it), whilst Ferrovial chose instead to maintain a presence in construction. Amey finds itself increasingly cooperating with the construction arm of Ferrovial (Ferrovial Agroman) in bidding for 'design, build and operate' contracts. The goal is to offer clients a 'one-stop' shop purchase, supplying architects and design consultants to design a project,

builders to complete it, and the services expertise of Amey to run it once completed.

Despite the potential apparent synergies from bringing the international group together to bid jointly on large contracts, Iñigo Meirás is adamant that the industry brand identities of national and regional players like Amey remain essential to this approach. Instead Meirás points to the increased collaboration and transfer of knowledge as another great benefit from Ferrovial's businesses working together. In addition, Ferrovial has since 2006 instigated an annual global group senior management conference and a global 'Ferrovial University' event to share best practice. Amey itself encourages all employees to learn Spanish.

Amey itself has pioneered a strategy of consulting-led 'end-to-end' selling, following the acquisition of Owen Williams, a specialist construction and engineering consulting firm in 2006. These moves suggest a new strategic direction where clients increasingly look to source a range of expertise ('Design, Build and Operate') from one group. In these contracts, Amey's consulting specialists are increasingly responsible for creating the 'architecture' of a single integrated solution for clients, on the assumption that many of the transaction costs of working in cooperation in a consortium might be eliminated. This market is expected to deliver double digit growth for the foreseeable future, evidenced by Amey's consulting arm increasing headcount by 60 per cent in 2009.

References:
[i] M.F. Guillen, *The Rise of the Spanish Multinationals: European Business in the Global Economy*. Cambridge: Cambridge University Press, 2005.
[ii] Ferrovial, *Presentation to Analysts*, London, 22 June 2005.
[iii] Ibid.

Who runs education now? Mergers and de-mergers in the public sector

Kevan Scholes

Mergers between different areas of government work to create new ministries or departments are very common. But this often requires at least one demerger from other areas of work too. So what should decide the best groupings within a ministry or department?

• • •

On 27 June 2007 the Labour Party's British Finance Minister, Gordon Brown, became Prime Minister, succeeding Tony Blair after 10 years of Labour[1] government. Like many new leaders he had some immediate changes to announce, amongst which was the creation of two new government departments to take over the work of the Department for Education and Skills (DfES). In an article entitled *Strategic Split or Messy Divorce?* Mike Baker, a BBC analyst, reported the announcement as follows:[i]

> If the Department for Education and Skills had been a family, then this week's momentous changes would amount to a divorce, with potentially serious implications for the children . . . The youngest child, called Schools, is staying with one parent. The oldest sibling, called Universities, is moving out with the other . . . The optimists see the splitting of the old DfES into two separate departments as an opportunity for education to double its voice within the Cabinet. One will be able to speak up purely for schools and the other for universities, skills and adult education.
>
> First there is the Department for Children, Schools and Families . . . the DCSF . . . The second voice at the Cabinet table will come from the Department for Innovation, Universities and Skills (DIUS).
>
> . . . Yet what about poor old Further Education? Forever the Cinderella of education, FE had finally looked set to go to the ball with the new Prime Minister's focus on skills . . . Now the department responsible for skills will have nothing to do with young people until

Source: Getty Images.

they are 19 – by which time, if they have been forced down an academic route, they will probably have lost interest in any sort of learning at all.

British education pre-1964[ii]

Since 1833 when British governments first took a role in the provision of education, through financial grants to support the work of voluntary bodies (including churches), there had been a progressive involvement of the state in policy, funding and the management of education in the UK. Until 1899 the use of funds voted by parliament was managed by the Education Committee of the Privy Council.[2] This

---

[1] In the 2000s Britain had three main political parties: Labour (left wing), Liberal Democrats (middle) and Conservative (right wing). During Tony Blair's premiership (1997–2007) the agendas of all three parties had moved towards the middle ground.

[2] In earlier days of the British monarchy the Privy Council was the main body that advised the monarch on matters of state. As Britain became a parliamentary democracy this role largely moved to parliament and government ministers. However, the Privy Council still meets monthly and at each meeting the Council will seek the monarch's formal approval to a number of Orders which have already been discussed and approved by Ministers.

---

work was carried out through an Education Department established within the Privy Council, under the leadership of the secretary of the Privy Council Education Committee. In 1856 this Department was detached from the Privy Council and constituted as a new Education Department, under the direction of a salaried vice-president. After 1872 the department was only responsible for education in England and Wales, with education policy in Scotland being transferred to a separate Committee for Education in Scotland.

The Board of Education Act 1899 replaced the Education Department with a Board of Education, headed by a President and principal ministers with responsibility for education policy in England and Wales. Following the Education Act 1944, the Board of Education was succeeded by a Ministry of Education, headed by a single Minister. Education policy in England and Wales was directed by this Ministry until 1964.

'Marriages and divorces' 1964–2010

From 1964 until the current day one of the most important policy issues for successive governments was deciding which other areas of government work were to be 'attached' to education. The remainder of this case study looks at the period from 1964 to 2010, in which time education had five 'marriages' and three 'divorces' (see Table 1). The 'logic' for each of these changes will be presented as it was reported at the time. It is also worth reflecting on the different 'positions' education has in the government of other European Union countries. A summary is given in Appendix 1.

Department of Education and Science (DES) 1964–92

In 1964 the Secretary of State for Education and Science Order 1964 merged the offices of Minister of Education and Minister of Science, to create a Department of Education

Table 1 Departments responsible for Education in England and Wales (1944–2010)

Years	Ministry/Department	Acronym
1944–64	Ministry of Education	
1964–92	Department of Education and Science	DES
1992–95	Department for Education	DFE
1995–2001	Department for Education and Employment	DfEE
2001–07	Department for Education and Skills	DfES
2007–09	Department for Children, Schools and Families *and*	DCSF
	Department for Innovation, Universities and Skills	DIUS
2009–	Department for Children, Schools and Families *and*	DCSF
	Department for Business, Innovation, and Skills	BIS

and Science, in line with the recommendations of the Trend Committee on Civil Science and the Robbins Committee on Higher Education.[iii] Although the new department was created in the last year of a Conservative government it was continued by the incoming Labour government. Indeed the new Prime Minister, Harold Wilson, famously remarked that the county's future would be 'forged in the white heat of [scientific] revolution'. The department survived for 28 years through three terms of Labour government (11 years) and four terms of Conservatives (17 years). A noteworthy Minister was Margaret Thatcher (1970–74), later to be Conservative Prime Minister (1979–90).

During these 28 years the country underwent massive change – particularly during the late 1970s and early 1980s which witnessed both economic and social turmoil in the UK. School leaving age was extended to 16 and the university sector grew from a small elitist provision by the creation of a new wave of universities in the 1960s and polytechnics in the early 1970s (which eventually became universities in 1992).

Over the course of its life the Department of Education and Science acquired the following responsibilities:

● Promoting education in England and post-secondary education in Wales. Most of the functions of the Department in respect of primary and secondary education in Wales were transferred to the Welsh Office by the Transfer of Functions (Wales) 1970. All remaining functions (except in regard to universities) were transferred to the Welsh Office in 1978.

● Relations between the government and universities in England, Wales and Scotland, including relations with the Universities Grants Committee.

● Fostering civil science in Great Britain and in collaboration with other nations. Following the Science and Technology Act 1965, this responsibility was channelled through research councils which were administered with the assistance of a Council on Scientific Policy.

● Support of the arts in Great Britain, including the Arts Council and most national museums. After 1979 this work was discharged by an Office of Arts and Libraries under the direction of the Minister for the Arts.

● Promoting sports through a Sports Council established in 1965.

Department for Education (DfE) 1992–95

In 1992 the Conservatives, led by John Major, won an unexpected and unprecedented fourth term in office. The science functions of the Department of Education and Science were transferred to the Cabinet Office's Office of Public Service. Education policy continued to be the responsibility of a renamed Department for Education until 1995.

Department for Education and Employment (DfEE) 1995–2001

In July 1995 the government scrapped its Employment Department and divided its duties between the Department for Education (renamed DfEE) and the Department for Trade and Industry. Perhaps significantly, the new DfEE minister (Gillian Shephard) was at the time the Minister for Employment. This merger to form DfEE was welcomed by senior leaders in both further and higher education. The *Times Higher Education* commented on the merger as follows:[iv]

> The creation of a single department is seen as one of the first outcomes of Mrs Shephard's review of higher education. Much of the evidence stressed the importance of lifelong learning and updating. Merger will make it easier to coordinate work on higher level National Vocational Qualifications and General NVQs, and break down barriers between academic and vocational qualifications.
>
> Mrs Shephard is regarded as the right person for the job because of her experience as Employment Secretary, and her enthusiasm for initiatives like NVQs. Ruth Gee, chief executive of the Association for Colleges, said: 'It looks as though this reconstruction of a party may lead at last to the construction of the first wholly integrated policy for education and training.'

Department for Education and Skills (DfES) 2001–07

After 18 years and four Conservative governments Labour regained power in 1997 under Prime Minister Tony Blair. Labour won a second term in 2001. Following this election the employment work of the DfEE and the Department of Social Security merged to form the Department for Work and Pensions (DWP). The new Department was set up, amongst other things, 'to carry out the Government's plans for helping people who want to work to find a job and keep it'.[v] The remaining part of DfEE was renamed the Department for Education and Skills (DfES). The department's early publications spelt out its challenges and priorities:

> The world in which people learn and work is changing rapidly. The gap between people and nations who have knowledge, skills and employment opportunities and those who have not is set to widen. Key factors affecting the development of the Department's policies for learning and skills are:
>
> • *globalisation*: the global economy is increasingly interconnected and knowledge-based. This means that goods, services, capital and information are highly mobile, and success depends on the skills of our people;

> • *information revolution*: the development of more powerful and cheaper digital technology has major implications for the way we communicate, manage information and educate ourselves;
>
> • *economic change*: rapid change in technology and the nature of work requires organisations and individuals to commit themselves to lifelong learning so their skills remain relevant;
>
> • *social and cultural changes*: an ageing population, increased early retirement, changes in family structures;
>
> • *concern about sustainable development*; and an increasing focus on the treatment of individuals.
>
> These factors all influence expectations and needs. Delivery of our agenda to address these issues depends on working with children, young people, adult learners, employers and a wide range of partners, particularly Non Departmental Public bodies.[vi]

During this second term of Labour government other factors started to impact on the management of education. Prime amongst these was the outcome of the public enquiry into the death of Victoria Climbié – an eight year old girl who was abused and murdered by her guardians. The report highlighted the lack of any proper coordination between the various public 'agencies' with which children have contact – primarily social services, schools and healthcare. This led to major changes in child protection policies and the Children Act of 2004. Amongst its many provisions this act required local authorities[3] to put in place an integrated strategy for the safeguard of children. This included the specific requirements to 'appoint a Director of Children's Services, and also a designated Lead Member [politician] . . . The Director and Lead Member will play a key leadership role in bringing together local partners . . . across a full range of local services'.[vii]

So, following a third election win in 2005 and the end of Tony Blair's 10 years as Prime Minister (2007) there was a mismatch between how education was 'positioned' in central and local government.

Department for Children, Schools and Families (DCSF) 2007–

Like many marriages and divorces there were both enthusiastic supporters and opponents of the changes of June 2007. The BBC website reported the government's reasons for creating the DCSF:[viii]

> The [DCSF] will have a 'coordinating role' on children's health, welfare and child poverty. The old Department

---

[3] Local Authorities in the UK run local government at city or county levels. This includes both the political process of local councils and the provision of local services (including schools).

for Education and Skills has traditionally looked after children right through to university. Its Sure Start programme offers support for families, including childcare and parenting classes. In a ministerial statement setting out the structural changes to government departments, Gordon Brown said the new department would for the first time bring together 'key aspects of policy affecting children and young people'.

'The new department will play a strong role both in taking forward policy relating to children and young people, and coordinating and leading work across government on youth and family policy.' It '. . . will assume responsibility for promoting the well-being, safety, protection and care of all young people – including through policy responsibility for children's social services', the statement said.

The department will take over the Respect agenda from the Home Office and 'lead a new emphasis across government on the prevention of youth offending'.

But Mike Baker of the BBC expressed concerns about the impact on Further Education:[ix]

'The rationale for the changes is that the DCSF will be able to deal with all aspects of childhood and families while the DIUS will be able to focus on productive skills and the educational needs of a competitive economy.

This has a certain logic. Yet it falls down with Further Education. Its involvement in 14–19 will now fall to one department while its post-19 interests will belong to another. Yet surely what has been long needed in vocational education has been some sense of a joined-up approach. Britain, especially England, has long failed to produce a coherent approach for children and young adults with a bent towards practical and vocational courses.'

Department for Innovation, Universities and Skills (DIUS) 2007–09

The other department created from the DfEE 'divorce' was the Department of Innovation, Universities and Skills (DIUS). It took over the science and innovation sections of the Department of Trade and Industry (DTI) which was disbanded.[4] The BBC reported some reasons for, and reactions to, the creation of DIUS:[x]

In his ministerial statement to the Commons, Gordon Brown said: 'The new department will be responsible for driving forward delivery of the government's long-term vision to make Britain one of the best places in the world for science, research and innovation, and to deliver the ambition of a world-class skills base'.

---

[4] The other DTI functions were taken over by the new Department for Business, Enterprise and Regulatory Reform.

Reaction to the shake up has been largely favourable. The higher education body – Universities UK – supports the changes, which bring universities together with innovation and skills. Its President, Drummond Bone, said: 'This is an exciting and forward-looking move, which we welcome. Universities are key to the generation and exploitation of new knowledge in the UK, so there is a clear rationale for moving science and innovation to the new department. We look forward to working with the new prime minister and new secretary of state John Denham to deliver not only the ideas – but also the skills – the UK needs'. Head teachers (of schools) and college leaders however, are concerned that colleges will be covered by both new departments. [see above]

Department for Business, Innovation and Skills (BIS) 2009–

Following a period of extreme political difficulty for the Prime Minister, Gordon Brown, the senior ministerial roles were 'reshuffled' in June 2009. One change was the merger of DIUS with the Department of Business, Enterprise and Regulatory Reform to create a major new Department for Business, Innovation and Skills (BIS) under the leadership of Lord Mandelson (who many commentators then regarded as the most powerful politician in the UK). Speaking to the BBC[xi] Sally Hunt, the General Secretary of the UCU lecturers' union expressed disappointment at the scrapping of DIUS:

she was 'very concerned' that the 'merger seems to signal that further and higher education are no longer considered important enough to have a department of their own. The fact they have been lumped in with business appears to be a clear signal of how the government views colleges and universities and their main roles in this country.'

Does it matter?

Structural change can be a passion of new leaders. So it is important to them that they can claim some underlying logic that 'justifies' these changes. However, commenting on the 2007 changes, Mike Baker of the BBC offered some words of warning:[xii]

'So, all in all, it is hard to see the rationale for the upheaval that will now hit the former DfES. Perhaps two separate departments will each be a more manageable size. Certainly one former Education Secretary's response was that they would love to have run a department like the new DCSF. But maybe, in the end, it is really all about sending out a signal that things will change now Gordon Brown is in charge – a way of drawing a line under the

Blair era. There is one other possible interpretation, albeit one that may be too cynical. By splitting the department into two smaller power-bases, Prime Minister Brown will ensure that he can more easily direct education policy from Number 10 [Downing Street].[5]

Postscript

Following the Labour Party defeat in the UK General Election in May 2010 the Conservatives and Liberal Democrats formed a coalition government (the first in peacetime for more than 70 years). The BBC website reported the immediate changes made in the field of education:

1 Michael Gove, the Education Secretary, decided to reverse Labour's rebranding of his department. The Department for Children, Schools and Families (DCSF) will be known once again as the Department for Education.
2 The DCSF's rainbow logo will disappear from the department's website and Westminster headquarters

although the Department is still in charge of children's services.
3 Higher education stays in the Department for Business, Innovation and Skills under Vince Cable.

References:
[i] Mike Baker, 'Strategic split or messy divorce', BBC website (www.bbc.co.uk), 30 June 2007.
[ii] The primary source for this section is the National Archives website: www.nationalarchives.gov.uk.
[iii] Ibid.
[iv] Tony Tysome, 'Shephard rounds on employment', *Times Higher Education*, 7 July 1995.
[v] DWP website: www.dwp.gov.uk.
[vi] From Department for Children, Schools and Families Website. Crown Copyright material is reproduced with permission under the terms of the Click-Use License.
[vii] www.everychildmatters.gov.uk.
[viii] 'Brown shakes up education arena', BBC website (www.bbc.co.uk), 28 June 2007.
[ix] Baker, 'Strategic Split'.
[x] BBC, 'Brown shakes up'.
[xi] 'Universities merged into business', BBC website (www.bbc.co.uk), 5 June 2009.
[xii] Baker, 'strategic split'.

APPENDIX 1 The position of education in the governments of European Union countries (2009)

EU country	Department/Ministry responsible for education	EU country	Department/Ministry responsible for education
Austria	Education, Science and Culture	*Latvia*	Education and Science
Belgium – Flemish	Education	*Lithuania*	Education and Science
Belgium – French	Education and Special Education	*Luxembourg*	National Education and Training
Belgium – German	Education and Research	*Malta*	Education, Culture, Youth and Sport
Bulgaria	Education and Science	*Netherlands*	Education, Culture and Science
Cyprus	Education and Culture	*Poland*	1. National Education and Sport 2. Science and Higher Education
Czech Republic	Education, Youth and Sport	*Portugal*	1. Education 2. Science, Technology and Higher Education
Denmark	Education	*Romania*	Education and Research
Estonia	Education	*Slovakia*	Education
Finland	Education	*Slovenia*	Education and Sport
France	National Education	*Spain*	Education, Culture and Sport
Germany	Education, Science, Research and Technology	*Sweden*	Education and Research
Greece	National Education and Religious Affairs	*UK – England and Wales*	1. Children, Schools and Families 2. Innovation, Universities and Skills
Hungary	Education	*UK – Scotland*	Education and Training
Ireland	Education and Science	*UK – Northern Ireland*	Education
Italy	Education		

Sources: National Government websites.

---

[5] This is the British Prime Minister's official residence.

Severstal

Eustathios Sainidis

The case study describes how one of the largest Russian steelmakers, Severstal, has developed its international strategy through a number of offshore acquisitions. With a strong vision to become one of the major global players in the industry the company has been successfully developing its strategic capability. However, the global economic crisis that began in mid-2007 may prove to be a turning point in the company's international strategy.

• • •

Introduction

In mid-2009, Severstal, Russia's third biggest steelmaker, announced further net losses due to a fragile global market. The company's recent international expansion in Europe and the US has proved more risky than initially planned. Although Severstal's business division in the US has been the main contributor to the company's $290 million net losses (€211m or £191m), Severstal insisted:

> We are committed to operating in North America, which is one of the world's most important long-term markets for steel, and will retain our most efficient units with a view to making them even more flexible and efficient.

Its main shareholder and CEO Alexei Mordashov has a strong belief in Severstal's international future. When interviewed by news provider Bloomberg in 2008 he said:

> The steel industry is still very fragmented and consolidation has proved very healthy. We should expect the continuation of fundamental trends, which consolidation is. You see a clear trend toward the creation of global companies, bigger companies, stronger companies.

A challenging and dynamic industry

Steel is an alloy made out of iron and small amounts of carbon, and is one of the most widely used materials. Its applications include the construction, energy, shipping and automotive markets. Its success as a product is based on its strong, resilient, versatile and recyclable properties.

Since the late 1980s the steel industry has become more global in terms of both competition and markets. Steel producers have also invested in production efficiencies leading to higher profit margins. Foreign direct investment

opportunities and the rapid growth of the emerging economies of China, Eastern Europe, Russia and South America have created a financially rewarding business environment. Steel production in 2008 reached just over 1.2 billion tonnes of crude steel, with China by far the biggest producer (502m tonnes), followed by Japan (119m tonnes), the US (91m tonnes), and Russia (68m tonnes). Demand for steel had been increasing year on year since the 1990s until the third quarter of 2008 when the industry was one of the first to feel the impact of the severe global economic slowdown beginning in 2007.

Major players in the industry include ArcelorMittal which is by far the largest producer of steel products and is led by the Indian-born Lakshmi Mittal, followed by Japanese Nippon Steel in second place. ArcelorMittal was the outcome of the acquisition of Luxembourg-based Arcelor by Mittal. The acquisition has become a milestone in the consolidation process of the steel industry. The newly formed company is nearly three times the size of Nippon Steel with a production capacity high enough to supply the entire automotive market. Table 1 gives an illustration of how the competition has changed between 2000 and 2008, with lower industry concentration and relatively smaller and fewer steel producers from China, Russia and India in 2000.

Although the industry has seen a great deal of merger and acquisition activity, it still remains highly fragmented in comparison to other manufacturing sectors. Steel producers use mergers and acquisitions as their preferred strategy to achieve growth. Organic development is expensive and environmental regulations can be a barrier for building new steel plants. Acquisitions act as a strategy to achieve synergies, and make sense when targeting niche markets. The acquisition of the Anglo-Dutch steel producer Corus by Indian-based Tata Steel is one such

Table 1 World steel producers 2000–08 by volume

2008		2000			
Rank	Crude steel output (million metric tons)	Rank	Crude steel output (million metric tons)	Company	Headquarters
1	103.3	4	22.4	ArcelorMittal	Luxembourg
2	37.5	1	28.4	Nippon Steel	Japan
3	35.4	8	19.1	Baosteel Group	China
4	34.7	2	27.7	POSCO	South Korea
5	33.3	–	–	Hebei Steel Group	China
6	33.0	9	29.0	JFE	Japan
7	27.7	26	6.7	Wuhan Steel Group	China
8	24.4	57	3.6	Tata Steel	India
9	23.3	–	–	Jiangsu Shagang Group	China
10	23.2	14	10.7	U.S. Steel	USA
11	21.8	64	3.0	Shandong Steel Group	China
12	20.4	16	10.0	Nucor	USA
13	20.4	25	7.1	Gerdau	Brazil
14	19.2	18	9.6	Severstal	Russia
15	17.7	59	3.6	Evraz	Russia
16	16.9	10	15.6	Riva	Italy
17	16.0	20	8.8	Anshan Steel	China
18	15.9	7	17.7	ThyssenKrupp	Germany
19	15.0	54	3.7	Maanshan Steel	China
20	14.1	12	11.6	Sumitomo Metal Industries	Japan
21	13.7	13	10.9	SAIL	India
22	12.2	22	8.0	Shougang Group	China
23	12.0	15	10.0	Magnitogorsk	Russia
24	11.3	21	8.2	Novolipetsk	Russia
25	11.3	–	–	Hunan Valin Group	China

Source: World Steel Association, www. worldsteel.org.

example. Professor Phanish Puram from London Business School commented on the acquisition: 'The Tata–Corus deal is different because it links low-cost Indian production and raw materials and growth markets to high-margin markets and high technology in the West.'

The vertical mergers and acquisitions activity has resulted in increased negotiating power for steelmakers over both their suppliers and customers. Steel producers see their supply chains as a source of creating value and reducing costs. This offers strong financial returns allowing for investment in quality and service with the aim to differentiate steel products and charge even higher premiums.

The most resourceful steel producers saw opportunities in investing in offshore operations to expand their product portfolio through related and unrelated acquisitions. The privatisation of government-owned assets in emerging economies such as Russia, Brazil, India, China and the Middle East allowed for foreign direct investment strategies. Owning a steel plant close to construction, shipping and automotive manufacturers in these locations offers competitive advantages in the rapidly growing local markets. Exchange rates are also in favour of Russian and Chinese steel producers with a weakening US dollar since the early 2000s, assisting cross-border acquisitions.

On the other hand, customers of steel producers are also pushing for structural changes in their own supply chain.

Automotive manufacturers, in particular, would like to see steel producers having a greater role in the production of their vehicles with the early stages of car assembly (e.g. stamping) taking place within the steel mills. Steel producers which have invested in such production facilities to fabricate custom-made parts can offer differentiated products attracting premium prices.

But there were signs of the steel industry reaching a tipping point even before the 2007 global economic crisis arrived. Gradual pricing pressures, gaps in product mix and asset concentration indicated that the industry had reached maturity by 2006. Industry analysts were already talking about evidence of hypercompetition from as early as 2002. The industry was changing rapidly with the dominant steel producers based in the US, Japan and Germany now under attack from new players in South Korea, Russia and India. The industry has experienced a cycle of global consolidation and fragmentation, and opportunistic short-term counterattack strategies.

After a good eight years of growth in the metals industry, September 2008 proved to be a turning point for steel producers. The global economic crisis had a severe effect on the industry and its markets. Demand for steel had fallen by 60 per cent and prices dropped to 2002 levels, a 70 per cent fall relative to their peak in 2007. Although some regional markets (China) were still experiencing growth, the lack of credit available to industrial consumers meant orders for steel products dried up. Financiers were reluctant to offer credit to businesses because of the troubles in the banking sector. With many steel producers continuing to operate at full capacity, very soon over-supply resulted in plummeting steel prices. As a result some companies had to reduce output by 90 per cent in the final quarter of 2008 and into 2009. Nonetheless, many steel producers could cope financially with the hit due to the pre-vious lucrative years of expanding sales, high steel prices, and market capitalisation of mergers and acquisitions.

Global market opportunities

The emerging markets of Africa, the Middle East and Asia are the main importing markets for steel. The expectation is they will continue to grow at a faster rate than the mature markets of North America, Europe and Japan. From 2000 to 2006 the global demand for steel products grew at an average annual rate of 6.8 per cent with demand from China growing at a rate of 19.3 per cent. The steel market is very cyclical with short 'peak to peak' periods. Huge demand variations exist between regional markets, which makes forecasting very difficult. Areas for growth for the future include China, Asia-Pacific, Africa and the Middle East (see Table 2). None of these markets is currently dominated by one single steel producer but all the major international steel players have strategies in place to target these lucrative markets.

China has become not only the major producer but also the largest consumer of steel products. The country's domestic production has increased annually by 15 per cent, However, there are only a small number of efficient Chinese producers capable of exporting steel. Overseas steel producers have used this gap in Chinese steel production

Table 2 Consumption versus production, forecast for 2013

Million tonnes by region	Production	Consumption	Imports
European Union (25 member countries)	205.0	207.3	2.3
Other Europe	45.6	60.1	14.5
Europe	**250.6**	**267.4**	**16.8**
CIS (Commonwealth of Independent States)	137.5	80.4	−57.1
North America	132.0	167.1	35.1
South America	65.0	51.5	−13.5
Asia (includes China)	1016.1	982.7	−33.4
China	743.1	673.6	−69.5
Africa	27.0	51.2	24.2
Middle East	39.0	67.1	28.1
World	**1676.8**	**1676.8**	
World excluding China	933.7	1003.2	

Source: HSBC Global Research, 'Emerging markets now drive global steel demand', 17 April 2008

capabilities as an attractive proposition for market opportunities and acquisitions in the country.

The US has a high level of steel consumption, mainly in the tooling and construction markets and at the same time has the most efficient steel-producing companies. As a market the US is attractive for its high demand, the low value of the US dollar, and growing inward foreign direct investment. On the other hand, the main barriers to invest in the US are the powerful trade unions and occasional federal protectionist measures.

South Korea has evolved as one of the major steel exporters with an increasing market share in the US, Japan and China. Significantly, South Korea is the biggest indirect exporter of steel, as a supplier of steel-based products such as auto-motive, shipping and electronic products. The country exports almost 60 per cent of its automotive production, 90 per cent of its shipping products and 60 per cent of its electronic products. This is about 10 times more than the European Union countries and three times more than Japan.

Severstal Group

Severstal was founded in 1955 as Cherepovets Steel Mill and remained under Soviet government ownership until the collapse of the Soviet Union in 1991. It was privatised in 1993 under the ownership and leadership of Alexei Mordashov when it was registered as the open joint stock company 'Severstal'. The city of Cherepovets located in north-west Russia, 600 kilometres north of Moscow, remains the global headquarters of the company under its latest form as Severstal Group.

Severstal's core businesses are steel and mining products but its portfolio also includes unrelated assets such a domestic airline, the Cherepovets local port, and a television channel. Since its privatisation in the 1990s it has become one of the most international Russian companies, with extensive overseas export activity and ownership of foreign assets. The company is listed on the Russian (RTS) and London (LSE) stock markets. Together with its Russian steel and mining operations, Severstal owns production facilities in the US, Canada, Europe (Italy, France and the UK), and Africa (see Figure 1). The range of products includes raw materials such as iron ore and coking coal which are supplied for in-house production of flat, rolled and long steel products as well as downstream products of steel pipes, wire ropes and metalware.

In 2008 Severstal produced 19.2 million tonnes of steel, becoming the third biggest producer in Russia and number 14 in the world, with revenues reaching US$22.4 billion (US$5.4bn EBITDA[1]). The group employs

---

[1] Earnings Before Interest, Taxes, Depreciation and Amortisation.

Figure 1 Severstal Group global presence

■ Steel and rolled products   ■ Metalware   ■ Mining   ■ Trade and services

Source: Severstal annual report, 2008.

over 100,000 staff with the majority based in its Cherepovets steel mill (CherMk). The years 2008 and 2009 saw a sharp drop in global demand for steel products and in the first quarter of 2009 Severstal suffered a reduction of almost 30 per cent in revenue as the price of steel fell by almost 40 per cent, down from its peak in August 2008. Orders for Severstal started to improve in the second quarter of 2009 in a still very volatile market.

Since 2002 Severstal has shifted its focus towards high value added steel products and in particular the lucrative, but also extremely difficult to enter, automotive steel market. To do so the company embarked on a series of acquisitions outside Russia starting with the acquisition of Rouge in the US, a historical supplier to automotive producer Ford. Rouge has been rebranded as Dearborn, now part of the Severstal North America subdivision.

Severstal has a very good relationship with the Russian government, easy access to capital for upgrading and extending its production facilities, and has a very positive public image in its hometown Cherepovets. However, investment in modernising its existing assets has been slow and its cost base is relatively high. Finally, a highly regulated steel industry has also delayed the company's global expansion.

Severstal Group divisions

With the aim to reduce cost and at the same time allow for a simplified and more efficient corporate reporting system, April 2008 saw the latest corporate restructuring of Severstal. Severstal Group became the management holding company built around three divisions: Severstal Russian Steel, Severstal Resources (mining assets) and Severstal International. The three divisions make a vertically integrated business entity with a global reach of related diversified products.

Severstal International includes Severstal North America Inc. in the US and Lucchini in Italy. Severstal North America Inc. is an integrated producer of high strength steel (AHSS) and flat-rolled steel products with a specific focus on the automotive steel market. In 2008 Severstal North America Inc. produced 5.1 million tonnes of steel products leading to US$5.3 million sales revenue. The majority of Severstal North America Inc. assets are the outcome of acquisitions, although the steel plant SeverCorr is an organic development built in 2007 at a cost of US$880 million. The US steel facilities are all strategically located near major customers producing highly efficient, low cost, high margin products.

Lucchini is split into two sites, Lucchini Piombino in Italy and Lucchini Ascometal in France. Lucchini is the second largest steel producer in Italy and one of the largest European producers of special quality long steel products. Sales revenues for 2008 were close to US$4 million. Lucchini's main markets include the automotive, rail, machinery and appliances industries and in 2009 it achieved a 20 per cent share of the European market. Its long term strategy is to diversify into high added value steel products and at the same time broaden its customer base.

Severstal's global strategy

Since 2002 Severstal Group has embarked on a number of international and domestic acquisitions with the aim to grow its global presence and increase in size, but also to use them as a defence mechanism against hostile acquisitions. Its CEO Alexei Mordashov is a strong believer in the consolidation of the steel industry and his vision is to make the company a globally recognised player and in particular in the automotive market. His ambition is to make Severstal Group one of the largest global steelmakers in the industry. He has pursued a number of aggressive and high risk offshore acquisitions in the US and Europe, taking over offshore loss-making steel mills with the objective to turn them into profitable businesses.

Although the company had, by 2009, some good experience in acquisitions as a method of pursuing its strategic direction, there is still a lack of a common practice within the business for integrating newly acquired assets. There is a strong dependency on the skills and knowledge of a very few senior managers who are able to negotiate and manage newly acquired businesses, but at a broader organisational level there is a lack of shared understanding and culture on how to incorporate such management competences. The strong leadership in certain business units has contributed to their efficient and rapid growth whereas other units which lacked similar management competences are under-performing. Moreover, the three Severstal Group divisions do not necessarily share the same culture. Coordination of global activities is heavily centralised, allowing for moderate flexibility. Steel mills in Russia, Europe and the US have enjoyed very little integration especially at operational level. The company has been investing in management development training programmes to act as enablers of a common 'Severstal thinking', although the results of this strategy may take some years to materialise.

In 2004 Severstal started a US$3 million five-year investment programme in corporate governance and corporate social responsibility as part of its strategy to enter the London Stock Exchange (LSE) in 2006. The LSE listing was a major success, raising global awareness of the Severstal brand and attracting investment capital. In Russia Severstal and its leader Alexei Mordashov were seen as the modern face of healthy and transparent Russian enterprises which could stand as equals with western companies. The investment into corporate governance and the LSE listing has so far successfully contributed in raising multi-billion-dollar funds by Russian and foreign creditors to support the company's global expansion strategy.

The future

By the end of 2009 steel demand forecasts were suggesting an extremely volatile market at least in the short term. The automotive steel market, which is the biggest market for steel producers in Europe and the US, has been undergoing considerable structural changes, with two major US car manufacturers General Motors and Chrysler having declared bankruptcy in June 2009. The Chinese steel market is expected to continue to grow, albeit at a slightly slower pace than in earlier years. This is at least some good news for Severstal, with its Cherepovets Steel Mill exporting two-thirds of its production to China. However, by mid-2009 the two major acquired US steel plants of Severstal, Dearborn in Michigan and Sparrows Point LLC in Maryland,

were operating at 70–75 per cent capacity and were unable to contribute to the holding company's much needed cash flow. Concerns have been raised amongst the company's shareholders regarding a possible sell-out of some of its US assets, although the management issued reassurances that Severstal has a long-term commitment to its US operations which serve as a vehicle for its global strategy. Still, at the beginning of 2010 there was talk of selling Severstal's two European subdivisions, Lucchini (Italy) and Carrington Wire (UK). Analysts are suggesting limited borrowing capability by Severstal given its financial situation in 2009 unless tough restructuring measures are taken in the near future.

Altogether the debt of Severstal Group in the first half of 2009 was US$7.5 billion and urgent measures are under way to reduce costs and conserve cash flow. Steel analyst Sergey Donskoy reported 'the lowest point in the company's history since its London share listing in September 2006'. Layoffs are expected to continue, although the managment has been under pressure from the Kremlin to keep redundancies at the Cherepovets Steel Mill to a minimum given that it employs at least a third of the local workforce.

Mergers and acquisitions activity in the steel industry is expected to resume, although at a slower pace than pre-2007 levels, with acquirers enjoying stronger negotiating power. Weak balance sheets and limited access to credit may dampen further mergers and acquisitions deals. Commentators on the industry are expecting that the activity may be less cross-border driven in the future, with more domestic acquisition deals. Very limited activity was reported throughout 2009, with acquirers putting on hold any proposed deals but at the same time giving away ground to new entrants from emerging markets (i.e. China) to become active buyers of foreign assets.

Finally, the steel industry is under pressure to act upon environmental concerns and to comply with the requirements of the Kyoto protocol and the European Union's target of reducing CO_2 emissions by at least 20 per cent by 2020. Energy consumption typically constitutes between 20 and 40 per cent of the cost of producing steel. With gas and electricity suppliers constantly pushing for higher prices, steel mills have no option but to invest in new production facilities to reduce harmful emissions. Exploiting the recyclable properties of steel may potentially act as a strategy to develop a competitive advantage.

References:
HSBC Global Research, 'Emerging markets now drive global steel demand', 17 April 2008.
KPMG International, 'What's ahead for the metal's industry in 2009?', April 2009.
PricewaterhouseCoopers, 'Forging ahead – first-quarter 2009 metals industry mergers and acquisitions analysis', 2009.
Severstal, *Annual Report*, 2008.
World Steel Association (www.worldsteel.org/).

CASE STUDY

Queensland Rail: QR Ltd (QR)

Kenneth Wiltshire

QR is currently Australia's largest national rail freight operator and an internationally competitive freight business. It has achieved this success, whilst remaining in government ownership and with a strong union presence, through strategic decisions on competition and investment and the formation of alliances. Recently, in response to the impact of the global financial crisis on its public finances, the Queensland Government has announced plans to privatise parts of the company, giving rise to a major protest campaign from unions, the media, the public and some coal companies. This case raises a number of key questions regarding strategy in government business settings.

● ● ●

Australia is an extremely large continent, larger than either the United States or Western Europe but with a relatively small population. Consequently it has fallen to state governments to provide the major transport and communication infrastructure, because private enterprise found the task uneconomic, especially as the population was very scattered across the nation. Another factor is the Australian belief, embedded in the nation's value system, that every citizen is entitled to the same standard of public services wherever they may live; a very costly goal for governments to deliver. Establishment of railways in the nineteenth century faced all of these challenges.

QR began as a colonial-style railway with the first train travelling from Ipswich to Grandchester on 1 July 1865. Queensland has always been the most decentralised state in Australia, the capital city Brisbane accounting for less than half the population of the state and the remainder scattered across vast distances between many provincial centres. So the railways were a major element in opening up the vast frontier. Indeed, the railways were seen as the key element of land settlement policy. The Queensland track was built to a gauge of only three foot six inches (i.e. a narrow gauge), rather than the standard gauge of four foot eight inches, to save costs in construction, and the railway remained the single largest cost item in the government's budget throughout the nineteenth century. Indeed the wages of all public servants often depended on the financial situation of the railways.

Over time a number of community service obligations were forced upon QR, including concessional freight rates for particular commodities or regions, concessions to some

Source: Alamy Images/Sindre Ellingsen.

passengers such as pensioners and school children, and free travel for politicians for life.

Organisational change has been a constant theme. QR has been through several institutional forms. It began as a government department operating under its own piece of legislation (The Railways Act). In 1991 QR began the commercialisation process with the creation of an independent Board of Directors (non-executive), appointed by the government to set strategic direction. In 1995 the entity was corporatised as a statutory Government Owned Corporation (GOC), and on I July 1995 became a company GOC which is very close to a Corporations Law Company, with two ministers as shareholders, namely the State Treasurer and the Minister responsible for Transport.

In government ownership QR has always confronted the classical governance dilemma of trying to run as a business but also remain a service to the public, with the main issue being how to maintain an 'arm's length' relationship with its owner, the Queensland Government. The role of the Board has never been clear – it formulates strategic directions without the actual power to implement them. The government then notes them as recommendations from the QR Board but retains the power to decide these matters. In reality this results in a 'disconnect' between strategic planning and execution. QR is required to pay an annual dividend to the government, which is set in a rather arbitrary fashion depending on annual results. It must receive government approval for its capital raising activities – a delicate aspect since competitive strategies in rail require large outlays on track and rolling stock. For most of its existence it has been subject to the full array of public sector accountability, including Auditor-General, Parliamentary Committee scrutiny, and Freedom of Information. In its corporate forms QR's Board has been comprised of people with business expertise, but the discretionary areas for the Board have been somewhat limited, with the Government retaining control over most aspects. QR has always been highly unionised, which has caused tensions regarding the introduction of modern business practices and has been a major force in keeping the railway in public ownership.

However, the dominant policy matter has been the need to cross-subsidise an unprofitable passenger network (especially in the urban areas) from profitable freight operations, especially haulage of coal. QR is also subject to regulation of its network access prices, often a source of tension. The same regulator, the Queensland Competition Authority, also oversees the ports, which have become bottlenecks in recent times, hindering QR's own freight haulage operations.

So, in summary, QR has a Board of non-executives, two shareholder ministers, service agreements with the State government, a requirement to pay a dividend, funded Community Service Obligations, and reports to a regulatory and accountability regime. It has six operating divisions:

- QR National – coal and bulk logistics, transport and general freight business
- Passenger Services – community, long distance and tourist passenger networks
- Network Access – managers of the Queensland railway network, including access to it and operations on it
- Infrastructure Services – construction, maintenance and management of the rail network
- Rolling Stock and Component Services – manufacture, heavy repair and overhaul of most of QR's rolling stock fleet
- Shared Services – internal business support across QR operations.[i]

In the last part of the twentieth century, as a result of sweeping national reforms to Australian Competition Policy, the 'business areas' of the public sector lost the traditional 'shield of the crown' and were forced to engage in open competition, including payment of full taxes, total transparency, and a requirement to provide third party access to its infrastructure. This had a major impact on the Australian railways which would now face competition from private freight companies that had to be given access to the track for their rolling stock at competitive prices.

Rather than take a defensive stance, QR took strategic advantage of this situation and won contracts in other Australian states (e.g. coal contracts in the Hunter Valley of NSW) and overseas, in competition with private bidders. This was quite an achievement for an organisation with a longstanding public service culture. A large part of the credit is given to the entrepreneurial skills of the CEO of the time, Bob Scheuber, who had a long career in QR having worked his way up the ladder. He had always retained his union membership, and the trust he had generated with the staff was considered to have been a vital factor in being able to introduce the new corporate and strategic focus, which did require some job cutting. It was also a key aspect of his leadership of a railway with the usual run of accidents which affect railways the world over. Scheuber has commented that in his major media appearances during such crises he regarded the interviews as a key avenue for communicating to his own workforce, just as much as to the public.

In 2006, QR signalled a more commercial future with the appointment of a former CEO of BHP, John Prescott, as Chairman. In 2007, leading steel company executive Lance Hockridge (formerly of Bluescope and BHP which are giant international mining companies and steelmakers) was appointed CEO to replace Bob Scheuber whose contract had expired.

QR's success has been aided by a set of strategic partnerships it has formed with linked operators in the transport and logistics supply chain. It has also had active Corporate Social Responsibility programmes with several community, not for profit organisations, and is the major sponsor of the 'Queensland Reds', the state's rugby union team.

In 2008, in a shock announcement, the State Labour government revealed that the global financial crisis had made a major dent in the State's finances; so much so that Queensland lost its longstanding Triple A credit rating and was facing intense difficulties in raising loans in the face of already mounting debt levels. In response to this crisis the government announced a privatisation programme which would include government forests, ports, and parts of QR, including its freight division and coal network. This produced a public outcry since privatisation had not even been mentioned during the election campaign. The unions immediately mounted a major protest campaign against privatisation in general but especially at the proposals for QR. This campaign gathered intensity and was backed by substantial media commentary, particularly when it became obvious that the government had not carefully thought through the privatisation goals or process and its likely ramifications.

Business generally welcomed the privatisation moves, citing various reasons why rail freight should be in private hands. The debate, it was argued, was about who is the best owner of QR's freight business: the government or the private sector; not an argument about individual managers but about structures and governance. 'Do we want QR's freight business owned by a government, which has a complex array of political and policy objectives, or do we want it owned by an entity with only a commercial focus?'[ii]

Three reasons for privatisation advanced were:

1 The freight business is capital intensive and it is extremely important that the required investments are made to transport Queensland's growing coal exports. A commercial entity that is well capitalised will generally invest when it sees sufficient demand for the services, but a government owner must weigh the more immediate political benefits of investing instead in possibly schools or hospitals.

2 It is more difficult for a government to run QR efficiently given that it is constantly lobbied by customers, unions and other stakeholders making demands that they might not make to a private operator.

3 QR needs to be responsive to commercial opportunities and such decisions regarding one customer, who might be prepared to pay, should not have to pass through a political filter.

On the other hand a group of leading economists attacked the privatisation plan, saying that the measures of costing and expected return had overstated the financial returns given the costs of dressing up the assets for sale, and undervalued the dividend stream that would have kept flowing to the government if the assets remained in public ownership. The coal industry expressed concerns at the plan to sell both QR track and rolling stock as one entity (i.e. an integrated operator like the Class 1 railways in the USA) which they claimed might lead to anticompetitive pricing and access decisions that would create inefficiencies and delay upgrades. The argument effectively complained that this would amount to replacing a public monopoly with a private one.

QR itself conducted a study of rail privatisations around the world and was unimpressed by experiences in Britain and New Zealand, but regarded Canadian experience more favourably. The British experience was believed to have brought some benefits, including possibly lower rail fares than might have been the case otherwise, but it also seemed that crowded trains, allegations of profiteering by the multitude of new rail service providers, paralysing crashes, and endless political friction had led to a bigger British government subsidy than had been the case when rail was in full British government ownership. Many argued that the splitting of the UK's train operating services from the track – i.e. above-rail assets (e.g. rolling stock such as locomotives and carriages) from below-rail assets (e.g. ownership of the track itself and responsibility for its maintenance) – was the source of many of the problems, because it led to a multitude of small train operators squabbling over access to lines that were controlled by a company that had no financial incentive to maintain or improve the infrastructure.

The main Australian competitor group to QR, Asciano, which operates the Pacific National group, an above-rail operator, expressed concerns to the competition regulator that the sale of a vertically integrated QR would give it incentives to discriminate against above-rail competitors.

As the debate wore on it became clear that the government had not taken many of these factors into account, especially the question of which body would have responsibility for track maintenance. Some 5000 workers in QR currently have this responsibility. It was not clear what the interface between the newly privatised parts of QR and the rest would be, and particularly why a government would continue to subsidise one part but not the other. The actual valuation of the assets and their split was another very difficult task. Moreover, QR had an enviable safety record, a reputation for good technical excellence, a sound customer/commercial balance, and a sense of corporate responsibility; the damage which could be done to the brand needed to be considered.

In the event the government responded to union and public concerns about ownership by announcing that the sale of QR's freight operations and coal network would be by a public flotation, with parcels of shares reserved for QR staff, and preferential access to shares for the Queensland public. (The government planned to offer QR National employees $1000[1] worth of free shares, and an additional $4000 worth on a discounted basis.) The government would also retain a 25–40 per cent initial shareholding which would be sold down over time. The Rollingstock Workshops, which services the freight rolling stock, and the track maintenance staff who build new track or maintain current track would be included in the new privatised freight entity called 'QR National'.

---

[1] $1000 Australian dollars = £605 or €666 or $915.

Therefore QR National was planned to be a fully integrated freight operator and track owner. This has produced strong opposition from a consortium of coal companies who fear such an entity would discriminate against users. Consequently they tried to convince the government to engage in a trade sale rather than a public float and have lodged a bid themselves to this effect.

With the split of freight from passenger operations, the plan also creates a new entity called Queensland Rail which will be a passenger business offering the suite of passenger services that QR currently provides. This new passenger Queensland Rail will stay in government ownership.

There are a number of key questions raised by the case. Is it possible for a government owned business to operate strategically and in an entrepreneurial manner given the political context in which it has to function? Is risk taking compatible with public sector accountability regimes? Can such an entity maintain a truly 'arm's length' relationship with its government owner to facilitate day to day business decision making? What are the potential advantages and disadvantages of the privatisation of a successful government business enterprise? Is there a case, in the transport and infrastructure sectors, for maintaining government ownership of networks and only privatising the value-added components? What can a government achieve, in the public interest, through public ownership, that it cannot achieve by privatisation plus regulation?

References:
[i] QR Annual Report, 2009.
[ii] *Australian Financial Review*, 30 November 2009.

CASE STUDY

The Changan–Ford joint venture: same bed but different dreams?

Valeriano Lencioni and Haoyue Huang

The case explores the cultural issues that can arise in an international joint venture where the cultural norms are very different. The Changan–Ford joint venture has been successful in terms of sales growth and building a significant market share but if it is to continue to thrive then cultural issues will have to be tackled. Many international joint ventures fail to survive because such issues remain unresolved.

• • •

At the start of 2010, China had become the largest world car market, overtaking the long-term dominance of the US, despite efforts by the federal government to help the domestic market through incentives, mainly a 'scrappage' scheme. China had come out of the severe recession of 2008 and 2009 relatively unhurt, while Western markets were still suffering. As a result its exports of consumer goods to the West had plummeted, but its internal market showed a robust demand, including cars. In China only about 20 per cent of people owned car – by comparison, in the US and Europe the ratio is about 50 per cent. The demand in China was especially heavy for cars that were perceived to be of higher quality than most of those produced by Chinese companies.

It is little surprise therefore that most Western car manufacturers devised strategies for expansion into the emerging Asian markets, particularly China. General Motors, Volkswagen, PSA Peugeot Citroen and Ford all had an important presence there, either through significant equity participation in Asian manufacturers – Suzuki, Mitsubishi, Nissan and Mazda were the leading ones – or by joint ventures (JVs) set up by Western manufacturers with Chinese companies. One such joint venture was set up in 2001 by Ford and Changan, a more than 100 year old Chinese car manufacturer. Changan Auto Co. Ltd employed 28,000 staff, working in three manufacturing plants in the People's Republic of China (PRC). Production and sales of cars grew at an impressive 30 per cent a year. Changan owned a 50 per cent stake in the JV, Ford owned 35 per cent and Mazda 15 per cent (see Figure 1).

The Ford Motor Company was a global leader in the automobile industry. Founded by Henry Ford in 1903, Ford was present in more than 200 countries and had 245,000 staff worldwide, manufacturing in about 100 factories around the world. Ford was the only manufacturer of the US 'big three' not to have had to borrow money from the government following the 2008–09 financial crisis. This was mainly because it had successfully negotiated, on favourable terms, a substantial loan just before the banking crisis became apparent. Subsequently, it sold a significant part of the stake it owned in Mazda, and later divested the Volvo brand, further reinforcing its balance sheet. Ford also owned a sound portfolio of models, many highly successful. Four of the best models were assembled by the Changan–Ford joint venture in Chongqing, in southwest China, and sold in the Chinese market: the small car Fiesta, the mid-sized Focus, the saloon Mondeo and the seven-seater S-Max.

The joint venture was proving to be successful: in 2009 it sold 319,000 units for revenue of £360 million[1] (≈ €400m or $540m) up from 210,000 units, revenue £270m in 2008. However, the very reasons for the success were also a source of concern. The models offered in the Chinese market sold well because they appealed to a sophisticated segment of buyers, who saw Western-designed cars as differentiated because of their overall superior quality, innovative technology and aesthetic appeal.

A powerful information system aimed at enhancing the JV's capabilities by better managing the entire value chain of the enterprise, including research, design, sourcing, production, marketing, sales and service, was designed in 2001 and completed in 2005. However, superior product quality and innovative capability require the integration of resources and capabilities, at the strategic as well as the

---

[1] £1 ≈ €1.10 ≈ $1.5.

Figure 1 Organisational structure of the joint venture

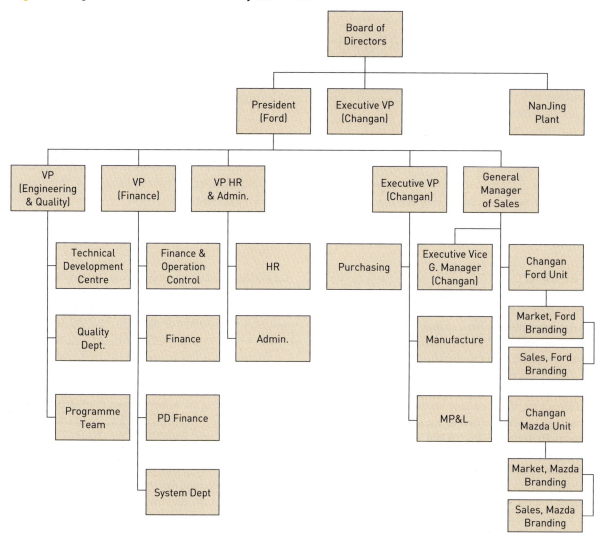

operational level. Cultural differences between Chinese and American managers pervaded all aspects of management, often generating friction and conflict, and there was concern that this would jeopardise the achievement of the joint venture's success in the medium term.

The main concerns of the top managers in the JV could be summarised as:

● Optimising output in terms of efficiency and quality, which is made more difficult by poor communication and different decision-making processes between the parties.
● Differences in understanding changes in the market and ways to deal with them led to a lack of effective product innovation and design, with serious implications for the JV's competitive advantage.

Early in January 2010, stories appeared in a number of financial media that put in doubt the future of the JV.[2] At

around that time, an external, independent, consultant was asked to explore the issues of concern. She was given access to senior managers to collect the necessary information, and asked to present, in a matter of days, an initial 'rough and ready' report for immediate consideration by the top managers.

Five senior managers were interviewed: the Human Resource Manager, the Marketing Manager, the General Manager, a Senior Manager and an Administration Manager. When interviewed, they expressed candid and revealing views about the cultural issues faced by the JV.

Below is the report that emerged from the investigation. The layout and style were designed to avoid any indication of a spurious clarity in a situation that is very complex

---

[2] For example, one in Reuters on 18 January 2010 carried the title 'Ford and Mazda say no to planning to break up China JV'.

THE REPORT

TO: The CEO of Changan-Ford Automobile Co.

FROM: The consultant

NOTE: The following comments are summaries of the responses from the interviews. The ones in italics are verbatim quotes.

1 Chinese traditional culture displays important differences to that of Western countries, and even to other Confucian cultures found in Japanese and other Asian countries' enterprises. Consequently, the managers of Changan–Ford, coming from two different national cultures, revealed largely different values, and the differences are likely to generate disruptive conflict, at least initially. With time and good management of the cultural processes, gradually a common ground can possibly be found to allow for a synergistic integration, or at least a constructive working arrangement.

Different points of view can produce new useful ideas and suggestions, with potential for improving managerial effectiveness. Exploring the American culture is an opportunity for Chinese managers to learn different ways of doing things.

2 The American culture espouses individualism. Many people think this is partly because the United States is a nation of immigrants, and from the 'Wild West' era onwards most American people believe individual rights and responsibilities are the basis of US society. Therefore Americans are great advocates of individualism and independence. Because of this individualistic trait, US managers tend to work in isolation. This does not mean that they do not help each other; they do, but, unless they are asked, managers may not take the initiative to help. Chinese employees think US managers are selfish, whilst US managers believe Chinese managers lack intuition and a sense of individual responsibility. In contrast with the individualistic US culture, collectivism is an important factor in the make-up of Chinese culture, where the group is the basic unit of society: a person's identity is realised in the group and through the group. Chinese people place emphasis on 'harmony' within the group, and they are good at using a balanced and harmonious approach to the resolution of conflict and to avoid confrontation. Chinese people also place emphasis on ethics and morality and pay attention to hierarchical order. They respect the spirit of collectivism and hard work whilst disdaining individualism and hedonistic ideas. Chinese people attach great importance to relationships and emotions: relationships are often more important than truth.

The JV needs to achieve a harmonious state. Managers must respect both cultures. Managers need to understand both cultures' characteristics, and need more communication with each other. In general, Western managers know more about Chinese culture than the Chinese know about Western culture and they also adapt more easily to working in Chinese contexts.

3 Culturally, Americans are inclined to use rather direct expressions; Chinese prefer to use tactful roundabout expressions. These different cultural habits tend to cause bad feelings and misunderstandings.

Yes, I have attempted to manage cultural conflict. You know . . . Chinese people believe in collectivism; they usually make decisions in a group or organisation, so . . . the process is too long, it takes a long time to make decisions. However, American people belong to an individualism characteristic, they make personal or individual decisions, so decision-making is very quick. Therefore, they often complain that Chinese managers make decisions too slowly. Given that, I called a meeting abut this issue and let American managers and Chinese managers discuss how to solve this problem. Finally, they found a consensus.

4 The Chinese subscribe to a high power distance approach to management: people readily accept the authority of organisational leadership and bureaucracy. On the other hand, in America people advocate flat organisational structures and the right to question decision making within the organisation. In US leaders' conversations with their subordinates it is not uncommon for employees to adopt a very direct way to point out what they see as mistakes, and voice frank criticism. Chinese managers, however, protect 'face' and find it very difficult to accept open criticism, which would result in conflict. Importantly, Chinese leaders will take subordinates' 'face' into account, because they want to maintain a good relationship with them, and they are careful to respect each other's 'face'.

In Chinese culture great importance is attached to respect for older people. In companies, employees respect the older staff members, because older people have a rich experience, knowledge and competence at work. Therefore, in JVs, Chinese managers still choose a 'seniority' system at work. Whilst in American culture managers attach great importance to respect for young people, and place emphasis on 'ability first'.

5 In the US, subordinates have the right to make recommendations and question their superiors. Subordinates have considerable autonomy in their own areas of responsibility. For Chinese employees the expression of different opinions is more implicit, so often they fail to clearly express their views. If there are different opinions these will not be stated directly, to avoid conflict, and avoid causing embarrassment to managers, especially in meetings. Only leaders state their views openly; employees are unlikely to do so. However, foreign workers have a tendency to go straight to the problem; people meet face to face to discuss and think about what to do, and even if a fierce conflict takes place as a result, afterwards they are still friends.

> *When Chinese managers make a decision on any project, they gather and evaluate other managers' points of view; that is they collect the 'group' point of view. American managers, when making a decision, prefer to do it individually.*
>
> *The Chinese make decisions as a 'group' or organisation; as a result the process is long. Americans tend to make decisions individually, so decision-making is quick. Therefore, they complain that Chinese managers make decisions too slowly. Furthermore the decision-making criteria between Chinese managers and American managers are not consistent.*

6 Chinese people pay attention to the 'Guan Xi' philosophy. They attach great importance to interorganisational and interpersonal relationships. These often influence each other. For example, in China exchanging gifts is a popular way to promote mutual understanding and friendship among people. On the other hand, US managers clearly differentiate between private and public relationships, and keep their private life separate from the professional life. Chinese managers respect the American approach, but still believe Americans should adapt to China's cultural conditions. The result is that US managers believe these approaches to be 'unreasonable'.

> *People need to understand the two countries' cultures. Understanding their own cultural strengths and weaknesses can help managers to objectively identify similarities and differences between the two cultures.*
>
> *Managers should be good at 'cultural empathy'. That is to be able to extricate themselves from their own culture.*

OTHER SIGNIFICANT ISSUES (reported by Chinese managers)

a Local development
There are many rules that need to be followed before a new vehicle can be introduced into China, such as the local requirements, safety certificate, exhaust rules and many more regulations. Chinese customers usually have different tastes about the vehicle's exterior and interior, on the vehicle's craftsmanship, and have different driving styles/habits and face different road conditions . . .

Ford engineers do not seem to want to help their Chinese colleagues to improve the product to get it much closer to their final customers. The reason is simply that the vehicle has been designed by Ford and Ford does not make available the engineering resources to their China JV partner.

This has led to several criticisms from the Chinese market concerning the Ford brand, e.g. rough ride, poor fuel economy.

b New vehicle introduction programme
Ford made key decisions on the vehicle introduction programme several years ago. It used the Indian market as a way to estimate consumption and consumer preferences in China. This led to the introduction of the wrong models for the Chinese market. The first local vehicle introduced was the Ford Ikon which had sold well in India and has a good driving performance but Chinese customers did not accept the Ikon (especially when they realised it had come from India). Another vehicle introduced by Ford in China (the S-max), despite its very good design and good sales record in Europe, did not sell well in China. The reason was that it did not meet Chinese customers' basic requirements – it seems it was too far ahead of what Chinese customers wanted and were prepared to pay for.

c Ford Engineering
As a trend in China, especially after China took the place of Germany as the second largest market in the world several years ago, many OEMs like GM & VW started to invest in local engineering, and improved their local design capability to get their company and product much closer to their target customers in China, and achieve very useful cost reductions through local development. Ford has an independent engineering centre in China, even though the JV has an engineering team; it seems they do not work closely with and help the JV. They just transfer the engineering voice/drawings and specifications from Ford, which leads to communication problems, lower efficiency and wastes human resources and blocks the local engineering improvement. As a result, the JV will lose competitive advantage without good local engineering, and cause their product to drift away from their customers.

with many 'soft' (cultural) issues. Care was also taken to avoid indicating any specific direction of enquiry, in order to foster and maintain creative thinking.

After reading the report, the CEO called a meeting of the senior managers to address the issues raised. Opening the meeting, he pointedly waved the report, and said: 'Ladies and Gentlemen, clear your diaries. We have some work to do!' The consultant offered to facilitate a workshop with the senior managers as a first step to tackle the cross-cultural issues in the JV.

TNK-BP: from Russia without love – a joint venture that almost fell apart

Phyl Johnson

The turbulent history of the joint venture between international oil company BP and a consortium of Russian billionaires recalls the title of the famous James Bond film. It even includes a role for the Russian security service. The case explores the many issues involved in the increasingly important area of international joint ventures and the difficulties involved in making them work.

● ● ●

Background

In June 2003, the then president of Russia (Vladimir Putin) and the Prime Minister of Britain (Tony Blair) stood in 10 Downing Street in London (the office of the UK Prime Minister) and witnessed the coming together of UK oil giant BP with the Russian consortium AAR (Alfa Group and Access-Renova Group). It was the start of a landmark joint venture that brought together BP's know-how with Russian natural resources. The deal, signed by BP's CEO, Lord John Browne, and his Russian counterparts from AAR, created a new enterprise called TNK-BP.

In return for a $6.8 billion (≈ €5.0bn or £4.4bn) investment, BP was getting access to oil reserves conservatively estimated at 4.1 billion barrels, a 13 per cent increase in its existing reserves.[1] The joint venture included: oil production in Siberia, oil refining, some gas interests and a network of 1400 filling stations in Russia and the Ukraine. It was to have its HQ in Moscow but see the majority of its 50,000 employees located across many regions of Russia and the Ukraine. TNK-BP was to be the third largest oil company in Russia.

The joint venture was owned 50–50 by BP on the one hand and the consortium of four billionaire Russian 'oligarchs' behind AAR on the other. BP would have the right to nominate a CEO and AAR would nominate the Chairman. The joint venture was to be incorporated in the British Virgin Islands which also allowed for disputes to be settled under British law, and any arbitration that became necessary would be carried out in Stockholm.

Source: Getty Images/Eightfish.

BP duly appointed as CEO Robert Dudley, an American BP executive with significant international experience, though none in Russia. Meanwhile, Alfa Group's Mikhail Fridman became the joint venture's Chairman.

BP was founded in 1909 and by 2010 was the second largest private sector oil company in the world. Listed on the London Stock Exchange, it has retailing operations in over 80 countries and oil exploration activities in 30 countries. Despite controversies in Alaska and elsewhere, BP has tried in recent years to present itself as committed to the highest ethical and environmental standards.

After Saudi Arabia, Russia is the largest oil exporting nation in the world. In the early twenty-first century, Russian oil technology was still relatively backward and the Russian industry was notorious for its environmental pollution. Rivers in the oil producing regions of Siberia are so polluted by oil leaks that 97 per cent of drinking water has been shown to be contaminated by oil. The head of

---

[1] This estimate follows conservative external guidelines: BP's own estimate was nearly twice that.

AAR, Mikhail Fridman, is one of the free-wheeling oligarchs who made their fortunes during the Russian privatisations of the 1990s. By 2010, he was estimated by *Forbes* magazine to be the second richest person in Russia. Fridman's Alfa Group has interests in banking, retail, telecommunications, media and vodka. The Alfa Group was accused by the US government of breaking UN sanctions against Iraq during the regime of Saddam Hussein and was refused a loan guarantee from the American Export–Import bank on national security grounds.

The early-to-mid 2000s saw considerable volatility in the international oil market. Whilst the oil companies were confronted with ever rising demand from China and other emerging markets, security issues in the Middle East were threatening supply. Oil firms began to look for new oil fields to explore in order to secure the provision of hydrocarbons (oil and gas) for the long term future. Russia has the largest oil and gas reserves on the planet and was already attracting investments from other leading energy companies such as Exxon, Shell and Total. Russia was a risky environment, but so were many of the alternatives. As BP's Lord Browne said: 'Industry players make different choices – whether to be in the Middle East, Nigeria or Russia. Each is different, but none is risk-free.'[i]

The evolution of TNK–BP

Indeed, BP already had experience with the Alfa Group and Russian oil. In 1997, BP had taken a 10 per cent stake in another Alfa oil company, Sidanco. But after the 1998 Russian financial crisis, Alfa had exploited local bankruptcy laws to seize complete control over Sidanco. BP had had to write off $200 million worth of investment. As he launched his latest partnership with the Alfa Group, Lord Browne commented: 'We have built a strong relationship tested by past difficulties, notably over Sidanco. We continue to build trust and less and less view each other's motives with suspicion.'[ii]

The TNK–BP joint venture got off to a good start, as world oil prices rose with the world economic boom. In 2003, oil prices were still around $20 per barrel, but surpassed $50 during 2005. In early 2005, Lord Browne told BP's investors that the joint venture had increased oil production by 14 per cent in the previous year and was planning to increase investment from just under $1 billion in 2003 to $1.8 billion in 2005. He continued:

> Now, over 18 months into the joint venture with Alfa Access-Renova, significant positive changes have taken place in TNK-BP's organization, the system of internal control, the ability to plan, the approach to safety and environmental issues, and the application of new technologies. While there are always uncertainties, our

constructive relationship with Russia and our joint ventures continues to strengthen.[iii]

By 2007, when Tony Hayward took over from Lord Browne as CEO of BP, TNK–BP was providing BP with a quarter of BP's oil production and accounted for a third of its oil reserves.

During 2006, the oil price approached $70 per barrel and two years later it peaked at over $130 per barrel. As oil became more valuable, Russian attitudes towards overseas ownership of their country's natural resources began to change. Essentially, Russia wanted control of Russian oil. Russian oil companies began to renegotiate the deals they had earlier made with the international oil giants. For instance, in 2006, Royal Dutch Shell and its Japanese partners were humiliated in a series of moves that resulted in state-controlled Gazprom, Russia's largest company, wrestling majority control of their Russian joint venture. Shell alone saw its stake in the joint venture sliced from 55 per cent to 27 per cent.

By 2007, TNK–BP was clearly the next target of the Russian mission to transfer assets from foreign to state ownership. Some of the pressure came again via Gazprom. Raising pollution concerns, Russia's environmental protection agency threatened to close down the huge Kovykta gasfield in which TNK–BP had a stake. During 2007, TNK–BP agreed to sell its Kovykta stake to Gazprom (though negotiations over the details of this continued into 2010). It was rumoured that the whole of the TNK–BP joint venture would have to be folded into Gazprom.

Meanwhile, TNK–BP's existing Russian partners from AAR were becoming more assertive too. The Russians complained that BP was restricting the growth of the joint venture. TNK–BP was in expansion talks in Kazakhstan, Turkmenistan and Venezuela, but by 2008 had still not committed to any investments outside its original Russian and Ukrainian sphere. Mikhail Fridman told the *Financial Times* that the joint venture was stagnating: 'because BP does not want it to grow into an international competitor and sees it simply as a vehicle for adding reserves to shore up its own stock price'.[iv]

AAR was also complaining at the cost of BP's expatriate managers and engineering experts. TNK–BP had about 110 foreign managers and 150 foreign technical experts at any one time. During 2008, a lawsuit by one of the AAR shareholders led to 148 foreign specialists being denied permits to work in Russia. Disputes also arose over dividend payments. As production levels had begun to flatten and as profits were taking a further hit from steep Russian taxes, it was reported that CEO Robert Dudley wanted to cut dividends and direct earnings into oilfields and equipment. The Russian side of the joint venture wanted to keep the dividend cash flowing. Dudley was called in for questioning by the Russian interior ministry with regard to alleged tax evasion. During April and May 2008, the Russian security services twice raided BP's Moscow offices. BP meanwhile launched a claim in the British courts against AAR with regard to the payment of tax liabilities incurred before 2003 that had been passed on to the new joint venture. Mikhail Fridman complained of BP's representation of the dispute:

> The attempt to portray this conflict as a dispute between a respectable western company and some Russian oligarchs who are trying to take control using dirty methods is completely cynical . . . There is a good English word: arrogance.[v]

In July 2008, Robert Dudley had to leave Russia after having been refused a work permit. In effect, he was banned from Russian soil. Dudley commented on his departure thus:

> In the light of the uncertainties surrounding the status of my work visa and the sustained harassment of the company and myself, I have decided to leave and work outside Russia temporarily.[vi]

Commentators were puzzled as to how he planned to manage more than 50,000 employees at such a distance. The *Tvoi Den* newspaper in Russia claimed, in a front-page story, that the Russian security service had unmasked a senior BP manager as a spy. It did not name the man but the negative feelings rumbled on as TNK–BP released a statement dismissing the spy allegations as 'absolutely ludicrous'.[vii]

Resolving the conflict

For BP's new CEO, Tony Haywood, resolving the conflict over such an important source of oil supply was crucial. BP's share price was trailing behind that of its principal rival Shell and there were rumours of a possible takeover bid by American giant Exxon. Russia, on the other hand, still needed Western expertise and capital to exploit its vast energy reserves, much of them in the technically demanding Arctic seas. Meanwhile, the economic crisis of 2008–09 had pushed oil prices down to around $30 a barrel.

In September 2008 TNK–BP's board moved into discussions to overhaul the governance structure of the joint venture. A new memorandum of understanding was signed by both parties that agreed to the appointment of three new directors to the board and that these three would be independent of either side in the dispute. Former German Chancellor Gerhard Schroeder, well connected to Vladimir Putin (now Russian Prime Minister), took one of these board positions. Robert Dudley would step down from his CEO post by the end of 2008. Mikhail Fridman

would serve as interim CEO while the joint venture looked for a permanent replacement. The new CEO would remain a BP nominee, but would now have to be a Russian speaker with significant Russian business experience. The memorandum of understanding included an option to make an initial public offering (IPO) on the Russian stock market of 20 per cent of the shares of TNK–BP.

The vacant spot at the top of TNK–BP was finally filled by the appointment in early 2010 of Maxim Barsky. Contrary to earlier expectations that the new CEO would be BP sponsored, he was the candidate favoured by the Moscow shareholders. Barsky was just 35 years old, and had made his career in the Russian oil business, where he had built up a successful company of his own. He was due to take up his appointment in January 2011 after six months' training at BP HQ in London and other parts of the BP business. BP's shares fell by 1.5 per cent on the news of the appointment. The press releases at the time from both interim CEO Mikhail Fridman and the new BP CEO Tony Hayward appeared keen to show a united front, whilst also leaving considerable room to read between the lines.

Mikhail Fridman, interim TNK-BP CEO, stated:

> This [Barsky's appointment] demonstrates that the shareholders are united on strategy, governance and support for the company's robust operational and financial performance. We are particularly grateful to the independent directors on our board, who played an instrumental role in helping the shareholders reach this important decision.[viii]

Tony Hayward, BP CEO, stated:

> I am pleased that the shareholders of TNK–BP have agreed this plan. We are all agreed that Maxim Barsky has the capabilities to lead the company into its next phase of development, and confident that the further experience he gains in the coming year will fully equip him for the task of CEO.

Now the governance and leadership issues at TNK–BP were publicly resolved, the joint venture could look to the future. The weak trading environment had pushed down earnings (EBITDA) in 2009 to $9.0 billion, from $10.1 billion in 2008. But, avoiding the Shell–Gazprom scenario, the 50–50 ownership remained in place. TNK–BP's total sales in 2009 were $35 billion, three times the level in 2003 (see Table 1). By early 2010, the oil price was back at $75 a barrel. In March 2010, TNK–BP announced they had increased their reserves by 13 per cent and that they intended to triple their exploration budget, aiming for a 40 per cent increase in drilling volumes.[ix] Was Lord Browne's 2003 bet finally coming good?

Table 1 TNK–BP's Performance

	2003	2004	2005	2006	2007	2008	2009
Proved reserves – crude oil and condensate (billion barrels; TNK–BP estimates)	7.9	8.0	8.2	7.5	7.9	7.4	7.7
Oil production – TNK–BP (thousand barrels per day)	1,242	1,418	1,554	1,494	1,451	1,453	1,489
Total sales (US$m)	12,079	17,226	30,180	35,725	38,926	51,886	34,753
Earnings before interest, tax, depreciation and amortisation (US$m)	3,971	6,386	9,143	11,255	9,565	10,103	9,007
Internally generated capital expenditures (US$m)	877	1,354	1,869	2,948	4,233	4,683	3,126

Source: www.TNK-BP.com.

References:
[i] Carl Mortishead, *The Times*, 17 October 2003.
[ii] Terry Macalister, *Guardian*, 17 October 2003.
[iii] *FD Wire*, 8 February 2005.
[iv] Ed Crooks, *The Financial Times*, 7 July 2008.
[v] Catherine Bolton and Ed Crooks, *The Financial Times*, 16 June 2008.
[vi] Andrew Kramer, *The New York Times*, 25 July 2008.
[vii] Tony Halpin, *The Times Online*, 31 May 2008.
[viii] Terry Macallister, *Guardian*, 19 November 2009.
[ix] Rachel Cooper, *Daily Telegraph*, 1 March 2010.

International HIV/AIDS Alliance

Gerry Johnson

The International HIV/AIDS Alliance is a network of organisations throughout the world dedicated to combating the spread and the effects of HIV and AIDS. This case explains how the Alliance has developed, the issues it faces and the choices it has to make to develop its future strategy.

● ● ●

Miriam M. Shamabobo runs a small shop on the outskirts of Lusaka, Zambia. A small sideroom decorated with posters about Anti Retroviral treatment (ART) and good nutrition is the base for NZP+, a partner of the Alliance Zambia's Community Education and Referral treatment support (ACER) project.

> I have three children. When I learned that I was HIV positive, I was devastated. Eventually I joined a support group. The NZP+ and ACER people came and showed me how to look after myself. Soon I realised I also wanted to help my fellow community members living with HIV. ACER taught us how to run a support group; about giving information and advice on HIV/AIDS, income-generating activities, supporting each other, problem sharing and administration. We also do a lot of social activities together such as playing football and going for picnics which help us forget about this whole thing.
>
> Now I look after seven support groups, with 20 people in each group. We share information about how group members can approach the clinic for testing and treatment. I feel really great with NZP+ and ACER's help. I am open with my status and people in the community can talk to me about things that they may fear about their health. I have met lots of people who were so scared. They didn't want to go for testing and I have helped them with that. I told them, knowing your status gives you power.

Miriam is one of 12,400 people living with HIV/AIDS supported by Alliance Zambia's ACER project. In 2007 an estimated 2.7 million people were newly infected with HIV. A total of 33 million people are living with HIV and this number will continue to increase through a combination of new infections and more people gaining access to life-saving ART. By 2010 there were 4 million people on ART

Source: Cristhian Marguez/International HIV/AIDS Alliance/Photovoice.

globally – a 36 per cent rise compared to 2008. Despite this success, for every person living with HIV who started ART in 2006, six other individuals may become infected with HIV. With 2 million people dying of HIV-related illnesses in 2007 alone – especially in Sub-Saharan Africa – there was a need for more scalable and cost effective community based models combining the prevention of new infections and support for adults and children living with/and or affected by HIV. The Alliance had pioneered integrated delivery models in close partnership with community health systems in Côte d'Ivoire, Uganda and Zambia and by 2009 was delivering similar models in 37 other countries.

The Alliance

The main purpose of the International HIV/AIDS Alliance is to take support to communities as part of 'well articulated national responses' to the spread of HIV/AIDS. Since 1994, the Alliance has been helping to do this in Africa,

---

Figure 1 Alliance coverage by region

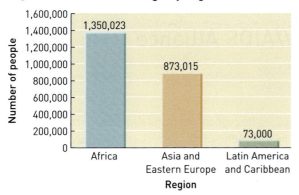

Asia, the Caribbean, Eastern Europe and Latin America. It has an international Secretariat in Brighton, UK, that provides global coordination for joint programmes, knowledge management and sharing of best practice, global policy platforms and resource mobilisation. The emphasis is, however, on developing a capacity for local responses, rather than providing support programmes centrally. This is done through linking organisations (LOs), of which there were 32 throughout the world in 2009. LOs support local communities. They are independent, not for profit organisations but of different sizes and different levels of sophistication and development.

The ACER project in Zambia is illustrative of the Alliance model. People like Miriam are supported by community based and non-governmental organisations such as NZP+, one of 1270 similar organisations supported by the Alliance across the globe. Such grassroots community action is coordinated and resourced at national level by Alliance LOs which support communities with capacity building and technical support, financial and material resources, advocacy and linkages to local and national government structures, donors and other international partners.

Coverage

The Alliance's 'IMPACT 2010' strategy, formulated in 2006, was to significantly scale up universal access to comprehensive HIV/AIDS services by 2010. By 2010 the Alliance had reached 2.3 million adults and children globally with HIV/AIDS prevention, care and support, sexual and reproductive health and treatment adherence programmes, a growth of 75 per cent compared to 2007.

The regional coverage by the Alliance is shown in Figure 1. Africa is hardest hit by the HIV/AIDS epidemic, with 67 per cent of the 33 million people living with HIV/AIDS in 2009. In most African countries there are high prevalence rates of HIV/AIDS in the population. In most countries in Asia, Eastern Europe and Latin America HIV/AIDS affects people living in population segments known as 'key populations' which have higher prevalence

rates than the general populations. These include injecting drug users (IDU), sex workers, men who have sex with men (MSM) and transgender.

Service areas

In all three regions the Alliance's work is in six generic areas, which vary depending on the nature of the epidemic in each country.

Prevention services

In 2008 the Alliance reached 894,000 people with prevention services – its single largest service type. More than 90 per cent of Alliance LOs have prevention programmes as part of their core services. In higher prevalence settings – such as Africa – the Alliance supports prevention activities and services aimed at the general population through local community structures, with the involvement of young people, with care initiatives that reach people living with HIV, and through sexual and reproductive health services. In lower prevalence countries the Alliance's work supports prevention programmes focusing on relevant members of key population groups such as MSM, IDUs and sex workers.

Care and support to orphans and vulnerable children

In 2008 in nine countries in Africa and Asia the Alliance supported 116,000 children orphaned by AIDS, living with HIV, currently caring for sick parents or who were in families that had taken in orphans. This included financial or material support – for example, school expenses, food, clothing and helping with legal issues such as inheritance and adoption as well as providing emotional and social support.

Care and support services

In 2008, the Alliance provided care and support services to 522,000 people in 14 countries. This included HIV testing and counselling, treatment, palliative care, support and reducing stigma and discrimination faced by people living with HIV/AIDS.

Treatment adherence

Even where anti-retroviral treatment becomes available, effective rollout requires people to believe that treatment is effective and to understand how it works. So the Alliance works to ensure that community structures and community leadership, especially from people living with HIV, support and endorse its introduction and use.

Technical support and capacity building

HIV affects people most when they do not have access to information, services, protection for their rights, or when they cannot act freely within their environment. In 2008, the Alliance provided 2630 civil society organisations with

Figure 2 Alliance income since 2004

technical support using expertise from the regions where it worked through a network of six technical support hubs managed by Alliance LOs.

Policy and advocacy

The Alliance aims to influence and improve the HIV policies of international policymakers and donors using the experiences of LOs and the lessons learnt about successful responses to HIV. Examples of partnerships at policy level include serving as a collaborating centre for the joint UNAIDS programme, working with the Global Fund to Fight AIDS, Tuberculosis and Malaria, a Programme Partnership Agreement with the UK Government's Department for International Development (DFID) and extensive policy work with the European Union and US Government amongst other policy initiatives.

Financial performance

During 2008, the Alliance's income rose by 12 per cent to US$72.7 million[1] (€53.4m or £48.5m). It spent 98 per cent of its income, with total expenditures amounting to $71.1 million, a 15 per cent increase on the previous year. This included a total of $57.4 million (or 81 per cent) in restricted and contract funding and the remaining $13.7 million (or 19 per cent) in unrestricted funding sources.

---

[1] The exchange rate used is £1 = €1.10 and £1 = $1.50.

The total number of donors funding the Alliance in 2008 reached 46 as compared with 38 in 2007 and 32 in 2006. New donor agreements were signed with the Australian and Swiss Governments for funding to be realised in 2009. The largest combined source of expenditure in 2008 was from governments, which provided 51.3 per cent of the Alliance's total income (as compared with 49.5 per cent in 2007). The single largest donor in 2008 remained the Global Fund, with 41 per cent of income coming from this source (as compared with 33 per cent in 2007). Figure 2 shows revenue sources and growth.

Most Alliance expenditure happens closest to where work is implemented. In 2008, the Alliance allocated a total of $27.5 million in small and mediumsized grants to 1270 implementing partners. Average size of grants increased to $17,875 from $10,800 in 2006. In addition, 40 per cent of all expenditures ($28.1 million) went towards supporting country operations and providing technical support to the 31 linking organisations and 2630 local community-based partners.

As LOs have developed, funds have increasingly gone direct to them (by 2009 amounting to some 50 per cent). There has therefore been a policy to set up regional centres (rather than one worldwide centre in Brighton) to support LOs. In consequence it became increasingly important to develop a clear Alliance strategy, not least to make clear who was doing what.

Governance

The Alliance has a central Council of Trustees. These are independent people from affected communities around the world involved in action on HIV/AIDS. They are supposed to represent beneficiaries rather than LOs or donors, although of course those beneficiaries are ultimately serviced by LOs. In terms of strategy development the Council is the ultimate decision-making body, but decisions are, of course, also influenced by both donors and by LOs. Indeed, once a year the directors of LOs meet to discuss what should be done in relation to the worldwide HIV/AIDS situation. This is not a decision making body, but a forum for consultation and an advisory body. However, by 2009 some of the LO directors were pushing to have governance representation on the Council.

Future challenges

As 2010 approached, there were significant issues that needed to be addressed. Sam McPherson, the Alliance's Head of Planning, Analysis and Learning, explained:

The changing donor environment

The donor environment is changing. There are those who think that the funding for HIV has been too great and that treating AIDS as an exceptional disease is wrong – the example of a village clinic with a very high level of provision for HIV/AIDS and no Aspirin. We argue that where there is a high level of provision for HIV/AIDS it has brought up the provision for other diseases. However, in practical terms it means that the overall funding for HIV/AIDS is going down and funding is shifting towards broader health systems: for malaria, TB, reproductive health and so on.

Bases of donor funding are also changing. There is money that comes through the Centre that is unrestricted – not allocated to particular projects or particular LOs. The Secretariat and ultimately the Council is responsible for this funding. There is also money that is given with specific targets attached; that is, therefore, restricted and where we have to account for every dollar spent. Essentially it is a contract often obtained through tenders. Increasingly in the HIV sector it is contract driven. In the past the Alliance has worked largely through unrestricted money so the accountability line for this has been fairly clear because most of the funding has gone through the Secretariat, who could hold the LOs accountable for what they did. But now increasingly funding goes directly to LOs, so the lines of accountability are more difficult to see. The LOs are not so accountable to us. For example, the Ukraine has $25 million direct funding so what the Board can say about that is limited.

All this is complicated by the diversity of expectations by donors. This highlights the importance of having a clear strategy as to what the Alliance is about. If donors do not agree with that strategy, even if they offered money, we would not take it. So for example, the Bush administration in the US up to 2009 insisted that we did abstinence-only programming; that means not talking about condoms. There was a big discussion about whether we could take money for that.

It's also important to remember that personalities matter. Donors might be government bodies but down the line it is an individual that we liaise with. And at the country level personal relations are vital. On the other hand, where we get Foundation money (e.g. from the Gates Foundation) it used to be personalised, but now they have professionals who manage it. But in all these cases, when it comes to auditing what goes on it is more formal.

Building capacity locally

How should we build capacity at a country level to deliver technical support? Take an organisation in Zambia, for example. It needs to deliver education programmes and organise condom distribution; to have robust accounting and financial systems; it needs monitoring and reporting systems to capture how they are operating; it needs good governance; and good quality programming. Many LOs have 'capacity gaps' in these respects. Traditionally we used to fly out and provide that support but it was decided in 2007 that that we could no longer afford that many people from the centre flying all over the world. It was also felt that the capacity to provide that support was increasingly available in the regions. So we decided that provision of services should be decentralised through hubs which would sit in certain LOs. The centre would support a team in a hub which would in turn support other LOs. Also we could get donors to agree to fund technical support through the hubs more easily than getting them to agree to such support in the centre. For example we have a country operation in Sudan which has big funding from the World Bank. It has clear capacity constraints around a finance system. Uganda has a hub and we would want to provide financial support from Uganda.

However, all this does require directors of LOs to take responsibility for it and there are reservations on the Council as to whether it will work. It is still under discussion.

What is the Alliance?

There is a good deal of reference to the Alliance as a 'family' and the idea that there has to be a joint agreement on key issues. There is also the idea of 'them and us' – our being together against external difficulties, trying to agree on important issues and the support of each other in these circumstances. The family metaphor is useful in terms of building this glue of an alliance. But I don't think anyone is kidding themselves: there are difficult dynamics as there are within any family.

The formally agreed alliance structure by which the 'family' operates emphasises both horizontal and vertical links that should provide a competitive advantage on tenders and other ways of accessing government support. Alliance LOs are committed to supporting organisation-wide initiatives that will help the Alliance as well as delivering their own national objectives. And the secretariat will continue to provide them with the support they need to do this. Underlying this is the point that the members of the alliance will have expectations of each other as well as from the Secretariat. But it also requires clarity on what services are provided from the centre and what from the hubs. Moreover, it is clear that there are those who do ask questions about the nature of the vertical relationships in the Alliance. Some directors of LOs have argued that the historic governance situation needs turning on its head so that the Secretariat becomes, as it were, the servant of the LOs – and the directors of LOs.

The role of the Centre

Typically the Centre is held responsible for performance and that may even be so if funding goes direct to the LOs. For example, Ukraine is part of the Alliance: if something went wrong in the Ukraine, we as an Alliance are bound to be answerable. In that respect it is rather like a franchise. So a fundamental question is: what is the Council responsible for? Is it responsible for the overall strategy; or is it responsible for funds that come through the Centre alone; or what?

There also remains an important need for central co-ordination and central services. Accreditation is a good example. Country X does not get accreditation if it does not meet the criteria set down by the Centre. That decision is ultimately taken by a sub-committee of the Board but that sub-committee does have representation from the LOs. Another example is that the list of available consultants to LOs is growing considerably. One of the concerns of the Secretariat is the quality control of these consultants, not all of whom are known to the Centre.

The switch to service provision through hubs has, however, meant that the role of the Centre has changed. As Sam explains:

It has meant a reduction from 130 to about 100 people. It hasn't so much been about cutting back the size as changing their type of work. The Centre now houses specialists in, for example, fund raising, knowledge management, not least on specialist technical aspects of HIV treatment, sharing and identifying the capacity gaps in LOs, arranging the resources to get that capacity filled from the hubs and helping the LOs report back to the donors. We don't need people who can go out and tell people about systems so much. We do need people to manage and monitor what's going on from the Centre.

Revising the strategy

In 2009, Sam McPherson was charged with coordinating a revision of the Alliance's strategy. There followed extensive consultation with LOs, Council members and members of the secretariat as well as some external stakeholders (donors and key leaders in the field), the outcome of which was a 'Summary of Strategic Options' intended as a framework for in-depth consultation across the Alliance. Extracts from it are reproduced below.

SUMMARY OF STRATEGIC OPTIONS

The paper focuses on a discussion of five '**strategic drivers**'[2] that that have emerged from the analysis of the consultation exercises to date and enable us to focus on the main issues that the Alliance needs to address in a new strategy. For each driver the paper outlines a range of **options** that are open to the organisation to address each of these strategic driver questions. These represent the critical strategic

decisions that will need to be made when formulating the new strategy. Although the options presented are in the most part NOT mutually exclusive, the current environment requires the Alliance to make hard choices about what we do and how we move forward. Resource constraints mean that we cannot 'do' everything and choices made in one area will necessarily limit choices in others. Choices made

---

[2] In the paper a 'strategic driver' means an overriding strategic priority area that:
• has been identified on the basis of a wide range of different facts, trends and issues;
• and must be addressed.

'under' one strategic driver will also necessarily impinge on choices that need to be made on others, in order for the overall strategy to be coherent. The paper describes the main options in a non-biased way. Intentionally what is presented is NOT a discussion of the pro's and con's of each option. The feedback received will ensure that the strategic decisions taken are informed by a range of stakeholder views. The emphasis is on generating feedback and comment that can be used by the Senior Management Team and ultimately, the Board of Trustees, as they formulate a new strategy.

Driver 1:
'Identifying a clear "focus" for the Alliance'

Key question: How do we leverage our strengths to best respond to the needs of individuals and communities affected by HIV/AIDS?

The majority of stakeholders consulted argued we must continue to place the needs of individuals and communities affected by HIV/AIDS first, renewing our commitment to supporting communities to reduce the spread of HIV and meet the challenges of AIDS.

Options

1a: The current model – the HIV lens
Keep a strong focus on HIV/AIDS and our identity as an HIV/AIDS organisation. Include other health-related issues in our programmed work but only those directly relevant to HIV: Tuberculosis, Hepatitis C, Sexual and Reproductive Health. Policy work remains focused on HIV/AIDS and bringing the voices of affected communities to policy arenas at different levels.

1b: The health lens
Broaden our focus to health issues to position ourselves as the leading organisation to channel funds and technical support to Community Based Organisations to respond to the health needs of their communities. This approach builds on a view that improving health and health systems generally is the only/best way to impact HIV in the long run.

1c: The human rights lens
Position ourselves as the leading organisation to build communities' capacities to claim their rights. Focus on empowering people to understand their rights, change legal frameworks and create mechanisms to monitor implementation. This approach builds on a view that improving people's abilities to claim their rights is the only/best way to impact HIV in the long run.

1d: The HIV lens with broader scope
Build on our capacity to mobilise and work with key populations, building their capacity and policy strengths to position ourselves as the leading organisation to support those most vulnerable to HIV. We use a 'HIV lens' to select the countries and the communities we work with; having done that we then work with them and focus on meeting their broader health needs as well as empowering them to claim their broader human rights. This approach builds on a view that focusing on protecting the rights and improving the overall health and lives of those most vulnerable to HIV is the only/best way to impact HIV in the long run.

Driver 2:
'Adapting to a changed financial environment'

Key question: How do we deliver our mission in a reduced and changed financial environment?

Given the increasing financial pressure, we need to deliver more for less. At the same time however, it is also important to identify new avenues and approaches to proactively increase revenue.

Options

Category 1: Increase income for the Alliance

2a: International advocacy/policy agenda
Align with global partners to drive the promotion of innovative funding mechanisms. The logic here is that we need to link with other organisations working in the broader field of development and health (such as Oxfam, etc.) to advocate global increases (or at least protect current levels) in funding for health and HIV/AIDS.

2b: National advocacy/policy agenda
Build national LO capacity to engage with governments for increasing the allocation of direct budget support to civil society. Here the logic is that (rightly) the available HIV/AIDS funding is increasingly coming under the control of governments within developing countries and therefore we need to build capacity of our organisations in these countries to lobby and advocate for these funds to be spent on the civil society response.

2c: Explore income generation responses at the LO and secretariat level

(i)   Engage in more commercial type activities to generate funds (e.g. link with corporates and/or 'sell' consultancy using the overheads/'profits' as an income stream).

(ii) Increase in-house capacity to manage large contracts (primarily on large-scale USAID contracts).

The logic here is that a significant amount of the available funding is now being delivered through these mechanisms and we need to adapt our organisation to be able to 'win' these contracts.

(iii) Explore new funding streams, i.e. funds from the general public (in the North), the corporate sector (CSR funds), high value donors and trusts.

2d: Building capacity of LOs to access increased in-country direct funding

Develop and devolve capacity and increase investment within LOs for successful resource mobilisation. The logic here is similar to point 2b: the money is increasingly in-country. Therefore we need to invest in building capacity in-country to access these funds. This might mean a concurrent reduction in resources being invested in secretariat (UK) fundraising efforts.

Category 2: Adjust to fit available resources

2e: Implement efficiency savings to maximise use and impact of available resources.

2f: Consolidate and/or increase focus on large LOs/ programmes, whilst reducing investment in LO/COs that are less cost effective and/or have less coverage. The logic here is that we might need to take hard decisions about investing only in those countries/programmes that we know have the most chance of increasing impact. This is very controversial since these decisions will mean people and countries will 'miss out'.

2g. Explore further devolution of Secretariat functions in order to pass on higher levels of unrestricted funds to LOs. This could be in the form of one or more regional secretariats. The logic here is that (arguably) resources go further through a devolved model since running costs are often less in developing countries than in the UK (think offshoring in the IT sector).

Category 3: Changing the Alliance model

2h: Explore expansions and/or mergers that offer skills and expertise in complementary areas which would expose the Alliance to new areas of work, new funders, and an expanded supporter base. Rather than try and build capacity in key areas from scratch we would explore mergers to 'acquire' capacity from other organisations.

The choices made here will necessarily depend on the strategic decisions made with respect to driver 1. The options are designed to capture the need to approach this question from several perspectives.

Options

Category 1: Geographical scope and coverage

3a: Increase the number of countries that are supported through the Alliance

3b: Maintain the current number of countries

3c: Reduce the number of countries that are supported through the Alliance

Category 2: A policy perspective

These options are not mutually exclusive but there is need to make some strategic choices as resources are limited.

3g: Focus on global policy work

Led by the Secretariat, focusing our policy work on ensuring that the Alliance voice is heard in the global policy arena and that LO experience and expertise is leveraged to impact on the global policy environment. The logic here is that we need to influence the global policy agenda on HIV/AIDS in order to ensure that 'our' constituency is well represented. This type of work (representation at global meetings, etc.) however is not cheap.

3h: Focus on regional policy work

The Secretariat and LOs together invest in policy work that focuses on regional policy issues. The logic here is that some of the key policy 'battles' are now taking place at the regional level. We need therefore to be investing in impacting in this area.

3i: Focus on national policy work

Focus on building the capacity of LOs and other civil society organisations to operate at the national level on national policy issues. The logic behind this option is that actually some of the most key policy issues are occurring at the local and national level (e.g. structural/ legal barriers are found undermining rights of people living with HIV). We need therefore to invest in building capacity of national level policy work to happen.

Driver 3:
'Making choices about where, how and with whom we work'

Key question: How should the Alliance make strategic choices about where to work, what to do and with whom?

Driver 4:
'Ensuring the provision of cutting-edge technical support'

Key question: What is the best model for technical support to enable the Alliance to achieve its mission?

▶

The purpose of investing in technical support is to ensure the delivery of quality programmes and support to communities. Communities receive direct support from Alliance LOs/COs and this will not change in the new strategy. The question is how best to provide technical support to LOs/COs so that they can maximise their technical strengthening role.

Since 2008, the Regional Technical Support Hubs have been the primary international technical support providers within the Alliance global partnership. LOs contact a Hub directly for technical support without going through the Secretariat. Significant progress has been made in terms of establishing the Hubs' ability to deliver quality technical support. However, the consultation raised significant concerns about how technical support delivery can be improved further to ensure that the quality of Alliance programming is maximised.

Options

4a: The current model
Technical support to civil society organisations is delivered by a Regional TS hub hosted by an Alliance Linking Organisation. This organisation mobilises expertise either from other linking organisations within the family or from consultants on an ad hoc or regular basis.

4b: Regional Secretariats
One to be created in each geographic region. Technical support is organised by the Alliance Regional Secretariat structure, drawing its expertise from the regional office itself, from LOs and from external consultants.

4c: Technical Support Department
A central mechanism with expertise to deliver technical support to civil society organisations. This can be located either at the Secretariat or localised in a geographic region.

Driver 5: 'Maintaining a strong Alliance global partnership'

Key question: How can we maintain a strong global Alliance that adds value to all its partners?

This question is not one which focuses exclusively on the 'value' of the Secretariat for the Alliance but rather on the question of how all members of the Alliance can contribute to maintaining a strong and dynamic global partnership.

Options

5a: Focus on the global core 'value' areas that being part of the Alliance brings
Investing in understanding and realising for all partners the five areas of 'value' identified by LOs/COs and the Secretariat as priorities:

- Knowledge management and technical support
- Working at a regional and global level
- Resource mobilisation
- Credibility and prestige
- Protection

5b: Develop different 'partnership' packages to meet different expectations of the Alliance
Build upon the core 'value' areas listed above but rather than try and agree universal Alliance-wide core values, focus on categorising organisations into groups that require/expect different value from being part of the Alliance. The Alliance family is made up of a diverse set of organisations that have different needs. We could therefore segment these organisations and deliver a more customised offering to these different segments . . . There would however be additional costs in taking this approach.

CASE STUDY

Doman Synthetic Fibres plc (B)

Peter Jones

The case describes a company in the chemical/synthetic fibres industry that is in 'strategic drift'. The patent on its established product is about to expire but the company has a potential replacement. The case presents three strategic options for the future which can be evaluated in resource planning and profitability terms.

● ● ●

'Over the past few years, as the results of major companies continue to show, textiles – and fibres in particular – have continued to be a difficult market and, although last year's results were up on the previous year, they were still very poor compared to other industries.'[i]

It was against this gloomy scene that Doman Synthetic Fibres (DSF) had been trading (see Appendices 1 and 2 which give details of the company's financial results for 2006–08). DSF was a small but technically successful company by the standards of the man-made fibre industry. Founded in 1946 by Wilfred Doman, grandfather of the present Managing Director, Wendy Doman, the company was heavily dependent on the sales of Britlene, which accounted in 2008 for some 95 per cent of total sales. This heavy dependence on a single product had been a familiar characteristic of the company for nearly 20 years, first with Aslene and then since 2000 with Britlene. It was only the patent protection on Britlene which had enabled DSF to survive the turbulent and difficult situation of recent years.

Synthetic Fibres as a whole represented some 40 per cent of the total UK textile production but, within that, Teklatite fibres, of which Britlene was the leading commercial type, accounted for only 3 per cent of total synthetic fibre production. Britlene was used mainly in the manufacture of heavy duty clothing although small quantities were used to produce industrial goods such as tyre cord and industrial belting.

In 2007, the R&D Department had developed a new product, Crylon, which like Britlene was a Teklatite fibre. Crylon had all the properties of Britlene but was superior in its heat resistant qualities. It was hoped that this additional property would open up new clothing uses (e.g. a substitute for asbestos clothing, adding to nightwear to improve its flame resistance) and new industrial uses in thermal and electrical insulation.

Wendy Doman expressed her attitude to Crylon:

For too long we've relied on Britlene as our only product. It's been a faithful friend to us but with patent protection running out in 2010, we must expand into something else and Crylon is the obvious candidate. We've got the technical experience in this area; it'll use our existing sales outlets; we could even convert some Britlene capacity to cut down on our capital costs and our agent has drawn up a watertight patent.

By mid-2008 the major technical and engineering problems associated with bulk production of Crylon seemed to have been solved but two years of the patent had already expired. Wendy Doman had set up a Capital Investment Working Party to put forward proposals on how the new product should be phased into the company's activities.

Production

The basic production method of Britlene and Crylon is similar to that of most man-made fibres. To produce a man-made fibre, an oil-based organic chemical is polymerised (a process of joining several molecules into a long chain) in conditions of intense pressure and heat, often by the addition of a suitable catalyst. This polymerisation takes place in large autoclaves (an industrial pressure-cooker). The polymer is then extruded (similar to being forced through the rose of a garden watering can), rapidly cooled and then either spun onto cones and bobbins or collected in bales. The spun material is known as filament yarn; the bales are called staple fibre.

For Britlene, DSF had bought the polymer, Polymutastine 15, as the raw material, which it chemically processed before the extrusion stage. However, for Crylon, it would be buying Hexatitanone, and polymerising this organic chemical itself. The raw materials for Britlene and Crylon were produced at Teesside by Hunters Chemicals. For both raw materials DSF took a low percentage of Hunters' production and Hunters was not a direct competitor of DSF in the fibre market.

Britlene facilities

Britlene was produced at three factories: Teesside, Bradford and Dumfries. The largest site was Teesside with three plants. There was one plant at each of the other two sites. The Teesside plant was next door to the raw material supplier and was not too far from the main markets in Lancashire and Yorkshire. Bradford was close to the main customers and as such proved a help for sorting out customer liaison on matters such as quality and rush orders.

All five production plants, purchased over the last eight years, had a design capacity of 5.5 million kilograms per annum of Britlene, independent of whether filament or staple was produced. However, after allowing for maintenance and an annual shutdown, expected output was 5 million kilograms per annum. Each plant was still in excellent order. Production was done on a five day a week, 24 hours a day (three shifts) basis. There was no weekend production, although Saturday had been worked occasionally in times of high demand, and the trade unions had agreed to allow members to work one Saturday per month at overtime rates.

Each plant employed about 52 people on production and 11 on maintenance. There was no difference in plant labour levels for the three shifts, but maintenance workers were mainly attached to the day shift.

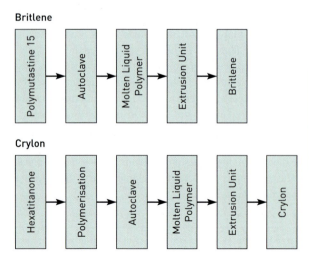

Britlene

Crylon

Figure 1

Proposed Crylon facilities

The distinctive features of Crylon were created in the new polymerisation process. When asked to explain the differences between the two products, the Research Director, Roger Tillotson, drew Figure 1:

> The key to Crylon is in the polymerisation. What we'll need is a new polymerisation-cum-autoclave unit to replace the old autoclave-only unit. The extrusion unit for Crylon is basically the same as we are using for Britlene. By the time we've reached the molten polymer state we've done the chemistry. Extrusion is just to get a storable and saleable product.

Together with Alpens, a major construction company, DSF has produced an acceptable plant design. A pilot plant was working very satisfactorily. This had provided valuable cost information. Jim Lewis explained:

> Our self-produced Crylon polymer should be about 10 per cent cheaper than Polymutastine 15, despite the extra costs of about 15 men on the new polymer plant and its extra depreciation. Of course these are only estimated from our pilot plant experience.

Acquiring Crylon capacity

There were two ways of acquiring Crylon capacity. DSF could convert a Britlene plant, or it could construct an entirely new plant.

For a *conversion* a new polymer unit would need to be constructed first; when complete it would be connected to the extrusion unit which would require minor conversion taking three months. Instrumentation and start-up checks would then be performed for a further three months, during which time there would be roughly half capacity. This meant that from the completion of the new polymer unit the whole plant would not be at full capacity for about six months. At least six months' planning and technical work was required by Alpens before construction could start.

Figure 2 sets out Alpens' estimated time scale for conversion of a Britlene unit to make Crylon.

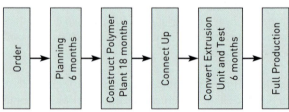

Figure 2

A *newly constructed* plant would mean building both a polymerisation and extrusion unit. Although no conversion was involved, such a plant could only operate at roughly half capacity for three months after start-up, while testing took place. Figure 3 shows Alpens' estimated time scale for a newly constructed unit.

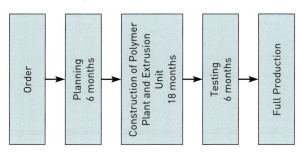

Figure 3

Preliminary market estimates for the new product made in 2008 indicated that an increase in the total number of plants might well be needed, especially if the predicted new industrial uses materialised. Wendy Doman, however, had gone on record saying:

> The creation of an entirely new site for operations would increase the complexities of multi-site operation to an unacceptable level. Conversely, the complete closure of one of the three existing sites is, I consider, a waste of the human and physical resources that we have invested in that location. I believe expansion could take place at one, two or all of the existing sites.

Estimated Crylon capital costs

The estimated costs and stage payments required by Alpens for a Crylon polymer plant and extrusion unit construction were:

for a Crylon polymer plant	£3,000,000[1]
for a new Crylon extrusion unit	£1,800,000
for a conversion of a Britlene extrusion unit to Crylon	£600,000

Thus the total cost of a new Crylon plant would be £4.8 million and a conversion £3.6 million.

The cost of the polymer plant was payable in three six monthly instalments of £1 million; the first being due one year after ordering.

The cost of new extrusion units or conversions was due on completion.

Land for two more plants was already available at Teesside and for one more at Bradford but any other developments would require an additional purchase.

Marketing

Since the late 1980s DSF had been a one-product company. Prior to the introduction of Britlene in 2000 the company

had relied on the patent protected product Aslene before moving into Teklatite fibres with Britlene. Experience with Aslene suggested that the near monopoly position held by Britlene could be eroded fairly rapidly once patent rights were removed at the end of 2010. One other UK manufacturer was producing Teklatite fibres and was rumoured to have plans to produce Britlene after that date. There were also fears that international competitors would enter the market after the Britlene patent expired.

Supply and demand

Britlene had carved out a secure niche in the man-made fibre market. Sluggish world trade in textiles and fibres had curtailed growth since 2005 but DSF had been able to produce and sell at virtually full capacity during 2005–08. The company had not needed nor had it tried to penetrate foreign markets with the exception of a small effort in 2001.

Peter Moore, DSF's Marketing Director, was confident that Crylon would enable DSF to regain a 90 per cent share in the UK Teklatite fibres market within three years of its introduction. He felt confident in the future of Crylon:

> We've moved customers once from Aslene to Britlene. I see no reason why we can't do it again. Crylon is a better product than Britlene. Initial customer trials have been most encouraging. With the right kind of effort I believe we can also generate sales of 5–10 million kg. of Crylon for use in thermal and electrical insulation. This is a mere flea-bite in comparison to sales of glass and mica for this purpose.

Pricing

Since 2006 prices for Britlene had only moved marginally. DSF had not attempted to pass on cost increases, as in the depressed textile market Peter Moore felt this would have been resisted by customers. In 2008 the list price for Britlene was 98 pence/kg.

There was considerable uncertainty about the price which could be obtained for Crylon. For textile uses it might command a premium (estimated at 10–20 per cent) over Britlene due to its improved qualities, but Peter Moore felt that this premium could well be used up in trying to shift customers onto the new product. Additionally, the increased competition anticipated once Britlene patents expired was expected to depress Teklatite prices.

The industrial market was a great unknown. Rough and ready calculations suggested that a price between 100p and 120p per kg ought to put it on a competitive basis with existing materials. However, the conservative nature of manufacturers taking a totally new material threw doubt on these estimates.

---

[1] £1 = $1.50 and £1 = €1.10 as at 1 March 2010.

Selling and promotion

In 2008 promotion expenditure was £50,000, spent on sales literature (£13,000) and limited advertising in newspapers and trade journals (£7000), and on the website (£30,000). This expenditure level was typical of the previous few years. For the launch of Britlene in 2000 the company had 'gone to town' by industry standards, spending £310,000 – on press advertising (£150,000) and a joint promotion with selected customers (£160,000). This had enabled the rapid acceptance of Britlene by the textile industry.

Peter Moore felt that once Crylon was established in the textile market its promotional needs would be similar to those for Britlene, but to break into the new industrial markets would require a much greater promotional effort, and the media mix would need to be different.

Personnel

In December 2008 DSF employed 414 people. Of these, weekly payroll employees, concerned mainly with production and maintenance, numbered 315. There were approximately 63 payroll employees on each of the five plants. The remaining 99 employees were monthly paid staff. Apart from supervisory production staff and commercial staff at the sales offices, all staff worked at the Teesside headquarters. Most payroll employees in DSF were unionised and John Williams described the company's relationship with the Union as 'good', although there was unease about possible plant closures. He was also concerned about labour relations in the construction industry, which he feared could delay building programmes and increase costs.

Unemployment

At all locations the general unemployment rate was higher than the national average, but the rate for chemically skilled workers was low at all sites. Supply of the particular skills DSF wanted was problematic and only at Teesside would extra demand for skilled labour be readily met.

Finance

Financial performance

The financial performance of the company during 2006–08 had been a cause of real concern (see Appendix 1). Up to five years previously the profit figures had been steady and a return on capital employed before tax of around 20 per cent was considered to be most satisfactory. As Mr Greenhaugh put it:

> In the early part of this century this company was considered a good investment by most analysts. We have always been financed solely by the share capital and retained earnings and this, coupled with our patent protection, made us a safe bet. In the last 2 or 3 years,

however, things haven't looked so good. Our share price has dropped to a disturbing level despite our continuing policy of maintaining the level of dividends. Our P/E ratio is now 7 and this is very disappointing. Investors are not sure where we are going as a company, but I believe the introduction of Crylon, if it comes through in time, will restore confidence.

Raising finance

Mr Greenhaugh compared the early 2009 situation to the similar position in 2000 when Britlene had been introduced to the market. Then, the initial development costs had been financed internally out of the previous profits as had about half the capital investment. Another £2.5 million had been required from external sources. This was a substantial amount for a company the size of DSF but confidence had been high, and a 1 for 1 rights issue at 62.5p had been fully subscribed. (The share price at the time had been standing at 68p.) Mr Greenhaugh wished confidence in DSF was as buoyant in 2008 and the share price as strong.

The first working party meeting

In setting up the working party in early 2009 to consider the Crylon case, Wendy Doman had picked one obviously up-and-coming manager from each major function. It was clear that she considered this exercise as part of their development, and success could easily mean rapid advancement on the back of Crylon expansion. As they sat down for their first meeting, the members of the working party realised that they all had a personal as well as a professional interest in how the study progressed.

There was general, albeit reluctant, agreement among the team that trends in production techniques and locations would necessitate a hard look at whether all three sites should continue, despite the MD's wish to preserve all three sites. However, there was considerably less consensus on the more strategic issue of whether to proceed with Crylon, and if so how fast and how much capacity to install.

Les Hill (from Finance) wondered whether they should develop it at all. He argued that Britlene was not yet a 'dog' in BCG terms. With suitable economies they could continue to make a profit from it, even if, as he acknowledged, the price might need to reduce in two years' time to deter new producers when the patent came off. He felt this was far less risky than significant capital investment which would stretch the company's resources and financial independence.

Chris Henson (from Sales and Marketing) viewed this as far too cautious and favoured what she called a 'two-horse' strategy. She believed some existing customers would prefer to continue with Britlene while others would switch to Crylon. With appropriate effort focused on industrial users she believed they could achieve a total of 30 million kg of sales, split between the two products.

Trevor Bryant (from Operations) felt both approaches lacked ambition. He argued that Crylon had been well received by customers and that the company should introduce it into both markets as soon as feasible. 'What is the point of being half-hearted and waiting?'

[2] This spreadsheet is available to tutors and students on the *Exploring Corporate Strategy* website. It will assist in the detailed resource planning needed to evaluate these options.

A simple EXCEL planning model[2] had been produced to look at the financial consequences of various scenarios. Brief results of the three views above are given in Appendix 3. The Henson and Bryant views also include the two possibilities of achieving or not a 15 per cent premium on the Crylon price over Britlene.

Reference:
[1] From an article in the textile trade press, July 2008.

APPENDIX 1 Profit and loss summary 2006–08

	2006 £ 000s		2007 £ 000s		2008 £ 000s	
Sales						
Products	23,602		23,840		24,042	
Licences	951		976		1,050	
		24,553		24,816		25,092
Cost of Goods Sold						
Raw Materials	6,086		6,592		7,230	
Direct Labour	6,391		6,940		7,521	
Prod. Overheads	2,177		2,602		2,869	
Depreciation	700		700		700	
		15,354		16,834		18,320
Gross Profit		9,199		7,982		6,772
Other Overheads						
Promotion and Sales	374		395		402	
Distribution	905		986		1,030	
General Admin.	2,738		3,009		3,320	
Research & Develop.	890		1,250		950	
		4,907		5,640		5,702
Operating Profit		4,292		2,342		1,070
Interest Payable		(189)		(231)		(240)
Net Profit Before Tax		4,481		2,573		1,310
Corporation Tax		1,814		1,146		704
Net Profit after tax		2,667		1,427		606
Dividend declared		750		750		750
Retained Earnings		1,917		677		(144)

APPENDIX 2 Balance sheet at 31 December 2008

Fixed Assets	£ 000s Cost	£ 000s Depreciation	£ 000s Net
Freehold Land and Buildings	8,010	(150)	7,860
Teesside 5,210			
Bradford 1,605			
Dumfries 1,195			
Plant and Machinery	8,790	(7,000)	1,790
Teesside 4,780			
Bradford 2,050			
Dumfries 1,960			
			9,650
Trade Investments at Cost			4,152
Working Capital			
Current Assets			
Work in Progress and Stock	2,720		
Debtors	2,980		
Cash	868		
		6,568	
Less Current Liabilities			
Creditors	2,307		
Taxation	436		
Dividend	510		
		3,253	
Net Working Capital			3,315
			17,117
Financed by:			
Share Capital			5,000
Capital Reserves			
Share Premium		500	
Revaluation Reserve		4,500	
			5,000
Retained Earnings			
Balance at 31.12.07		7,261	
Retained Profit 2008		(144)	
			7,117
			17,117

APPENDIX 3 Some results of possible future scenarios

Year	2009	2010	2011	2012	2013	2014
Option A – Hill						
Assumptions						
Price Britlene p/kg	1	1	0.9	0.9	0.9	0.9
Sales Vol. Britlene m kg	25	25	25	25	25	25
Key Results						
Net Profit before tax £m	2.0	2.2	0.6	0.6	0.6	0.6
Annual trading cash flow £m	1.6	1.6	−0.7	0.2	0.2	0.2
Capital payments £m	−	−	−	−	−	−
Net cash flow £m	1.6	1.6	−0.7	0.2	0.2	0.2
Cumulative cash balance £m (inc. trade investments at cost)	6.6	8.1	7.4	7.7	7.9	8.1
Option B1 – Henson (15 per cent premium)						
Assumptions						
Price Britlene p/kg	1	1	0.95	0.95	0.95	0.95
Price Crylon p/kg			1.10	1.10	1.10	1.10
Sales Vol. Britlene m kg	25	25	20	15	10	10
Sales Vol. Crylon m kg			5	11	17	20
Key Results						
Net Profit before tax £m	2.0	2.2	−1.1	−0.2	1.3	3.8
Annual trading cash flow £m	1.6	1.6	−1.8	0.5	2.1	4.3
Capital payments £m	−	2.0	5.6	6.3	1.4	−
Net cash flow £m	1.6	−0.4	−7.4	−5.8	0.7	4.3
Cumulative cash balance £m (inc. trade investments at cost)**	6.6	6.1	−1.2	−7.1	−6.4	−2.0
Option B2 – Henson (no premium)						
Assumptions						
Price Britlene p/kg	1	1	0.95	0.95	0.95	0.95
Price Crylon p/kg			0.95	0.95	0.95	0.95
Sales Vol. Britlene m kg	25	25	20	15	10	10
Sales Vol. Crylon m kg			5	11	17	20
Key Results						
Net Profit before tax £m	2.0	2.3	−1.5	−1.8	−1.3	0.5
Annual trading cash flow £m	1.6	1.6	−2.2	−1.0	−0.5	1.9
Capital payments £m	−	2.0	5.6	6.3	1.4	−
Net cash flow £m	1.6	−0.4	−7.8	−7.3	−1.9	1.9
Cumulative cash balance £m (inc. trade investments at cost)**	6.6	6.1	−1.6	−9.0	−10.8	−8.9
Option C1 – Bryant (15 per cent premium)						
Assumptions						
Price Britlene p/kg	1	1	0.95	0.95	−	−
Price Crylon p/kg			1.10	1.10	1.10	1.10
Sales Vol. Britlene m kg	25	25	16	5	−	−
Sales Vol. Crylon m kg			9	22	33	40
Key Results						
Net Profit before tax £m	2.0	2.2	−3.7	−0.8	3.6	6.9
Annual trading cash flow £m	1.6	1.6	−1.0	0.2	6.0	8.8
Capital payments £m	−	6.0	12.0	8.0	3.6	2.8
Net cash flow £m	1.6	−4.4	−13.0	−7.8	2.4	6.0
Cumulative cash balance £m (inc. trade investments at cost)**	6.6	2.1	−10.9	−18.7	−16.3	−10.3
Option C2 – Bryant (no premium)						
Assumptions						
Price Britlene p/kg	1	1	0.95	0.95	−	−
Price Crylon p/kg			0.95	0.95	0.95	0.95
Sales Vol. Britlene m kg	25	25	16	5	−	−
Sales Vol. Crylon m kg			9	22	33	40
Key Results						
Net Profit before tax £m	2.0	2.2	−5.0	−4.1	−1.7	0.3
Annual trading cash flow £m	1.6	1.6	−2.2	−3.0	1.0	4.1
Capital payments £m	−	6.0	12.0	8.0	3.6	2.8
Net cash flow £m	1.6	−4.4	−14.2	−11.0	−2.6	1.3
Cumulative cash balance £m (inc. trade investments at cost)**	6.6	2.1	−12.0	−23.0	−25.6	−24.3

** The lowest negative figure in this row indicates the maximum cash injection needed by DSF to fund the strategy, in addition to selling the trade investments of £4.2m.

CASE STUDY

Sony Corporation: restructuring continues, problems remain

Vivek Gupta and Indu Perepu

Sony, the electronics and media giant, has undertaken many restructuring exercises in the past in response to poor financial performance. This case focuses on the most recent restructuring of the Sony Group in 2009 when once again it found itself in a financial crisis. Why should this latest attempt be successful when previous attempts were not?

• • •

In crisis, again

In May 2009, Japan-based multinational conglomerate, Sony Corporation (Sony) announced that it had posted a loss of ¥98.9 billion[1] (£0.72bn or $1.09bn or €0.79bn) for the fiscal year ending March 2009. This was only Sony's second loss since 1958. The company had reported a net profit of ¥369 billion for the fiscal year ending March 2008. Sony also warned that with consumers worldwide cutting back on spending in the light of the economic recession, the losses could be up to ¥120 billion for the year ending March 2010.

Sony's announcement of losses came after its CEO, Howard Stringer (Stringer), had announced a major reorganisation plan in February 2009. The plan involved a new organisational structure for Sony, closure of eight of its 57 manufacturing sites, and a reduction of the workforce by 16,000. Through this plan, Sony expected to reduce costs by ¥300 billion.

On the reorganisation, Stringer said: 'This reorganisation is designed to transform Sony into a more innovative, integrated, and agile global company. (These changes and reorganization) will now make it possible for all of Sony's parts to work together.'[i]

Sony had gone through a series of reorganisation programmes starting from the year 1994, the aim being to improve the financial performance and competitiveness of the company. However, most of them failed to achieve the desired results. Analysts blamed the 'silo culture', which

Source: Getty Images/AFP.

prevented different divisions in Sony from communicating and cooperating with each other, for the company's problems.

Commenting on the reasons for the failure of earlier restructuring efforts, *Fortune* magazine, in June 2009, wrote:

> The culprit in nearly every case has been Sony's tradition-bound mentality, one that remained too focused on building excellent analog machines in an increasingly digital world. And though Stringer has been pushing for transformation since his first days in the top job, by his own admission he has been hamstrung by the management culture in Sony's home market and the repercussions of bad decisions made years ago that still haunt the company.[ii]

---

[1] €1 ≈ ¥125 and £1 ≈ ¥138 and $1 ≈ ¥90 as at March 2010.

Stringer's restructuring efforts

Stringer became the first non-Japanese CEO of Sony in March 2005. He identified five main challenges for Sony. These were: getting rid of its silo culture, attaining profitability across businesses, making products in line with industry standard technologies, improving the competencies in software and services, and divesting the company of its non-strategic assets. In order to deal with these challenges, Stringer announced a major reorganisation plan in September 2005.

According to the plan, Sony was reorganised into five business groups – the electronics business group, the games business group, the entertainment business group, the personal solutions business group, and the Sony financial holdings group. Through the new structure, Sony expected to achieve coordination across different areas including planning, technology, procurement, manufacturing, sales, and marketing. Sony also announced an internal slogan, 'Sony United', which outlined several measures that could be implemented to unite the company and enhance cross-company collaboration. The plan focused on revitalising the electronics business of the company and on improving profits by reducing business categories and product models. It also aimed at removing redundancies and overlaps in business processes by focusing resources only on the company's high growth business like HD products, mobile products, semiconductor/key component devices, and network-enabled products and appliances.

After the reorganisation plan announced in September 2005, Stringer went on to revamp Sony. One of Stringer's first tasks was to revive Sony's television business, which had suffered as the company had been late in launching flat panel televisions. The television business was brought under the charge of Katsumi Ihara, who discontinued production of CRT televisions and launched the Bravia brand of LCD TVs in late 2005.

One-third of Sony's 1000 subsidiaries and affiliates were involved in businesses that were different from the core electronics and entertainment business of the company. Sony then went on to discontinue businesses such as the Qualia line of luxury electronics, a cosmetics firm, a mail order shopping company and a chain of restaurants. Sony ended the production of around 600 of the total 3000 products it manufactured. By the first half of 2006, nine factories were closed down and over 5700 jobs were eliminated.

For the year ending March 2006, Sony's earnings had improved considerably; it reported a net profit of ¥123 billion. Though the electronics business remained a problem, the sales of flat panel televisions improved significantly and so did the sales of PCs and video cameras. In 2006, analysts were of the view that Stringer's efforts had succeeded in putting the company back on the right track.

On 29 March 2007, Sony announced that in order to strengthen its product development capability and improve profitability in the electronics segment, some more changes had to be made in its organisational structure. The company established the B2B Solutions Business Group, with the aim of enhancing its B2B business growth. On these changes, Sony announced:

> The 'B2B Solutions Business Group' will unite and streamline Sony's existing Broadcasting/Professional equipment businesses, B to B solution services, and FeliCa[2] business. At the same time, by utilizing Sony's broad-based research and development achievements in its B2B Solution Business, Sony hopes to develop new business that can drive sales and profit growth in the B to B business field.[iii]

As a part of the reorganisation, Ryoji Chubachi was made President of the B2B Solutions Business Group. Forming a part of the B2B Solutions Business Group were the B&P Business Group, the FeliCa Business division, and a part of the Personal Solutions Business Group. Two new groups, the TV Business Group and the Video Business Group, were also established.

The reorganisation plan started showing encouraging results. For the fiscal year ending March 2007, Sony's sales and operating revenue increased by 10.5 per cent to ¥8.29 trillion. The upward trend continued over the next year with revenues up to ¥8.87 trillion and profits up to ¥369 billion.

Challenges remain

The fiscal year 2008–09 witnessed several challenges for Sony. This period saw strengthening of the Yen vis-à-vis the US dollar coupled with global recession. The recession slowed down consumer spending considerably on premium electronics products, which meant Sony faced problems on the product front. Though the unit sales of Bravia televisions, one of Sony's top selling products, and VAIO PCs increased, the income from these products decreased. Moreover, the sales of digital cameras reduced from 23.5 million units to 22 million units and that of video cameras from 7.7 million units to 6.2 million units.

PlayStation 3 did not fare as well as expected and its sales were far behind those of Nintendo Wii and Microsoft's Xbox 360. The manufacturing costs on PlayStation 3 were also high. For example, Sony incurred US$840 as manufacturing costs on a PlayStation 3 that was sold for US$599, when it was launched in November 2006. By late 2008, the price of the PlayStation 3 had come down to US$399, while its manufacturing cost was still US$448. Though the sales

---
[2] FeliCa, which stands for Facility Card, is an RFID Smart card system by Sony.

of PlayStation 3 consoles increased from 9.12 million units to 10.06 million units, the sales of PlayStation 2 and PlayStation Portable had reduced considerably.

In October 2008, Sony slashed the net profit forecast for the fiscal year ending March 2009 from ¥520 billion to ¥150 billion. With the Yen appreciating and hitting a 13-year high against the US dollar at ¥94.62 per US dollar in October 2008, Japanese exports became uncompetitive. Sony expected this to have an adverse impact on its earnings. The company also said that the global economic downturn had affected the sales of LCD televisions and digital cameras. After the announcement, industry experts predicted that Sony was likely to post losses in the televisions, video gaming, mobile phone and computer segments.

In December 2008, Sony announced that a reduction in the workforce was inevitable along with a re-examination of businesses which were not profitable, in order to contain the losses. It announced that 8000 jobs would be slashed and that capital investment would be reduced by 30 per cent. It announced several measures to achieve cost savings to the extent of ¥100 billion – outsourcing production, closing plants, and reducing production.

At the same time, Sony announced initiatives to improve profitability and enhance operational efficiencies in the electronics business. The initiatives taken by the company included short-term measures like reducing operational expenses and lowering inventory costs. Other measures that it planned to take included adjusting product pricing to compensate for the increase due to the appreciating Yen against global currencies, withdrawing from or downsizing unprofitable businesses, delaying the investment in semiconductors and in a few television plants, and realigning domestic and overseas manufacturing sites.

In January 2009, Sony announced that its annual operating loss would be about ¥260 billion. Analysts opined that Sony had failed to deliver because of management related problems in the company. Atul Goyal, analyst at CLSA, said;

> Seven out of eight years, Sony has failed to meet its own initial operating profit forecast. This is probably the worst track record amongst most major exporters. That means that either management is not able to anticipate challenges . . . or they fail on execution almost every time. Either way, it does not reflect well on Sony's management.[iv]

In January 2009, industry experts pointed out that by giving more power to the CEO, Sony could be brought back onto a recovery path. In their opinion, a radical change was long overdue at Sony. According to Koya Tabata, analyst from Credit Suisse:

> 'The most important thing is that, to improve organizational strength in the areas of development, purchasing, and marketing, it will be necessary to further concentrate power in the hands of [Stringer] and unless this is achieved we believe [Sony] will be unable to close the gap with competitors such as Apple and Nintendo.'[v]

Reacting to the concerns expressed by analysts and other key stakeholders, Sony announced yet another reorganisation in February 2009.

Reorganisation in 2009

Sony announced a major reorganisation which was to be made effective from April 2009. The reorganisation concentrated on the electronics and game businesses of Sony, aiming to improve their profitability and strengthen competitiveness. Commenting on the reorganisation, Stringer said:

> This reorganization is designed to transform Sony into a more innovative, integrated, and agile global company with its next generation of leadership firmly in place. The changes we're announcing today will accelerate the transformation of the company that began four years ago. They will now make it possible for all of Sony's parts to work together to assume a position of worldwide leadership and, together, achieve great things.

The company proposed to form two business groups – the Networked Products & Services Group and the New Consumer Products Group.

Under the Networked Products & Services Group would be Sony Computer Entertainment, personal computers, mobile products including Walkman, and Sony Media Software and Services. The main aim of the group was to bring in new products using Sony's technologies and also to increase the pace of innovation at Sony that would lead to higher profitability. Forming a part of these processes was the expansion of the PlayStation network platform.

The New Consumer Products Group would include television, digital imaging, home audio, and the video business of the company. The focus of this group was on achieving profitability and growth through product innovation, and improving efficiency and speed of operations. Another area of interest for this group was development and growth in the emerging markets.

As a part of the reorganisation efforts, two cross-company units were created. One was the Common Software and Technology Team which was to develop and implement integrated technology and software solutions. The group was also required to provide coordinated software development services. The other unit was the Manufacturing/Logistics/Procurement team responsible for ensuring efficient supply chain solutions for the business groups.

The reorganisation was expected to speed up the production of networked products and services. Analysts were of the view that it would help different divisions in Sony like the PC, mobiles, and entertainment divisions, and also other divisions like television, digital imaging, home audio, and video to work in tandem. This would address the issue of the prevailing silo culture in the organisation.

The reorganisation also witnessed a reshuffle of some of the top executives in the company. Stringer assumed responsibility as the President of Sony, in addition to his existing positions of CEO and Chairman. Chubachi resigned from his post as President of Sony and CEO of the electronics components unit and became the Vice-Chairman of the company. After the reshuffle, the electronics division came under Stringer's direct purview.

Some analysts saw the latest reorganisation as Stringer's effort to unite different silos that existed in the organisation. According to Jonathan Nelson, Head of private equity firm Providence Equity:

The challenge of changing the culture of an iconic Japanese company is even more difficult than dealing with the current challenges of the consumer electronics industry. He's doing as well as anyone can under the circumstances.[vi]

However, some analysts remained sceptical about the efficacy of the proposed reorganisation plan. They opined that giving more powers to Stringer will neither change Sony's business model significantly nor strengthen the fundamentals of the company's operations. According to Kazuharu Miura of Daiwa Institute of Research: 'If the transformation failed, it would lose everything. It's like crossing the Rubicon.'[vii]

References:
[i] 'Howard Stringer gets president title, aims to save $3.1 billion over the coming fiscal year', www.sony.net, 27 February 2009.
[ii] Richard Siklos, 'Sony: lost in transformation', Fortune, 26 June 2009.
[iii] 'Sony announces personnel appointments and organizational changes effective April 01, 2007', www.sony.net, 29 March 2007.
[iv] Tina Wang, 'Earnings collapse looming for Sony', www.forbes.com, 13 January 2009.
[v] Leo Lewis, 'Sony on brink of upheaval as analysts back British chief', http://business.timesonline.co.uk, 5 January 2009.
[vi] Siklos, 'Sony: lost in transformation'.
[vii] 'Sony shares outstrip peers after shake-up', www.reuters.com, 2 March 2009.

LEAX: managing through a crisis

Anders Melander and Robert Radway

This case describes developments in the LEAX Group from the second half of 2008 until the summer of 2009. The case looks at the demand crisis in manufacturing industries through 'the eyes' of a typical medium sized subcontractor in the Swedish heavy vehicle industry. More specifically, LEAX is an established manufacturer which has displayed a growth of up to 34 per cent annually over recent years within a rather stable and predictable environment. However, this changed almost overnight and the company has had to cope with unprecedented problems. Some of the key issues include sensing and interpreting the environmental change, seizing opportunities that arise in the new landscape, and the long-term reconfiguration of resources and competences in order to take advantage of future changes. The case also provides an illustration of strategic leadership in crisis and what to learn from the experience.

● ● ●

'Every day, sudden and unprecedented events turned our plans inside out. We therefore made a decision to drop all long-term planning at the Annual Meeting in December [2008]. We were forced to focus on the daily needs, yet we had to look forward. I repeatedly asked myself "How shall we overcome this crisis in a better way than our competitors?"' [i]

Early in 2008, business was flourishing for the LEAX Group ('LEAX'). Having achieved an annual average growth of 35 per cent over the previous 15 years, the prognosis now indicated that the Swedish family-owned subcontractor's turnover would exceed SEK 1 billion[1] (~€103m, ~£94m or $141m) for the first time. The capacity utilisation within the Swedish heavy vehicle industry was reaching a record-high level and the projections of the two major Swedish original equipment manufacturers (OEMs), Volvo Trucks and Scania, looked very promising. Whilst the global car industry was facing severe problems caused by the global financial crisis of 2007/08 as well as a world of rising oil prices and increased awareness of traffic emissions,[ii] the Swedish heavy vehicle industry appeared to be safe and sound. Consequently, LEAX announced a new investment of around SEK 70 million (~€7.2m, ~£6.5m or $9.9m) in September 2008. In less than one month, however, the situation changed dramatically.

---

[1] Swedish Crown (SEK) ≈ €0.10 or £0.9 or $0.14.

A sudden crisis

On 24 October, when Volvo Trucks and Scania presented their third quarter results, it was evident that LEAX's optimistic prospect was drastically inaccurate. Most remarkably, Volvo Trucks announced that orders of heavy trucks in Europe had fallen from 21,948 (Q2) to 115 (Q3).[iii] In addition, Scania revealed a decrease of incoming orders on the European market from 9287 (Q2) to 5268 (Q3).[iv] Although Volvo Trucks had laid off around 1400 employees the previous month, this came as a shock to the Swedish subcontractors. The common belief had been that the original equipment manufacturers (OEMs) were making adjustments to 'normal' market conditions after a year of exceptional demand, but in reality the financial crisis had began manifesting itself across the globe. The effects of the financial crisis on the automotive industry were first felt in America, but quickly spread throughout the world. In essence, this meant that credit markets froze, which constrained potential customers from financing purchases of motor vehicles.

Among the Swedish heavy vehicle subcontractors, the severity and unpredictability of this demand shift caused alarming declines in cash flows and essentially paralysed production overnight and the troubles continued. In Q4, Scania's incoming orders decreased by a further 98 per cent, whilst Volvo Trucks saw cancellations induce an additional decline of 82 per cent.[v] Thus, in less than four months, the Swedish heavy vehicle industry went from enjoying the

---

upside of operating leverage (i.e. operating near capacity) to feeling severe pressure and the risks associated with high fixed costs. At LEAX, the question was no longer whether there would be a downturn but rather how drastic would it be. Concerns spread quickly within the organisation as approximately 70 per cent of turnover was derived from the heavy vehicle industry (and the remaining 30 per cent from the mining and electro-mechanical industries).

LEAX's history and business model

The LEAX business and concept was formed in the year 1982 by two mechanics, Lennart Berggren and Axel Seger. The idea was simple: LEAX would not have any products of its own but produce other companies' products more effectively than they could do it themselves. Unlike other suppliers of production services, LEAX offered a broad programme including grinding, lathing and milling. The distribution of a prospectus to a selected target group and previous business partners enabled LEAX to quickly achieve a customer base, and because the founders were very talented craftsmen, the company was soon established as a proficient subcontractor of mechanical components.

By 1991, LEAX had around 40 customers, 18 employees and a turnover exceeding SEK 10 million. The next year, however, a deep recession caused the Volvo Group to temporarily stop purchasing LEAX's components. Given that around 80 per cent of turnover derived from Volvo Trucks and that LEAX had invested SEK 10 million in a new factory, the company was now facing a severe crisis. Indeed, this crisis was similar to the one starting in October 2008, but it was far less severe (incoming orders decreased by around 30 per cent compared to 70 per cent in 2008). As a result of the crisis, Lennart and Axel restructured the company, cutting the workforce by seven people and decreasing the wages of members within the owner families. Drawing conclusions from the crisis, they also created four key strategic objectives to prevent similar occurrences in the future:

1 Reduce the dependency on individual customers – a single customer will not exceed 20 per cent of the company's turnover.
2 Concentrate on manufacturing specific components – develop economies of scale by expanding operation on shafts, cogwheels and yokes.
3 Focus on quality and IT solutions – develop more accurate quality systems with efficient and reliable IT services.
4 Enhance long-term strategic work – build resources and competences to achieve new opportunities.

The focus on quality led to the identification of opportunities to help other companies build up their environmental, quality and management systems. This, in turn, emerged as the foundation of a growing consultancy operation, known as Q-Control, which proved vital to LEAX's growth in the coming years.

In 1997, Lennart and Axel handed over the ownership of LEAX to their four sons who had been involved in key positions within the organisation for several years. At the time, the company had a turnover exceeding SEK 60 million and employed 67 people. Nevertheless, in his new position as CEO of LEAX, Roger Berggren (Lennart's youngest son) announced that LEAX was going to expand even faster in the coming years. His stated vision for the company was to become a 'one step partner' for their customers, comparable to a shopping centre with several specialist stores.

During Roger's first five years as CEO, LEAX achieved remarkable results as turnover increased by more than 300 per cent. Although part of this expansion occurred on an international level, the company maintained its major production in Sweden, where both the purchasing and sales departments remained located. Roger was, however, also aware that globalisation was opening new doors and that a lot was happening within mechanical manufacturing. He believed that planning ahead was crucial and stated the company's slogan: 'the day we cease getting better, is the day we stop being good'. He summarised the financial objectives for the group by the numbers '5-5-5', meaning that in 2005 the turnover should be SEK 500 million with profits of SEK 50 million.

The results of 2005 exceeded these objectives and in 2007 LEAX had become 19 times larger than it was before the change of leadership (10 years earlier). The company was now established as a leading service provider of mechanical and electro-mechanical solutions for the Swedish heavy vehicle, electro-mechanical and mining industries. The Group consisted of six active operative corporations that collectively offered an extensive range of services in flexible machining, assembly and testing of subsystems, as well as quality consultancy and measuring techniques. Yet each subsidiary had the same generic business strategy: contract manufacturing and supplies.

LEAX achieved its expansion by taking over factories from both suppliers and customers but also by growing organically in existing factories. The Group had also further improved its managerial processes. In June 2007, LEAX began the initial phase of taking over Scania's production unit for propeller shafts and other driveline components. Through this acquisition, LEAX further extended its production portfolio and attained access to parts of Scania's work with lean production. LEAX gained competence through a highly automated factory with new competence areas such as assembly and painting. The establishment opened up new possibilities for LEAX to continue to grow, and was a good complement to the company's other sites within the area of vehicle components. The acquisition of the site increased the Group's turnover by around 75 per cent and made Scania by far the largest customer, generating 20 per cent of the total turnover in 2007 (the maximum allowed for a single customer according to LEAX's strategic objectives).

Moreover, the larger volumes developed LEAX into a more powerful player with better purchasing conditions and the capability to offer cost efficient solutions. At this time, the firm competed with 5–6 other subcontractors for its share of the intended contracts, yet the most intense competitors were the customers themselves. For instance, as competition increased among specialised subcontractors in the capital-intensive heavy vehicle industry, the OEMs were increasingly facing make-or-buy decisions where LEAX competed with the OEMs' internal factories to produce their products more effectively than they could do themselves. LEAX was successful in doing this. Despite a comprehensive investment programme of SEK 300 million launched in 2007, LEAX struggled to supply the increased quantities demanded by the market during the first half of 2008. Further investments were, therefore, announced to increase production capacity. In June 2008, a second site in Latvia was inaugurated to allow further expansion in the east of Europe. However, the prospects for future expansion changed radically in the autumn of 2008.

Facing the crisis

Early in November 2008, LEAX made a decision to cut 50 people from its Swedish-based workforce over the coming three months. But the troubles continued; as cancellations of orders escalated, both Volvo Trucks and Scania – representing LEAX's two largest customers – declared that production facilities were to be shut down completely for one month during the first quarter in 2009. Regulations of the Swedish labour market, including a three month period of notice for redundancies, required LEAX to act carefully. Malena Bergenback, Human Resources Manager at LEAX, described how she tried to handle the situation:

> After a Board Meeting around Christmas, Roger approach me in the hallway saying 'It is not enough, we have to do more!'. We initiated negotiations with the union concerning adjustments in working hours. In January 2009, we reached an agreement in which personnel could be sent home with 48 hours notice on the condition that their missed working time [maximum of 370 hours] would be made use of in an economic upswing.

Nonetheless, in less than six months, LEAX was forced to reduce the number of employees from over 600 (excluding temporary employees) to around 400 and close one of its production premises. LEAX was facing a paradox: every bit of pressure was pulling the company to do everything that was necessary to cut costs in the short term, yet Roger realised that focusing too much on the short-term needs would undermine the company's success following the period of the crisis.

> The demand in the automotive industry will return sooner or later. We have to deal with the short-term needs without forgetting about the long-term. Our focus is trying to integrate them in order to strengthen what is unique about the company.

In the beginning of April 2009, LEAX reached an additional agreement with the union concerning reduction of wages. This contract involved 15 per cent temporary reduction for all employees, including top management and the board of directors. In parallel, however, the European Union approved LEAX's project worth SEK 4.6 million which meant that employees could use some of their free time for education.

> The idea is to encourage employees to update their knowledge in order to raise the core competences of the company. If this project arouses enthusiasm among employees, we are likely to be in a better position when demand returns. (Anna Wik, Project Manager at LEAX)

Later in the spring, the mining industry followed the same development as the automotive industry, but, fortunately, the electro-mechanical industry still demonstrated a strong performance in the first half of 2009. LEAX also resumed its consultancy business to compensate for the lower production levels and temporarily moved some of the employees into this business area. In addition, LEAX had employed a rather conservative financial strategy, which helped the organisation maintain a better cash flow. Unlike some subcontractors in the heavy vehicle industry, LEAX does not use factoring (i.e., selling its accounts receivable to a third party).

> A company that uses factoring will receive its customers' payments straight away, whereas we get our money 60–90 days later. Consequently, when the market froze, we still received money three months forward whilst many of our competitors experienced a complete stoppage of cash inflow. (Roger Berggren)

A vital element of the LEAX organisation has always been the consistent engagement in strategic planning and at the beginning of April 2009 long-term strategic planning was back on the agenda. New market opportunities were gradually presenting themselves as competitors struggled to deliver their orders, but LEAX adopted a cautious approach.

Frank Johansen, Head of Marketing, expressed why LEAX did not rush into new projects:

> The orders we accept now will stay with us for a long time. Accepting lower prices to cover our fixed costs will undermine long-term success when the market returns to normal. We need to be patient. The question, however, is how patient?

As of the Annual Meeting in 2007, LEAX's strategic objective was labelled '2212', corresponding to a turnover of SEK 2 billion and EBITDA[1] of SEK 200 million by the end of year 12 (2012). In October 2008, the organisation was well ahead of schedule as predictions suggested a turnover of SEK 1.2 billion. In 2009, however, the annual turnover was less than half of that. Nevertheless, LEAX's management is still determined to achieve the '2212 objective'; although in 2010 the work is centred on cutting costs and maintaining cash flow, there is also an optimism concerning new opportunities emerging as a result of the severe crisis.

For a recent update please visit www.leax.se.

---

[1] EBITDA = Earnings Before Interest, Taxes, Depreciation and Amortisation.

References:

[i] Roger Berggren, CEO, LEAX Group.

[ii] 'Antomotive industry crisis', *New York Times*, 2008, http://topics.nytimes.com/top/reference/timestopics/subjects/c/credit_crisis/auto_industry/index.html (accessed 26 November 2009).

[iii] Volvo Group, *Nine months ended September 30, 2008*, www3.volvo.com/investors/finrep/interim/2008/q3/q3_2008_eng.pdf (accessed 25 November 2009).

[iv] Scania Interim Report, *January–September 2008*, www.scania.com/Images/Scania%202008%20Q3%20report%20FINAL_tcm10-219196_50680.pdf (accessed 25 November 2009).

[v] Scania, *Annual Report 2008*, 2009, www.scania.com/Images/66684-EN_2008_lower s_tcm10-229950_50698.pdf (accessed 26 November 2009); Volvo Group, *Report on operations 2008*, 2009, www3.volvo.com/investors/finrep/interim/2008/q4/q4_2008_eng.pdf (accessed 25 November 2009).

Design and development of strategy processes at RACC

J. Ignacio Canales and Joaquim Vilà

RACC is an automobile club in Spain that has funded significant growth by reinvesting its profits due to its not-for-profit structure. This case study looks at the development of the strategy planning process at RACC over a 15-year period. The process had evolved by fostering managerial participation to achieve strategic goals. However, in 2005 and 2006, the organisation faced serious problems and significant changes were required. The question faced by RACC was whether the participative process of strategy development that had served it so well was compatible with these changes.

• • •

Introduction – the situation in 2008

In December 2008, the Strategy Development Unit of RACC (Reial Automòbil Club de Catalunya) was facing an important challenge. They needed to update the strategic planning process for the period 2008–13. The aim was to achieve the goals already established in the current strategic plan (notably the development of a multi-product and multi-channel strategy) while ensuring compatibility with the ongoing and revised strategy that had already begun to be implemented.

The previous strategic planning exercise, indeed all of them since 1995, had involved wide managerial participation coupled with a bottom-up approach. However, significant market changes in 2005 and 2006 combined with the changes to RACC's core businesses had identified some crucial and unavoidable issues that needed to be tackled to bring the businesses back into shape. Some key changes had to be imposed from top management that had not been foreseen at the time the plan had been developed in 2003.

During 2005 RACC detected symptoms of growth stagnation in the insurance business and this threatened RACC's position (as a broker) in the market and its relationship with insurance companies. As a reaction to these changes top management took corrective measures outside the normal strategic planning cycle. These measures brought changes to the ongoing strategy and organisational structure, in particular changing the structure of the insurance business. In effect RACC had to become more involved in producing insurance products and bearing some of the

Source: RACC.

risk rather than being just a broker. The objective of the change was to increase profitability and secure the survival of RACC in the insurance business.

RACC had an ad hoc strategic planning group which it called the 'strategy development unit'. This unit had the specific task of coordinating strategic planning and measuring achievement of targets. The Strategy Development Unit had no time to lose to develop the process that would define the new strategy. The multi-product and multi-channel strategy was made a key priority in order to increase cross-selling opportunities and to build both sales revenues and market share in a wider range of markets. The task at hand was to assess the pros and cons of different strategies and how best to implement changes in strategies and in particular how to incorporate the major changes that had occurred in the insurance business.

Background

RACC was founded in 1906, as a sports association in Catalonia, and is a 'not-for-profit' organisation. RACC's original core business was similar to that of other automobile clubs, such as AAA (US), ANWB (The Netherlands), RAC or AA (UK), and ADAC (Germany). Today, RACC offers a number of services to facilitate the daily use of the vehicle, such as full personal assistance (breakdown assistance, medical assistance, home assistance, legal assistance) to its members, and offers training, education, travel products and insurance services.

In 1995, Josep Mateu was appointed as CEO at RACC. From the outset he stressed a desire to build a talented professional management team, proactive and well trained in strategic management. Immediately after his arrival he hired a number of top executives from multinational firms. Mateu discarded the existing 1994 Strategic Plan for its lack of realism and practical usefulness due to over-ambitious goals and a non-existent plan for implementation. In 1997, Mateu and his management team invited a broader group of managers to come up with new ideas and to assess which products or services RACC should keep and which should be eliminated. Around 50 managers with business area or product line responsibilities participated (RACC had 700 employees and around 80 managers at that time). Opening up participation down the ranks in project generation proved useful in engaging organisational members in the development stage of strategy, and as RACC top managers recognised, it was even more relevant to facilitate carrying out projects and plans in the implementation phase. RACC had remained localised in Catalonia, a relatively wealthy region of Spain until 1998, when the company decided to expand to the rest of Spain and to expand its service offerings around a wider range of customer (member) requirements. These measures were fundamental in RACC's rapid growth and Mateu claimed the key reason for this successful expansion had been their strategic planning process and the commitment of RACC people to contribute to the strategy. This commitment had been achieved mainly via broad participation in the strategy process across the different stages that RACC had been through. RACC had achieved impressive growth, doubling its 1998 annual turnover by 2004 and having more than 1 million members.

In order to evaluate the planning systems at RACC it is necessary to review the way planning has developed under Josep Mateu's leadership.

Stage I: 2000–02

In 2000, Mateu decided a new strategic exercise was called for. With the aid of external consultants, the company carried out another participative process. To start the strategy process, 21 managers from levels 1 and 2 (senior managers), during one month and in small teams of about five people, carried out first an external analysis, focused on assessing the impact of external factors. The output of this initial step was to develop a shared set of aspirations in terms of goals and strategies that were not constrained by the weaknesses of the company prevailing at that time – this was termed the 'ideal strategy' ('writing a letter to Santa Claus' as it was called). Subsequently, the same teams undertook an internal analysis, to examine the feasibility of the initial thinking. The result of this activity was the identification of five corporate strategic priorities, with geographical expansion to the rest of Spain as the highest priority – this was termed the 'possible strategy'. Consultants provided guidance on how to put together tools of strategy analysis, organised the discussion within focus groups and made recommendations, which subsequently led to the adoption of a balanced scorecard to identify a wider range of goals and performance indicators.

Then 50 people from levels 1 to 4 (senior and middle managers) developed the external and internal analysis at the level of each business unit. This analysis generated about 40 projects across all business units. The executive committee, including the CEO and five top managers, was highly involved in the supervision of the process, and regularly met to judge the alignment of projects with corporate strategic priorities. By late 2000, resource allocation to the different projects and plans had taken place. The emphasis throughout the years 2001–02 was on geographical expansion, which was deemed successful, and by early 2003 RACC had achieved the figure of 900,000 members.

Stage II: 2003–06

In 2003, a new strategic exercise was scheduled to tackle the issue of how to capitalise on the successful expansion. This time, even more emphasis was given to middle management participation. The first step was an assessment of the previous 2001–03 strategic planning exercise, which was carried out by 25 people across the business units and support services. One hundred participants from levels 1 to 5 (senior, middle and junior management) carried out the external analysis and derived an 'ideal strategy' for the company as a whole which identified the company's aspirations for 2006. Subsequently they focused on the internal analysis, to progress towards a feasible RACC corporate strategy. The strategic planning department carried out the internal organising of groups, timetables and group tutors over a three-month period. All was progressing well and the successful planning routines of the previous period seemed to be working again, but suddenly things changed.

During 2005 RACC began to detect symptoms of stagnation in the insurance business and it was proving increasingly difficult to attract new customers (members). Taken together these two issues had a significant negative impact on keeping customer loyalty throughout the distribution channels. Unexpectedly, RACC faced increasing difficulties in maintaining revenue levels specifically in its business as broker of car insurance. A problem of scale had developed – from the significant growth over the previous years – insurance companies no longer wanted to bear the full risk of RACC's insurance policies and the only option seemed to be to become an insurance producer (and thus bear the risk) rather than a mere broker. This was, however, perceived to be extremely complicated and implied significant organisational changes – remembering that RACC is a not for profit organisation and most of its activities are low risk services. The urgency to take remedial action and abandon the insurance broker business to become an insurance producer became unavoidable in 2006.

In order to face such difficulties, several key action priorities were identified that would have to be implemented throughout 2007 that 2008. These revolved around the idea of guaranteeing the availability and control of a stable supply of car insurance products for RACC members in the medium and long run and on fostering cross-sales of the other products and services to increase turnover per member. All these measures were aimed at generating growth and helped RACC to establish a significant position in the car insurance market, while retaining its members at the centre of the business model. However, due to the urgent response required and the gravity of the situation, these measures had been decided on and implemented by top management and outside the normal planning systems that had served RACC so well in the past. The key question was whether RACC could retain its tried and trusted bottom-up system, with maximum involvement and participation, in an ever more difficult and complex environment.

Stage III: 2007–08

Senior management concentrated on reacting to the problems in the insurance business because they affected RACC's core business. They devoted significant effort to the formation of an insurance company and the development of RACC's own insurance products which involved major resource commitment and meant moving from being an intermediary to being an insurance company. While this effort gave RACC more independence and management discretion, it also forced the company to assume higher risks. RACC also reinforced the marketing channels with more sales offices and increased emphasis on direct sales via the internet and telephone. With the necessary resources

invested it strengthened RACC's capabilities to attract new business.

While these projects contributed to customer loyalty through the links between car insurance and road assistance, RACC's senior management also deployed additional initiatives to increase not only the number of members but also their frequency of interaction with RACC. Frequency of interaction was considered particularly important because it opened more business opportunities, i.e. cross-selling. In all, the business model transformation was geared towards giving the customers (members) more value.

Due to all these changes, and with all these projects, senior management deemed it necessary to trigger an update of RACC's strategic planning exercise to incorporate the impact and needs of these ongoing projects and to identify additional initiatives. They felt that carrying out a new strategic planning exercise would establish overall strategic coherence and help revamp projects that would ensure future financial stability. However, in contrast to the 2003 planning exercise, the 2008–13 planning exercise would be carried out with the help of external consultants. It was felt that these consultants could bring a more objective approach, working together with an RACC team of 10 top managers, whose dedication to the project was almost exclusive. The focus was on decisions about strategic development options (in particular the product range and alternative channels) and the feasibility of implementation plans. This process resulted in a new set of goals for the period 2008–13, which reinforced the concept of service to the car driver and established ambitious growth targets for RACC in car insurance.

The challenge

The development of strategy for the period from 2008 to 2013, due to the changes in the insurance business, put more emphasis on a multi-product and multi-channel strategy. This strategy focused on an expansion of services for the car driver and had to be designed with ambitious annual targets. RACC was proud of its approach to strategy which allowed it to operate its different businesses in different ways whilst producing synergies between them. It provided better customer service and fostered cross-sales as it encouraged better relationships between the businesses. However, in the current situation, this cross-selling strategy needed to be improved, which was a significant challenge. It required updating current and potential customer information, analysis of competitors and market trends, channel mix, geographic expansion, organisational restructuring, definition of commercial supervision, redistribution systems and probably many other issues that could arise. Analysis was needed for each business unit and in addition significant work in developing synergies and fruitful relationships between business units was required. The Strategic Development Unit was put in charge of the project and it had to be developed with urgency given how integral it was to the key ongoing developments in the insurance business.

Given the magnitude of the task and the tight schedule the Strategic Development Unit was focused on the following issues:

- Should the development of the strategy be carried out with broad participation or would it be better to keep it to a smaller team of senior managers?

- How to effectively manage the different interests and sensitivities of different business units within the organisation given that the insurance business was now much more important?
- How to ensure the strategy would develop and remain focused on the customer rather than a more inside-out perspective?
- How to balance volume growth rates with sustainable profits?

The answer to these questions would give the strategic development unit a clearer idea of how to go about the process of developing strategy in the future at RACC.

CASE STUDY

Consulting in MacFarlane Solutions

Seonaidh McDonald

A small, personally controlled company calls in a strategy consultant from a local business school. The consultant plans a series of strategy workshops based on scenario planning. After what seems like a successful initial workshop, the relationship is terminated and the consultant is left wondering why.

• • •

Twenty-seven years ago Bill MacFarlane left his job as an engineer in a major oil company to set up his own business. He saw an opportunity to set up a flexible, high-tech manufacturing facility which could produce and customise some of the very specialist components needed in the oil industry much more quickly than the larger manufacturers. He began by producing small batches of high specification parts for firms with drilling operations in the North Sea. Today, MacFarlane Solutions is an established firm with around 100 employees and a management team of nine. Like all companies in this sector, MacFarlane Solutions has suffered from the cyclical boom and bust of the oil industry. However, Bill's perpetual innovation and foresight in investing in new production technology and researching new materials have meant that his firm has been able to continue to secure orders from customers. More recently, his timely diversifications into specialist training and consultancy services have created new income streams which have helped the company survive leaner times.

Bill's approach to strategy is strongly grounded in his own expertise as an engineer. He is passionate about new technology and is a personal authority on both production processes and materials science. He also has nearly 40 years of experience in the oil industry and knows its limitations and opportunities well. His ideas for new products, services and processes all spring from this knowledge base. He is driven by the challenge of producing remedies for specific technical problems or overcoming limitations in current practice,

we are like the AA[1] of the industry. People bring us their problems because we have a certain reputation for

tackling anything, for delivering. I tell our customers, 'if my lot can't sort it out for you, it can't be done'.

The same strong leadership and intuitive strategy making that have for so long made MacFarlane Solutions a success now pose a major challenge: Bill is preparing to retire in two years' time. He has already decided which one of the managers will replace him as CEO. Although he has people on his management team who have expertise in all of the technical and management functions of the business, there is no one in the company who has any experience of strategy making. Bill decides that to prepare the company for his departure he is going to have to involve more people in strategy making. He believes that in order to do this, he will have to employ a more explicit and formal process than he has been used to.

With this in mind, he calls the local university Business School and asks a professor he met at a Chamber of Commerce meeting to recommend someone who could help. The professor recommends a colleague, Dr Jane Robertson, who has done strategy research in a number of companies in the past. Bill calls Jane and invites her to meet with him at MacFarlane Solutions. Over a couple of meetings, Bill explains his situation to Jane and asks her to design a new process for strategy making for himself and his management team.

Jane is a strategy lecturer in her early thirties. She is a sociologist by training. Her research is concerned with strategic processes and most of her studies have been in large organisations, so she is keen to see how strategy making works in practice in a small company. She is particularly interested in studying Bill's entrepreneurial style. In order to get to know the company better and understand how the management team see the impending challenge of taking on the task of strategy making, Jane carries out

---

[1] This stands for Automobile Association. The AA is the UK's original roadside assistance service for motorists who have broken down. The AAA is the US equivalent.

interviews with all of the managers. She finds that despite being considered a hard taskmaster, Bill is highly respected in the company. His constant innovation, understanding of the industry and gift for predicting how it will change are widely acknowledged to have saved the company from folding on a number of occasions. Graham Smith, the Operations Manager, has worked in MacFarlane Solutions for seven years since Bill poached him from a larger competitor. He tells Jane:

> I think if we hadn't had that ability, to see ahead and to move and to change, and that's largely down to Bill, we would have died or we wouldn't be 100 people, you know we would have been down to maybe 10 or 20, it wouldn't be the organisation that we have today and the vision is not just in services but investing in the facilities here.

Jonathon Blakeley is the Senior Materials Technologist whom Bill hired straight from university 25 years ago. He talks to Jane about his experience of working for Bill over the years and describes some of the risks that he had taken in the past in developing new capabilities within the company:

> Our Chief Executive . . . he's a very independent charac-ter and you know he very much leads from the top. He thinks the most important thing for us to be is agile, and this is what he's very good at. Bill is sort of ahead of the game. Sometimes you think, 'he's really gone out on a limb this time', there is no-one else in the UK that can do it and you know it's quite a risky strategy, but you know it's something that Bill's very good at, seeing a new market, seeing new opportunities, developing them and going off in new directions. You know I don't think we'd be here today if we'd relied on the old ways and carried on doing things as we did.

Almost everyone that Jane interviews expresses concern over how the company will survive without Bill's vision and drive.

Over the week following her interviews, Jane spends a lot of time thinking about what sort of strategy pro-cess would suit MacFarlane Solutions. Her only guidance from Bill has been that the process should be more inclusive than it has been in the past. Reviewing her interview notes, Jane finds that Bill's ability to imagine the future is regarded as the key competitive advantage for the company and that the removal of this skill from the firm is seen as the biggest single threat to its long-term survival. Jane is not sure that this is a complete or accurate statement of affairs, but as a qualitative researcher she understands that whether it is true or not, this strong belief about the company will need to be directly addressed by any new strategy-making process.

In order to meet Bill's criterion of involving more people, and to foster an ability to think creatively about the future, Jane plans a series of four strategy workshops, based on a Scenario Planning model:[1]

1 imagining different futures;
2 articulating current strategy;
3 critically examining fit between current strategy and different possible futures;
4 updating current strategy.

The first workshop is held in the company boardroom. Jeff Coutts, the Accounts Manager, turns up early and helps Jane to set up her laptop at the head of the huge boardroom table and arrange flip chart stands in each corner of the room. He tells her that 'the likes of him' is hardly ever in this room, which is only really used to impress important customers. Regular meetings are held with individual managers downstairs in Bill's office. He shows Jane some of the photos mounted on the wall: in some, Bill is pictured shaking hands with important customers, or receiving awards at business dinners; others feature shots of shiny, futuristic-looking, drilling components.

The workshop is attended by Bill and the whole man-agement team. Jane begins by giving a short presentation using PowerPoint on the history of Scenario Planning. She goes on to describe the process involved in building scenarios and using them as the basis of a strategic plan. Jane then outlines the agenda for the rest of the workshop and how this will fit with the other three workshops that have been planned.

Jane splits the management team and CEO up into small groups, taking care to include people with technical and business backgrounds in each group. She asks the groups to discuss current industry trends and then to begin to build up different pictures of which features of the environment might change, speed up or disappear in 10 or 20 years' time. Each team is given a flip chart and coloured pens to record their scenarios.

The managers are slightly reticent to share their ideas at first and their suggestions are very conservative. Jane notes that although the organisational chart in Bill's office suggests that each of these managers has equal status, those who oversee the business functions seem less willing to contribute than the technologists. Steve Riley, the newly appointed Marketing Manager, has ended up in Bill's team and looks particularly uncomfortable.

However, as the morning wears on the managers become more confident, creative and even slightly competitive. Each group produces an array of different ideas, ranging from the pessimistic to the visionary, and even the wildly unlikely. A number of the groups develop scenarios that centre on an oil industry which is hampered by crippling environ-mental legislation. In a similar vein, several groups imagine futures where oil and natural gas in more and more hostile locations are being sought out by the big drilling companies as more accessible reserves are exhausted. One group has turned these problems on their head and depicts an industry which has drawn on its ability to locate and service oil rigs in the North Sea to diversify completely out of oil and gas production into offshore wind farms and wave turbines. Another group sees big oil companies giving up production altogether to use their experience of worldwide operations management to become logistics specialists and globalisation consultants.

Jane then draws the groups back to the boardroom table, and invites each of them to describe their ideas of the future in turn. She encourages them to discuss the similarities and differences between their scenarios and to articulate the assumptions that lie beneath them. The scenarios from all the groups are met with good humour and are enthusiastically debated by the whole team.

After the workshop has ended Jane is invited to join some of the managers for lunch. Graham Smith tells her that he has enjoyed the morning, although he did not expect to. Pete MacFarlane, Bill's nephew and the IT Manager, asks Jane if she would come and do a more focused session with his department, who are just moving into software training provision for other SMEs. He jokingly asks her if 50 is too late to start wondering about doing an MBA at her Business School.

Jane is pleased with the progress that has been made during the first workshop. She feels that the pleasant atmosphere of the morning and the creative ideas produced by the teams will form the basis of a positive new era of strategy making for MacFarlane Solutions. She heads back to the university where she prepares a report for Bill which contains a summary of all the different ideas from the workshop. They meet, as planned, two weeks later to discuss the report and the next workshop. From the start of the meeting, Jane senses that Bill is being very cold towards her and does not want to discuss either the first workshop or the report. He cuts the meeting short after 20 minutes, saying that he has another appointment and that he doesn't feel that anything more can be achieved from this process. A week later, Jane gets a very formal letter from Jeff Coutts in his capacity as Company Secretary,

Dear Dr Robertson,
We acknowledge receipt of your report. Please accept this letter as formal notification that MacFarlane Solutions does not wish to proceed with any further strategy workshops. We thank you again for your contribution.

Reference:
[1] K. van der Heijden, *Scenarios: The Art of Strategic Conversation.* Chichester: John Wiley and Sons, 1996.

NHS Direct: managing in difficult times

Alex Murdock

The case looks at the continued development of NHS Direct and the roll-out of telephone and internet-based healthcare services. NHS Direct is now linked to NHS Choices – a new internet-based information medium. There is continuing innovation in the services provided and the case can be used to explore strategic development and change issues as well as resource capability and also elements of stakeholder analysis.

• • •

NHS Direct has been a leading example of the new modernised NHS based around the needs of patients. In five years it has grown from a small pilot scheme to a unique national service.[i]

On 28 April 2009 the *Guardian* newspaper reported that NHS Direct had received more than 1000 calls about swine flu in the previous 24 hours. Over a fifth of these calls were from people who had recently travelled to an infected area and were showing symptoms.

The telephone inquiries were also mirrored in internet-based contacts which, in particular, made use of a 'cold and flu assessment' tool available online from the website. Perhaps significantly, this marked increase in demand was ahead of any reported increase in demand for GP services. One of the key government agencies in medical emergencies, the Health Protection Agency, recommended that people with flu symptoms contact either NHS Direct or their GP.[ii]

In this way it can be argued that the swine flu outbreak showed that NHS Direct had established itself as a front line responder not just to minor health concerns but also in the case of a potential serious epidemic.

Arguably the statement of the Chair of NHS Direct in the Annual Report 2008/09 was a reassurance of its maturity and competence:

Since becoming a Trust in April 2007, NHS Direct has overcome initial scepticism and proven itself. Specifically, it has proven its ability to meet stringent performance standards while delivering a remote service which is safe, high quality and valued by patients. We are proud to be the only national provider of NHS services to patients, with the largest number of annual patient contacts of any NHS body as well as 17,000 public members.[iii]

Source: Alamy Images/Custom Medical Stock.

This had followed a complimentary report by the Healthcare Commission which observed in respect of NHS Direct that it:

delivers an important element of urgent and emergency care, including telephone-based assessments, advice about self-care, and acting as a gateway to other services. It has two targets for starting telephone-based assessments, similar to those for out-of-hours GP services: for more urgent ('priority 1') calls, to start the assessment within 20 minutes and for other urgent ('priority 2') calls to start the assessment within 60 minutes. During the data collection period, performance against these targets was 98% for priority 1 calls and 99% for priority 2 calls – both well above the 95% target agreed with the Department of Health.[iv]

The introduction of NHS Direct[v]

NHS Direct was the first step in a process that seeks to radically reconfigure the delivery of healthcare services and

Figure 1 Projected NHS spending and share of Gross Domestic Product (GPD)

Total NHS spending
£ billion, UK

Health's share of GDP
% of GDP, UK

Source: Derived from HM Treasury sources reported in 'NHS Five-Year Spending Plans 2003–2008', *Guardian*, 26 April 2002, copyright Guardian News & Media Ltd 2002.

Table 1 NHS Direct (England): costs and usage of various primary care services

	Cost without calling NHS Direct (£)	Cost including call to NHS Direct (£)	Usage without NHS Direct advice (%)	Usage with NHS Direct advice (%)
Self-care		15.11	17	35
GP in-hours contact	15.70	30.81	29	19
GP out of hours (urgent) contact	22.66	37.77	22	15
Accident and Emergency hospital attendance	64.96	80.77	3	3
Ambulance journey	141.54	156.65	8	8

Source: Derived from National Audit Office Report, 'NHS Direct in England', January 2002, HC 505.

healthcare information. It provided both opportunities and challenges. The UK Government intended that NHS Direct would become a well-used and well-regarded '24×7' gateway to the NHS from people's own homes.

NHS Direct call centres recruited nurses with a range of experience in hospital and community settings. About 60 per cent of the nurses worked part time for the service – often combining it with work elsewhere in the NHS. The provision of flexible hours and, in one case, a workplace crèche also had a positive impact on staff recruitment. A national competency framework had been developed together with a planned rotation of staff between call centres and walk-in centres.

NHS Direct was supported by considerable technology including extensive use of diagnostic software which prompted advisers to ask particular questions of callers and suggested possible diagnoses and recommended action.

The National Health Service and NHS Direct: size, finance and growth projections

The UK National Health Service (NHS) is one of the largest public sector organisations in Europe. It has over 1.3 million staff in the NHS Hospital and Community Health Services. The size and workforce trends are shown in Appendix 1.

NHS expenditure is the second biggest area of government spending after social security. Furthermore, NHS spending increased to over £100 billion[1] ($150bn or €110bn) in 2007–08. (see Figure 1). NHS spending is planned to increase, thus converging on the (higher) proportion of GDP spent on health by most other European countries. The severity and duration of the recession will impact on spending plans but traditionally the NHS has been regarded as 'the jewel in the crown' of the UK public sector and it is likely to be protected from the impact of cuts in public expenditure. Following the pre-budget report in December 2009 the NHS Confederation issued the following statement:

> As expected, the Chancellor has confirmed that spending on the NHS will continue to rise in line with inflation after 2011 and this is welcome, but the rising cost of providing healthcare means there are real challenges ahead.[vi]

In 2001 a university study assessed the cost of an NHS Direct call and calculated the impact on subsequent usage of other services. This suggested that NHS Direct saved about 45 per cent of its running costs through reduced usage of other services (see Table 1).

---
[1] £1 ≈ $1.50 or ≈ €1.10.

Figure 2 The NHS gateway to services

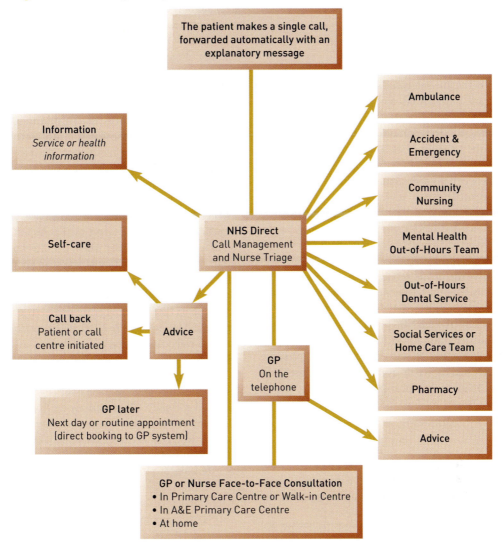

Source: 40th Report of Public Accounts Committee of House of Commons, 'NHS Direct in England', 2002.

NHS Direct: implementation and service relationships

The implementation of NHS Direct has been regarded as successful. The Public Accounts Committee Report noted that:

NHS Direct has quickly established itself as the world's largest provider of telephone healthcare advice, and is proving popular with the public. It has a good safety record, with very few recorded adverse events. Departments should consider what wider lessons they could learn from the successful introduction of this significant and innovative service.[vii]

The importance of the relationship to other parts of the NHS and related services is shown by Figure 2, which illustrates how NHS Direct functioned as a gateway.

The original intention that NHS Direct would have a significant impact upon reducing the demands upon GPs (family doctors), Accident and Emergency Hospital and Ambulance services has not been entirely fulfilled.

However, the Public Accounts Committee noted the challenge of integration with other NHS services. It cautioned the Department of Health to set a clear strategic direction for the service to avoid it trying to do too many things at once. Callers were waiting too long and the service needed to improve both its capacity and technical competence.

The NHS Direct Special Health Authority worked with Primary Care Health Trusts to ensure that locally relevant services were delivered.

NHS Direct Online

The growth of the internet based service has been particularly significant. This may be associated with the increased use of the internet and growth of home-based broadband access in the UK. Organisations such as NESTA[1] have highlighted the importance of online provision of public services and have stressed that this is actively expected by the majority of citizens accustomed to online banking and shopping services.[viii]

NHS Direct Online forms one element of the NHS's new National Knowledge Service. It is aimed primarily at the public, whereas the National Electronic Library for Health is aimed at health professionals.

The users of the online service are not necessarily the same as the users of the telephone service. Quite naturally the online service may be reaching a more IT literate user. It was quite likely (though NHS Direct does not provide any data) that the user group also includes health professionals.

NHS Direct has also developed a Digital TV presence which is expected to reach over 6 million households. This was launched in December 2006.

The further development of NHS Direct in England and Wales as an emergency response

The success of the service has led to proposals that it should be regarded as a response service with a more memorable number. The Police, Fire and Ambulance service in the

[1] NESTA is the National Endowment for Science, Technology and Arts; an independent body with a mission to make the UK more innovative.

UK has a simple number – 999. The suggestion is that NHS Direct has now evolved to the point where it should be given an equally simple access number. The suggestion is 111.

The 2008 Healthcare Commission report identified some key drivers of change associated with changes in emergency services (see Table 2).

Communication and understanding between the various emergency and related services would be critical to the success of effective response. The Healthcare Commission report drew attention to the importance of both networking and effective exchange of information. The recession could well impact on this as savings are sought in areas away from 'front line staff'. This may well involve a focus on savings in procurement of IT and other 'back office' provision.

NHS Direct, as a technology driven service, may be both a beneficiary and also a target in this respect. It will be seen as a 'front line' provider which has direct patient/user contact. However, its substantial overhead budget in terms of IT and other costs may well be put under pressure. The unit cost of a call to NHS Direct is not greatly different from that of a short GP phone call or surgery visit. The Coalition Government elected in May 2010 will be seeking efficiency gains and will be influenced by unit cost.

The increasing engagement of other stakeholders in the patient environment, such as pharmacists, continues to blur traditional boundaries. The issues over GP contracts, which led to many GPs withdrawing from out-of-hours cover, may provide a potential opportunity for NHS Direct, especially when concerns are raised about the competence and experience of agency medical staff brought in to cover.[ix] The extension of pharmacists' roles to cover prescribing activities, previously the province of GPs, represents a rather different challenge for NHS Direct.

NHS Direct can continue to expand its provision and range of coverage. A key question will be whether the up-front investment available for its set-up and initial expansion will

Table 2 Healthcare Commission assessment of change in emergency healthcare

Drivers of change	Changes to services
Long waits for services and treatment.	Changes to how patients are managed in hospital [for example, greater use of minor injury areas/units and emergency nurse practitioners, and improvements in how admissions are managed].
Increasing use of services.	
Pressures on facilities and staff [including changes to working arrangements].	Reorganisation of out-of-hours GP services.
Concerns over sustainability of GP services delivered in usual surgery hours and out-of-hours.	Changes to the responsibilities of GPs.
Increasing number of patients going to A&E departments and subsequently being admitted to hospital.	Introduction of walk-in centres [including commuter walk-in centres].
Rising expectations for convenient services.	Specialist roles for nurses and paramedics [for example, to enable more patients to be treated at home].
Fragmented working across services.	Increased resources and number of staff.
Variations in standards of care.	Introduction of NHS Direct [and extensions to other telephone advice services].
Patients going to 'the wrong service'.	

Source: Healthcare Commission, 'Not just a matter of time: A review of urgent and emergency care services in England', September 2008.

continue to be available and sufficient for further development. Research in Wales has suggested that some groups such as the elderly are relative under-users of NHS Direct Services. For a service which seeks to offer and demonstrate full reach and access such findings have to raise concerns.[x]

The review of the service in England by the National Audit Office focused on the need to address three key areas:

- Capacity – to meet the new demands the service will have to develop new human resource strategies, develop networks to deal with variations in demand between centres and be able to provide a justification for additional funding.
- Safety – to maintain or even improve on the current safety record whilst expanding services.
- Integration – to link with other healthcare providers to prevent duplication and inefficiencies and promote joint working. This will involve the need to develop further communication strategies and IT systems.

Variations in national development

The growth of devolution in the UK with a National Assembly in Wales and a separate Parliament in Scotland created the potential for different service developments.

Wales

In Wales the service was managed by one Health Authority (Swansea) on behalf of all of Wales. The majority of the advice was for home care, suggesting that the service was more likely to advise callers to pursue this option than in England. The service had also developed a significant role in the area of dental advice. The service also spearheaded relationships with voluntary organisations such as Samaritans (suicide prevention)and Childline (child abuse).

The service had sought to integrate its service strategy with the health plan priorities for Wales. The fact that the service was managed from one Health Authority may have encouraged this.

Scotland

In Scotland the service developed in a different direction. It had adopted a different name: NHS24. This could be seen as a departure from the UK Government image of developing a 'brand' for the service. The service was integrated into existing provision using a number of sites (as opposed to Wales). The service in Scotland had developed in close collaboration with health agencies and doctors while elsewhere it was heavily 'nurse led'.

Furthermore, Scotland had pioneered the extension of the service into a new area – that of lower priority ambulance calls. The fact that there was one Ambulance Service for the whole of Scotland had meant that this was easier to develop than elsewhere. The Ambulance Service in Scotland referred calls which were seen as neither life threatening nor serious (defined as Category C) to NHS24. This had required close collaboration between the two services and a high level of trust and mutual understanding.

The future?

The recession and its implications for Health Services in the UK will impact on NHS Direct and NHS24. The expectation that the service will continue to develop using the momentum of its progress to date may encounter the challenge of the expressed desire of the Government to 'protect front line services'.

NHS Direct and NHS24 (in Scotland) can be defined as 'front line services' but are not 'face-to-face' services as are GP and related services, Accident and Emergency and Ambulance provision. There will be a temptation to seek savings on the technology and overhead costs in order to protect front line professional services.

The growth of 'online provision' extolled by organisations such as NESTA perhaps does not take full account of the continued exclusion of certain categories of key and vulnerable NHS users from such provision. The suggestion that the elderly are less able to access online provision represents a potential challenge to NHS Direct if it seeks to demonstrate that it has full and equitable reach to all categories of user.

As the service expands into new areas such as dentistry, management of patient appointments and emergency service cover it is going to prove more complicated to deliver the prompt, safe and integrated service target set for it by key government reports. The increasingly complex and fast-moving technological milieu within which it has chosen to move is not always conducive to consolidation and reflection. Possibly the Scottish context is driven by a different imperative to that of England and Wales. It is possible that the plan for electronic linking of patient records enabling wider access by medical (and some other) NHS staff may prove to be a stumbling point. The need to make cost savings may well affect this very expensive and ambitious project.

The comment below from the NHS Direct 2008/09 Annual Report perhaps sums up both the challenge and opportunity which confronts NHS Direct in the fiscally constrained years ahead:

In common with the rest of the NHS, the public sector and the wider economy, we are entering a period of unprecedented pressure on public spending. This will become more severe over the coming years. However, we have the potential to help the public make more appropriate use of NHS services. Therefore, we must demonstrate that resources invested in NHS Direct save money for the wider NHS, thus supporting the whole system in providing patients with a high-quality, safe service while using dramatically fewer resources.[xi]

Postscript

As of September 2010 the new UK Coalition Government had indicated that it was considering changing NHS Direct and adopting a 111 number for incoming calls, with a reduction of medically qualified staff used to answer calls. The proposal has aroused considerable public concern and plans may change. There is a degree of uncertainty about Government policy regarding the future of NHS Direct in its current form.

References:
[i] Recruitment Material for NHS Direct.
[ii] James Sturcke 'Swine Flu fears boost NHS Direct queries' *Guardian* 28 April 2009.
[iii] NHS Direct Annual Report 2008/9 p. 7.
[iv] Healthcare Commission, 'Not just a matter of time: A review of urgent and emergency care services in England', September 2008, p. 26.
[v] The author acknowledges Munro et al. 'Evaluation of NHS Direct first wave sites', Second interim report to Dept of Health March 2000, as a background source.
[vi] NHS Confederation, 9 December 2009 (Statement by CEO, Steve Barnett).
[vii] 40th Report of Public Accounts Committee of House of Commons 'NHS Direct in England' (2002).
[viii] NESTA, 'Reboot Britain' 2009, see nesta.org.uk.
[ix] Care Quality Commission, Take care now – Interim report, October 2009.
[x] 'NHS Direct fails to reach the elderly', *Nursing Times*, 26 October 2009.
[xi] NHS Direct Annual Report 2008/09, p. 14.

APPENDIX 1 Size and trends in NHS workforce: NHS staffing changes 1999–2004

Increase in staff

	Sept 1999	Sept 2004	Increase since NHS plan[1]
Frontline staff of which:	926,200	1,119,600	193,400 (21%)
All doctors (excluding retainers)	94,000	117,000	23,100 (25%)
Nurses (including midwifery practice nurses and health visiting staff)	329,600	395,500	67,900 (21%)
Ambulance staff	14,800	17,300	2,500 (17%)
Scientific, therapeutic and technical staff	102,400	128,900	26,500 (26%)
Support to clinical staff	296,600	368,300	71,700 (24%)
Other frontline staff	88,800	90,600	1,800 (2.1%)
NHS infrastructure support[2]	171,200	211,500	40,300 (24%)
Total NHS workforce	1,097,400	1,331,100	233,700 (21%)

Increase in training numbers

	In 1999/2000	In 2004/05	Increase since NHS plan[3]
Medical school intake	3,970	6,290[4]	2,320 (58%)
Nursing and midwifery training commissions	18,710	25,020	6,310 (34%)

1 Change since the NHS Plan takes as a baseline the nearest annual figure before July 2000, compared to the latest annual position.
2 Includes practice staff (other than nurses) and other non-medical staff.
3 Includes central functions, properties and estates, and managers and senior managers.
4 Provisional information as July 2005 student numbers have not yet been continued.

Source: Chief Executive's Report to the NHS: December 2005, Reproduced under the terms of the Click-Use Licence.

GLOSSARY

Acceptability expected performance outcomes of a proposed strategy to meet the expectation of the stakeholders (p. 371)

Acquisition when one firm takes over the ownership ('equity') of another; hence the alternative term 'takeover' (p. 329)

Backward integration develop activities that involve the inputs into a company's current business (p. 240)

Balanced scorecards performance targets set according to a range of perspectives, not only financial (p. 447)

Barriers to entry factors that need to be overcome by new entrants if they are to compete in an industry (p. 55)

Blue Oceans new market spaces where competition is minimised (p. 73)

Boston Consulting Group (BCG) matrix uses market share and market growth criteria to determine the attractiveness and balance of a business portfolio (p. 249)

Business case provides the data and argument in support of a particular strategy proposal, e.g. investment in new equipment (p. 521)

Business-level strategy the plan of how an individual business should compete in its particular market(s) (p. 7)

Business model describes how an organisation manages incomes and costs through the structural arrangement of its activities (p. 301)

Buyers the organisation's immediate customers, not necessarily the ultimate consumers (p. 58)

CAGE framework emphasises the importance of cultural, administrative, geographical and economic distance (p. 278)

Cash cow a business unit within a portfolio that has a high market share in a mature market (p. 250)

Coercion the imposition of change or the issuing of edicts about change (p. 475)

Collaboration all those affected by strategic changes are active in setting the change agenda (p. 474)

Collaborative advantage the benefits received when a company achieves more by collaborating with other organisations than it would when operating alone (p. 338)

Collective strategy how the whole network of an alliance, of which an organisation is a member, competes against rival networks of alliances (p. 338)

Complementor (i) customers value your product more when they have another organisation's product than if they have your product alone; (ii) it's more attractive to suppliers to provide resources to you when they are also supplying another organisation than if they are supplying you alone (p. 62)

Competences the ways in which an organisation may deploy its assets effectively (p. 84)

Competitive advantage how a strategic business unit creates value for its users which is both greater than the costs of supplying them and superior to that of rival SBUs (p. 199)

Competitve strategy how a strategic business unit achieves competitive advantage in its domain of activity (p. 199)

Configurations the set of organisational design elements that interlink together in order to support the intended strategy (p. 453)

Conglomerate (unrelated) diversification diversifying into products or services that are not related to the existing business (p. 233)

Control systems the formal and informal ways of monitoring and supporting people within and around an organisation (p. 178)

Core competences the linked set of skillls, activities and resources that, together, deliver customer value, differentiate a business from its competitors and, potentially, can be extended and developed (p. 89)

Corporate entrepreneurship refers to radical change in an organisation's business, driven principally by the organisation's own capabilities (p. 328)

Corporate governance concerned with the structures and systems of control by which managers are held accountable to those who have a legitimate stake in an organisation (p. 123)

Corporate-level strategy concerned with the overall scope of an organisation and how value is added to the constituent businesses of the organisation as a whole (p. 7)

Corporate social responsibility (CSR) the commitment by organisations to behave ethically and contribute to economic development while improving the quality of life of the workforce and their families as well as the local community and society at large (p. 134)

Cost-leadership strategy this involves becoming the lowest-cost organisation in a domain of activity (p. 200)

Critical success factors (CSF) those factors that are either particularly valued by customers or which provide a significant advantage in terms of costs. [Sometimes called key success factors (KSF)] (p. 73)

Cultural systems these aim to standardise norms of behaviour within an organisation in line with particular objectives (p. 445)

Cultural web shows the behavioural, physical and symbolic manifestations of a culture (p. 176)

Differentiation involves uniqueness in some dimension that is sufficiently valued by customers to allow a price premium (p. 203)

Diffusion the process by which innovations spread amongst users (p. 303)

Direction the use of personal managerial authority to establish a clear strategy and how change will occur (p. 475)

Direct supervision direct control of strategic decisions by one or a few individuals, typically focused on the effort put into the business by the employees (p. 445)

Disruptive innovation this creates substantial growth by offering a new performance trajectory that, even if initially inferior to the performance of existing technologies, has the potential to become markedly superior (p. 309)

Diversification increasing the range of products or markets served by an organisation (p. 232)

Dogs business units within a portfolio that have a low share in static or declining markets (p. 250)

Dominant logic the set of corporate-level managerial competences applied across the portfolio of businesses (p. 238)

Dynamic capabilities an organisation's ability to renew and re-create its strategic capabilities to meet the needs of changing environments (p. 85)

Economies of scope efficiency gains made through applying the organisation's existing resources or competences to new markets or services (p. 237)

Education involves persuading others of the need for, and means of, strategic change (p. 473)

Emergent strategy a strategy that develops as a result of a series of decisions, in a pattern that becomes clear over time, rather than as a deliberate result of a 'grand plan' (p. 404)

Entrepreneurial life cycle this progresses through start-up, growth, maturity and exit (p. 311)

Exploring Strategy Model this includes understanding *the strategic position* of an organisation (context); assessing *strategic choices* for the future (content); and managing *strategy in action* (process) (p. 14)

Feasibility whether a strategy can work in practice (p. 383)

First-mover advantage where an organisation is better off than its competitors as a result of being first to market with a new product, process or service (p. 307)

Five forces framework *see* Porter's five forces framework

Focus strategy this targets a narrow segment of domain of activity and tailors its products or services to the needs of that specific segment to the exclusion of others (p. 205)

Forcefield analysis this provides an initial view of change problems that need to be tackled by identifying forces for and against change (p. 469)

Forward integration developing activities concerned with the output of a company's current business (p. 240)

Functional structure this divides responsibilities according to the organisation's primary specialist roles such as production, research and sales (p. 432)

Game theory this encourages an organisation to consider competitors' likely moves and the implications of these moves for its own strategy (p. 217)

Global–local dilemma the extent to which products and services may be standardised across national boundaries or need to be adapted to meet the requirements of specific national markets (p. 274)

Global sourcing purchasing services and components from the most appropriate suppliers around the world, regardless of their location (p. 272)

Global strategy this involves high coordination of extensive activities dispersed geographically in many countries around the world (p. 266)

Governance chain this shows the roles and relationships of different groups involved in the governance of an organisation (p. 124)

Hypercompetition this occurs where frequency, boldness and aggression of competitor interactions accelerate to create a condition of constant disequilibrium and change (p. 6)

Hypothesis testing a methodology used particularly in strategy projects for setting priorities in investigating issues and options; widely used by strategy consulting firms and members of strategy project teams (p. 521)

Industry a group of firms producing products and services that are essentially the same (p. 54)

Inimitable capabilities those capabilities that competitors find difficult to imitate or obtain (p. 91)

Innovation the conversion of new knowledge into a new product, process or service *and* the putting of this new product, process or service into actual use (p. 296)

Intended strategy a strategy that is deliberately formulated or planned by managers (p. 398)

International strategy a range of options for operating outside an organisation's country of origin (p. 266)

Key drivers for change the environmental factors likely to have a high impact on the success or failure of strategy (p. 50)

Leadership the process of influencing an organisation (or group within an organisation) in its efforts towards achieving an aim or goal (p. 471)

Learning organisation an organisation that is capable of continual regeneration due to a variety of knowledge, experience and skills within a culture that encourages questioning and challenge (p. 406)

Legitimacy this is concerned with meeting the expectations within an organisational field in terms of assumptions, behaviours and strategies (p. 171)

Logical incrementalism the development of strategy by experimentation and learning (p. 405)

Managing strategy in action this is about how strategies are formed and how they are implemented (p. 18)

Market a group of customers for specific products or services that are essentially the same (for example, a particular geographical market) (p. 54)

Market development this offers existing products to new markets (p. 253)

Market penetration this implies increasing share of the current markets with the current product range (p. 234)

Market segment a group of customers who have similar needs that are different from customer needs in other parts of the market (p. 71)

Market systems these typically involve some formalised system of 'contracting' for resources or inputs from other parts of an organisation and for supplying outputs to other parts of an organisation (p. 449)

Matrix structure this combines different structural dimensions simultaneously, for example product divisions and geographical territories or product divisions and functional specialisms (p. 436)

McKinsey 7-S framework this highlights the importance of fit between strategy, structure, systems, staff, style, skills and superordinate goals (p. 453)

Merger the combination of two previously separate organisations, typically as more or less equal partners (p. 329)

Mission statement this aims to provide the employees and stakeholders with clarity about the overriding purpose of the organisation (p. 120)

Monopoly formally an industry with just one firm and therefore no competitive rivalry (p. 60)

Multidivisional structure this is built up of separate divisions on the basis of products, services or geographical areas (p. 434)

Objectives statements of specific outcomes that are to be achieved (often expressed in financial terms) (p. 121)

Oligopoly a few firms dominate an industry, with the potential for limited rivalry and great power over buyers and suppliers (p. 60)

Open innovation this involves the deliberate import and export of knowledge by an organisation in order to accelerate and enhance its innovation (p. 300)

Operational strategies these are concerned with how the components of an organisation effectively deliver the corporate- and business-level strategies in terms of resources, processes and people (p. 7)

Organic development this is where a strategy is pursued by building on and developing an organisation's own capabilities (p. 328)

Organisational culture the taken-for-granted assumptions and behaviours that make sense of people's organisational context (p. 168)

Organisational field a community of organisations that interact more frequently with one another than with those outside the field and that have developed a shared meaning system (p. 169)

Organisational justice this refers to the perceived fairness of managerial actions, in terms of distribution, procedure and information (p. 337)

Organisational knowledge the collective intelligence, specific to an organisation, accumulated through both formal systems and the shared experience of people in that organisation (p. 94)

Organisational structures the roles, responsibilities and reporting relationships in organisations (p. 178)

Outsourcing activities that were previously carried out internally are subcontracted to external suppliers (p. 241)

Paradigm the set of assumptions held in common and taken for granted in an organisation (p. 174)

Parental developer an organisation that seeks to use its own central capabilities to add value to its businesses (p. 248)

Participation elements of the change process are delegated by a strategic leader, who still retains authority over, and coordinates, the processes of change (p. 475)

Path dependency where early events and decisions establish 'policy paths' that have lasting effects on subsequent events and decisions (p. 163)

Perfect competition this exists where barriers to entry are low, there are many equal rivals each with very similar products, and information about competitors is freely available (p. 60)

Performance targets these focus on the *outputs* of an organisation (or part of an organisation), such as product quality, revenues or profits (p. 446)

PESTEL framework this categorises environmental influences into six main types: political, economic, social, technological, environmental and legal (p. 50)

Planning systems these plan and control the allocation of resources and monitor their utilisation (p. 450)

Platform leadership this refers to how large firms consciously nurture independent companies through successive waves of innovation around their basic technological 'platform' (p. 300)

Political view of strategy development stategies develop as the outcome of bargaining and negotiation among powerful interest groups (or stakeholders) (p. 406)

Porter's Diamond this suggests that locational advantages may stem from local factor conditions; local demand conditions; local related and supporting industries; and from local firm strategy structure and rivalry (p. 271)

Porter's five forces framework this helps identify the attractiveness of an industry in terms of five competitive forces: the threat of entry; the threat of substitutes; the power of buyers; the power of suppliers; and the extent of rivalry between competitors (p. 54)

Portfolio manager he or she operates as an active investor in a way that shareholders in the stock market are either too dispersed or too inexpert to be able to do so (p. 247)

Power the ability of individuals or groups to persuade, induce or coerce others into following certain courses of action (p. 145, p. 177)

Project-based structure teams are created, undertake their work (e.g. internal or external contracts) and are then dissolved (p. 440)

Problem child *see* **Question mark**.

Product development organisations deliver modified or new products, or services, to existing markets (p. 234)

Profit pools the different levels of profit available at different parts of the value network (p. 102)

Question mark a business unit within a portfolio that is in a growing market but does not yet have high market share (also called 'problem child') (p. 250)

Rare capabilities those capabilities that are possessed uniquely by one organisation or by a few (p. 90)

Recipe a set of assumptions, norms and routines held in common within an organisational field about the appropriate purposes and strategies of organisational field members (p. 169)

Related diversification diversifying into products or services that are related to the existing business (p. 232)

Resource-based view (RBV) of strategy this states that the competitive advantage and superior performance of an organisation is explained by the distinctiveness of its capabilities (p. 83)

Resources assets possessed by an organisation, or that it can call upon (e.g. from partners or suppliers) (p. 84)

Returns the financial benefits that stakeholders are expected to receive from a strategy (p. 375)

Risk the extent to which the outcomes of a strategy can be predicted (p. 371)

Rituals particular activities or special events that emphasise, highlight or reinforce what is important in the culture (p. 177)

Rivals organisations with similar products and services aimed at the same customer group (NB not the same as substitutes) (p. 59)

Routines 'the way we do things around here' on a day-to-day basis (p. 177)

Scope indicates how far an organisation should be diversified in terms of products and markets (p. 231)

S-curve the shape of the curve reflects a process of initial slow adoption of an innovation, followed by a rapid acceleration in diffusion, leading to a plateau representing the limit to demand (p. 304)

Situational leadership successful leaders are able to adjust their style of leadership to the context they face (p. 473)

Social entrepreneurs individuals and groups who create independent organisations to mobilise ideas and resources to address social problems, typically earning revenues but on a not-for-profit basis (p. 315)

Staged international expansion model this proposes a sequential process whereby companies gradually increase their commitment to newly entered markets as they build market knowledge and capabilities (p. 282)

Stakeholder mapping this identifies stakeholder expectations and power, and helps in the understanding of political priorities (p. 141)

Stakeholders those individuals or groups that depend on an organisation to fulfil their own goals and on whom, in turn, the organisation depends (p. 119)

Star a business unit within a portfolio that has a high market share in a growing market (p. 250)

Statements of corporate values these communicate the underlying and enduring core 'principles' that guide an organisation's strategy and define the way that the organisation should operate (p. 121)

Strategic alliance where two or more organisations share resources and activities to pursue a strategy (p. 338)

Strategic business unit (SBU) this supplies goods or services for a distinct domain of activity (p. 198)

Strategic capabilities the capabilities of an organisation that contribute to its long-term survival or competitive advantage (p. 84)

Strategic choices these involve the options for strategy in terms of both the *directions* in which strategy might move and the *methods* by which strategy might be pursued (p. 17)

Strategic customer the person to whom the strategy is primarily addressed because they have the most influence over which goods or services are purchased (p. 72)

Strategic drift the tendency for strategies to develop incrementally on the basis of historical and cultural influences, but fail to keep pace with a changing environment (p. 158)

Strategic groups organisations within an industry or sector with similar strategic characteristics, following similar strategies or competing on similar bases (p. 69)

Strategic issue-selling the process of gaining attention and support of top management and other important stakeholders for strategic issues (p. 510)

Strategic lock-in this is where users become dependent on a supplier and are unable to use another supplier without substantial switching costs (p. 210)

Strategic plan this provides the data and argument in support of a strategy for the whole organisation (p. 521)

Strategic planners (also known as strategy directors or corporate managers): managers with a formal responsibility for coordinating the strategy process (p. 502)

Strategic planning systemised, step-by-step procedures to develop an organisation's strategy (p. 400)

Strategic position this is concerned with the impact on strategy of the external environment, the organisation's strategic capability (resources and competences), the organisation's goals and the organisation's culture (p. 16)

Strategy the long-term direction of an organisation (p. 3)

Strategy as design this views strategy development as a logical process of analysis and evaluation (p. 27)

Strategy as discourse the view that the language is important as a means by which managers communicate and explain and change strategy, but by which they also gain influence and power and establish their legitimacy and identity (p. 27)

Strategy as experience this views strategy development as the outcome of people's (not least managers) taken-for-granted assumptions and ways of doing things (p. 27)

Strategy as variety this is the view that strategy bubbles up from new ideas arising from the variety of people in and around organisations (p. 27)

Strategy canvas this compares competitors according to their performance on key success factors in order to develop strategies based on creating new market spaces (p. 73)

Strategy lenses ways of looking at strategy issues differently in order to generate many insights (p. 20)

Strategy maps these link different performance targets into a mutually supportive causal chain supporting strategic objectives (p. 447)

Strategy projects these involve teams of people assigned to work on particular strategic issues over a defined period of time (p. 520)

Strategy statements these should have three main themes: the fundamental *goals* that the organisation seeks, which typically draw on the organisation's stated mission, vision and objectives; the *scope* or domain of the organisation's activities; and the particular *advantages* or capabilities it has to deliver all of these (p. 8)

Strategy workshops (also called strategy away-days or off-sites): these involve groups of executives working intensively for one or two days, often away from the office, on organisational strategy (p. 518)

Structures these give people formally defined roles, responsibilities and lines of reporting with regard to strategy (p. 431)

Substitutes products or services that offer a similar benefit to an industry's products or services but by a different process (p. 57)

Suitability assessing which proposed strategies address the *key opportunities and restraints* an organisation faces (p. 364)

Suppliers those who supply the organisation with what it needs to produce the product or service (p. 58)

SWOT the strengths, weaknesses, opportunities and threats likely to impact on strategy development (p. 106)

Symbols objects, events, acts or people that convey, maintain or create meaning over and above their functional purpose (p. 177, p. 481)

Synergy the benefits gained where activities or assets complement each other so that their combined effect is greater that the sum of parts (p. 238)

Synergy manager a corporate parent seeking to enhance value for business units by managing synergies across business units (p. 248)

Systems these support and control people as they carry out structurally defined roles and responsibilities (p. 431)

Three horizons framework this suggests that every organization should think of itself as comprising three types of business or activity, defined by their 'horizons' in terms of years (p. 4)

Threshold capabilities those capabilities that are needed for an organisation to meet the necessary requirements to compete in a given market and achieve parity with competitors in that market (p. 87)

Tipping point this is here demand for a product or service suddenly takes off, with explosive growth (p. 304)

Transnational structure combines local responsiveness with high global coordination (p. 439)

Turnaround strategy here the emphasis is on speed of change and rapid cost reduction and/or revenue generation (p. 484)

Value strategic capabilities are of value when they provide potential competitive advantage in a market at a cost that allows an organisation to realise acceptable levels of return (p. 90)

Value chain the categories of activities within an organisation which, together, create a product or a service (p. 97)

Value curves a graphic depiction of how customers perceive competitors' relative performance across the critical success factors (p. 74)

Value innovation the creation of new market space by excelling on established critical success factors on which competitors are performing badly and/or by creating new critical success factors representing previously unrecognised customer wants (p. 74)

Value net a map of organisations in a business environment demonstrating opportunities for value-creating cooperation as well as competition (p. 62)

Value network inter-organisational links and relationships that are necessary to create a product or service (p. 97)

Vertical integration entering into activities where the organisation is its own supplier or customer (p. 240)

Vision statement concerned with the desired future state of the organisation (p. 121)

Yip's globalisation framework this sees international strategy potential as determined by market drivers, cost drivers, government drivers and competitive drivers (p. 268)

INDEX OF NAMES

GENERAL INDEX

Note: Page numbers in **bold** refer to definitions in the Glossary.

ACKNOWLEDGEMENTS

We are grateful to the following for permission to reproduce copyright material:

Figures

Figure 1 in Case Study 'The pharmaceutical industry' from *Medicines in Development: Biotechnology – 2006 Report* (2006), p. 51, Pharmaceutical Research and Manufacturers of America; Figure 1 in Case Study 'TUI and the European tour operators' from UNWTO, June 2009, © UNWTO, 9284402910, reproduced with permission; Figures 2 and 3 in Case Study 'TUI and the European tour operators' adapted from *The US Packaged Travel Landscape 2006–2010*, PhoCusWright Inc., any PhoCusWright data used in an article must be sourced as 'PhoCusWright Inc.' data and must use the exact 'source data' as noted above, all PhoCusWright Inc. publications are protected by copyright, it is illegal under US federal law (17USC 101 et seq.) to copy, fax or electronically distribute copyrighted material without explicit permission, any unauthorized use of the materials may violate copyright, trademark, and other applicable laws and could result in criminal or civil penalties, contact: Pam Carey, Manager, Marketing pcarey@phocuswright.com +1 860 350–4084 x540; Figures in Appendix 1 and Appendix 2 in Case Study 'Marks & Spencer' from www.marksandspencer.com, reproduced with permission; Figure 1 in Case Study 'NHS Direct' adapted from 'NHS five-year spending plans 2003–2008', *Guardian*, 26 April 2002, copyright Guardian News & Media Ltd 2002; Figure 2 in Case Study 'NHS Direct' from the 40th Report of Public Accounts Committee of House of Commons, NHS Direct in England, 2002, Crown Copyright material is reproduced with permission under the terms of the Click-Use License; Figures 2.2 and 6.9 adapted from Michael E. Porter (1998) *Competitive Strategy: Techniques for Analyzing Industries and Competitors*, adapted with the permission of The Free Press, a Division of Simon & Schuster, Inc., copyright © 1980, 1998 by The Free Press, all rights reserved; Figure 2.3 adapted from and reprinted by permission of *Harvard Business Review*, A. Brandenburger and B. Nalebuff (1996) 'The right game', July–August, pp. 57–64, copyright © 1996 by the Harvard Business School Publishing Corporation, Boston, MA, all rights reserved; Figure 2.6 adapted from Richard A. D'Aveni with Robert Gunther (1995) *Hypercompetitive Rivalries: Competing in Highly Dynamic Environments*, adapted with the permission of The Free Press, a Division of Simon & Schuster, Inc., copyright © 1994, 1995 by Richard A. D'Aveni, all rights reserved; Figures 3.4, 3.5 and 6.2 adapted from Michael E. Porter (1998) *Competitive Advantage: Creating and Sustaining Superior Performance*, adapted with the permissions of The Free Press, a Division of Simon & Schuster, Inc., copyright © 1985, 1998 by Michael E. Porter, all rights reserved; Figure 4.2 adapted from David Pitt-Watson, Hermes Fund Management; Figure 5.6 adapted from P. Grinyer and J.C. Spender (1979) *Turnaround:*

Managerial Recipes for Strategic Success, Associated Business Press, p. 203, reprinted with permission of Peter H. Grinyer and J.C. Spender; Figure in Illustration 6.5 from Avinash K. Dixit and Barry J. Nalebuff (1991) *Thinking Strategically: The Competitive Edge in Business, Politics, and Everyday Life*, copyright © 1991 Avinash K. Dixit and Barry J. Nalebuff, used by permission of W.W. Norton & Company, Inc.; Figure 6.5 adapted from D. Gursoy, M. Chen and H. Kim (2005) 'The US Airlines Relative Positioning', *Tourism Management*, 26(5), pp. 57–67, simplified from Figure 1 on p. 62, with permission from Elsevier; Figure 6.6 adapted from D. Faulkner and C. Bowman (1995) *The Essence of Competitive Strategy*, Prentice Hall, reproduced with permission; Figure 6.7 adapted from Richard D'Aveni with Robert Gunther (1994) *Hypercompetition: Managing the Dynamics of Strategic Manoeuvring*, with the permission of The Free Press, a Division of Simon & Schuster, Inc., copyright © 1994 by Richard D'Aveni, all rights reserved; Figure 6.8 reprinted by permission of *Harvard Business Review*, from N. Kumar (2006) 'A framework for responding to low-cost rivals', *Harvard Business Review*, December, Exhibit, copyright © 2006 by the Harvard Business School Publishing Corporation; Figure 7.2 adapted from H.I. Ansoff (1988) *Corporate Strategy*, Chapter 6, Penguin, with permission of the Ansoff Family Trust; Figures 7.5 and 7.9 adapted from M. Goold, A. Campbell and M. Alexander (1994) *Corporate Level Strategy: Creating value in the multibusiness company*, Wiley, copyright © 1994 John Wiley & Sons, Inc., reproduced with permission of John Wiley & Sons, Inc.; Chapter 7 References, p. 259, figure from H. Ansoff (1998) *The New Corporate Strategy*, John Wiley & Sons, Inc., copyright © 1988 (and owner), reproduced with permission of John Wiley & Sons, Inc., and the Ansoff Family Trust; Figure 8.1 from www.bigcharts.com, Marketwatch.Online by www.bigcharts.com, copyright 2006 by Dow Jones & Company, Inc., reproduced with permission of Dow Jones & Company, Inc. in the format Textbook via Copyright Clearance Center; Figure 8.3 adapted from Michael E. Porter (1990), *The Competitive Advantage of Nations*, Palgrave, reproduced with permission of Palgrave Macmillan in World territory excluding USA, Canada and Dependencies and with the permission of The Free Press, a Division of Simon & Schuster, Inc., copyright © 1990, 1998 by Michael E. Porter, all rights reserved in USA, Canada and Dependencies; Figure 8.4 adapted from M. Porter (1987) 'Changing patterns of international competition', pp. 9–39, Figure 5, copyright © 1987 by The Regents of the University of California, reprinted from the *California Management Review*, vol. 28, no. 2, by permission of The Regents; Figure 8.5 from M. Javidan, P. Dorman, M. de Luque and R. House (2006) *Academy of Management Perspectives*, copyright 2006 by Academy of Management (NY), reproduced with permission of Academy of Management (NY) in the format Textbook via Copyright Clearance Center; Figure 8.6 by permission of *Harvard Business Review*, Exhibit adapted from

I. Macmillan, S. van Putten and R. McGrath (2003) 'Global gamesmanship', May, copyright © 2003 by the Harvard Business School Publishing Corporation, Boston, MA, all rights reserved; Figure 8.8 reprinted by permission of Harvard Business School Press, from C.A. Bartlett and S. Ghoshal (1989) *Managing Across Borders: The Transnational Solution*, pp. 105–11, copyright © 1989 by the Harvard Business School Publishing Corporation, Boston, MA, all rights reserved; Figure in Chapter 8, Case Example, from http://finance.yahoo.com/echarts?s=LHL.F#chart7:symbol=lhl.f;range=20011224,20070102;compare=^ixic;indicator=ke_sd+volume;values=0;logscale=off, reproduced with permission of Yahoo! Inc. © 2010 Yahoo! Inc., YAHOO! and the YAHOO! logo are registered trademarks of Yahoo! Inc., data in the figure is reproduced with permission from the NASDAQ OMX Group, Inc.; Figure 9.2 adapted from W.J. Abernathy and J.M. Utterback (1975) 'A dynamic model of process and product innovation', *Omega*, 3(6), pp. 639–56, copyright © 1975, with permission from Elsevier; Figure 9.4 adapted and reprinted by permission of Harvard Business School Press, from C. Christensen and M.E. Raynor (2003) *The Innovator's Solution*, copyright © 2003 by the Harvard Business School Publishing Corporation, Boston, MA, all rights reserved; Figure 9.5 reprinted by permission of Harvard Business School Press from I. MacMillan and R.G. McGrath (2000) *The Entrepreneurial Mindset*, p. 176, copyright © 2000 by the Harvard Business School Publishing Corporation, Boston, MA, all rights reserved; unnumbered figure, Chapter 9, Case Example, from Phil Wolff (2010), *Skype Journal*, 8 March, reproduced with permission; Figure 10.2 from P. Haspeslagh and D. Jemison (1991) *Managing Acquisitions*, The Free Press, reproduced with permission from the authors; Figure 10.4 adapted from E. Murray and J. Mahon (1993) 'Strategic alliances: Gateway to the new Europe, *Long Range Planning*, 26, p. 109, copyright 1993, with permission from Elsevier; unnumbered figure in Illustration 13.2 from Proctor & Gamble, http://www.pg.com/en_US/company/global_structure_operations/corporate_structure.shtml, reproduced with permission; Figure 13.5 adapted and reprinted by permission of Harvard Business School Press from C.A. Bartlett and S. Ghoshal (1998) *Managing Across Borders: The Transnational Corporation*, 2nd Edition, copyright © 1998 by the Harvard Business School Publishing Corporation, Boston, MA, all rights reserved; Figure 13.6 from R. Lawson, W. Stratton and T. Hatch (2005) 'Achieving strategy with scorecarding', *Journal of Corporate Accounting and Finance*, March–April, p. 64 John Wiley & Sons Ltd, reproduced with permission; Figure 13.7 adapted from M. Goold and A. Campbell (1989) *Strategies and Styles*, Figure 3.1, p. 39, Wiley-Blackwell, reproduced with permission; Figure 13.8 from R. Waterman, T.J. Peters and J.R. Phillips (1980) 'Structure is not organization', *Business Horizons*, vol. 23, pp. 14–26, McKinsey & Company, reproduced with permission; Figures 14.2 and 14.3 adapted from J. Balogun and V. Hope Hailey (1999) *Exploring Strategic Change*, Prentice Hall, reproduced with permission; Figure 15.4 was published in G. Szulanski, J. Porac and Y. Doz (eds) (2005) 'An attention-based theory of strategy formulation: linking micro and macro perspectives in strategy processes', *Advances in Strategic Management, 22: Strategy Process*, December, pp. 39–62, copyright Elsevier (2005); unnumbered figure in Chapter 15, Case Example, from www.

msnbc.msn.com, MSNBC.COM (Online) (only staff-produced materials may be used) by MSNBC, copyright 2006 by MSNBC INTERACTIVE NEWS, LLC, reproduced with permission of MSNBC INTERACTIVE NEWS, LLC in the format Textbook via Copyright Clearance Center; .

Tables

Table 3 in Case Study 'Vodafone' from Pure Pricing, 'UK broadband, bundling and convergence update', July 2009, reproduced with permission; Table 4 in Case Study 'Vodafone' from Vodafone 2009 Annual Report, Vodafone Limited, reproduced with permission; Table 3 in Case Study 'TUI and the European tour operators', from *World Tourism Barometer*, June 2009, © UNWTO, 9284402910, reproduced with permission; Table 1 in Case Study 'The Hi-Fi Industry' from Euromonitor International Database, Euromonitor International, reproduced with permission; Table 2 in Case Study 'IKEA' from www.ikea.com, © Inter IKEA Systems B. V. 2010; Table 2 in Case Study 'Tesco' from N.M. Coe and N. Wrigley (2009) *The Globalisation of Retailing*, Vol. 1, p. xviii, Edward Elgar Publishing Ltd, reproduced with permission from the authors and publisher; Table 1 in Case Study 'Severstal' from World Steel Association; reproduced with permission; Table 2 in Case Study 'NHS Direct' from Healthcare Commission, *Not just a matter of time. A review of urgent and emergency care services in England*, September 2008, based on data from The Department of Health, reproduced with permission from The Care Quality Commission; Appendix 1 (Table) Case Study 'NHS Direct' from 'NHS Staffing: Changes 1999–2004: Chief Executive's report to the NHS', 7 December 2005, Department of Health, reproduced under the terms of the Click-Use Licence; Table C.i adapted and reprinted by permission of *Harvard Business Review*, from K.M. Eisenhardt and D.N. Sull (2001) 'Strategy as simple rules', January, Exhibit, copyright © 2001 by Harvard Business School Publishing Corporation, all rights reserved; Table 2.3 from *Strategies for Growth in an Increasingly Consolidated Global Beer Market*, Euromonitor International (2010) reproduced with permission; Table 14.1 adapted from J. Balogun *et al.* (2008) *Exploring strategic change*, 3rd Edition, FT/Prentice Hall, reproduced with permission; Table 15.1 from E. Sadler-Smith and E. Shefy (2004) 'The intuitive executive: understanding and applying "gut feel" in decision making', *Academy of Management Executive*, 18(4), pp. 76–91, copyright 2004 by the Academy of Management (NY), reproduced with permission of the Academy of Management (NY) in the format Textbook via Copyright Clearance Center; Table 15.2 adapted and reprinted by permission of *Harvard Business Review*, from S.A. Joni and D. Beyer (2009) 'How to pick a good fight', December, pp. 48–57, copyright © 2009 by the Harvard Business School Publishing Corporation, all rights reserved.

Text

Extract in Case Study 'IKEA' from Robert Crampton (2008) 'Why we love IKEA', *The Times*, 7 June, © the Times/The Sun/nisyndication.com; extracts in Case Study 'SAB Miller' from SABMiller Annual Report 1998, SABMiller Annual Report 2000 and SABMiller Annual Report 2003, SABMiller is one of the world's leading brewers, with brewing or major distribution operations in over 60 countries spread across six continents; extract 1 from Case Study 'Mergers and de-mergers in the public sector' from Tony Tysome 7 July 1995, 'Shephard rounds on employment', *Times Higher Education Supplement*, reproduced with kind permission of Times Higher Education; extract 2 in Case Study 'Mergers and de-mergers in the public sector' from the Department for Children, Schools and Families website, Crown Copyright material is reproduced with permission under the terms of the Click-Use License; Illustration 1.2 from www.ucc.ie, reproduced with permission; Illustration 1.2, extract from www.nokia.com, reproduced with permission; Illustration 3.1, extract from Tony Hall, Chief Executive of Royal Opera House, in *Royal Opera House Annual Review 2005/6*, p. 11, reprinted by permission of Royal Opera House; Illustration 3.3 adapted from www.smt.sandvik.com/sandvik, © AB Sandvik Materials Technology, reproduced with permission; Chapter 4, Case Example, extract from P. Vallely (2007) 'The Big Question: does the RED campaign help big eastern companies more than Africa?', *Independent*, 9 March, copyright *Independent*, 9 March 2007; Chapter 4, Case Example, p. 153 from Gerard Baker (2006) 'Mind the Gap: With this attack on globalization', *The Times*, 24 October, © The Times/The Sun/nisyndication.com; Illustration 4.2 from *The Times*, 16 September 2008, p. 2, © The Times/The Sun/nisyndication.com; Illustration 5.4 adapted from Mark Jenkins and Veronique Ambrosini (2002), *Strategic Management*, Palgrave, reproduced with permission of Palgrave Macmillan; Illustration 7.4 extracts adapted from 2009 Berkshire Hathaway, Inc.'s Annual Report, the material is copyrighted and used with permission of the author; Illustration 10.4 adapted from the document Oxfam's Partnership Policy at www.oxfam.org/uk/resources/accounts, reproduced with the permission of Oxfam GB, Oxfam House, John Smith Drive, Cowley, Oxford OX4 2JY, UK, www.oxfam.org.uk, Oxfam GB does not necessarily endorse any text or activities that accompany the materials; extract Chapter 14 p. 489 reprinted by permission from H. Tsoukas and R. Chia (2002) 'On organizational becoming: Rethinking organizational change', *Organization Science*, 13(5), pp. 578–9, copyright 2002, the Institute for Operations Research and the Management Sciences (INFORMS), 7240 Parkway Drive, Suite 310, Hanover, MD 21076, USA; quote in Illustration 14.3 (p. 475) from Sir Terry Leahy, in Chris Blackhurst (2004) *Management Today*, February, p. 32, reproduced with the permission of the copyright owner, Haymarket Business Publications Limited; Illustration 15.1 from 'Extracts from Strategy Unit job description for a team member: Band A',http://www.cabinetofficegov.uk/strategy/jobs/band_a.asp, Crown Copyright material is reproduced with permission under the terms of the Click-Use License.

The Financial Times
Illustration 6.2 from J. Leahy (2009) 'Volvo takes a lead in India', *Financial Times*, 31 August.

Screenshots
Screenshot in Case Study 'Web Reservations International' from www.hostelworld.com.

Photographs
Alamy Images: p. 739 Custom Medical Stock, p. 557 Rob Wilkinson, p. 697 Sindre Ellingsen; **Corbis:** p. 665 Helen King, p. 586 Michael Kim; **Getty Images:** pp. 650, 658 and 687, p. 724, AFT, p. 677 Bloomberg, p. 542 Dorling Kindersley, p. 705 Eightfish/Greg Pease; **Press Association Images:** p. 630 EMPICS Sports Photo Agency/Heribert Proepper/AP, p. 426 M. Spencer Green; **Reuters:** p. 619 Yves Herman.

All other images © Pearson Education.

In some instances we have been unable to trace the owners of copyright material, and we would appreciate any information that would enable us to do so.